SEVENTH EDITION

Entrepreneurship

theory | process | practice

Donald F. Kuratko
The Kelley School of Business
Indiana University—Bloomington

Richard M. Hodgetts (1942–2001)
College of Business Administration
Florida International University

THOMSON

SOUTH-WESTERN

Australia · Brazil · Canada · Mexico · Singapore · Spain · United Kingdom · United States

THOMSON
SOUTH-WESTERN

Entrepreneurship: Theory, Process, Practice

Seventh Edition

Donald F. Kuratko   Richard M. Hodgetts

VP/Editorial Director:
Jack W. Calhoun

VP/Editor-in-Chief:
Melissa Acuña

Executive Editor:
John Szilagyi

Developmental Editors:
Erin Denny
Joanne Vickers
Ohlinger Publishing

Sr. Marketing Manager:
Kimberly Kanakes

Sr. Production Project Manager:
Cliff Kallemeyn

Technology Project Editor:
Kristen Meere

Web Coordinator:
Karen Schaffer

Art Director:
Linda Helcher

Sr. Manufacturing Coordinator:
Doug Wilke

Production House:
Interactive Composition Corporation

Printer:
Quebecor World
Taunton, MA

Library of Congress Control Number:
2006921472

For more information about our
products, contact us at:

Thomson Learning Academic
Resource Center

1-800-423-0563

Thomson Higher Education
5191 Natorp Boulevard
Mason, OH 45040
USA

Brief Contents

Contents

16   Managing Entrepreneurial Growth   609

Preface

Entrepreneurship is the most powerful economic force known to humankind! The "entrepreneurial revolution" that captured our imagination during the late 1990s has now permeated every aspect of business thinking and planning. As exemplified by the "dynasty builders" of the previous decades, such as Sam Walton of Wal-Mart, Fred Smith of FedEx, Bill Gates of Microsoft, Michael Dell of Dell Computers, and Herb Kelleher of Southwest Airlines, the applications of creativity, risk taking, innovation, and passion lead the way to economic development far greater than anyone could imagine. The twenty-first century presents newer and sometimes more complex challenges than ever before conceived; however, the entrepreneurial drive and determination of our yet-to-be-discovered "dynasty builders" will be our greatest solution.

The process of transforming creative ideas into commercially viable businesses continues to be our major challenge. Successful entrepreneurship requires more than merely luck and money. It is a cohesive process of creativity, risk taking, and planning. Business students today need courses and programs that set forth a basic framework for understanding the process of entrepreneurship. We wrote this textbook to structure and illustrate the discipline of entrepreneurship in a manner that is as unique and creative as entrepreneurship itself. Text, cases, and exercises appear in *Entrepreneurship: Theory, Process, and Practice*, 7th edition, to bring together in one place the most significant resources for exploring the development of new and emerging ventures and to present them in an exciting, organized, and challenging manner.

Organization

The chapter sequence in *Entrepreneurship: Theory, Process, and Practice*, 7th edition, is systematically organized around the creation, assessment, growth development, and operation of new and emerging ventures. Each major part of the text contains chapters that specifically address these pertinent concepts of entrepreneurship.

Part 1 (Chapters 1–3) introduces the emerging world of entrepreneurship. The Internet and e-commerce are reviewed as they affect the entrepreneurial movement. Examining the entrepreneurial revolution throughout the world, this part reveals the evolving nature of entrepreneurship and its importance to the entire world economy. Finally, the concept of corporate entrepreneurship is introduced as an emerging corporate strategy to foster entrepreneurial creativity within the larger domain.

Part 2 (Chapters 4–6) addresses the entrepreneurial mind-set that resides within individuals. This part explores creativity for individuals and the concept of innovation. It also focuses on the ethical perspective that entrepreneurs need to take in developing a more socially conscious approach to business.

Part 3 (Chapters 7–11) focuses on the development of an entrepreneurial plan. This part includes the methods of assessing new ventures and business opportunities as well as a discussion of the assessment of industrial, competitive, and local environments and their effect on new and emerging ventures.

The issues of marketing that affect the preparing, planning, and operating of entrepreneurial start-ups as well as the financial tools that entrepreneurs need are also discussed. Finally, the development of a clear and comprehensive business plan is examined. A complete sample business plan appears in the Appendix following Chapter 11.

Part 4 (Chapters 12–14) examines the initiation of entrepreneurial ventures. The legal structures of organizations (sole proprietorships, partnerships, and corporations) as well as certain critical legal issues such as proprietary protections (patents, copyrights, and trademarks) and bankruptcy laws are examined. This part concludes with a thorough examination of the sources of capital formation available to entrepreneurs.

Part 5 (Chapters 15–18) focuses on the growth and development of entrepreneurial ventures, which are diverse yet interrelated areas. The need for strategic planning, the challenge of managing entrepreneurial growth, and the global opportunities available to entrepreneurs are all discussed in this part. Finally, the valuation process needed to acquire a business venture (or sell an existing firm) is discussed along with a presentation on harvest strategies for the entrepreneurial firm.

Distinguishing Features

Entrepreneurship: Theory, Process, and Practice is an organized, systematic study of entrepreneurship. Certain distinguishing features enhance its usefulness for both students and professors. Each chapter contains these specific learning items.

Opening Quotations for Each Chapter

Thought-provoking quotes capture the students' interest about the basic idea for the chapter.

Chapter Objectives

A clear set of learning objectives provides a preview of the chapter material and can be used by students to check whether they have understood and retained important points.

Figures and Tables

Numerous charts and tables illustrate specific text material, expand chapter ideas, or refer to outside source material.

Chapter Summary and Discussion Questions

Each chapter closes with a summary of key points to be retained. The discussion questions are a complementary learning tool that will enable students to check their understanding of key issues, to think beyond basic concepts, and to determine areas that require further study. The summary and discussion questions help students discriminate between main and supporting points and provide mechanisms for self-teaching.

Key Terms

The most important terms appearing in each chapter are shown in boldface where they first appear. A list of the key terms appears at the end of each chapter, and a complete glossary appears at the end of the book.

Cases

Short cases provide current material for student analysis and classroom discussion. These cases serve as an opportunity for students to sharpen their diagnostic skills, apply important chapter concepts, and determine the areas that require further research and study.

Video Cases

Ten cases within the text are video enriched, drawing on the experiences of business owners whose unique insights into how to start, run, and grow a business have been captured on video by the producers of the popular PBS television series *Small Business School*. The videos greatly enhance class discussion because students can see the company and more directly apply management concepts. Each case ends with questions for further analysis and discussion.

Experiential Exercises

A short exercise at the end of each chapter applies principles presented in the chapter, giving students practice on such topics as developing a business plan, analyzing funding sources, and taking self-tests to determine whether they are high achievers.

Challenging and Innovative Learning Tools

Entrepreneurship in Practice

Boxed items throughout the text illustrate one or more innovative ideas related to entrepreneurship. The topics range from finding an entrepreneurial niche to revealing the secrets of the entrepreneurial spirit. Each one is unique in its application to entrepreneurial activity.

The Entrepreneurial Process

Short vignettes about the entrepreneurial process are included throughout the text to show how practicing entrepreneurs handle specific challenges and opportunities that are considered the leading edge today.

Entrepreneurial Case Analyses

Comprehensive case studies that illustrate venture creations or managerial ideas confronted by actual firms culminate the five major parts of the text. The companies are real, so students can appreciate the value of analyzing the situations and data presented and compare their conclusions with the actual outcomes of the cases provided in the *Instructor's Resource Manual*.

Comprehensive Exercises

Comprehensive exercises that encourage students to go beyond the text material to apply the concepts and experience activities related to the entrepreneur are provided at the end of the parts.

Acknowledgments

Many individuals played an important role in helping to write, develop, and refine the text, and they deserve special recognition. First, my family, from whom I took so much time, deserves my deepest love and appreciation. Appreciation is extended to the staff at South-Western/Thomson Learning, in particular John Szilagyi.

A special acknowledgment goes to the always enthusiastic and successful Hattie Bryant. Ten selected vignettes from her PBS television series *Small Business School* were adapted into specialized video cases for this edition. I am extremely proud to have Hattie Bryant's work affiliated with this book.

The professionals who reviewed the manuscript and offered copious suggestions for improvement played a decisive role in the final result. I would first like to thank the reviewers for the earlier editions, including Michael Czinkota, Georgetown University; David H. Gobeli, Oregon State University; Charles C. Green, Frank Hoy, University of Texas at El Paso; Roger Hutt, Arizona State University; Richard Lorentz, University of Wisconsin-Eau Claire; Lorie L. Mazzaroppi, Fairleigh Dickinson University; Edward Miller, Montclair State University; Thomas Monroy, Baldwin Wallace College; Stephen Mueller, Florida International University; E.L. Murphree, Jr., George Washington University; David Olson, California State University–Bakersfield; James Powell, Amit Shah, Frostburg State University; Arthur Shriberg, Xavier University; Jack L. Sterrett, Southeast Missouri State University; Kim Stewart, University of Denver; Sherman Timmins, University of Toledo; Charles N. Toftoy, George Washington University; Warren Weber, California State Polytechnic University–Pomona; Anatoly V. Zhuplev, Loyola Marymount University; and Monica Zimmerman, Temple University.

I would especially like to thank the reviewers for this edition: Mary Allender, University of Portland; James Almeida, Fairleigh Dickinson University; Jeffrey Alves, Wilkes University; Joseph S. Anderson, Northern Arizona University; Lawrence Aronhime, Johns Hopkins University; Kenneth M. Becker, University of Vermont; Ted Berzinski, Mars Hill College; Thomas M. Box, Pittsburg State University; Stephen Braun, Concordia University; Martin Bressler, Houston Baptist University; Debbi Brock, Berea College; John Callister, Cornell University; Don Cassidy, Inver Hills Community College; A. A. Farhad Chowdhury, Mississippi Valley State University; James J. Chrisman, Mississippi State University; John E. Clarkin, College of Charleston; Teresa A. Daniel, Marshall University; Judy Dietert, Texas State University–San Marcos; Barbara Frazier, Western Michigan University; Barry Gilmore, University of Memphis; Judith Grenkowicz, Kirtland Community College; Stephanie Haaland, Linfield College; Peter Hackbert, Sierra Nevada College; David M. Hall, Saginaw Valley State University; Barton Hamilton, Olin School of Business, Washington University; Brenda Harper, Athens State University; Tim Hatten, Mesa State College; Daniel R. Hogan, Jr., Loyola University; Kathie K. Holland, University of Central Florida; Frank Hoy, University of Texas–El Paso; Rusty Juban, Southeastern Louisiana University; Ronald Kath, Life University; James T. Kilinski, Purdue University Calumet; Michael Krajsa, DeSales University; Stewart D. Langdon, Spring Hill College; Karl LaPan, Indiana University-Purdue University Fort Wayne; Hector Lopez, Hostos Community College/CUNY; Louis Marino, University of Alabama; Charles H. Matthews, University of Cincinnati; Todd Mick, Missouri Western State College; Angela Mitchell, Wilmington College; David

Mosby, UTA; Lynn Neeley, Northern Illinois University; Charles Nichols, Sullivan University; Terry W. Noel, California State University–Chico; John H. Nugent, Montana Tech of the University of Montana; Don Okhomina, Alabama State University; Joseph C. Picken, University of Texas at Dallas; Paul Preston, University of Montevallo; J. Harold Ranck, Jr., Duquesne University; Christina Roeder, James Madison University; William J. Rossi, University of Florida; Jonathan Silberman, Arizona State University West; Cynthia Simerly, Lakeland Community College; Ladd W. Simms, Mississippi Valley State University; Marsha O. Smith, Middle Tennessee State University; Richard L. Smith, Iowa State University; Marcene Sonneborn, Syracuse University; Timothy Stearns, California State University–Fresno; Charles Stowe, Sam Houston State University; Michael Stull, California State University San Bernardino; Thomas C. Taveggia, University of Arizona; Jill Thomas-Jorgenson, Lewis-Clark State College; Judy Thompson, Briar Cliff University; Charles N. Toftoy, George Washington University; Monica Zimmerman Treichel, Temple University; Henry T. Ulrich, Central Connecticut State University; Michael Wasserman, Clarkson University; Joan Winn, University of Denver; Amy Wojciechowski, West Shore Community College; Nicholas Young, University of St. Thomas; Raymond Zagorski, Kenai Peninsula College/University of Alaska; and Anatoly Zhuplev, Loyola Marymount University.

I would also like to thank Andrew M. Whisler, author of "The F1 Experience" business plan that appears as the Appendix following Chapter 11. In addition, I would like to thank Jason B. Correll, author of "Rockwood Lodge & Canoe Outfitters," the acquisition business plan located on the text website. Both individuals prepared excellent and comprehensive examples of business plans from which students are sure to benefit.

I would also like to express my appreciation of my colleagues at the Kelley School of Business at Indiana University–Bloomington for their tremendous support. In particular, I thank the staff at the Johnson Center for Entrepreneurship & Innovation at the Kelley School of Business, Indiana University–Bloomington, including Travis J. Brown, for assistance in research on various topics. A special thanks to Patricia P. McDougall, the Haeberle Professor of Entrepreneurship and Associate Dean at the Kelley School of Business, Indiana University, and Jeffrey G. Covin, The Glaubinger Professor of Entrepreneurship at the Kelley School of Business, Indiana University, both of whom have supported my efforts immensely. Finally, thanks to Daniel C. Smith, dean of the Kelley School of Business, Indiana University, for his leadership and enthusiastic support.

Donald F. Kuratko
The Kelley School of Business
Indiana University–Bloomington

About the Author

DR. DONALD F. KURATKO   Dr. Kuratko, or Dr. K, is the Jack M. Gill Chair of Entrepreneurship; Professor of Entrepreneurship and Executive Director, The Johnson Center for Entrepreneurship & Innovation, The Kelley School of Business, Indiana University– Bloomington. Dr. Kuratko is considered a preeminent scholar and national leader in the field of entrepreneurship. He has published over 150 articles on aspects of entrepreneurship, new venture development, and corporate entrepreneurship. His work has been published in journals such as *Strategic Management Journal, Academy of Management Executive, Journal of Business Venturing, Entrepreneurship Theory & Practice, Journal of Small Business Management, Journal of Small Business Strategy, Family Business Review,* and the *Journal of Business Ethics.* Dr. Kuratko has authored 22 books, including the leading entrepreneurship book in American universities today, *Entrepreneurship: Theory, Process, Practice,* 7th ed. (South-Western/Thomson Publishers, 2007), as well as *Strategic Entrepreneurial Growth,* 2nd ed. (South-Western/ Thomson Publishers, 2004), *Corporate Entrepreneurship & Innovation* (South-Western/ Thomson Publishers, 2007), and *Effective Small Business Management,* 7th ed. (Wiley & Sons Publishers, 2001). In addition, Dr. Kuratko has been consultant on corporate entrepreneurship and entrepreneurial strategies to a number of major corporations such as Anthem Blue Cross/Blue Shield, AT&T, United Technologies, Ameritech, The Associated Group (Acordia), Union Carbide Corporation, ServiceMaster and TruServ.

Under Dr. Kuratko's leadership with one of the largest and most prolific entrepreneurship faculties in the world, Indiana University's Entrepreneurship Program has recently been ranked #4 in the nation by *Entrepreneur* magazine, #11 in Graduate Business Schools for Entrepreneurship by *U.S. News & World Report,* #4 in Graduate Business Schools (Public Institutions) for Entrepreneurship by *U.S. News & World Report,* and one of the Top Five Entrepreneurial Business Schools by the *Princeton Review* as reported in *Forbes* magazine. Before coming to Indiana University Dr. Kuratko was the Stoops Distinguished Professor of Entrepreneurship and founding director of the Entrepreneurship Program at Ball State University. In addition, he was the Executive Director of The Midwest Entrepreneurial Education Center. Dr. Kuratko was the first professor ever to be named a Distinguished Professor for the College of Business at Ball State University and held that position for 15 years. The Entrepreneurship Program that Dr. Kuratko developed at Ball State University continually earned national rankings including: Top 20 in *Business Week* and *Success* magazines; Top 10 business schools for entrepreneurship research (*Journal of Management*); Top 4 in *U.S. News & World Report's* elite ranking (including the #1 public university for entrepreneurship); and the #1 Regional Entrepreneurship Program in *Entrepreneur* magazine.

Dr. Kuratko's honors include earning the Ball State University College of Business Teaching Award 15 consecutive years as well as being the only professor in the history of Ball State University to achieve all four of the university's major lifetime awards, which include Outstanding Young Faculty (1987); Outstanding Teaching Award (1990); Outstanding Faculty Award (1996); and Outstanding Researcher Award (1999). He was also honored as the Entrepreneur of the Year for the state of Indiana and was inducted into the Institute of American Entrepreneurs Hall of Fame (1990). He has been honored with The George Washington Medal of Honor, the Leavey Foundation Award for Excellence in Private Enterprise, the NFIB Entrepreneurship Excellence Award, and the National Model Innovative Pedagogy Award for Entrepreneurship. In addition, Dr. Kuratko was named the National Outstanding Entrepreneurship Educator by the U.S. Association for Small Business and Entrepreneurship, and he was selected one of the Top Three Entrepreneurship Professors in the U.S. by the Kauffman Foundation, Ernst & Young, *Inc.* magazine, and Merrill Lynch. He received the Thomas W. Binford Memorial Award for Outstanding Contribution to Entrepreneurial Development from the Indiana Health Industry Forum. Dr. Kuratko has been named a 21st Century Entrepreneurship Research Fellow by the National Consortium of Entrepreneurship Centers, as well as the U.S. Association for Small Business & Entrepreneurship Scholar for Corporate Entrepreneurship in 2003. Finally, he has been honored by his peers in *Entrepreneur* magazine as one of the Top Two Entrepreneurship Program Directors in the nation for three consecutive years including the #1 Entrepreneurship Program Director in 2003.

In Remembrance

DR. RICHARD M. HODGETTS (1942–2001)

On November 17, 2001, Dr. Richard M. Hodgetts passed away after a $3\frac{1}{2}$ year battle with bone marrow cancer. The field of Management lost one of its most significant contributors.

Dr. Hodgetts was a prolific author. He authored or coauthored over 45 college texts in numerous languages and published over 125 articles in some of the world's most highly regarded research journals. He was also the editor of *Journal of Leadership Studies* and served on a number of editorial boards.

Dr. Hodgetts was an active Academy of Management member his whole career, serving as program chair in 1991, chair of the Management History Division, editor of the New Time special issue of *Academy of Management Executive,* and on the Board of Governors from 1993–1996. For all of his dedicated service, he was inducted into the Academy Fellows. In 1999 Dr. Hodgetts received the prestigious Distinguished Educator Award from the Academy of Management.

Besides his tremendous contributions to the knowledge base of management, Dr. Hodgetts was a truly outstanding teacher. He won every Distinguished Teaching Award offered at both his first job of ten years at the University of Nebraska and his home school for 25 years at Florida International University, including Faculty Member of the Year by the Executive MBA students in the year of his passing. He literally developed thousands of students at all levels—undergraduate, MBA, executive development, and doctoral—and millions across the world were influenced by his texts and innovative distance education materials and courses. Simply put, he was the ultimate educator!

Dr. Hodgett's distinguished career as a scholar and educator was exemplified in his humor, his dedication to research, his genuine interest in his students, his compassion, and his true courage. Millions of students and practicing leaders have been and will continue to be influenced by his teaching and publications. His legacy will live forever!

Introduction

Theory, Process, and Practice

I have subtitled this book on entrepreneurship as *Theory, Process, and Practice* for two specific reasons, one of which is emotional and the other is logical. First, I wanted to honor my former mentor and coauthor, Dr. Richard M. Hodgetts, in selecting a subtitle that he developed for one of his most successful management books years ago. The loss of Dr. Hodgetts to cancer in 2001 will always remain a tragedy for all of us who knew him and recognized his powerful influence on the entire field of management in business schools. (See my remembrance of Dr. Hodgetts located just after the Preface.) The second reason I selected this subtitle is its representation of the book's focus. In studying entrepreneurship I believe that students must be exposed to the "theory development" of the field, the "processes" by which we now teach and study entrepreneurship, and the actual "practice" of entrepreneurship by those individuals and organizations that have been successful. Thus, in order to completely understand and appreciate this emerging discipline we call entrepreneurship, students must learn from theory, process, and practice. The subtitle represents the complete foundation of a discipline. Let's begin by briefly examining each facet.

The Theory of Entrepreneurship

Not too long ago the field of entrepreneurship was considered little more than an applied trade as opposed to an academic area of study. There was no "research" to be accomplished because it was thought that those who could not attend college would simply "practice" the concept of new business start-up. Yet our economy was actually based upon entrepreneurship, and history has proven that with each downturn in the economy it is entrepreneurial drive and persistence that bring us back. Thus, individual scholars began to examine entrepreneurship from a research perspective, and in doing so they initiated an academic field of scholarly pursuit. So we look back at some of the "believers" among the academic community, such as Arnold C. Cooper (Purdue University), Karl A. Vesper (University of Washington), Donald L. Sexton (Ohio State University), Robert C. Ronstadt (Babson College), and Howard H. Stevenson (Harvard University), who are all examples of the "pioneering" researchers in the embryonic days of entrepreneurship. Their wisdom, scholarship, and persistence guided the field of entrepreneurship from what was once considered a disrespected academic area to a field that has now gained unimaginable respect and admiration among business schools in the twenty-first century. Their willingness to delve into the research issues important to this developing discipline provided motivation for the next generation of scholars to pursue the entrepreneurship field with greater vigor.

Today we celebrate the immense growth in entrepreneurship research as evidenced by the number of academic journals devoted to entrepreneurship (44), the number of endowed professorships and chairs in entrepreneurship (more than 275), the development of the 21st Century Entrepreneurship Research Fellows by the National Consortium of Entrepreneurship Centers, and the increasing number of top scholars devoting much of their valuable research time and efforts to publishing on aspects of entrepreneurship in the top academic journals. It is indeed gratifying to see *Academy of Management Journal, Academy of Management Review, Academy of Management Executive, Strategic Management Journal,* and the *Journal of Management* publishing more entrepreneurship research; this increase is in direct proportion to the change in the journals' editorial review boards to include more scholars in the entrepreneurship field. Finally, many universities are now including certain entrepreneurship journals in their lists of top journals for the faculty to publish in. Many of the top business schools in the United States have accepted the *London Times* list of the top 35 academic journals, which includes the *Journal of Business Venturing, Entrepreneurship Theory & Practice,* and the *Journal of Small Business Management.* Additionally, a number of major academic institutions have developed programs in entrepreneurial research, and every year Babson College conducts a symposium titled "Frontiers in Entrepreneurship Research." Since 1981 the conference has provided an outlet for the latest developments in entrepreneurship.

In 1998 the National Consortium of Entrepreneurship Centers (NCEC) was founded for the purpose of continued collaboration among the established entrepreneurship centers, as well as the newer emerging centers, to work together to share information, develop special projects, and assist one another in advancing and improving their centers' impact. As mentioned above, this consortium also established the 21st Century Entrepreneurship Research Fellows, a growing collection of scholars in the field of entrepreneurship who have developed a mission to identify leading-edge research issues and domains and develop high-profile research initiatives that demonstrate the highest level of scholarship to entrepreneurship centers and the academic community at large. Research drives business schools. Today we see research in entrepreneurship as an accepted and respected part of this drive.

The Process of Entrepreneurship

Beginning with the "early adopters" of the discipline of entrepreneurship, such as the University of Southern California (USC), Babson College, and Harvard University, the number of schools teaching and researching entrepreneurship has exploded to more than 550 schools with majors in entrepreneurship, an additional 350 with concentrations in entrepreneurship, and at least one course in entrepreneurship now taught at over 1,600 universities worldwide! Some of the more prestigious research universities in the United States, such as Indiana University, University of Georgia, University of Colorado, and Syracuse University, have developed Ph.D. programs in entrepreneurship in order to prepare the next generation of scholars and researchers. The academic field of entrepreneurship has evolved dramatically over the last 30 years! In the midst of this huge expansion of courses remains the challenge of teaching entrepreneurship more effectively.

It has become clear that entrepreneurship, or certain facets of it, *can* be taught. Business educators and professionals have evolved beyond the myth that entrepreneurs are born, not made. Peter Drucker, recognized as one of the leading management thinkers of our time, has said, "The entrepreneurial mystique? It's not magic, it's not mysterious, and it has nothing to do with the genes. It's a discipline. And, like any discipline, it can be learned."[1] Additional support for this view comes from a ten-year (1985–1994) literature review of enterprise, entrepreneurship, and small-business management education that reported, "Most of the empirical studies surveyed indicated that entrepreneurship can be taught, or at least encouraged, by entrepreneurship education."[2]

Given the widely accepted notion that entrepreneurial ventures are the key to innovation, productivity, and effective competition, the question of whether entrepreneurship can be taught is obsolete. Robert C. Ronstadt posed the more relevant question regarding entrepreneurial education: What should be taught, and how should it be taught? He proposed that entrepreneurial programs should be designed so that potential entrepreneurs are aware of barriers to initiating their entrepreneurial careers and can devise ways to overcome them. He contended that an effective program must show students "how" to behave entrepreneurially and should also introduce them to people who might be able to facilitate their success.[3]

Four years later, researchers Robinson and Hayes conducted a survey of universities with enrollments of at least 10,000 students to determine the extent of the growth in entrepreneurship education.[4] While significant growth was cited, two specific challenges were pointed out: developing existing programs and personnel, thus improving the quality of the field. There are several obstacles that need to be overcome to facilitate the development of quality in the field. At the heart may be the lack of solid theoretical bases upon which to build pedagogical models and methods, and the lack of formal academic programs, representing a lack of commitment on the part of institutions. Robinson and Hayes believed that entrepreneurship education had come a long way in 20 years, yet there were several weak points in the field that were identified through their research. Of primary concern is the lack of depth in most of the programs that were then started. Further growth would depend upon how new programs were integrated with and nurtured by the established entrepreneurship education system. In the years that followed, we experienced a greater depth in the academic programs as well as newer initiatives to integrate entrepreneurship throughout the campuses.

In more recent times, researchers Solomon, Duffy, and Tarabishy conducted one of the most comprehensive empirical analyses on entrepreneurship education. In their review of entrepreneurship pedagogy, they stated, "A core objective of entrepreneurship education is that it differentiates from typical business education. Business entry is fundamentally a different activity than managing a business."[5] They concluded that pedagogy is changing based on a broadening market interest in entrepreneurial education. New interdisciplinary programs use faculty teams to develop programs for the nonbusiness student, and there is a growing trend in courses specifically designed for art, engineering, and science students. In addition to courses focused on preparing the future entrepreneur, instructional methodologies are being developed for those who manage entrepreneurs in organizations, potential resource people (accountants, lawyers, consultants) used by entrepreneurs, and top managers who provide vision and leadership for corporations, which must innovate in order to survive. Today's entrepreneurship educators are challenged with designing effective learning opportunities for entrepreneurship students.

The current trend in most universities is to develop or expand entrepreneurship programs and design unique and challenging curricula specifically designed for entrepreneurship students. More significantly, national recognition is now being given to the top entrepreneurial schools through awards such as the United States Association for Small Business and Entrepreneurship (USASBE) National Model Programs and the national rankings such as those done by *U.S. News & World Report* and *Entrepreneur* magazine. This kind of experience is offered to students in innovative entrepreneurship programs recognized by the USASBE. Highlights of these programs can be found at www.usasbe.org . These awarded model programs include undergraduate majors and concentrations, graduate-level programs, innovative pedagogy, and specialized programs. All of these universities have produced entrepreneurship education that has had real impact on students and a lasting impact on the entrepreneurship field.

The Practice of Entrepreneurship

The final aspect of entrepreneurship is its application in practice. We have seen this exhibited in the thousands of successful entrepreneurs throughout the last 20 years. They and their new ventures have changed our world . . . forever! However, it is important to understand the differences between mere opportunistic moneymaking and the real practice of entrepreneurship. For example, in the late 1990s we experienced the "dot-com" frenzy in which everyone thought they were entrepreneurs simply because they put a business title on the Internet. As I have pointed out many times, in the 1940s it cost $20 billion to invent the atomic bomb. It took another $20 billion to put man on the moon 20 years later. In 1999, the dot-coms burned right through $20 billion to achieve . . . well, nothing really. The dot-com bust hurt more than the cash-burning Internet start-ups and the venture capitalists that funded them. This plague spread like wildfire, collapsing the true entrepreneurial spirit of building one's dream into an enduring entity. Our classrooms became infatuated with the drive for investment and liquidity, fast cash, quick exits, and no real commitment. We pursued an "investment mentality" rather than facilitating the search for an "enduring enterprise." We have survived that time, but it did leave us a legacy to *learn* from. We must again focus on the real goals of entrepreneurs and the motivation that permeates from them. We must educate our next generation of entrepreneurs to learn from the dot-com evaporation and return to the roots of business formation and development. Exit strategies are fine, but they should not dominate the pursuit of entrepreneurial opportunity. One author referred to the dot-com individuals as "opportuneurs" rather than entrepreneurs because they uncoupled wealth from contribution, replaced risk taking with risk faking, and exploited external opportunity rather than pursuing inner vision.[6]

It should be the mission of all entrepreneurship educators to teach the students of today about the *true* entrepreneur. It is the mission of this book to provide an integration of entrepreneurs and their entrepreneurial pursuits into the text material. I want to be sure that today's practicing entrepreneurs and their interesting stories are presented in order to illustrate the real problems and issues involved with their ventures. Students need the exposure to those entrepreneurs who have paid the price, faced the challenges, and endured the failures. I want the lessons learned from our experienced entrepreneurs to "make a difference." It is only by reading about and studying their practices that we can truly learn the real application of the entrepreneurial theories and processes.

Final Thoughts before Venturing into the Text

After reviewing the major facets of theory, process, and practice that are so integral in the study of entrepreneurship, the question remains: So how do I approach this subject? The answer is neither complex nor profound. The answer is really an appreciation for your abilities and recognizing that each one of us can make a difference if we try. Remember, the journey of 10,000 miles always starts with the first step! Let this book and your entrepreneurial course be your first step.

Entrepreneurship is the new revolution, and it's about continual innovation and creativity. It is the future of our world economy. Today, the words used to describe the new innovation regime of the twenty-first century are: dream, create, explore, invent, pioneer, and imagine! I believe we are at a point in time when the gap between what can be imagined and what can be accomplished has never been smaller. This is the challenge for all of today's entrepreneurship students. To paraphrase the late Robert F. Kennedy in a speech made more than 30 years ago: You are living in one of the rarest moments in education history—a time when all around us the old order of things is crumbling, and a new world society is painfully struggling to take shape. If you shrink from this struggle and the many difficulties it entails, you will betray the trust that your own position forces upon you. You possess one of the most privileged positions; for you have been given the opportunity to educate and to lead. You can use your enormous privilege and opportunity to seek purely your tenure and security. But entrepreneurial history will judge you, and as the years pass, you will ultimately judge yourself on the extent to which you have used your abilities to pioneer and lead into new horizons. In your hands . . . is the future of your entrepreneurial world and the fulfillment of the best qualities of your own spirit.

Notes

1. P. F. Drucker, *Innovation and Entrepreneurship* (New York: Harper and Row, 1985).

2. G. Gorman, D. Hanlon, and W. King, "Some Research Perspectives on Entrepreneurship Education, Enterprise Education, and Education for Small Business Management: A Ten-Year Literature Review," *International Small Business Journal* 15 (1997): 56–77.

3. R. Ronstadt, "The Educated Entrepreneurs: A New Era of Entrepreneurial Education is Beginning," *American Journal of Small Business* 11(4) (1987): 37–53.

4. P. Robinson and M. Hayes, "Entrepreneurship Education in America's Major Universities," *Entrepreneurship Theory & Practice* 15(3) (1991): 41–52.

5. G. T. Solomon, S. Duffy, and A. Tarabishy, "The State of Entrepreneurship Education in the United States: A Nationwide Survey and Analysis," *International Journal of Entrepreneurship Education* 1(1) (2002): 65–86.

6. J. Useem, "The Risktaker Returns," *FSB* (May 2001): 70–71.

Entrepreneurship

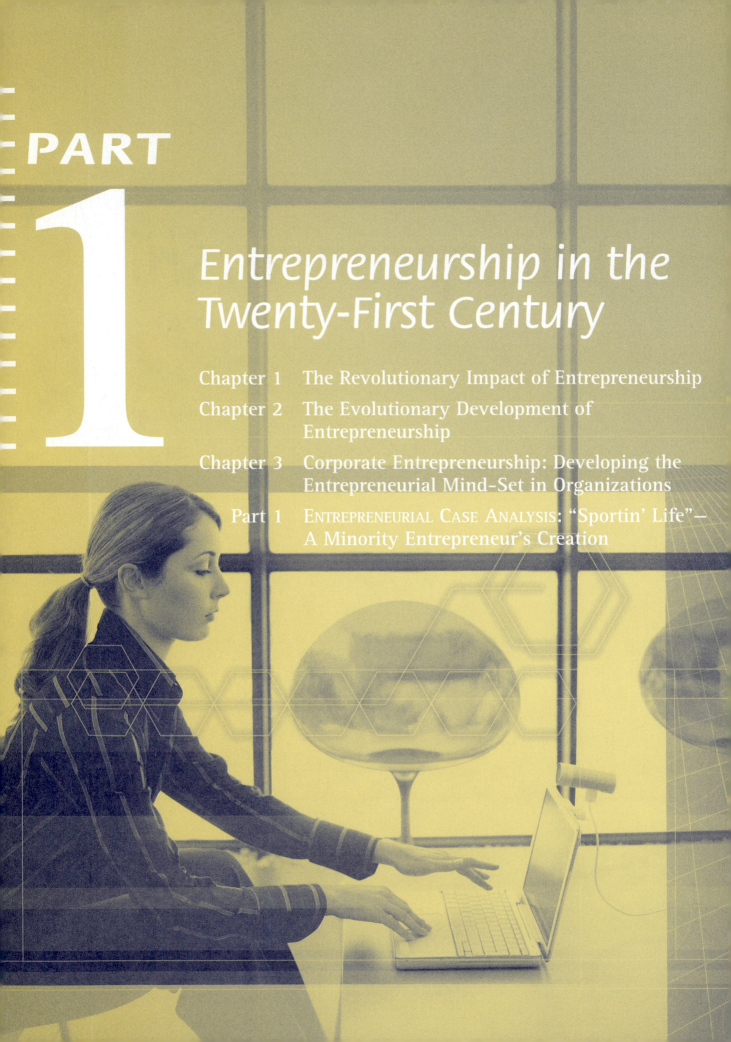

PART 1

Entrepreneurship in the Twenty-First Century

1

The Revolutionary Impact of Entrepreneurship

It's not the critic who counts, nor the observer who watches from a safe distance. Wealth is created only by doers in the arena who are marred with dirt, dust, blood, and sweat. These are producers who strike out on their own, who know high highs and low lows, great devotions, and who overextend themselves for worthwhile causes. Without exception, they fail more than they succeed and appreciate this reality even before venturing out on their own. But when these producers of wealth fail, they at least fail with style and grace, and their gut soon recognizes that failure is only a resting place, not a place in which to spend a lifetime. Their places will never be with those nameless souls who know neither victory nor defeat, who receive weekly paychecks regardless of their week's performance, who are hired hands in the labor in someone else's garden. These doers are producers and no matter what their lot is at any given moment, they'll never take a place beside the takers, for theirs is a unique place, alone, under the sun. They are entrepreneurs!

Joseph R. Mancuso

Center for Entrepreneurial Management

Chapter Objectives

1 To explain the importance of entrepreneurs for economic growth

2 To introduce the concept of an entrepreneurial perspective within individuals

3 To examine the Entrepreneurial Revolution taking place today

4 To illustrate the entrepreneurial environment

5 To highlight some of the latest trends in entrepreneurial research

6 To examine the emerging trends of e-commerce and the Internet in relation to entrepreneurship

Entrepreneurs—Challenging the Unknown

Entrepreneurs are individuals who recognize opportunities where others see chaos or confusion. They are aggressive catalysts for change within the marketplace. They have been compared to Olympic athletes challenging themselves to break new barriers, to long-distance runners dealing with the agony of the miles, to symphony orchestra conductors who balance the different skills and sounds into a cohesive whole, or to top-gun pilots who continually push the envelope of speed and daring. Whatever the passion, because they all fit in some way, entrepreneurs are the heroes of today's marketplace. They start companies and create jobs at a breathtaking pace. The U.S. economy has been revitalized because of the efforts of entrepreneurs, and the world has turned now to free enterprise as a model for economic development. The passion and drive of entrepreneurs move the world of business forward. They challenge the unknown and continuously create the future.

One anonymous quote sums up the realities for entrepreneurs. "Anyone [can be an entrepreneur] who wants to experience the deep, dark canyons of uncertainty and ambiguity; and who wants to walk the breathtaking highlands of success. But I caution, do not plan to walk the latter, until you have experienced the former."[1]

Entrepreneurs/Small-Business Owners: A Distinction

The terms *entrepreneur* and *small-business owner* are sometimes used interchangeably. Although some situations encompass both terms, it is important to note the differences in the titles. Small businesses are independently owned and operated, are not dominant in their fields, and usually do not engage in many new or innovative practices. They may never grow large, and the owners may prefer a more stable and less aggressive approach to running these businesses. In other words, they manage the businesses by expecting stable sales, profits, and growth. Because small firms include those purchased as already established businesses as well as franchises, small-business owners can be viewed as *managers* of small businesses.

On the other hand, entrepreneurial ventures are those for which the entrepreneur's principal objectives are innovation, profitability, and growth. Thus, the business is characterized by innovative strategic practices and sustainable growth. Entrepreneurs and their financial backers are usually seeking rapid growth and immediate profits. They may even seek the sale of their businesses if there is potential for large capital gains. Thus, entrepreneurs may be viewed as having a different perspective from small-business owners in the development of their firms.

In this book we concentrate on entrepreneurs and the effective development of entrepreneurship, including the entrepreneurial mind-set in established organizations. Some of the particular points in this book may apply to both small-business owners and entrepreneurs; however, keep in mind that our focus is on the aspects of innovation and growth associated with entrepreneurs.

Entrepreneurship: A Mind-Set

Entrepreneurship is more than the mere creation of business. Although that is certainly an important facet, it's not the complete picture. The characteristics of seeking opportunities, taking risks beyond security, and having the tenacity to push an idea through to reality combine into a special perspective that permeates entrepreneurs. As we will illustrate in Chapter 4, an entrepreneurial mind-set can be developed in individuals. This mind-set can be exhibited inside or outside an organization, in profit or not-for-profit enterprises, and in business or nonbusiness activities for the purpose of bringing forth creative ideas. Thus, entrepreneurship is an integrated concept that permeates an individual's business in an innovative manner. It is this mind-set that has revolutionized the way business is conducted at every level and in every country. *Inc.* magazine reported on the cover of one issue some time ago that "America is once again becoming a nation of risk takers and the way we do business will never be the same." So it is. The revolution has begun in an economic sense, and the entrepreneurial mind-set is the dominant force.

Our Entrepreneurial Economy—The Environment for Entrepreneurship

Entrepreneurship is the symbol of business tenacity and achievement. Entrepreneurs were the pioneers of today's business successes. Their sense of opportunity, their drive to innovate, and their capacity for accomplishment have become the standard by which free enterprise is now measured. This standard has taken hold throughout the entire world.

We have experienced an **Entrepreneurial Revolution** in the United States. This revolution will continue to be as powerful to the twenty-first century as the Industrial Revolution was to the twentieth century (if not more!).

Entrepreneurs will continue to be critical contributors to economic growth through their leadership, management, innovation, research and development effectiveness, job creation, competitiveness, productivity, and formation of new industry.

To understand the nature of entrepreneurship, it is important to consider from two perspectives the environment in which entrepreneurial firms operate. The first perspective is statistical, providing actual aggregate numbers to emphasize the importance of small firms in our economy. The second perspective examines some of the trends in entrepreneurial research and education so as to reflect the emerging importance of entrepreneurship in academic developments.

Predominance of New Ventures in the Economy

The past fifteen years have witnessed the powerful emergence of entrepreneurial activity in the United States. Many statistics illustrate this fact. For example, the U.S. Small Business Administration reported that during the past ten years, new business start-ups approached nearly 600,000 *per year.* Although many of these incorporations may have previously been sole proprietorships or partnerships, the trend still demonstrates the popularity of venture activity, whether it was through start-ups, expansions, or development. More specifically, in the new millennium we have witnessed the number of businesses in the United States soar to over 25 million, and that number is still growing at a rate of 2 percent. Collectively, U.S. businesses posted over $20 trillion in annual revenues.[2] Let's examine some of the historical numbers supporting this phenomenon.

Several methods are used to measure the impact of new ventures on the economy—for example, efforts to start a firm (which may not be successful), incorporation of a firm (which may never go into business), changes in net tax returns filed (reflecting new filings minus filings no longer received), and the amount of full-time and part-time self-employment might all be considered. According to the **National Federation of Independent Business (NFIB)**, approximately 12 million businesses have owners whose *principal* occupation is owning and operating them. Only 15,000 employ 500 or more people.[3] Small businesses are the most common form of enterprise-established relationships regardless of industry, and most small businesses consist of a single establishment. More than half of all businesses employ fewer than five people. More significantly, almost 90 percent of firms employ fewer than 20 people.

Despite these findings, it would seem safe to assume that new firms with employees may number more than 600,000 in a given year, and that another couple of million new business entities—in the form of self-employment—may also come into being each year. Approximately one new firm with employees is established every year for every 300 adults in the United States. As the typical new firm has at least two owners-managers, one of every 150 adults participates in the founding of a new firm each year. Substantially more—one in 12—are involved in trying to launch a new firm.

The net result, then, is that the United States has a very robust level of firm creation. Among the 6 million establishments (single- and multi-site firms) with employees, approximately 600,000 to 800,000 are added each year. That translates into an annual birthrate of 14 to 16 per 100 existing establishments.[4]

Initiated in 1999, the Global Entrepreneurship Monitor (GEM) is a unique, large-scale, long-term project developed jointly by Babson College, London Business School, and the Kauffman Foundation. Now reaching 40 countries worldwide, GEM provides annual assessment of the entrepreneurial environment of each country. According to the latest Global Entrepreneurship Monitor study, the United States outranks the rest of the world in important entrepreneurial support, such as entrepreneurship education training, financial support, and favorable social norms. The entrepreneurial sector is poised to be an even more important factor in the United State's future economic growth due to its adaptability to changing conditions and continued significant job creation. Entrepreneurs lead to economic growth in several different ways. Entrepreneurs enter and expand existing markets, thereby increasing competition and economic efficiency. Entrepreneurs also create entirely new markets by offering innovative products. These new markets also present profit opportunities to others, further spurring economic growth. A full 14 percent of entrepreneurs starting a business claimed their product had no direct competitor; this is a clear indication of new markets being created by entrepreneurs.

African Americans had the highest rate of total entrepreneurship activity with 16.5 percent, closely followed by Hispanic Americans with 15.2 percent. White Americans had the lowest TEA rate with only 10.8 percent. Total entrepreneurship activity (TEA) is measured in the Global Entrepreneurship Monitor, using survey data from all of the countries involved. It estimates the percentage of adult population involved in either starting up or managing a new business. This diversity is a strong contributor to the United States' past and future entrepreneurial tradition.

Some of the reasons cited for the exceptional entrepreneurial activity in the United States include: a culture that supports risk taking and seeking opportunities; Americans are relatively alert to unexploited economic opportunity and have a relatively low fear of failure; the United States is a leader in entrepreneurship education at both the undergraduate and graduate level; and the United States has a high percentage of individuals with professional, technological, or business degrees, a group that registers at the highest entrepreneurial activity rate.

Overall, every study continues to demonstrate that entrepreneurs' ability to expand existing markets and create new markets makes entrepreneurship important for individuals, firms, and entire nations.[5]

Entrepreneurial Firms' Impact

The United States has achieved its highest economic performance during the last ten years by fostering and promoting entrepreneurial activity. The U.S. success has at least three entrepreneurial components.

First, large firms that existed in mature industries have adapted, downsized, restructured, and reinvented themselves during the 1990s and are now thriving. Large businesses have adopted and learned and become more entrepreneurial. As large firms have become leaner, their sales and profits have increased sharply. For example, General Electric cut its workforce by 40 percent, from more than 400,000 20 years ago to fewer than 240,000 workers in 1996, while sales increased four-fold, from less than $20 billion to nearly $80 billion over the same period. This goal was accomplished in many cases by returning to the firm's "core competencies" and by contracting out functions formerly done in-house to small firms.

Second, while these large companies have been transforming themselves, new entrepreneurial companies have been blossoming. Twenty years ago, Nucor Steel was a small steel manufacturer with a few hundred employees. It embraced a new technology called thin slab casting, allowing it to thrive while other steel companies were stumbling. Nucor grew to 59,000 employees, with sales of $3.4 billion and a net income of $274 million. Newer entrepreneurial companies—some of which did not exist 25 years ago—have collectively created 1.4 million new jobs during the past decade.

Third, thousands of smaller firms have been founded, including many established by women, minorities, and immigrants. These new companies have come from every sector of the economy and every part of the country. Together these small firms make a formidable contribution to the economy, as many firms have hired one or two employees to create more than one million net new jobs in the last few years.

In summary, entrepreneurial firms make two indispensable contributions to the U.S. economy. First, they are an integral part of the renewal process that pervades and

Table 1.1   Small Business Job Generation

YEARS	NET NEW JOBS (000s)	<20 EMPLOYEES	SIZE OF BUSINESS 20–499 EMPLOYEES	500+ EMPLOYEES
1990–95	6,853	49.0%	27.5%	23.5%
1988–90	2,666	153.8	−31.9	−18.8
1986–88	6,169	24.1	20.8	55.1
1984–86	4,611	35.5	16.8	47.7
1982–84	4,318	48.8	27.9	23.3
1980–82	1,542	97.9	−2.4	4.5
1978–80	5,777	26.3	18.8	54.9
1976–78	6,062	38.2	34.5	27.3
1969–76	6,759	66.0	20.7	13.3

Source: *NFIB Small Business Policy Guide* (Washington, D.C., November 2000), 31.

defines market economies. Entrepreneurial firms play a crucial role in the innovations that lead to technological change and productivity growth. In short, they are about change and competition because they change market structure. The U.S. economy is a dynamic organic entity always in the process of "becoming," rather than an established one that has already arrived. It is about prospects for the future, not about the inheritance of the past.

Second, entrepreneurial firms are the essential mechanism by which millions enter the economic and social mainstream of American society. Small businesses enable millions of people, including women, minorities, and immigrants, to access the American Dream. The greatest source of U.S. strength has always been the American Dream of economic growth, equal opportunity, and upward mobility. In this evolutionary process, entrepreneurship plays the crucial and indispensable role of providing the "social glue" that binds together both high-tech and "Main Street" activities.[6]

New-business formations are the critical foundations for any net increase in U.S. employment. As a final note to the importance of small enterprises in a dynamic environment, we present Table 1.1 to outline how such businesses have bolstered U.S. employment. All of this detailed information provides insight into the U.S. economy, and our economic future may well lie in the development of our entrepreneurial abilities.

Trends in Research and Education

As we continue our study of entrepreneurship, it is important to note the research and educational developments that have occurred over the past few years. The major themes that characterize recent research about entrepreneurs and new-venture creation can be summarized as follows:

1. The entrepreneurial and managerial domains are not mutually exclusive but overlap to a certain extent. The former is more opportunity-driven, and the latter is more resource- and "conservation"-driven.[7]

the entrepreneurial
PROCESS

The Hot Trends to Watch

Authenticity—Consumers like the real thing (hand-crafted cheese made by a local organic dairy farmer versus Velveeta), and they like it when it is made locally. If you are local, advertise it, and even big companies can stress their involvement in the local community.

Age 35—Market to everybody as if they are 35 years old. Baby boomers refuse to accept they are getting older, and younger people are maturing quicker than past generations, making 35 a widely popular age to target.

Multitasking and Memory Loss—People are doing more at the same time, but remembering less. Consulting companies that deal with the negative effects of multitasking are a future growth opportunity.

Obesity—Not a new trend but still a hot one, markets to help people lose weight and help people live with overweight more comfortably are still underdeveloped markets.

The Third Place—Many 18- to 24-year-olds still live at home (56 percent of males and 43 percent of females) and thus need somewhere to escape from home (place one) and work (place two). Popular "third places" are Starbucks and Barnes & Noble, and more are coming.

Snobization—Americans are snobs, purchasing luxury items as status symbols. The $400 billion luxury market is expected to grow 15 percent annually until it reaches $1 trillion in 2010. Figure out a way to get on board, and your business could benefit in a big way.

Uniqueness—This trend goes hand in hand with the authenticity and snobization trends. People love being an early adopter. In a time of big-box retailers, it's up to entrepreneurs to fill this need.

Seniors—People over the age of 60 make up 16 percent of the U.S. population, and that percentage will grow to 20 percent as the baby boomers approach senior citizen status. Some businesses that stand to grow as more people age are senior-care consultants, nonmedical home care, senior meal delivery, and senior clothing and products.

Life Caching—Today's boomers have shoe boxes of fading Polaroids. Coming generations will save pictures/memories digitally. Some industrious entrepreneur will discover how to offer this type of service to the masses cheaply and conveniently.

Source: Adapted from Karen Axelton, Steve Cooper, Amanda C. Kooser, April Y. Pennington, Karen E. Spaeder, Laura Tiffany, Nichole L. Torres, and Sara Wilson, "Fever Pitch," *Entrepreneur* (January 2005): 72–89.

2. Venture financing, including both venture capital and angel capital financing as well as other innovative financing techniques, emerged in the 1990s with unprecedented strength, fueling another decade of entrepreneurship. [8]

3. Intrapreneurship (that is, entrepreneurship within large organizations) and the need for entrepreneurial cultures have gained much attention during the past few years.[9]

4. Entrepreneurial entry strategies have been identified that show some important common denominators, issues, and trade-offs.[10]

5. The great variety among types of entrepreneurs and the methods they have used to achieve success have motivated research on the psychological aspects that can predict future success.[11]

Best Business Schools for Entrepreneurship

Graduate

1. Babson College
2. Stanford University
3. University of Pennsylvania
4. Harvard University
5. Massachusetts Institute of Technology
6. University of Southern California
7. Northwestern University
8. University of Michigan–Ann Arbor
9. University of Texas–Austin
10. University of California–Berkeley
11. Indiana University–Bloomington
12. University of Virginia
13. University of Arizona
14. University of Colorado–Boulder
15. University of California–Los Angeles
16. Columbia University
17. New York University
18. Carnegie Mellon University
19. University of Chicago
20. University of Maryland–College Park

SOURCE: Adapted from *U.S News & World Report, Exclusive Graduate School Rankings for the Year 2006* (April 2005).

Undergraduate

1. Babson College
2. University of Pennsylvania (Wharton)
3. University of Southern California (Marshall)
4. Massachusetts Institute of Technology (Sloan)
5. Ball State University (IN)
6. Indiana University–Bloomington (Kelley)
7. University of California–Berkeley (Haas)
8. University of Arizona (Eller)
9. University of Texas–Austin (McCombs)
10. Baylor University (Hankamer)
11. New York University (Stern)
12. University of Michigan–Ann Arbor
13. University of Maryland–College Park (Smith)
14. University of North Carolina–Chapel Hill (Kenan-Flagler)
15. University of Washington
16. University of Oregon (Lundquist)
17. Wake Forest University (Calloway)
18. Washington University–St. Louis (Olin)

SOURCE: Adapted from *U.S News & World Report, Best Business School Rankings for the Year 2006* (September 2005).

6. The risks and trade-offs of an entrepreneurial career—particularly its demanding and stressful nature—have been a subject of keen research interest relevant to would-be and practicing entrepreneurs alike.[12]

7. Women and minority entrepreneurs have emerged in unprecedented numbers. They appear to face obstacles and difficulties different from those that other entrepreneurs face.[13]

8. The entrepreneurial spirit is universal, judging by the enormous growth of interest in entrepreneurship around the world in the past few years.[14]

9. The economic and social contributions of entrepreneurs, new companies, and family businesses have been shown to make immensely disproportionate

contributions to job creation, innovation, and economic renewal, compared with the contributions that the 500 or so largest companies make.[15]

10. Entrepreneurial education has become one of the hottest topics at U.S. business and engineering schools. The number of schools teaching a new-venture or similar course has grown from as few as two dozen 20 years ago to more than 500 at this time.[16]

Additionally, a number of major academic institutions have developed programs in entrepreneurial research, and every year a symposium titled "Frontiers in Entrepreneurship Research"[17] is conducted on one of the campuses. Since 1981 the conference has provided an outlet for the latest developments in entrepreneurship. Most of the university centers for entrepreneurship have focused on three major areas: (1) entrepreneurial education, (2) outreach activities with entrepreneurs, and (3) entrepreneurial research. These centers have been and will most likely continue to be the leaders in developing entrepreneurial research. Also, many universities are expanding programs and designing curricula specifically for entrepreneurship, with national recognition now given to the top entrepreneurial schools (see the Entrepreneurship in Practice box). For a complete, updated listing of university programs, see the National Consortium of Entrepreneurship Centers (NCEC) annual *Compendium of Entrepreneurship Programs* (www.nationalconsortium.org).

It is interesting to note that during the 1970s entrepreneurial courses were offered at only a handful of schools. Today that number has increased to more than 600, and schools are reporting a record number of students enrolling in such courses.

The Age of the Gazelles

New and smaller firms create the most jobs in the U.S. economy. The facts speak for themselves. The vast majority of these job-creating companies are fast-growing businesses. David Birch of Cognetics, Inc., has named these firms **gazelles**.[18] A gazelle, by Birch's definition, is a business establishment with at least 20 percent sales growth every year (for five years), starting with a base of at least $100,000.

Despite the continual downsizing in major corporations during the early 1990s, the gazelles produced 5 million jobs and brought the net employment growth to 4.2 million jobs. More recently, these gazelles (which currently number about 358,000, or 4 percent of all ongoing companies) generated practically as many jobs (10.7 million) as the entire U.S. economy (11.1 million) during the same period. Their extraordinary performance and contribution warrants their recognition.[19] (See Table 1.2 for myths associated with gazelles.)

Innovation

Gazelles are leaders in innovation, as shown by the following:

☐ New and smaller firms have been responsible for 55 percent of the innovations in 362 different industries and 95 percent of all radical innovations.

☐ Gazelles produce twice as many product innovations per employee as do larger firms.

☐ New and smaller firms obtain more patents per sales dollar than do larger firms.

Table 1.2 Mythology Associated with Gazelles

Gazelles are the goal of all entrepreneurs. Creating a gazelle can be rewarding not only financially, but professionally; however, not all entrepreneurs are suited for the high-stress environment that running a gazelle provides. The more successful a firm becomes, the more society scrutinizes the actions of the management. Once the world is watching, keeping a gazelle growing takes not only tenacity but composure under extreme pressure.

Gazelles receive venture capital. Although VC firms prefer to invest in gazelles, many gazelles have never received VC funding. With gazelles numbering close to 400,000, less than 2% of these companies have received funding, even in boom times.

Gazelles were never mice. By definition, gazelles are companies created with the intent of high growth and wealth creation, whereas mice are companies that are created with the goal of merely generating income and no intention of growth. Companies can be gazelles at birth; however, many businesses become gazelles later in life. As many as 20% of gazelles have been in operation for more than 30 years.

Gazelles are high-tech. To be classified as a gazelle, a company must have grown sales by 20% for at least a five-year period, which can include firms in any industry. This myth most likely stems from the high margins enjoyed by most technology-based companies; however, gazelles are commonly found in low-tech sectors. Two prevalent examples would be Best Buy and Starbucks.

Gazelles are global. The scope of a business has no role in its distinction as a gazelle, so even though some gazelles are operating on a global scale, it is not a necessary characteristic. Making the decision to expand overseas prematurely can just as quickly lead to the death of a business as it can lead to its success. Beyond the risks, international trade accounts for more than $800 billion annually in economic activity, but without careful planning, going global could lead to going out of business.

Growth

Note how these growth data indicate the current "Age of the Gazelles":

- ☐ During the past ten years, business startups have approached nearly 600,000 per year, according to the U.S. Small Business Administration.

- ☐ Of approximately 25 million businesses in the United States (based on IRS tax returns), only 17,000 qualify as "large" businesses.

- ☐ The compound growth rate in the number of businesses over a 12-year span is 3.9 percent.

- ☐ Each year about 14 percent of firms with employees drop from the unemployment insurance rolls while about 16 percent new and successor firms—firms with management changes—are added each year. This represents the disappearance or reorganization of half of all listed firms every five years!

- ☐ By the year 2010, demographers estimate 30 million firms will exist in the United States, up significantly from the 22.5 million firms existing in 2000.

Survival

How many gazelles survive? The simple answer is "none." Sooner or later, all companies wither and die. The more relevant question, therefore, is, "Over any particular

Table 1.3   Survival Rate of Firms by Age of Firm and Region, 1994–1998

	AGE IN 1994 (YEARS)					
REGION	1	2–5	6–10	11–19	20+	ALL
New England	70.4	75.4	79.7	80.4	83.8	80.6
Mid-Atlantic	67.0	70.8	76.3	77.9	81.5	77.6
South Atlantic	66.2	72.1	78.0	78.8	81.7	78.0
East-South Central	70.9	74.5	79.7	80.2	83.1	80.1
East-North Central	69.9	73.4	78.1	78.1	82.1	78.8
West-South Central	70.0	73.5	78.0	78.0	81.2	78.2
West-North Central	71.6	75.1	79.1	78.0	81.0	79.0
Mountain	69.6	73.1	78.8	79.3	81.4	78.6
Pacific	69.7	73.0	78.5	79.4	82.0	78.7
United States	68.9	73.0	78.1	78.7	81.9	78.6

Source: David Birch, Jan Gundersen, Anne Haggerty, and William Parsons, *Corporate Demographics* (Cambridge, MA: Cognetics, Inc., 1999), 8.

interval, how many firms die, and to what degree is it a function of their age at the beginning of the period?"

Table 1.3 provides some answers to that question. It focuses on younger companies, as a common variety of the question is, "How long will a start-up company last?"

The common myth that 85 percent of all firms fail in the first year (some versions of the myth have it in the first two years) is obviously not true. The origins of this myth have been traced by David Birch, formerly with MIT and then later his own firm, Cognetics, to a perfectly accurate piece of research stating that 85 percent of all firms fail. This finding may have been extended to become "85 percent of all small start-up firms fail in the first year."

Whatever the origin of this myth, the more accurate statement is that about half of all start-ups last between five and seven years, depending on economic conditions following the start. Table 1.3 picks up this tale in a slightly different way; note that more than two-thirds of all one-year-old firms made it from 1994 to 1998, and that the odds got better with age, with nearly 82 percent of the firms that were more than 20 years in age surviving.[20]

Emerging Trends: The Internet and E-Commerce

The late Peter F. Drucker had stated that the "truly revolutionary impact of the Information Revolution is just beginning to be felt . . . the explosive emergence of the Internet as a major, perhaps eventually the major, worldwide distribution channel for goods, for services, and, surprisingly, for managerial and professional jobs is profoundly changing economies, markets, and industry structures; products and services and their flow; consumer segmentation, consumer values, and consumer behavior; jobs and labor markets."[21]

Figure 1.1 The Internet Explosion

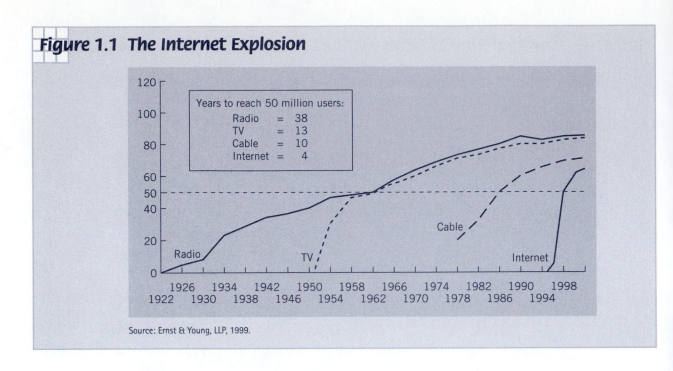

Source: Ernst & Young, LLP, 1999.

This quote summarizes quite succinctly the tremendous impact that the **Internet** is having on the global marketplace. The statistics appear to support this claim of profound change from the "Internet explosion" (see Figure 1.1).

U.S. businesses spent $85.7 billion on building up their Internet capabilities in 1999, according to International Data Corporation (IDC; Framingham, Massachusetts), up 39 percent from one year earlier. In 2000, total spending increased to $120 billion.

Manufacturers and financial services companies are pushing their electronic-commerce (e-commerce) initiatives especially aggressively. Media companies, retailers, and even utilities, however, are also spending billions of dollars in hopes of mastering the Internet's promise and turning it into a revenue- and profit-generating tool for themselves.

The allure of doing business on the Internet is simple. Online technology provides a low-cost, extremely efficient way to display merchandise, attract customers, and handle purchase orders. But getting all the parts of an e-commerce strategy to work smoothly can be a challenging experience. For every company that has it right, countless others are struggling to upgrade their websites and related infrastructure.

Internet use by small ventures is on the rise: The number of entrepreneurial businesses with access to the Internet nearly doubled over a two-year period, from 21.5 percent in 1996 to 41.2 percent in 1998. As many as 35 percent of small businesses maintain their own websites. Research shows that smaller organizations that utilize the web have higher annual revenues, averaging $3.79 million in 1998, compared with $2.72 million for all small ventures.[22]

Smaller ventures use the Internet for a variety of operations, including customer-based identification, advertising, consumer sales, business-to-business transactions, e-mail, and private internal networks for employees. Seventy-eight percent of small venture owners with a website have declared the ability to reach new and potential customers as their main reason for having one. (See Table 1.4 for further web facts.)

Table 1.4   Web Facts

- Fifty-seven percent of all small employers use the Internet for business-related activities. The most common business applications of the Internet in small firms are communicating by e-mail with suppliers and customers and gathering business-related information, such as prices, new products, etc.
- Sixty-one percent of small employers on the Internet (35 percent of all small employers) report they have a business website. Most were created recently. The average life span of small-business websites is just 21 months.
- Small-business websites most often generate income indirectly. They stimulate potential customers to buy, but the actual transaction usually occurs in the small employer's place of business or by phone, fax, or e-mail. Just 24 percent with a website reported sales made directly from their sites.
- The overwhelming majority of sales made directly over the Internet by small businesses are made to consumers and nonbusiness entities.
- The cost of creating and operating a website, both in direct outlays and employee hours, appears modest. However, about one in three does not know the cost, suggesting that the site is not a cost center or that the cost is negligible.
- The most frequent noted benefit of a website is additional customers. However, just 8 percent felt the site has increased business profits.
- The most frequently cited reason for not having a website is that their products or services don't lend themselves to sale on the Internet. The next most frequently mentioned reason is that they simply don't see any benefit in having a site. However, nearly half expected to have a website in the next 12 months.
- One-third of those not now using the Internet for business-related activities expect to be on the Internet within the next 12 months.

Source: Adapted from William J. Dennis, Jr., "The Use and Value of Web Sites," NFIB National Small Business Poll 1(2) (2001): 2.

The E-Commerce Challenge

Electronic commerce (**e-commerce**)—the marketing, promoting, buying, and selling of goods and services electronically, particularly via the Internet—is the new wave in transacting business. E-commerce encompasses various modes of Internet use:

- E-tailing (virtual storefronts), which is a site for shopping and making purchases.
- Electronic data interchange (EDI), which is business-to-business exchange of data.
- E-mail and computer faxing.
- Business-to-business buying and selling.
- Ensuring the security of data transactions.

It is simply the integration of business processes electronically via information and communication technologies.

According to the U.S. Small Business Administration, online retail marketing is currently experiencing about a 200 percent annual growth rate, with online traffic doubling every 100 days. In 2003 e-commerce, on a percentage basis, outperformed

Table 1.5 Advantages and Challenges of E-Commerce for Entrepreneurial Firms

ADVANTAGES

1. Ability of small firms to compete with other companies both locally and nationally (promotional tools)

2. Creation of the possibility and opportunity for more diverse people to start a business

3. Convenient and easy way of doing business transactions (not restricted to certain hours of operation, open 24 hours a day, seven days a week)

4. An inexpensive way (compared to the cost of paper, printing, and postage prior to the Internet) for small business to compete with larger companies and for U.S. firms to make American products available in other countries

5. Higher revenues for small businesses that utilize the Internet, averaging $3.79 million compared to $2.72 million overall (IDC research)

CHALLENGES

1. Managing upgrades (anticipating business needs/application)

2. Assuring security for a website and the back-in integration with existing company systems

3. Avoiding being a victim of fraudulent activities online

4. Handling the costs required to maintain the site

5. Finding and retaining qualified employees

Source: *E-Commerce: Small Business Ventures Online* (Washington, D.C.: U.S. Small Business Administration, Office of Advocacy, July 1999).

total U.S. economic activity in all four major economic sectors. Manufacturing led all industry sectors, accounting for $843 billion of total manufacturing shipments. U.S. retail e-commerce sales reached $56 billion in 2003, an increase of 25 percent over the previous year. Overall, 94 percent of all e-commerce was business to business (B-B). There is no question that e-commerce is now a major component of the economic activity throughout the world.[23]

Small firms encounter a number of barriers when pursuing the e-commerce route. These include initial start-up costs, difficulty in attracting and keeping technologically skilled personnel to service the site and customers, establishment of adequate security for a small business's (or its customers') data, and consumer trust. (See Table 1.5 for a list of advantages and challenges of e-commerce.)

The most immediate obstacle facing companies that seek to fully implement e-commerce is the cost. Experts estimate that a small business would need an initial investment of $10,000 to launch an e-commerce site and approximately 20 percent of the launching funds to maintain it annually. The technical barriers involve both personnel and data.[24]

E-Names: The Web Address

The most basic step in e-commerce is to choose an Internet name. Perhaps surprisingly, this step of choosing an Internet brand name isn't easy. Because customers are unlikely to remember long or awkward names, short and snappy web addresses are at a premium. Sometimes the most effective names have nothing to do with the business itself; for example, what *does* "eBay" mean?

The dot-com renderings of big portions of the English vocabulary have been used up already, as have obvious techno-permutations of those words. E-toys.com, Cyber-toys.com, and NetToys.com, for example, are all taken, as is Toys.com. By the beginning of 2005, over 33 million dot-com domains were in existence.[25]

Network Solutions, Inc., (a Herndon, Virginia, company that handles registration of **domain names**) was the first company to receive authorization from the National Science Foundation to dole out Internet addresses at no charge to registrants. In 1995, the company received permission from the federal government to begin charging domain name registrants. In 1998, as the commercial applications of the Internet became more apparent, the government formed the Internet Corporation for Assigned Names and Numbers (ICANN), the organization responsible for coordinating the domain name system. With the formation of ICANN, the monopoly once enjoyed by Network Solutions, Inc., was broken, and new registrars began to enter the market.[26] Today there are 462 ICANN-accredited registrars.[27]

Generally speaking, registering a domain name is as easy as checking with a domain name registrar to see whether the name has been registered and then paying a fee to register the name. At one time, Network Solutions, Inc., was able to charge an annual fee of $70 to register a .com, .net, or .org domain name, but that fee has now dropped to $34.99. Companies such as Dotster, Inc., charge as little as $14.95 for the same service. For additional fees, most registrars will provide e-mail support as well as web hosting services.

In many cases, however, the most desirable names have already been claimed. To allow for variations of the same domain name, 258 domain name extensions are now available, with the most recent introductions including .aero, .coop, and .museum.[28] To assist in the search for unique domain names, most registrars will provide a list of alternative, unregistered names for domain names already taken. In addition, individuals seeking ownership of an existing domain name can submit bids to the current owner in hopes that they can purchase the name. (See Table 1.6 for a list of the most expensive domain names sold.) At one time, individuals known as "cybersquatters" would purchase domain names that infringed on trademarks of existing or emerging businesses in order to extort high prices once the businesses decided to have an Internet presence. Issues such as these were curtailed by the Anticybersquatting Consumer Protection Act

Table 1.6   Five of the Most Expensive Domain Names Sold

DOMAIN	PRICE
Bingo.com (Bingo-based e-mail community)	$1.1 million
WallStreet.com (online "wagering" on stocks)	$1 million
Drugs.com (pharmaceutical and drug portal)	$823,456
University.com (a training and education "super-portal")	$530,000
Blackjack.com (online gambling)	$460,000

Source: *The Wall Street Journal* (E-Commerce Special, November 22, 1999). Copyright 1999 by Dow Jones & Co. Inc. Reproduced with permission of Dow Jones & Co. Inc.

Table 1.7   Use of Internet Sites

Company information	93%
Corporate image building	89
Product information	80
Advertising	78
Marketing	77
Customer communications	76
Recruiting	75
Customer service	72
Product sales	61
Business-to-business transactions	55
Business-to-employee communications	43

Source: Ernst & Young's 18th Annual Survey of Retail Information Technology, 1999.

of 1999, which enables trademark holders to force cybersquatters to release their domain names.

Developing a Website

Designing an attractive, useful **website** has its challenges. Some companies make their sites too flashy—in which case it can take ages to download, especially if customers aren't using high-speed modems to connect to the Internet. (See Table 1.7 for information about the use of Internet sites.)

Increased visitor traffic—which at first glance seems highly desirable—turns out to have its own headaches. Many first- or second-generation websites were patched together with data-management systems meant to handle only light loads. Now, busy websites may attract 500,000 visitors per day. Customers expect detailed information on thousands or even millions of products. In addition, pretty websites that don't

Figure 1.2   The Most Important Factors for Customers to Do Business Online

Source: *The Wall Street Journal* (E-Commerce special, November 22, 1999). Copyright 1999 by Dow Jones & Co. Inc. Reproduced with permission of Dow Jones & Co. Inc.

the entrepreneurial
PROCESS

Hard Lessons Learned About the Internet

1. **First movers always win.** Not necessarily. Those who sit back with their popcorn and refreshments (and readily available resources) get to watch the show, take notes, and make appropriate edits. Timing is everything, but strategy is still so utterly important in executing a plan well.

2. **Everything happens faster on Internet time.** Moore's Law may tell us that technology is fast. Murphy's Law tells us, however, that whatever can go wrong, will. Keep this in mind when a company changes its business model. The company may move fast, but will its customers? Consumer preferences don't change as quickly as technology allows.

3. **It's all about traffic; the site with the most page views wins.** Many Internet sites rely, or did rely, on hits to gain advertising revenue for sustainment. After the dot-com crash, 12 percent of Internet users lost their favorite site, and at least 17 percent have since been asked to pay for what used to be free. Fancy banner ads don't pay the bills if browsers don't have a reason to stick around and see what the site really has to offer.

4. **Advertising can build a brand in a hurry.** Never has been true, never will be. Some of the best-known online brands, Amazon, AOL, eBay, and Yahoo!, were all made household names by word-of-mouth and in essence, newsworthiness, good and bad. The Internet is an advertising and marketing tool, but not the only tool. Pure Internet companies that thought they could advertise their way to success were just plain wrong.

5. **The popularity of the Internet puts us on the brink of some great convergence between voice, data, computers, and television.** Technology makes for specialization and customization. The Internet's been developing for a few years now, but specialization between these four has been more divergent than convergent. Further, reliance of the four on each other could prove expensive and confusing.

SOURCE: Adapted from George Anders, "Five Things That Are Still True About the Internet" and "Five Things That Were Never True About the Internet," *Fast Company* (February 2001): 116, 120.

connect flawlessly to a company's inventory system and supply chain are considered failures[29] (see Figure 1.2).

The do-it-yourself approach for a website involves a simple, three-step process. First, build a website to display the merchandise and take orders electronically. That's not quite as easy as sending e-mail, but almost. Second, find someone to "host" your site, unless you have the programming skills and megabucks needed to buy and operate a web server of your own. Third, advertise and promote the store.

A number of products, such as IBM's HomePage Creator, will walk a small-business owner through the process of setting up an online store—complete with product catalog and a virtual shopping cart. For an extra fee, even the smallest online store can have real-time, online credit-card processing. First Data Corporation, Cardservice International, Inc., and other companies that specialize in authoring and billing credit-card purchases provide those services, often through a site builder.

A business website requires constant advertising and marketing. Internet shoppers can't go to a single source such as the Yellow Pages to find a web store selling what they want. Instead, there are hundreds of portals for entering the net, each with its own list of sites. As an online merchant, the trick is to get your web store listed, or cross-referenced, on as many portals as possible and to advertise the store and its products on the most popular portals. Once it's there, you must constantly check to ensure it remains there.

Lots of companies are eager to help. Microsoft Corporation's LinkExchange (http://www.microsoft.com/smallbusiness/hub.mspx) in San Francisco bills itself as a one-stop site for all the marketing needs of mom-and-pop stores online. For a yearly fee, Microsoft's Small Business Center Services will register a site with as many as 400 search engines and directories. The company also provides services that let Internet stores collect customer e-mail addresses and manage online mailing lists, and that help online merchants operate "affiliate" programs, which provide referral fees to other websites in return for generating sales leads.[30]

Sticking to Your Website

In the world of e-commerce, stickiness is everything. Loyalty is shallow when customers can click on a competing site and find a better deal. **Stickiness** refers to a host of potential value-adds, features, functions, and "gimmies"—all of which serve as electronic flypaper, of sorts, and make people want to stay at your site longer. The idea is that if potential customers stick around your site long enough, they're likely to buy something eventually and then return frequently to take advantage of your offerings.

Chat is an excellent way to increase stickiness, because customers love to speak their minds and swap ideas with fellow buyers. Unfortunately, chat can also be an expensive headache for small businesses: to make chat become a robust community-building feature for your site, you must integrate a variety of software products, purchase resources to create and maintain the infrastructure, and then monitor the chat for inappropriate activity. The last consideration is important, because inappropriate communications can taint an entire site or user community.

One way to create stickiness, without creating sticky technical situations for yourself, is to outsource the task to a company for chat technology and management. This option can be a safe, cost-effective, and efficient community experience. However, this service is expensive, with setup fees as high as $10,000 and ongoing fees of no less than $5,000 per month.[31]

Emerging E-Commerce Strategies

Numerous new strategies are being introduced to aid entrepreneurs who are entering the powerful Internet marketplace. A few of the strategies are worth summarizing.

The **3-P Growth Model**, introduced by Ernst & Young, defines three specific stages for a venture pursuing the e-commerce route:

1. *Presence*: the ramp-up stage where the entrepreneur needs to build an excitement about the specific capabilities or offerings of the venture in the marketplace.
2. *Penetration*: the "hypergrowth" stage where the entrepreneur focuses on gaining market share and establishing greater virtual integration.
3. *Profitability*: the managed growth stage where the entrepreneur needs to focus on expanding revenue via business-to-business transactions and increased operational efficiencies.

The Dot-Com Evaporation

In the 1940s, it cost $20 billion to invent the atomic bomb. It took another $20 billion to put man on the moon 20 years later. In 1999, the dot-coms burned right through $20 billion to achieve . . . well, nothing really. The dot-com bust hurt more than the cash-burning Internet start-ups and the VCs that funded them. This plague spread like wildfire, collapsing the front line *and* the support troops.

Scient Corporation, an Internet consulting firm, was founded in the late 1990s. Like so many others, it was enjoying the high tide, capitalizing on the demand, hiring the youngest and brightest employees, and spending cash before it knew what it had to spend. Growth was great, revenues and morale were high, and 1,140 employees were on the payroll. Then it happened. The rules changed; the tide shifted. The fuel of Scient's business model evaporated. Dot-com start-ups, which comprised 50 percent of its 1999 business engagements, disappeared from the revenue mix, offices were closed, and hundreds were laid off.

Scient, as well as the others, didn't expect "the worst" to happen so soon. It had noticed its client mix and their demands shifting in late 1999, but didn't realize what was on the horizon. Big enterprises, who were scared of the new, nimble companies and scrambling in the beginning, saw the mistakes the pure dot-coms were making and had re-focused on using technology as a commodity to improve existing systems and processes. Those who knew least about Internet technology and e-business were suddenly determining where the use of technology was headed. The tide shifted from "get the website up and worry about profits later" to "technology's a transforming agent, just a commodity."

The original push for conversion had been suddenly met by a push for integration. Fortunately Scient's strategies were able to quickly and accurately assess the new environment and prepare it for the age-old business philosophy of offering what the consumer wants. Now, Scient "delivers user-centered strategy, design, and technology projects specific to client needs in focused industry groups."

Scient is one of the lucky ones that is still around to tell its story. Perhaps this fact is due to the experience of its management—its executives are seasoned consulting veterans. Robert Howe, chairman and CEO, had built IBM Global Services; a top guy from Booz Allen and a Northwestern University Graduate School professor headed up the strategy department. A strong, weathered backbone may very well be what sustained Scient during the storm. Experience and big-business thinking would also be what kept Scient afloat after the storm. Once again, the basic rules and practices of business saved the day.

Scient Corporation has yet to yield a positive net income even though revenues are seven times that of its first year in business. After 39 acquisitions and an IPO, it remains a force in an industry characterized by consolidation. The horizon is clear for New York–based Scient, however, as the market for web services–based professional services is expected to reach $7.1 billion by 2006.

SOURCE: Adapted from Keith H. Hammonds, "Scient's Near-Death Experience," *Fast Company* (February 2001): 99–109; and Reshma Kapadia, "What Caused the Dot-Com Bust?" (February 2002), http://www.news24.com.

Another strategy aims at what is being considered the second generation of e-commerce—that is, the advancement from simply getting into e-commerce to pursuing competitive advantages through an understanding of the navigational challenges. Consultants Philip Evans and Thomas S. Wurster recommend three dimensions that should be understood for pursuit of competitive advantage: reach, richness, and affiliation.[32]

Reach relates to access and connection. It means, simply, how many customers with whom a business can connect and how many products it can offer to those customers. Reach is the most visible difference between electronic and physical business, and it has been the primary competitive differentiator for e-business thus far.

Richness focuses on the depth and detail of information that the business can give the customer, as well as the depth and detail of information it collects about the customer. It holds enormous potential for building close relationships with customers in a future dominated by e-commerce.

Affiliation is the specific interests that the business represents. Until now, affiliation hasn't been a serious competitive factor in physical commerce because, in general, no company ever devised a way to make money by taking the consumers' side. In contrast, it's a natural progression for pure navigators to affiliate with customers; they aren't selling anything—except, possibly, information—and therein could lie a huge competitive advantage.[33]

Entrepreneurial Opportunities

Free enterprise is the economic basis for all entrepreneurial activity. It means that any individual is free to transform an idea into a business. The opportunities for potential entrepreneurs are unlimited. The constantly changing economic environment provides a continuous flow of potential opportunities *if* an individual can recognize a profitable idea amid the chaos and cynicism that also permeates such an environment. Thousands of alternatives exist because every individual creates and develops ideas with a unique frame of reference.

Whether the motivation is profit or independence, or the challenge of developing one's own business, entrepreneurs are actively pursuing ideas and opportunities at a record pace. Consider the following facts:

☐ From 1966 to 2006, self-employment as a primary occupation increased by 50 percent (see Figure 1.3).

☐ Home-based business ownership has exploded into the economy and now represents 52 percent of all small firms and 10 percent of all revenue.

☐ Of the 24.8 million businesses in existence (5.5 million of which are employer businesses), 97 percent are considered small.

☐ Approximately 700,000 new employer firms will be added by 2010 (see Figure 1.4).

☐ Women's share of self-employment is expected to be about equal to that of men by 2005.

☐ The percentage of small businesses with access to the Internet nearly doubled from 1998 to 2005—from 21.5 percent to 41.2 percent, respectively.

☐ Online retail marketing is experiencing about 200 percent annual growth, and online traffic has been doubling every 100 days.

☐ By 2008, it is estimated that almost one-third of all business-to-business transactions will be performed via e-commerce.

Figure 1.3 Self-Employment, 1966–2006

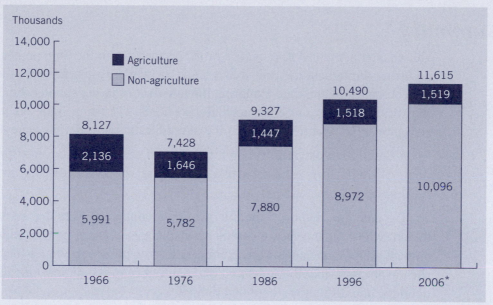

*Estimate.
Note: Data estimated from 1982–1988 Department of Labor data and 1989–1996 Bureau of the Census data. The rate of increase in new employer firms from 1982 to 1998 was used to both forecast subsequent years and impute data for prior years.
Source: Office of Advocacy, U.S. Small Business Administration, from data provided by the Bureau of Labor Statistics.

Figure 1.4 New Employer Firms, 1980–2010

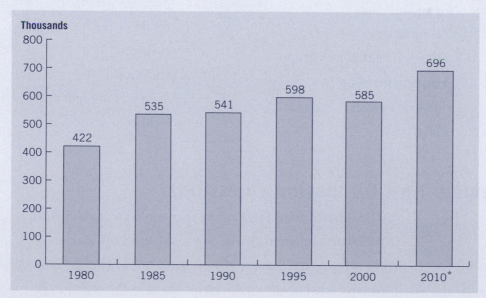

*Estimate.
Note: Data estimated from 1982–1988 Department of Labor data and 1989–1996 Bureau of the Census data. The rate of increase in new employer firms from 1982 to 1998 was used to both forecast subsequent years and impute data for prior years.
Source: Office of Advocacy, U.S. Small Business Administration, from data provided by the Department of Labor, Employment and Training Administration, and the Bureau of the Census, Statistics of U.S. Business.

The opportunities during this century will be immense. Entrepreneurial opportunities will continue to arise for individuals willing to take the risk. As we will see throughout the following chapters, the discipline of entrepreneurship can be learned to better prepare oneself to take advantage of such an entrepreneurial opportunity. Thus, your ability to act entrepreneurially may be enhanced. The decision to act is, and always will be, yours!

Summary

This chapter attempted to provide a broad perspective on the Entrepreneurial Revolution occurring throughout the United States and the world. Beginning with the concept of entrepreneurship and then exploring the mind-set of it, the chapter discussed important statistics supporting our entrepreneurial economy. The major forces in contemporary entrepreneurial research as well as the new educational programs were described.

A description of "gazelles" and their impact on the economy was presented. Gazelles are business establishments with at least 20 percent sales growth every year, starting from a base of $100,000.

The emerging trends of the Internet and e-commerce were discussed. Issues such as the growth of the Internet, e-commerce challenges, domain names, and website development and maintenance were examined. Contemporary strategies for e-commerce—such as the 3-P Growth Model and the importance of the dimensions of reach, richness, and affiliation—were highlighted.

Key Terms and Concepts

affiliation

domain name

e-commerce

Entrepreneurial Revolution

entrepreneurship

gazelle

Internet

National Federation of Independent Business (NFIB)

reach

richness

stickiness

3-P Growth Model

website

Review and Discussion Questions

1. Briefly describe what is meant by the term *entrepreneurship*.
2. Describe the predominance of new ventures in the economy.
3. What is the record number of new small firms being established?
4. How have most *net* new jobs been created in the economy?
5. Identify some of the promising trends for the new millennium.
6. Define a *gazelle* and discuss its importance.
7. Describe the increased use of the Internet by smaller firms.
8. Define the term *e-commerce* and describe all of the elements that it covers.
9. Briefly discuss the challenges facing companies as they seek domain names.
10. What does "stickiness" refer to in regard to a website?
11. Describe the 3-P Growth Model strategy for e-commerce.

Experiential Exercise

Separating Fact from Fiction

Many myths, or fictions, exist about the Internet and e-commerce for entrepreneurs. The following statements can be divided into two groups: fiction and facts. Place an FI before the fictions and an FA before the facts. Answers are provided at the end of the exercise.

1. _____ Building a website can be a complex undertaking.

2. _____ Traffic on a website will make you rich.

3. _____ The Internet is one of the most powerful tools for entrepreneurial businesses.

4. _____ Money is available for any Internet start-up.

5. _____ E-commerce refers to electronic commerce.

6. _____ Razzle-dazzle makes websites great.

7. _____ Domain names are always easy and inexpensive to obtain.

8. _____ Having a brand is everything on the Internet.

9. _____ A website's "stickiness" needs to be monitored.

10. _____ E-commerce does not include e-mail or electronic data interchange.

11. _____ Research shows that smaller ventures utilizing the web have higher annual revenues than those that do not.

12. _____ It has been estimated that a smaller venture may need an initial investment of $10,000 to launch an e-commerce site.

13. _____ ICANN oversees the registration of domain names.

14. _____ Only 20 percent of small firms have access to the Internet.

15. _____ Online retail marketing is currently growing at a rate of 200 percent per year.

Answers: 1. FA, 2. FI, 3. FA, 4. FI, 5. FA, 6. FI, 7. FI, 8. FI, 9. FA, 10. FI, 11. FA, 12. FA, 13. FA, 14. FI, 15. FA

Video Case 1.1

Entrepreneurship in Action
eHarmony with Dr. Neil Clark Warren

Finding a mate for life is something that most of us really desire . . . but how to go about doing it well is maybe one of the largest unmet consumer needs that was out there today. (Greg Forgatch)

Neil Clark Warren, a clinical psychologist and best-selling author, has long been concerned with the increasing numbers of failed marriages in the United States. "If you could reduce the divorce rate from where it is now [over 50 percent], it would be the greatest single social revolution in the history of the human race. And all of a sudden America would be a different country." His research into the key elements that produce happy and lasting marriages culminated in his 1993 book, *Finding the Love of Your Life*.

In 1995, still very much interested in increasing the marriage stability rate in this country, Warren teamed up with Greg Forgatch to provide seminars for single people on how to find a suitable mate that were based on the principles of his book. Warren describes what happened next: "And then . . . [the women] started coming to me and saying . . . 'are there any good men out there? I mean, now you told me how to choose between a bad man and a good man, but I don't meet very many men.' And men would say the same thing, 'Are there any good women out there?'"

Forgatch says that they knew they had some teaching tools, and they wanted to find the most effective way to make the tools available to the maximum number of single people possible. Dating services at the time were off-line, and Warren and Forgatch knew the difficulties involved in mass marketing for a brick and mortar business. So five years and 150 seminars later, they decided to start eHarmony.com, an Internet dating service that now attracts millions of people each year.

While the Internet now hosts many dating services, the distinctive success of eHarmony began with a well-thought-out research design and empirical research studies into the compatibility factors that produce successful marriages. Warren and Forgatch assembled a small number of associates who shared their interests and had key skills to offer the company. The team spent six months on a rudimentary questionnaire that they gave to approximately a thousand happily married people and then refined the questionnaire over the next several months to its current form, which has 436 questions. The team wanted to make sure that they could produce a questionnaire that had a sound scientific base.

"There's not one of those questions that is a duplicate. We don't replicate questions all over the place to just make it hard for you. But we ask you everything we can think of to ask you and, let me tell you, fundamentally, it goes down to this one theoretical point: Everybody gets married because of compatibility. Everybody does. . . . The only difference between the marriages that last and the marriages that don't last is how broad-based the compatibility is," says Warren.

On the practical level, answers to individual questions are grouped as responses to particular patterns, Forgatch explains. "It's all an intellectual-property based system. You can complete the questionnaire. We can assess it using our algorithms, in our modeling, and we can provide you the results online, and we can do it entirely automated so it has no human interaction." The questionnaire is offered to potential clients online free of charge.

Another key factor in its success is eHarmony's integrity. The dating service industry has been tainted with negative accusations that range from its careless superficiality and moneymaking promotions to its pornographic schemes. eHarmony is guided by its founders' interests in matching compatible couples. "We don't have any links going out of eHarmony. We take what users are—what they're doing at eHarmony, their experience—that seriously that we're going to take care of them. . . . We're going to respect their privacy . . . so we're not going to promote to them Club Med or some travel trip," says Forgatch.

Scientific modeling and a dedicated respect for their customers' interests are paying off for eHarmony. It takes 10 to 15 times longer to complete their questionnaire than those presented by other dating services, and their charges can be up to two and a half times more expensive. But they convert three times as many singles to their site because of what they offer.

Warren explains eHarmony's success: "I said, 'Dream a big dream for your marriage.' . . . And I think we've dreamed a big dream for our business. We would love to change the culture. For every 1 percent that you can reduce the divorce rate in America, it will affect a million people in one generation. That's our dream."

Questions

1. Explain how Neil Warren Clark made the transition from psychologist and author to entrepreneur.

2. What are the key elements to eHarmony's success?

3. What steps should eHarmony take in the future to ensure its success in the dating services arena?

Case 1.2

Gazelle . . . or Turtle?

Summit Software, Inc., recently celebrated its fifth year of business. Jim Mueller, the proprietor, started the software manufacturing and distribution company when he was still working as a professor at the local college, but now enjoys being in the fast-paced technology industry. Growth and expansion were easy for Jim thanks to his knowledge, his contacts, and the pool of readily available workers from which to choose. The company that originated in his den now occupies a nice space close to downtown.

Going into the sixth year, Jim continues to serve the same target market with customer support and lengthy projects. He acknowledges that technological advancements and new clientele are in the immediate future. All of the current and forecasted work leaves Jim and his three employees with little time to spend on administrative duties— let alone new accounts. Jim also realizes the company needs its own upgrades to continue its rate of success and to stay competitive. Looking at Summit's financials and the amount of work necessary to maintain the business, he's not sure where to go from here. Following is a snapshot of Jim's annual sales since inception:

Year 1	$112,000
Year 2	195,000
Year 3	250,000
Year 4	335,000
Year 5	487,000

Questions

1. Is Summit Software a gazelle? Support your answer.

2. What problems may Jim face owning such a fast-growing business?

3. Are gazelles more important to the economy than traditional growth businesses? Why or why not?

Case 1.3

To Web or Not To Web

Norah Mallory has been working at her tech-support job for almost three years and considers herself very fortunate to have landed such a perfect job right out of college. Always a go-getter, her ideas, effort, and tenacity got her promoted quickly. Throughout her career, however, she's been itching to get into business for herself. After working first-hand with customers and managing her own team, she believes she now possesses the technical, personal, and customer service skills needed to make the transition.

In her free time, Norah enjoys cooking and baking for herself, peers, and friends. What she really desires is to start a website out of her home devoted to various culinary aspects, including recipes to download and swap, kitchen tips, wine selection, a question-and-answer forum, and product sales and reviews. After reading up on the field, Norah thinks she can even make money by working with vendors to have links and displays on her site.

Norah knows she would need to take some vacation time and upgrade her system at home to create and maintain the site. A co-worker also informed her that most investors want to see an active and productive site before they'll provide any funding. Norah figures that with stocks, savings, friends, and family she could raise about $15,000. She wants to make a decision before another big project comes across her desk and prohibits her from taking any extended leave.

Questions

1. What problems will Norah likely face while trying to start the dot-com business?

2. What is the first step someone should take toward an Internet start-up?

3. Discuss Norah's possibilities given her knowledge and resources.

Notes

1. Jeffry A. Timmons, *New Venture Creation* (Burr Ridge, IL: McGraw-Hill/Irwin, 1999), 3.

2. http://www.bizstat.com, June 2005.

3. William J. Dennis, Jr., *Small Business Policy Guide* (Washington, D.C.: NFIB Foundation, 2000), 12–13.

4. Paul D. Reynolds, Michael Hay, and S. Michael Camp, *Global Entrepreneurship Monitor* (Kauffman Center for Entrepreneurial Leadership, 1999).

5. M. Minniti and W. D. Bygrave, *Global Entrepreneurship Monitor* (Kauffman Center for Entrepreneurial Leadership, 2004).

6. "The New American Revolution: The Role and Impact of Small Firms" (Washington, D.C.: U.S. Small Business Administration, Office of Economic Research, 1998); and William J. Dennis, Jr., and Lloyd W. Fernald, Jr., "The Chances of Financial Success (and Loss) from Small Business Ownership," *Entrepreneurship Theory and Practice* 26(1) (2000): 75–83.

7. Wayne H. Stewart, Warren E. Watson, Joan C. Carland, and James W. Carland, "A Proclivity for Entrepreneurship: A Comparison of Entrepreneurs, Small Business Owners and Corporate Managers," *Journal of Business Venturing* 14(2) (March 1999): 189–214.

8. Dean A. Shepherd and Andrew Zacharakis, "Speed to Initial Public Offering of VC-Backed Companies," *Entrepreneurship Theory and Practice* 25(3) (2001): 59–69; Dean A. Shepherd and Andrew Zacharakis, "Venture Capitalists' Expertise: A Call for Research into Decision Aids and Cognitive Feedback," *Journal of Business Venturing* 17(1)(2002): 1–20; and Lowell W. Busenitz, James O. Fiet, and Douglas D. Moesel, "Reconsidering the Venture Capitalists' 'Value Added' Proposition: An Interorganizational Learning Perspective," *Journal of Business Venturing* 19(6) (2004): 787–807.

9. Shaker A. Zahra, Donald F. Kuratko, and Daniel F. Jennings, "Corporate Entrepreneurship and Wealth Creation: Contemporary and Emerging Perspectives," *Entrepreneurship Theory and Practice* 24(2) (1999): 5–9; Donald F. Kuratko, R. Duane Ireland, and Jeffrey S. Hornsby, "Improving Firm Performance Through Entrepreneurial Actions: Acordia's Corporate Entrepreneurship Strategy," *Academy of Management Executive* 15(4) (2001): 60–71; G. Ahuja and C. M. Lampert, "Entrepreneurship in the Large Corporations: A Longitudinal Study of How Established Firms Create Breakthrough Inventions," *Strategic Management Journal* (special issue) 22(6) (2001): 521–544; and Donald F. Kuratko, Jeffrey S. Hornsby, and Michael G. Goldsby, "Sustaining Corporate Entrepreneurship: A Proposed Model of Perceived Implementation/Outcome Comparisons at

the Organizational and Individual Levels," *International Journal of Entrepreneurship and Innovation*, 5(2) (2004): 77–89.

10. R. Duane Ireland and Michael A. Hitt, "Achieving and Maintaining Strategic Competitiveness in the Twenty-First Century: The Role of Strategic Leadership," *Academy of Management Executive* (January 1999): 43–57; and Michael A. Hitt, R. Duane Ireland, S. Michael Camp, and Donald L. Sexton, "Strategic Entrepreneurship: Entrepreneurial Strategies for Wealth Creation," *Strategic Management Journal* (special issue) 22(6) (2001): 479–492.

11. Robert A. Baron, "Cognitive Mechanisms in Entrepreneurship: Why and When Entrepreneurs Think Differently Than Other People," *Journal of Business Venturing* (April 1998): 275–294; and Jill Kickul and Lisa K. Gundry, "Prospecting for Strategic Advantage: The Proactive Entrepreneurial Personality and Small Firm Innovation," *Journal of Small Business Management* 40(2) (2002): 85–97.

12. Rita G. McGrath, Ian C. MacMillan, and S. Scheinberg, "Elitists, Risk Takers and Rugged Individualists? An Exploratory Analysis of Cultural Differences Between Entrepreneurs and Non-entrepreneurs," *Journal of Business Venturing* (1992): 115–136; and Justin Tan, "Innovation and Risk-Taking in a Transitional Economy: A Comparative Study of Chinese Managers and Entrepreneurs," *Journal of Business Venturing* 16(4) (2001): 359–376.

13. Lisa K. Gundry and Harold P. Welsch, "The Ambitious Entrepreneur: High Growth Strategies of Women-Owned Enterprises," *Journal of Business Venturing* 16(5) (2001): 453–470; and Radha Chaganit and Patricia G. Greene, "Who Are Ethnic Entrepreneurs? A Study of Entrepreneurs' Ethnic Involvement and Business Characteristics," *Journal of Small Business Management* 40(2) (2002): 126–143.

14. Shaker A. Zahra, James Hayton, Jeremy Marcel, and Hugh O'Neill, "Fostering Entrepreneurship During International Expansion: Managing Key Challenges," *European Management Journal* 19(4) (2001): 359–369; Mike W. Peng, "How Entrepreneurs Create Wealth in Transition Economies," *Academy of Management Executive* 15(1) (2001): 95–110; and Paul Westhead, Mike Wright, and Deniz Ucbasaran, "The Internationalization of New and Small Firms: A Resource-Based View," *Journal of Business Venturing* 16(4) (2001): 333–358.

15. M. Minniti and W. D. Bygrave, *Global Entrepreneurship Monitor* (Kauffman Center for Entrepreneurial Leadership, 2004); and Nancy Upton, Elisabeth J. Teal, and Joe T. Felan, "Strategic and Business Planning Practices of Fast-Growing Family Firms," *Journal of Small Business Management* 39(4) (2001): 60–72.

16. Alberta Charney and Gary D. Libecap, "Impact of Entrepreneurship Education," *Insights: A Kauffman Research Series* (Kauffman Center for Entrepreneurial Leadership, 2000); Donald F. Kuratko, "The Emergence of Entrepreneurship Education: Development, Trends, Challenges," *Entrepreneurship Theory and Practice* 29(3) (2005): 577–598; and Jerry A. Katz "The Chronology and Intellectual Trajectory of American Entrepreneurship Education," *Journal of Business Venturing* 18(2) (2003): 283–300.

17. See, for example, *Frontiers of Entrepreneurship Research* (Wellesley, MA: Babson College, series of volumes, 1981–2005).

18. David Birch's research firm, Cognetics, Inc., traces the employment and sales records of some 14 million companies with a Dun & Bradstreet file.

19. David Birch, Jan Gundersen, Anne Haggerty, and William Parsons, *Corporate Demographics* (Cambridge, MA: Cognetics, Inc., 1999).

20. Ibid.

21. Peter F. Drucker, "Beyond the Information Revolution," *Atlantic Monthly* (October 1999): 47–57.

22. *E-Commerce: Small Business Ventures Online* (Washington, D.C.: U.S. Small Business Administration, Office of Advocacy, 1999) http://www.sba.gov/advo/research.

23. U.S. Department of Census, *E-Stats* (June 2005) http://www.census.gov/estats).

24. *E-Commerce: Small Business Ventures Online,* 1999.

25. http://www.zooknic.com/Domains/counts.html.

26. A. Michael Froomkin, "Wrong Turn in Cyberspace: Using ICANN to Route around the APA and the Constitution," *Duke Law Journal* 50(17) (2000): 17–184.

27. http://www.internic.net/alpha.html.

28. http://www.icann.org/tlds/.

29. George Anders, "Better, Faster, Prettier," *The Wall Street Journal* (E-Commerce special, November 22, 1999): R6.

30. Joelle Tessler, "Small Investment, Big Results," *The Wall Street Journal* (E-Commerce special, November 22, 1999): R16.

31. Steve Bennett and Stacey Miller, "The E-Commerce Plunge," *Small Business Computing* (February 2000): 48–52.

32. Philip Evans and Thomas S. Wurster, "Getting Real About Virtual Commerce," *Harvard Business Review* (November–December 1999): 85–94.

33. Philip Evans and Thomas S. Wurser, *Blown to Bits: The New Economics of Information Transforms Strategy* (Boston: Harvard Business School Press, 1999).

2

The Evolutionary Development of Entrepreneurship

Most of what you hear about entrepreneurship, says America's leading management thinker, is all wrong. It's not magic; it's not mysterious; and it has nothing to do with genes. It's a discipline and, like any discipline, it can be learned.

Peter F. Drucker

Innovation and Entrepreneurship

Chapter Objectives

1 To examine the historical development of entrepreneurship

2 To explore and debunk the myths of entrepreneurship

3 To define and explore the major schools of entrepreneurial thought

4 To explain the process approaches to the study of entrepreneurship

5 To set forth a comprehensive definition of entrepreneurship

The Evolution of Entrepreneurship

The word *entrepreneur* is derived from the French *entreprendre,* meaning "to undertake." The **entrepreneur** is one who undertakes to organize, manage, and assume the risks of a business. In recent years entrepreneurs have been doing so many things that it is necessary to broaden this definition. Today, an entrepreneur is an innovator or developer who recognizes and seizes opportunities; converts those opportunities into workable/marketable ideas; adds value through time, effort, money, or skills; assumes the risks of the competitive marketplace to implement these ideas; and realizes the rewards from these efforts.[1]

The entrepreneur is the aggressive catalyst for change in the world of business. He or she is an independent thinker who dares to be different in a background of common events. The literature of entrepreneurial research reveals some similarities, as well as a great many differences, in the characteristics of entrepreneurs. Chief among these characteristics are personal initiative, the ability to consolidate resources, management skills, a desire for autonomy, and risk taking. Other characteristics include aggressiveness, competitiveness, goal-oriented behavior, confidence, opportunistic behavior, intuitiveness, reality-based actions, the ability to learn from mistakes, and the ability to employ human relations skills.[2]

Although no single definition of *entrepreneur* exists and no one profile can represent today's entrepreneur, research is providing an increasingly sharper focus on the subject. A brief review of the history of entrepreneurship illustrates this.

America currently is in the midst of a new wave of business and economic development, and entrepreneurship is its catalyst. Yet the social and economic forces of entrepreneurial activity existed long before the new millennium. In fact, as noted in Chapter 1, the entrepreneurial spirit has driven many of humanity's achievements.

Humanity's progress from caves to campuses has been explained in numerous ways. But central to virtually all of these theories has been the role of the "agent of change," the force that initiates and implements material progress. Today we recognize that the agent of change in human history has been and most likely will continue to be the entrepreneur.[3]

The recognition of entrepreneurs dates back to eighteenth-century France when economist Richard Cantillon associated the "risk-bearing" activity in the economy with the entrepreneur. In England during the same period, the Industrial Revolution was evolving, with the entrepreneur playing a visible role in risk taking and the transformation of resources.[4]

The association of entrepreneurship and economics has long been the accepted norm. In fact, until the 1950s the majority of definitions and references to entrepreneurship had come from economists. For example, Cantillon (1725), just mentioned; Jean Baptiste Say (1803), the renowned French economist; and Joseph Schumpeter (1934), a twentieth-century economic genius, all wrote about entrepreneurship and its impact on economic development.[5] Over the decades writers have continued to try to describe or define what entrepreneurship is all about. Here are some examples:

> Entrepreneurship . . . consists in doing things that are not generally done in the ordinary course of business routine; it is essentially a phenomenon that comes under the wider aspect of leadership.[6]

> Entrepreneurship, at least in all nonauthoritarian societies, constitutes a bridge between society as a whole, especially the noneconomic aspects of that society, and the profit-oriented institutions established to take advantage of its economic endowments and to satisfy, as best they can, its economic desires.[7]

> In ... entrepreneurship, there is agreement that we are talking about a kind of behavior that includes: (1) initiative taking, (2) the organizing or reorganizing of social economic mechanisms to turn resources and situations to practical account, and (3) the acceptance of risk of failure.[8]

After reviewing the evolution of entrepreneurship and examining its varying definitions, Robert C. Ronstadt put together a summary description:

> Entrepreneurship is the dynamic process of creating incremental wealth. This wealth is created by individuals who assume the major risks in terms of equity, time, and/or career commitment of providing value for some product or service. The product or service itself may or may not be new or unique but value must somehow be infused by the entrepreneur by securing and allocating the necessary skills and resources.[9]

Entrepreneurship as a topic for discussion and analysis was introduced by the economists of the eighteenth century, and it continued to attract the interest of economists in the nineteenth century. In the twentieth century, the word became synonymous or at least closely linked with free enterprise and capitalism. Also, it was generally recognized that entrepreneurs serve as agents of change; provide creative, innovative ideas for business enterprises; and help businesses grow and become profitable.

Whatever the specific activity they engage in, entrepreneurs in the twenty-first century are considered the heroes of free enterprise. Many of them have used innovation and creativity to build multimillion-dollar enterprises from fledgling businesses—some in less than a decade! These individuals have created new products and services and have assumed the risks associated with these ventures. Many people now regard entrepreneurship as "pioneership" on the frontier of business.

In recognizing the importance of the evolution of entrepreneurship into the twenty-first century, we have developed an integrated definition that acknowledges the critical factors needed for this phenomenon.

> Entrepreneurship is a dynamic process of vision, change, and creation. It requires an application of energy and passion toward the creation and implementation of new ideas and creative solutions. Essential ingredients include the willingness to take calculated risks—in terms of time, equity, or career; the ability to formulate an effective venture team; the creative skill to marshal needed resources; the fundamental skill of building a solid business plan; and, finally, the vision to recognize opportunity where others see chaos, contradiction, and confusion.

The Myths of Entrepreneurship

Throughout the years many myths have arisen about entrepreneurship. These myths are the result of a lack of research on entrepreneurship. As many researchers in the field have noted, the study of entrepreneurship is still emerging, and thus "folklore" will tend to prevail until it is dispelled with contemporary research findings. Ten of the most notable myths with an explanation to dispel each myth appear next.

Myth 1: Entrepreneurs Are Doers, Not Thinkers

Although it is true entrepreneurs tend toward action, they are also thinkers. Indeed, they are often very methodical people who plan their moves carefully. The emphasis today on the creation of clear and complete business plans (Chapter 11) is an indication that "thinking" entrepreneurs are as important as "doing" entrepreneurs.

Myth 2: Entrepreneurs Are Born, Not Made

The idea that the characteristics of entrepreneurs cannot be taught or learned, that they are innate traits one must be born with, has long been prevalent. These traits include aggressiveness, initiative, drive, a willingness to take risks, analytical ability, and skill in human relations. Today, however, the recognition of entrepreneurship as a discipline is helping to dispel this myth. Like all disciplines, entrepreneurship has models, processes, and case studies that allow the topic to be studied and the knowledge to be acquired.

Myth 3: Entrepreneurs Are Always Inventors

The idea that entrepreneurs are inventors is a result of misunderstanding and tunnel vision. Although many inventors are also entrepreneurs, numerous entrepreneurs encompass all sorts of innovative activity.[10] For example, Ray Kroc did not invent the fast-food franchise, but his innovative ideas made McDonald's the largest fast-food enterprise in the world. A contemporary understanding of entrepreneurship covers more than just invention. It requires a complete understanding of innovative behavior in all forms.

Myth 4: Entrepreneurs Are Academic and Social Misfits

The belief that entrepreneurs are academically and socially ineffective is a result of some business owners having started successful enterprises after dropping out of school or quitting a job. In many cases such an event has been blown out of proportion in an attempt to "profile" the typical entrepreneur. Historically, in fact, educational and social organizations did not recognize the entrepreneur. They abandoned him or her as a misfit in a world of corporate giants. Business education, for example, was aimed primarily at the study of corporate activity. Today the entrepreneur is considered a hero—socially, economically, and academically. No longer a misfit, the entrepreneur is now viewed as a professional.

Myth 5: Entrepreneurs Must Fit the "Profile"

Many books and articles have presented checklists of characteristics of the successful entrepreneur. These lists were neither validated nor complete; they were based on case studies and on research findings among achievement-oriented people. Today we realize that a standard entrepreneurial profile is hard to compile. The environment, the venture itself, and the entrepreneur have interactive effects, which result in many different types of profiles. Contemporary studies conducted at universities across the United States will, in the future, provide more accurate insights into the various profiles of successful entrepreneurs. As we will show in Chapter 4, an "Entrepreneurial Mind-set" within individuals is more understandable than a particular profile.

Myth 6: All Entrepreneurs Need Is Money

It is true that a venture needs capital to survive; it is also true that a large number of business failures occur because of a lack of adequate financing. Yet having money is not the only bulwark against failure. Failure due to a lack of proper financing often is entrepreneurship IN PRACTICE

The E-Myth

Michael E. Gerber has written a book titled *The E-Myth: Why Most Businesses Don't Work and What to Do About It.* He clearly delineates the differences among the types of people involved with contemporary small businesses. These people are the following:

☐ The *entrepreneur* invents a business that works without him or her. This person is a visionary who makes a business unique by imbuing it with a special and exciting sense of purpose and direction. The entrepreneur's far-reaching perspective enables him or her to anticipate changes and needs in the marketplace and to initiate activities to capitalize on them.

☐ The *manager* produces results through employees by developing and implementing effective systems and, by interacting with employees, enhances their self-esteem and ability to produce good results. The manager can actualize the entrepreneur's vision through planning, implementation, and analysis.

☐ The *technician* performs specific tasks according to systems and standards management developed. The technician, in the best of businesses, not only gets the work done but also provides input to supervisors for improvement of those systems and standards.

Understanding these definitions is important, because Gerber contends that most small businesses *don't work;* their owners do. In other words, he believes that today's small-business owner works too hard at a job that he or she has created for himself or herself rather than working to create a business. Thus, most small businesses fail because the owner is more of a "technician" than an "entrepreneur." Working only as a technician, the small-business owner realizes too little reward for so much effort, and eventually, according to Gerber, the business fails.

The E-Myth is that today's business owners are not true entrepreneurs who create businesses but merely technicians who now have created a job for themselves. The solution to this myth lies in the owner's willingness to begin thinking and acting like a true entrepreneur: to imagine how the business would work without him or her. In other words, the owner must begin working on the business, in addition to working in it. He or she must leverage the company's capacity through systems development and implementation. The whole key is a person developing an "entrepreneurial perspective."

SOURCE: Adapted from Michael E. Gerber, *The E-Myth Revisited: Why Most Businesses Don't Work and What to Do about It* (New York: Harper Business, 1995); and personal interview, 1993.

an indicator of other problems: managerial incompetence, lack of financial understanding, poor investments, poor planning, and the like. Many successful entrepreneurs have overcome the lack of money while establishing their ventures. To those entrepreneurs, money is a resource but never an end in itself.

Myth 7: All Entrepreneurs Need Is Luck

Being at "the right place at the right time" is always an advantage. But "luck happens when preparation meets opportunity" is an equally appropriate adage. Prepared entrepreneurs who seize the opportunity when it arises often seem "lucky." They are, in fact, simply better prepared to deal with situations and turn them into successes. What appears to be luck really is preparation, determination, desire, knowledge, and innovativeness.

Myth 8: Ignorance Is Bliss for Entrepreneurs

The myth that too much planning and evaluation lead to constant problems—that overanalysis leads to paralysis—does not hold up in today's competitive markets, which demand detailed planning and preparation. Identifying a venture's strengths and weaknesses, setting up clear timetables with contingencies for handling problems, and minimizing these problems through careful strategy formulation are all key factors for successful entrepreneurship. Thus careful planning—not ignorance of it—is the mark of an accomplished entrepreneur.

Myth 9: Entrepreneurs Seek Success but Experience High Failure Rates

It is true that many entrepreneurs suffer a number of failures before they are successful. They follow the adage "If at first you don't succeed, try, try, again." In fact, failure can teach many lessons to those willing to learn and often leads to future successes. This is clearly shown by the **corridor principle**, which states that with every venture launched, new and unintended opportunities often arise. The 3M Corporation invented Post-it Notes using a glue that had not been strong enough for its intended use. Rather than throw away the glue, the company focused on finding another use for it and, in the process, developed a multimillion-dollar product. Yet, the statistics of entrepreneurial failure rates have been misleading over the years. In fact, one researcher, Bruce A. Kirchoff, has reported that the "high failure rate" most commonly accepted might be misleading. Tracing 814,000 businesses started in 1977, Kirchoff found that more than 50 percent were still surviving under their original owners or new owners. Additionally, 28 percent voluntarily closed down, and only 18 percent actually "failed" in the sense of leaving behind outstanding liabilities.[11]

Myth 10: Entrepreneurs Are Extreme Risk Takers (Gamblers)

As we will show in Chapter 4, the concept of risk is a major element in the entrepreneurial process. However, the public's perception of the risk most entrepreneurs assume is distorted. Although it may appear that an entrepreneur is "gambling" on a wild chance, the fact is the entrepreneur is usually working on a moderate or "calculated" risk. Most successful entrepreneurs work hard through planning and preparation to minimize the risk involved in order to better control the destiny of their vision.

These ten myths have been presented to provide a background for today's current thinking on entrepreneurship. By sidestepping the "folklore," we can build a foundation for critically researching the contemporary theories and processes of entrepreneurship.

Approaches to Entrepreneurship

To understand the nature of entrepreneurship, it is important to consider some of the theory development so as to better recognize the emerging importance of entrepreneurship. The research on entrepreneurship has grown dramatically over the years. As the field has developed, research methodology has progressed from empirical surveys of entrepreneurs to more contextual and process-oriented research. Theory development is what drives a field of study. Entrepreneurship theory has been developing over the last 20 years and it is apparent that the field is growing. More important, we need to understand some of that development in order to better appreciate the discipline of entrepreneurship. Also, the study of the basic theories in entrepreneurship helps to form a foundation upon which a student can build an understanding of the process and practice of entrepreneurship.

A theory of entrepreneurship is defined as a verifiable and logically coherent formulation of relationships, or underlying principles that either explain entrepreneurship, predict entrepreneurial activity (for example, by characterizing conditions that are likely to lead to new profit opportunities to the formation of new enterprises), or provide normative guidance (that is, prescribe the right action in particular circumstances).[12] As we are now in the new millennium, it has become increasingly apparent that we need to have some cohesive theories or classifications to better understand this emerging field.

In the study of contemporary entrepreneurship, one concept recurs: Entrepreneurship is interdisciplinary. As such it contains various approaches that can increase one's understanding of the field.[13] Thus we need to recognize the diversity of theories as an emergence of entrepreneurial understanding. One way to examine these theories is with a "schools of thought" approach that divides entrepreneurship into specific activities. These activities may be within a "macro" view or a "micro" view, yet all address the conceptual nature of entrepreneurship.

The Schools of Entrepreneurial Thought

In this section we will highlight the ideas emanating from the macro and micro views of entrepreneurial thought, and we will further break down these two major views into six distinct schools of thought, three within each entrepreneurial view (see Figure 2.1). Although this presentation does not purport to be all-inclusive, neither does it claim to limit the schools to these six, for a movement may develop for unification or expansion. Whatever the future holds, however, it is important to become familiar with these conceptual ideas on entrepreneurship to avoid the semantic warfare that has plagued general management thought for so many years.[14]

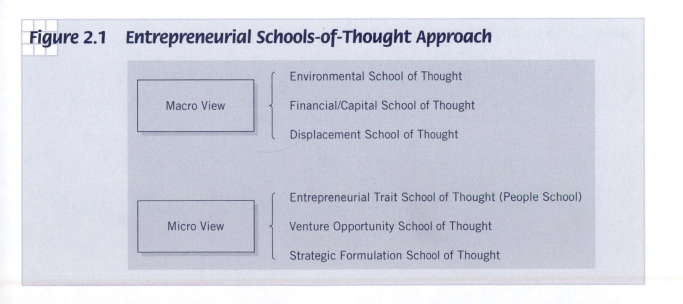

Figure 2.1   Entrepreneurial Schools-of-Thought Approach

Macro View
- Environmental School of Thought
- Financial/Capital School of Thought
- Displacement School of Thought

Micro View
- Entrepreneurial Trait School of Thought (People School)
- Venture Opportunity School of Thought
- Strategic Formulation School of Thought

The Macro View

The **macro view of entrepreneurship** presents a broad array of factors that relate to success or failure in contemporary entrepreneurial ventures. This array includes external processes that are sometimes beyond the control of the individual entrepreneur, for they exhibit a strong **external locus of control** point of view.

Three schools of entrepreneurial thought represent a breakdown of the macro view: (1) the environmental school of thought, (2) the financial/capital school of thought, and (3) the displacement school of thought. The first of these is the broadest and the most pervasive school.

The Environmental School of Thought   This school of thought deals with the external factors that affect a potential entrepreneur's lifestyle. These can be either positive or negative forces in the molding of entrepreneurial desires. The focus is on institutions, values, and mores that, grouped together, form a sociopolitical environmental framework that strongly influences the development of entrepreneurs.[15] For example, if a middle manager experiences the freedom and support to develop ideas, initiate contracts, or create and institute new methods, the work environment will serve to promote that person's desire to pursue an entrepreneurial career. Another environmental factor that often affects the potential development of entrepreneurs is their social group. The atmosphere of friends and relatives can influence the desire to become an entrepreneur.

The Financial/Capital School of Thought   This school of thought is based on the capital-seeking process. The search for seed and growth capital is the entire focus of this entrepreneurial emphasis. Certain literature is devoted specifically to this process, whereas other sources tend to treat it as but one segment of the entrepreneurial process.[16] In any case, the venture capital process is vital to an entrepreneur's development. Business-planning guides and texts for entrepreneurs emphasize this phase, and development seminars focusing on the funds application process are offered throughout the country on a continuous basis. This school of thought views the entire entrepreneurial venture from a financial management standpoint. As is apparent from Table 2.1, decisions involving finances occur at every major point in the venture process.

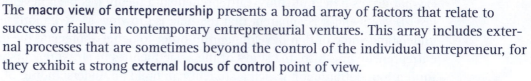

Table 2.1   Financial Analysis Emphasis

VENTURE STAGE	FINANCIAL CONSIDERATION	DECISION
Start-up or acquisition	Seed capital Venture capital sources	Proceed or abandon
Ongoing	Cash management Investments Financial analysis and evaluation	Maintain, increase, or reduce size
Decline or succession	Profit question Corporate buyout Succession question	Sell, retire, or dissolve operations

The Displacement School of Thought   This school of thought focuses on the negative side of group phenomena where someone feels "out of place" or is literally "displaced" from the group. It holds that the group hinders a person from advancing or eliminates certain critical factors needed for that person to advance. Due to such actions the frustrated individual will be projected into an entrepreneurial pursuit out of his or her own motivations to succeed. As Ronstadt has noted, individuals will not pursue a venture unless they are prevented or displaced from doing other activities.[17] Three major types of displacement illustrate this school of thought:

1. *Political displacement.* This is caused by factors ranging from an entire political regime that rejects free enterprise (international environment) to governmental regulations and policies that limit or redirect certain industries.

2. *Cultural displacement.* This deals with social groups precluded from professional fields. Ethnic background, religion, race, and sex are all examples of factors that figure in the minority experience. Increasingly, this experience will turn various individuals from standard business professions and toward entrepreneurial ventures. According to the U.S. government, the number of minority businesses grew by nearly half a million during the last ten years and represents one-tenth of all the nation's businesses.[18]

3. *Economic displacement.* This is concerned with the economic variations of recession and depression. Job loss, capital shrinkage, or simply "bad times" can create the foundation for entrepreneurial pursuits, just as it can affect venture development and reduction.

These examples of displacement illustrate the external forces that can influence the development of entrepreneurship. Cultural awareness, knowledge of political and public policy, and economic indoctrination will aid and improve entrepreneurial understanding under the displacement school of thought. The broader the educational base in economics and political science, the stronger the entrepreneurial understanding.

The Micro View

The **micro view of entrepreneurship** examines the factors that are specific to entrepreneurship and are part of the **internal locus of control**. The potential entrepreneur has the ability, or control, to direct or adjust the outcome of each major influence in this view. Although some researchers have developed this approach into various definitions and segments, as shown in Table 2.2, our approach presents the entrepreneurial trait theory (sometimes referred to as the "people school of thought"), the venture opportunity theory, and the strategic formulation theory. Unlike the macro approach, which focuses on events from the outside looking in, the micro approach concentrates on specifics from the inside looking out. The first of these schools of thought is the most widely recognized.

The Entrepreneurial Trait School of Thought   Many researchers and writers have been interested in identifying traits common to successful entrepreneurs.[19] This approach is grounded in the study of successful people who tend to exhibit similar characteristics that, if copied, would increase success opportunities for the emulators. For example, achievement, creativity, determination, and technical knowledge are four factors that *usually* are exhibited by successful entrepreneurs. Family development and

Table 2.2 Definitions and Criteria of One Approach to the Micro View

ENTREPRENEURIAL MODEL	DEFINITION	MEASURES	QUESTIONS
"Great Person"	"Extraordinary Achievers"	Personal principles Personal histories Experiences	What principles do you have? What are your achievements?
Psychological Characteristics	Founder Control over the means of production	Locus of control Tolerance of ambiguity Need for achievement	What are your values?
Classical	People who make innovations bearing risk and uncertainty "Creative destruction"	Decision making Ability to see opportunities Creativity	What are the opportunities? What is your vision? How do you respond?
Management	Creating value through the recognition of business opportunity, the management of risk taking . . . through the communicative and management skills to mobilize . . .	Expertise Technical knowledge Technical plans	What are your plans? What are your capabilities? What are your credentials?
Leadership	"Social architect" Promotion and protection of values	Attitudes, styles Management of people	How do you manage people?
Intrapreneurship	Those who pull together to promote innovation	Decision making	How do you change and adapt?

Source: Adapted from J. Barton Cunningham and Joe Lischeron, "Defining Entrepreneurship," *Journal of Small Business Management* (January 1991): 56.

educational incubation are also examined. Certain researchers have argued against educational development of entrepreneurs because they believe it inhibits the creative and challenging nature of entrepreneurship.[20] Other authors, however, contend that new programs and new educational developments are on the increase because they have been found to aid in entrepreneurial development.[21] The family development idea focuses on the nurturing and support that exist within the home atmosphere of an entrepreneurial family. This reasoning promotes the belief that certain traits established and supported early in life will lead eventually to entrepreneurial success.

The Venture Opportunity School of Thought   This school of thought focuses on the opportunity aspect of venture development. The search for idea sources, the development of concepts, and the implementation of venture opportunities are the important interest areas for this school. Creativity and market awareness are viewed as essential. Additionally, according to this school of thought, developing the right idea at the right time for the right market niche is the key to entrepreneurial success.

Another development from this school of thought is the previously described *corridor principle.* New pathways or opportunities will arise that lead entrepreneurs in different directions. The ability to recognize these opportunities when they arise and to implement the necessary steps for action are key factors. The maxim that preparation meeting opportunity equals "luck" underlies this corridor principle. Proponents of this school of thought believe that proper preparation in the interdisciplinary business segments will enhance the ability to recognize venture opportunities.

The Strategic Formulation School of Thought   George Steiner has stated that "strategic planning is inextricably interwoven into the entire fabric of management; it is not something separate and distinct from the process of management."[22] The strategic formulation approach to entrepreneurial theory emphasizes the planning process in successful venture development.[23]

Ronstadt views strategic formulation as a leveraging of unique elements.[24] Unique markets, unique people, unique products, or unique resources are identified, used, or constructed into effective venture formations. The interdisciplinary aspects of strategic adaptation become apparent in the characteristic elements listed here with their corresponding strategies:

- ☐ *Unique markets.* Mountain versus **mountain gap strategies**, which refers to identifying major market segments as well as interstice (in-between) markets that arise from larger markets.

- ☐ *Unique people.* **Great chef strategies**, which refers to the skills or special talents of one or more individuals around whom the venture is built.

- ☐ *Unique products.* **Better widget strategies**, which refers to innovations that encompass new or existing markets.

- ☐ *Unique resources.* **Water well strategies**, which refers to the ability to gather or harness special resources (land, labor, capital, raw materials) over the long term.

Without question, the strategic formulation school encompasses a breadth of managerial capability that requires an interdisciplinary approach.[25]

Schools of Entrepreneurial Thought: A Summary

Although the knowledge and research available in entrepreneurship are in an emerging stage, it is still possible to piece together and describe current schools of thought in the field. From this point we can begin to develop an appreciation for the schools and view them as a foundation for entrepreneurial theory. However, just as the field of management has used a "jungle" of theories as a basis for understanding the field and its capabilities, so too must the field of entrepreneurship use a number of theories in its growth and development.

the entrepreneurial
PROCESS

Patterns of Industry Evolution

The technological revolution connected people and markets much faster than ever, it led to lunacy in the stock market, and share prices were sweltering before companies were even in business. Soon after, stocks plunged 85 percent, leaving hundreds of companies and some banks broke. Does history repeat itself? You better believe it does. This description doesn't apply to the high-tech crash of 2000, but it does fit the steam-locomotion industry in England during the mid-1800s.

Much like the flair of dot-com start-ups, the new technology of 1850 was "Railway-Mania," and similar to the high-tech crash, the British stock market also bombed. However, only two decades later, railroads began carrying more than four times as many passengers than before. This pattern holds true for three other economic movements: the Industrial Revolution in the late 1700s, the cheap steel and electricity in the late 1800s, and the automobile and mass-production era in the early 1900s.

The Internet, however, is only the latest development in a much larger IT revolution, so it may not carry as much weight as the advent of electricity or the automobile. More important,

people's habits take years to change despite how compelling the technology may be.

Looking forward, the electronic commerce build-out will be relatively slow and encompass many more ups and downs. Just like the railroad industry prematurely pushing for rail lines between small towns, the Internet must coexist for some time with old methods until a payoff in lower costs and greater productivity is realized. People, companies, and government must adapt their work and lives in order to take advantage of these new technologies. Supportive technologies, such as broadband connections, will provide instant access to allow individuals to further integrate the Internet into their lives, making changes easier rather than forcing people to adapt. This is all more likely to happen when companies realize the Internet is a tool to improve business processes, not necessarily a business unto itself. New opportunities will only surface once people change how they do things. Time and time again, the surviving companies move on to produce their industry's greatest impact on society.

SOURCE: "How E-biz Rose, Fell, and Will Rise Anew," *BusinessWeek Online* (May 13, 2002).

Process Approaches

Another way to examine the activities involved in entrepreneurship is through a process approach. Although numerous methods and models attempt to structure the entrepreneurial process and its various factors, we shall examine three of the more traditional process approaches here.[26] First, we will discuss the "integrative" approach, as described by Michael H. Morris, P. Lewis, and Donald L. Sexton.[27] Their model incorporates theoretical and practical concepts as they affect entrepreneurship activity.

The second approach is an assessment process based on an entrepreneurial perspective developed by Robert C. Ronstadt. The third process approach, developed by William B. Gartner, is multidimensional and weaves together the concepts of individual, environment, organization, and process. All of these methods attempt to describe the entrepreneurial process as a consolidation of diverse factors, which is the thrust of this book.

An "Integrative" Approach

A more integrative picture of the entrepreneurial process is provided by Morris et al. (1994).[28] Presented in Figure 2.2, this model is built around the concepts of input to the entrepreneurial process and outcomes from the entrepreneurial process. The input component of Figure 2.2 focuses on the entrepreneurial process itself and identifies five key elements that contribute to the process. The first is environmental opportunities, such as a demographic change, the development of a new technology, or a modification to current regulations. Next is the individual entrepreneur, the person who assumes personal responsibility for conceptualizing and implementing a new venture. The entrepreneur develops some type of business concept to capitalize on the opportunity (e.g., a creative approach to solving a particular customer need). Implementing this business concept typically requires some type of organizational context, which could range from a sole proprietorship run out of the entrepreneur's home or a franchise of some national chain to an autonomous business unit within a large corporation. Finally, a wide variety of financial and nonfinancial resources are required on an ongoing basis. These key elements are then combined throughout the stages of the entrepreneurial process. Stated differently, the process provides a logical framework for organizing entrepreneurial inputs.

Figure 2.2 An Integrative Model of Entrepreneurial Inputs and Outcomes

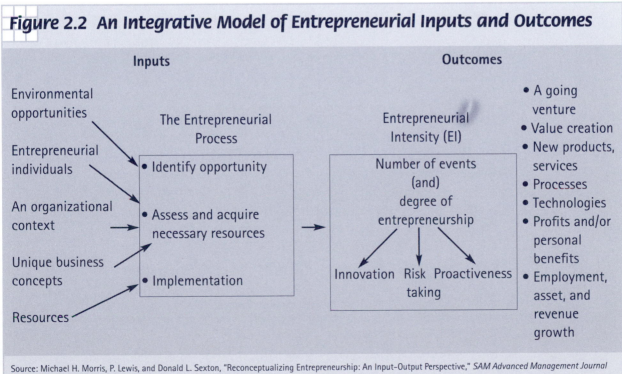

Source: Michael H. Morris, P. Lewis, and Donald L. Sexton, "Reconceptualizing Entrepreneurship: An Input-Output Perspective," *SAM Advanced Management Journal* 59(1) (winter 1994): 21–31.

The outcome component of Figure 2.2 first includes the level of entrepreneurship being achieved. As we shall discuss in more detail in the next chapter, entrepreneurship is a variable. Thus, the process can result in any number of entrepreneurial events and can produce events that vary considerably in terms of how entrepreneurial they are. Based on this level of "entrepreneurial intensity," final outcomes can include one or more going ventures, value creation, new products and processes, new technologies, profit, jobs, and economic growth. Moreover, the outcome can certainly be failure and thereby bring about the economic, psychic, and social costs associated with failure.

This model not only provides a fairly comprehensive picture regarding the nature of entrepreneurship, but can also be applied at different levels. For example, the model describes the phenomenon of entrepreneurship in both the independent start-up company and within a department, division, or strategic business unit of a large corporation.

Entrepreneurial Assessment Approach

Another model, developed by Robert C. Ronstadt, stresses making assessments qualitatively, quantitatively, strategically, and ethically in regard to the entrepreneur, the venture, and the environment.[29] (Figure 2.3 depicts this model.) To examine entrepreneurship, the results of these assessments must be compared to the stage of the entrepreneurial career—early, midcareer, or late. Ronstadt termed this process "the entrepreneurial perspective." We focus on this idea in Chapter 4 when we examine the individual characteristics of entrepreneurship.

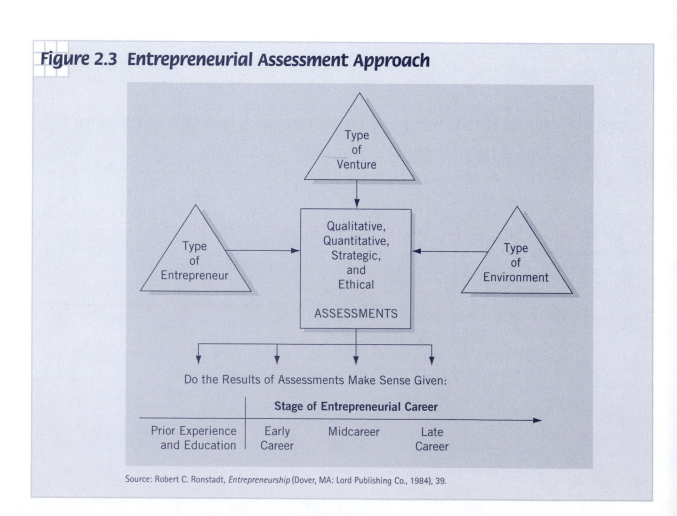

Figure 2.3 Entrepreneurial Assessment Approach

Type of Venture

Type of Entrepreneur

Qualitative, Quantitative, Strategic, and Ethical

ASSESSMENTS

Type of Environment

Do the Results of Assessments Make Sense Given:

Stage of Entrepreneurial Career

Prior Experience and Education | Early Career | Midcareer | Late Career

Source: Robert C. Ronstadt, *Entrepreneurship* (Dover, MA: Lord Publishing Co., 1984), 39.

Multidimensional Approach

A more detailed process approach to entrepreneurship is the **multidimensional approach**.[30] In this view entrepreneurship is a complex, multidimensional framework that emphasizes the individual, the environment, the organization, and the venture process. Specific factors that relate to each of these dimensions follow.

THE INDIVIDUAL

1. Need for achievement
2. Locus of control
3. Risk-taking propensity
4. Job satisfaction
5. Previous work experience
6. Entrepreneurial parents
7. Age
8. Education

THE ENVIRONMENT

1. Venture capital availability
2. Presence of experienced entrepreneurs
3. Technically skilled labor force
4. Accessibility of suppliers
5. Accessibility of customers or new markets
6. Governmental influences
7. Proximity of universities
8. Availability of land or facilities
9. Accessibility of transportation
10. Attitude of the area population
11. Availability of supporting services
12. Living conditions

THE ORGANIZATION

1. Type of firm
2. Entrepreneurial environment
3. Partners
4. Strategic variables
    a. Cost
    b. Differentiation
    c. Focus
5. Competitive entry wedges

THE PROCESS

1. Locating a business opportunity
2. Accumulating resources

Figure 2.4 Variables in New-Venture Creation

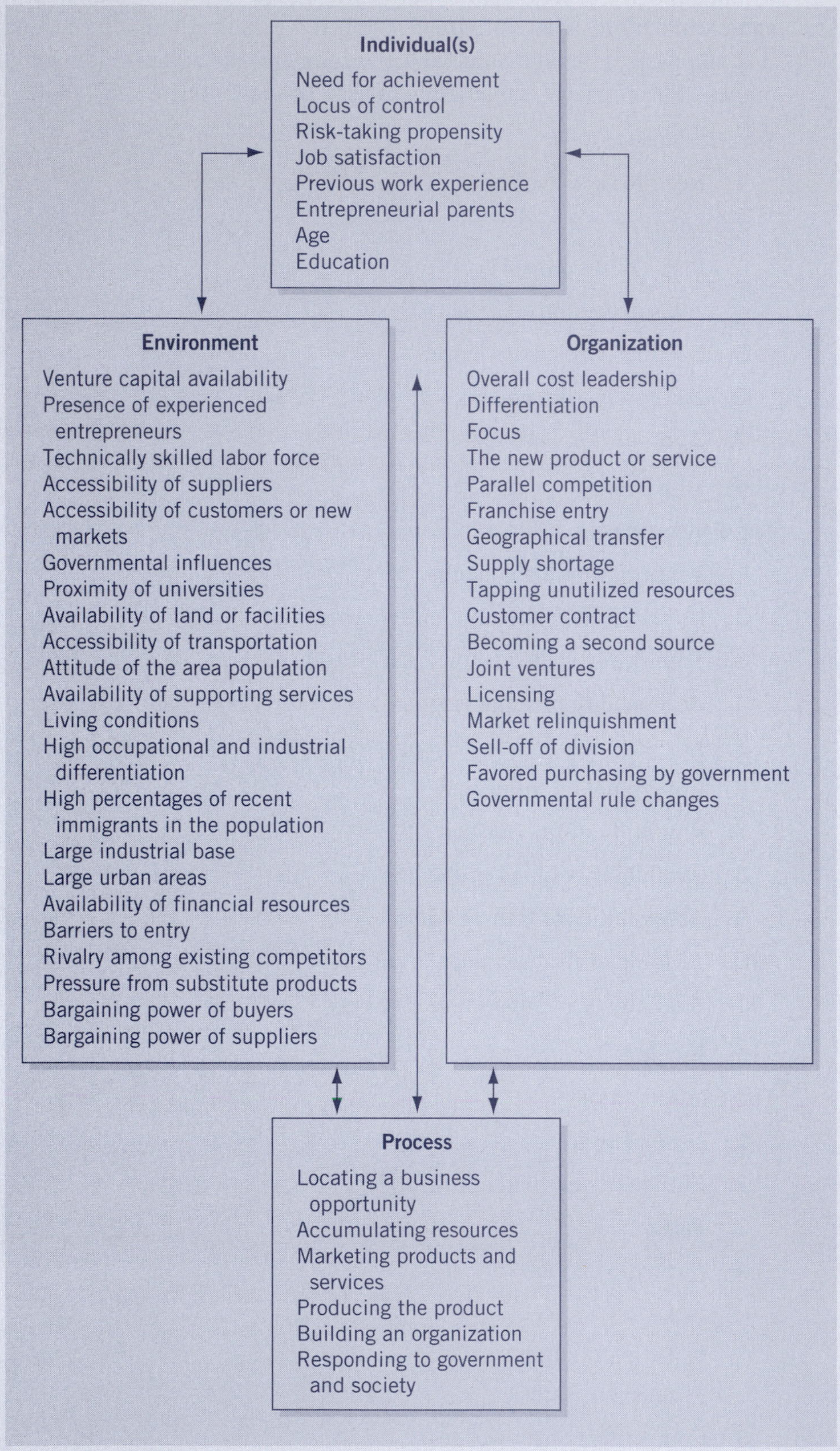

Individual(s)

Need for achievement
Locus of control
Risk-taking propensity
Job satisfaction
Previous work experience
Entrepreneurial parents
Age
Education

Environment

Venture capital availability
Presence of experienced
  entrepreneurs
Technically skilled labor force
Accessibility of suppliers
Accessibility of customers or new
  markets
Governmental influences
Proximity of universities
Availability of land or facilities
Accessibility of transportation
Attitude of the area population
Availability of supporting services
Living conditions
High occupational and industrial
  differentiation
High percentages of recent
  immigrants in the population
Large industrial base
Large urban areas
Availability of financial resources
Barriers to entry
Rivalry among existing competitors
Pressure from substitute products
Bargaining power of buyers
Bargaining power of suppliers

Organization

Overall cost leadership
Differentiation
Focus
The new product or service
Parallel competition
Franchise entry
Geographical transfer
Supply shortage
Tapping unutilized resources
Customer contract
Becoming a second source
Joint ventures
Licensing
Market relinquishment
Sell-off of division
Favored purchasing by government
Governmental rule changes

Process

Locating a business
  opportunity
Accumulating resources
Marketing products and
  services
Producing the product
Building an organization
Responding to government
  and society

Source: William B. Gartner, "A Conceptual Framework for Describing the Phenomenon of New Venture Creation," *Academy of Management Review* (October 1985): 702. Reprinted with permission.

3. Marketing products and services

4. Producing the product

5. Building an organization

6. Responding to government and society[31]

Figure 2.4 depicts the interaction of the four major dimensions of this entrepreneurial, or new-venture, process and lists more variables. This type of process moves entrepreneurship from a segmented school of thought to a dynamic, interactive process approach.

Intrapreneurship (Corporate Entrepreneurship)

Recently the term **intrapreneurship** has become popular in the business community, though very few executives thoroughly understand the concept. Gifford Pinchot has defined an intrapreneur as "any of the dreamers who do. . . ." However, he goes on to say, ". . . take hands-on responsibility for creating innovation of any kind within an organization. The intrapreneur may be the creator or the inventor but is always the dreamer who figures out how to turn an idea into a profitable reality."[32] This definition has definite similarities to entrepreneurship except that intrapreneurship takes place *within* an organization. The major thrust of intrapreneuring (also known as corporate entrepreneurship), then, is to create or develop the entrepreneurial spirit within corporate boundaries, thereby allowing an atmosphere of innovation to prosper.[33] More about this specific application of entrepreneurship is presented in Chapter 3.

Key Concepts

Before concluding our discussion of the nature of entrepreneurship, we need to put into perspective three key concepts: entrepreneurship, entrepreneur, and entrepreneurial management.

Entrepreneurship

Entrepreneurship is a process of innovation and new-venture creation through four major dimensions—individual, organizational, environmental, process—that is aided by collaborative networks in government, education, and institutions. All of the macro and micro positions of entrepreneurial thought must be considered while recognizing and seizing opportunities that can be converted into marketable ideas capable of competing for implementation in today's economy.

Entrepreneur

The **entrepreneur** is a catalyst for economic change who uses purposeful searching, careful planning, and sound judgment when carrying out the entrepreneurial process. Uniquely optimistic and committed, the entrepreneur works creatively to establish new resources or endow old ones with a new capacity, all for the purpose of creating wealth.

Entrepreneurial Management

The underlying theme of this book is the discipline of **entrepreneurial management**, a concept that has been delineated as follows:

> Entrepreneurship is based upon the same principles, whether the entrepreneur is an existing large institution or an individual starting his or her new venture single-handed. It makes little or no difference whether the entrepreneur is a business or a nonbusiness public-service organization, nor even whether the entrepreneur is a governmental or nongovernmental institution. The rules are pretty much the same, the things that work and those that don't are pretty much the same, and so are the kinds of innovation and where to look for them. In every case there is a discipline we might call Entrepreneurial Management.[34] The techniques and principles of this emerging discipline will drive the entrepreneurial economy in the twenty-first century.

Summary

This chapter examined the evolution of entrepreneurship, providing a foundation for further study of this dynamic and developing discipline. Exploring the early economic definitions as well as selected contemporary ones, the chapter presented a historical picture of how entrepreneurship has been viewed. In addition, the ten major myths of entrepreneurship were discussed to permit a better understanding of the folklore surrounding this newly developing field of study. Contemporary research is broadening the horizon for studying entrepreneurship and is providing a better focus on the what, how, and why behind this discipline.

The approaches to entrepreneurship were examined from two different perspectives: schools of thought and process. Six selected schools of thought were presented, and three approaches for understanding contemporary entrepreneurship as a process were discussed. The chapter concluded with definitions of entrepreneurship, entrepreneur, and entrepreneurial management.

Key Terms and Concepts

better widget strategies	great chef strategies
corridor principle	internal locus of control
displacement school of thought	intrapreneurship
entrepreneur	macro view of entrepreneurship
entrepreneurial assessment approach	micro view of entrepreneurship
entrepreneurial management	mountain gap strategies
entrepreneurial trait school of thought	multidimensional approach
entrepreneurship	strategic formulation school of thought
environmental school of thought	venture opportunity school of thought
external locus of control	water well strategies
financial/capital school of thought	

Review and Discussion Questions

1. Briefly describe the evolution of the term *entrepreneurship*.
2. What are the ten myths associated with entrepreneurship? Debunk each.
3. What is the macro view of entrepreneurship?

4. What are the schools of thought that use the macro view of entrepreneurship?

5. What is the micro view of entrepreneurship?

6. What are the schools of thought that use the micro view of entrepreneurship?

7. What are the three specific types of displacement?

8. In the strategic formulation school of thought, what are the four types of strategies involved with unique elements? Give an illustration of each.

9. What is the process approach to entrepreneurship? In your answer describe the entrepreneurial assessment approach.

10. What are the major elements in the framework for entrepreneurship presented in Figure 2.4? Give an example of each.

Experiential Exercise

Understanding Your Beliefs about Successful Entrepreneurs

Read each of the following ten statements, and to the left of each indicate your agreement or disagreement. If you fully agree with the statement, put a *10* on the line at the left. If you totally disagree, put a *1*. If you tend to agree more than you disagree, give a response between *6* and *9* depending on how much you agree. If you tend to disagree, give a response between *2* and *5*.

1. _____ Successful entrepreneurs are often methodical and analytical individuals who carefully plan out what they are going to do and then do it.

2. _____ The most successful entrepreneurs are born with special characteristics such as high achievement drive and a winning personality, and these traits serve them well in their entrepreneurial endeavors.

3. _____ Many of the characteristics needed for successful entrepreneurship can be learned through study and experience.

4. _____ The most successful entrepreneurs are those who invent a unique product or service.

5. _____ Highly successful entrepreneurs tend to have very little formal schooling.

6. _____ Most successful entrepreneurs admit that dropping out of school was the best thing they ever did.

7. _____ Because they are unique and individualistic in their approach to business, most successful entrepreneurs find it hard to socialize with others; they just do not fit in.

8. _____ Research shows that although it is important to have adequate financing before beginning an entrepreneurial venture, it is often more important to have managerial competence and proper planning.

9. _____ Successful entrepreneurship is more a matter of preparation and desire than it is of luck.

10. _____ Most successful entrepreneurs do well in their first venture, which encourages them to continue; failures tend to come later on as the enterprise grows.

Put your answers on the following list in this way: *(a)* Enter answers to numbers 1, 3, 8, and 9 just as they appear, and then *(b)* subtract the answers to 2, 4, 5, 6, 7, and 10 from 11 before entering them here. Thus, if you gave an answer of *8* to number 1, put an *8* before number 1 here. However, if you gave an answer of *7* to number 2 here, place a *4* before number 2 here. Then add both columns of answers and enter your total on the appropriate line.

_____1	_____6*	
_____2*	_____7*	
_____3	_____8	
_____4*	_____9	
_____5*	_____10*	_____Total

Interpretation: This exercise measures how much you believe the myths of entrepreneurship. The lower your total, the stronger your beliefs; the higher your total, the less strong your beliefs. Numbers 1, 3, 8, and 9 are accurate statements; numbers 2, 4, 5, 6, 7, and 10 are inaccurate statements. Here is the scoring key:

80–100   Excellent. You know the facts about entrepreneurs.

61–79   Good, but you still believe in a couple of myths.

41–60   Fair. You need to review the chapter material on the myths of entrepreneurship.

0–40   Poor. You need to reread the chapter material on the myths of entrepreneurship and study these findings.

■ Case 2.1

Paul's Four Shortcomings

Paul Enden has always been very reliable and a hard worker. For the past eight years Paul has been working in a large auto service garage. During this time he has made a number of recommendations to the owner regarding new services that could be provided to customers. One of these is called the "fast lube." With this service people who want to have their oil changed and their car lubricated do not have to leave the auto and come back later in the day. Three service racks handle this job. It generally takes less than 10 minutes to take care of a car, and most people can have the job completed within 25 minutes of the time they arrive. The service, which has become extremely popular with customers, resulted in an increase in overall profits of 5 percent last year.

Paul's wife believes he has a large number of ideas that could prove profitable. "You ought to break away and open your own shop," she has told him. Paul would like to do so, but he believes four things help account for entrepreneurial success, and he has none of them. Here is how he explained it to his wife:

"To be a successful entrepreneur, you have to be a thinker, not a doer. I'm a doer. Thinking bores me. I wouldn't like being an entrepreneur. Second, those guys who do best as entrepreneurs tend to be inventors. I'm not an inventor. If anything, I think of new approaches to old ways of doing business. I'm more of a tinkerer than an inventor. Third, you've got to be lucky to be a successful entrepreneur. I'm hard working; I'm not lucky. Fourth, you have to have a lot of money to do well as an entrepreneur. I don't have much money. I doubt whether $50,000 would get me started as an entrepreneur."

Questions

1. Does Paul need to be an inventor to be an effective entrepreneur? Explain your answer.

2. How important is it that Paul have a lot of money if he hopes to be an entrepreneur? Explain your answer.

3. What is wrong with Paul's overall thinking? Be sure to include a discussion of the myths of entrepreneurship in your answer.

Notes

1. For a compilation of definitions, see Robert C. Ronstadt, *Entrepreneurship* (Dover, MA: Lord Publishing, 1984), 28; Howard H. Stevenson and David E. Gumpert, "The Heart of Entrepreneurship," *Harvard Business Review* (March/April 1985): 85–94; and J. Barton Cunningham and Joe Lischeron, "Defining Entrepreneurship," *Journal of Small Business Management* (January 1991): 45–61.

2. See Calvin A. Kent, Donald L. Sexton, and Karl H. Vesper, *Encyclopedia of Entrepreneurship* (Englewood Cliffs, NJ: Prentice-Hall, 1982); Ray V. Montagno and Donald F. Kuratko, "Perception of Entrepreneurial Success Characteristics," *American Journal of Small Business* (winter 1986): 25–32; Thomas M. Begley and David P. Boyd, "Psychological Characteristics Associated with Performance in Entrepreneurial Firms and Smaller Businesses," *Journal of Business Venturing* (winter 1987): 79–91; and Donald F. Kuratko, "Entrepreneurship," *International Encyclopedia of Business and Management,* 2nd ed. (London: Routledge Publishers, 2002), 168–176.

3. Kent, Sexton, and Vesper, *Encyclopedia of Entrepreneurship,* xxix.

4. Israel M. Kirzner, *Perception, Opportunity, and Profit: Studies in the Theory of Entrepreneurship* (Chicago: University of Chicago Press, 1979), 38–39.

5. See Ronstadt, *Entrepreneurship,* 9–12.

6. Joseph Schumpeter, "Change and the Entrepreneur," in *Essays of J. A. Schumpeter,* ed. Richard V. Clemence (Reading, MA: Addison-Wesley, 1951), 255.

7. Arthur Cole, *Business Enterprise in Its Social Setting* (Cambridge, MA: Harvard University Press, 1959), 27–28.

8. Albert Shapero, *Entrepreneurship and Economic Development,* Project ISEED, Ltd. (Milwaukee, WI: Center for Venture Management, summer 1975), 187.

9. Ronstadt, *Entrepreneurship,* 28.

10. John B. Miner, Norman R. Smith, and Jeffrey S. Bracker, "Defining the Inventor-Entrepreneur in the Context of Established Typologies," *Journal of Business Venturing* (March 1992): 103–113.

11. "A Surprising Finding on New-Business Mortality Rates," *Business Week* (June 14, 1993): 22.

12. Ivan Bull and Gary E. Willard, "Towards a Theory of Entrepreneurship," *Journal of Business Venturing* (May 1993): 183–195; Ian C. MacMillan and Jerome A. Katz, "Idiosyncratic Milieus of Entrepreneurship Research: The Need for Comprehensive Theories," *Journal of Business Venturing* (January 1992): 1–8; Scott Shane and S. Venkataraman, "The Promise of Entrepreneurship as a Field of Research," *Academy of Management Review* (January 2000): 217–226; and Phillip H. Phan, "Entrepreneurship Theory: Possibilities and Future Directions," *Journal of Business Venturing* 19(5) (September 2004): 617–620.

13. William B. Gartner, "What Are We Talking about When We Talk about Entrepreneurship?" *Journal of Business Venturing* (January 1990): 15–28; see also Lanny Herron, Harry J. Sapienza, and Deborah Smith Cook, "Entrepreneurship Theory from an Interdisciplinary Perspective," *Entrepreneurship Theory and Practice* (spring 1992): 5–12; and Saras D. Sarasvathy, "The Questions We Ask and the Questions We Care About: Reformulating Some Problems in Entrepreneurship Research," *Journal of Business Venturing* 19(5) (September 2004): 707–717.

14. See Harold Koontz, "The Management Theory Jungle Revisited," *Academy of Management Review* (April 1980): 175–187; Richard M. Hodgetts and Donald F. Kuratko, "The Management Theory Jungle–Quo Vadis?" *Southern Management Association Proceedings* (November 1983): 280–283; J. Barton Cunningham and Joe Lischeron, "Defining Entrepreneurship," *Journal of Small Business Management* (January 1991): 45–61; Ian C. MacMillan and Jerome A. Katz, "Idiosyncratic Milieus of Entrepreneurship Research: The Need for Comprehensive Theories," *Journal of Business Venturing* (January 1992); and Murray B. Low, "The Adolescence of Entrepreneurship Research: Specification of Purpose," *Entrepreneurship Theory and Practice* 25(4) (2001): 17–25.

15. See Andrew H. Van de Ven, "The Development of an Infrastructure for Entrepreneurship," *Journal of Business Venturing* (May 1993): 211–230.

16. See David J. Brophy and Joel M. Shulman, "A Finance Perspective on Entrepreneurship Research," *Entrepreneurship Theory and Practice* (spring 1992): 61–71; and Truls Erikson, "Entrepreneurial Capital: The Emerging Venture's Most Important Asset and Competitive Advantage," *Journal of Business Venturing* 17(3) (2002): 275–290.

17. Ronstadt, *Entrepreneurship.*

18. Small Business Administration, *The State of Small Business: 1997: A Report of the President* (Washington, D.C.: Government Printing Office, 1997); and Matthew C. Sonfield, "Re-Defining Minority Businesses: Challenges and Opportunities," *Journal of Developmental Entrepreneurship* 6(3) (2001): 269–276.

19. Kelly G. Shaver and Linda R. Scott, "Person, Process, Choice: The Psychology of New Venture Creation," *Entrepreneurship Theory and Practice* (winter 1991): 23–45; and Ronald K. Mitchell, Lowell Busenitz, Theresa Lant, Patricia P. McDougall, Eric A. Morse, and J. Brock Smith, "The Distinctive and Inclusive Domain of Entrepreneurial Cognition Research," *Entrepreneurship Theory and Practice* 28(6) (winter 2004): 505–518.

20. See Magnus Aronsson, "Education Matters—But Does Entrepreneurship Education? An Interview with David Birch," *Academy of Management Learning & Education* 3(3) (2004): 289–292.

21. See Jerry A. Katz, "The Chronology and Intellectual Trajectory of American Entrepreneurship Education," *Journal of Business Venturing* 18(2) (2003): 283–300; Donald F. Kuratko, "The Emergence of Entrepreneurship Education: Development, Trends, and Challenges," *Entrepreneurship Theory and Practice* 29(5) (2005): 577–598; and Dean A. Shepherd, "Educating Entrepreneurship Students about Emotion and Learning from Failure," *Academy of Management Learning & Education* 3(3) (2004): 274–287.

22. George A. Steiner, *Strategic Planning* (New York: Free Press, 1979), 3.

23. See Marjorie A. Lyles, Inga S. Baird, J. Burdeane Orris, and Donald F. Kuratko, "Formalized Planning in Small Business: Increasing Strategic Choices," *Journal of Small Business Management* (April 1993): 38–50; and R. Duane Ireland, Michael A. Hitt, S. Michael Camp, and Donald L. Sexton, "Integrating Entrepreneurship and Strategic Management Actions to Create Firm Wealth," *Academy of Management Executive* 15(1) (2001): 49–63.

24. Ronstadt, *Entrepreneurship,* 112–115.

25. Michael A. Hitt, R. Duane Ireland, S. Michael Camp, and Donald L. Sexton, "Strategic Entrepreneurship: Entrepreneurial Strategies for Wealth Creation," *Strategic Management Journal* (special issue) 22(6) (2001): 479–492.

26. See the special issue, dealing with models, of *Entrepreneurship: Theory and Practice* 17(2) (1993); see also James J. Chrisman, Alan Bauerschmidt, and Charles W. Hofer, "The Determinants of New Venture Performance: An Extended Model," *Entrepreneurship Theory and Practice* (fall 1998): 5–30.

27. Michael H. Morris, P. Lewis, and Donald L. Sexton, "Reconceptualizing Entrepreneurship: An Input-Output Perspective," *Advanced Management Journal* 59(1) (winter 1994): 21–31.

28. Morris, et al., "Reconceptualizing Entrepreneurship."

29. Ronstadt, *Entrepreneurship,* 39.

30. Bradley R. Johnson, "Toward a Multidimensional Model of Entrepreneurship: The Case of Achievement Motivation and the Entrepreneur," *Entrepreneurship: Theory and Practice* (spring 1990): 39–54.

31. William B. Gartner, "A Conceptual Framework for Describing the Phenomenon of New Venture Creation," *Academy of Management Review* (October 1985): 702.

32. Gifford Pinchot III, *Intrapreneuring* (New York: Harper & Row, 1985), ix.

33. See R. Duane Ireland, Donald F. Kuratko, and Jeffrey G. Covin, "Antecedents, Elements, and Consequences of Corporate Entrepreneurship Strategy," *Best Paper Proceedings: Academy of Management,* (Annual Meeting: Seattle, Washington, 2003); Michael H. Morris and Donald F. Kuratko, *Corporate Entrepreneurship* (Mason, OH: Southwestern College Publishers, 2002); and Donald F. Kuratko, R. Duane Ireland, and Jeffrey S. Hornsby, "Improving Firm Performance through Entrepreneurial Actions: Acordia's Corporate Entrepreneurship Strategy," *Academy of Management Executive* 15(4): 60–71.

34. Peter F. Drucker, *Innovation and Entrepreneurship* (New York: Harper & Row, 1985), 143; see also Howard H. Stevenson and J. Carlos Jarillo, "A Paradigm of Entrepreneurship: Entrepreneurial Management," *Strategic Management Journal* (summer 1990): 17–27.

3

Corporate Entrepreneurship: Developing the Entrepreneurial Mind-Set in Organizations

There is nothing more difficult to take in hand, more perilous to conduct, than to take a lead in the introduction of a new order of things, because the innovation has for enemies all those who have done well under the old conditions and lukewarm defenders in those who may do well under the new.

Machiavelli

The Prince

Chapter Objectives

1   To define the term "corporate entrepreneurship"

2   To illustrate the need for corporate entrepreneuring

3   To describe the corporate obstacles preventing innovation from existing in corporations

4   To discuss the intrapreneurship considerations involved in reengineering corporate thinking

5   To describe the specific elements of an intrapreneurial strategy

6   To profile intrapreneurial characteristics and myths

7   To illustrate the interactive process of intrapreneurship

The global economy is creating profound and substantial changes for organizations and industries throughout the world. These changes make it necessary for business firms to carefully examine their purpose and to devote a great deal of attention to selecting and following strategies in their pursuit of the levels of success that have a high probability of satisfying multiple stakeholders. In response to rapid, discontinuous, and significant changes in their external and internal environments, many established companies have restructured their operations in fundamental and meaningful ways. In fact, after years of restructuring, some of these companies bear little resemblance to their ancestors in their business scope, culture, or competitive approach.[1]

The new century is seeing corporate strategies focused heavily on innovation. This new emphasis on entrepreneurial thinking developed during the **entrepreneurial economy** of the 1980s and 1990s.[2] Peter Drucker, the renowned management expert, described four major developments that explain the emergence of this economy. First, the rapid evolution of knowledge and technology promoted the use of high-tech entrepreneurial start-ups. Second, demographic trends such as two-wage-earner families, continuing education of adults, and the aging population added fuel to the proliferation of newly developing ventures. Third, the venture capital market became an effective funding mechanism for entrepreneurial ventures. Fourth, American industry began to learn how to manage entrepreneurship.[3]

The contemporary thrust of entrepreneurship as the major force in American business has led to a desire for this type of activity *inside* enterprises. Although some researchers have concluded that entrepreneurship and bureaucracies are mutually exclusive and cannot coexist,[4] others have described entrepreneurial ventures within the enterprise framework.[5] Successful corporate ventures have been used in many different companies, including 3M, Bell Atlantic, AT&T, Acordia, and Polaroid.[6] Today, a wealth of popular business literature describes a new "corporate revolution" taking place thanks to the infusion of entrepreneurial thinking into large bureaucratic structures.[7] This infusion is referred to as **corporate entrepreneurship**[8] or **intrapreneurship**.[9] Why has this concept become so popular? One reason is that it allows corporations to tap the innovative talents of their own workers and managers. Steven Brandt puts it this way:

> The challenge is relatively straightforward. The United States must upgrade its innovative prowess. To do so, U.S. companies must tap into the creative power of their members. Ideas come from people. Innovation is a capability of the many. That capability is utilized when people give commitment to the mission and life of the enterprise and have the power to do something with their capabilities. Noncommitment is the price of obsolete managing practices, not the lack of talent or desire.
>
> Commitment is most freely given when the members of an enterprise play a part in defining the purposes and plans of the entity. Commitment carries with it a de facto approval of and support for the management. Managing by consent is a useful managing philosophy if more entrepreneurial behavior is desired.[10]

Continuous innovation (in terms of products, processes, and administrative routines and structures) and an ability to compete effectively in international markets are among the skills that increasingly are expected to influence corporate performance in the twenty-first century's global economy. Corporate entrepreneurship is envisioned to be a process that can facilitate firms' efforts to innovate constantly and cope effectively with the competitive realities that companies encounter when competing in international markets. Entrepreneurial attitudes and behaviors are necessary for firms of all sizes to prosper and flourish in competitive environments.[11]

In recent years the subject of intrapreneurship has become quite popular, though very few people thoroughly understand the concept. Most researchers agree that the term refers to entrepreneurial activities that receive organizational sanction and resource commitments for the purpose of innovative results.[12] The major thrust of intrapreneuring is to develop the entrepreneurial spirit within organizational boundaries, thus allowing an atmosphere of innovation to prosper.

Defining the Concept

Operational definitions of corporate entrepreneurship have evolved over the last 30 years through scholars' work. For example, one researcher noted that corporate innovation is a very broad concept that includes the generation, development, and implementation of new ideas or behaviors. An innovation can be a new product or service, an administrative system, or a new plan or program pertaining to organizational members.[13] In this context, corporate entrepreneurship centers on reenergizing and enhancing the firm's ability to acquire innovative skills and capabilities.

Researcher Shaker A. Zahra observed that "corporate entrepreneurship may be formal or informal activities aimed at creating new businesses in established companies through product and process innovations and market developments. These activities may take place at the corporate, division (business), functional, or project levels, with the unifying objective of improving a company's competitive position and financial performance."[14] William D. Guth and Ari Ginsberg have stressed that corporate entrepreneurship encompasses two major phenomena: new venture creation within existing organizations and the transformation of organizations through strategic renewal.[15]

After a thorough analysis of the entrepreneurship construct and its dimensions, recent research has defined corporate entrepreneurship as a process whereby an individual or a group of individuals, in association with an existing organization, creates a new organization or instigates renewal or innovation within the organization. Under this definition, strategic renewal (which is concerned with organizational renewal involving major strategic and/or structural changes), innovation (which is concerned with introducing something new to the marketplace), and corporate venturing (corporate entrepreneurial efforts that lead to the creation of new business organizations within the corporate organization) are all important and legitimate parts of the corporate entrepreneurship process.[16]

As the field has further evolved, the concept of a corporate entrepreneurship strategy has developed. Researchers R. Duane Ireland, Jeffrey G. Covin, and Donald F. Kuratko define a corporate entrepreneurial strategy as "a vision-directed, organization-wide reliance on entrepreneurial behavior that purposefully and continuously rejuvenates the organization and shapes the scope of its operations through the recognition and exploitation of entrepreneurial opportunity."[17]

The Need for Corporate Entrepreneuring

Many companies today are realizing the need for corporate entrepreneuring. Articles in popular business magazines (*Business Week, Fortune, Success, U.S. News & World Report*) are reporting the infusion of entrepreneurial thinking into large bureaucratic structures. In fact, in many of his books, Tom Peters has devoted entire sections to innovation in the corporation.[18] Quite obviously, both business firms and consultants/ authors are recognizing the need for in-house entrepreneurship.

This need has arisen in response to a number of pressing problems, including rapid growth in the number of new and sophisticated competitors, a sense of distrust in the traditional methods of corporate management, an exodus of some of the best and brightest people from corporations to become small-business entrepreneurs, international competition, downsizing of major corporations, and an overall desire to improve efficiency and productivity.[19]

The first of these issues, the problem of competition, has always plagued businesses. However, today's high-tech economy is supporting a far greater number of competitors than ever before. In contrast to previous decades, changes, innovations, and improvements are now very common in the marketplace. Thus corporations must either innovate or become obsolete.

Another of these problems, losing the brightest people to entrepreneurship, is escalating as a result of two major developments. First, entrepreneurship is on the rise in terms of status, publicity, and economic development. This enhancement of entrepreneurship has made the choice more appealing to both young and seasoned employees. Second, in recent years venture capital has grown into a large industry capable of financing more new ventures than ever before. More significantly, as we will see in greater detail in Chapter 14, "angel investors" have emerged in unprecedented strength, which has opened a new opportunity for capital funding. These healthy capital funding markets have enabled new entrepreneurs to launch their ideas. This development is encouraging people with innovative ideas to leave large corporations and strike out on their own.

The modern corporation, then, is forced into seeking avenues for developing in-house entrepreneuring. To do otherwise is to wait for stagnation, loss of personnel, and decline. This new "corporate revolution" represents an appreciation for and a desire to develop intrapreneurs within the corporate structure.

Corporate Venturing Obstacles

The obstacles to corporate entrepreneuring usually reflect the ineffectiveness of traditional management techniques as applied to new-venture development. Although it is unintentional, the adverse impact of a particular traditional management technique can be so destructive that the individuals within an enterprise will tend to avoid corporate entrepreneurial behavior. Table 3.1 provides a list of traditional management techniques, their adverse effects (when the technique is rigidly enforced), and the recommended actions to change or adjust the practice.

Understanding these obstacles is critical to fostering corporate entrepreneuring because they are the foundation points for all other motivational efforts. To gain support and foster excitement for new-venture development, managers must remove the perceived obstacles and seek alternative management actions.[20]

After recognizing the obstacles, managers need to adapt to the principles of successful innovative companies. James Brian Quinn, an expert in the innovation field, found the following factors in large corporations that are successful innovators:

☐ *Atmosphere and vision.* Innovative companies have a clear-cut vision of and the recognized support for an innovative atmosphere.

☐ *Orientation to the market.* Innovative companies tie their visions to the realities of the marketplace.

Table 3.1   Sources of and Solutions to Obstacles in Corporate Venturing

TRADITIONAL MANAGEMENT PRACTICES	ADVERSE EFFECTS	RECOMMENDED ACTIONS
Enforce standard procedures to avoid mistakes	Innovative solutions blocked, funds misspent	Make ground rules specific to each situation
Manage resources for efficiency and ROI	Competitive lead lost, low market penetration	Focus effort on critical issues (e.g., market share)
Control against plan	Facts ignored that should replace assumptions	Change plan to reflect new learning
Plan for the long term	Nonviable goals locked in, high failure costs	Envision a goal, then set interim milestones, reassess after each
Manage functionally	Entrepreneur failure and/or venture failure	Support entrepreneur with managerial and multidiscipline skills
Avoid moves that risk the base business	Missed opportunities	Take small steps, build out from strengths
Protect the base business at all costs	Venturing dumped when base business is threatened	Make venturing mainstream, take affordable risks
Judge new steps from prior experience	Wrong decisions about competition and markets	Use learning strategies, test assumptions
Compensate uniformly	Low motivation and inefficient operations	Balance risk and reward, employ special compensation
Promote compatible individuals	Loss of innovators	Accommodate "boat rockers" and "doers"

Source: Reprinted by permission of the publisher from "Corporate Venturing Obstacles: Sources and Solutions," by Hollister B. Sykes and Zenas Block, *Journal of Business Venturing* (winter 1989): 161. Copyright © 1989 by Elsevier Science Publishing Co., Inc.

☐ *Small, flat organizations.* Most innovative companies keep the total organization flat and project teams small.

☐ *Multiple approaches.* Innovative managers encourage several projects to proceed in parallel development.

☐ **Interactive learning.** Within an innovative environment, learning and investigation of ideas cut across traditional functional lines in the organization.

☐ **Skunkworks.** (A nickname given to small groups that work on their ideas outside of normal organizational time and structure.) Every highly innovative enterprise uses groups that function outside traditional lines of authority. This eliminates bureaucracy, permits rapid turnaround, and instills a high level of group identity and loyalty.[21]

the entrepreneurial PROCESS

Innovation Inside Whirlpool

A sense of urgency set in at Whirlpool Corporation in 1999 when rival Maytag introduced the revolutionary front-loading washing machine; the retaliatory strategy—individual employee innovation.

Chairman and CEO David R. Whitwam believed that any one of Whirlpool's 55,000 employees could come up with innovative products or services given the proper guidance. Whitwam understands that most employees may not have the time or insight to develop an entire business or product line, but feels he must encourage all employees to at least *think* like entrepreneurs. The alternative option, according to Whitwam, is to resign the company to slow growth, diminishing margins, and faltering share prices.

The results have been a success. A KitchenAid division employee, Josh Gitlin, dreamt up a company specializing in in-home cooking classes taught by a network of branded chefs. The company, Inspired Chef, was launched and funded by Whirlpool and expanded to 33 states.

Whitwam now wants crazier ideas and more creative brainstorming. As a stimulus, he reserved 20 percent of Whirlpool's capital budget and is prepared to set away at least 35 percent. In order to motivate the executive-level employees, he has linked their pay to the revenue derived from these new product and service launches.

Because venture success is often determinate on a conducive environment, Whirlpool has created a network of mentors around the world to contribute to ideas and remove roadblocks. There are now 35 full-time "innovation consultants" and 177 part-time "innovation mentors" at the disposal of any employee with the next great idea. Once the idea is ready for financing, the employee and their innovative consultant are given 100 days and $100,000 to develop prototypes and conduct customer research.

The number of ventures continues to increase; the KitchenAid division is introducing a line of outdoor-grilling equipment, and Whirlpool is testing a mini-fridge that can be turned into an oven to cook the meal, all controlled via the Internet.

SOURCE: "Whirlpool Taps Its Inner Entrepreneur," *BusinessWeek Online* (February 7, 2002).

Reengineering Corporate Thinking

To establish corporate entrepreneuring, companies need to provide the freedom and encouragement intrapreneurs require to develop their ideas.[22] This is often a problem in enterprises because many top managers do not believe entrepreneurial ideas can be nurtured and developed in their environment. They also find it difficult to implement policies that encourage freedom and unstructured activity. But managers need to develop policies that will help innovative people reach their full potential. Five important steps for establishing this new thinking follow:

1. Set *explicit goals*. These need to be mutually agreed on by worker and management so that specific steps are achieved.

2. Create a system of *feedback* and *positive reinforcement*. This is necessary for potential inventors, creators, or intrapreneurs to realize that acceptance and reward exist.

3. Emphasize *individual responsibility*. Confidence, trust, and accountability are key features in the success of any innovative program.

4. Give *rewards* based on results. Reward systems should enhance and encourage others to risk and to achieve.[23]

5. *Do not punish failures.* Real learning takes place when failed projects are examined closely for what can be learned by individuals. In addition individuals must feel free to experiment without fear of punishment.

Although each enterprise must develop a philosophy most appropriate for its own entrepreneurial process, a number of key questions can assist in establishing the type of process an organization has. Organizations can use the following questions to assess their enterprise. Applying these questions helps them feed back to the planning process for a proper approach.

☐   *Does your company encourage self-appointed intrapreneurs?* Intrapreneurs appoint themselves to their role and receive the corporation's blessing for their self-appointed task. Despite this, some corporations foolishly try to appoint people to carry out an innovation.

☐   *Does your company provide ways for intrapreneurs to stay with their enterprises?* When the innovation process involves switching the people working on an idea—that is, handing off a developing business or product from a committed intrapreneur to whoever is next in line—that person is often not as committed as the originator of a project.

☐   *Are people in your company permitted to do the job in their own way, or are they constantly stopping to explain their actions and ask for permission?* Some organizations push decisions up through a multilevel approval process so that the doers and the deciders never even meet.

☐   *Has your company evolved quick and informal ways to access the resources to try new ideas?* Intrapreneurs need discretionary resources to explore and develop new ideas. Some companies give employees the freedom to use a percentage of their time on projects of their own choosing and set aside funds to explore new ideas when they occur. Others control resources so tightly that nothing is available for the new and unexpected. The result is nothing new.

☐   *Has your company developed ways to manage many small and experimental products and businesses?* Today's corporate cultures favor a few well-studied, well-planned attempts to hit a home run. In fact, nobody bats 1,000, and it is better to try more times with less careful and expensive preparation for each.

☐   *Is your system set up to encourage risk taking and to tolerate mistakes?* Innovation cannot be achieved without risk and mistakes. Even successful innovation generally begins with blunders and false starts.

☐   *Can your company decide to try something and stick with the experiment long enough to see if it will work, even when that may take years and several false starts?* Innovation takes time, even decades, but the rhythm of corporations is annual planning.

☐   *Are people in your company more concerned with new ideas or with defending their turf?* Because new ideas almost always cross the boundaries of existing patterns of organization, a jealous tendency to "turf protection" blocks innovation.

☐   *How easy is it to form functionally complete, autonomous teams in your corporate environment?* Small teams with full responsibility for developing an intraprise solve many of the basic innovation problems. But some companies resist their formation.

☐ *Do intrapreneurs in your company face monopolies, or are they free to use the resources of other divisions and outside vendors if they choose?* Entrepreneurs live in a multioption universe. If one venture capitalist or supplier can't or won't meet their needs, they have many more from which to choose. Intrapreneurs, however, often face single-option situations that may be called internal monopolies. They must have their product made by a certain factory or sold by a specific sales force. Too often these groups lack motivation or are simply wrong for the job, and a good idea dies an unnecessary death.[24]

Another way to create an innovative corporate atmosphere is to apply rules for innovation. The following rules can provide a hands-on guideline for developing the necessary innovative philosophy:

1. Encourage action.
2. Use informal meetings whenever possible.
3. Tolerate failure, and use it as a learning experience.
4. Persist in getting an idea to market.
5. Reward innovation for innovation's sake.
6. Plan the physical layout of the enterprise to encourage informal communication.
7. Expect clever **bootlegging** of ideas—secretly working on new ideas on company time as well as on personal time.
8. Put people on small teams for future-oriented projects.
9. Encourage personnel to circumvent rigid procedures and bureaucratic red tape.
10. Reward and promote innovative personnel.

When these rules are followed, they create an environment conducive to and supportive of potential entrepreneurs. The result is a corporate philosophy that supports intrapreneurial behavior.

What can a corporation do to reengineer its thinking to foster the entrepreneurial process? The organization needs to examine and revise its management philosophy. Many enterprises have obsolete ideas about cooperative cultures, management techniques, and the values of managers and employees. Unfortunately, doing old tasks more efficiently is not the answer to new challenges; a new culture with new values has to be developed.[25] Bureaucrats and controllers must learn to coexist with or give way to the designer and intrapreneur. Unfortunately, this is easier said than done. However, organizations can take some steps to help restructure corporate thinking and encourage an intrapreneurial environment: (1) early identification of potential intrapreneurs, (2) top management sponsorship of intrapreneurial projects, (3) creation of both diversity and order in strategic activities, (4) promotion of intrapreneurship through experimentation, and (5) development of collaboration between intrapreneurial participants and the organization at large.[26]

Developing a corporate entrepreneurial philosophy provides a number of advantages. One is that this type of atmosphere often leads to the development of new products and services and helps the organization expand and grow. A second is it creates a workforce that can help the enterprise maintain its competitive posture. A third is it promotes a climate conducive to high achievers and helps the enterprise motivate and keep its best people.

Conceptualizing Corporate Entrepreneurship Strategy

As mentioned earlier, a corporate entrepreneurship (CE) strategy is defined by us as a vision-directed, organization-wide reliance on entrepreneurial behavior that purposefully and continuously rejuvenates the organization and shapes the scope of its operations through the recognition and exploitation of entrepreneurial opportunity. As is true for all strategies, a corporate entrepreneurship strategy should be thought of in continuous, rather than dichotomous terms. Stated more directly, corporate entrepreneurship strategies vary in their degree of entrepreneurial intensity. Developed by researchers Jeffrey G. Covin, R. Duane Ireland, and Donald F. Kuratko, Figure 3.1 presents a model illustrating how a corporate entrepreneurship strategy is manifested

Figure 3.1 The Corporate Entrepreneurship Strategy Process

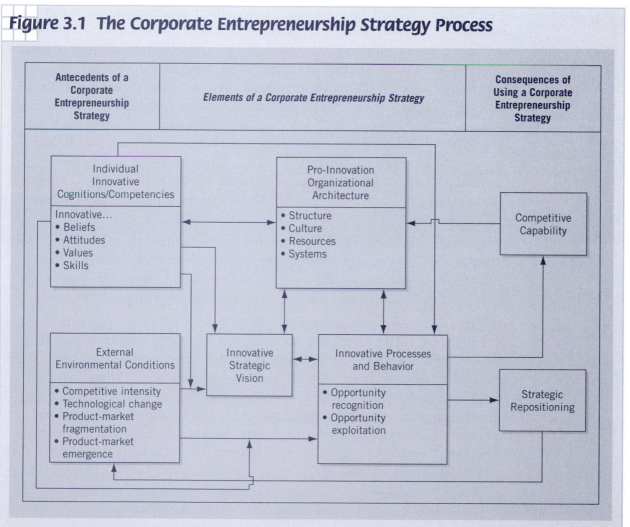

Source: Adapted from R. Duane Ireland, Donald F. Kuratko, and Jeffrey G. Covin, "Antecedents, Elements, and Consequences of Corporate Entrepreneurship," *Best Paper Proceedings: National Academy of Management* (August 2003) CD Rom: L1–L6; and R. Duane Ireland, Jeffrey G. Covin, and Donald F. Kuratko, *Corporate Entrepreneurship Strategy* (in press, 2007).

through the presence of three elements: an entrepreneurial strategic vision, a pro-entrepreneurship organizational architecture, and entrepreneurial processes and behavior as exhibited across the organizational hierarchy.[27] This model has several linkages which include: (1) individual entrepreneurial cognitions of the organization's members, (2) external environmental conditions that invite entrepreneurial activity, (3) top management's entrepreneurial strategic vision for the firm, (4) organizational architectures that encourage entrepreneurial processes and behavior, (5) the entrepreneurial processes that are reflected in entrepreneurial behavior, and (6) organizational outcomes resulting from entrepreneurial actions.

The model suggests that individual entrepreneurial cognitions and external environmental conditions are the initial impetus for adopting a CE strategy, and outcomes are assessed to provide justification for the strategy's continuance, modification, or rejection. The CE strategy, itself, is reflected in three elements: an entrepreneurial strategic vision, a pro-entrepreneurship organizational architecture, and entrepreneurial processes and behavior as exhibited throughout the organization. CE strategy cannot simply be consciously chosen and quickly enacted the way some strategies, such as acquisition, can be consciously chosen and quickly enacted. This is so because it requires more than just a decision, act, or event. It requires the creation of congruence between the entrepreneurial vision of the organization's leaders and the entrepreneurial actions of those throughout the organization, as facilitated through the existence of a pro-entrepreneurship organizational architecture. CE strategy is about creating self-renewing organizations through the unleashing and focusing of the entrepreneurial potential that exists throughout those organizations. It is also about consistency in approach and regularity in behavior. Firms engaging in CE strategies must encourage entrepreneurial behavior on a relatively regular or continuous basis. Obviously, how extensively firms must engage in entrepreneurial behavior before the presence of a CE strategy can be claimed is a matter of degree. At one end of the continuum is stability—the absence of innovation—with chaos—overwhelming innovation—being at the other. Researchers Charles Baden-Fuller and Henk Volberda rightfully assert that

> Resolving the paradox of change and preservation means recognizing that continuous renewal inside a complex firm is misleading. Too much change will lead to chaos, loss of cultural glue, fatigue, and organizational breakdown. While in the short-term, organizations that are chaotic can survive, in the longer term they are likely to collapse.[28]

Researchers Kathleen Eisenhardt, Shona Brown, and Heidi Neck perhaps best captured where firms with CE strategies lie along the "innovation" continuum in their observations concerning "competing on the entrepreneurial edge." Firms with CE strategies remain close to the "edge of time," judiciously balancing the exploitation of current entrepreneurial opportunities with the search for future entrepreneurial opportunities. Such firms are always near chaos, both strategically and structurally, but they have the wisdom and discipline to recognize the possibility of and avoid the extreme collapse referred to earlier.[29]

Thus for CE to operate as a strategy, it must "run deep" within organizations. Top managers are increasingly recognizing the need to respond to the entrepreneurial imperatives created by their competitive landscapes. Minimal responses to these entrepreneurial imperatives, reflecting superficial commitments to CE strategy, are bound to fail. Moreover, while top management can instigate the strategy, top management cannot dictate it. Those at the middle and lower ranks of an organization have a tremendous effect on and significant roles within entrepreneurial and strategic processes.[30] Without sustained and strong commitment from these lower levels of the organization, entrepreneurial behavior will never be a defining characteristic of the organization as is required by CE strategy.

CE strategy will be hard to create and, perhaps, even harder to perpetuate in organizations. The presence of certain external environmental conditions may be sufficient to prompt an organization's leaders into exploring the possibility of adopting a CE strategy. However, the commitment of individuals throughout the organization to making such a strategy work and the realization of personal and organizational entrepreneurial outcomes that reinforce this commitment will be necessary to assure that entrepreneurial behavior becomes a defining aspect of the organization. Thus, breakdowns in any of the three elements of CE strategy, or in linkages between or among these elements, would undermine the viability of such strategy. Moreover, alignments must be created in evaluation and reward systems such that congruence is achieved in the entrepreneurial behaviors induced at the individual and organizational levels. Thus, while external conditions may be increasingly conducive to the adoption of CE strategies, managers should harbor no illusions that the effective implementation of these strategies will be easily accomplished.

Corporations that create an entrepreneurial strategy find that the ethos of the original enterprise often changes dramatically.[31] Traditions are set aside in favor of new processes and procedures. Some people, unaccustomed to operating in this environment, will leave; others will discover a new motivational system that encourages creativity, ingenuity, risk taking, teamwork, and informal networking, all designed to increase productivity and make the organization more viable. Some people thrive in an entrepreneurial environment; others dislike it intensely.

The five critical steps of a corporate entrepreneurship strategy are: (1) developing the vision, (2) encouraging innovation, (3) structuring for an intrapreneurial climate, (4) developing individual managers for corporate entrepreneurship, and (5) developing venture teams. Each of these are now discussed in greater detail.

Developing the Vision

The first step in planning a corporate entrepreneurship strategy for the enterprise is sharing the vision of innovation that the corporate leaders wish to achieve.[32] The vision must be clearly articulated by the organization's leaders; however, the specific objectives are then developed by the managers and employees of the organization. Because it is suggested that corporate entrepreneuring results from the creative talents of people within the organization, employees need to know about and understand this vision. Shared vision is a critical element for a strategy that seeks high achievement (see Figure 3.2). This shared vision requires identification of specific objectives for corporate entrepreneuring strategies and of the programs needed to achieve those objectives. Author and researcher Rosabeth Moss Kanter has described three major objectives and their respective programs designed for venture development within companies. These are outlined in Table 3.2.

Encouraging Innovation

As will be discussed in Chapter 5, innovation is the specific tool of the entrepreneur. Therefore, corporations must understand and develop innovation as the key element in

Figure 3.2 Shared Vision

Source: Jon Arild Johannessen, "A Systematic Approach to the Problem of Rooting a Vision in the Basic Components of an Organization," *Entrepreneurship, Innovation, and Change* (March 1994): 47. Reprinted with permission from Plenum Publishing Corporation.

Table 3.2 Objectives and Programs for Venture Development

OBJECTIVES	PROGRAMS
Make sure that current systems, structures, and practices do not present insurmountable roadblocks to the flexibility and fast action needed for innovation.	Reduce unnecessary bureaucracy, and encourage communication across departments and functions.
Provide the incentives and tools for intrapreneurial projects.	Use internal "venture capital" and special project budgets. (This money has been termed **intracapital** to signify a special fund for intrapreneurial projects.) Allow discretionary time for projects (sometimes referred to as "bootlegging" time).
Seek synergies across business areas so new opportunities are discovered in new combinations.	Encourage joint projects and ventures among divisions, departments, and companies. Allow and encourage employees to discuss and brainstorm new ideas.

Source: Adapted by permission of the publisher from "Supporting Innovation and Venture Development in Established Companies," by Rosabeth Moss Kanter, *Journal of Business Venturing* (winter 1985): 56–59. Copyright © 1985 by Elsevier Science Publishing Co., Inc.

Figure 3.3 Radical versus Incremental Innovation

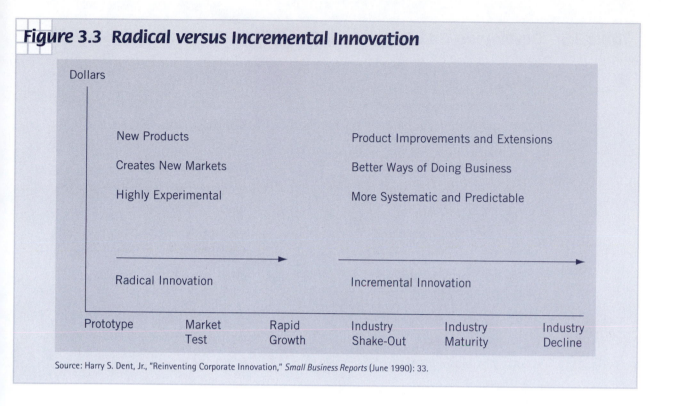

Source: Harry S. Dent, Jr., "Reinventing Corporate Innovation," *Small Business Reports* (June 1990): 33.

their strategy. Numerous researchers have examined the importance of innovation within the corporate environment.[33]

Innovation is described as chaotic and unplanned by some authors,[34] while other researchers insist it is a systematic discipline.[35] Both of these positions can be true depending on the nature of the innovation. One way to understand this concept is to focus on two different types of innovation: radical and incremental.[36]

Radical innovation is the launching of inaugural breakthroughs such as personal computers, Post-it Notes, disposable diapers, and overnight mail delivery. These innovations take experimentation and determined vision, which are not necessarily managed but *must* be recognized and nurtured.

Incremental innovation refers to the systematic evolution of a product or service into newer or larger markets. Examples include microwave popcorn, popcorn used for packaging (to replace Styrofoam), frozen yogurt, and so forth. Many times the incremental innovation will take over after a radical innovation introduces a breakthrough (see Figure 3.3). The structure, marketing, financing, and formal systems of a corporation can help implement incremental innovation. Jan Carlzon, CEO of SAS Airlines, has explained that his organization did not do one thing 1,000 percent better. Rather, his organization (referring to his people) did 1,000 things 1 percent better.

Both types of innovation require vision and support. This support takes different steps for effective development (see Table 3.3). In addition, they both need a **champion**—the person with a vision and the ability to share it.[37] And finally, both types of innovation require an effort by the top management of the corporation to develop and educate employees concerning innovation and intrapreneurship, a concept known as **top management support**.[38]

Table 3.3   Developing and Supporting Radical and Incremental Innovation

RADICAL	INCREMENTAL
Stimulate through challenges and puzzles.	Set systematic goals and deadlines.
Remove budgetary and deadline constraints when possible.	Stimulate through competitive pressures.
Encourage technical education and exposure to customers.	Encourage technical education and exposure to customers.
Allow technical sharing and brainstorming sessions.	Hold weekly meetings that include key management and marketing staff.
Give personal attention—develop relationships of trust.	Delegate more responsibility.
Encourage praise from outside parties.	Set clear financial rewards for meeting goals and deadlines.
Have flexible funds for opportunities that arise.	
Reward with freedom and capital for new projects and interests.	

Source: Adapted from Harry S. Dent, Jr., "Growth through New Product Development," *Small Business Reports* (November 1990): 36.

Encouraging innovation requires a willingness not only to tolerate failure but also to learn from it. For example, one of the founders of 3M, Francis G. Oakie, had an idea to replace razor blades with sandpaper. He believed men could rub sandpaper on their face rather than use a sharp razor. He was wrong, and the idea failed, but his ideas evolved until he developed a waterproof sandpaper for the auto industry, a blockbuster success!

Thus, 3M's philosophy was born. Innovation is a numbers game: the more ideas, the better the chances for a successful innovation. In other words, to master innovation companies must have a tolerance for failure. This philosophy has paid off for 3M. Antistatic videotape, translucent dental braces, synthetic ligaments for knee surgery, heavy-duty reflective sheeting for construction signs, and, of course, Post-it Notes are just some of the great innovations developed at 3M. Overall, the company has a catalog of 60,000 products.[39]

Today 3M follows a set of innovative rules that encourage employees to foster ideas. The key rules include the following:

☐ *Don't kill a project.* If an idea can't find a home in one of 3M's divisions, a staffer can devote 15 percent of his or her time to prove it is workable. For those who need seed money, as many as 90 Genesis grants of $50,000 are awarded each year.

☐ *Tolerate failure.* Encouraging plenty of experimentation and risk taking allows more chances for a new product hit. The goal: Divisions must derive 25 percent

The Champion Program at Bell Atlantic

An effective intrapreneurship program creates a management environment in which innovation can flourish, and it transforms ordinary people into successful intracorporate entrepreneurs. These intrapreneurs create new possibilities within the company in a way that neither they nor the company has dreamed possible. They may even do it first while handling their existing jobs. Experience has shown that intrapreneurial efforts develop a greater sense of ownership within the company.

One example of a successful intrapreneurial experience was the Bell Atlantic Champion Program. The program was structured into three phases: early business opportunity exploration, full business planning and trials, and commercial rollout.

These were the six major operating guidelines for the program:

1. Only five hours of company time per week were allowed on the project during the early phases. The rest of the time required had to be moonlighted out of the person's own time.

2. An expense-only budget of $1,000 per project was placed under the full discretionary control of the intrapreneur.

3. When ready, the project was presented to a cross-functional middle management review committee and either passed on to the next phase or terminated.

4. Regardless of whether the project was passed or terminated, the intrapreneur was eligible for up to $1,000 as an award for due diligence in evaluating the opportunity.

5. Candidates had a choice of either bringing their own ideas to the meeting or adopting one from the company's backlog.

6. The program was generally limited to lower and middle levels of management.

Thirty-five intrapreneurial candidates were put through an intensive four days of initial training and two sessions of follow-up training and coaching, each lasting two days. Between formal sessions the intrapreneurs were supported by the New Business Development Department as needed.

If, after three to four months of effort, candidates recommended more intensive effort to the screening committee—and were accepted—they then went through another three days of intensive training and coaching, followed by additional follow-up training days about six weeks apart. At this point, some were lent full-time to the New Business Group to work on their projects. Others negotiated roles within their home departments that permitted them to devote up to half of their time to their intrapreneurial projects.

If the project was then accepted for commercialization, Bell provided a compensation choice. Intrapreneurs were allowed to invest 10 percent of their salary, taken as a salary reduction, plus their individual performance award for a period of three years. In return, they received 5 percent of the pretax profits from their project up to a cap of ten times their investment. Alternatively, the intrapreneur could retain regular compensation and progress with the project.

Eight projects made it into the second phase of development, which was initiated by another three days of training and intensive coaching, ending with a presentation of a 90-day action plan for the project. Intrapreneurs whose projects did not make it through to the second phase could at their discretion either return to the drawing board for more investigation or terminate the project. Regardless, a celebration was held, and awards were given to the intrapreneurs.

The program expanded throughout the company, with more than 130 intrapreneurs championing more than 100 projects. At least 15 products went to market, and 15 patents were awarded. Potential revenues estimated for these projects total at least $100 million within five years.

SOURCE: Adapted from Austin K. Pryor and E. Michael Shays, "Growing the Business with Intrapreneurs," *Business Quarterly* (spring 1993): 43–50.

of sales from products introduced in the past five years. The target may be boosted to 30 percent in some cases.

☐ *Keep divisions small.* Division managers must know each staffer's first name. When a division gets too big, perhaps reaching $250 million to $300 million in sales, it is split up.

☐ *Motivate the champions.* When a 3M employee has a product idea, he or she recruits an action team to develop it. Salaries and promotions are tied to the product's progress. The champion has a chance to someday run his or her own product group or division.

☐ *Stay close to the customer.* Researchers, marketers, and managers visit with customers and routinely invite them to help brainstorm product ideas.

☐ *Share the wealth.* Technology, wherever it is developed, belongs to everyone.[40]

Structuring for a Corporate Entrepreneurial Environment

When reestablishing the drive to innovate in today's corporations, the final and possibly most critical step is to invest heavily in *entrepreneurial activities* that allow new ideas to flourish in an innovative environment. This concept, when coupled with the other elements of an innovation strategy, can enhance the potential for employees to become venture developers. To develop employees as a source of innovations for corporations, companies need to provide more nurturing and information-sharing activities.[41] In addition to establishing entrepreneurial ways and nurturing intrapreneurs, they need to develop an environment that will help innovative-minded people reach their full potential. Employee perception of an innovative environment is critical for stressing the importance of management's commitment not only to the organization's people but also to the innovative projects.

The importance of an organizational environment for corporate entrepreneurship is further emphasized by researcher Deborah V. Brazeal's model for internally developed ventures.[42] Figure 3.4 illustrates the model's focus on a joint function between innovative individuals and organizational factors. Brazeal defines corporate venturing as "an internal process that embraces the ultimate goal of growth through the development of innovative products, processes, and technologies" that should be institutionalized with an emphasis on long-term prosperity. Thus, for organizations to promote innovation among their employees, they must give careful attention to the melding of an individual's attitudes, values, and behavioral orientations with the organizational factors of structure and reward. Ultimately, the key objective is to enhance a firm's innovative abilities by developing an organizational environment supportive of individuals.

Developing Individual Managers for Corporate Entrepreneurship

As a way for organizations to develop key environmental factors for entrepreneurial activity, a corporate entrepreneurship training program (Corporate Breakthrough Training) often induces the change needed in the work atmosphere. It is not our intent to elaborate completely on the content of a training program here, but a brief summary of an actual program is presented to provide a general understanding of how such a program is designed to introduce an entrepreneurial environment in a company. This award-winning training program was intended to create an awareness of entrepreneurial opportunities in organizations. The Breakthrough Program consisted of six modules,

Figure 3.4 Intrapreneurial Development: Joint Function of Individual and Organizational Factors

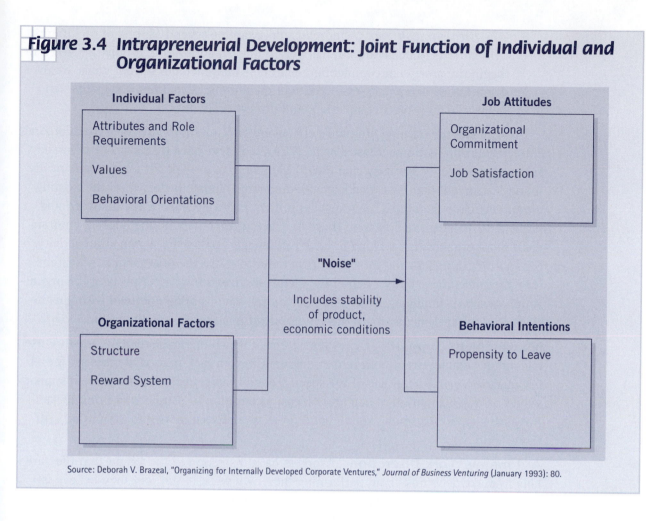

Source: Deborah V. Brazeal, "Organizing for Internally Developed Corporate Ventures," *Journal of Business Venturing* (January 1993): 80.

each designed to train participants to support corporate entrepreneurship in their own work area.[43] The modules and a brief summary of their contents follow:

1. *The Breakthrough Experience.* An enthusiastic overview of The Breakthrough Experience in which participants are challenged to think innovatively, and the need for "breaking out of the box" in today's organizations is emphasized.

2. *Breakthrough Thinking.* The process of thinking innovatively is foreign to most traditional organizations. The misconceptions about thinking innovatively are reviewed, and a discussion of the most common inhibitors is presented. After completing an innovation inventory, managers engage in several exercises designed to facilitate their own innovative thinking.

3. *Idea Acceleration Process.* Managers generate a set of specific ideas on which they would like to work. The process includes examining a number of aspects of the corporation including structural barriers and facilitators. Additionally, managers determine resources needed to accomplish their projects.

4. *Barriers and Facilitators to Innovative Thinking.* The most common barriers to innovative behavior are reviewed and discussed. Managers complete several exercises that will help them deal with barriers in the workplace. In addition, video case histories are shown that depict actual corporate innovators that have been successful in dealing with corporate barriers.

5. *Sustaining Breakthrough Teams.* Managers work together to form teams based on the ideas that have been circulating among the entire group. Team dynamics is reviewed for each group to understand.

6. *The Breakthrough Plan.* After managers examine several aspects of facilitators and barriers to behaving innovatively in their organization, groups are asked to begin the process of completing a plan. The plan includes setting goals, establishing a work team, assessing current conditions, developing a step-by-step timetable for project completion, and project evaluation.

To validate the training program's effectiveness, a questionnaire titled the "**Corporate Entrepreneurship Assessment Instrument**" (CEAI) was developed by researchers Donald F. Kuratko, Jeffrey S. Hornsby, and Ray V. Montagno to provide for a psychometrically sound instrument that measured key entrepreneurial climate factors from the existing intrapreneurship literature. The responses to the CEAI were statistically analyzed and resulted in five identified factors. These five factors are critical to the internal environment of an organization seeking to have its managers pursue entrepreneurial activity. It is important to understand these factors in order to assess the organization's "readiness" for entrepreneurial activity. Each of the factors discussed next are aspects of the organization over which management has some control. Each is briefly defined with illustrations of specific elements of a firm's environment relative to each dimension.

Management Support   This is the extent to which the management structure itself encourages employees to believe that innovation is, in fact, part of the role set for all organization members. Some of the specific conditions reflecting management support would be quick adoption of employee ideas, recognition of people who bring ideas forward, support for small experimental projects, and seed money to get projects off the ground.

Autonomy/Work Discretion   Workers have discretion to the extent that they are able to make decisions about performing their own work in the way they believe is most effective. Organizations should allow employees to make decisions about their work process and should avoid criticizing them for making mistakes when innovating.

Rewards/Reinforcement   Rewards and reinforcement enhance the motivation of individuals to engage in innovative behavior. Organizations must be characterized by providing rewards contingent on performance, providing challenges, increasing responsibilities, and making the ideas of innovative people known to others in the organizational hierarchy.

Time Availability   The fostering of new and innovative ideas requires that individuals have time to incubate these ideas. Organizations must moderate the workload of people, avoid putting time constraints on all aspects of a person's job, and allow people to work with others on long-term problem solving.

Organizational Boundary   These boundaries, real and imagined, prevent people from looking at problems outside their own jobs. People must be encouraged to look at the organization from a broad perspective. Organizations should avoid having standard operating procedures for all major parts of jobs and should reduce dependence on narrow job descriptions and rigid performance standards.[44]

The statistical results from the CEAI demonstrated support for this underlying set of internal environmental factors that organizations need to focus on when seeking to introduce an intrapreneurial strategy. These factors, as well as the previous research mentioned, are the foundation for the critical steps involved in introducing a corporate entrepreneurial climate.

Another researcher, Vijay Sathe, has suggested a number of areas on which corporations must focus if they are going to facilitate intrapreneurial behavior. The first is to encourage—not mandate—intrapreneurial activity. Managers should use financial rewards and strong company recognition rather than rules or strict procedures to encourage corporate entrepreneurship. This is actually a stronger internal control and direction method than traditional parameters.

Another area is the proper control of human resource policies. Managers need to remain in positions for a period long enough to allow them to learn an industry and a particular division. Rather than move managers around in positions, as is the case in many companies, Sathe suggests "selected rotation," in which managers are exposed to different but related territories. This helps managers gain sufficient knowledge for new-venture development.

A third factor is for management to sustain a commitment to intrapreneurial projects long enough for momentum to occur. Failures will inevitably occur, and learning must be the key aftermath of those failures. Thus, sustained commitment is an important element in managing corporate entrepreneurship.

A final element Sathe mentioned is to bet on people, not on analysis. Although analysis is always important to judge a project's progression, it should be done in a supportive rather than an imposed style. The supportive challenge can help intrapreneurs realize errors, test their convictions, and accomplish a self-analysis.[45]

It should be mentioned that the exact rewards for corporate entrepreneuring are not yet agreed on by most researchers.[46] Some believe allowing the inventor to take charge of the new venture is the best reward. Others say it is allowing the corporate entrepreneur more discretionary time to work on future projects. Still others insist that special capital, called *intracapital,* should be set aside for the corporate entrepreneur to use whenever investment money is needed for further research ideas.

In light of these climate elements, it is clear that change in the corporate structure is inevitable if intrapreneurial activity is going to exist and prosper. The change process consists of a series of emerging constructions of people, corporate goals, and existing needs. In short, the organization can encourage innovation by relinquishing controls and changing the traditional bureaucratic structure.[47] (See Table 3.4 for the Ten Commandments of an Intrapreneur.)

Developing Venture Teams

Venture teams and the potential they hold for producing innovative results are recognized as a productivity breakthrough for the new millennium. Certainly, no one doubts that their popularity is on the rise. Companies that have committed to a venture team approach often label the change they have undergone a "transformation" or a "revolution." This new breed of work team is a new strategy for many firms. It is referred to as self-directing, self-managing, or high-performing, although in reality a venture team includes all of those descriptions.[48]

In examining the entrepreneurial development for corporations, Robert Reich found that intrapreneurship is not the sole province of the company's founder or its top managers. Rather, it is diffused throughout the company, where experimentation and development occur all the time as the company searches for new ways to build on the knowledge already accumulated by its workers. Reich's definition of **collective entrepreneurship** follows:

In collective entrepreneurship, individual skills are integrated into a group; this collective capacity to innovate becomes something greater than the sum of its parts. Over time, as

Table 3.4   The Ten Commandments of an Intrapreneur

1. Come to work each day willing to be fired.
2. Circumvent any orders aimed at stopping your dream.
3. Do any job needed to make your project work, regardless of your job description.
4. Network with good people to assist you.
5. Build a spirited team: Choose and work with only the best.
6. Work underground as long as you can—publicity triggers the corporate immune mechanism.
7. Be loyal and truthful to your sponsors.
8. Remember it is easier to ask forgiveness than for permission.
9. Be true to your goals, but be realistic about the ways to achieve them.
10. Keep the vision strong.

Source: Adapted from *Intrapreneuring* by Gifford Pinchot III, 1985, 22. Copyright © Gifford Pinchot III. Adapted by permission of HarperCollins Publishers.

group members work through various problems and approaches, they learn about each other's abilities. They learn how they can help one another perform better, what each can contribute to a particular project, how they can best take advantage of one another's experience. Each participant is constantly on the lookout for small adjustments that will speed and smooth the evolution of the whole. The net result of many such small-scale adaptations, effected throughout the organization, is to propel the enterprise forward.[49]

In keeping with Reich's focus on collective entrepreneurship, venture teams offer corporations the opportunity to use the talents of individuals but with a sense of teamwork.

A **venture team** is composed of two or more people who formally create and share the ownership of a new organization.[50] The unit is semiautonomous in the sense it has a budget plus a leader who has the freedom to make decisions within broad guidelines. Sometimes the leader is called a "product champion" or an "intrapreneur." The unit is often separated from other parts of the firm—in particular, from parts involved with daily activities. This prevents the unit from engaging in procedures that can stifle innovative activities. If the venture proves successful, however, it eventually is treated the same as other outputs the organization produces. It is then integrated into the larger organization.[51]

In many ways, a venture team is a small business operating within a large business, and its strength is its focus on design (that is, structure and process) issues for innovative activities. One organization that operated successfully with the venture team concept was the Signode Corporation (see the Entrepreneurship in Practice box).

Specific intrapreneurship strategies vary from firm to firm. However, they all have similar patterns, seeking a proactive changing of the status quo and a new, flexible approach to operations management.

Signode's V-Teams

Robert F. Hettinger, a venture manager with Signode Industries, Inc., in Glenview, Illinois, smiles as he recounts the strategy initiated by Jack Campbell, director of corporate development. "He strongly believed," Hettinger says, "that you have to kiss a lot of frogs in order to find a prince. Most ideas in raw form aren't winners—you really have to work them out before success sets in."

Signode, a $750 million-a-year manufacturer of plastic and steel strapping for packaging and materials handling, wanted to chart new directions to become a $1 billion-plus firm by 1990. In pursuit of this goal, Signode set out in 1983 to devise an aggressive strategy for growth: developing "new legs" for the company to stand on. It formed a corporate development group to pursue markets outside the company's core businesses but within the framework of its corporate strengths.

Before launching the first of its venture teams, Signode's top management identified the firm's global business strengths and broad areas with potential for new product lines: warehousing/shipping; packaging; plastics for nonpackaging, fastening, and joining systems; and product identification and control systems. Each new business opportunity a venture team suggested was to have the potential to generate $50 million in business within five years. In addition, each opportunity had to build on one of Signode's strengths: industrial customer base and marketing expertise, systems sales and service capabilities, containment and reinforcement technology, steel and plastic process technology, machine and design capabilities, and productivity and distribution know-how.

The criteria were based on business-to-business selling only; Signode did not want to market directly to retailers or consumers. The basic technology to be employed in the new business had to already exist and had to have a strong likelihood of attaining a major market share within a niche. Finally, the initial investment in the new opportunity had to be $30 million or less.

Based on these criteria, Signode began to build its "V-Team" (venture team) approach to intrapreneurship. It took three months to select the first team members. The six initial teams had three common traits: high risk-taking ability, creativity, and the ability to deal with ambiguity. All were multidisciplinary volunteers who would work full-time on developing new consumer-product packaging businesses. The team members came from such backgrounds as design engineering, marketing, sales, and product development. They set up shop in rented office space five miles from the firm's headquarters. "We put them off-campus in order to create an entrepreneurial environment," Hettinger recalls.

The first venture team recommendation, complete with a business plan, was to produce plastic trays for frozen entrees that could be used in either regular or microwave ovens. The business potential for this product was estimated to be in excess of $50 million a year within five years.

Signode launched a total of six teams between October 1983 and April 1986. Two teams have already finished their strategic tasks and the other four are scheduled to make presentations to top management. All team volunteers passed a rigorous selection process. Typically, the employees are borrowed from operating divisions; after their team's work is finished, they either return to their old positions or take on positions with the newly formed business unit and further champion the new ideas.

According to Hettinger, the V-Team experience rekindled enthusiasm and affected morale overall. In every case a V-Team member became a better contributor to Signode. Most important, the V-Team approach became a strategy for members to invent their future rather than waiting for things to happen.

Source: Mark Frohman and Perry Pascarella, "Achieving Purpose-Driven Innovation," *Industry Week* (March 19, 1990): 20–26; and personal interviews, 2005.

Figure 3.5 An Interactive Model of Corporate Entrepreneuring

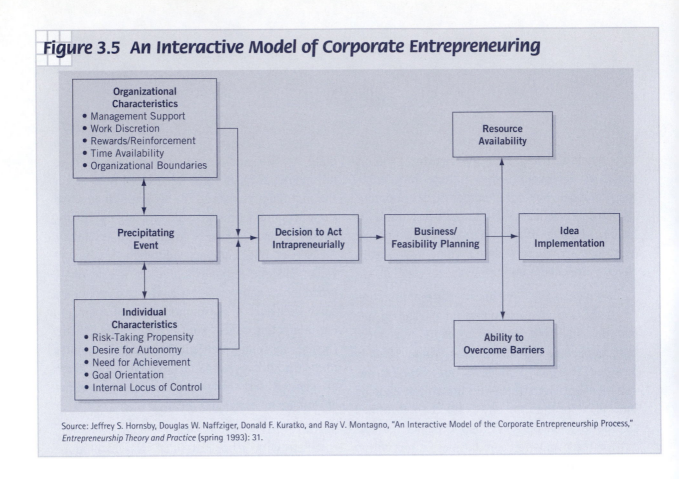

Source: Jeffrey S. Hornsby, Douglas W. Naffziger, Donald F. Kuratko, and Ray V. Montagno, "An Interactive Model of the Corporate Entrepreneurship Process," *Entrepreneurship Theory and Practice* (spring 1993): 31.

The Interactive Process of Corporate Entrepreneurship

As we emphasized in Chapter 2, the entire new-venture creation process is an interaction of many factors.[52] This is clear from the specific organizational strategies for intrapreneurship and the individual traits and characteristics of intrapreneurs. One research model was developed to illustrate the critical interaction of several activities rather than events that occur in isolation. Figure 3.5 illustrates the key elements of this process. Researchers Jeffrey S. Hornsby, Douglas W. Naffziger, Donald F. Kuratko, and Ray V. Montagno believe the decision to act intrapreneurially occurs as a result of interactions among organizational characteristics, individual characteristics, and some kind of precipitating event. The precipitating event provides the impetus to behave intrapreneurially when other conditions are conducive to such behavior.[53]

Researcher Shaker A. Zahra identified a number of influencing factors in corporate entrepreneurship that could be viewed as types of precipitating events. These include environmental factors such as hostility (threats to a firm's mission through rivalry), dynamism (instability of a firm's market because of changes), and heterogeneity (developments in the market that create new demands for a firm's products).[54]

These influencing factors seem to include some type of environmental or organizational change that precipitates or ignites the interaction of organizational and individual characteristics to cause intrapreneurial events. Some specific examples of precipitating events in the corporate entrepreneurship process could include the development of new procedures, a change in company management, a merger or acquisition, a competitor's move to increase market share, the development of new technologies, a cost reduction, a change in consumer demand, and economic changes.

The next major element after the decision to act intrapreneurially is to develop an effective feasibility plan (discussed in greater detail in Chapter 7) as well as an eventual complete business plan. The entire plan will encompass all phases of the start-up research needed to clarify the operations of a new internal venture. (A complete analysis of business plan development is covered later in Chapter 11.)

Although an accurate business plan is essential, its implementation and the ultimate success of the intrapreneurial idea depend on two factors. First, is the organization able to provide the needed resources? Second, can the intrapreneur overcome the organizational and individual barriers that may prohibit the new project?

The implementation of an intrapreneurial idea is the result of the interaction of the factors described in this chapter. After developing the feasibility analysis, acquiring the resources necessary for the new venture, and overcoming any existing organizational barriers, the intrapreneur is in a position to implement the idea and initiate the innovation.

In Chapter 2, we emphasized that understanding the process of entrepreneuring is more important than understanding the entrepreneur; likewise, understanding the intrapreneur is only one part of understanding the intrapreneurial process. The interactive nature of the process cannot be overstated. Intrapreneurship is multidimensional and relies on the successful interaction of several organizational and individual activities.[55] See the Entrepreneurial Process story on IBM.

Sustaining Corporate Entrepreneurship

An organization's sustained effort in corporate entrepreneurship is contingent upon individual members continuing to undertake innovative activities and upon positive perceptions of the activity by the organization's executive management, which will in turn support the further allocation of necessary organizational antecedents. Developed by researchers Donald F. Kuratko, Jeffrey S. Hornsby, and Michael G. Goldsby, Figure 3.6 illustrates the importance of perceived implementation/output relationships at the organizational and individual levels for sustaining corporate entrepreneurship.[56]

The first part of the model is based on theoretical foundations from previous strategy and entrepreneurship research. The second part of the model considers the comparisons made at the individual and organizational level on organizational outcomes, both perceived and real, that influence the continuation of the entrepreneurial activity.

The model demonstrates that a transformational trigger (something external or internal to the company that causes a change to take place) initiates the need for strategic adaptation or change. One such change that can be chosen is corporate entrepreneurial activity. Based on this choice of strategic direction, the proposed model centers around the individual's decision to behave entrepreneurially. Sustained entrepreneurial activity is the result of the perception of the existence of several organizational antecedents, such as top management support, autonomy, rewards, resources, and flexible organizational boundaries. The outcomes realized from this entrepreneurial activity are then compared at both the individual and organizational level to previous expectations. Thus, corporate entrepreneurial activities are a result of both an equity perception by the individual and the organization. Both must be satisfied with the outcomes for the entrepreneurial activities to continue from the

the entrepreneurial PROCESS

Corporate Entrepreneurship at IBM

In 1999 the CEO of IBM, Lou Gerstner, read in one of his division's monthly reports that quarterly pressure had forced a discontinuance of a promising new technology. He summoned J. Bruce Herreld, the senior vice president for strategy, who quickly analyzed the firm and found 22 other such cases! Even though IBM was known for its research labs that had obtained thousands of patents, upstarts like Oracle and Cisco built dynasties around those very same technologies. Why? The answer was old-guard thinking: rewarding short-term results in deference to any potential long-term risks. From that realization was born a company-wide corporate entrepreneurship effort four years later that aimed at finding new business opportunities. Under then CEO Samuel J. Palmisano and vice president Bruce Herreld, the Emerging Business Opportunity (EBO) Program was launched. Today the program stands as a model with a remarkable record of successes, such as the $2 billion Linux business, which charges for consulting on free software; a $1.7 billion digital media business, which helps companies manage video, audio, and images; and a $4.8 billion life sciences initiative focusing on "info-based medicine." While these successes are just the beginning, this new journey for IBM is making profound changes in its culture and its way of managing. Listed below are some of IBM's key rules for the EBO Program.

1. **Think big . . . really big.** Immerse into customer sector and examine what their needs and wishes are. Opportunities that EBOs search for have the potential to become billion-dollar businesses in five to seven years.

2. **Bring in the A-team.** Search for the star performers in some of the core areas, and recruit them to lead the EBO teams. They possess the experience, talent, and security to launch into the risky arena of new business development. Entrepreneurial growth is far too important for novices to tackle.

3. **Start small.** Use "pilot programs" to gain some clarity before launching full blast. "First of a kind" engagements with key customers will help resist the temptation to ramp up too fast.

4. **Establish unique measurement techniques.** Feedback from market trials, customer visits, partnership efforts, and the like are all areas for developing newer gauges of progress and success. Revenues and profits are the old guard, and they could easily kill an entrepreneurial effort early on. Look to set up the right parameters for judging the worthiness of the EBO effort.

Source: Adapted from Alan Deutschman, "Building a Better Skunk Works," *Fast Company* (March 2005): 68–73.

organizational perspective as well as the individual perspective. Satisfaction with performance outcomes serves as a feedback mechanism for either sustaining the current strategy or selecting an alternative one. Individuals, as agents of the strategic change, must also be satisfied with the intrinsic and extrinsic outcomes they receive for their entrepreneurial behavior. While it may be a "chicken-and-egg" question as to whether individual behavior or organizational strategy should change first, the model suggests that in a major strategic change, both are instrumental in making the change successful.

Figure 3.6 A Model of Sustained Corporate Entrepreneurship

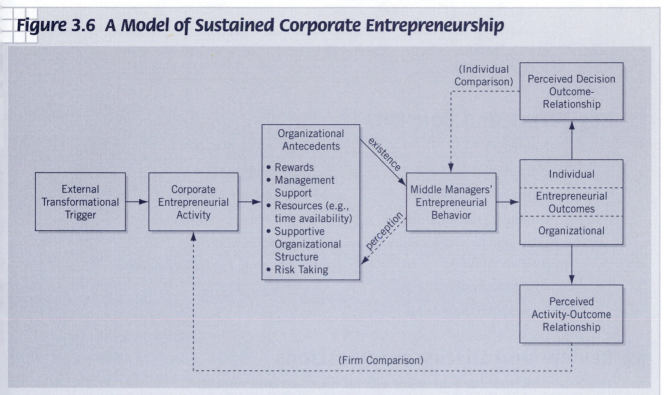

Source: Donald F. Kuratko, Jeffrey S. Hornsby, and Michael G. Goldsby, "Sustaining Corporate Entrepreneurship: Modeling Perceived Implementation and Outcome Comparisons at Organizational and Individual Levels," *International Journal of Entrepreneurship and Innovation* 5(2) (May 2004): 79.

■ Summary

Corporate entrepreneurship is the process of profitably creating innovation within an organizational setting. Most companies are realizing the need for corporate entrepreneuring (or *intrapreneuring*). This need has arisen as a response to (1) the rapidly growing number of new, sophisticated competitors, (2) a sense of distrust in the traditional methods of corporate management, and (3) an exodus of some of the best and brightest people from corporations to become small-business entrepreneurs.

When creating the climate for in-house entrepreneurial ways, companies must develop four climate characteristics: (1) explicit goals, (2) a system of feedback and positive reinforcement, (3) an emphasis on individual responsibility, and (4) rewards based on results. Organizations create intrapreneuring in a number of ways. The first step is to understand the obstacles to corporate venturing. These are usually based on the adverse impact of traditional management techniques. The next step is to adopt innovative principles that include atmosphere and vision, multiple approaches, interactive learning, and skunkworks.

Specific strategies for corporate entrepreneurship entail the development of a vision as well as the development of innovation. Two types of innovation exist: radical and incremental. To facilitate the development of innovation, corporations need to focus on the key factors of top management support, time, resources, and rewards. Thus, commitment to and support of intrapreneurial activity are critical.

Venture teams are the semiautonomous units that have the collective capacity to develop new ideas. Sometimes referred to as self-managing or high-performance teams, venture teams are emerging as the new breed of work teams formed to strengthen innovative developments.

At the end of this chapter we discussed the interactive process of intrapreneurship. In addition, we examined the role of individual and organizational characteristics that impact corporate entrepreneurship and discussed the concept of sustained corporate entrepreneurship.

Key Terms and Concepts

bootlegging

champion

collective entrepreneurship

corporate entrepreneurship

Corporate Entrepreneurship Assessment Instrument (CEAI)

entrepreneurial economy

incremental innovation

interactive learning

intracapital

intrapreneurship

radical innovation

skunkworks

top management support

venture team

Review and Discussion Questions

1. In your own words, what is corporate entrepreneurship?

2. What are two reasons that such a strong desire to develop corporate entrepreneurs has arisen in recent years?

3. What are some of the corporate obstacles that must be overcome to establish a corporate entrepreneurial environment?

4. What are some of the innovative principles identified by James Brian Quinn that companies need to establish?

5. A number of corporations today are working to reengineer corporate thinking and encourage an intrapreneurial environment. What types of steps would you recommend? Offer at least three and explain each.

6. What are five useful rules for innovation?

7. What are three advantages of developing an intrapreneurial philosophy?

8. Identify the four key elements on which managers should concentrate so as to develop a corporate entrepreneurship strategy.

9. Explain the differences between radical and incremental innovation.

10. Identify the five specific entrepreneurial climate factors that organizations need to address in structuring their environment.

11. Why are venture teams emerging as part of a new strategy for many corporations?

12. What exactly is the "interactive process" of intrapreneurship? Be specific.

13. Describe the elements that are involved in sustaining corporate entrepreneurship.

Experiential Exercise

Developing Corporate Entrepreneurship

Many ways of developing corporate entrepreneurship exist. Some of these are presented in the following list. Write *yes* next to those that would help develop corporate entrepreneurship and *no* next to those that would not help develop corporate entrepreneurship.

1. _____ Create an innovative climate.

2. _____ Set implicit goals.

3. _____ Provide feedback on performance.

4. _____ Provide positive reinforcement.

5. _____ Encourage structured activity.

6. _____ Develop a well-defined hierarchical structure, and stick to it.

7. _____ Tolerate failure.

8. _____ Encourage a bias for action.

9. _____ Make extensive use of formal meetings.

10. _____ Allow bootlegging of ideas.

11. _____ Reward successful personnel.

12. _____ Fire those who make mistakes as a way of creating a good example for others.

13. _____ Make extensive use of informal meetings.

14. _____ Encourage communication throughout the organization.

15. _____ Discourage joint projects and ventures among different departments.

16. _____ Encourage brainstorming.

17. _____ Encourage moderate risk taking.

18. _____ Encourage networking with others in the enterprise.

19. _____ Encourage personnel not to fear failing.

20. _____ Encourage personnel to be willing to succeed even if it means doing unethical things.

Answers: 1. Y, 2. N, 3. Y, 4. Y, 5. N, 6. N, 7. Y, 8. Y, 9. N, 10. Y, 11. Y, 12. N, 13. Y, 14. Y, 15. N, 16. Y, 17. N, 18. Y, 19. Y, 20. N

Video Case 3.1

An Environment for Intrapreneurship
INDUS with Shiv Krishnan

My desire to continue to learn and achieve and grow and help people and provide solutions to our customers, that is a constant, burning desire. (Shiv Krishnan)

Shiv Krishnan immigrated to the United States from India in 1979. He brought little with him except a burning desire to learn, to earn a living, and, in the process, to mentor and do good for people. Today, he is the owner of INDUS, an information technology corporation in Vienna, Virginia, that has 500 employees and does $80 million a year in sales.

His success story really begins with his family in India and the lessons he learned from them as a child. Shiv's grandfather, an educator and his most important mentor, dedicated his life to helping poor children. As a ten-year-old, Shiv remembers one day when a freshly appointed chief justice of the Indian Supreme Court came to the family's home and fell on his knees in front of his grandfather to pay him respect as his teacher. "That was very, very powerful. That showed that, when you do good things to people, it always comes back to you, and you have to give back to the community."

"The other message is, if you study hard and work hard, you can achieve almost anything in your life." Shiv took this message to heart. He earned a master's degree in chemical engineering in the United States, which led him to a job with the Commonwealth of Virginia in 1980. This work involved determining which chemicals were produced in the area and what quantities were hazardous to the air and water quality of the environment. In the process, Shiv realized that he could build a model to track these chemicals with a computer program.

Shiv's next job was as a consultant to a company called Versar that provided information products and services to the government. He continued to feel fascinated and challenged by the power of the computer to manage and present information, so he took additional computer courses. "And that's the time when probably my internal desire to . . . start a business of my own [formed]," he says. It was 1987, and he was 31 years old.

Next, Shiv worked for American Management Systems where he received his first management experience as a project manager. Three years later, he worked for a company called Vigyar and helped expand their offices to different states.

All of these experiences helped him gain confidence to start his own company. He worked from the second bedroom of his apartment. "You don't need a fancy office. You don't need a fancy anything . . . you need the tools, a computer, and maybe a printer or other storage. Then you need to have your brain. The ideas. I mean this is where it all evolves from," Shiv explains.

Shiv formed INDUS Corporation in 1993. He chose the name to honor his heritage, the Indus Valley civilization that flourished around 2500 BC in what today is Pakistan and western India. He also points out that the name, INDUS, combines the letters of his original homeland and his new country, the U.S.

INDUS, which specializes in web-enabling static information, grew over 1,000 percent in its first three years. Its initial break came with the development of MapQuest, but his customers now include commercial and government customers like SAIC, the U.S. General Services Administration, and the Departments of Commerce, Justice, and Transportation.

Shiv's wife, Meena, a systems engineer, was a strong supporter of his desire to form his own company. "My dear wife, Meena, she said, if you don't do it now, you will never do it."

Meena explains: "I know that he always had a passion of starting his own business, and we were very young at the time. A very important quality that I've come to learn about my husband is that he's very, very positive about anything and everything in life. He does not let little things bother him. . . . he just takes [something] . . . as it is, and, no matter how many times he falls, he has the energy and strength to get up and run again. And I think that is the single most quality, single most attribute that has enabled him to come up this far."

Shiv uses his positive attitude to mentor the people who work for him, and he acknowledges that his success is due to his employees. He believes that his responsibility is to challenge his employees, to bring them interesting problems and let them find useful solutions. "This is a people business that we are in. . . . The moment that you have the first employee, the challenges start. . . . We are [also] in the business of deploying the intellectual capital of our people to help our customers. So one of the basic tenants of INDUS is total employee satisfaction."

"I look at the strengths in people. I do not dwell on negatives or failures." He works hard to make sure that the work environment is friendly, not stressful. In fact, he is well known for walking around the offices with a smile on his face to encourage his employees, which they tease him about.

In addition to mentoring his employees, Shiv reaches out to help others in the community, such as new entrepreneurs. He also works with graduate students and the business leadership team at George Mason University.

The lessons that he learned from his boyhood in India have made Shiv Krishnan one of the most successful and respected entrepreneurs in the United States today.

Questions

1. Explain the attributes that make Shiv Krishnan a successful entrepreneur.

2. Explain the attributes that make Shiv Krishnan a good mentor for intrapreneurs at INDUS.

3. Would you like to work at INDUS? Explain your response.

Case 3.2

Southwest Airlines: Positively Outrageous Leadership

When Southwest Airlines first taxied onto the runway of Dallas's Love Field in 1971, industry gurus predicted it would be a short trip to bankruptcy for the Texas-based airline. But the first short-haul, low-fare, high-frequency, point-to-point carrier took a unique idea and made it fly. Today, Southwest Airlines is the most profitable commercial airline in the world.

But it took more than a wing and a prayer for Southwest to soar to such lofty altitudes. It took a maverick spirit. From the beginning, Southwest has flown against convention. Southwest's fleet of 737s—considered by many the safest in the industry— still makes only short hauls to 45 cities. The average flight distance is 394 miles. The airline does not give seat assignments, and the only food it serves passengers is a "snack pack." But what Southwest may lack in amenities, it seems to more than make up for in what could be called positively outrageous service. "FUN" is the company's mandate! Leading the way is founder and CEO, Herb Kelleher. "Herb Kelleher is defi- nitely the zaniest CEO in the world," Libby Sartain, vice president of Southwest Air- lines's People Department, admits. "Where else would you find a CEO who dresses up as Elvis Presley, who's on a first-name basis with 20,000 employees, and who has a heart as big as the state of Texas? His style has fostered an atmosphere where people feel comfortable being themselves—where they can have a good time when they work."

Legendary for his love of laughter, Kelleher calls his unique leadership style *management by fooling around.* "An important part of leadership, I think, is enjoying what you're doing and letting it show to the people that you work with," Kelleher reveals. "And I would much rather have a company that is bound by love, rather than bound by fear." Kelleher's philosophy has been enthusiastically embraced by a workforce that is 85 percent unionized. "Southwest's culture is designed to promote high spirit and avoid complacency. We have little hierarchy here. Our employees are encouraged to be creative and innovative, to break rules when they need to in order to provide good service to our customers," Sartain explains. "If you create the type of environment that a person really feels valued and they feel they make a difference, then they're going to be motivated. That's the type of environment we create here for our employees," Rita Bailey, Southwest's director of training, adds.

Beginning with its new-employee orientation, the airline nurtures intrapreneurship by grooming a workforce of leaders. "You can do whatever it takes to keep this airline on top," an orientation instructor tells his class of newly hired staffers. At Southwest Airlines's University for People, future managers and supervisors attend a course titled "Leading with Integrity." Through a series of role-playing exercises, employees learn that trust, cooperation, mutual respect, and good communication are the components of success. "An organization that has an esprit, that does things cooperatively and voluntarily rather than through coercion, is the most competitive organization you can have," Kelleher asserts. These guiding principles have earned Southwest Airlines the distinction of being named one of the ten best companies to work for in America.

Employees are valued and recognized in many ways for their achievements. Perhaps the most prestigious is Southwest's "Heroes of the Heart" award. Each year, one outstanding department has its name tattooed on a Southwest Jet. Southwest was the first airline to offer stock options to its employees. Today, employees own approximately 10 percent of the company.

In the lobby of Southwest Airlines's corporate headquarters is a prominent tribute to the men and women of Southwest. It reads: "The people of Southwest Airlines are the creators of what we have become—and what we will be. Our people transformed an idea into a legend. That legend will continue to grow only so long as it is nourished by our people's indomitable spirit, boundless energy, immense goodwill, and burning desire to excel. Our thanks and our love to the people of Southwest Airlines for creating a marvelous family and wondrous airline."

Questions

1. Describe some of the factors needed to reengineer corporate thinking that Southwest Airlines already exhibits.

2. What specific elements of a corporate entrepreneurial strategy are apparent within Southwest Airlines?

3. How has Herb Kelleher structured a climate conducive to entrepreneurial activity?

Notes

1. Shaker A. Zahra, Donald F. Kuratko, and Daniel F. Jennings, "Entrepreneurship and the Acquisition of Dynamic Organizational Capabilities," *Entrepreneurship Theory and Practice* (spring 1999): 5–10.

2. Peter F. Drucker, "Our Entrepreneurial Economy," *Harvard Business Review* (January/February 1984): 59–64.

3. Ibid., 60–61.

4. See, for example, C. Wesley Morse, "The Delusion of Intrapreneurship," *Long Range Planning* 19 (1986): 92–95; W. Jack Duncan et al., "Intrapreneurship and the Reinvention of the Corporation," *Business Horizons* (May/June 1988): 16–21; and Neal Thornberry, "Corporate Entrepreneurship: Antidote or Oxymoron?" *European Management Journal* 19(5) (2001): 526–533.

5. Robert A. Burgelman, "Designs for Corporate Entrepreneuring," *California Management Review* 26 (1984): 154–166; Rosabeth M. Kanter, "Supporting Innovation and Venture Developments in

Established Companies," *Journal of Business Venturing* (January 1985): 47–60; Donald F. Kuratko and Ray V. Montagno, "The Intrapreneurial Spirit," *Training and Development Journal* (October 1989): 83–86; Donald F. Kuratko and Jeffrey S. Hornsby, "Developing Entrepreneurial Leadership in Contemporary Organizations," *Journal of Management Systems* 8 (1997): 17–24; and Donald F. Kuratko, R. Duane Ireland, and Jeffrey S. Hornsby, "Improving Firm Performance Through Entrepreneurial Actions: Acordia's Corporate Entrepreneurship Strategy," *Academy of Management Executive* 15(4) (2001): 60–71.

6. For example, see Michael H. Morris and J. Don Trotter, "Institutionalizing Entrepreneurship in a Large Company: A Case Study at AT&T," *Industrial Marketing Management* 19 (1990): 131–134; Brian McWilliams, "Strength from Within–How Today's Companies Nurture Entrepreneurs," *Enterprise* (April 1993): 43–44; Donald F. Kuratko, Michael D. Houk, and Richard M. Hodgetts, "Acordia, Inc. Leadership Through the Transformation of Growing Small," *Journal of Leadership Studies* (spring 1998): 152–164; and Michael H. Morris and Donald F. Kuratko, *Corporate Entrepreneurship* (Mason, OH: South-Western, 2002): 77–100.

7. See, for example, Joseph H. Boyett and Henry P. Conn, *Workplace 2000* (New York: Dutton Books, 1991); Kenneth C. Green and Daniel T. Seymour, *Who's Going to Run General Motors?* (Princeton, NJ: Peterson's Guides, 1991); Robert L. Kuhn, *Generating Creativity and Innovation in Large Bureaucracies* (Westport, CT: Quorum Books, 1993); Zenas Block and Ian C. MacMillan, *Corporate Venturing* (Boston: Harvard Business School Press, 1993); and Gary Hamel, *Leading the Revolution* (Boston, MA: Harvard Business School Press, 2000).

8. Donald F. Kuratko, Jeffrey S. Hornsby, Douglas W. Naffziger, and Ray V. Montagno, "Implementing Entrepreneurial Thinking in Established Organizations," *Advanced Management Journal* (winter 1993): 28–34; Shaker A. Zahra, Daniel F. Jennings, and Donald F. Kuratko, "The Antecedents and Consequences of Firm-Level Entrepreneurship: The State of the Field," *Entrepreneurship Theory and Practice* 24(2) (1999): 45–65; and Michael H. Morris and Donald F. Kuratko, *Corporate Entrepreneurship* (Mason, OH: South-Western, 2002).

9. Gifford Pinchot III, *Intrapreneuring* (New York: Harper & Row, 1985).

10. Steven C. Brandt, *Entrepreneuring in Established Companies* (Homewood, IL: Dow-Jones-Irwin, 1986), 54.

11. Bruce R. Barringer and Alan C. Bluedorn, "Corporate Entrepreneurship and Strategic Management," *Strategic Management Journal* 20 (1999): 421–444; see also Jeffrey G. Covin and Morgan P. Miles, "Corporate Entrepreneurship and the Pursuit of Competitive Advantage," *Entrepreneurship Theory and Practice* (March 1999): 47–64.

12. See Robert A. Burgelman, "Designs for Corporate Entrepreneurship," *California Management Review* (winter 1984): 154–166; Rosabeth M. Kanter, "Supporting Innovation and Venture Development in Established Companies," *Journal of Business Venturing* (winter 1985): 47–60; and Donald F. Kuratko, "Intrapreneurship: Developing Innovation in the Corporation," *Advances in Global High Technology Management* 3 (1993): 3–14.

13. Fariborz Damanpour, "Organizational Innovation: A Meta-analysis of Determinant and Moderators," *Academy of Management Journal* 34 (1991): 355–390.

14. Shaker A. Zahra, "Predictors and Financial Outcomes of Corporate Entrepreneurship: An Exploratory Study," *Journal of Business Venturing* 6 (1991): 259–286.

15. William D. Guth and Ari Ginsberg, "Corporate Entrepreneurship," *Strategic Management Journal* (special issue) 11 (1990): 5–15.

16. Pramodita Sharma and James J. Chrisman, "Toward a Reconciliation of the Definitional Issues in the Field of Corporate Entrepreneurship," *Entrepreneurship Theory and Practice* (spring 1999): 11–28.

17. R. Duane Ireland, Donald F. Kuratko, and Jeffrey G. Covin, "Antecedents, Elements, and Consequences of Corporate Entrepreneurship," *Best Paper Proceedings: National Academy of Management* (August 2003) CD Rom: L1–L6; and R. Duane Ireland, Jeffrey G. Covin, and Donald F. Kuratko, *Corporate Entrepreneurship Strategy* (2007, forthcoming).

18. Tom Peters, *Liberation Management* (New York: Alfred A. Knopf, 1992); Tom Peters, *The Circle of Innovation* (New York: Alfred A. Knopf, 1997); and Tom Peters, *Re-Imagine! Business Excellence in a Disruptive Age,* (New York: DK Ltd., 2003).

19. Robert H. Hayes and William J. Abernathy, "Managing Our Way to Economic Decline," *Harvard Business Review* (July/August 1980): 67–77; see also Amanda Bennett, *The Death of the Organization Man* (New York: Simon and Schuster, 1990); and Donald F. Kuratko, "Developing Entrepreneurship within Organizations Is Today's Challenge," *Entrepreneurship, Innovation, and Change* (June 1995): 99–104.

20. Hollister B. Sykes and Zenas Block, "Corporate Venturing Obstacles: Sources and Solutions," *Journal of Business Venturing* (winter 1989): 159–167; Ian C. MacMillan, Zenas Block, and P. M. Subba Narasimha, "Corporate Venturing: Alternatives, Obstacles Encountered, and Experience Effects," *Journal of Business Venturing* (spring 1986): 177–191; Ari Ginsberg and Michael Hay, "Confronting the Challenges of Corporate Entrepreneurship: Guidelines for Venture Managers," *European Management Journal* 12 (1994): 382–389; and G. T. Lumpkin and Gregory G. Dess, "Linking Two Dimensions of Entrepreneurial Orientation to Firm Performance: The Moderating Role of Environment and Industry Life Cycle," *Journal of Business Venturing* 16(5) (2001): 429–452.

21. James Brian Quinn, "Managing Innovation: Controlled Chaos," Harvard Business Review (May/June 1985): 73–84; see also James Brian Quinn, Jordan J. Baruch, and Karen Anne Zien, *Innovation Explosion* (New York: The Free Press, 1997).

22. Dennis P. Slevin and Jeffrey G. Covin, "Juggling Entrepreneurial Style and Organizational Structure: How to Get Your Act Together," Sloan Management Review (winter 1990): 43–53; and Gregory G. Dess, G. T. Lumpkin, and Jeffrey E. McGee, "Linking Corporate Entrepreneurship to Strategy, Structure, and Process: Suggested Research Directions," *Entrepreneurship Theory and Practice* 23(3) (1999): 85–102.

23. See Susan R. Quinn, "Supporting Innovation in the Workplace," Supervision (February 1990): 3–5; Rick Brown and Joseph L. Meresman, "Balancing Stability and Innovation to Stay Competitive," *Personnel* (September 1990): 49–52; and Christine S. Koberg, Nikolaus Uhlenbruck, and Yolanda Sarason, "Facilitators of Organizational Innovation: The Role of Life Cycle Stage," *Journal of Business Venturing* 11 (1996): 133–149.

24. Pinchot III, *Intrapreneuring,* 198–199.

25. Robert Simons, "How Risky Is Your Company?" *Harvard Business Review* (May–June 1999): 85–94.

26. William E. Souder, "Encouraging Entrepreneurship in the Large Corporation," *Research Management* (May 1981): 18–22; see also Robert D. Russell, "An Investigation of Some Organizational Correlates of Entrepreneurship: Toward a Systems Model of Organizational Innovation," *Entrepreneurship, Innovation, and Change* (December 1995): 295–314; and Deborah Dougherty, "Managing Your Core Incompetencies for Corporate Venturing," *Entrepreneurship Theory and Practice* (spring 1995): 113–135.

27. R. Duane Ireland, Donald F. Kuratko, and Jeffrey G. Covin, "Antecedents, Elements, and Consequences of Corporate Entrepreneurship," *Best Paper Proceedings: Academy of Management* (August 2003), CD Rom: L1–L6.

28. Charles Baden-Fuller and Henk W. Volberda, "Strategic Renewal: How Large Complex Organizations Prepare for the Future, *International Studies of Management & Organization,* 27(2) (1997), 95–120.

29. Kathleen M. Eisenhardt, Shona L. Brown, and Heidi M. Neck, "Competing on the Entrepreneurial Edge." In G. D. Meyer and K. A. Heppard (eds.), *Entrepreneurship as Strategy*, 49–62 (Thousand Oaks, CA: Sage Publications, 2000).

30. See Donald F. Kuratko, R. Duane Ireland, Jeffrey G. Covin, and Jeffrey S. Hornsby, "A Model of Middle-Level Managers Corporate Entrepreneurial Behavior," *Entrepreneurship Theory and Practice* 29(6) (2005): 699–716.

31. See Gregory G. Dess, G. T. Lumpkin, and Jeffrey E. McGee, "Linking Corporate Entrepreneurship to Strategy, Structure, and Process: Suggested Research Directions," *Entrepreneurship Theory and Practice* (March 1999): 85–102.

32. James C. Collins and Jerry I. Porras, "Building Your Company's Vision," *Harvard Business Review* (September–October 1996): 65–77.

33. See, for example, Dean M. Schroeder, "A Dynamic Perspective on the Impact of Process Innovation upon Competitive Strategies," *Strategic Management Journal* 2 (1990): 25–41; and C. Marlene Fiol, "Thought Worlds Colliding: The Role of Contradiction in Corporate Innovation Processes," *Entrepreneurship Theory and Practice* (spring 1995): 71–90.

34. Thomas J. Peters, *Thriving on Chaos* (New York: Harper & Row, 1987).

35. Peter F. Drucker, "The Discipline of Innovation," *Harvard Business Review* (May/June 1985): 67–72.

36. Harry S. Dent, Jr., "Reinventing Corporate Innovation," *Small Business Reports* (June 1990): 31–42.

37. Jane M. Howell and Christopher A. Higgins, "Champions of Change: Identifying, Understanding, and Supporting Champions of Technology Innovations," *Organizational Dynamics* (summer 1990):

40–55; and Patricia G. Greene, Candida G. Brush, and Myra M. Hart, "The Corporate Venture Champion: A Resource-based Approach to Role and Process," *Entrepreneurship Theory and Practice* (March 1999): 103–122.

38. John A. Pearce II, Tracy Robertson Kramer, and D. Keith Robbins, "Effects of Managers' Entrepreneurial Behavior on Subordinates," *Journal of Business Venturing* 12 (1997): 147–160.

39. See Russell Mitchell, "Masters of Innovation," *Business Week* (April 1989), 58–63; *3M Annual Report*, 1995; and R. M. Kanter, J. Kao, and F. Wiersema, *Innovation: Breakthrough Ideas at 3M, DuPont, Pfizer, and Rubbermaid* (New York: HarperCollins Publishers, 1997).

40. Eric Von Hipple, Stefan Thomke, and Mary Sonnack, "Creating Breakthroughs at 3M," *Harvard Business Review* (September–October 1999): 47–57.

41. David Krackhardt, "Entrepreneurial Opportunities in an Entrepreneurial Firm: A Structural Approach," *Entrepreneurship Theory and Practice* (spring 1995): 53–70; and Morgan P. Miles and Jeffrey G. Covin, "Exploring the Practice of Corporate Venturing: Some Common Forms and Their Organizational Implications," *Entrepreneurship Theory and Practice* 26(3) (2002): 21–40.

42. Deborah V. Brazeal, "Organizing for Internally Developed Corporate Ventures," *Journal of Business Venturing* (January 1993): 75–90.

43. Kuratko and Montagno, "The Intrapreneurial Spirit," 83–87; see also Kuratko and Hornsby, "Developing Entrepreneurial Leadership in Contemporary Organizations," 17–24.

44. Donald F. Kuratko, Ray V. Montagno, and Jeffrey S. Hornsby, "Developing an Intrapreneurial Assessment Instrument for an Effective Corporate Entrepreneurial Environment," *Strategic Management Journal* 11 (1990): 49–58; and Jeffrey S. Hornsby, Donald F. Kuratko, and Shaker A. Zahra, "Middle Managers' Perception of the Internal Environment for Corporate Entrepreneurship: Assessing a Measurement Scale," *Journal of Business Venturing* 17(3) (2002): 253–273.

45. Vijay Sathe, "From Surface to Deep Corporate Entrepreneurship," *Human Resource Management* (winter 1988): 389–411.

46. Rosabeth M. Kanter, *Innovative Reward Systems for the Changing Workplace* (New York: McGraw-Hill, 1994).

47. See Kuratko, Hornsby, Naffziger, and Montagno, "Implementing Entrepreneurial Thinking," 28–33.

48. Chris Lee, "Beyond Teamwork," *Training* (June 1990): 25–32; Michael F. Wolff, "Building Teams— What Works," *Research Technology Management* (November/December 1989): 9–10; and Deborah H. Francis and William R. Sandberg, "Friendship Within Entrepreneurial Teams and Its Association with Team and Venture Performance," *Entrepreneurship Theory and Practice* 25(2) (2002): 5–25.

49. Robert B. Reich, "The Team as Hero," *Harvard Business Review* (May/June 1987): 81.

50. Judith B. Kamm and Aaron J. Nurick, "The Stages of Team Venture Formulation: A Decision-Making Model," *Entrepreneurship Theory and Practice* (winter 1993): 17–27; and Michael A. Hitt, Robert D. Nixon, Robert E. Hoskisson, and Rahul Kochhar, "Corporate Entrepreneurship and Cross-functional Fertilization: Activation, Process, and Disintegration of a New Product Design Team," *Entrepreneurship Theory and Practice* 23 (1999): 145–168.

51. Philip D. Olson, "Choices for Innovation-Minded Corporations," *Journal of Business Strategy* (January/February 1990): 42–46.

52. David B. Greenberger and Donald L. Sexton, "An Interactive Model of New Venture Creation," *Journal of Small Business Management* 26 (1988): 1–7.

53. Jeffrey S. Hornsby, Douglas W. Naffziger, Donald F. Kuratko, and Ray V. Montagno, "An Interactive Model of the Corporate Entrepreneurship Process," *Entrepreneurship Theory and Practice* (spring 1993): 29–37; and Hornsby, Kuratko, and Zahra, "Middle Managers' Perception of the Internal Environment for Corporate Entrepreneurship," 253–273.

54. Shaker A. Zahra, "Predictors and Financial Outcomes of Corporate Entrepreneurship: An Exploratory Study," *Journal of Business Venturing* 6 (1991): 259–285.

55. Stewart Thornhill and Raphael Amit, "A Dynamic Perspective of Internal Fit in Corporate Venturing," *Journal of Business Venturing* 16(1) (2001): 25–50.

56. Donald F. Kuratko, Jeffrey S. Hornsby, and Michael G. Goldsby, "Sustaining Corporate Entrepreneurship: Modeling Perceived Implementation and Outcome Comparisons at Organizational and Individual Levels," *International Journal of Entrepreneurship and Innovation* 5(2) (May 2004): 77–89.

Part 1

entrepreneurial
CASE ANALYSIS

"Sportin' Life"—

A Minority Entrepreneur's Creation

The Creator's Vision

In February 1988, a board of venture capitalists and private investors on the Emerging Business Forum in Indianapolis listened intently to artist/entrepreneur George Huggins describe his new cartoon creation—"Sportin' Life."

> . . . an idea whose time has come. "Sportin' Life" is an all-sports, antidrug, pro-ethics mascot. It is essential today that our children be continuously exposed to good sportsmanship, honesty, ethics, fair play, and, of course, the avoidance of drugs. "Sportin' Life" offers our youth a role model in cartoon characterization to address the needed values lacking in so many sports heroes. Children can become a "teammate" with "Sportin' Life" and learn that competition should always be fun and yet ethical. It's an individual effort to be all you can be, and it's best accomplished through unity. "Sportin' Life" is the ideal innovation to bring children together as part of a team that focuses on the highest values of sports and, in addition, works carefully to instill an antidrug atmosphere.
>
> In order to establish "Sportin' Life" in the marketplace, I am seeking to strategically place the concept in a toy doll format as well as posters for endorsement of antidrug or other virtuous themes. Eventually, I would like to license the character into other products if the market demands.
>
> Ladies and gentlemen, I need your support to launch this character.

The Forum's Reaction

The investors were impressed with the concept and the sincerity with which George Huggins presented it. However, a detailed business plan outlining the marketing, production, and financial projections would have to be developed before any of the investors would commit capital.

In the words of David C. Clegg, the president of the Indiana Institute for New Business Ventures, which sponsors the Emerging Business Forum, "One critical test for an entrepreneur's idea is the development of a complete business plan. It acts as a road map for outlining the venture's direction amid its opportunities. Thus, George must develop the concept further and attempt to substantiate the potential of the new character. If that can be done, I believe George will find capital sources more willing to commit to this project."

George realized then that he needed a complete business plan before seeking any more sources for seed capital. Even though he did not have the business background to understand a comprehensive business plan, George began the process of researching and developing information needed to confirm the viability of his idea. The following sections represent the pertinent segments researched and developed for the "Sportin' Life" character.

George Huggins: Artist/Entrepreneur

The place to start understanding the development of "Sportin' Life" is a little background on George Huggins. George is a black entrepreneur whose artistic talents are known in the Muncie, Indiana, area. He is currently an art teacher for the local high school. In addition, George owns and operates Geo-Graphic Art Productions, a small company that provides artwork of various kinds to agencies needing posters, banners, fliers, and so forth. Although not very profitable due to low volume (mostly

Source: This case was prepared by Dr. Donald F. Kuratko of the Kelley School of Business at Indiana University–Bloomington as a basis for class discussion rather than to illustrate either effective or ineffective handling of an administrative situation. All rights reserved. Copyright © 2005 by Donald F. Kuratko.

caused by George's limited time in the promotion of the business), the business has provided George another outlet to become known, especially in the black business community. On numerous occasions George has been the recipient of the community's minority achievement award for artistic talent.

Previous to his teaching and business operation, George spent ten years as a designer for the Ball Stores clothing department, also located in Muncie. This not only developed his artistic talents but also increased his visibility in the community.

George is 44 years old, married, and the father of four children. He holds a bachelor's degree in art education and has pursued graduate-level courses in computer art and journalism.

Since 1983 George has worked in his spare time developing this new cartoon character. A complete storyboard exists that depicts the beginning of "Sportin' Life" and why it has become an all-sports mascot representing sound values, good sportsmanship, and antidrugs.

> For the first time in my life I have used my teaching and artistic talent to create a concept needed in my community. The sports world is so pervasive in the lives of young children, and today that world is fraught with scandals, drugs, cheating, and cover-ups. Especially in the black community, young children seek to emulate the sports heroes and yearn to be part of a team. "Sportin' Life" offers a membership on a team that represents the values and ethics we need to develop in our children. In addition, he leads the team against the use of drugs. Thus, my character teaches the children what is missing from actual sports in the media. I believe this character represents everything I would like to accomplish in life. I believe in "Sportin' Life," and I want our children to become Teammates! (See Figure 1 for sketches of "Sportin' Life.")

Figure 1   All the Way "Live"

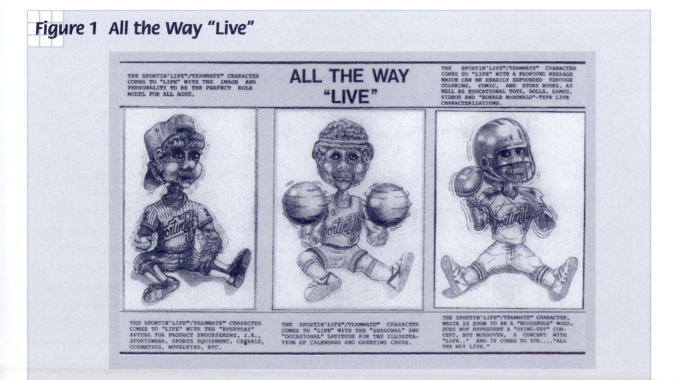

■ The Development of "Sportin' Life" (Niche, Competition, and Market)

The character "Sportin' Life" has some aspects no other character possesses. The idea that the character represents antidrugs is not the only outstanding quality. Being a sports figure gives the character a special identity, as do the values it represents. No other entity representing the antidrug campaign is a sports character; thus "Sportin' Life," the antidrug character, will be a special figure with its sports theme. In addition, the goals of the "Sportin' Life" concept are unprecedented because they address three specific areas: drug-free living, good sportsmanship, and moral/ethical behavior.

Although "Sportin' Life," as a doll, has no direct competition, it will have a great deal of indirect competition. The Hulk Hogan doll represents one sport, wrestling. Because this doll is small and made of plastic, it does not compete directly with the soft-bodied "Sportin' Life." Other indirect competitors are any soft or plastic dolls. These could be teddy bears, Cabbage Patch Kids, Barbies, or any stuffed animals. A consumer might consider any of these alternatives when purchasing a toy or present for a child instead of "Sportin' Life."

If "Sportin' Life" were to represent the drug-free theme, it would be up against three major competitors. The first major competitor is McGruff. McGruff has narrowed his anticrime campaign to the antidrug campaign. McGruff will be a tough competitor. He has prime TV advertising time plus a short video and theme song that have been out for almost two months as of this writing. Although McGruff is on the antidrug bandwagon, he does not represent the "Say No to Drugs" organization. According to a survey, which will be discussed later in this plan, people still think McGruff is an anticrime figure, not the new antidrug character. Thus "Sportin' Life" still has a chance to hit the market representing the drug-free theme and still be recognized as such. The second major competitor to "Sportin' Life" is Woodsy Owl. His new campaign against drugs follows the same direction as McGruff with the same advantages. The last major competitor is Ronald McDonald. When Ronald goes around to different towns to give his show, he presents safety, health, and antidrug themes. Because Ronald is a character and not a real person, children identify with him. Also, Ronald has been seen by many children over and over in the fast-food commercials. Being in the public eye, Ronald has quite a degree of credibility, like McGruff and Woodsy Owl. This strength would carry over if Ronald would decide to pursue the role of being a spokesperson for the drug-free campaign.

Two minor competitors to "Sportin' Life" are the characters Snoopy and Garfield. Although they are not full-time contenders to the "Say No to Drugs" program, they can get public awareness and could be competitors in the future. To find out more in this area, the "Just Say No" foundation was contacted. From its point of view, the drug-free program should be approached by letting children see actual people instead of characters saying no to drugs. People supporting this idea are Nancy Reagan, Isiah Thomas, and Dr. J. In the music industry, groups saying no to drugs are the Jets and Rock Against Drugs (RAD). They have an advantage over "Sportin' Life" because they are humans who communicate with children, not characters who speak at children. Using real persons as spokespeople for the "Say No to Drugs" program makes the topic more credible to children. Although, in this society, children identify with a character more often than with a real person, especially with "Come to Life" human dolls fashioned in toddler proportions and acting out everyday activities.

"Sportin' Life" would have an opportunity to widen its niche if his image were reproduced on a poster. For example, in the elementary schools no standard program represents the antidrug theme. However, individual teachers advocate the drug-free theme, but it is on their own accord and sporadic throughout the area schools. "Sportin' Life" could be introduced to the school system as a schoolwide mascot for the antidrug theme through a poster campaign.

Basically, the market for the doll and the antidrug campaign character is targeted at the same group. The target market for the antidrug character that will promote antidrugs and good sportsmanship campaigns will be elementary-level boys and girls 5 to 11 years of age. At these ages, children can be influenced not to use drugs and to participate in good sportsmanship. Also, "Sportin' Life," being a cartoon character, would probably appeal to elementary-aged children. The target market for the doll is slightly different in the respect that George wants to start to market the doll toward black elementary-aged children. Also, the doll will be marketed to families that have the discretionary income to purchase a doll like "Sportin' Life." Because "Sportin' Life" has black facial features and a dark complexion, the targeting of the doll at black children will be a good beginning. George plans to see if the concept of the doll will be accepted or rejected before expanding to all elementary-aged children. The idea is to start out small and move to a larger market.

Three main regions are currently being targeted: The first is Delaware County (located in central Indiana), the second is the state of Indiana, and the third is the Midwest. Delaware County has 9,871 children from the ages of 5 to 11 (kindergarten through the fifth grade), of which approximately 950 are black children. This information is from the 1988 statistics obtained from the Delaware County Planning Commission and from the public and private schools. Within the state of Indiana are 58,135 black children in the same age group. The last region is midwestern states consisting of Iowa, Illinois, Kentucky, Michigan, Minnesota, Ohio, Pennsylvania, West Virginia, and Wisconsin. Excluding Indiana, 6,468,800 children exist, and 786,763 of these are black children within the targeted age group. With all the regions combined, the total market is 7,083,910 children and, of that, 826,763 were black children.

The Survey

A survey was conducted to gain insight into the consumers' reaction to the "Sportin' Life" character as spokesperson for an antidrug campaign and also to the "Sportin' Life" doll. The survey took place at three sites in Muncie. The reason for three different sites was to gain a wide range of income levels and also racial status. One hundred four adults responded, as did a disappointing number of six children in the targeted age group. The survey showed a good reaction to the concept of the doll and the character to be used for antidrug campaigns. (The appendix contains complete survey results.)

The first question received a 94 percent affirmative response on whether the idea of a sports character advocating good sportsmanship and antidrugs is a good idea. The biggest answer why it is not a good idea is that drug problems are exploited by the media in the professional sports ranks as well as the amateur and college ranks. The character would be appealing to both boys and girls, as indicated by an 88 percent affirmative response.

The biggest response for what sport it should represent was basketball. The main reason for this was because of the dominant influence of basketball in Indiana. The next highest response was baseball, followed by football, and the fourth highest was for "Sportin' Life" to represent all sports. Many respondents said that the sports portrayed should depend on the area in which you are marketing (for example, basketball for Indiana). Eighty-eight percent of the people responded that "Sportin' Life" would be a good spokesperson for an antidrug theme, and of the 104 surveyed, 96 percent said that it would be effective within the target market age group. When the respondents were asked where they had noticed antidrug campaigns, television received 89 responses. Radio and billboards both received 24 responses, and the school setting followed with 12 responses. The newspaper, Nancy Reagan, posters, and magazines all had 8 responses or fewer.

A 79 percent affirmative response was given to the ability of the character to appeal to children if made into a doll; also, 72 percent said a need existed for a doll that represents antidrugs and good sportsmanship within the targeted age group. When asked if they knew of any doll to compete with "Sportin' Life," 88 percent of the surveys said no. In regard to competitive dolls, the responses included Teddy Ruxpin, Cabbage Patch, My Buddy, and, simply, all dolls.

The color of the character should pose no problem, since 79 percent responded favorably to the current color. Many responded that the uniform colors could be brighter. If the character is going to be successful it has to get in the public eye and be a memorable product. When asked in the survey if they heard about McGruff the dog, 73 percent responded yes. However, only 50 percent knew he represented anticrime, and only 11 percent knew of his campaigns against drug use. George must establish his character like McGruff and his campaign against crime. Because the public does not realize McGruff is against drugs, a gap exists in the public's perception of a character of this nature.

The results from the survey showed a possible modification of the target market for the doll. The antidrug sports character for promotion of an antidrug campaign would remain the same for all elementary children. The target market for the doll concept was aimed primarily at black children in elementary school. However, 90 percent of the people who responded to the two concepts of the doll and antidrug promotion were white, and the 10 percent that were black had parallel answers.

"Sportin' Life": Doll Manufacture

The most common dolls of today are made either of plastic or cloth. The plastic dolls can be either hard or soft. The cloth dolls can be all cloth, such as the Cabbage Patch dolls, or they can be a combination of cloth and plastic, such as the Teddy Ruxpin doll. The cloth dolls are not feasible for "Sportin' Life" because the distinctive facial features would be unattainable. Thus, attention was centered on the manufacturing of a plastic doll. Three manufacturing processes are available for plastic doll manufacturing. They are injection molding, blow molding, and rotational molding. Rotational molding would be the best for the "Sportin' Life" doll.

Three possible alternatives to manufacture the "Sportin' Life" doll are (1) set up a manufacturing site in the Muncie area, (2) license the doll to another manufacturing company, and (3) manufacture the doll overseas in the Orient.

The ideal doll George Huggins would manufacture has the following characteristics:

☐   14 inches in height.

☐   The doll will come in three possible outfits: basketball, baseball, and football.

☐   The head and all of the accessories will be constructed from a plastic material.

☐   The body will be made of a cloth and stuffed with a soft, cottonlike material.

☐   The outfits will be made out of a cottonlike material.

☐   The eyes will be painted on.

☐   The hands will have Velcro in them to hold onto the sports equipment.

After deciding on the type of doll he wanted to manufacture, George looked into the alternatives. He first examined a suitable manufacturing facility for that purpose and calculated all of the costs involved in the process. (See Table 1.) The cost figures are based on the average costs for the industry and related resources. The labor costs were derived from the average labor costs for the area according to the related jobs. The utility costs were based on past utility expenses at the facility and on the average utility costs for similar manufacturing facilities. The machinery costs were compiled from three different price lists obtained from equipment dealers. The mold costs were derived in the same manner.

After obtaining all of the necessary estimated production costs, George broke down the costs per doll. The estimated production cost for a local manufacturing site figured out to be approximately $38 per doll. This price could fluctuate a couple of dollars either way according to the accuracy of the estimates and according to the actual production output per day.

The second alternative was to license the doll to a doll manufacturer for production. Only a few places do this type of production, so the possibilities of an in-country manufacturing firm are limited. George contacted a doll manufacturing company in Ohio. After several weeks of discussion, it gave him an estimated price for the doll. The price range was $20–$25 per doll. This price would be according to the production amount desired, but the manufacturer believed at this point that its price per doll would be closer to the $20 amount. This doll would meet the same specifications mentioned earlier, and it would be shipped fully assembled and packaged.

The third alternative was to manufacture the doll overseas. Most of the dolls sold in the United States were produced in the Orient. However, the limited number of doll producers in America leads one to believe this is an inexpensive alternative. Because of George's lack of adequate connections to overseas producers, at this time, he has no estimated price per doll for this alternative.

A final alternative for manufacturing the "Sportin' Life" doll based on the information George was able to obtain was to license the doll to the Ohio Doll Company. While a doll may be produced fairly inexpensively, the concept of licensing creates an entirely new set of legal considerations.

Table 1　Local Manufacturing Facility Costs

ASSUMPTIONS

1. Average daily production will be 100 dolls.
2. Production facility will be 5,000 square feet.
3. Average production will be 22 days per month.
4. Equipment will be amortized over 5 years.

	MONTHLY	YEARLY
Rent	$416.67	$5,000.00
Utilities		
Gas (heat)	400.00	4,800.00
Electric	2,500.00	30,000.00
Sewage	80.00	960.00
Water	220.00	2,640.00
Phone	100.00	1,200.00
Total	$3,300.00	$39,600.00
Labor Costs		
Rotation molder (1) @ $10.34	$1,819.00	$21,828.00
Injection molder (1) @ 10.34	1,819.00	21,828.00
Sewers (6) @ 6.52	6,885.00	82,620.00
Painters (3) @ 7.69	4,060.00	48,720.00
Assemblers (3) @ 6.52	3,442.00	41,304.00
Pattern cutters (2) @ 5.60	1,971.00	23,652.00
Secretary @ 6.25	1,100.00	13,200.00
Operations manager's salary	2,166.00	26,000.00
Total	$23,262.00	$279,152.00
Material Costs		
Cloth	$24,000.00	$288,000.00
Plastic stock	16,000.00	192,000.00
Paints	600.00	7,200.00
Hair material	3,000.00	36,000.00
Body stuffing	6,000.00	72,000.00
Glue	600.00	7,200.00
Velcro	800.00	9,600.00
Packaging	2,200.00	26,400.00
Total	$53,200.00	$638,400.00

	ONE-TIME COST
Equipment Costs	
Rotation molding machine	$60,000.00
Injection molding machine	45,000.00
Pattern cutters (2)	8,000.00
Sewing machines (6)	12,000.00
Set-up cost	20,000.00

	ONE-TIME COST
Tables, chairs, storage bins	8,000.00
Office equipment/supplies	7,000.00
Total	$160,000.00

Mold Costs

	ONE-TIME COST
Head	$18,000.00
Baseball glove	6,000.00
Baseball cap	3,500.00
Baseball bat	2,500.00
Football helmet	7,000.00
Football mask	4,000.00
Football	4,000.00
Basketball	4,000.00
Football cleats	6,000.00
Baseball cleats	6,000.00
Basketball shoes	6,000.00
Total	$67,000.00

	MONTHLY	YEARLY
Total Costs		
Rent	$416.67	$5,000.00
Utilities	3,300.00	39,600.00
Labor	23,262.00	279,152.00
Raw materials	53,200.00	638,400.00
Amortized machine/ mold costs (5 years)	3,783.33	45,400.00
Total	$83,962.00	$1,007,552.00
Break-even price per doll	$38.16	

Total Capital Needed for Manufacturing Start-Up and First Month's/Year's Expenses without Any Income

	MONTHLY	YEARLY
Rent	$416.67	$5,000.00
Utilities	3,300.00	39,600.00
Labor	23,262.00	279,152.00
Materials	53,200.00	638,400.00
Equipment	160,000.00	160,000.00
Molds	67,000.00	67,000.00
Total	$307,178.67	$1,189,152.00

"Sportin' Life": Poster Production

The printing of posters may be an easy way to promote this idea. "Sportin' Life" needs to become a recognizable character to children and their parents. Therefore, posters may be a viable method for accomplishing that goal.

Several advantages to creating "Sportin' Life" posters exist. First, when George receives a sponsorship, his posters will have a message. This message is "say no to drugs." The adult consumer will support the idea of the poster, while children will love the actual "Sportin' Life." Because the poster appeals to both the parents and the children, it will have a high sales volume.

Also, the posters would be available in two different sizes. The 8½-inch × 11-inch poster is on high-quality paper, so it can be framed. The other poster, 11 inches × 17 inches, would be more appropriate for walls. "Sportin' Life" could be a positive image on a child's wall at home as well as on the walls at school (especially in the sport locker rooms).

Finally, "Sportin' Life" posters could be sold in literally hundreds of places. Unlike some products and services, posters are bought by almost all age groups. Several printing shops in the area were contacted to estimate the cost of the posters. The following depicts the costs.

300 (100 × 3 poses) 8½ inch × 11 inch	$36.95
1,500 (500 × 3 poses) 11 inch × 17 inch	83.80
3,000 (1,000 × 3 poses) 11 inch × 17 inch	132.50
	$253.25

Unit Cost Breakdown

300 total of 8½ inch × 11 inch	$.37
1,500 total of 11 inch × 17 inch	.17
3,000 total of 11 inch × 17 inch	.13

For a small investment of $253.25, "Sportin' Life" could be well on his way to becoming a poster character.

Pricing (Doll and Posters)

The doll market is an extremely tough market. Many different types, styles, and characteristics exist within the doll market. The doll prices range from $5.00 to $90.00 depending on the style and the type. The research done by George divided the doll market into three categories: low-priced, medium-priced, and high-priced dolls.

The low-priced dolls have the following characteristics. The prices range from $5.00 to $15.00. The dolls that fit into this range are Bert and Ernie, Nosy Bear, and Noid. The Bert and/or Ernie doll is a 10-inch × 5-inch doll dressed in Sesame Street clothes. The small amount of hair on the dolls does not appear authentic. The next doll that fits into this category is Nosy Bear. Priced at $13.00 and dressed in very bright colors, this doll looks like a bear and is 8 inches × 6 inches in size. The third and last doll to fit into this category is the Noid, which is the Domino's Pizza representative. This doll has hair and has the dimensions of 12 inches × 6 inches. It also has average clothing and a few facial features. The following characteristics are apparent when observing the low-priced dolls: They all have little hair, none is very soft, none has real facial features, and none comes with accessories.

The medium-priced doll range appeared to have many more dolls and many more features. The first is the Couch Potato. This doll resembles a potato and sits in a brown gunny sack. The doll is very soft and has a size of 12 inches × 6 inches. The next doll is called the Puffalumps. This doll is priced at $20.00 and comes with clothing. It is very soft and has dimensions of 12 inches × 8 inches. The next doll that fell into this range is Baby Talks Back. This doll is priced at $25.00 and has teeth and hair, is very soft, and has dimensions of 18 inches × 8 inches. Alf, another very popular medium-priced doll, is priced at $29.95. This doll is 20 inches × 9 inches and is big, soft, and hairy. The last doll is the Cabbage Patch Cornsilk Kids. This doll is priced at $35.00 and is approximately 18 inches × 9 inches. It is very soft, has nice clothes, has a full head of hair, and appears to be more appealing than the other dolls. The general noticeable characteristics in the medium-priced doll range are the higher cost, some accessories, and softer and larger dolls.

The dolls within the high-priced range are priced from $50.00 and up. Currently only the Cabbage Patch doll with the artificial intelligence fits into this category. The characteristics this doll has follow: talks, sings, nice clothing, beautiful hair, facial features, shoes, and adoption papers. This doll sells for $90.00 and appears to be the most popular doll of all the ones within these three categories.

In compliance with the production requirements of the "Sportin' Life" doll, George found the best fit was the medium-priced range. If the doll is subcontracted out, the doll will run a production cost of $25.00. With this in mind, the "Sportin' Life" doll would have to establish a market price between $45.00 and $50.00. Although "Sportin' Life" would be at the high end of the medium-price range, the size of the doll, its facial features, and its clothing may support a $50.00 price sticker.

In examining the poster market, George found that the market prices of posters are dependent on size as compared to the popularity of any one character. The poster market is divided into three categories broken down by size. A small poster has a size of 8½ inches × 11 inches; a medium, 11 inches × 17 inches; and a large, 22 inches × 18 inches. The characters found on the posters were Alf, Bud-Lite Dog, Alf 2, California Raisins, Argus, and Garfield. The small posters sold for $1.50, the medium-sized posters sold for $2.50, and the large posters sold for $4.00. (See Table 2 for full results.)

Table 2   Profit Margins

	DOLL	
LOW	**MEDIUM**	**HIGH**
$35.00	$45.00	$55.00
40% markup over production costs	80% markup over production costs	120% markup over production costs
	POSTERS: 8½" × 11"	
LOW	**MEDIUM**	**HIGH**
$1.00	$1.50	$1.75
170% markup over production costs	305% markup over production costs	372% markup over production costs
	POSTERS: 11" × 17"	
LOW	**MEDIUM**	**HIGH**
$2.00	$2.50	$2.75
1,000% markup	1,300% markup	1,500% markup

Table 2   (Continued)

DOLLS	PRICES
Cabbage Patch 1	$89.99
Couch Potato	24.99
Bert/Ernie	7.99
Puffalump	19.99
Nosy Bear	12.99
Alf	29.99
Cabbage Patch 2	34.99
Noid (Domino's Pizza)	13.00
Baby Talks Back	22.00

POSTERS	8½" × 11"	11" × 17"	22" × 18"
Alf	$1.50	$2.50	$3.99
Bud-Lite Dog	1.50	2.50	3.99
Alf 2	1.50	2.50	3.99
California Raisin	1.50	none	3.99
Noid (Domino's Pizza)	1.50	2.50	3.99
Argus	1.50	2.50	none
Garfield	1.50	2.95	none

Financial Segment

Table 3 provides a rough projection of the pro forma income statement developed by George Huggins for the first three years. Explanations are also provided to show how George estimated many of the figures. This section attempts to give some actual financial numbers to work with.

Income Statement First Year (Explanations)

☐ The pro forma income statement gross sales for the first year were obtained by combining the sales of dolls with the sales of both sizes of posters for the Delaware County area. The doll and poster sales were estimated, respectively, to be 10 percent and 50 percent of the 9,871 Delaware County children between the ages of 5 and 11. (Dolls: 10% × 9,871 = 987 × $45.00; posters: 50% × 9,871 = 4,935 × $1.50 and 4,935 × $2.50.) These figures may seem high, but the expectation is that sales will overflow into surrounding counties by the end of the year. It is also estimated that the posters will be sold to schools and other organizations that wish to promote antidrugs and sportsmanlike conduct.

☐ The gross monthly sales totals for the first year are established at 10 percent per month with the sixth and seventh months being the average. The gross sales for the year do not include an increase for the Christmas season because the business will still be in the early growth stage and have no real momentum.

Table 3   Pro Forma Income Statement For "Sportin' Life"

	YEAR 1	YEAR 2	YEAR 3
Sales Revenue			
A. Gross sales	$64,157	$292,179	$602,127
B. Discounts, returns, 1/2 allowance	(930)	(4,382)	(9,031)
C. Net sales	$63,227	$287,797	$593,096
D. Cost of goods sold			
Dolls	$25,950	$107,675	$177,100
Posters 8½" × 11"	841	5,384	12,040
Posters 11" × 17"	989	4,920	14,167
Total cost of goods sold	$27,780	$117,979	$203,307
Gross profit	$35,447	$169,818	$389,789
Operating Expenses			
E. Advertising	$1,325	$2,920	$6,020
F. Wages	57,600	68,200	82,000
G. Office supplies	3,660	4,250	4,250
H. Rent	3,000	3,000	4,200
I. Legal	1,000	3,000	3,000
J. Telephone	875	1,200	1,600
K. Miscellaneous	600	1,200	1,200
Total operating expenses	$68,060	$83,770	$102,270
Operating income/loss	$(35,621)	$86,048	$287,519
L. Other income	2,400	2,400	2,400
Other expenses			
Profit before taxes	$(33,221)	$88,448	$289,919
Taxes		29,385	95,673
M. Net income/loss	$(33,221)	$59,063	$194,246

☐ The discounts, returns, and allowances were estimated at about 1.5 percent of the year's gross sales. This figure is extremely safe compared with other industry figures.

☐ It is estimated that net sales for the first year will be $63,227.

☐ The manufacturing cost of the dolls was estimated to be $25 for each doll for the first three years; poster manufacturing costs were $.17 for the 8-inch × 11-inch size and $.20 for the 11-inch × 17-inch size.

The operating expenses follow:

☐ Advertising—an initial cost of $50 is estimated plus an additional outlay of $75 a month thereafter.

☐ Wages—for the first year estimates came to $57,600 for three employees. The three employees will be a manager (George Huggins), an accountant, and a graphic artist.

- ☐ Office supplies—including furniture, art supplies, a personal computer, ledgers, paper, and so on; these were estimated to be $3,000. (Depreciation was calculated on the balance sheet.)

- ☐ Rent—$250 a month includes utilities, and it will be paid three months in advance.

- ☐ Legal fees—These will cost approximately $1,000 a year.

- ☐ Phone—This is expected to run $200 for initial hookup and the first month's calls. Subsequent months are estimated to be between $50 and $75.

- ☐ Miscellaneous—$50 a month will be included for unforeseen expenses.

- ☐ Other income of $200 a month will come from such sources as sponsorship, videos, and miscellaneous sales. These sales minus the expenses and manufacturing costs will put the company at a loss.

- ☐ The company will recognize a $33,221 loss for the first year, and this is why it is estimated that an initial investment of $50,000 will be necessary to get started and an additional $25,000 loan will be needed after the first year.

Income Statement, Second Year

The plan for the second year is to expand the market area to include the entire state of Indiana. The marketing area would be enlarged to 615,110 children between the ages of 5 and 11. Projecting a market share of 0.5 percent of 615,110, 3,075 additional children would purchase the doll priced at $45.00. Also projecting a market share for posters of 4 percent of 615,110, 24,604 additional children would purchase the two posters.

The second year's gross sales will have the first and fourth quarters showing the average, with the second quarter showing 20 percent more sales because of the Christmas trade and the third quarter showing a 20 percent decline because of the after-Christmas slump.

Estimated sales figures for the second year are hoped to be about half of those of an established firm within the industry.

Advertising expenses for the second year are established at 1 percent of sales.

Wage increases will be given yearly to each employee assuming that the maximum number of staff remains at three. The yearly increases will be based on the amount of increased responsibilities these employees have taken on.

Income Statement, Third Year

In the third year the marketing area will be expanded to include ten states in the Midwest. This will increase the market area to 7,083,910 children in the current age group. This would give "Sportin' Life" an increase of 0.1 percent of that entire market for doll sales and a 1 percent share of that market for poster sales. In order to achieve this demand, the prices for the products for the first three years will remain constant.

The gross sales in the third year will have the first and fourth quarters showing the average, with the second quarter showing 20 percent more sales because of the Christmas trade and the third quarter showing a 20 percent decline because of the after-Christmas case slump.

Estimated sales figures by the end of the third year are projected to be $602,127, which is the industry average.

Advertising expenses for the third year are established at 1 percent of sales.

Operating expenses in the third year will increase because of plans for expansion into a ten-state Midwest area.

A projected net income of $194,246 is expected by the end of the third year. This should be enough to pay off debts and expand into new areas.

In conclusion, some important facts to note are that accounts receivable and inventory turnover will initially be three months but, thereafter, the turnover rate will be reduced to one month. Possibly, beginning expenses for renovation will include carpeting, blinds, and so forth.

Critical Risks (Product Safety and Liability)

A final consideration was given to the critical risks faced by George. Product liability was an immediate concern. Accidents involving consumer products cause 20 million injuries per year—110,000 causing permanent disability, 30,000 resulting in death. In facing these statistics, entrepreneurs must take responsibility for product safety and liability.

The existence and potential of product liability litigation are of great concern; the number of generous awards given to successful plaintiffs is rapidly increasing. A product-safety failure can have a potentially adverse effect on a new venture's reputation and sales. The need to comply with federal and state safety standards, as well as the need to monitor any potential for safety risks, are also concerns facing George.

No product is completely without risks, though, and George must judge whether his product's determined level of risk is acceptable on legal, political, moral, and economic grounds. For example, George may be more concerned with potential risks because he cannot bear the cost of litigation as easily as a multimillion-dollar corporation.

Many impediments and trends exist today concerning product safety of which George should remain aware. These impediments and trends are listed here.

Impediments to Improving Product-Safety Efforts

1. Regulations and regulators
2. Altering company attitudes
3. Increasing product complexity
4. Lack of proper organization
5. Product testing and evaluation
6. Costs and staffing problems
7. Product liability problems
8. Miscellaneous technical problems

Trends

1. Continued proliferation of product safety regulations
2. Additional increase in volume of product liability litigation
3. Increased management attention to financial impact of product failure

The "Sportin' Life" Dilemma—Then

George has prepared partial research needed to develop a business plan for his character. The dilemma he faces is threefold: First, is the information complete enough to structure a clear business plan for investors? Second, what investors should be approached—debt sources such as banks and other loan agencies or equity sources such as venture capitalists and informal investors? And, third, how can the sources be found to submit the "Sportin' Life" plan for consideration?

Additional Options Pursued

From 1989 to 1992, George Huggins struggled to get his character, "Sportin' Life," launched. In fact, he was not able to raise enough interest in the "Sportin' Life" characters to market them as a product line. He was able to develop an afterschool program for youth at local schools with his goal to teach the children a value system. Huggins conducted the program on a limited budget, mostly consisting of a $1,000 monthly grant from the "Just Say No to Drugs" program. Beyond 1992, Huggins considered other options, such as the Educational TASCC Force and Li'l TOTS Christian Child Care.

1992—Educational TASCC Force, Inc.

In 1992, George Huggins set out to start the Educational TASCC (Team Alliance of School, Community, and Church) Force (ETF). ETF intended to stress minority teamwork and build good sportsmanship, honesty, and fair play through a summer day camp series. This summer camp would utilize the "Sportin' Life" character to build these traits and values.

As George has stated:

Educational TASCC Force has developed a plan to raise the level of self-esteem in children of lower income families. Educational TASCC Force is a developmental program that will enhance a child's self-esteem with various group events. The use of a series of videotapes will teach the children to be goal-oriented, improve attitude and self-image, deal with stress among peers, and basic success. Tests will be given to evaluate the progress of all children (grades kindergarten through eighth). A set of characters known as "Sportin' Life" will be introduced to give the children a positive role model. The "Sportin' Life" characters' focus will be on the positive aspects of teamwork and group participation. They will be presented in the forms of posters and cartoons to help convey their message to others. The camp consists of five, two-week sessions during the summer months. Each session runs Monday through Friday. Participation is from 8:30 to 5:00 with lunch included. This time of day is while their parents are at work. The hopeful effects of this program could be everlasting on the children and inspire them to achieve greater heights.

George operated this camp out of a local church and submitted funding proposals to various organizations for this project (see Table 4 for the projected budget).

George envisioned his programs in summer day camp would generate interest in the "Sportin' Life" and teammates characters. Thus he would sell posters, t-shirts, and dolls of the characters. He also envisioned starting a comic strip on the characters from the notoriety that "Sportin' Life" would receive from the camps and other programs that he had initiated.

Table 4   *Educational TASCC Force, Inc., Year 1 Budget*

	SESSION COST	TOTAL COST
Personnel		
Theresa Huggins	$1,000.00	$5,000.00
George Huggins	1,000.00	5,000.00
Outside Services		
Dr. Necessary	800.00	4,000.00
Supplies		
Crafts	242.85	1,278.49
Reading and Math	191.35	986.45
Publications		
T-shirts	230.00	1,150.00
Posters	55.00	275.00
Certificates	7.50	37.50
Other Costs		
Snacks	297.90	1,489.50
Beverages	122.50	612.50
Rent and Utilities	240.00	1,200.00
Total Itemized Costs	$4,187.10	$21,029.44
Indirect Costs		
30% of Itemized Costs	1,256.13	6,308.83
Total Costs	$5,443.23	$27,338.27

1998—Li'l TOTS on TASCC Christian Child Care

In 1998, George set out to accomplish his goal of providing lower- to middle-income families with affordable Christian child care. He explored starting Li'l TOTS on TASCC Christian Child Care, a child care venture that would specialize in providing low-cost child care while providing character education.

As George describes the project:

☐ Purpose of Service. Li'l TOTS will provide quality child care services by incorporating a unique character development curriculum. The focus of Li'l TOTS is to provide child care service at an affordable price to those in the surrounding community.

☐ Stage of Development. Li'l TOTS child care services will begin on a small scale with no more than 15 children, combining infants and toddlers. The child care center will operate in an apartment complex. Facilities will be supported by funds that are generated by the apartment complex (see Table 5 for a projected budget).

☐ Service Limitation. Li'l TOTS growth will be limited to a maximum of 35 children. The size of the building limits the number of children that can be cared for due to regulations imposed by the licensing agency.

Table 5   Li'l TOTS Child Care Center

START-UP COSTS AND PRO FORMA INCOME STATEMENT YEAR 1 (BASED ON 15 CHILDREN)

Revenue:		
4 Infants @ $95/Week		$19,760
11 Toddlers @ $80/Week		45,760
Total Revenue		**$65,520**
Expenses:		
License and Permits		$400
Furniture, Educational, and Play Equipment		12,650
Curriculum and Staff Training		1,230
Total Start-up Costs		**$14,280**
Operating Budget:		
Rent		—
Maintenance		—
Telephone		1,800
Salaries		
Director	$20,000	
2 Teachers	38,000	
Part-time Aid	6,240	64,240
Payroll Taxes		7,163
Benefits (20% of salaries)		—
Insurance:		
General Liability		$750
Worker's Compensation	1,413	2,163
Substitutes		—
Food (@ $2 per child per day—pcpd)		7,800
Consumables ($.52 pcpd)		2,028
Kitchen and Paper Supplies ($.15 pcpd)		585
Office Supplies		1,000
Housekeeping		1,000
Miscellaneous (0.8% of total revenue)		524
Total Expenses		**$102,583**
Gross Income (Loss)		**$(37,063)**

☐ Proprietary Rights. Li'l TOTS unique curriculum will be portrayed through "Sportin' Life" cartoon characters. The characters have been trademarked and are exclusively used by George and whomever he permits.

☐ Government Approvals. Childcare Licensing is a complete document issued to a day nursery. This will authorize its operation at a specific location, specifying the number of children who may be cared for, the age range of the children, and the expiration date of the authorization. The following licensing and inspections will need to be obtained/performed:

- A special license for children under the age of two from the state department of public welfare (SDPW).

- A license for other children above the age of two from the SDPW.

- Inspections from the state board of health (SBH).

- Inspections from the fire marshall (SFM).

- Child Care Liability. Approximate cost of general liability insurance for the first year would be $750 annually for $1 million in coverage. After the first year, liability costs will be due to the expansion of the center. Liability insurance is approximately $50 per child annually.

2002—A Community Center

In 2002, George Huggins proposed an idea for a community center for Muncie, Indiana's youth. The main focus of the center would be to develop character within Muncie's "at risk" youth. He is in the process of developing programs for the center, in areas such as sports, activities, crafts, education, and character development. He is looking to purchase or lease a building of at least 5,000 square feet to house the center. He is also researching and evaluating the staffing and financial needs of the center. He would again use the "Sportin' Life" characters as examples to the local youth, with the goal of raising the interest of the characters to where a product line could be produced and marketed. George also plans to explore the possibility of opening a Christian bookstore within the center. This bookstore would serve as a profit center and a place to train teenagers for the job market. George is no longer considering day care as an option for the center. He is currently seeking funding to purchase a building and land, as well as supplies, equipment, furniture/fixtures, and other materials to use toward operating expenses the first three to five years.

The "Sportin' Life" Dilemma—Now

After years of relentless pursuit of his creation, George Huggins has proposed a number of options to further the recognition of "Sportin' Life." Even though none of the opportunities have provided George with the success he has hoped for, his resiliency remains strong. George sits back in his chair and ponders the future of "Sportin' Life." It's a concept he's worked on for over 15 years, and still the actual commercialization seems so far off. George says, "I believe in this character as a real tool for teaching our children. There must be a source of capital that would support it. It truly is an idea whose time has come. . . ."

Questions

1. As a consultant to George Huggins, evaluate the most viable opportunity and explain why.

2. Do entrepreneurial opportunities exist that George has not considered? What are they?

3. For developing a complete business plan, what information is needed or should be expanded for his "Sportin' Life" concept?

4. What other sources of capital should George pursue?

■ Appendix

"Sportin' Life" Survey (Adults)

1. Is the idea of an all-sports character advocating good sportsmanship and antidrugs a good idea?

   Yes _____   No _____

2. Do you believe that a character of this nature would appeal to both boys and girls?

   Yes _____   No _____

3. What sports do you think children would like the character to represent?

   _____

4. Would you like to see this character as a spokesperson for the antidrug theme?

   Yes _____   No _____

5. Would it be effective on children ages 5–11?

   Yes _____   No _____

6. If not, what ages should the idea concentrate on?

   _____

7. Where have you noticed antidrug campaigns? (TV, radio, billboard, etc.)

   _____

8. If this idea were made into a doll, do you think it would appeal to children?

   Yes _____   No _____

9. Is there a need by children for a doll like this?

   Yes _____   No _____

10. Do you know of any doll to compete with this one? If so, what is it?

    Yes _____   No _____   _____

11. Do you feel like the color of the character is appealing to all kids?

    Yes _____   No _____

12. Have you ever heard of McGruff? If so, what do you think he represents?

    Yes _____   No _____   _____

13. Would you buy the character if it were made into a doll?

    Yes _____   No _____

14. What size and type of doll would you prefer?

    _____

15. How much would you be willing to pay for the doll?

    _____

16. What range is your income in?

    $0–9,999   _____
    $10,000–24,999   _____
    $25,000–34,999   _____
    $35,000–above   _____

Survey Results

1. yes—94%

2. yes—88%

3.
Vball.	Footbl.	Bsktbl.	Basebl.	Bowl.	Gym.	Soc.	Ten.	All	Other
4	19	66	2	1	1	3	1	7	2

4. yes—88%

5. yes—96%

6. Teenagers

7.
TV	Radio	Billbds.	Posters	Newspr.	Nancy R.	Mag.	School
89	24	24	3	8	5	2	12

8. yes—79%

9. yes—72%

10. no—88%

11. yes—79%

12. yes—73% (over 50% associated with crime, only 11% with "Say No to Drugs")

13. yes—63% no—36% maybe—1%

14.
0–10 in.	11–15 in.	16–20 in.	21–25 in.	26+ in.
11%	3%	22%	4%	1%

Mostly soft and cuddly with hard plastic head.

15.
<$10	$10–15	$15–20	$25	$30+ (28% no answer)
8%	31%	18%	5%	10%

16.
$0–9,999	25%
$10,000–24,999	8%
$25,000–34,999	15%
$35,000+	13%
No Answer	39%

Part 1 Exercise

■ Determine Your EQ (Entrepreneurial Quotient)

☐ *Definition:* An "EN-TRE-PRE-NEUR" is an individual who creates, develops, and manages a business venture, with personal risk, for a potential profit.

☐ *Description:* The EQ, more commonly known as the Entrepreneur Quotient, is a self-directed learning tool. It is not a test, but rather a method by which an individual can compare his or her own personal characteristics with those of successful entrepreneurs.

☐ *Instructions:* Answer each question to the best of your ability. There is no time limit. Correct answers are given to each question to further stimulate your interest.

☐ *Interpretation:* Remember, this is not a test. If you cannot answer any of the questions, do not be alarmed. You can learn to be an entrepreneur. For those individuals who prefer a scoring format, the procedure below provides rough guidelines.

☐ *Correct Number:*

100   If you're not already an entrepreneur, you should be.

85   You're compatible. Get started.

70   You have potential. Study the rules.

55   You're behind, but you can still make it.

40   You don't seem to be interested, but that doesn't mean you can't make it.

25   You still have a chance. Go for it.

0   You're probably dead.

1. As a child, did you have a paper route, sell candy or magazine subscriptions, or shine shoes for money?

    Yes _____   No _____

2. Did you come from a family that owned a business?

    Yes _____   No _____

3. Do you have a relative who is in business?

    Yes _____   No _____

4. Have you ever worked for a small firm where you had close contact with the owner?

    Yes _____   No _____

5. Are you between the ages of 16 and 44?

    Yes _____   No _____

6. Have you ever worked for a large company where you worked closely with a top manager?

    Yes _____   No _____

Source: The EQ was created by James W. Kuntz for use by the Institute for the Development of Entrepreneur Abilities, Copyright 1984, App. H. From *Entrepreneurship Education*, ed. Kathryn Greenwood, Garry Bice, Raymond LaForge, and Dianne Wimberley (School of Occupational and Adult Education, College of Education, Oklahoma State University, Stillwater, OK 74078). Reprinted with permission.

7. Have you ever been fired from a job?

   Yes _____   No _____

8. Do you have experience in organization, planning, budgeting, personnel, marketing, advertising, administration, or evaluation?

   Yes _____   No _____

9. If you are married, is your spouse supportive of the personal and financial risks involved in starting a business?

   Yes _____   No _____

10. Do you have a library of "self-help" success books?

    Yes _____   No _____

11. Are you respected by your peers at work and by your friends in other areas of your life?

    Yes _____   No _____

12. Are you inquisitive, inventive, creative, innovative, and aggressive?

    Yes _____   No _____

13. Do you enjoy solving problems?

    Yes _____   No _____

14. Would you rather be your own boss?

    Yes _____   No _____

15. Do you like to make things happen?

    Yes _____   No _____

16. Do you enjoy taking personal and financial risks?

    Yes _____   No _____

17. Were you a first-born child in your family?

    Yes _____   No _____

18. Are you male or female?

    Male _____   Female _____

19. Are you married or single?

    Married _____   Single _____

20. Do you consider yourself a free and independent spirit?

    Yes _____   No _____

21. Do you have a high need for achievement?

    Ycs _____   No _____

22. Did you have a good relationship with your father?

    Yes _____   No _____

23. Small businesses employ more than 50 percent of the workforce, generate 50 percent of all new jobs, and account for 44 percent of the gross national product.

    True _____   False _____

24. Do you take rejection personally?

    Yes _____   No _____

25. Do you like to move around a lot?

    Yes _____   No _____

26. Is it true that entrepreneurs make good managers?

    Yes _____   No _____

27. To be a successful entrepreneur, an individual needs a lot of good luck.

    True _____   False _____

28. Successful entrepreneurs often use the advice of expert outside consultants.

    True _____   False _____

29. Do you believe that you can control your own destiny?

    Yes _____   No _____

30. Are you a consistent goal setter and a results-oriented individual?

    Yes _____   No _____

31. Have you ever been forced to move, gone through a divorce, or suffered a death of a spouse or parent?

    Yes _____   No _____

32. Do you have specific experience in the area of business you plan to go into?

    Yes _____   No _____

33. Personal savings is the most important source of start-up funds for entrepreneurs.

    True _____   False _____

34. Do you have managerial skills?

    Yes _____   No _____

35. Are you willing to work longer hours for the same salary you now make?

    Yes _____   No _____

36. Do you have a college degree or special skills and knowledge from a vocational or technical school?

    Yes _____   No _____

37. Do you know how to raise money for starting a business?

    Yes _____   No _____

38. Do you like people?

    Yes _____   No _____

39. Can you make quick decisions?

    Yes _____   No _____

40. Do you have a high energy level?

    Yes _____   No _____

41. Do your friends and acquaintances place a great deal of faith and trust in you?

    Yes _____   No _____

42. Do you follow through with implementation when a decision has been made?

    Yes _____   No _____

43. Do you believe in your own power to accomplish goals?

    Yes _____   No _____

44. Are you willing to change your negative habit patterns?

    Yes _____   No _____

45. Do you have high moral and ethical standards?

    Yes _____   No _____

46. Do you have a good idea or product and/or know how to get one?

    Yes _____   No _____

47. Do you know how to tap the power of your subconscious mind?

    Yes _____   No _____

48. Are you dedicated and committed to being in business for yourself?

    Yes _____   No _____

49. Do you know how to develop a business plan for presentation to a group of investors?

    Yes _____   No _____

50. Can you inspire and motivate other individuals?

    Yes _____   No _____

51. Do you know how to use radio, TV, direct mail, and space advertising?

    Yes _____   No _____

52. Do you know what the four Ps of marketing are?

    Yes _____   No _____

53. Are you familiar with the OPM principle?

    Yes _____   No _____

54. Do you know how to multiply your talents?

    Yes _____   No _____

55. Do you know how the 20/80 rule affects success?

    Yes _____   No _____

56. Have you ever made an assessment of your personality characteristics?

    Yes _____   No _____

57. Have you ever determined your net worth?

    Yes _____   No _____

58. Do you know what the 12 laws of universal success are?

    Yes _____   No _____

59. Have you ever explored your career potential?

    Yes _____   No _____

60. Do you believe in the power and success of self-directed learning?

    Yes _____   No _____

61. Do you wake up happy 99 percent of the time?

    Yes _____   No _____

62. Do you provide a period during each day for thinking, studying, planning, or relaxation?

    Yes _____   No _____

63. Do you consider yourself ambitious?

    Yes _____   No _____

64. Do you enjoy power, control, and authority?

    Yes _____   No _____

65. Would you be willing to quit your job today and start at the bottom?

    Yes _____   No _____

66. Do you know how to determine the "break-even" point?

    Yes _____   No _____

67. Do you know what motivates customer behavior and buying habits?

    Yes _____   No _____

68. Student organizations such as ATA, VICA, DECA, FFA, and others help students learn about entrepreneurship.

    Yes _____   No _____

69. Do you know where to get information on franchising?

    Yes _____   No _____

70. Do you know the rules of buying an existing business?

    Yes _____   No _____

71. Are you willing to follow a proven success system even if it differs from yours?

    Yes _____   No _____

72. The National Federation of Business is the largest small-business organization in the United States.

    Yes _____   No _____

73. Can you accept failure without admitting defeat?

    Yes _____   No _____

74. Do you know how to project cash flow?

    Yes _____   No _____

75. Do you know how to read a balance sheet and profit and loss statement?

    Yes _____   No _____

76. Are you familiar with the current business and tax laws?

    Yes _____   No _____

77. Are you familiar with the laws affecting recruitment and selection of personnel?

    Yes _____   No _____

78. Do you know, or are you willing to learn, how to sell?

    Yes _____   No _____

79. Do you consider yourself enthusiastic, imaginative, and tenacious?

    Yes _____   No _____

80. Are you willing to participate in both the profits and losses of a business?

    Yes _____   No _____

81. Do you know how to protect your ideas from thieves?

    Yes _____   No _____

82. Do you have a savings account?

    Yes _____   No _____

83. Are you familiar with the principles of bartering?

    Yes _____   No _____

84. Are you familiar with the rules and laws pertaining to investments?

    Yes _____   No _____

85. Are you familiar with the 30,000 occupational titles in the United States?

    Yes _____   No _____

86. Do you know how to get free publicity for your product or service?

    Yes _____   No _____

87. Are you dissatisfied with your present employment or schoolwork?

    Yes _____   No _____

88. Women entrepreneurs represent about 7 percent of all self-employed.

    True _____   False _____

89. Minority entrepreneurs represent about 5.5 percent of all self-employed.

    True _____   False _____

90. On the average, incorporated self-employed persons make more than self-employed proprietors.

    True _____   False _____

91. On the average, women entrepreneurs make less than men.

    True _____   False _____

92. Do you know where to find business and operating ratios for specific industries?

    Yes _____   No _____

93. Are you familiar with the differences between a general corporation, partnership, subchapter S, and proprietorship?

    Yes _____   No _____

94. Do you know how to find adult training programs in entrepreneurship?

    Yes _____   No _____

95. Are you familiar with the services offered by the SBA?

Yes _____   No _____

96. Are you familiar with the services offered by the Minority Business Development Agency and the Minority Business Development Centers?

Yes _____   No _____

97. Are you familiar with federal government contracting and R&D monies available to small business?

Yes _____   No _____

98. If you are a parent or teenager, are you familiar with entrepreneur programs available in high schools and colleges?

Yes _____   No _____

99. Are you familiar with business control systems such as accounting, record keeping, financial analysis, bookkeeping, profit center, collections, forecasting, and so on?

Yes _____   No _____

100. Do you know the secrets of working with bankers, accountants, and attorneys?

Yes _____   No _____

101. The failure rate of most small-business start-ups is about 80 percent within the first three years.

Yes _____   No _____

102. Immigrants have a high rate of entrepreneurship in the United States.

Yes _____   No _____

103. More than 90 percent of all businesses in the United States are small, employ fewer than 20 people, and are organized as sole proprietorships.

Yes _____   No _____

Correct Answers

1. Yes	22. Yes	43. Yes
2. Yes	23. True	44. Yes
3. Yes	24. No	45. Yes
4. Yes	25. Yes	46. Yes
5. Yes	26. No	47. Yes
6. Yes	27. True	48. Yes
7. Yes	28. True	49. Yes
8. Yes	29. Yes	50. Yes
9. Yes	30. Yes	51. Yes
10. Yes	31. Yes	52. Yes
11. Yes	32. Yes	53. Yes
12. Yes	33. True	54. Yes
13. Yes	34. Yes	55. Yes
14. Yes	35. Yes	56. Yes
15. Yes	36. Yes	57. Yes
16. Yes	37. Yes	58. Yes
17. Yes	38. Yes	59. Yes
18. Either	39. Yes	60. Yes
19. Either	40. Yes	61. Yes
20. Yes	41. Yes	62. Yes
21. Yes	42. Yes	63. Yes

64. Yes	78. Yes	92. Yes
65. Yes	79. Yes	93. Yes
66. Yes	80. Yes	94. Yes
67. Yes	81. Yes	95. Yes
68. True	82. Yes	96. Yes
69. Yes	83. Yes	97. Yes
70. Yes	84. Yes	98. Yes
71. Yes	85. Yes	99. Yes
72. True	86. Yes	100. Yes
73. Yes	87. Yes	101. True
74. Yes	88. True	102. True
75. Yes	89. True	103. True
76. Yes	90. True	
77. Yes	91. True	

PART 2

The Entrepreneurial Perspective

4 The Entrepreneurial Mind-Set in Individuals

For all we know about balance sheets, income statements, and cash flow accounting; for all of our understanding about marketing strategies, tactics, and techniques; and for everything we have learned about management principles and practices, there remains something essential, yet mysterious, at the core of entrepreneurship. It is so mysterious that we cannot see it or touch it; yet we feel it and know it exists. It cannot be mined, manufactured, or bought; yet it can de discovered. Its source is invisible; yet its results are tangible and measurable. This mysterious core is so powerful that it can make the remarkable appear ordinary, so contagious that it can spread like wildfire from one to another and so persuasive that it can transform doubt and uncertainty into conviction. This mysterious core is PASSION!

Ray Smilor, Ph.D.
Daring Visionaries

Chapter Objectives

1 To describe the entrepreneurial mind-set.

2 To present the major sources of information useful in profiling the entrepreneurial mind-set

3 To identify and discuss the most commonly cited characteristics found in successful entrepreneurs

4 To discuss the "dark side" of entrepreneurship

5 To identify and describe the different types of risk entrepreneurs face as well as the major causes of stress for these individuals and the ways they can handle stress

6 To examine entrepreneurial motivation

The Entrepreneurial Mind-Set

Today's current younger generation is sometimes referred to as Generation X because they feel "X-ed" out of traditional opportunities. This generation of the twenty-first century may become known as Generation E, however, because they are becoming the most entrepreneurial generation since the Industrial Revolution. As many as 5.6 million Americans younger than age 34 are actively trying to start their own businesses today. One-third of new entrepreneurs are younger than age 30, more than 60 percent of 18- to 29-year-olds say they want to own their own businesses, and nearly 80 percent of would-be entrepreneurs in the United States are between the ages of 18 and 34.[1]

Every person has the potential and free choice to pursue a career as an entrepreneur. Exactly what motivates individuals to make a choice for entrepreneurship has not been identified, at least not as one single event, characteristic, or trait. As we demonstrated in Chapter 2, researchers are continually striving to learn more about the entire entrepreneurial process to better understand the driving forces within entrepreneurs.[2] Throughout this book, the chapters are designed to concentrate on learning the discipline of entrepreneurship. However, this chapter is devoted to a more psychological look at entrepreneurs.

This chapter describes the most common characteristics associated with successful entrepreneurs as well as the elements associated with the "dark side" of entrepreneurship. In this manner we can become more acquainted with the complete perspective involved with **entrepreneurial behavior.** We call this the **entrepreneurial mind-set** an individual exhibits. Although certainly not an exact science, examining this mind-set provides an interesting look at the entrepreneurial potential within every individual.[3]

Who Are Entrepreneurs?

Frank Carney, the founder of Pizza Hut, Inc., once described entrepreneurs as the cornerstone of the American enterprise system, the self-renewing agents for our economic environment. Normally defined as risk takers in new-venture creations, entrepreneurs are uniquely optimistic, hard-driving, committed individuals who derive great satisfaction from being independent. Starting a new business requires more than just an idea; it requires a special person, an entrepreneur, who uses sound judgment and planning along with risk taking to ensure the success of his or her own business.

Entrepreneurs, driven by an intense commitment and determined perseverance, work very hard. They are optimists who see the cup as half full rather than half empty. They strive for integrity. They burn with the competitive desire to excel. They use failure as a tool for learning. They have enough confidence in themselves to believe they personally can make a major difference in the final outcome of their ventures.[4]

The substantial failure rate of new ventures attests to the difficulty of entrepreneurship. Inexperience and incompetent management are the main reasons for failure. But what are the factors for success? Do they apply to all components of entrepreneurship? These are some of the issues we shall explore in this chapter.

Sources of Research on Entrepreneurs

Three major sources of information supply data related to the entrepreneurial mind-set. The first source is publications, research-based as well as popular.[5] The following are among the more important of these publications:

1. *Technical and professional journals.* These are refereed journals that contain articles dealing with research—methodology, results, and application of results—that are well designed and tightly structured. Examples include the *Journal of Small Business Management, Entrepreneurship Theory and Practice, Journal of Business and Entrepreneurship, Journal of Business Venturing, Strategic Management Journal, Journal of Small Business Strategy, Academy of Management Review, Academy of Management Executive,* and *Academy of Management Journal.*

2. *Textbooks on entrepreneurship.* These texts typically address the operation of small firms and nonprofit organizations. Sections or chapters are frequently devoted to research on entrepreneurs. Examples include *New Venture Creation, Effective Small Business Management,* and *Strategic Entrepreneurial Growth.*[6]

3. *Books about entrepreneurship.* Most of these books are written as practitioners' "how-to" guides. Some deal with the problems facing the individual who starts a business; others deal with a specific aspect of the subject. Examples include *Startup, In the Owner's Chair, Small Business: An Entrepreneur's Plan,* and *The Business Planning Guide.*[7]

4. *Biographies or autobiographies of entrepreneurs.* Examples include *Business at the Speed of Thought* and *Radicals and Visionaries.*[8]

5. *Compendiums about entrepreneurs.* These are collections that deal with several selected individuals or that present statistical information or overviews of perceived general trends. Examples include *The Entrepreneurs,*[9] which is a compendium of information about selected living entrepreneurs; *The Enterprising Americans,*[10] which provides a summary of trends; and *The Venture Café,*[11] which examines strategies and stories from high-tech start-ups.

6. *News periodicals.* Many newspapers and news periodicals run stories on entrepreneurs either regularly or periodically. Examples include *Business Week, Forbes, Fortune, U.S. News and World Report,* and *The Wall Street Journal.*

7. *Venture periodicals.* A growing number of new magazines are concerned specifically with new business ventures. Most, if not all, of each issue's contents are related to entrepreneurship. Examples include *Black Enterprise, Entrepreneur, FSB, Inc.,* and *Family Business.*

8. *Newsletters.* A number of newsletters are devoted exclusively to entrepreneurship. The *Liaison* newsletter from the U.S. Association for Small Business and Entrepreneurship is an example.

9. *Proceedings of conferences.* Publications relating to annual or periodic conferences deal at least in part with entrepreneurship. Examples include *Proceedings of the Academy of Management, Proceedings of the International Council for Small Business, Proceedings of the U.S. Association for Small Business and Entrepreneurship,* and *Frontiers in Entrepreneurship Research* (proceedings of the Babson College Annual Entrepreneurship Conference).

10. *Government publications.* The U.S. government publishes a wealth of information on entrepreneurship, small-business operations, and specific small businesses. Examples include myriad Small Business Administration (SBA) pamphlets.

The second major source of information about the entrepreneurial mind-set is direct observation of practicing entrepreneurs. Through the use of interviews, surveys, and case studies, the experiences of individual entrepreneurs can be related. Analysis of these experiences can provide insights into the traits, characteristics, and personalities of individual entrepreneurs and leads to the discovery of commonalities that help explain the mind-set.

The final source of entrepreneurial information is speeches and presentations (including seminars) by practicing entrepreneurs. This source may not go as far in-depth as the other two do, but it does provide an opportunity to learn about the entrepreneurial mind-set. Entrepreneur-in-residence programs at various universities illustrate the added value oral presentations may have in educating people about entrepreneurship.

Common Characteristics Associated with Entrepreneurs

A review of the literature related to entrepreneurial characteristics reveals the existence of a large number of factors that can be consolidated into a much smaller set of profile dimensions. For example, if the work of John Kao is considered, 11 common characteristics can be identified:[12]

- ☐ Total commitment, determination, and perseverance
- ☐ Drive to achieve and grow
- ☐ Opportunity and goal orientation
- ☐ Taking initiative and personal responsibility
- ☐ Persistent problem solving
- ☐ Realism and a sense of humor
- ☐ Seeking and using feedback
- ☐ Internal locus of control
- ☐ Calculated risk taking and risk seeking
- ☐ Low need for status and power
- ☐ Integrity and reliability

Howard Stevenson and David Gumpert present an outline of the entrepreneurial organization that reveals such characteristics as imagination, flexibility, and willingness to accept risks.[13] William Gartner examined the literature and found a diversity of reported characteristics.[14] John Hornaday examined various research sources and formulated a list of 42 characteristics often attributed to entrepreneurs (see Table 4.1).

In the simplest of theoretical forms for studying entrepreneurship, entrepreneurs cause entrepreneurship. That is, $E + f(e)$ states that entrepreneurship is a function of the entrepreneur. Thus, the continuous examination of entrepreneurial characteristics does help in the evolving understanding of entrepreneurship.[15] One author provides the following description:

> Would-be entrepreneurs live in a sea of dreams. Their destinations are private islands—places to build, create, and transform their particular dreams into reality. Being an entrepreneur entails envisioning your island, and even more important, it means getting in the boat and rowing to your island. Some leave the shore and drift aimlessly in the shallow waters close to shore, while others paddle furiously and get nowhere, because they don't know how to paddle or steer. Worst of all are those who remain on the shore of the mainland, afraid to get in the boat. Yet, all those dreamers may one day be entrepreneurs if they can marshal the resources—external and internal—needed to transform their dreams into reality.
>
> Everyone has dreams. We all dream while asleep, even if we don't remember dreaming. Entrepreneurs' dreams are different. Their dreams are not limited to dreams about fantasy islands or fast cars. Theirs are about business.[16]

Table 4.1   Characteristics Often Attributed to Entrepreneurs

1. Confidence
2. Perseverance, determination
3. Energy, diligence
4. Resourcefulness
5. Ability to take calculated risks
6. Dynamism, leadership
7. Optimism
8. Need to achieve
9. Versatility; knowledge of product, market, machinery, technology
10. Creativity
11. Ability to influence others
12. Ability to get along well with people
13. Initiative
14. Flexibility
15. Intelligence
16. Orientation to clear goals
17. Positive response to challenges
18. Independence
19. Responsiveness to suggestions and criticism
20. Time competence, efficiency
21. Ability to make decisions quickly

22. Responsibility
23. Foresight
24. Accuracy, thoroughness
25. Cooperativeness
26. Profit orientation
27. Ability to learn from mistakes
28. Sense of power
29. Pleasant personality
30. Egotism
31. Courage
32. Imagination
33. Perceptiveness
34. Toleration for ambiguity
35. Aggressiveness
36. Capacity for enjoyment
37. Efficacy
38. Commitment
39. Ability to trust workers
40. Sensitivity to others
41. Honesty, integrity
42. Maturity, balance

Source: John A. Hornaday, "Research about Living Entrepreneurs," in *Encyclopedia of Entrepreneurship*, ed. Calvin Kent, Donald Sexton, and Karl Vesper, © 1982, 26–27. Adapted by permission of Prentice-Hall, Englewood Cliffs, NJ.

Entrepreneurship also has been characterized as the interaction of the following skills: inner control, planning and goal setting, risk taking, innovation, reality perception, use of feedback, decision making, human relations, and independence. In addition, many people believe successful entrepreneurs are individuals who are not afraid to fail.

Research is continuing to expand our understanding of the cognitions of entrepreneurs.[17] New characteristics are continually being added to this ever-growing list (see Table 4.2). At this point, however, let us examine some of the most often cited entrepreneurial characteristics. Although this list admittedly is incomplete, it does provide important insights into the entrepreneurial mind-set.

Commitment, Determination, and Perseverance

More than any other factor, total dedication to success as an entrepreneur can overcome obstacles and setbacks. Sheer determination and an unwavering commitment to succeed often win out against odds that many people would consider insurmountable. They also

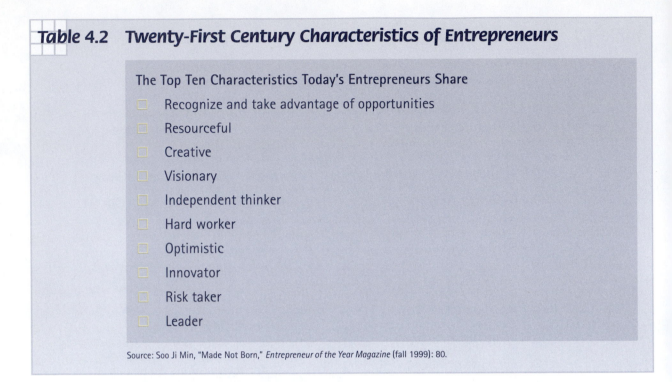

Table 4.2   Twenty-First Century Characteristics of Entrepreneurs

The Top Ten Characteristics Today's Entrepreneurs Share

☐ Recognize and take advantage of opportunities

☐ Resourceful

☐ Creative

☐ Visionary

☐ Independent thinker

☐ Hard worker

☐ Optimistic

☐ Innovator

☐ Risk taker

☐ Leader

Source: Soo Ji Min, "Made Not Born," *Entrepreneur of the Year Magazine* (fall 1999): 80.

can compensate for personal shortcomings. Often, entrepreneurs with a high-potential venture and a plan that includes venture capital financing can expect investors to measure their commitment in several ways. Examples include a willingness to mortgage their house, take a cut in pay, sacrifice family time, and reduce their standard of living.

Drive to Achieve

Entrepreneurs are self-starters who appear to others to be internally driven by a strong desire to compete, to excel against self-imposed standards, and to pursue and attain challenging goals. This need to achieve has been well documented in the entrepreneurial literature, beginning with David McClelland's pioneering work on motivation in the 1950s and 1960s.[18] High achievers tend to be moderate risk takers. They examine a situation, determine how to increase the odds of winning, and then push ahead. As a result, high-risk decisions for the average businessperson often are moderate risks for the well-prepared high achiever.

Opportunity Orientation

One clear pattern among successful, growth-minded entrepreneurs is their focus on opportunity rather than on resources, structure, or strategy. They start with the opportunity and let their understanding of it guide other important issues. They are goal oriented in their pursuit of opportunities. Setting high but attainable goals enables them to focus their energies, to selectively sort out opportunities, and to know when to say "no." Their goal orientation also helps them to define priorities and provides them with measures of how well they are performing.

Initiative and Responsibility

Historically, the entrepreneur has been viewed as an independent and highly self-reliant innovator. Most researchers agree that effective entrepreneurs actively seek and take the initiative. They willingly put themselves in situations where they are personally responsible for the success or failure of the operation. They like to take the initiative in solving a problem or in filling a vacuum where no leadership exists. They also like situations where their personal impact on problems can be measured. This is the action-oriented nature of the entrepreneur expressing itself.

Persistent Problem Solving

Entrepreneurs are not intimidated by difficult situations. In fact, their self-confidence and general optimism seem to translate into a view that the impossible just takes a little longer. Yet they are neither aimless nor foolhardy in their relentless attack on a problem or an obstacle that is impeding business operations. If the task is extremely easy or perceived to be unsolvable, entrepreneurs often will give up sooner than others. Simple problems bore them; unsolvable ones do not warrant their time. Moreover, although entrepreneurs are extremely persistent, they are realistic in recognizing what they can and cannot do and where they can get help in solving difficult but unavoidable tasks.

Seeking Feedback

Effective entrepreneurs often are described as quick learners. Unlike many people, however, they also have a strong desire to know how well they are doing and how they might improve their performance. In attempting to make these determinations, they actively seek out and use feedback. Feedback is also central to their learning from their mistakes and setbacks.

Internal Locus of Control

Successful entrepreneurs believe in themselves. They do not believe the success or failure of their venture will be governed by fate, luck, or similar forces. They believe their accomplishments and setbacks are within their own control and influence and they can affect the outcome of their actions. This attribute is consistent with a high-achievement motivational drive, the desire to take personal responsibility, and self-confidence.

Tolerance for Ambiguity

Start-up entrepreneurs face uncertainty compounded by constant changes that introduce ambiguity and stress into every aspect of the enterprise. Setbacks and surprises are inevitable; lack of organization, structure, and order is a way of life. Yet successful entrepreneurs thrive on the fluidity and excitement of such an ambiguous existence. Job security and retirement generally are of no concern to them.

Calculated Risk Taking

Successful entrepreneurs are not gamblers. When they decide to participate in a venture, they do so in a very calculated, carefully thought-out manner. They do everything possible to get the odds in their favor, and they often avoid taking unnecessary risks. These strategies include getting others to share inherent financial and business risks with them—for example, by persuading partners and investors to put up money, creditors to offer special terms, and suppliers to advance merchandise.

Integrity and Reliability

Integrity and reliability are the glue and fiber that bind successful personal and business relationships and make them endure. Investors, partners, customers, and creditors alike value these attributes highly. Integrity and reliability help build and sustain trust and confidence. Small-business entrepreneurs, in particular, find these two characteristics crucial to success.

Tolerance for Failure

Entrepreneurs use failure as a learning experience. The iterative, trial-and-error nature of becoming a successful entrepreneur makes serious setbacks and disappointments an

Perseverance and Commitment

"If at first you don't succeed, try and try again." "If you fall off the horse, you have to get back on." "What doesn't kill you only makes you stronger." Whatever adage you choose, Richard Schulze is "tenacious" personified. CEO and chairman of Best Buy Company, Inc., Schulze rightfully earned the title of Ernst & Young's Entrepreneur of the Year. His story, amazing enough to be a work of fiction, spans over three decades and defies the odds.

Richard Schulze dropped out of college to work for his father at his electronics distribution company. After gaining experience in the business, he began to pitch improvement ideas, only to find out his father was happy with the status quo. This ultimately drove Schulze to quit and start his own retail audio store, The Sound of Music. Founded in St. Paul, Minnesota, in 1966, the economy of the late 1960s and 1970s was agreeable with the small business, and the chain grew to nine stores.

In 1981, however, Schulze's largest and most profitable store was obliterated by a tornado. The sun did shine after the storm as the stock in the storeroom was left unscathed. Ever optimistic, Schulze rounded up his employees and held a "Tornado Sale" right in the store's parking lot. Hoping to liquidate the stock, the marketing budget was used to promote the event. Little did he know that the natural disaster would actually be a turn for the better. When the line to get into the lot exceeded two miles, Schulze was convinced he'd found a cash cow. The customers confirmed his theory when he questioned them on "what they truly wanted when shopping for technology products." The overall response: "A hassle-free shopping experience, broad selection of name-brand products readily available on shelves, informed sales assistance, service when needed, and a quick and easy checkout process." The overall result: Schulze utilized personal assets to reposition the company, included new product lines, and renamed the business Best Buy.

A relentless and savvy Schulze grew the chain to 251 stores by 1996. Life and business were good, and Schulze was probably working on his retirement portfolio. In fact, business was so good that Schulze decided to borrow $300 million to pad his computer inventory for the 1996 Christmas season. Much to his chagrin, disaster found him again when Intel introduced its new Pentium chip soon after the inventory purchase. Best Buy's stock fell from $22 per share to $5 as the company's earnings plummeted due to the obsolete assets. Apparently the experienced salesman was not proficient with the financial aspect of running a large business. The company was pricing its items too low, and operations were less than desirable. Debt, already at $271 million in 1995, encompassed 72 percent of equity.

After a second disaster, most would throw in the towel. But shareholders and family pressure didn't deter this entrepreneur from prevailing over the malcontent and saving the company. Drastic changes were made over a 14-month period, with the most important being the dismissal of the company's "no money down, no monthly payment, no interest" policy. Marketing, management, and inventory control were changed, and low-margin items were replaced with profitable ones. The textbook reconstruction yielded a 5,500 percent increase in earnings, rocketing them to $94.5 million in fiscal 1998. Schulze claims the happy ending was a result of his unwavering ethics, solid culture, and value system.

He never gave up, he got back on the horse, and his experiences certainly have made him stronger. The perseverance and commitment demonstrated over the years justify his designation as Entrepreneur of the Year, but his business acumen isn't the best reason for the title. In 1994, Schulze created the Best Buy Children's Foundation to support mentorship, leadership, and educational opportunities for the youth of Best Buy communities. Furthermore, amid the 1996 upheaval, he and his wife piloted the Schulze Family Fund—a fund appropriately created to provide crisis relief to company employees.

The story isn't over yet. New chapters will be written, as Best Buy now has 830 retail stores, 105,000 employees, and in 2002 it opened their first global sourcing office in China. E-commerce and international opportunities are also at the top of the agenda. With the electronics market on the rise, Best Buy has a front-row seat. Richard Schulze has plenty of experience to continually mold the story for the better, no matter what twists are thrown into the plot.

SOURCE: Ernst & Young, LLP, "Entrepreneur of the Year," *EOY Magazine* (1999): 13–15 and updated on website www.bestbuy.com, 2005.

integral part of the learning process. The most effective entrepreneurs are realistic enough to expect such difficulties. Furthermore, they do not become disappointed, discouraged, or depressed by a setback or failure. In adverse and difficult times, they look for opportunity. Many of them believe they learn more from their early failures than from their early successes.

High Energy Level

The extraordinary workloads and the stressful demands entrepreneurs face place a premium on energy. Many entrepreneurs fine-tune their energy levels by carefully monitoring what they eat and drink, establishing exercise routines, and knowing when to get away for relaxation.

Creativity and Innovativeness

Creativity was once regarded as an exclusively inherited trait. Judging by the level of creativity and innovation in the United States compared with that of equally sophisticated but less creative and innovative cultures, it appears unlikely this trait is solely genetic. An expanding school of thought believes creativity can be learned. Chapter 5 provides a comprehensive examination of this critical characteristic. New ventures often have a collective creativity that emerges from the joint efforts of the founders and personnel and produces unique goods and services.

Vision

Entrepreneurs know where they want to go. They have a vision or concept of what their firms can be. For example, Steve Jobs of Apple Computer fame wanted his firm to provide microcomputers that could be used by everyone from schoolchildren to businesspeople. The computer would be more than a machine. It would be an integral part of the person's life in terms of learning and communicating. This vision helped make Apple a major competitor in the microcomputer industry. Not all entrepreneurs have predetermined visions for their firms. In many cases this vision develops over time as the individual begins to realize what the firm is and what it can become.

Self-Confidence and Optimism

Although entrepreneurs often face major obstacles, their belief in their ability seldom wavers. During these down periods they maintain their confidence and let those around them know it. This helps the others sustain their own optimism and creates the level of self-confidence necessary for efficient group effort.

entrepreneurship IN PRACTICE

Entrepreneurs' Unheralded Characteristic—"Generosity"

Entrepreneurs' intentions go well beyond their watchful eye on the bottom line. In a recent survey of 809 owners/managers conducted by Princeton Survey Research Associates on behalf of the Better Business Bureau's Wise Giving Alliance, a whopping 91 percent of small businesses (business with 4 to 99 employees) actively support charities and community groups, an increase of 6 percent from the previous year.

The survey was conducted to determine small-business expectations regarding charity use of funds as well as to learn about the giving practices of small businesses.

The survey also revealed that the charitable practices of small businesses are identified by preferences to donate in their local community and carefully consider the use of donor funds when selecting a charity. In evaluation of charities, 92 percent consider the opinions of the community at large, while 50 percent regard it as the most important consideration. Eighty-two percent use the recommendations of the business owners and 72 percent use their clients' or customers' suggestions.

A focus on the charity's expenditure of funds is given high regard by 83 percent of respondents followed by the clarity of the vision or description of the program (63 percent). "These contributors are always mindful of their own bottom line, so perhaps that's why they want charities to observe strict limits on use of donated funds. A majority of small-business givers expect 80 percent or more of a charity's total expenditures to go toward programs, as opposed to fundraising or administrative costs," said Art Taylor, president and CEO of the BBB Wise Giving Alliance.

Sixty-three percent of donors contributed through in-kind contributions of products or services while 85 percent of small businesses indicated that they had supported a charity by participating in at least one fundraising or promotional event.

"At a time when many charities at the local level are struggling to raise funds and deliver critical services, it is good news indeed to see the widespread support that small businesses provide to local nonprofit organizations. We tend to think of large corporations when we talk about business giving, but this survey clearly shows that small-business giving is in itself an important force in philanthropy and one that should be recognized and encouraged," said Taylor.

SOURCE: "Good Deeds and Watchful Eyes," *BusinessWeek Online* (March 7, 2002); and *BBB Wise Giving Alliance: Donor Expectations Survey*, (Princeton Survey Research Associates Inc., September 2001). http://www.give.org/news/.

Independence

The desire for independence is a driving force behind contemporary entrepreneurs. Their frustration with rigid bureaucratic systems, coupled with a sincere commitment to "make a difference," adds up to an independent personality trying to accomplish tasks his or her own way. This is not to say entrepreneurs must make *all* the decisions; however, they do want the authority to make the important ones.

Team Building

The desire for independence and autonomy does not preclude the entrepreneur's desire to build a strong entrepreneurial team. Most successful entrepreneurs have highly qualified, well-motivated teams that help handle the venture's growth and development. In fact, although the entrepreneur may have the clearest vision of where the firm is (or should be) headed, the personnel are often more qualified to handle the day-to-day implementation challenges.[19]

The Dark Side of Entrepreneurship

A great deal of literature is devoted to extolling the rewards, successes, and achievements of entrepreneurs. However, a **dark side of entrepreneurship** also exists. This aspect of the entrepreneurial mind-set has a destructive source that exists within the energetic drive of successful entrepreneurs. In examining this dual-edged approach to the entrepreneurial personality, researcher Manfred Kets de Vries has acknowledged the existence of certain negative factors that may envelop entrepreneurs and dominate their behavior.[20] Although each of these factors possesses a positive aspect, it is important for entrepreneurs to understand the potential destructive vein of these factors.

The Entrepreneur's Confrontation with Risk

Starting or buying a new business involves **risk.** The higher the rewards, the greater the risk entrepreneurs usually face. This is why entrepreneurs tend to evaluate risk very carefully.

In an attempt to describe the risk-taking activity of entrepreneurs, researchers Thomas Monroy and Robert Folger developed a typology of entrepreneurial styles.[21] Figure 4.1 illustrates the classifications in terms of the financial risk endured when undertaking a new venture. In this model, the financial risk is measured against the level of profit motive (defined as the desire for monetary gain or return from the venture), with the characteristic or risk coupled with the type of activity. Profit-seeking activity is associated with the strong desire to maximize profit, and activity seeking

Figure 4.1 Typology of Entrepreneurial Styles

		Level of Personal Financial Risk	
		Low	**High**
Level of Profit Motive	**Low**	Risk avoiding Activity seeking	Risk accepting Activity seeking
	High	Risk avoiding Profit seeking	Risk accepting Profit seeking

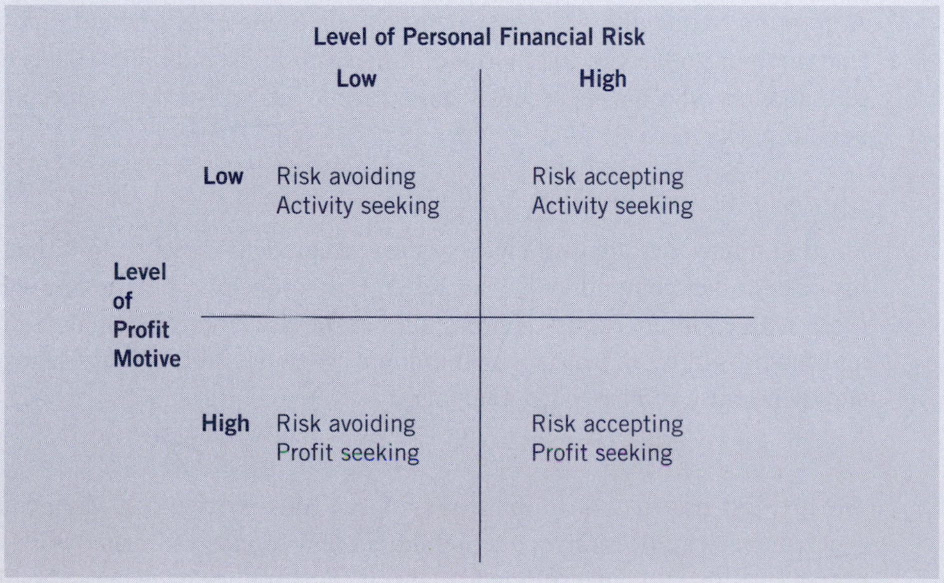

Source: Thomas Monroy and Robert Folger, "A Typology of Entrepreneurial Styles: Beyond Economic Rationality," *Journal of Private Enterprise* IX(2) (1993): 71.

refers to other activities associated with entrepreneurship, such as independence or the work of the venture itself. The thrust of this theory argues that entrepreneurs vary in the relation between risk and financial return. This typology highlights the need to explore in economic theory the styles or entrepreneurial motivations that deviate from the styles most characterizing the rational person.

"If different entrepreneurial styles exist, then not every person who founds a new business enterprise does so by seeking to minimize financial risk and maximize financial return. Models of organization formation would thus have to be adjusted for differences among those who form organizations."[22] Thus, not all entrepreneurs are driven solely by monetary gain, and the level of financial risk cannot be completely explained by profit opportunity. Entrepreneurial risk is a far more complex issue than a simple economic risk-versus-return explanation.

It should be noted that "people who successfully innovate and start businesses come in all shapes and sizes. But they do have a few things others do not. In the deepest sense, they are willing to accept risk for what they believe in. They have the ability to cope with a professional life riddled by ambiguity, a consistent lack of clarity. Most have a drive to put their imprint on whatever they are creating. And while unbridled ego can be a destructive thing, try to find an entrepreneur whose ego isn't wrapped up in the enterprise."[23]

Entrepreneurs face a number of different types of risk. These can be grouped into four basic areas.[24]

Financial Risk

In most new ventures the individual puts a significant portion of his or her savings or other resources at stake. This money or these resources will, in all likelihood, be lost if the venture fails. The entrepreneur also may be required to sign personally on company obligations that far exceed his or her personal net worth. The entrepreneur is thus exposed to personal bankruptcy. Many people are unwilling to risk their savings, house, property, and salary to start a new business.

Career Risk

A question frequently raised by would-be entrepreneurs is whether they will be able to find a job or go back to their old job if their venture should fail. This is a major concern to managers who have a secure organizational job with a high salary and a good benefit package.

Family and Social Risk

Starting a new venture uses much of the entrepreneur's energy and time. Consequently, his or her other commitments may suffer. Entrepreneurs who are married, and especially those with children, expose their families to the risks of an incomplete family experience and the possibility of permanent emotional scars. In addition, old friends may vanish slowly because of missed get-togethers.

Psychic Risk

The greatest risk may be to the well-being of the entrepreneur. Money can be replaced; a new house can be built; spouse, children, and friends can usually adapt. But some entrepreneurs who have suffered financial catastrophes have been unable to bounce back, at least not immediately. The psychological impact has proven to be too severe for them.

Stress and the Entrepreneur

Some of the most common entrepreneurial goals are independence, wealth, and work satisfaction. Research studies of entrepreneurs show that those who achieve these goals often pay a high price.[25] A majority of entrepreneurs surveyed had back problems, indigestion, insomnia, or headaches. To achieve their goals, however, these entrepreneurs were willing to tolerate these effects of stress. The rewards justified the costs.

What Is Entrepreneurial Stress?

In general, **stress** can be viewed as a function of discrepancies between a person's expectations and ability to meet demands, as well as discrepancies between the individual's expectations and personality. If a person is unable to fulfill role demands, then stress occurs. To the extent entrepreneurs' work demands and expectations exceed their abilities to perform as venture initiators, they are likely to experience stress. One researcher has pointed out how entrepreneurial roles and operating environments can lead to stress. Initiating and managing a business require taking significant risk. As previously mentioned, these risks may be described as financial, career, family, social, or psychic. Also, entrepreneurs must engage in constant communication activities, interacting with relevant external constituencies including customers, suppliers, regulators, lawyers, and accountants, which is stressful.

Lacking the depth of resources, entrepreneurs must bear the cost of their mistakes while playing a multitude of roles, such as salesperson, recruiter, spokesperson, and negotiator. These simultaneous demands can lead to role overload. Owning and operating a business require a large commitment of time and energy, often at the expense of family and social activities. Finally, entrepreneurs are often working alone or with a small number of employees and therefore lack the support from colleagues that may be available to managers in a large corporation.[26]

In addition to the roles and environment entrepreneurs experience, stress can result from a basic personality structure. Referred to as "type A" behavior, this personality structure describes people who are impatient, demanding, and overstrung. These individuals gravitate toward heavy workloads and find themselves completely immersed in their business demands. Some of the distinguishing characteristics associated with type A personalities follow:

- [ ] Chronic and severe sense of time urgency. For instance, type A people become particularly frustrated in traffic jams.

- [ ] Constant involvement in multiple projects subject to deadlines. Somehow type A people take delight in the feeling of being swamped with work.

- [ ] Neglect of all aspects of life except work. These workaholics live to work rather than work to live.

- [ ] A tendency to take on excessive responsibility, combined with the feeling that "only I am capable of taking care of this matter."

- [ ] Explosiveness of speech and a tendency to speak faster than most people. Type A people are thus prone to ranting and swearing when upset. A widespread belief in the stress literature is that type A behavior is related to coronary heart disease and that stress is a contributor to heart disease.[27]

Thus, to better understand stress, entrepreneurs need to be aware of their particular personality as well as the roles and operating environments that differentiate their business pursuits.[28]

Sources of Stress

Researchers David P. Boyd and David E. Gumpert have identified four causes of entrepreneurial stress: (1) loneliness, (2) immersion in business, (3) people problems, and (4) the need to achieve.[29]

Loneliness   Although entrepreneurs are usually surrounded by others—employees, customers, accountants, and lawyers—they are isolated from people in whom they can confide. Long hours at work prevent them from seeking the comfort and counsel of friends and family members. Moreover, they tend not to participate in social activities unless they provide a business benefit.

Immersion in Business   One of the ironies of entrepreneurship is that successful entrepreneurs make enough money to partake of a variety of leisure activities, but they cannot take that exotic cruise, fishing trip, or skiing vacation because their business will not allow their absence. Most entrepreneurs are married to their business. They work long hours, leaving little time for civic organizations, recreation, or further education.

People Problems   Entrepreneurs must depend on and work with partners, employees, customers, bankers, and professionals. Most experience frustration, disappointment, and aggravation in their experiences with these people. Successful entrepreneurs are to some extent perfectionists and know how they want things done; often they spend a lot of time trying to get lackadaisical employees to meet their performance standards. And, frequently, because of irreconcilable conflict, many partnerships are dissolved.

Need to Achieve   Achievement brings satisfaction. During the Boyd and Gumpert study, however, it became clear that a fine line exists between attempting to achieve too much and failing to achieve enough. More often than not, the entrepreneur was trying to accomplish too much. Many are never satisfied with their work no matter how well it was done. They seem to recognize the dangers (for example, to their health) of unbridled ambition, but they have a difficult time tempering their achievement need. They seem to believe that if they stop or slow down, some competitor is going to come from behind, and everything they have built will fall apart.

Dealing with Stress

It is important to point out that not all stress is bad. Certainly, if stress becomes overbearing and unrelenting in a person's life, it wears down the body's physical abilities. However, if stress can be kept within constructive bounds, then it could increase a person's efficiency and improve performance.[30]

Boyd and Gumpert made a significant contribution to defining the causes of entrepreneurial stress, but what makes their study particularly noteworthy is the presentation of stress reduction techniques—ways entrepreneurs can improve the quality of their business and personal lives.[31] Although classic stress-reduction techniques such as meditation, biofeedback, muscle relaxation, and regular exercise help reduce stress, Boyd and Gumpert suggest that another important step entrepreneurs can take is to clarify the causes of their stress. Having identified these causes, entrepreneurs then can combat excessive stress by (1) acknowledging its existence, (2) developing coping mechanisms, and (3) probing unacknowledged personal needs.

Presented here are six specific ways entrepreneurs can cope with stress.

Networking   One way to relieve the loneliness of running a business is to share experiences by networking with other business owners. The objectivity gained from hearing about the triumphs and errors of others is itself therapeutic.

Getting Away from It All   The best antidote to immersion in business, report many entrepreneurs, is a holiday. If vacation days or weeks are limited by valid business constraints, short breaks still may be possible. Such interludes allow a measure of self-renewal.

Communicating with Employees   Entrepreneurs are in close contact with employees and can readily assess the concerns of their staffs. The personal touches often unavailable in large corporations, such as company-wide outings, flexible hours, and small loans to tide workers over until payday, are possible. In such settings employees often are not only more productive than their counterparts in large organizations but also experience much less stress due to the personal touches that are applied.

Finding Satisfaction Outside the Company   Countering the obsessive need to achieve can be difficult because the entrepreneur's personality is inextricably bound in the company fabric. Entrepreneurs need to get away from the business occasionally and become more passionate about life itself; they need to gain some new perspectives.

Delegating   Implementation of coping mechanisms requires implementation time. To gain this time, the entrepreneur has to delegate tasks. Entrepreneurs find delegation difficult, because they think they have to be at the business all of the time and be involved in every aspect of the operation. But if time is to be gained for alleviation of stress, then appropriate delegatees must be found and trained.

Exercising Rigorously   Researchers Michael G. Goldsby, Donald F. Kuratko, and James W. Bishop examined the relationship between exercise and the attainment of personal and professional goals for entrepreneurs.[32] The study addressed the issue by examining the exercise regimens of 366 entrepreneurs and the relationship of exercise frequency with the company's sales and the entrepreneur's personal goals. Specifically, the study examined the relationship that two types of exercise—running and weightlifting—had with sales volume, extrinsic rewards, and intrinsic rewards. The results indicated that running is positively related to all three outcome variables while weightlifting is positively related to extrinsic and intrinsic rewards. This study demonstrates the value of exercise regimens on relieving the stress associated with entrepreneurs.

The Entrepreneurial Ego

In addition to the challenges of risk and stress, the entrepreneur also may experience the negative effects of an inflated ego. In other words, certain characteristics that usually propel entrepreneurs into success also can be exhibited to their extreme. We examine four of these characteristics that may hold destructive implications for entrepreneurs.[33]

Overbearing Need for Control

Entrepreneurs are driven by a strong desire to control both their venture and their destiny. This internal focus of control spills over into a preoccupation with controlling everything. An obsession for autonomy and control may cause entrepreneurs to work in structured situations *only* when they have created the structure on *their* terms. This, of course, has serious implications for networking in an entrepreneurial team, since entrepreneurs can visualize the external control by others as a threat of subjection or infringement on their will. Thus, the same characteristic that entrepreneurs need for successful venture creation also contains within it a destructive side.

Entrepreneurial Fear 101

The fear an entrepreneur experiences has its own taste, its own smell, and its own gut-wrenching pain. And it does not go away as long as the person remains an entrepreneur. It becomes an education entrepreneurs experience—Entrepreneurial Fear 101. Although the course is very exclusive, admission is automatic; permission is neither needed nor sought, and tenure is indefinite. The fear entrepreneurs experience cannot be expected, cannot be escaped, and cannot be prepared against. Because most entrepreneurs do not admit they have experienced this entrepreneurial fear, it remains a deep, dark secret. And because it is not talked about, most entrepreneurs feel they are the only ones who have ever experienced it.

According to Wilson Harrell, an entrepreneur from Jacksonville, Florida, this entrepreneurial fear is much different from simple fear. Fear is usually accidental, unexpected, and short lived, such as the sudden rush of adrenaline experienced when you almost get hit by a bus, he explains. On the other hand, entrepreneurial fear is self-inflicted. It is a private world where no sleep occurs, and wide-awakening nightmares filled with monsters constantly try to destroy every morsel of the entrepreneur's being.

What causes this fear? Well, it is not the money, for any entrepreneur will explain that money is just a bonus of the accomplishment, and losing money is one of the risks taken. Fear of failure has a lot to do with it. Entrepreneurs do not want to become just another businessperson and pass into oblivion without leaving their mark. What induces this complex fear has yet to be determined.

For Harrell, the fear came while starting his own food brokerage business to sell products on military bases in Europe. Harrell was appointed a representative of Kraft Food Company and did so well increasing its sales that he sold himself out of a job. Because he had made his job look so easy, it was suggested to Kraft's management team that its own salespeople could do the work better and cheaper. So what did Harrell do? Because losing the Kraft account would put him out of business, he put everything on the line and proposed that if Kraft kept brokering through his company and took over the brokering in Germany, then Harrell would help it take over the food industry everywhere. After Harrell experienced 30 days of immeasurable terror, Kraft made the decision to trust Harrell and continue brokering through his company. Although he later sold his business, 30 years later the company still represents Kraft, Inc., not only in Europe but also in the Far East and many other countries. The company has grown into the largest military-representative organization in the field and was sold in 1985 for more than $40 million.

What is the secret to entrepreneurship, given such fear? It's reward. No matter what pain is experienced through the fear, the elation felt from success surmounts it. That high, along with fear, is an emotion reserved for entrepreneurs and becomes food for the spirit. Addicting? It is more like a roller-coaster ride. In the beginning, imagine pulling yourself up the incline very slowly, making any tough decisions with a growing sense of excitement and foreboding. Then when you hit the top, for a brief moment it is frightening, and the anticipation accelerates before you lose all feelings of control. As you go screaming into the unknown, fear takes over. At first, all you feel is fear; then, suddenly, the ride is over, the fear is gone, but the exhilaration remains. What is next for the entrepreneur? He or she buys another ticket.

So what is the key ingredient for entrepreneurial success? According to Wilson Harrell, it is the ability to handle fear. For he believes it is the lonely entrepreneur living with his or her personal fear who breathes life and excitement into an otherwise dull and mundane world.

Source: Wilson Harrell, "Entrepreneurial Terror," *Inc.* (February 1987): 74–76.

Sense of Distrust

To remain alert to competition, customers, and government regulations, entrepreneurs are continually scanning the environment. They try to anticipate and act on developments that others might recognize too late. This distrustful state can result in their focusing on trivial things, causing them to lose sight of reality, to distort reasoning and logic, and to take destructive actions. Again, distrust is a dual-edged characteristic.

Overriding Desire for Success

The entrepreneur's ego is involved in the desire for success. Although many of today's entrepreneurs believe they are living on the edge of existence, constantly stirring within them is a strong desire to succeed in spite of the odds. Thus the entrepreneur rises up as a defiant person who creatively acts to deny any feelings of insignificance. The individual is driven to succeed and takes pride in demonstrating that success. Therein lie the seeds of possible destructiveness. If the entrepreneur seeks to demonstrate achievement through the erection of a monument—such as a huge office building, an imposing factory, or a plush office—then the danger exists that the individual will become more important than the venture itself. Losing perspective like this can, of course, be the destructive side of the desire to succeed.

Unrealistic Optimism

The ceaseless optimism that emanates from entrepreneurs (even through the bleak times) is a key factor in the drive toward success. Entrepreneurs maintain a high enthusiasm level that becomes an **external optimism** that allows others to believe in them during rough periods. However, when taken to its extreme, this optimistic attitude can lead to a fantasy approach to the business. A self-deceptive state may arise in which entrepreneurs ignore trends, facts, and reports and delude themselves into thinking everything will turn out fine. This type of behavior can lead to an inability to handle the reality of the business world.

These examples do not imply that *all* entrepreneurs fall prey to these scenarios nor that each of the characteristics presented always gives way to the "destructive" side. Nevertheless, all potential entrepreneurs need to know that the dark side of entrepreneurship exists.

Entrepreneurial Motivation

Examining why people start businesses and how they differ from those who do not (or those who start unsuccessful businesses) may help explain how the motivation entrepreneurs exhibit during start-up is linked to the sustaining behavior exhibited later. Lanny Herron and Harry J. Sapienza have stated, "Because motivation plays an important part in the creation of new organizations, theories of organization creation that fail to address this notion are incomplete."[34]

Researcher Bradley R. Johnson, in his review of achievement motivation and the entrepreneur, stated, "It remains worthwhile to carefully study the role of the individual, including his or her psychological profile. Individuals are, after all, the energizers of the entrepreneurial process."[35]

Thus, although research on the psychological characteristics of entrepreneurs has not provided an agreed-on "profile" of an entrepreneur, it is still important to recognize the contribution of psychological factors to the entrepreneurial process.[36] In fact,

Figure 4.2 A Model of Entrepreneurial Motivation

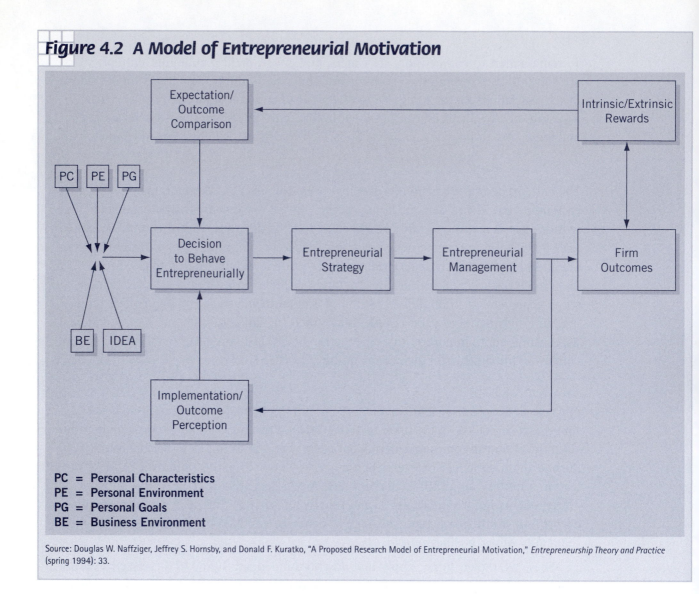

PC = Personal Characteristics
PE = Personal Environment
PG = Personal Goals
BE = Business Environment

Source: Douglas W. Naffziger, Jeffrey S. Hornsby, and Donald F. Kuratko, "A Proposed Research Model of Entrepreneurial Motivation," *Entrepreneurship Theory and Practice* (spring 1994): 33.

the quest for new-venture creation as well as the willingness to *sustain* that venture is directly related to an **entrepreneur's motivation.**[37] One research study examined the importance of satisfaction to an entrepreneur's willingness to remain with the venture. Particular goals, attitudes, and backgrounds were all important determinants of an entrepreneur's eventual satisfaction.[38] In that vein, one research approach examines the motivational process an entrepreneur experiences.[39] Figure 4.2 illustrates the key elements of this approach.

The decision to behave entrepreneurially is the result of the interaction of several factors. One set of factors includes the individual's personal characteristics, the individual's personal environment, the relevant business environment, the individual's personal goal set, and the existence of a viable business idea.[40] In addition, the individual compares his or her perception of the probable outcomes with the personal expectations he or she has in mind. Next, an individual looks at the relationship between the entrepreneurial behavior he or she would implement and the expected outcomes.

According to the model, the entrepreneur's expectations are finally compared with the actual or perceived firm outcomes. Future entrepreneurial behavior is based on the results of all of these comparisons. When outcomes meet or exceed expectations, the entrepreneurial behavior is positively reinforced, and the individual is motivated to continue to behave entrepreneurially, either within the current venture or possibly through the initiation of additional ventures, depending on the existing entrepreneurial goal. When outcomes fail to meet expectations, the entrepreneur's motivation will be lower and will have a corresponding impact on the decision to continue to act entrepreneurially. These perceptions also affect succeeding strategies, strategy implementation, and management of the firm.[41]

Summary

In attempting to explain the "entrepreneurial mind-set within individuals, this chapter presented the most common characteristics exhibited by successful entrepreneurs. Then a review of the "dark side" of entrepreneurship revealed certain factors that possess a destructive vein for entrepreneurs. Finally, a motivational model of entrepreneurship was discussed.

First, it is important to recognize that a number of sources of information relating to the entrepreneurial mind-set exist. Three major ones are publications, direct observation, and presentations by or case studies of practicing entrepreneurs.

Several studies have been conducted to determine the personal qualities and traits of successful entrepreneurs. Some of these were examined in the chapter: commitment, determination, and perseverance; drive to achieve; opportunity orientation; initiative and responsibility; persistent problem solving; seeking feedback; internal locus of control; tolerance for ambiguity; calculated risk taking; integrity and reliability; tolerance for failure; high energy level; creativity and innovativeness; vision; self-confidence and optimism; independence; and team building.

The next part of the chapter focused on the dark side of entrepreneurship, including the confrontation with risk, the problems of stress, and the particular traits that may permeate the entrepreneurial ego.

Finally, the chapter introduced a model of entrepreneurial motivation. Recognizing the contribution of psychological factors to the process of entrepreneurship, this model demonstrated the importance of entrepreneurs' perceived expectations and actual outcomes in their motivation to start and sustain a venture.

Key Terms and Concepts

calculated risk taking	immersion in business
career risk	loneliness
dark side of entrepreneurship	need for control
delegating	networking
drive to achieve	opportunity orientation
entrepreneurial behavior	psychic risk
entrepreneurial mind-set	risk
entrepreneurial motivation	stress
external optimism	tolerance for ambiguity
family and social risk	tolerance for failure
financial risk	vision

Review and Discussion Questions

1. Identify and describe the three major sources of information that supply data related to the entrepreneurial mind-set.

2. How do the following traits relate to entrepreneurs: desire to achieve, opportunity orientation, initiative, and responsibility?

3. Some of the characteristics attributed to entrepreneurs include persistent problem solving, continuous seeking of feedback, and internal locus of control. What does this statement mean? Be complete in your answer.

4. Entrepreneurs have a tolerance for ambiguity, are calculated risk takers, and have a high regard for integrity and reliability. What does this statement mean? Be complete in your answer.

5. Is it true that most successful entrepreneurs have failed at some point in their business careers? Explain.

6. In what way is "vision" important to an entrepreneur? Self-confidence? Independence?

7. Entrepreneurship has a "dark side." What is meant by this statement? Be complete in your answer.

8. What are the four specific areas of risk that entrepreneurs face? Describe each.

9. What are four causes of stress among entrepreneurs? How can an entrepreneur deal with each of them?

10. Describe the factors associated with the entrepreneurial ego.

11. What is the concept of entrepreneurial motivation?

12. How does the model depicted in the chapter illustrate an entrepreneur's motivation? Be specific.

Experiential Exercise

Are You a High Achiever?

One of the most important characteristics of a successful entrepreneur is the desire to be a high achiever. The following ten questions are designed to help identify your achievement drive. Write the letter preceding your answer in the blank to the left of each. Scoring information is provided at the end of the exercise.

1. _____ An instructor in one of your college classes has asked you to vote on three grading options: (*a*) Study the course material, take the exams, and receive the grade you earn; (*b*) roll a die and get an A if you roll an odd number and a D if you roll an even number; (*c*) show up for all class lectures, turn in a short term paper, and get a C. Which of these options would you choose?

2. _____ How would you describe yourself as a risk taker? (*a*) high, (*b*) moderate, (*c*) low.

3. _____ You have just been asked by your boss to take on a new project in addition to the many tasks you are already doing. What would you tell your boss? (*a*) Since I'm already snowed under, I can't handle any more.

(*b*) Sure, I'm happy to help out; give it to me. (*c*) Let me look over my current workload and get back to you tomorrow about whether I can take on any more work.

4. _____ Which one of these people would you most like to be? (*a*) Steve Jobs, founder of Apple Computers, (*b*) Lee Iacocca of Chrysler fame, (*c*) Jack Welch, former CEO of General Electric.

5. _____ Which one of these games would you most like to play? (*a*) Monopoly, (*b*) bingo, (*c*) roulette.

6. _____ You have decided to become more physically active. Which one of these approaches has the greatest attraction for you? (*a*) join a neighborhood team, (*b*) work out on your own, (*c*) join a local health club.

7. _____ With which one of these groups would you most enjoy playing poker? (*a*) friends, (*b*) high-stake players, (*c*) individuals who can challenge you.

8. _____ Which one of these persons would you most like to be? (*a*) a detective solving a crime, (*b*) a politician giving a victory statement, (*c*) a millionaire sailing on his or her yacht.

9. _____ Which one of these activities would you prefer to do on an evening off? (*a*) visit a friend, (*b*) work on a hobby, (*c*) watch television.

10. _____ Which one of these occupations has the greatest career appeal for you? (*a*) computer salesperson, (*b*) corporate accountant, (*c*) criminal lawyer.

Scoring: Transfer each of your answers to the following scoring key by circling the appropriate number (for example, if your answer to question 1 is *c*, you will circle the number *2* in row 1). Then total all three columns to arrive at your final score.

	a	b	c
1.	10	0	2
2.	2	10	2
3.	6	2	10
4.	7	10	5
5.	10	0	0
6.	2	10	6
7.	4	2	10
8.	10	7	4
9.	4	10	4
10.	10	5	10
	_____ +	_____ +	_____ = _____

High achievers	76–100
Moderate achievers	50–75
Low achievers	Less than 50

INTERPRETATION:

1. High achievers take personal responsibility for their actions. They do not like to rely on luck. The third option *(c)* assumes the class time saved by not having to study for exams will be used to study for other classes; otherwise the answer would be a zero.

2. High achievers are moderate risk takers in important situations.

3. High achievers like to study a situation before committing themselves to a course of action.

4. Jobs is a high-achieving individual but is more interested in design and engineering than in goal accomplishment; Iacocca is an extremely high-achieving salesperson/executive; Jack Welch is more driven by the need for power than the need to achieve.

5. Monopoly allows the high achiever to use his or her skills; bingo and roulette depend on luck.

6. The high achiever would work out on his or her own. The second-best choice is to join a health club, which allows less individual freedom but gives the chance to get feedback and guidance from individuals who understand how to work out effectively.

7. High achievers like challenges but not high risks. If you are a very good poker player and you chose *(b)*, you then can raise your score on this question from 2 to 10.

8. Because high achievers like to accomplish goals, the detective would have the greatest appeal for them. The politician is more interested in power, and the millionaire is simply enjoying himself or herself.

9. High achievers like to do constructive things that help them improve themselves, so working on a hobby would be their first choice.

10. The computer salesperson and the criminal lawyer have a much higher need to achieve than does the corporate accountant.

Video Case 4.1

Understanding the Entrepreneurial Perspective
Ken Done, Artist

You have to get the best out of every day. If you live this day well, then the memories that you have of this day are great, and the expectation that you have of the next day is great. (Ken Done)

Ken Done, Australia's most famous artist, accidentally created a business when he realized how much people enjoyed his work—in any medium he offered it. "I suppose artists paint because that's what they do to try to communicate to people. And it is a great joy to be confronted by a big, blank canvas and to then have the opportunity to put down something. But I wanted to be a Monday painter, not a Sunday painter." And he made that happen.

Done held his first public art exhibition in 1980 when he was 40 years old. As an advertising gimmick, he made 12 tee-shirts for the press with the hope that the shirts would remind reporters to cover his show. The shirts were such a huge success that other people wanted to know how they could get one. And that's how Ken Done went from artist to entrepreneur.

"So it's a very straightforward exercise, isn't it? If you make something and it's well priced and people like it, almost inevitably you realize you can make more. . . . I'm a painter. That's how I spend all my time. But the concept of repeating the singular effort or taking one part of a piece of design and multiplying it is, essentially, you know, what business . . . is about."

Done grew up on the southern coast of Australia, an area well known for its dramatic natural colors from the sea and the earth. His parents had a subscription to *The Saturday Evening Post,* which, at the time, featured glossy covers from the work of Norman Rockwell. Because contemporary periodicals in Australia were in black and white and sepia tones, Done became drawn to Rockwell's paintings, which he claims were "very influential in my life."

Done's paintings are full of light, bold color, and keen detail, and they well capture and transform the bright landscapes of his environment. Since the 1960s, when he became interested in the techniques of Japanese artists, Done has adopted a similar simplicity of design for some of his paintings. Perhaps his most well-known painting is "Postcard from God," which incorporates this statement: "I'm thinking of you always."

The transition from art to business has been easy for Done because, whatever he does, he does with both with passion and discipline. His wife, Judy, a fashion designer, is his partner. "I'm not afraid of business. And, in fact, I see business in a sense as the most creative act of all," he maintains. From those original 12 tee-shirts, he has developed an enterprise that employs 100 people to make swimwear, sportswear, and accessories, all of which are based on his original paintings and drawings.

However pleased Done is with people's response to his art and his clothing designs, however, he has a clear and determined focus for his business, which he won't compromise. Creativity and integrity are vital to him. The way he works with his employees is one indication of how he wants his business to run. "People in the office start at about 8:30, and they finish at 5:00. . . . I want them to go home to their families. I don't want people there at night. That's not what I think business is about, nor do I think that's what life is about. . . . that's not how you get . . . the most creativity out of people."

Another indication of Done's uncompromising approach is how he dealt with successful licensing arrangements once he was able to bring his work to the United States. He realized that his designs were being changed to suit the colder climates of North America, and that did not fit his plan. "The clothing or the stuff wasn't looking exactly like our stuff. So we decided at that point in time we would cut out all wholesaling and all licensing, and we cut our business by 50 percent in one hit because we couldn't control it. . . . You will see, hopefully, more of our stuff in America, but it will be ours, the way that we can control it."

Done continues to paint each day in his studio, and he has a clear idea of why he is there. "Certain paintings . . . have the great ability to give you pleasure over a long period of time . . . and I think art should be about beauty basically. . . . Art . . . teaches you more about failure than success because you always want to go further. You always have the challenge . . . no matter how much talent you have. . . . you really have to work hard at it. . . ."

As for creating a successful business, he maintains: "You simply have to make something that somebody else wants. That's all. And you have to price it properly, and you have to present it properly."

Questions

1. Name the characteristics of an entrepreneur that Ken Done demonstrates.

2. Which characteristic do you think is most important to his business success?

3. Identify the risks that Ken Done has faced and the ones he might face in the future.

Case 4.2

Jane's Evaluation

Paul Medwick is a commercial banker. In the past month he has received loan applications from three entrepreneurs. All three have fledgling businesses with strong potential. However, Paul believes it is important to look at more than just the business itself; the individual also needs close scrutiny.

The three entrepreneurs are (1) Robin Wood, owner of a small delicatessen located in the heart of a thriving business district; (2) Richard Trumpe, owner of a ten-minute oil-change-and-lube operation; and (3) Phil Hartack, owner of a bookstore that specializes in best sellers and cookbooks. Paul has had the bank's outside consultant, Professor Jane Jackson, interview each of the three entrepreneurs. Jane has done a lot of work with entrepreneurs and after a couple of hours of discussion is usually able to evaluate a person's entrepreneurial qualities. In the past Jane has recommended 87 people for loans, and only two of these ventures have failed. This success rate is much higher than that for commercial loans in general. Here is Jane's evaluation of the three people whom she interviewed.

CHARACTERISTIC	ROBIN WOOD	RICHARD TRUMPE	PHIL HARTACK
Perseverance	H	M	M
Drive to achieve	M	H	M
Initiative	M	H	M
Persistent problem solving	M	M	H
Tolerance for ambiguity	L	M	H
Integrity and reliability	H	M	H
Tolerance for failure	H	H	H
Creativity and innovativeness	M	H	M
Self-confidence	H	H	H
Independence	H	H	H

H = High

M = Medium

L = Low

Questions

1. Which of the three applicants do you think comes closest to having the mind-set of an ideal entrepreneur? Why?

2. To which applicant would you recommend that the bank lend money? (Assume each has asked for a loan of $50,000.) Defend your answer.

3. Can these three entrepreneurs do anything to improve their entrepreneurial profile and their chances for success? Be specific in your answer.

Case 4.3

To Stay or to Go?

Mary Gunther has been a sales representative for a large computer firm for seven years. She took this job after graduation from a large university, where she had majored in computer science. Recently Mary has been thinking about leaving the company and starting her own business. Her knowledge of the computer field would put her in an ideal position to be a computer consultant.

Mary understands computer hardware and software, is knowledgeable about the strong and weak points of all the latest market offerings, and has a solid understanding of how to implement a computer system throughout an organization. Mary believes many medium-sized firms around the country would like to introduce computer technology but do not know how to do so. The large manufacturers, such as the one for which she works, are more interested in selling hardware than in helping their clients develop a fully integrated, company-wide computer system. Small consulting firms have to be brought in to do this. Mary feels that as a consultant she not only would be able to evaluate a computer's effectiveness, but also would know how to set up these machines so they would provide maximum benefit to the company.

Mary estimates that if she were to leave the computer firm tomorrow, she could line up ten clients immediately. This would provide her with sufficient income for six months. She is sure that during this period she would have little difficulty getting more clients. Six of these ten firms are located on the East Coast, two of them are in the Midwest, and the remaining two are in California. Mary estimates that it would take about two weeks to install a system and have it working, and it would probably take another two days to correct any problems that occur later on. These problems would be handled on a follow-up visit, usually 10 to 14 days later.

The idea of starting her own venture appeals to Mary. However, she is not sure she wants to leave her job and assume all the responsibilities associated with running her own operation. Before going any further, she has decided to evaluate her own abilities and desires and make certain this is the right career move for her.

Questions

1. Identify three major characteristics Mary should have if she hopes to succeed in this new venture. Defend your choices.

2. How can Figure 4.1 help Mary decide if she is sufficiently entrepreneurial to succeed in this new venture? Which quadrant would she have to be in to succeed in the new venture?

Notes

1. Bruce Tulgan, "Generation X: The Future Is Now," *Entrepreneur of the Year Magazine* (fall 1999): 42.

2. See, for example, William D. Bygrave and Charles W. Hofer, "Theorizing about Entrepreneurship," *Entrepreneurship Theory and Practice* (winter 1991): 12–22; Ivan Bull and Gary E. Willard, "Towards a Theory of Entrepreneurship," *Journal of Business Venturing* 8 (May 1993): 183–196; and William B. Gartner, "Is There an Elephant in Entrepreneurship? Blind Assumptions in Theory Development," *Entrepreneurship Theory and Practice* 25(4) (2001): 27–39.

3. See Robert A. Baron, "Cognitive Mechanisms in Entrepreneurship: Why and When Entrepreneurs Think Differently Than Other People," *Journal of Business Venturing* (April 1998): 275–294.

4. Melissa S. Cardon, Charlene Zietsma, Patrick Saparito, Brett P. Matherne, and Carolyn Davis, "A Tale of Passion, New Insights into Entrepreneurship from a Parenthood Metaphor," *Journal of Business Venturing* 20(1) (January 2005): 23–45.

5. For more on publications, see John A. Hornaday, "Research about Living Entrepreneurs," *Encyclopedia of Entrepreneurship,* ed. Calvin Kent, Donald Sexton, and Karl Vesper (Englewood Cliffs, NJ: Prentice-Hall, 1982), 21–22.

6. Jeffry A. Timmons, *New Venture Creation* (Homewood, IL: Irwin, 1990); Richard M. Hodgetts and Donald F. Kuratko, *Effective Small Business Management* (Fort Worth, TX: Harcourt College Publishers, 2001); Donald F. Kuratko and Harold P. Welsch, *Entrepreneurial Strategy* (Fort Worth, TX: The Dryden Press, 1994); and Donald F. Kuratko and Harold P. Welsch, *Strategic Entrepreneurial Growth* (Mason, OH: South-Western, 2001).

7. William J. Stolze, *Startup: An Entrepreneur's Guide to Launching and Managing a New Venture* (Hawthorne, NJ: Career Press, 1992); Ronald W. Torrence, *In the Owner's Chair* (Englewood Cliffs, NJ: Prentice-Hall, 1992); Lee A. Eckert, J. D. Ryan, and Robert J. Ray, *Small Business: An Entrepreneur's Plan* (Fort Worth, TX: The Dryden Press, 1993); and David N. Bangs, *The Business Planning Guide,* 7th ed. (Chicago: Upstart Publishing, 1995).

8. Bill Gates, *Business at the Speed of Thought* (New York: Time Warner, 1999); and Thaddeus Wawro, *Radicals and Visionaries: The True Life Stories Behind the Entrepreneurs Who Revolutionized the 20th Century* (Irvine, CA: Entrepreneur Media, 2000).

9. Robert L. Shook, *The Entrepreneurs* (New York: Harper & Row, 1980); see also Robert Sobel, *The Entrepreneurs: Explorations within the American Business Tradition* (New York: Weybright and Talley, 1974).

10. John Chamberlin, *The Enterprising Americans: A Business History of the United States* (New York: Harper & Row, 1963).

11. Teresa Esser, *The Venture Café,* (New York: Warner Books, 2002).

12. John J. Kao, *The Entrepreneur* (Englewood Cliffs, NJ: Prentice-Hall, 1991).

13. Howard H. Stevenson and David E. Gumpert, "The Heart of Entrepreneurship," *Harvard Business Review* (March/April 1985): 85–94.

14. See William B. Gartner, "Some Suggestions for Research on Entrepreneurial Traits and Characteristics," *Entrepreneurship Theory and Practice* (fall 1989): 27–38.

15. Ibid.

16. Lloyd E. Shefsky, *Entrepreneurs Are Made Not Born* (New York: McGraw-Hill, Inc., 1994).

17. Robert J. Sternberg, "Successful Intelligence as a Basis for Entrepreneurship," *Journal of Business Venturing* 19(2) (March 2004): 189–201; Robert A. Baron, "The Cognitive Perspective: A Valuable Tool for Answering Entrepreneurship's Basic 'Why' Questions," *Journal of Business Venturing* 19(2) (March 2004): 221–239; Ronald K. Mitchell, Lowell Busenitz, Theresa Lant, Patricia P. McDougall, Eric A. Morse, and J. Brock Smith, "The Distinctive and Inclusive Domain of Entrepreneurial Cognition Research," *Entrepreneurship Theory and Practice* 28(6) (winter 2004): 505–518; and Robert A. Baron and Thomas B. Ward, "Expanding Entrepreneurial Cognition's Toolbox: Potential Contributions from the Field of Cognitive Science," *Entrepreneurship Theory and Practice* 28(6) (winter 2004): 553–574.

18. David C. McClelland, *The Achieving Society* (New York: Van Nostrand, 1961); and "Business Drive and National Achievement," *Harvard Business Review* (July/August 1962): 99–112.

19. For some articles on entrepreneurial characteristics, see John B. Miner, Norman R. Smith, and Jeffrey S. Bracker, "Defining the Inventor-Entrepreneur in the Context of Established Typologies," *Journal of*

Business Venturing (March 1992): 103–113; Rita Gunther McGrath, Ian C. MacMillan, and Sari Scheinberg, "Elitists, Risk Takers, and Rugged Individualists? An Exploratory Analysis of Cultural Differences between Entrepreneurs and Non-Entrepreneurs," *Journal of Business Venturing* (March 1992): 115–136; Ellen A. Fagenson, "Personal Value Systems of Men and Women Entrepreneurs versus Managers," *Journal of Business Venturing* (September 1993): 409–430; and Jill Kickul and Lisa K. Gundry, "Prospecting for Strategic Advantage: The Proactive Entrepreneurial Personality and Small Firm Innovation," *Journal of Small Business Management* 40(2) (2002): 85–97.

20. Manfred F. R. Kets de Vries, "The Dark Side of Entrepreneurship," *Harvard Business Review* (November/December 1985): 160–167.

21. Thomas Monroy and Robert Folger, "A Typology of Entrepreneurial Styles: Beyond Economic Rationality," *Journal of Private Enterprise* IX(2) (1993): 64–79.

22. Ibid., 75–76.

23. Michael O'Neal, "Just What Is an Entrepreneur?" *Business Week* (special enterprise issue 1993): 104–112.

24. Patrick R. Liles, *New Business Ventures and the Entrepreneur* (Homewood, IL: Irwin, 1974), 14–15.

25. Adebowale Akande, "Coping with Entrepreneurial Stress," *Leadership & Organization Development Journal* 13(2) (1992): 27–32; and E. Holly Buttner, "Entrepreneurial Stress: Is It Hazardous to Your Health?" *Journal of Managerial Issues* (summer 1992): 223–240.

26. Buttner, "Entrepreneurial Stress"; see also M. Afzalur Rabin, "Stress, Strain, and Their Moderators: An Empirical Comparison of Entrepreneurs and Managers," *Journal of Small Business Management* (January 1996): 46–58.

27. See K. A. Mathews and S. C. Haynes, "Type A Behavior Pattern and Coronary Disease Risk," *American Journal of Epistemology* 123 (1986): 923–960.

28. Akande, "Coping with Entrepreneurial Stress."

29. David P. Boyd and David E. Gumpert, "Coping with Entrepreneurial Stress," *Harvard Business Review* (March/April 1983): 46–56.

30. J. M. Ivancevich and M. T. Matteson, *Stress and Work: A Managerial Perspective* (Glenview, IL: Scott, Foresman & Co., 1980).

31. Boyd and Gumpert, "Coping with Entrepreneurial Stress."

32. Michael G. Goldsby, Donald F. Kuratko, and James W. Bishop, "Entrepreneurship and Fitness: An Examination of Rigorous Exercise and Goal Attainment among Small Business Owners," *Journal of Small Business Management,* 43(1) (January 2005): 78–92.

33. Kets de Vries, "The Dark Side of Entrepreneurship."

34. Lanny Herron and Harry J. Sapienza, "The Entrepreneur and the Initiation of New Venture Launch Activities," *Entrepreneurship Theory and Practice* (fall 1992): 49–55.

35. Bradley R. Johnson, "Toward a Multidimensional Model of Entrepreneurship: The Case of Achievement Motivation and the Entrepreneur," *Entrepreneurship Theory and Practice* (spring 1990): 39–54.

36. See Kelly G. Shaver and Linda R. Scott, "Person, Process, Choice: The Psychology of New Venture Creation," *Entrepreneurship Theory and Practice* (winter 1991): 23–45.

37. Don E. Bradley and James A. Roberts, "Self-Employment and Job Satisfaction: Investigating and Role of Self-Efficacy, Depression, and Seniority," *Journal of Small Business Management* 42(1) (January 2004): 37–58.

38. Arnold C. Cooper and Kendall W. Artz, "Determinants of Satisfaction for Entrepreneurs," *Journal of Business Venturing* (November 1995): 439–458.

39. Douglas W. Naffziger, Jeffrey S. Hornsby, and Donald F. Kuratko, "A Proposed Research Model of Entrepreneurial Motivation," *Entrepreneurship Theory and Practice* (spring 1994): 29–42.

40. A. Rebecca Reuber and Eileen Fischer, "Understanding the Consequences of Founders' Experience," *Journal of Small Business Management* (February 1999): 30–45.

41. Donald F. Kuratko, Jeffrey S. Hornsby, and Douglas W. Naffziger, "An Examination of Owner's Goals in Sustaining Entrepreneurship," *Journal of Small Business Management* (January 1997): 24–33.

5 *Creativity and Innovation*

The era of the intelligent man/woman is almost over and a new one is emerging—the era of the creative man/woman.

Pinchas Noy

Chapter Objectives

1 *To examine the role of creativity and to review the major components of the creative process: knowledge accumulation, incubation process, idea experience, evaluation, and implementation*

2 *To present ways of developing personal creativity: recognize relationships, develop a functional perspective, use your "brains," and eliminate muddling mind-sets*

3 *To introduce the four major types of innovation: invention, extension, duplication, and synthesis*

4 *To define and illustrate the sources of innovation for entrepreneurs*

5 *To review some of the major myths associated with innovation and to define the ten principles of innovation*

Entrepreneurs: Imagination and Creativity

Entrepreneurs blend imaginative and creative thinking with a systematic, logical process ability. This combination is a key to success. In addition, potential entrepreneurs are always looking for unique opportunities to fill needs or wants. They sense economic potential in business problems by continually asking "What if . . . ?" or "Why not . . . ?" They develop an ability to see, recognize, and create opportunity where others find only problems. It has been said that the first rule for developing entrepreneurial vision is to recognize that problems are to solutions what demand is to supply. Applying this rule means an entrepreneur will analyze a problem from every possible angle: What is the problem? Whom does it affect? How does it affect them? What costs are involved? Can it be solved? Would the marketplace pay for a solution? This is the type of analysis that blends creative thinking with systematic analysis.[1]

In order to give a better perspective of this entrepreneurial vision, this chapter is devoted to examining the role of creativity and the innovation process. These two major topics are keys to understanding opportunity and its development for entrepreneurs.

The Role of Creativity

It is important to recognize the role of creativity in the innovative process. **Creativity** is the generation of ideas that result in the improved efficiency or effectiveness of a system.[2]

Two important aspects of creativity exist: process and people. The process is goal oriented; it is designed to attain a solution to a problem. The people are the resources that determine the solution. The process remains the same, but the approach that the people use will vary. For example, sometimes they will adapt a solution, and at other times they will formulate a highly innovative solution.[3] Table 5.1 compares these two approaches.

One study examined the validity of these two approaches for distinguishing innovative entrepreneurs from adaptive entrepreneurs and found their application very effective.[4] Thus, understanding the problem-solving orientation of individuals helps develop their creative abilities.

The Nature of the Creative Process

Creativity is a process that can be developed and improved.[5] Everyone is creative to some degree. However, as is the case with many abilities and talents (for example, athletic, artistic), some individuals have a greater aptitude for creativity than others. Also, some people have been raised and educated in an environment that encouraged them to develop their creativity. They have been taught to think and act creatively. For others the process is more difficult because they have not been positively reinforced, and, if they are to be creative, they must learn how to implement the creative process.[6]

Table 5.1   Two Approaches to Creative Problem Solving

ADAPTOR	INNOVATOR
Employs a disciplined, precise, methodical approach	Approaches tasks from unusual angles
Is concerned with solving, rather than finding, problems	Discovers problems and avenues of solutions
Attempts to refine current practices	Questions basic assumptions related to current practices
Tends to be means oriented	Has little regard for means; is more interested in ends
Is capable of extended detail work	Has little tolerance for routine work
Is sensitive to group cohesion and cooperation	Has little or no need for consensus; often is insensitive to others

Source: Michael Kirton, "Adaptors and Innovators: A Description and Measure," *Journal of Applied Psychology* (October 1976): 623. Copyright © 1976 by The American Psychological Association.

Many people incorrectly believe that only a genius can be creative.[7] Most people also assume some people are born creative and others are not, or only the gifted or highly intelligent person is capable of generating creative ideas and insights. Yet, the real barriers to creative thinking are sometimes the inadvertent "killer phrases" we use in our communications. Table 5.2 lists the 15 key "idea stoppers" we use. People may not intentionally stop a creative idea, but these simple negative phrases prohibit people from thinking any further.[8]

Creativity is not some mysterious and rare talent reserved for a select few. It is a distinct way of looking at the world that is oftentimes illogical. The creative process involves seeing relationships among things others have not seen (for example, modems—using telephones to transfer data among computers).[9]

The creative process has four commonly agreed-on phases or steps. Most experts agree on the general nature and relationships among these phases, although they refer to them by a variety of names.[10] Experts also agree that these phases do not always occur in the same order for every creative activity. For creativity to occur, chaos is necessary but a structured and focused chaos. We shall examine this four-step process using the most typical structural development.

Phase 1: Background or Knowledge Accumulation

Successful creations are generally preceded by investigation and information gathering. This usually involves extensive reading, conversations with others working in the field, attendance at professional meetings and workshops, and a general absorption of information relative to the problem or issue under study. Additional investigation in both related and unrelated fields is sometimes involved. This exploration provides the individual with a variety of perspectives on the problem, and it is particularly important to the entrepreneur, who needs a basic understanding of all aspects of the development of a new product, service, or business venture.

Table 5.2 The Most Common Idea Stoppers

1. "Naah."
2. "Can't" (said with a shake of the head and an air of finality).
3. "That's the dumbest thing I've ever heard."
4. "Yeah, but if you did that . . ." (poses an extreme or unlikely disaster case).
5. "We already tried that—years ago."
6. "We've done all right so far; why do we need that?"
7. "I don't see anything wrong with the way we're doing it now."
8. "That doesn't sound too practical."
9. "We've never done anything like that before."
10. "Let's get back to reality."
11. "We've got deadlines to meet—we don't have time to consider that."
12. "It's not in the budget."
13. "Are you kidding?"
14. "Let's not go off on a tangent."
15. "Where do you get these weird ideas?"

Source: Adapted from *The Creative Process*, ed. Angelo M. Biondi, The Creative Education Foundation, 1986.

People practice the creative search for background knowledge in a number of ways. Some of the most helpful follow: (1) read in a variety of fields; (2) join professional groups and associations; (3) attend professional meetings and seminars; (4) travel to new places; (5) talk to anyone and everyone about your subject; (6) scan magazines, newspapers, and journals for articles related to the subject; (7) develop a subject library for future reference; (8) carry a small notebook and record useful information; and (9) devote time to pursue natural curiosities.[11]

Phase 2: The Incubation Process

Creative individuals allow their subconscious to mull over the tremendous amounts of information they gather during the preparation phase. This incubation process often occurs while they are engaged in activities totally unrelated to the subject or problem. It happens even when they are sleeping. This accounts for the advice frequently given to a person who is frustrated by what appears to be an unsolvable problem: "Why don't you sleep on it?"[12] Getting away from a problem and letting the subconscious mind work on it allows creativity to spring forth. Some of the most helpful steps to induce incubation follow: (1) engage in routine, "mindless" activities (cutting the grass, painting the house); (2) exercise regularly; (3) play (sports, board games, puzzles); (4) think about the project or problem before falling asleep; (5) meditate or practice self-hypnosis; and (6) sit back and relax on a regular basis.[13]

Phase 3: The Idea Experience

This phase of the creative process is often the most exciting. It is when the idea or solution the individual is seeking is discovered. Sometimes referred to as the "eureka factor," this phase is also the one the average person incorrectly perceives as the only component of creativity.[14]

As with the incubation process, new and innovative ideas often emerge while the person is busy doing something unrelated to the enterprise, venture, or investigation (for example, taking a shower, driving on an interstate highway, leafing through a newspaper).[15] Sometimes the idea appears as a bolt out of the blue. In most cases, however, the answer comes to the individual incrementally. Slowly but surely, the person begins to formulate the solution. Because it is often difficult to determine when the incubation process ends and the idea experience phase begins, many people are unaware of moving from Phase 2 to Phase 3.

In any event, here are ways to speed up the idea experience: (1) daydream and fantasize about your project, (2) practice your hobbies, (3) work in a leisurely environment (for example, at home instead of the office), (4) put the problem on the back burner, (5) keep a notebook at bedside to record late-night or early-morning ideas, and (6) take breaks while working.[16]

Phase 4: Evaluation and Implementation

This is the most difficult step of a creative endeavor and requires a great deal of courage, self-discipline, and perseverance. Successful entrepreneurs can identify ideas that are workable and that they have the skills to implement. More important, they do not give up when they run into temporary obstacles.[17] Often they will fail several times before they successfully develop their best ideas. In some cases entrepreneurs will take the idea in an entirely different direction or will discover a new and more workable idea while struggling to implement the original idea. Another important part of this phase is the reworking of ideas to put them into final form. Because frequently an idea emerges from Phase 3 in rough form, it needs to be modified or tested to put it in final shape. Some of the most useful suggestions for carrying out this phase follow: (1) increase your energy level with proper exercise, diet, and rest; (2) educate yourself in the business-planning process and all facets of business; (3) test your ideas with knowledgeable people; (4) take notice of your intuitive hunches and feelings; (5) educate yourself in the selling process; (6) learn about organizational policies and practices; (7) seek advice from others (for example, friends, experts); and (8) view the problems you encounter while implementing your ideas as challenges.[18]

Figure 5.1 illustrates the four phases of the creative thinking process. If a person encounters a major problem while moving through the process, it is sometimes helpful to go back to a previous phase and try again. For example, if an individual is unable to formulate an idea or solution (Phase 3), a return to Phase 1 often helps. By immersing him- or herself in the data, the individual allows the unconscious mind to begin anew processing the data, establishing cause-effect relationships, and formulating potential solutions.

Developing Your Creativity

You can do a number of things to improve your own creative talents. Becoming aware of some of the habits and mental blocks that stifle creativity is one of the most helpful.[19] Of course, as with most processes, your development will be more effective if you regularly practice exercises designed to increase your creative abilities. The following section is designed to improve your awareness of some of the thought habits that limit your creativity and to assist you in developing a personalized creativity improvement program.

Figure 5.1 *The Creative Thinking Process*

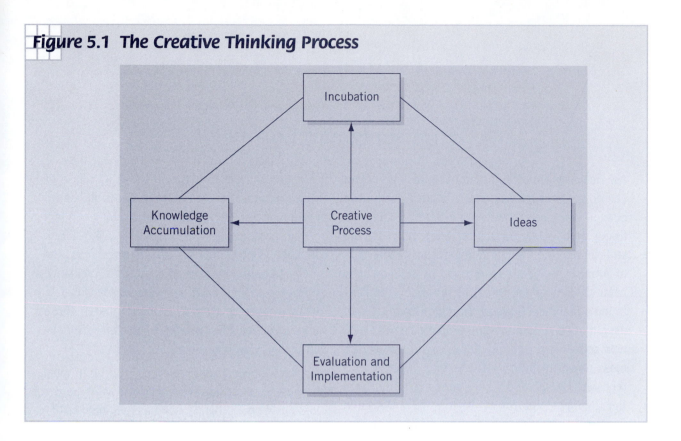

Recognizing Relationships

Many inventions and innovations are a result of the inventor's seeing new and different relationships among objects, processes, materials, technologies, and people.[20] Examples range widely and include (1) adding fruit juice to soft drinks to create Slice, (2) combining combustion engine technology with the wheel to create the automobile, and (3) using a 330-pound defensive football player as a running back and pass receiver.

If you wish to improve your creativity, it helps to look for different or unorthodox relationships among the elements and people around you. This activity involves *perceiving in a relational mode.* You can develop this talent by viewing things and people as existing in a complementary or **appositional relationship** with other things and people. Simply stated, things and people exist in the world in relation to other things and people. Creative people seem to be intuitively aware of this phenomenon and have developed a talent for recognizing new and different relationships. These relationships often lead to visions that result in new ideas, products, and services.[21] In order to develop the ability to recognize new relationships, you must practice perceiving in a relational mode. The following exercise helps with this development.

A Creative Exercise   Analyze and elaborate on how the following pairs relate to each other in a complementary way: nut and bolt, husband and wife, chocolate cake and vanilla ice cream, grass clippings and tomato plants, peanut butter and jelly, athlete and coach, humanity and water, winning and losing, television and overhead projectors, and managers and production workers.

Developing a Functional Perspective

If expanded, the principle of perceiving in a relational mode helps develop a **functional perspective** toward things and people. A creative person tends to view things and people in terms of how they can satisfy his or her needs and help complete a project.

entrepreneurship IN PRACTICE

Terrorism Ignites Creativity

Ask not how America can innovate; ask what you can do to innovate America. It might as well have been a war poster with Uncle Sam pointing his finger at us. Only days after September 11, the still-smoldering Pentagon advertised for the help of American citizens to respond by sending new ideas to combat the threat of terrorism. The Pentagon's Technical Support Working Group (TSWG) usually receives around 900 proposals a year with new technology and new ideas to aid the world's most powerful military force; that October they received 12,500. The TSWG agencies range from the Energy Department to the FBI, CIA, and Federal Aviation Administration, and local police and fire departments. The group sends out an annual list of problems it is interested in solving, and then evaluates the proposals it receives. They will then choose only 100 to 200 proposals for research each year and fund $50 to $100 million for the projects.

One company proposing their products to TSWG is Equator Technologies, Inc. Equator makes super-fast digital signal processors used in video cameras and is creating an automated baggage inspection system that would use a database of images of weapons rotated on all possible planes of vision. It has been shown that a gun, when laid on end, has been mistaken for a shaving-cream can when using traditional baggage scanners. Another company envisions the use of surveillance cameras equipped with software to identify terrorists whose facial measurements match those found in police files, photos of known terrorists, and possibly FBI records.

Many of the TSWG's projects end up in local firehouses, police stations, airports, and border crossings. Some projects, such as handheld radiation detectors and bomb resistant building plans, have proven successful during the 2002 Olympics and at the Pentagon.

However, the group isn't without failure. They once funded a special radio antenna that picked up signals no better than a chain link fence. The unofficial motto at TSWG—"If you fail, fail right. . . . don't just fail because you didn't try everything or you stopped short."

SOURCE: "Small Biz vs. the Terrorists," *BusinessWeek Online* (March 2, 2002).

For example, the homemaker who cannot find a screwdriver often will use a butter knife to tighten a loose screw. Or the cereal manufacturer will add fruit to its product to create a new product line that appeals to a health-conscious market.

If you wish to become more innovative and creative, you need to visualize yourself in complementary relationships to the things and people of the world. You must learn to look at them in terms of how they complement you in your attempts to satisfy your own needs and to complete your projects. You must begin to look at things and people in nonconventional ways and from a different perspective.[22] The following exercise is designed to help you develop a functional perspective.

A Creative Exercise   Think of and write down all the functions you can imagine for the following items (spend five minutes on each item):

- ☐ An egotistical staff member
- ☐ A large pebble

- ☐ A fallen tree branch
- ☐ A chair
- ☐ A computer "whiz kid"
- ☐ An obsessively organized employee
- ☐ The office "gossip"
- ☐ An old hubcap
- ☐ A new secretary
- ☐ An empty roll of masking tape
- ☐ A yardstick
- ☐ An old coat hanger
- ☐ The office tightwad
- ☐ This exercise

Using Your Brains

Ever since split-brain studies were conducted in the 1950s and 1960s, experts on creativity, innovation, and self-development have emphasized the importance of developing the skills associated with both hemispheres of the brain.[23]

The **right brain** hemisphere helps an individual understand analogies, imagine things, and synthesize information. The **left brain** hemisphere helps the person analyze, verbalize, and use rational approaches to problem solving. Although the two brain hemispheres (right and left) process information differently and are responsible for different brain activities and skills (see Table 5.3), they are integrated through a group of connecting nerve fibers called the corpus callosum. Because of this connection and the nature of the relationship between the activities of each hemisphere, each hemisphere should be viewed as existing and functioning in a complementary relationship with the other hemisphere.[24]

The creative process involves logical and analytical thinking in the knowledge accumulation, evaluation, and implementation stages. In addition, it calls for imagination, intuition, analogy conceptualization, and synthesizing in the incubation and idea creation stages. So to become more creative, it is necessary to practice and develop

Table 5.3   *Processes Associated with the Two Brain Hemispheres*

LEFT HEMISPHERE	RIGHT HEMISPHERE
Verbal	Nonverbal
Analytical	Synthesizing
Abstract	Seeing analogies
Rational	Nonrational
Logical	Spatial
Linear	Intuitive
	Imaginative

Source: Betty Edwards, *Drawing on the Right Side of the Brain* (Los Angeles: Tarcher, 1979).

the entrepreneurial PROCESS

Developing Creativity

What color is the sky when you dream? Do you consider yourself to be creative? "Creativity" has been defined as having the quality or power of creating. People are innately creative. Really. Let your creativity out of the playpen! Millions of dollars are made from creative endeavors that are truly simple. You can cash in too if you use some of these methods to boost your creativity.

1. **Brainstorm!** This is the old-school way to drum up creative ideas and solve problems, but it's still by far the best. The corporate world was woken up when Alex Osborn introduced this concept in the 1950s. Established rules were easy to follow:

   ☐ *Shout out or write down every solution that comes to mind.*

   ☐ *Off-the-wall ideas are welcome.*

   ☐ *Criticize nothing.*

   ☐ *Organize later.*

2. **Opposites attract.** Here's an interesting concept. Synectics. Similar to the word itself, synectics involves putting two "nonsensical" things together to see what happens. Examples. "Imagine a restaurant with no waiters, tables, or silverware." It's McDonald's. "Imagine a bookstore with no books—and no store." Isn't that Amazon.com? "Moving trucks with no movers": U-Haul. Don't hesitate to explore that which is strange!

3. **THINKubate.** Gerald Haman created (there's that word again) the "THINKubator"—a playground where businesspeople, entrepreneurs, and the like can go to escape the humdrum environment of offices and "can't doers." The playground houses comfortable seating, toys, fun pictures, and overall, offers an environment that favors brain stimulation and idea creation. It must work, because Haman has

developed numerous products for Procter & Gamble and Arthur Andersen.

4. **Trigger great ideas.** Triggers are everyday items that can be used to stimulate the brain: abstract photos, inspiring quotes, uncompleted ideas, tips, and so on. Place trigger items in various places you look or visit often—the refrigerator door, your dashboard, your phone. You never know when a connection will be made.

5. **Connect.** Every person you meet or place you visit might be an opportunity waiting to happen. The key is to be prepared for that opportunity when it arises. Creativity consultant Jordan Ayan suggests building up your C.O.R.E.: curiosity, openness, risk, and energy. These traits can be enhanced by reading up on trends, attending trade shows, browsing, and trying new things. Spotting open windows isn't necessarily easy, but increasing the number of the windows can be.

6. **Always celebrate failure.** Try and try again. What doesn't kill you only makes you stronger. Dare to be great! Get the idea? Don't suffer from insanity! Enjoy every minute of it!

7. **Make 'em laugh.** Humor is a great way to relieve stress. Use it in your creative endeavors. Can you imagine Dennis the Menace helping you build your prototype? How about letting the Disney World characters coauthor your business plan? Let your youngest relative in on your invention. Humor and laughter certainly encourage creativity.

8. **Sweat it.** Yes! Sweat it out! Exercise gets the creative juices—endorphins—flowing. Let the mind wander while you're jogging or ride the exercise bike while reading the year-end

reports. Just be sure to keep a notepad handy to jot down all of your great ideas!

9. **Remember your wildest dreams.** Has anyone ever replied to you with this statement: "In your dreams!" Well, go figure. Dreams are a great place to start when it comes to unleashing creativity. Elias Howe once had a dream in which cannibals were piercing his flesh with spears. Thus the sewing machine was invented. Don't ignore daydreams or spur-of-the-moment ideas, either. Your subconscious could be trying to tell you something.

SOURCE: Adapted from Nick D'Alto, "Think Big," *Business Start Ups* (January 2000): 61–65.

both right- and left-hemisphere skills. The following problem-solving exercise is designed to demonstrate the effectiveness of combining the skills of both hemispheres when solving problems.

A Creative Exercise   Assume you have an idea that will save your organization time and money on processing customer complaints. Your supervisor has been extremely busy and has been unwilling to stop and listen to your idea.

1. Write down all the left-hemisphere-type solutions to this problem you can think of in five minutes.

2. Write down all the right-hemisphere-type solutions to this problem you can think of in five minutes.

3. Compare these lists and combine two or more solutions from each list that will result in a unique and innovative way to solve this problem.

4. Repeat steps 1, 2, and 3 using a current problem you are facing at work or at home.

Our society and its educational institutions reward individuals who have been successful at developing their logical, analytical, and rational left-brain skills. Little emphasis, however, has been placed on practicing and using right-brain skills. Table 5.4 represents some ways you can practice developing both left- and right-hemisphere skills.[25]

Eliminating Muddling Mind-Sets

A number of mental habits block or impede creative thinking. It has been estimated that adults use only 2 to 10 percent of their creative potential.[26] For example, many individuals tend to make quick judgments about new things, people, and ideas. Another inclination is to point out the negative components of a new or different idea because of the psychological discomfort associated with change. Some common mental habits that inhibit creativity and innovation are "either/or" thinking, security hunting, stereotyping, and probability thinking. These habits tend to muddle creative thought processes, and different thought processes must be used to enhance creative thinking.[27]

Either/Or Thinking   Because of the speed of change in the modern world, personal lives are filled with a great deal of uncertainty and ambiguity. People often get bogged down with striving for an unreasonable amount of certainty in their lives. But the creative person learns to accept a reasonable amount of ambiguity in his or her work and life. In fact, many exceptionally creative people thrive in an uncertain environment and find it exhilarating.[28]

Security Hunting   Many people try to make the right decision or take the correct action every time. In doing so, they rely on averages, stereotypes, and probability theory to minimize their risks. Although this strategy often is appropriate, at times a

Table 5.4   Ways to Develop Left- and Right-Hemisphere Skills

LEFT-HEMISPHERE SKILLS	RIGHT-HEMISPHERE SKILLS
1. Step-by-step planning of your work and life activities	1. Using metaphors and analogies to describe things and people in your conversations and writing
2. Reading ancient, medieval, and scholastic philosophy, legal cases, and books on logic	2. Taking off your watch when you are not working
3. Establishing timetables for all of your activities	3. Suspending your initial judgment of ideas, new acquaintances, movies, TV programs, and so on
4. Using and working with a computer program	4. Recording your hunches, feelings, and intuitions and calculating their accuracy
	5. Detailed fantasizing and visualizing things and situations in the future
	6. Drawing faces, caricatures, and landscapes

creator or innovator must take some calculated risks.[29] Sometimes these risks result in the innovator's being wrong and making mistakes. Yet by recognizing this as part of the innovation game, the creative person learns from his or her mistakes and moves on to create bigger and better things. We all know Thomas Edison failed numerous times when searching for the correct materials to use inside the incandescent lightbulb.

Stereotyping   It is ironic that although averages and stereotypes are abstractions that people fabricate, people act and make decisions based on them as if these were data entities existing in the real world. For example, one could hypothesize that the average homemaker is female, 38 years old, and 5′4″ tall; weighs 120 pounds; and has two children, a part-time job, and 14.5 years of formal education. If one tried to find a person who fits this description, however, the chances of success would be small. In short, the more descriptive the abstraction or stereotype, the less real it becomes. Predicating actions from stereotypes and averages can cause an individual to act on the basis of a distorted picture of reality. More important, relying on these abstractions can limit a person's perception of the real entities and possibilities in the world. Edward deBono argues that people must alter their thinking to enhance their creativity. Only new patterns of thinking will lead to new ideas and innovations.[30]

Probability Thinking   In their struggle to achieve security, many people also tend to rely on probability theory to make decisions. An overreliance on this decision-making method, however, can distort reality and prohibit one from taking calculated risks that may lead to creative endeavors.

Probability experts report that the predictive power of probability theory increases in proportion to the number of times an event is repeated. If a person wishes to predict the probability of tossing the number *3* when rolling dice a certain number of times, probability theory is extremely useful. However, if the person wishes to know the likelihood of rolling a *4* with one roll of the dice, the predictive ability of probability theory is much less valuable.

In the creative game, often an individual is looking at an opportunity or situation that may occur only once in a lifetime. In a single-event situation, intuition and educated guesses are just as useful, if not more useful, than logic and probability.[31] One way of increasing your creative capacities is to practice looking at some of the situations in your life as a 50/50 game, and then begin to take some risks. Additionally, the following problem-solving exercises are designed to help eliminate muddling mind-sets:

- ☐ Practice taking small risks in your personal life and at work, relying on your intuition and hunches. Keep a log of these risks and chart their accuracy and consequences. For example, try to draw to an inside straight in your next family poker game.

- ☐ Go out of your way to talk to people who you think conform to a commonly accepted stereotype.

- ☐ Take on a number of complex projects at work and at home that do not lend themselves to guaranteed and predictable results. Allow yourself to live with a manageable amount of ambiguity. Notice how you react to this ambiguity.

- ☐ When an idea is presented to you, first think of all the positive aspects of the idea, then of all the negative aspects, and finally of all the interesting aspects of the idea.

- ☐ When listening to people, suspend initial judgment of them, their ideas, and their information, and simply listen.

- ☐ Try making some decisions in the present. That is, do not let your personal history or your estimates about the future dominate your decision-making process.[32]

Arenas in Which People Are Creative

Remember, people are inherently creative. Some act on that creativity all of the time while others stifle it, and most of us fall somewhere in between the two. The reality is that people often do not recognize when or how they are being creative. Further, they fail to recognize the many opportunities for creativity that arise within their jobs on a daily basis. Creativity researcher William Miller argues that people often do not recognize when they are being creative, and they frequently overlook opportunities to be creative. He suggests that the path to creativity begins by first recognizing all of the ways in which we are or can be creative. People in organizations can channel their creativity into seven different arenas:

- ☐ **Idea creativity**: thinking up a new idea or concept, such as an idea for a new product or service or a way to solve a problem.

- ☐ **Material creativity**: Inventing and building a tangible object such as a product, an advertisement, a report, or a photograph.

- ☐ **Organization creativity**: organizing people or projects and coming up with a new organizational form or approach to structuring things. Examples could include organizing a project, starting a new type of venture, putting together or reorganizing a work group, and changing the policies and rules of a group.

- ☐ **Relationship creativity**: innovative approach to achieving collaboration, cooperation, and win-win relationships with others. The person who handles a difficult situation well or deals with a particular person in an especially effective manner is being creative in a relationship or one-on-one context.

- ☐ **Event creativity**: producing an event such as an awards ceremony, team outing, or annual meeting. The creativity here also encompasses décor, ways in which people are involved, sequence of happenings, setting, and so forth.

- ☐ **Inner creativity**: changing one's inner self. Being open to new approaches to how we do things and thinking about ourselves in different ways. Achieving a change of heart or finding a new perspective or way to look at things that is a significant departure from how one has traditionally looked at them.

- ☐ **Spontaneous creativity**: acting in a spontaneous or spur-of-the-moment manner such as coming up with a witty response in a meeting, an off-the-cuff speech, a quick and simple way to settle a dispute, or an innovative appeal when trying to close a sale.[33]

The Creative Climate

Creativity is most likely to occur when the business climate is right. No enterprise will have creative owners and managers for long if the right climate is not established and nurtured. Some of the important characteristics of this climate follow:

- ☐ A trustful management that does not overcontrol the personnel
- ☐ Open channels of communication among all business members
- ☐ Considerable contact and communication with outsiders
- ☐ A large variety of personality types
- ☐ A willingness to accept change
- ☐ An enjoyment in experimenting with new ideas
- ☐ Little fear of negative consequences for making a mistake
- ☐ The selection and promotion of employees on the basis of merit
- ☐ The use of techniques that encourage ideas, including suggestion systems and brainstorming
- ☐ Sufficient financial, managerial, human, and time resources for accomplishing goals[34]

Innovation and the Entrepreneur

Innovation is a key function in the entrepreneurial process. Researchers and authors in the field of entrepreneurship are, for the most part, in agreement with Peter F. Drucker about the concept of innovation:

> Innovation is the specific function of entrepreneurship. . . . It is the means by which the entrepreneur either creates new wealth-producing resources or endows existing resources with enhanced potential for creating wealth.[35]

Innovation is the process by which entrepreneurs convert opportunities into marketable ideas. It is the means by which they become catalysts for change.[36]

The innovation process is more than just a good idea. The origin of an idea is important, and the role of creative thinking may be vital to that development.[37] However, a major difference exists between an idea arising from mere speculation and one that is the product of extended thinking, research, experience, and work. More important, a prospective entrepreneur must have the desire to bring a good idea through the development stages. Thus innovation is a combination of the vision to create a good idea and the perseverance and dedication to remain with the concept through implementation.

The Innovation Process

Most innovations result from a conscious, purposeful search for new opportunities.[38] This process begins with the analysis of the sources of new opportunities. Drucker has noted that because innovation is both conceptual and perceptual, would-be innovators must go out and look, ask, and listen. Successful innovators use both the right and left sides of their brains. They look at figures. They look at people. They analytically work out what the innovation has to be to satisfy the opportunity. Then they go out and look at potential product users to study their expectations, values, and needs.[39]

Most successful innovations are simple and focused. They are directed toward a specific, clear, and carefully designed application. In the process they create new customers and new markets. Today's cameras combined in a cell phone are a good example. Although these cameras are highly sophisticated, they are easy to use and appeal to a specific market niche: people who want instant photography.

Above all, innovation often involves more work than genius. As Thomas Edison once said, "Genius is 1 percent inspiration and 99 percent perspiration." Moreover, innovators rarely work in more than one area. For all his systematic innovative accomplishments, Edison worked only in the electricity field.

Types of Innovation

Four basic types of innovation exist (see Table 5.5). These extend from the totally new to modifications of existing products or services. In order of originality, these are the four types:

- ☐ **Invention:** the creation of a new product, service, or process, often one that is novel or untried. Such concepts tend to be "revolutionary."

- ☐ **Extension:** the expansion of a product, service, or process already in existence. Such concepts make a different application of a current idea.

- ☐ **Duplication:** the replication of an already existing product, service, or process. The duplication effort, however, is not simply copying but adding the entrepreneur's own creative touch to enhance or improve the concept to beat the competition.

- ☐ **Synthesis:** the combination of existing concepts and factors into a new formulation. This involves taking a number of ideas or items already invented and finding a way so together they form a new application.[40]

Table 5.5   Innovation in Action

TYPE	DESCRIPTION	EXAMPLES
Invention	Totally new product, service, or process	Wright brothers—airplane Thomas Edison—lightbulb Alexander Graham Bell—telephone
Extension	New use or different application of an already existing product, service, or process	Ray Kroc—McDonald's Nolan Bushnell—Atari Kemmons Wilson—Holiday Inn
Duplication	Creative replication of an existing concept	Wal-Mart—department stores Gateway—personal computers Pizza Hut—pizza parlor
Synthesis	Combination of existing concepts and factors into a new formulation or use	Fred Smith—Federal Express Merrill Lynch—home equity financing

Sources of Innovation

Innovation is a tool by which entrepreneurs typically exploit change rather than create change.[41] Although some inventions have created change, these are rare. It is more common to find innovations that take advantage of change. The internal and external areas that serve as innovation sources are presented next.

Unexpected Occurrences

These are successes or failures that, because they were unanticipated or unplanned, often end up proving to be a major innovative surprise to the firm.

Incongruities

These occur whenever a gap or difference exists between expectations and reality. For example, when Fred Smith proposed overnight mail delivery, he was told, "If it were that profitable, the U.S. Post Office would be doing it." It turned out Smith was right. An incongruity existed between what Smith felt was needed and the way business was currently conducted.

Process Needs

These exist whenever a demand arises for the entrepreneur to innovate and answer a particular need. The creation of health foods and time-saving devices are examples.

Industry and Market Changes

Continual shifts in the marketplace occur, caused by developments such as consumer attitudes, advancements in technology, industry growth, and the like. Industries and markets are always undergoing changes in structure, design, or definition. An example is found in the health care industry, where hospital care has undergone radical change and where home health care and preventive medicine have replaced hospitalization and surgery as primary focus areas. The entrepreneur needs to be aware of and seize these emerging opportunities.

Demographic Changes

These arise from trend changes in population, age, education, occupations, geographic locations, and similar factors. Demographic shifts are important and often provide new entrepreneurial opportunities. For example, as the average population age in Florida has increased (due largely to the influx of retirees), land development, recreational, and health care industries all have profited.

Perceptual Changes

These changes occur in people's interpretation of facts and concepts. They are intangible yet meaningful. Perception can cause major shifts in ideas to take place. The current fitness craze, caused by the perceived need to be healthy and physically fit, has created a demand for both health foods and health facilities throughout the country.

Knowledge-Based Concepts

These are the basis for the creation or development of something brand new, tying into our earlier discussion of invention as a type of innovation. Inventions are knowledge-based; they are the product of new thinking, new methods, and new knowledge. Such innovations often require the longest time period between initiation and market implementation because of the need for testing and modification. For example, today's cameras in cell phones have revolutionized the way we use instant photography. This concept was not even thought possible just five years ago.

Some examples of these innovation sources are presented in Table 5.6.

Major Innovation Myths

Presented next is a list of the commonly accepted innovation myths, along with reasons why these are myths and not facts.[42]

Table 5.6   Sources of Innovation

SOURCE	EXAMPLES
Unexpected occurrences	Unexpected success: Apple Computer (microcomputers) Unexpected failure: Ford's Edsel
Incongruities	Overnight package delivery
Process needs	Sugar-free products Caffeine-free coffee Microwave ovens
Industry and market changes	Health care industry: changing to home health care
Demographic changes	Rest homes or retirement centers for older people
Perceptual changes	Exercise (aerobics) and the growing concern for fitness
Knowledge-based concepts	Video industry; robotics

Myth 1: Innovation Is Planned and Predictable

This myth is based on the old concept that innovation should be left to the research and development (R&D) department under a planned format. In truth, innovation is unpredictable and may be introduced by anyone.

Myth 2: Technical Specifications Should Be Thoroughly Prepared

Thorough preparation often takes too long. Quite often it is more important to use a try/test/revise approach.

Myth 3: Creativity Relies on Dreams and Blue-Sky Ideas

Accomplished innovators are very practical people and create from the opportunities left by reality—not daydreams.

Myth 4: Big Projects Will Develop Better Innovations Than Smaller Ones

This myth has been proven false time and time again. Larger firms are now encouraging their people to work in smaller groups, where it often is easier to generate creative ideas.

Myth 5: Technology Is the Driving Force of Innovation and Success

Technology is certainly one source for innovation, but it is not the only one. Moreover, the customer or market is the driving force behind any innovation. Market-driven or customer-based innovations have the highest probability of success. A good example is found in Polaroid's Polarvision, a television camera that allowed for instant playback of the film. Polaroid hit the market with this technological advance at the same time videocassette recorders arrived. The result: Polaroid's product was rejected, and the company lost millions of dollars.

Principles of Innovation

Potential entrepreneurs need to realize innovation principles exist. These principles can be learned and, when combined with opportunity, can enable individuals to innovate. The major motivation principles follow:

- ☐ *Be action oriented.* Innovators always must be active and searching for new ideas, opportunities, or sources of innovation.

- ☐ *Make the product, process, or service simple and understandable.* People must readily understand how the innovation works.

- ☐ *Make the product, process, or service customer-based.* Innovators always must keep the customer in mind. The more an innovator has the end-user in mind, the greater the chance the concept will be accepted and used.

- ☐ *Start small.* Innovators should not attempt a project or development on a grandiose scale. They should begin small and then build and develop, allowing for planned growth and proper expansion in the right manner and at the right time.

- ☐ *Aim high.* Innovators should aim high for success by seeking a niche in the marketplace.

- ☐ *Try/test/revise.* Innovators always should follow the rule of try, test, and revise. This helps work out any flaws in the product, process, or service.

- ☐ *Learn from failures.* Innovation does not guarantee success. More important, failures often give rise to innovations.[43]

the entrepreneurial
PROCESS

Five Types of Innovators

Gatekeepers—These people collect and channel information about changes in the technical environment. They stay current with events and ideas through personal contacts, professional meetings, and the news media. When gatekeepers find relevant information, they send it to the appropriate person or unit for follow-up.

Idea Generators—This role involves analysis of information about new technologies, products, or procedures in order to yield a new idea for the company. The fresh idea may be an innovative solution to an existing problem in product or business development or the identification of a new marketplace opportunity.

Champions—Champions advocate and push for the new idea. This role involves obtaining and applying the resources and staff to demonstrate the idea's feasibility. Champions are concerned about results, not risk, and do not spend time studying the consequences of failure. Their mission is to remove obstacles.

Project Managers—Someone has to draw up schedules and budgets; arrange periodic information sessions and status reports; coordinate labor, equipment, and other resources; and monitor progress against the plan. Project managers integrate and administer the tasks, people, and physical resources necessary to move an idea into practice.

Coaches—This function addresses the technical and interpersonal aspects of the work in the innovation process. Coaches provide technical training related to new developments and help people work together to turn an idea into a tangible result.

SOURCE: Mark Frohman and Perry Pascarella, "Achieving Purpose-Driven Innovation," *Industry Week* (March 19, 1990): 20–26.

☐ *Follow a milestone schedule.* Every innovator should follow a schedule that indicates milestone accomplishments. Although the project may run ahead or behind schedule, it still is important to have the schedule in order to plan and evaluate the project.

☐ *Reward heroic activity.* This principle applies more to those involved in seeking and motivating others to innovate. Innovative activity should be rewarded and given the proper amount of respect. This also means tolerating and, to a limited degree, accepting failures as a means of accomplishing innovation. Innovative work must be seen as heroic activity that will reveal new horizons for the enterprise.

☐ *Work, work, work.* This is a simple but accurate exhortation with which to conclude the innovation principles. It takes work—not genius or mystery—to innovate successfully.[44]

Summary

This chapter examined the importance of creativity and innovation to the entrepreneur. The creativity process was described, and ways of developing creativity were presented. Exercises and suggestions were included to help the reader increase the development of his or her creativity. The nature of the creative climate also was described.

The four basic types of innovation—invention, extension, duplication, and synthesis—were explained, and the sources of innovation were outlined and examined. The last part of the chapter reviewed the myths commonly associated with innovation, and presented the major innovation principles.

Key Terms and Concepts

appositional relationship	invention
creative process	left brain
creativity	muddling mind-sets
duplication	probability thinking
extension	right brain
functional perspective	stereotyping
incongruities	synthesis
innovation	

Review and Discussion Questions

1. In your own words, state what is meant by the term *innovation*.
2. What is the difference between an adaptor and an innovator?
3. What are four major components in the creative process?
4. What are the four steps involved in developing personal creativity?
5. What are four major types of innovation?
6. What are the major sources of innovation? Explain and give an example of each.
7. Briefly describe the five major myths commonly associated with innovation.
8. Identify and describe five of the innovation principles.

Experiential Exercise

Developing Your Personal Creativity

This exercise is designed to help you develop your personal creativity. To enhance your creativity, you should make improvements in the following areas:

1. *Personal development* (self-discipline, self-awareness, self-confidence, improvement in energy level)
2. *Problem-solving skills* (problem recognition)
3. *Mental fluency* (quantity of thoughts/ideas)
4. *Mental flexibility* (switching gears/approaches)
5. *Originality* (unusual thoughts and ideas)

It is best to start small and work on a few things at a time. Follow the step-by-step approach listed next. Use the accompanying worksheet to help you design a personal creativity program.

1. Choose one of the five areas for improvement listed (for example, mental fluency).
2. Establish a specific objective for this area (for example, to increase your ability to generate logical and intuitive solutions to problems at work).

3. Decide how much time you will give to this program (for example, three hours per week).

4. Decide how long you will work in this area (for example, one month, two months).

5. Decide what actions you will take and what exercises you will perform to improve in this area (for example, sentence-creation exercises, usage ideas, meditation, suspension of initial judgments).

6. Set up an outline of your program (that is, day of week, time of day, place, and what you will do during this time).

7. Review your program after completion, and write a similar program for another one of the five areas for improvement.

Personal Creativity Program Worksheet

Area of improvement _____

Specific objective _____

_____

_____

Number of hours per week _____

Duration of program _____

Actions/exercises _____

_____

_____

_____

Outline of Program

Day of the week   _____   _____   _____   _____

Time of day   _____   _____   _____   _____

Place   _____   _____   _____   _____

Actions that day _____   _____   _____   _____

                  _____   _____   _____   _____

Case 5.1

Post–it Notes

One way new products are developed is to take a current product and modify it in some way. Another way is to determine how a previously developed product can be marketed or used by a particular group of customers.

The 3M Company is famous for many products, among them adhesives and abrasives. In one of 3M's most famous innovative stories from the 1980s, a 3M manager, who was a member of a church choir, wanted to mark the pages of his hymnal so he could quickly find them. A bookmark would not do because the piece of paper could easily fall out. The manager needed something that would adhere to the page but not tear it. Back at work, the manager asked one of the members of the research and development department if an adhesive existed that would do this. One did, but it never had been marketed because the company found that the adhesive was not strong enough for industrial use. At the manager's request, a batch of the glue was prepared and applied to small pieces of paper that could be used as bookmarks.

As the manager who had requested the product began to think about the new product, he concluded it had uses other than as a bookmark. Secretaries could use it to attach messages to files, and managers could use it to send notes along with letters and memos. In an effort to spur interest in the product, the manager had a large batch of these "attachable" notes, now called Post-it Notes, made and began distributing them to secretaries throughout the company. Before long more people began to ask for them. The manager then ordered the supply cut off and told everyone who wanted them that they would have to contact the marketing department. When that department became inundated with calls for Post-it Notes, it concluded that a strong demand existed throughout industry for these notes, and full production began. Today Post-it Notes is one of the largest and most successful product lines at the 3M Company.

Questions

1. In the development of this product, how did the creative thinking process work? Describe what took place in each of the four steps.

2. Why did the manager have the Post-its sent to secretaries throughout the company? What was his objective in doing this?

3. What type of innovation was this—invention, extension, duplication, or synthesis? Defend your answer.

4. Which of the innovation sources discussed in the chapter help account for this product's success? Explain in detail.

Notes

1. Lloyd W. Fernald, Jr., "The Underlying Relationship between Creativity, Innovation, and Entrepreneurship," *Journal of Creative Behavior* 22(3) (1988): 196–202; and Thomas B. Ward, "Cognition, Creativity, and Entrepreneurship," *Journal of Business Venturing* 19(2) (March 2004): 173–188.

2. Timothy A. Matherly and Ronald E. Goldsmith, "The Two Faces of Creativity," *Business Horizons* (September/October 1985): 8; see also Bruce G. Whiting, "Creativity and Entrepreneurship: How Do They Relate?" *Journal of Creative Behavior* 22(3) (1988): 178–183.

3. Michael Kirton, "Adaptors and Innovators: A Description and Measure," *Journal of Applied Psychology* (October 1976): 622–629.

4. E. Holly Buttner and Nur Gryskiewicz, "Entrepreneurs' Problem-Solving Styles: An Empirical Study Using the Kirton Adaption/Innovation Theory," *Journal of Small Business Management* (January 1993): 22–31.

5. See Edward deBono, *Serious Creativity: Using the Power of Creativity to Create New Ideas* (New York: Harper Business, 1992).

6. Eleni Mellow, "The Two Conditions View of Creativity," *Journal of Creative Behavior* 30(2) (1996): 126–143.

7. H. J. Eysenck, *Genius: The Nature of Creativity* (New York: Cambridge University Press, 1995); and B. Taylor, *Into the Open: Reflections on Genius and Modernity* (New York: New York University Press, 1995).

8. Teresa Amabile, "How to Kill Creativity," *Harvard Business Review* 76 (September–October 1998): 77–87.

9. See Dale Dauten, *Taking Chances: Lessons in Putting Passion and Creativity in Your Work Life* (New York: New Market Press, 1986).

10. Edward deBono, *Six Thinking Hats* (Boston: Little, Brown, 1985); and Edward deBono, "Serious Creativity," *The Journal for Quality and Participation* 18(5) (1995): 12.

11. For a discussion of the development of creativity, see Eugene Raudsepp, *How Creative Are You?* (New York: Perigee Books, 1981); Arthur B. Van Gundy, *108 Ways to Get a Bright Idea and Increase Your Creative Potential* (Englewood Cliffs, NJ: Prentice-Hall, 1983); and Roger L. Firestien, *Why Didn't I Think of That?* (Buffalo, NY: United Education Services Inc., 1989).

12. T. A. Nosanchuk, J. A. Ogrodnik, and Tom Henigan, "A Preliminary Investigation of Incubation in Short Story Writing," *Journal of Creative Behavior* 22(4) (1988): 279–280. (This study reported that an eight-day incubation period was associated with significantly elevated story-writing creativity.)

13. W. W. Harman and H. Rheingold, *Higher Creativity: Liberating the Unconscious for Breakthrough Insights* (Los Angeles: Tarcher, 1984); and Daniel Goleman, Paul Kaufman, and Michael Ray, *The Creative Spirit* (New York: Penguin Books USA Inc., 1993).

14. See J. Conrath, "Developing More Powerful Ideas," *Supervisory Management* (March 1985): 2–9; Denise Shekerjian, *Uncommon Genius: How Great Ideas Are Born* (New York: Viking Press, 1990); and Keng L. Siau, "Group Creativity and Technology," *Journal of Creative Behavior* 29(3) (1996). Siau argues that electronic brainstorming instead of in-person brainstorming eliminates "evaluation apprehension" among group participants.

15. Deborah Funk, "I Was Showering When . . . ," *Baltimore Business Journal* 12(46) (March 1995): 13–14.

16. For more on idea development, see A. F. Osborn, *Applied Imagination*, 3rd ed. (New York: Scribners, 1963); William J. Gordon, *Synectics* (New York: Harper & Row, 1961); and Ted Pollock, "A Personal File of Stimulating Ideas, Little-Known Facts and Daily Problem-Solvers," *Supervision* 4 (April 1995): 24.

17. Martin F. Rosenman, "Serendipity and Scientific Discovery," *Journal of Creative Behavior* 22(2) (1988): 132–138.

18. For more on implementation, see John M. Keil, *The Creative Mystique: How to Manage It, Nurture It, and Make It Pay* (New York: Wiley, 1985); and James F. Brandowski, *Corporate Imagination Plus: Five Steps to Translating Innovative Strategies into Action* (New York: The Free Press, 1990).

19. J. Wajec, *Five Star Minds: Recipes to Stimulate Your Creativity and Imagination* (New York: Doubleday, 1995); and Frank Barron, *No Rootless Flower: An Ecology of Creativity* (New Jersey: Hampton Press, Inc., 1995).

20. See Dale Dauten, *Taking Chances: Lessons in Putting Passion and Creativity into Your Work Life* (New York: Newmarket Press, 1986); and Gary A. Davis, *Creativity Is Forever* (Dubuque, IA: Kendall/Hunt, 1986).

21. Sidney J. Parnes, *Visionizing: State-of-the-Art Processes for Encouraging Innovative Excellence* (East Aurora, NY: D.O.K., 1988).

22. See E. Paul Torrance, *The Search for Sartori and Creativity* (Buffalo, NY: Creative Education Foundations, 1979); Erik K. Winslow and George T. Solomon, "Further Development of a Descriptive Profile of Entrepreneurs," *Journal of Creative Behavior* 23(3) (1989): 149–161; and Roger von Oech, *A Whack on the Side of the Head* (New York: Warner Books, 1998).

23. Tony Buzan, *Make the Most of Your Mind* (New York: Simon and Schuster, 1984).

24. Weston H. Agor, *Intuitive Management: Integrating Left and Right Brain Management Skills* (Englewood Cliffs, NJ: Prentice-Hall, 1984); Tony Buzan, *Using Both Sides of Your Brain* (New York: Dutton, 1976); and D. Hall, *Jump Start Your Brain* (New York: Warner Books, 1995).

25. For more on this topic, see Jacquelyn Wonder and Priscilla Donovan, *Whole-Brain Thinking* (New York: Morrow, 1984), 60–61.

26. Doris Shallcross and Anthony M. Gawienowski, "Top Experts Address Issues on Creativity Gap in Higher Education," *Journal of Creative Behavior* 23(2) (1989): 75.

27. Vincent Ryan Ruggiero, *The Art of Thinking: A Guide to Critical and Creative Thought* (New York: Harper Collins, 1995).

28. David Campbell, *Take the Road to Creativity and Get Off Your Dead End* (Greensboro, NC: Center for Creative Leadership, 1985).

29. James O'Toole, *Vanguard Management: Redesigning the Corporate Future* (New York: Berkley Books, 1987).

30. Edward deBono, *Lateral Thinking: Creativity Step by Step* (New York: Harper & Row, 1970).

31. Zoa Rockenstein, "Intuitive Processes in Executive Decision Making," *Journal of Creative Behavior* 22(2) (1988): 77–84.

32. Adapted from deBono, *Lateral Thinking;* and Eugene Raudsepp, *How to Create New Ideas: For Corporate Profit and Personal Success* (Englewood Cliffs, NJ: Prentice-Hall, 1982).

33. William C. Miller, *Flash of Brilliance* (Reading, PA: Perseus Books, 1999).

34. Karl Albrecht, *The Creative Corporation* (Homewood, IL: Dow Jones-Irwin, 1987); see also William C. Miller, *The Creative Edge: Fostering Innovation Where You Work* (New York: Addison-Wesley Publishing, 1987); K. Mark Weaver, "Developing and Implementing Entrepreneurial Cultures," *Journal of Creative Behavior* 22(3) (1988): 184–195; American Management Association, *Creative Edge: How Corporations Support Creativity and Innovation* (New York, 1995); D. Leonard and S. Straus, "Putting the Company's Whole Brain to Work," *Harvard Business Review* 75 (July–August 1997): 111–121; and J. Hirshberg, *The Creative Priority* (New York: Harper Books, 1998).

35. Peter F. Drucker, *Innovation and Entrepreneurship* (New York: Harper & Row, 1985), 20.

36. Jane M. Howell and Christopher A. Higgins, "Champions of Change: Identifying, Understanding, and Supporting Champions of Technological Innovations," *Organizational Dynamics* (summer 1990): 40–55; see also Dean M. Schroeder, "A Dynamic Perspective on the Impact of Process Innovation upon Competitive Strategies," *Strategic Management Journal* 11 (1990): 25–41.

37. Peter F. Drucker, "The Discipline of Innovation," *Harvard Business Review* (May/June 1985): 67–72.

38. See Peter L. Josty, "A Tentative Model of the Innovation Process," *R & D Management* (January 1990): 35–44.

39. Drucker, "The Discipline of Innovation," 67.

40. Adapted from Richard M. Hodgetts and Donald F. Kuratko, *Effective Small Business Management,* 7th ed. (Fort Worth, TX: Harcourt College Publishers, 2001), 21–23.

41. See Jane M. Howell and Chris A. Higgins, "Champions of Change," *Business Quarterly* (spring 1990): 31–36; and Dean A. Shepherd and Dawn DeTienne, "Prior Knowledge, Potential Financial Reward, and Opportunity Identification," *Entrepreneurship Theory and Practice* 29(1) (January 2005): 91–112.

42. Adapted from Drucker, *Innovation and Entrepreneurship;* and Thomas J. Peters and Nancy J. Austin, *A Passion for Excellence* (New York: Random House, 1985).

43. For a good example, see Ronald A. Mitsch, "Three Roads to Innovation," *Journal of Business Strategy* (September/October 1990): 18–21.

44. William Taylor, "The Business of Innovation," *Harvard Business Review* (March/April 1990): 97–106.

6 Entrepreneurial Ethics

Ownership is hope. It's curiosity, openness, an eagerness to learn and grow. It's caring about yourself and the people around you. It's wanting to contribute, to make a difference. It's the courage and conviction to face the future. It's confidence, self-esteem, and pride. It's the ability to handle diversity. It's giving back to your community and appreciating the gifts you've received. Those are great qualities to have in a business . . . and they're the qualities we need now more than ever!!

Jack Stack, CEO, SRC Holdings Corp.

A Stake in the Outcome

Chapter Objectives

1 To discuss the importance of ethics for entrepreneurs

2 To define the term "ethics"

3 To study ethics in a conceptual framework for a dynamic environment

4 To review the constant dilemma of law versus ethics

5 To examine the role of ethics in the free enterprise system

6 To present strategies for establishing ethical responsibility

7 To introduce the challenge of social responsibility

8 To emphasize the importance of entrepreneurs taking a position of ethical leadership

The Ethical Side of Enterprise

Ethical issues in business are of great importance today. And why not? The prevalence of scandals, fraud, and various forms of executive misconduct in corporations has spurred the watchful eye of the public.[1]

Ethics is not a new topic, however. It has figured prominently in philosophical thought since the time of Socrates, Plato, and Aristotle. Derived from the Greek word *ethos,* meaning custom or mode of conduct, ethics has challenged philosophers for centuries to determine what exactly represents right or wrong conduct. For example, business executive Vernon R. Loucks, Jr., notes that "it was about 560 B.C. . . . when the Greek thinker Chilon registered the opinion that a merchant does better to take a loss than to make a dishonest profit. His reasoning was that a loss may be painful for a while, but dishonesty hurts forever—and it's still timely."[2]

Today's entrepreneurs are faced with many ethical decisions, especially during the early stages of their new ventures. And, as Sir Adrian Cadbury observed, "There is no simple universal formula for solving ethical problems. We have to choose from our own codes of conduct whichever rules are appropriate to the case in hand; the outcome of these choices makes us who we are."[3]

The purpose of this chapter is to examine some of the issues surrounding ethics and entrepreneurship. It is our hope that aspiring entrepreneurs will realize the powerful impact integrity and ethical conduct have on creating a successful venture.

Defining Ethics

In the broadest sense, **ethics** provide the basic rules or parameters for conducting any activity in an "acceptable" manner. More specifically, ethics represent a set of principles prescribing a behavioral code that explains what is good and right or bad and wrong; ethics may, in addition, outline moral duty and obligations.[4] The problem with most definitions of the term is not in the description but rather in the implications for implementation. The definition is a static description that implies society agrees on certain universal principles. With society operating in a dynamic and ever-changing environment, however, such a consensus does not exist.[5] In fact, continual conflict over the ethical nature of decisions is quite prevalent.

This conflict arises for a number of reasons. First, business enterprises are confronted by many interests both inside and outside the organization—for example, stockholders, customers, managers, the community, the government, employees, private interest groups, unions, peers, and so on. Second, society is undergoing dramatic change. Values, mores, and societal norms have gone through a drastic evolution in the past few decades. A definition of ethics in such a rapidly changing environment must be based more on a process than on a static code. Figure 6.1 illustrates a conceptual framework for viewing this process. As one ethicist states, "Deciding what is good or right or bad and wrong in such a dynamic environment is necessarily 'situational.' Therefore, instead of relying on a set of fixed ethical principles, we must now develop an ethical process."[6]

Figure 6.1 Classifying Decisions Using a Conceptual Framework

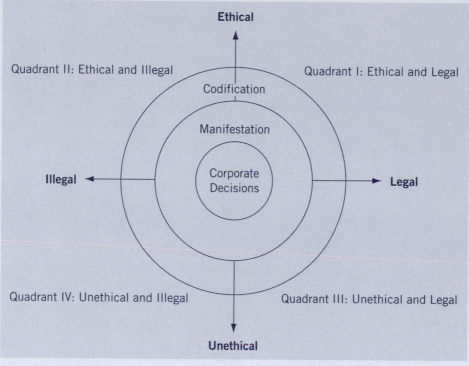

Source: Verne E. Henderson, "The Ethical Side of Enterprise," *Sloan Management Review* (spring 1982): 42.

The quadrants depicted in Figure 6.1 demonstrate the age-old dilemma between law and ethics. Moving from the ideal ethical and legal position (Quadrant I) to an unethical and illegal position (Quadrant IV), one can see the continuum of activities within an ethical process. Yet legality provides societal standards but not definitive answers to ethical questions.

Ethics and Laws

For the entrepreneur the dilemma of legal versus ethical is a vital one. Just how far can an entrepreneur go in order to establish his or her venture? Survival of the venture is a strong motivation for entrepreneurs, and although the law provides the boundaries for what is illegal (even though the laws are subject to constant interpretation), it does not supply answers for ethical considerations.

Managerial Rationalizations

One researcher suggests that legal behavior represents one of four **rationalizations** managers use for justifying questionable conduct. The four rationalizations are believing (1) that the activity is not "really" illegal or immoral; (2) that it is in the individual's or the corporation's best interest; (3) that it will never be found out; and (4) that because it helps the company, the company will condone it.[7]

These rationalizations appear realistic, given the behavior of many business enterprises today. However, the legal aspect can be the most dubious. This is because the business world (and society) relies heavily on the law to qualify the actions of various

Table 6.1   Types of Morally Questionable Acts

TYPE	DIRECT EFFECT	EXAMPLES
Nonrole	Against the firm	Expense account cheating Embezzlement Stealing supplies
Role failure	Against the firm	Superficial performance appraisal Not confronting expense account cheating Palming off a poor performer with inflated praise
Role distortion	For the firm	Bribery Price fixing Manipulating suppliers
Role assertion	For the firm	Investing in South Africa Using nuclear technology for energy generation Not withdrawing product line in face of initial allegations of inadequate safety

Source: James A. Waters and Frederick Bird, "Attending to Ethics in Management," *Journal of Business Ethics* 5 (1989): 494.

situations. The law interprets the situations within the prescribed framework. Unfortunately, this framework does not always include ethical or moral behavior. This is left up to the individual, which is the precise reason for the dilemma.

In any examination of the realm of managerial rationalizations, the idea of morally questionable acts becomes a major concern for understanding ethical conduct. One research study developed a typology of morally questionable acts.[8] Table 6.1 summarizes the distinctions made in this typology. Morally questionable acts are either "against the firm" or "on behalf of the firm." In addition, the managerial role differs for various acts. **Nonrole** acts are those the person takes outside of his or her role as manager, yet they go against the firm. Examples would include expense account cheating and embezzlement. **Role failure** acts are also against the firm, but they involve a person failing to perform his or her managerial role, including superficial performance appraisals (not totally honest) and not confronting someone who is cheating on expense accounts. **Role distortion** acts and **role assertion** acts are rationalized as being "for the firm." These acts involve managers/entrepreneurs who rationalize that the long-run interests of the firm are foremost. Examples include bribery, price fixing, manipulating suppliers, and failing to withdraw a potentially dangerous product from the market. Role distortion is the behavior of individuals thinking they are acting in the best interests of the firm, so their roles are "distorted." Role assertion is the behavior of individuals asserting their roles beyond what they should be, thinking (falsely) that they are expanding their personal roles to "help" the firm.

All four of these roles involved in the morally questionable acts, whether "for" or "against" the firm, illustrate the types of rationalizations that can occur. In addition, this typology presents an interesting insight into the distinctions involved with managerial rationalization.

Figure 6.2 *Overlap between Moral Standards and Legal Requirements*

The Matter of Morality

Ethical conduct may reach beyond the limits of the law.[9] As one group of noted legal writers has pointed out, morals and law are not synonymous but may be viewed as two circles partially superimposed on each other (see Figure 6.2). The area covered by both the moral standards circle and the legal requirements circle represents the body of ideas that are both moral and legal. Yet the largest expanse of area is outside this overlapping portion, indicating the vast difference that sometimes exists between morality (ethics) and law.[10]

LaRue Hosmer has pointed out three conclusions regarding the relationship between legal requirements and moral judgment. First, as noted earlier, the requirements of law may overlap at times but do not duplicate the moral standards of society. Some laws have no moral content whatsoever (for example, driving on the right side of the road), some laws are morally unjust (for example, racial segregation laws before the 1960s), and some moral standards have no legal basis (for example, telling a lie). Second, legal requirements tend to be negative (forbidding acts), whereas morality tends to be positive (encouraging acts). Third, legal requirements usually lag behind the acceptable moral standards of society.[11]

In addition, even if the argument were made that laws are supposed to be the collective moral judgment of society, inherent problems arise when people believe laws represent morality. Whether it is lack of information on issues, misrepresentation of the values or laws, or an imprecise judicial system, the legal environment has difficulty encompassing all ethical and moral expectations. Thus the issue of law and ethics will continue to be a dilemma for entrepreneurs (see Table 6.2).

Economic Trade-Offs

Innovation, risk taking, and venture creation are the backbone of the free enterprise system. From this system emerge the qualities of individualism and competition. These qualities have produced an economic system that creates jobs (approximately 20 million jobs in the past decade) and enormous growth in ventures (more than 600,000 incorporations each year). However, these same qualities also have produced complex trade-offs between economic profits and social welfare, as revealed by the following situations:

☐ Advertisements for Marlboro and Vantage cigarettes show young, athletic, outdoorsy men and women, yet cigarettes place hundreds of thousands of people in hospital intensive care units and cause about 350,000 deaths per year.

Table 6.2 Major Problems Regarding Laws Reflecting Ethical Standards

1. *The moral standards of members of society may be based on a lack of information relative to issues of corporate conduct.* Most people were apparently unaware of the payments of large foreign bribes until the revelations of the Lockheed case and the subsequent Securities and Exchange Commission study. Many people now may be unaware of the magnitude of the toxic-waste disposal problem, with 231 million metric tons of waste being produced annually. It is difficult for personal moral standards to influence the law if relevant information is missing.

2. *The moral standards of members of society may be diluted by the formation of small groups.* People with similar norms, beliefs, and values tend to become associated in small groups, but these standards generally are not precisely similar among all members, and compromises have to be made. Further, many small groups act from motives other than morality; economic benefits and professional prestige often seem to be stressed. It is difficult for personal moral standards to influence the law if they are not conveyed accurately.

3. *The moral standards of members of society may be misrepresented in the consensus of large organizations.* Many organizations do share norms, beliefs, and values, but no evidence indicates each individual and each group within the organization has equal influence, or even equal weighted influence, in determining that consensus. This can be seen in the norms, beliefs, and values of many nonprofit organizations, such as hospitals and universities; the standards of the professional personnel—the physicians and the faculty—often seem to predominate.

4. *The moral standards of members of society may be misrepresented in the formulation of the laws.* This is the same point made about shaping the consensus of an organization, though on a larger scale. No guarantees exist that all organizations have equal influence, or even equal influence weighted by size, in determining the law. This can be seen in the provisions of much tax legislation; certain organizations always seem to be favored.

5. *The legal requirements formed through the political process are often incomplete or imprecise and have to be supplemented by judicial court decisions or administrative agency actions.* This can be seen in both product liability cases and equal employment reviews; the meaning and the application of the law have to be clarified outside of the legislative process. It is difficult for personal moral standards to influence the law if they are considered only indirectly—if at all—in two of the means of formulating that law.

Source: Reproduced with permission from LaRue T. Hosmer, *The Ethics of Management,* 2nd ed. (Homewood, IL: Richard D. Irwin, 1991), 91–92.

☐ Among the 50,000 toxic-waste dump sites in the United States, more than 1,000 are considered very dangerous. Every day, more steel drums rust through, their toxic contents running into streams and lakes and contaminating drinking water.

☐ During an economic downturn, a manager at Bank of America was faced with laying off, by seniority, most of the more recently hired black and women employees.

entrepreneurship IN PRACTICE

An Entrepreneur's Success Turns into Disaster

Stew Leonard, an entrepreneur and retail legend from Norwalk, Connecticut, featured by Tom Peter's *In Search of Excellence* as the wizard who transformed a small dairy farm into a $200 million-a-year supermarket Disneyland, shocked the business world when he pleaded guilty to tax fraud in 1993.

Federal agents say he conspired to defraud the government of taxes on $17.5 million. How? He developed a computer software program that allowed him to reduce sales data on an item-by-item basis and skim $17 million in cash over a period from 1981 to 1991. Computer tapes that contained the real financial figures were destroyed, and the company's auditors were given the understated books. In order to divert even more money, Leonard had customers buy gift certificates with cash.

Each day the cash was emptied from the registers into a "money room" where it was counted, placed in bags, and dropped down a chute into the "vault room." Most of the unreported money was taken to the Caribbean, where Leonard owns a second home. Another executive, Leonard's brother-in-law, kept $484,000 hidden behind a false panel in his basement. The computer program itself was also hidden.

The government apparently began investigating Leonard after he was stopped in June 1991 by customs agents as he boarded a flight to the Caribbean with $80,000 in cash. He had not filed the required government forms for taking that amount of money out of the country.

IRS agents identified Leonard's actions as the largest criminal tax evasion in Connecticut's history and as the largest case in the country's history involving a computer program as part of the conspiracy.

Leonard had achieved the pinnacle of success in his industry. Two hundred thousand customers visit his two stores every week. His Norwalk store has the highest sales per square foot, $3,470 compared to the industry average of $300 to $500, and it sells 10 million quarts of milk and 8 million ears of corn annually. A former recipient of the Presidential Award for Entrepreneurial Achievement, Leonard now stands disgraced after receiving a sentence that included a prison term, community service, and repayment of $15 million in restitution. For an in-depth look at Stew Leonard's story, see the Entrepreneurial Case Analysis following this chapter.

SOURCE: Richard Behar, "Skimming the Cream," *Time* (August 2, 1993): 49; and Clifford J. Levy, "Founder of Renowned Store Pleads Guilty in Fraud Case," *The New York Times* (July 23, 1993): A11.

☐ Young financial wizard Dennis Levine made millions of dollars in personal profits using information obtained from those who were a party to proposed mergers. He purchased stock before the news became public, and the stock increased in price.[12]

These vignettes demonstrate the conflicting needs inherent in the free enterprise system. On the one hand is the generation of profits, jobs, and efficiency. On the other hand is the quest for personal and social respect, honesty, and integrity. A utilitarian ethical norm would calculate what the greatest good for the greatest number would be. This calculation also would take into account future generations.[13] Unfortunately, although the calculation sounds easy, in practice it borders on the impossible. To illustrate, one study reported that 65 percent of the public said executives would do everything they could to make a profit, even if it meant ignoring society's needs.[14] Another study reported that a Darwinian ethic was now prevailing in business that spreads a "profit-at-any-price" attitude among business owners and managers.[15]

Yet the public's perception may be based more on a misunderstanding of the free enterprise system than a condemnation of it. One ethicist, Margaret Maxey, reminds us that in a complex world of changing technology and valuable innovations, we cannot blame single individuals for the ethical problems of free enterprise. Rather, we must understand the total, systematic impact that free enterprise has on the common good.[16]

In spite of these misconceptions, the fact remains that unethical behavior does take place. Why? A few possible explanations include (1) greed, (2) distinctions between activities at work and activities at home, (3) a lack of a foundation in ethics, (4) survival (bottom-line thinking), and (5) a reliance on other social institutions to convey and reinforce ethics. Whatever the reasons, ethical decision making is a challenge that confronts every businessperson involved in large or small enterprises.[17]

Establishing a Strategy for Ethical Responsibility

Because the free enterprise system in which the entrepreneur flourishes is fraught with myriad conflicts, entrepreneurs need to commit to an established strategy for ethical responsibility.

Ethical Practices and Codes of Conduct

A **code of conduct** is a statement of ethical practices or guidelines to which an enterprise adheres. Many such codes exist—some related to industry at large and others related directly to corporate conduct. These codes cover a multitude of subjects, ranging from misuse of corporate assets, conflict of interest, and use of inside information to equal employment practices, falsification of books or records, and antitrust violations.

How prevalent are codes of conduct today? The Conference Board found that 227 out of 300 firms surveyed had codes of conduct.[18] Based on the results of such research, two important conclusions can be reached. First, codes of conduct are becoming more prevalent in industry. Management is not just giving lip service to ethics and moral behavior; it is putting its ideas into writing and distributing these guidelines for everyone in the organization to read and follow. Second, in contrast to earlier codes, the more recent ones are proving to be more meaningful in terms of external legal and social development, more comprehensive in terms of their coverage, and easier to implement in terms of the administrative procedures used to enforce them.[19]

Of course, the most important question still remains to be answered: Will management really adhere to a high moral code? Many managers would respond to this question by answering "yes." Why? The main reason is that it is good business. One top executive put the idea this way: "Singly or in combination, unethical practices have a corrosive effect on free markets and free trade, which are fundamental to the survival of the free enterprise system. They subvert the laws of supply and demand,

and they short-circuit competition based on classical ideas of product quality, service, and price. Free markets become replaced by contrived markets. The need for constant improvement in products or services is thus removed."[20]

A second, related reason is that by improving the moral climate of the enterprise, the corporation can eventually win back the public's confidence. This would mark a turnaround in that many people today question the moral and ethical integrity of companies and believe that businesspeople try to get away with everything they can. Only time will tell whether codes of conduct will serve to improve business practices. Current trends indicate, however, that the business community is working hard toward achieving this objective.[21]

Approaches to Managerial Ethics

When focusing on an ethical position, entrepreneurs should analyze various organizational characteristics. One study examined ethical norms, motives, goals, orientation toward law, and strategy and used these characteristics to define three distinct types of management: **immoral management, amoral management,** and **moral management.**[22] Table 6.3 provides a summary of each characteristic within each of the ethical types. These characteristics are important for gaining insight into the continuum of behaviors that can be exhibited. Before entrepreneurs set forth any strategy, it is imperative that they analyze their own reactions to these characteristics and thus their own ethical styles.

Moving from an immoral or amoral position to a moral position requires a great deal of personal effort. Whether it is a commitment to sending employees to training seminars on business ethics, establishing codes of conduct, or exhibiting tighter operational controls, the entrepreneur needs to develop particular areas around which a strategy can be formulated.

A Holistic Approach

One author has suggested a holistic management approach that encompasses ethics in its perspective. This dual-focused approach includes "knowing how" and "knowing that." Admittedly, it is an aesthetic, philosophical perspective, but the understanding of it "reminds the administrator that there exist complementary forms of acquiring managerial knowledge."[23] In other words, managerial practices as well as the ethical implications of those practices need to be acquired.

To apply a holistic approach, entrepreneurs can develop specific principles that will assist them in taking the right external steps as their ventures develop. Presented here are one executive's four principles for ethical management:[24]

☐ Principle 1: *Hire the right people.* Employees who are inclined to be ethical are the best insurance you can have. They may be the only insurance. Look for people with principles. Let them know that those principles are an important part of their qualifications for the job.

☐ Principle 2: *Set standards more than rules.* You can't write a code of conduct airtight enough to cover every eventuality. A person inclined to fraud or misconduct isn't going to blink at signing your code anyway. So don't waste your time on heavy regulations. Instead, be clear about standards. Let people know the level of performance you expect—and that ethics is not negotiable.

Table 6.3   Approaches to Managerial Ethics

ORGANIZATIONAL CHARACTERISTICS	IMMORAL MANAGEMENT	AMORAL MANAGEMENT	MORAL MANAGEMENT
Ethical norms	Managerial decisions, actions, and behavior imply a positive and active opposition to what is moral (ethical). Decisions are discordant with accepted ethical principles. An active negation of what is moral is implied.	Management is neither moral nor immoral, but decisions lie outside the sphere to which moral judgments apply. Managerial activity is outside or beyond the moral order of a particular code. A lack of ethical perception and moral awareness may be implied.	Managerial activity conforms to a standard of ethical, or right, behavior. Managers conform to accepted professional standards of conduct. Ethical leadership is commonplace on the part of management.
Motives	Selfish: Management cares only about its or the company's gains.	Well-intentioned but selfish: The impact on others is not considered.	Good: Management wants to succeed but only within the confines of sound ethical precepts (fairness, justice, due process).
Goals	Profitability and organizational success at any price.	Profitability; other goals not considered.	Profitability within the confines of legal obedience and ethical standards.
Orientation toward law	Legal standards are barriers management must overcome to accomplish what it wants.	Law is the ethical guide, preferably the letter of the law. The central question is what managers can do legally.	Obedience is toward the letter and spirit of the law. Law is a minimal ethical behavior. Managers prefer to operate well above what the law mandates.
Strategy	Exploit opportunities for corporate gain. Cut corners when it appears useful.	Give managers free rein. Personal ethics may apply but only if managers choose. Respond to legal mandates if caught and required to do so.	Live by sound ethical standards. Assume leadership position when ethical dilemmas arise. Enlightened self-interest prevails.

Source: Archie B. Carroll, "In Search of the Moral Manager," *Business Horizons* (March/April 1987): 12. Copyright © 1987 by the Foundation for the School of Business at Indiana University. Reprinted by permission.

□   Principle 3: *Don't let yourself get isolated.* You know managers can lose track of markets and competitors by moving into the ivory tower. But they also can lose sight of what's going on in their own operations. The only problem is you are responsible for whatever happens in your office or department or corporation, whether or not you know about it.

the entrepreneurial
PROCESS

Shaping an Ethical Strategy

The development of an organizational climate for responsible and ethically sound behavior requires continuing effort and investment of time and resources. A code of conduct, ethics officers, training programs, and annual ethics audits do not necessarily add up to a responsible, ethical organization. A formal ethics program can serve as a catalyst and a support system, but organizational integrity depends on the integration of the company's values into its driving systems.

Here are a few key elements entrepreneurs should keep in mind when developing an ethical strategy.

☐ *The entrepreneur's guiding values and commitments must make sense and be clearly communicated.* They should reflect important organizational obligations and widely shared aspirations that appeal to the organization's members. Employees at all levels must take them seriously, feel comfortable discussing them, and have a concrete understanding of their practical importance.

☐ *Entrepreneurs must be personally committed, credible, and willing to take action on the values they espouse.* They are not mere mouthpieces. They must be willing to scrutinize their own decisions. Consistency on the part of leadership is key. Entrepreneurs must assume responsibility for making tough calls when ethical obligations conflict.

☐ *The espoused values must be integrated into the normal channels of the organization's critical activities:* planning innovation, resource allocation, information communication, and personnel promotion and advancement.

☐ *The venture's systems and structures must support and reinforce its values.* Information systems, for example, must be designed to provide timely and accurate information. Reporting relationships must be structured to build in checks and balances to promote objective judgment.

☐ *Employees throughout the company must have the decision-making skills, knowledge, and competencies needed to make ethically sound decisions every day.* Ethical thinking and awareness must be part of every employee's skills.

SOURCE: Adapted from Lynn Sharp Paine, "Managing for Organizational Integrity," *Harvard Business Review* (March/April 1994): 106–117.

☐ Principle 4: *The most important principle is to let your ethical example at all times be absolutely impeccable.* This isn't just a matter of how you act in matters of accounting, competition, or interpersonal relationships. Be aware also of the signals you send to those around you. Steady harping on the importance of quarterly gains in earnings, for example, rather easily leads people to believe you don't care much about how the results are achieved.

Mark Twain once said, "Always do the right thing. This will surprise some people and astonish the rest." It will also motivate them to do the right thing. Indeed, without a good example from the top, ethical problems (and all the costs that go with them) are probably inevitable within your organization.

Ethical Responsibility

It must be kept in mind that establishing a strategy for ethical responsibility is not an easy task for entrepreneurs. No single ideal approach to organizational ethics exists. Entrepreneurs need to analyze the ethical consciousness of their organization, the process and structure devised to enhance ethical activity, and, finally, their own commitment to institutionalize ethical objectives in the company.[25] Keeping these points in mind, entrepreneurs eventually can begin to establish a strategy for ethical responsibility. This strategy should encompass three major elements: ethical consciousness, ethical process and structure, and institutionalization.[26]

Ethical Consciousness   The development of ethical consciousness is the responsibility of the entrepreneur because his or her vision created the venture. The key figure to set the tone for ethical decision making and behavior is the entrepreneur. An open exchange of issues and processes within the venture, established codes of ethics for the company, and the setting of examples by the entrepreneur are all illustrations of how this is done. One interesting example from a large corporation involves Motorola. When the company's CEO discovered bookkeeping discrepancies in one of the departments, he directed the 20 implicated employees to make retribution by donating $8,500 to charity.[27] This action commanded positive ethical action and set the tone for ethical expectations.

Ethical Process and Structure   Ethical process and structure refer to the procedures, position statements (codes), and announced ethical goals designed to avoid ambiguity. Having all key personnel read the venture's specific ethical goals and sign affidavits affirming their willingness to follow those policies is a good practice for ventures.

Institutionalization   Institutionalization is a deliberate step to incorporate the entrepreneur's ethical objectives with the economic objectives of the venture. At times an entrepreneur may have to modify policies or operations that become too intense and infringe on the ethics of the situation. This is where the entrepreneur's commitment to ethics and values is tested. Constant review of procedures and feedback in operations are vital to institutionalizing ethical responsibility.

Ethics and Business Decisions

In addition to the normal challenges of business decisions, the entrepreneur is faced with specific ethical dilemmas. Figure 6.3 illustrates four main themes of ethical dilemmas—conflict of interests, personality traits, responsibility to stakeholders, and level of openness.[28] The conflict of interests theme deals with much of what was mentioned earlier in the chapter concerning morality and economic trade-offs. It involves the constant tension of trying to separate the "person" from the "business decision." Personality traits relate more specifically to relationships and personal issues. In many instances, the personal issues or individual personalities cause the dilemma. The responsibility to stakeholders theme incorporates the pressure of managerial rationalization discussed earlier and emphasizes the importance of having a code of conduct. Finally, the level of openness suggests that entrepreneurs need to be more public about their values and expectations. Once again, the value of a code of conduct is evident with this theme.

Amid these dilemmas, entrepreneurs are challenged by the need to make business decisions each day. Many of these decisions are complex and raise ethical considerations.

Figure 6.3 Four Main Themes of Ethical Dilemmas for Entrepreneurs

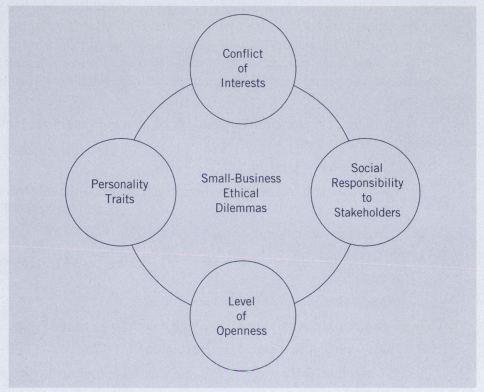

Source: Shailendra Vyakarnam, Andy Bailey, Andrew Myers, and Donna Burnett, "Towards an Understanding of Ethical Behavior in Small Firms," *Journal of Business Ethics* 16(15) (1977): 1625–1636.

Complexity of Decisions

The business decisions of entrepreneurs are highly complex for five reasons. First, ethical decisions have extended consequences. They often have a ripple effect in that the consequences are felt by others outside the venture. For example, the decision to use inexpensive but unsafe products in operations will affect both workers and consumers of the final good.

Second, business decisions involving ethical questions have multiple alternatives. It is not always "do" or "don't do." Many decisions have a wide range of alternatives that may allow a mixture of less important decisions. In reference to the first example about the use of unsafe products, the entrepreneur may have the alternative of using still less expensive but nevertheless safe products.

Third, ethical business decisions often have mixed outcomes. Social benefits as well as costs are involved with every major business decision, as are financial revenues and expenses.

Fourth, most business decisions have uncertain ethical consequences. It is never absolutely certain what actual consequence(s) a decision will have even when it appears logical; in other words, a decision is never without ethical risk.

Finally, most ethical business decisions have personal implications. It is difficult for an entrepreneur to divorce himself or herself from a decision and its potential outcome. Venture success, financial opportunity, and new-product development are all areas that may be affected by decisions having ethical consequences. The entrepreneur often will find it impossible to make a purely impersonal decision.[29]

These five statements about business decisions need to be considered when an entrepreneur is developing a new venture. They indicate the need to grasp as much information as possible about each major decision. One ethicist, who believes this implies understanding the characteristic features of a venture's activities, which in turn allows for a stronger sensitivity to the outcomes, has noted that "someone in business needs to know its general tendencies—the special tracks it leaves—to anticipate points of crisis, and of special concern to us, to increase the possibility of intelligent moral actions."[30]

Some of the pertinent questions that can be used to examine the ethics of business decisions are listed here:

1. Have you defined the problem accurately?

2. How would you define the problem if you stood on the other side of the fence?

3. How did this situation occur in the first place?

4. To whom and to what do you give your loyalty as a person and as a corporation member?

5. What is your intention in making this decision?

6. How does this intention compare with the probable results?

7. Whom could your decision or action injure?

8. Can you discuss the problem with the affected parties before you make your decision?

9. Are you confident your position will be as valid over a long period of time as it seems now?

10. Could you disclose without qualms your decision or action to your boss, your CEO, the board of directors, your family, and society as a whole?

11. What is the symbolic potential of your action if understood? If misunderstood?

12. Under what conditions would you allow exceptions to your stand?[31]

Although this is not a conclusive list, it does provide a frame of reference for entrepreneurs wrestling with the complexity of decisions concerning their venture.

Ethics, as we have seen, is extremely difficult to define, codify, and implement because of its surfacing of personal values and morality. Yet the importance of ethics when initiating new enterprises must be stressed. As one writer has noted, "The singular importance of enterprises to our daily lives and our collective future demands our careful attention and finest efforts."[32]

The Social Responsibility Challenge

Over the past three decades, social responsibility has emerged as a major issue. Although it takes different forms for different industries and companies, the basic challenge exists for all.

Social responsibility consists of obligations a business has to society. These obligations extend to many different areas. Table 6.4 presents some of them. The diversity of

Table 6.4　*What Is the Nature of Social Responsibility?*

Environment	Pollution control
	Restoration or protection of environment
	Conservation of natural resources
	Recycling efforts
Energy	Conservation of energy in production and marketing operations
	Efforts to increase the energy efficiency of products
	Other energy-saving programs (for example, company-sponsored car pools)
Fair Business Practices	Employment and advancement of women and minorities
	Employment and advancement of disadvantaged individuals (disabled, Vietnam veterans, ex-offenders, former drug addicts, mentally retarded, and hardcore unemployed)
	Support for minority-owned businesses
Human Resources	Promotion of employee health and safety
	Employee training and development
	Remedial education programs for disadvantaged employees
	Alcohol and drug counseling programs
	Career counseling
	Child day-care facilities for working parents
	Employee physical fitness and stress management programs
Community Involvement	Donations of cash, products, services, or employee time
	Sponsorship of public health projects
	Support of education and the arts
	Support of community recreation programs
	Cooperation in community projects (recycling centers, disaster assistance, and urban renewal)
Products	Enhancement of product safety
	Sponsorship of product safety education programs
	Reduction of polluting potential of products
	Improvement in nutritional value of products
	Improvement in packaging and labeling

Source: Richard M. Hodgetts and Donald F. Kuratko, *Management,* 3rd ed. (San Diego, CA: Harcourt Brace Jovanovich, 1991), 670.

social responsibility opens the door for questions concerning the *extent* corporations should be involved.

An examination of the stages or levels of social responsibility behavior that corporations exhibit reveals that distinct differences exist in the way corporations respond. S. Prakesh Sethi, a researcher in social responsibility, has established a framework that classifies the social actions of corporations into three distinct

Table 6.5   Classifying Corporate Social Behavior

DIMENSION OF BEHAVIOR	STAGE ONE: SOCIAL OBLIGATION	STAGE TWO: SOCIAL RESPONSIBILITY	STAGE THREE: SOCIAL RESPONSIVENESS
Response to social pressures	Maintains low public profile, but if attacked, uses PR methods to upgrade its public image; denies any deficiencies; blames public dissatisfaction on ignorance or failure to understand corporate functions; discloses information only where legally required	Accepts responsibility for solving current problems; will admit deficiencies in former practices and attempt to persuade public that its current practices meet social norms; attitude toward critics conciliatory; freer information disclosures than stage one	Willingly discusses activities with outside groups; makes information freely available to the public; accepts formal and informal inputs from outside groups in decision making; is willing to be publicly evaluated for its various activities
Philanthropy	Contributes only when direct benefit to it clearly shown; otherwise, views contributions as responsibility of individual employees	Contributes to noncontroversial and established causes; matches employee contributions	Activities of stage two, *plus* support and contributions to new, controversial groups whose needs it sees as unfulfilled and increasingly important

Source: Excerpted from S. Prakash Sethi, "A Conceptual Framework for Environmental Analysis of Social Issues and Evaluation of Business Patterns," *Academy of Management Journal* (January 1979): 68. Copyright 1979 by the Academy of Management. Reproduced with permission of the Academy of Management.

categories: social obligation, social responsibility, and social responsiveness (see Table 6.5).

This framework illustrates the range of corporate intensity about social issues. Some firms simply react to social issues through obedience to the laws—**social obligation;** others respond more actively, accepting responsibility for various programs—**social responsibility;** still others are highly proactive and are even willing to be evaluated by the public for various activities—**social responsiveness.**

Only a few studies have examined different features of social responsibility by entrepreneurs.[33] For example, one researcher examined the perspectives of 180 small-business owners on social responsibility and found that 88 percent recognized social responsibility as part of their business role.[34] In another study, the researchers used a random telephone survey to explore the general public's perceptions of social responsibility in large versus small businesses. Their findings indicated that entrepreneurs were more critical of their own performance than was the general public.[35]

Environmental Awareness

The decade of the 1990s was one of greater environmental concern. This reawakening of the need to preserve and protect our natural resources motivated businesses into a stronger **environmental awareness.** As illustrated in Table 6.4, the environment stands out as one of the major challenges of social responsibility. In June 1992, 140 world leaders, along with 30,000 additional participants, gathered in Rio de Janeiro for the Earth Summit to discuss worldwide environmental problems. Our recent "throwaway" culture has endangered our natural resources from soil to water to air.

Researchers Paul Hawken and William McDonough state: "Industry is being told that if it puts its hamburgers in coated-paper wrappers, eliminates emissions, and plants two trees for every car sold, we will be on the way to an environmentally sound world. Nothing could be further from the truth. The danger lies not in the half measures but in the illusions they foster, the belief that subtle course corrections can guide us to a good life that will include a 'conserved' natural world and cozy shopping malls."[36]

This quote illustrates the enormous challenges entrepreneurs confront as they attempt to build socially responsible organizations for the future. Of the 100 million enterprises worldwide, a growing number are attempting to redefine their social responsibilities because they no longer accept the notion that the business of business is business. Because of an international ability to communicate information widely and quickly, many entrepreneurs are beginning to recognize their responsibility to the world around them. Entrepreneurial organizations, the dominant inspiration throughout the world, are beginning the arduous task of addressing social-environmental problems.

Entrepreneurs need to take the lead in designing a new approach to business in which everyday acts of work and life accumulate as a matter of course into a better world. One theorist has developed the term "ecovision" to describe a possible leadership style for innovative organizations.[37] **Ecovision** encourages open and flexible structures that encompass the employees, the organization, and the environment, with attention to evolving social demands.

The environmental movement consists of many initiatives connected primarily by values rather than by design. A plan to create a sustainable future should realize its objectives through a practical, clearly stated strategy. Some of the key steps recommended by Hawken and McDonough follow:[38]

1. Eliminate the concept of waste. Seek newer methods of production and recycling.

2. Restore accountability. Encourage consumer involvement in making companies accountable.

3. Make prices reflect costs. Reconstruct the system to incorporate a "green fee" where taxes are added to energy, raw materials, and services to encourage conservation.

4. Promote diversity. Continue researching the needed compatibility of our ever-evolving products and inventions.

5. Make conservation profitable. Rather than demanding "low prices" to encourage production shortcuts, allow new costs for environmental stewardship.

6. Insist on accountability of nations. Develop a plan for every trading nation of sustainable development enforced by tariffs.

Even though the results of studies specific to ethics, social responsibility, and entre-preneurs are still emerging, a number of views are already agreed on. The research is showing differences in the ethical environment, ethical precepts, and ethical perceptions between large firms and small firms. The reasons relate to the structure of smaller firms, which have fewer professional specialists, less formality, and a stronger influence by the owner-entrepreneur.

the entrepreneurial
PROCESS

Avoiding an Enron Disaster

Enron, Tyco, Arthur Andersen, and Computer Associates: why was the recent boom period plagued with so many unethical practices among companies? Historically, misconduct and bad judgment have often coincided with periods of great prosperity. When attitudes are characterized by "anything goes," and the market is typified with expanding profits and stocks at full-throttle, the economy is at peak danger. It is because of such greed and prosperity that the line between right and wrong becomes blurred.

The greatest equivalent of today's ethical lapses is the Roaring Twenties and the stock market crash of 1929. This period was made notorious by, among other people, Ivar Kreuger. Kreuger founded an international conglomerate in wooden matches by lending money to foreign governments in return for nationwide match monopolies—the money from such loans came from the sale of stock. Later, an audit of his books revealed that $250 million in assets never really existed. Eventually, all this activity led to the creation of the Securities and Exchange Commission (SEC).

Today the possibilities to create spectacular financial debacles have increased due to more complex financial vehicles that take advantage of the "gray" areas in accounting. The following lists five ways investors are demanding more information from companies to ensure corporate accounting is not finagling the financials.

1. *Bring hidden liabilities back onto the balance sheet.* It was the disclosure of billions of dollars in off-balance-sheet debt tucked away in "special purpose entities" or SPEs (entities created to hide potential losses or debt from public view) that brought Enron's problems to the front. Though legitimate, SPEs have been controversial for nearly 30 years. Current practices allow removal of an SPE from the balance sheet if an investor is willing to contribute just 3 percent of its capital.

2. *Highlight the things that matter.* Anything less than 5 or 10 percent of earnings or assets was generally considered immaterial to overall performance and allowed to be left off the statements. Now the SEC and the Financial Accounting Standards Board are evaluating the qualitative factors in addition to the quantitative factors.

3. *List the risks and assumptions built into the numbers.* Corporate "guesstimations" can play a large role in corporate earnings; from future demand of a product line to discounted rates due to risk factors, investors are demanding to know the assumptions.

4. *Standardize operating income.* Standard & Poor's has made a proposal for what should be included and excluded from pro forma operating earnings. Currently, there is no uniformity to detail what companies added and subtracted from the net income to generate their pro formas.

5. *Provide aid in figuring free-cash flow.* Analysts currently calculate free-cash flow themselves by utilizing past results. Investors are, therefore, left to guess what information should be used.

SOURCES: "The Dirt a Bull Market Leaves Behind," *BusinessWeek Online* (June 13, 2002); and "Commentary: Five Ways to Avoid More Enrons," *BusinessWeek Online* (February 18, 2002).

Ethical Considerations in Corporate Entrepreneurship

Corporate entrepreneurs—described in the academic literature as those managers or employees who do not follow the status quo of their co-workers—are depicted as visionaries who dream of taking the company in new directions. As a result, though, in overcoming internal obstacles to reaching their professional goals they often walk a fine line between clever resourcefulness and outright rule breaking. Researchers Donald F. Kuratko and Michael G. Goldsby developed a framework as a guideline for managers and organizations seeking to impede unethical behaviors in the pursuit of entrepreneurial activity (see Figure 6.4).[39] They examined the barriers that middle managers face in trying to be entrepreneurial in less supportive environments, the unethical consequences that can result, and a suggested assessment and training program for averting such dilemmas.

The barriers include the organizational obstacles under two major categories: internal network issues and leadership issues. The specific barriers to innovative actions include systems, structures, policies and procedures, culture, strategic direction, and people. Based on these barriers and the managerial dilemmas that can be caused, the researchers advise companies that embrace corporate entrepreneurship to: (1) establish the needed flexibility, innovation, and support of employee initiative and risk taking; (2) remove the barriers that the entrepreneurial middle manager may face to more closely align personal and organizational initiatives and reduce the need to behave un- ethically; and (3) include an ethical component to corporate training that will provide

Figure 6.4   Ethical Considerations in Corporate Entrepreneurship

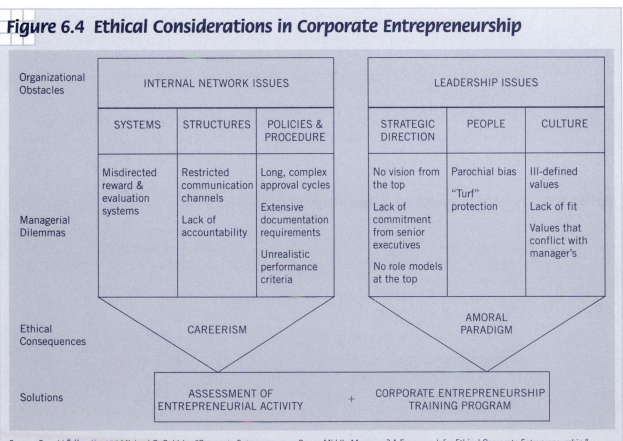

Source: Donald F. Kuratko and Michael G. Goldsby, "Corporate Entrepreneurs or Rogue Middle Managers? A Framework for Ethical Corporate Entrepreneurship," *Journal of Business Ethics* 55 (2004): 18.

guidelines for instituting compliance and values components into state-of-the-art corporate entrepreneurship programs. However, even if corporate entrepreneurship is supported, some managers may still pose ethical risks to the company. Unfortunately, rarely will everyone in an organization do the right thing. For this reason, it would be wise to include an ethical component in corporate training programs to insure everyone is aware of the expectations and vision of senior management. It is believed that a more complete training program and approach to corporate entrepreneurship will make for a better future for both the organization and its members and prevent future ethical crises.

Ethical Leadership by Entrepreneurs

Even though ethics and social responsibility present complex challenges for entrepreneurs, the value system of an owner-entrepreneur is the key to establishing an ethical organization.[40] An owner has the unique opportunity to display honesty, integrity, and ethics in all key decisions. The owner's actions serve as a model for all other employees to follow.

In small businesses the ethical influence of the owner is more powerful than in larger corporations because his or her leadership is not diffused through layers of management. Owners are easily identified, and usually employees constantly observe them in a small business. Therefore, entrepreneurs possess a strong potential to establish high ethical standards in all business decisions.

To illustrate, one study examined the ethical concern of owner-entrepreneurs regarding specific business issues.[41] Table 6.6 provides a list of the issues owners believed needed a strong ethical stance, as well as the issues the same entrepreneurs viewed with greater tolerance in regard to demanding ethics. It verifies that ethical decision making is a complex challenge due to the nature and personal perception of various issues.[42]

In another research study, it was found that an owner's value system was a critical component of the ethical considerations that surround a business decision.

Table 6.6   Issues Viewed by Small-Business Owners

DEMANDS STRONG ETHICAL STANCE	GREATER TOLERANCE REGARDING ETHICAL POSITION
Faulty investment advice	Padded expense account
Favoritism in promotion	Tax evasion
Acquiescing in dangerous design flaw	Collusion in bidding
Misleading financial reporting	Insider trading
Misleading advertising	Discrimination against women
Defending healthfulness of cigarette smoking	Copying computer software

Source: Justin G. Longenecker, Joseph A. McKinney, and Carlos W. Moore, "Ethics in Small Business," *Journal of Small Business Management* (January 1989): 30.

entrepreneurship IN PRACTICE

Software Piracy

When you hear the words "business ethics," do you think about software piracy? From Fortune 500 corporations to sole proprietorships, companies of all shapes and sizes can fall victim to the ethical seesaw that is software piracy. For many, piracy is not a goal or an intended action. There are enough problems for a business manager or owner to face without having to keep track of who is using what software on what computers and whether the company paid for its use. And those who are aware they are committing an illegal act may not realize the problems they're creating for themselves and their businesses should they get caught. Software manufacturers lose an estimated $2.3 billion in revenue annually because ethical standards are not practiced or enforced in the workplace.

The Business Software Alliance (BSA) is a collaboration of software manufacturers aimed at stopping companies from illegally using, and making money from, copyrighted software. The BSA, on average, catches and threatens with legal proceedings one company per day. Over the past six years, the alliance of companies such as Novell and Microsoft has recovered $37 million in lost revenues. Currently, it is striving to make the job easier by providing businesses with the tools necessary to help them stay legal. BSA offers free audit software on its Web site, www.bsa.org, so companies can fix themselves before it's too late.

Larry Lightman, vice president of sales and marketing at Elliot Laboratories, admits that his company may have been a little naïve. "Whenever people wanted to purchase software, they were reimbursed for it, and anyone could install it. Some software was purchased, and some wasn't. There wasn't any rhyme or reason behind it."

Ad hoc installation of software is one of the main reasons piracy exists. Legally, for every computer in use, separate software packages should be bought, registered, and recorded. While this may sound very expensive, the cost will pale in comparison to the fines incurred should you get caught. Elliot Laboratories was fined only $60,000 for its mistake. If the case had gone to court, the company may have been fined $100,000 for each copyright infringement. Furthermore, the BSA member may also be granted a portion of the profits the offending company earned from use of its software.

How can this punishment be avoided? Elliot created a Filemaker database that keeps track of all of its computers, their users, and the serial numbers and licensing information of each installed application. Having one person keep control of the computer and software use is the best way to avoid an avalanche. Purchasing PCs without the bundled software may also help curb the problem. The packages, as alluring as they are, often do not include the licenses needed for protection.

Stopping piracy at its source is the safest option. It is always better to be proactive than reactive. It's true that if it weren't for disgruntled employees, many companies would be "home free." The no-piracy hotline is a great way for unhappy workers to get revenge when they're feeling cheated or abused. No business owner wants to see the U.S. Marshals at his or her front door, so don't give them a reason to be there.

SOURCE: Adapted from David G. Propson, "Cease and Desist," *Small Business Computing* (December 1999): 61–6.

This study also had implications for entrepreneurs who are seeking to establish an ethical environment within which employees and other constituents can work. For example, it was shown that the preparation of a specific policy statement on ethics (code of ethics) by the owner and his or her other employees may provide the clear understanding needed for administrative decision making. Small-business owners may also need to specifically address administrative decision-making processes. In addition, they may need to spend some time developing benchmarks or guidelines concerning ethical behaviors of employees. While these guidelines cannot be expected to cover every possible scenario, they will nevertheless help address the business development/profit motive dimension. Finally, if entrepreneurs can carefully establish explicit rewards and punishments that are based upon ethical behaviors (and enforced), then the concerns of crime and theft can begin to be addressed.[43]

With the growing number of female entrepreneurs, companies are now examining the ethics of caring. Caring is a feminine alternative to the more traditional and masculine ethics that are based on rules and regulations.[44] The focus of feminist philosophies is the fostering of positive relationships in all areas of life, or, as Milton Mayeroff states, "To care for another person, in the most significant sense, is to help him grow and actualize himself."[45] Following laws may not lead to building relationships as strong as one could. However, by considering the interests of others and maintaining healthy relationships, caring, according to feminists, can lead to more genuinely moral climates.

Overall, entrepreneurs must realize that their personal integrity and ethical example will be the key to their employees' ethical performance. Their values can permeate and characterize the organization. This unique advantage creates a position of ethical leadership for entrepreneurs.[46]

Summary

Ethics is a set of principles prescribing a behavioral code that explains right and wrong; it also may outline moral duty and obligations. Because it is so difficult to define the term, it is helpful to look at ethics more as a process than as a static code. Entrepreneurs face many ethical decisions, especially during the early stages of their new ventures.

Decisions may be legal without being ethical, and vice versa. As a result, entrepreneurs can make four types of decisions: legal and ethical, legal and unethical, illegal and ethical, and illegal and unethical. When making decisions that border on the unethical, entrepreneurs commonly rationalize their choices. These rationalizations may be based on morally questionable acts committed "against the firm" or "on behalf of the firm" by the managers involved. Within this framework are four distinct types of managerial roles: nonrole, role failure, role distortion, and role assertion.

Sometimes the entrepreneur must make decisions that involve economic trade-offs. In some situations the company will make a profit but others in society may suffer. To establish ethical strategies, some corporations create codes of conduct. A code of conduct is a statement of ethical practices or guidelines to which an enterprise adheres. Codes are becoming more prevalent in organizations today, and they are proving to be more meaningful in their implementation.

Some ethicists have attempted to provide a clearer view of morality by examining organizational behavior along a continuum that includes immoral, amoral, and moral management. However, entrepreneurs need to focus on a holistic approach that places ethics in perspective and that allows personnel to understand what they can and cannot do. In this way the blurred line between ethical and unethical behavior becomes clearer.

It is also important for entrepreneurs to realize that many decisions are complex and that it can be difficult to deal with all of a decision's ethical considerations. Some of them may be overlooked, and some may be sidestepped because the economic cost is too high. In the final analysis, ethics is sometimes a judgment call, and what is unethical to one entrepreneur is viewed as ethical to another.

The challenge of social responsibility has emerged as a major issue for entrepreneurs. Social responsibility consists of obligations that a business has to society. The social actions of corporations are classified into three categories: social obligation, social responsibility, and social responsiveness. Studies have revealed that entrepreneurs recognize social responsibility as part of their role and that the structure of smaller firms allows entrepreneurs to more personally influence the organization. This opportunity for entrepreneurs to exert ethical influence on their ventures creates a unique challenge of ethical leadership for all entrepreneurs. Despite the ever-present lack of clarity and direction in ethics, however, ethics will continue to be a major issue for entrepreneurs during the new century.

Key Terms and Concepts

amoral management	rationalizations
code of conduct	role assertion
ecovision	role distortion
environmental awareness	role failure
ethics	social obligation
immoral management	social responsibility
moral management	social responsiveness
nonrole	

Review and Discussion Questions

1. In your own words, what is meant by the term *ethics*?

2. Ethics must be based more on a process than on a static code. What does this statement mean? Do you agree? Why or why not?

3. A small pharmaceutical firm has just received permission from the Food and Drug Administration (FDA) to market its new anticholesterol drug. Although the product has been tested for five years, management believes serious side effects may still result from its use, and a warning to this effect is being printed on the label. If the company markets this FDA-approved drug, how would you describe its actions from an ethical and legal standpoint? Use Figure 6.1 to help you.

4. Marcia White, the leading salesperson for a small manufacturer, has been giving purchasing managers a kickback from her commissions in return for their buying more of the company's goods. The manufacturer has a strict rule against this practice. Using Figure 6.1, how would you describe Marcia's behavior? What would you suggest the company do about it?

5. Explain the four distinct roles managers may take in rationalizing morally questionable acts "against the firm" or "on behalf of the firm." Be complete in your answer.

6. What is a code of conduct, and how useful is it in promoting ethical behavior?

7. Describe carefully the differences between immoral, amoral, and moral management. Use Table 6.3 in your answer.

8. Why do complex decisions often raise ethical considerations for the entrepreneur?

9. Social responsibility can be classified into three distinct categories. Describe each category, and discuss the efforts of entrepreneurs to become more socially responsible.

10. Describe the critical threat to our environment as a major challenge of social responsibility.

11. What is "ecovision"? Outline some specific recommendations for entrepreneurs to consider that promote environmental awareness.

12. How can entrepreneurs develop a position of ethical leadership in business today?

13. Cal Whiting believes entrepreneurs need to address the importance of ethics in their organizations. However, in his own company he is unsure of where to begin because the entire area is unclear to him. What would you suggest? Where can he begin? What should he do? Be as practical as you can in your suggestion.

Experiential Exercise

Knowing the Difference

Most entrepreneurial actions are ethical and legal. Sometimes, however, they are unethical and/or illegal. The four categories of ethical/legal actions and a list of examples of each category (*a* through *h*) follow. Match them up by placing the number of the category next to appropriate examples from the list (two are given for each category).

1. Ethical and legal

2. Unethical and legal

3. Ethical and illegal

4. Unethical and illegal

a. _____ Giving a gift of $50,000 to a foreign minister to secure a business contract with his country (a customary practice in his country) and then writing off the gift as a tax-deductible item

b. _____ Knowing that 1 percent of all tires have production defects but shipping them anyway and giving mileage allowances to anyone whose tires wear out prematurely

c. _____ Manufacturing a new fuel additive that will increase gas mileage by 10 percent

d. _____ Offering a member of the city council $100,000 to vote to give the entrepreneur the local cable television franchise

e. _____ Publishing a newspaper story that wrongly implies but does not openly state that the governor (a political opponent of the newspaper) is deliberately withholding state funds for education in the newspaper's effort to win nomination support for its candidate from the state teachers union

f. _____ Obtaining inside information from another brokerage that results in the entrepreneur netting more than $2 million

g. _____ Producing a vaccine, already approved by the Food and Drug Administration, that will retard the growth of bone cancer

h. _____ Producing and selling a drug that will reduce heart attacks but failing to complete all of the paperwork that must be filed with the government prior to selling the product

Answers: a. 3, b. 2, c. 1, d. 4, e. 2, f. 4, g. 1, h. 3

Video Case 6.1

**Ethical and Social Responsibility Challenges for Entrepreneurs
On Target Supplies and Logistics with Albert Black**

> We have to be leaders in organizations, not because of our positions but because of the contributions that we can make to that organization. (Albert Black)

What perhaps is so remarkable about Albert Black is not the fact that he was born in a ghetto and then grew up to make millions of dollars; it is the fact that, having achieved his goal, he has returned to the ghetto to help others reach success.

Albert grew up in Frasier Courts, an inner-city ghetto in Dallas, Texas. But his parents instilled in him a sense of pride and determination that he could become anything he wanted to be. His father talked to him about becoming a businessman. "My mother is a driver. She expected nothing but the best. . . . We had to speak correctly. We had to walk correctly. We had to make the best grades in school. . . . We lived in the ghetto, but my mother wouldn't permit us to think that way." And from his grandmother, Albert learned to treat people with "Christian passion" and to "do what you say you're gonna do."

Albert took their lessons to heart. At eight years of age, he began to rent a lawnmower to cut yards for fifty cents. He won a football scholarship that enabled him to earn a college degree and then went on to earn an MBA from Southern Methodist University in 1995.

Albert started On Target Supplies and Logistics in 1982. The company provides copy and computer paper to its customers as well as virtual warehousing for the paper so that it arrives on the customer's desk when the customer is actually ready to use it.

He started the company the hard way. He did it while working another job. From 5:00 PM until 1:00 AM every night, he worked in the computer operations area of Texas Utilities, and then he would start his own business day at 7:00 AM. His wife, Gwynith, also worked a job to support the business. Albert maintained this regimen for ten years while On Target formed its customer base. "We roamed the streets of Dallas looking for customers under highways, rocks, byways, anywhere we could find them." Today his customer list includes EDS, Texas Instruments, Southwestern Bell, Texas Utilities, American Airlines, and Verizon and has generated $10.2 million in sales.

Albert feels an ethical responsibility to help the people from his early neighborhood find their own success. "The reason I went into business is the same reason I'm in business today. We wanted to create jobs and to hire people. We think that's God's work, and that's what we wanted to be involved in. We also wanted to improve the infrastructure of inner cities in communities that we were doing business in." In fact, On Target's offices are located in Albert's old neighborhood.

Albert's concern shows directly in the way he treats his 114 employees. He pays his employees well above the industry average. "We have come into a neighborhood and taken tax users and made them tax producers." He encourages employees to save their money in the company 401(k) plan. He offers frequent seminars that teach people how to spend money and how to save it. "We also encourage people to continue their education. As a company, we're willing to pay for it. . . . I think everybody around here knows that when Albert's sitting down with you and gives you that old . . . south Dallas smile and . . . suggests that you go to college, I think they get the message," says one employee.

Every Friday at 7:00 AM, Albert holds a staff meeting that begins with a hot breakfast. "We like for people to come in, get comfortable, enjoy a good breakfast, and open up their hearts and minds, so that we can do that teaching . . . and counseling [about how to succeed]. There's nothing against the rules in helping people have better lives." Part of the staff meeting includes discussing the operational plans of the company and sharing its financial statements on costs and sales.

Albert explains that On Target promises its employees three benefits; the first is an educational income. "If you come to work with us, you will know how to run a business."

"We'll also pay you a psychological income. We want you to feel good about what you're doing at On Target Supplies and Logistics . . . that attitude that says, 'together we can climb mountains and win battles.'" The last benefit is a financial income. "We will pay you above market."

Because his business is service oriented, Albert Black realizes that his employees are his best asset and that working together will make everyone a success. "Small business leaders . . . take risks. . . . We actually go out there and make a difference in people's lives."

Questions

1. Explain the ethical principles that Albert Black exemplifies.

2. Would you like to work for Albert Black? Explain your response.

3. Identify any problems Black might encounter in the way that he manages people.

Case 6.2

Letting the Family In

When Carmine Guion started his retail company three years ago, he had more than enough working capital to keep operations going. This abundance of money helped him grow rapidly, and today he has outlets in 16 states. In order to become larger, however, he is going to have to secure outside funding. Carmine has decided to issue stock. The investment house advising him has suggested that he float an issue of 1 million shares at $5 each. After all expenses, he will clear $4.50 per share. Carmine and his wife intend to hold on to 250,000 shares and sell 750,000 shares. Carmine feels that with his shares and those that will be bought by his relatives and friends, he need have little concern about the firm's being taken over by outside investors.

Carmine talked to his father, who agreed to buy 10,000 shares at $5. Carmine's two uncles are each buying 5,000 shares at $5. A group of 20 other relatives is going to buy an additional 5,000 shares.

Earlier this week Carmine received some good news from his accountant. His profit estimate for next year is going to be at least double what he had previously estimated. When Carmine shared this information with the investment brokers, they were delighted. "When this news gets out," one of them told him, "your stock will rise to between $13 and $15 per share. Anyone who gets in on the original offering at $5 will do very well indeed."

Carmine has told only his father and two uncles the good news. Based on this information, the three of them have decided to buy three times as much stock as previously planned. "When it rises to around $12," his father said, "I'll sell 10,000 shares and hang on to the other 20,000." His uncles intend to do the same thing. Carmine is delighted. He also intends to tell some of his other relatives about the improved profit picture prior to the time the initial stock offering is made.

Questions

1. Has Carmine been unethical in his conduct? What is your reasoning?

2. Is it ethical for Carmine to tell his other relatives the good news? Why or why not?

3. If you were advising Carmine, what would you tell him? Why?

Case 6.3

A Friend for Life

The Glades Company is a small manufacturer. It has produced and marketed a number of different toys and appliances that have done very well in the marketplace. Late last year the product designer at the company, Tom Berringer, told the president, Paula Glades, that he had invented a small, cuddly, talking bear that might have a great deal of appeal. The bear is made of fluffy brown material that simulates fur and has a tape inside that contains 50 messages.

The Glades Company decided to find out exactly how much market appeal the bear would have. Fifty of them were produced and placed in kindergartens and nurseries around town. The results were better than the firm had hoped. One of the nurseries reported: "The bear was so popular that most of the children wanted to take it home for an evening." Another said the bear was the most popular toy in the school.

Based on these data, the company decided to manufacture and market 1,000 of the bears. At the same time, a catchy marketing slogan was formulated: "A Friend for Life." The bear was marketed as a product a child could play with for years and years. The first batch of 1,000 bears sold out within a week. The company then scheduled another production run. This one was for 25,000 bears. Last week, in the middle of the production run, a problem was uncovered. The process of making the bear fur is much more expensive than had been anticipated. The company is faced with two options: it can absorb the extra cost and have the simulated fur produced, or it can use a substitute fur that will not last as long. Specifically, the original simulated fur will last for up to seven years of normal use; the less-expensive simulated fur will last for only eight months.

Some of the managers at Glades believe most children are not interested in playing with the same toy for more than eight months, so substituting the less-expensive simulated fur for the more-expensive fur should be no problem. Others believe the company will damage its reputation if it opts for the substitute fur. "We are going to have complaints within eight months, and we are going to rue the day we agreed to a cheaper substitute," the production manager argues. The sales manager disagrees, contending that "the market is ready for this product, and we ought to provide it." In the middle of this crisis, the accounting department issued its cost analysis of the venture. If the company goes with the more-expensive simulated fur, it will lose $2.75 per bear. If it chooses the less-expensive simulated fur, it will make a profit of $4.98 per bear.

The final decision on the matter rests with Paula Glades. People on both sides of the issue have given her their opinion. One of the last to speak was the vice president of manufacturing, who said, "If you opt for the less-expensive fur, think of what this is going to do to your marketing campaign of 'A Friend for Life.' Are you going to change this slogan to 'A Friend for Eight Months'?" But the marketing vice president urged a different course of action: "We have a fortune tied up in this bear. If you stop production now or go to the more-expensive substitute, we'll lose our shirts. We aren't doing anything illegal by substituting the fur. The bear looks the same. Who's to know?"

Questions

1. Is the recommendation of the marketing vice president legal? Is it ethical? Why or why not?

2. Would it be ethical if the firm used the less-expensive simulated fur but did not change its slogan of "A Friend for Life" and did not tell the buyer about the change in the production process? Why or why not?

3. If you were advising Paula, what would you recommend?

■ Notes

1. Janean Chun, "Code of Honor," *Entrepreneur* (August 1996): 112–118; Bruce Horovitz, "Scandals Shake Public Trust," *USA Today* (July 16, 2002): 1A–2A; John A. Byrne, Michael Arndt, Wendy Zellner, and Mike McNamee, "Restoring Trust in Corporate America: Business Must Lead the Way to Reform," *Business Week* (June 24, 2002): 31–39; and Amey Stone, "Putting Teeth in Corporate Ethics," *Business Week* (February 19, 2004).

2. Vernon R. Loucks, Jr., "A CEO Looks at Ethics," *Business Horizons* (March/April 1987): 2.

3. Sir Adrian Cadbury, "Ethical Managers Make Their Own Rules," *Harvard Business Review* (September/October 1987): 64.

4. Verne E. Henderson, "The Ethical Side of Enterprise," *Sloan Management Review* (spring 1982): 38.

5. Richard Evans, "Business Ethics and Changes in Society," *Journal of Business Ethics* 10 (1991): 871–876.

6. Henderson, "The Ethical Side," 40.

7. Saul W. Gellerman, "Why Good Managers Make Bad Ethical Choices," *Harvard Business Review* (July/August 1986): 85.

8. James A. Waters and Frederick Bird, "Attending to Ethics in Management," *Journal of Business Ethics* 5 (1989): 493–497.

9. Christopher D. Stone, *Where the Law Ends: The Social Control of Corporate Behavior* (New York: Harper & Row, 1975).

10. Al H. Ringlab, Roger E. Meiners, and Frances L. Edwards, *Managing in the Legal Environment,* 3rd ed. (St. Paul, MN: West, 1996), 12–14; see also Roger LeRoy Miller and Frank B. Cross, *The Legal Environment Today* (St. Paul, MN: West, 1996), 33–37.

11. LaRue T. Hosmer, *The Ethics of Management,* 2nd ed. (Homewood, IL: Richard D. Irwin, 1991), 81–83.

12. Gerald F. Cavanaugh and Philip J. Chmielewski, "Ethics and the Free Market," *America* (January 31, 1987): 79.

13. Ibid., 81.

14. Edward L. Hennessy, "Business Ethics—Is It a Priority for Corporate America?" *Financial Executive* (October 1986): 14–15.

15. Myron Magnet, "The Decline and Fall of Business Ethics," *Fortune* (December 8, 1986): 65–72.

16. Margaret N. Maxey, "Bioethical Reflections on the Case for Private/Free Enterprise," in *The Future of Private Enterprise,* ed. Craig E. Aronoff, Randall B. Goodwin, and John L. Ward (Atlanta: Georgia State University Publications, 1986), 145–164.

17. Charles R. Stoner, "The Foundation of Business Ethics: Exploring the Relationship between Organization Culture, Moral Values, and Actions," *SAM Advanced Management Journal* (summer 1989): 38–43; James B. Lucas, "How to Avoid Enronism," *American Management Association MWorld* (spring 2002): 6–11; and Charles Haddad, Dean Foust, and Steve Rosenbush, "WorldCom's Sorry Legacy," *Business Week* (July 8, 2002): 38–41.

18. Susan J. Harrington, "What Corporate America Is Teaching about Ethics," *Academy of Management Executive* (February 1991): 21–30.

19. For more on this topic, see Donald R. Cressey and Charles A. Moore, "Managerial Values and Corporate Codes of Conduct," *California Management Review* (summer 1983): 121–127; Steven Weller, "The Effectiveness of Corporate Codes of Ethics," *Journal of Business Ethics* (July 1988): 389–395; and Diane E. Kirrane, "Managing Values: A Systematic Approach to Business Ethics," *Training & Development Journal* (November 1990): 53–60.

20. Reported in Darrell J. Fashing, "A Case of Corporate and Management Ethics," *California Management Review* (spring 1981): 84.

21. Amitai Etzioni, "Do Good Ethics Ensure Good Profits?" *Business and Society Review* (summer 1989): 4–10; L. J. Brooks, "Corporate Ethical Performance: Trends, Forecasts, and Outlooks," *Journal of Business Ethics* 8 (1989): 31–38; Harrington, "What Corporate America Is Teaching about Ethics"; and Simcha B. Werner, "The Movement for Reforming American Business Ethics: A Twenty Year Perspective," *Journal of Business Ethics* 11 (1992).

22. Archie B. Carroll, "In Search of the Moral Manager," *Business Horizons* (March/April 1987): 7–15.

23. F. Neil Brady, "Aesthetic Components of Management Ethics," *Academy of Management Review* (April 1986): 344.

24. Adapted from Vernon R. Loucks, Jr., "A CEO Looks at Ethics," *Business Horizons* (March/April 1987): 6. Copyright © 1987 by the Foundation for the School of Business at Indiana University. Reprinted by permission.

25. Patrick E. Murphy, "Creating Ethical Corporate Structures," *Sloan Management Review* (winter 1989): 81–87.

26. Joseph A. Raelin, "The Professional as the Executive's Ethical Aide-de-Camp," *The Academy of Management Executive* (August 1987): 176.

27. Ibid., 177.

28. Shailendra Vyakarnam, Andy Bailey, Andrew Myers, and Donna Burnett, "Towards an Understanding of Ethical Behavior in Small Firms," *Journal of Business Ethics* 16(15) (1997): 1625–1636.

29. LaRue T. Hosmer, *The Ethics of Management* (Homewood, IL: Richard D. Irwin, 1987), 13–15.

30. Wade L. Robison, "Management and Ethical Decision-Making," *Journal of Business Ethics* (spring 1984): 287.

31. Laura L. Nash, "Ethics without the Sermon," *Harvard Business Review* (November/December 1981). Copyright © 1981 by the President and Fellows of Harvard College; all rights reserved. For additional questions, see Diane E. Kirrane, "Managing Values: A Systematic Approach to Business Ethics," *Training & Development Journal* (November 1990): 53–60.

32. Henderson, "The Ethical Side," 46.

33. Judith Kenner Thompson and Howard L. Smith, "Social Responsibility and Small Business: Suggestions for Research," *Journal of Small Business Management* (January 1991): 30–44.

34. Erika Wilson, "Social Responsibility of Business: What Are the Small Business Perspectives?" *Journal of Small Business Management* (July 1980): 17–24.

35. James J. Chrisman and Fred L. Fry, "Public versus Business Expectations: Two Views on Social Responsibility for Small Business," *Journal of Small Business Management* (January 1982): 19–26.

36. Paul Hawken and William McDonough, "Seven Steps to Doing Good Business," *Inc.* (November 1993): 79–92.

37. Reginald Shareef, "Ecovision: A Leadership Theory for Innovative Organizations," *Organizational Dynamics* 20 (summer 1991): 50–63.

38. Hawken and McDonough, "Seven Steps," 81–88.

39. Donald F. Kuratko and Michael G. Goldsby, "Corporate Entrepreneurs or Rogue Middle Managers? A Framework for Ethical Corporate Entrepreneurship," *Journal of Business Ethics* 55 (2004): 13–30.

40. Elisabeth J. Teal and Archie B. Carroll, "Moral Reasoning Skills: Are Entrepreneurs Different?" *Journal of Business Ethics* (March 1999): 229–240.

41. Justin G. Longenecker, Joseph A. McKinney, and Carlos W. Moore, "Ethics in Small Business," *Journal of Small Business Management* (January 1989): 27–31.

42. Neil Humphreys, Donald P. Robin, R. Eric Reidenbach, and Donald L. Moak, "The Ethical Decision Making Process of Small Business Owner/Managers and Their Customers," *Journal of Small Business Management* (July 1993): 9–22; and Jeffrey S. Hornsby, Donald F. Kuratko, Douglas W. Naffziger, William R. LaFollette, and Richard M. Hodgetts, "The Ethical Perceptions of Small Business Owners: A Factor Analytic Study," *Journal of Small Business Management* (October 1994): 9–16.

43. Hornsby, Kuratko, Naffziger, LaFollette, and Hodgetts, "The Ethical Perceptions of Small Business Owners," 9–16.

44. Nel Noddings, *Caring: A Feminine Approach to Ethics and Moral Education* (Berkeley: University of California Press, 1984).

45. Milton Mayeroff, *On Caring* (New York: Harper & Row, 1971), 1.

46. Justin G. Longenecker, Joseph A. McKinney, and Carlos W. Moore, "Do Smaller Firms Have Higher Ethics?" *Business and Society Review* (fall 1989): 19–21; Paul J. Serwinek, "Demographic and Related Differences in Ethical Views among Small Businesses," *Journal of Business Ethics* (July 1992): 555–566; Donald F. Kuratko, "The Ethical Challenge for Entrepreneurs," *Entrepreneurship, Innovation, and Change* (December 1995): 291–294; and Donald F. Kuratko, Michael G. Goldsby, and Jeffrey S. Hornsby, "The Ethical Perspectives of Entrepreneurs: An Examination of Stakeholder Salience," *Journal of Applied Management and Entrepreneurship* 9(4) (October 2004): 19–42.

Part 2

entrepreneurial CASE ANALYSIS

Stew Leonard's Dairy

Stewart (Stew) J. Leonard's father, Leo Leonard, owned and operated a small dairy route with four milk trucks. As a young boy, Stew often helped his father with deliveries. By the time Stew was in high school he was operating his own milk route.[1] Stew pursued a college education in hopes that it would prepare him to one day run the dairy. After Stew's graduation from college, his father passed away and Stew took over the dairy.

In the late 1960s, the state of Connecticut decided to build a highway through the land used for the dairy. Furthermore, the proliferation of supermarkets and refrigerators had made the cost of running a milk delivery route prohibitive. So Stew decided to move and start a new store. In 1968 the Small Business Administration loaned Stew $500,000, the largest loan granted to that date, to start a dairy store in Norwalk, Connecticut. Stew and his wife, Marianne, knew they were risking their net worth of $100,000, but on the basis of his experience selling dairy products since he was a child, he was convinced his ideas would work. He expected to be competitive with other area stores by stocking mostly his own products in a specialized dairy store.[2]

Stew Leonard and his wife formed a partnership. He refused to form a corporation because he wanted to be liable for any losses.[3] Before opening, he visited many food stores across the country gathering information on what worked and what did not.[4] During one visit he met a farmer who was bottling and selling milk on the premises.[5] Stew decided his store would do the same. Calculating the cost of the SBA loan and other credit, Stew estimated he needed to sell $20,000 a week to survive. Through long hours and attention to detail, Stew realized $21,850 in his first week in business. By mid-week he was so optimistic about reaching the $20,000 mark that he took his wife on a trip to Grenada in the Caribbean.

The following week, an incident occurred that was to become the foundation of the Stew Leonard management philosophy. The incident began when a customer complained that the eggnog she recently purchased was sour. Stew tasted the eggnog and concluded that the customer was wrong. He told her so and added, "We sold over 300 half-gallons of eggnog this week, and you're the only one who's complained." The customer angrily left the store and stated she would never come back.[6] Later that evening Stew could not get the scene out of his mind. Upon reflection, he acknowledged that not only had he failed to empathize with the customer, but he had ignored the potential repercussions of the complaint. His wife, Marianne, said that her husband had just lost a valuable customer over a $.99 carton of eggnog. This was a customer who may have later spent thousands of dollars on groceries, money that Stew Leonard's dairy store would now never see. This mistake led Stew Leonard to a mission statement for his business:

Rule 1: The customer is always right!

Rule 2: If the customer is ever wrong, reread Rule 1!

These rules, which were engraved on a 6,000-pound boulder and placed at the entrance of the store, became the credo upon which Stew Leonard built his business.[7] By the end of the 1980s, the store had grown from two cash registers, 6,000 square feet,

---

Source: This case was prepared by Charles B. Shrader, Steven A. Rallis, and Joan L. Twenter of Iowa State University and is intended to be used as a basis for classroom discussion rather than to illustrate either effective or ineffective management practices. Partial support for writing the case was provided by the Murray G. Bacon Center for Ethics in Business. Faculty members in nonprofit institutions are encouraged to reproduce this case for distribution to their own students without charge or written permission. All other rights reserved jointly to the authors and the Society for Case Research. Copyright © 1998 by the *Business Case Journal* and Charles B. Shrader, Steven A. Rallis, and Joan L. Twenter.

and $20,000 a week in sales to a retail grocery with more than two dozen registers, 37,000 square feet, and annual sales in excess of $100 million.[8] By 1991, a second store had been opened on a 40-acre complex in Danbury, Connecticut. Although the mission statement formed the backbone of the strategy that enabled the organization to expand 27 times in roughly 20 years, Stew Leonard implemented additional strategies to achieve his business's remarkable growth—a growth so remarkable that Stew Leonard's did more business per square foot than any business of any kind in the world.[9]

Marketing and Customer Relations

Initially, Stew Leonard stocked his dairy store with just under a dozen items. Eventually, the store topped out at 800 items (the typical supermarket stocked 15,000). Stew differentiated his store by eliminating the middleman and passing the savings on to his customers.[10]

Stew also sold the idea of freshness. Customers knew they could count on the freshest produce, milk, cheese, meats, and baked goods. A glass-enclosed milk processing plant was located in the center of the store, where customers could see their milk being produced.[11] Beth Leonard, Stew's daughter, ran the bakery, which filled the store with the aroma of croissants, cookies, and muffins.[12] Free samples and recipes were always made available to customers.

To further distinguish itself from other food stores, Stew Leonard's added entertainment to the marketing mix.[13] A petting zoo with barnyard animals was placed in the parking lot, encouraging parents to bring children. Animated singing animals filled the store and employees roamed the aisles in cow, chicken, and duck costumes.[14] All of this was part of Leonard's emphasis on making grocery shopping an enjoyable experience.[15]

Building on the mission statement, *The Customer Is Always Right,* Stew Leonard's adopted other customer service systems. A liberal return policy provided internal checks and balances, which required employees to constantly monitor quality. Even if a Stew Leonard "team member" knew that a customer was returning an item the store did not sell, the customer got his or her money back.[16] Stew once said: Our attitude is that everybody's honest. If we occasionally run into someone who isn't, we just take it on the chin. But the important point is that 999 out of 1,000 customers are honest. We simply refuse to let one dishonest customer determine how we are going to treat the other 999.[17]

Stew Leonard's exhibited a special commitment to following up on customers' comments. A suggestion box was filled to capacity each day.[18] By 11:00 A.M. each morning, all the complaints and suggestions were typed and submitted to the appropriate department. Managers held weekly meetings to report what had been done with the customers' suggestions.

Customer feedback was also gathered through in-store focus groups. Each month ten specially selected customers were given $20 worth of store gift certificates in return for which they met with store managers and offered suggestions on what items should be stocked and how items should be displayed.[19]

There were other small acts of kindness, as well. For example, free ice cream cones were given randomly to customers, customers' pictures with Stew Leonard's shopping bags were posted near the entrance, and elderly customers were given free rides to the dairy in a bus provided by the store.[20] By conducting business in this manner, Stew Leonard's earned tremendous customer trust and loyalty over the years.[21]

Employee Relations

Employees, referred to as team members, were well trained in customer relations. Many employees were also Leonard family members.

The large number of family members working for the company contributed to the company's culture. Of the company's 1,200+ employees, 25 percent had worked at Stew Leonard's for at least five years and over half had family as co-workers.[22] Stew believed in nepotism.[23] He was an ardent supporter of employing relatives as team members; he believed they worked much harder because the presence of a relative was like another boss watching over them.[24]

Team members understood that a job at Stew Leonard's required that they provide superior customer service.[25] The company's two stores were open 364 days a year, and team members were required to work during various times of the day and on holidays. Also, team members were expected to be well groomed and display positive attitudes. As a result of Stew's hiring practices, the store had a 60 percent turnover rate—much better than the supermarket industry average of 82 percent.[26]

Curiosity about Stew Leonard's training and customer relations methods ran strong among business firms. Inquiries from companies like Kraft, Citibank, and IBM led to the creation of Stew Leonard University by Stew's daughter, Jill.[27] "Stew U" was a four-hour seminar intended to give insight into Stew Leonard's operation. Throughout the seminar, attendees were taught methods of how to handle dissatisfied customers, appropriate behaviors of team members, and management tips for motivating team members.[28]

Stew Leonard's offered its employees a variety of incentive programs to heighten the level of customer service, such as:

1. A monthly "One Idea Club," where ten team members and a department manager went to other supermarkets and on the basis of that experience made suggestions for improving store departments.[29]

2. A "Superstar of the Month," nominated by co-workers and department managers for achievement of safety, cleanliness, and attendance. Winners had their photographs posted in the store and were awarded $100.[30]

3. "Ladders of Success" charts placed near checkout lanes demonstrating team members' career progressions. Stew Leonard's company fully supported a promotion-from-within policy.[31]

4. Retail gift certificates valued up to $500 if team members' ideas were implemented.[32]

5. Fifty dollar awards to team members who referred new hires.[33]

6. An ABCD (Above and Beyond the Call of Duty) award—a polo shirt embroidered with "ABCD Award"—to employees who performed beyond the duties of their jobs.[34]

7. A "Hall of Fame," which consisted of workers who performed admirably during their careers.[35]

8. An "Outstanding Performance Award" given to three high achievers at the annual Christmas party.[36]

9. A recreation program, supplemented by employee vending machine funds, providing outings and trips to workers at discount rates.[37]

10. A "Stew's News" company newsletter—called the ultimate company newsletter by *Inc.* magazine—filled with information about bonus plans, contests, and customer comments. Births, parties, anniversaries, illnesses, and organization successes were included.[38]

11. A "Name Game" reward for cashiers who thanked customers by name. Customers dropped cashiers' names in a box, and at the end of each week, the three cashiers who thanked the most customers by name received $30.[39]

These activities were used by Stew Leonard Dairy to focus team members on the mission statement. Stew knew everybody was motivated by different things. Occasionally, Stew would place extra dollars in pay envelopes along with thank-you notes (which he wrote hundreds of every year) for employees who performed exceptionally well.[40] Impromptu inducements were often granted to team members. It was not uncommon for Stew Leonard or the other managers to hand out lunch or dinner certificates for special performance such as coming in on a day off.[41]

The Organization

Stew Leonard's overall company goal—customer satisfaction—determined the design of the organization. It was a simple, relatively informal structure. Because the business was a partnership, there was no board of directors or shareholders. There were also no required annual reports or meetings. The partners gained and lost in proportion to the success of the business, and were personally liable for financial obligations. The partnership paid no taxes as an entity; rather, Stew and Marianne were taxed directly for their portion of the business's income.

All four of Stew Leonard's children were actively involved in the business and held corporate titles. Stew Jr., the oldest, was president. He originally planned on working for an accounting firm after earning his M.B.A. at UCLA, but became involved in every detail of the company. Tom managed the Danbury store, which opened in the fall of 1991. Beth, after obtaining her master's degree in French and working for a croissant distributor, originated and managed the high-volume in-store bakery.[42] Jill Leonard was the vice president of human resources.[43] And, of course, Marianne, Stew Sr.'s wife, continued to provide support as she had from the beginning.

Marianne's brothers Frank H. Guthman and Stephen F. Guthman served as executive vice president and vice president of finance, respectively.[44] Most company decisions were made by the family. However, lower-level employees were allowed a great deal of discretion, especially in the area of customer service.

The company preferred "in-house" control practices. Customers were asked to pay cash for gift certificates and were encouraged to use cash for other purchases.[45] Stew did not make much use of outside consultants in his business. He preferred using the in-house customer focus groups for business advice. Being privately held, the company did not publicly reveal its profits.[46] Profits, however, were significant enough to fund the store's numerous expansions as well as a large second home for Stew and his children. The second home, located in St. Maarten in the Caribbean, was named "Carpe Diem" (Latin for "seize the day").[47]

As the business grew from a small dairy to super retailer to world's largest dairy store, the Stew Leonard's story was one of customer satisfaction, employee development, and tremendous growth. Over the years the store received numerous awards and accolades. For example:

- [ ] An award for entrepreneurial excellence from President Ronald Reagan
- [ ] The Connecticut Small Business Advocate of the Year Award
- [ ] A citation from the *Guinness Book of World Records* for doing more business per square foot than any store of any kind in the world

In addition, a certified in-house Dale Carnegie training school, attended by Fortune 500 firms, was operated in conjunction with Stew Leonard University. In 1991, Stew Leonard's Dairy was nominated for the Malcolm Baldridge National Quality Award in the service category in 1991, and might have become the first retail organization ever to win the award had not the company decided to withdraw from the competition.

In addition to all other awards, a 1993 issue of *Chief Information Officer* (*CIO*), a publication for data processing and computer programming professionals, named Stew Leonard's as one of the 21 recipients of their customer service award.[48] Criteria for winning this award included a company's successful integration of management information systems and customer service. The store was commended for its ability in tracking sales and using point-of-sale data. The sophisticated system also helped managers anticipate heavy traffic periods so that cash registers could be staffed adequately and product shortages avoided.

Trouble Looms

On August 25, 1991, Stew Leonard, Sr., was questioned by a Norwalk, Connecticut, reporter about a visit from the Criminal Investigation Division of the Internal Revenue Service. On August 9, 1991, the IRS raided the homes of several company officers, seizing boxes of records and cash.[49] Stew Leonard said that the raid "came out of the blue" and that he was "as surprised as anyone else."[50] But U.S. customs agents had stopped him back in June 1991 when, with $80,000 in cash, he boarded a flight to St. Maarten in the Caribbean.[51] Leonard had not filled out the forms required for taking large sums of money out of the country, and this eventually led to the IRS confiscation of store records.[52] Nevertheless, Leonard maintained that he did not know what prompted the IRS agents to enter the store with a search warrant on August 9th.[53]

Leonard and his son Tom, manager of the Danbury store, told the news reporters and the public that the IRS was simply conducting a routine audit. However, the Criminal Investigation Division of the IRS did not conduct "audits," which involved possible civil violations; it investigated possible criminal violations of internal revenue laws.[54]

Most people in the community reacted with disbelief to news of the investigation. Many of Stew Leonard's customers found it impossible to believe that any wrongdoing had taken place, regarding the Leonard family as a pillar of honesty in the community. Ironically, it was Stew Leonard's sophisticated computer system that gave the IRS the primary evidence it needed to charge Stew and other executives with tax evasion.

The Guilty Plea

On July 22, 1993, the U.S. Department of Justice announced that Stewart J. Leonard, Sr., Frank H. Guthman, Stephen F. Guthman, and company general manager, Tiberio (Barry) Belardinelli, had pleaded guilty in federal court to federal tax conspiracy charges. The four defendants admitted that between 1981 and August 9, 1991, they had defrauded the IRS by skimming more then $17 million from Stew Leonard's Dairy in Norwalk, Connecticut. It had taken the IRS almost two years to determine the full extent of the tax evasion scheme. Along with paper records and large sums of cash, the IRS found other items indicating the executives' aversion to paying taxes.[55]

According to the IRS, Stew Leonard had avoided $6.7 million in taxes between 1981 and 1991 by not reporting $17 million in sales during that period.[56] They also reported that it was the largest computer-driven criminal tax evasion case in United States history, calling the fraud a crime of the twenty-first century.[57]

Stew Leonard, Jr., president of the Norwalk store, was cited as having knowledge of the tax conspiracy.[58] A *New York Times* article reported that part of the plea bargain arrangement was that no charges would be brought against Stew Jr.[59] Observers speculated that the IRS may have given Stew Jr. immunity in order to persuade his father to plead guilty. According to the IRS, Stew Sr. was initially turned in by an employee who had recently been fired.[60]

The "Equity Program"—Skimming

In Frank Guthman's basement, in a hollowed-out edition of the 1982 *New England Business Directory,* the Criminal Investigation Division of the IRS discovered a computer program that the executives had named "Equity."[61] Apparently, the program had been developed in the latter part of 1981 by Jeffrey Pirhalla, Stew Leonard's computer programmer. Frank Guthman had instructed the programmer to create the program in order to reduce sales data stored on Stew Leonard's computer. Frank Guthman had also directed Pirhalla to write the program so that it would reduce Stew Leonard's financial and bank deposit data.

Witnesses in the court proceedings testified that Stew Leonard, Sr., and the other executives were informed of the use of this tax evasion tool. In general, the program enabled the defendants to enter a dollar figure that matched a cash receipt withdrawal for the day. Typical cash diversions were $10,000 to $15,000 per day. Furthermore, the program allowed the company to keep dual books that generated accounting spreadsheets disclosing "actual" and "reported" sales. To appease previous IRS auditors, Stew Leonard's had provided "reported" sales data while the actual sales were utilized only for store operations.

As part of the scheme, Belardinelli and the Guthmans set up a system that transferred Universal Product Code (UPC) scanner information from the cash registers to two different computer record systems. One set of records systematically understated sales by a predetermined amount. Belardinelli destroyed the tapes with the "real" sales data generated daily from the cash registers. Then he secretly removed cash from bank deposit bags in his office, and the skimmed cash was hidden in "vaults" and "fireplaces" constructed specifically for the execution of this crime. Correspondingly, investigators identified personal and partnership tax forms that were falsely submitted to the IRS.

Shortweighting

To make matters worse, on July 23, 1993, a day after the tax evasion announcement, the Connecticut State Consumer Products Department charged Stew Leonard's with violating state labeling laws.[62] A series of inspections involving a check of 2,658 products in the Norwalk store revealed that 730 of the products checked weighed less than what the label stated—they were "shortweighted"—and 500 items carried no labels or were improperly labeled.[63] The Consumer Products Commissioner reported that this rejection rate, 46.3 percent, was much greater than the statewide average of 5 percent.[64]

Some industry experts believed that shortweighting charges were not fair and were merely the bureaucratic attempt of a vengeful state to embarrass the family.[65] They maintained that store scales were accurate and that the variance noted by investigators was not atypical of other stores. Stew Jr. argued that because the company sold so many hand-packed and precooked items, product weight could not always be perfectly accurate.[66]

Each of the 1,230 violations was subject to a $500 maximum fine.[67] Stew Leonard's had already been assessed fines of $10,500 for similar violations at the Danbury store. The company planned to appeal the Danbury store fines as well as the potentially costly fines on the alleged 1,230 violations.[68]

The Aftermath

News of the crime drew harsh criticism from industry professionals and the media, but caused only a minor decline in sales.[69] Some customers condemned the elder Leonard and the store for being hypocritical.[70] The majority of Stew Leonard's clientele was angrier about the shortweighting than the tax evasion. Indeed, many people believed that the tax fraud was a private rather than a business issue.[71] Several shoppers even expressed sympathy for Stew and his family and pledged they would continue to support the company.[72] As had happened early in the investigation, in 1991, some community members thought the IRS was overreacting, even harassing the company. One customer stated that it was okay for the store to cheat the government because everybody else does it.[73] *The Danbury News Times* polled 5,323 of its readers and 4,556 said they would continue to shop at Stew Leonard's.[74] Employees of Stew Leonard's, including Stew Jr., stated that business was good and that they were 100 percent behind the fallen founder.[75]

Stew Leonard was sentenced to 52 months in prison and ordered to pay $15 million in back taxes, penalties, and interest.[76] He was also fined $850,000 for court and probation costs, but this fine was later reduced to $650,000 by a federal appeals court judge.[77] The resulting $650,000 was still much larger than the usual $100,000 fine for tax fraud, because Stew had profited so greatly from the scheme.[78] Leonard's brothers-in-law, Frank H. Guthman and Stephen F. Guthman, were sentenced to 41-month and 18-month prison terms, respectively.[79] Frank Guthman's plea agreement provided that he pay $335,000 in tax, penalties, and interest. Stephen Guthman was not fined. Belardinelli received no prison sentence but was fined $15,000 and put on probation for two years.[80]

Stew gave no reason for the crime he committed, although he did apologize to customers and employees. At one point, the Leonards insinuated that the tax scheme had been suggested by their lawyer (now deceased) as a way to raise capital for expansion.[81] Later, in 1994, after reflecting on the crisis while in prison, Stew commented that "Somehow, I just lost sight of my core values."[82] After the incident, the company continued to grow, and was even planning to open a third store. Stew Leonard was scheduled to be released from a Schuylkill, Pennsylvania, prison in December 1997.[83]

Damage Control

Once Stew Sr. was in prison, Stew Jr. had to step up and fill the leadership void. Stew Jr. began running the Norwalk store, which was still in his mother's name. Stew Jr., Tom, and their sisters, Jill and Beth, owned and operated the new Danbury store.[84] They were now faced with monumental decisions regarding damage control. How would they be able to maintain the business? How could they regain goodwill and customer confidence? How could they overcome the stigma associated with skimming and shortweighting? Would they be able to get along without Stew Sr.? What steps could they take to ensure that wrongdoing like this wouldn't happen again? How could they restore the company's reputation?

There were other worries as well. Stew Sr.'s health was in question. Prior to entering prison, he had to have a heart valve and hip replaced.[85]

To make matters worse, in early 1996, it was reported that Tom was under a grand jury investigation for skimming cash from store vending machines.[86] According to investigators, Tom had been skimming cash from pop machines, hot dog vendors, and other vending locations in the store. Stew Jr. would almost certainly be called to testify before the grand jury.

Stew Jr. had been responsible for withdrawing from the Baldridge Award competition in 1991, a move he had made only because of the criminal inverstiations.[87] Now he wondered if he could put the store back into contention for the prestigious award.

Young Stew Jr. knew he must direct his attention immediately to the challenges facing him. He knew his father would want to return to store management and that it was his mission to pave the way. He pondered how he would be able to regain customers' faith and redeem the Leonard family name.

Questions

1. Why do you think Stew Leonard's Dairy has been so successful?

2. Why would someone like Stew Leonard, who was doing so many things right, do something so terribly wrong?

3. Who are the stakeholders in this case? And how much of a stake does each group have in the failure of the company?

4. In your opinion, what were the "moral hazards" that might have helped lead to the wrongdoing? Were there any hints of Stew's proclivity for wrongdoing?

5. You have been hired as a consultant to the Leonard family to give advice on what actions the company should now take. What are your recommendations for restoring customer confidence?

Notes

1. S. Leonard Jr., "The Customer Is Always Right," *Executive Excellence* 10(8) (1993): 16–17.

2. Davis K. Fishman, *Stew Leonard's—The Disney World of Supermarkets* (New York: Curtis Brown Publishers, 1985).

3. Ibid.

4. Les Slater, Interview in *Review of Business* 13 (summer/fall 1991): 10–12.

5. Fishman, *Stew Leonard's*.

6. S. Leonard, "Love That Customer!" *Management Review* 76(10) (October 1987): 36–39.

7. Ibid.

8. E. Penzer, "Secrets from the Supermarket," *Incentive* 165(8) (August 1991): 67–69.

9. M. Raphel, "Confidence Is Number One," *Direct Marketing* 52(5) (September 1989): 30, 32.

10. E. T. Suters, "Stew Leonard: Soul of a Leader," *Executive Excellence* 8(6) (June 1991): 13–14.

11. Fishman, *Stew Leonard's.*

12. M. Adams, "The Udder Delights of Stew U," *Successful Meetings* 403 (March 1991): 59–61.

13. T. Englander, "Stew Leonard's: In-store Disneyland," *Incentive* 163(1) (January 1989): 26–30.

14. Leonard, "The Customer Is Always Right."

15. Slater, Interview.

16. Adams, "The Udder Delights of Stew U."

17. Leonard, "Love That Customer!"

18. Englander, "Stew Leonard's."

19. S. Bennett, "What Shoppers Want," *Progressive Grocer* 71(10) (October 1992): 73–78.

20. Englander, "Stew Leonard's"; and D. Feldman, "Companies Aim to Please," *Management Review* 78(5) (May 1989): 8–9.

21. J. M. Hill, "Supermarkets Can Beat Warehouse Clubs, But Not on Price Alone," *Brandweek* 34(1) (January 1993): 25.

22. Leonard, "The Customer Is Always Right."

23. Slater, Interview.

24. Fishman, *Stew Leonard's.*

25. S. Weinstein, "How to Hire the Best," *Progressive Grocer* 72(7) (July 1993): 119–122.

26. Ibid.

27. Adams, "The Udder Delights of Stew U."

28. Ibid.

29. Englander, "Stew Leonard's.

30. B. Bolger, "Stew Leonard: Unconventional Wisdom," *Incentive* 162(11) (November 1988): 36–40; and Englander, "Stew Leonard's."

31. Ibid.

32. Bolger, "Stew Leonard."

33. Ibid.

34. Ibid.

35. Ibid.

36. Englander, "Stew Leonard's."

37. Ibid.

38. Adams, "The Udder Delights of Stew U."

39. Penzer, "Secrets from the Supermarket."

40. Ibid.

41. Ibid.

42. Fishman, *Stew Leonard's.*

43. Weinstein, "How to Hire the Best."

44. R. Pastore, "A Virtual Shopping Spree," *CIO* (August 6, 1993): 70–74.

45. C. J. Levy, "Store Founder Pleads Guilty in Fraud," *The New York Times* (July 23, 1993): B1, B4.

46. Bolger, "Stew Leonard."

47. J. Steinberg, "Papers Show Greed Calculation and Betrayal in Stew Leonard Case," *The New York Times* (October 22, 1993).

48. Pastore, "A Virtual Shopping Spree."

49. B. Kanner, "Spilled Milk," *New York* 26(42) (October 25, 1993): 68–74.

50. J. Heller, "At Stew Leonard's Business as Usual Despite IRS Audit," *The Fairpress* (Norwalk, weekly edition), sec. CG (August 15, 1991): 54.

51. Kanner, "Spilled Milk."

52. Levy, "Store Founder Pleads Guilty."

53. "IRS Crime Unit Probing Records," *The Advocate* (August 22, 1991).

54. Heller, "At Stew Leonard's."

55. Steinberg, "Papers Show Greed Calculation and Betrayal."

56. C. H. Wamae, "Leonard Checks in at Federal Hospital," *Connecticut Post* (November 30, 1993): A7.

57. Levy, "Store Founder Pleads Guilty."

58. Kanner, "Spilled Milk."

59. Steinberg, "Papers Show Greed Calculation and Betrayal."

60. P. Berman, "Like Father, Like Son," *Forbes* (May 20, 1996): 44–45.

61. B. Ingram, "Stew, We Hardly Knew Ye," *Supermarket Business* (September 1993): 157–158.

62. J. Barron, "Stew Leonard's Is Cited for Shorting Customers," *The New York Times* (July 24, 1993): L24.

63. M. Tosh, "Mislabeling Charge May Be More Taxing," *Supermarket News* (August 2, 1993): 43.

64. Ingram, "Stew, We Hardly Knew Ye."

65. H. O'Neill, Telephone interview with consultant who worked with Stew Leonard's in making the Baldridge Award application (August 1996).

66. Kanner, "Spilled Milk"; and R. Zemke, "Piling On," *Training* 30(10) (October 1993): 10.

67. Barron, "Stew Leonard Is Cited."

68. Barron, "Stew Leonard Is Cited"; and E. Zwiebach, "Stew Leonard's Reports Sales Dip," *Supermarket News* (August 2, 1993): 42–43.

69. Zwiebach, "Stew Leonard's Reports Sales Dip."

70. Ingram, "Stew, We Hardly Knew Ye."

71. Ibid.

72. J. Crispens, "The Reaction from Shoppers: Luke-Warm to Mildly Stewed," *Supermarket News* (August 2, 1993): 42.

73. Ibid.

74. Kanner, "Spilled Milk."

75. Ingram, "Stew, We Hardly Knew Ye."

76. IRS, Telephone interview with Larry Marini, state investigator, Criminal Investigation Division, Connecticut (March 1995).

77. S. Silvers, "Judge Reduces Stew's Fine," *Connecticut Post* (October 27, 1994): A1, A13.

78. Ibid.

79. Wamae, "Leonard Checks in at Federal Hospital."

80. Ibid.

81. Kanner, "Spilled Milk."

82. Silvers, "Judge Reduces Stew's Fine."

83. Telephone interview with E. Suters, *The Unnatural Act of Management* (April 1995); and Berman, "Like Father, Like Son."

84. Berman, "Like Father, Like Son."

85. P. T. Farrelly, Jr., "Leonard to Begin Sentence Today at Medical Facility," *The Hour* (November 29, 1993): 1–2.

86. Berman, "Like Father, Like Son."

87. O'Neill, Telephone interview.

Part 2 Exercise

How Ethical Are You?

Directions: Please read the following business situations and write the number in the blank that shows the degree to which you personally feel they are ethically acceptable.

Never Acceptable			Indifferent		Always Acceptable	
1	2	3	4	5	6	7

1. An executive earning $50,000 per year padded his expense account by almost $1,500 per year. _____

2. In order to increase profits, a general manager used a production process that exceeded legal limits for environmental pollution. _____

3. Because of pressure from his brokerage firm, a stockbroker recommended a type of bond that he did not consider to be a good investment. _____

4. A small business received one-fourth of its gross revenue in the form of cash. The owner reported only one-half of the cash receipts for income tax purposes. _____

5. A company paid a $350,000 "consulting" fee to an official of a foreign country. In return, the official promised assistance in obtaining a contract that should produce a $10 million profit for the contracting company. _____

6. A company president found that a competitor had made an important scientific discovery that would sharply reduce the profits of his own company. He then hired a key employee of the competitor in an attempt to learn the details of the discovery. _____

7. A highway building contractor deplored the chaotic bidding situation and cutthroat competition. He reached an understanding with other major contractors to permit bidding that would provide a reasonable profit. _____

8. A company president recognized that sending expensive Christmas gifts to purchasing agents might compromise their positions. However, he continued the policy since it was common practice and changing it might result in loss of business. _____

9. A corporate director learned that his company intended to announce a stock split and increase its dividend. On the basis of this information, he bought additional shares and sold them at a gain following the announcement. _____

10. A corporate executive promoted a loyal friend and competent manager to the position of divisional vice president in preference to a better-qualified manager with whom he had no close ties. _____

11. An engineer discovered what he perceived to be a product design flaw that constituted a safety hazard. His company declined to correct the flaw. The engineer decided to keep quiet, rather than taking his complaint outside the company. _____

12. A comptroller selected a legal method of financial reporting that concealed some embarrassing financial facts that would otherwise have become public knowledge. _____

13. An employer received applications for a supervisor's position from two equally qualified applicants but hired the male

applicant because he thought some employees might resent being supervised by a female. _____

from the Surgeon General's office that cigarette smoking is harmful to the smoker's health. _____

14. As part of the marketing strategy for a product, the producer changed its color and marketed it as "new and improved" even though its other characteristics were unchanged. _____

16. An owner of a small firm obtained a free copy of a copyrighted computer software program from a business friend rather than spending $500 to obtain his own program from the software dealer. _____

15. A cigarette manufacturer launched a publicity campaign challenging new evidence

Survey Results: Here Is How 240 Small-Business Owners Responded

1. Mean response = 2.0
2. Mean response = 1.5
3. Mean response = 1.7
4. Mean response = 2.7
5. Mean response = 3.3
6. Mean response = 3.9
7. Mean response = 3.2
8. Mean response = 3.2
9. Mean response = 2.8
10. Mean response = 3.5
11. Mean response = 2.3
12. Mean response = 4.1
13. Mean response = 3.1
14. Mean response = 3.2
15. Mean response = 3.5
16. Mean response = 3.6

PART 3

Developing the Entrepreneurial Plan

7 Assessment of Entrepreneurial Opportunities

To avoid all mistakes in the conduct of a great enterprise is beyond man's powers. . . . But, when a mistake has once been made, to use his reverses as lessons for the future is the part of a brave and sensible man.

Minucius (AD 209)

Chapter Objectives

1 To explain the challenge of new-venture start-ups

2 To review common pitfalls in the selection of new-venture ideas

3 To present critical factors involved in new-venture development

4 To examine why new ventures fail

5 To study certain factors that underlie venture success

6 To analyze the evaluation process methods: profile analysis, feasibility criteria approach, and comprehensive feasibility method

7 To outline the specific activities involved in a comprehensive feasibility evaluation

The Challenge of New-Venture Start-Ups

During the past few years, the number of new-venture start-ups has been consistently high. It is reported that more than 600,000 new firms have emerged in the United States every year since the early 1990s. That works out to approximately 1,500 business start-ups per day. In addition, the ideas for potential new businesses are also surfacing in record numbers; the U.S. Patent Office currently reviews more than 375,000 patent applications per year.[1]

The reasons for entrepreneurs starting up new ventures are numerous. One study reported seven components of new-venture motivation: the need for approval, the need for independence, the need for personal development, welfare (philanthropic) considerations, perception of wealth, tax reduction and indirect benefits, and following role models.[2] These components are similar to the characteristics discussed in Chapter 4 concerning the "entrepreneurial mind-set." Although researchers agree that many reasons exist for starting a venture, the entrepreneurial motivations of individuals usually relate to the *personal characteristics* of the entrepreneur, the *environment,* and the *venture* itself. The complexity of these key factors makes the assessment of new ventures extremely difficult. One recent study examined the importance of start-up activities to potential entrepreneurs (those attempting to start a venture). Entrepreneurs who successfully started a business "were more aggressive in making their business real; that is, they undertook activities that made their businesses tangible to others: they looked for facilities and equipment, sought and got financial support, formed a legal entity, organized a team, bought facilities and equipment, and devoted full time to the business. Individuals who started businesses seemed to act with a greater level of intensity. They undertook more activities than those individuals who did not start their businesses. The pattern of activities seems to indicate that individuals who started firms put themselves into the day-to-day process of running an ongoing business as quickly as they could and that these activities resulted in starting firms that generated sales (94 percent of the entrepreneurs) and positive cash flow (50 percent of the entrepreneurs)."[3] Another study examined the quantitative and qualitative managerial factors that contribute to the success or failure of a young firm. It was found that firms do not have equal resources starting out. More important, the successful firms made greater use of professional advice and developed more detailed business plans.[4] Yet another recent study examined the importance of obtaining legitimacy with the early stakeholders as a prerequisite to venture survival.[5] As researcher Arnold C. Cooper points out, the challenges to predicting new-firm performance include environmental effects (the risk of new products or services, narrow markets, and scarce resources), the entrepreneur's personal goals and founding processes (reasons for start-up), and the diversity of the ventures themselves (differing scales and potential).[6] (See Figure 7.1 for illustration.)

In addition to the problems presented by the complexity of the factors in new-venture performance, it is difficult to obtain reliable data concerning start-up, performance, and failure. Surveys by phone and mail have been used with owners, employees, and competitors to obtain measures of sales, profit, technology, market share, and so forth.[7] The results are not completely comparable to all ventures or all industries. It is from this pioneering work, however, that more and better data are being gathered for the evaluation of new ventures.

It should be understood that new-venture assessment begins with the idea and venture selection stage. However, most studies of new-venture development deal with

Figure 7.1 The Elements Affecting New-Venture Performance

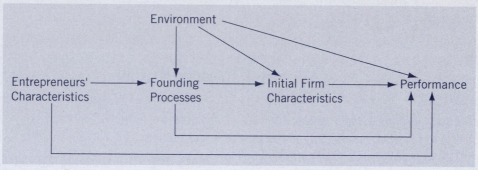

Source: Arnold C. Cooper, "Challenges in Predicting New Firm Performance," *Journal of Business Venturing* (May 1993): 243.
Reprinted with permission.

established start-up businesses. Researchers Paul Reynolds and Brenda Miller describe a "fully developed new firm" as one that requires the full-time commitment of one or more individuals, is selling a product or service, has formal financial support, and has hired one or more individuals.[8]

Therefore, as ideas develop into new-venture start-ups, the real challenge is for those firms to survive and grow. In order to do this, they need to have a clear understanding of the critical factors for selecting ventures, the known reasons for venture failure, and an effective evaluation process for new ventures.

Pitfalls in Selecting New Ventures

The first key area of analysis is the selection of a new venture. This stage of transition from an idea to a potential venture can be the most critical for understanding new-venture development. Presented here are six of the most important pitfalls commonly encountered in the process of selecting a new venture.

Lack of Objective Evaluation

Many entrepreneurs lack objectivity. Engineers and technically trained people are particularly prone to falling in love with an idea for a product or service. They seem unaware of the need for the scrutiny they would give to a design or project in the ordinary course of their professional work. The way to avoid this pitfall is to subject all ideas to rigorous study and investigation.[9]

No Real Insight into the Market

Many entrepreneurs do not realize the importance of developing a marketing approach in laying the foundation for a new venture. They show a managerial shortsightedness.[10] Also, they do not understand the life cycle that must be considered when introducing a new product or service.

No product is instantaneously profitable, nor does its success endure indefinitely. Entrepreneurs must not only project the life cycle of the new product, but also recognize that introducing the product at the right time is important to its success. Timing is critical. Action taken too soon or too late will often result in failure.

entrepreneurship IN PRACTICE

World-Class Failures

Ford's Diesel It had innovations galore—and quality problems from stuck hoods to defective power steering. Estimated loss per car was almost $1,117, or a total of $250 million.

DuPont's Corfam A synthetic leather supposed to do for shoes what nylon did for stockings. Leather was just better. Cost: $80 million to $100 million.

Polaroid's Polavision Edwin Land used Polaroid's wet-chemistry technology to develop an instant movie camera. But videotape technology was far better.

United Artists' "Heaven's Gate" Almost $30 million over budget, this Western movie bombed so badly it almost destroyed UA.

RCA's Videodisc This innovation was supposed to capture the video-recorder market, but it couldn't tape television shows. Loss: $500 million.

Time's TV-Cable Week This was a bid to compete with TV Guide. Cause of death: ballooning costs to customize editions for each cable system. Loss: $47 million.

IBM's PCjr The awkward Chiclet keyboard, the slow microprocessor, an unattractive price, and a late launch caused a major disaster. Cost: $40 million.

New Coke Coca-Cola's answer to Pepsi's sweeter formula provoked a national uproar from old-formula loyalists.

R. J. Reynolds' Premier This cigarette didn't burn or emit smoke, but it simply didn't taste good. Its failure persuaded CEO Ross Johnson to launch his equally disastrous buyout attempt.

NutraSweet's Simplesse This fat substitute was meant to change the way we eat. However, the market is swamped with substitutes, and many consumers like fat.

SOURCE: "Flops," *Business Week* (August 16, 1993): 80.

Inadequate Understanding of Technical Requirements

The development of a new product often involves new techniques. Failure to anticipate the technical difficulties with developing or producing a product can sink a new venture. Entrepreneurs cannot be too thorough when studying the project before initiating it. Encountering unexpected technical difficulties frequently poses time-consuming and costly problems.

Poor Financial Understanding

A common difficulty with the development of a new product is an overly optimistic estimate of the funds required to carry the project to completion. Sometimes entrepreneurs are ignorant of costs or are victims of inadequate research and planning. Quite often they tend to underestimate development costs by wide margins. It is not unusual for estimates to be less than half of what is eventually required.

Lack of Venture Uniqueness

A new venture should be unique. **Uniqueness** is the special characteristics and design concepts that draw the customer to the venture, which should provide performance or service that is superior to competitive offerings. The best way to ensure customer awareness of differences between the company's product and competitors' products is through product differentiation. Pricing becomes less of a problem when the customer sees the product as superior to its competitors. A product that is unique in a significant way can gain the advantage of differentiation.

Ignorance of Legal Issues

Business is subject to many legal requirements. One is the need to make the workplace safe for employees. A second is to provide reliable and safe products and services. A third is the necessity for patents, trademarks, and copyrights to protect one's inventions and products. When these legal issues are overlooked, major problems can result. (See the Entrepreneurship in Practice box on world-class failures.)

Critical Factors for New-Venture Development

A number of **critical factors** are important for new-venture assessment. One way to identify and evaluate them is with a checklist (see Table 7.1). In most cases, however, such a questionnaire approach is too general. The assessment must be tailor-made for the specific venture.

Table 7.1   A New-Venture Idea Checklist

Basic Feasibility of the Venture

1. Can the product or service work?
2. Is it legal?

Competitive Advantages of the Venture

1. What specific competitive advantages will the product or service offer?
2. What are the competitive advantages of the companies already in business?
3. How are the competitors likely to respond?
4. How will the initial competitive advantage be maintained?

Buyer Decisions in the Venture

1. Who are the customers likely to be?
2. How much will each customer buy, and how many customers are there?
3. Where are these customers located, and how will they be serviced?

Marketing of the Goods and Services

1. How much will be spent on advertising and selling?
2. What share of market will the company capture? By when?
3. Who will perform the selling functions?
4. How will prices be set? How will they compare with the competition's prices?
5. How important is location, and how will it be determined?
6. What distribution channels will be used—wholesale, retail, agents, direct mail?

Table 7.1   (Continued)

7. What are the sales targets? By when should they be met?

8. Can any orders be obtained before starting the business? How many? For what total amount?

Production of the Goods and Services

1. Will the company make or buy what it sells? Or will it use a combination of these two strategies?

2. Are sources of supplies available at reasonable prices?

3. How long will delivery take?

4. Have adequate lease arrangements for premises been made?

5. Will the needed equipment be available on time?

6. Do any special problems with plant setup, clearances, or insurance exist? How will they be resolved?

7. How will quality be controlled?

8. How will returns and servicing be handled?

9. How will pilferage, waste, spoilage, and scrap be controlled?

Staffing Decisions in the Venture

1. How will competence in each area of the business be ensured?

2. Who will have to be hired? By when? How will they be found and recruited?

3. Will a banker, lawyer, accountant, or other advisers be needed?

4. How will replacements be obtained if key people leave?

5. Will special benefit plans have to be arranged?

Control of the Venture

1. What records will be needed? When?

2. Will any special controls be required? What are they? Who will be responsible for them?

Financing the Venture

1. How much will be needed for development of the product or service?

2. How much will be needed for setting up operations?

3. How much will be needed for working capital?

4. Where will the money come from? What if more is needed?

5. Which assumptions in the financial forecasts are most uncertain?

6. What will be the return on equity, or sales, and how does it compare with the rest of the industry?

7. When and how will investors get their money back?

8. What will be needed from the bank, and what is the bank's response?

Source: Karl H. Vesper, *New Venture Strategies*, copyright © 1990, 172. Adapted by permission of Prentice-Hall, Inc., Englewood Cliffs, New Jersey.

the entrepreneurial
PROCESS

An Employee Self-Assessment

When planning for new opportunities, the SWOT (strengths, weaknesses, opportunities, and threats) has long been the tried-and-tested format in assessing a company. However, the intellectual talent among a company's employees can be just as rich in opportunities as the environmental strengths of the company. Ask employees to use the same strategic planning techniques for themselves to assess the past year and years ahead.

If all else fails, the employees of your company will strengthen their own skills, which will strengthen the company in the long run.

1. **Have each employee do a personal SWOT analysis.** Convey the importance of the analysis, and allow employees several hours or even days to complete the SWOT.

2. **Have employees go over their SWOT analyses together.** If employees share their self-analyses, team members can learn how to support one another. Their analyses should lay out specific objectives and tactics in meeting those objectives. During this meeting, owners or managers will have the chance to evaluate the plans of employees, determine the practicality of their objectives, and capitalize on interests previously unknown.

3. **Acknowledge the good in each plan.** Inevitably an employee will set an unattainable goal. Try to focus on other goals in the analysis that are attainable and assist the organization. Let the employee know he or she should first focus on the attainable objectives.

4. **Revisit the plan monthly or quarterly.** This shouldn't become a flavor-of-the-month idea. Each plan's progress should be reevaluated often enough to keep the goals as important as they were when they were established. Revisiting the plans on a monthly basis will keep employees on track.

Remember that the strengths and weaknesses focus on the internal aspect of the employee, while the opportunities and threats refer to the external factors in the company, such as lack of managers in a division. The following are some questions for creating a successful personal SWOT analysis:

1. **Assess your strengths.**
   - ☐ Where do you excel?
   - ☐ What makes you particularly useful to your organization?
   - ☐ What unusual skill(s) do you bring to your job?
   - ☐ What experience provides you depth of understanding for the work you do?
   - ☐ What particular needs of your organization do you meet?
   - ☐ What standards do you adhere to that benefit your company?

2. **Assess your weaknesses.**
   - ☐ Where do you fall short?
   - ☐ What types of tasks do you fail to get done on time?
   - ☐ In what ways do you not work well with fellow staff?
   - ☐ What skills do you lack that would help you do your job more effectively?
   - ☐ In what areas have you failed to provide what your organization needs to serve its customers more efficiently and make more profit?

3. **Assess your opportunities.**
   - ☐ How does your job contribute to the bottom line of the organization?
   - ☐ How might technology provide you a "leg up" in helping your organization?

☐ How can you help your organization capitalize on the economic downturn?

☐ How can you and your job benefit from the growing immigrant population?

☐ What is going on in your market, your city, your county, and your state that can benefit you and the job you do?

4. **Assess your threats.**

☐ How does the current economy affect your position?

☐ How is your organization changing, and will any of those changes make what you do less important?

☐ Do you need to change your function in the organization or take on new

responsibilities to remain as useful as before?

☐ Do you offer the same level of skill that new employees bring to the organization?

☐ Do you perform a particular task that no one has realized is obsolete, but will?

5. **Make a plan.**

☐ An effective plan should use strengths and confront weaknesses while taking advantage of the opportunities and neutralizing the threats.

SOURCE: Scott Miller, "Have You Done Your SWOT Analysis Lately?" *Entrepreneur.com—Your Business* (January 14, 2002) http://www.entrepreneur.com.

A new venture goes through three specific phases: prestart-up, start-up, and poststart-up. The prestart-up phase begins with an idea for the venture and ends when the doors are opened for business. The start-up phase commences with the initiation of sales activity and the delivery of products and services and ends when the business is firmly established and beyond short-term threats to survival. The poststart-up phase lasts until the venture is terminated or the surviving organizational entity is no longer controlled by an entrepreneur.

The major focus in this chapter is on the prestart-up and start-up phases, because these are the critical segments for entrepreneurs. During these two phases five factors are critical: (1) the relative uniqueness of the venture, (2) the relative investment size at start-up, (3) the expected growth of sales and/or profits as the venture moves through its start-up phase, (4) the availability of products during the prestart-up and start-up phases, and (5) the availability of customers during the prestart-up and start-up phases.

Uniqueness

A new venture's range of uniqueness can be considerable, extending from fairly routine to highly nonroutine. What separates the routine from the nonroutine venture is the amount of innovation required during prestart-up. This distinction is based on the need for new process technology to produce services or products and on the need to service new market segments. Venture uniqueness is further characterized by the length of time a nonroutine venture will remain nonroutine. For instance, will new products, new technology, and new markets be required on a continuing basis? Or will the venture be able to "settle down" after the start-up period and use existing products, technologies, and markets?

Investment

The capital investment required to start a new venture can vary considerably. In some industries less than $50,000 may be required, whereas in other industries millions of dollars are necessary. Moreover, in some industries only large-scale start-ups are feasible. For example, in the publishing industry one can start a small venture that can remain small or grow into a larger venture. By contrast, an entrepreneur attempting to break into the airline industry will need a considerable upfront investment.

Another finance-related critical issue is the extent and timing of funds needed to move through the venture process. To determine the amount of needed investment, entrepreneurs must answer questions such as these: Will industry growth be sufficient to maintain break-even sales to cover a high fixed-cost structure during the start-up period? Do the principal entrepreneurs have access to substantial financial reserves to protect a large initial investment? Do the entrepreneurs have the appropriate contacts to take advantage of various environmental opportunities? Do the entrepreneurs have both industry and entrepreneurial track records that justify the financial risk of a large-scale start-up?[11]

Growth of Sales

The **growth of sales** through the start-up phase is another critical factor. Key questions are as follows: What is the growth pattern anticipated for new-venture sales and profits? Are sales and profits expected to grow slowly or level off shortly after start-up? Are large profits expected at some point with only small or moderate sales growth? Or are both high sales growth and high profit growth likely? Or will initial profits be limited with eventual high profit growth over a multiyear period? In answering these questions, it is important to remember that most ventures fit into one of the three following classifications.

Lifestyle ventures appear to have independence, autonomy, and control as their primary driving forces. Neither large sales nor profits are deemed important beyond providing a sufficient and comfortable living for the entrepreneur.

In **small profitable ventures**, financial considerations play a major role. Additionally, autonomy and control are important in the sense that the entrepreneur does not want venture sales (and employment) to become so large that he or she must relinquish equity or an ownership position and thus give up control over cash flow and profits, which, it is hoped, will be substantial.

In **high-growth ventures**, significant sales and profit growth are expected to the extent that it may be possible to attract venture capital money and funds raised through public or private placements.[12]

Product Availability

Essential to the success of any venture is **product availability**, the availability of a salable good or service, at the time the venture opens its doors. Some ventures have problems in this regard because the product or service is still in development and needs further modification or testing. Other ventures find that because they bring their product to market too soon, it must be recalled for further work. A typical example is the software firm that rushes the development of its product and is then besieged by customers who find "bugs" in the program. Lack of product availability in finished form can affect the company's image and its bottom line.

Customer Availability

If the product is available before the venture is started, the likelihood of venture success is considerably better than otherwise. Similarly, venture risk is affected by **customer availability** for start-up. At one end of the risk continuum is the situation where customers are willing to pay cash for products or services before delivery. At the other end of the continuum is the enterprise that gets started without knowing exactly who will buy its product. A critical consideration is how long it will take to determine who the customers are and what their buying habits are. As researcher Robert C. Ronstadt notes:

> The decision to ignore the market is an extremely risky one. There are, after all, two fundamental criteria for entrepreneurial success. The first is having a customer who is willing to pay you a profitable price for a product or a service. The second is that you must actually produce and deliver the product or service. The farther a venture removes itself from certainty about these two rules, the greater the risk and the greater the time required to offset this risk as the venture moves through the prestart-up and start-up periods.[13]

Why New Ventures Fail

Every year many millions of dollars are spent on starting new enterprises. Many of these newly established businesses vanish within a year or two; only a small percentage is successful. Most studies have found that the factors underlying the failure of new ventures are, in most cases, within the control of the entrepreneur. Some of the major reasons for the failure of new ventures follow.

Researchers Albert V. Bruno, Joel K. Leidecker, and Joseph W. Harder examined 250 high-tech firms and found three major categories of causes for failure: product/market problems, financial difficulties, and managerial problems.[14]

Product/market problems involved the following factors:

- □ *Poor timing.* In 40 percent of the cases studied, a premature entry into the marketplace contributed to failure.

- □ *Product design problems.* Although these may be related to timing, product design and development became key factors at earlier stages of the venture, and when the essential makeup of the product or service was changed, failure resulted.

- □ *Inappropriate distribution strategy.* Whether it was based on commissioned sales representatives or direct sales at trade shows, the distribution strategy had to be geared toward the product and customer.

- □ *Unclear business definition.* Uncertainty about the "exact" business they were in caused these firms to undergo constant change and to lack stabilization.

- □ *Overreliance on one customer.* This resulted in a failure to diversify and brought about the eventual demise of some of the firms.

In the financial difficulties category were the following factors:

- □ *Initial undercapitalization.* In 30 percent of the case studies, undercapitalization contributed to failure.

- □ *Assuming debt too early.* Some of the firms attempted to obtain debt financing too soon and in too large an amount. This led to debt service problems.

- □ *Venture capital relationship problems.* Differing goals, visions, and motivations of the entrepreneur and the venture capitalist resulted in problems for the enterprise.

Managerial problems involved two important factors:

- □ *Concept of a team approach.* These problems associated with the managerial team were found: (1) hirings and promotions on the basis of nepotism rather than qualifications, (2) poor relationships with parent companies and venture capitalists, (3) founders who focused on their weaknesses rather than on their strengths (though weakening the company, they supposedly were building their skills), and (4) incompetent support professionals (for example, attorneys who were unable to read contracts or collect on court judgments that already had been made).

☐ *Human resource problems.* Inflated owner ego, employee-related concerns, and control factors were all problems leading to business failure. The study also revealed such interpersonal problems as (1) kickbacks and subsequent firings that resulted in an almost total loss of customers, (2) deceit on the part of a venture capitalist in one case and on the part of a company president in another, (3) verbal agreements between the entrepreneur and the venture capitalists that were not honored, and (4) protracted lawsuits around the time of discontinuance.

In a more recent study of successful ventures (firms listed in the *Inc.* 500 group of fastest-growing privately held companies), the most significant problems encountered at start-up were researched in order to systematically sort them into a schematic. Table 7.2 lists the types and classes of problems identified during the first year of operation. The researcher also surveyed the current problems the owners of these successful firms

Table 7.2   Types and Classes of First-Year Problems

1. *Obtaining external financing*
   Obtaining financing for growth
   Other or general financing problems

2. *Internal financial management*
   Inadequate working capital
   Cash-flow problems
   Other or general financial management
     problems

3. *Sales/marketing*
   Low sales
   Dependence on one or few clients/
     customers
   Marketing or distribution channels
   Promotion/public relations/advertising
   Other or general marketing problems

4. *Product development*
   Developing products/services
   Other or general product development
     problems

5. *Production/operations* management
   Establishing or maintaining quality
     control
   Raw materials/resources/supplies

   Other or general production/
     operations management
     problems

6. *General management*
   Lack of management experience
   Only one person/no time
   Managing/controlling growth
   Administrative problems
   Other or general management
     problems

7. *Human resource management*
   Recruitment/selection
   Turnover/retention
   Satisfaction/morale
   Employee development
   Other or general human resource
     management problems

8. *Economic environment*
   Poor economy/recession
   Other or general economic
     environment problems

9. *Regulatory environment*
   Insurance

Source: David E. Terpstra and Philip D. Olson, "Entrepreneurial Start-up and Growth: A Classification of Problems," *Entrepreneurship Theory and Practice* (spring 1993): 19.

encountered in order to explore the possible changes in problem patterns of new firms. It was found that dominant problems at **start–up** related to sales/marketing (38 percent), obtaining external financing (17 percent), and internal financial management (16 percent). General management problems were also frequently cited in the start-up stage (11 percent). In the **growth stage**, sales/marketing remained the most dominant problem (22 percent), but it was less important than in the start-up stage. Internal financial management (21 percent) continued to be a dominant problem, as were human resource management (17 percent) and general management (14 percent). Additionally, more regulatory environment problems occurred in the growth stage (8 percent) than were mentioned in the start-up stage (1 percent). Finally, organizational structure/design (6 percent) emerged as a problem in the growth stage.[15] It is important for entrepreneurs to recognize these problem areas at the outset because they remain challenges to the venture as it grows.

Another study of 645 entrepreneurs focused on the classification of start-up and growth problems experienced internally versus externally.[16] Figure 7.2 depicts the types of problems and the percentage of firms that reported these problems. **Internal problems**

Figure 7.2 Internal and External Problems Experienced by Entrepreneurs

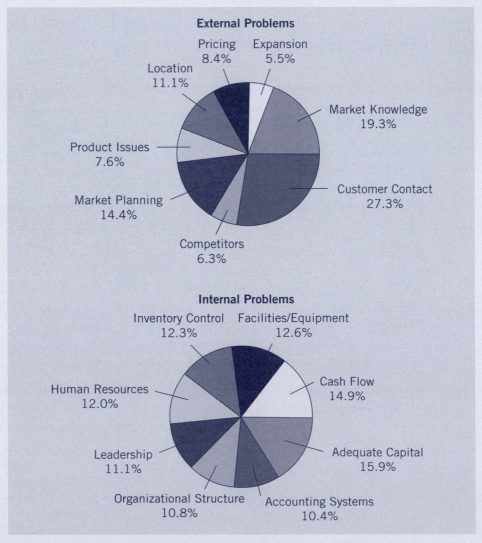

External Problems

Pricing 8.4%
Expansion 5.5%
Location 11.1%
Market Knowledge 19.3%
Product Issues 7.6%
Customer Contact 27.3%
Market Planning 14.4%
Competitors 6.3%

Internal Problems

Inventory Control 12.3%
Facilities/Equipment 12.6%
Human Resources 12.0%
Cash Flow 14.9%
Leadership 11.1%
Adequate Capital 15.9%
Organizational Structure 10.8%
Accounting Systems 10.4%

Source: H. Robert Dodge, Sam Fullerton, and John E. Robbins, "Stage of Organization Life Cycle and Competition as Mediators of Problem Perception for Small Businesses," *Strategic Management Journal* 15 (1994): 129. Reprinted by permission of John Wiley & Sons, Ltd.

Table 7.3   Determinants of New-Venture Failures

ENTREPRENEUR	RANK	VENTURE CAPITALIST	RANK
I—Lack of management skill	1	I—Lack of management skill	1
I—Poor management strategy	2	I—Poor management strategy	2
I—Lack of capitalization	3	I—Lack of capitalization	3
I—Lack of vision	4	E—Poor external market conditions	4
I—Poor product design	5	I—Poor product design	5
I—Key personnel incompetent	6	I—Poor product timing	6

E = External factor

I = Internal factor

Source: Andrew L. Zacharakis, G. Dale Meyer, and Julio DeCastro, "Differing Perceptions of New Venture Failure: A Matched Exploratory Study of Venture Capitalists and Entrepreneurs," *Journal of Small Business Management* (July 1999): 8.

involved adequate capital, cash flow, facilities/equipment, inventory control, human resources, leadership, organizational structure, and accounting systems. **External problems** were related to customer contact, market knowledge, marketing planning, location, pricing, product considerations, competitors, and expansion. The researchers found that the "intensity of competition" rather than life cycle stages was crucial in changing the relative importance of the problem areas. Thus, entrepreneurs need to recognize not only that **start-up problems** remain with the venture but also that the increasing competition will adjust the relative importance of the problems.

In a recent study conducted by researchers Andrew Zacharakis, G. Dale Meyer, and Julio DeCastro, the differing perceptions of new-venture failure were examined. Internal and external factors were identified and ranked by a sample of venture capitalists as well as a sample of entrepreneurs. Entrepreneurs attributed new venture failure in general to *internal* factors 89 percent of the time. In the same vein venture capitalists overwhelmingly attributed the failure of most new ventures to *internal* causes (84 percent).[17] (See Table 7.3.)

A fourth "failure" or problem study dealt with a proposed **failure prediction model** based on financial data from newly founded ventures. The study assumed the financial failure process was characterized by too much initial indebtedness and too little revenue financing. As shown by the failure process schematic in Table 7.4, the risk of failure can be reduced by using less debt as initial financing and by generating enough revenue in the initial stages. Further, the study recognized the risk associated with the initial size of the venture being developed. Specific applications of the model included the following:[18]

1. *Role of profitability and cash flows.* The entrepreneur and manager should ensure that the products are able to yield positive profitability and cash flows in the first years.

2. *Role of debt.* The entrepreneur and manager should ensure that enough stockholders' capital is in the initial balance sheet to buffer future losses.

3. *Combination of both.* The entrepreneur and manager should not start a business if the share of stockholders' capital in the initial balance sheet is low and if negative cash flows in the first years are probable.

Table 7.4   The Failure Process of a Newly Founded Firm

1. Extremely high indebtedness (poor static solidity) and small size

2. Too slow velocity of capital, too fast growth, too poor profitability (as compared to the budget), or some combination of these

3. Unexpected lack of revenue financing (poor dynamic liquidity)

4. Poor static liquidity and debt service ability (dynamic solidity)

A. Profitability

1. Return on investment ratio defined on end-of-the-year basis

$$= \frac{\text{Net Profit} + \text{Interest Expenses}}{\text{Total Capital at the End of the Year}} \times 100$$

B. Liquidity
Dynamic

2. Cash flow to net sales

$$= \frac{\text{Net Profit} + \text{Depreciations}}{\text{Net Sales}} \times 100$$

Static

3. Quick ratio

$$= \frac{\text{Financial Assets}}{\text{Current Debt}}$$

C. Solidity
Static

4. Stockholders' capital to total capital

$$= \frac{\text{Total Capital} - \text{Debt Capital}}{\text{Total Capital}} \times 100$$

Dynamic

5. Cash flow to total debt

$$= \frac{\text{Net Profit} + \text{Depreciations}}{\text{Total Debt}} \times 100$$

D. Other Factors
Growth or Dynamic Size

6. Rate of annual growth in net sales

$$= \frac{\text{Net Sales in Year } t}{\text{Net Sales in Year } t - 1} \times 100$$

Size

7. Logarithmic net sales

$$= \ln(\text{Net Sales})$$

Velocity of Capital

8. Net sales to total capital

$$= \frac{\text{Net Sales}}{\text{Total Capital at the End of the Year}}$$

Source: Erkki K. Laitinen, "Prediction of Failure of a Newly Founded Firm," *Journal of Business Venturing* (July 1992): 326–328. Reprinted with permission.

4. *Role of initial size.* The entrepreneur and manager should understand that the more probable the negative cash flows and the larger the debt share in the initial balance sheet, the smaller the initial size of the business should be.

5. *Role of velocity of capital.* The entrepreneur and manager should not budget for fast velocity of capital in the initial years if the risk of negative cash flows is

high. More sales in comparison to capital means more negative cash flows and poorer profitability.

6. *Role of control.* The entrepreneur and manager should monitor financial ratios from the first year, especially the cash-flow-to-total-debt ratio. Risky combinations of ratios (Z-scores)—especially negative cash flows, a low stockholders' capital-to-total-capital ratio, and a high velocity of capital—should be monitored and compared with industrial standards. The entrepreneur should try to identify the reasons for poor ratios and pay special attention to keeping profitability at the planned level (with control ratios).

The Evaluation Process

A critical task of starting a new business enterprise is conducting solid analysis and evaluation of the feasibility of the product/service idea getting off the ground. Entrepreneurs must put their ideas through this analysis in order to discover if the proposals contain any fatal flaws.

Asking the Right Questions

Many important evaluation-related questions should be asked. Ten sets of preliminary questions that can be used to screen an idea are presented here.

1. Is it a new product/service idea? Is it proprietary? Can it be patented or copyrighted? Is it unique enough to get a significant head start on the competition? Or can it be easily copied?

2. Has a prototype been tested by independent testers who try to blow the system or rip the product to shreds? What are its weak points? Will it stand up? What level of research and development should it receive over the next five years? If it is a service, has it been tested on guinea pig customers? Will they pay their hard-earned money for it?

3. Has it been taken to trade shows? If so, what reactions did it receive? Were any sales made? Has it been taken to distributors? Have they placed any orders?

4. Is the product or service easily understood by customers, bankers, venture capitalists, accountants, lawyers, and insurance agents?

5. What is the overall market? What are the market segments? Can the product penetrate these segments? Can any special niches be exploited?

6. Has market research been conducted? Who else is in the market? How big is the market? How fast is it growing? What are the trends? What is the projected life cycle of the product or service? What degree of penetration can be achieved? Are there any testimonials from customers and purchasing agents? What type of advertising and promotion plan will be used?

7. What distribution and sales methods will be used—jobbers, independent sales representatives, the company sales force, direct mail, door-to-door sales, supermarkets, service stations, company-owned stores? How will the product be transported: company-owned trucks, common carriers, postal service, or air freight?

8. How will the product be made? How much will it cost? For example, will it be produced in-house or by others? Will production be by job shop or continuous process? What is the present capacity of company facilities? What is the break-even point?

9. Will the business concept be developed and licensed to others or developed and sold away?

10. Can the company get—or has it already lined up—the necessary skills to operate the business venture? Who will be the workers? Are they dependable and competent? How much capital will be needed now? How much more in the future? Have major stages in financing been developed?[19]

Profile Analysis

A single strategic variable seldom shapes the ultimate success or failure of a new venture. In most situations a combination of variables influences the outcome. Thus it is important to identify and investigate these variables before the new idea is put into practice. The results of such a profile analysis enable the entrepreneur to judge the business's potential.

The internal profile analysis in the Experiential Exercise at the end of this chapter is one method of determining the resources available to a new venture. This checklist approach allows entrepreneurs to identify major strengths and weaknesses in the financial, marketing, organizational, and human resource factors needed for the venture to progress successfully. In this manner entrepreneurs can prepare for possible weaknesses that may inhibit the growth of their ventures. More important, many of the reasons cited for venture failure earlier in this chapter can be avoided through a careful profile analysis.

Feasibility Criteria Approach

Another method, the **feasibility criteria approach**, was developed as a criteria selection list from which entrepreneurs can gain insights into the viability of their venture and is based on the following questions:

☐ *Is it proprietary?* The product does not have to be patented, but it should be sufficiently proprietary to permit a long head start against competitors and a period of extraordinary profits early in the venture to offset start-up costs.

☐ *Are the initial production costs realistic?* Most estimates are too low. A careful, detailed analysis should be made so no large, unexpected expenses arise.

☐ *Are the initial marketing costs realistic?* This answer requires the venture to identify target markets, market channels, and promotional strategy.

☐ *Does the product have potential for very high margins?* This is almost a necessity for a fledgling company. Gross margins are one thing the financial community understands. Without them, funding can be difficult.

☐ *Is the time required to get to market and to reach the break-even point realistic?* In most cases, the faster the better. In all cases, the venture plan will be tied to this answer, and an error here can spell trouble later on.

☐ *Is the potential market large?* In determining the potential market, entrepreneurs must look three to five years into the future because some markets take this long to emerge. The cellular telephone, for example, had an annual demand of approximately 400,000 units in 1982. However, by the late 1990s this market was estimated to grow by at least 45 percent annually.

☐ *Is the product the first of a growing family?* If it is, the venture is more attractive to investors. If they do not realize a large return on the first product, they might on the second, third, or fourth.

☐ *Does an initial customer exist?* It is certainly impressive to financial backers when a venture can list its first ten customers by name. This pent-up demand also means the first quarter's results are likely to be good and the focus of attention can be directed to later quarters.

☐ *Are the development costs and calendar times realistic?* Preferably, they are zero. A ready-to-go product gives the venture a big advantage over competitors. If costs exist, they should be complete and detailed and tied to a month-by-month schedule.

☐ *Is this a growing industry?* This is not absolutely essential if the profits and company growth are there, but it means less room for mistakes. In a growing industry, good companies do even better.

☐ *Can the product and the need for it be understood by the financial community?* If the financiers can grasp the concept and its value, the chances for funding will increase. For example, a portable heart-monitoring system for postcoronary monitoring is a product many will understand. Undoubtedly, some of those hearing the presentation will have already had coronaries or heart problems of some sort.[20]

This criteria selection approach provides a means of analyzing the internal strengths and weaknesses that exist in a new venture by focusing on the marketing potential and industry potential critical to assessment. If the new venture meets fewer than six of these criteria, it typically lacks feasibility for funding. If the new venture meets seven or more of the criteria, it may stand a good chance of being funded.

Comprehensive Feasibility Approach

A more comprehensive and systematic feasibility analysis, a **comprehensive feasibility approach**, incorporates external factors in addition to those in the criteria questions. Figure 7.3 presents a breakdown of the factors involved in a comprehensive feasibility study of a new venture—technical, market, financial, organizational, and competitive. A more detailed feasibility analysis guide is provided in Table 7.5, which identifies the specific activities involved in each feasibility area. Although all five of the areas

Figure 7.3 Key Areas for Assessing the Feasibility of a New Venture

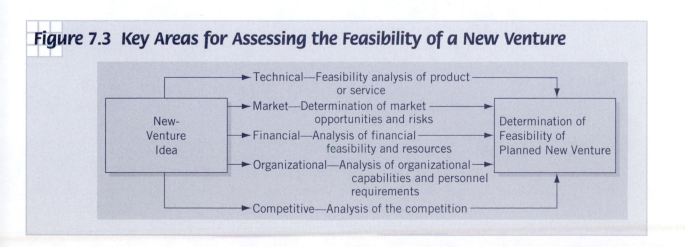

Table 7.5 *Specific Activities of Feasibility Analyses*

TECHNICAL FEASIBILITY ANALYSIS	MARKET FEASIBILITY ANALYSIS	FINANCIAL FEASIBILITY ANALYSIS	ANALYSIS OF ORGANIZATIONAL CAPABILITIES	COMPETITIVE ANALYSIS
Crucial technical specifications	*Market potential*	*Required financial resources for:*	*Personnel requirements*	*Existing competitors*
Design	Identification of potential customers and their dominant characteristics (e.g., age, income level, buying habits)	Fixed assets	Required skill levels and other personal characteristics of potential employees	Size, financial resources, market entrenchment
Durability		Current assets		Potential reaction of competitors to newcomer by means of price cutting, aggressive advertising, introduction of new products, and other actions
Reliability		Necessary working capital		
Product safety		*Available financial resources*	*Managerial requirements*	
Standardization	Potential market share (as affected by competitive situation)	Required borrowing	Determination of individual responsibilities	
Engineering requirements		Potential sources for funds		
Machines		Cost of borrowing	Determination of required organizational relationships	Potential new competitors
Tools	Potential sales volume	Repayment conditions		
Instruments		Operation cost analysis		
Work flow	Sales price projections		Potential organizational development	
Product development	*Market testing*	Fixed costs		
Blueprints	Selection of test	Variable costs	*Competitive analysis*	
Models	Actual market test	Projected cash flow		
Prototypes	Analysis of market	Projected profitability		
Product testing	*Marketing planning issues*			
Lab testing	Preferred channels of distribution, impact of promotional efforts, required distribution points (warehouses), packaging considerations, price differentiation			
Field testing				
Plant location				
Desirable characteristics of plant site (proximity to suppliers, customers), environmental regulations				

Source: Hans Schollhammer and Arthur H. Kuriloff, *Entrepreneurship and Small Business Management* (New York: John Wiley & Sons, 1979): 56. Copyright © 1979 by John Wiley & Sons, Inc. Reprinted by permission of John Wiley & Sons, Inc.

Facing Your Fears!

The inner journey to the creation of an entrepreneurial venture can be even more fearful than the external process of developing a business plan and searching for capital. Building up the courage to quit a job and start a new venture can sound easy and yet pose enormous emotional challenges when the actual events are about to unfold. One consultant, Suzanne Mulvehill, author of *Employee to Entrepreneur* and host of her own radio talk show, suggests particular strategies to follow in confronting the emotional challenges of entrepreneurial start-ups. She coined the term "Emotional Endurance" to signify the inner strength that is needed to make the jump from job to venture. Listed below are a few of the more significant strategies that may help in moving through the emotional journey.

1. **Say yes to your yearning.** In other words acknowledge the desire you are experiencing to venture out on your own. It all begins with accepting the possibility that it could happen.

2. **Visualize your success.** Creating a vision of what could be may be a powerful motivator to what will be. It is important to write down this vision so it has tangible reality to it in this early stage.

3. **Evaluate your beliefs.** On a sheet of paper list all of your beliefs about money, business, and yourself. Then in a similar column write down how you would like to view money, business, and yourself. Compare these beliefs and decide how far apart they are and why.

4. **Do what you love.** There is no replacement for passion. What you love is what will drive you to succeed even in the tough times. Develop your business ideas around the types of things that you absolutely love to do.

5. **Get educated.** Avoid the myths that education saps out any desire to be an entrepreneur.

That may have been true 20 years ago but we have come a long way in our approaches to business education. Entrepreneurship education is the hottest subject in universities worldwide. Remember, knowledge is power.

6. **Eliminate excuses.** Whenever you hear yourself make an excuse for not doing something, write it down and examine it later. Become aware of common excuses you may be using that have no real foundation. Turn your "I can'ts" into open-ended questions that allow you to explore the possibilities rather than shut the door.

7. **Know that there is no "right time."** Waiting for the proverbial perfect time is a trap that many people fall into only to find later that time passed them by. The only guarantee we have about time is that it continues on with or without us. Rather than wait, you need to proactively move on your idea.

8. **Start small.** It is always better to be realistic and reach for what you can accomplish in the near future. The longer-term future may hold greater things for the venture, but at the beginning you need to avoid being overwhelmed.

9. **Answer the "what ifs."** Stop for a moment and write down all of the "what ifs" that you question yourself with. See if you can begin to logically answer the questions. It's amazing how much courage will be gained by analyzing these contingencies.

10. **Ask for help.** Reach out and find help. The maverick entrepreneur is a myth of the past. Today there is so much assistance available if you are willing to seek it out. Ignorance is not asking the questions; rather ignorance is being arrogant to think you have all the answers.

SOURCE: Adapted from Suzanne Mulvehill, "Fear Factor," *Entrepreneur* (April 2005): 104–111.

presented in Figure 7.3 are important, two merit special attention: technical and market.

Technical Feasibility

The evaluation of a new-venture idea should start with identifying the technical requirements, the **technical feasibility**, for producing a product or service that will satisfy the expectations of potential customers. The most important of these are:

- ☐ Functional design of the product and attractiveness in appearance
- ☐ Flexibility, permitting ready modification of the external features of the product to meet customer demands or technological and competitive changes
- ☐ Durability of the materials from which the product is made
- ☐ Reliability, ensuring performance as expected under normal operating conditions
- ☐ Product safety, posing no potential dangers under normal operating conditions
- ☐ Reasonable utility—an acceptable rate of obsolescence
- ☐ Ease and low cost of maintenance
- ☐ Standardization through elimination of unnecessary variety among potentially interchangeable parts
- ☐ Ease of processing or manufacture
- ☐ Ease in handling and use[21]

The results of this investigation provide a basis for deciding whether a new venture is feasible from a technical point of view.

Marketability

Assembling and analyzing relevant information about the **marketability** of a new venture are vital for judging its potential success. Three major areas in this type of analysis are (1) investigating the full market potential and identifying customers (or users) for the goods or service, (2) analyzing the extent to which the enterprise might exploit this potential market, and (3) using market analysis to determine the opportunities and risks associated with the venture. To address these areas, a variety of informational sources must be found and used. For a market feasibility analysis, general sources would include the following:

- ☐ *General economic trends:* various economic indicators such as new orders, housing starts, inventories, and consumer spending
- ☐ *Market data:* customers, customer demand patterns (for example, seasonal variations in demand, governmental regulations affecting demand)
- ☐ *Pricing data:* range of prices for the same, complementary, and substitute products; base prices; and discount structures
- ☐ *Competitive data:* major competitors and their competitive strength

More attention is given to marketing issues in Chapter 9. At this point it is important to note the value of marketing research in the overall assessment and evaluation of a new venture.[22]

Thus, as demonstrated by Table 7.5, the comprehensive feasibility analysis approach is closely related to the preparation of a thorough business plan (covered in detail in Chapter 11). The approach clearly illustrates the need to evaluate each segment of the venture *before* initiating the business or presenting it to capital sources.

In order to assist in understanding feasibility analysis, Appendix 7A illustrates a template used for a complete feasibility plan. This template, created in a format to answer specific questions about the proposed venture idea, allows entrepreneurs the ability to analyze each important segment before moving forward with an idea. Venture capitalists generally agree that the risks in any entrepreneurial venture are you, your management team, and any apparent fundamental flaws in your venture idea. Therefore, you need to make a reasonable evaluation of these risks.

Summary

The complexity of factors involved in new-venture start-up (as shown in Figure 7.1) makes it difficult to clearly assess and evaluate each one. In addition, the difficulty of obtaining reliable data on failed firms adds to this dilemma. Improvements are being made, however, and new-venture assessment is becoming a stronger process.

A number of pitfalls may occur in the selection of a new venture: lack of an objective evaluation of the venture, lack of insight into the market, inadequate understanding of technical requirements, poor financial understanding, lack of venture uniqueness, and failure to be aware of legal issues.

When assessing a new venture, an entrepreneur needs to consider several critical factors: the uniqueness of the good or service, the amount of capital investment required to start the venture, the growth of sales, and the availability of the product.

Some major reasons new ventures fail are inadequate knowledge of the market, faulty product performance, ineffective marketing and sales effort, inadequate awareness of competitive pressures, rapid product obsolescence, poor timing, and undercapitalization. In drawing together these and other reasons, recent research reveals three major categories of causes for failure: product/market problems, financial difficulties, and managerial problems. In addition, entrepreneurs face internal and external problems.

The feasibility of the entrepreneur's product or service can be assessed by asking the right questions, by making a profile analysis of the venture, and by carrying out a comprehensive feasibility study.

Key Terms and Concepts

comprehensive feasibility approach	failure prediction model
critical factors	feasibility criteria approach
customer availability	growth of sales
external problems	growth stage

high-growth venture   small profitable venture

internal problems   start-up problems

lifestyle venture   technical feasibility

marketability   uniqueness

product availability

Review and Discussion Questions

1. Explain the challenges involved in new-venture development.

2. Describe some of the key factors involved in new-venture performance (use Figure 7.1).

3. Many entrepreneurs lack objectivity and have no real insight into the market. Why are these characteristics considered pitfalls of selecting new ventures?

4. Many entrepreneurs have a poor understanding of the finances associated with their new venture and/or have a venture that lacks uniqueness. Why are these characteristics considered pitfalls of selecting new ventures?

5. Describe each of the five critical factors involved in the prestart-up and start-up phases of a new venture.

6. Identify and discuss three examples of product/market problems that can cause a venture to fail.

7. Identify and discuss two examples of financial difficulties that can cause a venture to fail.

8. Identify and discuss two examples of managerial problems that can cause a venture to fail.

9. List four major types of problems new ventures confront.

10. Describe the proposed "failure prediction" model for newly founded firms.

11. How can asking the right questions help an entrepreneur evaluate a new venture? What types of questions are involved?

12. Explain how a feasibility criteria approach works.

13. Explain how a comprehensive feasibility approach works.

Experiential Exercise

Internal Profile Analysis

Choose any emerging company with which you are familiar. If you are not familiar with any, consult magazines such as *Entrepreneur, Fortune,* and *Business Week,* and gather information on one firm. Then complete the following internal profile analysis by placing a check mark (√) in the appropriate column.

INTERNAL RESOURCE	STRONG WEAKNESS	SLIGHT WEAKNESS	NEUTRAL	SLIGHT STRENGTH	STRONG STRENGTH
Financial					
Overall performance	_____	_____	_____	_____	_____
Ability to raise capital	_____	_____	_____	_____	_____
Working capital	_____	_____	_____	_____	_____
Position	_____	_____	_____	_____	_____
Marketing					
Market performance	_____	_____	_____	_____	_____
Knowledge of markets	_____	_____	_____	_____	_____
Product	_____	_____	_____	_____	_____
Advertising and promotion	_____	_____	_____	_____	_____
Price	_____	_____	_____	_____	_____
Distribution	_____	_____	_____	_____	_____
Organizational and Technical					
Location	_____	_____	_____	_____	_____
Production	_____	_____	_____	_____	_____
Facilities	_____	_____	_____	_____	_____
Access to suppliers	_____	_____	_____	_____	_____
Inventory control	_____	_____	_____	_____	_____
Quality control	_____	_____	_____	_____	_____
Organizational structure	_____	_____	_____	_____	_____
Rules, policies, and procedures	_____	_____	_____	_____	_____
Company image	_____	_____	_____	_____	_____
Human					
Number of employees	_____	_____	_____	_____	_____
Relevancy of skills	_____	_____	_____	_____	_____
Morale	_____	_____	_____	_____	_____
Compensation package	_____	_____	_____	_____	_____

Based on your analysis, what three recommendations would you make to the company's management?

1. _____

_____

2. _____

_____

3. _____

_____

Video Case 7.1

Assessing and Developing Entrepreneurial Opportunities
Wahoo's with Wing Lam, Ed Lee, Mingo Lee, and Steve Karfaridis

> We are a bunch of laid-back surfers at heart. . . . the key to our success is taking everybody's natural abilities and talents and inclinations and . . . keeping them on track. (Steve Karfaridis)

Wing Lam, Ed Lee, and Mingo Lee opened the first Wahoo's Fish Tacos in 1988 on the southern California coast where they love to surf and just hang out. The sons of Chinese immigrant restaurateurs, themselves born in Brazil, they didn't want to take over their parents' business, nor did they want to go to work in corporate America. But their parents told them it was time to start earning their own paychecks.

Talking over their knowledge of the restaurant business and their love of surfing among themselves and friends, the brothers came up with the idea of opening up little beach places that served simple, delicious surfer food. Wing explains how they made it happen: "Literally, the day before we opened, I actually sat in the kitchen and wrote things down, and tried a couple of things, and said, 'We're opening tomorrow.'"

Initially, they felt pretty comfortable in starting this new venture because of their background. Mingo explains: "We literally grew up over the restaurant. We lived on the third floor over our restaurant. From the day you're able to walk, you knew what was going on in the operation. We stood on Coke crates peeling shrimp and washing dishes."

Cooking tasty food was easy for them, but they also wanted to offer their customers a "great hangout place" that captured the feel of the surfer spots along the Baja coast. Their target customers, of course, were surfers, mostly males between 18 and 24 years old who, according to research from the National Restaurant Association, eat out 5.9 times a week. With good food served generously and at low prices, they had no trouble attracting a faithful clientele.

Their development plans also started out simply. Again, Mingo explains: "Initially, it was a single concept. We have three brothers, we can probably get ourselves up to three stores, and we each run our own store." As for operational plans, they followed their father's "old school methods . . . that you keep everything between the ears. And you just put it together."

As the opportunities to expand further appeared, the brothers realized that they needed some help and brought on a fourth partner, Steve Karfaridis, an old friend and an emigrant from Greece who also had a restaurant background. Steve was attracted to the brothers' concepts of serving fresh and uncomplicated food in simple and clean restaurants. He helped them keep their original vision and put various financial and operational plans in place, for example, an inventory control system and a computerized payroll. His goal was standardization of every aspect involved in the restaurants.

Together, the four of them have built a company that now has 300 employees in 22 locations, each generating over $1 million in revenue. In addition to the original tribe of surfboarders, they have targeted snowboarders (two of the restaurants are in Denver), skateboarders, and various other sports enthusiasts.

Now, each of the four partners is responsible for a particular aspect of the business that reflects their particular strengths. Mingo is CEO and handles all corporate finances.

Steve is the operations manager and handles the daily questions at the restaurant level. Ed works on development, finding new locations to expand, and Wing handles marketing and promotions.

Wing's marketing approach reflects the nature of a small business that prides itself on being part of the community. Instead of some expensive corporate marketing strategy, he gives "tons of food" away at various sporting events such as the U.S. Open of Surfing in Huntington Beach or the opening of the first rock climbing gym in Costa Mesa.

"If you go out there, and they sample your product, that's the cheapest way. Because once they taste it, they see it, they smell it, they touch it . . . they connect it to you. Everybody wants to support a local businessman. . . . they see you being a part of the community. . . . they want to support you back because you are supporting the community. The giving comes back tenfold," says Wing.

Another aspect of the business that the partners take pride in is their training program for managers. To keep good employees, they decided to let them take over leadership roles in the restaurants; they believe that these employees know all of the components involved and can bring an effective team together. "We needed to give them a place to grow," says Mingo, "so we basically created the Wahoo's farm system like a baseball team." When new managers are ready, they are sent off to open new units.

Although Wahoo's Fish Tacos has expanded enormously, its owners remain focused on their simple concept of providing simple, good food in comfortable, surfer-joint locations. And their customers keep coming in.

Questions

1. Although opening the first Wahoo's sounds simple enough, what knowledge about product, competition, customer base, location, and finance did the brothers bring to the business?

2. Discuss elements that make Wahoo's still successful and able to expand.

3. Discuss the entrepreneurial qualities of the partners that make them an effective management team.

Case 7.2

Nothing Unique to Offer

Over the past four months, George Vazquez has been putting together his plan for a new venture. George wants to open a pizzeria near the local university. The area has three pizza enterprises, but George is convinced demand is sufficient to support a fourth.

The major competitor is a large national franchise unit that, in addition to its regular food-service menu of pizzas, salads, soft drinks, and desserts, offers door-to-door delivery. This delivery service is very popular with the university students and has helped the franchise unit capture approximately 40 percent of the student market. The second competitor is a "pizza wagon" that carries precooked pizzas. The driver circles the university area and sells pizzas on a first-come, first-served basis. The pizza wagon starts the evening with 50 pizzas of all varieties and sizes and usually sells 45 of them at full price. The last 5 are sold for whatever they will bring. It generally takes the wagon all evening to sell the 50 pizzas, but the profit markup is much higher than that obtained from the typical pizza sales at the franchise unit.

The other competitor offers only in-house services, but it is well known for the quality of its food.

George does not believe it is possible to offer anything unique. However, he does believe that a combination of door-to-door delivery and high-quality, in-house service can help him win 15 to 20 percent of the local market. "Once the customers begin to realize that 'pizza is pizza,'" George told his partner, "we'll begin to get more business. After all, if there is no difference between one pizza place and another, they might just as well eat at our place."

Before finalizing his plans, George would like to bring in one more partner. "You can never have too much initial capital," he said. "You never know when you'll have unexpected expenses." But the individual whom George would like as a partner is reluctant to invest in the venture. "You really don't have anything unique to offer the market," he told George. "You're just another 'me too' pizzeria, and you're not going to survive." George hopes he will be able to change the potential investor's mind, but if he is not, George believes he can find someone else. "I have 90 days before I intend to open the business, and that's more than enough time to line up the third partner and get the venture under way," he told his wife yesterday.

Questions

1. Is there any truth to the potential investor's comment? Is the lack of uniqueness going to hurt George's chances of success? Explain.

2. If George were going to make his business venture unique, what steps might he take? Be complete in your answer.

3. In addition to the uniqueness feature, what other critical factors is George overlooking? Identify and describe three, and give your recommendations for what to do about them.

Case 7.3

A Product Design Problem

When Billie Aherne learned that the government was soliciting contracts for the manufacture of microcomputer components, she read the solicitation carefully. Billie's knowledge of microcomputers is extensive, and for the past five years she has been a university professor actively engaged in research in this area. If she could land this government contract, Billie felt certain she would be well on her way to going into business designing microcomputer components.

Billie asked for a leave of absence so she could bid on the microcomputer contract. She then worked up a detailed proposal and submitted it to the government. Eight months ago she learned she had been awarded the contract. For the next four months, Billie and two university colleagues who had joined her worked on completing their state-of-the-art components. When private firms learned of their contract, Billie was inundated with requests for components. She realized that as soon as she completed her government contract, she would be free to enter into contracts with private firms. Two months ago Billie shipped the components to the government. The next week she began signing contracts with firms in the private sector. In all, Billie signed agreements with six firms to provide each of them an average of $400,000 worth of components over the next four months. Last week the first shipment of components was delivered to one of the private firms.

In the mail earlier today Billie received a letter from the government. The communication informed her of quality problems with the components she had manufactured and shipped. Part of the letter read, "It took approximately four weeks of use before it became evident your components have a quality flaw. We believe the problem is in the basic design. We would like to meet with you at the earliest possible time to discuss your design and to agree on which steps must be taken in order for you to comply with the terms of your contract." Billie hoped to keep this news quiet until she could talk to the government representatives and find out what is going wrong. However, an hour ago she received a call from one of the private firms. "We hear that the microcomputer components you shipped to the government had a quality flaw," the speaker told Billie. "Could you tell us exactly what the problem is?"

Questions

1. What happened? What mistake did Billie make in terms of the new venture?

2. How could this problem have been prevented? Defend your answer.

3. What lesson about new-venture assessment does this case provide? Be complete in your answer.

Notes

1. William J. Dennis, *Business Starts and Stops* (Washington, D.C.: National Federation of Independent Business, November 1999); and Michael S. Malone, "The 200 Year Old U.S. Patent Office Is Beginning to Show Its Age," *Forbes* (June 24, 2002): 33–40.

2. Sue Birley and Paul Westhead, "A Taxonomy of Business Start-Up Reasons and Their Impact on Firm Growth and Size," *Journal of Business Venturing* (January 1994): 7–32.

3. Nancy M. Carter, William B. Gartner, and Paul D. Reynolds, "Exploring Start-Up Event Sequences," *Journal of Business Venturing* (May 1996): 151–166.

4. Robert N. Lussier, "A Nonfinancial Business Success versus Failure Prediction Model for Young Firms," *Journal of Small Business Management* (January 1995): 8–20.

5. Frédéric Delmar and Scott Shane, "Legitimating First: Organizing Activities and the Survival of New Ventures," *Journal of Business Venturing* 19(3) (May 2004): 385–410.

6. Arnold C. Cooper, "Challenges in Predicting New Firm Performance," *Journal of Business Venturing* (May 1993): 241–253.

7. Candida G. Brush and Pieter A. Vanderwerf, "A Comparison of Methods and Sources for Obtaining Estimates of New Venture Performance," *Journal of Business Venturing* (March 1992): 157–170; see also Gaylen N. Chandler and Steven H. Hanks, "Measuring the Performance of Emerging Businesses: A Validation Study," *Journal of Business Venturing* (September 1993): 391–408; and Scott L. Newbert, "New Firm Formation: A Dynamic Capability," *Journal of Small Business Management* 43(1) (January 2005): 55–77.

8. Paul Reynolds and Brenda Miller, "New Firm Gestation: Conception, Birth, and Implications for Research," *Journal of Business Venturing* (September 1992): 405–417.

9. Bhaskar Chakravorti, "The New Rules for Bringing Innovations to the Market," *Harvard Business Review* (March 2004): 58–67.

10. Theodore Levitt, "Marketing Myopia," *Harvard Business Review* (July/August 1960): 45–56.

11. Robert C. Ronstadt, *Entrepreneurship* (Dover, MA: Lord Publishing, 1984), 74.

12. Adapted from Ronstadt, *Entrepreneurship*, 75.

13. Ibid., 79.

14. Albert V. Bruno, Joel K. Leidecker, and Joseph W. Harder, "Why Firms Fail," *Business Horizons* (March/April 1987): 50–58. For more recent comparisons, see Fahri Karakaya and Bulent Kobu, "New Product Development Process: An Investigation of Success and Failure in High Technology and Non-High Technology Firms," *Journal of Business Venturing* (January 1994): 49–66; and Timothy Bates, "Analysis of Young, Small Firms that have Closed: Delineating Successful from Unsuccessful Closures," *Journal of Business Venturing* 20(3) (May 2005): 343–358.

15. David E. Terpstra and Philip D. Olson, "Entrepreneurial Start-up and Growth: A Classification of Problems," *Entrepreneurship Theory and Practice* (spring 1993): 5–20.

16. H. Robert Dodge, Sam Fullerton, and John E. Robbins, "Stage of the Organizational Life Cycle and Competition as Mediators of Problem Perception for Small Businesses," *Strategic Management Journal* 15 (1994): 121–134.

17. Andrew L. Zacharakis, G. Dale Meyer, and Julio DeCastro, "Differing Perceptions of New Venture Failure: A Matched Exploratory Study of Venture Capitalists and Entrepreneurs," *Journal of Small Business Management* (July 1999): 1–14.

18. Erkki K. Laitinen, "Prediction of Failure of a Newly Founded Firm," *Journal of Business Venturing* (July 1992): 323–340.

19. John G. Burch, *Entrepreneurship* (New York: John Wiley & Sons, 1986), 68–69.

20. Gordon B. Baty, *Entrepreneurship: Playing to Win* (Reston, VA: Reston Publishing, 1974), 33–34.

21. Hans Schollhammer and Arthur H. Kuriloff, *Entrepreneurship and Small Business Management* (New York: John Wiley & Sons, 1979), 58; see also Kwaku Atuahene-Gima and Haiyang Li, "Strategic Decision Comprehensiveness and New Product Development Outcomes in New Technology Ventures," *The Academy of Management Journal* 47(4) (August 2004): 583–597.

22. Gerald E. Hills, "Marketing Analysis in the Business Plan: Venture Capitalists' Perceptions," *Journal of Small Business Management* (January 1985): 38–46; see also Frans J. H. M. Verhees and Matthew T. G. Meulenberg, "Market Orientation, Innovativeness, Product Innovation, and Performance in Small Firms," *Journal of Small Business Management* 42(2) (April 2004): 134–154.

Appendix 7A

Feasibility Plan Outline

This outline provides the needed aspects of a complete feasibility plan. Each section has some of the key material that needs to be included. Following this outline will help the entrepreneur recognize the actual feasibility of the proposed venture as well as the areas that need to be further developed before the concept could ever be considered for potential funding.

Title Page

Name of proposed company: _____

Names and titles of the founding team members:

_____

_____

_____

_____

_____

Relevant contact information (name, title, address, phone, email):

_____

_____

_____

_____

_____

Table of Contents

Make sure all of the contents in the feasibility plan have page numbers and are listed carefully in the table of contents.

The Sections of a Feasibility Plan

Executive Summary

Explanation: Include the most important highlights from each section of the feasibility study. Be sure to include a clear and concise description of the venture, whatever proprietary aspects it may possess, the target market, the amount of financing needed, and the type of financing that is being requested.

_____

_____

_____

_____

_____

_____

The Business Concept

Explanation: Using the following directions, articulate a compelling story for why this is an excellent concept. This section allows the reader to understand what concept is being proposed and why it has true potential in the marketplace. It also provides an opportunity for the entrepreneur to prove that he or she can articulate this concept in clear and comprehensible terms to people outside their circle of friends and close associates.

Key Concepts

Describe whether the proposed concept is a retail, wholesale, manufacturing, or service business. Identify the current stage of development for the venture (concept stage, start-up, initial operations, or expansion).

_____

_____

_____

_____

Include a clear description of the targeted customer, the value proposition (in terms of benefits gained) for that customer, and what the potential growth opportunities.

_____

_____

_____

_____

Summarize any proprietary rights associated with this concept whether that be patents, copyrights, licenses, royalties, distribution rights, or franchise agreements.

▪ Industry/Market Analysis

Explanation: The industry/market analysis is critical. Is there a market for the product or service resulting from the venture? What are the current trends in this industry? What are the predicted trends for this industry? Can any of this be substantiated? The market for the product/service may be so obvious, yet the feasibility analysis must validate its existence. In the venture feasibility analysis, it may enough to prove that a sufficient market exists for the venture and, therefore, further in depth research is warranted. However, entrepreneurs should always study their competitors in their marketplace. Lessons learned from competitors provide opportunities for entrepreneurs to find the real unique distinctions in their own concept.

Key Concepts

Explain the industry that this concept is focusing on as well as whatever trends may exist in that particular industry today.

Discuss the target market analysis that has been used and what specific market niche that has produced. In addition, identify the market size, its growth potential, and your plan for market penetration based on research.

Explain the customer profile in terms of who the specific customer is and again what value proposition (in terms of benefits) is being offered the customer.

Finally, be sure to include a competitor analysis that describes thoroughly the competition existing today and how specifically your concept will match up or exceed the competition and why.

_____

_____

_____

_____

Management Team

Explanation: Keep in mind that all new ventures must stand the scrutiny of whether the founding team can really move this idea to market. The experience of the management team may end up being one of the most critical factors to outside investors. Many times venture capitalists have expressed their belief that they prefer a "B" idea with an "A" team as opposed to an "A" idea with a "B" team. In other words there is a real concern as to the implementation phase of a proposed concept. Does this founding team have the background, experience, skills, and networks to make the concept operationally successfully?

Key Concepts

Identify the founding team members and the key personnel in place to guide the proposed company.

_____

_____

_____

_____

Explain the team's qualifications and how the critical tasks are being assigned. Also include any board of directors/advisors that are in place.

_____

_____

_____

_____

Finally, outline any "gaps" in the management team (in terms of skills and abilities) and explain how those will be addressed.

_____

_____

_____

Product/Service Development Analysis

Explanation: Before going any further with a conceptual idea, the entrepreneur must determine if the concept has any practical feasibility. One of the most important questions in this section of the feasibility analysis would be: "What unique features distinguish your product/service?" The more unique features of a product or service, the better chance the business concept has of being successful.

Key Concepts

Provide a detailed description of the proposed concept including any unique features that make it distinctive.

_____

_____

_____

_____

Explain the current status of the project with a clear timeline of the key tasks to complete.

_____

_____

_____

_____

Identify any intellectual property involved with this potential venture, and discuss the proprietary protection that exists. Any proposed or completed prototype testing should be described here as well.

_____

_____

_____

_____

Finally identify any anticipated critical risks in terms of potential product liability, governmental regulations, or raw material issues that may hinder this project at any stage.

_____

_____

_____

Financial Analysis

Explanation: Summarize the critical assumptions upon which the financial information is Based; in other words, show how the numbers have been derived. A pro forma income statement and a statement of cash flows are the two most critical financial documents to add here—even though they may include preliminary outside sources needed to get some idea of the generation of revenue and the cash position of the venture during the first three years. If possible, provide a break even analysis to demonstrate where the venture moves from survival to growth.

Key Concepts

Assumptions:

_____

_____

_____

Pro Forma Income Statement:

_____

_____

_____

Pro Forma Cash Flow Statement:

_____

_____

_____

Break Even Analysis:

_____

_____

_____

_____

Timeline

Explanation: Use a graphic representation of the dates and the related tasks in order of their completion until actual concept launch.

_____

_____

_____

_____

Bibliography

Explanation: Provide any key endnotes, footnotes, sources, or extra information that would be critical for a funding source to see in relation to the work you performed in creating this feasibility study.

_____

_____

_____

8 Environmental Assessment of Entrepreneurial Ventures

Most firms face external environments that are growing more turbulent, complex, and global—conditions that make interpretation increasingly difficult. To cope with what are often ambiguous and incomplete environmental data and to increase their understanding of the general environment, successful firms engage in a process called external environmental analysis.

Michael A. Hitt, R. Duane Ireland, and Robert E. Hoskisson

Strategic Management: Competitiveness and Globalization

Chapter Objectives

1 *To examine some of the major ways of assessing the economic environment*

2 *To review the regulatory environment within which a new venture must exist*

3 *To examine the industry environment from a competitive market analysis and strategic point of view*

4 *To present the community environmental perspective to ensure an understanding of the local impact*

5 *To examine community support in terms of reliance and deservedness*

6 *To review the nature of business incubators and their importance to emerging ventures*

Sustainable Competitive Advantage

True competitiveness requires every entrepreneur to prepare his or her potential venture in light of all the forces surrounding it. Therefore an entrepreneur must formulate and eventually implement a value-creating strategy. This value must be determined in consideration of the external environment in which the new venture will exist. In order for any new venture to survive it must pursue a course that leads to a **sustainable competitive advantage.** This is when a venture has implemented a strategy that other companies simply cannot duplicate or find it too costly to compete with that particular element. However, every sustainable competitive advantage can only be maintained for a certain amount of time depending upon the speed with which competitors are able to duplicate or substitute. While it is dynamic in nature, the pursuit of a sustainable competitive advantage is a full complement of commitments, decisions, and actions by the entrepreneur. As we saw in Chapter 7, the initial assessment of the proposed venture is critical. The specifics of strategic planning will be covered in Chapter 15; however, at this point we begin the external assessment process of examining the environment.

The Environment for New Ventures

Many ways of making an **environmental assessment** for a new venture exist.[1] In the main, however, these approaches are neither highly sophisticated nor heavily quantitative. Being neither an economist nor a quantitative analyst, the average new-venture entrepreneur will stay within the confines of what he or she can understand and use for conducting this assessment. This often entails evaluating the general economic environment and determining which governmental regulations, both national and local, will impact the venture. A more detailed evaluation of the industry is then made, with primary consideration given to such areas as common industry characteristics, barriers to entry, and competitive analysis. The overall economic method of analysis moves from general considerations to specific considerations.

The last part of the analysis focuses on the community perspective—that is, local conditions. The entrepreneur will examine location factors, the fit between the business and the local environment, and, if the situation warrants, the use of a business incubator. Throughout the analysis the entrepreneur will concentrate on gathering practical and useful information that will help answer the question: What do I need to know in getting ready for this new venture?

Environmental Scanning

Environmental scanning refers to the efforts by which an owner-entrepreneur examines the external and internal environments before making a decision.[2]

As shown in Figure 8.1, a new venture's external environment is divided into three major areas: the general, industry, and competitor environments. The general environment is composed of elements in the broader society that influence an

Figure 8.1 The External Environment

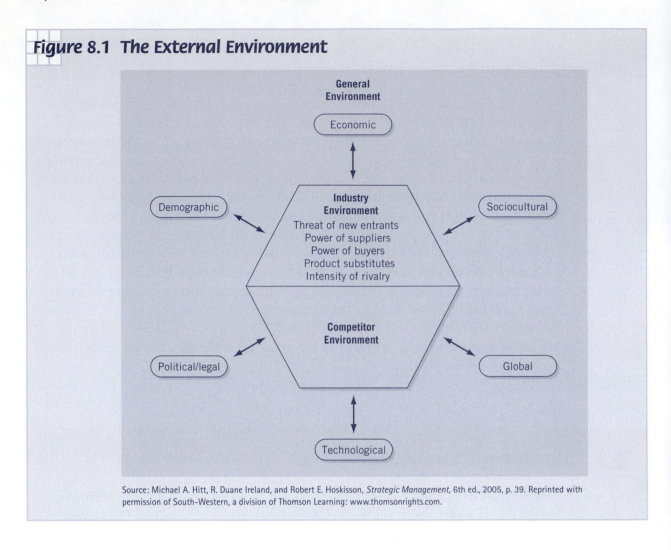

Source: Michael A. Hitt, R. Duane Ireland, and Robert E. Hoskisson, *Strategic Management*, 6th ed., 2005, p. 39. Reprinted with permission of South-Western, a division of Thomson Learning: www.thomsonrights.com.

industry and the firms within it. These are grouped into six environmental segments: demographic, economic, political/legal, sociocultural, technological, and global. Examples of elements analyzed in each of these segments are presented in Table 8.1.

New ventures cannot directly control the general environment's segments and elements so gathering information required for understanding each segment is necessary. A new venture will have very little individual effect on the U.S. economy, yet the economy will have a major effect on the venture's ability to operate or even survive. Thus, learning as much as possible about the general environment before launching the venture may be a substantial benefit to the entrepreneur.

The industry environment is a set of factors that directly influences a new venture's competitive actions and responses: the threat of new entrants, the power of suppliers, the power of buyers, the threat of product substitutes, and the intensity of rivalry among competitors. Working together, the interactions of these factors determines an industry's profit potential. More will be covered on this as we look at the macro view and assess the industry. The challenge for an entrepreneur is to find a position within an industry where it can favorably influence one or more of those factors and successfully defend against their influence.

The competitor environment is how a new venture's competitors are positioned within the industry. Exactly how new ventures gather and interpret information about

Table 8.1   The Environmental Variables

Demographic Segment	☐ Population size	☐ Ethnic mix
	☐ Age structure	☐ Income distribution
	☐ Geographic distribution	
Economic Segment	☐ Inflation rates	☐ Personal savings rate
	☐ Interest rates	☐ Business savings rates
	☐ Trade deficits or surpluses	☐ Gross domestic product
	☐ Budget deficits or surpluses	
Political/Legal Segment	☐ Antitrust laws	☐ Labor training laws
	☐ Taxation laws	☐ Educational philosophies and policies
	☐ Deregulation philosophies	
Sociocultural Segment	☐ Women in the workforce	☐ Concerns about the environment
	☐ Workforce diversity	☐ Shifts in work and career preferences
	☐ Attitudes about quality of work life	☐ Shifts in preferences regarding product and service characteristics
Technological Segment	☐ Product innovations	☐ Focus of private and government-supported R&D expenditures
	☐ Process innovations	
	☐ Applications of knowledge	☐ New communication technologies
Global Segment	☐ Important political events	☐ Newly industrialized countries
	☐ Critical global markets	☐ Different cultural and institutional attributes

Source: Michael A. Hitt, R. Duane Ireland, and Robert E. Hoskisson, *Strategic Management*, 6th ed., 2005, p. 40. Reprinted with permission of South-Western, a division of Thomson Learning: www.thomsonrights.com.

their potential competitors is referred to as competitor analysis. Understanding a new venture's competitive environment complements the insights gained by analyzing the general and industry environments.

In combination, the results of the three analyses help an entrepreneur establish his or her strategic course of action in seeking that sustainable competitive advantage.[3] The research usually begins with a general macro view of the economic and industry environments.

A Macro View: The Economic and Industry Environments

Two major areas of the macro view warrant consideration: (1) the overall economic environment and (2) the specific industry environment.

Assessing the Economic Environment

The economic environment plays a vital role in the success or failure of any new venture. Too often it becomes obvious that an entrepreneur made little effort to determine whether the economic environment was friendly or hostile to his or her specific venture.[4] Additionally, entrepreneurs often commit funds to a business without adequate preliminary investigation. An assessment of the economic environment can help them avoid these pitfalls. Some of the most important questions to be answered follow: What is the current state of the economy? What is the condition of the labor market? Are the interest rates rising or stable? How many firms are in this industry? Do the firms vary in size and general characteristics, or are they all similar? What is the geographic concentration of firms in the industry; that is, are they in one area, or are they widely dispersed? Do the firms serve only the domestic market? Do opportunities to serve foreign markets exist as well? What federal, state, and local government regulations affect this type of business? What is the competitive nature of this business?

Answers to these questions provide an overall picture of the business climate within which a new venture will operate. In addition, entrepreneurs with emerging new ventures must realize that certain attitudes and skills are needed for proper assessment of the environment. The following are the most important, presented from a management point of view:

☐ A broadened awareness of influences in the external environment that affect the corporation and management decision making

☐ The ability to integrate traditional business concerns about influences from the external environment into a comprehensive decision-making framework based on a holistic view of business and its relationship to the larger society in which it functions

☐ Political skills (compromise, negotiation) to resolve the conflicting interests among different constituencies that have diverse values and objectives

☐ Communication skills to articulate a business position on a very complex public issue and to persuade people that this position has merit and deserves serious consideration

☐ Intellectual skills to analyze and understand complex public issues—the ability to think clearly about these issues and exchange ideas with the various business publics[5]

Understanding the Regulatory Environment

A business must comply with governmental rules and regulations. Costs and profits can be affected as much by a government directive as by a management decision from the front office or a customer decision at the checkout counter. Fundamental entrepreneurial decisions—such as what lines of business to go into, what products and services to produce, which investments to finance, how and where to make goods and how to market them, and what prices to charge—are increasingly subject to governmental control.[6]

The government (both federal and state) has increasingly become a partner to business in America. Although everyone tends to focus on the size of the federal government, the realm of state and local governments in the United States is also huge. There are 50 state governments plus more than 39,000 "all-purpose" governments (cities, counties, and towns) and another 45,000 jurisdictions with some governmental responsibilities (districts); together, these governments employ more than 11 million Americans. From 1970 to 1995, grants from the federal government to the state and local level increased from $24 billion to $228 billion.[7] Therefore, understanding and communicating with government is not only a key to success, but in the case of entrepreneurial ventures, may be essential for survival.

To deal with this greater role of government, a coalition to advocate the interests of small firms and new ventures has emerged. In addition, a network of state commerce departments, trade and professional associations, the National Chamber of Commerce, the Small Business Administration (SBA), and certain universities is developing a stronger voice for the entrepreneur.

Over the past few decades many legislators focused their attention on big business and expected little firms to fall into line. Although some aid and benefits were provided to small-business entrepreneurs, most governmental efforts were directed at regulation. In the process, the small firm became saddled with the same amount of regulatory red tape as the giant corporation. Today it appears the tide has turned. Over the years there has been a significant shift in the attitudes and actions of legislators. A number of reasons can be cited for this shift: an awareness of the need to strengthen the small-business sector of the economy; an effort by Washington to increase national employment by promoting small-business interests; and the growth of foreign multinationals in the United States, which unleashed a renewed pride in the country's innovative and entrepreneurial spirit.

Despite conflicting theories and policies, everyone agrees on one thesis: If small businesses are to survive successfully as an American institution, there needs to be continual review of the regulatory policies and their unfair impact on smaller firms.[8] Governmental regulation is one of the most discernible influences on businesses today. Since it encompasses so many regulatory acts and agencies, this aspect of the environment is the first new ventures must consider (see Figure 8.2).

Although the ways in which public policy affects America's business environment are being continually explored, the differential effect of public policy issues on smaller businesses today is becoming increasingly important as the nation looks to the entrepreneurial sector for economic growth and job creation.[9] After two decades of economic revitalization (due to the successful birth, growth, and development of entrepreneurial ventures), we are now entering an era characterized by new regulations, taxes, and policies that will affect smaller firms. As new legislation is adopted, the government is beginning to establish new "ground rules" by which smaller businesses must attempt to prosper in a world of regulatory compliance.

Over the past 25 years, government regulation of business has increased at a rapid rate. For example, approximately 210,000 legislative bills are introduced in state legislatures in a typical two-year cycle, many of which will affect smaller firms in some way. Until recently, the burden on a smaller business, in terms of the impact compliance, was never considered. Instead, what was demanded from the larger corporate sector was simply expected from small businesses in the same industry. The following quote by George McGovern, a former U.S. Senator turned entrepreneur, may

Figure 8.2 Impact of Regulatory Agencies on the Typical Business

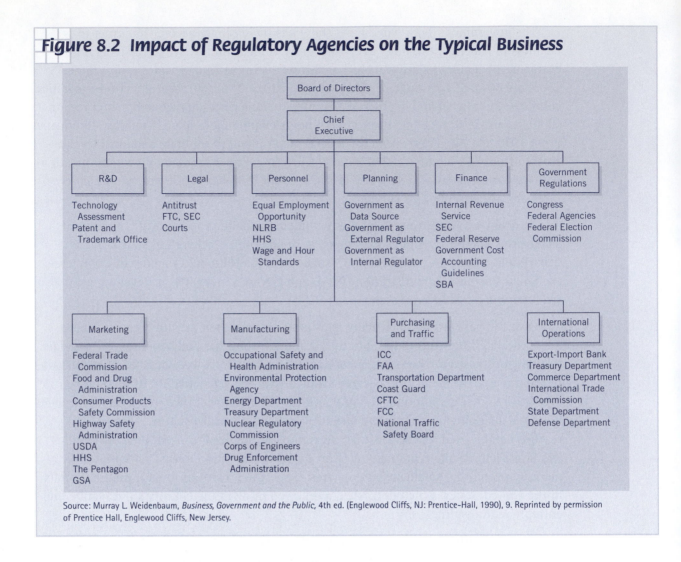

Source: Murray L. Weidenbaum, *Business, Government and the Public,* 4th ed. (Englewood Cliffs, NJ: Prentice-Hall, 1990), 9. Reprinted by permission of Prentice Hall, Englewood Cliffs, New Jersey.

capture the feelings of many owner-entrepreneurs concerning the role of government regulations in the operations of their firms:

> In retrospect, I wish I had known more about the hazards and difficulties of business. . . . I wish that during the years I was in public office I had first-hand experience about the difficulties businesspeople face every day. That knowledge would have made me a better senator. . . . To create job opportunities we need entrepreneurs who will risk their capital against an expected payoff. Too often, however, public policy does not consider whether we are choking off those opportunities.[10]

This feeling is supported by the following statistics: the Code of Federal Regulations has 65,000 pages of new and modified regulations each year; 52 federal agencies employ more than 122,000 workers to administer 5,000 regulations; the federal regulatory cost for these agencies fell from $443 billion in 1997 to $397 billion by 2001, but recent increases in government activity have brought that figure back to more than $800 billion.[11]

Governmental regulations affect smaller ventures in a variety of ways:

- ☐ *Prices:* Small businesses are often forced to raise their prices to absorb the costs of regulatory compliance.

- ☐ *Cost inequities:* Financially, small companies feel the brunt of regulatory burdens more than large corporations.

- □ *Competitive restriction:* Putting a greater burden on small business tends to favor big business, thereby subtly encouraging large companies while discouraging small ones.

- □ *Managerial restriction:* Due to time devoted to paperwork-imposed duties, the small-business person must sacrifice valuable managerial time in complying with governmental regulations.

- □ *Mental burden:* Postponed projects, wasted time, and managerial failure due to lack of time and energy all begin to take their toll on the small-business person. Frustration leading to depression may spell failure for the business.

Smaller firms (fewer than 20 employees) face an annual regulatory burden of $6,975 per employee, a burden nearly 60 percent above that facing a firm employing over 500 employees.[12] Public policy experts agree that one of the most serious consequences of federal regulation of business is the threat to the continued existence of the small firm.[13] Regulatory burdens may surface not only in compliance costs but also in the paperwork burden that becomes the ancillary aspect of governmental policies:

> The small firm, unlike its large firm counterpart, does not have a professional staff to respond to heavy paperwork and reporting requirements. Often the owner/entrepreneur is the only individual with sufficient knowledge to respond to an agency's requirement for information. Reporting costs, like the other more severe burdens of federal regulation, are not proportioned to the size of the firm.[14]

Some outside observers have suggested that small businesses simply ignore governmental compliance orders. The penalties for such actions are stiff, however, and the consequences are serious. Noncompliance can result in the failure of the entire venture.[15] A more reasonable approach is for entrepreneurs to turn to the public sector and demand assistance with easing the regulatory burden. This is now being done. Figure 8.3 illustrates an entrepreneur's contingency decision model for identifying and assessing key issues affecting the venture.

Trends in Policy Formation

The political influence of entrepreneurs has been steadily growing over the past 25 years. Indeed, it appears to be the growing trend in the political structure today. Any regulator or congressperson who ignores this group does so at personal peril. As a result, regulatory reform legislation has established milestone laws that offer small businesses some objective considerations. Several of these acts are highlighted next.

The Regulatory Flexibility Act   The Regulatory Flexibility Act (Reg. Flex), enacted in 1982, recognized that the size of a business has a bearing on its ability to comply with federal regulation. The law puts the burden of review on the government to ensure that legislation does not unfairly affect small business. According to the SBA, the major goals of this act are (1) to increase agency awareness and understanding of the impact of agency regulations on small business, (2) to require that agencies communicate and explain their findings to the public, and (3) to encourage agencies to provide regulatory relief to small entities. The chief council for advocacy is the Small Business Administration, which monitors the agencies for compliance.

The Equal Access to Justice Act   The Equal Access to Justice Act (Equal Access), also enacted in 1982, provides greater equity between small businesses and regulatory bodies. According to this act, if a small business challenges a regulatory agency and

Figure 8.3 An Entrepreneur's Contingency Decision Model for Public Policy

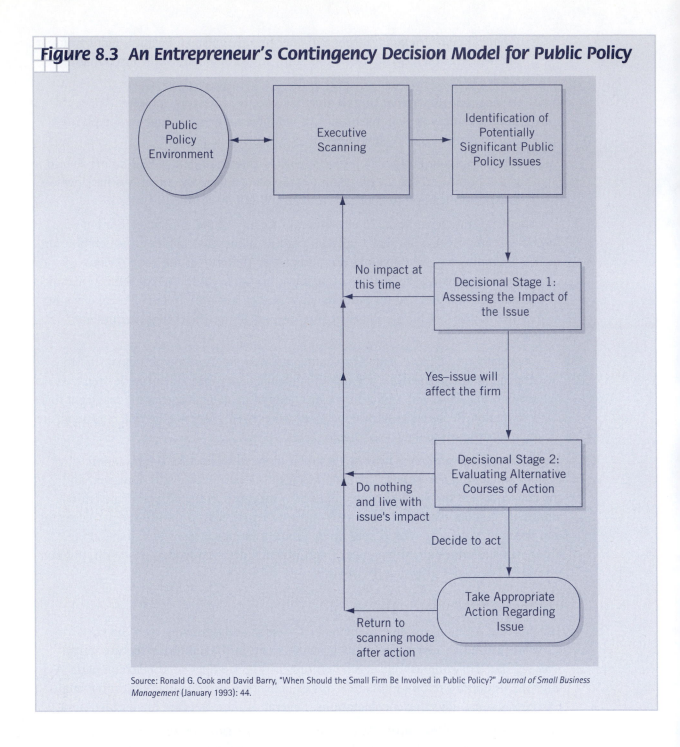

Source: Ronald G. Cook and David Barry, "When Should the Small Firm Be Involved in Public Policy?" *Journal of Small Business Management* (January 1993): 44.

wins, the regulatory agency must pay the legal costs of the small business. Equal Access has five stipulations that help ensure equal justice for small business: (1) The government or the small business may initiate litigation; (2) bad faith by the governmental agency does *not* have to be proven; (3) substantially justified actions must be demonstrated by the agency; (4) to receive an award, the business does not have to prevail on all issues; and (5) no dollar limit to the awards exists.

The Congressional Review Act   Enacted in 1997, the **Congressional Review Act** requires agencies to send their final regulations to Congress for review 60 days before they take effect. This mandatory review enables Congress to make the final decision on the need for specific regulations and makes agencies more sensitive to congressional intent. Congress can kill a regulation if (1) it passes a joint resolution of disapproval within the review period and the president signs it, or (2) the president vetoes the resolution and Congress overrides the veto.

The Small Business Regulatory Enforcement Fairness Act   Enacted in 1996, the Small Business Regulatory Enforcement Fairness Act eases regulatory costs and burdens on small business. It requires agencies issuing regulations and the SBA to assist small-business operators in understanding and complying with the rules. Agencies are authorized to reduce or waive civil penalties for violations of statutory or regulatory requirements. Under certain circumstances, attorney fees and court costs may be awarded for unreasonable actions brought against small entities by federal agencies.

The Paperwork Reduction Act   This act, which was enacted in 1995, required modest reductions annually for six years in paperwork burdens imposed by federal government agencies.

The Unfunded Mandates Reform Act   Enacted in 1995, the Unfunded Mandates Reform Act requires Congress and federal agencies to consider the actual costs of new federal mandates. Agencies must prepare cost-benefit and other analyses, unless prohibited by law, for any rule that will likely result in costs of $100 million or more in any year.[16]

The government must seek the appropriate balance between regulation and freedom. As one SBA official stated, "By mitigating the impact of government regulation on small business, the viability of small business will be determined in the marketplace, not in a federal office building."[17] That is, we must begin to focus on measuring and improving the "quality of business life" for tomorrow's microenterprises. "Looking ahead, our nation's economic destiny will not be determined solely by management. Much of U.S. industry is locked into a global competitive struggle, which is intensifying daily. To succeed, U.S. industry must enjoy a competitive quality of business life. To a major extent that quality is dependent upon national, state, and local government policy toward business."[18]

Other Significant Public Policy Developments

During the past 25 years, the U.S. government has been grappling with some of the major policy issues of our lifetime. Trade, taxes, regulations, the environment, job training, immigration, and health care reform are among the issues on which governmental decisions will affect U.S. businesses.

In 1980 the White House inaugurated a special small-business conference, which eventually led to a breakfast series that began in November 1982. The major objective of these meetings was to analyze the unique problems confronting small businesses. These meetings included entrepreneurs, small-business people, and small-business lobbyists, brought together by the administration to begin formulating entrepreneurial policy. In 1986 another White House conference convened to reassess the policies of the previous five years and to make recommendations for future policy decisions. These conferences have been successful because they have encouraged an informal exchange of ideas *before* overall policy was officially decided. In June 1995 the third White House Conference on Small Business revisited the concerns of small firms.[19] The results of that conference were significant as numerous recommendations were implemented by the government. Table 8.2 provides a listing of the legislation that occurred as a direct result of the White House conference.

Table 8.2 Legislation Implementing Recommendations of the 1995 White House Conference on Small Business

1999

☐ American Inventors Protection Act

☐ SBIC Technical Corrections Act

☐ Small Business Year 2000 Readiness Act

1998

☐ Internal Revenue Service Restructuring and Reform Act

☐ Department of Defense Reform Act

☐ Federal Activities Inventory Reform Act

☐ Omnibus Budget Reconciliation Act

☐ Paperwork Reduction Act Amendments

1997

☐ Balanced Budget Act

☐ Taxpayer Relief Act

☐ HUBZone Act

1996

☐ Small Business Regulatory Enforcement Fairness Act

☐ Small Business Job Protection Act

☐ Health Insurance Portability and Accountability Act

☐ Economic Growth and Regulatory Paperwork Reduction Act

☐ Telecommunications Act

☐ Federal Acquisition Reform Act

☐ National Securities Markets Improvement Act

☐ Small Business Programs Improvement Act

1995

☐ Small Business Lending Enhancement Act

Source: *Building the Foundation for a New Century: Final Report on the Implementation of the Recommendations of the 1995 White House Conference on Small Business* (Washington, DC: U.S. Small Business Administration, 2000).

These conferences and meetings have created an atmosphere of respect and understanding for the entrepreneur/small-business person in all future federal and state policies. Certainly, they have been a step in the right direction.

Examining the Industry Environment

Noted strategic consultant Michael E. Porter has suggested that at its root, environmental assessment involves asking two critical questions. First, what is the structure of your industry, and how is it likely to evolve over time? If the business the entrepreneur is in

Location, Location, Location

Every year, Dun & Bradstreet and *Entrepreneur* magazine, in a collaborative effort, assess the nation's most favorable homes for entrepreneurs. It goes without saying that location is a major factor in a business's success. Scenery, availability of labor, new markets, economies of scale, and quality of life, among other things, all affect the decision to enter into business or relocate a growing firm in any given city. Experts recommend that entrepreneurs do their homework and visit a potential site before taking any actions. Thorough planning is also essential to ensure the most cost-effective move.

The following ranks the top cities in each region, based on four criteria: (1) entrepreneurial activity—*number of businesses less than five years old;* (2) small-business growth—*significant employment growth in one year;* (3) job growth—*changes in nonagricultural job growth and business incorporations;* and (4) risk—*the probability of a company becoming insolvent within two years.*

Entrepreneur and D&B's Best Cities for Entrepreneurs

1. Minneapolis/St. Paul MN/WI
2. Washington, DC, MD/VA/WV
3. Atlanta, GA
4. Fort Lauderdale, FL
5. Salt Lake City/Ogden, UT
6. West Palm Beach/Boca Raton, FL
7. Norfolk/Virginia Beach/Newport News, VA/NC
8. Miami, FL
9. Charlotte/Gastonia/Rock Hill, NC/SC
10. Orlando, FL

Best Bets for . . .

Entrepreneurial Activity

1. Las Vegas, NV/AZ
2. Atlanta, GA
3. Orlando, FL
4. Austin/San Marcos, TX
5. Phoenix/Mesa/AZ

Small-Business Growth

1. Louisville, KY/IN
2. Indianapolis, IN
3. Minneapolis/St. Paul, MN/WI
4. Salt Lake City/Ogden, UT
5. Kansas City, MO/KS

Job Growth

1. Las Vegas, NV/AZ
2. West Palm Beach/Boca Raton, FL
3. Phoenix/Mesa, AZ
4. Riverside/San Bernardino, CA
5. Providence/Fall River/Warwick, RI

Risk

1. Nassau/Suffolk, NY
2. Bergen/Passaic, NJ
3. Hartford, CT
4. New York City, NY
5. Washington, DC/MD/VA/WV

Although they were not considered in this evaluation, other attributes are also important when determining a city's attitude toward small business:

- ☐ *Business performance* includes company failure rates and payment delinquencies.
- ☐ *Quality of life* is based on per capita income and cost-of-living data.
- ☐ *The state's attitude toward small business* is revealed in the Corporation for Economic Development's annual Development Report Card for the states. It measures economic performance, business vitality, and development capacity. State-sponsored small-business support programs should also be considered.

SOURCE: "Hot Cities for Entrepreneurs," http://www.entrepreneur.com/bestcities, 2005.

Figure 8.4 Elements of Industry—The Five Forces Model

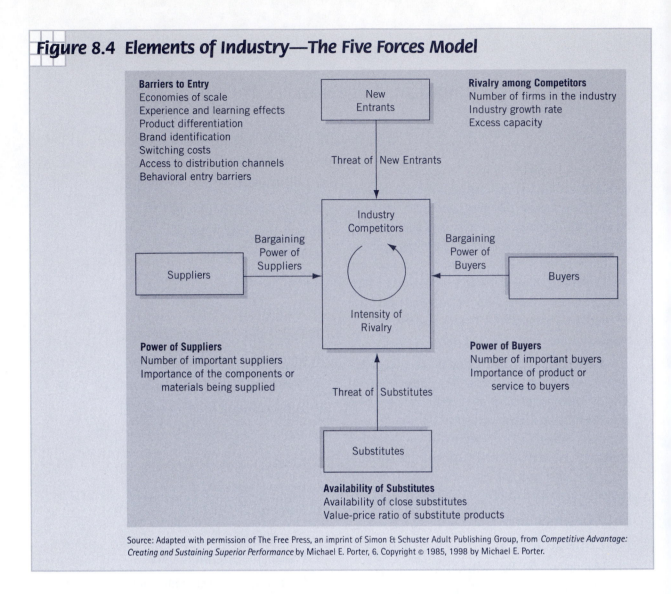

Barriers to Entry
Economies of scale
Experience and learning effects
Product differentiation
Brand identification
Switching costs
Access to distribution channels
Behavioral entry barriers

Rivalry among Competitors
Number of firms in the industry
Industry growth rate
Excess capacity

New Entrants

Threat of New Entrants

Industry Competitors

Bargaining Power of Suppliers

Bargaining Power of Buyers

Suppliers

Buyers

Intensity of Rivalry

Power of Suppliers
Number of important suppliers
Importance of the components or
    materials being supplied

Power of Buyers
Number of important buyers
Importance of product or
    service to buyers

Threat of Substitutes

Substitutes

Availability of Substitutes
Availability of close substitutes
Value-price ratio of substitute products

Source: Adapted with permission of The Free Press, an imprint of Simon & Schuster Adult Publishing Group, from *Competitive Advantage: Creating and Sustaining Superior Performance* by Michael E. Porter, 6. Copyright © 1985, 1998 by Michael E. Porter.

is not very attractive—and we will soon show how to measure its attractiveness—then the person may want to get out of it or redefine it.

Second, what is the company's relative position in the industry? No matter how attractive the game is, an entrepreneur will not do well if his or her company does not hold a good position in it. Conversely, the business can be in a lackluster industry with low-average profitability, yet if it occupies exactly the right niche, it can perform very well.

"Most small companies, of course, cannot change an industry's structure. What they can do, however, is establish a good position in the industry, a position based on sustainable competitive advantage," Porter says.[20]

Evaluation of the industry environment is the second critical step in the overall economic assessment of a new venture. A number of major elements of industry structure exist, as depicted in Figure 8.4.[21] As Figure 8.5 illustrates, the process of assessing the entire industry structure is detailed and comprehensive.[22] For our purposes here, however, we shall examine only those segments of which entrepreneurs need to be aware.

Common Industry Characteristics

Although industries vary in size and development, certain characteristics are common to new and emerging industries. The most important of these are discussed next.

Figure 8.5 Guide to Using the Five Forces Model for Industry Analysis

New Entrants

a. What are the barriers to entry? Are we able to raise them? What factors are tending to lower them?
b. What firms are potential or imminent new entrants? What are their characteristics (size, number, growth, customer base, and so on)?
c. What are the entrants' competitive strategies likely to be? How might the new entrants and their strategies reshape the industry?
d. When will they enter our market(s)?

Suppliers

a. What firms are suppliers, and how large or concentrated are they?
b. How concentrated is our industry (their buyers) relative to them? That is, how many of us buy what percent of the output?
c. Can firms in the industry switch suppliers easily?
d. What percent of their total output is purchased by our industry? How large are the quantities?
e. How important is their product or service to the quality of ours?
f. How much of our cost does their product or service represent?
g. What is the threat of forward integration by each supplier? (Conversely, what is the opportunity for backward integration by one or more of us?)
h. What is their relative bargaining power over us?

Industry Competitors

a. What firms are the major competitors (today)? What are their basic characteristics (size, growth, product lines, customer base, geographic coverage, and so on)?
b. What are their relative positions in the industry?
c. What is the competitive advantage of each? (What "switching costs" or strategies does each use?)
d. How do they compete? What "weapons" or strategies does each use?
e. What form does competition take—open warfare, polite détente, secrecy, open signaling?
f. How is product differentiation achieved?
g. How competitive is the industry? Are any competitors attempting to shape the industry? How?

Buyers

a. What firms are the customers for this industry? How concentrated are they?
b. How fast is demand growing overall and in different segments? What is the potential for finding or creating new markets or niches?
c. What are the switching costs? How high are they?
d. How price sensitive is each customer segment for each of the industry's services?
e. How large is the threat of backward integration (that is, buyer's self-supplying our products or services)?
f. What is the customer's relative bargaining power?

Substitutes

a. What are the substitutes or alternatives for our product or service?
b. How big an impact will the substitutes have? (That is, how viable are they as direct replacements for our product or service?)
c. How quickly will they penetrate?
d. Which players in the industry will consider substitutes as an opportunity for diversification?

Source: Adapted and reprinted by permission of *Harvard Business Review.* Michael E. Porter, "How Competitive Forces Shape Strategy," *Harvard Business Review* (February 1979): 137–145. Copyright © 1979 by the Harvard Business School Publishing Corporation; all rights reserved.

Technological Uncertainty   A great deal of uncertainty usually exists about the technology in an emerging industry: Which product configuration will ultimately prove to be the best? Which production technology will prove to be the most efficient? How difficult will it be to develop this technology? How difficult will it be to copy technological breakthroughs in the industry?

Strategic Uncertainty   Related to technological uncertainty are a wide variety of strategic approaches often tried by industry participants. Since no "right" strategy has been clearly identified, industry participants will formulate different approaches to product positioning, advertising, pricing, and the like, as well as different product configurations or production technologies.

First–Time Buyers   Buyers of an emerging industry's products or services are perforce first-time buyers. The marketing task is thus one of substitution, or getting the buyer to make the initial purchase of the new product or service.

Short Time Horizons   In many emerging industries the pressure to develop customers or produce products to meet demand is so great that bottlenecks and problems are dealt with expediently rather than on the basis of an analysis of future conditions. Short-run results are often given major attention, while long-run results are given little consideration.

Barriers to Entry

In addition to the structural components of an emerging industry, **barriers to entry** exist. These barriers may include proprietary technology (expensive to access), access to distribution channels (limited or closed to newcomers), access to raw materials and other inputs (for example, skilled labor), cost disadvantages due to lack of experience (magnified with the technological and competitive uncertainties), or risk (which raises the effective opportunity cost of capital). Other barriers to entry are presented in Table 8.3. Some of these barriers will decline or disappear as the industry develops. However, it is still important for entrepreneurs to be aware of these barriers.

Competitive Analysis

Another important area is the analysis of the competition in the industry.[23] Both the quality and quantity of the competition must be carefully scrutinized. This **competitive analysis** involves consideration of the number of competitors as well as the strength of each. Figure 8.6 provides an illustrative grid that can be used to analyze the competition.

In assessing the competition, it is important to keep in mind the various elements that will affect the profile. Figure 8.7 illustrates the components of a competitive analysis from the standpoint of (1) what drives the competition and (2) what the competition can do. The competition's current strategy and future goals will help dictate its response. So too will the assumptions that each competitor has about itself as well as its perceived strengths and weaknesses.

Figure 8.7 provides a framework that allows an entrepreneur to better assess the competition. A good competitive analysis is vital to the ultimate success of any new venture.

Taking the Right Steps

In addition to the analytical process already discussed, a number of useful steps can assist an entrepreneur in examining the industry. The following are five of the most helpful:

1.   *Clearly define the industry for the new venture.* The key here is to develop a relevant definition that describes the focus of the new venture. Definitions will vary, of course, depending on the venture and its specific target market. The more clearly the entrepreneur can define the industry for the new venture, the better the chance the venture will get off to a sound start.

2.   *Analyze the competition.* An analysis of the number, relative size, traditions, and cost structures of direct competitors in the industry can help establish the nature of the competition. Will competition become more or less intense as the number and characteristics of competitors change over time? This question also can be answered through detailed analysis. For instance, what will happen to the

Table 8.3   Possible Constraints to Industry Development

CONSTRAINT	EXPLANATION
Inability to obtain raw materials and components	The development of an emerging industry requires that new suppliers be established or existing suppliers expand output or modify raw materials and components to meet the industry's needs. In the process, severe shortages of raw materials and components are very common.
Period of rapid escalation of raw materials prices	Because of burgeoning demand and inadequate supply, prices for key raw materials often skyrocket in the early phases of an emerging industry. This situation is partly the simple economics of supply and demand and partly the result of suppliers realizing the value of their products to the desperate industry.
Absence of infrastructure	Emerging industries are often faced with difficulties, such as those of material supply, caused by the lack of appropriate infrastructure: distribution channels, service facilities, trained mechanics, complementary products.
Perceived likelihood of obsolescence	An emerging industry's growth will be impeded if buyers perceive that second- or third-generation technologies will significantly make currently available products obsolete. Buyers will wait instead for the pace of technological progress to slow down and prices to fall as a consequence.
Erratic product quality	For many newly established firms, the lack of standards and technological uncertainty often cause erratic product quality in emerging industries. This erratic quality, even if caused by only a few firms, can negatively affect the image and credibility of the entire industry.
Image and credibility with the financial community	As a result of newness, the high level of uncertainty, customer confusion, and erratic quality, the emerging industry's image and credibility with the financial community may be poor. This result can affect not only the ability of firms to secure low-cost financing but also the ability of buyers to obtain credit.

Source: Adapted with permission of The Free Press, an imprint of Simon & Schuster Adult Publishing Group, from *Competitive Strategy: Techniques for Analyzing Industries and Competitors* by Michael E. Porter, 6. Copyright © 1985, 1998 by Michael E. Porter.

degree of competition if (a) market growth increases rapidly, (b) direct competitors equalize in size, (c) one or two direct competitors become substantially larger in size, or (d) product/service differentiation slows down?

3. *Determine the strength and characteristics of suppliers.* The important factor here is to establish the stance of the venture in relation to the suppliers. How

Figure 8.6 Competitive Profile Analysis

Instructions
Place an *X* to denote any competitive factor that a competitor has or can provide/perform better than you.

	Competitive Firms			
Competitive Factor	Company A	Company B	Company C	Your Company
Product uniqueness				
Relative product quality				
Price				
Service				
Availability/convenience				
Reputation/image				
Location				
Advertising and promotional policies/ effectiveness				
Product design				
Caliber of personnel				
Raw material cost				
Financial condition				
Production capability				
R&D position				
Variety/selection				

will the new firm be treated compared to other, more established firms? Do many suppliers offering diverse services exist, or must the new venture be prepared to accept limited services from a few?

4. *Establish the value-added measure of the new venture.* The concept of **value added** is a basic form of contribution analysis in which sales minus raw material costs equals the value added. The purpose behind this measure is to determine how much value the entrepreneur is adding to the product or service. This introduces the concept of *integration*—backward or forward. Backward integration is the movement of a buyer to acquire supplier services. Forward integration is the movement of a supplier to absorb the duties of a buyer. The likelihood of integration occurring is determined substantially by the degree to which the value added is essential to the final processing and user consumption.

Figure 8.7 Components of a Competitive Analysis

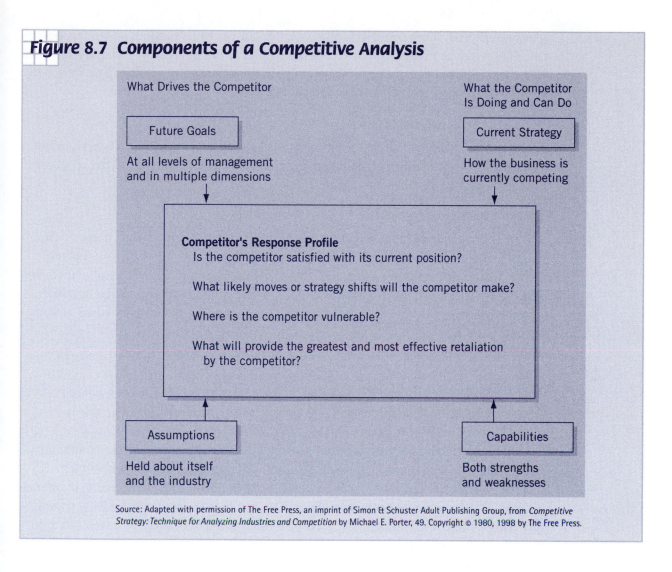

What Drives the Competitor

Future Goals

At all levels of management
and in multiple dimensions

What the Competitor
Is Doing and Can Do

Current Strategy

How the business is
currently competing

Competitor's Response Profile

Is the competitor satisfied with its current position?

What likely moves or strategy shifts will the competitor make?

Where is the competitor vulnerable?

What will provide the greatest and most effective retaliation
by the competitor?

Assumptions

Held about itself
and the industry

Capabilities

Both strengths
and weaknesses

Source: Adapted with permission of The Free Press, an imprint of Simon & Schuster Adult Publishing Group, from *Competitive Strategy: Technique for Analyzing Industries and Competition* by Michael E. Porter, 49. Copyright © 1980, 1998 by The Free Press.

5. *Project the market size for the particular industry.* Markets are dynamic and prone to change over time. Therefore, it is important to examine the historical progression of the market, establish its present size, and extrapolate the data to project the market growth potential. This can be done in terms of the industry life cycle, consumers (numbers and trends), product/service developments, and competitive analysis.

These five key points are not all-inclusive. However, they do represent an initial analysis of the industry environment that a new venture faces. This type of macroanalysis is important for establishing the framework within which a venture will start, grow, and, it is hoped, prosper. Once this analysis is complete, attention can be turned to the microenvironment, which provides a community perspective.

A Micro View: The Community Perspective

After analyzing the macroenvironment of the economy and the industry, the entrepreneur needs to focus on microenvironmental assessment. This analysis is directed toward the community where the new venture is to be launched.[24] For a new venture, searching and identifying a target market is one of the most important reasons for utilizing the micro view. A target market refers to the limited group of individuals (consumers) that a new venture is attempting to attract to its product or service. Because there are so many benefits to the new firm if it can successfully identify the most effective target market, we begin by examining the community location as a means to gather information regarding the eventual market.

Researching the Location

Assessing the local community environment is as vital to the success of a new venture as assessing the regulatory economy and the industry. We shall now discuss a number of major community facets to consider.

Community Demographics

A study of **community demographics** helps entrepreneurs determine the composition or makeup of consumers who live within the community. These data typically include such statistics as community size; the residents' purchasing power (disposable income), average educational background, and types of occupations; the percentage of residents who are professionals and nonprofessionals; and the extent of entrepreneurial activity in the community.

A few factors may be of special concern in this data analysis. One is the size of the new venture relative to the community itself and to other businesses in the community. Analysis of this factor helps the entrepreneur evaluate the new venture's potential in terms of sales, growth, employment, and attraction of customers. Each variable is directly related to the size factor, and all variables are interrelated. For example, a new venture may actually increase the total sales of all competitive firms in the community. A new furniture store located opposite an established furniture store often will serve to increase overall sales by drawing more business to the locale. People from other communities will come to comparison shop and will stay to buy. People from the local community will be more likely to purchase their furniture from one of these two stores than to drive to other communities to do so. The major reason is that furniture is a comparison good, and most people like to look at the offerings of at least two stores before they buy.

Another important demographic characteristic is the amount of entrepreneurial activity in the community. To assess this factor, it is important to count the number of entrepreneurs in the community, to examine their types of business ventures, and to establish their track records with suppliers (within and outside the region), their success with local banks, and their customer base. If the community has a lot of entrepreneurial activity, it will be more receptive to new ventures, and doors will be more easily opened. For example, local banks will be more accustomed to reviewing entrepreneurial loan applications and will have developed expertise in evaluating such applications and dealing with follow-up business.

Economic Base

The extent of an entrepreneur's opportunity may be determined, in part, by the **economic base** of the community. This base includes the nature of employment, which influences the size and distribution of income, and the purchasing trends of consumers in the area. Additionally, it is wise to examine any community dependence on one large firm or industry that may be affected by seasonal or cyclical fluctuations.

Population Trends

It is important to examine population trends in order to identify expanding communities as opposed to long-term declining or static populations. Growth usually indicates solid, aggressive civic leadership with opportunities available for budding entrepreneurial ventures. Favorable signs of a growing community typically include chain or department store branches throughout the area, branch plants of large industrial firms, a progressive chamber of commerce, a good school system, transportation facilities (air, rail, highway), construction activity, and an absence of vacant buildings. In addition, many entrepreneurs supplement this information with selected sources of environmental data. Table 8.4 describes some of these sources.

Table 8.4   Selected Sources of Environmental Data

SOURCE	DESCRIPTION
The Census of Population (Census Bureau)	Taken every ten years, these data present information on age, race, sex, marital status, family status, ethnic origin, migration, education, income, occupation, employment, and other characteristics of the population. This information is available for states and counties and for every city, town, or village. For cities of 50,000 or more, inhabitants' data have been tabulated by census tracts—small areas with an average population of 4,000 or 5,000; summary information is available for the entire metropolitan area in which such a city is located, as well as for individual blocks within the city.
The Census of Manufacturers (Census Bureau)	Taken every four years, these data include the number of manufacturing establishments, the number of production and other employees, value added by manufacture, cost of materials, value of shipments, and recent capital expenditures for each of the nation's manufacturing industries. These data also are compiled for each of the states, and much of the information is available for counties as well.
The Census of Business (Census Bureau)	Taken every four years, this census provides information on all types of retail and wholesale trade and services. Included are data on the number of establishments, gross annual sales or receipts, the number of employees, annual payroll, and the number of active proprietors of unincorporated enterprises. These data are compiled for each state and county and for all communities with a population of 2,500 or more.
Department of Commerce publications	Each state's department of commerce has various publications that track the business activity of counties and cities, as well as state employment and industry data.
Sales Management magazine's "Buying Power Index"	Published annually, this publication contains a wealth of information helpful in setting sales quotas, planning distribution, locating warehouses, and studying sales potential. It includes information on population and income for every state by county and city, including per capita and per household incomes. Retail sales estimates are also made for every state by county and city. This information is combined and weighted to produce a buying power index useful for predicting sales in a particular locality.

Overall Business Climate

A summary view of the community from the business perspective includes consideration of transportation, banking, professional services, the economic base, growth trends, and the solidity of the consumer income base. It is important to make an assessment of the general business climate before deciding on the location of a new venture. (See the "Experiential Exercise: A Sample Community Analysis" for more on this subject.)

Determining Reliance and Deservedness

Another method of evaluating a community is in terms of **reliance** and **deservedness.** In such an evaluation the following questions are particularly important:

1. How familiar is the entrepreneur with the community where the venture will be located?

2. Will the proposed venture make any special positive or negative impacts on the community during the prestart-up period or during the start-up period?

3. Does the entrepreneur have special skills in human relations with which to nurture key local contacts?

4. What active steps can be taken to strengthen local support and maximize local opportunities during the start-up period?

5. What active steps can be taken to reduce local opposition and minimize local problems during the start-up period?

Answers to these questions help determine the level of support likely to exist in a given community. Entrepreneurs can gain exceptional community support in two major ways. The first is based on (1) the strength of the community's reliance on or need for the entrepreneur's venture and (2) the entrepreneur's willingness to make a commitment to the community. Figure 8.8 illustrates this idea.

The second way entrepreneurs may gain exceptional community support is through the community perception of their "deservedness." People generally identify with those who they think deserve their support. Thus, the strength of the relationship between this perceived deservedness and the community's identification with the new venture will influence the possibility of exceptional community support. Figure 8.9 illustrates this relationship.

Examining the Use of Business Incubators

In some locales, it is possible for a new venture to use an incubator approach in getting started. Although many definitions of the term **business incubator** exist, most agree it is a facility with adaptable space that small businesses can lease on flexible terms and at reduced rents. Support services—financial, managerial, technical, and administrative—are available and shared, depending on the size and nature of tenants' needs. Most incubators limit the amount of time, ranging from two to five years, a small business may occupy space in the facility.

The basic purpose of an incubator is to increase the chances of survival for new start-up businesses.[25] Four major types of incubators exist, and the objectives of each type tend to vary:

1. *Publicly sponsored:* These incubators are organized through city economic development departments, urban renewal authorities, or regional planning and

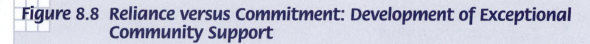

Figure 8.8 *Reliance versus Commitment*: Development of Exceptional Community Support

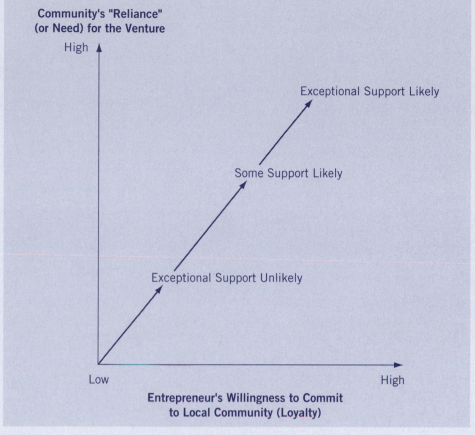

Source: Adapted from Robert C. Ronstadt, *Entrepreneurship* (Natick, MA: Lord Publishing, Inc., 1984), 84. Reprinted with permission.

development commissions. Job creation is the main objective of the publicly sponsored incubator.

2. *Nonprofit-sponsored:* These incubators are organized and managed through industrial development associations of private industry, chambers of commerce, or community-based organizations with broad community support or a successful record in real estate development. Area development is the major objective of nonprofit-sponsored incubators.

3. *University-related:* Many of these incubator facilities are spin-offs of academic research projects. Most are considered science and technology incubators. The major goal of university-related incubators is to translate the findings of basic research and development into new products or technologies.[26]

4. *Privately sponsored:* These incubators are organized and managed by private corporations. The major goal is to make a profit and, in some cases, to make a contribution to the community.[27]

Regardless of their type, however, most incubators provide the following kinds of services:

☐ Below-market-rate rental space on flexible terms. The rates are negotiable but usually range from $1.50 to $4.00 per square foot.

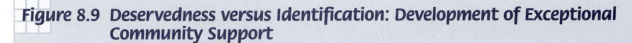

Figure 8.9 *Deservedness versus Identification: Development of Exceptional Community Support*

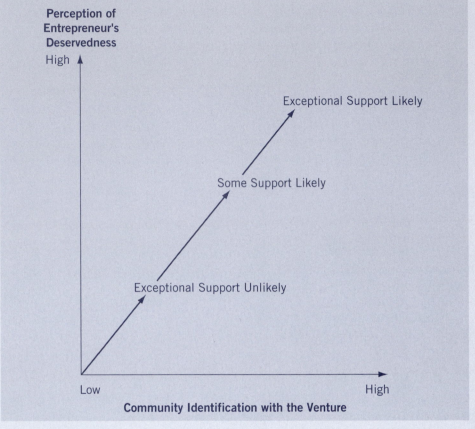

Source: Adapted from Robert C. Ronstadt, *Entrepreneurship* (Natick, MA: Lord Publishing, Inc., 1984), 85. Reprinted with permission.

☐ Elimination of building maintenance responsibilities. This allows new entrepreneurs freedom from maintenance of furniture and equipment and of such areas as loading docks, lunch areas, conference rooms, and reception areas.

☐ Sharing of equipment and services that would otherwise be unavailable or unaffordable. Such services are typically divided into three major categories: (1) offices and communications services such as typing, photocopying, and phone answering; (2) business services such as business planning and financial planning; and (3) facilities and equipment services, including a reception area, conference rooms, and computers.

☐ Additional information on and access to various types of financial and technical assistance.

☐ Provision of an environment where small businesses are not alone, thereby reducing the anxiety of starting a new venture.

☐ Increased business tenants' visibility to the community.

Figure 8.10 shows how an incubator works. Differences do exist between publicly sponsored and privately sponsored incubators. Table 8.5 gives some statistics on incubators.

Incubators are targeted toward providing benefits for small businesses that are incapable of generating their own managerial, technical, financial, or administrative

Figure 8.10 How Does the Incubator Work?

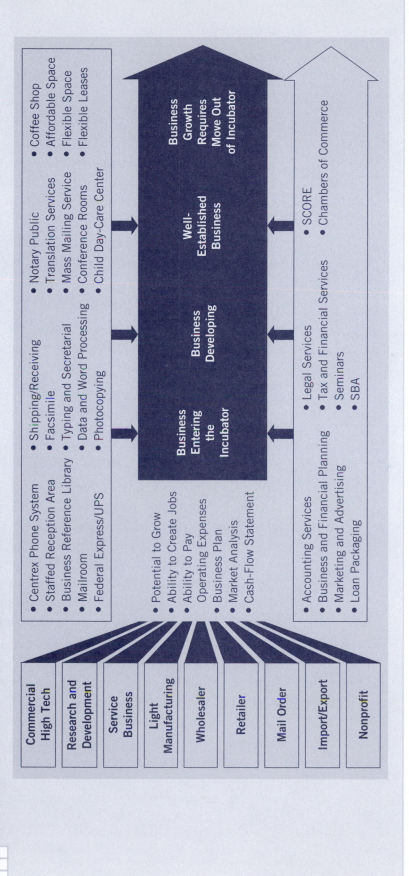

Table 8.5   Privately and Publicly Sponsored Incubators: A Comparison

CHARACTERISTICS	DIFFERENCES
Size and tenant capacity	Privately sponsored facilities are twice the size of publicly sponsored facilities and have a median tenant capacity of 45 compared to 14 for public initiatives.
Incubator governance	Publicly sponsored incubators have executive or advisory boards, while privately sponsored do not.
Tenant selection	The criterion of publicly sponsored incubators is job creation potential with strict entry standards, while privately sponsored incubators seek profit potential in their tenants and thus do not have strict entry barriers.
Exit policy	Public facilities have a time limit on tenant residency, while private incubators tend to allow residents to stay or grow out of the facility.
Rent	Private incubators charge higher rents (usually two or three times more than public facilities) per square foot.
Services	While both sectors have centralized services, the concentration is different. Privately sponsored incubators tend to provide physical and human services (for example, space, secretarial, maintenance, conference rooms), whereas publicly sponsored facilities concentrate more on financial and business services.
Financial sources	Privately sponsored incubators have a majority of the financing sources in the private sector, whereas the publicly sponsored initiatives are widely distributed among private, governmental, and industrial development financial sources.
Operating revenue	Both types of incubators use the revenue from rent and services for their operating income. The difference arises in the nonrent revenue that is needed to operate the incubator. Publicly sponsored incubators receive most of this revenue from government sources. Privately sponsored incubators rely to a great extent on private sources, which allows them to receive, on average, more money.
Staff	Privately sponsored incubators have larger staffs than do publicly sponsored facilities (mean size of 5 as opposed to 1.7). Consulting staff size tends to be about the same; however, the incubator managers of privately sponsored facilities possess more business experience than do their public counterparts.
Growth patterns	Publicly sponsored incubators place a greater emphasis on job creation and have registered a higher level of growth in employment (157%) than privately sponsored incubators (31%). However, in sales growth the privately sponsored facilities, which emphasize net profit of the tenants, have demonstrated a larger increase (75%) than the publicly sponsored facilities (35.2%).

Source: Data from David N. Allen and Syedur Rahman, "Small Business Incubators: A Positive Environment for Entrepreneurship," *Journal of Small Business Management* (July 1985): 12–22. Copyright 1985 by Blackwell Publishing. Reproduced with permission of Blackwell Publishing. See also The National Business Incubator Association (Athens, Ohio) http://www.nbia.org.

the entrepreneurial PROCESS

Evaluating Environmental Trends

Environmental trends come in all forms and usually they are difficult to recognize early. Correctly quantifying any type of trend has been a challenge for centuries; when it comes to the bottom line, credibility then becomes the dominant factor in evaluating trends. In examining various sources that report on surveys, polls, and trends, experts recommend the following when discerning the truths in trends:

☐ *Gauge the Source:* Media critic Jon Katz thinks most social trends and analyses are laughable, but respect the data in business publications more than studies cited in the mainstream press because the business audience is more demanding.

☐ *Investigate the Facts:* Read the news items very closely. Look at two criteria: who responded to the survey, and how representative was the sample. Website surveys often fail on both counts because respondents are self-selecting; possibly because they have an interest in the outcome. These respondents are also less likely to represent the public, largely because not everyone has access to computers. Also, take caution when considering conditional surveys. These typically claim people would be willing to pay $X for a particular service they do not already have.

☐ *Bear in Mind When the Survey Was Conducted:* Events alter human behavior, thus polls are more of a snapshot in time instead of a concrete change. Values and beliefs take a very long time to change.

☐ *Dig Deeper:* Find out what information the source left out. If you find a blurb on a survey in a local paper, go to the source and find out all the numbers. Spend a proportional amount of time on researching the information, as you would rely upon it.

☐ *When You Find the Source, Ask the Questions Good Journalists Ask:* Find out what you should ask by reading "20 Questions a Journalist Should Ask about Poll Results," written by former journalist G. Evan Witt available at http://www.ncpp.org/qajsa.htm.

☐ *Beware the Hockey Stick:* Market projections with a sudden up-tick at the end are known as hockey sticks. At the point of the jump it notes, "estimated"; for the most part, you'll do a better job predicting the future based on recent facts or even a psychic.

☐ *Don't Be Too Skeptical:* Try not to discount a trend because it doesn't coincide with everything else you know. If the information is accurate and you choose to disregard it, it could spell doom for your business.

SOURCE: Adapted from Chris Sandlund, "Plug in the Numbers," *Entrepreneur* (June 2002): 19–21.

services. A less obvious but recently realized focus is the community benefits from establishing incubators. The latest research in this area reveals the following important community benefits:

☐ Transformation of underused property into a center of productivity

☐ Creation of opportunities for public/private partnerships

☐   Diversification of the local economic base

☐   Enhancement of the locality's image as a center of innovation and entrepreneurship

☐   Increased employment opportunities[28]

Thus business incubators have become appealing to small businesses and community developers alike. Public, private, and nonprofit groups have all demonstrated a willingness to develop this concept. In the process, supporters have arisen among the public, the media, and the financial community. In particular, the goal of this communal positioning of new businesses under one roof for the purpose of providing low rent and shared on-site services will increase entrepreneurial success and thus enhance the economic development of local communities.

Summary

In assessing a new venture, entrepreneurs consider a number of different environments. Typically, they begin with the macro and then move on to the micro, focusing on data that help them decide how to establish the venture. Two major macro areas warrant their consideration. One is the overall economic environment; the other is the specific industry environment. The overall economic environment analysis assesses the nature of the industry and the regulatory environment that exists there. The specific industry environment entrepreneurs address includes common industry characteristics, barriers to entry, and competitive analysis.

The microanalysis focuses on examining the location, determining reliance and deservedness, and studying the feasibility of using business incubators. When examining the location, entrepreneurs consider areas such as community demographics, the economic base, population trends, and the overall business climate. To determine reliance and deservedness, entrepreneurs look for the right fit between the business and the community. When exploring business incubators, they focus attention on the presence of these facilities in the local area and the benefits they would hold for the specific enterprise.

Key Terms and Concepts

barriers to entry

business incubator

community demographics

competitive analysis

Congressional Review Act

deservedness

economic base

environmental assessment

Equal Access to Justice Act

Regulatory Flexibility Act

reliance

Small Business Regulatory Enforcement Fairness Act

sustainable competitive advantage

Unfunded Mandates Reform Act

value added

Review and Discussion Questions

1.   To assess the economic environment of a venture, an entrepreneur would like a number of questions answered. Identify and discuss five of these questions.

2.   Briefly discuss each of the following effects of governmental regulations on small ventures: prices, cost inequities, competitive restrictions, managerial restrictions, mental burdens.

3. How does each of the following legislative acts affect small ventures: (a) the Regulatory Flexibility Act, (b) the Equal Access to Justice Act, (c) the Small Business Regulatory Enforcement Fairness Act, (d) the Unfunded Mandates Reform Act?

4. Of what value is Figure 8.4 to helping an entrepreneur make a new-venture assessment?

5. What are barriers to entry? How do they affect new-venture assessment?

6. How could an entrepreneur use Figure 8.7 to conduct a competitive profile analysis? What would the results provide? What types of decisions could the individual make from the analysis?

7. Identify and describe four of the steps to take when making an industry assessment.

8. How can an entrepreneur go about researching the location for a venture? What information can community demographics and population trends provide?

9. Discuss this statement: One method of evaluating a community is in terms of reliance and deservedness.

10. What is a business incubator? What are the four major types of incubators?

11. Of what value is a business incubator to a new venture? Explain in detail.

Experiential Exercise

A Sample Community Analysis

Assume you are in the process of opening a small retail hardware store. Choose a site location in your community, and then answer the following questions about the community, potential customers, competition, and location.

Potential of the Trading Area

1. How big is the trading area? _____ sq. mi.

2. What is the customer potential within five miles? _____ customers

3. What is the density of population? _____ people per sq. mi.

4. Is transportation adequate for supplies? _____ yes _____ no

5. What is the income level of the trading area? _____ per capita

6. What is the local employment pattern, based on number of people employed? _____ % people employed

7. What is the general makeup of the community? _____ residential _____ old _____ growing

8. What are the trends in population and income? _____ up _____ down

9. Is new construction on the increase? _____ yes _____ no

10. Are school enrollments up? _____ yes _____ no

11. Are retail sales on the increase? _____ yes _____ no

12. Have average business improvements been made recently? _____ yes _____ no

13. Does business property have a high vacancy rate? _____ yes _____ no

14. Have shopping patterns changed drastically in recent years? _____ yes _____ no

15. Are customers moving to or away from the potential location? _____ to _____ from

16. What are the present zoning restrictions?_____

_____

Can Customers Get to the Location?

1. Is the area served by adequate public transportation? _____ yes _____ no

2. How broad an area does the transportation service encompass? _____ sq. mi.

3. Is the area generally attractive to shoppers? _____ yes _____ no

4. Can it be easily reached by automobile? _____ yes _____ no

5. Is public parking adequate and relatively inexpensive? _____ yes _____ no

6. How many spaces in the available nearby parking lot are taken up by all-day parkers? _____ many _____ few

7. If located on a highway, is the location easily accessible from the main traffic flow? _____ yes _____ no

8. What are restrictions on signs and store identification?

_____

9. If the location is on a limited access road, how close is the nearest interchange? _____ miles

10. Is the location accessible to delivery trucks? _____ yes _____ no

11. Is the traffic speed too fast to encourage entrance by automobile? _____ yes _____ no

12. Are most customers who drive past the location on their way to work or on shopping trips? _____ on way to work _____ on shopping trips

13. Will nearby stores help you? Are the other stores in the shopping center, neighborhood, or highway location of a nature that will attract customers who also will become patrons of your store? _____ yes _____ no _____ maybe _____ likely

14. What are the prospects for changes in traffic flow in the near future? _____ slight _____ likely

15. Will anticipated changes improve or damage the location? _____ improve _____ damage

16. Are zoning changes planned that would affect accessibility of the location? _____ yes _____ no

Judging the Competition

1. How many other businesses of the same kind exist between the prospective location and the most highly populated area? _____ stores

2. Is this spot the most convenient store location in the area? _____ yes _____ no

3. How many other stores of the same kind are in this trading area? _____ stores

4. How many of them will compete with you for customers? _____ stores

5. Do these other stores have better parking facilities? _____ yes _____ no

6. Do these other stores offer the same type of merchandise? _____ yes _____ no

7. Do you consider these other stores more aggressive or less aggressive than your own operation will be? _____ more _____ less

8. What other competing stores are planned for this trading area in the near future?
_____

9. Are other potential sites that are closer to the majority of customers likely to be developed in the near future? _____ yes _____ no

10. Are your major competitors well-known, well-advertised stores? _____ yes _____ no

11. Does a need for another store of this kind in the area actually exist? _____ yes _____ no

12. How well is the demand for this product being met in the area? _____ very well _____ moderately well

13. If any empty stores or vacant lots are near the location, is a competitive store planned for them? _____ yes _____ no

Can the Location Attract New Business?

1. Is the location in an attractive district? _____ yes _____ no

2. Do numerous stores exist that will draw potential customers for you into the area? _____ yes _____ no

3. Is the location near well-known and well-advertised stores? _____ yes _____ no

4. Is this location the most attractive one in the area? _____ yes _____ no

5. Is the location on the side of the street with the busiest customer traffic? _____ yes _____ no

6. Is the location nearer to the general parking area than locations of competing firms? _____ yes _____ no

7. Is the location in the center of or on the fringe of the shopping district? _____ center _____ fringe

8. Is it near common meeting places for people, such as public offices? _____ yes _____ no

9. Are most of the people passing the store prospective customers? _____ yes _____ no

10. Are the people who pass usually in a hurry, or are they taking time to shop? _____ in a hurry _____ taking time to shop

Cost of the Location

1. What will your rent be? $ _____ per month

2. Who will pay the utility costs? _____ you _____ others

3. Who pays additional costs, such as taxes, public services, and costs of improvements? _____ you _____ others

4. What are the possibilities for eventual expansion? _____ good _____ poor

5. Are good employees available? _____ yes _____ no

6. Will your potential income justify your costs? _____ yes _____ no

Based on your analysis, is this a good community in which to open a retail hardware store? Explain.

Video Case 8.1

Environmental and Marketing Assessment
Rodgers' Chevrolet with Pamela Rodgers

> I was going against the grain. . . . I was a woman, I was minority. . . . they thought this business was too challenging—too competitive. (Pamela Rodgers)

Pamela Rodgers had an unusual dream. She wanted to become an automobile dealer. Because of her tenacious determination and focus on working hard, she now owns a successful Chevrolet dealership; it employs 85 people and generates 73 million dollars in revenue by selling approximately 200 cars a month and by servicing as many as 1,200 cars a month. And her success happened in a quiet suburb just south of Detroit, Michigan, the automobile hub of the United States.

Pamela explains how she made her dream a reality. She worked in the corporate offices of Ford and earned an MBA in finance. At Ford, she developed a relationship with a mentor. "I don't know what he saw, but whatever it is, thank God for it. Maybe just my willingness to work, my tenacity for work, my willingness to come early, stay late, do whatever it takes to get the job done. Follow-through. Discipline . . . because I volunteered to do things."

With assistance from Ford's Minority Dealer Program, Pamela was able to open a dealership in Flint, Michigan. But Flint, with its nine GM plants, is a GM town. "It was a very tough market, and we went in right in 1990. . . . the economy was not very strong at that time. So, of course, it was impossible to make that boat float."

When the dealership was liquidated, Pamela went back to work for her mentor as general manager of his GM dealership. When he moved on to a dealership in Detroit in 1993 and took his clientele with him, she bought the store, which no one else wanted. "I bought the 'ugly duckling.' Yes . . . it was cash poor and really didn't have a huge following."

Pamela was thankful that GM gave her this opportunity, and she set out to transform the "ugly duckling" into a profitable dealership. Part of her plan was to hire a good team. Joe Posby, her general manager, is a valuable player on that team with his skills in marketing and marketing research. Joe says, "With an automobile dealership we do know . . . we will sell, primarily, all of our new and pre-owned cars within a 15-mile radius of the dealership. . . . predominately that's my market," Joe says.

He explains further: "Most people will either buy from where they live or where they work. Again, within 15 miles of the dealership. So that's where I primarily will put all my efforts in marketing." Joe allocates 50 percent of his budget in direct mail marketing, 20 percent on newspaper ads, and the rest in different mediums.

Every week, the dealership sends out targeted mailings of between 7,500 to 10,000 pieces to the people who live within that 15-mile radius. This marketing strategy has worked well for Rodgers Chevrolet.

Pamela has also put considerable effort into building the service department in her dealership, which she says is not "the backend [but] the backbone." She maintains: "This is certainly not your father's car dealership where sell, sell, sell was the mantra. Yes, you have to sell, but everyone at Rodgers knows that service is what brings customers back over and over and over again." She wants service advisors to fully inform customers about maintenance needs, repairs required, the time needed to repair a car, and when the customer can expect to be called to pick up a car. "Those things are very important. Communication with the customers," she says and smiles, "The service department is abuzz. They know they're good."

In fact, employees in every department exhibit an enthusiasm for working with Pamela in this dealership; her one important guideline for everyone is to take care of the customer who comes in the door. Pamela is keen on giving other women an opportunity in the automobile business. "We have women salespeople, we have a woman parts manager, F&I manager, controller. We have women at all ranks of our business, which is unusual for a car dealership." Promoting women in her dealership makes good marketing sense as well. Pamela is well aware of the statistics that identify women as purchasing 50 percent of all automobiles sold and influencing 85 to 90 percent of all automobile sales.

Pamela doesn't overlook any possible way to make both men and women customers feel welcome and comfortable in her dealership. When she decided to renovate the building several years ago, she used the Chevrolet racing reputation as her inspiration. She hired a set designer and builder from a theatre to create a customer lounge with a speedway setting. "Customers love it," she says, "and the kids really seem to enjoy it, too."

Pamela is enjoying her success in the exciting arena of automobiles, but she doesn't take it for granted. She acknowledges that she spends more time at work than at home and that she considers her employees part of her extended family. She has no plans to change this pattern because she enjoys it. "If I am comfortable, shoot me—I never want to be comfortable. I don't want to become complacent."

Questions

1. Which attributes did Pamela Rodgers bring from her corporate experience to her dealership that contributed to her success?

2. Name the factors that contribute to her continuing success as a dealer.

3. Discuss the dealership's marketing and marketing research strategies.

4. Would you buy a car from a dealership owned by a woman? Explain your response.

Case 8.2

Examining the Industry

John Hargan and Rita Maylor decided to launch a new business to produce and distribute noncarbonated, high-quality soft drinks. They decided on a location in Colorado partly because they believed access to high-quality, pure water would provide them with a competitive edge. A business consultant recommended they construct a comprehensive business plan that would include a clear and thorough assessment of the beverage industry. This exercise should help them understand their challenges and help position this new product. The two partners have spent two months of their spare time (because they both work for another employer full-time) trying to gather research to validate their idea. Because their current employer is not in the beverage industry, they are struggling to find sources of information. John and Rita realize that before any type of viable business plan can be developed, the beverage industry needs to be assessed. The specific elements of this type of assessment are unclear to both of them, however.

Questions

1. What elements of the industry should John and Rita examine?

2. How would the five forces model (Figure 8.4) help them?

3. Describe what potential barriers to entry they might encounter.

Case 8.3

An Incubator Investigation

For the past four years Darlene Danforth has worked for a large office-fixture and supply company. The local area sales representative for one of the company's major suppliers recently announced he was retiring. The man had experienced a heart attack and decided to find a less strenuous job. Unexpectedly one day, Darlene received a call from the supplier. "For the past ten years we have been selling your company a lot of office fixtures and supplies," the supplier told Darlene. "And for the past two years we've been working directly with you. We now have an opening for a sales rep in your city. If you take the job, we can guarantee you'll make 25 percent more money than you're making now. Your job will be to call on other office-fixture and supply companies in the state, in addition to your present company, of course. We pay 2 percent on all sales and have 125 active accounts you would be taking over. In addition, we know that more than 2,000 companies in the state are potential customers. So there's plenty of room for growth. Would you like the job?"

Darlene thought about the offer for a week, talked it over with her employer, and decided to take the job. Because her state is not very large, she can reach most of her customers in two to three hours. This means she has little likelihood of being away from home very often. However, she will need to set up an office, maintain records, and have some general office functions performed for her. Since Darlene has never run her own business before, she is concerned about her ability to manage the operation. Her boss has suggested she look into a business incubator. "For your particular needs, this can be exactly what you need. It will provide you an office, a secretary, and some support help while you are on the road selling." The idea sounds fine to Darlene, but she really does not know much about incubators. She has decided the place to start is to investigate what incubators are all about and what functions they can perform for her.

Questions

1. Give a detailed description of a business incubator.

2. Identify and describe three benefits that a business incubator would offer Darlene.

3. Would an incubator be of value to Darlene? Why or why not?

Notes

1. Arnold C. Cooper, Timothy B. Folta, and Carolyn Woo, "Entrepreneurial Information Search," *Journal of Business Venturing* (March 1995): 95–106.

2. See Sumaria Indra Mohan-Neill, "The Influence of Firm's Age and Size on Its Environmental Scanning Activities," *Journal of Small Business Management* (October 1995): 10–21; James J. Lang, Roger J. Calantone, and Donald Gudmundson, "Small Firm Information Seeking as a Response to Environmental Threats and Opportunities," *Journal of Small Business Management* (January 1997): 11–23; and Reginald M. Beal, "Competing Effectively: Environmental Scanning,

Competitive Strategy, and Organizational Performance in Small Manufacturing Firms," *Journal of Small Business Management* (January 2000): 27–47.

3. Michael A. Hitt, R. Duane Ireland, and Robert E. Hoskisson, *Strategic Management: Competitiveness and Globalization*, 5th ed. (Mason, OH: South-Western/Thomson Learning, 2005), 39–41.

4. See Andrew H. Van de Ven, "The Development of an Infrastructure for Entrepreneurship," *Journal of Business Venturing* (May 1993): 211–230; see also Thomas M. Begley, Wee-Liang Tan, and Herbert Schoch, "Politico-Economic Factors Associated with Interest in Starting a Business: A Multi-Country Study," *Entrepreneurship Theory and Practice* 29(1) (January 2005): 35–56.

5. Rogene A. Buchholz, *Business Environment and Public Policy: Implications for Management & Strategy Formulation,* 4th ed. (1992), 15. Reprinted by permission of Prentice-Hall, Inc., Englewood Cliffs, New Jersey.

6. Ronald G. Cook and David Barry, "When Should the Small Firm Be Involved in Public Policy?" *Journal of Small Business Management* (January 1993): 39–50.

7. M. Silverstein, "The Public Entrepreneurship Revolution," *Business and Society Review* (fall 1996): 15–183.

8. Donald F. Kuratko, Jeffrey S. Hornsby, and Douglas W. Naffziger, "The Adverse Impact of Public Policy on Microenterprises: An Exploratory Study of Owners' Perceptions," *Journal of Developmental Entrepreneurship* (spring/summer 1999): 81–93.

9. John G. Udell and Robert W. Pricer, "Reengineering of Public Policy Toward Private Enterprise," *Journal of Private Enterprise* (summer 1994): 1–12.

10. E. J. Fueler, "Regulated to Death," *Chief Executive* (May 1993): 14–15.

11. D. Warner, "Regulations' Staggering Costs," *Nation's Business* (June 1992): 50–53; and W. Mark Crain and Thomas D. Hopkins, "The Impact of Regulatory Costs on Small Firms," *A Report for the Office of Advocacy,* U.S. Small Business Administration, 2005, http://www.sba.gov.

12. Crain and Hopkins, "The Impact of Regulatory Costs on Small Firms."

13. See Murray L. Weidenbaum, *Business and Government in the Global Marketplace* (Upper Saddle River, NJ: Prentice-Hall, 1999).

14. Kenneth Chilton and Murray Weidenbaum, "Government Regulation: The Small Business Burden," *Journal of Small Business Management* (January 1982): 4–10.

15. Robert F. Scherer, Daniel J. Kaufman, and M. Fall Ainina, "Complaint Resolution by OSHA in Small and Large Manufacturing Firms," *Journal of Small Business Management* (January 1993): 73–82.

16. Rogelio Garcia, "Federal Regulatory Reform: An Overview," *Congressional Research,* Library of Congress (May 11, 1998), 3–8, as reported in Lawrence M. Lesser, *Business Public Policy and Society* (Fort Worth, TX: Harcourt Publishers, 2000).

17. *Small Business Advocate* (Washington, D.C.: U.S. Small Business Administration, 1994).

18. John G. Udell, "Entrepreneurs, Public Policy and the Quality of Business Life," *Journal of Private Enterprise* (winter 1993): 1–18.

19. See *Building the Foundation for a New Century: Final Report on the Implementation of the Recommendations of the 1995 White House Conference on Small Business* (Washington, D.C.: U.S. Small Business Administration, 2000).

20. Michael E. Porter, "Knowing Your Place—How to Assess the Attractiveness of Your Industry and Your Company's Position in It," *Inc.* (September 1991): 90.

21. See, for example, Michael E. Porter, *Competitive Strategy* (New York: Free Press, 1980); Michael E. Porter, *Competitive Advantage* (New York: Free Press, 1985); and Michael E. Porter, "From Competitive Advantage to Corporate Strategy," *Harvard Business Review* (May/June 1987): 43–59.

22. Kenneth Charles Robinson, "An Examination of the Influence of Industry Structure on Eight Alternative Measures of New Venture Performance for High Potential Independent New Ventures," *Journal of Business Venturing* (February 1999): 165–188.

23. For a detailed discussion of this topic, see Porter, *Competitive Strategy;* Michael E. Porter and Victor E. Millar, "How Information Gives You Competitive Advantage," *Harvard Business Review* (July/August 1985): 149–160; and Michael A. Hitt, R. Duane Ireland, and Robert E. Hoskisson, *Strategic Management: Competitiveness and Globalization*, 5th ed. (Mason, OH: South-Western/ Thomson Learning, 2002).

24. William H. Hudnut III, "The Rise of the Entrepreneurial City: An Urban Agenda for the 1990s," *Hudson Institute Briefing Paper* (November 1993): 158; see also John Case, "Place Matters," *Inc.: The State of Small Business* (1996 special issue): 94–95.

25. Fred L. Fry, "The Role of Incubators in Small Business Planning," *American Journal of Small Business* (summer 1987): 51–62; Mark P. Rice, Jana B. Matthews, Laura Kilcrease, and Susan Matlock, *Growing New Ventures, Creating New Jobs* (Westport, CT: Greenwood Publishing Group, 1995); and Bart Clarysse, Mike Wright, Andy Lockett, Els Van de Velde, and Ajay Vohora, "Spinning Out New Ventures: A Typology of Incubation Strategies from European Research Institutions," *Journal of Business Venturing* 20(2) (March 2005): 183–216.

26. Phillip H. Phan, Donald S. Siegel, and Mike Wright, "Science Parks and Incubators: Observations, Synthesis and Future Research," *Journal of Business Venturing* 20(2) (March 2005): 165–182; and Sang Suk Lee and Jerome S. Osteryoung, "A Comparison of Critical Success Factors for Effective Operations of University Business Incubators in the United States and Korea," *Journal of Small Business Management* 42(4) (October 2004): 418–426.

27. See The National Business Incubator Association (Athens, OH) http://www.nbia.org.

28. See the following for a detailed discussion of incubators: David N. Allen and Syedur Rahman, "Small Business Incubators," *Journal of Small Business Management* (July 1985): 12–22; Donald F. Kuratko and William R. LaFollette, "Examining the Small Business Incubator Explosion," *Mid-American Journal of Business* (September 1986): 29–34; Richard Steffens, "What Incubators Have Hatched," *Planning* (May 1992): 28–30; Brian Walker, "Incubator Fundamentals," *NBIA Review* 18(3) (June 2002): 6–9; Phillip H. Phan, Donald S. Siegel, and Mike Wright, "Science Parks and Incubators: Observations, Synthesis and Future Research," *Journal of Business Venturing* 20(2) (March 2005): 165–182; and Bart Clarysse, Mike Wright, Andy Lockett, Els Van de Velde, and Ajay Vohora, "Spinning Out New Ventures: A Typology of Incubation Strategies from European Research Institutions," *Journal of Business Venturing* 20(2) (March 2005): 183–216.

9 Marketing Research for Entrepreneurial Ventures

The generation and use of market research enables a management team to learn about changes in the market faster than the competition, making it a major component of competitive rationality and competitive advantage.

Peter R. Dickson

Marketing Management

Chapter Objectives

1 To review the importance of marketing research for new ventures

2 To present factors that inhibit the use of marketing

3 To examine the marketing concept: philosophy, segmentation, and consumer orientation

4 To establish the areas vital to marketing planning

5 To highlight the questions concerning hazards in marketing

6 To characterize the marketing stages of growing ventures

7 To discuss telemarketing as a potential tool for marketing

8 To discuss the key features of a pricing strategy

9 To present the emerging use of Internet marketing for entrepreneurial firms

Table 9.1   Common Elements in the Marketing Skills of Great Entrepreneurs

1. They possess unique environmental insight, which they use to spot opportunities that others overlook or view as problems.

2. They develop new marketing strategies that draw on their unique insights. They view the status quo and conventional wisdom as something to be challenged.

3. They take risks that others, lacking their vision, consider foolish.

4. They live in fear of being preempted in the market.

5. They are fiercely competitive.

6. They think through the implications of any proposed strategy, screening it against their knowledge of how the marketplace functions. They identify and solve problems that others do not even recognize.

7. They are meticulous about details and are always in search of new competitive advantages in quality and cost reduction, however small.

8. They lead from the front, executing their management strategies enthusiastically and autocratically. They maintain close information control when they delegate.

9. They drive themselves and their subordinates.

10. They are prepared to adapt their strategies quickly and to keep adapting them until they work. They persevere long after others have given up.

11. They have clear visions of what they want to achieve next. They can see further down the road than the average manager can see.

Source: Peter R. Dickson, *Marketing Management* (Fort Worth, TX: The Dryden Press, 1994), 8. Reprinted with permission of South-Western, a division of Thomson Learning: http://www.thomsonrights.com.

A **market** is a group of consumers (potential customers) who have purchasing power and unsatisfied needs.[1] A new venture will survive only if a market exists for its product or service.[2] This is so obvious that it would seem every entrepreneur would prepare thoroughly the market analysis needed for establishing a target market. However, many entrepreneurs know very little about their market, and some even attempt to launch new ventures without identifying any market. (See Table 9.1 concerning the marketing skills of great entrepreneurs.)

A number of techniques and strategies can assist entrepreneurs with effectively analyzing a potential market. By using them, entrepreneurs can gain in-depth knowledge about the specific market and can translate this knowledge into a well-formulated business plan. Effective marketing analysis also can help a new venture position itself and make changes that will result in increased sales.[3] The key to this process is marketing research.

Marketing Research

Marketing research involves the gathering of information about a particular market, followed by analysis of that information.[4] A knowledge and understanding of the procedures involved in marketing research can be very helpful to the entrepreneur in gathering, processing, and interpreting market information.

Defining the Research Purpose and Objectives

The first step in marketing research is to define precisely the informational requirements of the decision to be made. Although this may seem too obvious to mention, the fact is needs are too often identified without sufficient probing. If the problem is not defined clearly, the information gathered will be useless.

In addition, specific objectives should be established. For example, one study has suggested the following set of questions for establishing objectives for general marketing research:

- ☐ Identify where potential customers go to purchase the good or service in question.
- ☐ Why do they choose to go there?
- ☐ What is the size of the market? How much of it can the business capture?
- ☐ How does the business compare with competitors?
- ☐ What impact does the business's promotion have on customers?
- ☐ What types of products or services are desired by potential customers?[5]

Gathering Secondary Data

Information that has already been compiled is known as **secondary data**. Generally speaking, secondary data are less expensive to gather than are new, or primary, data. The entrepreneur should exhaust all the available sources of secondary data before going further into the research process. Marketing decisions often can be made entirely with secondary data.

Secondary data may be internal or external. Internal secondary data consist of information that exists within the venture. The records of the business, for example, may contain useful information. External secondary data are available in numerous periodicals, trade association literature, and government publications.

Unfortunately, several problems accompany the use of secondary data. One is that such data may be outdated and, therefore, less useful. Another is that the units of measure in the secondary data may not fit the current problem. Finally, the question of validity is always present. Some sources of secondary data are less valid than others.

Gathering Primary Data

If the secondary data are insufficient, a search for new information, or **primary data**, is the next step. Several techniques can be used to accumulate primary data. These are often classified as observational methods and questioning methods. Observational methods avoid contact with respondents, whereas questioning methods involve respondents in varying degrees. Observation is probably the oldest form of research in existence. Observational methods can be used very economically. Furthermore, they avoid a potential bias that can result from a respondent's awareness of his or her participation under questioning methods. A major disadvantage of observational methods, however, is that they are limited to descriptive studies.

Surveys and experimentation are two questioning methods that involve contact with respondents. **Surveys** include contact by mail, telephone, and personal interviews. Mail surveys are often used when respondents are widely dispersed; however, these are characterized by low response rates. Telephone surveys and personal interview surveys involve verbal communication with respondents and provide higher response rates. Personal interview surveys, however, are more expensive than mail and telephone surveys.

Moreover, individuals often are reluctant to grant personal interviews because they feel a sales pitch is forthcoming. (Table 9.2 describes the major survey research techniques.)

Experimentation is a form of research that concentrates on investigating cause-and-effect relationships. The goal is to establish the effect an experimental variable has on a dependent variable. For example, what effect will a price change have on sales? Here the price is the experimental variable, and sales volume is the dependent variable. Measuring the relationship between these two variables would not be difficult if it were not for the many other variables involved.[6]

Developing an Information-Gathering Instrument

The questionnaire is the basic instrument for guiding the researcher and the respondent through a survey. The questionnaire should be developed carefully before it is used. Several major considerations for designing a questionnaire are listed here:

- ☐ Make sure each question pertains to a specific objective in line with the purpose of the study.

- ☐ Place simple questions first and difficult-to-answer questions later in the questionnaire.

- ☐ Avoid leading and biased questions.

- ☐ Ask: "How could this question be misinterpreted?" Reword questions to reduce or eliminate the possibility they will be misunderstood.

- ☐ Give concise but complete directions in the questionnaire. Succinctly explain the information desired, and route respondents around questions that may not relate to them.

- ☐ When possible, use scaled questions rather than simple yes/no questions to measure intensity of an attitude or frequency of an experience. For example, instead of asking: "Do we have friendly sales clerks?" (yes/no), ask: "How would you evaluate the friendliness of our sales clerks?" Have respondents choose a response on a five-point scale ranging from "Very unfriendly" (1) to "Very friendly" (5).[7]

Interpreting and Reporting the Information

After the necessary data have been accumulated, they should be developed into usable information. Large quantities of data are merely facts. To be useful, they must be organized and molded into meaningful information. The methods of summarizing and simplifying information for users include tables, charts, and other graphic methods. Descriptive statistics, such as the mean, mode, and median, are most helpful in this step of the research procedure.

Marketing Research Questions

The need for marketing research before and during a venture will depend on the type of venture. However, typical research questions might include the following, which are divided by subject:

Sales

1. Do you know all you need to know about your competitors' sales performance by type of product and territory?

2. Do you know which accounts are profitable and how to recognize a potentially profitable one?

Table 9.2   Comparison of Major Survey Research Techniques

CRITERIA	DIRECT/COLD MAILING	MAIL PANELS	TELEPHONE	PERSONAL IN-HOME	MALL INTERCEPT
Complexity and versatility	Not much	Not much	Substantial, but complex or lengthy scales difficult to use	Highly flexible	Most flexible
Quantity of data	Substantial	Substantial	Short, lasting typically between 15 and 30 minutes	Greatest quantity	Limited, 25 minutes or less
Sample control	Little	Substantial, but representative-ness may be a question	Good, but nonlisted households can be a problem	In theory, provides greatest control	Can be problematic; sample representativeness may be questionable
Quality of data	Better for sensitive or embarrassing questions; however, no interviewer is present to clarify what is being asked		Positive side, interview can clear up any ambiguities; negative side, may lead to socially accepted answers	There is the chance of cheating	Unnatural testing environment can lead to bias
Response rates	In general, low; as low as 10%	70–80%	60–80%	Greater than 80%	As high as 80%
Speed	Several weeks; completion time will increase with follow-up mailings	Several weeks with no follow-up mailings, longer with follow-up mailings	Large studies can be completed in 3 to 4 weeks	Faster than mail but typically slower than telephone surveys	Large studies can be completed in a few days
Cost	Inexpensive; as low as $2.50 per completed interview	Lowest	Not as low as mail; depends on incidence rate and length of questionnaire	Can be relatively expensive, but considerable variability	Less expensive than in-home, but higher than telephone; again, length and incidence rate will determine cost
Uses	Executive, industrial, medical, and readership studies	All areas of marketing research, particularly useful in low-incidence categories	Particularly effective in studies that require national samples	Still prevalent in product testing and other studies that require visual cues or product prototypes	Pervasive-concept tests, name tests, package tests, copy test

Source: Peter R. Dickson, *Marketing Management* (Fort Worth, TX: The Dryden Press, 1994), 114. Reprinted with permission of South-Western, a division of Thomson Learning: http://www.thomsonrights.com.

the entrepreneurial
PROCESS

Elements of Marketing Success

Leadership—As the owner or manager of a business, it is up to you to ensure your vision is clearly defined for all employees. The marketing programs your employees initiate must support the goals of the company. If the expectations are not clear, they will most likely not be met.

Listening—Customers are always more than willing to criticize a business. They will let you know what they want, what they need, and what they are willing to pay for it. If you ask nicely, they'll even tell you which marketing efforts they like best. Whether it's surveys, focus groups, polls, or feedback cards, you must first learn to listen to the customers' preferences.

Teamwork—Enroll your entire company into your marketing plan. Solicit their ideas, share your plans for new marketing efforts, and keep them posted on the company's progress. If a marketing plan is going to work, you must include everyone—from the janitor to the controller. Employees can produce great referrals, provide positive public relations, and even generate sales.

Coordination—Out-of-stock problems, delivery complications, and pricing inconsistencies are all barriers to sales. Open communication among all departments and individuals is a prerequisite to solving these types of problems. Once personnel can support rather than hinder each other, your marketing program will have a better success rate.

Focus—Unlike major conglomerations where there is internal battle over market share, a small business has the luxury of narrowly focusing on a defined audience. Attempting to take on too many target markets will diffuse your efforts and sabotage your results.

Accountability: Begin by setting quantifiable goals for each program or initiative. Each new program should build upon the previous. In order to achieve success, the actions must be measured and tracked. Examine each approach and then reproduce what works best.

Flexibility—Consumers are fickle; the successful companies are the ones who respond quickly to changes in the marketplace. If a marketing program stops working, investigate the problem and fix it . . . fast.

Continuity—Despite fast changes in the market, a consistent presentation of your brand and image are essential to your company's long-term growth. The names, logos, and slogans should be the basis of every marketing program.

Insight—Some companies always seem to be up on the changes in the market. They're the ones leading the industry in forecasting trends, evaluating competition, and developing new products and technology. You may not have the resources large companies do; however, the real secret isn't in the amount of resources you have, but what you do to look like you have what it takes to stay ahead of the pack.

SOURCES: Kim T. Gordon, "And Another Thing . . . " *Entrepreneur* (April 2002): 85–86.

3. Is your sales power deployed where it can do the most good, maximizing your investment in selling costs?

Distribution

1. If you are considering introducing a new product or line of products, do you know all you should about distributors' and dealers' attitudes toward it?

2. Are your distributors' and dealers' salespeople saying the right things about your products or services?

3. Has your distribution pattern changed along with the geographic shifts of your markets?

Markets

1. Do you know all that would be useful about the differences in buying habits and tastes by territory and kind of product?

2. Do you have as much information as you need on brand or manufacturer loyalty and repeat purchasing in your product category?

3. Can you now plot, from period to period, your market share of sales by products?

Advertising

1. Is your advertising reaching the right people?

2. Do you know how effective your advertising is in comparison to that of your competitors?

3. Is your budget allocated appropriately for greater profit—according to products, territories, and market potentials?

Products

1. Do you have a reliable quantitative method for testing the market acceptability of new products and product changes?

2. Do you have a reliable method for testing the effect on sales of new or changed packaging?

3. Do you know whether adding higher or lower quality levels would make new profitable markets for your products?

Inhibitors to Marketing Research

Despite the fact most entrepreneurs would benefit from marketing research, many fail to do it. A number of reasons for this exist, among them cost, complexity, level of need for strategic decisions, and irrelevancy. A number of articles have dealt with the lack of marketing research by entrepreneurs in the face of its obvious advantages and vital importance to the success of small businesses.[8]

Cost

Marketing research can be expensive, and some entrepreneurs believe that only major organizations can afford it. Indeed, some high-level marketing research is expensive, but smaller companies can also use very affordable marketing techniques.

Complexity

A number of marketing research techniques rely on sampling, surveying, and statistical analysis. This complexity, especially the quantitative aspects, is frightening to many entrepreneurs, and they shun it. The important point to remember is that the key concern is interpretation of the data, and an entrepreneur always can obtain the advice and counsel of those skilled in statistical design and evaluation by calling on the services of marketing research specialists or university professors trained in this area.

Strategic Decisions

Some entrepreneurs feel that only major strategic decisions need to be supported through marketing research. This idea is tied to the cost and complexity issues already mentioned. The contention is that because of the cost and statistical complexity of marketing research, it should be conducted only when the decisions to be made are major. The problem lies not only in the misunderstanding of cost and complexity but also in the belief that marketing research's value is restricted to major decisions. Much of the entrepreneur's sales efforts could be enhanced through the results of such research.[9]

Irrelevancy

Many entrepreneurs believe marketing research data will contain either information that merely supports what they already know or irrelevant information. Although it is true that marketing research does produce a variety of data, some of which may be irrelevant, it is also a fact that much of the information is useful. In addition, even if certain data merely confirm what the entrepreneur already knows, it is knowledge that has been tested and thus allows the individual to act on it with more confidence.

As indicated by these inhibitors, most of the reasons for entrepreneurs not using marketing research center either on a misunderstanding of its value or on a fear of its cost. However, the approach to marketing does not have to be expensive and can prove extremely valuable.

Developing the Marketing Concept

Effective marketing is based on three key elements: marketing philosophy, market segmentation, and consumer behavior. A new venture must integrate all three elements when developing its marketing concept and its approach to the market. This approach helps set the stage for how the firm will seek to market its goods and services.

Marketing Philosophy

Three distinct types of marketing philosophies exist among new ventures: production driven, sales driven, and consumer driven.

The **production-driven philosophy** is based on the belief "produce efficiently and worry about sales later." Production is the main emphasis; sales follow in the wake of production. New ventures that produce high-tech, state-of-the-art output sometimes use a production-driven philosophy. A **sales-driven philosophy** focuses on personal selling and advertising to persuade customers to buy the company's output. When an overabundance of supply occurs in the market, this philosophy often surfaces. New auto dealers, for example, rely heavily on a sales-driven philosophy. A **consumer-driven philosophy** relies on research to discover consumer preferences, desires, and needs *before* production actually begins. This philosophy stresses the need for marketing research in order to better understand where or who a market is and to develop a strategy targeted toward that group. Of the three philosophies, a consumer-driven orientation is often most effective, although many ventures do not adopt it.

Three major factors influence the choice of a marketing philosophy:

1. *Competitive pressure.* The intensity of the competition will many times dictate a new venture's philosophy. For example, strong competition will force many entrepreneurs to develop a consumer orientation in order to gain an edge over competitors. If, on the other hand, little competition exists, the entrepreneur may remain with a production orientation in the belief that what is produced will be sold.

2. *Entrepreneur's background.* The range of skills and abilities entrepreneurs possess varies greatly. While some have a sales and marketing background, others possess production and operations experience. The entrepreneur's strengths will influence the choice of a market philosophy.

3. *Short-term focus.* Sometimes a sales-driven philosophy may be preferred due to a short-term focus on "moving the merchandise" and generating sales. Although this focus appears to increase sales (which is why many entrepreneurs pursue this philosophy), it also can develop into a hard-selling approach that soon ignores customer preferences and contributes to long-range dissatisfaction.

Any one of the three marketing philosophies can be successful for an entrepreneur's new venture. It is important to note, however, that over the long run the consumer-driven philosophy is the most successful. This approach focuses on the needs, preferences, and satisfactions of the consumer and works to serve the end-user of the product or service.

Market Segmentation

Market segmentation is the process of identifying a specific set of characteristics that differentiate one group of consumers from the rest. For example, although many people eat ice cream, the market for ice cream can be segmented based on taste and price. Some individuals prefer high-quality ice cream made with real sugar and cream because of its taste; many others cannot tell the difference between high-quality and average-quality ingredients and, based solely on taste, are indifferent between the two types. The price is higher for high-quality ice cream such as Häagen-Daz or Ben & Jerry's, so the market niche is smaller for these offerings than it is for lower-priced competitors. This process of segmenting the market can be critical for new ventures with very limited resources.

To identify specific market segments, entrepreneurs need to analyze a number of variables. As an example, two major variables that can be focused on are demographic and benefit variables. Demographic variables include age, marital status, sex, occupation, income, location, and the like. These characteristics are used to determine a geographic and demographic profile of the consumers and their purchasing potential. The benefit variables help to identify unsatisfied needs that exist within this market. Examples may include convenience, cost, style, trends, and the like, depending on the nature of the particular new venture. Whatever the product or service, it is extremely valuable to ascertain the benefits a market segment is seeking in order to further differentiate a particular target group.

the entrepreneurial
PROCESS

Competitive Information

Felicia Lindau and Jason Monberg run an online retailer of greeting cards. Business was going well when the opportunity to set up a strategic alliance arose. Much to their chagrin, a copy of their business plan also made it to the meeting—but they didn't bring it. It had been obtained by the potential partner from someone they thought they could trust with the confidential information.

Following is a list of techniques to use to assess your competition and avoid paying a high-priced market research firm to collect information for you.

1. **Networking.** According to business professor Philip Anderson, talking to people in the field will help you get a feel for what's going on in your industry. Vendors, customers, and anyone who does business with companies in your field may have information on emerging competition. Lindau states that venture capitalists are a wonderful source of information because of the due diligence they must perform with pending venture loans. Much like what happens during the start-up phase of a business, a person can become so immersed in a project that he or she develops tunnel vision. Social networking also can provide a fresh view of the industry.

2. **Related products.** This market is the obvious place to look. Companies that can provide anything that complements your product or service are primed to become competition, because they also know what the customers' needs are and how to fulfill them. Large companies whose customers are businesses will assess this issue very differently from a small business with the average person as its primary consumer. A good example of a complementary relationship is the one existing among cameras, film, photo disks, and so on. The number and type of photographic

products available have increased substantially in recent years, and different fields have capitalized on this trend.

3. **Value chain.** Whereas related products fall on the horizontal axis of an industry, exploring the value chain forces a vertical assessment of potential entrants into your competitive pool. The value chain for a given product or service offers many opportunities for expansion, both for you and the potential competition. In this situation, the potential competition is fully aware of, and understands, the business environment in which you operate. They already have easy access to suppliers, buyers, and services that you deal with on a daily basis.

4. **Companies with related competencies.** One of the more ignored avenues involves companies that can take their expertise and apply it to an indirectly related field. Competencies can be both technological and nontechnological. Just because one company has unparalleled customer service and sales in the cellular industry doesn't mean the company couldn't use the same spectacular service in the cable business. The perfect example for expanding on technological similarities is Motorola. Its original intent was to focus on the defense industry. Surely that was not an area cellular providers were examining when trying to anticipate potential competition!

5. **Internet.** It goes without saying that the Internet is one of the premiere sources of information available to anyone who knows how to use it. Using search engines to access the 800 million web pages allows a business to easily scope out anyone that offers similar products or services. Searches can be both broad and defined. Most

important, they can be done cheaply and as often as desired. Anderson suggests using words that customers might use and avoiding technological or industry jargon when surfing, but points out that brainstorming all possible relations should ensure a thorough and more effective search.

Once the sufficient information has been gathered, a plan to beat the current and emerging competition should be prepared. The plan created will be analogous to the business's strengths and resources. Issues such as losing sales to another company could be addressed, a SWOT (strengths, weaknesses, opportunities, threats) analysis could be executed, or the plan to offer a new product or change price points could be outlined.

SOURCE: Adapted from Mark Henricks, "Friendly Competition?" *Entrepreneur* (December 1999): 114–117.

Consumer Behavior

Consumer behavior is defined by the many types and patterns of consumer characteristics. However, entrepreneurs can focus their attention on only two considerations: personal characteristics and psychological characteristics. Table 9.3 provides an example by tying these characteristics to the five types of consumers: innovators, early adopters, early majority, late majority, and laggards.

In the table the differences in social class, income, occupation, education, housing, family influence, and time orientation are illustrated. So, too, are the psychological characteristics labeled as needs, perceptions, self-concept, aspiration groups, and reference groups. This breakdown can provide an entrepreneur with a visual picture of the type of consumer to target for the sales effort.

The next step is to link the characteristic makeup of potential consumers with buying trends in the marketplace. Table 9.4 shows the changing priorities that shaped buying decisions during the 1990s. Each of these factors relates to consumer attitudes and behaviors based on education, the economy, the environment, and/or societal changes. By tying together the data in Tables 9.3 and 9.4, the entrepreneur can begin to examine consumer behavior more closely.

An analysis of the way consumers view the venture's product or service provides additional data. Entrepreneurs should be aware of five major consumer classifications:

1. *Convenience goods*—whether staple goods (foods), impulse goods (checkout counter items), or emergency goods and services, consumers will want these goods and services but will not be willing to spend time shopping for them.

2. *Shopping goods* are products consumers will take time to examine carefully and compare for quality and price.

3. *Specialty goods* consist of products or services consumers make a special effort to find and purchase.

4. *Unsought goods* are items consumers do not currently need or seek. Common examples are life insurance, encyclopedias, and cemetery plots. These products require explanation or demonstration.

5. *New products* are items that are unknown due to lack of advertising or are new products that take time to be understood. When microcomputers were first introduced, for example, they fell into this category.

Table 9.3 Consumer Characteristics

Personal Characteristics	INNOVATORS (2–3%)	EARLY ADOPTERS (12–15%)	EARLY MAJORITY (33%)	LATE MAJORITY (34%)	LAGGARDS (12–15%)
1. Social class	Lower upper	Upper middle	Lower middle	Upper lower	Lower lower
2. Income	High income (inherited)	High income (earned from salary and investment)	Above-average income (earned)	Average income	Below-average income
3. Occupation	Highest professionals Merchants Financiers	Middle management and owners of medium-sized businesses	Owners of small businesses Nonmanagerial office and union managers	Skilled labor	Unskilled labor
4. Education	Private schooling	College	High school Trade school	Grammar school, some high school	Very little–some grammar school
5. Housing	Inherited property Fine mansions	Large homes—good suburbs or best apartments	Small houses Multiple-family dwellings	Low-income housing in urban-renewal projects	Slum apartments
6. Family influence	Not family oriented Children in private school or grown	Children's social advancement important Education important	Child centered and home centered	Children taken for granted	Children expected to raise themselves
7. Time orientation	Present oriented, but worried about impact of time	Future oriented	Present oriented	Present (security) oriented	Tradition oriented, live in the past

Psychological Characteristics					
1. Nature of needs	Self-actualization needs (realization of potential)	Esteem needs (for status and recognition by others)	Belonging needs (with others and groups)	Safety needs (freedom from fear)	Survival needs (basic needs)
2. Perceptions	Cosmopolitan in outlook	Prestige Status conscious Aspire to upper class	Local aspirations and local social acceptance	Home and product centered	Live from day to day
3. Self-concept	Elite	Social strivers, peer group leaders, venturesome	Respectability from own reference groups and home	Security, home centered, aggressive, apathetic, no hope	Fatalistic, live from day to day
4. Aspiration groups	British upper class	Innovator class	In own social strata, dissociated from upper lower	Others in this classification and in early majority, dissociated from lower lower	Don't aspire
5. Reference groups	Sports, social, and travel groups	Dominate industry and community organizations Golf, college, and fraternity	Social groups of this strata: chambers of commerce, labor unions, family, church, P.T.A., auxiliaries	Family, labor unions	Ethnic group oriented

SOURCE: Roy A. Lindberg and Theodore Cohn, *The Marketing Book for Growing Companies That Want to Excel* (New York: Van Nostrand Reinhold, 1986), 80–81. Reprinted with permission.

Table 9.4   Changing Priorities and Purchases in the Family Life Cycle

STAGE	PRIORITIES	MAJOR PURCHASES
Fledgling: teens and early 20s	Self; socializing; education	Appearance products, clothing, automobiles, recreation, hobbies, travel
Courting: 20s	Self and other; pair bonding; career	Furniture and furnishings, entertainment and entertaining, savings
Nest building: 20s and early 30s	Babies and career	Home, garden, do-it-yourself items, baby-care products, insurance
Full nest: 30–50s	Children and others; career; midlife crisis	Children's food, clothing, education, transportation, orthodontics; career and life counseling
Empty nest: 50–75	Self and others; relaxation	Furniture and furnishings, entertainment, travel, hobbies, luxury automobiles, boats, investments
Sole survivor: 70–90	Self; health; loneliness	Health care services, diet, security and comfort products, TV and books, long-distance telephone services

SOURCE: Peter R. Dickson, *Marketing Management* (Fort Worth, TX: The Dryden Press, 1994), 91. Reprinted with permission of South-Western, a division of Thomson Learning: http://www.thomsonrights.com.

Marketing Stages for Growing Ventures

Most emerging ventures will evolve through a series of marketing stages. In each stage the marketing functions will differ; thus each requires a specific type of marketing strategy.[10]

A growing venture has four distinct stages: entrepreneurial marketing (Stage 1), opportunistic marketing (Stage 2), responsive marketing (Stage 3), and diversified marketing (Stage 4).[11] Table 9.5 provides a breakdown of each stage in relation to marketing strategy, marketing organization, marketing goals, and critical success factors. Notice that the strategy in each stage relates closely to the marketing goals. For example, entrepreneurial marketing (Stage 1) has a strategy of developing a market niche and a goal of attaining credibility in the marketplace. Stage 2, opportunistic marketing, seeks a strategy of market penetration for the purpose of attaining sales volume, thereby demonstrating the logical progression depicted in the table. Stage 3, responsive marketing, seeks to develop the product market and create customer satisfaction. Stage 4, diversified marketing, focuses on new-business development and seeks to manage the product life cycle.

Table 9.5   The Evolution of the Marketing Function

	STAGE 1: ENTREPRENEURIAL MARKETING	STAGE 2: OPPORTUNISTIC MARKETING	STAGE 3: RESPONSIVE MARKETING	STAGE 4: DIVERSIFIED MARKETING
Marketing Strategy	Market niche	Market penetration	Product-market development	New-business development
Marketing Organization	Informal, flexible	Sales management	Product-market management	Corporate and divisional levels
Marketing Goals	Credibility in the marketplace	Sales volume	Customer satisfaction	Product life-cycle and portfolio management
Critical Success Factors	A little help from your friends	Production economies	Functional coordination	Entrepreneurship and innovation

Source: Reprinted by permission of the *Harvard Business Review* (exhibit 1) from "Growing Ventures Can Anticipate Marketing Stages," by Tyzoon T. Tyebjee, Albert V. Bruno, and Shelby H. McIntyre (January/February 1983) 64. Copyright © 1983 by the Harvard Business School Publishing Corporation; all rights reserved.

It is important to realize that these stages are developed with a growing venture in mind. The idea of growth as a strategic planning factor, discussed in Chapter 15, is also presented here as a marketing factor.

Marketing Planning

Marketing planning is the process of determining a clear, comprehensive approach to the creation of customers. For developing this plan, the following elements are critical:

☐ *Marketing research:* determining who the customers are, what they want, and how they buy

☐ *Sales research:* promoting and distributing products according to marketing research findings

☐ *Marketing information system:* collecting, screening, analyzing, storing, retrieving, and disseminating marketing information on which to base plans, decisions, and actions

☐ *Sales forecasting:* coordinating personal judgment with reliable market information

☐ *Marketing plans:* formulating plans for achieving long-term marketing and sales goals

☐ *Evaluation:* identifying and assessing deviations from marketing plans[12]

Marketing Research

The purpose of marketing research is to identify customers—target markets—and to fulfill their desires. For marketing research, the following areas warrant consideration:

☐ *The company's major strengths and weaknesses.* These factors offer insights into profitable opportunities and potential problems and provide the basis for effective decision making.

Out-Marketing the Giants

In today's business world, everything appears to be focused on the "superstore" concept. The Wal-Marts, Kmarts, Lowes, and Meijers all mass market and, of course, all have the "lowest price guaranteed!" How does an entrepreneur compete within this multimedia blitz of supersizes and compressed prices? It's not easy, but, as always, the entrepreneurial spirit devises opportunities on which to capitalize. Here is one company's story, followed by some tips for outwitting the giants.

Kleenex and AstroTurf have one thing in common: they've been genericized by consumers. When you sneeze or need to wipe away tears, you want a Kleenex, not a facial tissue. When you think of indoor sports floors, you think of AstroTurf, not synthetic grass. AstroTurf currently owns 75 percent of the North American synthetic playing surface market, and Jim Savoca, chief operating officer of the Texas-based company, doesn't feel threatened by new competition. He should, however, because the small business FieldTurf has penetrated the market and is competing well against the dominant brand-name product.

FieldTurf differs from AstroTurf in that the synthetic fibers are woven into a carpet filled with alternating layers of sand and ground-up rubber. The sand provides stability, and the rubber provides resilience. For school districts and professional organizations, the most important attributes of synthetic floors are price and quality. FieldTurf costs less than half as much as its counterpart. Its $500 annual upkeep cost pales in comparison to AstroTurf's hefty $60,000, $25,000 of which goes for watering. That's how FieldTurf was able to get samples on floors and in front of the right people. Furthermore, FieldTurf drains water that can act as a host to infection when it remains stagnant—a likely event on AstroTurf's nonporous surface. Revenues for the company

were $19 million in 1999, up more than 1,000 percent from FieldTurf's $1.3 million in revenues in 1997. If the lack of injuries and positive feedback continue to promote the small business, it will certainly make a bigger dent into AstroTurf's current $250 million share of the market.

Jean Prevost and her partner, ex-Canadian Football League quarterback John Gilman, were canny enough to expect AstroTurf to introduce a knock-off of their invention once the word got out about its resemblance to real grass, resistance to rips and tears, and softness. Although they were not truly able to afford it, they poured money into 37 pending patents and patent litigation insurance—one case has already been settled. AstroTurf thus focused its marketing efforts on its eight-year warranty, keying in on the company's stable existence and longevity. FieldTurf answered that with an eight-year warranty backed by Lloyd's of London.

The two managers have also concocted a great strategy to promote their already-proven product and fend off inferior product allegations thrown out by AstroTurf. Ex-athletes such as Eddie Firmani (soccer), Steve Furness, Dick and Steve Khoury, and Neil Lomax (all football) are singing the artificial carpet's praises nationwide. FieldTurf couldn't ask for a better marketing campaign, with Furness literally sliding on the turf at trade shows and getting up without a friction burn.

Why is Prevost so sure that her product will stand the test of time and the monopolistic competition? She's got evidence of the rubber/sand necessity and plenty of support from coaches and field caretakers all over the United States. The maintenance crew at Dick Biven's Stadium in Texas was challenged to put the turf through the wringer—no complaints. The team doctor deemed it safer than grass. After 74 football games,

59 soccer games, and 80 marching band shows, the FieldTurf was "better than the day it was laid down." Biven's was the only stadium still playable after torrential rains washed out all of the other playing fields. After all, FieldTurf is the result of 20 years of research and development.

Tips

☐ Tap your database: Use purchase data to customize incentives, and use direct mail based on demographics, location, product preference, and price.

☐ Excel at "guerrilla marketing": Use local promotions to get close to customers and break through advertising clutter.

☐ Create store-specific marketing programs: Win retailer loyalty, differentiate your product, and build local sales.

☐ Search for missed opportunities: Small marketers can often focus on a relatively neglected product—such as duct tape or dental floss—and take market share from a bigger player or increase sales in a tired category.

☐ Apply the personal touch: Small-business marketers can get a big payoff when top executives pay personal attention to customers' letters, retailers' queries, and sales staffs' suggestions.

☐ Utilize today's technology: The cost of database technology is dropping, making direct-mail marketing a viable tactic for small-business marketers with tight budgets.

SOURCE: Adapted from Edward O. Welles, "Turf Wars," *Inc.* (February 2000): 90–98; and Christopher Power, "How to Get Closer to Your Customers," *Business Week*, Enterprise Issue (1993): 42–45.

☐ *Market profile.* A market profile helps a company identify its current market and service needs: How profitable are existing company services? Which of these services offer the most potential? Which (if any) are inappropriate? Which will customers cease to need in the future?

☐ *Current and best customers.* Identifying the company's current clients allows management to determine where to allocate resources. Defining the best customers enables management to more directly segment this market niche.

☐ *Potential customers.* By identifying potential customers, either geographically or with an industry-wide analysis of its marketing area, a company increases its ability to target this group, thus turning potential customers into current customers.

☐ *Competition.* By identifying the competition, a company can determine which firms are most willing to pursue the same basic market niche.

☐ *Outside factors.* This analysis focuses on changing trends in demographics, economics, technology, cultural attitudes, and governmental policy. These factors may have substantial impact on customer needs and, consequently, expected services.

☐ *Legal changes.* Marketing research performs the important task of keeping management abreast of significant changes in governmental rates, standards, and tax laws.[13]

Marketing research need not be extremely expensive. Presented next are some useful tips regarding low-cost research. These tips can be valuable to entrepreneurs needing research but lacking the funds for sophisticated measures.

Tip 1:   Establish a contest requiring entrants to answer a few simple questions about the quality of your products or services. The entry form is dropped into a convenient deposit box at the exit door of your store or service department with the drawing at month's end.

Tip 2:   Piggyback a questionnaire about the quality of your products or services onto a company catalog or sales brochure. Be sure also to ask what other items the customer would like to see the organization offering. Such a system functions as an ongoing program of organizational evaluation.

Tip 3:   Every organization receives the occasional complaint from a disgruntled customer. Instead of treating such situations casually, many organizations now adopt a management-by-exception philosophy and give grievances a high priority. Management follow-up with an in-depth interview often results in the revelation of unsuspected problems.

Tip 4:   Develop a standard set of questions regarding the quality of your organization's product and services suitable for administration by telephone. Have a secretary or part-time employee set aside a half-day each month in which 20 to 30 customers are called. Such a program often reminds customers to place an order. Many clients feel flattered their opinions are sought.

Tip 5:   Some organizations have succeeded by including research questionnaires in various products' packages. In this way they attempt to determine how a buyer heard about an item, why it was purchased from the firm, and so on. The only difficulty with this approach is that it focuses on customers and neglects research about the potential of sales to those who have not bought.[14]

Sales Research

An entrepreneur needs to continually review the methods employed for sales and distribution in relation to the market research that has been conducted. Matching the correct customer profile with sales priorities is a major goal in sales research. The following is a list of potential questions to be answered by this research:

- ☐ Do salespeople call on their most qualified prospects on a proper priority and time-allocation basis?
- ☐ Does the sales force contact decision makers?
- ☐ Are territories aligned according to sales potential and salespeople's abilities?
- ☐ Are sales calls coordinated with other selling efforts, such as trade publication advertising, trade shows, and direct mail?
- ☐ Do salespeople ask the right questions on sales calls? Do sales reports contain appropriate information? Does the sales force understand potential customers' needs?
- ☐ How does the growth or decline of a customer's or a prospect's business affect the company's own sales?

Marketing Information System

A marketing information system compiles and organizes data relating to cost, revenue, and profit from the customer base. This information can be useful for monitoring the strategies, decisions, and programs concerned with marketing. As with all information systems designs, the key factors affecting the value of such a system are (1) data reliability, (2) data usefulness or understandability, (3) reporting system timeliness, (4) data relevancy, and (5) system cost.

Sales Forecasting

Sales forecasting is the process of projecting future sales through historical sales figures and the application of statistical techniques. The process is limited in value due to its reliance on historical data, which many times fail to reflect current market conditions. As a segment of the comprehensive marketing-planning process, however, sales forecasting can be very valuable.

Marketing Plans

Marketing plans are part of a venture's overall strategic effort.[15] To be effective, these plans must be based on the venture's specific goals. Here is an example of a five-step program designed to help entrepreneurs follow a structured approach to developing a market plan:

Step 1: Appraise marketing strengths and weaknesses, emphasizing factors that will contribute to the firm's "competitive edge." Consider product design, reliability, durability, price/quality ratios, production capacities and limitations, resources, and need for specialized expertise.

Step 2: Develop marketing objectives along with the short- and intermediate-range sales goals necessary to meet those objectives. Next, develop specific sales plans for the current fiscal period. These goals should be clearly stated, measurable, and within the company's capabilities. To be realistic, these goals should require only reasonable efforts and affordable expenditures.

Step 3: Develop product/service strategies. The product strategy begins with identifying the end-users, wholesalers, and retailers, as well as their needs and specifications. The product's design, features, performance, cost, and price then should be matched to these needs.

Step 4: Develop marketing strategies. Strategies are needed to achieve the company's intermediate- and long-range sales goals and long-term marketing objectives. These strategies should include advertising, sales promotion campaigns, trade shows, direct mail, and telemarketing. Strategies also may be necessary for increasing the size of the sales force or marketing new products. Contingency plans will be needed in the event of technological changes, geographic market shifts, or inflation.

Step 5: Determine a pricing structure. A firm's pricing structure dictates which customers will be attracted, as well as the type or quality of products/services that will be provided. Many firms believe the market dictates a "competitive" pricing structure. But this is not always the case—many companies with a high price structure are very successful. Regardless of the strategies, customers must believe that the product's price is appropriate. The price of a product or service, therefore, should not be set until marketing strategies have been developed.[16]

Evaluation

The final critical factor in the marketing planning process is evaluation. Since a number of variables can affect the outcome of marketing planning, it is important to evaluate performance. Most important, reports should be generated from a customer analysis—attraction or loss of customers with reasons for the gain or loss, as well as established customer preferences and reactions. This analysis can be measured against performance in sales volume, gross sales dollars, or market share. It is only through this type of evaluation that flexibility and adjustment can be incorporated into marketing planning.

Telemarketing

Telemarketing is the use of telephone communications to sell merchandise directly to consumers. It is one of the fastest-growing direct market channels available to entrepreneurs and has become a direct marketing tool.

Revenues generated by telephone sales are growing at an annual rate of 25 percent to 35 percent, according to the Direct Marketing Association. It is estimated that during the 1990s the average household received at least 19 telemarketing calls per year and placed 16 orders for products and services via the telephone. In some cases, firms actually switched to fully automated telemarketing systems. Telemarketing systems now can use automatic-dialing and recorded-message players (ADRMPs) to dial numbers and play advertising messages that are voice activated and even that record orders from customers or forward the call to an operator.[17] However, keep in mind that many states have instituted "no call" lists, which means consumers may be able to shut out telemarketers from reaching their phones. The use of telemarketing is still in force, but it seems to be losing its impact due to the combination of the "no call" regulations and the widespread use of the Internet as a source to reach consumers. In any event, there are still advantages and pitfalls to be aware of with telemarketing.

Advantages

A telemarketing program can assist a venture in its marketing functions in a number of ways. A firm may be able to increase potential customer sales, upgrade sales or encourage multiple orders, reactivate old accounts, and support the current sales staff through an effective telemarketing program. Some of the specific advantages of telemarketing follow:

☐ *Receptiveness.* Most prospects are more receptive to telephone calls than to personal contact. This is true, in part, because potential customers expect less sales pressure over the phone.

☐ *Impressions.* First impressions, although often biased, can affect sales success. The telephone can help reduce many of the prospect's biases, since prejudgments can be based only on the caller's voice.

☐ *More presentations.* A conscientious field salesperson may obtain one high-quality prospect out of four contacts, while a telemarketer may reach only one high-quality prospect out of eight calls. However, a telephone salesperson can make 30 to 40 calls per hour, resulting in four to five presentations.

☐ *Unlimited geographic coverage.* Telephone salespeople can penetrate markets anywhere in the world where telephones are available.

☐ *Better time management.* The average field salesperson spends only three out of eight hours actually selling. The balance of the day is occupied in traveling or waiting for appointments. The telemarketer, on the other hand, uses the majority of the workday to sell. When a potential customer is unavailable, the salesperson simply makes a note to call later and dials another prospect.

☐ *Immediate feedback.* Telemarketing is the quickest means of assessing new sales strategies and allows them to be readily tested, adjusted, and retested before they are applied in the field. Some firms take advantage of telephone sales' immediate feedback by including marketing research questions in sales presentations.

☐ *Better control.* An inside sales force can be supervised more easily than a field staff. Typically, one supervisor for every five telephone salespeople monitors the sales team's performance.

☐ *Less "piracy."* Since inside sales personnel do not meet the customers or the competition's salespeople, they are less likely to receive job offers.

☐ *Lower salary and commissions.* Typically, compensation for a telemarketer is approximately 50 percent that of a field salesperson.

☐ *Other lower expenses.* A telemarketer can perform such diverse duties as handling marginal accounts, canvassing, and simple order taking more quickly than an outside salesperson by generating more customer calls per hour. The resulting savings in both expenses and time is telemarketing's greatest advantage.[18]

Pitfalls

Although telemarketing has numerous advantages, an entrepreneur also should be aware of potential pitfalls. First, poor telephone techniques can defeat the telemarketing strategy. Bad habits such as vagueness, impersonal attitude, overaggressiveness, rudeness, dishonesty, and long-winded discussions have to be avoided. This can be done through effective training programs.

Second, dissension between the field sales staff and the telephone sales personnel can arise. In order for the two groups to cooperate and work together effectively, both groups must have clear guidelines as well as open lines of communication between them. In addition, current customers need to be aware of the sales force's joint effort so they never feel discontent when the field representatives turn an account over to the telephone staff. A venture's management needs to address the coordination of leads, sales calls, follow-ups, and resulting commissions.

Third, entrepreneurs must be aware of the ever-present problem of rapid turnover of telephone staff. The work can be very monotonous, with people frequently leaving to find more interesting, challenging work. Additionally, the stigma of "phone peddling" often makes the workers feel their jobs are unimportant. To overcome these problems, management must make a sincere effort to create a professional, satisfied, and well-trained telemarketing staff.

Finally, the growing adoption of "no call" lists by many states as well as the eventual national "no call" list has dramatically hampered the efforts of telemarketers. These lists have been the direct result of consumer hostility toward telemarketing. Entrepreneurs should be aware of this growing trend as well as the huge popularity of Internet-based marketing.

Internet Marketing

The Internet can assist a new venture's overall marketing strategy in a number of ways. First, the Internet allows the firm to increase its presence and brand equity in the marketplace. Company and brand sites provide the opportunity to communicate the overall mission of the company/brand, to provide information on attributes and/or ratings of the company/brand, and to give information on the history of the company/brand. In addition, firms can easily communicate information on the marketing mix offered.

Second, the Internet allows the company to cultivate new customers. Providing important information about both the attributes of the firm's product and those of competitive products can aid in the decision-making process. In addition, the website can demonstrate products in actual use. This kind of information builds interest in the brand.

In addition, the Internet allows website visitors to match their needs with the offerings of the company. It is extremely important to remember that while traditional marketing techniques tend to be push-oriented (the company decides what the consumer will see and where), the Internet is pull-oriented (the consumer chooses what, when, and how to look in greater detail). This technique requires website designers to think differently about what should or should not appear in the site offering.

Third, the Internet can improve customer service by allowing customers to serve themselves when and where they choose. As more consumers begin to use the Internet, companies can readily serve these individuals without incurring expensive distribution costs. The expansion of the number of customers served requires only that the organization have enough servers available.

The fourth benefit to marketers relates to information transfer. Traditionally, companies have gathered information via focus groups, mail surveys, telephone surveys, and personal interviews. These techniques can be very expensive to implement, however. In contrast, the web offers a mechanism for the company to collect similar information at a fraction of the cost.

Not only can information be gathered from consumers, but information can also be shared with them. For example, the web can be used to provide expensive or specialized materials to consumers who request such information. The fulfilling of information requests via the web can offer substantial savings to the company (see Table 9.6 for web tips).

Table 9.6   Web Design Tips

THINGS TO DO	THINGS TO AVOID
Provide a description of the firm	Scrolling
Ensure fast loading times	Large graphic files
Create consistent navigation pathways	Reliance on one browser
Make the site interactive	Broken links
Register with search engines	Excessive use of plug-ins
Register the domain name	Obscure URLs
Use trademarks appropriately	Copycatting other sites
Market the site in other materials	Allowing the website to grow stale

Source: John H. Lindgren, Jr., "Marketing on the Internet," *Marketing Best Practices* (Fort Worth, TX: Harcourt College Publishers, 2000), 559.

The greatest potential for the future is probably in direct marketing, where catalogs can be offered online. These catalogs can be changed with ease if prices and/or product offerings change, resulting in substantial savings for organizations that would otherwise print new catalogs and mail them to consumers.

Although numerous advantages are available to companies that market via the Internet, two major concerns have also arisen: the limited target audience and consumer resistance to change. In regard to the first concern, the Internet is popular but not accessible by everyone. Although Internet use is increasing rapidly, until the demographics of Internet usage mirror our society as a whole, companies must use caution in overemphasizing this medium in their overall marketing mix. In regard to the second concern, resistance to change, it should be remembered that changing behavior patterns is difficult and sometimes time-consuming.

The change in behavior that will be necessary for Internet marketing to really take off requires that firms understand how to make consumers feel more confident when purchasing over the Internet. One simple solution is to educate consumers about the process—but achieving that goal will take time. Warranties, security measures, and other methods to reduce the perceived risk to consumers must be evaluated by companies that are bent on overcoming consumers' resistance to change.[19]

Pricing Strategies

One final marketing issue that needs to be addressed is that of pricing strategies. Many entrepreneurs, even after marketing research is conducted, are unsure of how to price their product or service. A number of factors affect this decision: the degree of competitive pressure, the availability of sufficient supply, seasonal or cyclical changes in demand, distribution costs, the product's life-cycle stage, changes in production costs, prevailing economic conditions, customer services provided by the seller, the amount of promotion done, and the market's buying power. Obviously, the ultimate price decision will balance many of these factors and, usually, will not satisfy *all* conditions. However, awareness of the various factors is important.

Other considerations, sometimes overlooked, are psychological in nature:

☐ The quality of a product in some situations is interpreted by customers according to the level of the item's price.

☐ Some customer groups shy away from purchasing a product where no printed price schedule is available.

☐ An emphasis on the monthly cost of purchasing an expensive item often results in greater sales than an emphasis on total selling price.

☐ Most buyers expect to pay even-numbered prices for prestigious items and odd-numbered prices for commonly available goods.

☐ The greater the number of meaningful customer benefits the seller can convey about a given product, generally the less will be the price resistance.[20]

Table 9.7   Pricing for the Product Life Cycle

Customer demand and sales volume will vary with the development of a product. Thus pricing for products needs to be adjusted at each stage of their life cycle. The following outline provides some suggested pricing methods that relate to the different stages in the product life cycle.

PRODUCT LIFE–CYCLE STAGE	PRICING STRATEGY	REASONS/EFFECTS
Introductory Stage		
☐ Unique product	**Skimming**—deliberately setting a high price to maximize short-term profits	Initial price set high to establish a quality image, to provide capital to offset development costs, and to allow for future price reductions to handle competition
☐ Nonunique product	**Penetration**—setting prices at such a low level that products are sold at a loss	Allows quick gains in market share by setting a price below competitors' prices
Growth Stage	**Consumer pricing**—combining penetration and competitive pricing to gain market share; depends on consumer's perceived value of product	Depends on the number of potential competitors, size of total market, and distribution of that market
Maturity Stage	**Demand-oriented pricing**—a flexible strategy that bases pricing decisions on the demand level for the product	Sales growth declines; customers are very price-sensitive
Decline Stage	**Loss leader pricing**—pricing the product below cost in an attempt to attract customers to other products	Product possesses little or no attraction to customers; the idea is to have low prices bring customers to newer product lines

Source: Adapted from Colleen Green, "Strategic Pricing," *Small Business Reports* (August 1989): 27–33.

Pricing procedures differ depending on the nature of the venture—retail, manufacturing, or service. Pricing for the product life cycle as presented in Table 9.7, however, might be applied to any type of business. The table demonstrates the basic steps of developing a pricing system and indicates how that system should relate to the desired pricing goals.

With this general outline in mind, potential entrepreneurs can formulate the most appropriate pricing strategy. Table 9.8 provides a thorough analysis of pricing strategies, outlining when each strategy is generally used, what the procedures are, and the advantages and disadvantages associated with each. This checklist can provide entrepreneurs with reference points for establishing and evaluating pricing strategies for their ventures.

Table 9.8 Pricing Strategy Checklist

STRATEGY OBJECTIVE	WHEN GENERALLY USED	PROCEDURE	ADVANTAGES	DISADVANTAGES
Skim the cream of the market for high short-term profit (without regard for long term).	No comparable competitive products. Drastically improved product or new product innovation. Large number of buyers. Little danger of competitor entry due to high price, patent control, high R&D costs, high promotion costs, and/or raw material control. Uncertain costs. Short life cycle. Inelastic demand.	Determine preliminary customer reaction. Charge premium price for product distinctiveness in short run, without considering long-run position. Some buyers will pay more because of higher present value to them. Then gradually reduce price to tap successive market levels (i.e., skimming the cream of a market that is relatively insensitive to price). Finally, tap more sensitive segments.	Cushions against cost overruns. Requires smaller investment. Provides funds quickly to cover new-product promotion and initial development costs. Limits demand until production is ready. Suggests higher value in buyer's mind. Emphasizes value rather than cost as a guide to pricing. Allows initial feeling out of demand before full-scale production.	Assumes that a market exists at high price. Results in ill will in early buyers when price is reduced. Attracts competition. Likely to underestimate ability of competitors to copy product. Discourages some buyers from trying the product (connotes high profits). May cause long-run inefficiencies.
Slide down demand curve to become established as efficient manufacturer at optimum volume before competitors become entrenched, without sacrificing long-term objective (e.g., obtain satisfactory share of market).	By established companies launching innovations. Durable goods. Slight barriers to entry by competition. Medium life span.	Tap successive levels of demand at highest prices possible. Then slide down demand curve faster and farther than forced to in view of potential competition. Rate of price change is slow enough to add significant volume at each successive price level, but fast enough to prevent large competitor from becoming established on a low-cost volume basis.	Emphasizes value rather than cost as a guide to pricing. Provides rapid return on investment. Provides slight cushion against cost overruns.	Requires broad knowledge of competitive product developments. Requires much documented experience. Results in ill will in early buyers when price is reduced. Discourages some buyers from buying at initial high price.
Compete at the market price to encourage others to produce and promote the product to stimulate primary demand.	Several comparable products. Growing market. Medium to long product life span. Known costs.	Start with final price and work back to cost. Use customer surveys and studies of competitors' prices to approximate final price. Deduct selling margins. Adjust product, production, and selling methods to sell at this price and still make necessary profit margins.	Requires less analysis and research. Existing market requires fewer promotion efforts. Causes no ill will in early buyers since price will not be lowered soon.	Limited flexibility. Limited cushion for error. Slower recovery of investment. Must rely on other differentiating tools.

(Continued)

Table 9.8 (Continued)

STRATEGY OBJECTIVE	WHEN GENERALLY USED	PROCEDURE	ADVANTAGES	DISADVANTAGES
Market penetration to stimulate market growth and capture and hold a satisfactory market share at a profit through low prices. Become strongly entrenched to generate profits over long term.	Long product life span. Mass market. Easy market entry. Demand is highly sensitive to price. Unit costs of production and distribution decrease rapidly as quantity of output increases. Newer product. No "elite" market willing to pay premium for newest and best.	Charge low prices to create a mass market, resulting in cost advantages derived from larger volume. Look at lower end of demand curve to get price low enough to attract a large customer base. Also review past and competitor prices.	Discourages actual and potential competitor inroads because of apparent low profit margins. Emphasizes value more than cost in pricing. Allows maximum exposure and penetration in minimum time. May maximize long-term profits if competition is minimized.	Assumes volume is always responsive to price reductions, which isn't always true. Relies somewhat on glamour and psychological pricing, which doesn't always work. May create more business than production capacity available. Requires significant investment. Small errors often result in large losses.
Preemptive pricing to keep competitors out of market or eliminate existing ones	Used more often in consumer markets. Manufacturers may use this approach on one or two products, with other prices meeting or higher than those of competitors.	Price at low levels so that market is unattractive to possible competitors. Set prices as close as possible to total unit cost. As increased volume allows lower cost, pass advantage to buyers via lower prices. If cost declines rapidly with increases in volume, can start price below cost (can use price approaching variable costs).	Discourages potential competitors because of apparent low profit margins. Limits competitive activity and expensive requirements to meet them.	Must offer other policies that permit lower price (limited credit, delivery, or promotions). Small errors can result in large losses. Long-term payback period.

Source: Roy A. Lindberg and Theodore Cohn, *The Marketing Book for Growing Companies That Want to Excel* (New York: Van Nostrand Reinhold, 1986), 116–117. Reprinted with permission.

Summary

Marketing research involves the gathering of information about a particular market, followed by analysis of that information. The marketing research process has five steps: (1) Define the purpose and objectives of the research, (2) gather secondary data, (3) gather primary data, (4) develop an information-gathering instrument (if necessary), and (5) interpret and report the information.

Entrepreneurs do not carry out marketing research for four major reasons: (1) cost, (2) complexity of the undertaking, (3) belief that only major strategic decisions need to be supported through marketing research, and (4) belief that the data will be irrelevant to company operations. Usually they misunderstand the value of marketing research or fear its cost.

Developing a marketing concept has three important areas. One area is the formulation of a marketing philosophy. Some entrepreneurs are production-driven, others are sales-driven, and still others are consumer-driven. The entrepreneur's values and the market conditions will help determine this philosophy. A second area is market segmentation, which is the process of identifying a specific set of characteristics that differentiate one group of consumers from the rest. Demographic and benefit variables are often used in this process. A third area is an understanding of consumer behavior. Since many types and patterns of consumer behavior exist, entrepreneurs need to focus on the personal and psychological characteristics of their customers. In this way they can determine a tailor-made, consumer-oriented strategy. This customer analysis focuses on such important factors as general buying trends in the marketplace, specific buying trends of targeted consumers, and the types of goods and services being sold.

Most emerging ventures go through the four marketing stages of entrepreneurial marketing, opportunistic marketing, responsive marketing, and diversified marketing. Each stage requires a different strategy, and the entrepreneur must adjust accordingly.

Marketing planning is the process of determining a clear, comprehensive approach to the creation of customers. For developing this plan, the following elements are critical: marketing research, sales research, a marketing information system, sales forecasting, marketing plans, and evaluation.

Two other critical areas in marketing for new ventures are telemarketing and the Internet. Telemarketing is the use of telephone communications to directly contact and sell merchandise to consumers. The cost/benefit ratio of telecommunications was so high that it was one of the most important marketing tools utilized during the 1990s. However, by 2006, the growth of consumer hostility toward their invasion of privacy with these telemarketers lead to the development of "no call" lists by many states and even the development of a national "no call" list. The Internet is fast becoming one of the greatest marketing tools of the twenty-first century. It offers numerous benefits for the overall marketing strategy of a company, including brand recognition, information transfer, and customer services. Nevertheless, some concerns have arisen regarding the Internet's limited target audience and the potential for customer resistance to change.

Pricing strategies are a reflection of marketing research and must consider such factors as marketing competitiveness, consumer demand, life cycle of the goods or services being sold, costs, and prevailing economic conditions.

■ Key Terms and Concepts

consumer pricing	penetration
consumer-driven philosophy	primary data
demand-oriented pricing	production-driven philosophy
experimentation	sales-driven philosophy
Internet marketing	secondary data
loss leader pricing	skimming
market	surveys
marketing research	telemarketing
market segmentation	

■ Review and Discussion Questions

1. In your own words, what is a market? How can marketing research help an entrepreneur identify a market?

2. What are the five steps in the marketing research process? Briefly describe each.

3. Which is of greater value to the entrepreneur, primary or secondary data? Why?

4. Identify and describe three of the primary obstacles to undertaking marketing research.

5. How would an entrepreneur's new-venture strategy differ under each of the following marketing philosophies: production-driven, sales-driven, consumer-driven? Be complete in your answer.

6. In your own words, what is market segmentation? What role do demographic and benefit variables play in the segmentation process?

7. Identify and discuss three of the most important personal characteristics that help an entrepreneur identify and describe customers. Also, explain how the product life cycle will affect the purchasing behavior of these customers.

8. Identify and discuss three of the psychological characteristics that help an entrepreneur identify and describe customers. Also, explain how the product life cycle will affect the purchasing behavior of these customers.

9. How does the way consumers view a venture's product or service affect strategy? For example, why would it make a difference to the entrepreneur's strategy if the consumers viewed the company as selling a convenience good as opposed to a shopping good?

10. Identify and describe four of the major forces shaping buying decisions in the new century.

11. Most emerging ventures evolve through a series of marketing stages. What are these stages? Identify and describe each.

12. What does the entrepreneur of an emerging venture need to know about sales research and a marketing information system?

13. For developing a marketing plan, what are the five steps that are particularly helpful? Identify and describe each.

14. How does telemarketing work? What are its advantages? What are its pitfalls? What is the greatest detriment to this marketing tool being used in the twenty-first century?

15. Describe the benefits and concerns of marketing on the Internet. Be specific in your answer.

16. What are some of the major environmental factors that affect pricing strategies? What are some of the major psychological factors that affect pricing? Identify and discuss three of each.

Experiential Exercise

Identifying the Customer

One of the most important activities of entrepreneurs is identifying their customers. A list of the five basic types of consumers (A through E) and a list of descriptions of these types (a through o) follow. Identify the order in which people adopt new goods by ranking the first list from 1 (first adopters) to 5 (last adopters). Then match the descriptions with the types of consumer by placing a *1* next to those that describe initial adopters, on down to a *5* next to those that describe final adopters. (Three descriptions are listed for each of the five types of consumer.) Answers are provided at the end of the exercise.

A. _____ Early adopters

B. _____ Early majority

C. _____ Laggards

D. _____ Innovators

E. _____ Late majority

a. _____ High-income people who have inherited their wealth

b. _____ Future oriented

c. _____ Below-average-income wage earners

d. _____ Present (security) oriented

e. _____ High-income people who have incomes from salary and investment

f. _____ Highest professionals, including merchants and financiers

g. _____ Present oriented

h. _____ Average-income wager earners

i. _____ Middle managers and owners of medium-sized businesses

j. _____ Above-average-income wage earners

k. _____ Present oriented, but worried about the impact of time

l. _____ Unskilled labor

m. _____ Skilled labor

n. _____ Owners of small businesses; nonmanagerial office and union managers

o. _____ Tradition-oriented people who often live in the past

Answers: A. 2, B. 3, C. 5, D. 1, E. 4, a. 1, b. 2, c. 5, d. 4, e. 2, f. 1, g. 3, h. 4, i. 2, j. 3, k. 1, l. 5, m. 4, n. 3, o. 5

Case 9.1

Dealing with the Competition

Six months ago Roberta O'Flynn opened a small office supply store. Roberta sells a wide range of general office merchandise, including photocopying and typing paper, writing tablets, envelopes, writing instruments, and computer diskettes, as well as a limited range of office desks, chairs, and lamps.

Several office supply stores in the local area are, in Roberta's opinion, competitors. In an effort to better understand the competition, Roberta has visited four of these stores and pretended to be a customer so she could get information regarding their prices, product offerings, and service. Each has a different strategy. For example, one of them sells strictly on price. It is the customer's responsibility to pick up the merchandise and carry it away. Another relies heavily on service, including a 90-day credit plan for those purchasing equipment in excess of $500. This company's prices are the highest of the four stores Roberta visited. The other two stores use a combination of price and service strategies.

Roberta believes that in order to get her new venture off the ground, she must develop a marketing strategy that helps her effectively compete with these other firms. Since her store is extremely small, Roberta believes that a certain amount of marketing research could be of value. On the other hand, her budget is extremely limited, and she is not sure how to collect the information. Roberta believes that what she needs to do is develop a market niche that will be loyal to her. In this way, no matter how extensive the competition, she always will have a group of customers who buy from her. Roberta also believes that the focus of this research has to be in two general directions. First, she has to find out what customers look for from an office supply store. How important is price? Service? Quality? Second, she has to determine the general strategy of each of her major competitors so she can develop a plan of action for preventing them from taking away her customers. Right now, however, her biggest question is: How do I go about getting the information I need?

Questions

1. Will the information Roberta is seeking be of value to her in competing in this market? Why or why not?

2. How would you recommend Roberta put together her marketing research plan? What should be involved? Be as complete as possible in your answer.

3. How expensive will it be for Roberta to follow your recommendations for her marketing research plan? Describe any other marketing research efforts she could undertake in the near future that would be of minimal cost.

Case 9.2

A New Spin on Music

After graduation from an excellent university with a degree in entrepreneurship, Brian Wright was eager to launch a business. Brian always enjoyed working with new technologies as well as watching movies, playing video games, and listening to music. So, with the proliferation of online movie and video game rental services, he believed that a service providing the online rental of CDs made perfect sense.

Brian was confident that the success of the other online rental services proved that there was a market for the online rental of entertainment media; therefore, renting CDs online would be an easy concept for customers to grasp. Although MP3s and MP3 players were growing in popularity, Brian knew that he and his friends preferred to listen to an album in its entirety; after all, Brian believed that "any true fan of an artist would want the entire album."

When calculating potential revenue, Brian concluded that the average retail price of a CD was approximately $14. If he charged $2 per CD per rental, which would be an 85 percent savings to the customer based on the full retail price of a CD, he could recoup his costs within seven rentals. In addition, Brian believed that he could negotiate contracts with the music labels to purchase CDs in bulk at a discount, which would in turn reduce the time it would take for him to reach break-even. He knew enough about music encryption technologies to know that restrictions could be built into the CDs to deter people from copying songs from them. He decided that taking such precautions would alleviate any concerns that the music labels might have regarding piracy.

As Brian began discussing his idea with his friends, their enthusiasm convinced him that he needed to act quickly before someone else seized the opportunity. At $2 per rental and an estimated two rentals per customer per month, he would only need a little over 20,000 customers to reach $1,000,000 in annual revenue. Looking at his financial forecasts, Brian decided that it was time to bring his online CD rental service to market.

Questions

1. Has Brian completed the proper marketing research for this potential opportunity? Why or why not? Explain.

2. Based on the case, are there key mistakes that you would caution Brian about? Explain.

3. What specific steps would you recommend to Brian in order for him to better assess this opportunity?

Notes

1. For a discussion of markets, see E. Jerome McCarthy and William D. Perreault, *Basic Marketing: A Managerial Approach,* 8th ed. (Homewood, IL: Irwin, 1984), Chapter 2; and Peter R. Dickson, *Marketing Management* (Fort Worth, TX: The Dryden Press, 1994).

2. Harriet Buckman Stephenson, "The Most Critical Problem for the Fledgling Small Business: Getting Sales," *American Journal of Small Business* (summer 1984): 26–33.

3. Alfred M. Pelham, "Market Orientation and Other Potential Influences on Performance in Small and Medium-Sized Manufacturing Firms," *Journal of Small Business Management* (January 2000): 48–67.

4. For a thorough presentation, see Stephen W. McDaniel and A. Parasuraman, "Practical Guidelines for Small Business Marketing Research," *Journal of Small Business Management* (January 1986): 1–7.

5. Robert T. Justis and Bill Jackson, "Marketing Research for Dynamic Small Business," *Journal of Small Business Management* (October 1978): 10–20; see also Timothy M. Baye, "Relationship Marketing: A Six-Step Guide for the Business Start-Up," *Small Business Forum* (spring 1995): 26–41.

6. Thomas J. Callahan and Michael D. Cassar, "Small Business Owners' Assessments of Their Abilities to Perform and Interpret Formal Market Studies," *Journal of Small Business Management* (October 1995): 1–9.

7. McDaniel and Parasuraman, "Practical Guidelines," 5.

8. As an example, see Alan R. Andreasen, "Cost-Conscious Marketing Research," *Harvard Business Review* (July/August 1983): 74–75.

9. John A. Pearce II and Steven C. Michael, "Marketing Strategies That Make Entrepreneurial Firms Recession-Resistant," *Journal of Business Venturing* (July 1997): 301–314.

10. Richard B. Robinson, Jr. and John A. Pearce II, "Product Life-Cycle Considerations and the Nature of Strategic Activities in Entrepreneurial Firms," *Journal of Business Venturing* (spring 1986): 207–224.

11. Tyzoon T. Tyebjee, Albert V. Bruno, and Shelby H. McIntyre, "Growing Ventures Can Anticipate Marketing Stages," *Harvard Business Review* (January/February 1983): 62–66.

12. "Marketing Planning," *Small Business Reports* (April 1986): 68–72.

13. Ibid., 70.

14. *Marketing Tactics Master Guide for Small Business* by Gerald B. McCready, © 1982, 8. Reprinted by permission of the publisher, Prentice-Hall, a division of Simon & Schuster, Englewood Cliffs, New Jersey.

15. Avraham Shama, "Marketing Strategies during Recession: A Comparison of Small and Large Firms," *Journal of Small Business Management* (July 1993): 62–72.

16. "Marketing Planning," 71.

17. Philip Kotler, *Marketing Management,* 9th ed. (Upper Saddle River, NJ: Prentice-Hall, 1997), 729–730.

18. "Telemarketing: Designing a Profitable Program," *Small Business Reports* (August 1987): 23–24.

19. For a thorough review of Internet marketing, see John H. Lindgren, Jr., "Marketing on the Internet," *Marketing Best Practices* (Fort Worth, TX: Harcourt College Publishers, 2000), 540–564; see also Charles W. Lamb, Jr., Joseph F. Hair, Jr., and Carl McDaniel, *Essentials of Marketing* (Mason, OH: South-Western/Thomson Learning, 2005), Chapter 14.

20. McCready, *Marketing Tactics,* 79.

Financial Preparation for Entrepreneurial Ventures

Small company managers are too inclined to delegate to outside accountants every decision about their companies' financial statements. Indeed, it is most unfair to suppose that accountants can produce—without management's advice and counsel—the perfect statement for a company. Instead, I contend, top managers of growing small companies must work with their independent accountants in preparing company financial statements to ensure that the right message is being conveyed. . . .

James McNeill Stancill
"Managing Financial Statements: Image and Effect"
Growing Concerns

Chapter Objectives

1 To explain the principal financial statements needed for any entrepreneurial venture: the balance sheet, income statement, and cash-flow statement

2 To outline the process of preparing an operating budget

3 To discuss the nature of cash flow and to explain how to draw up such a document

4 To describe how pro forma statements are prepared

5 To explain how capital budgeting can be used in the decision-making process

6 To illustrate how to use break-even analysis

7 To describe ratio analysis and illustrate the use of some of the important measures and their meanings

Today's entrepreneur operates in a competitive environment characterized by the constraining forces of governmental regulation, competition, and resources. In regard to the latter, no firm has access to an unlimited amount of resources. So in order to compete effectively, the entrepreneur must allocate resources efficiently. Three kinds of resources are available to the entrepreneur: human, material, and financial. This chapter focuses on financial resources in the entrepreneurial environment, beginning with a discussion of financial statements as a managerial planning tool. How the budgeting process translates into the preparation of pro forma statements is presented, and attention is also given to break-even analysis and ratio analysis as profit-planning tools.

The Importance of Financial Information for Entrepreneurs

Financial information pulls together all the information presented in the other segments of the business: marketing, distribution, manufacturing, and management. It quantifies all the assumptions and historical information concerning business operations.[1]

It should be remembered that entrepreneurs make assumptions to explain how numbers are derived and correlate these assumptions with information presented in other parts of the business operations. The set of assumptions on which projections are based should be clearly and precisely presented. Without these assumptions, numbers will have little meaning. It is only after carefully considering such assumptions that the entrepreneur will be able to assess the validity of financial projections. Because the rest of the financial plan is an outgrowth of these assumptions, they are the most integral part of any financial segment. (See Table 10.1 for a financial glossary for entrepreneurs.)

In order for entrepreneurs to develop the key components of a financial segment, they should follow a clear process, described in the next section.

Table 10.1   A Financial Glossary for the Entrepreneur

Accrual system of accounting A method of recording and allocating income and costs for the period in which each is involved, regardless of the date of payment or collection. For example, if you were paid $100 in April for goods you sold in March, the $100 would be income for March under an accrual system. (Accrual is the opposite of the cash system of accounting.)

Asset Anything of value that is owned by you or your business.

Balance sheet An itemized statement listing the total assets and liabilities of your business at a given moment. It is also called a *statement of condition.*

Capital (1) The amount invested in a business by the proprietor(s) or stockholders. (2) The money available for investment or money invested.

Cash flow The schedule of your cash receipts and disbursements.

Cash system of accounting A method of accounting whereby revenue and expenses are recorded when received and paid, respectively, without regard for the period to which they apply.

Collateral Property you own that you pledge to the lender as security on a loan until the loan is repaid. Collateral can be a car, home, stocks, bonds, or equipment.

Cost of goods sold This is determined by subtracting the value of the ending inventory from the sum of the beginning inventory and purchases made during the period. Gross sales less cost of goods sold gives you gross profit.

Current assets Cash and assets that can be easily converted to cash, such as accounts receivable and inventory. Current assets should exceed current liabilities.

Current liabilities Debts you must pay within a year (also called short-term liabilities).

Depreciation Lost usefulness; expired utility; the diminution of service yield from a fixed asset or fixed asset group that cannot or will not be restored by repairs or by replacement of parts.

Equity An interest in property or in a business, subject to prior creditors. An owner's equity in his or her business is the difference between the value of the company's assets and the debt owed by the company. For example, if you borrow $30,000 to purchase assets for which you pay a total of $50,000, your equity is $20,000.

Expense An expired cost; any item or class of cost of (or loss from) carrying on an activity; a present or past expenditure defraying a present operating cost or representing an irrecoverable cost or loss; an item of capital expenditures written down or off; or a term often used with some qualifying expression denoting function, organization, or time, such as a selling expense, factory expense, or monthly expense.

Financial statement A report summarizing the financial condition of a business. It normally includes a balance sheet and an income statement.

Gross profit Sales less the cost of goods sold. For example, if you sell $100,000 worth of merchandise for which you paid $80,000, your gross profit would be $20,000. To get net profit, however, you would have to deduct other expenses incurred during the period in which the sales were made, such as rent, insurance, and sales staff salaries.

Interest The cost of borrowing money. It is paid to the lender and is usually expressed as an annual percentage of the loan. That is, if you borrow $100 at 12%, you pay 1% (.01 × $100 = $1) interest per month. Interest is an expense of doing business.

Income statement Also called *profit and loss statement.* A statement summarizing the income of a business during a specific period.

Liability Money you owe to your creditors. Liabilities can be in the form of a bank loan, accounts payable, and so on. They represent a claim against your assets.

Loss When a business's total expenses for the period are greater than the income.

Net profit Total income for the period less total expenses for the period. (See *Gross profit.*)

Net worth The same as *equity.*

Personal financial statement A report summarizing your personal financial condition. Normally it includes a listing of your assets, liabilities, large monthly expenses, and sources of income.

Profit (See *Net profit* and *Gross profit.*) "Profit" usually refers to net profit.

Profit and loss statement Same as *income statement.*

Variable cost Costs that vary with the level of production on sales, such as direct labor, material, and sales commissions.

Working capital The excess of current assets over current liabilities.

Understanding the Key Financial Statements

Financial statements are powerful tools entrepreneurs can use to manage their ventures.[2] The basic financial statements an entrepreneur needs to be familiar with are the balance sheet, the income statement, and the cash-flow statement. The following sections examine each of these in depth, providing a foundation for understanding the books of record all ventures need.

The Balance Sheet

A **balance sheet** is a financial statement that reports a business's financial position at a specific time. Many accountants like to think of it as a picture taken at the close of business on a particular day, such as December 31. The closing date is usually the one that marks the end of the business year for the organization.

The balance sheet is divided into two parts: the financial resources owned by the firm and the claims against these resources. Traditionally, these claims against the resources come from two groups: creditors who have a claim to the firm's assets and can sue the company if these obligations are not paid and owners who have rights to anything left over after the creditors' claims have been paid.

The financial resources the firm owns are called *assets*. The claims creditors have against the company are called *liabilities*. The residual interest of the firm's owners is known as *owners' equity*. When all three are placed on the balance sheet, the assets are listed on the left, and the liabilities and owners' equity are listed on the right.

An asset is something of value the business owns. In order to determine the value of an asset, the owner-manager must do the following:

1. Identify the resource
2. Provide a monetary measurement of that resource's value
3. Establish the degree of ownership in the resource

Most assets can be identified easily. They are tangible, such as cash, land, and equipment. However, *intangible assets* also exist. These are assets that cannot be seen; examples include copyrights and patents.

Liabilities are the debts of the business. These may be incurred either through normal operations or through the process of obtaining funds to finance operations. A common liability is a short-term account payable in which the business orders some merchandise, receives it, and has not yet paid for it. This often occurs when a company receives merchandise during the third week of the month and does not pay for it until it pays all of its bills on the first day of the next month. If the balance sheet was constructed as of the end of the month, the account still would be payable at that time.

Liabilities are divided into two categories: short term and long term. **Short-term liabilities** (also called *current liabilities*) are those that must be paid during the coming 12 months. **Long-term liabilities** are those that are not due and payable within the next 12 months, such as a mortgage on a building or a five-year bank loan.

Owners' equity is what remains after the firm's liabilities are subtracted from its assets. It is the claim the owners have against the firm's assets. If the business loses money, its owners' equity will decline. This will become clearer when we explain why a balance sheet always balances.[3]

Understanding the Balance Sheet

In order to fully explain the balance sheet, it is necessary to examine a typical one and determine what each entry means. Table 10.2 provides an illustration. Note that it has three sections: assets, liabilities, and owners' equity. Within each of these classifications are various types of accounts. The following sections examine each type of account presented in the table.

Table 10.2   Kendon Corporation Balance Sheet for the Year Ended December 31, 2006

ASSETS		
Current Assets		
Cash		$200,000
Accounts receivable	$375,000	
Less: Allowance for uncollectible accounts	$25,000	350,000
Inventory		150,000
Prepaid expenses		35,000
Total current assets		$735,000
Fixed Assets		
Land		$330,000
Building	$315,000	
Less: Accumulated depreciation of building	80,000	
Equipment	410,000	
Less: Accumulated depreciation of equipment	60,000	
Total fixed assets		915,000
Total assets		$1,650,000
LIABILITIES		
Current Liabilities		
Accounts payable	$150,000	
Notes payable	25,000	
Taxes payable	75,000	
Loan payable	50,000	
Total current liabilities		$300,000
Bank loan		200,000
Total liabilities		$500,000
OWNERS' EQUITY		
Contributed Capital		
Common stock, $10 par, 40,000 shares	$400,000	
Preferred stock, $100 par, 500 shares		
Authorized, none sold	--------	
Retained earnings	750,000	
Total owners' equity		1,150,000
Total liabilities and owners' equity		$1,650,000

Current Assets

Current assets consist of cash and other assets that are reasonably expected to be turned into cash, sold, or used up during a normal operating cycle. The most common types of current assets are those shown in Table 10.2.

Cash refers to coins, currency, and checks on hand. It also includes money the business has in its checking account and savings account.

Accounts receivable are claims of the business against its customers for unpaid balances from the sale of merchandise or the performance of services. For example, many firms sell on credit and expect their customers to pay by the end of the month. Or, in many of these cases, they send customers a bill at the end of the month and ask for payment within ten days.

The *allowance for uncollectible accounts* refers to accounts receivable judged to be uncollectible. How does a business know when receivables are not collectible? This question can be difficult to answer; it is not known. However, assume the business asks all of its customers to pay within the first ten days of the month following the purchase. Furthermore, an aging of the accounts receivable shows that the following amounts are due the firm:

NUMBER OF DAYS OUTSTANDING	AMOUNT OF RECEIVABLES
1–10	$325,000
11–20	25,000
21–30	20,000
31–60	5,000
61–90	7,500
91+	17,500

In this case, the firm might believe that anything more than 60 days old will not be paid and will write it off as uncollectible. Note in Table 10.2 that the allowance for uncollectible accounts is $25,000, the amount that has been outstanding more than 60 days.

Inventory is merchandise held by the company for resale to customers. Current inventory in our example is $150,000, but this is not all of the inventory the firm had on hand all year. Naturally, the company started the year with some inventory and purchased more as sales were made. This balance sheet figure is what was left at the end of the fiscal year.

Prepaid expenses are expenses the firm already has paid but that have not yet been used. For example, insurance paid on the company car every six months is a prepaid-expense entry because it will be six months before all of the premium has been used. As a result, the accountant would reduce this prepaid amount by one-sixth each month. Sometimes supplies, services, and rent are also prepaid, in which case the same approach is followed.

Fixed Assets

Fixed assets consist of land, building, equipment, and other assets expected to remain with the firm for an extended period. They are not totally used up in the production of the firm's goods and services. Some of the most common types are shown in Table 10.2.

Land is property used in the operation of the firm. This is not land that has been purchased for expansion or speculation; that would be listed as an investment rather than a fixed asset. Land is listed on the balance sheet at cost, and its value usually is changed only periodically. For example, every five years, the value of the land might be recalculated so that its value on the balance sheet and its resale value are the same.

Building consists of the structures that house the business. If the firm has more than one building, the total cost of all the structures is listed.

Accumulated depreciation of building refers to the amount of the building that has been written off the books due to wear and tear. For example, referring to Table 10.2, the original cost of the building was $315,000, but accumulated depreciation is $80,000, leaving a net value of $235,000. The amount of depreciation charged each year is determined by the company accountant after checking with the Internal Revenue Service rules. However, a standard depreciation is 5 percent per year for new buildings, although an accelerated method sometimes is used. In any event, the amount written off is a tax-deductible expense. Depreciation therefore reduces the amount of taxable income to the firm and helps lower the tax liability. In this way, the business gets the opportunity to recover part of its investment.

Equipment is the machinery the business uses to produce goods. This is placed on the books at cost and then depreciated and listed as the *accumulated depreciation of equipment*. In our example, it is $60,000. The logic behind equipment depreciation and its effect on the firm's income taxes is the same as that for accumulated depreciation on the building.

Current Liabilities

Current liabilities are obligations that will become due and payable during the next year or within the operating cycle. The most common current liabilities are listed in Table 10.2.

Accounts payable are liabilities incurred when goods or supplies are purchased on credit. For example, if the business buys on a basis of net 30 days, during that 30 days the bill for the goods will constitute an account payable.

A **note payable** is a promissory note given as tangible recognition of a supplier's claim or a note given in connection with an acquisition of funds, such as for a bank loan. Some suppliers require that a note be given when a company buys merchandise and is unable to pay for it immediately.

Taxes payable are liabilities owed to the government—federal, state, and local. Most businesses pay their federal and state income taxes on a quarterly basis. Typically, payments are made on April 15, June 15, and September 15 of the current year and January 15 of the following year. Then the business closes its books, determines whether it still owes any taxes, and makes the required payments by April 15. Other taxes payable are sales taxes. For example, most states and some cities levy a sales tax. Each merchant must collect the taxes and remit them to the appropriate agency.

A **loan payable** is the current installment on a long-term debt that must be paid this year. As a result, it becomes a part of the current liabilities. The remainder is carried as a long-term debt. Note that in Table 10.2 $50,000 of this debt was paid in 2006 by the Kendon Corporation.

Long-Term Liabilities

As we have said, long-term liabilities consist of obligations that will not become due or payable for at least one year or not within the current operating cycle. The most common are bank loans.

A *bank loan* is a long-term liability due to a loan from a lending institution. Although it is unclear from the balance sheet in the table how large the bank loan originally was, it is being paid down at the rate of $50,000 annually. Thus, it will take four more years to pay off the loan.

Contributed Capital

The Kendon Corporation is owned by individuals who have purchased stock in the business. Various kinds of stock can be sold by a corporation, the most typical being common stock and preferred stock. Only common stock has been sold by this company.

Common stock is the most basic form of corporate ownership. This ownership gives the individual the right to vote for the board of directors. Usually, for every share of common stock held, the individual is entitled to one vote. As shown in Table 10.2, the corporation has issued 40,000 shares of $10 par common stock, raising $400,000. Although the term *par value* may have little meaning to most stockholders, it has legal implications; it determines the legal capital of the corporation. This legal capital constitutes an amount that total stockholders' equity cannot be reduced below except under certain circumstances (the most common is a series of net losses). For legal reasons, the total par value of the stock is maintained in the accounting records. However, it has no effect on the *market value* of the stock.

Preferred stock differs from common stock in that its holders have preference to the assets of the firm in case of dissolution. This means that, after the creditors are paid, preferred stockholders have the next claim on whatever assets are left. The common stockholders' claims come last. Table 10.2 shows 500 shares of preferred stock were issued, each worth a par value of $100, but none has been sold. Therefore, it is not shown as a number on the balance sheet.

Retained Earnings

Retained earnings are the accumulated net income over the life of the business to date. In Table 10.2, the retained earnings are shown as $750,000. Every year this amount increases by the profit the firm makes and keeps within the company. If dividends are declared on the stock, they, of course, are paid from the total net earnings. Retained earnings are what remain after that.

Why the Balance Sheet Always Balances

By definition, the balance sheet always balances.[4] If something happens on one side of the balance sheet, it is offset by something on the other side. Hence, the balance sheet remains in balance. Before examining some illustrations, let us restate the balance-sheet equation:

Assets = Liabilities + Owners' Equity

With this in mind, let us look at some typical examples of business transactions and their effect on the balance sheet.

A Credit Transaction

The Kendon Corporation calls one of its suppliers and asks for delivery of $10,000 of materials. The materials arrive the next day, and the company takes possession of them.

The bill is to be paid within 30 days. How is the balance sheet affected? *Inventory* goes up by $10,000, and *accounts payable* rise by $10,000. The increase in current assets is offset by an increase in current liabilities.

Continuing this illustration, what happens when the bill is paid? The company issues a check for $10,000, and *cash* declines by this amount. At the same time, *accounts payable* decrease by $10,000. Again, these are offsetting transactions, and the balance sheet remains in balance.

A Bank Loan

Table 10.2 shows the Kendon Corporation had an outstanding bank loan of $200,000 in 2006. Assume the company increases this loan by $100,000 in 2007. How is the balance sheet affected? *Cash* goes up by $100,000, and *bank loan* increases by the same amount; again balance is achieved. However, what if the firm uses this $100,000 to buy new machinery? In this case, *cash* decreases by $100,000 and *equipment* increases by a like amount. Again, a balance exists. Finally, what if Kendon decides to pay off its bank loan? In this case, the first situation is reversed; *cash* and *bank loan* (long-term liabilities) decrease in equal amounts.

A Stock Sale

Suppose the company issues and sells another 40,000 shares of $10 par *common* stock. How does this action affect the balance sheet? (This answer is rather simple.) *Common stock* increases by $400,000, and so does *cash*. Once more, a balance exists.

With these examples in mind, it should be obvious why the balance sheet always balances. Every entry has an equal and offsetting entry to maintain this equation:

Assets = Liabilities + Owners' Equity

Keep in mind that, in accounting language, the terms *debit* and *credit* denote increases and decreases in assets, liabilities, and owners' equity. The following chart relates debits and credits to increases and decreases.

CATEGORY	A TRANSACTION INCREASING THE AMOUNT	A TRANSACTION DECREASING THE AMOUNT
Asset	Debit	Credit
Liability	Credit	Debit
Owners' equity	Credit	Debit

Applying this idea to the preceding examples results in the following:

	DEBIT	CREDIT
Credit Transaction		
Inventory	$10,000	
Accounts payable		$10,000
Bank Loan		
Cash	100,000	
Bank Loan		100,000
Stock Sale		
Cash	400,000	
Common Stock		400,000
	$510,000	$510,000

The Income Statement

The **income statement** is a financial statement that shows the change that has occurred in a firm's position as a result of its operations over a specific period. This is in contrast to the balance sheet, which reflects the company's position at a particular point in time.

The income statement reports the success (or failure) of the business during the period. In essence, it shows whether revenues were greater than or less than expenses. These *revenues* are the monies the small business has received from the sale of its goods and services. The *expenses* are the costs of the resources used to obtain the revenues. These costs range from the cost of materials used in the products the firm makes to the salaries it pays its employees.

Most income statements cover a one-year interval, but it is not uncommon to find monthly, quarterly, or semiannual income statements. All of the revenues and expenses accumulated during this time are determined, and the net income for the period is identified. Many firms prepare quarterly income statements but construct a balance sheet only once a year. This is because they are interested far more in their profits and losses than in examining their asset, liability, and owners' equity positions. However, it should be noted that the income statement drawn up at the end of the year will coincide with the firm's fiscal year, just as the balance sheet does. As a result, at the end of the business year, the organization will have both a balance sheet and an income statement. In this way, they can be considered together and the interrelationship between them can be studied. A number of different types of income and expenses are reported on the income statement. However, for purposes of simplicity, the income statement can be reduced to three primary categories: (1) revenues, (2) expenses, and (3) net income.

Revenues are the gross sales the business made during the particular period under review. Revenue often consists of the money actually received from sales, but this need not be the case. For example, sales made on account still are recognized as revenue, as when a furniture store sells $500 of furniture to the Adams family today, delivers it tomorrow, and will receive payment two weeks from now. From the moment the goods are delivered, the company can claim an increase in revenue.

Expenses are the costs associated with producing goods or services. For the furniture store in the preceding paragraph, the expenses associated with the sale would include the costs of acquiring, selling, and delivering the merchandise. Sometimes these are expenses that will be paid later. For example, the people who deliver the furniture may be paid every two weeks, so the actual outflow of expense money in the form of salaries will not occur at the same time the work is performed. Nevertheless, it is treated as an expense.

Net income is the excess of revenue over expenses during the particular period under discussion. If revenues exceed expenses, the result is a *net profit*. If the reverse is true, the firm suffers a *net loss*. At the end of the accounting period, all of the revenues and expenses associated with all of the sales of goods and services are added together, and then the expenses are subtracted from the revenues. In this way, the firm knows whether it made an overall profit or suffered an overall loss.[5]

Understanding the Income Statement

In order to explain the income statement fully, it is necessary to examine one and determine what each account is. Table 10.3 illustrates a typical income statement. It

Table 10.3   Kendon Corporation Income Statement for the Year Ended December 31, 2006

Sales Revenue	$1,750,000	
Less: Sales returns and allowances	50,000	
Net sales	_____	$1,700,000
Cost of Goods Sold		
Inventory, January, 2005	$ 150,000	
Purchases	1,050,000	
Goods available for sale	$1,200,000	
Less: Inventory, December, 2005	200,000	
Cost of goods sold		1,000,000
Gross margin		$ 700,000
Operating Expenses		
Selling expenses	$ 150,000	
Administrative expenses	100,000	
Total operating expenses		250,000
Operating income		$ 450,000
Financial Expenses		$ 20,000
Income before income taxes		$ 430,000
Estimated Income Taxes		172,000
Net profit		$ 258,000

has five major sections: (1) sales revenue, (2) cost of goods sold, (3) operating expenses, (4) financial expense, and (5) income taxes estimated.

Revenue

Every time a business sells a product or performs a service, it obtains revenue. This often is referred to as *gross revenue* or *sales revenue*. However, it is usually an overstated figure because the company finds that some of its goods are returned or some customers take advantage of prompt-payment discounts.

In Table 10.3, sales revenue is $1,750,000. However, the firm also has returns and allowances of $50,000. These returns are common for companies that operate on a "satisfaction or your money back" policy. In any event, a small business should keep tabs on these returns and allowances to see if the total is high in relation to the total sales revenue. If so, the firm will know something is wrong with what it is selling, and it can take action to correct the situation.

Deducting the sales returns and allowances from the sales revenue, the company finds its *net sales*. This amount must be great enough to offset the accompanying expenses in order to ensure a profit.

Cost of Goods Sold

As the term implies, the cost of goods sold section reports the cost of merchandise sold during the accounting period. Simply put, the cost of goods for a given period equals the beginning inventory plus any purchases the firm makes minus the inventory on hand at the end of the period. Note in Table 10.3 the beginning inventory was $150,000 and the purchases totaled $1,050,000. This gave Kendon goods available for sale of $1,200,000. The ending inventory for the period was $200,000, so the cost of goods sold was $1,000,000. This is what it cost the company to buy the inventory it sold. When this cost of goods sold is subtracted from net sales, the result is the *gross margin*. The gross margin is the amount available to meet expenses and to provide some net income for the firm's owners.

Operating Expenses

The major expenses, exclusive of costs of goods sold, are classified as **operating expenses.** These represent the resources expended, except for inventory purchases, in generating the revenue for the period. Expenses often are divided into two broad subclassifications: selling expenses and administrative expenses.

Selling expenses result from activities such as displaying, selling, delivering, and installing a product or performing a service. Expenses for displaying a product include rent for storage space, depreciation on fixtures and furniture, property insurance, and utility and tax expenses. Sales expenses, salaries, commissions, and advertising also fall into this category. Costs associated with getting the product from the store to the customer also are considered selling expenses. Finally, if the firm installs the product for the customer, all costs, including the parts used in the job, are considered in this total. Taken as a whole, these are the selling expenses.

Administrative expenses is a catchall term for operating expenses not directly related to selling or borrowing. In broad terms, these expenses include the costs associated with running the firm. They include salaries of the managers, expenses associated with operating the office, general expenses that cannot be related directly to buying or selling activities, and expenses that arise from delinquent or uncollectible accounts.

When these selling and administrative expenses are added together, the result is *total operating expenses*. Subtracting them from gross margin gives the firm its *operating income*. Note in Table 10.3 that selling expenses are $150,000, administrative expenses are $100,000, and total operating expenses are $250,000. When subtracted from the gross margin of $700,000, the operating income is $450,000.

Financial Expense

The **financial expense** is the interest expense on long-term loans. As seen in Table 10.3, this expense is $20,000. Additionally, many companies include their interest expense on short-term obligations as part of their financial expense.

Estimated Income Taxes

As noted earlier, corporations pay estimated income taxes, and then, at some predetermined time (for example, December 31), the books are closed, actual taxes are determined, and any additional payments are made (or refunds claimed). When these taxes are subtracted from the income before income taxes, the result is the *net profit*. In our example, the Kendon Corporation made $258,000.

The Cash-Flow Statement

The **cash-flow statement** (also known as *statement of cash flows*) shows the effects of a *company's operating, investing, and financing activities on its cash balance.* The principal purpose of the statement of cash flows is to provide relevant information about a company's cash receipts and cash payments during a particular accounting period. It is useful in answering such questions as:

- ☐ How much cash did the firm generate from operations?
- ☐ How did the firm finance fixed capital expenditures?
- ☐ How much new debt did the firm add?
- ☐ Was the cash from operations sufficient to finance fixed asset purchases?

The statement of cash flows is a supplement to the balance sheet and income statements. One of the limitations of the income and balance sheet statements is that they are based on accrual accounting. In accrual accounting, revenues and expenses are recorded when incurred—not when cash changes hands. For example, if a sale is made for credit, under accrual accounting the sale is recognized but cash has not been received. Similarly a tax expense may be shown in the income statement but it may not be paid until later. The statement of cash flows reconciles the accrual-based figures in the income and balance sheet statements to the actual cash balance reported in the balance sheet.

The statement of cash flows is broken down into *operating, investing,* and *financing* activities. Table 10.4 provides an outline of a statement of cash flows. *Operating cash flows* refer to cash generated from or used in the course of business operations of the firm. For most firms the net operating cash flows will be positive because their operating inflows (primarily from revenue collections) will exceed operating cash outflows (for example, payment for raw materials and wages).

Investing activities refer to cash flow effects from long-term investing activities, such as purchase or sale of plant and equipment. The net cash flow from investing activities can be either positive or negative. A firm that is still in the growth phase would be building up fixed assets (installing new equipment or building new plants) and therefore show negative cash flows from investing activities. On the other hand a firm that is divesting unprofitable divisions may realize cash inflows from the sale of assets and therefore show a positive cash flow from investing activities.

Financing activities refer to cash flow effect of financing decisions of the firm, including sale of new securities, such as stocks and bonds, repurchase of securities, and payment of dividends. Note that payment of interest to lenders is *not* included under financing activities. Accounting convention in determining the statement of cash flows assumes that interest payments are part of operating cash flows. Once the cash flows

Table 10.4 Format of Statement of Cash Flows

Cash flows from operating activities	$
Cash flows from investing activities	$
Cash flows from financing activities	$
Net increase (decrease) in cash	$
Cash at beginning of period	$
Cash at end of period	$

from the three different sources—operating, investing, and financing—are identified, the beginning and ending cash balances are reconciled.

Because this statement is most frequently used by those analyzing the firm, the use of a cash budget may be the best approach for an entrepreneur starting up a venture. The cash budget procedure will be covered in the next section.

Preparing Financial Statements

One of the most powerful tools the entrepreneur can use in planning financial operations is a **budget**.[6] The *operating budget* is a statement of estimated income and expenses over a specified period of time. Another common type of budget is the *cash budget*, which is a statement of estimated cash receipts and expenditures over a specified period of time. It is typical for a firm to prepare both types of budgets by first computing an operating budget and then constructing a cash budget based on the operating budget. A third common type of budget is the *capital budget*, which is used to plan expenditures on assets whose returns are expected to last beyond one year. This section examines all three of these budgets: operating, cash flow, and capital. Then the preparation of pro forma financial statements from these budgets is discussed.

The Operating Budget

Typically, the first step in creating an **operating budget** is the preparation of the **sales forecast**.[7] An entrepreneur can prepare the sales forecast in several ways. One way is to implement a statistical forecasting technique such as **simple linear regression**. Simple linear regression is a technique in which a linear equation states the relationship among three variables:

$$Y = a + bx$$

Y is a dependent variable (it is dependent on the values of a, b, and x), x is an independent variable (it is not dependent on any of the other variables), a is a constant (in regression analysis, Y is dependent on the variable x, all other things held constant), and b is the slope of the line (the change in Y divided by the change in x). For estimating sales, Y is the variable used to represent the expected sales, and x is the variable used to represent the factor on which sales are dependent. Some retail stores may believe their sales are dependent on their advertising expenditures, whereas other stores may believe their sales are dependent on some other variable, such as the amount of foot traffic past the store.

When using regression analysis, the entrepreneur will draw conclusions about the relationship between, for example, product sales and advertising expenditures. Presented next is an example of how Mary Tindle, owner of a clothing store, used regression analysis.

Mary began with two initial assumptions: (1) If no money is spent on advertising, total sales will be $200,000, and (2) for every dollar spent on advertising, sales will be increased by two times that amount. Relating these two observations yields the following simple linear regression formula:

$$S = \$200,000 + 2A$$

where

   S = Projected Sales

   A = Advertising Expenditures

Figure 10.1 Regression Analysis

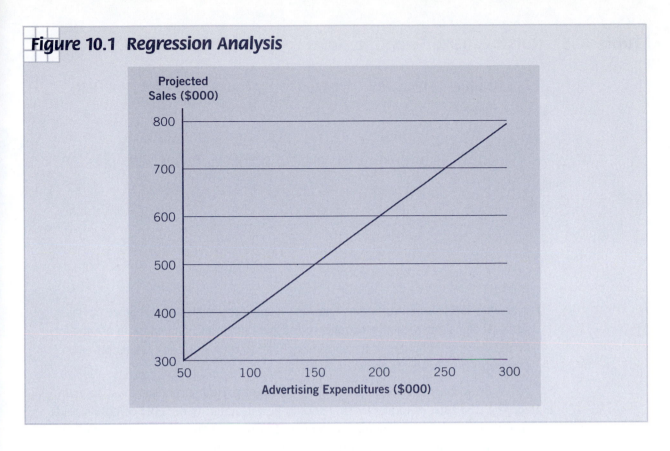

(Note that it is often easier to substitute more meaningful letters into an equation. In this case, the letter S was substituted for the letter Y simply because the word sales starts with that letter. The same is true for the letter A, which was substituted for the letter X.) In order to determine the expected sales level, Mary must insert different advertising expenditures and complete the simple linear regression formula for each different expenditure. The following data and Figure 10.1 demonstrate the results.

SIMPLE LINEAR REGRESSION ($000)

A	2A	S = $200 + 2A
$ 50	$100	$300
100	200	400
150	300	500
200	400	600
250	500	700
300	600	800

Another commonly used technique for the preparation of a sales forecast is the estimation that current sales will increase a certain percentage over the prior period's sales. This percentage is based on a trend line analysis that covers the five preceding sales periods and assumes that the seasonal variations will continue to run in the same pattern. Obviously, since it needs five preceding sales periods, trend line analysis is used for more established ventures. It is nevertheless an important tool that entrepreneurs should be aware of as the venture grows and becomes more established. Here is an example of how John Wheatman, owner of North Central Scientific, used trend line analysis to forecast sales for his computer retail store:

After considerable analysis of his store's sales history, John Wheatman decided to use trend line analysis and estimated that sales would increase 5 percent during the next

Table 10.5   North Central Scientific: Sales Forecast for 20XX ($000)

	JANUARY	FEBRUARY	MARCH	APRIL	MAY	JUNE
Sales	$300	$350	$400	$375	$500	$450
× 1.05	315	368	420	394	525	473
	JULY	AUGUST	SEPTEMBER	OCTOBER	NOVEMBER	DECEMBER
Sales	$475	$480	$440	$490	$510	$550
× 1.05	499	504	462	515	536	578

year, with the seasonal variations following roughly the same pattern. Since he has a personal computer with an electronic spreadsheet program, John chose to use the input of last year's sales figures in the spreadsheet and to then increase each month by 5 percent. The results are shown in Table 10.5.

After a firm has forecast its sales for the budget period, expenses must be estimated. The first type of expenses that should be estimated is the cost of goods sold, which follows sales on the income statement. For retail firms this is a matter of projecting purchases and the corresponding desired beginning and ending inventories. Many firms prefer to have a certain percentage of the next month's sales on hand in inventory. Here is how John Wheatman determines his store's expected purchases and inventory requirements:

> For determining his purchase requirements, John Wheatman believes his gross profit will represent 20 percent of his sales dollar. This is based on analysis of the past five years' income statement. Consequently, cost of goods sold will represent 80 percent of the sales for the current month. In addition, John wants to have approximately one week's inventory on hand. Thus the ending inventory is estimated to be 25 percent of next month's sales. The results are shown in Table 10.6.

A manufacturing firm, on the other hand, will need to establish its production budget, a material purchases budget based on the production budget, and the corresponding direct labor budget. The production budget is management's estimate of the number of units that need to be produced in order to meet the sales forecast. This budget is prepared by working backward through the cost of goods sold section. First, the predicted number of units that will be sold during that month is determined. Then the desired ending-inventory-level balance is added to this figure. The sum of these two figures is the number of units that will be needed in inventory. Once the inventory requirements have been determined, the entrepreneur must determine how many of these units will be accounted for by the beginning inventory (which is the prior month's ending inventory) and how many units will have to be produced. The production requirement is calculated by subtracting the period's beginning inventory from the inventory needed for that period. For example:

> Tom B. Good, president and founder of General Manufacturing, has decided to implement a budget in order to help plan for his company's growth. After receiving the unit sales forecast from his sales manager, Tom examined last year's product movement reports and determined

Table 10.6   North Central Scientific: Purchase Requirements Budget for 20XX ($000)

	JAN.	FEB.	MAR.	APR.	MAY	JUNE	JULY	AUG.	SEPT.	OCT.	NOV.	DEC.
Sales revenue	$315	$368	$420	$394	$525	$473	$499	$504	$462	$515	$536	$578
Cost of goods sold												
Beginning inventory	$ 63	$ 74	$ 84	$ 79	$105	$ 95	$100	$101	$ 92	$103	$107	$116
Purchases	263	305	331	341	410	383	400	395	380	416	437	413
Cost of goods available	$326	$379	$415	$420	$515	$478	$500	$496	$472	$519	$544	$529
Ending inventory	74	85	79	105	95	100	101	92	102	107	116	66
Cost of goods sold	$252	$294	$336	$315	$420	$378	$399	$403	$370	$412	$428	$462
Gross profit	$ 63	$ 74	$ 84	$ 79	$105	$ 95	$100	$101	$ 92	$103	$108	$116

Cost of goods sold = Current period sales × .80

Ending inventory = Next month's sales × (.80)(.25) (since inventory is carried at cost)

Cost of goods available = Cost of goods sold + Ending inventory

Beginning inventory = Prior month's ending inventory or current month's sales × (.80)(.25)

Purchases = Cost of goods available − Beginning inventory

Gross profit = Sales − Cost of goods sold

Table 10.7   General Manufacturing: Production Budget Worksheet for 20XX ($000)

	JAN.	FEB.	MAR.	APR.	MAY	JUNE	JULY	AUG.	SEPT.	OCT.	NOV.	DEC.
Projected sales (units)	125	136	123	143	154	234	212	267	236	345	367	498
Desired ending inventory	14	12	14	15	23	21	27	24	35	37	50	26
Available for sale	139	148	137	158	177	255	239	291	271	382	417	524
Less: Beginning inventory	12	14	12	14	15	23	21	27	24	35	37	50
Total production requirements	127	134	125	144	162	232	218	264	247	347	380	474

that he would like to have 10 percent of the next month's sales on hand as a buffer against possible fluctuations in demand. He has also received a report from his production manager that his ending inventory this year is expected to be 12,000 widgets, which will also be the beginning inventory for the budget period. Table 10.7 shows the results.

After the production budget has been calculated, the materials required for producing the specified number of units can be determined from an analysis of the bill of materials for the product being manufactured. In addition, by examining the amount of direct labor needed to produce each unit, management can determine the amount of direct labor that will be needed during the forthcoming budget period.

The last step in preparing the operating budget is to estimate the operating expenses for the period. Three of the key concepts in developing an expense budget are fixed, variable, and mixed costs. A **fixed cost** is one that does not change in response to changes in activity for a given period of time. Rent, depreciation, and certain salaries are examples. A **variable cost** is one that changes in the same direction as, and in direct proportion to, changes in operating activity. Direct labor, direct materials, and sales commissions are examples. **Mixed costs** are a blend of fixed and variable costs. An example is utilities, since part of this expense would be responsive to change in activity, and the rest would be a fixed expense, remaining relatively stable over the budget period. Mixed costs can present a problem for management in that it is sometimes difficult to determine how much of the expense is variable and how much is fixed.

After the expenses have been budgeted, the sales, cost of goods, and expense budget are combined to form the operating budget. Table 10.8 outlines North Central Scientific's anticipated expenses for the budget year and the completed operating budget for the period. Each month represents the pro forma, or projected, income and expenses for that period.

The Cash-Flow Budget

After the operating budget has been prepared, the entrepreneur can proceed to the next phase of the budget process, the **cash-flow budget**. This budget, which is often prepared with the assistance of an accountant, provides an overview of the cash inflows and outflows during the period. By pinpointing cash problems in advance, management can make the necessary financing arrangements.[8]

The first step in the preparation of the cash-flow budget is the identification and timing of cash inflows. For the typical business, cash inflows will come from three sources: (1) cash sales, (2) cash payments received on account, and (3) loan proceeds. Not all of a firm's sales revenues are cash. In an effort to increase sales, most businesses will allow some customers to purchase goods on account. Consequently, part of the funds will arrive in later periods and will be identified as cash payments received on account. Loan proceeds represent another form of cash inflow that is not directly tied to the sales revenues. A firm may receive loan proceeds for several reasons—for example, the planned expansion of the firm (new building and equipment) or meeting cash-flow problems stemming from an inability to pay current bills.

Some businesses have a desired minimum balance of cash indicated on the cash-flow budget, highlighting the point at which it will be necessary to seek additional financing. Table 10.9 provides an example of how North Central Scientific prepared its cash-flow budget.

Table 10.8 North Central Scientific: Expense and Operating Budgets

In order to identify the behavior of the different expense accounts, John Wheatman decided to analyze the past five years' income statements. Following are the results of his analysis:

- ☐ Rent is a constant expense and is expected to remain the same over the next year.

- ☐ Payroll expense changes in proportion to sales, since the more sales the store has, the more people it must hire to meet increased consumer demands.

- ☐ Utilities are expected to remain relatively constant over the budget period.

- ☐ Taxes are based primarily on sales and payroll and are therefore considered a variable expense.

- ☐ Supplies will vary in proportion to sales. This is because most of the supplies will be used to support sales.

- ☐ Repairs are relatively stable and are a fixed expense. John has maintenance contracts on the equipment in the store, and the cost is not scheduled to rise during the budget period.

NORTH CENTRAL SCIENTIFIC: EXPENSE BUDGET FOR 20XX ($000)

	JAN.	FEB.	MAR.	APR.	MAY	JUNE	JULY	AUG.	SEPT.	OCT.	NOV.	DEC.
Anticipated operating expenses												
Rent	$ 2	$ 2	$ 2	$ 2	$ 2	$ 2	$ 2	$ 2	$ 2	$ 2	$ 2	$ 2
Payroll	32	37	42	39	53	47	50	50	46	51	54	58
Utilities	5	5	5	5	5	5	5	5	5	5	5	5
Taxes	3	4	4	4	5	5	5	5	5	5	5	6
Supplies	16	18	21	20	26	24	25	25	23	26	27	29
Repairs	2	2	2	2	2	2	2	2	2	2	2	2
Total expenses	$ 60	$ 68	$ 76	$ 72	$ 93	$ 85	$ 89	$ 89	$ 83	$ 91	$ 95	$102
Sales revenue	$315	$368	$420	$394	$525	$473	$499	$504	$462	$515	$536	$578
Cost of goods sold												
Beginning inventory	$ 63	$ 74	$ 84	$ 79	$105	$ 95	$100	$101	$ 92	$103	$107	$116
Purchases	263	305	331	341	410	383	400	395	380	416	437	413
Cost of goods available	$326	$379	$415	$420	$515	$478	$500	$496	$472	$519	$544	$529
Ending inventory	74	85	79	105	95	100	101	92	102	107	116	66
Cost of goods sold	$252	$294	$336	$315	$420	$378	$399	$403	$370	$412	$428	$462
Gross profit	$ 63	$ 74	$ 84	$ 79	$105	$ 95	$100	$101	$ 92	$103	$108	$116
Operating expenses												
Rent	$ 2	$ 2	$ 2	$ 2	$ 2	$ 2	$ 2	$ 2	$ 2	$ 2	$ 2	$ 2
Payroll	32	37	42	39	53	47	50	50	46	51	54	58
Utilities	5	5	5	5	5	5	5	5	5	5	5	5
Taxes	3	4	4	4	5	5	5	5	5	5	5	6
Supplies	16	18	21	20	26	24	25	25	23	26	27	29
Repairs	2	2	2	2	2	2	2	2	2	2	2	2
Total expenses	$ 60	$ 68	$ 76	$ 72	$ 93	$ 85	$ 89	$ 89	$ 83	$ 91	$ 95	$102
Net profit	$ 3	$ 6	$ 8	$ 7	$ 12	$ 10	$ 11	$ 12	$ 9	$ 12	$ 12	$ 14

Table 10.9   North Central Scientific: Cash-Flow Budget

John Wheatman has successfully completed his operating budget and is now ready to prepare his cashflow worksheet. After analyzing the sales figures and the cash receipts, John has determined that 80 percent of monthly sales are in cash. Of the remaining 20 percent, 15 percent is collected in the next month, and the final 5 percent is collected in the month following (see the cash receipts worksheet below). Wheatman's purchases are typically paid during the week following the purchase. Therefore, approximately one-fourth of the purchases are paid for in the following month. Rent expense is paid a month in advance. However, since it is not expected to go up during the budget period, the monthly cash outlay for rent remains the same. All the other expenses are paid in the month of consumption (see the cash disbursements worksheet below). Finally, the cash-flow worksheet is constructed by taking the beginning cash balance, adding the cash receipts for that month, and deducting the cash disbursements for the same month.

NORTH CENTRAL SCIENTIFIC: CASH RECEIPTS WORKSHEET FOR 20XX ($000)

	JAN.	FEB.	MAR.	APR.	MAY	JUNE	JULY	AUG.	SEPT.	OCT.	NOV.	DEC.
Sales	$315	$388	$420	$394	$525	$473	$499	$504	$462	$515	$536	$578
Current month	$252	$294	$336	$315	$420	$378	$399	$403	$370	$412	$428	$462
Prior month	82	47	55	63	59	79	71	75	76	69	77	80
Two months back	26	28	16	18	21	19	26	24	24	25	24	26
Cash receipts	$360	$369	$407	$396	$500	$476	$496	$502	$470	$506	$529	$568

NORTH CENTRAL SCIENTIFIC: CASH DISBURSEMENTS WORKSHEET FOR 20XX ($000)

	JAN.	FEB.	MAR.	APR.	MAY	JUNE	JULY	AUG.	SEPT.	OCT.	NOV.	DEC.
Purchases	$263	$305	$331	$341	$410	$383	$400	$395	$380	$416	$437	$413
Current month	$197	$228	$248	$256	$307	$287	$300	$296	$285	$312	$328	$309
Prior month	98	66	76	83	85	102	96	100	99	95	104	109
Purchase payments	$295	$294	$324	$339	$392	$396	$396	$396	$384	$407	$432	$419
Operating expenses	$ 60	$ 68	$ 76	$ 72	$ 93	$ 85	$ 89	$ 89	$ 83	$ 91	$ 95	$102
Cash payments	$355	$362	$400	$412	$485	$481	$485	$485	$467	$498	$527	$521

NORTH CENTRAL SCIENTIFIC: CASH-FLOW WORKSHEET FOR 20XX ($000)

	JAN.	FEB.	MAR.	APR.	MAY	JUNE	JULY	AUG.	SEPT.	OCT.	NOV.	DEC.
Beginning cash	$122	$127	$134	$141	$127	$141	$143	$154	$170	$173	$181	$184
Add: Receipts	360	369	407	396	500	476	496	502	470	506	529	568
Cash available	$482	$496	$541	$537	$627	$617	$639	$656	$640	$679	$710	$752
Less: Payments	355	362	400	411	485	481	485	485	467	498	527	521
Ending cash	$127	$134	$141	$126	$142	$136	$154	$171	$173	$181	$183	$231

the entrepreneurial
PROCESS

Sharpen Your Financials

Many people wonder what the most important part of a business plan really is. As technology continues to make the world smaller, a solid, competent, and tenacious management team will make a business. Second only to the management section, however, is the financial segment. Financials serve no purpose if an investor has no confidence in the owner's ability to execute, financially, the plan laid out before him or her. A sharp set of financials will exhume these qualities and set yours apart from the rest.

1. Thoroughness—Including an income statement and only an income statement is not enough. Investors and bankers want to see a balance sheet and cash-flow statement as well. They want to see exactly when you'll be able to pay them back.

2. Realism—Monthly projections are fine for the first year of operations. Beyond that, stick to quarterly or yearly data. The financial gurus know how tough it is to be accurate.

3. Simplicity—Other than adjusting for seasonality as needed, avoid becoming too worrisome about the probability of your projections. Include the "most likely" statements and keep an addendum handy showing the "break-even" statements.

4. Good Editing—Sales and cost of goods sold numbers should focus primarily on major product lines. For expenditures, pinpoint those that consume more than 10 percent of the total revenue.

5. Street Smarts—Double-check to make sure interest and tax rates are correct and taken into consideration. The simplest of expenses, such as interest payments, become easy to overlook when creating a full set of financials. An oversight in this area will send a bad signal to the investor.

SOURCE: Paul A. Broni, "Winning Numbers," *Success* (May 1999): 69.

Pro Forma Statements

The final step in the budget process is the preparation of **pro forma statements,** which are projections of a firm's financial position over a future period (pro forma income statement) or on a future date (pro forma balance sheet). In the normal accounting cycle, the income statement is prepared first and then the balance sheet. Similarly, in the preparation of pro forma statements, the pro forma income statement is followed by the pro forma balance sheet.

In the process of preparing the operating budget, the firm will have already prepared the pro forma income statements for each month in the budget period. Each month presents the anticipated income and expense for that particular period, which is what the monthly pro forma income statements do. In order to prepare an annual pro forma income statement, the firm combines all months of the year.

The process for preparing a pro forma balance sheet is more complex. The last balance sheet prepared before the budget period began, the operating budget, and the cash-flow budget are needed in preparing a pro forma balance sheet. Starting with the beginning balance sheet balances, the projected changes as depicted on the budgets are added to create the projected balance sheet totals.

After preparing the pro forma balance sheet, the entrepreneur should verify the accuracy of his or her work with the application of the traditional accounting equation:

Assets = Liabilities + Owner's Equity

Table 10.10   North Central Scientific: Pro Forma Statements

At this point in the budget process, John Wheatman has the information necessary to prepare pro forma financial statements. The first set he has decided to prepare are the pro forma income statements. To do this, John simply copies the information from the operating budget (see the comparative income statements below and compare with the operating budget). The next set of pro forma statements is the pro forma balance sheets. In order to compile these, John uses the following information along with the operating budget and the cash-flow worksheet he has prepared:

Cash: the ending cash balance for each month from the cash-flow worksheet

Accounts receivable: 20 percent of the current month's sales plus 5 percent of the preceding month's sales

Inventory: the current month's ending inventory on the pro forma income statements

Prepaid rent: the $2,000 is expected to remain constant throughout the budget period and is always paid one month in advance

Building and equipment: no new acquisitions are expected in this area, so the amount will remain constant

Accumulated depreciation: since no new acquisitions are anticipated, this will stay the same; all buildings and equipment are fully depreciated

Accounts payable: 25 percent of current purchases

Capital: prior month's capital balance plus current month's net income

NORTH CENTRAL SCIENTIFIC: COMPARATIVE PRO FORMA INCOME STATEMENTS FOR 20XX ($000)

	JAN.	FEB.	MAR.	APR.	MAY	JUNE	JULY	AUG.	SEPT.	OCT.	NOV.	DEC.
Sales	$315	$388	$420	$394	$525	$473	$499	$504	$462	$515	$536	$578
Cost of goods sold												
Beginning inventory	$ 63	$ 74	$ 84	$ 79	$105	$ 95	$100	$101	$ 92	$103	$107	$116
Purchases	263	305	331	341	410	383	400	395	380	416	437	413
Cost of goods available	$326	$379	$415	$420	$515	$478	$500	$496	$472	$519	$544	$529
Ending inventory	74	85	79	105	95	100	101	92	102	107	116	66
Cost of goods sold	$252	$294	$336	$315	$420	$378	$399	$403	$370	$412	$428	$462
Gross profit	$ 63	$ 74	$ 84	$ 79	$105	$95	$100	$101	$ 92	$103	$108	$116
Operating expenses												
Rent	$ 2	$ 2	$ 2	$ 2	$ 2	$ 2	$ 2	$ 2	$ 2	$ 2	$ 2	$ 2
Payroll	32	37	42	39	53	47	50	50	46	51	54	58
Utilities	5	5	5	5	5	5	5	5	5	5	5	5
Taxes	3	4	4	4	5	5	5	5	5	5	5	6
Supplies	16	18	21	20	26	24	25	25	23	26	27	29
Repairs	2	2	2	2	2	2	2	2	2	2	2	2
Total expenses	$ 60	$ 68	$ 76	$ 72	$ 93	$ 85	$ 89	$ 89	$ 83	$ 91	$ 95	$102
Net profit	$ 3	$ 6	$ 8	$ 7	$ 12	$ 10	$ 11	$ 12	$ 9	$ 12	$ 12	$ 14

Table 10.10   (Continued)

	JAN.	FEB.	MAR.	APR.	MAY	JUNE	JULY	AUG.	SEPT.	OCT.	NOV.	DEC.
Assets												
Cash	$127	$134	$141	$126	$142	$136	$154	$171	$173	$181	$183	$231
Accounts receivable	91	89	102	100	125	121	123	126	117	126	133	142
Inventory	74	84	79	105	95	100	101	92	103	107	116	66
Prepaid rent	2	2	2	2	2	2	2	2	2	2	2	2
Building and equipment	350	350	350	350	350	350	350	350	350	350	350	350
Less: Accumulated depreciation	−350	−350	−350	−350	−350	−350	−350	−350	−350	−350	−350	−350
Total assets	$294	$309	$324	$333	$364	$359	$380	$391	$395	$416	$434	$441
Liabilities												
Accounts payable	$ 66	$ 76	$ 83	$ 85	$102	$ 96	$100	$ 99	$ 95	$104	$109	$103
Capital	228	234	242	249	261	270	280	292	300	312	326	339
Total liabilities and equity	$294	$310	$325	$334	$363	$366	$380	$391	$395	$416	$435	$442

If the equation is not in balance, the work should be rechecked. Table 10.10 provides a brief account of the process of preparing pro forma financial statements for North Central Scientific.

Capital Budgeting

Entrepreneurs may be required to make several investment decisions in the process of managing their firms. The impact of some of these decisions will be felt primarily within one year. On other investments, however, the returns are expected to extend beyond one year. Investments that fit into this second category are commonly referred to as capital investments or capital expenditures. A technique the entrepreneur can use to help plan for capital expenditures is **capital budgeting**.[9]

The first step in capital budgeting is to identify the cash flows and their timing. The inflows, or returns as they are commonly called, are equal to net operating income before deduction of payments to the financing sources but after the deduction of applicable taxes and with depreciation added back, as represented by the following formula:

Expected Returns = $X(1 - T)$ + Depreciation

X is equal to the net operating income, and T is defined as the appropriate tax rate. An illustration follows.

John Wheatman is faced with a dilemma. He has two mutually exclusive projects, both of which require an outlay of $1,000. The problem is that he can afford only one of the projects. After discussing the problem with his accountant, John discovered that the first step he needs to take is to determine the expected return on each project. In order to gather this information, he has studied the probable effect on the store's operations and has developed the data shown in Table 10.11.

Table 10.11   North Central Scientific: Expected Return Worksheet

PROPOSAL A

YEAR	X	(1 − T) (T = .40)	X(1 + T)	DEPRECIATION	X(1 − T) + DEPRECIATION
1	$500	$0.60	$ 300	$200	$500
2	333	0.60	200	200	400
3	167	0.60	100	200	300
4	−300	0.60	−180	200	20
5	−317	0.60	−190	200	10

PROPOSAL B

YEAR	X	(1 − T) (T = .40)	X(1 − T)	DEPRECIATION	X(1 − T) + DEPRECIATION
1	−$167	$0.60	−$100	$200	$100
2	0	0.60	100	200	200
3	167	0.60	100	200	300
4	333	0.60	200	200	400
5	500	0.60	300	200	500

X = Anticipated change in net income

T = Applicable tax rate (.40)

Depreciation = Depreciation (computed on a straight-line basis) = Cost/Life = 1,000/5

Table 10.11 provides a good illustration of the expected returns for John Wheatman's two projects. At this point, however, the cash inflows of each year are shown without consideration of the time value of money. The cash outflow is used to refer to the initial cash outlay that must be made in the beginning (the purchase price). When gathering data to estimate the cash flows over the life of a project, it is imperative to obtain reliable estimates of the savings and expenses associated with the project.

The principal objective of capital budgeting is to maximize the value of the firm. It is designed to answer two basic questions:

1. Which of several mutually exclusive projects should be selected? (Mutually exclusive projects are alternative methods of doing the same job. If one method is chosen, the other methods will not be required.)

2. How many projects, in total, should be selected?[10]

The three most common methods used in capital budgeting are the payback method, the net present value (NPV) method, and the internal rate of return (IRR) method. Each has certain advantages and disadvantages. In this section, the same proposal will be used under each method to more clearly illustrate each technique.

Payback Method

One of the easiest capital-budgeting techniques to understand is the **payback method** or, as it is sometimes called, the payback period. In this method the length of time required to "pay back" the original investment is the determining criterion. The entrepreneur will select a maximum time frame for the payback period. Any project that requires a longer period will be rejected, and projects that fall within the time frame will be accepted. Here is an example of the payback method used by North Central Scientific:

John Wheatman has a decision to make. He would like to purchase a new cash register for his store but is unsure which of two proposals to accept. Each machine costs $1,000. An analysis of the projected returns reveals the following information:

YEAR	PROPOSAL A	PROPOSAL B
1	$500	$100
2	400	200
3	300	300
4	20	400
5	10	500

After careful consideration, John decides to use the payback method with a cutoff period of 3 years. In this case he discovers that Proposal A would pay back his investment in 2 1/3 years; $900 of the original investment will be paid back in the first 2 years and the last $100 in the third year. Proposal B, on the other hand, will require 4 years for its payback. Using this criterion John chooses Proposal A and rejects Proposal B.

One of the problems with the payback method is that it ignores cash flows beyond the payback period. Thus, it is possible for the wrong decision to be made. Nevertheless, many companies, particularly entrepreneurial firms, continue to use this method for several reasons: (1) It is very simple to use in comparison to other methods, (2) projects with a faster payback period normally have more favorable short-term effects on earnings, and (3) if a firm is short on cash, it may prefer to use the payback method because it provides a faster return of funds.

Net Present Value

The **net present value (NPV) method** is a technique that helps to minimize some of the shortcomings of the payback method by recognizing the future cash flows beyond the payback period. The concept works on the premise that a dollar today is worth more than a dollar in the future. How much more depends on the applicable cost of capital for the firm. The cost of capital is the rate used to adjust future cash flows to determine their value in present period terms. This procedure is referred to as discounting the future cash flows, and the discounted cash value is determined by the present value of the cash flow.

To use this approach, the entrepreneur must find the present value of the expected net cash flows of the investment, discounted at the appropriate cost of capital, and subtract from it the initial cost outlay of the project. The result is the net present value of the proposed project. Many financial accounting and finance textbooks have tables (called present value tables) that list the appropriate discount factors to multiply by the future cash flow to determine the present value. In addition, financial calculators are available that will compute the present value given the cost of capital, future cash flow, and the year of the cash flow. Finally, given the appropriate data, electronic spreadsheet programs can be programmed to determine the present value. After the net present value has been calculated for all of the proposals, the entrepreneur can select the project with the highest net present value. Here is an example of the NPV method used by North Central Scientific:

Not really satisfied with the results he has obtained from the payback method, John Wheatman has decided to use the NPV method to see what result it would produce. After conferring with his accountant, John learned that the cost of capital for his firm is 10 percent. He then prepared the following tables:

PROPOSAL A

YEAR	CASH FLOW	DISCOUNT FACTOR	PRESENT VALUE
1	$500	0.9091	$454.55
2	400	0.8264	330.56
3	300	0.7513	225.39
4	20	0.6830	13.66
5	10	0.6209	6.21
			$1,030.37
Less: Initial outlay			−1,000.00
Net present value			$30.37

PROPOSAL B

YEAR	CASH FLOW	DISCOUNT FACTOR	PRESENT VALUE
1	$100	0.9091	$90.91
2	200	0.8264	165.28
3	300	0.7513	225.39
4	400	0.6830	273.20
5	500	0.6209	310.45
			$1,065.23
Less: Initial outlay			−1,000.00
Net present value			$65.23

Since Proposal B has the higher net present value, John selected Proposal B and rejected Proposal A.

Internal Rate of Return

The **internal rate of return (IRR) method** is similar to the net present value method in that the future cash flows are discounted. However, they are discounted at a rate that makes the net present value of the project equal to zero. This rate is referred to as the internal rate of return of the project. The project with the highest internal rate of return is then selected. Thus a project that would be selected under the NPV method also would be selected under the IRR method.

One of the major drawbacks to the use of the IRR method is the difficulty that can be encountered when using the technique. Under the NPV method, it is quite simple to look up the appropriate discount factors in the present value tables. When using the IRR concept, however, the entrepreneur must begin with a net present value of zero and work backward through the tables. What this means, essentially, is that the entrepreneur must estimate the approximate rate and eventually try to track the actual internal rate of return for the project. Although this may not seem too difficult for projects with even cash flows (that is, cash flows that are fairly equal over the business periods), projects with uneven cash flows (fluctuating periods of cash inflow and cash outflow) can be a nightmare. Unfortunately, reality dictates that most projects will probably have uneven cash flows. Fortunately, electronic calculators and spreadsheet programs are available that can determine the actual internal rate of return, given the cash flows, initial cash outlays, and the appropriate cash-flow periods. Here is an example of the IRR method used by North Central Scientific:

> Having obtained different results from the payback period and the NPV method, John Wheatman is confused about which alternative to select. To alleviate this confusion, he has decided to use the internal rate of return to evaluate the two proposals and has decided that the project with the higher IRR will be selected (after all, it would win two out of three times). Accordingly, he has prepared the following tables with the help of his calculator:

PROPOSAL A (11.83% IRR)

YEAR	CASH FLOW	DISCOUNT FACTOR	PRESENT VALUE
1	$500	0.8942	$447.10
2	400	0.7996	319.84
3	300	0.7151	214.53
4	20	0.6394	12.80
5	10	0.5718	5.73
			$1,000.00
Less: Initial outlay			−1,000.00
Net present value			$0.00

PROPOSAL B (12.01% IRR)

YEAR	CASH FLOW	DISCOUNT FACTOR	PRESENT VALUE
1	$100	0.8928	$89.27
2	200	0.7971	159.42
3	300	0.7117	213.51
4	400	0.6354	254.15
5	500	0.5673	283.65
			$1,000.00
Less: Initial outlay			−1,000.00
Net present value			$0.00

> Proposal B is selected because it has the higher IRR. This conclusion supports the statement that the project with the higher NPV will also have the higher IRR.

The North Central Scientific examples illustrate the use of all three capital-budgeting methods. Even though Proposal A was chosen by the first method (payback), under the other two methods (net present value and internal rate of return) Proposal B surfaced as the better proposal. It is important for entrepreneurs to understand all three methods and to use the one that best fits their needs. If payback had been John Wheatman's only consideration, then Proposal A would have been selected. When future cash flows beyond payback are to be considered, the NPV and the IRR are the methods to determine the best proposal.

The budgeting concepts discussed so far are extremely powerful planning tools. But how can entrepreneurs monitor their progress during the budget period? How can they use the information accumulated during the course of the business to help plan for future periods? Can this information be used for pricing decisions? The answer to the third question is "yes," and the rest are answered in the following sections.

Break-Even Analysis

In today's competitive marketplace, entrepreneurs need relevant, timely, and accurate information that will enable them to price their products and services competitively and yet be able to earn a fair profit. **Break-even analysis** supplies this information.

Break-Even Point Computation

Break-even analysis is a technique commonly used to assess expected product profitability. It helps determine how many units must be sold in order to break even at a particular selling price.

Contribution Margin Approach

A common approach to break-even analysis is the **contribution margin approach**. Contribution margin is the difference between the selling price and the variable cost per unit. It is the amount per unit that is contributed to covering all other costs.[11] Since the break-even point occurs where income equals expenses, the contribution margin approach formula is

$$0 = (SP - VC)S - FC \text{ or } FC = (SP - VC)S$$

where

SP = Unit selling price

VC = Variable costs per unit

S = Sales in units

FC = Fixed cost

This model also can be used for profit planning by including the desired profit as part of the fixed cost.

Graphic Approach

Another approach to break-even analysis taken by entrepreneurial firms is the graphic approach. In order to use this approach, the entrepreneur needs to graph at least two numbers: total revenue and total costs. The intersection of these two lines (that is, where total revenues are equal to the total costs) is the firm's break-even point. Two additional costs—variable costs and fixed costs—also may be plotted. Doing so enables the entrepreneur to visualize the various relationships in the firm's cost structure.

Handling Questionable Costs

Although the first two approaches are adequate for situations in which costs can be broken down into fixed and variable components, some firms have expenses that are difficult to assign. For example, are repairs and maintenance expenses fixed or variable expenses? Can firms facing this type of problem use break-even analysis for profit planning? The answer is "yes," thanks to a new technique designed specifically for entrepreneurial firms. This technique calculates break-even points under alternative assumptions of fixed or variable costs to see if a product's profitability is sensitive to cost behavior. The decision rules for this concept follow: If expected sales exceed the higher break-even point, then the product should be profitable, regardless of the other break-even point; if expected sales do not exceed the lower break-even point, then the product should be unprofitable. Only if expected sales are between the two break-even points is further investigation of the questionable cost's behavior needed.[12]

entrepreneurship IN PRACTICE

Bad Credit? No Credit? You've Got a Problem!

You're getting a degree from a good school, you've saved up some money, you're working on that fool-proof business plan, and you may even have some experience in the industry—but you forgot about the dings on your credit report.

With Americans ever-relying on credit cards, it is not uncommon for wanna-be entrepreneurs to have a poor personal credit history. Because of this, you may have to wait a while for that small-business loan. An increase in outstanding consumer debt, particularly credit card debt, has been cited as a significant contributor to the increased rate of filing bankruptcy according to the FDIC.

Doug Tatum, CEO of Atlanta-based Tatum CFO Partners, said most loans under the $1 million price tag are based on personal assets and the credit history of the entrepreneur. There also lies a gap between financing the person and financing the business; it is usually not until the needed capital surpasses the assets of an individual that a lender begins to consider financing the business.

Experts say the best strategy for an entrepreneur with a tarnished credit history is to continue saving while establishing good credit. Credit counselors and credit-repair companies can help with bad credit, or you can attempt to negotiate bills directly with the lenders. Seek out nonprofit credit counselors such as American Consumer Credit Counseling (http://www.consumercredit.com) or contact a local Better Business Bureau. The goal is to solve the problem that created the bad credit in the first place.

According to the American Collectors Association, the nation's 151.9 million credit card holders owned an average of 9.1 cards with an average outstanding balance of $405 per card. They also estimate that bad debt costs every adult in the United States more than $680 a year. So although it may be difficult to consider putting your plans on hold, taking the time to repair or rework your credit should polish up your business financial savvy. You can also spend extra time in researching your industry and saving money before taking that big leap.

SOURCES: Karen Klein, "The Need for a Clean Credit History," *BusinessWeek Online* (April 9, 2002); and The Association of Credit and Collection Professionals, http://www.collector.com.

The concept works by substituting the cost in question (QC) first as a fixed cost and then as a variable cost. The break-even formulas presented earlier would have to be modified to determine the break-even levels under the two assumptions. Under the fixed-cost assumption, the entrepreneur would use the following equation:

$$0 = (SP - VC)S - FC - QC$$

To calculate the break-even point assuming QC is variable, the following equation would be used:

$$0 = [SP - VC - (QC/U)]S - FC$$

U is the number of units for which the questionable cost normally would be appropriate. What the entrepreneur is determining is the appropriate unit cost that should be used if the cost is a variable cost. Given next is an example of how an entrepreneur could use the technique:

Tim Goodman, president of General Manufacturing, a small manufacturer of round widgets, has decided to use break-even analysis as a profit-planning tool for his company. He

Figure 10.2 General Manufacturing: Fixed-Cost Assumption

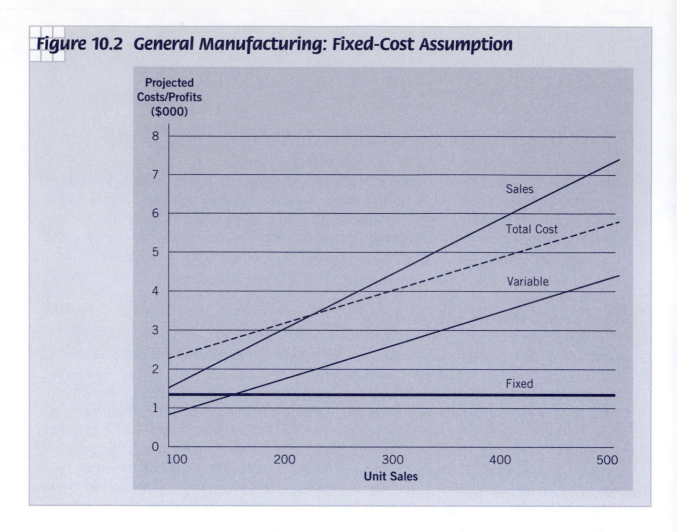

believes using this technique will enable his firm to compete more effectively in the marketplace. From an analysis of the operating costs, Tim has determined that the variable cost per unit is $9, while fixed costs are estimated to be $1,200 per month. The anticipated selling price per unit is $15. He also has discovered he is unable to classify one cost as either variable or fixed. It is a $200 repair and maintenance expense allocation. This $200 is appropriate for an activity level of 400 units; therefore, if the cost were variable, it would be $.50 per unit ($200/400). Finally, sales are projected to be 400 units during the next budget period.

The first step in this process is to determine the break-even point assuming the cost in question is fixed. Consequently, Tim would use the following equation:

$$0 = (SC - VC)S - FC - QC$$
$$= (15 - 9)S - 1,200 - 200$$
$$= 6S - 1,400$$
$$1,400 = 6S$$
$$234 = S$$

Figure 10.2 provides a graphic illustration of the results. The final quantity was rounded up to the next unit, because a business normally will not sell part of a unit.

The next step in the process is to calculate the break-even point assuming the cost in question is a variable cost. Tim would use the following equation to ascertain the second break-even point:

Figure 10.3 General Manufacturing: Variable-Cost Assumption

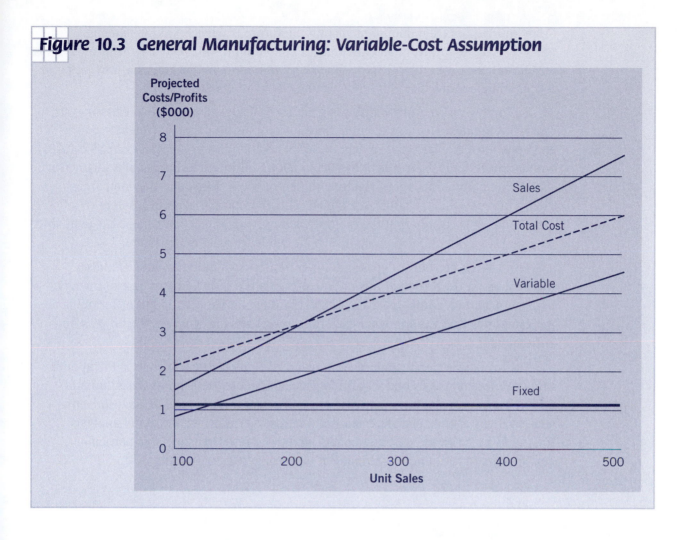

$$0 = [SC - VC - (QC/U)]S - FC$$
$$= [15 - 9 - (200/400)]S - 1,200$$
$$= (6 - .50)S - 1,200$$
$$1,200 = 5.50S$$
$$219 = S$$

Figure 10.3 presents a graphic illustration of the results.

Now that the two possible break-even points have been established, Tim must compare them to his projected sales. The variable-cost sales of 400 units are greater than the larger break-even point of 234 units. Therefore, the product is assumed to be profitable regardless of the cost behavior of the repair and maintenance expense. It does not matter whether the cost is variable or fixed; the firm still will be profitable.

Ratio Analysis

Financial statements report both on a firm's position at a point in time and on its operations over some past period. However, the real value of financial statements lies in the fact that they can be used to help predict the firm's earnings and dividends.

From an investor's standpoint, predicting the future is what financial statement analysis is all about; from an entrepreneur's standpoint, financial statement analysis is useful both as a way to anticipate conditions and, more important, as a starting point for planning actions that will influence the course of events.

An analysis of the firm's ratios is generally the key step in a financial analysis. The **ratios** are designed to show relationships among financial statement accounts. For example, Firm A might have a debt of $6,250,000 and interest charges of $520,000, while Firm B might have a debt of $62,800,000 and interest charges of $5,840,000. Which company is stronger? The true burden of these debts, and the companies' ability to repay them, can be ascertained (1) by comparing each firm's debt to its assets and (2) by comparing the interest each must pay to the income it has available for interest payment. Such comparisons are made by ratio analysis.[13]

Table 10.12 has been prepared as an entrepreneur's guide to understanding the various ratios. Note that this outline presents the ratio's importance to owners, managers, and creditors. More important than the simple calculation of formulas are the categories that explain what each ratio *measures* and what each ratio *tells* an entrepreneur.

Ratio analysis can be applied from two directions. **Vertical analysis** is the application of ratio analysis to one set of financial statements. Here, an analysis "up and down" the statements is done to find signs of strengths and weaknesses. **Horizontal analysis** looks at financial statements and ratios over time. In horizontal analysis, the trends are critical: Are the numbers increasing or decreasing? Are particular components of the company's financial position getting better or worse?[14]

Table 10.12 Financial Ratios

RATIO	FORMULA	WHAT IT MEASURES	WHAT IT TELLS YOU
Owners			
Return on investment (ROI)	$\dfrac{\text{Net Income}}{\text{Average Owner's Equity}}$	Return on owner's capital; when compared with return on assets, it measures the extent financial leverage is being used for or against the owner	How well is this company doing as an investment?
Return on assets (ROA)	$\dfrac{\text{Net Income}}{\text{Average Total Assets}}$	How well assets have been employed by management	How well has management employed company assets? Does it pay to borrow?
Managers			
Net profit margin	$\dfrac{\text{Net Income}}{\text{Sales}}$	Operating efficiency; the ability to create sufficient profits from operating activities	Are profits high enough, given the level of sales?
Asset turnover	$\dfrac{\text{Sales}}{\text{Average Total Assets}}$	Relative efficiency in using total resources to produce output	How well are assets being used to generate sales revenue?

RATIO	FORMULA	WHAT IT MEASURES	WHAT IT TELLS YOU
Return on assets	$\dfrac{\text{Net Income}}{\text{Sales}} \times \dfrac{\text{Sales}}{\text{Total Assets}}$	Earning power on all assets; ROA ratio broken into its logical parts; turnover and margin	How well has management employed company assets?
Average collection period	$\dfrac{\text{Average Accounts Receivable}}{\text{Annual Credit Sales}} \times 365$	Liquidity of receivables in terms of average number of days receivables are outstanding	Are receivables coming in too slowly?
Inventory turnover	$\dfrac{\text{Cost of Goods Sold Expense}}{\text{Average Inventory}}$	Liquidity of inventory; the number of times it turns over per year	Is too much cash tied up in inventories?
Average age of payables	$\dfrac{\text{Average Accounts Payable}}{\text{Net Purchases}} \times 365$	Approximate length of time a firm takes to pay its bills for trade purchases	How quickly does a prospective customer pay its bills?

Short-Term Creditors

RATIO	FORMULA	WHAT IT MEASURES	WHAT IT TELLS YOU
Working capital	Current Assets − Current Liabilities	Short-term debt-paying ability	Does this customer have sufficient cash or other liquid assets to cover its short-term obligations?
Current ratio	$\dfrac{\text{Current Assets}}{\text{Current Liabilities}}$	Short-term debt-paying ability without regard to the liquidity of current assets	Does this customer have sufficient cash or other liquid assets to cover its short-term obligations?
Quick ratio	$\dfrac{\text{Cash} + \text{Marketable Securities} + \text{Accounts Receivable}}{\text{Current Liabilities}}$	Short-term debt-paying ability without having to rely on inventory sales	Does this customer have sufficient cash or other liquid assets to cover its short-term obligations?

Long-Term Creditors

RATIO	FORMULA	WHAT IT MEASURES	WHAT IT TELLS YOU
Debt-to-equity ratio	$\dfrac{\text{Total Debt}}{\text{Total Equity}}$	Amount of assets creditors provide for each dollar of assets the owners provide	Is the company's debt load excessive?
Times interest earned	$\dfrac{\text{Net Income} + \text{Interest} + \text{Taxes}}{\text{Interest Expense}}$	Ability to pay fixed charges for interest from operating profits	Are earnings and cash flows sufficient to cover interest payments and some principal repayments?
Cash flow to liabilities	$\dfrac{\text{Operating Cash Flow}}{\text{Total Liabilities}}$	Total debt coverage; general debt-paying ability	Are earnings and cash flows sufficient to cover interest payments and some principal repayments?

Source: Kenneth M. Macur and Lyal Gustafson, "Financial Statements as a Management Tool," *Small Business Forum* (fall 1992): 24.

■ Summary

Three principal financial statements are important to entrepreneurs: the balance sheet, the income statement, and the cash-flow statement. The budgeting process facilitates financial statement preparation. Some key budgets entrepreneurs should prepare are the operating budget, the cash-flow budget, and the capital budget. The operating budget typically begins with a sales forecast, followed by an estimation of operating expenses. A cash-flow budget provides an overview of the inflows and outflows of cash during a specific period. Pro forma financial statements then are prepared as projections of the firm's financial position over a future period (pro forma income statement) or on a future date (pro forma balance sheet). The operating and cash-flow budgets often are used to prepare these pro forma statements. The capital budget is used to help entrepreneurs make investment decisions. The three most common methods of capital budgeting are the payback period, the net present value method, and the internal rate of return method.

Another commonly used decision-making tool is break-even analysis, which tells how many units must be sold in order to break even at a particular selling price. It is possible to use this analysis even when fixed or variable costs can only be estimated. The last part of the chapter examined ratio analysis, which can be a helpful analytical tool for entrepreneurs. Ratios are designed to show relationships between financial statement accounts.

■ Key Terms and Concepts

accounts payable	long-term liabilities
accounts receivable	mixed cost
administrative expenses	net income
balance sheet	net present value (NPV) method
break-even analysis	notes payable
budget	operating budget
capital budgeting	operating expenses
cash	owners' equity
cash-flow budget	payback method
cash-flow statement	prepaid expenses
contribution margin approach	pro forma statement
expenses	ratios
financial expense	retained earnings
fixed assets	revenue
fixed cost	sales forecast
horizontal analysis	short-term liabilities (current liabilities)
income statement	simple linear regression
internal rate of return (IRR) method	taxes payable
inventory	variable cost
liabilities	vertical analysis
loan payable	

Review and Discussion Questions

1. What is the importance of financial information for entrepreneurs? Briefly describe the key components.

2. What are the benefits of the budgeting process?

3. How is the statistical forecasting technique of simple linear regression used in making a sales forecast?

4. Describe how an operating budget is constructed.

5. Describe how a cash-flow budget is constructed.

6. What are pro forma statements? How are they constructed? Be complete in your answer.

7. Describe how a capital budget is constructed.

8. One of the most popular capital-budgeting techniques is the payback method. How does this method work? Give an example.

9. Describe the net present value method. When would an entrepreneur use this method? Why?

10. Describe the internal rate of return method. When would an entrepreneur use this method? Why?

11. When would an entrepreneur be interested in break-even analysis?

12. If an entrepreneur wants to use break-even analysis but has trouble assigning some costs as either fixed or variable, can break-even analysis still be used? Explain.

13. What is ratio analysis? How is horizontal analysis different from vertical analysis?

Experiential Exercise

The Project Proposal

Bill Sergent has just received a request for proposal (RFP) from a large computer firm. The firm is looking for a supplier to provide it with high-tech components for a super-computer being built for the Department of Defense. Bill's firm, which is only eight months old, was founded by a group of scientists and engineers whose primary expertise is in the area of computers and high technology. Bill is thinking about making a reply to the RFP, but first he wants to conduct a break-even analysis to determine how profitable the venture will be. Here is the information he will be using in his analysis:

☐ The computer firm wants 12 different components built, and the purchase price will be $10,000 per component.

☐ The total cost of building the first component will be $20,000.

☐ The cost of building each of the 11 other components will be $8,000, $6,000, $5,000, $4,000, $5,000, $6,000, $8,000, $10,000, $28,000, $40,000, and $40,000, respectively.

☐ Bill's company will not accept any proposal that will give it less than a 10 percent return on sales.

On the basis of this information, complete the following break-even chart, and then answer the two questions.

Revenues ($000)

$150 _____

140 _____

130 _____

120 _____

110 _____

100 _____

90 _____

80 _____

70 _____

60 _____

50 _____

40 _____

30 _____

20 _____

10 _____

    1   2   3   4   5   6   7   8   9   10   11   12

Units

1. Should Bill bid on the contract? Why or why not?_____

_____

2. If Bill has some room for negotiation with the computer firm, what would you recommend he do? Why?_____

_____

_____

Case 10.1

It's All Greek to Her

When Regina McDermott opened her auto repair shop, she thought her 15 years of experience with cars was all she would need. To a degree she was right. Within six months her shop had more work than it could handle, thanks to her widening reputation. At the same time, however, Regina has found it necessary to spend more and more time dealing with financial planning.

Three weeks ago her accountant came by to see her to discuss a number of finance-related matters. One of these is the need for cash budgeting. "I can work up a cash budget for you," he explained. "However, I think you should understand what I'm doing so you will realize the importance of the cash budget and be able to visualize your cash inflows and outflows. I think you also need to make a decision regarding the new equipment you are planning to purchase. This machinery is state of the art, but, as we discussed last week, you can buy a number of different types of machinery. You are going to have to decide which is the best choice."

Regina explained to her accountant that she was indifferent about which equipment to buy. "All of this machinery is good. Perhaps I should purchase the cheapest." At this point the accountant explained to her that she could use a number of ways to evaluate this type of decision. "You can base your choice on the payback method—how long it takes to recover your investment in each of these pieces of equipment. You can base it on net present value by discounting future cash flows to the present. Or you can base it on internal rate of return, under which the cash flows are discounted at a rate that makes the net present value of the project equal to zero."

Regina listened quietly and when the accountant was finished, she told him, "Let me think about the various ways of evaluating my capital investment, and I'll get back to you. Then, perhaps, you and I can work out the numbers together." Her accountant said this sounded fine to him and he left. Regina began to wish she had taken more accounting courses while in college. As she explained to her husband, "When the accountant begins to talk, it's all Greek to me."

Questions

1. What is the purpose of a cash-flow budget? What does it reveal? Of what value would it be to Regina?

2. How does the payback method work? How does the net present value method work? How would you explain each of these methods to Regina?

3. How does the internal rate of return method work? How would you explain it to Regina?

Case 10.2

The Contract Proposal

Dennis Darby owns a small manufacturing firm that produces electronic components for use in helicopters. Most of his business is a result of military and aircraft manufacturer contracts, although 10 percent of revenues come from firms that own or rent helicopters. The latter are typically large Fortune 500 companies or leasing/rental firms that work on a contractual basis for clients.

Dennis would like to increase his revenues from sales to private corporations that own their own helicopters. Specifically, he would like to do more business with oil companies that maintain helicopter fleets for ferrying people to and from oil rigs in the Gulf of Mexico and other offshore locations. Early this week Dennis received a request from an oil company for 120 electronic components. He turned the order over to his chief estimator, who estimates that the fixed costs associated with producing these components will be $35,000, the unit variable cost will be $400, and the unit selling price will be $800.

Dennis will not accept any order on which the return on sales is less than 20 percent. Additionally, the estimator has told him that a $1,000 expense can be classified as either fixed or variable. Dennis intends to take this information and make a decision whether to accept the contract from the oil company. He has to make a decision within the next three days.

Questions

1. What is the break-even point for this project? Will the company make money if it manufactures the components? Show your calculations.

2. If the project will be profitable, will it provide Dennis with the desired 20 percent return? Explain.

3. Of what value is break-even analysis to Dennis? Be complete in your answer.

■ Notes

1. See Richard G. P. McMahon and Leslie G. Davies, "Financial Reporting and Analysis Practices in Small Enterprises: Their Association with Growth Rate and Financial Performance," *Journal of Small Business Management* (January 1994): 9–17.

2. Kenneth M. Macur and Lyal Gustafson, "Financial Statements as a Management Tool," *Small Business Forum* (fall 1992): 23–34; see also Robert Dove, "Financial Statements," *Accountancy* (January 2000): 7.

3. See Billie M. Cunningham, Loren A. Nikolai, and John D. Bazley, *Accounting: Information for Business Decisions* (Ft. Worth, TX: Harcourt College Publishers, 2000).

4. See Jacqueline Emigh, "Balance Sheet," *ComputerWorld* (Nov. 15, 1999): 86.

5. See Cunningham, Nikolai, and Bazley, *Accounting;* and John Capel, "Balancing the Books," *Supply Management* (November 1999): 94.

6. Neil C. Churchill, "Budget Choice: Planning vs. Control," *Harvard Business Review* (July/August 1984): 151.

7. Fred A. Shelton and Jack C. Bailes, "How to Create an Electronic Spreadsheet Budget," *Management Accounting* (July 1986): 42.

8. Fred Waedt, "Understanding Cash Flow Statements, or What You Need to Know Before You Ask for a Loan," *Small Business Forum* (spring 1995): 42–51.

9. See Scott Besley and Eugene F. Brigham, *Essentials of Managerial Finance,* 12th ed. (Fort Worth, TX: The Dryden Press, 2000), 335–353.

10. Ibid., 403.

11. Cunningham, Nikolai, and Bazley, *Accounting: Information for Business Decisions,* 63–70.

12. Kenneth P. Sinclair and James A. Talbott, Jr., "Using Break-Even Analysis When Cost Behavior Is Unknown," *Management Accounting* (July 1986): 53; see also Cunningham, Nikolai, and Bazley, *Accounting: Information for Business Decisions,* 70–74.

13. See Besley and Brigham, *Essentials of Managerial Finance,* 95–110.

14. Kenneth M. Macur and Lyal Gustafson, "Financial Statements as a Management Tool," *Small Business Forum* (fall 1992): 23–34.

11

Developing an Effective Business Plan

It is well established that you can't raise money without a business plan. . . . a business plan is a work of art in its own right. It's the document that personifies and expresses your company. Each plan, like every snowflake, must be different. Each is a separate piece of art. Each must be reflective of the individuality of the entrepreneur. Just as you wouldn't copy someone else's romancing techniques, so should you seek to distinguish your plan for its differences.

Joseph R. Mancuso
How to Write a Winning Business Plan

Chapter Objectives

1 To examine the critical factors that should be addressed in planning

2 To explore the planning pitfalls that plague many new ventures

3 To outline the importance of a business plan and describe the benefits derived from it

4 To set forth the viewpoints of those who read a business plan and describe the six steps followed in the reading process

5 To emphasize the importance of coordinating the business plan segments

6 To review key recommendations by venture capital experts for the development of a plan

7 To present a complete outline of an effective business plan and a discussion of each segment

8 To present some helpful hints for writing an effective business plan

9 To highlight points to remember in the presentation of a business plan

Planning is essential to the success of any undertaking. Planning entails the formulation of goals and directions for the future of a venture.[1] A number of critical factors must be addressed when planning:

1. *Realistic goals.* These must be specific, measurable, and set within time parameters.

2. *Commitment.* The venture must be supported by all involved—family, partners, employees, team members.

3. *Milestones.* Subgoals must be set for continual and timely evaluation of progress.

4. *Flexibility.* Obstacles must be anticipated, and alternative strategies must be formulated.

The comprehensive business plan, which should be the result of meetings and reflections on the direction of the new venture, is the major tool for determining the essential operation of a venture. It also is the primary document for managing the venture. One of the major benefits of this plan is that it helps the enterprise avoid common pitfalls that often undo all previous efforts. The following section describes these pitfalls.

Pitfalls to Avoid in Planning

A number of pitfalls in the business plan process should be avoided. The five pitfalls presented in this section represent the most common errors committed by entrepreneurs. To make these danger areas more easily recognizable, certain indicators or warning signs are presented. Each pitfall then has a possible solution introduced that will help entrepreneurs avoid the particular trap that limits a new venture's opportunity to succeed.

Pitfall 1: No Realistic Goals   Although this pitfall may sound self-explanatory, the following indicators demonstrate how common and well disguised it can be: lack of any attainable goals, lack of a time frame to accomplish things, lack of priorities, and lack of action steps.

One way to avoid this pitfall is to set up a timetable with specific steps to be accomplished during a specific period.

Pitfall 2: Failure to Anticipate Roadblocks   One of the most common pitfalls occurs when the entrepreneur is so immersed in his or her idea that objectivity goes out the window. In other words, the person does not recognize the possible problems that may arise. Indicators are no recognition of future problems, no admission of possible flaws or weaknesses in the plan, and no contingency or alternative plans.

The best way to avoid this pitfall is to list (1) the possible obstacles that may arise and (2) the alternatives that state what might have to be done to overcome the obstacles.

Pitfall 3: No Commitment or Dedication   Too many entrepreneurs appear to lack real commitment to their ventures. Although ventures may have started from a hobby or part-time endeavor, entrepreneurs must be careful to avoid the impression they do not take their ventures seriously. Indicators are excessive procrastination, missed appointments, no desire to invest personal money, and appearance of making a "fast buck" from a hobby or a "whim."

The easiest way to avoid this pitfall is to act quickly and to be sure to follow up all professional appointments. Also, be ready and willing to demonstrate a financial commitment to the venture.

Pitfall 4: Lack of Demonstrated Experience (Business or Technical) Since many investors weigh very heavily the entrepreneur's actual experience in a venture, it is important that entrepreneurs demonstrate what background they possess. Because too many beginners attempt to promote ideas they really have no true knowledge of, they are doomed to fail simply because they are perceived as ignorant of the specifics in the proposed business. Indicators are no experience in business, no experience in the specific area of the venture, lack of understanding of the industry in which the venture fits, and failure to convey a clear picture of how and why the venture will work and who will accept it.

To avoid this pitfall, entrepreneurs need to give evidence of personal experience and background for this venture. If they lack specific knowledge or skills, they should obtain assistance from those who possess this knowledge or these skills. Demonstrating a team concept about those who will be helping out also may be useful.

Pitfall 5: No Market Niche (Segment) Many entrepreneurs propose an idea without establishing who the potential customers will be. Just because the entrepreneur likes the product or service does not mean others will buy it. Numerous inventions at the U.S. Patent Office never reached the marketplace because no customers were targeted to buy them—no market was ever established. Indicators are uncertainty about who will buy the basic idea(s) behind the venture, no proof of a need or desire for the good or product proposed, and assumption that customers or clients will purchase just because the entrepreneur thinks so.

The best possible way to avoid this pitfall is to have a market segment specifically targeted and to demonstrate why and how the specific product or service will meet the needs or desires of this target group. (More specific information on market research was developed in Chapter 9.)

The five pitfalls detailed here represent the most common points of failure entrepreneurs experience *before* their business plan ever gets reviewed. In other words, these critical areas must be carefully addressed before developing a business plan. If these pitfalls can be avoided, then the entire business plan will be written more carefully and thus will be reviewed more thoroughly. This preparation helps entrepreneurs establish a solid foundation on which to develop an effective business plan.

What Is a Business Plan?

A **business plan** is the written document that details the proposed venture. It must describe current status, expected needs, and projected results of the new business.[2] Every aspect of the venture needs to be covered: the project, marketing, research and development, manufacturing, management, critical risks, financing, and milestones or a timetable. A description of all of these facets of the proposed venture is necessary to demonstrate a clear picture of what that venture is, where it is projected to go, and how the entrepreneur proposes it will get there. The business plan is the entrepreneur's roadmap for a successful enterprise.[3]

the entrepreneurial
PROCESS

Overlooked Research Sources for Business Plans

The first obstacle to overcome when preparing a business plan is a lack of in-depth research resources. The following sources are recommended for entrepreneurs to pursue when seeking some of the basic information needed to prepare the business plan.

Track the Code. Begin by finding out what NAICS (North American Industry Classification System) code your company may fall under. Look up the appropriate NAICS or SIC code at LogLink (http://loglink.com/sic.asp). You can now use this code to gain important information on your industry at sites like Hoover's (http://www.hoovers.com) and ThomasNet (http://www.thomasnet.com/index.html). These sites will offer access to essential statistics and comparisons with both public and private companies for free.

Additional industry sites would include Yahoo's finance guide (http://finance.yahoo.com), industry guide (http://biz.yahoo.com/industry), and their list of newspapers and magazines (http://dir.yahoo.com/News_and_Media/Newspapers/By_Region). Chambers of commerce are also a valuable source of information for specific markets. You can begin at the U.S. Chamber of Commerce to find a local chamber's site (http://www.uschamber.com).

Check Your Competition. The art of competitive research has really taken off. Specialized firms now charge exorbitant fees for in-depth research, but you can extract valuable information on your own just by browsing their company website. You can gain insight on their strategies by perusing their job listings, finding strategic partnerships, and assessing customer relationships. Venture Consult also suggests scanning resumes of people who have worked for your competition; you can gain insight into strategies and weaknesses of the company from the job-hunter's accomplishments.

Search Out Government Resources. Start with FirstGov (http://www.firstgov.com) and the U.S. Small Business Administration (http://www.sba.gov). There is also a site where you can buy the annual U.S. industry and trade outlook (http://www.ita.doc.gov/td/industry/otea/outlook/index.html).

Don't Forget Your Customers. Private companies typically have the most in-depth research available; however, most of the research is not available to the public. Private associations, industry organizations, and trade shows can offer much of the valuable research that private companies spend thousands to gain. Find your industry's website that covers your market, and you will find the top trade shows that cover your company's niche and market. It is often much less expensive to purchase a report than to commission research through a firm. A couple of companies' sites worth checking out are http://www.InfoTechTrends.com and http://www.MarketResearch.com. The absolute best source of information is your current and prospective customers. Listen to what they want, and find out what problems they have with other companies and what they would like to see happen with your company.

SOURCE: Karen Klein, "Research Resources for Beginners," *BusinessWeek Online* (January 14, 2002).

In some professional areas the business plan is referred to as a venture plan, a loan proposal, or an investment prospectus. Whatever the name, the business plan is the minimum document required by any financial source. The business plan allows the entrepreneur entrance into the investment process. Although it should be used as a working document once the venture is established, the major thrust of the business plan is to encapsulate the strategic development of the project in a comprehensive document for outside investors to read and understand.

The business plan describes to investors and financial sources all of the events that may affect the proposed venture. Details are needed for various projected actions of the venture, with associated revenues and costs outlined. It is vital to explicitly state the assumptions on which the plan is based. For example, increases/decreases in the market or upswings/downswings in the economy during the start-up period of the new venture should be stated.

The emphasis of the business plan always should be the final implementation of the venture. In other words, it's not just the writing of an effective plan that is important but also the translation of that plan into a successful enterprise.[4]

Benefits of a Business Plan

The entire business planning process forces the entrepreneur to analyze all aspects of the venture and to prepare an effective strategy to deal with the uncertainties that arise. Thus a business plan may help an entrepreneur avoid a project doomed to failure. As one researcher states, "If your proposed venture is marginal at best, the business plan will show you why and may help you avoid paying the high tuition of business failure. It is far cheaper not to begin an ill-fated business than to learn by experience what your business plan could have taught you at a cost of several hours of concentrated work."[5]

It is important that entrepreneurs prepare their own business plan. If an entrepreneurial team is involved, then all of the key members should be part of writing the plan; in this case it is important that the lead entrepreneur understand the contribution of each team member. If consultants are sought to help prepare a business plan, the entrepreneur must remain the driving force behind the plan. Seeking the advice and assistance of outside professionals is always wise, but entrepreneurs need to understand every aspect of the business plan, since it is they who come under the scrutiny of financial sources. Thus the business plan stands as the entrepreneur's description and prediction for his or her venture, and it must be defended by the entrepreneur—simply put, it is the entrepreneur's responsibility.[6]

Other benefits are derived from a business plan for both the entrepreneur and the financial sources that read it and evaluate the venture. Specifically for the entrepreneur, the following benefits are gained:

- ☐ The time, effort, research, and discipline needed to put together a formal business plan force the entrepreneur to view the venture critically and objectively.

- ☐ The competitive, economic, and financial analyses included in the business plan subject the entrepreneur to close scrutiny of his or her assumptions about the venture's success.

☐ Since all aspects of the business venture must be addressed in the plan, the entrepreneur develops and examines operating strategies and expected results for outside evaluators.

☐ The business plan quantifies objectives, providing measurable benchmarks for comparing forecasts with actual results.

☐ The completed business plan provides the entrepreneur with a communication tool for outside financial sources as well as an operational tool for guiding the venture toward success.[7]

The financial sources that read the plan derive the following benefits from the business plan:

☐ The business plan provides for financial sources the details of the market potential and plans for securing a share of that market.

☐ Through prospective financial statements, the business plan illustrates the venture's ability to service debt or provide an adequate return on equity.

☐ The plan identifies critical risks and crucial events with a discussion of contingency plans that provide opportunity for the venture's success.

☐ By providing a comprehensive overview of the entire operation, the business plan gives financial sources a clear, concise document that contains the necessary information for a thorough business and financial evaluation.

☐ For a financial source with no prior knowledge of the entrepreneur or the venture, the business plan provides a useful guide for assessing the individual entrepreneur's planning and managerial ability.[8]

Developing a Well-Conceived Business Plan

Most investors agree that only a well-conceived and well-developed business plan can gather the necessary support that will eventually lead to financing. The business plan must describe the new venture with excitement and yet with complete accuracy.

Who Reads the Plan?

It is important to understand the audience for whom the business plan is written. Although numerous professionals may be involved with reading the business plan, such as venture capitalists, bankers, investors, potential large customers, lawyers, consultants, and suppliers, entrepreneurs need to clearly understand three main viewpoints when preparing the plan.[9]

The first viewpoint is, of course, the entrepreneur's, since he or she is the one developing the venture and clearly has the most in-depth knowledge of the technology or creativity involved. This is the most common viewpoint in business plans and it is essential. However, too many plans emphasize this viewpoint and neglect the viewpoints of potential customers and investors.

More important than high technology or creative flair is the marketability of a new venture. Referred to as "market-driven," this type of enterprise convincingly demonstrates the benefits to users—the particular group of customers it is aiming for—and the existence of a substantial market. This viewpoint—that of the marketplace—is the second critical emphasis that an entrepreneur must incorporate into a business plan. Yet although the actual value of this information is considered high, too many entrepreneurs tend to deemphasize in-depth marketing information in their business plans.[10] Establishing an actual market (determining who will buy the product or use the service) and documenting that the anticipated percentage of this market is appropriate for the venture's success are valuable criteria for the business plan.

The third viewpoint is related to the marketing emphasis just discussed. The investor's point of view is concentrated on the financial forecast. Sound financial projections are necessary if investors are to evaluate the worth of their investment. This is not to say an entrepreneur should fill the business plan with spreadsheets of figures. In fact, many venture capital firms employ a "projection discount factor," which merely represents the belief of venture capitalists that successful new ventures usually reach approximately 50 percent of their projected financial goals.[11] However, a three- to five-year financial projection is essential for investors to use in making their judgment of a venture's future success.

These three viewpoints have been presented in an order of decreasing significance to point out the emphasis needed in a well-conceived business plan. If they are addressed carefully in the plan, then the entrepreneur has prepared for what experts term the **five-minute reading**. The following six steps represent the typical business plan reading process many venture capitalists use (less than one minute is devoted to each step):

Step 1: Determine the characteristics of the venture and its industry.

Step 2: Determine the financial structure of the plan (amount of debt or equity investment required).

Step 3: Read the latest balance sheet (to determine liquidity, net worth, and debt/equity).

Step 4: Determine the quality of entrepreneurs in the venture (sometimes *the* most important step).

Step 5: Establish the unique feature in this venture (find out what is different).

Step 6: Read the entire plan over lightly (this is when the entire package is paged through for a casual look at graphs, charts, exhibits, and other plan components).[12]

These steps provide insight into how the average business plan is read. It appears somewhat unjust that so much of the entrepreneur's effort is put into a plan that is given only a five-minute reading. However, that's the nature of the process for many venture capitalists. Other financial or professional sources may devote more time to analyzing the plan. But keep in mind that venture capitalists read through numerous business plans; thus, knowing the steps in their reading process is valuable for developing any plan. Related to the process of venture capitalists is this updated version of an old quote that links entrepreneurs and venture capitalists: "The people who manage people manage people who manage things, *but* the people who manage money manage the people who manage people."[13]

Putting the Package Together

When presenting a business plan to potential investors, the entrepreneur must realize that the entire package is important. Presented next is a summary of key issues that the entrepreneur needs to watch for if the plan is going to be viewed successfully. A business plan gives financiers their first impressions of a company and its principals.

Potential investors expect the plan to look good, but not too good; to be the right length; to clearly and concisely explain early on all aspects of the company's business; and not to contain bad grammar and typographical or spelling errors.

Investors are looking for evidence that the principals treat their own property with care—and will likewise treat the investment carefully. In other words, form as well as content is important, and investors know that good form reflects good content and vice versa.

Among the format issues we think most important are the following:

Appearance—The binding and printing must not be sloppy; neither should the presentation be too lavish. A stapled compilation of photocopied pages usually looks amateurish, while bookbinding with typeset pages may arouse concern about excessive and inappropriate spending. A plastic spiral binding holding together a pair of cover sheets of a single color provides both a neat appearance and sufficient strength to withstand the handling of a number of people without damage.

Length—A business plan should be no more than 50 pages long. The first draft will likely exceed that, but editing should produce a final version that fits within the 40-page ideal. Adherence to this length forces entrepreneurs to sharpen their ideas and results in a document likely to hold investors' attention.

Background details can be included in an additional volume. Entrepreneurs can make this material available to investors during the investigative period after the initial expression of interest.

The Cover and Title Page—The cover should bear the name of the company, its address and phone number, and the month and year in which the plan is issued. Surprisingly, a large number of business plans are submitted to potential investors without return addresses or phone numbers. An interested investor wants to be able to contact a company easily and to request further information or express an interest, either in the company or in some aspect of the plan.

Inside the front cover should be a well-designed title page on which the cover information is repeated and, in an upper or a lower corner, the legend "Copy number" provided. Besides helping entrepreneurs keep track of plans in circulation, holding down the number of copies outstanding—usually to no more than 20—has a psychological advantage. After all, no investor likes to think that the prospective investment is shopworn.

The Executive Summary—The two to three pages immediately following the title page should concisely explain the company's current status, its products or services, the benefits to customers, the financial forecasts, the venture's objectives in three to seven years, the amount of financing needed, and how investors will benefit.

This is a tall order for a two-page summary, but it will either sell investors on reading the rest of the plan or convince them to forget the whole thing.

The Table of Contents—After the executive summary, include a well-designed table of contents. List each of the business plan's sections and mark the pages for each section.[14]

An attractive appearance, an effective length, an executive summary, a table of contents, proper grammar, correct typing, and a cover page—all are important factors when putting together a complete package. These points many times separate successful plans from unacceptable ones.

Guidelines to Remember

The following points are a collection of recommendations by experts in venture capital and new-venture development.[15] These guidelines are presented as tips for successful business plan development. Entrepreneurs need to adhere to them in order to understand the importance of the various segments of a business plan they are creating, which will be discussed in the next section.

Keep the Plan Respectably Short

Readers of business plans are important people who refuse to waste time. Therefore entrepreneurs should explain the venture not only carefully and clearly but also concisely. (The plan should be no more than 50 pages long, excluding the appendix.)

Organize and Package the Plan Appropriately

A table of contents, an executive summary, an appendix, exhibits, graphs, proper grammar, a logical arrangement of segments, and overall neatness are elements critical to the effective presentation of a business plan.

Orient the Plan toward the Future

Entrepreneurs should attempt to create an air of excitement in the plan by developing trends and forecasts that describe what the venture *intends* to do and what the opportunities are for the use of the product or service.

Avoid Exaggeration

Sales potentials, revenue estimates, and the venture's potential growth should not be inflated. Many times a best-case, worst-case, and probable-case scenario should be developed for the plan. Documentation and research are vital to the plan's credibility. (See Table 11.1 for business plan phrases.)

Highlight Critical Risks

The critical-risks segment of the business plan is important in that it demonstrates the entrepreneur's ability to analyze potential problems and develop alternative courses of action.

Give Evidence of an Effective Entrepreneurial Team

The management segment of the business plan should clearly identify the skills of each key person as well as demonstrate how all such people can effectively work together as a team in managing the venture.

Do Not Overdiversify

Focus the attention of the plan on one main opportunity for the venture. A new business should not attempt to create multiple markets or pursue multiple ventures until it has successfully developed one main strength.

Identify the Target Market

Substantiate the marketability of the venture's product or service by identifying the particular customer niche being sought. This segment of the business plan is pivotal to the success of the other parts. Market research has to be included to demonstrate how this market segment has been identified.

Keep the Plan Written in the Third Person

Rather than continually stating "I," "we," or "us," the entrepreneur should phrase everything as "he," "she," "they," or "them." In other words, avoid personalizing the plan, and keep the writing objective.

Table 11.1   Common Business Plan Phrases: Statement versus Reality

STATEMENT	REALITY
We conservatively project . . .	We read a book that said we had to be a $50 million company in five years, and we reverse-engineered the numbers.
We took our best guess and divided by 2.	We accidentally divided by 0.5.
We project a 10 percent margin.	We did not modify any of the assumptions in the business plan template that we downloaded from the Internet.
The project is 98 percent complete.	To complete the remaining 2 percent will take as long as it took to create the initial 98 percent but will cost twice as much.
Our business model is proven . . .	. . . if you take the evidence from the past week for the best of our 50 locations and extrapolate it for all the others.
We have a six-month lead.	We tried not to find out how many other people have a six-month lead.
We need only a 10 percent market share.	So do the other 50 entrants getting funded.
Customers are clamoring for our product.	We have not yet asked them to pay for it. Also, all of our current customers are relatives.
We are the low-cost producer.	We have not produced anything yet, but we are confident that we will be able to.
We have no competition.	Only IBM, Microsoft, Netscape, and Sun have announced plans to enter the business.
Our management team has a great deal of experience . . .	. . . consuming the product or service.
A select group of investors is considering the plan.	We mailed a copy of the plan to everyone in *Pratt's Guide*.
We seek a value-added investor.	We are looking for a passive, dumb-as-rocks investor.
If you invest on our terms, you will earn a 68 percent internal rate of return.	If everything that could ever conceivably go right does go right, you might get your money back.

Source: Reprinted by permission of *Harvard Business Review.* Adapted from William A. Sahlman, "How to Write a Great Business Plan," (July–August 1997): 106. Copyright © 1997 by the Harvard Business School Publishing Corporation; all rights reserved.

Capture the Reader's Interest

Because of the numerous business plans submitted to investors and the small percentage of business plans funded, entrepreneurs need to capture the reader's interest right away by stating the uniqueness of the venture. Use the title page and executive summary as key tools for capturing the reader's attention and creating a desire to read more.

These guidelines are helpful for entrepreneurs preparing to write a business plan. The following section analyzes the ten major segments of a business plan.

Elements of a Business Plan

A detailed business plan usually has ten sections. The ideal length of a plan is 50 pages, although depending on the need for detail, the overall plan can range from 25 to more than 50 pages if an appendix is included.[16] Table 11.2 provides an outline of a typical plan. The remainder of this section describes the specific parts of the plan. A complete business plan for The Fl Experience appears in Appendix 11A at the end of this chapter.

Executive Summary

Many people who read business plans (bankers, venture capitalists, investors) like to see a summary of the plan that features its most important parts. Such a summary gives a

Table 11.2   Complete Outline of a Business Plan

Section I: Executive Summary

Section II: Business Description

    A. General description of the business

    B. Industry background

    C. Goals and potential of the business and milestones (if any)

    D. Uniqueness of product or service

Section III: Marketing

    A. Research and analysis

        1. Target market (customers) identified

        2. Market size and trends

        3. Competition

        4. Estimated market share

    B. Marketing plan

        1. Market strategy—sales and distribution

        2. Pricing

        3. Advertising and promotions

Section IV: Operations

    A. Identify location

        1. Advantages

        2. Zoning

        3. Taxes

    B. Proximity to supplies

    C. Access to transportation

Section V: Management

    A. Management team—key personnel

    B. Legal structure—stock agreements, employment agreements, ownership

    C. Board of directors, advisors, consultants

Table 11.2 (Continued)

Section VI: Financial

A. Financial forecast
1. Profit and loss
2. Cash flow
3. Break-even analysis
4. Cost controls
5. Budgeting plans

Section VII: Critical Risks

A. Potential problems
B. Obstacles and risks
C. Alternative courses of action

Section VIII: Harvest Strategy

A. Transfer of asset
B. Continuity of business strategy
C. Identify successor

Section IX: Milestone Schedule

A. Timing and objectives
B. Deadlines and milestones
C. Relationship of events

Section X: Appendix or Bibliography

Source: Donald F. Kuratko, Ray V. Monatgno, and Frank J. Sabatine, *The Entrepreneurial Decision* (Muncie, IN: The Midwest Entrepreneurial Education Center, College of Business, Ball State University, 2002).

brief overview of what is to follow, helps put all of the information into perspective, and should be no longer than two to three pages. The summary should be written only after the entire business plan has been completed. In this way particular phrases or descriptions from each segment can be identified for inclusion in the summary. Since the summary is the first, and sometimes the only, part of a plan read, it must present the quality of the entire report. The summary must be a clever snapshot of the complete plan.

The statements selected for a summary segment should briefly touch on the venture itself, the market opportunities, the financial needs and projections, and any special research or technology associated with the venture. And this should be done in such a way that the evaluator or investor will choose to read on. If this information is not presented in a concise, competent manner, the reader may put aside the plan or simply conclude the project does not warrant funding.

Business Description

First, the name of the venture should be identified, with any special significance related (for example, family name, technical name). Second, the industry background should be presented in terms of current status and future trends. It is important to note any special industry developments that may affect the plan. If the company has an existing business or franchise, this is the appropriate place to discuss it. Third, the new venture should be thoroughly described along with its proposed potential. All key terms should be defined and made comprehensible. Functional specifications or descriptions should be provided. Drawings and photographs also may be included.

Fourth, the potential advantages the new venture possesses over the competition should be discussed at length. This discussion may include patents, copyrights, and trademarks, as well as special technological or market advantages.

Marketing Segment

In the **marketing segment** of the plan the entrepreneur must convince investors that a market exists, that sales projections *can be achieved,* and that the competition can be beaten.

This part of the plan is often one of the most difficult to prepare. It is also one of the most critical because almost all subsequent sections of the plan depend on the sales estimates developed here. The projected sales levels, based on the market research and analysis, directly influence the size of the manufacturing operation, the marketing plan, and the amount of debt and equity capital required.

Most entrepreneurs have difficulty preparing and presenting market research and analyses that will convince investors the venture's sales estimates are accurate and attainable. The following are aspects of marketing that should be addressed when developing a comprehensive exposition of the market.

Market Niche and Market Share

A **market niche** is a homogeneous group with common characteristics—that is, all the people who have a need for the newly proposed product or service. In describing this niche, the writer should address the bases of customer purchase decisions: price, quality, service, personal contacts, or some combination of these factors.

Next, a list of potential customers who have expressed interest in the product or service, together with an explanation for their interest, should be included. If it is an existing business, the current principal customers should be identified and the sales trend should be discussed. It is important to describe the overall potential of the market. Sales projections should be made for at least three years, and the major factors affecting market growth (industry trends, socioeconomic trends, governmental policy, and population shifts) should be discussed. A review of previous market trends should be included, and any differences between past and projected annual growth rates should be explained. The sources of all data and methods used to make projections should be indicated. Then, if any major customers are willing to make purchase commitments, they should be identified, and the extent of those commitments should be indicated. On the basis of the product or service advantages, the market size and trends, the customers, and the sales trends in prior years, the writer should estimate market share and sales in units and dollars for each of the next three years. The growth of the company's sales and its estimated market share should be related to the growth of the industry and the customer base.

Competitive Analysis

The entrepreneur should make an attempt to assess the strengths and weaknesses of the competing products or services. Any sources used to evaluate the competition should be cited. This discussion should compare competing products or services on the basis of price, performance, service, warranties, and other pertinent features. It should include a short discussion of the current advantages and disadvantages of competing products and services and why they are not meeting customer needs. Any knowledge

entrepreneurship IN PRACTICE

Tips for the Ultimate Business Plan

To obtain financing for your business, you would rather:

1. Jump out of an airplane.

2. Write a business plan.

More often than not, people will choose (1). As crazy as it sounds, potential entrepreneurs are frequently dismayed by the prospect of having to put together a plan and the accompanying financials. But when written well and as accurately as possible, business plans not only become key to obtaining financing, but also become the vehicle that drives the business throughout its start-up phase. A good plan enables the entrepreneur to target the right market, reduce risk, and ultimately make the correct, informed decision.

Why Business Plans Fail

☐ The plan is constructed around strategies that are defined inaccurately.

☐ The plan, while substantial, cannot be described clearly by management.

☐ The plan lacks detailed information about job responsibilities and operating schedules.

☐ The plan does not state goals and objectives lucidly and in professional terms.

☐ The plan is incomplete.

Business Plan Do's and Don'ts

Executive Summary

Do: Get right to the point.

Don't: Write more than a page and a half.

Management

Do: Play up your previous successes.

Don't: Paper over the gaps in your team.

Marketing

Do: Send a product sample, if you can.

Don't: Underprice your services because you failed to get good market data.

Financials

Do: Run cash-flow models at different growth rates.

Don't: Inflate or understate your margins.

Overall

Do: Have a friend proofread your plan.

Don't: Forget to use feedback.

SOURCE: C. J. Prince, "The Ultimate Business Plan," *Success* (January 2000): 44–49.

---

of competitors' actions that could lead to new or improved products and an advantageous position also should be presented.

Finally, a review of competing companies should be included. Each competitor's share of the market, sales, and distribution and production capabilities should be discussed. Attention should be focused on profitability and the profit trend of each competitor. Who is the pricing leader? Who is the quality leader? Who is gaining? Who is losing? Have any companies entered or dropped out of the market in recent years?

Marketing Strategy

The general marketing philosophy and approach of the company should be outlined in the **marketing strategy**. These should be developed from market research and evaluation data and should include a discussion of (1) the kinds of customer groups to be targeted by the initial intensive selling effort; (2) the customer groups to be targeted for later selling efforts; (3) methods of identifying and contacting potential customers in these groups; (4) the features of the product or service (quality, price, delivery, warranty, and so on) to be emphasized to generate sales; and (5) any innovative or unusual marketing concepts that will enhance customer acceptance (for example, leasing where only sales were previously attempted).

This section also should indicate whether the product or service will initially be introduced nationally or regionally. Consideration also should be given to any seasonal trends and what can be done to promote contraseasonal sales.

Pricing Policy

The price must be "right" in order to penetrate the market, maintain a market position, and produce profits. In this discussion a number of pricing strategies should be examined, and then one should be convincingly presented. This pricing policy should be compared with the policies of the major competitors. The gross profit margin between manufacturing and final sales costs should be discussed, and consideration should be given as to whether this margin is large enough to allow for distribution, sales, warranty, and service expenses; for amortization of development and equipment costs; and for profit. Attention also should be given to justifying any price increases over competitive items on the basis of newness, quality, warranty, or service.

Advertising Plan

For manufactured products, the preparation of product sheets and promotional literature; the plans for trade show participation, trade magazine advertisements, and direct mailings; and the use of advertising agencies should be presented. For products and services in general, a discussion of the advertising and promotional campaign contemplated to introduce the product and the kind of sales aids to be provided to dealers should be included. Additionally, the schedule and cost of promotion and advertising should be presented, and, if advertising will be a significant part of the expenses, an exhibit showing how and when these costs will be incurred should be included.

These five subsets of the marketing segment are needed to detail the overall marketing plan, which should describe *what* is to be done, *how* it will be done, and *who* will do it.

Research, Design, and Development Segment (Applicable Only If R&D Is Involved)

The extent of any research, design, and development in regard to cost, time, and special testing should be covered in this segment. Investors need to know the status of the project in terms of prototypes, lab tests, and scheduling delays.

In order to have a comprehensive section, the entrepreneur should have (or seek out) technical assistance in preparing a detailed discussion. Blueprints, sketches, drawings, and models are often important.

It is equally important to identify the design or development work that still needs to be done and to discuss possible difficulties or risks that may delay or alter the project. In this regard, a developmental budget that shows the costs associated with labor, materials consulting, research, design, and the like should be constructed and presented.

Operations Segment

This segment always should begin by describing the location of the new venture. The chosen site should be appropriate in terms of labor availability, wage rate, proximity to suppliers and customers, and community support. In addition, local taxes and zoning requirements should be sorted out, and the support of area banks for new ventures should be touched on.

Specific needs should be discussed in terms of the facilities required to handle the new venture (plant, warehouse storage, and offices) and the equipment that needs to be acquired (special tooling, machinery, computers, and vehicles).

Other factors that might be considered are the suppliers (number and proximity) and the transportation costs involved in shipping materials. Also, the labor supply, wage rates, and needed skilled positions should be presented.

Finally, the cost data associated with any of the operation factors should be presented. The financial information used here can be applied later to the financial projections.

Management Segment

This segment identifies the key personnel, their positions and responsibilities, and the career experiences that qualify them for those particular roles. Complete résumés should be provided for each member of the management team. Also, this section is where the entrepreneur's role in the venture should be clearly outlined. Finally, any advisors, consultants, or members of the board should be identified and discussed.

The structure of payment and ownership (stock agreements, consulting fees, and so on) should be described clearly in this section. In summary, the discussion should be sufficient so that investors can understand each of the following critical factors that have been presented: (1) organizational structure, (2) management team and critical personnel, (3) experience and technical capabilities of the personnel, (4) ownership structure and compensation agreements, and (5) board of directors and outside consultants and advisors.

Financial Segment

The financial segment of a business plan must demonstrate the potential viability of the undertaking. In this part of the plan, three basic financial statements must be presented: the pro forma balance sheet, the income statement, and the cash-flow statement.

The Pro Forma Balance Sheet

Pro forma means projected, as opposed to actual. The pro forma balance sheet projects what the financial condition of the venture will be at a particular point in time. Pro forma balance sheets should be prepared at start-up, semiannually for the first years, and at the end of each of the first three years. The balance sheet details the assets required to support the projected level of operations and shows how these assets are to be financed (liabilities and equity). Investors will want to look at the projected balance sheets to determine if debt/equity ratios, working capital, current ratios, inventory turnover, and so on are within the acceptable limits required to justify the future financings projected for the venture.

The Income Statement

The income statement illustrates the projected operating results based on profit and loss. The sales forecast, which was developed in the marketing segment, is essential to this document. Once the sales forecast (earnings projection) is in place, production costs must be budgeted based on the level of activity needed to support the projected earnings. The materials, labor, service, and manufacturing overhead (fixed and variable) must be considered, in addition to such expenses as distribution, storage, advertising, discounts, and administrative and general expenses—salaries, legal and accounting, rent, utilities, and telephone.

The Cash-Flow Statement

In new-venture creation, the cash-flow statement may be the most important document because it sets forth the amount and timing of expected cash inflows and outflows. This section of the business plan should be carefully constructed.

Given a level of projected sales and capital expenditures over a specific period, the cash-flow forecast will highlight the need for and the timing of additional financing and will indicate peak requirements for working capital. Management must decide how this additional financing is to be obtained, on what terms, and how it is to be repaid. The total amount of needed financing may be supplied from several sources: part by equity financing, part by bank loans, and the balance by short-term lines of credit from banks. This information becomes part of the final cash-flow forecast.

A detailed cash flow, if understood properly, can direct the entrepreneur's attention to operating problems before serious cash crises arise.

In the financial segment it is important to mention any assumptions used for preparing the figures. Nothing should be taken for granted. Also, it should include how the statements were prepared (by a professional CPA or by the entrepreneur) and who will be in charge of managing the business's finances.

The final document that should be included in the financial segment is a break-even chart, which shows the level of sales (and production) needed to cover all costs. This includes costs that vary with the production level (manufacturing labor, materials, sales) and costs that do not change with production (rent, interest charges, executive salaries).

Critical-Risks Segment

In this segment potential risks such as the following should be identified: effect of unfavorable trends in the industry, design or manufacturing costs that have gone over estimates, difficulties of long lead times encountered when purchasing parts or materials, and unplanned-for new competition.

In addition to these risks, it is wise to cover the what-ifs. For example, what if the competition cuts prices, the industry slumps, the market projections are wrong, the sales projections are not achieved, the patents do not come through, or the management team breaks up?

Finally, suggestions for alternative courses of action should be included. Certainly, delays, inaccurate projections, and industry slumps all can happen, and people reading the business plan will want to know the entrepreneur recognizes these risks and has prepared for such critical events.

Harvest Strategy Segment

Every business plan should provide insights into the future harvest strategy. It is important for the entrepreneur to plan the orderly transition of the venture as it grows and develops. This section needs to deal with such issues as management succession

Writing the Business Plan

Your desk is covered with pieces of information that you want to put into your business plan. You've had your coffee. Your phone is off the hook. But you spend the next 15 minutes staring out the window . . . unable to get going.

You're not alone. Most people experience some form of writer's block when faced with a particularly important or large-scale job.

Why? Most researchers who study the act of writing currently believe that many of our writing problems are caused by our approach. They say that all writers—whether they are conscious of it or not—go through a five-stage process when they write: prewriting, writing, revising, editing, and proofreading. The majority of writing problems are caused, the researchers say, when the writer tries to do all of the steps at once. Let's take a closer look at each of these steps.

Prewriting

This is the stage where you decide what you're going to say. You may write or review your notes, assemble facts, organize your thoughts, establish your goals, or draft an outline. The more you have to say, the more important this stage is. Generally, the more time you spend here, the less time you will spend in the revising stage.

Writing

After you know in broad terms what you need to say, you can start saying it. This is the stage where you just get it down. Resist the temptation to try to say everything perfectly. Don't correct grammar or punctuation. Don't stop after every sentence to critique yourself. Just keep going.

Revising

When you're done, you can start revising for clarity. Rework your sentences until you are sure that your reader will understand them.

Then, take a break from the project. At the very least, return a phone call or stand up and stretch. The next stage will require you to switch gears dramatically, and it will be much easier if you approach it from a fresh perspective.

Editing

This is the most crucial—and most difficult—stage of the writing process. At this point, you should take a very objective look at your business plan and ask yourself:

- ☐ Does it do what it should do?
- ☐ Is it convincing?
- ☐ Do I need to include more information? Less?
- ☐ Have I supported all of my most important statements?
- ☐ Is it well organized?
- ☐ Is it readable?
- ☐ Is the tone appropriate? Is the style appropriate?

Proofreading

All that is left to do now is to look for typographical errors and minor grammatical errors, and to make sure that the business plan is spaced correctly on the page. It helps if someone else can take a look. Keep in mind that minor errors could undermine the impact of the whole business plan.

The most important applications of the process approach are: Don't correct yourself while you write, and don't wait for "the perfect opening sentence" to come to you.

Speaking from my own experience as a professional writer (who hates to write), this process approach makes a lot of sense. I consciously go through the steps about 90 percent of the time.

While I taught this at University of Wisconsin–Milwaukee, about 75 percent of my students said that this approach saved them time and was especially helpful when they had tight deadlines.

SOURCE: Catherine Stover, "A Common Stumbling Block: The Writing Process," *Small Business Forum* (Winter 1990/1991): 35.

and investor exit strategies. In addition, some thought should be given to change management—that is, the orderly transfer of the company assets if ownership of the business changes; continuity of the business strategy during the transition; and designation of key individuals to run the business if the current management team changes. With foresight, entrepreneurs can keep their dreams alive, ensure the security of their investors, and usually strengthen their businesses in the process. For this reason, a harvest strategy for this business is essential.

Milestone Schedule Segment

The **milestone schedule segment** provides investors with a timetable for the various activities to be accomplished. It is important to show that realistic time frames have been planned and that the interrelationship of events within these time boundaries is understood. Milestone scheduling is a step-by-step approach to illustrating accomplishments in a piecemeal fashion. These milestones can be established within any appropriate time frame, such as quarterly, monthly, or weekly. It is important, however, to coordinate the time frame not only with such early activities as product design and development, sales projections, establishment of the management team, production and operations scheduling, and market planning but with other activities as well:

- ☐ Incorporation of the venture
- ☐ Completion of design and development
- ☐ Completion of prototypes
- ☐ Hiring of sales representatives
- ☐ Product display at trade shows
- ☐ Signing up distributors and dealers
- ☐ Ordering production quantities of materials
- ☐ Receipt of first orders
- ☐ First sales and first deliveries (dates of maximum interest because they relate directly to the venture's credibility and need for capital)
- ☐ Payment of first accounts receivable (cash in)

These items are the types of activities to be included in the milestone schedule segment. The more detailed the schedule, the more likely the entrepreneur will persuade potential investors that he or she has thought things out and is therefore a good risk.

Appendix and/or Bibliography Segment

The final segment is not mandatory, but it allows for additional documentation that is not appropriate in the main parts of the plan. Diagrams, blueprints, financial data, vitae of management team members, and any bibliographical information that supports the other segments of the plan are all examples of material that can be included. It is up to the entrepreneur to decide which, if any, items to put into this segment. However, the material should be limited to relevant and supporting information.

Table 11.3 provides an important recap of the major segments of a business plan, using helpful hints as practical reminders for entrepreneurs. By reviewing this, entrepreneurs can gain a macroview of the planning process. Table 11.4 is a personal checklist that gives entrepreneurs the opportunity to evaluate their business plan for each segment. The step-by-step evaluation is based on coverage of the particular segment, clarity of its presentation, and completeness.

Table 11.3   Helpful Hints for Developing the Business Plan

I. Executive Summary

☐ No more than three pages. This is the most crucial part of your plan because you must capture the reader's interest.

☐ What, how, why, where, and so on must be summarized.

☐ Complete this part after you have a finished business plan.

II. Business Description Segment

☐ The name of your business.

☐ A background of the industry with history of your company (if any) should be covered here.

☐ The potential of the new venture should be described clearly.

☐ Any uniqueness or distinctive features of this venture should be clearly described.

III. Marketing Segment

☐ Convince investors that sales projections and competition can be met.

☐ Use and disclose market studies.

☐ Identify target market, market position, and market share.

☐ Evaluate all competition and specifically cover why and how you will be better than your competitors.

☐ Identify all market sources and assistance used for this segment.

☐ Demonstrate pricing strategy since your price must penetrate and maintain a market share to produce profits. Thus the lowest price is not necessarily the best price.

☐ Identify your advertising plans with cost estimates to validate proposed strategy.

IV. Operations Segment

☐ Describe the advantages of your location (zoning, tax laws, wage rates). List the production needs in terms of facilities (plant, storage, office space) and equipment (machinery, furnishings, supplies).

☐ Describe the access to transportation (for shipping and receiving).

☐ Indicate proximity to your suppliers.

☐ Mention the availability of labor in your location.

☐ Provide estimates of operation costs—be careful; too many entrepreneurs underestimate their costs.

V. Management Segment

☐ Supply résumés of all key people in the management of your venture.

☐ Carefully describe the legal structure of your venture (sole proprietorship, partnership, or corporation).

☐ Cover the added assistance (if any) of advisors, consultants, and directors.

☐ Give information on how and how much everyone is to be compensated.

VI. Financial Segment

☐ Give actual estimated statements.

☐ Describe the needed sources for your funds and the uses you intend for the money.

☐ Develop and present a budget.

☐ Create stages of financing for purposes of allowing evaluation by investors at various points.

Table 11.3   (Continued)

VII. Critical–Risks Segment

- ☐ Discuss potential risks before investors point them out—for example,
  - ☐ Price cutting by competitors.
  - ☐ Any potentially unfavorable industry-wide trends.
  - ☐ Design or manufacturing costs in excess of estimates.
  - ☐ Sales projections not achieved.
  - ☐ Product development schedule not met.
  - ☐ Difficulties or long lead times encountered in the procurement of parts or raw materials.
  - ☐ Greater than expected innovation and development costs to stay competitive.
  - ☐ Provide some alternative courses of action.

VIII. Harvest Strategy Segment

- ☐ Outline a plan for the orderly transfer of company assets (ownership).
- ☐ Describe the plan for transition of leadership.
- ☐ Mention the preparations (insurance, trusts, and so on) needed for continuity of the business.

IX. Milestone Schedule Segment

- ☐ Develop a timetable or chart to demonstrate when each phase of the venture is to be completed. This shows the relationship of events and provides a deadline for accomplishment.

X. Appendix or Bibliography

Source: Donald F. Kuratko, Ray V. Monatgno, and Frank J. Sabatine, *The Entrepreneurial Decision* (Muncie, IN: The Midwest Entrepreneurial Education Center, College of Business, Ball State University, 2002).

Table 11.4   Business Plan Assessment: Complete Evaluation of Each Component

The Components

There are ten components of a business plan. As you develop your plan, you should assess each component. Be honest in your assessment since the main purpose is to improve your business plan and increase your chances of success. For instance, if your goal is to obtain external financing, you will be asked to submit a complete business plan for your venture. The business plan will help a funding source to more adequately evaluate your business idea.

Assessment

Directions: The brief description of each component will help you write that section of your plan. After completing your plan, use the scale provided to assess each component.

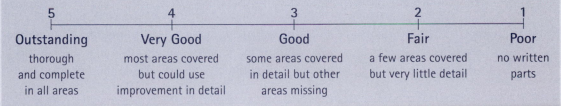

5	4	3	2	1
Outstanding	**Very Good**	**Good**	**Fair**	**Poor**
thorough and complete in all areas	most areas covered but could use improvement in detail	some areas covered in detail but other areas missing	a few areas covered but very little detail	no written parts

Table 11.4   (Continued)

The Ten Components of a Business Plan

1. **Executive Summary.** This is the most important section because it has to convince the reader that the business will succeed. In no more than three pages, you should summarize the highlights of the rest of the plan. This means that the key elements of the following components should be mentioned.

   The executive summary must be able to stand on its own. It is not simply an introduction to the rest of the business plan, but rather discusses who will purchase your product or service, what makes your business unique, and how you plan to grow in the future. Because this section summarizes the plan, it is often best to write it last.

   Rate this component:

5	4	3	2	1
Outstanding	Very Good	Good	Fair	Poor

2. **Description of the Business.** This section should provide background information about your industry, a history of your company, a general description of your product or service, and your specific mission that you are trying to achieve. Your product or service should be described in terms of its unique qualities and value to the customer. Specific short-term and long-term objectives must be defined. You should clearly state what sales, market share, and profitability objectives you want your business to achieve.

Key Elements	Have you covered this in the plan?	Is the answer clear? (yes or no)	Is the answer complete? (yes or no)
a. What type of business will you have?			
b. What products or services will you sell?			
c. Why does it promise to be successful?			
d. What is the growth potential?			
e. How is it unique?			

   Rate this component:

5	4	3	2	1
Outstanding	Very Good	Good	Fair	Poor

3. **Marketing.** There are two major parts to the marketing section. The first part is research and analysis. Here, you should explain who buys the product or service—in other words, identify your target market. Measure your market size and trends, and estimate the market share you expect. Be sure to include support for your sales projections. For example, if your figures are based on published marketing research data, be sure to cite the source. Do your best to make realistic and credible projections. Describe your competitors in considerable detail, identifying their strengths and weaknesses. Finally, explain how you will be better than your competitors.

   The second part is your marketing plan. This critical section should include your market strategy, sales and distribution, pricing, advertising, promotion, and public awareness efforts. Demonstrate how your pricing strategy will result in a profit. Identify your advertising plans, and include cost estimates to validate your proposed strategy.

Table 11.4 (Continued)

Key Elements	Have you covered this in the plan?	Is the answer clear? (yes or no)	Is the answer complete? (yes or no)
a. Who will be your customers? (*target market*)			
b. How big is the market? (*number of customers*)			
c. Who will be your competitors?			
d. How are their businesses prospering?			
e. How will you promote sales?			
f. What market share will you want?			
g. Do you have a pricing strategy?			
h. What advertising and promotional strategy will you use?			

Rate this component:

5	4	3	2	1
Outstanding	Very Good	Good	Fair	Poor

4. **Operations.** In this segment you describe the actual operations and outline their advantages. Zoning, taxes, access to transportation, and proximity to supplies should all be considered in this section.

Key Elements	Have you covered this in the plan?	Is the answer clear? (yes or no)	Is the answer complete? (yes or no)
a. Have you identified a specific location?			
b. Have you outlined the advantages of this location?			
c. Any zoning regulations or tax considerations?			
d. Will there be access to transportation?			
e. Will your suppliers be conveniently located?			

Rate this component:

5	4	3	2	1
Outstanding	Very Good	Good	Fair	Poor

5. **Management.** Start by describing the management team, their unique qualifications, and your plans to compensate them (including salaries, employment agreements, stock purchase plans, levels of ownership, and other considerations). Discuss how your organization is structured; consider including a diagram illustrating who reports to whom. Also include a discussion of the potential contribution of the board of directors, advisors, or consultants. Finally, carefully describe the legal structure of your venture (sole proprietorship, partnership, or corporation).

Table 11.4   (Continued)

Key Elements	Have you covered this in the plan?	Is the answer clear? (yes or no)	Is the answer complete? (yes or no)
a. Who will manage the business?			
b. What qualifications do you have?			
c. How many employees will you have?			
d. What will they do?			
e. How much will you pay your employees and what type of benefits will you offer them?			
f. What consultants or specialists will you use?			
g. What legal form of ownership will you have?			
h. What regulations will affect your business?			

Rate this component:

5	4	3	2	1
Outstanding	Very Good	Good	Fair	Poor

6. **Financial.** Three key financial statements must be presented: a balance sheet, an income statement, and a cash-flow statement. These statements typically cover a one-year period. Be sure you state any assumptions and projections made when calculating the figures.

Determine the stages where your business will require external financing and identify the expected financing sources (both debt and equity sources). Also, clearly show what return on investment these sources will achieve by investing in your business. The final item to include is a break-even analysis. This analysis should show what level of sales will be required to cover all costs.

If the work is done well, the financial statements should represent the actual financial achievements expected from your business plan. They also provide a standard by which to measure the actual results of operating your business. They are a very valuable tool to help you manage and control your business.

Key Elements	Have you covered this in the plan?	Is the answer clear? (yes or no)	Is the answer complete? (yes or no)
a. What is your total expected business income for the first year? Quarterly for the next two years? (*forecast*)			
b. What is your expected monthly cash flow during the first year?			

Table 11.4   (Continued)

Key Elements	Have you covered this in the plan?	Is the answer clear? (yes or no)	Is the answer complete? (yes or no)
c. Have you included a method of paying yourself?			
d. What sales volume will you need to make a profit during the three years?			
e. What will be the break-even point?			
f. What are your projected assets, liabilities, and net worth?			
g. What are your total financial needs?			
h. What are your funding sources?			

Rate this component:

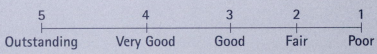

5	4	3	2	1
Outstanding	Very Good	Good	Fair	Poor

7. **Critical Risks.** Discuss potential risks before they happen. Here are some examples: price cutting by competitors, potentially unfavorable industry-wide trends; design or manufacturing costs that could exceed estimates; sales projections that are not achieved. The idea is to recognize risks and identify alternative courses of action. Your main objective is to show that you can anticipate and control (to a reasonable degree) your risks.

Key Elements	Have you covered this in the plan?	Is the answer clear? (yes or no)	Is the answer complete? (yes or no)
a. What potential problems have you identified?			
b. Have you calculated the risks?			
c. What alternative courses of action exist?			

Rate this component:

5	4	3	2	1
Outstanding	Very Good	Good	Fair	Poor

8. **Harvest Strategy.** Ensuring the survival of a venture is hard work. A founder's protective feelings for an idea built from scratch make it tough to grapple with issues such as management succession and harvest strategies. With foresight, however, an entrepreneur can keep the dream alive, ensure the security of his or her venture, and usually strengthen the business in the process. Thus a written plan for succession of your business is essential.

Table 11.4   (Continued)

Key Elements	Have you covered this in the plan?	Is the answer clear? (yes or no)	Is the answer complete? (yes or no)
a. Have you planned for the orderly transfer of the venture assets if ownership of the business is passed to this corporation?			
b. Is there a continuity of business strategy for an orderly transition?			

Rate this component:

5	4	3	2	1
Outstanding	Very Good	Good	Fair	Poor

9. **Milestone Schedule.** This section is an important segment of the business plan because it requires you to determine what tasks you need to accomplish to achieve your objectives. Milestones and deadlines should be established and monitored on an ongoing basis. Each milestone is related to all others, and together all of them provide a timely representation of how your objective is to be accomplished.

Key Elements	Have you covered this in the plan?	Is the answer clear? (yes or no)	Is the answer complete? (yes or no)
a. How have you set your objectives?			
b. Have you set deadlines for each stage of your growth?			

Rate this component:

5	4	3	2	1
Outstanding	Very Good	Good	Fair	Poor

10. **Appendix.** This section includes important background information that was not included in the other sections. It is where you would put such items as résumés of the management team, names of references and advisors, drawings, documents, licenses, agreements, and any materials that support the plan. You may also wish to add a bibliography of the sources from which you drew information.

Key Elements	Have you covered this in the plan?	Is the answer clear? (yes or no)	Is the answer complete? (yes or no)
a. Have you included any documents, drawings, agreements, or other materials needed to support the plan?			
b. Are there any names of references, advisors, or technical sources you should include?			
c. Are there any other supporting documents?			

Table 11.4   (Continued)

Rate this component:	5	4	3	2	1
	Outstanding	Very Good	Good	Fair	Poor

Summary: Your Plan

Directions: For each of the business plan sections that you assessed earlier, circle the assigned points on this review sheet and then total the circled points.

Components			Points		
1. Executive summary	5	4	3	2	1
2. Description of the business	5	4	3	2	1
3. Marketing	5	4	3	2	1
4. Operations	5	4	3	2	1
5. Management	5	4	3	2	1
6. Financial	5	4	3	2	1
7. Critical risks	5	4	3	2	1
8. Harvest strategy	5	4	3	2	1
9. Milestone schedule	5	4	3	2	1
10. Appendix	5	4	3	2	1

Total Points: _____

Scoring: 50 pts. — **Outstanding!** The ideal business plan. Solid!

45–49 pts. — **Very Good.**

40–44 pts. — **Good.** The plan is sound with a few areas that need to be polished.

35–39 pts. — **Above Average.** The plan has some good areas but needs improvement before presentation.

30–34 pts. — **Average.** Some areas are covered in detail yet other areas show weakness.

20–29 pts. — **Below Average.** Most areas need greater detail and improvement.

Below 20 pts. — **Poor.** Plan needs to be researched and documented much better.

Source: Donald F. Kuratko, *Developing an Effective Entrepreneurial Plan* (Bloomington: Kelley School of Business, Indiana University, 2006).

Presentation of the Business Plan

Once a business plan is prepared, the next major challenge is presenting the plan to either a single financial person or, in some parts of the country, a forum where numerous financial investors have gathered.[17] In any situation the oral presentation is a key step in selling the business plan to potential investors.

The presentation should be organized, well prepared, interesting, and flexible. Entrepreneurs should develop an outline of the significant highlights that will capture the audience's interest. Although the outline should be followed, they also must feel free to add or remove certain bits of information as the presentation progresses—a memorized presentation lacks excitement, energy, and interest.

Suggestions for Preparation

The following steps in preparing an oral presentation are suggested for entrepreneurs:

1. Know the outline thoroughly.

2. Use key words in the outline that help recall examples, visual aids, or other details.

3. Rehearse the presentation in order to get the feel of its length.

4. Be familiar with any equipment to be used in the presentation—such as an overhead projector, a slide projector, or a VCR.

5. The day before, practice the complete presentation using all visual aids and equipment.

6. The day of the presentation, arrive early in order to set up, test any equipment, and organize notes and visual aids.[18]

What to Expect

Entrepreneurs should realize that the audience reviewing their business plan is antagonistic. The venture capital sources pressure them in order to test their venture as well as the entrepreneurs. Thus, entrepreneurs must expect and prepare for a critical, sometimes skeptical audience of financial sources. As an example, the following comments from Joseph R. Mancuso, president of the Center for Entrepreneurial Management, illustrate the reality of what entrepreneurs face:

> When you finally do hand over your plan, the venture source will glance at it briefly and begin his preliminary comments. No matter how good you think your plan is, he's not going to look at it and say, "This is the greatest plan I've ever seen!" so don't go in looking for praise. It's highly likely that his remarks will be critical, and even if they aren't, they'll seem that way. Don't panic. Even if it seems like an avalanche of objections, bear in mind that Digital Equipment Corporation (DEC) was turned down by everyone before American Research & Development (AR&D) in Boston decided to take a $70,000 chance on them. That might not seem like much now, but at the time it made all the difference. And Fred Adler didn't put $25,000 into Data General until all of the other established venture capitalists had turned down the deal. These are two of the best venture capital deals of all time and they almost didn't happen, so don't expect results in the first twenty minutes.[19]

Entrepreneurs must be prepared to handle the questions from the evaluators and learn from the criticism. They should never feel defeated but rather should make a commitment to improving the business plan for future review. Table 11.5 outlines some of the key questions that might be asked when a business plan is turned down. Entrepreneurs should use the answers to these questions to revise, rework, and improve their business plan. The goal is not so much to succeed the *first* time as it is to *succeed*.

Table 11.5   What to Do When a Venture Capitalist Turns You Down: Ten Questions

1. *Confirm the decision:* "That means you do not wish to participate at this time?"

2. *Sell for the future:* "Can we count you in for a second round of financing, after we've completed the first?"

3. *Find out why you were rejected:* "Why do you choose not to participate in this deal?" (Timing? Fit? All filled up?)

4. *Ask for advice:* "If you were in my position, how would you proceed?"

5. *Ask for suggestions:* "Can you suggest a source who invests in this kind of deal?"

6. *Get the name:* "Whom should I speak to when I'm there?"

7. *Find out why:* "Why do you suggest this firm, and why do you think this is the best person to speak to there?"

8. *Work on an introduction:* "Who would be the best person to introduce me?"

9. *Develop a reasonable excuse:* "Can I tell him that your decision to turn us down was based on _____ ?"

10. *Know your referral:* "What will you tell him when he calls?"

Source: Joseph R. Mancuso, *How to Write a Winning Business Plan* (Englewood Cliffs, NJ: Prentice-Hall, 1985), 37. Reprinted with the permission of Simon & Schuster Adult Publishing Group. Copyright © 1985 by Prentice-Hall, Inc.

Summary

This chapter provided a thorough examination of an effective business plan. The critical factors in planning and the pitfalls to be avoided were discussed. Indicators of these pitfalls and ways to avoid them were also presented.

Next, a business plan was defined, and benefits for both entrepreneurs and financial sources were discussed. Developing a well-conceived plan was presented from the point of view of the audience for whom the plan is written. The typical six-step reading process of a business plan was presented to help entrepreneurs better understand how to put the business plan together. Ten guidelines in developing a business plan were provided, collated from the advice of experts in venture capital and new-business development.

The next section illustrated some of the major questions that must be answered in a complete and thorough business plan. The business plan was outlined with every major segment addressed and explained.

The chapter then presented some helpful hints for preparing a business plan, along with a self-analysis checklist for doing a careful critique of the plan before it is presented to investors.

Finally, the chapter closed with a review of how to present a business plan to an audience of venture capital sources. Some basic presentation tips were listed, together with a discussion of what to expect from the plan evaluators.

Key Terms and Concepts

business plan

five-minute reading

market niche

marketing segment

marketing strategy

milestone schedule segment

Review and Discussion Questions

1. What are the critical factors to be considered when preparing a business plan?

2. Describe each of the five planning pitfalls entrepreneurs often encounter.

3. Identify an indicator of each pitfall named in question 2. What would you do about each?

4. Identify the benefits of a business plan (a) for an entrepreneur and (b) for financial sources.

5. What are the three major viewpoints to be considered when developing a business plan?

6. Describe the six-step process venture capitalists follow when reading a business plan.

7. What are some components to consider in the proper packaging of a plan?

8. Identify five of the ten guidelines to be used for preparing a business plan.

9. Briefly describe each of the major segments to be covered in a business plan.

10. Why is the summary segment of a business plan written last? Why not first?

11. What are five elements included in the marketing segment of a business plan?

12. What are some critical factors covered in the management segment of a business plan?

13. What is the meaning of the term *critical risks?*

14. Describe each of the three financial statements that are mandatory for the financial segment of a business plan.

15. Why are milestones important to a business plan?

Experiential Exercise

Putting Together a Business Plan

The ten major segments of a business plan are listed in the following left column. Identify the order in which each segment will appear in the plan by placing a *1* next to the first part, and so on down to a *10* next to the last part.

Then match each of the 20 items or descriptions on the right with the segment in which it would appear. For example, if an item would appear in the first segment, put a *1* next to this description. Two items or descriptions are listed for each segment of the report.

Answers are provided at the end of the exercise.

Segments of the Report	Contents of the Segments
_____ 1. Financial segment	_____ a. Describes the potential of the new venture
_____ 2. Marketing segment	_____ b. Discusses the advantages of location

_____ 3. Management segment   _____ c. Discusses price cutting by the
                                                      competition

_____ 4. Summary   _____ d. Provides bibliographical information

_____ 5. Operations segment   _____ e. Most crucial part of the plan

_____ 6. Business description segment _____ f. Describes any prototypes developed

_____ 7. Critical-risks segment   _____ g. Analyzes case if any sales projections
                                                      are not attained

_____ 8. Appendix   _____ h. Shows the relationship between events
                                                      and deadlines for accomplishment

_____ 9. Harvest strategy segment   _____ i. Provides résumés of all key personnel

_____ 10. Milestone schedule segment _____ j. Contains support material such as
                                                      blueprints and diagrams

                                        _____ k. Discusses pricing strategy

                                        _____ l. Should be written after the business
                                                      plan is completed

                                        _____ m. Provides a budget

                                        _____ n. Explains proximity to suppliers

                                        _____ o. Sets forth timetables for completion
                                                      of major phases of the venture

                                        _____ p. Provides industry background

                                        _____ q. Explains costs involved in testing

                                        _____ r. Identifies target markets

                                        _____ s. Describes legal structure of the venture

                                        _____ t. Provides balance sheet and income
                                                      statement

Answers: 1. 6, 2. 3, 3. 5, 4. 1, 5. 4, 6. 2, 7. 7, 8. 10, 9. 7, 10. 9, a. 2, b. 4, c. 7, d. 10, e. 1, f. 2, g. 7, h. 9, i. 5, j. 10, k. 3, l. 1, m. 6, n. 4, o. 9, p. 2, q. 2, r. 3, s. 5, t. 6

Case 11.1

It's Just a Matter of Time

Pedro Santini has been a computer analyst for five years. In his spare time he has developed a word processing software program that is more comprehensive and powerful than any on the market. Since he does not have a great deal of money, Pedro believes the first step in producing and marketing this product should be to get the necessary venture capital.

The software program has been written and trial-tested by Pedro and a handful of friends to whom he gave the material. Two of these friends are full-time typists who told him that the program is faster and easier to use than anything on the market. Pedro believes that these kinds of testimonials point out the profit potential of the product. However, he still needs to get financial support.

One of Pedro's friends has suggested a meeting with a venture capitalist. "These guys have all sorts of money to lend for new ventures," the friend told Pedro. "All you have to do is explain your ideas and sell them on giving you the money. They are always looking to back a profitable idea, and yours is certain to be one of the best they have seen in a long time."

Pedro agrees with his friend but believes he should not discuss the matter with a venture capitalist until he has thought through answers to the various types of questions likely to be asked. In particular, Pedro believes he should be able to provide the venture capitalist with projected sales for the first three years and be able to explain the types of expenses that would be incurred. Once he has done this, Pedro feels he will be ready to talk to the individual. "Right now," he told his friend, "it's just a matter of time. I'd think that within seven to ten days I'll be ready to present my ideas and discuss financial needs."

Questions

1. In addition to financial questions, what other questions is the venture capitalist likely to ask Pedro?

2. Would a business plan be of any value to Pedro? Why or why not?

3. How would you recommend Pedro get ready for his meeting with the venture capitalist? Be complete in your answer.

Case 11.2

The Incomplete Plan

When Joan Boothe drew up her business plan, she was certain it would help her get venture capital. Joan is in the throes of putting together a monthly magazine directed toward executive women in the workplace. The objective of the periodical is to provide information useful to women who are pursuing careers. The first issue is scheduled to go to press in 90 days. Some of the articles included in this issue are "Managing Your Time for Fun and Profit," "What You Need to Know about Dressing for Success," and "Money Management: Do It Like the Experts." A section also is devoted to successful women at work. It is titled "Women in the News." Other features include a question-and-answer section that responds to letters and inquiries from readers (the first issue's questions were submitted by a group of women executives, each of whom had been asked to help get the column started by sending in a question); a stock market section that reviews industries or companies and points out the benefits and risks associated with investing in them; and a column on the state of the economy and the developments or trends expected over the next 12 months.

Joan's business plan consisted of six parts: a summary, a business description, a manufacturing segment, a management segment, a milestone schedule segment, and an appendix. When it was returned to her with the rejection letter, the venture-capital firm wrote, "Without a marketing segment, attention to critical risks, and a financial segment, this plan is incomplete and cannot be favorably reviewed by us. If you would provide us with this additional information and submit the rewritten plan within the next 60 days, we will be happy to review the plan and give you our opinion within 10 working days."

Questions

1. What should Joan put in the marketing segment? What types of information will she need?

2. For the critical-risks assessment segment, what key areas does Joan have to address? Discuss two of these.

3. For the financial segment, what suggestions would you make to Joan regarding the kinds of information to include? Be as specific as possible.

Notes

1. See Douglas W. Naffziger and Donald F. Kuratko, "An Investigation into the Prevalence of Planning in Small Business," *Journal of Business and Entrepreneurship* (fall 1991): 99–110.

2. Fred L. Fry and Charles R. Stoner, "Business Plans: Two Major Types," *Journal of Small Business Management* (January 1985): 1–6.

3. Donald F. Kuratko and Arnold Cirtin, "Developing a Business Plan for Your Clients," *National Public Accountant* (January 1990): 24–28.

4. James W. Henderson, *Obtaining Venture Financing* (Lexington, MA: Lexington Books, 1988), 13–14; see also Stephen C. Perry, "The Relationship Between Written Business Plans and the Failure of Small Businesses in the U.S.," *Journal of Small Business Management* 39(3) (2001): 201–208.

5. Joseph R. Mancuso, *How to Write a Winning Business Plan* (Englewood Cliffs, NJ: Prentice-Hall, 1985), 44.

6. See Donald F. Kuratko, "Demystifying the Business Plan Process: An Introductory Guide," *Small Business Forum* (winter 1990/1991): 33–40.

7. Adapted from Henderson, *Obtaining Venture Financing*, 14–15; and Mancuso, *How to Write*, 43.

8. Henderson, *Obtaining Venture Financing*, 15.

9. Stanley R. Rich and David E. Gumpert, "How to Write a Winning Business Plan," *Harvard Business Review* (May/June 1985): 156–166.

10. Gerald E. Hills, "Market Analysis in the Business Plan: Venture Capitalists' Perceptions," *Journal of Small Business Management* (January 1985): 38–46.

11. Rich and Gumpert, "How to Write," 159.

12. Mancuso, *How to Write*, 52.

13. Ibid., 65.

14. Reprinted by permission of the *Harvard Business Review*. An exhibit from "How to Write a Winning Business Plan," by Stanley R. Rich and David E. Gumpert, May/June 1985, 162. Copyright © 1985 by the President and Fellows of Harvard College; all rights reserved.

15. These guidelines are adapted from Jeffry A. Timmons, "A Business Plan Is More Than a Financing Device," *Harvard Business Review* (March/April 1980): 25–35; W. Keith Schilt, "How to Write a Winning Business Plan," *Business Horizons* (September/October 1987): 13–22; William A. Sahlman, "How to Write a Great Business Plan," *Harvard Business Review* (July–August 1997): 98–108; and Donald F. Kuratko, Ray V. Montagno, and Frank J. Sabatine, *The Entrepreneurial Decision* (Muncie, IN: The Midwest Entrepreneurial Education Center, Ball State University, 2002), 40–50.

16. See Donald F. Kuratko, "Cutting through the Business Plan Jungle," *Executive Female* (July/August 1993): 17–27.

17. For example, the Massachusetts Institute of Technology sponsors a business plan forum in Boston, and the Venture Club of Indiana sponsors a monthly meeting with presentations.

18. For more on oral presentations, see Scot Ober, *Contemporary Business Communication*, 3rd ed. (Boston, MA: Houghton Mifflin Company, 1998), 416–440.

19. Mancuso, *How to Write*, 34.

A Business Plan Prepared by Andrew M. Whisler

The F1 Experience

The F1 Experience

I. Executive Summary

Statement of Purpose

The following business plan has been developed by Mr. Andrew M. Whisler to obtain $1,500,000 in start-up capital for the development and operation of Indiana's premiere indoor kart racing facility. This plan will also serve as the financial and operational outline and plan for the first three years of the venture's operation. Mr. Whisler will obtain a loan through Key Bank in the amount of $1,000,000. Additionally, four investors will be offered 500 shares of stock at a price of $100 per share. This will result in a capital fund of $200,000, which will total approximately 13 percent of the total $1,500,000 start-up capital needed for the venture. Mr. Whisler will retain 3,000 shares of stock by investing funds from a grant by the Midwest Entrepreneurial Education Center in the amount of $250,000, and $50,000 in capital from a relative.

The F1 Experience and Its Founder

The F1 Experience will be an indoor kart racing center focused on providing customers with an exhilarating rush of adrenaline and excitement through the use of high-speed, European-style go-karts. Operations will primarily focus on servicing walk-in customers and corporate and event clients through racing sessions and facility rentals, but also will serve smaller niches with adult racing leagues and youth camps. Walk-in business will be generated through members of the local community, trade show attendees, conventioneers, and tourists/visitors of the city. Corporate outings and events will be sold to business establishments and organizations within the Indianapolis and metropolitan surrounding area (MSA), and leagues will be geared toward repeat customers of the facility. Finally, youth camps will be available to children between the ages of 10 and 17.

The grand opening of The F1 Experience is scheduled for October 1, 2002. The center will be located on the northeast side of Indianapolis, Indiana, at 8603 Allisonville Road, in the Castle Creek Plaza. This plaza is located at the corners of Allisonville Road and 86th Street, directly behind the Castleton Mall. Mr. Whisler will operate The F1 Experience as a Subchapter S corporation.

Mr. Andrew M. Whisler, founder of the venture, will receive a bachelor's of science degree in Entrepreneurship and Small Business Management from Ball State University, Muncie, Indiana, on May 4, 2002. Mr. Whisler has over three years of successful sales and managerial experience, and was certified in Track and Club Operations at the Track and Club Workshop during the International Karting Expo in St. Charles, Illinois, in February 2002. Additionally, he has participated in this sport for several years, and has spent months researching the industry and observing the operations of other similar facilities. With his love of racing and desire to succeed, Mr. Whisler will develop The F1 Experience into Indiana's premiere indoor karting facility.

Competitive Advantage

Mr. Whisler will face direct competition from three indoor karting centers already operating in the Indianapolis market. He is confident that the unique approach and competitive advantages of The F1 Experience will set it apart from the competition. The existing centers in the market are solely focused on providing customers with entertainment and enjoyment through kart racing sessions. This will also be the primary focus of The F1 Experience, but customers will have the option of alternative forms of entertainment through the use of a full arcade, retail novelty shop, concessions stand, and safe viewing and television entertainment.

Additionally, The F1 Experience will feature Indiana's longest and widest kart racing track allowing for safer racing conditions. The track will also enhance each customer's enjoyment of a road racing experience through the use of a banked turn and two sections of rolling hills. The F1 Experience will feature a newly designed kart that will allow the facility to increase the market size by offering new racing programs to more age categories. This feature is not available, and cannot be readily made available, at the competing facilities.

Financial Forecasts

All financial projections for The F1 Experience show the potential for success and growth in the existing market. In the second year of operation, $50,000 in dividends will be paid to stockholders for a 10 percent return on investment, and $75,000 will be paid in year three for a 15 percent return. The following table represents the projected sales and profit of The F1 Experience for its first three fiscal years of operation.

PROJECTED SALES AND PROFIT

YEAR ENDING	GROSS SALES	NET INCOME (LOSS)
September 2003	$1,258,749	$(69,112)
September 2004	$2,017,247	$352,696
September 2005	$2,608,543	$669,857

II. Business Description

General Description of Business

The F1 Experience will focus on providing customers with an exhilarating rush of adrenaline and excitement through the use of high-speed, European-style go-karts. The main attraction of the business will be an indoor, concession kart racing track to be opened on the northeast side of Indianapolis, Indiana, at 8603 Allisonville Road. The building stands at the corner of 86th Street and Allisonville Road, behind the Castleton Mall. The F1 Experience has been chosen for the name of the business, as the Formula One racing circuit is what has inspired the development of these indoor facilities, and patrons will get to experience the thrill of racing in a safe, controlled atmosphere.

The main attraction of the facility will be the 1,000-foot karting track. "But don't be fooled by the name and appearance. At 2 inches off the ground and with top speeds of [45] M.P.H., these karts are a far cry from the bumpy rides of youth. Drivers need concentration and nerve as well as helmets, race gear and instruction. . . . 'These things drive and feel very much like a race car.'"[1] The F1 Experience will offer a wide array of racing opportunities, ranging from arrive-and-drive formats, facility rentals, leagues, camps, and other racing options. In addition to racing, there will be conference rooms, arcade games, a snack bar, and a retail shop featuring apparel from NASCAR, Formula One and the Indy Racing League. Business will be geared toward adult patrons with karts that will reach up to 45 mph in the straights. However, adjustable speed control devices on each of the karts will allow for specified dates and times to be set aside for youth driving camps and youth racing events. The experience will allow each customer to become a race car driver for a short time period as they suit up in a protective uniform, strap on a helmet, and compete with as many as 12 other drivers for the fastest lap. After the race, each driver will receive a computer generated printout with a wealth of information, from position in the race, lap by lap times, highest speed achieved, average speed, and other interesting statistics from their race. Each customer's name will be posted in lights for everyone to see on a scoreboard hung over the winner's circle podium.

Mr. Andrew M. Whisler believes that this new venture will attract interest from the local residents of the community, as well as visiting tourists and businesses seeking new forms of corporate entertainment. Customers will be attracted to The F1 Experience because of its location, themed décor, added attractions, and unique track layout. The F1 Experience will feature a newly developed kart that is unlike any other in the market, and the track will feature a banked turn, two sections of rolling hills, and several long straightways to further enhance the experience of racing on a road course setup. Additionally, The F1 Experience will offer year-round entertainment that is not dependent upon the weather. This will provide an added benefit as the weather in Indiana is highly unpredictable, and offers poor conditions for the majority of the year.

Industry Information

Entertainment

We live in a society that revolves around entertainment. People are always looking for things to do and new places to experience. From 1997 to 2000, consumer expenditures on entertainment in the United States saw an average annual growth rate of 8 percent, totaling $595 billion in 2000.[2] Entertainment businesses thrive on the disposable personal income of consumers in the local community for the success of their companies. In 2000, disposable personal income rose 5.3 percent, and Standard & Poor's [projected] that it would increase by an additional 5.5 percent in 2001.[3]

History of Karting

Though the basic concept of indoor karting has been in existence for some time, very little information is readily available as to the current trends and statistics of the industry. Indoor karting originated in Great Britain during the 1970s as outdoor karters became frustrated with dealing with the horrible weather conditions they were going through.[4] Races were originally run in huge halls with the original "indoor karts" consisting of outdoor karts with few modifications. This meant that karts were very noisy and put out large amounts of smoke. The floors of the buildings were often slick, so contact was a common problem. Facilities began renting out karts rather than having people bring in their own karts, and indoor karting has since grown and progressed to its current state.

Indoor karting experienced its first real growth in popularity in 1994, when Michael Schumacher became the world champion in the Formula One series for the first time. Before 1994, the number of tracks in Germany could be counted on one hand, but Schumacher triggered a boom in the industry, which could never have been predicted by anyone.[5] Unofficial estimates stated there were approximately 500 indoor karting tracks established in Germany within one year, from the end of 1994 to 1996. Most of these facilities were unprofessionally operated, and were run in warehouse facilities with outdoor karts. This lack of experience in the operation of the facilities led to a high failure rate, and now, approximately half of these facilities are still in existence today.

The industry has seen a facelift, as karting centers now feature specially designed karts, are equipped for safety, use ventilation systems to remove the gases, and offer many other features to their patrons. In 1999, the Association of Indoor and Outdoor Kart Track Operators (IOKV) was formed by Mr. Reinhard Menath to enhance the future of the industry in Europe. These new facilities have taken a new approach to generating revenues, with the primary focus being on company events. "The most important aspect of successful operation is the 'seller of the track.' Today, more than 60% of the tracks make 60% or more of their money from company (corporate) or event business," says Menath.[6] Virtually every track operator around the world backs this statement. Mr. Jan Wessel, owner of The Hamburg Fun and Speed Kartbahn (one of Germany's most successful facilities), states, "Almost 70% of our money is made from companies, for whom we organize sports events, staff incentives, or even kick-off meetings."[7]

The Industry in America

While indoor karting has seen an explosion of centers across Europe, the industry is still very new, and has a huge potential for growth here in America. One of the biggest problems, though, is that no organizations have successfully formed to aide in the development and future success of the industry. Mr. Whisler did extensive research in an effort to find information as to the current state, and relative information on the market in the United States. Contacts were made with the International Kart Federation (IKF), World Karting Association (WKA), and the North American Karting Association (NAKA). Representatives from all three stated that they have no information as to any statistics of karting, but these numbers need to be found. Fred Marik, of the NAKA, told Mr. Whisler, "We do not have any statistical information on the industry, but it is sorely needed. A demographic study, sales tracking system, and establishing government relations are high on the NAKA list of priorities for the year. We are also looking into how we might assist the indoor operators. . . . We will look to start a new branch of the association for indoor karting facilities."[8]

Mr. Whisler also contacted Mr. Anthony Peterson, owner of Kartz indoor karting center and head of the National Indoor Karting Association (NIKA). Mr. Peterson stated that he has just started the organization this year, and he too had no information he could provide for Mr. Whisler. "The indoor karting industry is new to the United States, and subsequently very little data is available publicly. Information is fiercely guarded and protected. . . ."[9]

Although Mr. Peterson has stated that he has started, and was chosen to head, the National Indoor Karting Association, there was no mention made of this organization at the Indoor Kart Racing Conference, which Mr. Whisler attended at the 2002 Karting Expo held in St. Charles, Illinois. This conference was held to discuss the current state of indoor karting, and was used to establish an initial launch to make an indoor karting association as a part of the NAKA. The conference was headed by Mr. Dick Valentine, former professional race car driver and primary founder of F1 Boston, which is considered to be the premier indoor karting center in the United States. "Though no official statistics exist, it is estimated that there are currently approximately 25 to 30 indoor karting centers in the United States," stated Mr. Valentine. "It is estimated that there will be approximately 300 to 400 of these facilities in the near future."[10] The primary purpose of the seminar was to establish a list of operators and prospective operators, as Mr. Valentine is looking to head the efforts to join the NAKA in establishing an official organization for indoor track operators.

Consumer Spending

Currently, concession race tracks are classified under SIC code 7948, which is Racing, Including Track Operation. Unfortunately, this includes "promoters and participants in racing activities, including racetrack operators, operators of racing stables, jockeys, racehorse trainers, and race car owners and operators."[11] This means that the current industry estimates with regard to sales are irrelevant to The F1 Experience.

Mr. Whisler used market research to project the current market for the Indianapolis MSA region. The method of projection is further broken down in the Marketing Segment, but Mr. Whisler established a current projected market of $4,678,160 in walk-in business sales, and $5,771,855 in corporate outing/event sales. However, the 2001 infoUSA report listed current Indianapolis establishments Stefan Johansson Karting Center and Racers at $10 to 20 million and $5 to 10 million in annual sales, respectively. The market in Indianapolis has also seen consistent growth throughout the years. "Johansson's Karting Center has been growing 30% annually since it opened in 1996."[12]

Although there is currently no information available as to the number of people or companies currently using indoor facilities in the United States, limited information is available on the numbers and demographics on kart racing. "In kart racing, approximately 96% of participants are male with 48% being between the ages of 22 and 35. The Midwest has the most participants at 45% with the next closest region being the South East at 25%."[13] While males are the predominant kart racers, females also are enjoying indoor kart racing. "Coronel [owner of Coronel Kartracing] estimates that about 30% of his guests are female, and the number is growing."[14]

Another astounding figure is the number of businesses and corporations that are using these facilities for their outings and events. A majority of the current indoor track operators state that their corporate rental revenues make up anywhere from 50 to 80 percent of their yearly sales receipts. "Johansson's Karting Center . . . relies on corporate bookings for 85% of its business."[15] This trend is also seen at Racers, which relies on corporate clients for about 70 percent of its business.[16] Businesses are increasingly trying to find new forms of entertainment for their employees. "It's the sound of a new generation of high-performance go-karts, which are gaining popularity as an alternative to golf and tennis at those spirit-building corporate outings. . . . Companies are shelling out an average of $15,000 to $20,000 to hold [company outings and] sales meetings at these [facilities]."[17]

Products and Services

The F1 Experience is primarily a service facility, with the main focus on providing customers with a racing experience. The following list of products and services will be offered through the establishment of the business:

- ☐ Arrive and Drive Racing
- ☐ Arcade Games
- ☐ Corporate Outings/Private Events
- ☐ Concessions
- ☐ League Racing
- ☐ Retail Novelty Shop
- ☐ Youth Kart Racing Camps
- ☐ Advertising Packages
- ☐ Safe Viewing Areas and Television Entertainment

Arrive and Drive Racing will be open to the public during specified weekly hours further discussed in the Operations Segment. Anyone who is 18 years of age or older will be able to enter the facility, sign all necessary waivers, and purchase entrance passes into the desired number of race sessions. They will then receive a suit, helmet, and head sock; listen to pre-race instructions; and participate in a 20-lap race for the fastest lap. After each race session, patrons will receive a statistical printout of their performance. Walk-in customers will account for roughly 43 percent of the annual revenues for the center.

Corporate Outings and Private Events will be focused on providing entertainment while being used for team building, networking, staff incentives, client entertainment, product launches, fund raisers, or convention kick-off parties. Three primary racing formats will be available, or companies/groups will be able to submit their own idea of the racing formats they would like to use. The first format, the Le Mans, will primarily be used for team building events. The Super Prix will be geared toward groups with no more than 10 drivers, and the Exclusive Sprints will be the primary racing format for larger groups of 100 or more. Catering will be available through local restaurants, and can be arranged by The F1 Experience. As the main focus of The F1 Experience, corporate outings and private events will generate approximately 43 percent of revenues.

Leagues will be formed throughout the year and raced on a weekly basis. Up to 24 drivers will be accepted into each league, and customers will be able to form their own leagues with a minimum of 12 drivers. Leagues will offer an attractive form of racing, as customers will receive a minimum of twice the amount of racing time as their dollar could buy them on a walk-in basis. Each league will run one night a week, with more than one league being able to race per night. A typical league will last five weeks, and points will be awarded to each racer by best lap positioning. League winners will receive an engraved plate to be displayed on a designated wall of The F1 Experience. Revenues generated through weekly league racing will account for 4 percent of the center's revenues.

Youth Racing Camps will be available several times throughout the year for children ages 10 to 17. After both parents have filled out the appropriate forms and waivers, campers will participate in a two-hour camp, one day a week for five weeks. Campers will receive classroom as well as hands-on instruction to kart racing and proper techniques. Throughout the camp, campers will be given opportunities to compete against one another on the track. If the child passes all tests of the training camp, they will be awarded a special racing license, which will allow them to participate in special sessions of open practice and designated junior races. Youth camps will only provide a small portion of the overall revenues, at just over 1 percent.

The F1 Experience will offer an **Arcade** area as an alternative form of entertainment for customers not participating in the racing, or waiting between races. Games will vary throughout the year, as provided by Shaffer Distributing Company. One multi-driver, racing simulation game will always be present to allow for racing enjoyment to be experienced by all customers, even if they do not wish to suit up. The arcade will account for roughly 1 percent of the facility's revenues, after splitting the agreed portion of the income generated from the games with the supplier.

A **Concession Stand** will feature an assortment of candies, suckers, chips, cookies, sodas, sports drinks, and bottled water. The stand will account for 1 percent of The F1 Experience's revenues, and will be located in conjunction with the **Retail Novelty Shop**, which will generate roughly 5 percent of revenues. The shop will feature clothes and products of the top drivers in the NASCAR, Formula One, and Indy Racing League racing series. An assortment of clothing items will be available, including coats, jackets, long-sleeve tee shirts, tee shirts, and hats. These items will be offered in adult and children's sizes. Other items will include flags, license plates, decals, key chains, and signs. Inventory will be adjusted to meet the buyer's needs during the three professional races that visit Indianapolis throughout each year.

The F1 Experience will also promote the safety of its patrons by offering **Safe Viewing Areas and Television Entertainment** throughout the facility. All customers entering the facility will be required to sign spectator's waivers or participant's waivers. Nobody under the age of 18 will be admitted into the race area for any reason (with exception to children's camps and racing). Because of this, The F1 Experience will feature large glass walls allowing visitors to watch the racing without entering the race area. Two sets of bleachers will also be located in the enclosed track area, allowing for adult visitors to have a place to view the ongoing races or children's camps while they wait. Also, six television monitors throughout the facility will show race standings, as well as participants in the upcoming race. Six more television monitors throughout the facility will allow customers to watch a variety of television stations. Tables and chairs will be placed in an open area in front of the retail shop, and will feature a 36″ television for customers to enjoy while they wait for their race session to begin, or wait for their friends and family to finish up.

Finally, The F1 Experience will offer **Advertising Packages** to companies in the community. This sales tactic is widely used by other indoor karting centers as another means of generating revenues. Advertising fees will be paid on a monthly basis to the center, and the purchasing company will receive the agreed upon benefits. These fees will make up a small portion of the center's revenues at 2 percent of the total year's revenues in the first year of operation.

Strategy to Differentiate

There are currently three indoor karting centers in the Indianapolis area. Racers is located in the Union Station building, in downtown Indianapolis; Stefan Johansson Karting Center is located on the west side of Indianapolis, by the Lafayette Square Mall; and FasTimes is located near Keystone at the Crossing, on the north side of Indianapolis. With the differentiation that will be used by The F1 Experience, Mr. Whisler is confident that the new facility will be prosperous and become the premiere indoor karting center in the state. The company will look to acquire a share of the existing market as well as increase the market size by offering unique programs to new age groups.

The main strengths of The F1 Experience will lie in the highly differentiated approach of the facility. In addition to kart racing, The F1 Experience will offer a wide array of entertainment activities from a full arcade to snack shop, retail store featuring items from the top racing circuits, and several areas to relax and watch television. Themed decorations will also make patrons feel like they are at a real racetrack. This will be done with the architectural changes made to the facility as well as pictures, signs, banners, and other decorations. The F1 Experience will offer entertainment for the whole family by offering racing camps for children, which will lead to interest from parents and their participation in the sport. The facility will encourage its customers to gain an interest in other motor sports, and will allow them convenient shopping for apparel of their favorite driver in the retail shop.

Mr. Whisler is confident that The F1 Experience will appeal to the local community and visiting tourists, and will capture a significant portion of the current market as well as increase the market size. With his experience in sales and educational background, Mr. Whisler is determined to make The F1 Experience Indiana's premiere facility for indoor karting.

III. Marketing Segment

Indianapolis—Racing Capital of the World

Indianapolis hosts hundreds of sporting events and conventions, which generate over a billion dollars for the local communities on an annual basis. "Each year, an estimated 5 million visitors visit Indianapolis, bringing $1.5 billion in revenues."[18] Incoming visitors range from individuals from conventions and religious conferences, to participants in sporting events like the World Police & Fire Games, to the 2002 World Basketball Championships for Men.

In the mid-1970s, Indianapolis city leaders chose to use sports as an economic and community tool, and backed the construction of sports facilities and marketing strategies to attract top sporting events.[19] With this help from the community, Indianapolis has become known as the Racing Capital of the World, hosting the three largest single-day sporting events in the world with the Indianapolis 500, Brickyard 400, and SAP United States Grand Prix. The economic impact of these three events alone is equivalent to the city hosting three NFL Super Bowls annually.[20] Numerous other motor sport–related functions are held throughout the city on an annual basis, including events like the Carquest World of Wheels, EA Sports Supercross, International Powersport Dealers Expo, Four Wheel Jamboree Nationals, NHRA Nationals, and more.

Additionally, the city has launched an initiative to attract more motor sport businesses to the area through Indy Motorforce. This is a civil taskforce of more than 100 volunteers from public and private sectors dedicated to helping motor sports–related businesses prosper in regional Indianapolis.[21]

Through the years, Indianapolis has been given the reputation of being the "Cross-roads of America," due to the fact that it is located within a 600-mile distance of half the United States population.[22] Indianapolis is located in Marion County, which is Indiana's largest county with a population of 860,454.[23] Marion County also ranks third in the state for income per capita. The F1 Experience will be located in Marion County, and is less than $1/2$ mile outside of Hamilton County, which is Indiana's fastest growing county at a current population of 182,740. Hamilton County is also Indiana's wealthiest county per capita, and just became the nation's sixth-most affluent county with a median household income of $72,530.[24]

Primary Research

To determine feasibility, marketing strategies, and other critical information, Mr. Whisler conducted 100 surveys at a competing facility in Indianapolis (Racers at Union Station) to better understand the market of individuals already using these facilities. He also conducted phone interviews or mailed questionnaires to an additional 250 businesses in the Indianapolis region to determine the market and community desire for a facility of this type. A final set of interviews was conducted of current indoor karting facilities to better understand the industry and help project marketing figures. Critical figures from each of these surveys are covered in depth in the following sections.

Kart Racing Demographics

Mr. Whisler found that indoor karting appeals to a broad demographic through evenly spread percentages in the categories of age, education, and income.

A majority of the walk-in market for indoor karting consists of people between the ages of 18 and 34 at a total of 76 percent. However, a good percentage of customers aged 35 and older also participate in these activities.

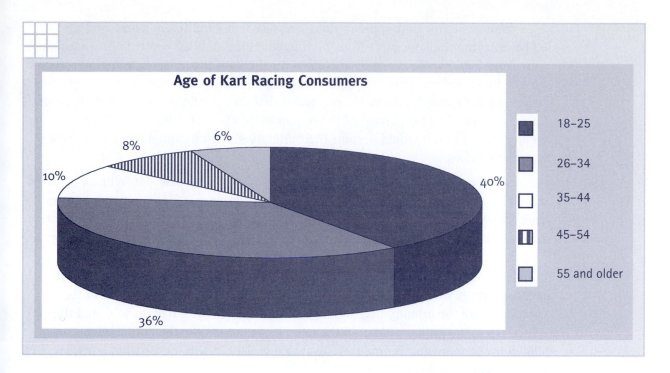

Age of Kart Racing Consumers

6%

8%

10%

40%

36%

- 18–25
- 26–34
- 35–44
- 45–54
- 55 and older

There is a very even spread in the household incomes of indoor karting participants. The top bracket was a $50,000 to $74,999 income, making up 22 percent of the market, followed by a vastly different $20,000 to $29,999 at 16 percent. The other six categories all fell within 4 percent of each other.

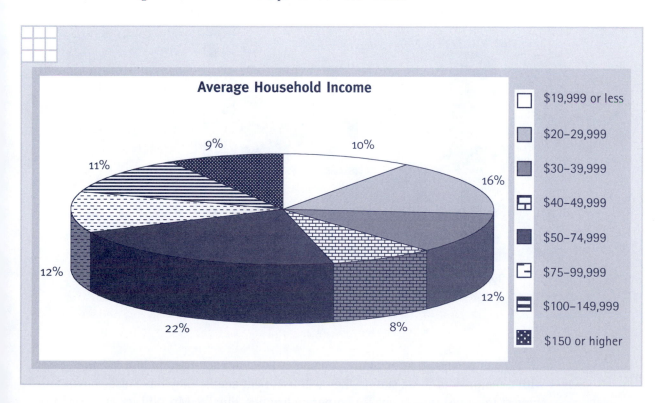

Average Household Income

9%

11%

10%

16%

12%

12%

8%

22%

- $19,999 or less
- $20–29,999
- $30–39,999
- $40–49,999
- $50–74,999
- $75–99,999
- $100–149,999
- $150 or higher

Finally, Mr. Whisler found that indoor karting center customers are willing to travel long distances to use the service. Fifty-five percent of the respondents said they were willing to travel 20 miles or more to visit the center, with an additional 15 percent willing to go 16 to 20 miles, and 14 percent responding they would travel 11 to 15 miles. Only 16 percent would travel a distance 10 miles or less.

Customers participating in the survey represented 13 different states, and the 62 percent from Indiana came from 28 different cities. Only 22 percent of the customers were from Indianapolis, Carmel, or Noblesville. Perhaps the most encouraging statistics for The F1 Experience came through data for the viability of a new center. Thirty-five percent of the survey participants responded that they would use a new facility in the Castleton area. Over 90 percent of the respondents who stated they would use this facility agreed that it would become their primary site for karting if they were happy with the services.

A good response was received from the corporate market also. Mr. Whisler obtained data from an evenly spread set of companies with fewer than 25 employees or sales under $0.99 million, to corporations with 100+ employees or more than $25 million in annual sales. Mr. Whisler found that on average, males make up 65 percent and females 35 percent of the labor force, and on average, 73 percent of employees attend the outings/events that are held. Also, 27 percent of companies sponsor smaller depart-mental outings with an average budget of $650. The president/CEO/owner of the companies are the primary decision makers in what activities will be held, and the type of activity is the primary factor in the criteria used to choose the outing/event. As shown in the following figure, there is a wide variety in why or for what purposes outings/events are held.

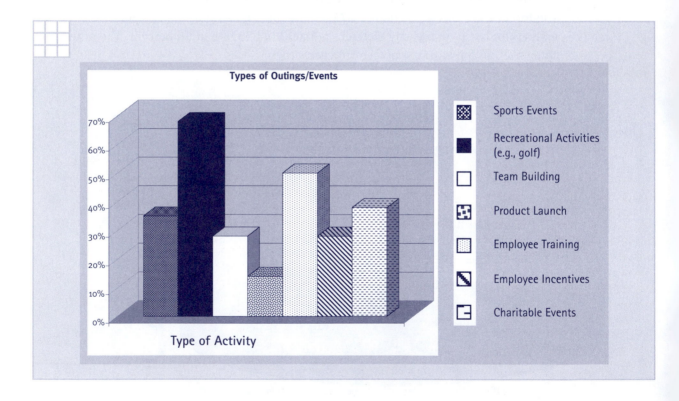

As will be shown later, many companies have already used indoor karting centers, with a majority of these stating they will use them again. They have also shown an interest in sponsoring teams for corporate leagues. Finally, Mr. Whisler also tried to conduct a survey of employees within these corporations to see if there is an interest for this type of activity. Of the companies he surveyed, only two were willing to allow Mr. Whisler to conduct these interviews, and only if he mailed them the surveys. In both cases, Mr. Whisler mailed the surveys, and tried to conduct a follow up, but neither returned the information.

Target Markets

By using the data gathered in primary research and studying the current facilities around the country, Mr. Whisler identified two primary markets that will be targeted as well as several secondary markets to help boost revenues. The trend in the industry is that a majority of sales come from the use of the facility for corporate outings or special events. This avenue can generate anywhere from 50 to 80 percent of the annual sales receipts of the facilities revenues. Mr. Whisler, along with the events coordinator at The F1 Experience, will develop and sell outings and events for companies and groups of all sizes in the Indianapolis MSA area.

The second primary market to be targeted, walk-in racers, consists of members of the local community, city visitors, and trade show/convention attendants. As noted in the previous survey analysis, walk-in customers represent a wide array of ages and demographics. Therefore, marketing campaigns will need to address the interests of a broad category of people, or several smaller marketing campaigns will need to be conducted to attract each of the noted groups separately. Walk-in sales make up the majority of the revenue besides corporate events.

Secondary markets will be made up of community and national business chains, for the purchase of advertising packages within the facility, and patrons of the center for snacks and concessions, arcade games, and retail sales. Also in this category would be children ages 10 to 17 for youth kart racing camps, and any individuals 18 years of age and older for participation in weekly kart racing leagues.

Market Share Analysis—Primary Sources

Walk-In Sales

Market Size   The current facilities in Indianapolis were not willing to help Mr. Whisler in his efforts to determine the current market size, so he made contacts with facilities in Charlotte, North Carolina, and Roswell, Georgia, to project these figures. To do this, Mr. Whisler used statistics from the latest census to determine the population of individuals 18 to 65 years of age in each market. He then divided the number of walk-ins per month by the population, and used this ratio to determine the walk-in market size for Indianapolis. The following results were obtained through this projection.

49,908	Population of Indianapolis (18–65)
×0.21698	Walk-in ratio in other cities
10,829	Walk-ins/month
×12	Months
129,949	Walk-ins/year

With the projected number of walk-in visitors per year determined to be 129,949 for the Indianapolis market, Mr. Whisler then applied his primary research to find the number of sessions per year for the total market.

129,949 CUSTOMERS PER YEAR = TOTAL MARKET

% OF TOTAL MARKET	×	SESSIONS	=	TOTAL SESSIONS
43%		1 session		55,878
42%		2 sessions		109,157
11%		3 sessions		42,883
4%		5 sessions		25,990
			Total sessions	233,908

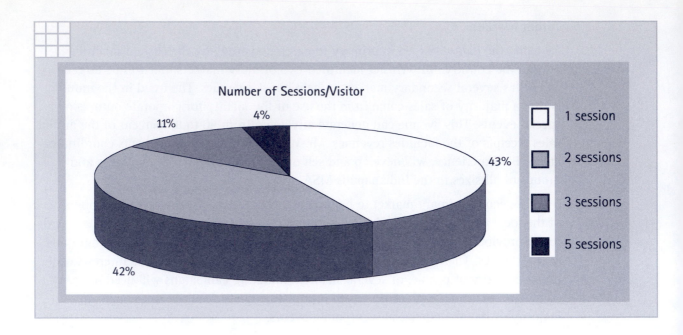

Number of Sessions/Visitor

- 1 session — 43%
- 2 sessions — 42%
- 3 sessions — 11%
- 5 sessions — 4%

This data shows that the projected current market size for Indianapolis is 233,908 sessions, including both first time and repeat customers. Of the respondents, 93 percent stated that they use an indoor karting center three times or less per month. Mr. Whisler estimated that half of the individuals making three visits per month or less on the survey are repeat visit customers, and the other half visit one time only. This leads to a calculation of 107,598 of the sessions coming from one-time visitors, and 126,310 from repeat customers.

233,908	Total market (sessions)
× 46%	One-time visitors
107,598	**Sessions from one-time visitors**

233,908	Total market (sessions)
− 107,598	Sessions from one-time visitors
126,310	**Sessions from repeat visitors**

Market Share   Primary research gathered from individuals at an indoor karting facility in Indianapolis indicates that The F1 Experience would be able to obtain 32 percent of the overall market. This was calculated by using 100 percent of the individuals responding that a new indoor karting facility located in the Castleton area would be their primary site for karting if they were happy with the services. However, Mr. Whisler does not believe that it would be possible for this new facility to obtain this share of the market in the first year of operation. With this in mind, a five-year goal for obtaining 32 percent of the market share was set. In the first year, it is estimated that The F1 Experience will be able to capture just over one-third of the five-year goal, for a total of 11 percent of the current overall walk-in market. With this information, Mr. Whisler is projecting the following revenues from walk-in customers in the first year of operation.

129,949	Total market (customers)	233,908	Total market (sessions)
×11%	F1's share	×11%	F1's share
14,294	Total customers (F1)	25,730	Sessions
		×$20	Price/session
		$514,600	**Total revenue**

A total of 25,730 sessions will be purchased from 14,294 customers visiting The F1 Experience in the first year of operation. The 25,730 sessions represent approximately 12 percent of the maximum capacity The F1 Experience would be able to handle if running all walk-in traffic all the time. In the second year of operation, The F1 Experience will reach over half of its five-year projection for a total of 18 percent of the market, and in year three, the business will be almost three-quarters of the projection, for a total of 23 percent of the market. Total market growth rate has been determined by taking the average growth rate of the population in Indianapolis between the ages of 18 and 65 and applying it to the current population of this same age category. This annual growth rate is 0.007 percent.

Corporate Outings/Events

Market Size   In an effort to determine the current market size for corporate outings and events in Indianapolis, Mr. Whisler had to derive another formula, as the current facilities were not willing to help. This projection was based on the number of business establishments in the Indianapolis metropolitan surrounding area (MSA) and the statistics derived from the primary research Mr. Whisler conducted of business spending and trends for outings and events. The U.S. Bureau of Census showed 41,537 establishments in 1998, with an average growth rate of 1.9 percent per year from 1994 to 1998 for the Indianapolis MSA region. Mr. Whisler used this growth rate to project the current number at 44,774 establishments. Understanding that not all of these establishments could be considered a viable market, Mr. Whisler projected that only 10 percent would be a marketable share to even consider this type of activity. He then used his primary data to determine the current market by using all of the companies that said they had used an indoor karting facility before and would use one again (19 percent), and a projected number of companies that have not used an indoor karting center, but would possibly use one. These calculations resulted in the following statistics.

44,774	Establishments
× 10%	Marketable share
4,477	**Total marketable establishments**

4,477	Establishments	4,477	Establishments
× 19%	Have used—would use again	× 12%	Have not used—would possibly use
851	Establishment	538	Establishments

851	Establishments
+ 538	Establishments
1,389	**Total market**

After determining the current market at 1,389 business establishments, Mr. Whisler was able to use his primary data to determine that the total spending on outings/events at indoor karting facilities results in $5,771,855 in total revenues.

1,389 = TOTAL MARKET FOR OUTINGS/EVENTS

% OF TOTAL OUTINGS	=	BUSINESSES	×	SPENDING/EVENT	=	TOTAL REVENUES
35%		486		$745/event		$362,070
42%		583		$3,645/event		2,125,035
15%		209		$7,750/event		1,619,750
8%		111		$15,000/event		$1,665,000
					Total revenues	$5,771,855

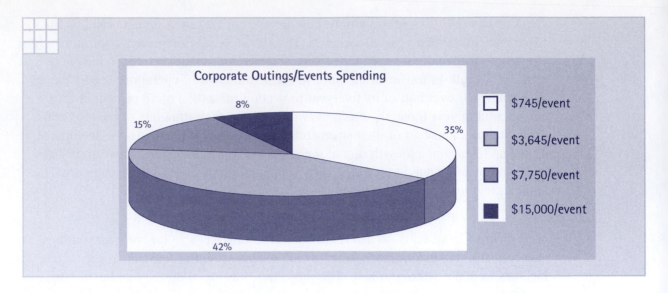

Corporate Outings/Events Spending

- $745/event
- $3,645/event
- $7,750/event
- $15,000/event

35% 8% 15% 42%

Market Share   Mr. Whisler projected that The F1 Experience will attempt to capture 28 percent of the overall market for outings/events within a five-year time frame. This projection is based on the total number of indoor karting centers in the market, and the increased interest in the new facility due to its competitive advantages. Mr. Whisler believes that this figure is conservative, yet realistic. With this in mind, Mr. Whisler projected that The F1 Experience will capture roughly one-third of this projected goal during the first year of operation. This results in a first-year projection of 9 percent of the current market.

1,389	Total market
×9%	F1's share
125	**Outings/events**

After determining that The F1 Experience would hold 125 outings/events in the first year of operation, Mr. Whisler did two separate calculations to determine the revenues generated from this source. The first calculation shows the revenues generated from outings/events that would not use catering service. Primary research showed that 20 percent of these companies would not want catering. This resulted in the following revenues.

25 = TOTAL OUTINGS/EVENTS AT F1 WITHOUT CATERING

% OF TOTAL OUTINGS =	BUSINESSES ×	SPENDING/EVENT =	TOTAL REVENUE
35%	9	$600/event	$5,400
42%	10	$3,300/event	$33,000
15%	4	$7,000/event	$28,000
8%	2	$13,500/event	$27,000
		Total revenues	**$93,400**

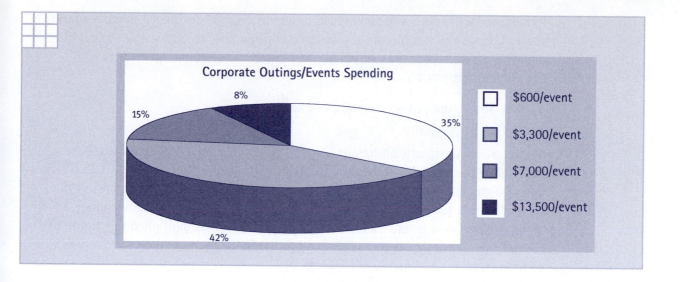

Next, calculations were made to determine revenues from outings/events with catering, as well as the cost of providing the catering service. Of the businesses surveyed, 80 percent responded that they would want catering in the form of an informal meal, like pizza. Results of the calculations are shown in the following tables.

99 = TOTAL OUTINGS/EVENTS AT F1 WITH CATERING

% OF TOTAL OUTINGS	=	BUSINESSES	×	SPENDING/EVENT	=	TOTAL SALES
35%		34		$600/event		$25,330
42%		42		$3,300/event		153,090
15%		15		$7,000/event		116,250
8%		8		$13,500/event		120,000
					Total sales	$414,670

COST OF GOODS SOLD FOR OUTINGS/EVENTS AT F1

BUSINESSES	×	COGS/EVENT	=	TOTAL COGS
34		$150/event		5,100
42		$350/event		14,700
15		$750/event		11,250
8		$1,500/event		12,000
			Total COGS	$43,050

$414,670	Sales
−43,050	COGS
Total revenue $371,620	

These calculations show that The F1 Experience will net $465,020 from both outings/events without catering, and outings/events with catering combined ($93,400 + $371,620). Of the outings/events per year, 124 represent approximately 6 percent of the maximum capacity for these activities if The F1 Experience were to solely run operations on outings/events. During the second year of operation, it is projected that The F1 Experience will reach just over one-half of its five-year goal for 14 percent of the total market, and by the end of year three, The F1

Experience will reach almost three-quarters of its goal for an 18 percent market share. Increase in the overall market size is projected by increasing the number of business establishments in Indianapolis MSA by the average growth rate of 1.9 percent per year.

Market Share Analysis—Secondary Markets

Advertising Revenue

Market Size   Currently, all indoor karting centers that Mr. Whisler visited sell advertising packages for signage/sponsorships within the facilities. The F1 Experience will also capitalize on this market as a secondary source of income. To project the current market for advertising within the centers, Mr. Whisler used an average advertising package cost from other indoor karting centers, and multiplied this figure by the current number of businesses advertising in the Indianapolis centers. The results were as follows.

$1,200	Average advertising package price/month
×21	Businesses currently advertising in Indianapolis centers
$25,200	Advertising revenue/month
×12	Months
$302,400	Total advertising package market/year

Market Share   There are currently 21 businesses advertising in three indoor karting centers in the Indianapolis market. This means that each facility averages seven advertising packages per year, generating average revenues of $8,400 per month. Mr. Whisler projected that The F1 Experience will be able to reach this seven-package average by the third year of operation. In getting to that point, The F1 Experience will sell two packages in year one, four in year two, and seven in year three. This means that in the first year of operation, The F1 Experience will have the following revenues from the sale of advertising packages within the facility.

$1,200	Average advertising package price/month
×2	Packages sold in Year 1—F1
$2,400	Advertising revenue/month
×12	Months
$28,800	Total advertising package market/year

Two advertising packages represent approximately 9 percent of the total market in the first year of operation. This is calculated by taking the total number of advertising packages in the entire market (23) and dividing it by the number of packages The F1 Experience will hold (2). In year two, this will see an increase to 16 percent of the total market, and the projected goal of 25 percent in year three.

Concessions

Primary research gathered by Mr. Whisler showed that customers would like to have concessions available while visiting an indoor karting center. The facility where the surveys were conducted does not offer concessions, so answers were skewed, but the overall response showed positive results. Of the people surveyed, 69 percent currently spend $0 on food and concessions, but a total of 45 percent of the respondents marked that they would use a snack bar at an indoor karting center.

To determine the revenue generated from this source, Mr. Whisler used the total visitors to The F1 Experience, including repeat business, knowing that most customers who purchase food/concessions will purchase the goods with each visit. The projected figure is conservative since no consideration was given to the number of visitors not participating in racing activities, visitors participating in leagues or camps, visitors participating in a corporate outing/event, or children brought to the facility with their parents (over 34 percent of people with children stated they would bring them to the facility). With this in mind, the following sales projections were given for the first year.

14,294 = TOTAL F1 CUSTOMERS PER YEAR

% OF TOTAL CUSTOMERS	=	PEOPLE	×	PURCHASES	=	SALES	−	COGS (AVG = 51%)
69%		9,863		$0		$0		$0
24%		3,431		$4		13,724		6,999
5%		714		$8		5,712		2,913
2%		286		$12		3,432		1,750
					Total sales	$22,868		
						COGS	$11,663	
						Total profit	$11,205	

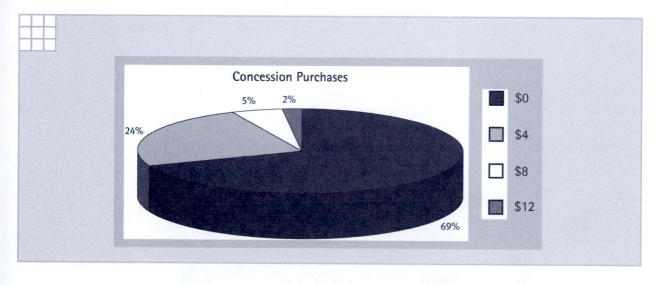

Arcade

The F1 Experience will expand the market for arcade revenues at indoor karting facilities as none of the competitors offer this feature. Again, the facility where the surveys were conducted does not offer an arcade, so spending patterns do not reflect the total revenue that could be generated. A total of 34 percent of the people surveyed responded that they would use an arcade at an indoor facility.

Mr. Whisler used the primary research he gathered to determine his revenue generated through games/arcade. The total that was figured is conservative, because, as mentioned in the previous section, no consideration was given to the number of visitors not participating in races, visitors participating in a corporate outing/event, league or camp participants, or children brought by their parents. Mr. Whisler believes that the last mentioned category, children brought by their parents, could account for a substantial increase in revenues generated through the games/arcade as the children look for a source of entertainment while they wait for their parents to finish racing. In the 20 hours Mr. Whisler spent at Racers observing operations and surveying customers, he noticed that on numerous occasions, one parent was forced to sit in the hallway/lobby monitoring their children with no source of entertainment while the other parent was enjoying their time on the track. With little children this can be an annoyance as the whole process, from sign-in to the end of one race, usually takes roughly 30 minutes or more.

The following revenue projection was made by staying with the initial responses on the surveys of how much customers are currently spending on games/arcade, even though this is not currently available to them at the Indianapolis locations.

14,294 = TOTAL F1 CUSTOMERS PER YEAR

% OF TOTAL CUSTOMERS	=	PEOPLE	×	PURCHASES	=	SALES	−	COGS (50%)
84%		12,008		$0		$0		$0
9%		1,286		$5		6,430		3,215
2%		286		$8		2,288		1,144
5%		714		$12		8,568		4,284
					Total sales	$17,286		
						COGS		$8,643
						Total profit		$8,643

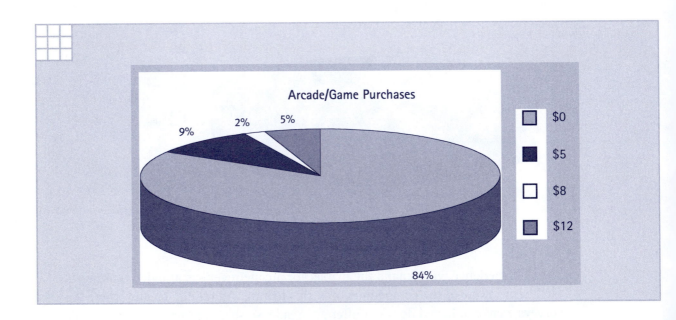

Arcade/Game Purchases

Legend: $0, $5, $8, $12

9%   2%   5%

84%

Retail Merchandise

By offering a retail merchandise store within the facility, The F1 Experience will again be expanding the market, instead of taking the market from the competing facilities. Mr. Whisler determined the interest for this feature with his primary research. Of the respondents, 16 percent marked that they would use a retail shop at a karting facility to purchase racing apparel/collectibles, and another 9 percent slightly agreed. These figures, in combination with the responses on spending per year, were used to determine the revenues from the retail shop for The F1 Experience. Mr. Whisler did take into account the number of repeat visitors, so they would not be counted more than once. To do this, he applied the calculations to the number of one-time customers visiting the facility each year. Repeat visitors are projected at 54 percent of the total visitors to the facility. To project the number of these individuals who would actually purchase items, Mr. Whisler used 100 percent of the people responding they would use this retail shop, and 50 percent of the people who responded they slightly agreed, for a total of 20 percent of the marketable number of visitors. The projected revenues are as follows.

14,294	=	Total F1 customers per year
7,719		Less repeat visitors (54%)
6,575	=	Total retail customers at F1

% OF TOTAL RETAIL CUSTOMERS	=	PEOPLE	×	PURCHASES	=	SALES	−	COGS (AVG = 52%)
80%		5,654		$0		$0		$0
9%		460		$25		11,500		5,980
4		197		$75		14,775		7,683
2		66		$175		11,550		6,006
3%		132		$325		42,900		22,308
2%		66		$400		26,400		13,728
				Total sales		$107,125		
						COGS		$55,705
						Total profit		$51,420

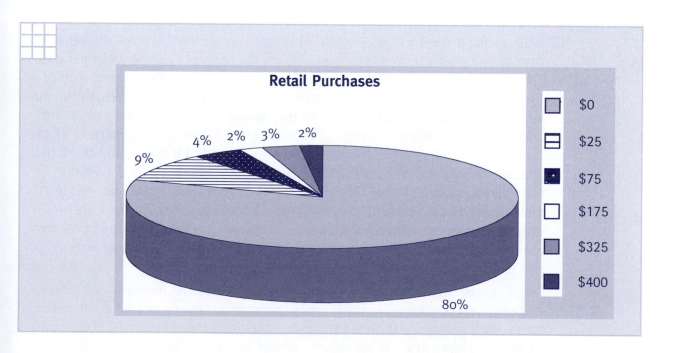

Retail Purchases

Legend: $0, $25, $75, $175, $325, $400

Youth Racing Camps

Youth racing camps will be implemented throughout the year as an additional source of revenue, as well as a way to increase the awareness of the sport and to promote The F1 Experience. This program will also be a way for The F1 Experience to increase the total market, as none of the competitors currently offer this format or are equipped to offer it. Of the people who were surveyed at Racers, 38 percent of the respondents had children. Later in the survey, 21 percent of these individuals with children responded that they would enroll them in a weekly junior karting school, and an additional 8 percent responded they slightly agreed with this statement.

Using these figures, Mr. Whisler projected that 525 visitors (excluding repeat customers) would enroll their children in a kart racing camp. He calculated this by using 100 percent of the individuals responding they agreed. If each of these individuals enrolled only one child in a five-week camp at $20 per week, the total possible revenues would be $52,469. This excludes families who would enroll multiple children, or children who would attend more than one camp. Mr. Whisler understands that it would not be possible for The F1 Experience to put 525 children through a five-week camp during the course of one year. With this in mind, he established that the center would offer five (5) five-week camps throughout the first year of operation, with 24 children enrolled in each camp. Each camper will pay a fee of $100, or $20 per week, to participate in the camp. This means that The F1 Experience will generate the following revenues from youth camps in the first year of operation.

5	Camps in Year 1
×5	Weeks per camp
×24	Children per camp
×$20	Price per child (per week)
$12,000	Total revenue in Year 1

Adult Racing Leagues

Adult racing leagues will also be offered throughout the year. Leagues will offer customers a chance to race with more time on the track at a cheaper price per visit. The F1 Experience will offer leagues arranged through the facility, leagues formed by customers, and will work with area businesses to form corporate leagues. Of the survey respondents, 35 percent agreed that they would enroll in a weekly kart racing league, and an additional 15 percent slightly agreed. These figures jumped to 47 percent agreeing and 13 percent slightly agreeing when asked if they would enroll in a league if sponsored by their employer. Of the businesses that were surveyed by Mr. Whisler, 6 percent stated they were very likely to sponsor a corporate team(s), and another 12 percent stated they were probable on the issue. Other responses showed that several companies are willing to sponsor multiple teams, and they are also willing to pay the current weekly fees per individual that The F1 Experience will be charging.

With these figures, Mr. Whisler projected that 2,301 visitors (based on numbers excluding repeat customers) would enroll in a kart racing league by taking 100 percent of the people responding they would enroll (not counting increase in interest if sponsored by their employer). If 2,301 individuals enrolled in one five-week kart racing league throughout the course of a year, at a fee of $40 per week, the total revenues that could be generated by The F1 Experience would be $92,040.

However, Mr. Whisler understands that it would not be feasible for the facility to run this many leagues throughout the course of the year, so he has established that in the first year of operation, The F1 Experience will host ten five-week leagues (two leagues will run in the same night, five times during the year) with 24 entrants per league, at a fee of $40 per week, per entrant. This results in the following revenues for Year 1.

10	Leagues in Year 1
×5	Weeks per league
×24	Entrants per league
×$40	Price per entrant (per week)
$48,000	**Total revenue in Year 1**

Pricing

The F1 Experience will utilize pricing that will be consistent with the other facilities in the local market. Each walk-in racing session will cost the consumer $20 for a 20-lap session. In addition to racing, they will receive the use of one head sock, driving suit, and helmet. They will also receive a computer-generated statistical read-out of their performance after each session. Additionally, each customer will receive a complimentary license upon their first visit, which will speed up their check-in time with each additional visit. Unlike other facilities, Mr. Whisler has chosen not to charge customers for these licenses, which will cost the center under $1 per each new visitor.

Corporate outings and special events will be priced on an individual basis, depending on the total package of services that the company or group is seeking. In general, events will cost $100 per person with catering of an informal meal included. If a company does not want catering for the outing, a general fee of $90 per person will be used. Smaller groups, of less than 20, requiring less time can be accommodated for prices as low as $50 per person.

Youth kart racing camps and adult kart racing leagues will be attractive to customers as they allow more time behind the wheel for a lower cost than arrive and drive racing. Youth camps will be priced at $20 per week for each five-week camp, and adult racing leagues will have entry fees of $40 per week for each five-week league.

Retail clothing merchandise will be priced at the manufacturer's suggested retail price, with an average profit margin of 48 percent, and snack foods and drinks will be priced slightly above these suggested prices with an average profit margin of 49 percent. Even at this higher mark-up, costs will be below that of other facilities. A good example of this is the pricing on drinks. Racers only offers drinks to their customers, and they charge $2 for every bottle. The F1 Experience will sell a majority of their bottled drinks for $1.25 and candy bars will carry a $0.75 price tag. This will allow them a candy bar and drink at an even $2 cost.

Competition

Direct Competition

Racers, Inc.

302 S. Meridian St.

Indianapolis, IN 46225

Racers at Union Station began operation in October of 2000 after struggling to get approval for operations. The conflict came with the current tenants of the facility opposed to the center opening because of a misunderstanding of what the indoor karting industry is really like. Racers is currently the largest facility in Indiana with total space of 45,730 square feet. The center features two tracks, and space to accommodate up to 500 individuals for events. The center has a 1,200 square foot meeting room, 1,000 square foot meeting room, and deck area of 5,000 square feet. The main track is roughly 900 feet in length and is set up in a road course layout. The secondary track is less than 600 feet in length, and is an oval. The strengths of Racers include a very friendly staff, size of facilities, appearance of equipment, and location.

Some of these strengths can also be viewed as weaknesses. Mr. John Combs, partner of Racers, told Mr. Whisler that their location can be a weakness due to the parking situation in downtown Indianapolis.[25] Parking is very limited around the city, and customers must pay for parking. Other weaknesses included a high investment to meet requirements of the city. Union Station is owned by the city of Indianapolis, and part of the agreement to allow Racers to open was that the facility maintain a strict appearance standard. To meet this, Racers had to make high investments in items like the track barrier. The barrier at Racers cost just over $250,000. This money could have been spent in racing décor or other items to enhance the facility. (Mr. Whisler will utilize a new barrier system that is widely used in the top centers in Europe. It has a very classy look, and is nowhere near the investment of Racers.) Mr. Whisler believes that they also invested too much money in karts that will not be used. In several visits to the facility, the secondary oval track has never been open. This results in almost 20 karts at a cost of nearly $10,000 each sitting idle. This secondary track also meant a major investment into a secondary timing system. Representatives of ROC Timing quoted Mr. Whisler a project cost of almost $200,000 at the Racers' facility.

The two-track setup is also a weakness because of the space requirements. To fit two tracks of any significant length into the available area, track width had to be compromised. This means in its widest points, the track can only fit two karts side by side. The result is racing conditions that are not as safe, and a lack of passing zones, leaving customers unsatisfied with the visit if they are stuck behind a lagging driver the entire race. Other weaknesses of Racers include no snack bar, as only one soft drinks vending machine is available. Also, the building is plain, with very little racing décor or theme-related items. There are no other attractions to participate in, other than racing, so patrons are forced to stand and wait their turn to race, and any accompanying children must be attended in the empty hallway in front of the main entrance of the center. This can become very tiring for parents when the facility is busy. Finally, the only clothing item that can be purchased is a hat with the Racers' logo.

Stefan Johansson

Karting Center

3649 Lafayette Rd.

Indianapolis, IN 46222

Stefan Johansson Karting Center is the oldest facility in Indiana, and the first indoor karting center opened in the United States. It was established in 1996, but Mr. Whisler is convinced that this facility will not provide overwhelming competition to The F1 Experience. The biggest strength of Stefan Johansson is the name. The 35,000 square foot facility is owned by former race car driver Stefan Johansson, which can be used as a selling point. However, there are many weaknesses to this facility. Their long standing in the community is also a strength, since word of mouth is the primary source of advertisement in the industry.

A primary weakness is that the center is located in a building that is beginning to show its age, and is located in a poor area of the community. The stores around the center are very run down, and the neighborhood is of poor quality. Stefan Johansson does offer corporate events and parties at their facility, but all functions are held in the lobby area, and the glass windows are covered with moveable curtains. The track is an unfinished, concrete floor, which makes for slick driving conditions, and an unsafe environment. Another weakness of the facility is the size. At 35,000 square feet, there is minimal room for their short 800-foot track, and lobby/meeting areas. In Mr. Whisler's experiences at the facility, the staff was not friendly, and again, there were limited attractions besides racing. They do offer one single video game in the corner of the lobby, and they also have a counter with soft drinks and a small selection of sandwiches. Finally, the only retail items that they sell have their Stefan Johansson logo embroidered on them.

FasTimes

Indoor Karting

3455 Harper Rd.

Indianapolis, IN 46240

The third facility, FasTimes, is unique, but not a significant threat to The F1 Experience. FasTimes pride themselves on being "the only multi-level, indoor karting facility in the Midwest." While this is a unique feature, it alone is not a strong enough selling point to keep customers coming back after they have experienced it. The biggest advantage of FasTimes is that they are a subsidy of the Royal Pins Leisure Centers, so they have financial backing other than the karting center, and a high traffic medium for advertisement.

Mr. Whisler views this facility as having the least amount of threat in competition, in spite of its proximity to The F1 Experience. The multi-level track is 900 feet in length, but the overall facility size is small, allowing groups of no more than 130 people to visit at a time. Also, due to the multi-level design, the floors to the lobby and conference areas vibrate heavily when the karts run on the track underneath. The facility only offers one four-seat racing simulator video game. They do offer beverages to customers and have the capability to provide in-house catering of pizza and soda available during rental of the facility.

FasTimes also sits in a poor location. The building is located just off of Interstate 465, but is not visible from the road. It can only be seen from the interstate during the winter months when leaves have fallen, but even then, you need to know where it sits in order to see it clearly. FasTimes' facility is also hard to find from the road that runs directly in front of it. There is no signage from the front road, and the small access road is hard to see. The building is surrounded by car dealerships on all sides, preventing a clear view of its location.

The most disappointing aspect of the facility is their customer service. Mr. Whisler has frequently visited the facility and the service is always the same. FasTimes primarily uses teenagers to run the front desk and lobby, and they are typically standing in a group talking as you walk in. Customers do not receive any acknowledgement that they are there, and the first time Mr. Whisler attended it took 18 minutes before he was even asked if he wanted to race or needed any help. Mr. Whisler has also witnessed three occasions in two visits where individuals were in asking about renting the facility. In each case the teens at the counter handed them the standard brochure and stated that they might want to call in if they had any questions. Mr. Whisler talked to one of these individuals who said they were planning on renting the facility for an outing, and the individual then stated they would now look elsewhere.

Indirect Competition

Mr. Whisler understands that there will be several competitors to The F1 Experience including more than the other centers in Indianapolis. Competition will come in the form of any other venue where potential customers can spend their entertainment dollar.

For walk-in customers, this would include things like video rental stores, bowling alleys, movie theaters, or even nice restaurants. Other competition might come from professional sporting events, or even high school sporting events during the school year, as parents want to watch their children participate in these activities. Mr. Whisler will strive to set The F1 Experience apart by making it an experience the whole family can enjoy in a safe, friendly environment.

Competition for the corporate outing and event market will come from other types of activities. This might include things like golfing, sporting events, or even nice banquet facilities. To combat this, The F1 Experience will be sold as an activity and center where all employees will be able to have a good time. With sporting outings like golf, everyone is not able to participate because of issues like equipment needs, interest, and skill or experience. With an indoor karting center, everyone is able to participate, the equipment is provided, and it does not require any skill for an enjoyable time. Understanding that not all people will find this type of activity attractive, other entertainment sources are available for people who do not want to drive the karts. On a golf course, there are no other activities available, whereas The F1 Experience will offer relaxing areas to sit and watch television while socializing with other employees.

The F1 Experience will also face indirect competition for its other forms of entertainment, including the retail shop, adult leagues, and youth camps. Adult racing leagues and youth camps face indirect competition from other leagues, sports activities, or other camps. The retail store will have competition from other stores carrying racing circuit apparel or any type of sportswear.

Advantages of The F1 Experience

The F1 Experience

Indoor Karting Center

8603 Allisonville Rd.

Indianapolis, IN 46350

The F1 Experience has been designed with several unique advantages and features to set itself apart from the competition. With a combination of these factors, the facility will establish itself as the premiere indoor karting center in Indiana.

One of the primary advantages of The F1 Experience is the **size of the facility.** Before the addition of the office space at the back of the facility, total square footage will be 49,800. This will make it the largest facility in Indiana. It will also feature the largest conference/multi-purpose room, which can be used in an open format at 3,940 square feet, or divided in the middle, offering two 1,970 square foot rooms.

Instead of using the size to create two mid-size tracks, Mr. Whisler has decided to develop a **single track** that will be **wider, allow for more customers at one time,** and be designed with the customers' enjoyment as the priority. The track width will allow for five karts of comfortable space racing side-by-side at its widest points, compared to competing facilities where it is very tight at a maximum of three karts wide. Also, the track barrier is flexible and moveable, so the track can be redesigned to add variety to the racing experience. Mr. Whisler has also developed the track with uniqueness in mind by using a tarmac surface, much like pavement, for better traction, a banked turn, and two sections of rolling hills. This will set the track apart from the competing center, and enhance the experience of true road course racing. The track has also been designed with speed in mind, allowing customers to achieve a top speed of 45 mph in the straights, compared to a top speed of 38 mph experienced at Racers. All of these features will be incorporated on what will be the **longest indoor karting track in the state** at over 1,000 feet.

Another advantage for The F1 Experience will be the **location.** Customers will have easy points of access from both Allisonville Road and 86th Street, and the center will be highly visible to over 66,000 vehicles traveling these roads each day. The center is also located directly behind the Castleton Mall, which is Indiana's largest mall, and home to over 11 million customers per year.[26] The F1 Experience's location is also directly in Marion County, Indiana's largest county, and just outside of Hamilton County, Indiana's fastest growing, most affluent county.

A variety of services and programs will also set the center apart from the competition. None of the competing indoor karting centers have as wide an offering of entertainment sources or unique programs. The racing themed décor will provide a special atmosphere, and customers will have a variety of activities to participate in if they do not want to race or if there is a long wait until, or between, their races. The F1 Experience will be the only center to offer a **full arcade, retail novelty shop,** and vast choice of **concession items.** Also, the unique kart that has been chosen for the facility will offer availability to a new market with children's camps. Each kart is equipped with a speed transponder and pedal extenders, so children can safely learn the proper techniques of racing and driving through the multiple youth camps offered throughout the year. Youth kart racing camps will be exclusive to The F1 Experience as none of the other centers offer, or are equipped to offer, this service.

Other advantages of the facility will be the investment made and overall cost of starting the operation. By designing the track with the format previously explained, Mr. Whisler will be able to reduce his overall investment in the number of karts to half of his largest competitor, Racers. Also, The F1 Experience will be using a new kart design by Bowman Karts that will offer distinct advantages. Unlike the karts at the competing facilities, which run on methanol racing fuel, these karts will run on propane. The average price per gallon of methanol is nearly twice that of propane, and it does not burn as cleanly. "Propane burns cleaner, is almost odorless, and is non-toxic. Methanol does not burn completely, has a very distinct odor, and is toxic."[27] Due to the fact that the propane burns cleaner, the large expense of added fans and ventilation in the track area will be greatly reduced. This new kart design will also allow The F1 Experience to reduce their maintenance costs. Unlike other karts where the engine is located directly to the right of the driver's seat, the Bowman Storm kart is equipped with an engine in the rear of the chassis. This means that there are fewer and smaller parts used to make the kart run. It also reduces the risk that a customer will touch a hot engine part.

This strong combination of unique products and services offered will assist the facility as it quickly propels itself to the top of the market. As customers use the facility, and share the memories of their experiences with family and friends, The F1 Experience will become known as the premiere site for indoor karting in Indiana.

Advertising and Promotion

Advertisement

Mr. Whisler will have to carefully develop an advertising campaign to promote The F1 Experience, as a majority of the customers are obtained through word-of-mouth. Through survey analysis, Mr. Whisler found the following statistics in regards to how customers had learned about the facility.

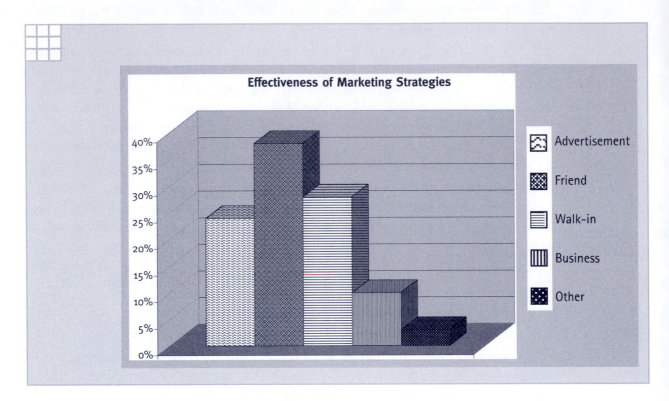

Only 23 percent of the customers had heard about the facility through advertisement mediums compared to 42 percent and 28 percent coming from a referral by friend or walk-in business, respectfully. Mr. Whisler will start advertising for The F1 Experience as construction gets under way, and will heavily promote the unique features of the facility. The following advertising methods will be the primary avenues used in spreading the word of the new facility and increasing the public's knowledge of this form of entertainment.

Phone Book   The first form of advertisement that The F1 Experience will use is the Ameritech Phone Book yellow pages for Indianapolis, Indiana. This will cost $144 per month for a 1″ listing with color in the phone book, and a full-page display on yellowpages.com. New phone books are published in October, so payments will start during the first month of operation.

Flyers   Flyers will be the primary source of advertisement for The F1 Experience. These will be passed out throughout the city on a regular basis, and will be heavily used on and before days when racing events are held in the area. Flyers will be distributed at the local hotels during these events, as well as near the racing venues themselves. The flyers will also be distributed through the local schools to promote upcoming youth camps at the facility. They will be printed and copied in one-quarter sections of standard-sized paper. Colored paper costs $3.99 per 500-sheet ream, so

2,000 flyers can be printed for this same price. Expense for flyers is included in the office supplies expense.

Newspaper   Mr. Whisler will occasionally run a $2'' \times 3''$ advertisement in The Indianapolis Star to increase public awareness of the facility. One $2'' \times 3''$ ad will cost $155 per week to run from Thursday to Saturday, and this same ad will cost $288 per week to run on a Sunday. The F1 Experience will run weekly Thursday through Sunday advertisements during the month prior to opening, and will run Thursday through Sunday advertisements two weeks of each month in which a major race is held (May, August, and September). Additionally, Mr. Whisler will run one $2'' \times 3''$ Thursday through Saturday ad, one time per month during all other months.

Radio   The F1 Experience will advertise on WFMS, 95.5 FM, one month prior to the grand opening of the center, and on a quarterly basis throughout the year. A representative of WFMS has developed a plan for The F1 Experience that will include four, 30-second commercials to run on Thursdays, Fridays, and Saturdays during the specified months for a cost of $6,000 per month.

Promotions

Mr. Whisler will use a variety of promotional avenues to gain more interest from the community and ensure that they will continue to use The F1 Experience for their indoor karting and racing apparel needs. Promotions to be used are as follows.

Free Tee Shirts   The F1 Experience will mail postcards offering one free tee shirt, with the purchase of one racing session at full price, to any individual presenting the postcard at their session purchase. The cards will be mailed two times per year, with 2,000 sent in each mailing in year one, 3,000 in year two, and 4,000 in year three. These tee shirts will feature a four-color design, including the center's name and location, to be designed later, and will cost The F1 Experience $2.99 apiece. In addition to the postcard mailings, Mr. Whisler will give free tee shirts to the first 500 customers. Price calculations are located in the Financial Segment.

Newsletter   A newsletter will be sent on a quarterly basis to frequent customers of the facility to inform them of happenings and upcoming events of the facility. The newsletter will also contain league results, upcoming league opportunities, youth camp information, and any other information that Mr. Whisler finds relevant. Newsletters will be sent to 2,000 of the previous customers on a quarterly basis. This will start after the first six months of operation. In year two of operations, 3,000 newsletters will be sent each quarter, and 4,000 in year three. Price calculations for the newsletter are located in the Financial Segment.

Press Releases   Mr. Whisler will frequently utilize press releases as a free method of promoting The F1 Experience. After the completion of each adult racing league or youth racing camp, Mr. Whisler will submit press releases with participants' names and standings. This will enhance the enjoyment of the customer's experience as well as promote the facility.

Awards   The F1 Experience will give awards after select races to further enhance the enjoyment of the experience. Small, engraved plaques will be placed on a specified wall within the facility, recognizing league winners and corporate guests. Each plaque will cost The F1 Experience $199. In addition to this recognition, the top three finishers at corporate outings/events, leagues, and youth camps will receive medals. These medals will cost The F1 Experience $3 apiece.

■ IV. Operations Segment

Location

The F1 Experience will operate on the northeast side of Indianapolis at the corner of Allisonville Road and 86th Street, in the Castle Creek Plaza. This location will enhance the likelihood of walk-in traffic, as it is highly visible to thousands of people each day. The average daily traffic count of Allisonville Road is 49,143 vehicles, and 86th Street has approximately 16,876 vehicles on a daily basis. The Castle Creek Plaza is located approximately $1/4$ mile north of Interstate 465 and $1\,1/2$ miles west of Interstate 69, and is within two miles of two malls and numerous restaurants. This location offers a population of 56,540 within three miles and 165,614 within five miles, while the average household income within these same radii is approximately $82,308 and $83,412, respectively. Other tenants of the Castle Creek Plaza include two restaurants (The Ale Emporium and The Melting Pot), Cookies by Design, Hollywood Video, Mail Boxes Etc., Tuchman Cleaners, and two small specialty shops. There are also approximately 35 hotels within a five-mile radius of this location.

Mr. Whisler will deal with Mr. Mark Perlstein, of The Linder Company, to finalize the lease on the building. The F1 Experience will lease two adjoining sections of the building with 49,800 accumulated square feet of space at a lease price of $9 per square foot, per year. Leasehold improvements will be designed and constructed through Indianapolis-based Entertainment Architecture, which has designed and constructed nearly 25 percent of the indoor karting centers existing in the United States today. Internal remodeling will include construction of the track; construction of walls to secure the track area; bathroom remodeling; and construction of the retail shop, conference room, and office areas. New carpeting and tile will be laid, and the walls will receive fresh coats of paint or wallpaper. Construction and improvements will be themed around making the facility look and feel like a racing venue, through the use of signage, pictures, banners, and construction materials. The total investment into leasehold improvements will be $735,932, as quoted by Mr. Robert McGuffey of Entertainment Architecture in Indianapolis, Indiana.

Zoning Regulations

Mr. Whisler will be leasing 49,800 square feet of the Castle Creek Plaza for the development of The F1 Experience. The building is currently zoned as C-4. Mr. Larry Williams of the Department of Metropolitan Development stated that a C-4 classification includes indoor recreational activities, so no zoning change would need to be made for an indoor karting facility.

Labor Supply

The F1 Experience will employ 15 part-time personnel as general staff members, with each working an average of 20 hours per week. These staff members will primarily consist of college students or young adults who are 18 years or older. In addition to the general staff members, The F1 Experience will employ two part-time mechanics, working an average of 14 hours per week. These individuals will be hired from a local technical college, and will be attracted with a strong hourly wage and short, morning-hour staffing. Mr. Whisler will also hire four race directors, with each working an average of 23 hours per week. These individuals will also be 18 years or older, and will initially be selected from the most qualified of the applicants. As the business continues in operation, general staff members will be promoted to race director as the opportunities arise. Ideally, staff members will have a strong passion for, and knowledge of, racing. This will make the job more interesting for them, and it will be more natural for them to assist the customers in enjoying the experience to the fullest.

In addition to the part-time personnel, The F1 Experience will also hire two assistant facilities directors and one events coordinator. More detailed descriptions of each position and the included work duties can be found in the Management Segment.

Business Operations

The F1 Experience indoor karting center will be open year-round, with the only closings being on Christmas Day and Thanksgiving. The normal business hours will be seven days a week, from 11 AM to 11 PM, with guaranteed walk-in karting on Fridays from 6 PM to 11 PM, Saturdays from 2 PM to 11 PM, and Sundays from 11 AM to 4 PM. This schedule can be adjusted to accommodate groups renting the facilities and special events like youth racing camps, which will be held on Saturday mornings throughout the year. The F1 Experience will see the most walk-in and facility rental traffic from Labor Day to Memorial Day.[28] Therefore, the following personnel schedules show a typical work week's scheduling, but hours and staffing numbers can be adjusted appropriately with the traffic flow throughout the year.

SALARY PERSONNEL

	MONDAY	TUESDAY	WEDNESDAY	THURSDAY	FRIDAY	SATURDAY	SUNDAY
Facilities director	4 pm–12 am	4 pm–12 am	8 am–5 pm	8 am–1 pm	4 pm–12 am	8 am–5 pm	OFF
Assistant facilities director	8 am–5 pm	8 am–5 pm	OFF	4 pm–12 am	8 am–5 pm	OFF	4 pm–12 am
Assistant facilities director	4 pm–12 am	OFF	4 pm–12 am	8 am–5 pm	OFF	4 pm–12 am	8 am–5 pm
Events coordinator	8 am–5 pm	8 am–5 pm	8 am–5 pm	8 am–5 pm	8 am–5 pm	OFF	OFF

PART-TIME PERSONNEL

	MONDAY	TUESDAY	WEDNESDAY	THURSDAY	FRIDAY	SATURDAY	SUNDAY	TOTAL HOURS
8 am–12 pm	1 GS 1 ME	1 ME	1 GS 1 ME	1 ME	1 GS 1 ME	2 GS 1 ME	1 ME	20 GS 28 ME
11 am–6 pm	3 GS 1 RD	3 GS 1 RD	3 GS 1 RD	3 GS 1 RD	3 GS 1 RD	3 GS 1 RD	3 GS 1 RD	147 GS 49 RD
6 pm–12 am	3 GS 1 RD	3 GS 1 RD	3 GS 1 RD	3 GS 1 RD	3 GS 1 RD	3 GS 1 RD	3 GS 1 RD	126 GS 42 RD

GS = General staff   293 total work hours per week
ME = Mechanic   28 total work hours per week
RD = Race director   91 total work hours per week

The following lists are the standard procedures for opening and closing The F1 Experience for each day's operations. The duties will be divided among all of the staff members working the current shift, with exception to the mechanics and events coordinator.

Opening

1. Unlock doors
2. Turn off alarm system
3. Adjust the building temperature controls
4. Check the parking lot for litter
5. Check track and adjust barrier
6. Clean windows, restrooms, conference rooms
7. Straighten and re-organize the retail shop and snack bar
8. Get cash drawers from safe and verify the money count
9. Put "Open Racing" sign by the road (if an open racing day)
10. Distribute flyers in the community
11. Final visual check that everything is in place for opening

Closing

1. Remove cash drawers from registers and verify money to sales receipts
2. Move karts to storage area for refueling and maintenance check
3. Empty all trash cans
4. Bring sign in from the road
5. Mop all tiled surfaces and sweep all carpeted areas
6. Shut down all computers and turn on voice mail
7. Turn down building temperature controls
8. Turn off all lights
9. Set the alarm
10. Lock all doors

Suppliers

Suppliers for The F1 Experience will include the following:

- **Cornerstone Propane** (Indianapolis, Indiana): will provide and fill mass propane storage as needed.

- **Buyers Wholesale Distributor** (Indianapolis, Indiana): will provide all snack bar items including candies, chips, and beverages.

- **Action Performance–Charlotte** (Charlotte, North Carolina): will provide all items for retail shop. This includes jackets, shirts, hats, flags, and other collectibles. Featured items will be from the top drivers of the NASCAR, Formula One, and Indy Racing League racing circuits.

- **Bowman Karts** (Braintree, Maine): will provide supplies for kart maintenance. If shipping or parts costs can be found at a better price locally, service will be switched.

- **Keysan** (Greensburg, Pennsylvania): supplier for janitorial supplies. If better costs can be found with a local janitorial supply company, service will be switched.

- **Shaffer Distributing Company** (Indianapolis, Indiana): will provide and service video games, simulators, and pinball machines for the arcade in return for 50 percent of revenues generated by these devices.

Further details of costs and profit margins for supplies and inventories can be found in the Marketing and Financial Segments.

V. Management Segment

Legal Structure

The F1 Experience indoor karting center will be developed as an S Corporation. This structure will be used so Mr. Whisler can use investors to raise the necessary start-up capital, still maintain a limited liability status, and have income taxed through personal income.

Management/Personnel

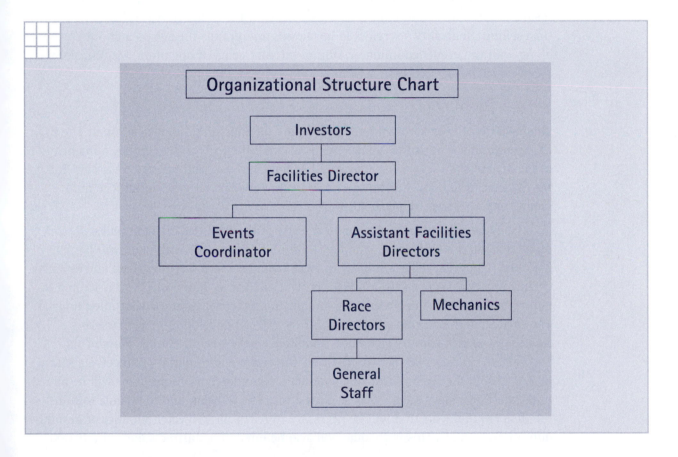

One of the biggest factors to the success of any business is the staff that is employed. A great facility may attract numbers of visitors initially, but if they have a bad experience they will neither return with more business nor favorably promote the experience to friends and acquaintances. With this in mind, Mr. Whisler will carefully select the most qualified applicants in any hiring period. The F1 Experience will employ a total of 25 personnel, including Mr. Whisler. The following job descriptions cover all positions that will be hired at The F1 Experience.

Facilities Director

As the majority owner of the business, Mr. Whisler will assume the position and responsibilities of facilities director. With his experience in sales and educational background, Mr. Whisler, along with the support of his staff, will have a strong foundation on which to run the business. Mr. Whisler has received a degree in Entrepreneurship and Small Business Management from Ball State University, and has over three years of successful sales and managerial experience. He was also certified in Track and Club Operations at the Track and Club Workshop during the International Karting Expo in St. Charles, Illinois, in February 2002.

Mr. Whisler will be in charge of ordering inventory, marketing efforts, and all administrative functions of the business. He will look for support in some of these areas from other staff members, and will delegate duties to the appropriate individuals. More importantly, Mr. Whisler will spend a majority of his time further enhancing his knowledge of the industry and assisting customers in having the most enjoyable experience possible. He will also take an active role in trying to establish an association for indoor kart track operators, which could lead to government relations, bulk insurance discounts, and other support services for the industry. Mr. Whisler will spend time selling the facility's services to businesses and groups for events and outings, along with the events coordinator. During the first years of operation, Mr. Whisler will receive a salary of $30,000.

Events Coordinator

The position of events coordinator is arguably the most important position at The F1 Experience. If the business follows trends of other indoor karting centers, a majority of the business will come through rental of the facility. It will be very important for Mr. Whisler to find an individual who has experience in sales, an interest in auto racing, and an outgoing personality.

The events coordinator will report directly to the facilities director, and will work on an 8 AM to 5 PM schedule, Mondays through Fridays. This individual will be expected to develop relationships with local businesses and organizations, and establish events on a consistent basis. Mr. Whisler will look for an individual who is willing to put in the extra effort to make sales, and not simply come in at the scheduled hours. The events coordinator will also assist Mr. Whisler in developing new marketing techniques to attract more customers and increase the overall market share of the business. In return of his/her work efforts, the events coordinator will receive a salary of $38,000. In the second year of operation, a second events coordinator will be added to the staff, to relieve some of these duties from Mr. Whisler, and to be able to fulfill the time requirements that will be necessary to reach the projected number of monthly outings and events. This individual will also be hired at a starting salary of $38,000.

Assistant Facilities Director

Two assistant facilities directors will be hired to assist Mr. Whisler in the daily operation of the track. Mr. Whisler will count on these individuals for assistance in all aspects of operation, so each will need to have a strong work ethic, an interest in motor sports, and a desire to succeed.

Assistant facilities directors will perform the administrative duties of the business while Mr. Whisler is not present, or if he is in need of assistance. They will be in charge of standard procedures for opening and closing the facility each day, as well as arranging schedules and making sure employees are at the right places at the right times. Mr. Whisler will seek out local community members with past managerial experience to fill these positions. These individuals will work an average of 42 hours per week, and will receive monetary compensation in the amount of $32,000. The assistant facilities directors will report directly to Mr. Whisler.

Mechanic

The F1 Experience will employ two part-time mechanics for the maintenance of the 15-kart fleet. Mr. Whisler will look to hire these individuals as students of the local technical school, and they will each work an average of 14 hours per week in daily shifts from 8 AM to 12 PM. During this time, the mechanic will perform safety checks of each kart on a daily basis, and do repair and maintenance work as needed. The F1 Experience will carry three extra karts, which will not be used on a regular basis, unless a kart needs to be kept down for an extended period of time for repairs. For their time and efforts, the mechanics will be paid an hourly rate of $10. They will also be allowed one free session per day on a noncumulative basis. The mechanics will report to the facilities director and assistant facilities directors.

Race Director

Mr. Whisler will hire four individuals for the position of race director. These individuals will work an average of 23 hours per week for an hourly rate of $10. They will also receive one free session per workday on a noncumulative basis. The race director will be in charge of briefing customers on the rules and regulations of the track, as well as getting the races started on time. They will also direct the safe operation of the track, and will be in constant radio communication with other personnel working the track area, to accurately assess and enforce penalties. These individuals will work at the computer timing system terminal during the race, and will be available to answer any questions customers may have. The race director will report to the facilities director and assistant facilities directors. Mr. Whisler will selectively choose the individuals hired to these positions from the most qualified applicants in the initial hiring period. As the business continues in operation, these positions will be filled by general staff members as the opportunities arise.

General Staff

The F1 Experience will also employ 15 individuals to work as general staff members. General staff members will be looked to for help in assisting with track operation, check-in assistance, retail shop and food stand operation, facilities cleaning and maintenance, flyer distribution, and other duties as they arise. Each individual will average 20 hours of work per week at an hourly rate of $8, and will receive one free race session per workday on a noncumulative basis. In addition to their assigned tasks, general staff members will assist customers in having an entertaining and exciting experience. Mr. Whisler will hire these individuals as members of the local community who are 18 years of age and older. He will primarily focus on hiring individuals who are enrolled in the local colleges. General staff members will report to race directors when they are working the track area, and will report to the assistant facilities directors on all other occasions.

Professional Support

The following individuals will provide professional assistance to The F1 Experience:

- ☐ **Accountant:** Michael Whisler, Summers, Carroll, Whisler, LLC, Muncie, Indiana
- ☐ **Attorney:** David Karnes, Dennis, Wenger & Abrell, P.C., Muncie, Indiana
- ☐ **Insurance Agent:** Toni Freemento, Allied Specialty Insurance, Treasure Island, Florida
- ☐ **Consultant:** Davey Jones, Davey Jones KartZone, Houston, Texas

Mr. Jones is the owner of Davy Jones KartZone in Houston, Texas. He comes from a successful racing background, finishing second in the second closest finish at the

Indianapolis 500, and was part of the winning team of the 24 Hours of Le Mans, both in 1996. In 2000, Mr. Jones opened the first and only indoor karting center in Houston, Texas. Mr. Whisler met Mr. Jones at the 2002 International Karting Expo in February, and the two discussed the need for support from other facilities in order for this new sport to reach its potential. Mr. Whisler and Mr. Jones will use each others' support and ideas to improve their position in their respective markets.

Regulations

Due to the nature of the sport, federal regulations have been put in place that could affect the business. Currently, concession go-kart track operators must adhere to the rules of the American Society of Testing and Materials (ASTM). However, indoor kart racing does not fall under this category, and rules are determined on a state-by-state basis. Indiana is one of the most lenient states in this regard, and tracks are not required to operate under ASTM standards. Regulations could play a role in the future of the business, though, unless an organization can be formed to enhance legislative knowledge of the sport and how safe it really is. If current ASTM standards for recreational go-karting were to be placed on indoor kart racing tracks in Indiana, changes would need to be made to the karts. This would include a roll bar, seat belts, head restraint, steering wheel pad, and colored pedals. This upgrade package would be purchased through the kart manufacturer, Bowman Karts. The costs of this upgrade would run The F1 Experience $360 per kart, for a total of $5,400 for the 15-kart fleet.

With the current push by operators to form a new classification, called concession racing, there have been proposed standards that would be recommended to the ASTM for the industry. These proposed standards would include the required use of helmets, neck brace, suit, gloves, and signed waiver for all patrons. The F1 Experience will already be using helmets, suits, and waivers, so upgrade costs would be minimal. Equipping the facility with gloves and neck braces would cost $2,816. One might have concern over the lack of seat belts and roll bars as required or proposed equipment for the karts, but current track operators and individuals with years of experience in the field hold a strong stance that this would be more dangerous than the current setup. The ASTM has established a goal of having rules and regulations in place by 2007.

Mr. Whisler understands that with high-speed sports comes a danger factor, and unfortunately the degree of this danger factor is in the control of the customer behind the wheel. With this in mind, strict rules will be in place and strictly enforced without question. The first rule in place will be that all individuals, from employees to visitors, will be required to sign liability waivers before entering the facility. Patrons not wishing to participate in races will sign a spectator waiver, and everyone else will sign a participant's waiver. After the individual has signed a waiver, he or she will only be required to sign a separate sign-in waiver upon every following visit. This measure will be in place so customers cannot say they did not read the waiver when they first visited the facility. If an accident were to occur, several signed waivers will help The F1 Experience maintain their innocence. These documents will relieve the liability of The F1 Experience for any injury or accidents incurred. In addition to waivers, The F1 Experience also will carry insurance to cover any costs if liability is assigned to the center.

Secondly, individuals under the age of 18 will not be allowed to enter the race area for any reason, with exception of youth driving camps and youth racing. Under these two conditions, they will be allowed to enter the area only with a waiver signed by both parents, and with one of the parents present. The parent who is present will be required to sign a liability waiver for the child with each visit. The only way a child will be able to participate is with a signature from both parents and one parent present at all times. The attorney for The F1 Experience will draw up final copies of all waivers.

Track rules and regulations will also be in place, and patrons will be verbally reminded of these rules before each session, as well as with various signs hung in the racing area. The first rule is that The F1 Experience will run under no contact with no exceptions, strictly enforced. This includes contact with other karts and contact with the walls. The track will run on a three-strike policy. Staff members placed strategically around the track will watch for contact, and if any is seen, it will be radioed to the race director. After they have confirmed there was contact, the driver will be assessed a black-flag and sent to the course penalty box. On the first infraction, a timing clock will count down a 10-second penalty before they can return to the racing area. Upon the second infraction will come a 20-second penalty, and a third infraction will result in removal from the track, and no more sessions that day. The customer will not receive a refund in this situation.

A final regulation in place will be a break-it, buy-it policy for track barriers. All customers will be informed of this before the race, and The F1 Experience will charge $100 per section that is broken. This is not too harsh of a penalty, as it would take an extreme hit and recklessness to break one of the three-foot sections.

VI. Critical Risks Segment

Inaccurate Sales Projections

Mr. Whisler is confident that the sales projections and market share are accurate portrayals of the business The F1 Experience will do in the first years of operation. His confidence is based on his research of the industry and experiences at the competing businesses. As the sport continues to grow and become more widely known, the market will continue to increase at a steady pace. Also, if an association of indoor kart track operators comes into existence, it will assist in cost reductions with things like reduced insurance costs through bulk purchasing.

If sales projections do not meet expectations, several steps can be taken to avoid or reduce potentially devastating problems. An initial step to increase cash flow would be to sell inventory at reduced prices. The advertising budget can also be cut back to help ease expenses, and creative, low-cost advertising techniques can be used. The most effective method of advertisement will be word of mouth, so Mr. Whisler will need to find creative ways to get new customers into the facility, so they will in turn tell their friends and family. An open line of credit has also been established with Key Bank so additional funds will be available when necessary.

Failure to reach the projected revenues could also be offset by aggressively pursuing the youth market, with more camps in the yearly schedule, and more times devoted to youth racing. As parents watch their youth get involved in the sport, their interest might grow, and it could develop into an activity the whole family could enjoy.

Weak Economy

With the nature of the business revolving highly around corporate entertainment and special events, a weak economy could pose a risk to the success of the venture. During downturns in the economy, businesses will be more likely to make cuts in the entertainment aspects of their budgets than in any other area. Mr. Whisler strongly believes that an aggressive sales approach from the events coordinator(s) and himself will be able to generate the number of event/outing bookings per year that will be needed to succeed, but additional time and effort will need to be spent selling these functions in times of weak economic conditions. A stronger effort will be needed to pursue more companies in order to meet the sales goals.

If businesses are not willing to spend the money for company-wide events during these periods, more focus can be put on selling gift certificates for companies to give out as rewards or incentives, or selling smaller group outings for the businesses to utilize as reward programs for their employees.

A more focused approach to walk-in sales, leagues, and youth programs can also be used to offset inadequate corporate sales. This will require more time devoted to these areas by the events coordinator instead of through general advertising to the walk-in customers and flyer handouts from the other staff members.

Construction Delays

With the size of the initial investment being made into The F1 Experience, and the monthly costs involved with running the business, construction delays could potentially pose a big risk. The architect and construction supervisor, Mr. Robert McGuffey of Entertainment Architecture, has assured Mr. Whisler that all construction will be completed within the four-month time projection that was quoted. However, any significant delay will cost tens of thousands of dollars in lost revenues and expenses.

Steps can be taken to minimize the loss if a construction delay were to occur. By constructing the track and ordering the barriers, karts, and equipment in the early stages of development, events can be held and walk-in traffic can be accepted even if construction is not completed. Mr. Whisler can advertise around this "problem" as a promotional tool. Discounted rates can be given to attract customers and they can check out the facility in production. Mr. Whisler will use the same approach that competitor Racers used as they finished the remodeling of their facilities at Union Station. They held three large events of 300 or more individuals, generating a large amount of revenue to offset the expenses still being incurred during construction.

Additionally, Mr. Whisler will hold enough cash to cover three months worth of expenses for the facility. This capital will be raised as part of the initial start-up capital for the venture.

Injury to Visitors

With the high-speed nature of the sport, and the control of safety in the hands of the driver, injury to visitors could affect the operation of The F1 Experience. A significant injury to any patron or staff member may cause a decrease in attendance due to fears of safety issues. This might also bring about lawsuits from the injured party.

Mr. Whisler will implement several procedural standards and guidelines to keep the facility as safe an environment as possible. A series of waivers, as well as verbal instruction will be utilized to keep all patrons informed of the risks. Several safety measures will be taken in the choice of equipment and track construction as well. Each member of the staff will be thoroughly trained in the actions to be taken in case of an accident. Medical attention will be called immediately, and staff members will be instructed not to touch anyone or anything at the site. Mr. Whisler will personally follow up with anyone who may be injured without implying or admitting any guilt or responsibility.

An extra investment into the insurance expense will be used to ensure an appropriate amount of insurance coverage in the event that injuries were to occur. The staff of The F1 Experience will continually address all patrons with the need for safety, and will have full authority to remove anyone from the track who is viewed as a potential hazard to the safety of fellow customers.

VII. Milestone Schedule

2002

JANUARY
Establish conceptual ideas of Indoor Karting Center
Begin research of industry and trends
Initialize conversation with indoor karting centers

FEBRUARY
Find location
Conduct survey research at Racers
Design layout of facility
Attend International Karting Expo in St. Charles, Illinois
Complete and receive certification in Kart Track and Club Operations
Mail 250 surveys to area businesses and conduct phone interviews

MARCH
Analyze survey data
Start writing business plan
Establish costs and determine potential market
Complete rough drafts of plan segments

APRIL
Finalize costs and develop final copy of plan
Turn in finished plan
Present plan for The F1 Experience to investors

MAY
Receive bachelor's degree in Entrepreneurship and Small Business Management from Ball State University
Submit state ACDR applications
Obtain financing
Sign lease for building

JUNE
Begin construction of track and leasehold improvements

JULY
Order karts, barrier system, racing suits, helmets, and head socks

AUGUST
Hire events coordinator and assistant facilities directors
Begin scheduling outings and events

SEPTEMBER
Hire mechanics, race directors, and general staff members
Train employees on all aspects of the business

OCTOBER
October 1, 2002—Grand Opening
Begin first youth kart racing camp

NOVEMBER
Begin first series of adult kart racing leagues

2003–2004

YEARLY
August 2003—Hire second events planner
Continue with normal operations
Seek new marketing avenues
Establish relationships within the community

FUTURE

Develop community racing events
Implement extreme teen package
Hold fundraising events for local charities
Host seminars and luncheons with celebrities from the top racing circuits

■ VIII. Financial Segment

Proposal

Total start-up costs for The F1 Experience will be $1,500,000. This includes costs to purchase the necessary equipment and supplies, leasehold improvements, and beginning cash on hand. The start-up period for the venture will run from May 2002 to October 2002. Lease signing will be on May 31, and opening day for the facility will be October 1.

Financing Plan

The F1 Experience will require a total of $1,500,000 in start-up capital. The following chart will break down the start-up costs and sources of capital.

SOURCES	
AMOUNT	**SOURCE**
$1,000,000	Key Bank (7.5% for 20 years)
250,000	Midwest Entrepreneurial Education Center
200,000	Private investors
50,000	Contributed capital from relative
$1,500,000	Total start-up capital
USES	
$735,932	Leasehold improvements
257,902	Purchase of assets
251,905	Start-up operating expenses
7,292	Principle payments
$240,969	Beginning cash on hand

Financial Assumptions—Income Statement

Operating Revenue

Sales   All sales figures are projected as discussed in the Marketing Segment. Walk-in sales will be 11 percent of the total market in year one, 18 percent in year two, and 23 percent in year three. Corporate/event sales will account for 9 percent of the total market in year one, 14 percent in year two, and 18 percent in the third year of operation. League sales will remain constant from year one to year three, as the same number of leagues will be run in each year. Advertising packages will see growth in all three years. Mr. Whisler is projecting the sale of two packages in year one, four in year two, and seven in year three. Camp sales will also remain constant through the first three years of operation, as the same number of camps will be run in each year. Retail, concession, and arcade purchases are based on the number of patrons using the center each year and their spending patterns. All sales per month have been adjusted to reflect the monthly trends of the industry.

Cost of Goods Sold   Corporate/events costs are based on an average outing attendance and food price per individual. Food and drink costs were based on a rate of $10 per person. Mr. Whisler used primary research to project that 80 percent of visiting groups and companies would use catering services. Costs of goods sold for retail items are based on an average of 52 percent per item. Concessions costs average 51 percent of sales, and 50 percent of arcade sales will be given to the supplying company.

Gross Profit   This represents the total sales less the total costs of goods sold.

Operating Expenses

Yellow Pages   Mr. Whisler will purchase a 1″ advertising column in the Ameritech Indianapolis Yellow Pages for a monthly fee of $144.[29]

Radio   The F1 Experience will use radio advertisement one month prior to the opening of the business, and on a quarterly basis throughout the year. This will cost the center $6,000 per month.[30]

Newspaper   Newspaper advertising will alternate from month to month as discussed in the Marketing Segment. One, 2″ × 3″ advertisement will cost $155 to run on Thursday through Saturday, and $288 per week to run in the Sunday paper.[31]

Salary   This figure represents a cumulative total of all the salaries that will be paid on a monthly basis.

Facilities Director

Mr. Whisler will receive an annual salary of $30,000 through the first three years of operation.

Events Coordinator

The F1 Experience will employ one events coordinator in year one, at a salary of $38,000. A raise will be given to $40,000 after 12 months, $42,000 after 24 months, and $43,000 after 36 months. One year after the initial hiring of the events coordinator, a second events coordinator will be hired at a salary of $38,000 and will follow through the same raise system.

Assistant Facilities Directors

Two assistant facilities directors will be hired to assist Mr. Whisler with the daily operations. In year one, they will each receive a salary of $32,000, with an increase to $33,500 after 12 months of employment. Additional raises will be given at 24 and 36 months of employment, to $35,000 and $36,000, respectively.

Wages   This figure represents the cumulative total of monthly wages for the hourly employees of The F1 Experience. Mr. Whisler will employ two mechanics at $10 per hour, with average workweeks of 14 hours. Four race directors will be hired at $10 per hour, with average workweeks of 23 hours, and 15 general staff members will be employed for $8 per hour at an average of 20 hours per week.

Payroll Taxes   Payroll taxes are figured at 7.65 percent of the first $80,400 per employee for Social Security, 2.7 percent of the first $7,000 for State Unemployment, and 0.8 percent of the first $7,000 for Federal Unemployment. These calculations begin with the initial hiring of each staff member and start over at the beginning of each calendar year. Mr. Whisler has calculated these taxes on the cumulative wages for hourly employees.

Rent   Mr. Whisler will be leasing a total of 49,800 square feet of the Castle Creek Plaza, which is currently zoned C-4. Mr. Mark Perlstein, of The Linder Company, has quoted Mr. Whisler a yearly lease rate of $9 per square foot, which will only include general area maintenance. Mr. Whisler will sign a 10-year lease for the building.

Insurance   Insurance for The F1 Experience has been quoted at $48,000 for the first year of operation by Allied Specialty Insurance. Mrs. Toni Freemento told Mr. Whisler to base the following years' expenses on 4 percent of total sales. She also stated that this would be in line with packages that have been developed for other indoor karting centers.

Utilities   The utilities for the building were based upon past billings to the site, and an expert witness. A representative of Indianapolis Power and Light Company quoted an average billing of $1,300 for this site's electric expense, and Mr. Robert McGuffey, of Entertainment Architecture, quoted an average gas bill of $2,500. The monthly calculations have been adjusted to show seasonality trends.

Telephone   Telephone service will incur a cost of $79 for hookup and $66 for monthly service. This will include two lines and a toll-free number.[32]

Legal/Accounting Fees   Mr. Whisler quoted accounting at $450 per month for book-keeping and payroll, and a yearly fee of $350 for tax preparation. Mr. David Karnes, of Dennis, Wenger & Abrell, P.C., will file the appropriate forms for becoming an S Corporation and prepare all liability waivers for a fee of $850.

Copier Rental   The F1 Experience will lease a copier from Integrated Business Systems for a fee of $60 per month. Mr. Phil Hagen quoted Mr. Whisler an additional charge of $295 per year for service and supplies (toner) for the unit.

Office Supplies   Mr. Whisler will be purchasing office supplies from Staples. These initial supplies will cost $1,347, and a monthly fee of $50 has been allocated for additional office supply purchases.

Trash Removal   The F1 Experience will use Republic Trash Services for trash pick-up on a bi-weekly basis. This will cost $29 per month.[33]

Association Dues   Mr. Whisler will purchase a gold membership to the Indianapolis Chamber of Commerce on a yearly basis. This will run the company $940 per year.[34]

Satellite Dish   The F1 Experience will feature satellite service on multiple televisions throughout the facility. Four receivers will be purchased at a cost of $50 each, and monthly service will cost $42 ($22 for Total Choice Package + $5 per receiver).[35]

Fire Extinguisher Service   Mr. Whisler will purchase 12 fire extinguishers from Koorsen Protective Services, during the initial start-up phase, for $561. Additionally, there will be a yearly service-check fee of $155.[36]

Propane   Mr. Whisler has derived fuel consumption at 0.165 gallons per session, based on statistical information provided by Bowman Karts. Cornerstone Propane will provide a 1,000-gallon tank with pumping station, and will charge Mr. Whisler the current cost of propane plus an additional $0.30 per gallon for use of the tank and pumps. Mr. Pete Noreika has quoted Mr. Whisler an average annual price of $1.00 per gallon for propane.

Janitorial Supplies   The initial janitorial supplies will be purchased during the start-up period at a cost of $907. Additionally, a monthly fee of $60 has been set aside to replenish these supplies.

Kart Maintenance   Mr. Vic Hollman, of Bowman Karts, told Mr. Whisler to allocate $75 per month, per kart for maintenance. This includes oil changes every 100 hours, and body, chassis, and engine work. Mr. Whisler will also need to replace the engines of all karts at the beginning of year three. Engines will cost $615 apiece for a total cost of $9,225.

ADT Security Monitoring   Mr. Whisler will use the security system currently installed in the building for monthly monitoring. ADT will provide monthly services of intrusion detection and control, asset protection, access management, video surveillance, and fire and life safety. Mr. Alan Kirchain has quoted a monthly price of $30 for these services.

Promotion Materials   The F1 Experience will use promotional materials as explained in the Marketing Segment. Costs of paper for flyers are included in the office supplies expense. Four-color tee shirts will be printed by Dark Star at a cost of $2.99 each. Mainwaring Group Advertising will print postcards at $300 per 2,000 and postage is figured at a rate of $0.21 per card. Mr. Whisler will have enough shirts printed to cover 80 percent of the postcards shipped. Medals for race winners will be purchased through Advantage Promotions. These will cost The F1 Experience $3 each. Additionally, Mr. Whisler will purchase plaques through Advantage Promotions at a price of $199 each.

Web Page Design/Maintenance   A website will be designed and maintained by Mr. Bonnier Moulton of 307 Webworks. Initial design fees for the ten-page site will be $750, and Mr. Whisler will update the site once a month with information like league standings and camp participants. Updates to the site will cost The F1 Experience $35 per month.

Web Page Hosting   Web page hosting will be provided by Half-Price-Hosting at a cost of $17 per month.

Licenses   The F1 Experience will provide all first-time patrons to the facility with a free license. This will allow for easier check-in with repeat visits. Licenses will cost The F1 Experience $0.91 per person, and supplies will be purchased through ROC Timing.[37]

Credit Card Service Charge   Mr. Jamie Moss, of Key Bank, quoted a monthly fee of $14 for a credit card terminal and printer. An additional fee of 1.99 percent of credit card sales will be paid to Key Bank on a monthly basis.

Maintenance   Mr. Whisler has set aside $500 per month for general maintenance of the facility.

Discount   A discount expense of 1 percent of sales was used to cover retail discounts, coupons, and free or discounted sessions throughout the course of each month.

Charitable Contributions   Mr. Whisler has set aside a quarterly expense for charitable contributions to community organizations, fund-raisers, and other groups. This expense will be shown in the months of March, June, September, and December. In the first year of operation, The F1 Experience will have a charitable contribution expense of $2,000. In the second year of operation, $5,000 will be paid out, and in year three, the expense will be $10,000.

Interest Expense   Interest expense is the amount of each month's loan payment that goes toward the interest of the loan.

Property Tax   The current property tax rate for Washington Township is 0.041682. Property taxes are not included in the terms of the lease, so The F1 Experience will pay taxes on a $869,200 value for the land, and $2,522,400 value for the building.[38] Additionally, property taxes will be paid on the depreciated value of leasehold improvements to the building, machinery and equipment, and full value of inventory.

Total Cash Expense   This represents the total of all cash expenses for the month or the year.

Depreciation   The F1 Experience will depreciate assets using a straight-line method. Depreciation will be figured by taking the initial value and dividing by the expected life in months.

Total Operating Expenses   This represents the total amount of both cash and non-cash expenses.

Income (Loss) from Operations   This represents the amount of money made or lost after subtracting the total operating expenses from the monthly or yearly gross profits.

Tax Distribution to Shareholders   The tax distribution to shareholders represents the total amount of state and federal taxes paid on the monthly income from operations. State tax rates are figured at 5 percent and federal rates are figured at 20 percent.

Net Income (Loss) This represents the total gain of dollars or loss of dollars after taxes have been subtracted.

Financial Assumptions—Statement of Cash Flows

Beginning Cash Balance The beginning cash balance represents the amount of cash on hand at the beginning of each month. The initial cash flow for The F1 Experience is the remainder of the start-up capital less the cost of the leasehold improvements, pre-opening expenses, and purchase of assets.

Operating Activities

Cash Receipts from Operations This represents the total of all cash inflows for each month.

Total Cash Available Total cash available is the total of each month's beginning cash balance, plus the cash receipts from operations for the same month.

Total Operating Disbursements This represents the total monthly or yearly outflow of cash for operating expenses, costs of goods sold, tax distribution, and dividends paid. The calculations for all figures (with exception to dividends paid) are the same as discussed in the Financial Assumptions for the Income Statement. Mr. Whisler will pay dividends to investors in the final month of the fiscal year of the business, starting in year two. In year two, Mr. Whisler will pay dividends of 10 percent of investment to investors, and 15 percent in year three.

Financing Activities

Bank Loan A loan in the amount of $1,000,000 will be acquired from Key Bank in Indianapolis. Mr. Bill Stamper quoted an interest rate of 7.5 percent for the loan to be amortized over a 20-year period. This rate will be fixed for the first five years of operation, and is then subject to change.

Line of Credit Mr. Whisler will also have an open line of credit established with Key Bank. Mr. Stamper quoted an interest rate of 4.24 percent for the first three months, and then the rate will adjust to the current prime rate.

Sale of Common Stock This represents the gains from the sale of stock. The F1 Experience will issue 2,000 shares of stock to four private investors. Each investor will acquire 500 shares at a cost of $100 per share. This will raise a total of $200,000 in capital for The F1 Experience, and these individuals will hold a cumulative total of 40 percent ownership of the company. A total of 5,000 shares will be issued, and Mr. Whisler will retain the remaining 3,000 shares through his investment of the Midwest Entrepreneurial Education Center grant and contributed capital.

Midwest Entrepreneurial Education Center The Midwest Entrepreneurial Education Center will provide The F1 Experience with $250,000 in capital. This represents approximately 17 percent of the total start-up capital required.

Contributed Capital: This represents the $50,000 that Mr. Whisler will be receiving from a relative.

Investment Activities

Cash Disbursements from Investments This represents the total amount of cash disbursed for the purchase of assets in the start-up period of the venture. Leasehold improvements will be designed and constructed through Entertainment Architecture, the timing system will be purchased and installed through ROC Timing, and the karts and barrier system will be purchased through Bowman Karts. Additionally, the track will be constructed through Milestone Paving; the retail shop inventory through Action Performance; and suits, helmets, and head socks through RG Racewear. Other investments, including office furnishings, multimedia equipment, kart maintenance and storage equipment, snack bar inventory, phone system, signs, and fire extinguishers, will be purchased through miscellaneous suppliers.

Net Cash Flow   Represents the positive or negative cash flow for each month after subtracting total operating disbursements and cash disbursements from activities, and adding cash receipts from financing to the cash receipts from operation.

Ending Cash Balance   This represents the previous month's ending cash balance plus the net cash flow of the current month.

Financial Assumptions—Balance Sheet

Assets

Cash   Current cash available to The F1 Experience.

Retail Shop Inventory   Inventory will feature an array of team/driver jackets, shirts, hats, and more, in a variety of adult and youth sizes. Inventory will be maintained at a level valued at $30,723.[39]

Snack Bar Inventory   Mr. Whisler will offer a wide array of candy and snack type items through the snack bar. Total value will be $2,134.[40]

Leasehold Improvements   Leasehold improvements will encompass renovations to the current facility. Improvements are valued at $735, 932.[41]

ROC Timing System   Includes timing system, cash drawer and check-in system, and licensing system. The total ROC package is valued at $65,679.[42]

Karts   Includes a 15-kart fleet of 9.5 horsepower, propane fueled, European-style go-karts. Total value of the karts is $61,695.[43]

Track   The F1 Experience will feature a paved, tarmac racing surface, valued at $40,665.[44]

Barrier   A flexible, moveable barrier system will be purchased with a value of $16,150.[45]

Suits, Helmets, Head Socks   The F1 Experience will purchase a supply of suits, helmets, and head socks to be used by all drivers. Youth sizes will also be purchased. Total value for these items is $11,759.[46]

Miscellaneous Needs   Miscellaneous needs include two bleacher systems, all computer terminals, washer and dryer, televisions, and track communication systems. The total value of these items is $11,248.

Office Furnishings   Office furnishings will be purchased for the office area. This includes all items from desks to time clock, and is valued at $3,978.

Multimedia Equipment   Multimedia equipment will be purchased for use in the conference room. This will include a digital video projector, retractable screen, and lectern. The value of these items is $2,887.

Kart Maintenance/Storage Equipment   The F1 Experience will fully equip a kart maintenance and storage area with tools, kart-lifts, cabinets, and shelves. The total value of these items is $2,293.

Phone System   A new phone system with eight-line capabilities will be installed at The F1 Experience. This system will consist of one base system, three corded handsets, and two cordless handsets. Total value for the system will be $1,090.

Signs   Mr. Whisler will purchase signs through Sign Craft, Inc., of Indianapolis. This will include two signs for the front of the building, new panels for the plaza pylon sign, and two road signs that can be stored in the facility at night. Total sign value will be $7,040.[47]

Fire Extinguishers   The F1 Experience will purchase 11 5-pound fire extinguishers and 1 20-pound fire extinguisher with signs. Total value for all 12 units will be $561.[48]

Total Assets   Total assets are determined by adding the current assets (cash) to the fixed assets, and subtracting the accumulated depreciation of the fixed assets.

Liability and Stockholders' Equity

Liabilities   This represents the amount of money owed on the bank loan and any money owed to the line of credit.

Retained Earnings   This is the accumulated total of net income or loss recorded in the income statement. This dollar figure continually accumulates throughout the life of the venture unless any amount of the earnings is expensed or paid out in dividends to investors.

Total Stockholders' Equity   This represents the total amount of common stock less the retained earnings of the business.

THE F1 EXPERIENCE
START-UP COSTS INCURRED
(MAY 2002–SEPTEMBER 2002)

ASSETS	COST	OPERATING EXPENSES	COST
Leasehold Improvements	$735,932	Rent	$149,400
ROC Timing System	65,679	Office Supplies	1,347
Karts	61,695	Janitorial Supplies	907
Track	40,665	Web Page Design	750
Retail Shop Inventory	30,723	Web Page Hosting	17
Barrier	16,150	Utilities	13,680
Suits, Helmets, Head Socks	11,759	Telephone	343
Miscellaneous—Other		Legal/Accounting Fees	1,300
Purchase Needs	11,248	Copier Rental	60
Office Furnishings	3,978	Copier Service Fee	295
Multimedia Equipment	2,887	Trash Removal	116
Kart Maintenance/Storage—		Association Dues	940
Supplies and Tools	2,293	ADT—Security Monitoring	120
Snack Bar Inventory	2,134	Newspaper Advertisement	1,772
Phone System	1,090	Radio Advertisement	6,000
Fire Extinguishers with Signs	561	Salary	27,464
Signs	7,040	Wages	7,200
Total	**$993,834**	Payroll Tax—Salary	2,964
		Payroll Tax—Wages	803
		Insurance	16,000
		Interest Expense	24,932
		Promotional Materials	1,495
		Total	**$257,905**

Total start-up costs	$1,251,739
Add: Principle payments	7,292
Add: Beginning cash on hand	240,969
Total Start-up Capital	**$1,500,000**

The F1 Experience
Income Statement
Fiscal Period Ending September 30, 2003

	Start-Up Period	October	November	December	January	February	March	April	May	June	July	August	September	TOTALS
Operating Revenue														
Walk-in	—	$30,880	$30,880	$51,460	$36,020	$61,760	$46,300	$36,020	$51,460	$30,880	$25,720	$61,760	$51,460	$514,600
Corporate/Event	—	28,525	42,865	74,055	49,870	40,565	29,355	36,960	64,430	28,810	15,725	38,080	58,830	508,070
Leagues	—	0	7,680	1,920	5,760	3,840	3,840	5,760	0	9,600	0	5,760	3,840	48,000
Advertising	—	2,400	2,400	2,400	2,400	2,400	2,400	2,400	2,400	2,400	2,400	2,400	2,400	28,800
Camps	—	480	1,920	0	1,920	480	1,440	960	480	1,920	0	1,920	480	12,000
Retail	—	6,500	6,500	10,825	7,475	12,575	9,725	7,475	10,825	6,500	5,325	12,575	10,825	107,125
Concessions	—	1,372	1,372	2,288	1,600	2,744	2,060	1,600	2,288	1,372	1,140	2,744	2,288	22,868
Arcade	—	1,037	1,037	1,729	1,210	2,074	1,556	1,210	1,729	1,037	864	2,074	1,729	17,286
Total Sales	—	71,194	94,654	144,677	106,255	126,438	96,676	92,385	133,612	82,519	51,174	127,313	131,852	1,258,749
COGS: Corporate/Event	—	2,850	4,100	5,900	4,350	3,900	2,550	3,500	4,750	2,250	1,350	3,400	4,150	43,050
Retail	—	3,380	3,380	5,629	3,887	6,539	5,057	3,887	5,629	3,380	2,769	6,539	5,629	55,705
Concessions	—	700	700	1,167	816	1,399	1,051	816	1,167	700	581	1,399	1,167	11,663
Arcade	—	518	518	865	605	1,037	778	605	865	518	432	1,037	865	8,643
Total COGS	—	7,448	8,698	13,561	9,658	12,875	9,436	8,808	12,411	6,848	5,132	12,375	11,811	119,061
Gross Profit	—	63,746	85,956	131,116	96,597	113,563	87,240	83,577	121,201	75,671	46,042	114,938	120,041	1,139,688

(continued)

	Start-Up Period	October	November	December	January	February	March	April	May	June	July	August	September	TOTALS
Operating Expenses														
Cash														
Advertising														
Yellow Pages	–	144	144	144	144	144	144	144	144	144	144	144	144	1,728
Radio	6,000	6,000	–	–	6,000	–	–	6,000	–	–	6,000	–	–	24,000
Newspaper	1,772	360	155	155	155	155	155	155	886	155	155	886	886	4,258
Personnel														
Salary	27,464	10,152	12,696	10,152	12,696	10,152	10,152	10,152	12,696	10,152	10,152	16,830	13,460	139,442
Wages	7,200	14,400	18,000	14,400	18,000	14,400	14,400	14,400	18,000	14,400	14,400	18,000	14,400	187,200
Payroll Tax–Salary	2,964	894	972	777	1,416	1,132	957	777	972	777	777	1,416	1,132	11,999
Payroll Tax–Wages	803	1,606	2,007	1,606	2,007	1,606	1,606	1,606	2,007	1,606	1,606	2,007	1,606	20,876
Operational														
Rent	149,400	37,350	37,350	37,350	37,350	37,350	37,350	37,350	37,350	37,350	37,350	37,350	37,350	448,200
Insurance	16,000	4,000	4,000	4,000	4,000	4,000	4,000	4,000	4,000	4,000	4,000	4,000	4,000	48,000
Utilities	13,680	2,280	3,990	5,130	5,130	3,990	2,280	2,280	2,280	3,990	5,130	5,130	3,990	45,600
Telephone	343	66	66	66	66	66	66	66	66	66	66	66	66	792
Legal/Accounting Fees	1,300	450	450	450	450	450	450	800	450	450	450	450	450	5,750
Copier Rental	60	60	60	60	60	60	60	60	60	60	60	60	60	720
Copier Service Fee	295	–	–	–	–	–	–	–	–	–	–	–	–	–
Office Supplies	1,347	50	50	50	50	50	50	50	50	50	50	50	50	600
Trash Removal	116	29	29	29	29	29	29	29	29	29	29	29	29	348
Association Dues	940	–	–	–	–	–	–	–	–	–	–	–	–	–
Satellite Dish	–	242	42	42	42	42	42	42	42	42	42	42	42	704
Fire Extinguisher Service	–	–	–	–	–	–	–	–	–	–	–	–	–	–
Propane	907	506	742	923	736	982	816	777	789	744	399	1,053	892	9,359
Janitorial Supplies	–	60	60	60	60	60	60	60	60	60	60	60	60	720
Kart Maintenance	–	900	900	900	900	900	900	900	900	900	900	900	900	10,800
ADT–Security Monitoring	120	30	30	30	30	30	30	30	30	30	30	30	30	360
Promotional Materials	1,495	72	352	316	5,648	506	135	1,213	72	560	6,229	117	479	15,699
Web Page Design/Maintenance	750	35	35	35	35	35	35	35	35	35	35	35	35	420
Web Page Hosting	17	17	17	17	17	17	17	17	17	17	17	17	17	204
Licenses–1st time customers	–	421	421	703	492	843	632	492	703	421	350	843	703	7,024
CC Service Charge	–	192	192	311	222	370	281	222	311	192	162	370	311	3,136
Maintenance	–	500	500	500	500	500	500	500	500	500	500	500	500	6,000
Discount	–	886	1,021	1,318	1,033	1,277	1,164	925	1,201	821	622	1,208	1,196	12,672
Charitable Contributions	–	–	–	500	–	–	500	–	–	500	–	–	500	2,000
Interest Expense	24,932	6,204	6,193	6,181	6,169	6,158	6,146	6,134	6,122	6,110	6,098	6,085	6,073	73,673
Property Tax	–	1,139	1,139	1,139	1,139	1,139	1,139	1,139	1,139	1,139	1,139	1,139	1,139	13,668
Total Cash Expenses	257,905	89,045	91,613	87,344	104,576	86,443	84,096	90,355	90,911	85,300	96,952	98,817	90,500	1,095,952
Non-Cash														
Depreciation	–	9,404	9,404	9,404	9,404	9,404	9,404	9,404	9,404	9,404	9,404	9,404	9,404	112,848
Total Operating Expenses	257,905	98,449	101,017	96,748	113,980	95,847	93,500	99,759	100,315	94,704	106,356	108,221	99,904	1,208,800
Income (Loss) from Operations	(257,905)	(34,703)	(15,061)	34,368	(17,383)	17,716	(6,260)	(16,182)	20,886	(19,033)	(60,314)	6,717	20,137	(69,112)
Tax Distribution to Shareholders	–	–	–	–	–	–	–	–	–	–	–	–	–	–
Net Income (Loss)	(257,905)	(34,703)	(15,061)	34,368	(17,383)	17,716	(6,260)	(16,182)	20,886	(19,033)	(60,314)	6,717	20,137	(69,112)

The F1 Experience
Statement of Cash Flows
Fiscal Period Ending September 30, 2003

	Start-Up Period	October	November	December	January	February	March	April	May	June	July	August	September	Year
Beginning Cash Balance	–	$240,969	$213,818	$206,298	$248,195	$238,329	$263,551	$264,785	$256,085	$284,441	$272,866	$219,998	$234,148	$240,969
Operating Activities														
Cash Received (Inflows)														
Walk-in	–	30,880	30,880	51,460	36,020	61,760	46,300	36,020	51,460	30,880	25,720	61,760	51,460	514,600
Corporate/Event	–	28,525	42,865	74,055	49,870	40,565	29,355	36,960	64,430	28,810	15,725	38,080	58,830	508,070
Leagues	–	–	7,680	1,920	5,760	3,840	3,840	5,760	–	9,600	–	5,760	3,840	48,000
Advertising	–	2,400	2,400	2,400	2,400	2,400	2,400	2,400	2,400	2,400	2,400	2,400	2,400	28,800
Camps	–	480	1,920	–	1,920	480	1,440	960	480	1,920	0	1,920	480	12,000
Retail	–	6,500	6,500	10,825	7,475	12,575	9,725	7,475	10,825	6,500	5,325	12,575	10,825	107,125
Concessions	–	1,372	1,372	2,288	1,600	2,744	2,060	1,600	2,288	1,372	1,140	2,744	2,288	22,868
Arcade	–	1,037	1,037	1,729	1,210	2,074	1,556	1,210	1,729	1,037	864	2,074	1,729	17,286
Cash Receipts from Operations	–	71,194	94,654	144,677	106,255	126,438	96,676	92,385	133,612	82,519	51,174	127,313	131,852	1,258,749
Total Cash Available	–	312,163	308,472	350,975	354,450	364,767	360,227	357,170	389,697	366,960	324,040	347,311	366,000	1,499,718
Cash Disbursements (Outflows)														
Operating Expenses	$257,905	$89,045	$91,613	$87,344	$104,576	$86,443	$84,096	$90,355	$90,911	$85,300	$96,952	$98,817	$90,500	$1,095,952
Cost of Goods Sold	–	7,448	8,698	13,561	9,658	12,875	9,436	8,808	12,411	6,848	5,132	12,375	11,811	119,061
Rounding	–	–	–	–	–	–	–	–	–	–	–	–	–	–
Tax Distribution	–	–	–	–	–	–	–	–	–	–	–	–	–	–
Dividends Paid	–	–	–	–	–	–	–	–	–	–	–	–	–	–
Total Operating Disbursements	257,905	96,493	100,311	100,905	114,234	99,318	93,532	99,163	103,322	92,148	102,084	111,192	102,311	1,215,013

(continued)

	Start-Up Period	October	November	December	January	February	March	April	May	June	July	August	September	Year
Financing Activities														
Cash Receipts														
Bank Loan	1,000,000	–	–	–	–	–	–	–	–	–	–	–	–	–
Add: Interest Expense	24,932	6,204	6,193	6,181	6,169	6,158	6,146	6,134	6,122	6,110	6,098	6,085	6,073	73,673
Less: Loan Payment	(32,224)	(8,056)	(8,056)	(8,056)	(8,056)	(8,056)	(8,056)	(8,056)	(8,056)	(8,056)	(8,056)	(8,056)	(8,056)	(96,672)
Line of Credit	–	–	–	–	–	–	–	–	–	–	–	–	–	–
Sale of Common Stock	200,000	–	–	–	–	–	–	–	–	–	–	–	–	–
Midwest Entrepreneurial Center	250,000	–	–	–	–	–	–	–	–	–	–	–	–	–
Contributed Capital	50,000	–	–	–	–	–	–	–	–	–	–	–	–	–
Cash Receipts from Financing	1,492,708	(1,852)	(1,863)	(1,875)	(1,887)	(1,898)	(1,910)	(1,922)	(1,934)	(1,946)	(1,958)	(1,971)	(1,983)	(22,999)
Investment Activities														
Cash Disbursements														
Leasehold Improvements	735,932	–	–	–	–	–	–	–	–	–	–	–	–	–
ROC Timing System	65,679	–	–	–	–	–	–	–	–	–	–	–	–	–
Karts	61,695	–	–	–	–	–	–	–	–	–	–	–	–	–
Track	40,665	–	–	–	–	–	–	–	–	–	–	–	–	–
Retail Shop Inventory	30,723	–	–	–	–	–	–	–	–	–	–	–	–	–
Barrier	16,150	–	–	–	–	–	–	–	–	–	–	–	–	–
Suits, Helmets, Head Socks	11,759	–	–	–	–	–	–	–	–	–	–	–	–	–
Miscellaneous	11,248	–	–	–	–	–	–	–	–	–	–	–	–	–
Office Furnishings	3,978	–	–	–	–	–	–	–	–	–	–	–	–	–
Multi-Media Equipment	2,887	–	–	–	–	–	–	–	–	–	–	–	–	–
Kart Maintenance/Storage Equip.	2,293	–	–	–	–	–	–	–	–	–	–	–	–	–
Snack Bar Inventory	2,134	–	–	–	–	–	–	–	–	–	–	–	–	–
Phone System	1,090	–	–	–	–	–	–	–	–	–	–	–	–	–
Signs	7,040	–	–	–	–	–	–	–	–	–	–	–	–	–
Fire Extinguishers	561	–	–	–	–	–	–	–	–	–	–	–	–	–
Cash Disbursements from Investments	993,834	–	–	–	–	–	–	–	–	–	–	–	–	–
Net Cash Flows	240,969	(27,151)	(7,520)	41,897	(9,866)	25,222	1,234	(8,700)	28,356	(11,575)	(52,868)	14,150	27,558	20,737
Ending Cash Balance	240,969	213,818	206,298	248,195	238,329	263,551	264,785	256,085	284,441	272,866	219,998	234,148	261,706	261,706

The F1 Experience
Balance Sheet
Fiscal Period Ending September 30, 2003

	Start-Up Period	October	November	December	January	February	March	April	May	June	July	August	September
Assets													
Current Assets													
Cash	$240,969	$213,818	$206,298	$248,195	$238,329	$263,551	$264,785	$256,085	$284,441	$272,866	$219,998	$234,148	$261,706
Retail Shop Inventory	30,723	30,723	30,723	30,723	30,723	30,723	30,723	30,723	30,723	30,723	30,723	30,723	30,723
Snack Bar Inventory	2,134	2,134	2,134	2,134	2,134	2,134	2,134	2,134	2,134	2,134	2,134	2,134	2,134
Total Current Assets	273,826	246,675	239,155	281,052	271,186	296,408	297,642	288,942	317,298	305,723	252,855	267,005	294,563
Fixed Assets													
Leasehold Improvements	735,932	735,932	735,932	735,932	735,932	735,932	735,932	735,932	735,932	735,932	735,932	735,932	735,932
ROC Timing System	65,679	65,679	65,679	65,679	65,679	65,679	65,679	65,679	65,679	65,679	65,679	65,679	65,679
Karts	61,695	61,695	61,695	61,695	61,695	61,695	61,695	61,695	61,695	61,695	61,695	61,695	61,695
Track	40,665	40,665	40,665	40,665	40,665	40,665	40,665	40,665	40,665	40,665	40,665	40,665	40,665
Barrier	16,150	16,150	16,150	16,150	16,150	16,150	16,150	16,150	16,150	16,150	16,150	16,150	16,150
Suits, Helmets, Head Socks	11,759	11,759	11,759	11,759	11,759	11,759	11,759	11,759	11,759	11,759	11,759	11,759	11,759
Miscellaneous	11,248	11,248	11,248	11,248	11,248	11,248	11,248	11,248	11,248	11,248	11,248	11,248	11,248
Office Furnishings	3,978	3,978	3,978	3,978	3,978	3,978	3,978	3,978	3,978	3,978	3,978	3,978	3,978
Multi-Media Equipment	2,887	2,887	2,887	2,887	2,887	2,887	2,887	2,887	2,887	2,887	2,887	2,887	2,887
Kart Maintenance/Storage Equip.	2,293	2,293	2,293	2,293	2,293	2,293	2,293	2,293	2,293	2,293	2,293	2,293	2,293
Phone System	1,090	1,090	1,090	1,090	1,090	1,090	1,090	1,090	1,090	1,090	1,090	1,090	1,090
Signs	7,040	7,040	7,040	7,040	7,040	7,040	7,040	7,040	7,040	7,040	7,040	7,040	7,040
Fire Extinguishers	561	561	561	561	561	561	561	561	561	561	561	561	561
Less: Accumulated Depreciation	—	(9,404)	(18,808)	(28,212)	(37,616)	(47,020)	(56,424)	(65,828)	(75,232)	(84,636)	(94,040)	(103,444)	(112,848)
Total Fixed Assets	960,977	951,573	942,169	932,765	923,361	913,957	904,553	895,149	885,745	876,341	866,937	857,533	848,129
Total Assets	1,234,803	1,198,248	1,181,324	1,213,817	1,194,547	1,210,365	1,202,195	1,184,091	1,203,043	1,182,064	1,119,792	1,124,538	1,142,692
Liability and Stockholders' Equity													
Liabilities													
Line of Credit	—	—	—	—	—	—	—	—	—	—	—	—	—
Bank Loan	992,708	990,856	988,993	987,118	985,231	983,333	981,423	979,501	977,567	975,621	973,663	971,692	969,709
Total Liabilities	992,708	990,856	988,993	987,118	985,231	983,333	981,423	979,501	977,567	975,621	973,663	971,692	969,709
Stockholders' Equity													
Common Stock	500,000	500,000	500,000	500,000	500,000	500,000	500,000	500,000	500,000	500,000	500,000	500,000	500,000
Retained Earnings	(257,905)	(292,608)	(307,669)	(273,301)	(290,684)	(272,968)	(279,228)	(295,410)	(274,524)	(293,557)	(353,871)	(347,154)	(327,017)
Total Stockholders' Equity	242,095	207,392	192,331	226,699	209,316	227,032	220,772	204,590	225,476	206,443	146,129	152,846	172,983
Total Liabilities and Stockholders' Equity	1,234,803	1,198,248	1,181,324	1,213,817	1,194,547	1,210,365	1,202,195	1,184,091	1,203,043	1,182,064	1,119,792	1,124,538	1,142,692

The F1 Experience
Income Statement
Fiscal Period Ending September 30, 2004

	October	November	December	January	February	March	April	May	June	July	August	September	TOTALS
Operating Revenue													
Walk-in	$50,880	$50,880	$84,800	$59,340	$101,760	$76,320	$59,340	$84,800	$50,880	$42,400	$101,760	$84,800	$847,960
Corporate/Event	51,610	51,500	95,230	48,355	64,040	66,360	53,805	91,690	51,555	34,410	91,890	109,100	809,545
Leagues	1,920	7,680	0	7,680	1,920	3,840	5,760	1,920	7,680	0	5,760	3,840	48,000
Advertising	4,800	4,800	4,800	4,800	4,800	4,800	4,800	4,800	4,800	4,800	4,800	4,800	57,600
Camps	960	1,440	480	1,920	0	1,440	960	960	1,440	480	1,920	0	12,000
Retail	10,325	10,325	17,775	12,500	21,125	16,125	12,500	17,775	10,325	8,275	21,125	17,775	175,950
Concessions	2,261	2,261	3,768	2,638	4,523	3,392	2,636	3,776	2,256	1,885	4,524	3,768	37,688
Arcade	1,711	1,711	2,852	1,996	3,415	2,563	1,996	2,852	1,711	1,430	3,415	2,852	28,504
Total Sales	124,467	130,597	209,705	139,229	201,583	174,840	141,797	208,573	130,647	93,680	235,194	226,935	2,017,247
COGS: Corporate/Event	4,450	4,950	7,800	4,600	6,000	6,500	4,050	7,850	4,600	3,150	6,950	7,950	68,850
Retail	5,369	5,369	9,243	6,500	10,985	8,385	6,500	9,243	5,369	4,303	10,985	9,243	91,494
Concessions	1,153	1,153	1,922	1,346	2,307	1,730	1,344	1,926	1,151	961	2,307	1,922	19,222
Arcade	855	856	1,426	998	1,707	1,282	998	1,426	855	715	1,708	1,426	14,252
Total COGS	11,827	12,328	20,391	13,444	20,999	17,897	12,892	20,445	11,975	9,129	21,950	20,541	193,818
Gross Profit	112,640	118,269	189,314	125,785	180,584	156,943	128,905	188,128	118,672	84,551	213,244	206,394	1,823,429

(continued)

Operating Expenses	October	November	December	January	February	March	April	May	June	July	August	September	TOTALS
Cash													
Advertising													
Yellow Pages	144	144	144	144	144	144	144	144	144	144	144	144	1,728
Radio	6,000	–	–	6,000	–	–	6,000	–	–	6,000	–	–	24,000
Newspaper	360	155	155	155	155	155	155	886	155	155	886	886	4,258
Personnel													
Salary	16,830	13,460	13,460	16,830	13,460	13,460	16,830	13,460	13,460	16,830	13,999	13,999	176,078
Wages	18,000	14,400	14,400	18,000	14,400	14,400	18,000	14,400	14,400	18,000	14,400	14,400	187,200
Payroll Tax–Salary	1,303	1,030	1,030	1,877	1,501	1,195	1,287	1,030	1,030	1,288	1,071	1,071	14,713
Payroll Tax–Wages	2,007	1,606	1,606	2,007	1,606	1,606	2,007	1,606	1,606	2,007	1,606	2,007	21,277
Operational													
Rent	37,350	37,350	37,350	37,350	37,350	37,350	37,350	37,350	37,350	37,350	37,350	37,350	448,200
Insurance	6,724	6,724	6,724	6,724	6,724	6,724	6,724	6,724	6,724	6,724	6,724	6,724	80,688
Utilities	2,280	3,990	5,130	5,130	3,990	2,280	2,280	2,280	3,990	5,130	5,130	3,990	45,600
Telephone	66	66	66	66	66	66	66	66	66	66	66	66	792
Legal/Accounting Fees	450	450	450	450	450	450	800	450	450	450	450	450	5,750
Copier Rental	60	60	60	60	60	60	60	60	60	60	60	60	720
Copier Service Fee	295												295
Office Supplies	50	50	50	50	50	50	50	50	50	50	50	50	600
Trash Removal	29	29	29	29	29	29	29	29	29	29	29	29	348
Association Dues	940												940
Satellite Dish	42	42	42	42	42	42	42	42	42	42	42	42	504
Fire Extinguisher Service	155												155
Propane	917	1,030	1,414	1,131	1,503	1,200	1,089	1,404	1,009	671	1,668	1,425	14,461
Janitorial Supplies	60	60	60	60	60	60	60	60	60	60	60	60	720
Kart Maintenance	900	900	900	900	900	900	900	900	900	900	900	900	10,800
ADT–Security Monitoring	30	30	30	30	30	30	30	30	30	30	30	30	360
Promotional Materials	1,137	569	171	9,505	343	153	1,562	180	560	9,216	406	352	24,154
Web Page Design/Maintenance	35	35	35	35	35	35	35	35	35	35	35	35	420
Web Page Hosting	17	17	17	17	17	17	17	17	17	17	17	17	204
Licenses–1st time customers	694	694	1,158	810	1,389	1,042	810	1,158	694	579	1,389	1,158	11,575
CC Service Charge	308	308	503	356	601	454	356	503	308	259	601	503	5,060
Maintenance	500	500	500	500	500	500	500	500	500	500	500	500	6,000
Discount	1,267	1,637	1,914	1,567	1,987	1,891	1,590	1,912	1,303	1,009	2,137	1,987	20,201
Charitable Contributions			1,250		1,250	1,250				1,250		1,250	5,000
Interest Expense	6,061	6,048	6,036	6,023	6,010	5,998	5,985	5,972	5,959	5,946	5,932	5,919	71,889
Property Tax	4,897	4,897	4,897	4,897	4,897	4,897	4,897	4,897	4,897	4,897	4,897	4,897	58,764
Total Cash Expenses	109,908	96,281	99,581	120,745	98,299	96,438	109,655	96,145	97,078	118,444	100,579	100,301	1,243,454
Non-Cash													
Depreciation	9,404	9,404	9,404	9,404	9,404	9,404	9,404	9,404	9,404	9,404	9,404	9,404	112,848
Total Operating Expenses	119,312	105,685	108,985	130,149	107,703	105,842	119,059	105,549	106,482	127,848	109,983	109,705	1,356,302
Income (Loss) from Operations	(6,672)	12,584	80,329	(4,364)	72,881	51,101	9,846	82,579	12,190	(43,297)	103,261	96,689	467,127
Tax Distribution to Shareholders	–	–	(4,925)	–	(19,699)	(14,692)	(2,831)	(23,741)	(3,505)	–	(17,240)	(27,798)	(114,431)
Net Income (Loss)	(6,672)	12,584	75,404	(4,364)	53,182	36,409	7,015	58,838	8,685	(43,297)	86,021	68,891	352,696

The F1 Experience
Statement of Cash Flows
Fiscal Period Ending September 30, 2004

	October	November	December	January	February	March	April	May	June	July	August	September	Year
Beginning Cash Balance	$261,706	$262,443	$282,423	$365,211	$368,218	$428,758	$472,513	$486,861	$553,019	$569,011	$533,008	$626,309	$261,706
Operating Activities													
Cash Received (Inflows)													
Walk-in	50,880	50,880	84,800	59,340	101,760	76,320	59,340	84,800	50,880	42,400	101,760	84,800	847,960
Corporate/Event	51,610	51,500	95,230	48,355	64,040	66,360	53,805	91,690	51,555	34,410	91,890	109,100	809,545
Leagues	1,920	7,680	–	7,680	1,920	3,840	5,760	1,920	7,680	–	5,760	3,840	48,000
Advertising	4,800	4,800	4,800	4,800	4,800	4,800	4,800	4,800	4,800	4,800	4,800	4,800	57,600
Camps	960	1,440	480	1,920	–	1,440	960	960	1,440	480	1,920	–	12,000
Retail	10,325	10,325	17,775	12,500	21,125	16,125	12,500	17,775	10,325	8,275	21,125	17,775	175,950
Concessions	2,261	2,261	3,768	2,638	4,523	3,392	2,636	3,776	2,256	1,885	4,524	3,768	37,688
Arcade	1,711	1,711	2,852	1,996	3,415	2,563	1,996	2,852	1,711	1,430	3,415	2,852	28,504
Cash Receipts from Operations	124,467	130,597	209,705	139,229	201,583	174,840	141,797	208,573	130,647	93,680	235,194	226,935	2,017,247
Total Cash Available	386,173	393,040	492,128	504,440	569,801	603,598	614,310	695,434	683,666	662,691	768,202	853,244	2,278,953
Cash Disbursements (Outflows)													
Operating Expenses	109,908	96,281	99,581	120,745	98,299	96,438	109,655	96,145	97,078	118,444	100,579	100,301	1,243,454
Cost of Goods Sold	11,827	12,328	20,391	13,444	20,999	17,897	12,892	20,445	11,975	9,129	21,950	20,541	193,818
Rounding	–	–	–	–	–	–	–	–	–	–	–	–	–
Tax Distribution	–	–	4,925	–	19,699	14,692	2,831	23,741	3,505	–	17,240	27,798	114,431
Dividends Paid	–	–	–	–	–	–	–	–	–	–	–	50,000	50,000
Total Operating Disbursements	121,735	108,609	124,897	134,189	138,997	129,027	125,378	140,331	112,558	127,573	139,769	198,640	1,601,703

(continued)

	October	November	December	January	February	March	April	May	June	July	August	September	Year
Financing Activities													
Cash Receipts													
Bank Loan	—	—	—	—	—	—	—	—	—	—	—	—	—
Add: Interest Expense	6,061	6,048	6,036	6,023	6,010	5,998	5,985	5,972	5,959	5,946	5,932	5,919	71,889
Less: Loan Payment	(8,056)	(8,056)	(8,056)	(8,056)	(8,056)	(8,056)	(8,056)	(8,056)	(8,056)	(8,056)	(8,056)	(8,056)	(96,672)
Line of Credit	—	—	—	—	—	—	—	—	—	—	—	—	—
Sale of Common Stock	—	—	—	—	—	—	—	—	—	—	—	—	—
Midwest Entrepreneurial Center	—	—	—	—	—	—	—	—	—	—	—	—	—
Contributed Capital	—	—	—	—	—	—	—	—	—	—	—	—	—
Cash Receipts from Financing	(1,995)	(2,008)	(2,020)	(2,033)	(2,046)	(2,058)	(2,071)	(2,084)	(2,097)	(2,110)	(2,124)	(2,137)	(24,783)
Investment Activities													
Cash Disbursements													
Leasehold Improvements	—	—	—	—	—	—	—	—	—	—	—	—	—
ROC Timing System	—	—	—	—	—	—	—	—	—	—	—	—	—
Karts	—	—	—	—	—	—	—	—	—	—	—	—	—
Track	—	—	—	—	—	—	—	—	—	—	—	—	—
Retail Shop Inventory	—	—	—	—	—	—	—	—	—	—	—	—	—
Barrier	—	—	—	—	—	—	—	—	—	—	—	—	—
Suits, Helmets, Head Socks	—	—	—	—	—	—	—	—	—	—	—	—	—
Miscellaneous	—	—	—	—	—	—	—	—	—	—	—	—	—
Office Furnishings	—	—	—	—	—	—	—	—	—	—	—	—	—
Multi-Media Equipment	—	—	—	—	—	—	—	—	—	—	—	—	—
Kart Maintenance/Storage Equip.	—	—	—	—	—	—	—	—	—	—	—	—	—
Snack Bar Inventory	—	—	—	—	—	—	—	—	—	—	—	—	—
Phone System	—	—	—	—	—	—	—	—	—	—	—	—	—
Signs	—	—	—	—	—	—	—	—	—	—	—	—	—
Fire Extinguishers	—	—	—	—	—	—	—	—	—	—	—	—	—
Cash Disbursements from Investments													
Net Cash Flows	737	19,980	82,788	3,007	60,540	43,755	14,348	66,158	15,992	(36,003)	93,301	26,158	390,761
Ending Cash Balance	262,443	282,423	365,211	368,218	428,758	472,513	486,861	553,019	569,011	533,008	626,309	652,467	652,467

The F1 Experience
Balance Sheet
Fiscal Period Ending September 30, 2004

	October	November	December	January	February	March	April	May	June	July	August	September
Assets												
Current Assets												
Cash	262,443	282,423	365,211	368,218	428,758	472,513	486,861	553,019	569,011	533,008	626,309	652,467
Retail Shop Inventory	30,723	30,723	30,723	30,723	30,723	30,723	30,723	30,723	30,723	30,723	30,723	30,723
Snack Bar Inventory	2,134	2,134	2,134	2,134	2,134	2,134	2,134	2,134	2,134	2,134	2,134	2,134
Total Current Assets	295,300	315,280	398,068	401,075	461,615	505,370	519,718	585,876	601,868	565,865	659,166	685,324
Fixed Assets												
Leasehold Improvements	735,932	735,932	735,932	735,932	735,932	735,932	735,932	735,932	735,932	735,932	735,932	735,932
ROC Timing System	65,679	65,679	65,679	65,679	65,679	65,679	65,679	65,679	65,679	65,679	65,679	65,679
Karts	61,695	61,695	61,695	61,695	61,695	61,695	61,695	61,695	61,695	61,695	61,695	61,695
Track	40,665	40,665	40,665	40,665	40,665	40,665	40,665	40,665	40,665	40,665	40,665	40,665
Barrier	16,150	16,150	16,150	16,150	16,150	16,150	16,150	16,150	16,150	16,150	16,150	16,150
Suits, Helmets, Head Socks	11,759	11,759	11,759	11,759	11,759	11,759	11,759	11,759	11,759	11,759	11,759	11,759
Miscellaneous	11,248	11,248	11,248	11,248	11,248	11,248	11,248	11,248	11,248	11,248	11,248	11,248
Office Furnishings	3,978	3,978	3,978	3,978	3,978	3,978	3,978	3,978	3,978	3,978	3,978	3,978
Multi-Media Equipment	2,887	2,887	2,887	2,887	2,887	2,887	2,887	2,887	2,887	2,887	2,887	2,887
Kart Maintenance/Storage Equip.	2,293	2,293	2,293	2,293	2,293	2,293	2,293	2,293	2,293	2,293	2,293	2,293
Phone System	1,090	1,090	1,090	1,090	1,090	1,090	1,090	1,090	1,090	1,090	1,090	1,090
Signs	7,040	7,040	7,040	7,040	7,040	7,040	7,040	7,040	7,040	7,040	7,040	7,040
Fire Extinguishers	561	561	561	561	561	561	561	561	561	561	561	561
Less: Accumulated Depreciation	(122,252)	(131,656)	(141,060)	(150,464)	(159,868)	(169,272)	(178,676)	(188,080)	(197,484)	(206,888)	(216,292)	(225,696)
Total Fixed Assets	838,725	829,321	819,917	810,513	801,109	791,705	782,301	772,897	763,493	754,089	744,685	735,281
Total Assets	1,134,025	1,144,601	1,217,985	1,211,588	1,262,724	1,297,075	1,302,019	1,358,773	1,365,361	1,319,954	1,403,851	1,420,605
Liability and Stockholders' Equity												
Liabilities												
Line of Credit	–	–	–	–	–	–	–	–	–	–	–	–
Bank Loan	967,714	965,706	963,686	961,653	959,607	957,549	955,478	953,394	951,297	949,187	947,063	944,926
Total Liabilities	967,714	965,706	963,686	961,653	959,607	957,549	955,478	953,394	951,297	949,187	947,063	944,926
Stockholders' Equity												
Common Stock	500,000	500,000	500,000	500,000	500,000	500,000	500,000	500,000	500,000	500,000	500,000	500,000
Retained Earnings	(333,689)	(321,105)	(245,701)	(250,065)	(196,883)	(160,474)	(153,459)	(94,621)	(85,936)	(129,233)	(43,212)	(24,321)
Total Stockholders' Equity	166,311	178,895	254,299	249,935	303,117	339,526	346,541	405,379	414,064	370,767	456,788	475,679
Total Liabilities and Stockholders' Equity	1,134,025	1,144,601	1,217,985	1,211,588	1,262,724	1,297,075	1,302,019	1,358,773	1,365,361	1,319,954	1,403,851	1,420,605

The F1 Experience
Income Statement
Fiscal Period Ending September 30, 2005

	October	November	December	January	February	March	April	May	June	July	August	September	TOTALS
Operating Revenue													
Walk-in	$65,460	$65,460	$109,120	$76,380	$130,940	$98,200	$76,380	$109,120	$65,460	$54,520	$130,940	$109,120	$1,091,100
Corporate/Event	94,250	67,885	111,015	79,240	83,870	81,765	63,325	111,840	45,335	64,905	113,530	128,190	1,045,150
Leagues	–	9,600	–	5,760	3,840	1,920	7,680	1,920	7,680	–	7,680	1,920	48,000
Advertising	8,400	8,400	8,400	8,400	8,400	8,400	8,400	8,400	8,400	8,400	8,400	8,400	100,800
Camps	1,440	960	–	2,400	–	1,440	960	960	1,440	–	1,920	480	12,000
Retail	13,475	13,475	22,575	16,125	27,175	20,600	16,125	22,425	13,475	11,375	27,175	22,350	226,350
Concessions	2,912	2,912	4,848	3,392	5,816	4,364	3,392	4,848	2,912	2,420	5,816	4,848	48,480
Arcade	2,200	2,200	3,669	2,563	4,403	3,289	2,563	3,669	2,200	1,835	4,403	3,669	36,663
Total Sales	188,137	170,892	259,627	194,260	264,444	219,978	178,825	263,182	146,902	143,455	299,864	278,977	2,608,543
COGS: Corporate/Event	8,700	6,550	9,400	7,700	7,750	8,450	4,600	9,000	4,100	5,550	8,400	8,450	88,650
Retail	7,007	7,007	11,739	8,385	14,131	10,712	8,385	11,661	7,007	5,915	14,131	11,622	117,702
Concessions	1,485	1,485	2,472	1,730	2,966	2,226	1,730	2,472	1,485	1,234	2,966	2,472	24,723
Arcade	1,100	1,100	1,834	1,282	2,202	1,644	1,283	1,834	1,100	918	2,201	1,834	18,332
Total COGS	18,292	16,142	25,445	19,097	27,049	23,032	15,998	24,967	13,692	13,617	27,698	24,378	249,407
Gross Profit	169,845	154,750	234,182	175,163	237,395	196,946	162,827	238,215	133,210	129,838	272,166	254,599	2,359,136

(continued)

	October	November	December	January	February	March	April	May	June	July	August	September	TOTALS
Operating Expenses													
Cash													
Advertising													
Yellow Pages	144	144	144	144	144	144	144	144	144	144	144	144	1,728
Radio	6,000	–	–	6,000	–	–	6,000	–	–	6,000	–	–	24,000
Newspaper	360	155	155	155	155	155	155	886	155	155	886	886	4,258
Personnel													
Salary	17,500	13,999	17,500	14,575	13,999	13,999	17,500	13,999	13,999	17,500	14,230	14,230	183,030
Wages	18,000	14,400	18,000	14,400	14,400	14,400	18,000	14,400	14,400	18,000	14,400	14,400	187,200
Payroll Tax—Salary	1,339	1,071	1,339	1,581	1,561	1,296	1,339	1,071	1,071	1,339	1,089	1,089	15,185
Payroll Tax—Wages	2,007	1,606	2,007	1,606	1,606	1,606	2,007	1,606	1,606	2,007	1,606	1,606	20,876
Operational													
Rent	37,350	37,350	37,350	37,350	37,350	37,350	37,350	37,350	37,350	37,350	37,350	37,350	448,200
Insurance	8,695	8,695	8,695	8,695	8,695	8,695	8,695	8,695	8,695	8,695	8,695	8,695	104,340
Utilities	2,280	3,990	5,130	5,130	3,990	2,280	2,280	2,280	3,990	5,130	5,130	3,990	45,600
Telephone	66	66	66	66	66	66	66	66	66	66	66	66	792
Legal/Accounting Fees	450	450	450	450	450	450	800	450	450	450	450	450	5,750
Copier Rental	60	60	60	60	60	60	60	60	60	60	60	60	720
Copier Service Fee	295	–	–	–	–	–	–	–	–	–	–	–	295
Office Supplies	50	50	50	50	50	50	50	50	50	50	50	50	600
Trash Removal	29	29	29	29	29	29	29	29	29	29	29	29	348
Association Dues	940	–	–	–	–	–	–	–	–	–	–	–	940
Satellite Dish	42	42	42	42	42	42	42	42	42	42	42	42	504
Fire Extinguisher Service	155	–	–	–	–	–	–	–	–	–	–	–	155
Propane	1,165	1,320	1,747	1,386	1,981	1,578	1,437	1,726	1,227	874	2,126	1,758	18,325
Janitorial Supplies	60	60	60	60	60	60	60	60	60	60	60	60	720
Kart Maintenance	10,125	900	900	900	900	900	900	900	900	900	900	900	20,025
ADT—Security Monitoring	30	30	30	30	30	30	30	30	30	30	30	30	360
Promotional Materials	1,531	605	198	12,483	397	225	1,956	189	587	12,176	243	569	31,159
Web Page Design/Maintenance	35	35	35	35	35	35	35	35	35	35	35	35	420
Web Page Hosting	17	17	17	17	17	17	17	17	17	17	17	17	204
Licenses—1st time customers	894	894	1,489	1,042	1,786	1,340	1,042	1,489	894	746	1,786	1,489	14,891
CC Service Charge	392	392	644	455	770	581	455	644	392	329	770	644	6,468
Maintenance	500	500	500	500	500	500	500	500	500	500	500	500	6,000
Discount	1,842	2,013	2,540	2,015	2,562	2,330	1,921	2,401	1,587	1,405	2,747	2,498	25,861
Charitable Contributions	–	–	2,500	–	2,500	2,500	–	2,500	2,500	–	–	2,500	10,000
Interest Expense	5,906	5,892	5,879	5,865	5,852	5,838	5,824	5,810	5,796	5,782	5,768	5,753	69,965
Property Tax	4,768	4,768	4,768	4,768	4,768	4,768	4,768	4,768	4,768	4,768	4,768	4,768	57,216
Total Cash Expenses	123,027	99,533	112,324	119,889	102,255	101,324	113,462	99,697	101,400	124,639	103,977	104,608	1,306,135
Non-Cash													
Depreciation	9,404	9,404	9,404	9,404	9,404	9,404	9,404	9,404	9,404	9,404	9,404	9,404	112,848
Total Operating Expenses	132,431	108,937	121,728	129,293	111,659	110,728	122,866	109,101	110,804	134,043	113,381	114,012	1,418,983
Income (Loss) from Operations	37,414	45,813	112,454	45,870	125,736	86,218	39,961	129,114	22,406	(4,205)	158,785	140,587	940,153
Tax Distribution to .50 Shareholders	(10,757)	(13,171)	(32,331)	(13,188)	(36,149)	(24,788)	(11,489)	(37,120)	(6,442)	–	(44,442)	(40,419)	(270,296)
Net Income (Loss)	26,657	32,642	80,123	32,682	89,587	61,430	28,472	91,994	15,964	(4,205)	114,343	100,168	669,857

The F1 Experience
Statement of Cash Flows
Fiscal Period Ending September 30, 2005

	October	November	December	January	February	March	April	May	June	July	August	September	Year
Beginning Cash Balance	$652,467	$686,378	$726,260	$813,610	$853,505	$950,292	$1,018,908	$1,054,552	$1,153,704	$1,176,812	$1,179,737	$1,301,196	$652,467
Operating Activities													
Cash Received (Inflows)													
Walk-in	65,460	65,460	109,120	76,380	130,940	98,200	76,380	109,120	65,460	54,520	130,940	109,120	1,091,100
Corporate/Event	94,250	67,885	111,015	79,240	83,870	81,765	63,325	111,840	45,335	64,905	113,530	128,190	1,045,150
Leagues	–	9,600	0	5,760	3,840	1,920	7,680	1,920	7,680	–	7,680	1,920	48,000
Advertising	8,400	8,400	8,400	8,400	8,400	8,400	8,400	8,400	8,400	8,400	8,400	8,400	100,800
Camps	1,440	960	–	2,400	0	1,440	960	960	1,440	0	1,920	480	12,000
Retail	13,475	13,475	22,575	16,125	27,175	20,600	16,125	22,425	13,475	11,375	27,175	22,350	226,350
Concessions	2,912	2,912	4,848	3,392	5,816	4,364	3,392	4,848	2,912	2,420	5,816	4,848	48,480
Arcade	2,200	2,200	3,669	2,563	4,403	3,289	2,563	3,669	2,200	1,835	4,403	3,669	36,663
Cash Receipts from Operations	188,137	170,892	259,627	194,260	264,444	219,978	178,825	263,182	146,902	143,455	299,864	278,977	2,608,543
Total Cash Available	840,604	857,270	985,887	1,007,870	1,117,949	1,170,270	1,197,733	1,317,734	1,300,606	1,320,267	1,479,601	1,580,173	3,261,010
Cash Disbursements (Outflows)													
Operating Expenses	123,027	99,533	112,324	119,889	102,255	101,324	113,462	99,697	101,400	124,639	103,977	104,608	1,306,135
Cost of Goods Sold	18,292	16,142	25,445	19,097	27,049	23,032	15,998	24,967	13,692	13,617	27,698	24,378	249,407
Rounding	–	–	–	–	–	–	–	–	–	–	–	–	–
Tax Distribution	10,757	13,171	32,331	13,188	36,149	24,788	11,489	37,120	6,442	–	44,442	40,419	270,296
Dividends Paid	–	–	–	–	–	–	–	–	–	–	–	75,000	75,000
Total Operating Disbursements	152,076	128,846	170,100	152,174	165,453	149,144	140,949	161,784	121,534	138,256	176,117	244,405	1,900,838

	October	November	December	January	February	March	April	May	June	July	August	September	Year
Financing Activities													
Cash Receipts													
Bank Loan	—	—	—	—	—	—	—	—	—	—	—	—	—
Add: Interest Expense	5,906	5,892	5,879	5,865	5,852	5,838	5,824	5,810	5,796	5,782	5,768	5,753	69,965
Less: Loan Payment	(8,056)	(8,056)	(8,056)	(8,056)	(8,056)	(8,056)	(8,056)	(8,056)	(8,056)	(8,056)	(8,056)	(8,056)	(96,672)
Line of Credit	—	—	—	—	—	—	—	—	—	—	—	—	—
Sale of Common Stock	—	—	—	—	—	—	—	—	—	—	—	—	—
Midwest Entrepreneurial Center	—	—	—	—	—	—	—	—	—	—	—	—	—
Contributed Capital	—	—	—	—	—	—	—	—	—	—	—	—	—
Cash Receipts from Financing	(2,150)	(2,164)	(2,177)	(2,191)	(2,204)	(2,218)	(2,232)	(2,246)	(2,260)	(2,274)	(2,288)	(2,303)	(26,707)
Investment Activities													
Cash Disbursements													
Leasehold Improvements	—	—	—	—	—	—	—	—	—	—	—	—	—
ROC Timing System	—	—	—	—	—	—	—	—	—	—	—	—	—
Karts	—	—	—	—	—	—	—	—	—	—	—	—	—
Track	—	—	—	—	—	—	—	—	—	—	—	—	—
Retail Shop Inventory	—	—	—	—	—	—	—	—	—	—	—	—	—
Barrier	—	—	—	—	—	—	—	—	—	—	—	—	—
Suits, Helmets, Head Socks	—	—	—	—	—	—	—	—	—	—	—	—	—
Miscellaneous	—	—	—	—	—	—	—	—	—	—	—	—	—
Office Furnishings	—	—	—	—	—	—	—	—	—	—	—	—	—
Multi-Media Equipment	—	—	—	—	—	—	—	—	—	—	—	—	—
Kart Maintenance/Storage Equip.	—	—	—	—	—	—	—	—	—	—	—	—	—
Snack Bar Inventory	—	—	—	—	—	—	—	—	—	—	—	—	—
Phone System	—	—	—	—	—	—	—	—	—	—	—	—	—
Signs	—	—	—	—	—	—	—	—	—	—	—	—	—
Fire Extinguishers	—	—	—	—	—	—	—	—	—	—	—	—	—
Cash Disbursements from Investments													
Net Cash Flows	33,911	39,882	87,350	39,895	96,787	68,616	35,644	99,152	23,108	2,925	121,459	32,269	680,998
Ending Cash Balance	686,378	726,260	813,610	853,505	950,292	1,018,908	1,054,552	1,153,704	1,176,812	1,179,737	1,301,196	1,333,465	1,333,465

The F1 Experience
Balance Sheet
Fiscal Period Ending September 30, 2005

	October	November	December	January	February	March	April	May	June	July	August	September
Assets												
Current Assets												
Cash	$686,378	$726,260	$813,610	$853,505	$950,292	$1,018,908	$1,054,552	$1,153,704	$1,176,812	$1,179,737	$1,301,196	$1,333,465
Retail Shop Inventory	30,723	30,723	30,723	30,723	30,723	30,723	30,723	30,723	30,723	30,723	30,723	30,723
Snack Bar Inventory	2,134	2,134	2,134	2,134	2,134	2,134	2,134	2,134	2,134	2,134	2,134	2,134
Total Current Assets	719,235	759,117	846,467	886,362	983,149	1,051,765	1,087,409	1,186,561	1,209,669	1,212,594	1,334,053	1,366,322
Fixed Assets												
Leasehold Improvements	735,932	735,932	735,932	735,932	735,932	735,932	735,932	735,932	735,932	735,932	735,932	735,932
ROC Timing System	65,679	65,679	65,679	65,679	65,679	65,679	65,679	65,679	65,679	65,679	65,679	65,679
Karts	61,695	61,695	61,695	61,695	61,695	61,695	61,695	61,695	61,695	61,695	61,695	61,695
Track	40,665	40,665	40,665	40,665	40,665	40,665	40,665	40,665	40,665	40,665	40,665	40,665
Barrier	16,150	16,150	16,150	16,150	16,150	16,150	16,150	16,150	16,150	16,150	16,150	16,150
Suits, Helmets, Head Socks	11,759	11,759	11,759	11,759	11,759	11,759	11,759	11,759	11,759	11,759	11,759	11,759
Miscellaneous	11,248	11,248	11,248	11,248	11,248	11,248	11,248	11,248	11,248	11,248	11,248	11,248
Office Furnishings	3,978	3,978	3,978	3,978	3,978	3,978	3,978	3,978	3,978	3,978	3,978	3,978
Multi-Media Equipment	2,887	2,887	2,887	2,887	2,887	2,887	2,887	2,887	2,887	2,887	2,887	2,887
Kart Maintenance/Storage Equip.	2,293	2,293	2,293	2,293	2,293	2,293	2,293	2,293	2,293	2,293	2,293	2,293
Phone System	1,090	1,090	1,090	1,090	1,090	1,090	1,090	1,090	1,090	1,090	1,090	1,090
Signs	7,040	7,040	7,040	7,040	7,040	7,040	7,040	7,040	7,040	7,040	7,040	7,040
Fire Extinguishers	561	561	561	561	561	561	561	561	561	561	561	561
Less: Accumulated Depreciation	(235,100)	(244,504)	(253,908)	(263,312)	(272,716)	(282,120)	(291,524)	(300,928)	(310,332)	(319,736)	(329,140)	(338,544)
Total Fixed Assets	725,877	716,473	707,069	697,665	688,261	678,857	669,453	660,049	650,645	641,241	631,837	622,433
Total Assets	1,445,112	1,475,590	1,553,536	1,584,027	1,671,410	1,730,622	1,756,862	1,846,610	1,860,314	1,853,835	1,965,890	1,988,755
Liability and Stockholders' Equity												
Liabilities												
Line of Credit	–	–	–	–	–	–	–	–	–	–	–	–
Bank Loan	942,776	940,612	938,435	936,244	934,040	931,822	929,590	927,344	925,084	922,810	920,522	918,219
Total Liabilities	942,776	940,612	938,435	936,244	934,040	931,822	929,590	927,344	925,084	922,810	920,522	918,219
Stockholders' Equity												
Common Stock	500,000	500,000	500,000	500,000	500,000	500,000	500,000	500,000	500,000	500,000	500,000	500,000
Retained Earnings	2,336	34,978	115,101	147,783	237,370	298,800	327,272	419,266	435,230	431,025	545,368	570,536
Total Stockholders' Equity	502,336	534,978	615,101	647,783	737,370	798,800	827,272	919,266	935,230	931,025	1,045,368	1,070,536
Total Liabilities and Stockholders' Equity	1,445,112	1,475,590	1,553,536	1,584,027	1,671,410	1,730,622	1,756,862	1,846,610	1,860,314	1,853,835	1,965,890	1,988,755

The F1 Experience
Financial Ratios (2003–2005)

	2003	2004	2005	Racing Including Track Operation 2001 SIC 7948 Industry Standards			Amusement and Recreation NEC 2001 SIC 7999 Industry Standards		
				Upper Q	Med	Lower Q	Upper Q	Med	Lower Q
Quick Ratio	0.27	0.69	1.45	1.7	0.8	0.4	2.2	0.6	0.1
Current Ratio	0.30	0.73	1.49	3.1	2.0	0.9	3.8	1.5	0.7
Current Liabilities to Net Worth	560.6	198.6	85.8	6.8	21.2	37.5	13.3	38.2	117.4
Total Liabilities to Net Worth	560.6	198.6	85.8	13.2	37.7	117.2	26.4	84.9	215.9
Fixed Assets to Net Worth	490.3	154.6	58.1	45.7	105.6	154.6	44.8	88.8	176.6
Sales to Inventory	38.31	61.39	79.39	305.2	231.5	175.5	70.3	24.0	7.6
Sales to Net Working Capital	(1.86)	(7.77)	5.82	7.6	5.9	2.1	15.9	7.6	3.5
Return on Sales	-5.5%	17.5%	25.7%	7.1%	3.7%	0.2%	8.7%	3.9%	-3.4%
Return on Assets	-6.0%	24.8%	33.7%	9.7%	7.2%	0.2%	16.4%	5.4%	-5.9%
Return on Net Worth	-40.0%	74.1%	62.6%	21.3%	9.8%	0.3%	38.7%	12.3%	-8.4%
Net Worth	$172,983	$475,679	$1,070,536						
Net Working Capital	$(675,146)	$(259,602)	$448,103						

Break-Even Analysis

Fixed Costs	2002			2003								
	October	November	December	January	February	March	April	May	June	July	August	September
Salary	$10,152	$12,696	$10,152	$12,696	$10,152	$10,152	$10,152	$12,696	$10,152	$10,152	$16,830	$13,460
Wages	14,400	18,000	14,400	18,000	14,400	14,400	14,400	18,000	14,400	14,400	18,000	14,400
Payroll Tax—Salary	894	972	777	2,007	1,132	957	777	972	777	777	1,416	1,132
Payroll Tax—Wages	1,606	2,007	1,606	2,007	1,606	1,606	1,606	2,007	1,606	1,606	2,007	1,606
Rent	37,350	37,350	37,350	37,350	37,350	37,350	37,350	37,350	37,350	37,350	37,350	37,350
Insurance	4,000	4,000	4,000	4,000	4,000	4,000	4,000	4,000	4,000	4,000	4,000	4,000
Utilities	2,280	3,990	5,130	5,130	3,990	2,280	2,280	2,280	3,990	5,130	5,130	3,990
Telephone	66	66	66	66	66	66	66	66	66	66	66	66
Legal/Accounting Fees	450	450	450	450	450	450	800	450	450	450	450	450
Copier Rental	60	60	60	60	60	60	60	60	60	60	60	60
Copier Service Fee	–	–	–	–	–	–	–	–	–	–	–	–
Office Supplies	50	50	50	50	50	50	50	50	50	50	50	50
Trash Removal	29	29	29	29	29	29	29	29	29	29	29	29
Association Dues	–	–	–	–	–	–	–	–	–	–	–	–
Satellite Dish	242	42	42	42	42	42	42	42	42	42	42	42
Fire Extinguisher Service	–	–	–	–	–	–	–	–	–	–	–	–
Janitorial Supplies	60	60	60	60	60	60	60	60	60	60	60	60
Kent Maintenance	900	900	900	900	900	900	900	900	900	900	900	900
ADT—Security Monitoring	30	30	30	30	30	30	30	30	30	30	30	30
Web Page Design/Maintenance	35	35	35	35	35	35	35	35	35	35	35	35
Web Page Hosting	17	17	17	17	17	17	17	17	17	17	17	17
Maintenance	500	500	500	500	500	500	500	500	500	500	500	500
Interest Expense	6,204	6,193	6,181	6,169	6,158	6,146	6,134	6,122	6,110	6,098	6,085	6,073
Property Tax	1,139	1,139	1,139	1,139	1,139	1,139	1,139	1,139	1,139	1,139	1,139	1,139
Depreciation	9,404	9,404	9,404	9,404	9,404	9,404	9,404	9,404	9,404	9,404	9,404	9,404
Yellow Pages	144	144	144	144	144	144	144	144	144	144	144	144
Total Fixed Costs	90,012	98,134	92,522	99,694	91,714	89,817	89,975	96,353	91,311	92,439	103,744	94,937

(continued)

	2002			2003								
	October	November	December	January	February	March	April	May	June	July	August	September
Variable Costs												
Cost of Goods Sold	7,448	8,698	13,561	9,658	12,875	9,436	8,808	12,411	6,848	5,132	12,375	11,811
Propane	527	763	902	757	982	878	777	748	784	441	971	829
Promotional Materials	72	352	316	5,648	506	135	1,213	72	560	6,229	117	479
Licenses–1st time customers	421	421	703	492	843	632	492	703	421	350	843	703
CC Service Charge	192	192	311	222	370	281	222	311	192	162	370	311
Discount	886	1,021	1,318	1,033	1,277	1,164	925	1,201	821	622	1,208	1,196
Charitable Contributions	–	–	500	–	–	500	–	–	500	–	–	500
Tax Distribution to Shareholders	–	–	–	–	–	–	–	–	–	–	–	–
Radio	6,000	–	–	6,000	–	–	6,000	–	–	6,000	–	–
Newspaper	360	155	155	155	155	155	155	886	155	155	886	886
Total Variable Costs	15,906	11,602	17,766	23,965	17,008	13,181	18,592	16,332	10,281	19,091	16,770	16,715
Total Costs (Fixed + Variable)	105,918	109,736	110,288	123,659	108,722	102,998	108,567	112,685	101,592	111,530	120,514	111,652
Sales												
Total Sales	$71,194	$94,654	$144,677	$106,255	$126,438	$96,676	$92,385	$133,612	$82,519	$51,174	$127,313	$131,852

(continued)

Break-Even Analysis

	2003			2004								
	October	November	December	January	February	March	April	May	June	July	August	September
Fixed Costs												
Salary	$16,830	$13,460	$13,460	$16,830	$13,460	$13,460	$16,830	$13,460	$13,460	$16,830	$13,999	$13,999
Wages	18,000	14,400	14,400	18,000	14,400	14,400	18,000	14,400	14,400	18,000	14,400	14,400
Payroll Tax–Salary	1,303	1,030	1,030	1,877	1,501	1,195	1,287	1,030	1,030	1,288	1,071	1,071
Payroll Tax–Wages	2,007	1,606	1,606	2,007	1,606	1,606	2,007	1,606	1,606	2,007	1,606	2,007
Rent	37,350	37,350	37,350	37,350	37,350	37,350	37,350	37,350	37,350	37,350	37,350	37,350
Insurance	6,883	6,883	6,883	6,883	6,883	6,883	6,883	6,883	6,883	6,883	6,883	6,883
Utilities	2,280	3,990	5,130	5,130	3,990	2,280	2,280	2,280	3,990	5,130	5,130	3,990
Telephone	66	66	66	66	66	66	66	66	66	66	66	66
Legal/Accounting Fees	450	450	450	450	450	450	800	450	450	450	450	450
Cop er Rental	60	60	60	60	60	60	60	60	60	60	60	60
Cop er Service Fee	295	–	–	–	–	–	–	–	–	–	–	–
Office Supplies	50	50	50	50	50	50	50	50	50	50	50	50
Trash Removal	29	29	29	29	29	29	29	29	29	29	29	29
Association Dues	940	–	–	–	–	–	–	–	–	–	–	–
Satellite Dish	42	42	42	42	42	42	42	42	42	42	42	42
Fire Extinguisher Service	155	–	–	–	–	–	–	–	–	–	–	–
Janitorial Supplies	60	60	60	60	60	60	60	60	60	60	60	60
Kart Maintenance	900	900	900	900	900	900	900	900	900	900	900	900
ADT–Security Monitoring	30	30	30	30	30	30	30	30	30	30	30	30
Web Page Design/Maintenance	35	35	35	35	35	35	35	35	35	35	35	35
Web Page Hosting	17	17	17	17	17	17	17	17	17	17	17	17
Maintenance	500	500	500	500	500	500	500	500	500	500	500	500
Interest Expense	6,061	6,048	6,036	6,023	6,010	5,998	5,985	5,972	5,959	5,946	5,932	5,919
Property Tax	4,897	4,897	4,897	4,897	4,897	4,897	4,897	4,897	4,897	4,897	4,897	4,897
Depreciation	9,404	9,404	9,404	9,404	9,404	9,404	9,404	9,404	9,404	9,404	9,404	9,404
Yellow Pages	144	144	144	144	144	144	144	144	144	144	144	144
Total Fixed Costs	108,788	101,451	102,579	110,784	101,884	99,856	107,656	99,665	101,362	110,118	103,055	102,303

(continued)

	2003			2004								
	October	November	December	January	February	March	April	May	June	July	August	September
Variable Costs												
Cost of Goods Sold	11,827	12,328	20,391	13,444	20,999	17,897	12,892	20,445	11,975	9,129	21,950	20,541
Propane	793	967	1,229	1,048	1,359	1,200	1,028	1,157	948	629	1,400	1,178
Promotional Materials	1,137	569	171	9,505	343	153	1,562	180	560	9,216	406	352
Licenses—1st time customers	694	694	1,158	810	1,389	1,042	810	1,158	694	579	1,389	1,158
CC Service Charge	308	308	503	356	601	454	356	503	308	259	601	503
Discount	1,267	1,637	1,914	1,567	1,987	1,891	1,590	1,912	1,303	1,009	2,137	1,987
Charitable Contributions	–	–	1,250	–	–	1,250	–	–	1,250	–	–	1,250
Tax Distribution to Shareholders	–	–	10,301	–	20,854	15,399	3,318	25,012	4,109	–	18,965	29,569
Radio	6,000	–	–	6,000	–	–	6,000	–	–	6,000	–	–
Newspaper	360	155	155	155	155	155	155	886	155	155	886	886
Total Variable Costs	22,386	16,658	37,072	32,885	47,687	39,441	27,711	51,253	21,302	26,976	47,734	57,424
Total Costs (Fixed + Variable)	131,174	118,109	139,651	143,669	149,571	139,297	135,367	150,918	122,664	137,094	150,789	159,727
Sales												
Total Sales	$124,467	$130,597	$209,705	$139,229	$201,583	$174,840	$141,797	$208,573	$130,647	$93,680	$235,194	$226,935

(continued)

Break-Even Analysis

Fixed Costs	2004			2005								
	October	November	December	January	February	March	April	May	June	July	August	September
Salary	$17,500	$13,999	$17,500	$14,575	$13,999	$13,999	$17,500	$13,999	$13,999	$17,500	$14,230	$14,230
Wages	18,000	14,400	18,000	14,400	14,400	14,400	18,000	14,400	14,400	18,000	14,400	14,400
Payroll Tax—Salary	1,339	1,071	1,339	1,581	1,561	1,296	1,339	1,071	1,071	1,339	1,089	1,089
Payroll Tax—Wages	2,007	1,606	2,007	1,606	1,606	1,606	2,007	1,606	1,606	2,007	1,606	1,606
Rent	37,350	37,350	37,350	37,350	37,350	37,350	37,350	37,350	37,350	37,350	37,350	37,350
Insurance	8,902	8,902	8,902	8,902	8,902	8,902	8,902	8,902	8,902	8,902	8,902	8,902
Utilities	2,280	3,990	5,130	5,130	3,990	2,280	2,280	2,280	3,990	5,130	5,130	3,990
Telephone	66	66	66	66	66	66	66	66	66	66	66	66
Legal/Accounting Fees	450	450	450	450	450	450	800	450	450	450	450	450
Copier Rental	60	60	60	60	60	60	60	60	60	60	60	60
Copier Service Fee	295	–	–	–	–	–	–	–	–	–	–	–
Office Supplies	50	50	50	50	50	50	50	50	50	50	50	50
Trash Removal	29	29	29	29	29	29	29	29	29	29	29	29
Association Dues	940	–	–	–	–	–	–	–	–	–	–	–
Satellite Dish	42	42	42	42	42	42	42	42	42	42	42	42
Fire Extinguisher Service	155	–	–	–	–	–	–	–	–	–	–	–
Janitorial Supplies	60	60	60	60	60	60	60	60	60	60	60	60
Kart Maintenance	10,125	900	900	900	900	900	900	900	900	900	900	900
ADT—Security Monitoring	30	30	30	30	30	30	30	30	30	30	30	30
Web Page Design/Maintenance	35	35	35	35	35	35	35	35	35	35	35	35
Web Page Hosting	17	17	17	17	17	17	17	17	17	17	17	17
Maintenance	500	500	500	500	500	500	500	500	500	500	500	500
Interest Expense	5,906	5,892	5,879	5,865	5,852	5,838	5,824	5,810	5,796	5,782	5,768	5,753
Property Tax	4,768	4,768	4,768	4,768	4,768	4,768	4,768	4,768	4,768	4,768	4,768	4,768
Depreciation	9,404	9,404	9,404	9,404	9,404	9,404	9,404	9,404	9,404	9,404	9,404	9,404
Yellow Pages	144	144	144	144	144	144	144	144	144	144	144	144
Total Fixed Costs	120,454	103,765	112,662	105,964	104,215	102,226	110,107	101,973	103,669	112,565	105,030	103,875

(continued)

Variable Costs	2004			2005								
	October	November	December	January	February	March	April	May	June	July	August	September
Cost of Goods Sold	18,292	16,142	25,445	19,097	27,049	23,032	15,998	24,967	13,692	13,617	27,698	24,378
Propane	1,145	1,403	1,685	1,426	1,940	1,641	1,478	1,645	1,288	935	2,063	1,674
Promotional Materials	1,531	605	198	12,483	397	225	1,956	189	587	12,176	243	569
Licenses—1st time customers	894	894	1,489	1,042	1,786	1,340	1,042	1,489	894	746	1,786	1,489
CC Service Charge	392	392	644	455	770	581	455	644	392	329	770	644
Discount	1,842	2,013	2,540	2,015	2,562	2,330	1,921	2,401	1,587	1,405	2,747	2,498
Charitable Contributions	–	–	2,500	–	–	2,500	–	–	2,500	–	–	2,500
Tax Distribution to Shareholders	11,857	23,456	32,048	16,983	35,158	30,577	16,707	31,861	11,501	–	39,443	33,357
Radio	6,000	–	–	6,000	–	–	6,000	–	–	6,000	–	–
Newspaper	360	155	155	155	155	155	155	886	155	155	886	886
Total Variable Costs	42,313	45,060	66,704	59,656	69,817	62,381	45,712	64,082	32,596	35,363	75,636	67,995
Total Costs (Fixed + Variable)	162,767	148,825	179,366	165,620	174,032	164,607	155,819	166,055	136,265	147,928	180,666	171,870
Sales												
Total Sales	$188,137	$170,892	$259,627	$194,260	$264,444	$219,978	$178,825	$263,182	$146,902	$143,455	$299,864	$278,977

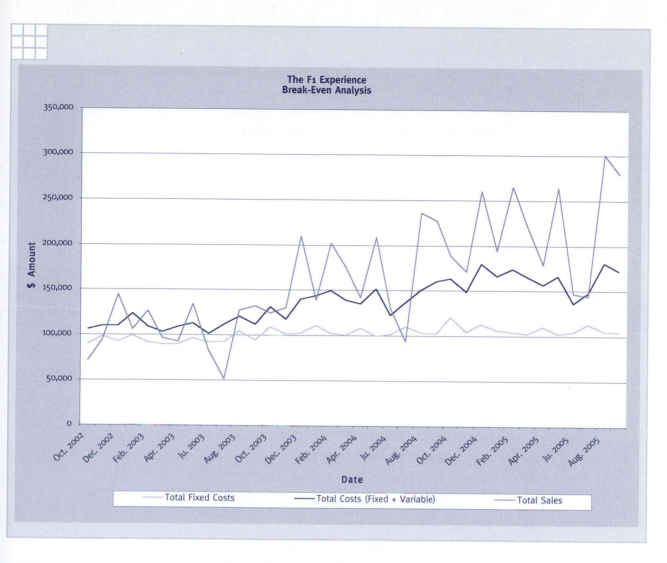

The F1 Experience
Break-Even Analysis

Legend: Total Fixed Costs · Total Costs (Fixed + Variable) · Total Sales

Critical Analysis for Students

This complete business plan was prepared and presented for potential funding. How would you evaluate the value of this business plan if you were a funding source? Using Table 11.4 from Chapter 11, (Business Plan Assessment: Complete Evaluation of Each Component), prepare a thorough analysis of each segment and then a final grade for this plan. This case study exercise is unique in that students are able to gain experience in evaluating a business plan before ever attempting to develop a plan of their own.

Notes

1. Sarah Sturmon Dale, "Go-Karting for Executives," *Time* (July 30, 2001).

2. "Retailing Specialty," Standard & Poor's Industry Survey (July 26, 2001).

3. Ibid.

4. "The History of Indoor Karting," http://www.karting.co.nz/indoorgrandprix/historykart/.

5. "Amusement Technology Management," http://www.e-kmi.com (February 1999).

6. Ibid.

7. Ibid.

8. Interview with Fred Marlk, NAKA (February 2, 2002).

9. Interview with Anthony Peterson, NIKA (February 5, 2002).

10. Dick Valentine, Indoor Kart Racing Conference, 2002 International Karting Expo (February 24, 2002).

11. http://www.Zapdata.com.

12. Anthony Schoettle, "Union Station as a Racing Venue?" *Indianapolis Business Journal* (November 15, 1999).

13. Darrell Sitarz, "Now That I Have Your Attention," http://www.e-kmi.com (February 1, 2001).

14. Bob Cycon, "Indoor Kart Racing," *Inside Info* (January 1, 2001).

15. Schoettle, "Union Station as a Racing Venue?"

16. Doug Sword, "Vibration at Station gets the Green Flag," *Indianapolis Star* (February 10, 2001).

17. Sturmon Dale, "Go-Karting for Executives."

18. Interview with Diane Whitsitt, Indiana Convention and Visitors Association (February 4, 2002).

19. "Special Events and Conventions," http://www.indy.org.

20. Ibid.

21. "Indy Motorforce," The Indy Partnership, http://www.indypartnership.com.

22. Michael Evans and Barry Barovick, *The Ernst & Young Almanac and Guide to U.S. Businesses and Cities* (Dallas, TX: Ernst & Young, 1994).

23. "Census 2000 Supplementary Survey," U.S. Census, http://www.census.gov.

24. The Associated Press, "Census Shows a Wide Gap Between Rich and Poor Counties," *The Star Press* (January 14, 2002).

25. Interview with John Combs, Racers (February 8, 2002).

26. Interview with Jennifer Stark, Simon Properties (March 19, 2002).

27. Interview with Matt Dibble, Technical Director, G&G Oil (January 29, 2002).

28. Interview with John Combs, Racers (February 8, 2002).

29. Quote from Vronda Cox, Ameritech representative.

30. Quote from WFMS representative.

31. Quote from Indianapolis Star representative.

32. Quote from Ameritech representative.

33. Quote from Dana Bishop, Republic Trash Services representative.

34. Quote from Indianapolis Chamber of Commerce representative.

35. Quote from Circuit City representative.

36. Quote from Don Workman, Koorsen Protective Services representative.

37. Quote from Martin Knowles, ROC Timing representative.

38. Quote from Washington Township Assessor representative.

39. Quote from Stacy Lunsford, Action Performance—Charlotte representative.

40. Quote from Buyer's Wholesale Distributors.

41. Quote from Robert McGuffey, owner of Entertainment Architecture.

42. Quote from Martin Knowles, ROC Timing representative.

43. Quote from Vic Hollman, Bowman Karts representative.

44. Quote from Gary Sparks, Milestone Construction representative.

45. Quote from Vic Hollman, Bowman Karts representative.

46. Quote from Max Tyler, RG Racewear representative.

47. Quote from Steve McVicker, Sign Craft Incorporated representative.

48. Quote from Don Workman, Koorsen Protective Services representative.

Part 3

CommunityWeb.com—

An Internet Firm's Effort to Survive

Introduction

Dan Pale, a 30-year-old CEO of an Internet start-up company, CommunityWeb.com, was faced with the most important decision of his business career. After more than a year of operation that was funded with approximately $1.6 million in start-up capital, his company was experiencing difficult times. Pale and cofounder, Jim Mack, were faced with some tough decisions. A lack of cash flow to the business coupled with rapidly increasing debt were causing mounting financial pressures. Potential legal problems were also on the horizon. Sitting at his desk on June 8, 2001, Pale now ponders a decision to sign a funding agreement with Wall Street Venture Capital.

Formation of the Initial Business Concept—CommunityWeb.com

Dan Pale had talked about and researched the idea of a localized Internet portal for many months. In the fall of 1999, Pale, determined that the idea seemed technologically feasible, visited Jim Mack, owner of a financial planning firm in Seymour, Indiana. After three meetings Mack agreed to join the venture. They contacted the Information and Communication Sciences' Applied Research Institute at Ball State University to conduct further research on the concept. In March 2000, CommunityWeb, Inc., was officially established. Jim Mack served as the CEO and chairman of the board of directors while Dan Pale served as the president/COO.

The basic idea behind the business concept was to localize the Internet. This would be done through a website that would allow users to narrow information found on the web to a localized and specific geographic area. In turn, the website would then generate advertisements specific to the same geographic area from where the user had originated his or her visit. The idea was to contain these capabilities within one national website. This site would also give users the ability to interact by posting stories about local sporting and news events.

Building the Organization and Its Product

Dan Pale recruited and hired a talented, young team at CommunityWeb. For several months employees mined and categorized an extensive database of URLs and built a model for taking CommunityWeb.com to market. The firm used in-house software to locate, capture, and categorize these website addresses. Pale and Mack planned to take their concept of localized Internet utilization to market via franchising. Franchisees would buy the rights to sell CommunityWeb.com advertising (banner ads, e-mail marketing, pop-up ads) to specific territories. Each franchise would sell for $35,000 and would cover a geographic region populated by approximately 100,000 people. Pale and Mack expected to use the franchise fees to fund CommunityWeb's further growth. The company planned on retaining ownership of the 50 largest metropolitan markets in the United States.

Jim Mack and Dan Pale initially estimated that the company would need $2 million in start-up equity. Raising this amount of money as an Internet start-up, especially in a small, midwestern city, was not an easy task. Jim Mack tapped his extensive base of financial planning clients and raised nearly all of the company's angel capital. However, the fundraising efforts proved to be quite costly. A great deal of money was spent promoting CommunityWeb to potential investors. The amount contributed by each investor averaged between $25,000 and $50,000. By mid-January 2001, the company had raised $1.6 million of its original $2 million target but had sold only two franchises. Pale and Mack developed the company's business plan for the sole purpose of attracting investors (see Appendix). CommunityWeb's business model and the projected financial forecasts seemed to change on a near-weekly basis, making it difficult to constantly update the business plan. Very few changes were ever made to the firm's original business plan. As the business model began to change, financial projections were hastily adapted, and the business plan was never adjusted accordingly. The firm's first set of pro forma financial statements estimated that revenues would exceed $1 billion within two years. After consulting venture capital firms and other dot-com businesses that had already been in operation, CommunityWeb reduced its estimations to a more conservative figure. The projected third-year revenues would be just over $160 million. The company's June 2001 projected financial statements business plan addendum shows the earnings estimates too had been scaled back even further (see Table 1).

Because the firm's historical financial statements had not been audited, communication with potential institutional investors and venture capitalists was difficult.

There was also the issue that Jim Mack never registered the distribution of equities for private placement with the Securities and Exchange Commission (SEC). Therefore, the

Table 1 Financial Projections CommunityWeb, Inc.

PROJECTED PROFIT AND LOSS 2002–2004

INCOME STATEMENT	2002	2003	2004
Sales	$1,761,201.00	$7,508,323.00	$26,240,359.00
Direct Cost of Sales	$1,190,785.00	$5,508,538.00	$ 8,817,481.00
Other	—	—	—
Total Cost of Sales	$1,190,785.00	$5,508,538.00	$ 8,817,481.00
Gross Margin	$ 570,416.00	$1,999,785.00	$17,422,878.00
Gross Margin %	32.39%	26.63%	66.40%
Operating Expenses			
Accountant Fees	$ 2,400.00	$ 2,700.00	$ 3,000.00
Attorney Fees	12,000.00	12,300.00	12,600.00
Commissions or Referrals	111,322.80	386,265.00	597,412.50
Equipment Leases	67,608.00	67,608.00	67,608.00
Insurance—General Liability, WC, etc.	1,344.00	1,644.00	1,944.00
Insurance—Auto	2,208.00	2,508.00	2,808.00
Internet Connection	4,254.00	4,554.00	4,854.00
Web Hosting and Security	24,000.00	24,300.00	24,600.00
Advertising/Marketing	18,250.00	75,083.00	93,854.04
Miscellaneous	6,000.00	6,300.00	6,600.00
Office Supplies	6,000.00	6,300.00	6,600.00

Table 1   (Continued)

INCOME STATEMENT	PROJECTED PROFIT AND LOSS 2002–2004		
	2002	2003	2004
Professional Dev./Subscription/ Membership Fees	2,400.00	2,700.00	3,000.00
Payroll	568,795.02	812,557.50	934,441.13
Payroll Burden	170,069.71	243,767.25	280,332.34
Rent	22,200.00	22,200.00	22,200.00
Telephone	21,600.00	22,680.00	23,760.00
Trade Shows	6,000.00	6,300.00	6,600.00
Travel	4,250.00	4,550.00	4,850.00
Utilities	6,000.00	6,300.00	6,600.00
Total Overhead	$1,056,701.53	$1,710,616.75	$ 2,103,664.01
Total Operating Expense	$2,247,486.53	$7,219,154.75	$10,921,145.01
Profit before Interest and Taxes	$ (486,285.53)	$ 289,168.25	$15,319,213.99
Interest Expense (Short-term)	—	—	—
Interest Expense (Long-term)	—	—	—
Taxes Incurred	0	0	4,940,000.00
Net Profit	$ (486,286.00)	$ 289,168.00	$10,379,213.99

legality of these securities could be in question. (The SEC provides Regulation D for selling stock to private parties. Rules 504a, 504, 505, and 506 cover the specific requirements.)

The Founders and the Management Team

Dan Pale's business career began at age 23 when he founded a clothing store that quickly grew to more than $1.2 million in annual sales. Pale was also co-owner of his family's business, a True Value hardware store and Just Ask Rental Center. In 1998, he repositioned himself in telecommunications and took over management of WKBY-AM talk radio in Seymour, Indiana. In less than two years, he increased the station's revenue by 600 percent. He also helped position WKBY as the largest talk-format station in southern Indiana. He served in a management role in Indiana Regional Radio Partners, Inc., through April 2000.

Jim Mack was a certified financial planner and registered financial consultant. He had 13 years experience in the financial services industry. He was cofounder and president of the Financial Investors Group based in Seymour, Indiana, and had clients in 17 states. Mack hosted a weekly radio program at WKBY and was a contributor to *The Roaring 2000's Investor's Guide*, one of *The New York Times* business best sellers. He also served on the advisory board of the H. S. Dent Foundation and was a noted speaker in areas of business development and fundamental economic trends.

The rest of the management team was very young and energetic. Most of the team members were recent college graduates. The following were the original management team at CommunityWeb and their credentials as of spring 2001:[1]

Jeffrey Lehm

Director of Database Development and Technology
Lehm left his position as Computer Information Systems Regional Program Chair for Ivy Tech State College in Seymour, Indiana, to join CommunityWeb.

Michael Hunt

Chief Information Officer
Hunt completed his master's degree in Information and Communication Sciences from Ball State University in December 2000.

Jonathan Lester

Director of Communications
Lester earned degrees in both advertising and marketing from Ball State University and is currently completing a master's degree in Public Relations.

Tony Baker

Director of Franchise Sales and Business Development
Baker was the director of marketing for the largest franchise of BD's Mongolian Barbecue restaurants.

Jim McDuffy

Director of Special Markets
McDuffy had over ten years of management experience in various business environments ranging from the entertainment industry to web development.

John Taylor

Director of Wireless Strategies/Research and Development
Taylor received his bachelor of arts in Marketing from Ball State University with a double minor in Japanese and Asian Studies. He was also pursuing a master's degree in Information and Communication Sciences.

Troy Simon

Director of Indianapolis Operations
Simon completed his master's degree in Information and Communication Sciences from Ball State University in 1998. Simon then served as a business development representative at Intelliseek, a leading provider in personalized Internet services.

Business, Industry, and Economic Conditions

The Internet had a significant impact on the global business climate between 1999 and 2001. By 2001, there were more than 160 million Internet users worldwide, and they were beginning to spend a significant amount of time online, averaging over 18 hours connected monthly. Internet retailing had also become a dominant business force in the American economy, as monthly Internet spending was approaching $4 billion, averaging $270 per consumer.[2]

The economic conditions during 2001 made it difficult for growing businesses, especially Internet-based, to obtain funding. The Internet boom of 1999 and 2000, where Internet companies received equity investment at alarming rates, was definitely a thing of the past. Many venture capitalists had gone back to basic business fundamentals, and only considered firms with sound business models and solid business plans. In addition, private investors were becoming more cautious because of the recent plunge ("tech wreck") of the Nasdaq stock market (see Figure 1).

Figure 1 Nasdaq Composite

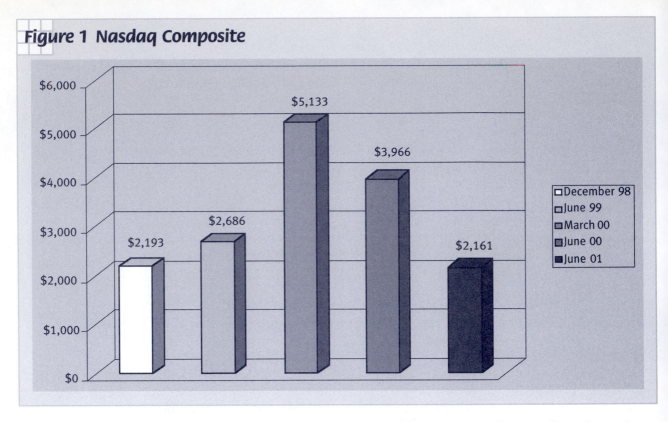

The Nasdaq composite peaked at a value of $5,133 in March 2000. Since that point, the Nasdaq composite value had declined to its June 2001 level of $2,161.[3] According to emarketer.com, over 555 Internet businesses worldwide closed in the first half of 2001.

Internet firms such as Citysearch.com, localbusiness.com, and cityworks.com, among others, began to make major cutbacks or ceased operations. Double Click, the largest online ad broker, continued to lose more than $100 million per quarter. In addition, most companies, including dot-coms, were cutting their advertising budgets across the board. Competitive Media Reporting estimated that 2001 advertising spending across all media would fall more than $102.4 billion from 2000 levels.[4] While there still seemed to be interest in specialized and localized Internet ads, many industry factors were causing negative pressures on ad revenue–based business models. According to John Groth, CEO of BeaconVentureCapital (Bethesda, Maryland), the capital markets were not looking favorably on firms with the majority of revenues coming from Internet advertising sales.

The Competitive Landscape

By June 2001, CommunityWeb faced competition from firms such as DigitalCity.com, OneMain.com, MyCity.com, Yahoo! Get Local, Visionvibes.com, Wowtown.com, URL-Surfer.com, Citysearch.com, megago.com, move.com, busyreceptionist.com, usaonline.com, switchboard.com, relocationcentral.com, MyWay.com, and numerous yellow pages websites, among others. CommunityWeb believed, however, that none of these sites truly provided local information across the nation. They contended that these sites were geared toward larger cities or were restricted to very small regions. Thus, CommunityWeb never viewed any of these competitors as major threats to the success of its business model. DigitalCity.com and Citysearch.com, however, were engaged in significant national advertising campaigns and had developed the greatest name recognition among localized Internet sites. CommunityWeb considered its main competitors to be local newspapers and radio stations. The firm saw these traditional media forms as its greatest rivals.

CommunityWeb.com in Operation

The CommunityWeb.com website was officially launched on January 28, 2001. Visitors to the site could read and post local news and sports stories, check the local weather forecast, and search for URLs (Uniform Resource Locators, or website addresses) tailored to specific locales and business categories. The URL searches used Community-Web's tool and its database, which by April 2001 included more than 200,000 URLs.

During the first few months of 2001, CommunityWeb was able to establish partnerships and alliances with several strong companies such as AT&T, Infospace.com, and Hargiss Communication. CommunityWeb, however, soon realized that many of these partners did not fit into its vision and broke all ties with most of these partners to pursue other partnerships with companies like LocaLine and valupage.com.

CommunityWeb continued to struggle to get its business concept off the ground. Tony Baker, the person hired as director of franchise sales, had managed to sell just two franchises, leaving Dan Pale and Jim Mack contemplating their next move. They were faced with the immediate need to generate positive cash flow within the next two to three months.

CommunityWeb's workforce had peaked to approximately 175 employees in March 2001, causing the company to incur over $200,000 of payroll expenses. Pale and Mack had expected to sign more than 100 franchisees in the first year, but their efforts produced only failed prospects. Running short of funds in April 2001 they imposed major cutbacks, leaving only 15 key employees and a monthly expenditure of about $75,000 (see Table 2). Pale and Mack saw these cuts as a necessary move to keep their firm

Table 2   Summary Financial Information as Provided by Management

	MARCH 2001	APRIL 2001
Professional and consulting fees	$ 9,500	$ 2,000
Equipment lease and depreciation	19,000	3,000
Software/Connectivity/Hosting	35,000	–
Employee/Payroll expenses:		
CEO—Mack	10,000	6,250
President—Pale	10,000	5,000
Staff—Other	142,500	25,850
Contract labor—Mining	20,000	–
Taxes	14,300	3,265
Training	10,000	–
Other	2,600	2,500
Employee/Payroll expenses—total	209,400	42,865
Marketing expenses	20,050	5,000
Rent/Utilities	3,655	2,100
Website maintenance/design	14,000	13,000
Office supplies	4,000	3,100
Interest/Other	5,400	4,400
Total expenses	$320,005	$75,465

Table 3   Timeline of Critical Events

- ☐ **January–February 2000**—Dan Pale researches the possibility of localizing the Internet.

- ☐ **February 2000**—Pale meets with Jim Mack of the Financial Investors Group to discuss the possibility of building a localized Internet portal.

- ☐ **March 2000**—Mack and Pale agree to start the business, which they name CommunityWeb. They incorporate as a C corporation and begin staffing the company.

- ☐ **April 2000–January 2001**—The large staff of "miners" collect and capture a comprehensive database of URLs.

- ☐ **January 28, 2001**—The website, http://www.CommunityWeb.com, is officially launched.

- ☐ **February–May 2001**—CommunityWeb management worked on developing business relationships that would strengthen its position in the marketplace. The firm also worked on raising equity and selling franchises.

- ☐ **April 2001**—Due to mounting financial pressures, Mack is forced to make major cutbacks in workforce and expenditures.

- ☐ **May 2001**—CommunityWeb changes its business model to sell its Website tools to ISPs. The firm discontinued the use of its URL database. Mack steps down as CEO and chairman of the board, while Pale takes over as CEO. Mack remains on the board of directors.

- ☐ **June 2001**—CommunityWeb considers entering a deal with Wall Street Venture Capital of New York.

alive. With no incoming revenue, mounting debt, and a failing business model, they began to panic and felt the cutbacks across the board were their only option.

At this point CommunityWeb had abandoned its original business plan and now focused on selling its website tools to ISPs (Internet service providers). They believed CommunityWeb's tools could be used by the ISPs in their default browsers and portals (gateways). CommunityWeb would become their provider of local information and their "face" to users. However, the firm was forced to drop its URL database from its set of tools offered to ISPs, due to significant technical errors which reduced both the effectiveness and size (reduced to under 40,000 URLs) of the database. This was a major setback to CommunityWeb, but the company just did not have the financial resources needed to fix the database errors (see Table 3 for a timeline of critical events). To generate additional revenues CommunityWeb also introduced a web development division to its business. In addition, the company also attempted to market itself as an ISP.

■ Mounting Financial Pressure and Internal Conflict

Jim Mack and Dan Pale recognized their financial crisis. They believed CommunityWeb had only a few months to establish a positive cash flow. Mack planned to continue raising funds through his client base and personal network while Pale and his staff feverishly marketed their new business model to ISPs. Capital markets had become tighter and Mack seemingly had exhausted his personal resources. By the end of April 2001, Mack and Pale resorted to "bootstrapping" for short-term financing, pushing several of their own credit cards to their limits, delaying payments to most of the company's creditors, and falling more than $200,000 behind in remitting payroll taxes and employee withholdings to the IRS. The company had also accrued other debts in excess of $1 million (see Table 4). Pale and Mack's personal debt had grown to over $300,000. Employees also started to feel the pinch of the firm's cash flow problems as the issuance of paychecks was often delayed by as much as three to four weeks.

Amid the financial pressures, personal conflicts arose between Mack and the employees. Mack was often criticized for being too controlling. Key management personnel had questioned his desire to make all of the company's strategic decisions. Because of Mack's constant changing of the business model, employees rarely knew the "latest" direction of the company. Conflict between Mack and Pale also began to surface. Mack and Pale often did not see "eye to eye" on strategic or financial issues. Pale felt as though Mack, the CEO, was taking control over the daily activities, which Pale considered his job as president and COO. In May 2001, due to the mounting conflicts and Mack's apparent mismanagement of the company, the board of directors removed Jim Mack as CEO and chairman of the board and appointed Pale as his replacement. Mack would remain on the board of directors, but would relinquish all day-to-day operations of the company to Dan Pale. Mack maintained his role in raising capital for the company.

Table 4   Balance Sheet—Fiscal Year Ending February 2002

ASSETS		
Current Assets		
Checking Account	$ 41.09	
Expense Account	237.11	
Client Fees Receivable	904.94	
Investments	50,000.00	
Total Current Assets		$ 51,183.14
Property and Equipment		
Furniture and Fixtures	$ 21,804.26	
Computer Equipment	257,960.30	
Leasehold Improvements	19,275.25	
Accum. Depreciation—Furniture	(7,014.80)	
Accum. Depreciation—Computer Equipment	(112,411.33)	
Accum. Depreciation—Leasehold	(6,203.74)	
Total Property and Equipment		$173,409.94
Total Assets		$224,593.08

Table 4 (Continued)

LIABILITIES AND CAPITAL

Current Liabilities

Accounts Payable	$ 355,748.64	
Deductions Payable	785.71	
Federal Payroll Taxes Payable	266,406.50	
FUTA Tax Payable	4,450.64	
State Payroll Taxes Payable	32,715.16	
SUTA Payable	8,907.29	
Local Payroll Taxes Payable	7,630.73	
Employee Benefits Payable	18,705.47	
Total Current Liabilities		$ 695,350.14

Long-term Liabilities

Loan from Shareholder—Dan Pale	$ 304,929.20	
Loan from Shareholder—Jim Mack	68,500.00	
Long-term Liabilities		$ 373,429.20
Total Liabilities		$1,068,779.34

Capital

Treasury Stock	$ (7,545.00)	
Paid-In Capital	1,892,008.68	
Retained Earnings	(1,017,263.51)	
Net Income	(1,711,386.43)	
Total Capital		$(844,186.26)
Total Liabilities and Capital		$ 224,593.08

The Wall Street Venture Capital Deal

Over the past several months of funding efforts, Mack and Pale had been working on developing a relationship with a relatively unknown firm named Wall Street Venture Capital from New York City. In June 2001, Pale and Mack capitalized on an invitation to present their business model to this venture capital firm. After seeing their presentation, Wall Street Venture Capital agreed to raise funding for CommunityWeb through a partnership. If CommunityWeb accepted the agreement, Wall Street Venture Capital would acquire 30 percent equity of the company, and CommunityWeb would be charged a $20,000 commitment fee. CommunityWeb would then be limited to raising an additional $500,000 outside of Wall Street Venture Capital over the next six months to fund current operations. Wall Street Venture Capital would agree to raise $5 million for CommunityWeb within six months, as well as position the firm for a buyout. CommunityWeb would also be able to use its relationship with Wall Street Venture Capital as leverage in meeting financial obligations to current investors and for forming new partnerships.

For almost two months Jim Mack and Dan Pale attempted to investigate the viability of this New York–based venture capital firm. However, as of June 2001, Mack and Pale had been unable to establish whether or not Wall Street Venture Capital had a proven track record with multimillion-dollar start-up investing. Any information on the firm was hard to obtain. As an example, its website was not functional and the New York Chamber of Commerce did not have any information on the firm. When Mack and Pale asked the president of Wall Street Venture Capital, Joseph McElroys, to give documentation of the firm's successfully funded projects, the response was that most of Wall Street's deals were international and documentation was not readily available.

The Dilemma

Dan Pale now faces his toughest decision as CEO of CommunityWeb. He has the mounting pressures of sinking deeper and deeper into debt, risking more and more invested capital, and facing the legal issues associated with the debt to the IRS and the improper sale of securities. Pale is seriously considering entering the agreement with Wall Street Venture Capital. The following issues plague Pale as he considers his next move.

☐ *Federal Tax Liability*—The company owes the Internal Revenue Service an amount in excess of $200,000. The company has filed with the IRS form 656 "Offer in Compromise" to settle this debt. There is no assurance that the IRS will accept this offer in compromise. The IRS may counteroffer or reject the offer completely. In this case, CommunityWeb may not have sufficient funds to pay the delinquent taxes, interest, and any penalties. Furthermore, the IRS can even foreclose on the company's assets if it chooses.

☐ *Indiana State Tax Liability*—The company owes the state of Indiana an amount in excess of $20,000. The company has entered into a payment agreement with the State of Indiana on this debt. If the company fails to make the required payments to the State of Indiana, the Indiana Department of Revenue could foreclose on the company's assets.

☐ *Securities Violations*—The company has previously sold investments in the company in excess of $1.6 million. The sale of these securities may not have been in compliance with all federal and state securities laws. They face the probability that a rescission offer would be made to all purchasers and that an action could be filed by the securities regulatory agencies. In addition, the company's officers could possibly face criminal charges for these SEC violations.

☐ *Failure to Make a Profit*—The company, since its inception in 2000, has been primarily involved in the research and development of its Internet technology and has had no chance of developing revenues. Currently the company has not made a profit and there is no future assurance it ever will. The company is operating with a "burn rate" (a popular term used to denote expenditures without sufficient revenue to at least approach a break-even point) and has yet to establish a working business model that can successfully show a profit. Much of the initial $1.6 million of raised capital was spent on developing the URL database, marketing franchises to potential buyers, and for attracting potential investors.

Dan Pale needs to make a move to save his company. Taking into account all of these issues, the agreement with Wall Street Venture Capital may be the best choice—or is it?

■ Notes

1. See Appendix for more detailed management biographies.

2. http://www.clickz.com/stats/.

3. www.nasdaq.com.

4. http://www.emarketer.com.

APPENDIX: BUSINESS PLAN

Executive Summary

CommunityWeb, Inc. is the Internet with local flavor and a personal touch. With CommunityWeb's unique search technology and full range of connectivity and other web-related solutions, it enables businesses, nonprofit organizations, and individuals to interact in a specific geographic locale via the Internet. People who use the CommunityWeb portal to search CommunityWeb's website database find content that is most relevant to them, from news and sports scores to classified ads and even a community calendar. The free, simple search process is based on the individual needs of each end user, which allows them to search for information, goods, and services in their hometown or almost any specific area without wading through the useless links that traditional search engines yield as results.

While optimizing localized web searches for private citizens, CommunityWeb provides area businesses the same luxury for specific geographic areas. A business knows with reasonable certainty that someone who searches a specific location either lives in that community or plans to visit it. CommunityWeb enables businesses of all sizes to participate in Internet advertising. CommunityWeb's dynamic one-to-one marketing enables businesses to market toward specific geographic areas as well as to specific age groups, income ranges, and interests. To motivate end users to register, CommunityWeb offers them the free Local Rewards program. Registered members earn points for visiting local advertisers' sites. They can then redeem accumulated points for services and merchandise, or donate them to a local charity. Becoming a member is simple and free; in less than one minute, a user can join by providing basic geographic, demographic, and psychographic information. For example, a user may like music but have no interest in apparel. Businesses spend over $2 billion per quarter on marketing on the World Wide Web, but they collect little to no information about end users. Local Rewards addresses that issue. CommunityWeb's Local Rewards program demonstrates yet another way CommunityWeb provides a win-win scenario for businesses and residents of communities it services.

CommunityWeb provides a human approach to the Internet. Through its franchise model, CommunityWeb will place community coordinators around the country in communities of all sizes. This provides a name and a face for people to call upon when things get confusing and technology changes, as it always does. CommunityWeb brings the Internet together for the individual and the community. CommunityWeb provides a customized browser that carries its name, Internet services from dial-up to high-speed connectivity solutions (through an alliance with AT&T), and web design, hosting, and other related services (from alliances with various web-design firms).

Many companies have attempted to enter local communities from an Internet perspective. More than 20 companies have succeeded in tier-one cities that are defined as *metropolitan statistical areas* (MSAs). MSAs contain over 1 million residents each and represent more than one-third of the American population in 42 distinct areas. Companies venturing into tier-two and tier-three markets have failed from a global perspective. Individual community sites exist in these markets, but without continuity, they do nothing for commerce or community development in their respective areas.

Source: Prepared by the Management at CommunityWeb, January 2001.

CommunityWeb is the platform that combines these communities, serving as the cord that provides individuality while binding communities together to provide true business relevance. CommunityWeb plans to corporately maintain these MSA market operations, but will focus on initially proving its product through fully operational corporately owned test markets. CommunityWeb has partially funded the Indianapolis MSA as a test market and is seeking funding to start one corporately owned mid-market franchise each month, which started in April 2001.

CommunityWeb's success depends upon a loyal number of users and massive name brand recognition. CommunityWeb will employ three immediate strategies to gather these members and create product awareness. All three of these models provide built-in loyalty of membership as well as the opportunity for quick-start franchises. CommunityWeb will also allow select entrepreneurs to acquire franchise rights.

CommunityWeb will continue to franchise the business model in small-to-midsize markets nationwide. Franchisees can come from four different business backgrounds: (1) companies currently providing Internet service on a more local and/or regional basis; (2) traditional media outlets that have built-in membership loyalty that provides a profitable alliance for both the company and CommunityWeb; (3) companies currently involved in website design; and (4) existing "specific community" websites with an identifiable user base.

CommunityWeb's main attack toward the franchise marketplace is through regional Internet service providers (ISPs). CommunityWeb has found in its preliminary research that there are over 600 regional ISPs in the Midwest that have less than 50,000 subscribers. CommunityWeb has also found that this will add very little to its current cost structure. These ISPs generally have somewhere around 5,000 subscribers, but they typically only generate approximately $2 per month toward their bottom line per customer. Community-Web's offer to these ISPs is simple: CommunityWeb will provide them with a Community-Web franchise in exchange for their conversion to the CommunityWeb system. This includes automatically registering their subscribers as CommunityWeb.com memberships, converting their subscribers' accounts to the CommunityWeb/AT&T virtual ISP, and selling CommunityWeb.com advertising in their markets. CommunityWeb has contacted over fifty of these ISPs in Indiana alone and has gotten appointments with nearly all of them.

CommunityWeb is designed to be profitable by August 2001 and remain that way. The company uses Internet technology but is truly an interactive communications company focusing on dynamic one-to-one marketing.

Based on current Internet standards for usage and advertising, CommunityWeb can generate $15.60 per month per member. The business model and current plan calls for $2 million of initial investment with a positive cash flow of over $17 million in the second year of operations.

CommunityWeb has also recently seen the value of its unique URL database come to fruition. The database is proving to be highly marketable to thousands of websites at a monthly licensing fee of anywhere from $500 to $5,000.

CommunityWeb has over 35 potential franchisees and has raised over $1,400,000. CommunityWeb is currently seeking an additional $600,000 in first-round funding and another $2 million in bridge financing. CommunityWeb is currently offering shares at $4 per share with the minimum investment of $25,000. That investment represents 6,250 voting-class shares controlling 1/8th percent (.00125) of the company.

The CommunityWeb Business Model

The CommunityWeb business model revolves around four main areas: members, community coordinators, content, and advertising. These four areas are simple in nature, but drive the success of CommunityWeb.

Members

The most important aspect of the CommunityWeb.com is membership. CommunityWeb has put a great deal of emphasis on the development of a dedicated user base. Member interaction through viewing advertisements, submitting content, and using the exclusive *CommunityWeb Directory*[1] drives the success of CommunityWeb. Members are encouraged to submit local content of interest to them.

Community Coordinators

Community coordinators, which exist both as franchisees and as MSA coordinators, provide a local "heartbeat" to the Internet for each community. These community coordinators and their sales force will have established relationships with community businesses, not-for-profits, and the general population, which allows for fast membership growth and accelerated advertising sales.

Content

Content, such as calendar events, local sports stories, local news stories, local press releases, and the *CommunityWeb Directory,* is what makes CommunityWeb.com an attractive, useful, informative, and successful website. While CommunityWeb will provide the *CommunityWeb Directory* as well as localized content through news and sports stories, calendar events, and press releases, members are encouraged to submit the bulk of this local content and represent their community on the Internet.

Advertising

Localized advertising is the main revenue engine of CommunityWeb.com. Very specifically targeted and localized advertising is what makes CommunityWeb's advertising system unique to the Internet. Local advertising will be utilized in the community section through promotional windows, CommunityWeb's *CommunityWeb Directory,* targeted e-mail marketing, and follow-up e-mail.

Strategic Alliances

CommunityWeb has developed several key technological and business relationships to better position itself in the marketplace.

AT&T: CommunityWeb has formed a strategic alliance with global communications giant AT&T in several areas. AT&T expects to better reach local markets through CommunityWeb, and CommunityWeb will utilize AT&T's resources to host the CommunityWeb.com website and provide private-labeled Internet connectivity services through a virtual ISP (VISP) system. This alliance will enable CommunityWeb to act as an ISP without having the initial capital expenses usually associated with launching local Internet services. Income from this alliance will come from every home or business that signs up for Internet access service. CommunityWeb's wholesale cost for dial-up accounts will be $13.95 per month. CommunityWeb plans to re-sell this service at a very competitive rate of $18.95 per month. This alliance should prove to be very powerful, given AT&T's position in the ISP market. AT&T is the world's largest and highest rated ISP.[2]

Hargiss Communication/Quad Entertainment: The proprietary Set Top Box that Hargiss Communication has developed is a hardware and software solution that provides "Movies-On-Demand," Internet access, games, digital cable TV, and a local guide to the surrounding area (through CommunityWeb) to hotel or resort amenities, hospitals, and homes. CommunityWeb has entered into a strategic partnership with Hargiss Communication to provide a local guide portal for their interface using the CommunityWeb index of local URLs and its local content. CommunityWeb currently has a 15 percent ownership in a new subsidiary company formed with Hargiss Communication, called Quad Entertainment, and will be an integral part of developing the Set Top Box business model. In addition, Jed Delke of CommunityWeb will serve as CEO of Quad Entertainment and CommunityWeb will occupy three of the six board of directors spots on the company.

InfoSpace.com: CommunityWeb has partnered with InfoSpace.com to increase the options and content that CommunityWeb can provide to members. InfoSpace is one of the largest information sources on the web, thus providing a very powerful resource to CommunityWeb members. The information resources that InfoSpace provides enhance CommunityWeb's content, allowing CommunityWeb to concentrate on its core business. InfoSpace will provide these resources on contract through a co-branded system. CommunityWeb members will see the CommunityWeb website, color scheme, and structure when navigating the InfoSpace content through CommunityWeb.com. This partnership also provides CommunityWeb with a revenue source through the advertising revenue sharing model.

Legal, Professional, Accounting, and Technical Partners and Associates

Thomas Reardon, partner of James, Austin, Cooper, and Burr Law Offices, located in Seymour, Indiana, heads the legal counsel. Reardon's role is to help determine any specialized counsel that CommunityWeb will need along the business development process. In addition, CommunityWeb has partnered with franchise attorney Mark Jacoby of Indianapolis.

CommunityWeb will work with the Commercial Services Group of Crowe Chizek LLP for assistance with SEC and accounting issues. As a leading accounting and consulting organization, Crowe Chizek offers specialized services with a client-focused relationship culture. Crowe is the leading member firm of Howarth International, an international network of independent accounting and consulting firms, with more than 100 members and 400 offices in 372 cities throughout the world. Crowe Chizek's clients include IBM, Microsoft, Oracle, and Onyx Software. Specifically, Crowe Chizek will provide CommunityWeb assistance in finding an appropriate enterprise accounting package. They will also provide independent audits of CommunityWeb's financial statements. Crowe Chizek will be able to provide consulting expertise should the need arise in the future. Four different individuals handle the accounting department. Donald Hager is chief advisor. He has contributed to acquisition planning and stock distribution. Jim Mack is serving in the capacity of controller. Gregory Borst, CPA, will handle current payroll and day-to-day taxation issues.

Technology Expertise—Internal and External

CommunityWeb has a team of highly educated and experienced database developers, programmers, and system architects. In addition, CommunityWeb has partnered with several higher-education institutions in the area as well. CommunityWeb has developed a dynamic site, which requires expertise from several different technology sectors. A commercially viable product was released on January 28, 2001, and is continuing to be built and improved. CommunityWeb has accomplished this mission by using its own talented employees and by contracting for services from Joseph A. Graves and Associates (JGA). Michael Hunt has led this team through the development phases and will continue to lead this team through continuous improvement phases. JGA has provided project management and programming expertise on different components of the site. Jeff Lehm has provided the database expertise.

CommunityWeb Associates

CommunityWeb has assembled a very talented, energetic, and enthusiastic group of entrepreneurial, business, and creative minds to drive this venture. Associate education backgrounds range from marketing, entrepreneurship, political science, communication, journalism, and information sciences at both the undergraduate and graduate levels. Experiences range from financial planning, retail management, franchise development, business development, education, and mass media management.

Officers, Board of Directors, Principals, and Significant Associates

James A. Mack, CFP, RFC

Chairman, Board of Directors and CEO

Jim Mack is a certified financial planner and registered financial consultant. Mack serves as president and cofounder of the Financial Investors Group, based in Seymour, Indiana, with clients in 17 states. He has spent 13 years in the financial services industry creating and evaluating business and succession plans. He hosted a weekly radio show for five years and helped contribute to *The Roaring 2000s Investor: Strategies for the Life You Want*. Mack sits on the advisory board to the H. S. Dent Foundation and speaks nationally to thousands on business development concepts that focus on fundamental trends that drive the U.S. economy.

Daniel E. Pale

President

Dan Pale has over ten years of experience in retail business operations. At the age of 23, he started a retail clothing business that quickly grew to generate over $1.2 million in sales per year. Pale also co-owns a True Value hardware store and Just Ask Rental Center. In 1998, he entered the broadcast industry, taking over the management of WKBY Talk Radio in Seymour, Indiana. In less than two years, he increased station revenue by 600 percent and increased listenership, making the station the number one talk radio format in southern Indiana. He is also a member of the adjunct faculty at a local university's telecommunications program, and through April 2000, maintained a management role with Indiana Regional Radio Partners, Inc.

Greg Dent

Board of Directors

Greg Dent is currently president and CEO of Healthx.com. Dent has over 20 years experience in the health care and technology industries. In 1987, Greg founded First Benefit Corp., a Midwest-based third-party administrator (TPA) that appeared in *Inc.* magazine's top 500 growth companies in 1991, 1992, and 1993. He also founded Qubic, a nationwide organization comprised of 12 independently owned TPAs. In 1993,

First Benefit Corp. was acquired by CoreSource. In 1995, Dent founded a new company, Intermark, and began development of what is now the Healthx.com product. In 1998, the company officially became Healthx.com.

Dominic Mancino

Board of Directors

A native of Southern California, and a current resident of Indiana for the past eight years, Dominic Mancino has been with AT&T for several years and works as a sales director for business services in Indiana. He comes with a wealth of industry knowledge having worked within telecommunications for twenty years for companies like Western Electric and Pacific Bell. His responsibilities have taken him from sales and engineering to his current position as sales director. Mancino has consulted with companies all around the United States to define Internet strategies, and the practical application of IP-based solutions for business development. Mancino is a graduate of Ricks College, which is now known as Brigham Young University of Idaho.

Dr. Nathan Walker

Board of Directors

Nathan Walker was recently with the National Association of Broadcasters in Washington, D.C., where he was vice president of television operations. He currently teaches courses in technology, business aspects, and regulatory issues at the Center for Information and Communication Sciences at Ball State University, along with serving as codirector of the Applied Research Institute. His work includes the development of the network, interactive Kiosk system. Dr. Walker regularly consults with AT&T Bell Labs, U.S. West Advanced Technologies, Ameritech, McDonald's Corporation, and GTE Labs.

Sheri Waters

Board of Directors

Sheri Waters is a motivational speaker, trainer, and coach. She is the president/owner of the Waters Connection, Inc., a Midwest-based national consulting firm that specializes in improving organizational performance through leadership development, sales and customer services coaching/training, team building, and organizational development. Waters developed her expertise through years of service at Ameritech Corporation. Her responsibilities included training, developing, coaching, and supporting over 3,000 senior managers and 4,000 associates in the Consumer Market Unit, which includes 17 Customer Care Centers across the states of Indiana, Illinois, Michigan, Wisconsin, and Ohio. Her most recent clients include Ameritech Consumer Services, Ameritech New Media, Cheap Tickets, Inc., and 21st Century Telecom, among others. Waters is a "Gold" member of the Indianapolis Chamber of Commerce.

Michael A. Marell

Board of Directors

Mike Marell is the owner of Michael A. Marell & Associates, a consulting firm established to assist businesses in continuous improvement strategies using statistical methods. The firm uses many improvement methods, including the methods of Dr. W. Edwards Deming, Dr. Donald Wheeler, Dr. Genichi Taguchi, and William Conway. The firm's objective for its clients is to train and support them to make their business processes and customer services more effective. Marell was employed at Delco Remy Division of General Motors and Delphi Automotive Systems for over 31 years in engineering, quality, and statistical assignments. For 18 years Marell trained employees from all areas of the company to make improvements and to assist in the application of statistical process control, machine qualification, supplier development, design of experiments, and robust engineering. Marell is a licensed professional engineer and certified quality engineer.

William Vacarro, M.D.

Board of Directors

William Vacarro has served the public through the practice of family medicine since 1973. Dr. Vacarro currently serves as the president and CEO of Community Hospital in Seymour, Indiana. Dr. Vacarro is on the board of directors for the Anderson Chamber of Commerce and the Corporation for Economic Development. Dr. Vacarro serves on the Executive Committee, Health Status Committee, and the Facilities and Technology Committee for the Madison Health Partners.

Dr. Michael Foster

Board of Directors

Michael Foster received his bachelor's degree in accounting from the University of Wisconsin–Whitewater and his master's degree in guidance and counseling, also from Wisconsin–Whitewater. Dr. Foster went on to earn his doctoral degree in higher education from Indiana University in 1984. Since that time Dr. Foster has consulted for several organizations, both for-profit and nonprofit in nature. Dr. Foster has also served since 1982 as a professor of management in Seymour University's School of Business. Dr. Foster served as the president and CEO of Marcon, Inc., in Seymour, Indiana, from 1995 to 1997.

Dr. Stephan Reece

Principal

Stephan Reece is the codirector of the Applied Research Institute at Ball State University and an associate professor at the Center for Information and Communication Sciences, also at Ball State University. He was the owner of Communications and Digital Services, Inc., for ten years and engineered all system installations, data networks, and peripheral equipment (T-1, E&M, DID, voice processing, call sequencers, call accounting systems, CLID, ACDs, Centrex, ISDN services and products).

Jeffrey Lehm

Director of Database Development and Technology

Jeff Lehm, as owner of Valcour Computer Group, Inc., constructed data management systems for government agencies and entities such as the Indiana Department of Workforce Development, and associations such as the National Free Flight Association. He is the Computer Information Systems regional program chair for Ivy Tech State College in Seymour, Indiana, and has extensive knowledge in database research and technology as it applies to the Internet. Lehm played an instrumental role in the development of the E-commerce Certification Program at Ivy Tech State College.

Michael Hunt

Chief Information Officer

Michael Hunt is a 1995 graduate of Ball State University's Entrepreneurship and Small Business Management program. In addition, Hunt recently completed his master's degree in Information and Communication Sciences at the Center for Information and Communication Sciences at Ball State University. Hunt contributed to the Network Integration Center (NIC), the Ball-Foster Unified Messaging Team, and the VPN Forum project. From 1995 to 1997, Hunt wrote the business plan and helped start Escapades, Inc., a family entertainment center in Marion, Indiana. After leaving Escapades in 1997, he worked at Knapp Supply Co., Inc., as the network administrator and purchasing agent.

Jonathan Lester

Director of Communications

Jon Lester earned degrees in both advertising and marketing from Ball State University and is currently finishing a master's degree in public relations. As owner and operator of a successful advertising agency, JL Unlimited, Lester built a reputation within the small-to-midsize business market, winning several Addy Awards and Citations of Excellence. Clients include Alltrista; Community Hospitals, Indianapolis; and Community Hospital, Seymour, among others. Realizing the impact the Internet is having on the advertising industry, Lester established webaxis, LLC, a high-end e-solutions provider, to coexist with his agency. Under his direction, webaxis has achieved several large strides in just under a year—user window for controlling their e-environment (Executive Dashboard Systems), web leasing financing, Perpetual Marketing Systems, and more.

Tony Baker

Director of Franchise Sales and Business Development

Tony Baker was the director of marketing for the largest franchise of BD's Mongolian Barbeque restaurants, one of the fastest growing casual dining concepts in America. Baker strengthened and advanced the growth of BD's Mongolian Barbeque, while spending less than 2 percent of its marketing budget on conventional advertising mediums. His local, or neighborhood, marketing techniques have brought franchises as much as 20 percent growth in sales in an industry that marvels at anything over 5 percent. Baker has designed and executed five record openings for franchisees. He has overseen marketing and operations for this $10 million franchise for three years.

Jim McDuffy

Director of Special Markets

McDuffy has over ten years of management experience in various business environments ranging from the entertainment industry to web development. He has served as lead developer and consultant for many web-based projects including the web strategy of Connecticut Electric, one of the world's largest suppliers of replacement circuit breakers. McDuffy's leadership enabled the Degerberg Academy in Chicago to grow to a 600 percent student increase over a four-year period, resulting in a national award from the United States Martial Arts Association in 1993. He studied theatre and film-making at Indiana University and has worked in several production venues in Chicago between 1987 and 1997. McDuffy has also served as a radio personality, hosting a weekly computer talk show "Computer Digest."

John Taylor

Director of Wireless Strategies/Research and Development

John Taylor received his bachelor of arts in marketing from Ball State University with a double minor in Japanese and Asian Studies. He has demonstrated success in international relationship building, developing promotional material, marketing media, and project management. Taylor also recently completed his graduate degree at the Ball State University Center for Information and Communication Sciences. His project experience includes work with a leading wireless manufacturer and network hardware manufacturers and web development for industry, nonprofit, and research organizations. His web development portfolio includes the Applied Research Institute, the Virtual Private Network Forum, the Ohana Foundation, and the Institute for Wireless Innovation, among others.

Troy Simon

Director of Indianapolis Operations

Troy Simon is a 1997 graduate of Ball State University, where he earned a degree in corporate management and financial institutions as a scholar athlete. In December 1998, he completed his master's of science degree in information and communication sciences at the Center for Information and Communication Sciences, also at Ball State University. Simon then served as a business development representative at Intelliseek, a leading provider in personalized Internet services. He implemented over 40 partnerships and created an estimated user count of 6 million. He brings knowledge of search technologies and experience in working with start-up companies to CommunityWeb.

Stock Distribution

The following chart details the stockholders in CommunityWeb and their ownership percentage. Five million shares have been authorized, while another 2.3 million shares are being held for future authorizations, issued as follows:

OWNER	NUMBER OF SHARES
Investors	2,300,000
Dan Pale	850,000
Jim Mack	850,000
Associates	600,000
Board of Directors	200,000
Stephan Reece	100,000
Nathan Walker	100,000

Of the 2.3 million investor shares, 1.8 million are being held for future placements and 500,000 are dedicated to the current placement.

It will be the practice of CommunityWeb to allow all employees to participate in stock ownership. Each of the directors has the opportunity to earn 50,000 options each year. The board of directors will determine the execution price on a year-by-year basis. For the year August 1, 2000 through July 31, 2001, the price will be $10 per share.

Each new full-time employee will receive 1,000 options at the same price provided to the directors.

Each board of directors member will receive 5,000 shares per year of participation.

Partners

Ball State University—Center for Information and Communication Sciences

Ball State University has contributed extensively to this project. Over 150 students at Ball State University have tested and developed concepts to further the scopes of the CommunityWeb website. Ball State has also elected to use CommunityWeb in a senior-level public relations curriculum. Six students were initially assigned to CommunityWeb to help in micro and macro development of the company. Their emphasis was in creating partnerships with local nonprofit and government organizations, as well as national firms. CommunityWeb has access to over 150 undergraduate and graduate students from the Applied Research Institute Laboratory at Ball State University's Center for Information and Communication Sciences for research, testing, and employee recruitment. Present clients of the center include Ameritech, Cisco, Ericsson, First Consulting Group, Lucent, McDonald's, and Nortel.

Ivy Tech State College—Computer Science Laboratory

Ivy Tech State College has created an entire curriculum for a two-year degree to help provide assistance in development as well as provide CommunityWeb with a long-term employee pool. Ivy Tech students, under the direction of professors and Community-Web staff, provide developmental solutions to assure that CommunityWeb is the most technologically advanced local web portal.

CommunityWeb.com Exclusive Features

Geographically and Categorically Searchable CommunityWeb Directory

CommunityWeb's valuable directory of locally based websites is searchable by state, city, category, and subcategory. Searches by zip code and county are also planned for future search tool revisions. According to research conducted at the Center for Information and Communication Sciences at Ball State University, *no search index of this kind currently exists on the Internet.* Research has shown that the major local search engines today catalog only half of the URLs in existence. This would help to explain why just 6.86 percent of global website referrals are through traditional search engines.[3] A poll recently taken by Roper Starch found that 71 percent of all users view their search engine experiences as being very frustrating.[4] CommunityWeb gathers URLs in a unique manner that enables CommunityWeb to gather and catalog more URLs than any other search engine site. This "data-mining" method of gathering URLs also enables CommunityWeb to screen the contents of the websites to *avoid any adult-oriented or other objectionable material.* The directory offers unique web marketing opportunities for the future development of business-to-business and business-to-consumer sales.

Local Rewards Program

CommunityWeb has created a unique free membership program to businesses, nonprofit organizations, and individuals that accepts press releases, sports scores, editorials, birth announcements, calendar events, and more. The membership program will allow members to be rewarded with "Local Rewards" points for visiting advertisers' websites, interacting with promotions geared at driving traffic to a retailer's website and physical storefront location, and submitting content to CommunityWeb. Local Rewards points can then be redeemed in the CommunityWeb Online Prize Catalog to win products, services, merchandise, and more. The technology that powers this membership program will allow for advertising by specific geographic locations and demographic/psychographic groupings with the delivery of targeted banner advertising to a viewer's interest. *This membership program has demonstrated click-through rates of more than 5,000 times the national average.*[5]

CommunityWeb.com Unique Features

- ☐ An events community calendar for display of event times, locations, and other information specific by location and category classification. End users can customize the calendar to only display events that they have identified as important to them.

☐ A News and Sports section featuring national, state, and local content.

☐ Weather forecasts dynamically generated by CommunityWeb from data supplied by the National Weather Service. Forecasts can be viewed by geographic location and can be delivered via e-mail daily to the end user. The ABC affiliate weatherman for Indianapolis, Paul Poteet, will provide a human face to the site as the National Forecaster on CommunityWeb.com.

☐ Direct links to local media sites with local radio and TV broadcast listings.

☐ A web directory of community-based websites searchable by geographic location and keyword search. The web directory consists of the website name, categorization and subcategory listing, site description, and a direct link to the site.

Industry Background

Without a doubt, the world has been turned upside down since the Internet became commercialized in the early 1990s. An estimated 57 million people used the Internet in 1997, according to CyberAtlas. Internet usage grew to 200 million in 1999 and is expected to reach over 300 million by the year 2005, which is approximately 5 percent of the world's population. Internet usage patterns are reported by CyberAtlas every month on their website.

A typical Internet user:

☐ Uses the Internet 19 times per month

☐ Views 671 pages per month

☐ Visits 11 unique sites per session

☐ Views an average of 36 pages per session

According to the Census Bureau, 80 percent of the people who use the Internet use it for e-mail or to find government, business, health, or education information. The next most sought-after information is news, weather, and sports. People access the Internet primarily through analog phone lines. The U.S. market for Internet service providers generated $32.5 billion in revenue in 2000, a 37 percent increase over 1999. Twelve million homes accessed the Internet through high-speed services in 2000. High-speed Internet access is expected to surpass dial-up services by the year 2005.[6]

Online Advertising Market

This newer medium has created another avenue for businesses to reach customers. Advertising on the Internet started with simple websites and links to a company's website from other websites. Online advertisements have become the way to reach customers on the Internet. Contrary to popular myth, online advertising is still growing at a significant rate. Internet advertising increased over 63 percent in the third quarter of 2000 compared to the third quarter of 1999.[7] In addition, online advertising revenues grew over 53 percent in 2000. Those revenues from online advertisements exceeded $8 billion in 2000 and are expected to reach $32 billion by 2005.[8]

▮ Market Analysis

Target Market

CommunityWeb is targeting its product to the "baby boomer" market, aged 35 to 54. This target group provides the best base to grow CommunityWeb into a profitable business. Demographics of this age group include:

- ☐ 83% Caucasian, 12% African American
- ☐ 50% male/female
- ☐ 70% married
- ☐ 30% attended or graduated from college
- ☐ 34% have an income above $75,000
- ☐ 76% work full-time
- ☐ over 30% are in professional and/or managerial positions

Internet usage:

- ☐ 66% have Internet access at home and/or work
- ☐ 15% use the Internet on a daily basis
- ☐ 9% use the Internet three to six times per week
- ☐ 52% prefer products that offer the latest technology

"Older" Internet users now comprise the fastest growing demographic group in the Internet market. Approximately 20 percent of U.S. Internet users are aged 45 to 64. This same group is on the Internet more often, stays on longer, and visits more sites than their younger counterparts. Baby boomers typically use the Internet to communicate with friends and family as well as to search for health- and lifestyle-related information.

CommunityWeb will reach this target market through key community influences. These influencing individuals include nonprofit organization leaders and constituents, public opinion leaders, and community coordinators (franchisees). CommunityWeb has developed an aggressive grass roots marketing plan that will drive membership through localized community influences. CommunityWeb's presence in each community will show these community leaders how their organizations and communities can benefit from CommunityWeb.com.[9]

Market Position

According to Media Metrix, baby boomers and seniors are the fastest growing section of the online population. Last year, this demographic grew by 18.4 percent and outpaced the 18- to 24-year-old demographic, which had a 17.5 percent growth rate. The report by Media Metrix also shows that this group stays online longer and views more pages. On average, they access the Internet 6.3 more days per month and stay logged on 235.7 minutes longer. Lifestyle- and health-related sites are the most popular among the baby boomers. CommunityWeb will capture this market by catering to this demographic group's desire for localized lifestyle information. CommunityWeb is pursuing a franchise model for market penetration. This grassroots effort will help establish the heartbeat in a local community that has been lacking from most Internet websites.

Competition

CommunityWeb is positioning itself to be the premier local content provider and largest local search index in the world. Current attempts at localizing content and services on the web are being made by Internet service providers, search engines, media sites, local government, and others.

☐ Current attempts at providing this content and service have primarily been limited to only major market cities with populations over one million. America Online's Digital City, Yahoo!, Citysearch.com, and many others have maintained a narrow focus with limited community information and no content for small- to medium-size cities and towns.

☐ The competition on providing Internet services and e-commerce solutions is intense. *CommunityWeb's niche is the "human factor," putting real people in their own communities as a franchise owner.* While most companies depend heavily on costly national advertising and direct mail campaigns, CommunityWeb will launch a grassroots effort that will provide the highest level of customer service available today.

The following chart details the competitive strengths and weaknesses of CommunityWeb's competition.

	COMMUNITYWEB	ONEMAIN	MYCITY	DIGITALCITY	YAHOO!
Local Calendar	√				
Local News	√	√		√	
Local Sports	√			√	
Movie Times	√	√	√	√	√
Dining	√	√	√		
Maps	√	√	√	√	√
Local Advertisement	√			√	
Reward System	√	√			
Personalization	√	√	√	√	√

Marketing Plan

☐ Goal 1—To establish CommunityWeb as the leading supplier of local content and Internet-related services on the web.

☐ Goal 2—To maintain and continually grow the world's deepest and most comprehensible index of local, regional, national, and global URLs in existence.

☐ Goal 3—To create the most extensive database of individuals classified geographically, demographically, and psychographically available on the web.

Brand Evaluation

CommunityWeb is the first company on the Internet to compile all of the necessary tools that enables users to stay in touch with their local environment in such an in-depth manner. CommunityWeb makes all of these tools available in an easy-to-understand web portal specifically designed to provide local content and services to individual communities.

Brand Awareness

CommunityWeb strives to be the decisive winner in providing a public forum and information source for specific communities and/or geographic regions. The website strives to relate reliable data and provide a place for community interaction on issues that are most important to individual families. "Community for You" will instantly be associated with family-friendly content and user-friendly navigation. "The community portal on the web" is the branding stance CommunityWeb will take. The company is a step ahead of its competition because of the focus on depth of information in conjunction with breadth of local information, interaction, and community services. While others try to do a little of everything, CommunityWeb focuses on providing the most comprehensive source of content that is user perpetuated.

Customer Promise

"We strive to be your one stop comprehensive resource for providing insight into your local environment and in doing so, never creating a disappointing experience."

Consumer Market

In terms of target markets, CommunityWeb will focus its efforts on those markets it believes will not only benefit greatly from its technology, but which are likely to be the most receptive to its products and services, notably:

- Educational sector
- Corporate sector
- Small business sector
- Nonprofit sector
- Government

CommunityWeb market share will be achieved through:

- Grassroots efforts with the local franchisees
- Volunteers within each community helping the grassroots effort to take hold
- Direct competition in the marketplace
- Affiliations with other companies with dominant positions in their fields
- High-profile, local, regional, and national marketing and advertising campaigns

Technology Plan

CommunityWeb has developed and continues to further develop a dynamic site, which requires expertise from several different technology sectors. CommunityWeb has accomplished this mission by using its own talented employees and by contracting for services from Joseph A. Graves and Associates (JGA). Michael Hunt has led this team through the development phases and will continue to lead this team through continuous improvement phases. JGA has provided project management and programming expertise on different components of the website. Jeff Lehm has provided the databases expertise. A commercially viable product was released on January 28, 2001. This product is continuing to be built and improved.

☐ CommunityWeb will populate the directory database with over one million URLs representing a broad range of community-based websites across the nation by April 1, 2001. This index will be the most comprehensive of its kind when compared to the Open Directory Project (approximately 300,000 URLs as of January 31, 2001) at www.dmoz.org. To accomplish this, CommunityWeb hired over 100 full-time employees that harvest this data. A custom application was written to aid these data miners to ensure the quality and quantity of the information collected.

☐ The 100 full-time employees will be responsible for maintaining and adding new URLs after the initial population of the database has occurred. They will also be responsible for screening content that is submitted to our community pages.

The design, testing, and implementation of this website took place in approximately 12 weeks, starting October 17, 2000.

Financial Segment

Online Advertising—Per User Revenue

A typical Internet user accesses the Internet an average of 19 times per month, visits 17 unique sites per month, and views an average of 36 pages per session.[10] CommunityWeb has projected that a user of the site will visit it 15 times per month and view 6 pages on each of the 11 community sections (2 on the *CommunityWeb Directory*) per month. CommunityWeb has designed a website that has the capability to show a user five online advertisements per page. Each ad "impression" will result in an average of 3 cents of revenue. The result, coupled with one page of national advertising, is $15.60 in revenue from each member from online advertising. CommunityWeb has the ability to dynamically display advertising by geographic regions and in targeted categories of information. This will allow advertising customers to target not only a specific demographic, but also a specific geographic region as small as a zip code. CommunityWeb has used these numbers to generate all of its monthly revenue projections.

AT&T Internet Services

Dial-up access will continue to be the main method of accessing the Internet over the next few years. High-speed access subscription is increasing and is expected to take over the dial-up access market by the year 2005.[11] CommunityWeb is currently developing a high-speed Internet access program with AT&T. The alliance with AT&T will provide CommunityWeb with the ability to offer both dial-up access (short-term) and high-speed connectivity solutions (long-term) to the Internet. Franchisees will be able to sell dial-up access to users at $18.95 per month, which costs CommunityWeb $13.95 per month. CommunityWeb will have the luxury of a constant one-month cash float from revenues of this service through AT&T. CommunityWeb has projected that 5 percent of its members, in addition to an undetermined amount of nonmembers, will use CommunityWeb for Internet access.

InfoSpace.com Advertising Revenues

Although CommunityWeb will outsource the InfoSpace content for a $5,000 monthly fee, CommunityWeb expects to recover and exceed this cost with advertising revenue gains once a member navigates the InfoSpace content through CommunityWeb.com. CommunityWeb will receive 35 percent of the banner advertising revenues on the co-branded pages once a unique visitor per day threshold of 10,000 is met.

Franchise Sales and Fees

Revenue from franchising is generated in two ways: (1) through a one-time fee for the sale of franchises, and (2) through a continuous revenue stream from fees charged to the franchise owner on a monthly basis. The average starting sale price for a franchise will be $35,000 per 100,000 capita. This price will increase as membership numbers are established in given areas. In other words, a market with an established membership will result in a larger investment for a potential franchisee. This is because CommunityWeb has already increased the value and potential of the market by providing an established membership, thus providing revenue existing streams to the franchisee. The sale of franchises will provide a great deal of revenue during the infancy and growth stage of the company. Each franchisee will also pay 12.5 percent of revenues as a royalty fee to CommunityWeb.

Quad Entertainment

Everyone who stays in a hotel or resort that is Hi-5 Set Top Box equipped will receive a free membership to CommunityWeb.com. From the free memberships provided, CommunityWeb expects that 5 percent will continue to use CommunityWeb's website when they return home. The hotel and resort industry experiences a 67.5 percent utilization of the rooms available and the average stay is 2.75 days. Given that there will be 40,000 rooms available, 27,000 will be occupied during a one-month period. Each of those rooms will accommodate 11 distinct visitors (30 days/2.75), resulting in 297,000 visitors and free memberships.[12] Five percent of those visitors, or 14,850, will continue to use CommunityWeb.com upon their return home. Revenue models for Internet access, the membership program, and normal website usage will apply to these end users as well. Revenue projections for the first month (starting in August 2001) are as follows:

Internet Access = $3,712 ($5.00 $\times$ 14,850 $\times$ 5%)

Online Advertising = $220,522 ($14.85 $\times$ 14,850)

Memberships will increase exponentially after the first month. Quad will continue to add boxes each month and each box in place will provide CommunityWeb with two additional members per month.

Licensing of the CommunityWeb Directory

Another revenue opportunity has recently surfaced for CommunityWeb. Community-Web has recently taken offers to lease its database of categorized URLs. Through research and its contact with the CEO of MyCoupons.com, Randy Conrad, Community-Web has learned that there are more than 7,500 websites that would be willing to pay an average of more than $500 per month to lease the *CommunityWeb Directory* (as it exists today) in a co-branded environment. The directory is currently populated with over 400,000 URLs—this number and the marketable value of the directory stands to increase drastically due to relationships that CommunityWeb has developed with NUOS and ListGuy. CommunityWeb is in the process of partnering with the two to further develop and market its database of URLs. ListGuy specializes in business mailing lists, has a database with more than 4 million URLs, and wishes to be the marketing and brokering arm of the *CommunityWeb Directory*. NUOS was started by two Harvard professors and has been very involved in the creation and maintenance of Dunn and Bradstreet's online database. They have more than 6 million URLs, which can be loaded into CommunityWeb's database. NUOS and ListGuy see value in merging the databases while utilizing CommunityWeb's expertise and search tool. Commission levels are still in negotiation, but CommunityWeb expects to retain 60 percent of the profits from this venture. (See the financial projection highlights that follows.)

FINANCIAL PROJECTION HIGHLIGHTS (CORPORATE)

$ MILLIONS	YEAR 1	YEAR 2	YEAR 3
Revenues	2.22	30.83	182.15
Net Income	(.41)	19.08	148.64
Cash Flow	2.87	19.08	148.64

NOTE: Net Income and Cash totals merely represent earning potential, as the majority of the positive cash flow and net profit earned will be utilized to further market the CommunityWeb name and product. Year one cash flow of $2.87 million includes $3.38 million in investment capital.

Milestone Schedule

Goal: 10 MSAs, 100 Franchises

CommunityWeb believes the Midwest is the best market to penetrate using our "warm marketing" approach. We will use marketing dollars and the loyalty of the Midwest to attack to the west and east coasts.

Franchises Rollout—Year 1:

- ☐ Phase 1: 12 franchises by March 31, 2001
- ☐ Phase 2: 28 franchises by June 31, 2001
- ☐ Phase 3: 30 franchises by September 31, 2001
- ☐ Phase 4: 30 franchises by December 31, 2001

First Year Franchise Rollout by Region:

- ☐ 40 franchises in Indiana, Illinois, and Michigan (Midwest)
- ☐ 20 franchises in California
- ☐ 20 franchises on East Coast

MSA Phase 1:

- ☐ Indianapolis—currently in operation
- ☐ Detroit—currently in operation
- ☐ Cleveland—currently in operation
- ☐ Louisville—April 1, 2001

CommunityWeb knows a large part of the online community in the United States is located in the state of California. CommunityWeb's plan is to develop the three largest MSAs in California to capture this market early in our development. Silicon Valley is the cradle of many technology companies. This region's ability to duplicate CommunityWeb's concept and develop its own version is the primary reason California is in the second phase of the rollout. California also has 10 percent of the total population of the United States within its borders. CommunityWeb's marketing plans will reach more users more cost-effectively in this highly populated state. CommunityWeb will focus its marketing efforts on the MSAs. The marketing mediums in these MSAs are expected to bleed into the rest of the state.

MSA Phase 2:

- ☐ Los Angeles—April 1, 2001
- ☐ San Diego—March 1, 2001
- ☐ San Francisco—May 1, 2001

MSA Phase 3:

- ☐ New York—June 1, 2001
- ☐ Washington—July 1, 2001
- ☐ Philadelphia—August 1, 2001
- ☐ Boston—September 1, 2001

MSA Phase 4:

- ☐ Dallas—November 1, 2001
- ☐ Houston—December 1, 2001
- ☐ San Antonio—January 1, 2002

Questions

1. Should CommunityWeb utilize Wall Street Venture Capital as its primary funding source? If not, why and what should the firm's next step be?

2. Assess the company's burn rate (cash expenditure without any notable cash inflow) and financial outlook.

3. What are some critical mistakes made by CommunityWeb?

4. Are there any ethical and/or legal concerns in this case?

5. What were some of the major reasons that CommunityWeb was having problems taking its business model to market?

6. What were some of the reasons that CommunityWeb was having trouble obtaining financing?

7. Evaluate the CommunityWeb business plan as an effective tool for raising capital.

▓ Notes

1. See "CommunityWeb.com Exclusive Features" section.

2. AT&T Promotional Literature.

3. "Banners Effective Even When People Don't Click," *Media* (January 2001): 7.

4. http://www.nua.com/surveys/.

5. Based on Media Rewards, LLC, and CommunityWeb research and beta testing.

6. http://www.clickz.com/stats/.

7. "Search Engines Refer Just 7% of Traffic," *Media* (January 2001): 6.

8. www.clickz.com/stats/.

9. EchoPoint Media Research—MRI Data.

10. http://www.clickz.com/stats/.

11. http://www.clickz.com/stats/.

12. Hargiss Communication Business Plan.

Part 3 Exercise

Recognizing Financial Terminology

The Accounting Equation

Step A: Identify the accounting equation.

_____ = _____ + _____

Step B: Apply the accounting equation to find the missing number.

Total Assets   = $346,700

Total Liabilities =   196,300

Owner's Equity   =   _____

Step C: Apply the accounting equation again to find the missing number.

Total Assets   = $_____

Total Liabilities =   110,000

Owner's Equity   =   57,400

Financial Terminology

Directions: The following is a list of financial terms. Identify each as an asset (A), liability (L), owner's equity (OE), revenue (R), or expense (E). In addition, place the correct identification letter in the appropriate statement column (balance sheet or income statement).

TERMS	BALANCE SHEET	INCOME STATEMENT
Cash in bank		
Accounts receivable		
Accounts payable		
Inventory on hand		
Payroll deductions payable		
Notes payable		
Capital stock		
Sales (credit)		
Sales (cash)		
Payroll		
Taxes		
Supplies		
Rent		
Building		
Equipment		
Purchases		
Cost of goods sold		
Gross profit		
Retained earnings		

PART 4

Initiating Entrepreneurial Ventures

12 Legal Structures for New Business Ventures

No one legal form of organization, or for that matter no combination of two or more of them, is suited to each and every small business. To try to say what is the best form for all enterprises would be like trying to select an all-purpose suit for a man.

In choosing a legal form of organization, consideration to the parties concerned must be made—their likes, dislikes and dispositions, their immediate and long-range needs and their tax situations. Seldom, if ever, does any one factor completely determine which is best.

U.S. Small Business Administration
"Selecting a Legal Structure for Your Firm"

Chapter Objectives

1 To examine the legal forms of organization—sole proprietorship, partnership, corporation, and franchising

2 To illustrate the advantages and disadvantages of each of these four legal forms

3 To compare the characteristics of a sole proprietorship, partnership, and a corporation

4 To explain the nature of the limited partnership and limited liability partnerships (LLPs)

5 To examine how an S corporation works

6 To define the additional classifications of corporations, including limited liability companies (LLCs)

7 To review the costs and benefits associated with the corporate form of organization

8 To examine the franchise structure, benefits, and drawbacks

Identifying Legal Structures

Before deciding how to organize an operation, prospective entrepreneurs need to identify the legal structure that will best suit the demands of the venture. The necessity for this derives from changing tax laws, liability situations, the availability of capital, and the complexity of business formation.[1]

Three primary legal forms of organization are the sole proprietorship, the partnership, and the corporation. Because each form has specific advantages and disadvantages, it is impossible to recommend one form over the other. The entrepreneur's specific situation, concerns, and desires will dictate this choice.[2]

Sole Proprietorships

A **sole proprietorship** is a business that is owned and operated by one person. The enterprise has no existence apart from its owner. This individual has a right to all of the profits and bears all of the liability for the debts and obligations of the business. The individual also has **unlimited liability,** which means his or her business and personal assets stand behind the operation. If the company cannot meet its financial obligations, the owner can be forced to sell the family car, house, and whatever assets that would satisfy the creditors.

To establish a sole proprietorship, a person merely needs to obtain whatever local and state licenses are necessary to begin operations. If the proprietor should choose a fictitious or assumed name, he or she also must file a "certificate of assumed business name" with the county. Because of its ease of formation, the sole proprietorship is the most widely used legal form of organization.[3]

Advantages of Sole Proprietorships

Some of the advantages associated with sole proprietorships follow:

- ☐ *Ease of formation.* Less formality and fewer restrictions are associated with establishing a sole proprietorship than with any other legal form. The proprietorship needs little or no governmental approval, and it usually is less expensive than a partnership or corporation.

- ☐ *Sole ownership of profits.* The proprietor is not required to share profits with anyone.

- ☐ *Decision making and control vested in one owner.* No co-owners or partners must be consulted in the running of the operation.

- ☐ *Flexibility.* Management is able to respond quickly to business needs in the form of day-to-day management decisions as governed by various laws and good sense.

- ☐ *Relative freedom from governmental control.* Except for requiring the necessary licenses, very little governmental interference occurs in the operation.

- ☐ *Freedom from corporate business taxes.* Proprietors are taxed as individual taxpayers and not as businesses.

Disadvantages of Sole Proprietorships

Sole proprietorships also have disadvantages. Some of these follow:

☐ *Unlimited liability.* The individual proprietor is personally responsible for all business debts. This liability extends to *all* of the proprietor's assets.

☐ *Lack of continuity.* The enterprise may be crippled or terminated if the owner becomes ill or dies.

☐ *Less available capital.* Ordinarily, proprietorships have less available capital than other types of business organizations, such as partnerships and corporations.

☐ *Relative difficulty obtaining long-term financing.* Because the enterprise rests exclusively on one person, it often has difficulty raising long-term capital.

☐ *Relatively limited viewpoint and experience.* The operation depends on one person, and this individual's ability, training, and expertise will limit its direction and scope.

Partnerships

A **partnership** is an association of two or more persons acting as co-owners of a business for profit. Each partner contributes money, property, labor, or skills, and each shares in the profits (as well as the losses) of the business.[4]

The **Uniform Partnership Act** is generally followed by most states as the guide for legal requirements in forming a partnership.[5] Though not specifically required in the act, written articles of partnership are usually executed and are always recommended. This is because, unless otherwise agreed to in writing, the courts assume equal partnership—that is, equal sharing of profits, losses, assets, management, and other aspects of the business.

The articles of partnership clearly outline the financial and managerial contributions of the partners and carefully delineate the roles in the partnership relationship. The following are examples of the types of information customarily written into the agreement:

☐ Name, purpose, domicile

☐ Duration of agreement

☐ Character of partners (general or limited, active or silent)

☐ Contributions by partners (at inception, at later date)

☐ Division of profits and losses

☐ Draws or salaries

☐ Rights of continuing partner(s)

☐ Death of a partner (dissolution and windup)

☐ Release of debts

☐ Business expenses (method of handling)

☐ Separate debts

☐ Authority (individual partner's authority on business conduct)

☐ Books, records, and method of accounting

Advice You Should Take

Managing growth is a major challenge for large and small companies alike. An increasing number of small companies are acknowledging that outside help can be invaluable in this respect. By forming an advisory board of corporate executives and industry veterans, savvy entrepreneurs are able to map out growth plans, develop sophisticated management structures, and venture into new markets. "Been there, done that" helps keep entrepreneurs from making avoidable mistakes. Advisory boards are especially helpful because the entrepreneur's attitude toward recommendations and disagreements represents a gauge of his or her willingness to acknowledge investors', and shareholders', value.

Advisory boards differ from a board of directors in that they have no legal or fiduciary responsibility for the actions of the business. Protection should still be provided for the board, however. Follow these four steps:

1. Include provisions in the company's bylaws that outline the responsibilities and term of office for advisors.

2. Ask advisors to make no public statements for or about the company.

3. Advise the board to avoid undisclosed conflicts of interest.

4. Demand that proprietary information about the company be kept confidential.

Although the expertise of advisors becomes particularly important when a business faces a major crisis or issue, this should not be the only time that the resource is tapped. After a business has survived the initial start-up phase and is ready to pursue other significant goals, having a well-connected board can really boost results. An effective group that insists on detailed financial and marketing information serves as a good sounding board when making strategic plans. Additionally, sudden problems can be quickly resolved with just a few phone calls. The balance of information and credibility an advisory board provides ensures that the decisions made are sound ones, whether financial, strategical, or operational.

Here are a few suggestions for recruiting advisory board members:

1. Make it known that you are looking. Headhunters, the National Association of Corporate Directors, and SCORE are good places to start. Ask for referrals, but only from people you trust: bankers, lawyers, professional colleagues.

2. Don't be afraid to aim high and contact executives at companies that are larger and more successful than your own. Getting top names on your board will only help you land more top names.

3. Search for people who excel in areas where you are weak. Interviews enable you to not only assess their technical and personable skills, but also examine the likelihood that a trustful relationship can be forged.

4. Prep new members about the market and management challenges and issues your company faces before asking them to join. Also, inform them of the tone you'll maintain: they are there to protect the business, not your ego.

5. Money isn't the draw for most advisory board members—rather, interest in the person, business, and product is key. Capitalize on that idea and use products, stock options, and investment interest to keep them working on the puzzle if you think they're going to stray.

SOURCE: Lester A. Picker, "Hatch Ideas with Outside Advisors to Boost Profits," *Your Company* (June/July 1996): 32–35; Anne Ashby Gilbert, "Playing the Board Game," *Fortune Small Business* (February/March 2000): 50–55; and Joanne Cleaver, "Friendly Advice," *Success* (May 1999): 26–27.

- ☐ Sale of partnership interest
- ☐ Arbitration
- ☐ Settlement of disputes
- ☐ Additions, alterations, or modifications of partnership
- ☐ Required and prohibited acts
- ☐ Absence and disability
- ☐ Employee management

In addition to the written articles, entrepreneurs must consider a number of different types of partnership arrangements. Depending on the needs of the enterprise, one or more of these may be used. It is important to remember that in a typical partnership arrangement at least one partner must be a general partner who is responsible for the debts of the enterprise and who has unlimited liability.[6]

Advantages of Partnerships

The advantages associated with the partnership form of organization follow:

- ☐ *Ease of formation.* Legal formalities and expenses are few compared with those for creating a more complex enterprise, such as a corporation.
- ☐ *Direct rewards.* Partners are motivated to put forth their best efforts by direct sharing of the profits.
- ☐ *Growth and performance facilitated.* In a partnership it often is possible to obtain more capital and a better range of skills than in a sole proprietorship.
- ☐ *Flexibility.* A partnership often is able to respond quickly to business needs in the form of day-to-day decisions.
- ☐ *Relative freedom from governmental control and regulation.* Very little governmental interference occurs in the operation of a partnership.
- ☐ *Possible tax advantage.* Most partnerships pay taxes as individuals, thus escaping the higher rate assessed against corporations.

Disadvantages of Partnerships

Partnerships also have disadvantages. Some of these follow:

- ☐ *Unlimited liability of at least one partner.* Although some partners can have limited liability, at least one must be a general partner who assumes unlimited liability.
- ☐ *Lack of continuity.* If any partner dies, is adjudged insane, or simply withdraws from the business, the partnership arrangement ceases. However, operation of the business can continue based on the right of survivorship and the possible creation of a new partnership by the remaining members or by the addition of new members.
- ☐ *Relative difficulty obtaining large sums of capital.* Most partnerships have some problems raising a great deal of capital, especially when long-term financing is involved. Usually the collective wealth of the partners dictates the amount of total capital the partnership can raise, especially when first starting out.

☐ *Bound by the acts of just one partner.* A general partner can commit the enterprise to contracts and obligations that may prove disastrous to the enterprise in general and to the other partners in particular.

☐ *Difficulty of disposing of partnership interest.* The buying out of a partner may be difficult unless specifically arranged for in the written agreement.

Partnership Success

The desire and decision to form partnerships appear to be fairly well understood. However, very little information exists regarding the processes required to develop and nurture the partnership beyond the initial decision to establish the relationship. Given both the costs and risks associated with a failed partnership, insight into the factors affecting partnership success is quite useful. One research study attempted to shed light on these issues and to offer an improved understanding of the form and substance of the interaction between or among partners.

The study suggested that trust, the willingness to coordinate activities, and the ability to convey a sense of commitment to the relationship are key. Critical also are the communications strategies the trading parties use. (See Figure 12.1 for an illustration of the key factors.)

Figure 12.1 Factors Associated with Partnership Success

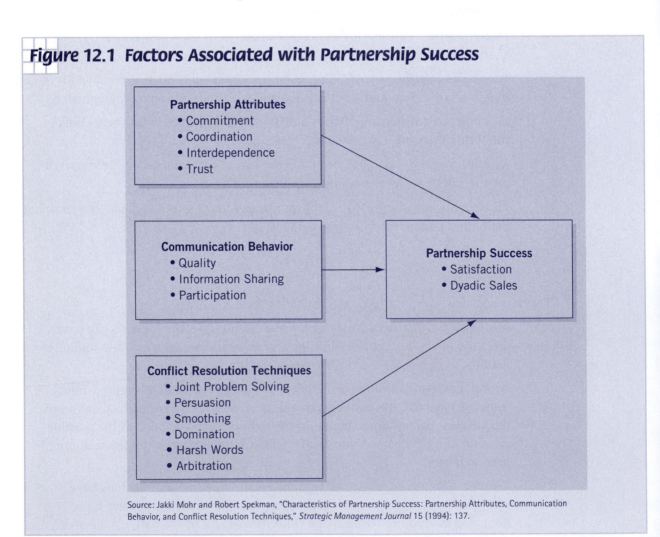

Source: Jakki Mohr and Robert Spekman, "Characteristics of Partnership Success: Partnership Attributes, Communication Behavior, and Conflict Resolution Techniques," *Strategic Management Journal* 15 (1994): 137.

Joint participation enables all parties to better understand the strategic choices facing them. The researchers found that trust, commitment, communication quality, joint planning, and joint problem resolution all serve to better align partners' expectations, goals, and objectives. The challenge lies in developing a management philosophy or corporate culture under which independent trading parties can relinquish some control, while also engaging in planning and organizing that takes into account the needs of all parties.[7]

Corporations

A **corporation** is "an artificial being, invisible, intangible, and existing only in contemplation of the law" (Supreme Court Justice John Marshall, 1819). As such, a corporation is a separate legal entity apart from the individuals who own it. A corporation is created by the authority of state laws and is usually formed when a transfer of money or property by prospective shareholders (owners) takes place in exchange for capital stock (ownership certificates) in the corporation.[8] The procedures ordinarily required to form a corporation are (1) subscriptions for capital stock must be taken and a tentative organization created, and (2) approval must be obtained from the secretary of state in the state in which the corporation is to be formed. This approval is in the form of a charter for the corporation, stating the powers and limitations of the particular enterprise. Corporations that do business in more than one state must comply with federal laws regarding interstate commerce and with the varying state laws that cover foreign (out-of-state) corporations.

Advantages of Corporations

Some of the advantages associated with corporations follow:

- ☐ *Limited liability.* The stockholder's liability is limited to the individual's investment. This is the most money the person can lose.

- ☐ *Transfer of ownership.* Ownership can be transferred through the sale of stock to interested buyers.

- ☐ *Unlimited life.* The company has a life separate and distinct from that of its owners and can continue for an indefinite period of time.

- ☐ *Relative ease of securing capital in large amounts.* Capital can be acquired through the issuance of bonds and shares of stock and through short-term loans made against the assets of the business or personal guarantees of the major stockholders.

- ☐ *Increased ability and expertise.* The corporation is able to draw on the expertise and skills of a number of individuals, ranging from the major stockholders to the professional managers who are brought on board.

Disadvantages of Corporations

Corporations also have disadvantages. Some of these follow:

- ☐ *Activity restrictions.* Corporate activities are limited by the charter and by various laws.

the entrepreneurial PROCESS

Incorporating on the Web

Today forming a corporation is easier than ever. Individuals wishing to form a corporation can simply access the services of one of the many companies that provide online incorporation services. While one has always been able to incorporate in states outside of his or her residence, online incorporation service providers have made this process much more simple. Delaware has been the favorite of many out-of-state incorporations over the past several years. This is due, in large part, to the state's limited restrictions on the formation and operation of corporations.

Web Incorporation Firms

There are literally hundreds of firms that offer online incorporation services. Most of these firms offer a very simple process for incorporation in any state. Most of these sites also offer valuable information, such as the various forms of corporation and the positives and negatives of the different options, FAQs on incorporation, the cost of incorporation and maintenance of a corporation, and advantages and disadvantages of incorporation. Harvard Business Services (http://www.delawareinc.com), The Company Corporation (http://www.incorporate.com), and American Incorporators Ltd. (http://www.ailcorp.com) are a few examples of these online incorporation firms. Entrepreneurs also can simply search using a search engine by typing in the word "incorporation" to locate other online incorporation firms.

Considerations for the Entrepreneur

The entrepreneur must consider the future of the business that he or she wishes to incorporate. While in most cases online incorporation is fine for individuals who are interested in starting smaller businesses with limited growth potential, other avenues are recommended for entrepreneurs who plan to start a business with higher growth potential. If high growth is possible and large amounts of funding is likely necessary, then entrepreneurs are recommended to seek legal counsel through the process of incorporation.

How to Incorporate on the Web

In most cases, filing for incorporation on the web is as simple as filling out an online incorporation form on one of these firm's websites. These firms then take this information and file the necessary forms at the state office in which the entrepreneur wishes to incorporate. The given state will then issue a certificate of incorporation.

☐ *Lack of representation.* Minority stockholders are sometimes outvoted by the majority, who force their will on the others.

☐ *Regulation.* Extensive governmental regulations and reports required by local, state, and federal agencies often result in a great deal of paperwork and red tape.

☐ *Organizing expenses.* A multitude of expenses are involved in forming a corporation.

☐ *Double taxation.* Income taxes are levied both on corporate profits and on individual salaries and dividends.

Table 12.1 compares the characteristics of sole proprietorships, partnerships, and corporations.

Table 12.1   Comparison of the Major Forms of Business

CHARACTERISTIC	SOLE PROPRIETORSHIP	PARTNERSHIP	CORPORATION
1. Method of Creation	Created at will by owner	Created by agreement of the parties	Charter issued by state—created by statutory authorization
2. Legal Position	Not a separate entity; owner is the business	Not a separate legal entity in many states	Always a legal entity separate and distinct from its owners—a legal fiction for the purposes of owning property and being a party to litigation
3. Liability	Unlimited liability	Unlimited liability (except for limited partners in a limited partnership)	Limited liability of shareholders—shareholders are not liable for the debts of the corporation
4. Duration	Determined by owner; automatically dissolved on owner's death	Terminated by agreement of the partners, by the death of one or more of the partners, by withdrawal of a partner, by bankruptcy, and so forth	Can have perpetual existence
5. Transferability of Interest	Interest can be transferred, but individual's proprietorship then ends	Although partnership interest can be assigned, assignee does not have full rights of a partner	Share of stock can be transferred
6. Management	Completely at owner's discretion	Each general partner has a direct and equal voice in management unless expressly agreed otherwise in the partnership agreement	Shareholders elect directors who set policy and appoint officers
7. Taxation	Owner pays personal taxes on business income	Each partner pays pro rata share of income taxes on net profits, whether or not they are distributed	Double taxation—corporation pays income tax on net profits, with no deduction for dividends, and shareholders pay income tax on disbursed dividends they receive
8. Organizational Fees, Annual License Fees, and Annual Reports	None	None	All required
9. Transaction of Business in Other States	Generally no limitation	Generally no limitation	Normally must qualify to do business and obtain certificate of authority

Table 12.1   (Continued)

CHARACTERISTIC	LIMITED PARTNERSHIP	LIMITED LIABILITY COMPANY	LIMITED LIABILITY PARTNERSHIP
1. Method of Creation	Created by agreement to carry on a business for a profit; at least one party must be a general partner and the others limited partners; a certificate of limited partnership is filed; a charter must be issued by the state	Created by an agreement of the owner-members of the company; articles of organization are filed; a charter must be issued by the state	Created by agreement of the partners; a certificate of a limited liability partnership is filed; a charter must be issued by the state
2. Legal Position	Treated as a legal entity	Treated as a legal entity	Generally, treated the same as a general partnership
3. Liability	Unlimited liability of all general partners; limited partners are liable only to the extent of capital contributions	Member-owners' liability is limited to the amount of capital contributions or investment	Varies from state to state but usually limits liability of a partner for certain acts committed by other partners
4. Duration	By agreement in certificate, or by termination of the last general partner (withdrawal, death, or other reason) or last limited partner	Unless a single-member LLC, can have perpetual existence (same as a corporation)	Terminated by agreement of partners, by death or or withdrawal of a partner, by law (such as bankruptcy)
5. Transferability of Interest	Interest can be assigned (same as general partnership), but if assignee becomes a member with consent of other partners, certificate must be amended	Member interests are freely transferable	Interest can be assigned the same as in a general partnership
6. Management	General partners have equal voice or by agreement; limited partners may not retain limited liability if they actively participate in management	Member-owners can fully participate in management, or management is selected by owner-members who manage on behalf of the members	Same as a general partnership
7. Taxation	Generally taxed as a partnership	LLC is not taxed, and members are taxed personally on profits "passed through" the LLC	Same as a general partnership
8. Organizational Fees, Annual License Fees, and Annual Reports	Organizational fee required; usually not others	Organizational fee required; others vary with states	Organizational fee required (such as a set amount per partner); usually not others
9. Transaction of Business in Other States	Generally, no limitations	Generally, no limitation but may vary depending on state	Generally, no limitation, but state laws vary as to formation and limitation of liability

Source: Kenneth W. Clarkson, Roger LeRoy Miller, Gaylord A. Jentz, and Frank B. Cross, West's *Business Law: Legal, Ethical, International, and E-Commerce Environment,* 8th ed. (Mason, OH: South-Western, a division of Thomson Learning: http://www.thomsonrights.com © 2001), 722–723. Reprinted with permission.

Specific Forms of Partnerships and Corporations

A number of specific forms of partnerships and corporations warrant special attention. The following sections examine these.

Limited Partnerships

Limited partnerships are used in situations where a form of organization is needed that permits capital investment without responsibility for management *and* without liability for losses beyond the initial investment. Such an organization allows the right to share in the profits with limited liability for the losses.

Limited partnerships are governed by the **Uniform Limited Partnership Act (ULPA)**, which was formulated in 1916 and revised in 1976, with amendments added in 1985.[9] The act contains 11 articles and 64 sections of guidelines covering areas such as (1) general provisions, (2) formation, (3) limited partners, (4) general partners, (5) finance, (6) distributions and withdrawals, (7) assignment of partnership interest, (8) dissolution, (9) foreign limited partnerships, (10) derivative actions, and (11) miscellaneous. If a limited partnership appears to be the desired legal form of organization, the prospective partners must examine these ULPA guidelines.

The creation of a limited partnership is a formal proceeding, as opposed to the voluntary approach a general partnership uses. A limited partnership must involve two or more partners, and they must sign a certificate that sets forth, at a minimum, the following information:

1. Name of the firm
2. Type of business
3. Location of the principal place of business
4. Name and place of residence of each member and whether each is a general or a limited partner
5. Duration of the partnership
6. Amount of cash and a description and agreed-on valuation of any other property contributed by each limited partner
7. Additional contributions (if any) each limited partner is to make and the times at which the partner is to make them
8. Methods for changes in personnel (if any) and subsequent continuance of the business
9. Share of profits or other compensation each limited partner is entitled to receive

The content of the certificate and the method of filing resemble those of the corporate charter. Additionally, private, informal agreements often are made covering matters not addressed in the certificate, such as the sharing of profits by the partners.[10]

Limited Liability Partnerships

The **limited liability partnership (LLP)** is a relatively new form of partnership that allows professionals the tax benefits of a partnership while avoiding personal liability for the malpractice of other partners. If a professional group organizes as an LLP, innocent partners are not personally liable for the wrongdoing of the other partners.

The LLP is similar to the *limited liability company* (*LLC*) discussed later. The difference is that LLPs are designed more for professionals who normally do business as a partnership. As with limited liability companies, LLPs must be formed and operated in compliance with state statutes.

One of the reasons why LLPs are becoming so popular among professionals is that most statutes make it relatively easy to establish an LLP. This is particularly true for an already formal partnership. For example, to become an LLP in Texas, all a partnership must do is fulfill the following requirements:

1. File the appropriate form with the secretary of state

2. Pay an annual fee of $200 per partner

3. Maintain at least $100,000 in professional liability insurance

4. Add either "L.L.P." or "Registered Limited Liability Partnership" to its name

Converting from a partnership to an LLP is easy also because the firm's basic organizational structure remains the same. Additionally, all of the statutory and common-law rules governing partnerships still apply (apart from those modified by the LLP statute). Normally, LLP statutes are simply amendments to a state's already existing partnership law.[11]

S Corporations

Formerly termed a Subchapter **S corporation**, the S corporation takes its name from Subchapter S of the Internal Revenue Code, under which a business can seek to avoid the imposition of income taxes at the corporate level yet retain some of the benefits of a corporate form (especially the limited liability).

Commonly known as a "tax option corporation," an S corporation is taxed similarly to a partnership.[12] Only an information form is filed with the IRS to indicate the shareholders' income. In this manner the double-taxation problem of corporations is avoided. Corporate income is not taxed but instead flows to the personal income of shareholders of businesses and is taxable at that point.

Although this is very useful for small businesses, strict guidelines must be followed:

1. The corporation must be a domestic corporation.

2. The corporation must not be a member of an affiliated group of corporations.

3. The shareholders of the corporation must be individuals, estates, or certain trusts. Corporations, partnerships, and nonqualifying trusts cannot be shareholders.

4. The corporation must have 100 or fewer shareholders.

5. The corporation must have only one class of stock, although not all shareholders need have the same voting rights.

6. No shareholder of the corporation may be a nonresident alien.

Benefits from Electing S Corporations

The S corporation offers a number of benefits. For example, when the corporation has losses, Subchapter S allows the shareholders to use these losses to offset taxable income. Also, when the stockholders are in a tax bracket lower than that of the corporation, Subchapter S causes the company's entire income to be taxed in the shareholders' bracket, whether or not it is distributed. This is particularly attractive when the corporation wants to accumulate earnings for some future business purposes.

The taxable income of an S corporation is taxable only to those who are shareholders at the end of the corporate year when that income is distributed.

The S corporation can choose a fiscal year that will permit it to defer some of its shareholders' taxes. This is important because undistributed earnings are not taxed to the shareholders until after the corporation's (not the shareholders') fiscal year. In addition, the shareholder in an S corporation can give some of his or her stock to other members of the family who are in a lower tax bracket. Also, up to six generations of one family may elect to be treated as one shareholder. Finally, an S corporation can offer some tax-free corporate benefits. These benefits typically mean federal tax savings to the shareholders.

Limited Liability Companies

Since 1977, an increasing number of states have authorized a new form of business organization called the **limited liability company (LLC)**. The LLC is a hybrid form of business enterprise that offers the limited liability of a corporation but the tax advantages of a partnership.

A major advantage of the LLC is that it does not pay taxes on an entity; rather, profits are "passed through" the LLC and paid personally by company members. Another advantage is that the liability of members is limited to the amount of their investments. In an LLC, members are allowed to participate fully in management activities, and, under at least one state's statute, the firm's managers need not even be LLC members. Yet another advantage is that corporations and partnerships, as well as foreign investors, can be LLC members. Also, no limit exists on the number of LLC shareholder members.

The disadvantages of the LLC are relatively few. Perhaps the greatest disadvantage is that LLC statutes differ from state to state, and thus any firm engaged in multistate operations may face difficulties. In an attempt to promote some uniformity among the states in respect to LLC statutes, the National Conference of Commissioners on Uniform State Laws drafted a uniform limited liability company statute for submission to the states to consider for adoption. Until all the states have adopted the uniform law, however, an LLC in one state will have to check the rules in the other states in which the firm does business to ensure it retains its limited liability.[13]

Other Corporation Classifications

Corporations also can be classified by location, fund sources, objectives, corporate activities, and ownership arrangements.

Domestic and Foreign Corporations

A corporation must be incorporated in a particular state. The corporation is referred to as a **domestic corporation** by its home state (the state in which it incorporated). By contrast, a corporation operating in any other state in the United States is known as a **foreign corporation**. (This discussion does not refer to international corporations; the terms *domestic* and *foreign* apply only to status within the United States.)

Public and Private Corporations

A **public corporation** is one formed by the government to meet some political or governmental purpose. Cities and towns that incorporate are common examples. In addition, many organizations of the federal government are public corporations. **Private corporations** are created either wholly or in part for private benefit. Most business corporations are private. Private corporations can serve a public purpose, as a public utility does, for example, but they are nonetheless owned by private people rather than by the government.

Nonprofit Corporations

A familiar form of **nonprofit corporation** (or not-for-profit) is the religious, charitable, or educational corporation. Its purpose is not to make a profit, but it is permitted to do so if the profit is left within the corporation. Nonprofit corporations are organized under state statutes that usually provide for different formation and operating policies. Such corporations can issue shares of stock but cannot pay dividends to share owners. Most nonprofit corporations are private.

Professional Corporations

Most **professional corporations** are private corporations involving practitioners of professions such as law, accounting, or medicine. The professional corporation has become extremely popular because its tax benefits (pension plan, medical benefits, and so forth) are often better than those provided by a partnership form of organization.

Close Corporations

The **close corporation**, or closely held corporation, is typically one in which all shares of stock are held either by a single shareholder or a small number of shareholders (the actual number is usually established by state law). These shares are not available for purchase by the general public. Close-corporation shareholders manage the firm directly.[14]

Costs Associated with Incorporation

Just about anyone can start a corporation. However, numerous expenses are associated with starting and running such a venture:

- ☐ *Lawyers' fees.* These can range from $1,500 to $5,000.
- ☐ *Accountants' fees.* It can cost from $1,000 to $2,500 to establish a bookkeeping system for a corporation.
- ☐ *Fees to the state.* The state can require an annual corporate fee of several hundred dollars.
- ☐ *Unemployment insurance taxes.* Even if the corporation has only one employee, it must still pay unemployment insurance taxes, either to the state in which it is registered or to the federal government.
- ☐ *Employer's contribution to Social Security.* If a person is a salaried employee of some other company in addition to being an employee of his or her own corporation, he or she must pay an employer's "contribution" to Social Security. This contribution is nonrefundable.
- ☐ *Annual legal and accounting fees.* A variety of forms must be filed for corporations in different states. In addition, corporate records and minute books must be maintained. Typically, an accountant or a lawyer does this. Annual fees for such services can run into many hundreds of dollars.

Franchising

Today, more than a third of all retail sales and an increasing part of the gross domestic product are generated by private franchises. A **franchise** is any arrangement in which the owner of a trademark, trade name, or copyright has licensed others to use it in selling goods or services. A *franchisee* (a purchaser of a franchise) is generally legally independent but economically dependent on the integrated business system of the *franchisor* (the seller of the franchise). In other words, a franchisee can operate as an independent businessperson but still realize the advantages of a regional or national organization.[15]

Advantages of Franchising

A number of advantages are associated with franchising.[16]

Training and Guidance

Perhaps the greatest advantage of buying a franchise, as compared to starting a new business or buying an existing one, is that the franchisor will usually provide both training and guidance to the franchisee. As a result, the likelihood of success is much greater for national franchisees who have received this assistance than for small-business owners in general. For example, it has been reported that the ratio of failure for small enterprises in general to franchised businesses may be as high as four or five to one.

Brand-Name Appeal

An individual who buys a well-known national franchise, especially a big-name one, has a good chance to succeed. The franchisor's name is a drawing card for the establishment. People are often more aware of the product or service offered by a national franchise and prefer it to those offered by lesser-known outlets.

A Proven Track Record

Another benefit of buying a franchise is that the franchisor has already proved the operation can be successful. Of course, if someone is the first individual to buy a franchise, this is not the case. However, if the organization has been around for five to ten years and has 50 or more units, it should not be difficult to see how successful the operations have been. If all of the units are still in operation and the owners report they are doing well financially, one can be certain the franchisor has proved that the layout and location of the store, the pricing policy, the quality of the goods or service, and the overall management system are successful.

Financial Assistance

Another reason a franchise can be a good investment is that the franchisor may be able to help the new owner secure the financial assistance needed to run the operation. In fact, some franchisors have personally helped the franchisee get started by lending money and not requiring any repayment until the operation is running smoothly. In short, buying a franchise is often an ideal way to ensure assistance from the financial community.

Disadvantages of Franchising

The prospective franchisee must weigh the advantages of franchising against the accompanying disadvantages. Some of the most important drawbacks follow:

1. Franchise fees
2. The control exercised by the franchisor
3. Unfulfilled promises by some franchisors

The following sections examine each of these disadvantages.

Franchise Fees

In business, no one gets something for nothing. The larger and more successful the franchisor, the greater the franchise fee. For a franchise from a national chain, it is not uncommon to be faced with a fee of $5,000 to $100,000. Smaller franchisors or those who have not had great success charge less. Nevertheless, entrepreneurs deciding whether or not to take the franchise route into small business should weigh the fee against the return they could get putting the money into another type of business. Also, remember that this fee covers only the benefits discussed in the previous section. The prospective franchisee also must pay for building the unit and stocking it, although the franchisor may provide assistance in securing a bank loan. Additionally, a fee is usually tied to gross sales. Typically, the franchise buyer pays an initial franchise fee, spends his or her own money to build a store, buys the equipment and inventory, and then pays a continuing royalty based on sales, usually between 5 and 12 percent. Most franchisors require buyers to have 25 to 50 percent of the initial costs in cash. The rest can be borrowed, in some cases, from the franchising organization itself.[17] Table 12.2 presents a list of the costs involved in buying a franchise.

Franchisor Control

When one works in a large corporation, the company controls the employee's activities. If an individual has a personal business, he or she controls his or her own activities. A franchise operator is somewhere between these extremes. The franchisor generally exercises a fair amount of control over the operation in order to achieve a degree of uniformity. If entrepreneurs do not follow franchisor directions, they may not have their franchise license renewed when the contract expires.

Unfulfilled Promises

In some cases, especially among less-known franchisors, the franchisees have not received all they were promised.[18] For example, many franchisees have found themselves with trade names that have no drawing power. Also, many franchisees have found that the promised assistance from the franchisor has not been forthcoming. For example, instead of being able to purchase supplies more cheaply through the franchisor, many operators have found themselves paying exorbitant prices for supplies. If franchisees complain, they risk having their agreement with the franchisor terminated or not renewed.

Franchise Law

The growth in franchise operations has outdistanced laws about franchising. A solid body of appellate decisions under federal or state laws relating to franchises has yet to be developed.[19] In the absence of case law that precisely addresses franchising, the courts tend to apply general common-law principles and appropriate federal or state

Table 12.2 The Costs of Franchising

Don't let the advantages of franchising cloud the fact that significant costs are involved. Although the franchise fee may be $75,000, the actual cost of "opening your doors for business" can be more than $200,000! Depending on the type of franchise, the following expenditures are possible:

1. **The Basic Franchise Fee**   For this, you may receive a wide range of services: personnel training, licenses, operations manuals, training materials, site selection and location preparation assistance, and more. Or you may receive none of these.

2. **Insurance**   You will need coverage for a variety of items, such as plate glass, office contents, vehicles, and others. You should also obtain so-called umbrella insurance. It is inexpensive and is meant to help out in the event of crippling million- or multimillion-dollar lawsuits.

3. **Opening Product Inventory**   If initial inventory is not included in your franchise fee, you will have to obtain enough to open your franchise.

4. **Remodeling and Leasehold Improvements**   In most commercial leases, you are responsible for these costs.

5. **Utility Charges**   Deposits to cover the first month or two are usually required for electricity, gas, oil, telephone, and water.

6. **Payroll**   This should include the costs of training employees before the store opens. You also should include a reasonable salary for yourself.

7. **Debt Service**   This includes principal and interest payments.

8. **Bookkeeping and Accounting Fees**   In addition to the services the franchisor may supply in this area, it is always wise to use your own CPA.

9. **Legal and Professional Fees**   The cost of hiring an attorney to review the franchise contract, file for and obtain any necessary zoning or planning ordinances, and handle any unforeseen conflicts must be factored into your opening-costs projections.

10. **State and Local Licenses, Permits, and Certificates**   These run the gamut from liquor licenses to building permits for renovations.

Source: Donald F. Kuratko, "Achieving the American Dream as a Franchisee," *Small Business Network* (July 1987): 2.

statutory definitions and rules. Characteristics associated with a franchising relationship are similar in some respects to those of principal/agent, employer/employee, and employer/independent-contractor relationships, yet a franchising relationship does not truly fit into any of these traditional classifications. (See the Entrepreneurship in Practice box.)

Much franchise litigation has arisen over termination provisions. Because the franchise agreement is normally a form contract the franchisor draws and prepares, and because the bargaining power of the franchisee is rarely equal to that of the franchisor, the termination provisions of contracts are generally more favorable to the franchisor. This means the franchisee, who normally invests a substantial amount of time and money in the franchise operation to make it successful, may receive little or nothing for the business upon termination. The franchisor owns the trademark and hence the business.[20]

entrepreneurship IN PRACTICE

The Uniform Franchise Offering Circular

In 1979 the Federal Trade Commission established a Franchise Disclosure Rule requiring franchisors to make full presale disclosure nationwide. To comply with this ruling, the **Uniform Franchise Offering Circular (UFOC)** was developed.

The UFOC is divided into 23 items that provide different segments of information for prospective franchisees. In summary form, here are the major sections:

Sections I–IV: cover the franchisor, the franchisor's background, and the franchise being offered.

Sections V–VI: delineate the franchise fees, both initial and ongoing.

Section VII: sets forth all of the initial expenses involved to establish the entire franchise.

Sections VIII–IX: detail the franchisee's obligation to purchase specific goods, supplies, services, and so forth from the franchisor.

Section X: provides information on any financing arrangements available to franchisees.

Section XI: describes in detail the contractual obligations of the franchisor to the franchisee.

Section XII: clearly outlines the geographic market within which the franchisee must operate.

Sections XIII–XIV: disclose all pertinent information regarding trademarks, trade names, patents, and so forth.

Section XV: outlines the franchisor's expectations of the franchisee (day-to-day operations).

Section XVI: explains any restrictions or limitations.

Section XVII: sets forth the conditions for the franchise's renewal, termination, or sale.

Section XVIII: discloses the actual relationship between the franchise and any celebrity figure used in advertising for the franchise.

Section XIX: provides a factual description of any potential "earnings claims," including their assumptions and actual figures.

Section XX: lists the names and addresses of all existing franchises in the state where the proposed franchise is to be located.

Sections XXI–XXIII: provide certified financial statements for the previous three fiscal years and a copy of the actual franchise contract.

The UFOC must be given to a prospective franchisee at least ten days prior to the payment of any fees or contracts signed. It is the responsibility of the franchisee to read and understand the various sections delineated in this document.

SOURCE: Adapted from David J. Kaufmann and David E. Robbins, "Now Read This," *Entrepreneur* (January 1991): 100–105.

Final Thoughts

As mentioned earlier, an entrepreneur always should seek professional legal advice in order to avoid misunderstanding, mistakes and, of course, added expenses.

The average entrepreneur encounters many diverse problems and stumbling blocks in venture formation. Since he or she does not have a thorough knowledge of law, accounting, real estate, taxes, and governmental regulations, an understanding of certain basic concepts in these areas is imperative.

The material in this chapter is a good start toward understanding the legal forms of organizations. It can provide entrepreneurs with guidelines for seeking further and more specific advice on the legal form that appears most applicable to their situation. (See Table 12.3 for a good review of an entrepreneur's options.)

Table 12.3   The Entrepreneur's Options

ESSENTIAL CHARACTERISTICS

Major Traditional Business Forms

1. *Sole proprietorships:* the simplest form of business, used by anyone who does business without creating an organization. The owner is the business. The owner pays personal income taxes on all profits and is personally liable for all business debts.

2. *Partnerships*

a) *General partnerships:* created by agreement of the parties; not treated as an entity except for limited purposes. Partners have unlimited liability for partnership debts, and each partner normally has an equal voice in management. Income is "passed through" the partnership to the individual partners, who pay personal taxes on the income.

b) *Limited partnerships:* must be formed in compliance with statutory requirements. A limited partnership consists of one or more general partners, who have unlimited liability for partnership losses, and one or more limited partners, who are liable only to the extent of their contributions. Only general partners can participate in management.

3. *Corporations:* must be formed in compliance with statutory requirements: a legal entity separate and distinct from its owners that can have perpetual existence. The shareholder/owners elect directors, who set policy and hire officers to run the day-to-day business of the corporation. Shareholders normally are not personally liable for the corporation's debts. The corporation pays income tax on net profits; shareholders pay income tax on disbursed dividends.

Limited Liability Companies

The limited liability company (LLC) is a hybrid form of business organization that offers the limited liability of corporations but the tax benefits of partnerships. Unlike limited partners, LLC members participate in management. Unlike shareholders in S corporations, members of LLCs may be corporations or partnerships, are not restricted in number, and may be residents of other countries.

Other Organizational Forms

1. *Joint venture:* an organization created by two or more persons in contemplation of a limited activity or a single transaction; otherwise, similar to a partnership.

2. *Syndicate:* an investment group that undertakes to finance a particular project; may exist as a corporation or as a general or limited partnership.

Table 12.3   (Continued)

ESSENTIAL CHARACTERISTICS

3. *Joint stock company:* a business form similar to a corporation in some respects (transferable shares of stock, management by directors and officers, perpetual existence) but otherwise resembling a partnership.

4. *Business trust:* created by a written trust agreement that sets forth the interests of the beneficiaries and obligations and powers of the trustee(s). Similar to a corporation in many respects. Beneficiaries are not personally liable for the debts or obligations of the business trust.

5. *Cooperative:* an association organized to provide an economic service, without profit, to its members. May take the form of a corporation or a partnership.

Private Franchises

1. *Types of franchises*

   a) Distributorship (for example, automobile dealerships)

   b) Chain-style operation (for example, fast-food chains)

   c) Manufacturing/processing-plant arrangement (for example, soft-drink bottling companies, such as Coca-Cola)

2. *Laws governing franchising:* governed by contract law, occasionally by agency law, and by federal and state statutory and regulatory laws.

3. *The franchise contract*

   a) Ordinarily requires the franchisee (purchaser) to pay a price for the franchise license.

   b) Specifies the territory to be served by the franchisee's firm.

   c) May require the franchisee to purchase certain supplies from the franchisor at an established price.

   d) May require the franchisee to abide by certain quality standards relating to the product or service offered but cannot set retail resale prices.

   e) Usually provides for the date and conditions of termination of the franchise arrangement. Both federal and state statutes attempt to protect certain franchisees from franchisors who unfairly or arbitrarily terminate franchises.

Source: From *Business Law Today, Text & Summarized Cases, Legal, Ethical, Regulatory, and International Environment*, 4th ed. by Miller/Jentz. Copyright © 1997. Reprinted with permission of South-Western, a division of Thomson Learning: http://www.thomsonrights.com.

The following key questions can be helpful for placing legal forms of business in perspective:

1. What is the size of the risk? What is the amount of the investor's liability for debts and taxes?

2. What would the continuity (life) of the firm be if something happened to the principal(s)?

3. What legal structure would ensure the greatest administrative adaptability for the firm?

4. What effects will federal, state, and local laws have on the operation?

5. What are the possibilities of attracting additional capital?

6. What are the needs for and possibilities of attracting additional expertise?

7. What are the costs and procedures associated with starting the operation?

8. What is the ultimate goal and purpose of the enterprise, and which legal structure can best serve this purpose?

Summary

This chapter examined the three major forms of legal organization: sole proprietorship, partnership, and corporation. The advantages and disadvantages of each form were highlighted and compared. In addition, the characteristics and tax considerations of partnerships were compared with those of corporations.

The specific forms of partnerships and corporations were examined. In particular, the requirements and benefits of limited partnerships, limited liability partnerships, S corporations, and limited liability companies were presented.

Additional corporation classifications were reviewed, and a section was devoted to the corporate considerations of costs. Franchising also was discussed, with emphasis on the advantages and disadvantages as well as concerns over legal protections. Finally, a checklist of key questions for entrepreneurs to consider before structuring their venture was provided.

Key Terms and Concepts

close corporation

corporation

domestic corporation

foreign corporation

franchise

limited liability company (LLC)

limited liability partnership (LLP)

limited partnership

nonprofit corporation

partnership

private corporation

professional corporation

public corporation

S corporation

sole proprietorship

Uniform Franchise Offering Circular (UFOC)

Uniform Limited Partnership Act (ULPA)

Uniform Partnership Act

unlimited liability

Review and Discussion Questions

1. Identify the legal forms available for entrepreneurs structuring their ventures.

2. Define each of the following: sole proprietorship, partnership, and corporation.

3. What are the specific advantages and disadvantages associated with each primary legal form of organization?

4. Compare the major tax considerations of a partnership with those of a corporation.

5. What is the ULPA? Describe it.

6. Name three specific types of partners. How do they differ?

7. Explain the limited liability partnership.

8. What is the double taxation corporations face?

9. How does a limited partnership work? Give an example.

10. What is the nature of an S corporation? List five requirements for such a corporation.

11. Define each of the following: foreign corporation, nonprofit corporation, professional corporation, and close corporation.

12. What is a limited liability company?

13. What are the advantages and disadvantages of franchising?

14. Identify the UFOC. Explain why it is important in franchising.

15. What are four key questions to be considered by entrepreneurs before structuring their venture?

Experiential Exercise

Get It Right

The following list of advantages and disadvantages is associated with sole proprietorships, partnerships, and corporations. Place an S next to those that relate to sole proprietorships, a P next to those that relate to partnerships, and a C next to those that relate to corporations. If the advantage or disadvantage applies to more than one type of organizational form, put all answers on the accompanying line. Answers are provided at the end of the exercise.

Advantages	Disadvantages
1. Limited liability _____	1. Unlimited liability _____
2. Sole ownership of profits _____	2. Governmental regulation _____
3. Unlimited life _____	3. Lack of continuity _____
4. Ease of formation _____	4. Double taxation _____
5. Flexibility _____	5. Difficulty obtaining large sums of capital _____
6. Transfer of ownership _____	6. Organizing expenses _____
7. Relative freedom from governmental control _____	7. Relatively limited viewpoint and experience _____
8. Increased ability and expertise _____	8. Activity restrictions _____

Answers: Advantages: 1. C; 2. S; 3. C; 4. S, P; 5. S, P; 6. C; 7. S, P; 8. C
Disadvantages: 1. S, P; 2. C; 3. S, P; 4. C; 5. S, P; 6. C; 7. S; 8. C

Video Case 12.1

Legal Structures for Developing Ventures
Biosite with Kim Blickenstaff, Ken Buechler, and Gunars Valkirs

> We solve problems together. Nobody gets mad at each other; we've never had a shouting contest. We just recognize that we're in the middle of a problem, and we have to solve it. (Ken Buechler)

Biosite, a medical technology company that produces testing and diagnostic equipment, got its start when a large drug corporation tried to rein in three of its intrapreneurs. Biosite founders Kim Blickenstaff, CEO, Dr. Ken Buechler, president and chief scientific officer, and Dr. Gunars Valkirs, senior vice president for Biosite Discovery, were a complementary team who enjoyed the intellectual challenge of discovering biotechnology tools that would improve health care. When their corporate employer took over Hybritech, the firm they originally worked for, it wanted them to work within a prescribed system. The threesome decided it was time to go out on their own.

Blickenstaff explains their corporate situation: "It wasn't really any fun anymore. We weren't really able to be innovative in what we wanted to do. It was more of a situation where we were told what to do. We couldn't really be scientists I guess is the best way to say it."

Based on their experience, the Biotech founders believed that the market needed a portable, rapid diagnostic tool to test for drugs of abuse, and they had developed such a tool. Initially, however, no one in the health care industry was interested.

Blickenstaff says: "Let me tell you what it's like to have ten out of ten Harvard MBAs . . . look to your business plan and say it's a stupid idea. I mean that gets to be tough."

Valkirs adds: "I think what we did right was we identified the first product opportunity correctly when even some of the experts in the drug-testing field said this market does not exist. . . . we're talking about the CEO of a company that was the leading drug testing company in the world [who] said there's no market for this product."

Initially, the threesome didn't have much money or a solid business plan. But two senior people at Hybritech, Ted Greene and Tim Wollaeger, knew what they had accomplished in the laboratories in the past and were willing to invest in them. The process of developing their product through continued research and more venture-capital money took from 1988 to 1992. They had to continually prove progress toward their goal in order to persuade venture capitalists to keep giving them more money. Their project required a 21 million dollar investment before the product got launched, but once it did, sales began to climb quickly. The company went public in 1997, and the investors were happy.

Blickenstaff, Buechler, and Valkirs did not anticipate going beyond their drug-testing idea to develop a public corporation. They thought they had a one-product idea, the rapid drug-testing idea, and they would probably be bought out by a large corporation. However, their original investors, Greene and Wollaeger, challenged them to think beyond their first success.

Blickenstaff remembers: "I have to admit I was scared of the thought of ever having to go public or run a public company. It was sort of the business equivalent of Mount Everest."

They considered their options; they had a product that was becoming more and more successful, and they could have walked away with millions in their pockets and looked for other ways to spend their time.

Buechler says they soon decided "that wouldn't have been a fun thing to do." They decided to reinvest their profits into researching, designing, and producing new diagnostic technology, and to set up the public corporation to do so. "We recognized that there was this need, a totally new technology had to be developed. Technology that hadn't existed at all anywhere and it was that challenge and that's what made it fun to continue to work." One of their best sellers today is the Triage BNP Test, which is an aid in the diagnosis of congestive heart failure.

Their first action once the corporation went public was to find a person who could capably serve as a chief operating officer managing a 150 to 200 million-dollar business in the health care industry. They secured intellectual property rights on the products they developed. They also developed a management team that was equally committed to health care issues. As for the founders of Biosite, they dedicated their time to diagnostic problem solving in the laboratory.

Valkirs explains their current status—and the probable reason for their success: "We haven't even scratched the surface on the potential of diagnostics. We're really probably the first diagnostics company to take a very global perspective and treat diagnostics more like the pharmaceutical company treats the pharmaceutical business."

Questions

1. What did the original investors, Ted Greene and Tim Wollaeger, see in Blickenstaff, Buechler, and Valkirs that made them want to invest in their research?

2. Why did the Biotech founders hire a COO and a management team to run their corporation?

3. What are the advantages and the disadvantages for the three founders to form a public corporation?

Case 12.2

Gina's Decision

When Gina Wilson opened her boutique six years ago, she had only one full-time employee. Since then Gina has added two general partners and greatly expanded the operation. Over the past year it has become obvious that the group could open another boutique that would be equally successful. The problem is money. The partnership lacks funds for expansion.

Gina's banker has suggested that the company borrow $200,000 from the bank and pledge the firm's assets as collateral. "This will get you the money you need, and once you have the boutique going, you can repay the money," he told them. The idea sounds fine to the partners, although they are concerned about the risk involved. If the second boutique does not do well, it could affect the success of the first boutique by siphoning off funds to repay the loan.

Gina has been thinking about incorporating the business, selling stock, and using these funds for expansion purposes. She has not shared this idea with her banker because she wants to give it more thought, but she intends to talk it over with her partners later in the week. She is also pondering the value of an S corporation. She has heard her accountant talk about this type of corporation, although she is unsure of the type of legal arrangement it involves.

Questions

1. What are the benefits of the company's becoming a corporation? Is this a better idea than the banker's proposal of taking a $200,000 loan? Why or why not?

2. How does an S corporation work? Would this be a good idea for the firm? Why or why not?

3. What would you recommend to Gina? Explain in detail.

Case 12.3

A Question of Incorporation

The Harlow family opened its first motel in 1982. Initially, business was slow. It took almost 11 months to break even and three years for the Harlows to feel that the operation was going to be a success. They stuck with it, and by 1987 they were able to increase the size of the motel from 28 to 50 rooms. They expanded again in 1989, this time to 100 rooms. In each case, the motel's occupancy rate was so high that the Harlows had to turn people away during the months of April to September, and the occupancy rate was 85 percent during the other months. By industry standards, their business was one of the most successful motels in the country.

As they entered the 1990s, Harold and Becky Harlow decided that, rather than expanding, they would be better off buying another motel, perhaps in a nearby locale. They chose to hire someone to run their current operation and spend most of their time at the new location until they had it running properly. In 1992, they made their purchase. Like their first motel, the second location was an overwhelming success within a few years. From then on, the Harlows bought a number of new motels. By 1999, they had seven motels with an average of 100 rooms per unit.

During all of this time, Becky and Harold kept their own financial records, bringing in a certified public accountant only once a year to close the books and prepare their income tax returns. Last week the new accountant asked them how long they intended to keep running seven motels. The Harlows told him that they enjoyed the operation and hoped to keep at it for another ten years, when they planned to sell out and retire.

Harold admitted that trying to keep all of the motels going at the same time was difficult but noted that he had some excellent managers working for him. The accountant asked him whether he would consider incorporating. "If you incorporate," he said, "you could sell stock and use the money to buy more motels. Additionally, you could keep some of the stock for yourself so you could maintain control of the operation, sell some for expansion purposes, and sell the rest to raise some money you can put aside in a savings account or some conservative investment. That way, if things go bad, you still will have a nest egg built up." The accountant also explained to Harold and Becky that, as a partnership, they are currently responsible for all business debts. With a corporation, they would have limited liability; that is, if the corporation failed, the creditors could not sue them for their personal assets. In this way, their assets would be protected, so the money Harold would get for selling the stock would be safely tucked away.

The Harlows admitted that they had never really considered another form of organization. They always assumed that a partnership was the best form for them. Now they are willing to examine the benefits of a corporation, and they will go ahead and incorporate their business if this approach promises them greater advantages.

Questions

1. What are the advantages and disadvantages of a partnership?
2. Contrast the advantages and disadvantages of a partnership with those of a corporation.
3. Provide your opinion on whether the Harlows should incorporate.
4. Would the LLC option be of value to them? Explain.

◼ Notes

1. Kent Royalty, Robert Calhoun, Radie Bunn, and Wayne Wells, "The Impact of Tax Reform on the Choice of Small Business Legal Form," *Journal of Small Business Management* (January 1988): 9–17; and David S. Hulse and Thomas R. Pope, "The Effect of Income Taxes on the Preference of Organizational Form for Small Businesses in the United States," *Journal of Small Business Management* (January 1996): 24–35.

2. For a detailed discussion of each form, see Kenneth W. Clarkson, Roger LeRoy Miller, Gaylord A. Jentz, and Frank B. Cross, *West's Business Law,* 9th ed. (Mason, OH: South-Western, a division of Thomson Learning, 2004), 615–737.

3. For more on the sole proprietorship, see Roger LeRoy Miller, Frank B. Cross, and Gaylord A. Jentz, *Essentials of the Legal Environment* (Mason, OH: Thomson Learning, 2005).

4. For a good analysis of partnerships, see Roger LeRoy Miller and Gaylord A. Jentz, *Business Law Today* (Mason, OH: Thomson Learning, 2006).

5. The Uniform Partnership Act appears in full in Clarkson et al., *West's Business Law,* Appendix E, A-215–A-227.

6. For detailed coverage on limited partnership, see Roger LeRoy Miller and Gaylord A. Jentz, *Business Law Today,* 7th ed. (Mason, OH: Thomson Learning, 2006), Appendix D, A-111–A-117. For coverage of the Uniform Limited Partnership Act (ULPA), see Clarkson, et al., *West's Business Law,* Appendix G, A-228–A-238.

7. Jakki Mohr and Robert Spekman, "Characteristics of Partnership Success: Partnership Attributes, Communication Behavior, and Conflict Resolution Techniques," *Strategic Management Journal* 15 (1994): 135–152.

8. For detailed presentations of corporate laws and regulations, see Clarkson et al., *West's Business Law,* Appendix H, "The Revised Model Business Corporation Act," A-239–A-249.

9. The complete revised Uniform Limited Partnership Act may be found in Clarkson et al., *West's Business Law,* Appendix G, A-228–A-238.

10. For more detail on limited partnerships, see Richard A. Mann and Barry S. Roberts, *Smith and Roberson's Business Law,* 13th ed. (Mason, OH: Thomson Learning, 2006).

11. Miller and Jentz, *Business Law Today,* 686–687.

12. For details on S corporations, see Miller and Jentz, *Business Law Today,* 720–721.

13. Miller and Jentz, *Business Law Today,* 414; see also Mary Sprouse, "The Lure of Limited Liability Companies," *Your Company* (fall 1995): 19.

14. For a detailed account of close corporations, see Clarkson et al., *West's Business Law,* 641–642.

15. Clarkson et al., *West's Business Law,* 730.

16. See Alden Peterson and Rajiv P. Dant, "Perceived Advantages of the Franchise Option from the Franchisee Perspective: Empirical Insights from a Service Franchise," *Journal of Small Business Management* (July 1990): 46–61; Richard M. Hodgetts and Donald F. Kuratko, *Effective Small Business Management,* 7th ed. (Fort Worth, TX: The Dryden Press, 2001), 112–141; Scott A. Shane and Frank Hoy, "Franchising: A Gateway to Cooperative Entrepreneurship," *Journal of Business Venturing* (September 1996): 325–328; Frank Hoy and Scott Shane, "Franchising as an Entrepreneurial Venture Form," *Journal of Business Venturing* (March 1998): 91–94; and Patricia J. Kaufmann, "Franchising and the Choice of Self-Employment," *Journal of Business Venturing* (July 1999): 345–362.

17. Bryce Webster, The Insider's Guide to Franchising (New York: Macmillan, 1986); and Lloyd T. Tarbutton, *Franchising: The How-To Book* (Englewood Cliffs, NJ: Prentice-Hall, 1986).

18. Russell M. Knight, "Franchising from the Franchisor's and Franchisee's Points of View," *Journal of Small Business Management* (July 1986): 8–15.

19. See Steven C. Michael, "To Franchise or Not to Franchise: An Analysis of Decision Rights and Organizational Form Shares," *Journal of Business Venturing* (January 1996): 59–71.

20. Clarkson, et al., *West's Business Law,* 734–735.

13

Legal Issues Related to Emerging Ventures

A major difficulty for the inexperienced entrepreneur is the host of strange terms and phrases which are scattered throughout most legal documents. The novice in this kind of reading should have some understanding not only of what is contained in such documents, but also why these provisions have been included.

If an entrepreneur cannot find the time or take the interest to read and understand the major contracts into which his company will enter, he should be very cautious about being an entrepreneur at all.

Patrick R. Liles

Harvard Business School

Chapter Objectives

1 To introduce the importance of legal issues to entrepreneurs

2 To examine patent protection, including definitions and preparation

3 To review copyrights and their relevance to entrepreneurs

4 To study trademarks and their impact on new ventures

5 To present the major segments of the bankruptcy law that apply to business

6 To highlight some cost-saving legal tips

Entrepreneurs cannot hope to have the legal expertise or background of a lawyer, of course, but they should be sufficiently knowledgeable about certain legal concepts that have implications for the business venture.[1]

Table 13.1 sets forth some of the major legal concepts that can affect entrepreneurial ventures. These concepts can be divided into three groups: (1) those that relate to the inception of the venture, (2) those that relate to the ongoing venture, and (3) those

Table 13.1 Major Legal Concepts and Entrepreneurial Ventures

I. Inception of an Entrepreneurial Venture
  A. Laws governing intellectual property
    1. Patents
    2. Copyrights
    3. Trademarks
  B. Forms of business organization
    1. Sole proprietorship
    2. Partnership
    3. Corporation
    4. Franchise
  C. Tax considerations
  D. Capital formation
  E. Liability questions

II. An Ongoing Venture: Business Development and Transactions
  A. Personnel law
    1. Hiring and firing policies
    2. Equal Employment Opportunity Commission
    3. Collective bargaining
  B. Contract law
    1. Legal contracts
    2. Sales contracts
    3. Leases

III. Growth and Continuity of a Successful Entrepreneurial Venture
  A. Tax considerations
    1. Federal, state, local
    2. Payroll
    3. Incentives
  B. Governmental regulations
    1. Zoning (property)
    2. Administrative agencies (regulatory)
    3. Consumer law
  C. Continuity of ownership rights
    1. Property laws and ownership
    2. Wills, trusts, estates
    3. Bankruptcy

that relate to the growth and continuity of the venture. In this chapter the focus will be on the legal concepts related to the first and third groups. Specifically, we shall examine intellectual property protection (patents, copyrights, trademarks) and bankruptcy law.

Patents

A **patent** provides the owner with exclusive rights to hold, transfer, and license the production and sale of the product or process. Design patents last for 14 years; all others last for 20 years. The objective of a patent is to provide the holder with a temporary monopoly on his or her innovation and thus to encourage the creation and disclosure of new ideas and innovations in the marketplace. Securing a patent, however, is not always an easy process.

A patent is an **intellectual property right.** It is the result of a unique discovery, and patent holders are provided protection against infringement by others. In general, a number of items can qualify for patent protection, among them processes, machines, products, plants, compositions of elements (chemical compounds), and improvements on already existing items.[2]

Securing a Patent

Because quite often the patent process is complex (see Figure 13.1), careful planning is required. For pursuing a patent, the following basic rules are recommended by the experts:

Rule 1:   Pursue patents that are broad, are commercially significant, and offer a strong position. This means that relevant patent law must be researched in order to obtain the widest coverage possible on the idea or concept. In addition, there must be something significantly novel or proprietary about the innovation. Record all steps or processes in a notebook and have them witnessed so that documentation secures a strong proprietary position.

Rule 2:   Prepare a patent plan in detail. This plan should outline the costs to develop and market the innovation as well as analyze the competition and technological similarities to your idea. Attempt to detail the precise value of the innovation.

Rule 3:   Have your actions relate to your original patent plan. This does not mean a plan cannot be changed. However, it is wise to remain close to the plan during the early stages of establishing the patent. Later, the path that is prepared may change—for example, licensing out the patent versus keeping it for yourself.

Rule 4:   Establish an **infringement budget.** Patent rights are effective only if potential infringers fear legal damages. Thus it is important to prepare a realistic budget for prosecuting violations of the patent.

Rule 5:   Evaluate the patent plan strategically. The typical patent process takes three years. This should be compared to the actual life cycle of the proposed innovation or technology. Will the patent be worth defending in three years or will enforcement cost more than the damages collected?[3]

These rules relating to proper definition, preparation, planning, and evaluation can help entrepreneurs establish effective patent protection. In addition, they can help the patent attorney conduct the search process.

Figure 13.1   The Patent Process: From Application to Allowance and Issue

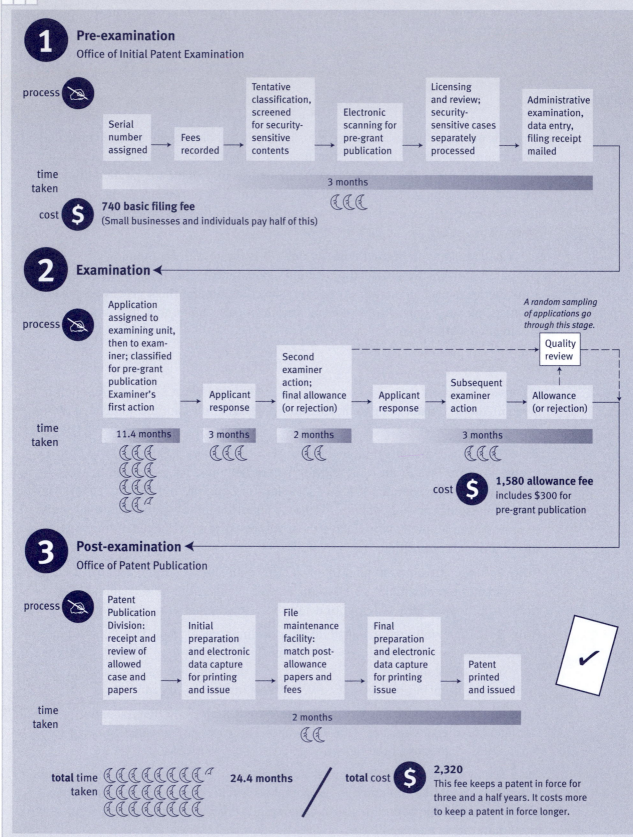

1 **Pre-examination**
Office of Initial Patent Examination

process

Serial number assigned → Fees recorded → Tentative classification, screened for security-sensitive contents → Electronic scanning for pre-grant publication → Licensing and review; security-sensitive cases separately processed → Administrative examination, data entry, filing receipt mailed

time taken   3 months

cost   **$**   **740 basic filing fee**
(Small businesses and individuals pay half of this)

2 **Examination**

process

Application assigned to examining unit, then to examiner; classified for pre-grant publication Examiner's first action → Applicant response → Second examiner action; final allowance (or rejection) → Applicant response → Subsequent examiner action → Allowance (or rejection) → Quality review

A random sampling of applications go through this stage.

time taken   11.4 months   3 months   2 months   3 months

cost   **$**   **1,580 allowance fee**
includes $300 for pre-grant publication

3 **Post-examination**
Office of Patent Publication

process

Patent Publication Division: receipt and review of allowed case and papers → Initial preparation and electronic data capture for printing and issue → File maintenance facility: match post-allowance papers and fees → Final preparation and electronic data capture for printing issue → Patent printed and issued

time taken   2 months

total time taken   **24.4 months**   /   **total** cost   **$**   **2,320**
This fee keeps a patent in force for three and a half years. It costs more to keep a patent in force longer.

Source: United States Patent Office, 2005.

Patent applications must include detailed specifications of the innovation that any skilled person in the specific area can understand. A patent application has two parts:

1. **Specification** is the text of a patent and may include any accompanying illustrations. Because its purpose is to teach those fluent in this area of technology all they need to understand, duplicate, and use the invention, it may be quite long. The specification typically includes:

   a. An introduction explaining why the invention will be useful.

   b. Description of all prior art that you are aware of and that could be considered similar to the invention. The specification usually lists other patents, by number, with a brief description of each, but you can cite and describe unpatented technology as well.

   c. A summary of the invention that describes the essence of the new technology and emphasizes its difference from prior art, while including all its requisite features, whether novel or not.

   d. A detailed description of the invention, including anything that could be remotely relevant, reference to all reasonable variations, and number bounds. Take as much space as you like. Use as many numbers as reasonable, including close or tight limits based on experience, as well as loose ones based on what might be possible. This section should be detailed enough to really teach a skilled practitioner.

   e. Examples and/or experimental results, in full detail.

   f. The specification is inherently broad because its intent is to teach and also, as a practical matter, to allow some flexibility in the claims that are based on it.

2. **Claims** are a series of short paragraphs, each of which identifies a particular feature or combination of features that is protected by the patent. The entire claims section, at the end of the patent, is typically about one page long or less.

   Claims define and limit the patented invention. The invention can be broad (a process requiring an "inorganic, nonmetal solid" would cover a lot of possibilities, for example) but sharply limited not to cover anything in prior art (other existing processes that use organics or metals).[4]

Once the application is filed with the **Patent and Trademark Office** of the Department of Commerce, an examiner will determine whether the innovation qualifies for patentability. The examiner will do this by researching technical data in journals as well as previously issued patents. Based on the individual's findings, the application will be rejected or accepted.

Only a small percentage of issued patents are commercially valuable. Consequently, the entrepreneur must weigh the value of the innovation against the time and money spent to obtain the patent. Also, it is important to remember that many patents granted by the Patent and Trademark Office have been declared invalid after being challenged in court. This occurs for several reasons. One is that the patent holder waited an unreasonable length of time before asserting his or her rights. A second is that those bringing suit against the patent holder are able to prove the individual misused the patent rights—for example, by requiring certain purchases of other goods or services as part of the patent-use arrangement. A third is that other parties are able to prove the patent itself fails to meet tests of patentability and is therefore invalid.[5]

entrepreneurship IN PRACTICE

Patent Protection—A Practical Perspective

Most people do not realize that just 2 percent of all patents ever realize any profits. Considering the cost of the patent process and the amount of time and resources it takes to protect patents, actually getting patent protection may not even be the best way to go. Because of this, many experts suggest that inventors consider licensing their product rather than marketing it themselves. In addition, many experts suggest that a venture capitalist, financially secure business partner, or consultant may be the best way to ensure success. The United States Patent and Trademark Office (USPTO) also gives priority to individuals who can prove that they came up with an idea first. This is difficult to prove, and again, the bigger, more established companies likely have an advantage on the average inventor. Just $10 allows the inventor to file a disclosure agreement with the USPTO. The next step is to file for a "patent pending" status, or a "provisional patent." This filing is just $80 and lasts for one year. It allows the inventor to further test the product and seek legal advice regarding the product. More information regarding provisional patents can be found on the USPTO website at http://www.uspto.gov/web/offices/pac/provapp.htm. Avoid the TV commercials offering patent assistance for as much as a $13,000 fee. They usually only offer a design patent (when a utility patent is most often needed). They also offer to submit the invention to industry. However, this does not mean that they will submit the invention to the correct industry or really do any "legwork" for the inventor. Finally, examine the many resources on the Internet that can help inventors take the best route toward success. Some examples are:

http://www.patentcafe.com

http://www.inventnet.com

http://www.inventorfraud.com

http://www.wini2.com

http://www.inventorfraud.com/helpers.htm

http://www.uspto.gov

SOURCE: Adapted from Michael Boland, "ASAP Inventor's Guide to the Fast Lane," *Forbes* (June 24, 2002): 72.

If, after careful review, an entrepreneur concludes that the innovation will withstand any legal challenge and is commercially worthwhile, a patent should be pursued. If a challenge is mounted, legal fees may be sizable, but a successful defense can result in damages sufficient to compensate for the infringement plus court costs and interest. In fact, the court may award damages of up to three times the actual amount. In addition, a patent infringer can be liable for all profits resulting from the infringement as well as for legal fees.[6]

Copyrights

A **copyright** provides exclusive rights to creative individuals for the protection of their literary or artistic productions. It is not possible to copyright an idea, but the particular mode for expression of that idea often can be copyrighted. This expression can take many forms, including books, periodicals, dramatic or musical compositions, art, motion pictures, lectures, sound recordings, and computer programs.

Any works created after January 1, 1978, and receiving a copyright are protected for the life of the author plus 70 years. The owner of this copyright may (1) reproduce the work, (2) prepare derivative works based on it (for example, a condensation or movie version of a novel), (3) distribute copies of the work by sale or otherwise, (4) perform the work publicly, and (5) display the work publicly. Each of these rights, or a portion of each, also may be transferred.[7]

Understanding Copyright Protection

For the author of creative material to obtain copyright protection, the material must be in a tangible form so it can be communicated or reproduced. It also must be the author's own work and thus the product of his or her skill or judgment. Concepts, principles, processes, systems, or discoveries are not valid for copyright protection until they are put in tangible form—written or recorded.

Formal registration of a copyright with the Copyright Office of the Library of Congress is a requirement before an author can begin a lawsuit for infringement. In addition, an author can find his or her copyright invalidated if proper notice isn't provided.

Anyone who violates an author's exclusive rights under a copyright is liable for infringement. However, because of the **fair use doctrine**, it is sometimes difficult to establish infringement. Fair use is described as follows:

> [Reproduction of a copyrighted work for] purposes such as criticism, comment, news reporting, teaching (including multiple copies for classroom use), scholarship, or research is not an infringement of copyright. In determining whether the use made of a work in any particular case is a fair use, the factors to be considered shall include (1) the purpose and character of the use, including whether such use is of a commercial nature or is for nonprofit educational purposes; (2) the nature of the copyrighted work; (3) the amount and substantiality of the portion used in relation to the copyrighted work as a whole; and (4) the effect of the use upon the potential market for a value of the copyrighted work.[8]

If, however, an author substantiates a copyright infringement, the normal remedy is recovery of actual damages plus any profits the violator receives. The following guidelines for copyright protection are from a lawyer's point of view:

1. There is absolutely no cost or risk involved in protecting material which you generate by copyright. Therefore, as a matter of course, any writings that you prepare and spend a lot of time on should be copyrighted by putting the copyright notice (©) on it.

2. It is not necessary to register copyrights with the Copyright Office unless and until you want to sue somebody for infringement. Therefore, in the overwhelming majority of cases, assuming you are not in the publishing business, simply use the copyright notice and do not bother spending the time and effort necessary to register copyrights with the U.S. Copyright Office.

3. In buying material and using it yourself, I suggest that you take a commercial view of fair use. For example, if you buy a subscription to a periodical, you can duplicate various articles, or indeed, a complete issue on some occasions, for use within your own organization. There may be some technical arguments as to the extent of the fair use exception under the copyright laws, but I know of no case, nor any circumstance whatsoever, where a publisher has objected to a subscriber's making copies of something for internal use. At the other extreme,

entrepreneurship IN PRACTICE

Watch What You Say

The government can't help protect your business from the competition if your employees are willingly sharing valuable information. Copious amounts of sensitive and confidential information are being made public every day by business travelers who pay no heed to the fact that people have ears. Carrying on a seemingly harmless conversation with a co-worker on an airplane, in a bus, or in a restaurant has wreaked havoc for more than one company. An employee of Fuld & Company, a management consulting firm, was riding a shuttle bus when he heard every bit of a company's distribution strategy being discussed in the seat in front of him. Luckily for the two talkers, he wasn't competition. He did, however, let it be known what had just occurred.

Protecting trade secrets is not a new concept, but with the amount of businesspeople traveling every day and the development of technology, the smallest slip can be dangerous. Leonard Fuld, a competitive intelligence expert, states that it's common for companies to overlook the human factor when it comes to information leaking out. He emphasizes the point by talking about the "Nerd Bird," a frequent shuttle flight from Austin, Texas, to San Jose, California, that carries mostly engineers and executives from the semiconductor and software industries. "I was even told an anecdote about an executive who waited until passengers had disembarked and then quickly roamed the aisle to see if any documents had been left behind." "I know of people in firms who justify booking first-class airfare based on the quality of information they might be able to pick up that way," states a Silicon Valley businessperson.

Verbal exchanges aren't the only way travelers are hurting themselves. Rental car trunks, stolen briefcases, and the simple misplaced memo are known to be gold mines as well.

Business travelers should keep these things in mind to protect intellectual property that can't be protected by the government:

1. **Avoid talking shop in public areas where competitors are likely to be present.** Business jargon isn't a code when the executive sitting right beside you is in the same industry.

2. **Never expose laptop screens on airplanes, buses, or other conveyances when working on confidential facts and figures.** If the work is unavoidable, ask for a window seat and use smaller font sizes.

3. **Be particularly vigilant at trade shows.** Proprietary technology, new product releases, and the like should be discussed in detail only behind closed doors.

4. **Pay phones and cell phones pose an amazing opportunity for others to partake in the conversation.** Be cautious of your surroundings when making important phone calls.

5. **Protect the files on your computer by purchasing a cable lock or security software.** Help deter computer theft by labeling both the case and computer and never letting them out of your sight.

6. **Keep unnecessary documentation back at the office.** Also check your work area and account for all paperwork after handling important documents to see if anything has "mysteriously" landed on the floor.

SOURCE: David Barber, "Loose Lips Sink You," *Inc.* (June 1999), www.inc.com.

the entrepreneurial
PROCESS

Post-Internet Copyright Protection

Intellectual property has become increasingly difficult to protect since the rise of the Internet. Before the net, intellectual property protection was not as common, because of the time it took to do so and the lower quality of reproductions. The Internet has drastically changed this. Digital reproductions of intellectual property are now transferred quickly and seamlessly, with little or no compromise to quality. The market for copyrighted works is much different than it is for typical products and services. The price for the average product or service is calculated by marking up the actual cost of production. In the case of copyrighted materials, there are usually low production costs but very high research and development costs. Such works are at very high risk to be pirated. According to the Business Software Alliance, half of the worldwide software market is distributed through pirated means. Likewise, the International Federation of the phonographic industry estimates that 20 percent of all music is pirated. Another problem that exists is that of the global nature of the Internet. Considering that current copyright laws are national in nature and that countries enforce those laws in varying degrees, international protection of works is very difficult. Ambiguity exists, however, due to a significant portion of piracy being altruistic in nature. In other words, the individuals giving away or transferring the copies of software or music are doing so at no charge just to do someone a favor. Current copyright laws also cause some confusion. Works can be reproduced for public use (which requires permission) and for private use (which may not require permission). The ambiguity between these two distinctions has caused confusion on when reproduction is acceptable.

Given these issues, the legal protection of copyrighted works is unlikely to change in the near future. Many companies, however, are taking steps to try to give themselves as much protection as possible. Technologies and tools such as online database searching, secure bundling and transmission of software packages, and "digital detectives" are currently being used by companies to combat this problem. Companies like Cyveillance, Ewatch, and Cybercheck are using search tools to monitor the unauthorized usage of copyrighted works, such as software and music files.

Even when companies are able to detect piracy, the problem is still the enforcement of the law. Cease and desist warnings can be issued, court action can be taken, or licenses may be issued. Swallowing their pride and issuing a license to the abuser is often the most sensible solution to these firms because the first two options are very difficult to enforce. Even if infringing websites are shut down, mirror sites have usually already been created and are ready to backup the site that was shut down.

The government, in an effort to further protect copyrighted works, passed the No Electronic Theft Act (NET) and Digital Millennium Copyright Act. The NET Act now holds individuals criminally responsible even if they do not profit from an act of piracy, while the Digital Millennium Copyright Act holds individuals criminally responsible for trying to circumvent technologies put in place to prevent piracy, such as software encryption.

Entrepreneurs must understand that the Internet has created an environment in which piracy can thrive, and therefore, there is a significant risk that their works will be pirated from the Internet. Entrepreneurs should make a decision as to exactly what kind of funds they want to budget toward fighting piracy. Because legal battles are often costly and time-consuming, entrepreneurs may find that they cannot fight every case of piracy that they encounter.

if you systematically make copies of other people's copyrighted material and thereby clearly deprive the copyright owner of additional subscriptions that he or she would otherwise have, or if you use copyrighted material in something you are going to sell for profit yourself, I think you are asking for trouble.

4. Be especially careful of catalogs and other similar materials that may have been compiled at some expense by other companies. Many times these catalogs will have so-called trap lines, which are fictitious items of information designed to trap someone who was simply copying the information. If a competitor of yours has put together an excellent catalog and spent a lot of time and money gathering the necessary information, you cannot simply copy it yourself and save all that time and money without running a risk under the copyright laws. This, of course, runs both ways, and that is why I suggest that you copyright everything that you spend a lot of time and money preparing. You may want to use trap lines also.

5. There may be some slight advantage in copyrighting advertisements. . . . In some situations it might be desirable to include the copyright notice on any advertisement you prepare if it seems possible to you that a competitor may want to try to use it. For example, a lawyer who was putting on seminars on product liability cases developed an excellent advertisement in the form of a very short article about the important aspects of minimizing product liability exposure. It was a mail-order-type advertisement consisting of a half a dozen pages or so, and I noticed it was copyrighted. The lawyer obviously had spent a lot of time in developing that ad, and did not want other people to be able to use his work to promote competitive seminars.

6. There are some things that cannot be copyrighted, such as U.S. government publications, which are in the public domain. Also, statutes, cases, congressional history, congressional debates, and all such things that are generated by government agencies generally cannot be copyrighted. However, it is possible to copyright the arrangement of those things on a page. Thus, if a publisher has gone to the trouble of setting particular statutes in type, you cannot capitalize on this time and expense by simply cutting the page out of the published work and using that for duplication. You can, of course, retype the material and use it freely.

7. Ideas cannot be copyrighted. Therefore, if someone writes an article and copyrights it, you are certainly free to read that article, digest it, take the ideas from that article and other sources, and weave them into your own material

without any copyright problems. On the other hand, if someone has copyrighted an article, you cannot simply rephrase it or change minor words and claim it as your own. Exactly where the line is to be drawn is not clear. However, a little common sense will give the appropriate answer in most of these cases.[9]

Protected Ideas?

The Copyright Act specifically excludes copyright protection for any "idea, procedure, process, system, method of operation, concept, principle, or discovery, regardless of the form in which it is described, explained, illustrated, or embodied." Note that it is not possible to copyright an *idea*. The underlying ideas embodied in a work may be freely used by others. What is copyrightable is the particular way an idea is expressed. Whenever an idea and an expression are inseparable, the expression cannot be copyrighted.

Generally, anything that is not an original expression will not qualify for copyright protection. Facts widely known to the public are not copyrightable. Page numbers are not copyrightable because they follow a sequence known to everyone. Mathematical calculations are not copyrightable. Compilations of facts, however, are copyrightable. The Copyright Act defines a compilation as "a work formed by the collection and assembling of preexisting materials of data that are selected, coordinated, or arranged in such a way that the resulting work as a whole constitutes an original work of authorship."[10]

Trademarks

A **trademark** is a distinctive name, mark, symbol, or motto identified with a company's product(s) and registered at the Patent and Trademark Office. Thanks to trademark law, no confusion should result from one venture's using the symbol or name of another.

Specific legal terms differentiate the exact types of marks. For example, trademarks identify and distinguish goods. Service marks identify and distinguish services. Certification marks denote the quality, materials, or other aspects of goods and services and are used by someone other than the mark's owner. Collective marks are trademarks or service marks members of groups or organizations use to identify themselves as the source of goods or services.[11]

Usually, personal names or words that are considered generic or descriptive are not trademarked, unless the words are in some way suggestive or fanciful or the personal name is accompanied by a specific design. For example, English Leather may not be trademarked to describe a leather processed in England; however, English Leather is trademarked as a name for aftershave lotion, since this constitutes a fanciful use of the words. Consider also that even the common name of an individual may be trademarked if that name is accompanied by a picture or some fanciful design that allows easy identification of the product, such as Smith Brothers Cough Drops.[12]

In most cases the Patent and Trademark Office will reject an application for marks, symbols, or names that are flags or insignias of governments, portraits or signatures of living persons, immoral or deceptive, or items likely to cause problems due to resemblance to a previously registered mark.[13] Once issued, the trademark is listed in the Principal Register of the Patent and Trademark Office. This listing offers several advantages: (1) nationwide constructive notice of the owner's right to use the mark (thus eliminating the need to show that the defendant in an infringement suit had notice of the mark), (2) Bureau of Customs protection against importers using the mark, and (3) incontestability of the mark after five years.[14]

In 1988, the Trademark Revision Act was passed by Congress. This act significantly altered the prior registration scheme, which required use of the mark before filing an application. The 1988 act, in contrast, allows a person to file on the basis either of use or of a bona fide intention to use the mark in commerce. This is the "intent-to-use" provision, which requires putting the mark into commerce within six months after filing with the U.S. Patent and Trademark Office. At the end of the six months, the person must provide proof the mark was put into commerce and that the application was not opposed. Under extenuating circumstances, the six-month period can be extended by 30 months, giving the applicant a total of three years from the date of notice of trademark approval to use the mark and file the required use statement. The new provision has considerably cut the costs of developing and marketing a new product. It has particularly benefited small companies.[15]

In 1995, Congress amended the Trademark Act by passing the Federal Trademark Dilution Act, which extended the protection available to trademark owners by creating a federal cause of action for trademark dilution. Until the passage of this amendment, federal trademark law only prohibited the unauthorized use of the same mark on competing—or on noncompeting but "related"—goods or services when such use would likely confuse consumers as to the origin of those goods and services. Trademark dilution laws that also have been enacted by about half of the states protect "distinctive" or "famous" trademarks (such as Jergens, McDonald's, RCA, and Macintosh) from certain unauthorized uses of the marks *regardless* of a showing of competition or a likelihood of confusion.[16]

Historically, a trademark registration lasted 20 years; however, the current registrations are good for only ten years with the possibility for continuous renewal every ten years. It is most important to understand that a trademark may be invalidated in four specific ways:

1. **Cancellation proceedings** are a third party's challenge to the mark's distinctiveness within five years of its issuance.

2. **Cleaning-out procedure** refers to the failure of a trademark owner to file an affidavit stating it is in use or justifying its lack of use within six years of registration.

3. **Abandonment** is the nonuse of a trademark for two consecutive years without justification or a statement regarding the trademark's abandonment.

4. **Generic meaning** is the allowance of a trademark to represent a general grouping of products or services. For example, cellophane has come to represent plastic wrap, and scotch tape has come to represent adhesive tape. Xerox is currently seeking, through national advertising, to avoid having its name used to represent copier machines.

the entrepreneurial
PROCESS

Nike vs. Mike: A Parody on Trademark Infringement

Mike Stanard had a great idea for his daughter to try during summer vacation: Establish an enterprise called "Just Did It" (a spoof on Nike's "Just Do It" slogan) and sell tee shirts with the famous swoosh design (identical to Nike's) but accompanied by the word "Mike" instead of Nike. The tee shirts would be sold for $19.95 and long-sleeved ones for $24.95. They would send out 1,400 brochures to college athletes and celebrities named Michael. What a great idea!

Nike did not think so. From 1971 to 1994, Nike had invested more than $300 million advertising its trademarks. Aggregate sales revenues from Nike trademarked apparel had exceeded $10 billion. The "Just Do It" slogan alone produced 1989–1994 revenue exceeding $15 million. Nike sued Stanard for trademark infringement.

Stanard's defense was parody. A parody must convey two simultaneous and contradictory messages: that it is the original, but also that it is not the original and is instead a parody. The customer must be amused and not confused.

To assess whether a trademark infringement has occurred, the courts consider seven factors: (1) the degree of similarity between the trademarks, (2) the similarity of the products for which the name is used, (3) the area and manner of concurrent use, (4) the degree of care likely to be exercised by consumers, (5) the strength of the complainant's trademark, (6) whether actual product confusion exists among buyers, and (7) an intent on the part of the alleged infringer to palm off his or her products as those of another.

Since Stanard sold the shirts by mail (customers had to write a check to "Just Did It") and he had no apparent intent to copy Nike's products specifically, the court concluded no confusion existed. Thus, the parody defense succeeded. The parody defense doesn't always work, however. Marketers will have to decide whether the legal risk involved in parody marketing is worth unknown sales results.

Some examples of court rulings include these:

- ☐ Miami Mice was a valid parody of Miami Vice.
- ☐ Hard Rain Cafe was likely to confuse consumers regarding the Hard Rock Cafe.
- ☐ Enjoy Cocaine was not a valid parody of Enjoy Coca-Cola, where both used the familiar red-and-white logo.
- ☐ Stop the Olympic Prison, using the five-interlocking-rings logo, was considered not confusing with the Olympic Committee's trademark.
- ☐ Lardash was considered a valid parody of Jordache.
- ☐ Mutant of Omaha and the subtitle Nuclear Holocaust Insurance was not a valid parody of Mutual of Omaha.
- ☐ Bagzilla was a permissible pun of Godzilla and would not confuse consumers.
- ☐ Spy Notes was a valid parody of Cliff Notes.

SOURCE: Maxine S. Lans, "Parody as a Marketing Strategy," *Marketing News* (January 3, 1994): 20.

If a trademark is properly registered, used, and protected, the owner can obtain an injunction against any uses of the mark that are likely to cause confusion. (See the Part 4 Playboy Emblem case study on page 571, for an excellent example of a company seeking to protect its trademark.) Moreover, if infringement and damages can be proven in court, a monetary award may be given to the trademark holder.

the entrepreneurial PROCESS

Internet Intellectual Property Information Sources

http://www.uspto.gov

The United States Patent and Trademark Office website provides a wealth of valuable information for entrepreneurs. Users can locate patent and trademark information, such as registration forms, international patents, legal issues, and FAQs. Users can also check the status of a trademark or patent application on this site.

http://www.patents.com

This site, provided by the law offices of Oppedahl and Larson, provides basic patent information in a very organized manner. It is also updated frequently.

http://www.bustpatents.com

This site, sponsored by Source Translation and Optimization, offers assistance with Internet, biotech, and e-commerce patents. Users also can sign up for the free daily information e-mail, Internet Patent News Service, at this site.

http://www.copyright.gov/

The United States Copyright Office at the Library of Congress website provides information on copyright protecting works, licensing, and legal issues. Users also can search copyright records on the site.

http://www.law.cornell.edu/wex/index.php/Copyright

The Legal Information Institute in the Cornell School of Law website provides legal documentation and a history of copyright law. It also offers information on international copyrights and links to other copyright information resources.

http://www.findlaw.com

This site allows the user to look up any topic in a search and yield returns of the actual written law, court precedence, and current cases and interpretations. The site also gives topical searches that aide the user in getting started as well as a business section to help put the laws into more practical applications.

http://www.swlearning.com/blaw/wbl/chooseyourbook.html

West's Business Law textbook's website offers an overview of the book, cases, and updates that allow surfers the ability to check contents before purchasing.

Avoiding the Pitfalls

Trademark registration and search can be costly, sometimes ranging into the thousands of dollars. Trademark infringement can be even more expensive. To avoid these pitfalls, one author has noted five basic rules entrepreneurs should follow when selecting trademarks for their new ventures.

Rule 1:   Never select a corporate name or a mark without first doing a trademark search.

Rule 2:   If your attorney says you have a potential problem with a mark, trust that judgment.

Rule 3:   Seek a coined or a fanciful name or mark before you settle for a descriptive or a highly suggestive one.

Rule 4:   Whenever marketing or other considerations dictate the use of a name or a mark that is highly suggestive of the product, select a distinctive logotype for the descriptive or suggestive words.

Rule 5:   Avoid abbreviations and acronyms wherever possible, and when no alternative is acceptable, select a distinctive logotype in which the abbreviation or acronym appears.[17]

Trade Secrets

Certain business processes and information cannot be patented, copyrighted, or trademarked. Yet they may be protected as **trade secrets**. Customer lists, plans, research and development, pricing information, marketing techniques, and production techniques are examples of potential trade secrets. Generally, anything that makes an individual company unique and has value to a competitor could be a trade secret.[18]

Protection of trade secrets extends both to ideas and to their expression. For this reason, and because a trade secret involves no registration or filing requirements, trade-secret protection is ideal for software. Of course, the secret formula, method, or other information must be disclosed to key employees. Businesses generally attempt to protect their trade secrets by having all employees who use the process or information agree in their contracts never to divulge it. Theft of confidential business data by industrial espionage, such as stealing a competitor's documents, is a theft of trade secrets without any contractual violation and is actionable in itself.

The law clearly outlines the area of trade secrets: Information is a trade secret if (1) it is not known by the competition, (2) the business would lose its advantage if the competition were to obtain it, and (3) the owner has taken reasonable steps to protect the secret from disclosure.[19] Keep in mind that prosecution is still difficult in many of these cases.

Trademark Protection on the Internet

Because of the unique nature of the Internet, its use creates unique legal questions and issues—particularly with respect to intellectual property rights. The emerging body of law governing cyberspace is often referred to as *cyberlaw*.

One of the initial trademark issues involving intellectual property in cyberspace has been whether domain names (Internet addresses) should be treated as trademarks or simply as a means of access, similar to street addresses in the physical world. Increasingly, the courts are holding that the principles of trademark law should apply to domain names. One problem in applying trademark law to Internet domain names, however, is that trademark law allows multiple parties to use the same mark—as long as the mark is used for different goods or services and will not cause customer confusion. On the Internet as it is currently structured, only one party can use a particular domain name, regardless of the type of goods or services offered. In other words, although two or more businesses can own the trademark Entrevision, only one business can operate on the Internet with the domain name "Entrevision.com." Because of this restrictive feature of domain names, a question has arisen as to whether domain names should function as trademarks. To date, the courts that have considered this question have held that the unauthorized use of another's mark in a domain name may constitute trademark infringement.[20]

Table 13.2 provides a comprehensive outline of the forms of intellectual property protection.

Table 13.2   Forms of Intellectual Property

	PATENT	COPYRIGHT	TRADEMARKS (SERVICE MARKS AND TRADE DRESS)	TRADE SECRETS
DEFINITION	A grant from the government that gives an inventor exclusive rights to an invention.	An intangible property right granted to authors and originators of a literary work or artistic production that falls within specified categories.	Any distinctive word, name, symbol, or device (image or appearance), or combination thereof, that an entity uses to identify and distinguish its goods or services from those of others.	Any information (including formulas, patterns, programs, devices, techniques, and processes) that a business possesses and that gives the business an advantage over competitors who do not know the information or process.
REQUIREMENTS	An invention must be: 1. Novel. 2. Not obvious. 3. Useful.	Literary or artistic works must be: 1. Original. 2. Fixed in a durable medium that can be perceived, reproduced, or communicated. 3. Within a copyrightable category.	Trademarks, service marks, and trade dresses must be sufficiently distinctive (or must have acquired a secondary meaning) to enable consumers and others to distinguish the manufacturer's, seller's, or business user's products or services from those of competitors.	Information and processes that have commercial value, that are not known or easily ascertainable by the general public or others, and that are reasonably protected from disclosure.
TYPES OR CATEGORIES	1. Utility (general). 2. Design. 3. Plant (flowers, vegetables, and so on).	1. Literary works (including computer programs). 2. Musical works. 3. Dramatic works. 4. Pantomime and choreographic works. 5. Pictorial, graphic, and sculptural works. 6. Films and audiovisual works. 7. Sound recordings.	1. Strong, distinctive marks (such as fanciful, arbitrary, or suggestive marks). 2. Marks that have acquired a secondary meaning by use. 3. Other types of marks, including certification marks and collective marks. 4. Trade dress (such as a distinctive decor, menu, or style or type of service).	1. Customer lists. 2. Research and development. 3. Plans and programs. 4. Pricing information. 5. Production techniques. 6. Marketing techniques. 7. Formulas. 8. Compilations.
HOW ACQUIRED	By filing a patent application with the U.S. Patent and Trademark Office and receiving that office's approval.	Automatic (once in tangible form); to recover for infringement, the copyright must be registered with the U.S. Copyright Office.	1. At common law, ownership is created by use of mark. 2. Registration (either with the U.S. Patent and Trademark Office or with the appropriate state office) gives constructive notice of date of use.	Through the originality and development of information and processes that are unique to a business, that are unknown by others, and that

Table 13.2   (Continued)

	PATENT	COPYRIGHT	TRADEMARKS (SERVICE MARKS AND TRADE DRESS)	TRADE SECRETS
			3. Federal registration is permitted if the mark is currently in use *or* if the applicant intends use within six months (period can be extended to three years). 4. Federal registration can be renewed between the fifth and sixth years and, thereafter, every ten years.	would be valuable to competitors if they knew of the information and processes.
RIGHTS	An inventor has the right to make, use, sell, assign, or license the invention during the duration of the patent's term. The first to invent has patent rights.	The author or originator has the exclusive right to reproduce, distribute, display, license, or transfer a copyrighted work.	The owner has the right to use the mark or trade dress and to exclude others from using it. The right of use can be licensed or sold (assigned) to another.	The owner has the right to sole and exclusive use of the trade secrets and the right to use legal means to protect against misappropriation of the trade secrets by others. The owner can license or assign a trade secret.
DURATION	20 years from the date of application; for design patents, 14 years.	1. For authors: the life of the author, plus 70 years. 2. For publishers: 95 years after the date of publication or 120 years after creation.	Unlimited, as long as it is in use. To continue notice by registration, the registration must be renewed by filing.	Unlimited, as long as not revealed to others.
CIVIL REMEDIES FOR INFRINGEMENT	Monetary damages, which include reasonable royalties and lost profits, *plus* attorneys' fees. (Treble damages are available for intentional infringement.)	Actual damages, plus profits received by the infringer; *or* statutory damages of not less than $500 and not more than $20,000 ($100,000, if infringement is willful); *plus* costs and attorneys' fees.	1. Injunction prohibiting future use of mark. 2. Actual damages, *plus* profits received by the infringer (can be increased to three times the actual damages under the Lanham Act). 3. Impoundment and destruction of infringing articles. 4. *Plus* costs and attorneys' fees.	Monetary damages for misappropriation (the Uniform Trade Secrets Act permits punitive damages up to twice the amount of actual damages for willful and malicious misappropriation); *plus* costs and attorneys' fees.

Source: Kenneth W. Clarkson, Roger LeRoy Miller, Gaylord A. Jentz, and Frank B. Cross, *West's Business Law: Legal, Ethical, International, and E-Commerce Environment,* 8th ed. (Mason, OH: South-Western, a division of Thomson Learning: http://www.thomsonrights.com, © 2001), 125–126. Reprinted with permission.

Bankruptcy

Bankruptcy occurs when a venture's financial obligations are greater than its assets. No entrepreneur intentionally seeks bankruptcy. Although occasionally problems can arise out of the blue, here are several ways to foresee impending failure: (1) New competition enters the market, (2) other firms seem to be selling products that are a generation ahead, (3) the research and development budget is proportionately less than the competition's, and (4) retailers always seem to be overstocked.[21]

Other early warning signs of bankruptcy follow:

- ☐ Financial management is lax. No one knows how the company's money is spent.

- ☐ Company officers, too busy to keep tabs on the bookkeeping, have trouble providing information or documentation of corporate transactions to the accountant.

- ☐ Officers and family members make repeated emergency loans to the company. This usually means the business cannot get credit from banks.

- ☐ Customers are given large discounts if they pay more promptly. Products are put on sale to generate cash. This puts a faltering company in greater jeopardy by reducing needed markups.

- ☐ Contracts are accepted below standard price to generate cash. This is only a temporary—and eventually suicidal—answer to cash-flow problems.

- ☐ The bank wants loans subordinated. If a business owner lends money to the company, the bank wants a guarantee the company will not pay back the owner before the bank. In other words, the bank suspects the business is in danger.

- ☐ Sales decrease without an accompanying cutback in the amount of inventory ordered. A business owner who lets this inequity mount will inevitably suffer big cash-flow problems.

- ☐ Key personnel depart suddenly.

- ☐ An inadequate supply of materials delays or halts the company's product shipments. This may indicate suppliers have not received payment for some time and are not extending further credit.

- ☐ Payroll taxes are not paid. This, done in the belief the IRS's lag time in catching such delinquencies will give the business time to recover, spells disaster.[22]

In addition, specific financial ratios can assist in detecting impending bankruptcy. Table 13.3 lists these ratios, how they are derived, and what change to watch for.

In spite of many warning signs, numerous ventures are confronted with bankruptcy each year.[23] As can be seen in Table 13.4, the rate of business bankruptcies has steadily declined since 1991, with the exception of 2001, where a small increase took place. The rate of consumer bankruptcies has continued to climb and has consistently been the largest percentage of bankruptcy filings since 1990. It is interesting to note, however, that of the ten largest business bankruptcies in U.S. history (shown in Table 13.5), seven have occurred since 2001. Thus, while the overall trend in business bankruptcies has not demonstrated an alarming increase, some of the largest bankruptcies ever witnessed in the United States have been recent occurrences. Entrepreneurs must therefore be aware of some basics involved with the bankruptcy codes.

Table 13.3 Bankruptcy-Detecting Financial Ratios

	DERIVATION	CHANGE TO WATCH FOR
Liquidity Ratios		
Net working capital (sometimes called risk)	Current assets less current liabilities	Fewer dollars
Cash flow versus current liabilities	Net income plus depreciation and other noncash expenses divided by current liabilities	Lower ratio
Debt Ratios		
Cash-flow coverage	Cash flow divided by fixed charges, including interest and dividends	Lower ratio
Times interest earned	Income before interest and taxes divided by interest charges	Lower ratio
Short-term debt to assets	Current liabilities divided by total assets	Higher ratio
Activity Ratios		
Inventory turn	Sales divided by inventory	Lower ratio
Average collection period	Accounts receivable divided by average daily sales	Higher ratio
Profitability Ratios		
Profit margin	Net income divided by sales	Lower ratio

Source: Adapted from Harlan D. Platt, *Why Companies Fail* (Lexington, MA: Lexington Books, 1985), 86.

The Bankruptcy Act

The **Bankruptcy Act** is a federal law that provides for specific procedures for handling *insolvent debtors*. An insolvent debtor is one who is unable to pay debts as they become due. The initial act of 1912 was amended in 1938 and then completely revised in 1978. Significant amendments were added in 1984. The purposes of the Bankruptcy Act are (1) to ensure that the property of the debtor is distributed fairly to the creditors, (2) to protect creditors from having debtors unreasonably diminish their assets, and (3) to protect debtors from extreme demands by creditors. The law was set up in order to provide assistance to both debtors and creditors.

Each of the various types of bankruptcy proceedings has its own particular provisions. For purposes of business ventures, the three major sections are called straight bankruptcy (Chapter 7), reorganization (Chapter 11), and adjustment of debts (Chapter 13). Table 13.6 provides a comparison of these three types of bankruptcies. The following sections examine each type.

Chapter 7: Straight Bankruptcy

Sometimes referred to as **liquidation**, Chapter 7 bankruptcy requires the debtor to surrender all property to a trustee appointed by the court. The trustee then sells the assets and turns the proceeds over to the creditors. The remaining debts,

Table 13.4   Business and Consumer Bankruptcies since 1990

YEAR	TOTAL FILINGS	BUSINESS FILINGS	NON-BUSINESS FILINGS	CONSUMER FILINGS AS A PERCENTAGE OF TOTAL FILINGS
1990	782,960	64,853	718,107	91.72%
1991	943,987	71,549	872,438	92.42%
1991	971,517	70,643	900,874	92.73%
1993	875,202	62,304	812,898	92.88%
1994	832,829	52,374	780,455	93.71%
1995	926,601	51,959	874,642	94.39%
1996	1,178,555	53,549	1,125,006	95.46%
1997	1,404,145	54,027	1,350,118	96.15%
1998	1,442,549	44,367	1,398,182	96.92%
1999	1,319,465	44,367	1,281,581	97.12%
2000	1,253,444	35,472	1,217,972	97.17%
2001	1,492,129	40,099	1,452,030	97.31%
2002	1,577,651	38,540	1,539,111	97.56%
2003	1,660,245	35,037	1,625,208	97.89%
2004	1,597,462	34,317	1,563,145	97.85%

Source: http://www.abiworld.org, 2002.

Table 13.5   The Ten Largest Business Bankruptcies in U.S. History

COMPANY	BANKRUPTCY DATE	TOTAL ASSETS PRE-BANKRUPTCY
Worldcom, Inc.	07/21/2002	$103,914,000,000
Enron Corp.	12/2/2001	$ 63,392,000,000
Texaco, Inc.	4/12/1987	$ 35,892,000,000
Financial Corp. of America	9/9/1988	$ 33,864,000,000
Global Crossing Ltd.	1/28/2002	$ 25,511,000,000
Adelphia Communications	6/25/2002	$ 24,409,662,000
Pacific Gas and Electric Co.	4/6/2001	$ 21,470,000,000
MCorp	3/31/1989	$ 20,228,000,000
Kmart Corp.	1/22/2002	$ 17,007,000,000
NTL, Inc.	5/8/2002	$ 16,834,200,000

Source: http://www.bankruptcy.com, 2002.

with certain exceptions, are then discharged, and the debtor is relieved of his or her obligations.

A liquidation proceeding may be voluntary or involuntary. In a voluntary bankruptcy, the debtor files a petition with the bankruptcy court that provides a list of all creditors, a statement of financial affairs, a list of all owned property, and a list of current income and expenses. In an involuntary bankruptcy, the creditors force the debtor into bankruptcy. For this to occur, 12 or more creditors with at least 3 of them

Table 13.6   Bankruptcy: A Comparison of Chapters 7, 11, and 13

	CHAPTER 7	CHAPTER 11	CHAPTER 13
PURPOSE	Liquidation	Reorganization	Adjustment
WHO CAN PETITION	Debtor (voluntary) or creditors (involuntary)	Debtor (voluntary) or creditors (involuntary)	Debtor (voluntary) only
WHO CAN BE A DEBTOR	Any "person" (including partnerships and corporations) except railroads, insurance companies, banks, savings and loan institutions, and credit unions. Farmers and charitable institutions cannot be involuntarily petitioned.	Any debtor eligible for Chapter 7 relief; railroads are also eligible.	Any individual (not partnerships or corporations) with regular income who owes fixed unsecured debt of less than $290,525 or secured debt of less than $871,550.
PROCEDURE LEADING TO DISCHARGE	Nonexempt property is sold with proceeds to be distributed (in order) to priority groups. Dischargeable debts are terminated.	A plan is submitted and, if it is approved and followed, debts are discharged.	A plan is submitted (must be approved if debtor turns over disposable income for three-year period) and, if it is approved and followed, debts are discharged.
ADVANTAGES	On liquidation and distribution, most debts are discharged, and the debtor has an opportunity for a fresh start.	The debtor continues in business. Creditors can accept the plan, or it can be "crammed down" on them. The plan allows for a reorganization and liquidation of debts over the plan period.	The debtor continues in business or keeps possession of assets. If the plan is approved, most debts are discharged after a three-year period.

Source: Roger LeRoy Miller and Gaylord A. Jentz, *Fundamentals of Business Law*, 6th ed. (Mason, OH: South-Western, a division of Thomson Learning: http://www.thomsonrights.com, © 2005), 438. Reprinted with permission.

having a total of $5,000 of claims must exist; or if fewer than 12 exist, 1 or more creditors must have a claim of $5,000 against the debtor.[24]

Chapter 11: Reorganization

Reorganization is the most common form of bankruptcy. Under this format, a debtor attempts to formulate a plan to pay a portion of the debts, have the remaining sum discharged, and continue to stay in operation. The plan is essentially a contract between the debtor and creditors. In addition to being viewed as "fair and equitable," the plan must (1) divide the creditors into classes, (2) set forth how each creditor will be satisfied, (3) state which claims or classes of claims are impaired or adversely affected by the plan, and (4) provide the same treatment to each creditor in a particular class.

The same basic principles that govern Chapter 7 bankruptcy petitions also govern the Chapter 11 petitions. The proceedings may be either voluntary or involuntary, and the provisions for protection and discharge are similar to the Chapter 7 regulations.

Once an order for relief (the petition) is filed, the debtor in a Chapter 11 proceeding continues to operate the business as a **debtor-in-possession**, which means the court appoints a trustee to oversee the management of the business. The plan is then submitted to the creditors for approval. Approval generally requires that creditors holding two-thirds of the amount and one-half of the number of each class of claims impaired by the plan must accept it. Once approved, the plan goes before the court for confirmation. If the plan is confirmed, the debtor is responsible for carrying it out.[25]

Once the plan is confirmed by the creditors, it is binding for the debtor. This type of bankruptcy provides an alternative to liquidating the entire business and thus extends to the creditors and debtor the benefits of keeping the enterprise in operation.

Chapter 13: Adjustment of Debts

Under this arrangement individuals are allowed to (1) avoid a declaration of bankruptcy, (2) pay their debts in installments, and (3) be protected by the federal court. Individuals or sole proprietors with unsecured debts of less than $100,000 or secured debts of less than $350,000 are eligible to file under a Chapter 13 procedure. This petition must be voluntary only; creditors are not allowed to file a Chapter 13 proceeding. In the petition the debtor declares an inability to pay his or her debts and requests some form of extension through future earnings (longer period of time to pay) or a composition of debt (reduction in the amount owed).

The individual debtor then files a plan providing the details for treatment of the debts. A Chapter 13 plan must provide for (1) the turnover of such future earnings or income of the debtor to the trustee as is necessary for execution of the plan, (2) full payment in deferred cash payments of all claims entitled to priority, and (3) the same treatment of each claim within a particular class (although the 1984 amendments permit the debtor to list codebtors, such as guarantors or sureties, as a separate class).[26] The plan must provide for payment within three years unless the court specifically grants an extension to five years.

Once the debtor has completed all payments scheduled in the plan, the court will issue a discharge of all other debts provided for in the plan. As always, some exceptions to the discharge exist, such as child support and certain long-term debts. In addition, the debtor can be discharged even though he or she does not complete the payments within the three years if the court is satisfied that the failure is due to circumstances for which the debtor cannot justly be held accountable. During a Chapter 13 proceeding, no other bankruptcy petition (Chapter 7 or 11) may be filed against the debtor. Thus an individual has an opportunity to relieve a debt situation without liquidation or the stigma of bankruptcy. In addition, the creditors may benefit by recovering a larger percentage than through a liquidation.

Keeping Legal Expenses Down

Throughout any legal proceedings, the entrepreneur can run up large legal bills. Presented next are some suggestions for minimizing these expenses:

- ☐ Establish the fee structure with an attorney before any legal matters are handled. This structure may be based on an hourly charge, a flat fee (straight contract fee), or a contingent fee (percentage of negotiated settlement).

- [ ] Always compromise and attempt to settle any dispute rather than litigate.
- [ ] Have your lawyer design forms that you can use in routine transactions.
- [ ] Use a less expensive lawyer for small collections.
- [ ] Suggest cost-saving methods to your attorney for ordinary business matters.
- [ ] See your lawyer during normal business hours.
- [ ] Consult with your lawyer on several matters at one time.
- [ ] Keep abreast of legal developments in your field.
- [ ] Handle some matters yourself.
- [ ] Shop around, but don't lawyer-hop. Once you find a good lawyer, stick with that person. A lawyer who's familiar with your business can handle your affairs much more efficiently than a succession of lawyers, each of whom must research your case from scratch.[27]

■ *Summary*

A patent is an intellectual property right that is a result of a unique discovery. Patent holders are provided protection against infringement by others. This protection is for 14 years in the case of design patents and for 20 years in all other cases.

Securing a patent can be a complex process, and careful planning is required. Some of the useful rules to follow in acquiring a patent were set forth in the chapter.

A patent may be declared invalid for several reasons: failure to assert the property right for an unreasonable length of time, misuse of the patent, and inability to prove the patent meets patentability tests. On the other hand, if a patent is valid, the owner can prevent others from infringing on it; if they do infringe on it, the owner can bring legal action to prevent the infringement as well as, in some cases, obtain financial damages.

A copyright provides exclusive rights to creative individuals for the protection of their literary or artistic productions. This protection extends for the life of the author plus 70 years. In case of infringement, the author (or whoever holds the copyright) can initiate a lawsuit for infringement. This action can result in an end to the infringement and, in some cases, the awarding of financial damages.

A trademark is a distinctive name, mark, symbol, or motto identified with a company's product(s). When an organization registers a trademark, it has the exclusive right to use that mark. The registration before 1989 lasts for 20 years. However, after 1989 the registration is for ten years and is renewable every ten years thereafter. In case of infringement, the trademark holder can seek legal action and damages.

For more than a decade numerous business failures have occurred, but business bankruptcy cases have been decreasing the past few years since 1991. Three major sections of the Bankruptcy Act are of importance to entrepreneurs. Chapter 7 deals with straight bankruptcy and calls for a liquidation of all assets in order to satisfy outstanding debts. Chapter 11 deals with reorganization, a format wherein a business continues operating and attempts to formulate a plan to pay a portion of the debts, to have the remaining sum discharged, and to continue to pay the debt in installments. Chapter 13 deals with individual debtors who file a plan for adjustment of their debts. This would apply to sole proprietorships because they are individually owned. More business bankruptcies are handled under Chapter 11 than under the other two sections.

Key Terms and Concepts

abandonment	generic meaning
bankruptcy	infringement budget
Bankruptcy Act	intellectual property right
cancellation proceedings	liquidation
claims	patent
cleaning-out procedure	Patent and Trademark Office
copyright	specification
debtor-in-possession	trade secrets
fair use doctrine	trademark

Review and Discussion Questions

1. In your own words, what is a patent? Of what value is a patent to an entrepreneur? What benefits does it provide?

2. What are four basic rules entrepreneurs should remember about securing a patent?

3. When can a patent be declared invalid? Cite two examples.

4. If a patent is infringed on by a competitor, what action can the patent holder take? Explain in detail.

5. In your own words, what is a copyright? What benefits does a copyright provide?

6. How much protection does a copyright afford the owner? Can any of the individual's work be copied without paying a fee? Explain in detail. If an infringement of the copyright occurs, what legal recourse does the owner have?

7. In your own words, what is a trademark? Why are generic or descriptive names or words not given trademarks?

8. When may a trademark be invalidated? Explain.

9. What are three of the pitfalls individuals should avoid when seeking a trademark?

10. How can an entrepreneur find out if the business is going bankrupt? What are three early warning signs?

11. What type of protection does Chapter 7 offer to a bankrupt entrepreneur?

12. What type of protection does Chapter 11 offer to a bankrupt entrepreneur? Why do many people prefer Chapter 11 to Chapter 7?

13. What type of protection does Chapter 13 offer to a bankrupt entrepreneur? How does Chapter 13 differ from Chapter 7 or Chapter 11?

Experiential Exercise

Protecting Your Legal Interests

Entrepreneurs need to know how to legally protect their interests in a property or work. The most effective way to gain legal protection is to obtain a copyright or a trademark. Two definitions are given here. Place a C next to the one that defines a copyright;

place a *T* next to the one that defines a trademark. Then, on the list below (a through j), place a *C* next to each item that could be protected with a copyright and a *T* next to each item that could be protected with a trademark. Answers are provided at the end of the exercise.

1. _____ A distinctive name, mark, symbol, or motto identified with a company's product

2. _____ An exclusive protection of a literary or an artistic production

   a. _____ Best-selling novel

   b. _____ Logo

   c. _____ Company's initials (such as IBM or ITT)

   d. _____ Motion picture

   e. _____ Word (such as Coke or Pepsi)

   f. _____ Computer program

   g. _____ Musical comedy

   h. _____ Slogan

   i. _____ Stage play

   j. _____ Symbol

Answers: 1. T, 2. C, a. C, b. T, c. T, d. C, e. T, f. C, g. C, h. T, i. C, j. T

Case 13.1

A Patent Matter

Technological breakthroughs in the machine industry are commonplace. Thus, whenever one company announces a new development, some of the first customers are that company's competitors. The latter will purchase the machine, strip it down, examine the new technology, and then look for ways to improve it. The original breakthroughs always are patented by the firm that discovers them, even though the technology is soon surpassed.

A few weeks ago Tom Farrington completed the development of a specialized lathe machine that is 25 percent faster and 9 percent more efficient than anything currently on the market. This technological breakthrough was a result of careful analysis of competitive products. "Until I saw some of the latest developments in the field," Tom told his wife, "I didn't realize how easy it would be to increase the speed and efficiency of the machine. But once I saw the competition's products, I knew immediately how to proceed."

Tom has shown his machine to five major firms in the industry, and all have placed orders with him. Tom has little doubt he will make a great deal of money from his invention. Before beginning production, however, Tom intends to get a patent on his invention. He believes his machine is so much more sophisticated and complex than any other machine on the market that it will take his competitors at least four years to develop a better product. "By that time I hope to have improved on my invention and continue to remain ahead of them," he noted.

Tom has talked to an attorney about filing for a patent. The attorney believes Tom should answer two questions before proceeding: (1) How long will it take the competition to improve on your patent? (2) How far are you willing to go in defending your patent right? Part of the attorney's comments were as follows: "It will take us about three years to get a patent. If, during this time, the competition is able to come out with something that is better than what you have, we will have wasted a lot of time and effort. The patent will have little value since no one will be interested in using it. Since some of your first sales will be to the competition, this is something to which you have to give serious thought. Second, even if it takes four years for the competition to catch up, would you be interested in fighting those who copy your invention after, say, two years? Simply put, we can get you a patent, but I'm not sure it will provide you as much protection as you think."

Questions

1. Given the nature of the industry, how valuable will a patent be to Tom? Explain.

2. If Tom does get a patent, can he bring action against infringers? Will it be worth the time and expense? Why or why not?

3. What do you think Tom should do? Why?

Case 13.2

All She Needs Is a Little Breathing Room

When Debbie Dawson started her business 12 months ago, she estimated it would be profitable within 8 months. That is not what happened. During the first six months she lost $18,000, and during the next six months she lost an additional $14,000. Debbie believes the business is going to get better during the next six months and that she will be able to break even by the end of the second year. However, her creditors are not sure. Debbie's business owes the two largest creditors a total of $48,000. The others are owed a total of $38,000.

Debbie believes that if she can postpone paying her creditors for a period of one year, her company will be strong enough to pay off all of its debts. On the other hand, if she has to pay the creditors now, she will be too weak financially to continue and will have to declare bankruptcy. "I really think it's in everyone's best interest to give me 12 months of breathing room," she explained to her husband. "If they will do this, everyone is going to come out on top. Otherwise, we are all going to take a financial bath."

Debbie has considered broaching the subject with her two major creditors. However, she is not sure whether this suggestion would be accepted or would be used as a basis for their bringing legal action against her. "If they think I am trying to stall them, they just might demand repayment immediately and force me into bankruptcy," she explained to a close friend. "Of course, if they see things my way, that's a different story. In any event, I'm reluctant to pursue this line of action without talking to my attorney."

Debbie hopes she and her lawyer, Juan, can work out a plan of action that will prevent her having to declare bankruptcy and liquidate the firm. During her phone call to set up a meeting with Juan, she commented, "If everyone remains calm and looks the situation over very carefully, I think they'll agree that my suggestion is a good one. After all, I'm not asking them to put any more money in the business, so the most they can lose is what they are owed currently. On the other hand, if they force my hand, they'll probably be lucky to get 40 cents on the dollar. If they wait, they could end up with all of their money. All I'm asking for is a little breathing room." Juan suggests they meet later this week to talk about it. "I'm sure we can think of something," he told her.

Questions

1. What type of bankruptcy agreement would you recommend? Why?

2. Why would you not recommend the other types of bankruptcy? Be complete in your answer.

3. When selling the creditors on your recommendation, what argument(s) would you use?

Notes

1. Marianne M. Jennings, *Business: Its Legal, Ethical, and Global Environment,* 7th ed., (Mason, OH: Thomson Learning, 2006).

2. Al H. Ringleb, Roger E. Meiners, and Frances L. Edwards, *Managing in the Legal Environment* (St. Paul, MN: West, 1996), 212–213; see also John R. Allison and Robert A. Prentice, *Business Law,* 6th ed. (Fort Worth, TX: The Dryden Press, 1994), 194–197.

3. Reprinted by permission of the *Harvard Business Review.* An excerpt from "Making Patents Work for Small Companies," by Ronald D. Rothchild, July/August 1987, 24–30. Copyright © 1987 by the President and Fellows of Harvard College; all rights reserved.

4. Ibid., 28.

5. Robert A. Choate and William H. Francis, *Patent Law: Trade Secrets—Copyright—Trademarks* (St. Paul, MN: West, 1981), 1024–1025; and Kenneth W. Clarkson, Roger LeRoy Miller, Gaylord A. Jentz, and Frank B. Cross, *West's Business Law: Legal, Ethical, International, and E-Commerce Environment,* 8th ed. (Mason, OH: South-Western/Thomson Learning, 2001), 131–136.

6. Roger LeRoy Miller and Gaylord A. Jentz, *Business Law Today* (St. Paul, MN: West, 1997), 168–169.

7. Ibid., 170–171; and Choate and Francis, *Patent Law,* 932–945.

8. Clarkson et al., *West's Business Law,* 134–135.

9. William A. Hancock, *The Small Business Legal Advisor* (New York: McGraw-Hill, 1982), 205–208. Copyright © 1982 McGraw-Hill Book Company. Reprinted with permission.

10. Clarkson et al., *West's Business Law,* 134–135.

11. See Thomas G. Field, Jr., *Trademarks and Business Goodwill* (Washington, D.C.: Office of Business Development, Small Business Administration, 1990).

12. Clarkson et al., *West's Business Law,* 128.

13. For a complete discussion, see Choate and Francis, *Patent Law,* 992–1042.

14. Dorothy Cohen, "Trademark Strategy," *Journal of Marketing* (January 1986): 61–74.

15. Clarkson et al., *West's Business Law,* 128–129.

16. Ibid., 128.

17. Thomas M. S. Hemnes, "How Can You Find a Safe Trademark?" *Harvard Business Review* (March/April 1985): 40–48; see also Michael Finn, "Everything You Need to Know about Trademarks and Publishing," *Publishers Weekly* (January 6, 1992): 41–44.

18. Clarkson et al., *West's Business Law,* 137.

19. Ringleb, Meiners, and Edwards, *Managing in the Legal Environment,* 213.

20. Clarkson et al., *West's Business Law,* 544–563.

21. Harlan D. Platt, *Why Companies Fail* (Lexington, MA: Lexington Books, 1985), 83.

22. Reuben Abrams, "Warning Signs of Bankruptcy," *Nation's Business* (February 1987): 22.

23. *The State of Small Business: A Report to the President* (Washington, D.C.: Government Printing Office, 1997), 39–41; and *The Business Failure Record* (Washington, D.C.: The Dun & Bradstreet Corp., 1997), 1–3.

24. Clarkson et al., *West's Business Law*, 545–555.

25. For a detailed discussion of Chapter 11 bankruptcy, see Clarkson et al., *West's Business Law*, 555–557.

26. Ibid., 557–559.

27. Adapted from Fred S. Steingold, "*18 Ways to Cut Legal Costs,*" *Inc.*, special issue on small-business success, 1985.

14

Sources of Capital for Entrepreneurs

Money is like a sixth sense without which you cannot make a complete use of the other five.

William Somerset Maugham

Of Human Bondage

Chapter Objectives

1 To differentiate between debt and equity as methods of financing

2 To examine commercial loans and public stock offerings as sources of capital

3 To discuss private placements as an opportunity for equity capital

4 To study the market for venture capital and to review venture capitalists' evaluation criteria for new ventures

5 To discuss the importance of evaluating venture capitalists for a proper selection

6 To examine the existing informal risk-capital market ("angel capital")

Every entrepreneur planning a new venture confronts the dilemma of where to find start-up capital. Entrepreneurs usually are not aware that numerous possibilities and combinations of financial packages may be appropriate for new ventures.

It is important, therefore, to understand not only the various sources of capital but also the expectations and requirements of these sources. Without this understanding, an entrepreneur may be frustrated with attempts to find appropriate start-up capital.

Commercial loans, public offerings, private placements, convertible debentures, venture capital, and informal risk capital are some of the major terms used in the search for capital. But what exactly are they, and what is expected of an entrepreneur applying for these funds?

Studies have investigated the various sources of capital preferred by entrepreneurs.[1] These sources range from debt to equity depending upon the type of financing that is arranged. As illustrated in Figure 14.1, entrepreneurs have a number of sources of capital as their ventures develop. Notice that the level of risk and the stage of the firm's development impact the appropriate source financing for the entrepreneurial ventures.

In this chapter we examine the various sources of capital available to new ventures, with some insights into the processes expected of the entrepreneur. We begin with an examination of the differences between debt and equity financing.

Figure 14.1 Who Is Funding Entrepreneurial Start-Up Companies?

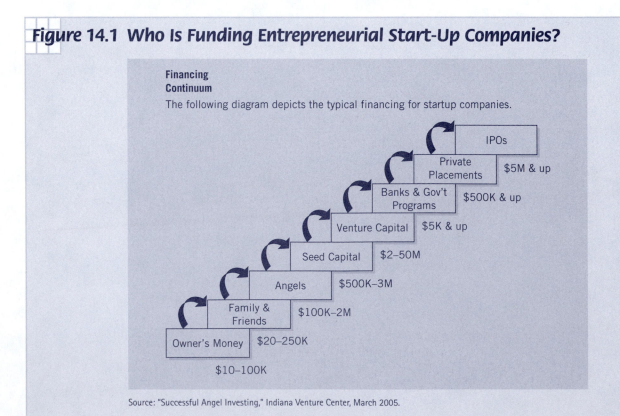

Financing Continuum

The following diagram depicts the typical financing for startup companies.

- IPOs
- Private Placements — $5M & up
- Banks & Gov't Programs — $500K & up
- Venture Capital — $5K & up
- Seed Capital — $2–50M
- Angels — $500K–3M
- Family & Friends — $100K–2M
- Owner's Money — $20–250K
- $10–100K

Source: "Successful Angel Investing," Indiana Venture Center, March 2005.

Debt versus Equity

The use of *debt* to finance a new venture involves a payback of the funds plus a fee (interest) for the use of the money. *Equity* financing involves the sale of some of the ownership in the venture. Debt places a burden of repayment and interest on the entrepreneur, while equity financing forces the entrepreneur to relinquish some degree of control. In the extreme, the choice for the entrepreneur is (1) to take on debt without giving up ownership in the venture or (2) to relinquish a percentage of ownership in order to avoid having to borrow. In most cases, a combination of debt and equity proves most appropriate.

Debt Financing

Many new ventures find that **debt financing** is necessary. Short-term borrowing (one year or less) is often required for working capital and is repaid out of the proceeds from sales. Long-term debt (term loans of one to five years or long-term loans maturing in more than five years) is used to finance the purchase of property or equipment, with the purchased asset serving as collateral for the loans. The most common sources of debt financing are commercial banks.[2]

Commercial Banks

About 7,769 commercial banks operate in the United States today.[3] Although some banks will make unsecured short-term loans, most bank loans are secured by receivables, inventories, or other assets. Commercial banks also make a large number of intermediate-term loans with maturities of one to five years. In about 90 percent of these cases, the banks require collateral, generally consisting of stocks, machinery, equipment, and real estate, and systematic payments over the life of the loan are required. Apart from real estate mortgages and loans guaranteed by the SBA or a similar organization, commercial banks make few loans with maturities greater than five years. Banks also may offer a number of services to a new venture, including computerized payroll preparation, letters of credit, international services, lease financing, and money market accounts.

To secure a bank loan, an entrepreneur typically will have to answer a number of questions. Five of the most common questions, together with descriptive commentaries, follow.

1. *What do you plan to do with the money?* Do not plan on using funds for a high-risk venture. Banks seek the most secure venture possible.

2. *How much do you need?* Some entrepreneurs go to their bank with no clear idea of how much money they need. All they know is that they want money. The more precisely the entrepreneur can answer this question, the more likely the loan will be granted.

3. *When do you need it?* Never rush to the bank with immediate requests for money with no plan. Such a strategy shows that the entrepreneur is a poor planner, and most lenders will not want to get involved.

4. *How long will you need it?* The shorter the period of time the entrepreneur needs the money, the more likely he or she is to get the loan. The time at which the loan will be repaid should correspond to some important milestone in the business plan.

5. *How will you repay the loan?* This is the most important question. What if plans go awry? Can other income be diverted to pay off the loan? Does collateral exist? Even if a quantity of fixed assets exists, the bank may be unimpressed because it knows from experience that assets sold at a liquidation auction bring only a fraction of their value. Five to ten cents on the dollar is not unusual.[4]

Banks are not the only source of debt financing. Sometimes a new venture can obtain long-term financing for a particular piece of equipment from the manufacturer, which will take a portion of the purchase price in the form of a long-term note. Manufacturers are most willing to do this when an active market exists for their used equipment, so if the machinery must be repossessed, it can be resold. Also, new ventures sometimes can obtain short-term debt financing by negotiating extended credit terms with suppliers. However, this kind of trade credit restricts the venture's flexibility with selecting suppliers and may reduce its ability to negotiate supplier prices.

Debt financing has both advantages and disadvantages.

Advantages

- [ ] No relinquishment of ownership is required.
- [ ] More borrowing allows for potentially greater return on equity.
- [ ] During periods of low interest rates, the opportunity cost is justified since the cost of borrowing is low.

Disadvantages

- [ ] Regular (monthly) interest payments are required.
- [ ] Continual cash-flow problems can be intensified because of payback responsibility.
- [ ] Heavy use of debt can inhibit growth and development.

Other Debt-Financing Sources

In addition to commercial banks, other debt-financing sources include trade credit, accounts receivable factoring, finance companies, leasing companies, mutual savings banks, savings and loan associations, and insurance companies. Table 14.1 provides a summary of these sources, the business types they often finance, and their financing terms.

Trade credit is credit given by suppliers who sell goods on account. This credit is reflected on the entrepreneur's balance sheet as accounts payable, and in most cases it must be paid in 30 to 90 days. Many small, new businesses obtain this credit when no other form of financing is available to them. Suppliers typically offer this credit as a way of attracting new customers.

Accounts receivable financing is short-term financing that involves either the pledge of receivables as collateral for a loan or the sale of receivables (factoring). Accounts receivable loans are made by commercial banks, whereas factoring is done primarily by commercial finance companies and factoring concerns.

Accounts receivable bank loans are made on a discounted value of the receivables pledged. A bank may make receivable loans on a notification or non-notification plan. Under the notification plan, purchasers of goods are informed that their accounts have been assigned to the bank. They then make payments directly to the bank, which credits them to the borrower's account. Under the non-notification plan, borrowers collect their accounts as usual and then pay off the bank loan.

Table 14.1   Common Debt Sources

SOURCE	BUSINESS TYPE FINANCED			FINANCING TERM	
	START-UP FIRM	EXISTING FIRM	SHORT TERM	INTERMEDIATE TERM	LONG TERM
Trade credit	Yes	Yes	Yes	No	No
Commercial banks	Sometimes, but only if strong capital or collateral exists	Yes	Frequently	Sometimes	Seldom
Finance companies	Seldom	Yes	Most frequent	Yes	Seldom
Factors	Seldom	Yes	Most frequent	Seldom	No
Leasing companies	Seldom	Yes	No	Most frequent	Occasionally
Mutual savings banks and savings-and-loan associations	Seldom	Real estate ventures only	No	No	Real estate ventures only
Insurance companies	Rarely	Yes	No	No	Yes

Factoring is the sale of accounts receivable. Under this arrangement, the receivables are sold, at a discounted value, to a factoring company. Some commercial finance companies also do factoring. Under a standard arrangement the factor will buy the client's receivables outright, without recourse, as soon as the client creates them by its shipment of goods to customers. Factoring fits some businesses better than others, and it has become almost traditional in industries such as textiles, furniture manufacturing, clothing manufacturing, toys, shoes, and plastics.

Finance companies are asset-based lenders that lend money against assets such as receivables, inventory, and equipment. The advantage of dealing with a commercial finance company is that it often will make loans that banks will not. The interest rate varies from 2 to 6 percent over that charged by a bank. New ventures that are unable to raise money from banks and factors often turn to finance companies.

Other financial sources include equity instruments (discussed in the next section), which give investors a share of the ownership. Examples of these follow.

☐ *Loan with warrants* provide the investor with the right to buy stock at a fixed price at some future date. Terms on the warrants are negotiable. The warrant customarily provides for the purchase of additional stock, such as up to 10 percent of the total issue at 130 percent of the original offering price within a five-year period following the offering date.

☐ *Convertible debentures* are unsecured loans that can be converted into stock. The conversion price, the interest rate, and the provisions of the loan agreement are all areas for negotiation.

☐ *Preferred stock* is equity that gives investors a preferred place among the creditors in the event the venture is dissolved. The stock also pays a dividend and can increase in price, thus giving investors an even greater return. Some preferred stock issues are convertible to common stock, a feature that can make them even more attractive.

☐ *Common stock* is the most basic form of ownership. This stock usually carries the right to vote for the board of directors. If a new venture does well, common-stock investors often make a large return on their investment. These stock issues often are sold through public or private offerings.

Equity Financing

Equity financing is money invested in the venture with no legal obligation for entrepreneurs to repay the principal amount or pay interest on it. The use of equity funding thus requires no repayment in the form of debt. It does, however, require sharing the ownership and profits with the funding source. Since no repayment is required, equity capital can be much safer for new ventures than debt financing. Yet the entrepreneur must consciously decide to give up part of the ownership in return for this funding.[5]

Over the past 20 years, there has been a tremendous boom in the private equity industry. The pool of U.S. private equity funds—partnerships specializing in venture capital, leveraged buyouts, mezzanine investments, build-ups, distressed debt, and related investments—grew from $5 billion in 1980 to more than $225 billion in 2002.[6]

Equity capital can be raised through two major sources: public stock offerings and private placements. In both cases, entrepreneurs must follow the state laws pertaining to the raising of such funds and must meet the requirements set forth by the Securities and Exchange Commission (SEC). This entire process can be difficult, expensive, and time-consuming. The laws and regulations are complex and often vary from state to state. On the other hand, successful stock offerings can help a fledgling enterprise raise a great deal of money.

Public Offerings

Going public is a term used to refer to a corporation's raising capital through the sale of securities on the public markets. Here are some of the advantages to this approach.

☐ *Size of capital amount.* Selling securities is one of the fastest ways to raise large sums of capital in a short period of time.

☐ *Liquidity.* The public market provides liquidity for owners since they can readily sell their stock.

☐ *Value.* The marketplace puts a value on the company's stock, which in turn allows value to be placed on the corporation.

☐ *Image.* The image of a publicly traded corporation often is stronger in the eyes of suppliers, financiers, and customers.[7]

Over the last decade many new ventures have sought capital through the public markets. The term **initial public offering (IPO)** is used to represent the registered public offering of a company's securities for the first time. In 2002, for example there were 81 IPOs accounting for $19.2 billion. The year 2003 had the same number of IPOs (81) yet the amount raised was only $13.5 billion. Many times the number of companies "going public" does not vary much, but the amount of financing raised certainly does. Also the economy has a major effect on the IPO markets as evidenced by the huge upswing in IPOs from 1995 to 1999 when 2,994 companies went "public" during an economic period of continual growth and prosperity. The year 2000 introduced a correction on the economy, and everything began to constrict, including the IPO market. By 2001 there were only 91 firms that went public, raising $37.1 billion. That was quite a slump from the all-time high of 868 IPOs in 1996. Today we see much more stable and conservative activity among the IPO markets.[8]

These figures reflect the tremendous *volatility* that exists within the stock market and, thus, entrepreneurs should be aware of the concerns confronting them when pursuing the IPO market. In addition, many new ventures have begun to recognize some other disadvantages of going public. A few of these follow.

☐ *Costs.* The expenses involved with a public offering are significantly higher than for other sources of capital. Accounting fees, legal fees, and prospectus printing and distribution, as well as the cost of underwriting the stock, can result in high costs.

☐ *Disclosure.* Detailed disclosures of the company's affairs must be made public. New-venture firms often prefer to keep such information private.

☐ *Requirements.* The paperwork involved with SEC regulations, as well as continuing performance information, drains large amounts of time, energy, and money from management. Many new ventures consider these elements better invested in helping the company grow.

☐ *Shareholder pressure.* Management decisions are sometimes short term in nature in order to maintain a good performance record for earnings and dividends to the shareholders. This pressure can lead to a failure to give adequate consideration to the company's long-term growth and improvement.[9]

The advantages and disadvantages of going public must be weighed carefully. If the decision is to undertake a public offering, then it is important the entrepreneur understand the process involved. Chapter 18 presents some of the complex requirements involved in the IPO process.

Here we summarize by saying that entrepreneurs who pursue the public securities route should be prepared for reporting requirements, disclosure statements, and the shared control and ownership with outside shareholders.

Private Placements

Another method of raising capital is through the **private placement** of securities. Small ventures often use this approach.

The SEC provides **Regulation D,** which eases the regulations for the reports and statements required for selling stock to private parties—friends, employees, customers, relatives, and local professionals. Regulation D defines four separate exemptions, which are based on the amount of money being raised. Along with their accompanying rule, these exemptions follow.

1. *Rule 504a—placements of less than $500,000*: No specific disclosure/information requirements and no limits on the kind or type of purchasers exist. This makes marketing offerings of this size easier than it was heretofore.

2. *Rule 504—placements up to $1,000,000*: Again, no specific disclosure/information requirements and no limits on the kind or type of purchasers exist.

3. *Rule 505—placements of up to $5 million*: The criteria for a public offering exemption are somewhat more difficult to meet than those for smaller offerings. Sales of securities can be made to not more than 35 nonaccredited

the entrepreneurial
PROCESS

Going Public: The Acid Test

Public versus private is a major decision, and one not to be taken lightly or made hastily. IPOs are complex and time-consuming transactions, and not all have favorable endings. Following are six questions that will provide an idea as to if your company is best suited for the public or private scene.

1. **Are you building a company that can run without you?**

   The work leading up to a public offering is so intensive and detailed that it will take an entrepreneur's focus away from the everyday operations, ultimately hurting the business. Unless you have a strong management team, consider hiring a CFO that has experience taking companies, preferably small ones, through the rigors of going public.

2. **Can you get to a market capitalization of $100 million within three years of going public?**

   Your financials can answer this question for you. The value of a public company is a multiple of what it earns. Take the average price-earnings ratio for your industry and apply it to the earnings you project for the third year after your company goes public. If the result isn't near $100 million, staying private may be best. This number is a good indicator because it is the level of earnings at which the company will *begin* attracting brokers and investors.

3. **Are you building a company with high gross and operating margins?**

   A high sales volume will be reached only if the company has access to adequate funding to promote and finance sales. The bottom line truly rests on the top line, and a public company cannot afford to lose its most important number. High margins will help curb any unexpected losses.

4. **Can your business deliver double-digit sales and earnings growth, year in and year out?**

   The competition among public companies, mutual funds, and other investment networks is fierce. Investors won't look twice at a company that doesn't grow fast enough to warrant the use of their time and money.

5. **Are you building a family business?**

   If the succession plan for the business is set in stone to be passed on to the kids, don't go public. Families measure the success of a business generation by generation. Money movers are interested in the quarter-to-quarter progress. Going public will eventually be the end of any succession strategy.

6. **Can the business be built inexpensively?**

   The main reason companies go public is to raise initial funds for major growth. As a result, sales and growth *need* to reflect the use of the first round of financing. If it's perceived that another round of financing will be necessary to achieve the original plan, investors will look elsewhere.

In the information age, it seems only fitting that "going public" is also possible on the Internet. The rules just outlined can be thrown to the wayside when it comes to the amazing things happening with Internet business funding. Since the first *direct public offering* (*DPO*) in 1995, more than 200 companies have been able to avoid underwriters in their quest for stock options. For example, Andrew Klein raised $1.6 million for his New York City–based online brewing company, causing quite a stir in the venture capital arena. It was once thought that the "website IPO" would radically change the securities market. Perhaps companies selling their own stock on their own websites, bypassing brokers, would become common practice. This practice started with Spring Street Brewing Company's stock offering through its website in 1996. The SEC set the precedence by allowing Spring Street to trade shares in this manner.

Although several firms have traded their stock from their websites, the success in doing so has been limited. The most significant hurdle that these firms face is following the registration requirements for IPOs, which are rather time-consuming and expensive. Thus, entrepreneurs have found it difficult to raise initial capital needs from the web. Another problem has been that of a lack of secondary markets.

Foreign firms are required to register securities with the SEC before offering them to the U.S. public, but this has been difficult to enforce on Internet transactions. The SEC further interpreted this rule in 1998, saying that foreign firms were required to avoid "targeting" U.S. investors. These foreign firms may avoid problems with the SEC by stating on their sites that they have not registered with the SEC.

Firms are also required to report information accurately on their websites. Companies are responsible for updates to correct historical financial statements, financial projections, press releases, or even stories that they have linked on their site.

SOURCE: David Evanson and Art Beroff, "Burnt Offerings?" *Entrepreneur* (July 1999): 56–59; and Bethany McLean, "Direct Public Offerings: Cash for Low-Profile Firms," *Fortune Small Business* (February/March 2000): 31–33; see also Kenneth W. Clarkson, Roger LeRoy Miller, Gaylord A. Jentz, and Frank B. Cross, *West's Business Law: Legal, Ethical, International, and E-Commerce Environment*, 8th ed. (Mason, OH: South-Western/Thomson Learning, 2001).

purchasers and to an unlimited number of accredited purchasers. If purchasers are nonaccredited as well as accredited, then the company must follow specified information disclosure requirements. Investors must have the opportunity to obtain additional information about the company and its management.

4. *Rule 506—placements in excess of $5 million:* Sales can be made to no more than 35 nonaccredited purchasers and an unlimited number of accredited purchasers. However, the nonaccredited purchasers must be "sophisticated" in investment matters. Also, the specific disclosure requirements are more detailed than those for offerings between $500,000 and $5 million. Investors must have the opportunity to obtain additional information about the company and its management.[10]

As noted in Rules 505 and 506, Regulation D uses the term **accredited purchaser.** Included in this category are the following.

☐ Institutional investors such as banks, insurance companies, venture capital firms, registered investment companies, and small-business investment companies (SBICs)

☐ Any person who buys at least $150,000 of the offered security and whose net worth, including that of his or her spouse, is at least five times the purchase price

☐ Any person who, together with his or her spouse, has a net worth in excess of $1 million at the time of purchase

☐ Any person whose individual income was in excess of $200,000 in each of the past two years and who expects the same income for the current year

☐ Directors, executive officers, or general partners of the company or partnership selling the securities

☐ Certain tax-exempt organizations with more than $500,000 in assets

Everyone not covered in these descriptions is regarded as a nonaccredited purchaser.

Strategies for Negotiating Loans

The process of negotiating a loan does not begin and end in a couple of visits to your local bank. Instead it is a multifaceted approach that begins with a personal relationship before an application is made and continues through the life of your business. Consider using these seven strategies when negotiating with commercial bankers—gaining even the slightest edge over your banker could save you thousands.

Call Early and Often: Strong personal relationships are just as essential as they were in the past. Start by inviting a banker to your place of business; show your company's sense of pride, offer a lunch, or let the banker try some product samples. Consider including him or her on a board of advisors.

Get the Book: Robert Morris Associates' Annual Statement Studies (now known as The Risk Management Association or RMA; http://www.rmahq.org) is the bankers' bible. The crucial operating parameters in which bankers make their loan decisions are all based on this guide to over 600 industries. It contains common financial ratios and statements compiled from a national survey of commercial loan accounts.

Offer More: Most banks desire depository accounts and other fee-generating services. The more business you offer the bank, the more likely they will stretch to approve your loan. These could include payroll accounts, wire transfers, and credit card processing.

Anticipate Failure: Make a list of pitfalls in your company and then provide a strategy to overcome those problems. This not only shows the bank you have thought thoroughly about your business, but also gives your banker the information he or she needs to go in front of the review committee. Start with the loss of key personnel. In order to provide a proactive solution to the loss of the owner, assure the bank that the loan could be repaid through the addition of a large insurance policy.

Plan Pessimistically: In order to get a loan approved, clear deadlines and projections are needed. For safety sake, plan for larger expenses than normal to provide that extra financial cushion.

Negotiate Smartly: Know what is important to you in a loan. If your business would fail, you may not wish to lose your home, pension, or retirement plan. It may be wiser to consider a higher interest rate or tougher terms for added security.

Stay Vigilant: Remember, most loans must be reevaluated each year and the loan's covenants can change every quarter. But once you put together a solid relationship, a shining business plan, and a level of risk coverage for your lender, anything is negotiable.

SOURCE: David Worrell, "Attacking a Loan," *Entrepreneur* (July 2002): 51–52.

"*Sophisticated*" investors are wealthy individuals who invest more or less regularly in new and early- and late-stage ventures. They are knowledgeable about the technical and commercial opportunities and risks of the businesses in which they invest. They know the kind of information they want about their prospective investment, and they have the experience and ability needed to obtain and analyze the data provided.

The objective of Regulation D is to make it easier and less expensive for small ventures to sell stock. However, many states have not kept pace with these rules. Consequently, many new ventures still find it costly and time-consuming to try to clear their offerings in some states. In addition, many are discouraged by the disclosure requirements for offerings of $500,000 and over, which are cited under Rules 505 and 506. In spite of these difficulties, Regulation D does a lot to simplify small-company financing.[11]

The Venture Capital Market

Venture capitalists are a valuable and powerful source of equity funding for new ventures. These experienced professionals provide a full range of financial services for new or growing ventures, including the following.

- ☐ Capital for start-ups and expansion
- ☐ Market research and strategy for businesses that do not have their own marketing departments
- ☐ Management-consulting functions and management audit and evaluation
- ☐ Contacts with prospective customers, suppliers, and other important businesspeople
- ☐ Assistance in negotiating technical agreements
- ☐ Help in establishing management and accounting controls
- ☐ Help in employee recruitment and development of employee agreements
- ☐ Help in risk management and the establishment of an effective insurance program
- ☐ Counseling and guidance in complying with a myriad of government regulations

Recent Developments in Venture Capital

Venture Capital reversed a three-year downward trend by investing $21 billion into 2,873 deals in 2004. The annual investment had fallen every year since 2001 culminating in a six-year low of $18.9 billion in 2003 (see Table 14.2). However, it should be understood that the Venture Capitalists (commonly referred to as VCs) raised their investments in later-stage companies and not start-ups or early-stage ventures. Table 14.3 illustrates the stages of VC investment in the first quarter of 2005. Notice the smaller amount of activity associated with the start-up and seed-stage companies. There were only 32 deals compared to 267 expansion deals. Table 14.4 emphasizes this

Table 14.2 Venture Capital Investment by Year

YEAR	NUMBER OF DEALS	AVERAGE PER DEAL (MILLIONS)	INVESTMENT (BILLIONS)
2000	7832	$13.38	$104.87
2001	4451	9.17	40.80
2002	3042	7.09	21.58
2003	2825	6.69	18.91
2004	2873	7.31	21.00

Source: PricewaterhouseCoopers/Thomas Venture Economics/National Venture Capital Association, MoneyTree™ Survey, 2005.

Table 14.3   Venture Capital Investment by Stage of Development—Q1 2005

	AMOUNT (MILLIONS)	% OF TOTAL	DEALS
Expansion	$1969	42.56%	267
Later Stage	1831	39.56%	175
Early Stage	752	16.26%	200
Startup/Seed	75	1.62%	32
Total	$4627	100%	674

Source: PricewaterhouseCoopers/Thomas Venture Economics/National Venture Capital Association, MoneyTree™ Survey, 2005.

Table 14.4   Venture Capital Investments Comparison (Later Stage versus Early Stage)

	AMOUNT (MILLIONS)	% OF TOTAL	DEALS
Expansion	$1969	42.56%	267
Later Stage	1831	39.56%	175
Early Stage	752	16.26%	200
Startup/Seed	75	1.62%	32
Total	$4627	100%	674

Source: PricewaterhouseCoopers/Thomas Venture Economics/National Venture Capital Association, MoneyTree™ Survey, 2005.

point as it shows the comparison of VC investments at the later stage versus the early stage since the first quarter of 2004. Once again, the early stage deals are far less than the later stage deals in every quarter. So it must be understood that today's venture capitalists are far less inclined to finance a start-up firm as opposed to a firm in its more mature stages of development.

In addition to these developments, a number of major trends have been occurring in venture capital over the last few years.

First, the predominant investor class is changing from individuals, foundations, and families to pension institutions. Therefore, sources of capital commitments will continue to shift away from the less-experienced venture capital firm (less than three years) to the more-experienced firm (greater than three years). Second, funds are becoming more specialized and less homogeneous. The industry has become more diverse, more specialized, and less uniform than is generally thought. Sharp differences are apparent in terms of investing objectives and criteria, strategy, and focusing on particular stages, sizes, and market technology niches.[12]

Third, feeder funds are emerging. Accompanying this specialization is a new farm team system. Large, established venture capital firms have crafted both formal and informal relationships with new funds as feeder funds. Often, one general partner of the established fund will provide time and know-how to the new fund. The team may share deal flow and coinvest in a syndicated deal. More often than not, these new funds focus on seed-stage or start-up deals that can feed later deals to the more conventional, mainstream venture capital firm with which they are associated.[13]

Fourth, small start-up investments are drying up. Many venture capital firms have numerous troubled ventures in their portfolios. As a result, general partners, who are often the most experienced and skillful at finding and nurturing innovative technological ventures, are allocating premium time to salvaging or turning around problem ventures. In addition, because start-up and first-stage investing demands the greatest intensity of involvement by venture capital investors, this type of venture has felt the greatest effects. Finally, other venture capital funds lack professionals who have experience with start-ups and first-stage ventures. Consequently, the level of seed and start-up financing is lower in comparison to the financing available for early stages, expansion, and acquisition.[14]

Fifth, the trend is toward a new legal environment. The heated competition for venture capital in recent years has resulted in a more-sophisticated legal and contractual environment. The frequency and extent of litigation are rising. As an example, the final document governing the inventory/entrepreneur relationship—called the investment agreement—can be a few inches thick and can comprise two volumes. In this regard, legal experts recommend that the following provisions be carefully considered in the investment agreement: choice of securities (preferred stock, common stock, convertible debt, and so forth), control issues (who maintains voting power), evaluation issues and financial covenants (ability to proceed with mergers and acquisitions), and remedies for breach of contract (rescission of the contract or monetary damages).[15]

Dispelling Venture Capital Myths

Because many people have mistaken ideas about the role and function of venture capitalists, a number of myths have sprung up about them. Some of these, along with their rebuttals, follow.

Myth 1: Venture Capital Firms Want to Own Control of Your Company and Tell You How to Run the Business   No venture capital firm intentionally sets out to own control of a small business. Venture capitalists have no desire to run the business. They do not want to tell entrepreneurs how to make day-to-day decisions and have the owner report to them daily. They want the entrepreneur and the management team to run the company profitably. They do want to be consulted on any major decision, but they want no say in daily business operations.[16]

Myth 2: Venture Capitalists Are Satisfied with a Reasonable Return on Investments   Venture capitalists expect very high, exorbitant, unreasonable returns. They can obtain reasonable returns from hundreds of publicly traded companies. They can obtain reasonable returns from many types of investments not having the degree of risk involved in financing a small business. Because every venture capital investment involves a high degree of risk, it must have a correspondingly high return on investment.[17]

Myth 3: Venture Capitalists Are Quick to Invest   It takes a long time to raise venture capital. On the average, it will take six to eight weeks from the initial contact to raise venture capital. If the entrepreneur has a well-prepared business plan, the investor will be able to raise money in that time frame. A venture capitalist will see from 50 to 100 proposals a month. Out of that number, ten will be of some interest. Out of those ten, two or three will receive a fair amount of analysis, negotiation, and investigation.

the entrepreneurial
PROCESS

The Dos and Don'ts of Approaching Venture Capitalists

So you want a piece of the venture capital pie? Venture capitalists are busy people, constantly inundated with business plans that range from pipe dreams to the next software giant. Keep these things in mind if you want to capture their attention.

Do

☐ Prepare all materials before soliciting firms.

☐ Send a business plan and cover letter first.

☐ Solicit several firms.

☐ Keep phone conversations brief.

☐ Remain positive and enthusiastic about your company, product, and service.

☐ Know your minimum deal and walk away if necessary.

☐ Negotiate a deal you can live with.

☐ Investigate the venture capitalist's previous deals and current portfolio structure.

Don't

☐ Expect a response.

☐ Dodge questions.

☐ Give vague answers.

☐ Hide significant problems.

☐ Expect immediate decisions.

☐ Fixate on pricing.

☐ Embellish facts or projections.

☐ Bring your lawyer.

SOURCE: Adapted from Paul DeCeglie, "The Truth about Venture Capital," *Business Start-Ups* (February 2000): 40–47.

Of the two or three, one may be funded. This funneling process of selecting 1 out of 100 takes a great deal of time. Once the venture capitalist has found that one, he or she will spend a significant amount of time investigating possible outcomes before funding it.

Myth 4: Venture Capitalists Are Interested in Backing New Ideas or High-Technology Inventions—Management Is a Secondary Consideration   Venture capitalists back only good management. If an entrepreneur has a bright idea but a poor managerial background and no experience in the industry, the individual should try to find someone in the industry to bring onto the team. The venture capitalist will have a hard time believing that an entrepreneur with no experience in that industry and no managerial ability in his or her background can follow through on a business plan. A good idea is important, but a good management team is even more important.[18]

Myth 5: Venture Capitalists Need Only Basic Summary Information before They Make an Investment   A detailed and well-organized business plan is the only way to gain a venture capital investor's attention and obtain funding. Every venture capitalist, before becoming involved, wants the entrepreneur to have thought out the entire business plan and to have written it down in detail.[19]

Venture Capitalists' Objectives

Venture capitalists have different objectives from most others who provide capital to new ventures. Lenders, for example, are interested in security and payback. As partial owners of the companies they invest in, venture capitalists, however, are most concerned with return on investment. As a result, they put a great deal of time into weighing the risk of a venture against the potential return. They carefully measure both the product/service and the management. Figure 14.2 illustrates an evaluation system for measuring these two critical factors—status of product/service and status of management—on four levels. The figure demonstrates that ideas as well as entrepreneurs are evaluated when the viability of a venture proposal is determined.

Venture capitalists are particularly interested in making a large return on investment (ROI). Table 14.5 provides some commonly sought targets. Of course, these targets are flexible. They would be reduced, for example, in cases where a company has a strong market potential, is able to generate good cash flow, or the management has invested

Figure 14.2 Venture Capitalist System of Evaluating Product/Service and Management

Status of Product/Service		Level 1	Level 2	Level 3	Level 4
	Level 4 Fully developed product/service Established market Satisfied users	4/1	4/2	4/3	4/4
	Level 3 Fully developed product/service Few users as of yet Market assumed	3/1	3/2	3/3	3/4
Riskiest	**Level 2** Operable pilot or prototype Not yet developed for production Market assumed	2/1	2/2	2/3	2/4
	Level 1 Product/service idea Not yet operable Market assumed	1/1	1/2	1/3	1/4
		Level 1 Individual founder/ entrepreneur	**Level 2** Two founders Other personnel not yet identified	**Level 3** Partial management team Members identified to join company when funding is received	**Level 4** Fully staffed, experienced management team

◄———— **Riskiest** ————

Status of Management

Source: Stanley Rich and David Gumpert, *Business Plans That Win $$$*, 160. Reprinted by permission of Sterling Lord Literistic, Inc. Copyright © 1985 by Stanley Rich and David Gumpert.

Table 14.5   Returns on Investment Typically Sought by Venture Capitalists

STAGE OF BUSINESS	EXPECTED ANNUAL RETURN ON INVESTMENT	EXPECTED INCREASE ON INITIAL INVESTMENT
Start-up business (idea stage)	60% +	10–15 × investment
First-stage financing (new business)	40%–60%	6–12 × investment
Second-stage financing (development stage)	30%–50%	4–8 × investment
Third-stage financing (expansion stage)	25%–40%	3–6 × investment
Turnaround situation	50% +	8–15 × investment

Source: W. Keith Schilit, "How to Obtain Venture Capital," *Business Horizons* (May/June 1987): 78. Copyright © 1987 by the Foundation for the School of Business at Indiana University. Reprinted by permission.

a sizable portion of its own funds in the venture.[20] However, an annual goal of 20 to 30 percent ROI would not be considered too high, regardless of the risks involved.

Criteria for Evaluating New–Venture Proposals

In addition to the evaluation of product ideas and management strength, numerous criteria are used to evaluate new-venture proposals. Researcher Dean A. Shepherd developed a list of eight critical factors that venture capitalists use in the evaluation of new ventures. Timing of entry, key success factor stability, educational capability, lead time, competitive rivalry, entry wedge imitation, scope, and industry-related competence were all considered factors that are used by venture capitalists.[21] Each factor was defined from the high/low perspective. (See Table 14.6 for the definitions.)

Another group of researchers developed 28 of these criteria, grouped into six major categories: (1) entrepreneur's personality, (2) entrepreneur's experience, (3) product or service characteristics, (4) market characteristics, (5) financial considerations, and (6) nature of the venture team.[22] The study surveyed more than 100 venture capitalists regarding these criteria and found that they most frequently rated ten of the criteria as essential when reviewing new-venture proposals (see Table 14.7). Six of these ten relate to the entrepreneur personally, three deal with the investment in and growth of the project, and one relates to the venture's patent or copyright position.

Other researchers have uncovered similar results. For example, John Hall and Charles W. Hofer examined the criteria venture capitalists use during a proposal screening and evaluation. Table 14.8 outlines the factors used in the study.[23] Their results showed that venture capitalists reached a "go/no go" decision in an average of 6 minutes on the initial screening and less than 21 minutes on the overall proposal evaluation. They found that the venture capital firm's requirements and the long-term growth and profitability of the proposed venture's industry were the critical factors for initial screening. In the more-detailed evaluation, the background of the entrepreneurs as well as the characteristics of the proposal itself were important.

In a study examining the "demand side" of venture capital, researchers surveyed 318 private entrepreneurs who sought out venture capital in amounts of $100,000 or more. The study found that entrepreneurs' success with acquiring funding is related to four general, variable categories: (1) characteristics of the entrepreneurs, including

Table 14.6   Factors in Venture Capitalists' Evaluation Process

ATTRIBUTE	LEVEL	DEFINITION
Timing of entry	Pioneer	Enters a new industry first
	Late follower	Enters an industry late in the industry's stage of development
Key success factor stability	High	Requirements necessary for success will not change radically during industry development
	Low	Requirements necessary for success will change radically during industry development
Educational capability	High	Considerable resources and skills available to overcome market ignorance through education
	Low	Few resources or skills available to overcome market ignorance through education
Lead time	Long	An extended period of monopoly for the first entrant prior to competitors entering the industry
	Short	A minimal period of monopoly for the first entrant prior to competitors entering this industry
Competitive rivalry	High	Intense competition among industry members during industry development
	Low	Little competition among industry members during industry development
Entry wedge mimicry	High	Considerable imitation of the mechanisms used by other firms to enter this, or any other, industry—for example, a franchisee
	Low	Minimal imitation of the mechanisms used by other firms to enter this, or any other, industry—for example, introducing a new product
Scope	Broad	A firm that spreads its resources across a wide spectrum of the market—for example, many segments of the market
	Narrow	A firm that concentrates on intensively exploiting a small segment of the market—for example, targeting a niche
Industry-related competence	High	Venturer has considerable experience and knowledge with the industry being entered or a related industry
	Low	Venturer has minimal experience and knowledge with the industry being entered or related industry

Source: Dean A. Shepherd, "Venture Capitalists' Introspection: A Comparison of 'In Use' and 'Espoused' Decision Policies," *Journal of Small Business Management* (April 1999): 76–87; and "Venture Capitalists' Assessment of New Venture Survival," *Management Science* (May 1999): 621–632. Reprinted by permission. Copyright 1999, the Institute for Operation Research and the Management Sciences (INFORMS), 7240 Parkway Drive, Suite 310, Hanover MD 21076 USA.

education, experience, and age; (2) characteristics of the enterprise, including stage, industry type, and location (for example, rural or urban); (3) characteristics of the request, including amount, business plan, and prospective capital source; and (4) sources of advice, including technology, preparation of the business plan, and places to seek funding.[24]

Table 14.7   Ten Criteria Most Frequently Rated Essential in New-Venture Evaluation

CRITERION	PERCENTAGE
Capable of sustained intense effort	64
Thoroughly familiar with market	62
At least ten times return in five to ten years	50
Demonstrated leadership in past	50
Evaluates and reacts to risk well	48
Investment can be made liquid	44
Significant market growth	43
Track record relevant to venture	37
Articulates venture well	31
Proprietary protection	29

Source: Reprinted by permission of the publisher from "Criteria Used by Venture Capitalists to Evaluate New Venture Proposals," by Ian C. MacMillan, Robin Siegel, and P. N. Subba Narasimha, *Journal of Business Venturing* (winter 1985): 123. Copyright © 1985 by Elsevier Science Publishing Co., Inc.

The business plan is a critical element in a new-venture proposal and should be complete, clear, and well presented. Venture capitalists will generally analyze five major aspects of the plan: (1) the proposal size, (2) financial projections, (3) investment recovery, (4) competitive advantage, and (5) company management.

The evaluation process typically takes place in stages. The four most common stages follow.

Stage 1: Initial Screening   This is a quick review of the basic venture to see if it meets the venture capitalist's particular interests.

Stage 2: Evaluation of the Business Plan   This is where a detailed reading of the plan is done in order to evaluate the factors mentioned earlier.

Stage 3: Oral Presentation   The entrepreneur verbally presents the plan to the venture capitalist.

Stage 4: Final Evaluation   After analyzing the plan and visiting with suppliers, customers, consultants, and others, the venture capitalist makes a final decision.

This four-step process screens out approximately 98 percent of all venture plans. The rest receive some degree of financial backing.

Evaluating the Venture Capitalist

The venture capitalist will evaluate the entrepreneur's proposal carefully, and the entrepreneur should not hesitate to evaluate the venture capitalist. Does the venture capitalist understand the proposal? Is the individual familiar with the business? Is the person someone with whom the entrepreneur can work? If the answers reveal a poor fit, it is best for the entrepreneur to look for a different venture capitalist.

One researcher found that venture capitalists do add value to an entrepreneurial firm beyond the money they supply, especially in high-innovation ventures. Because of this finding, entrepreneurs need to choose the appropriate venture capitalist at the outset and, most important, they must keep the communication channels open as the firm grows.[25]

Table 14.8   *Venture Capitalists' Screening Criteria*

Venture Capital Firm Requirements

Must fit within lending guidelines of venture firm for stage and size of investment
Proposed business must be within geographic area of interest
Prefer proposals recommended by someone known to venture capitalist
Proposed industry must be kind of industry invested in by venture firm

Nature of the Proposed Business

Projected growth should be relatively large within five years of investment

Economic Environment of Proposed Industry

Industry must be capable of long-term growth and profitability
Economic environment should be favorable to a new entrant

Proposed Business Strategy

Selection of distribution channel(s) must be feasible
Product must demonstrate defendable competitive position

Financial Information on the Proposed Business

Financial projections should be realistic

Proposal Characteristics

Must have full information
Should be a reasonable length, be easy to scan, have an executive summary, and
    be professionally presented
Proposal must contain a balanced presentation
Use graphics and large print to emphasize key points

Entrepreneur/Team Characteristics

Must have relevant experience
Should have a balanced management team in place
Management must be willing to work with venture partners
Entrepreneur who has successfully started previous business given special consideration

Source: John Hall and Charles W. Hofer, "Venture Capitalists' Decision Criteria in New Venture Evaluation," *Journal of Business Venturing* (January 1993): 37.

On the other hand, it is important to realize that the choice of a venture capitalist can be limited. Although funds are available today, they tend to be controlled by fewer groups, and the quality of the venture must be promising. Even though two and one-half times more money is available today for seed financing than was available ten years ago, the number of venture capital firms is not increasing. In addition, the trend toward concentration of venture capital under the control of a few firms is increasing.[26]

Nevertheless, the entrepreneur should not be deterred from evaluating prospective venture capitalists. The following Entrepreneurship in Practice box provides a list of important questions that a prospective venture capital firm should answer. Evaluating and even negotiating with the venture capitalist are critical to establishing the best equity funding:

You may worry that if you rock the boat by demanding too much, the venture capital firm will lose interest. That's an understandable attitude; venture capital is hard to

entrepreneurship IN PRACTICE

Asking the Right Questions

There are a number of important questions that entrepreneurs should ask of venture capitalists. Here are seven of the most important along with their rationales.

1. Does the venture capital firm in fact invest in your industry? How many deals has the firm actually done in your field?

2. What is it like to work with this venture capital firm? Get references. (An unscreened list of referrals, including CEOs of companies that the firm has been successful with as well as those it has not, can be very helpful.)

3. What experience does the partner doing your deal have, and what is his or her clout within the firm? Check out the experiences of other entrepreneurs.

4. How much time will the partner spend with your company if you run into trouble? A seed-stage company should ask, "You guys

are a big fund, and you say you can seed me a quarter of a million dollars. How often will you be able to see me?" The answer should be at least once a week.

5. How healthy is the venture capital fund, and how much has been invested? A venture firm with a lot of troubled investments will not have much time to spare. If most of the fund is invested, there may not be much money available for your follow-on rounds.

6. Are the investment goals of the venture capitalists consistent with your own?

7. Have the venture firm and the partner championing your deal been through any economic downturns? A good venture capitalist won't panic when things get bad.

SOURCE: Reprinted from Marie-Jeanne Juilland, "What Do You Want from a Venture Capitalist?" August 1987 issue of *Venture, For Entrepreneurial Business Owners & Investors*, by special permission. Copyright © 1987 Venture Magazine, Inc., 521 Fifth Ave., New York, NY 10175-0028.

get and if you've gotten as far as the negotiating process, you're already among the lucky few.

But that doesn't mean you have to roll over and play dead. A venture capital investment is a business deal that you may have to live with for a long time. Although you'll have to give ground on many issues when you come to the bargaining table, there is always a point beyond which the deal no longer makes sense for you. You must draw a line and fight for the points that really count.[27]

Informal Risk Capital—"Angel" Financing

Not all venture capital is raised through formal sources such as public and private placements. Many wealthy people in the United States are looking for investment opportunities. They are referred to as **business angels** or **informal risk capitalists**. These individuals constitute a huge potential investment pool, as the following calculations show.

☐ The *Forbes* 400 richest people in America represent a combined net worth of approximately $125 billion (an average of $315 million per person).

☐ Forty percent of the 400 are self-made millionaires, with a combined net worth of approximately $50 billion.

☐ If 10 percent of the self-made wealth were available for venture financing, the pool of funds would amount to $5 billion.

☐ More than 500,000 individuals in America have a net worth in excess of $1 million. If 40 percent of these individuals were interested in venture financing, 200,000 millionaires would be available.

☐ Assuming only one-half of those 200,000 millionaires would actually consider investment in new ventures at a rate of $50,000 per person, 100,000 investors would provide a pool of $5 billion.

☐ If the typical deal took four investors with $50,000 each (from the pool of $5 billion), then a potential 25,000 ventures could be funded at $200,000 apiece.[28]

William E. Wetzel, Jr., a noted researcher in the field of informal risk capital, has defined this type of investor as someone who has already made his or her money and now seeks out promising young ventures to support financially. "Angels are typically entrepreneurs, retired corporate executives, or professionals who have a net worth of more than $1 million and an income of more than $100,000 a year. They're self-starters. And they're trying to perpetuate the system that made them successful."[29] If entrepreneurs are looking for such an angel, Wetzel advises them, "Don't look very far away—within 50 miles or within a day's drive at most. And that's because this is not a full-time profession for them."[30]

Why would individuals be interested in investing in a new venture from which professional venture capitalists see no powerful payoff? It may be, of course, that the reduced investment amount reduces the total risk involved in the investment. However, informal investors seek other, nonfinancial returns, among them the creation of jobs in areas of high unemployment, development of technology for social needs (for example, medical or energy), urban revitalization, minority or disadvantaged assistance, and personal satisfaction from assisting entrepreneurs.[31] Table 14.9 describes the major differences between business angels and venture capitalists.

How do informal investors find projects? Research studies indicate that they use a network of friends. Additionally, many states are formulating venture capital networks, which attempt to link informal investors with entrepreneurs and their new or growing ventures.

Table 14.9   Main Differences Between Business Angels and Venture Capitalists

MAIN DIFFERENCES	BUSINESS ANGELS	VENTURE CAPITALISTS
Personal	Entrepreneurs	Investors
Firms funded	Small, early-stage	Large, mature
Due diligence done	Minimal	Extensive
Location of investment	Of concern	Not important
Contract used	Simple	Comprehensive
Monitoring after investment	Active, hands-on	Strategic
Exiting the firm	Of lesser concern	Highly important
Rate of return	Of lesser concern	Highly important

Source: Mark Van Osnabrugge and Robert J. Robinson, *Angel Investing* (San Francisco: Jossey-Bass, 2000), 111. This material is used by permission of John Wiley & Sons, Inc.

Types of Angel Investors

Angel investors can be classified into five basic groups:

☐   **Corporate angels.** Typically, so-called corporate angels are senior managers at *Fortune* 1000 corporations who have been laid off with generous severances or have taken early retirement. In addition to receiving the cash, an entrepreneur may persuade the corporate angel to occupy a senior management position.

☐   **Entrepreneurial angels.** The most prevalent type of investors, most of these individuals own and operate highly successful businesses. Because these investors have other sources of income, and perhaps significant wealth from IPOs or partial buyouts, they will take bigger risks and invest more capital. The best way to market your deal to these angels, therefore, is as a synergistic opportunity. Reflecting this orientation, entrepreneurial angels seldom look at companies outside of their own area of expertise and will participate in no more than a handful of investments at any one time. These investors almost always take a seat on the board of directors but rarely assume management duties. They will make fair-sized investments— typically $200,000 to $500,000—and invest more as the company progresses.

☐   **Enthusiast angels.** Whereas entrepreneurial angels tend to be somewhat calculating, enthusiasts simply like to be involved in deals. Most enthusiast angels are age 65 or older, independently wealthy from success in a business they started, and have abbreviated work schedules. For them, investing is a hobby. As a result, they typically play no role in management and rarely seek to be placed on a board. Because they spread themselves across so many companies, the size of their investments tends to be small—ranging from as little as $10,000 to perhaps a few hundred thousand dollars.

☐   **Micromanagement angels.** Micromanagers are very serious investors. Some of them were born wealthy, but the vast majority attained wealth through their own efforts. Unfortunately, this heritage makes them dangerous. Because most have successfully built a company, micromanagers attempt to impose the tactics that worked for them on their portfolio companies. Although they do not seek an active management role, micromanagers usually demand a seat on the board of directors. If business is not going well, they will try to bring in new managers.

☐   **Professional angels.** The term "professional" in this context refers to the investor's occupation, such as doctor, lawyer and, in some very rare instances, accountant. Professional angels like to invest in companies that offer a product or service with which they have some experience. They rarely seek a board seat, but they can be unpleasant to deal with when the going gets rough and may believe that a company is in trouble before it actually is. Professional angels will invest in several companies at one time, and their capital contributions range from $25,000 to $200,000.[32]

The importance of understanding the role of informal risk capital is illustrated by the fact that the pool of today's angel capital is five times the amount in the institutional venture capital market, providing money to 20 to 30 times as many companies. Angels invest more than $20 billion a year in 30,000 to 40,000 companies nationwide, twice the amount of money and twice the number of companies ten years ago.[33]

Recent research by Jeffrey Sohl, who worked with William E. Wetzel, Jr., on "Angel Capital," shows a marked increase in angel investing activity over the past few years. A total of 48,000 entrepreneurial ventures received angel funding in 2004. In addition there were 225,000 individual angel investors active in 2004, which demonstrates the huge expansion of angel activity in the United States over the last few years.[34]

Another important consideration for **angel capital** is that 60 percent of informal investment is devoted to seed a start-up business as opposed to 28 percent of venture capital. Of those initial deals, 82 percent were for less than $500,000 whereas only 13 percent of venture capital handled deals that small. The average size of an informal investment is $250,000, which indicates the importance of informal risk capital to entrepreneurs seeking small amounts of start-up financing.[35] (See Table 14.10 for some "angel stats.") Obviously, informal networks are a major potential capital source for entrepreneurs. However, every entrepreneur should be careful and thorough in his or her approach to business angels. There are advantages and disadvantages associated with "angel financing." Figure 14.3 illustrates some of the critical pros and cons of dealing with business angels. It is only through recognition of these issues that entrepreneurs will be able to establish the best relationship with a business angel.

Table 14.10   "Angel Stats"

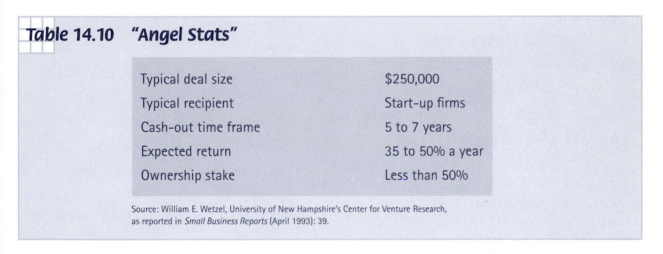

Typical deal size	$250,000
Typical recipient	Start-up firms
Cash-out time frame	5 to 7 years
Expected return	35 to 50% a year
Ownership stake	Less than 50%

Source: William E. Wetzel, University of New Hampshire's Center for Venture Research, as reported in *Small Business Reports* (April 1993): 39.

Figure 14.3 The Pros and Cons of Business Angel Investments

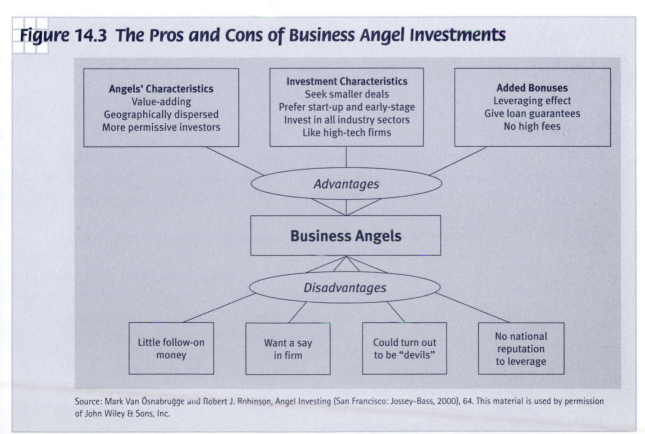

Angels' Characteristics
Value-adding
Geographically dispersed
More permissive investors

Investment Characteristics
Seek smaller deals
Prefer start-up and early-stage
Invest in all industry sectors
Like high-tech firms

Added Bonuses
Leveraging effect
Give loan guarantees
No high fees

Advantages

Business Angels

Disadvantages

Little follow-on money

Want a say in firm

Could turn out to be "devils"

No national reputation to leverage

Source: Mark Van Osnabrugge and Robert J. Robinson, Angel Investing (San Francisco: Jossey-Bass, 2000), 64. This material is used by permission of John Wiley & Sons, Inc.

the entrepreneurial
PROCESS

Why Are Angels Joining Angel Organizations?

Angel Investing in the '80s

In the 1980s, networking was very difficult. Deal flow was low and syndication impossible. In addition, the process was not very well defined. Consequently:

- ☐ Angel investing was too much work
- ☐ Angels hid from entrepreneurs
  - ☐ To avoid reading 100 plans per year
  - ☐ Preferring deals from trusted sources only

Angel Investing Now

Today the process is well documented with an explosive growth in angel organizations, from 10 to 200 angel groups in the United States in eight years! Consequently:

- ☐ Deal flow is up, encouraged by new originations and high-profile successes
- ☐ Angels are rather easy to access in multiple markets

- ☐ Training and education is available for both entrepreneurs and angels
- ☐ VCs are more willing to work with angels (love/hate relationship)
- ☐ Significantly more capital in play

Outcomes

The proliferation of formal angel networks results in:

- ☐ Increased visibility of angels
  - ☐ Understanding level of activity
  - ☐ Recruiting new angel members
- ☐ Finding quality angels more easily, thereby increasing deal flow
- ☐ Availability of best practices and organizational models
- ☐ Avoiding burnout through division of labor
- ☐ Eliminating the need to fly solo

SOURCE: "Successful Angel Investing," Indiana Venture Center, March 2005.

Summary

This chapter has examined the various forms of capital formation for entrepreneurs. Initial consideration was given to debt and equity financing in the form of commercial banks, trade credit, accounts receivable financing, factoring and finance companies, and various forms of equity instruments.

Public stock offerings have advantages and disadvantages as a source of equity capital. Although large amounts of money can be raised in short periods of time, the entrepreneur must sacrifice a degree of control and ownership. In addition, the Securities and Exchange Commission has myriad requirements and regulations that must be followed.

Private placements are an alternative means of raising equity capital for new ventures. This source is often available to entrepreneurs seeking venture capital in amounts of less than $500,000, although it is possible that up to $5 million could be raised with no more than 35 nonaccredited purchasers. The SEC's Regulation D clearly outlines the exemptions and requirements involved in a private placement. This placement's greatest advantage to the entrepreneur is limited company disclosure and only a small number of shareholders.

In recent years the venture capital market has grown dramatically. Billions of dollars are now invested annually to seed new ventures or help fledgling enterprises grow. The individuals who invest these funds are known as venture capitalists. A number of myths that have sprung up about these capitalists were discussed and refuted.

Venture capitalists use a number of different criteria when evaluating new-venture proposals. In the main these criteria focus on two areas: the entrepreneur and the investment potential of the venture. The evaluation process typically involves four stages: initial screening, business plan evaluation, oral presentation, and final evaluation.

In recent years informal risk capital has begun to play an important role in new-venture financing. Everyone with money to invest in new ventures can be considered a source for this type of capital. Some estimates put the informal risk capital pool at more than $5 billion. Entrepreneurs who are unable to secure financing through banks or through public or private stock offerings will typically turn to the informal risk capital market by seeking out friends, associates, and other contacts who may have (or know of someone who has) money to invest in a new venture.

Key Terms and Concepts

accounts receivable financing	finance companies
accredited purchaser	informal risk capitalists
angel capital	initial public offering (IPO)
business angel	private placement
debt financing	Regulation D
equity financing	trade credit
factoring	venture capitalists

Review and Discussion Questions

1. Using Figure 14.1 describe some of the sources of capital available to entrepreneurs, and discuss how they correlate to the varying levels of risk involved with each stage of the venture.

2. What are the benefits and drawbacks of equity and of debt financing? Briefly discuss both.

3. Identify and describe four types of debt financing.

4. If a new venture has its choice between long-term debt and equity financing, which would you recommend? Why?

5. Why would a venture capitalist be more interested in buying a convertible debenture for $50,000 than in lending the new business $50,000 at a 10 percent interest rate?

6. What are some of the advantages of going public? What are some of the disadvantages?

7. What is the objective of Regulation D?

8. If a person inherited $100,000 and decided to buy stock in a new venture through a private placement, how would Regulation D affect this investor?

9. How large is the venture capital pool today? Is it growing or shrinking?

10. Is it easier or more difficult to get new-venture financing today? Why?

11. Some entrepreneurs do not like to seek new-venture financing because they feel that venture capitalists are greedy. In your opinion, is this true? Do these capitalists want too much?

12. Identify and describe three objectives of venture capitalists.

13. How would a venture capitalist use Figure 14.2 to evaluate an investment? Use an illustration in your answer.

14. Identify and describe four of the most common criteria venture capitalists use to evaluate a proposal.

15. Of what practical value is Table 14.5 to new-venture entrepreneurs?

16. In a new-venture evaluation, what are the four stages through which a proposal typically goes? Describe each in detail.

17. An entrepreneur is in the process of contacting three different venture capitalists and asking each to evaluate her new business proposal. What questions should she be able to answer about each of the three?

18. An entrepreneur of a new venture has had no success in getting financing from formal venture capitalists. He now has decided to turn to the informal risk capital market. Who is in this market? How would you recommend the entrepreneur contact these individuals?

19. How likely is it that the informal risk capital market will grow during the next five years? Defend your answer.

20. Of all the sources of capital formation, which is ideal? Why?

■ Experiential Exercise

Analyzing the Funding Sources

For each funding source, write down what the text says about its usefulness for small firms. Then seek out and interview a representative of each source to find out the person's point of view of his or her relationship to small firms.

SOURCE	WHAT THE TEXT SAYS	SOURCE'S POINT OF VIEW
Banks		
Long-term loans		
Short-term loans		
Intermediate-term loans		
Private placement (Regulation D)		
Public offerings (IPO)		
Finance company		
Factor		
Trade credit		
State or local development companies		
Small Business Investment Company (SBIC)		
Informal risk capital (seed capital network)		
Venture capitalist		

Video Case 14.1

Planning and Financing an Entrepreneurial Venture
Office Pavilion with Vicky Carlson

You see this smile on my face. . . . it's called cash flow.   (Vicky Carlson)

Vicky Carlson, owner of Office Pavilion in San Diego, California, graduated from the University of Wyoming in 1986 with a lot of confidence, determination, and energy but no job prospects. She grew up in Gillette, Wyoming, a small town of 20,000 people at the time. "I know that my core self and values stem from the environment I grew up in. . . . we did have magazines, and we did have television, and we had books when I grew up [in Gillette]. So I could see the world, and I always knew that I wanted to experience the world."

With some reluctance, Vicky took a temp job as a receptionist in Denver at Office Pavilion, a Herman Miller office systems dealership known for its classic furniture designs. Office Pavilion was just getting started as a gallery and showroom, and they were looking for good employees. Vicky made it clear to management that she did not want to be pigeonholed in the receptionist's job for long. She also made it a point to ask questions, get training, and demonstrate her interest in the company in any way possible; her hard work paid off because, in short order, she became a showroom manager.

"I had the luxury, I would say, in getting into this industry—or the opportunity to be able to work through every department, so that I understood everything about the business, the whole detail," Vicky explains. Within five and a half years, she had advanced to vice president of operations in a business doing $30 million in sales.

At that point, Vicky was approached by a company in Los Angeles that needed some help with their operations. She decided to make the move, but only temporarily. She knew that she wanted her own Herman Miller/Office Pavilion store, and, three and a half years later, in 1994, she was able to buy an open dealership in San Diego.

She approached Herman Miller executives for initial financial backing to buy the store and convinced them that she could make it a success. Although Miller executives were reluctant to finance a new, independent dealership at that time, Vicky wrote a proposal that persuaded them that she would be a good investment. "It's like I know I can do it, and I know I will do it. And you know what, there will be things that I don't see now that I'll run into, but I'll figure it out."

Vicky also convinced the owner of the San Diego store to sell it for a reasonable price. She knew that the operation had been on the market for several years, and the owner wanted to move into a different market. "Herman Miller lent me the money for my working capital and my initial note [to the owner] . . . because the way we negotiated the deal is I paid him some money up front, and then I paid him the balance over a four-year period of time."

The store became very successful, and Vicky decided that, in order to expand the operation, she needed to move into a larger facility. Only months later, early in 2001, the economy started to decline, and Vicky's projected sales forecast became a nightmare. She knew she had to respond to the economic downturn quickly, especially because she had a seven-year lease on the larger building.

Vicky remembers, "Sales dropped off the charts. I had to cut a million dollars out of my budget. . . . I had a meeting with my management team, and I had looked at the financials, and I knew what revenue we were generating. I had to make some good assumptions based on an unknown future [about] what we probably could do, and, based on that, I had to look at where our expenses were. . . ." The management team trimmed any expenses possible and were also forced to make some layoffs. But when the 9/11 tragedy struck and the economy declined even more, the organization did not have to make any additional adjustments. They already had a steady course.

Under Vicky's leadership over the past decade, Office Pavilion has become a "support center for progressive workplace environments in San Diego County." Today's sales clearly indicate that the firm has rebounded successfully; it employs 45 people, and annual revenue is over $20 million. Vicky affirms, "Each year gets better and better." Her advice to aspiring entrepreneurs is very practical: "Know the benchmarks" and act on them. "Things sometimes take longer than you think, but you just keep moving forward."

Questions

1. Discuss possible critical factors involved in the Herman Miller organization's decision to invest in Vicky Carlson's business.

2. Discuss Vicky Carlson's plans for new-venture financing. What were the possible advantages and potential disadvantages to her plans?

Case 14.2

Looking for Capital

When Joyce and Phil Abrams opened their bookstore one year ago, they estimated it would take them six months to break even. Because they had gone into the venture with enough capital to keep them afloat for nine months, they were sure they would need no outside financing. However, sales have been slower than anticipated, and most of their funds now have been used to purchase inventory or meet monthly expenses. On the other hand, the store is doing better each month, and the Abramses are convinced they will be able to turn a profit within six months.

At present, Joyce and Phil want to secure additional financing. Specifically, they would like to raise $100,000 to expand their product line. The store currently focuses most heavily on how-to-do-it books and is developing a loyal customer following. However, this market is not large enough to carry the business. The Abramses feel that if they expand into an additional market such as cookbooks, they can develop two market segments that, when combined, would prove profitable. Joyce is convinced that cookbooks are an important niche, and she has saved a number of clippings from national newspapers and magazines reporting that people who buy cookbooks tend to spend more money per month on these purchases than does the average book buyer. Additionally, customer loyalty among this group tends to be very high.

The Abramses own all of their inventory, which has a retail market value of $280,000. The merchandise cost them $140,000. They also have at a local bank a line of credit of $10,000, of which they have used $4,000. Most of their monthly expenses are covered out of the initial capital with which they started the business ($180,000 in all). However, they will be out of money in three months if they are not able to get additional funding.

The owners have considered investigating a number of sources. The two primary ones are a loan from their bank and a private stock offering to investors. They know nothing about how to raise money, and these are only general ideas they have been discussing with each other. However, they do have a meeting scheduled with their accountant, a friend, who they hope can advise them on how to raise more capital. For the moment, the Abramses are focusing on writing a business plan that spells out their short business history and objectives and explains how much money they would like to raise and where it would be invested. They hope to have the plan completed before the end of the week and take it with them to the accountant. The biggest problem they are having in writing the plan is that they are unsure of how to direct their presentation. Should they aim it at a banker or a venture capitalist? After their meeting with the accountant, they plan to refine the plan and direct it toward the appropriate source.

Questions

1. Would a commercial banker be willing to lend money to the Abramses? How much? On what do you base your answer?

2. Would this venture have any appeal for a venture capitalist? Why or why not?

3. If you were advising the Abramses, how would you recommend they seek additional capital? Be complete in your answer.

Case 14.3

The $3 Million Venture

The Friendly Market is a large supermarket located in a city in the Southwest. "Friendly's," as it is popularly known, has more sales per square foot than any of its competitors because it lives up to its name. The personnel go out of their way to be friendly and helpful. If someone asks for a particular brand-name item and the store does not carry it, the product will be ordered. If enough customers want a particular product, it is added to the regular line. Additionally, the store provides free delivery of groceries for senior citizens, check-cashing privileges for its regular customers, and credit for those who have filled out the necessary application and have been accepted into the "Friendly Credit" group.

The owner, Charles Beavent, believes that his marketing-oriented approach can be successfully used in any area of the country. He is therefore thinking about expanding and opening two new stores, one in the northern part of the city and the other in a city located 50 miles east. Locations have been scouted, and a detailed business plan has been drawn up. However, Charles has not approached anyone about providing the necessary capital. He estimates he will need about $3 million to get both stores up and going. Any additional funding can come from the current operation, which throws off a cash flow of about $100,000 monthly.

Charles feels two avenues are available to him: debt and equity. His local banker has told him the bank would be willing to look over any business plan he submits and would give him an answer within five working days. Charles is convinced he can get the bank to lend him $3 million. However, he does not like the idea of owing that much money. He believes he would be better off selling stock to raise the needed capital. Doing so would require him to give up some ownership, but this is more agreeable to him than the alternative.

The big question now is, How can the company raise $3 million through a stock offering? Charles intends to check into this over the next four weeks and make a decision within eight weeks. A number of customers have approached him over the past year and have asked him if he would consider making a private stock offering. Charles is convinced he can get many of his customers to buy into the venture, although he is not sure he can raise the full $3 million this way. The other approach he sees as feasible is to raise the funds through a venture capital company. This might be the best way to get such a large sum, but Charles wonders how difficult it would be to work with these people on a long-term basis. In any event, as he said to his wife yesterday, "If we're going to expand, we have to start looking into how we can raise more capital. I think the first step is to identify the best source. Then we can focus on the specifics of the deal."

Questions

1. What would be the benefits of raising the $3 million through a private placement? What would be the benefits of raising the money through a venture capitalist?

2. Of these two approaches, which would be best for Charles? Why?

3. What would you recommend Charles do now? Briefly outline a plan of action he can use to get the financing process started.

Notes

1. Albert V. Bruno and Tyzoon T. Tyebjee, "The Entrepreneur's Search for Capital," *Journal of Business Venturing* (winter 1985): 61–74; see also Howard E. Van Auken and Richard B. Carter, "Acquisitions of Capital by Small Business," *Journal of Small Business Management* (April 1989): 1–91; and Gavin Cassar, "The Financing of Business Start-Ups," *Journal of Business Venturing* 19(2) (March 2004): 261–283.

2. *The State of Small Business: A Report of the President,* 1997 (Washington, D.C.: Government Printing Office, June 1997), 277–280; see also Jerry Feigen, "Financing Sources for Small Businesses," *In-Business* (July/August 1990): 43–44; and http://www.sba.gov (Financing), 2005.

3. http://www.fdic.gov, 2005.

4. A complete explanation can be found in Ralph Alterowitz and Jon Zonderman, *Financing Your New or Growing Business* (Canada: Entrepreneur Press, 2002); see also Bruce G. Postner, "How to Finance Anything," *Inc.* (February 1993): 54–68.

5. Truls Erikson, "Entrepreneurial Capital: The Emerging Venture's Most Important Asset and Competitive Advantage," *Journal of Business Venturing* 17(3) (2002): 275–290.

6. PriceWaterhouseCoopers, MoneyTree™ Survey, 2005 (http://www.nvca.com).

7. See *Going Public* (New York: The NASDAQ Stock Market, Inc., 1999), 5–9.

8. http://www.ipomonitor.com, 2005.

9. See *Going Public* (New York: The NASDAQ Stock Market, Inc., 1999), 5–9.

10. A summary can be found in business law texts such as Kenneth W. Clarkson, Roger LeRoy Miller, Gaylord A. Jentz, and Frank B. Cross, *West's Business Law: Legal, Ethical, International, and E-Commerce Environment,* 8th ed. (Mason, OH: South-Western/Thomson Learning, 2001), 692–695.

11. For a good source of firms involved in private placements, see David R. Evanson, *Where to Go When the Bank Says No: Alternatives for Financing Your Business* (Princeton, NJ: Bloomberg Press, 1998); see also T. B. Folta and J. J. Janney, "Strategic Benefits to Firms Issuing Private Equity Placements," *Strategic Management Journal* 25(3) (March 2004): 223–242.

12. Edgar Norton and Bernard H. Tenenbaum, "Specialization versus Diversification as a Venture Capital Investment Strategy," *Journal of Business Venturing* (September 1993): 431–442.

13. Edgar Norton and Bernard H. Tenenbaum, "Factors Affecting the Structure of U.S. Venture Capital Deals," *Journal of Small Business Management* (July 1992): 20–29.

14. S. Michael Camp and Donald L. Sexton, "Trends in Venture Capital Investment: Implications for High Technology Firms," *Journal of Small Business Management* (July 1992): 11–19; Raphael Amit, James Brander, and Christoph Zott, "Why Do Venture Capital Firms Exist? Theory and Canadian Evidence," *Journal of Business Venturing* 6 (1998): 441–466; and PriceWaterhouseCoopers, MoneyTree™ Survey, 2005 (http://www.nvca.com).

15. Ghislaine Bouillet-Cordonnier, "Legal Aspects of Start-Up Evaluation and Adjustment Methods," *Journal of Business Venturing* (March 1992): 91–102; and PriceWaterhouseCoopers, MoneyTree™ Survey, 2005 (http://www.nvca.com).

16. Ian C. MacMillan, David M. Kulow, and Roubina Khoylian, "Venture Capitalists' Involvement in Their Investments: Extent and Performance," *Journal of Business Venturing* (January 1989): 27–47; and Sharon Gifford, "Limited Attention and the Role of the Venture Capitalist," *Journal of Business Venturing* 6 (1997): 459–482.

17. Gregory F. Chiampou and Joel J. Kallet, "Risk/Return Profile of Venture Capital," *Journal of Business Venturing* (January 1989): 1–10.

18. Howard E. Van Auken, "Financing Small Technology-Based Companies: The Relationship Between Familiarity with Capital and Ability to Price and Negotiate Investment," *Journal of Small Business Management* 39(3) (2001): 240–258.

19. David J. Gladstone, *Venture Capital Handbook* (Reston, VA: Reston, 1983), 21–24.

20. Keith Schilit, "How to Obtain Venture Capital," *Business Horizons* (May/June 1987): 76–81.

21. Dean A. Shepherd, "Venture Capitalists' Introspection: A Comparison of 'In Use' and 'Espoused' Decision Policies," *Journal of Small Business Management* (April 1999): 76–87; and "Venture Capitalists' Assessment of New Venture Survival," *Management Science* (May 1999): 621–632.

22. Ian C. MacMillan, Robin Siegel, and P. N. Subba Narasimha, "Criteria Used by Venture Capitalists to Evaluate New Venture Proposals," *Journal of Business Venturing* (winter 1985): 119–128.

23. John Hall and Charles W. Hofer, "Venture Capitalist's Decision Criteria in New Venture Evaluation," *Journal of Business Venturing* (January 1993): 25–42.

24. Ronald J. Hustedde and Glen C. Pulver, "Factors Affecting Equity Capital Acquisition: The Demand Side," *Journal of Business Venturing* (September 1992): 363–374.

25. Harry J. Sapienza, "When Do Venture Capitalists Add Value?" *Journal of Business Venturing* (January 1992): 9–28; see also Juan Florin, "Is Venture Capital Worth It? Effects on Firm Performance and Founder Returns," *Journal of Business Venturing* 20(1) (January 2005): 113–135; and Lowell W. Busenitz, James O. Fiet, and Douglas D. Moesel, "Reconsidering the Venture Capitalists' 'Value Added' Proposition: An Interorganizational Learning Perspective," *Journal of Business Venturing* 19(6) (November 2004): 787–807.

26. B. Elango, Vance H. Fried, Robert D. Hisrich, and Amy Polonchek, "How Venture Capital Firms Differ," *Journal of Business Venturing* (March 1995): 157–179; Dean A. Shepherd and Andrew L. Zacharakis, "Venture Capitalists' Expertise: A Call for Research into Decision Aids and Cognitive Feedback," *Journal of Business Venturing* 17(1) (2002): 1–20; and Dick De Clercq and Harry J. Sapienza, "When Do Venture Capitalists Learn from Their Portfolio Companies?" *Entrepreneurship Theory and Practice* 29(4) (2005): 517–535.

27. Harold M. Hoffman and James Blakey, "You Can Negotiate with Venture Capitalists," *Harvard Business Review* (March/April 1987): 16; Andrew L. Zacharakis and Dean A. Shepherd, "The Nature of Information and Overconfidence on Venture Capitalist's Decision Making," *Journal of Business Venturing* 16(4) (July 2001): 311–332; James C. Brau, Richard A. Brown and Jerome S. Osteryoung, "Do Venture Capitalists Add Value to Small Manufacturing Firms? An Empirical Analysis of Venture and Nonventure Capital-Backed Initial Public Offerings," *Journal of Small Business Management* 42(1) (January 2004): 78–92; and Lowell W. Busenitz, James O. Fiet, and Douglas D. Moesel, "Signaling in Venture Capitalist–New Venture Team Funding Decisions: Does It Indicate Long-Term Venture Outcomes?" *Entrepreneurship Theory and Practice* 29(1) (January 2005): 1–12.

28. William E. Wetzel, Jr., "Informal Risk Capital: Knowns and Unknowns," in *The Art and Science of Entrepreneurship,* ed. Donald L. Sexton and Raymond W. Smilor (Cambridge, MA: Ballinger, 1986), 88.

29. William E. Wetzel, Jr., as quoted by Dale D. Buss, "Heaven Help Us," *Nation's Business* (November 1993): 29.

30. William E. Wetzel, Jr., "Angel Money," *In-Business* (November/December 1989): 44.

31. William E. Wetzel, Jr., "Angels and Informal Risk Capital," *Sloan Management Review* (summer 1983); see also John Freear, Jeffrey E. Sohl, and William E. Wetzel, Jr., "Angels and Non-angels: Are There Differences?" *Journal of Business Venturing* (March 1994): 109–123.

32. Evanson, *Where to Go When the Bank Says No,* 40–44.

33. Buss, "Heaven Help Us," 29–30; see also John Freear, Jeffrey E. Sohl, and William E. Wetzel, Jr., "Angels: Personal Investors in the Venture Capital Market," *Entrepreneurship & Regional Development* 7 (1995): 85–94; and Jeffrey Sohl, "The Angel Investor Market in 2004," Center for Venture Research, University of New Hampshire, May 2005.

34. Jeffrey Sohl, "The Angel Investor Market in 2004," Center for Venture Research, University of New Hampshire, May 2005.

35. Wetzel, "Angel Money," 42–44; and Colin M. Mason and Richard T. Harrison, "Is It Worth It? The Rates of Return from Informal Venture Capital Investments," *Journal of Business Venturing* 17(3) (2002): 211–236.

entrepreneurial
CASE ANALYSIS

The Playboy Emblem—

A Case of Trademark Infringement

The Letter

On August 26, 1982, a disturbing and almost unbelievable letter arrived certified mail (return receipt requested) at the tavern. The letter to John P. Browne stated:

Re: RABBIT HEAD Design Trademark Infringement—Bunny's Tavern, Brookfield, Illinois

Gentlemen:

It has been brought to our attention that Bunny's Tavern has painted on the outside wall of its establishment a rabbit head design virtually identical to our company's RABBIT HEAD Design trademark. The RABBIT HEAD Design is a trademark owned by Playboy Enterprises, Inc., and Bunny's unauthorized use of our mark constitutes trademark infringement and unfair competition. Bunny's continued use of our mark is likely to cause confusion to the general public, in that the public could consider Bunny's Tavern as being in some way sponsored by or otherwise associated with our company.

Unless Bunny's Tavern immediately and permanently ceases and desists its unauthorized use of our company's RABBIT HEAD Design trademark or any other mark or design similar thereto owned by or associated with our company within ten days of the date of this letter, we will recommend to management that legal action be taken against it to protect our company's rights.

Should Bunny's Tavern wish to avoid the possibility of future unpleasantness and the needless expense of litigation, please have an authorized representative sign, date, and return the enclosed copy of this letter. Such signature will evidence Bunny's agreement to settle this matter according to the terms of this letter.

Should Bunny's Tavern continue its unauthorized use of our company's mark, it does so at its own risk.

Very truly yours,

PLAYBOY ENTERPRISES, INC.

Harriet E. Earle

Trademarks Coordinator

Background: John P. Browne and His Tavern

In November 1948 John P. Browne opened a neighborhood tavern of modest means. Located on 47th Street in Brookfield, Illinois (a western suburb of Chicago), the small building provided a room with 16 bar stools and no tables. A few arcade games (bowling and pinball) were available for entertainment of the clientele.

For over 34 years the tavern operated successfully (by standards of a lifestyle venture, that is, John P. Browne was able to make a profit and provide for his family). The customers were local neighborhood friends and workers from the surrounding factories located down the street (e.g., Electro-Motive and Materials Service). The clientele was loyal, and a strong rapport was established through the years with owner/operator John P. Browne and his customers, since he handled most of the bartending duties himself. In his later years his father, Patrick J., also bartended, which provided the clientele with a family influence at the Browne establishment.

Source: This case was prepared by Dr. Donald F. Kuratko of the Kelley School of Business at Indiana University, and is intended to be used as a basis for class discussion. Presented and accepted by the refereed Midwest Society for Case Research Workshop, 1986. All rights reserved to the author and to the Midwest Society for Case Research. Copyright © 2005 by Donald F. Kuratko.

Throughout the continuous operation of this tavern business and loyal development of the clientele, John P. Browne became a well-liked and well-respected businessman in the local community. The Brookfield community (now with a population of 21,000) knew the purpose of his business and his clientele, which was to provide a local gathering spot for beer and alcohol consumption combined with a neighborhood atmosphere.

John P. Browne is known by all as "Bunny Browne" and has been all of his life. Sixty-three years ago a nurse in a Chicago hospital coined the nickname when she thought he was as "cute as a bunny." The nickname remained through his early years, and when John developed into a lightweight boxer in the Chicago area "Golden Gloves," the nickname characterized his bouncing style in the ring.

Thus, it was only fitting that John use his popular name for his neighborhood establishment in 1948. Therefore, "Bunny" Browne's Tap was named officially.

The Rabbit Head Emblem

The idea of painting an emblem on the side of Bunny Browne's tavern was conceived five years after the tavern opened. In 1954, one of the tavern's patrons, Joe Karasek, developed the idea as a gesture of friendship and gratitude to his friend Bunny Browne.

After discussing various caricatures that could be painted on the wall, both Bunny Browne and Joe Karasek agreed that a simple rabbit's head would be the easiest to distinguish from a distance and would clearly represent the nickname "Bunny."

Thus, in the summer of 1954 Joe began his task of painting the east side of the tavern black and then drawing the rabbit's head in white (see Figure 1).

Figure 1

Figure 2

Note: Playboy Enterprises developed its rabbit head design in 1953. It was designed by Arthur Paul, and it has stood for over 40 years as the Playboy symbol. In addition, Playboy had its emblem registered as a trademark that same year—1953. Thus, it became a protected property item of the Playboy domain (see Figure 2).

Bunny's Response

Bunny Browne was astounded that Playboy would ever consider his emblem any type of threat to its powerful sexual domain, especially considering that his type of tavern could never be misconstrued as a copy, replica, or even a poor imitation of the Playboy Clubs. Thus, how could a sole proprietor of a small local tavern in existence before Playboy started its empire in 1953 be guilty of "unfair competition" through a trademark infringement?

"I thought it was a joke," Bunny Browne said. "After all, it has been up there for nearly 30 years, and I am unaware of anyone ever having confused my establishment with the Playboy Club."

According to Bunny, he himself has never owned a copy of *Playboy* magazine, and, noting that at age 63 he is often the youngest person in the bar, his clientele wouldn't have any use for that kind of bunny. "Basically, I feel I'm absolutely no threat to their organization. They are simply nitpicking!" Bunny stated.

It seemed appropriate that a letter of clarification to Playboy's chief executive officer—Christine Hefner—would be the simplest approach. Surely there was a misunderstanding of Bunny Browne's tavern and once Christine Hefner understood, there would probably be no further action.

The return letter from Bunny Browne to Christine Hefner was sent on September 3, 1982. It read:

Dear Ms. Hefner:

Enclosed is a copy of a letter I received by certified mail from the office of your general counsel. As you see, it is addressed to Bunny's Tavern and says that my modest tavern, place of business, is guilty of unfair competition, and the use of a rather tired-looking emblem I have on the side wall could confuse the public, and cause the public to believe that my little tavern is associated with Playboy Enterprises, Inc.

In a way it is flattering to be considered a competitor of a giant enterprise, but it is disturbing to read the reference to expensive litigation and unpleasantness.

When you read what is involved (and I hope you will be given this letter), you too may feel that your lawyer's letter does not express your feeling and does not reflect favorably on Playboy Enterprises.

I was first called Bunny by a nurse in the hospital where I was born over 63 years ago. I have been known as Bunny all of my life. I have lived my life in Brookfield (pop. 21,000) and very few of the people in the village know me as John. I began my business as Bunny's in November 1948 and have operated it continuously since that time. My tavern is not large (16 stools and no tables). My trade is from Brookfield and the surrounding neighborhood. The emblem of Bunny has been on the wall since the 1950s. It is inconceivable that anyone would confuse my emblem and tavern with the Playboy Club. My patrons and the people of Brookfield would, I know, be astonished to learn of Playboy's fears and I am sure would be upset to learn that I have fears of future unpleasantness and expensive litigation.

Ms. Hefner, I hope you will inform me that you consider the action of your lawyers to be unnecessary and in this case not in the best interest of Playboy.

Sincerely,

John P. Browne

Bunny's Tavern

9536 W. 47th Street

Brookfield, Illinois 60513

Playboy's Response

The letter from John "Bunny" Browne did apparently reach Christine Hefner and, through her counsel Howard Shapiro, she replied in a letter dated September 13, 1982. It read:

Dear Mr. Browne:

Christine Hefner has asked me to reply to your letter to her of September 3, 1982.

Although our "Bunny" is not quite as old as you, we take quite a paternal interest in protecting it. Since 1953, when it was created for Playboy by Arthur Paul, it has become a symbol of our company and like an overprotective parent, we have gone to great lengths to keep it from harm.

It seems that a lot of our readers are also very protective of our Rabbit Head Design mark. Several of them, evidently, drove past your tavern and contacted us to inquire why our mark was on the side of your building. This is how your establishment came to our attention. It's obvious from this contact that people saw your "tired-looking personal emblem" and thought of our company, and it is for this reason that Ms. Earle sent her letter.

It's obvious that you have a lot of pride in your tavern and in your reputation in the community. If someone else moved into your community, opened a tavern and utilized the name "Bunny's," we would hope that you would feel that something that belonged to you was being taken away, just as we feel that the use of a Rabbit Head Design on the side of your building is taking something away from us.

Litigation is expensive and we have no desire to go that route unless it becomes absolutely necessary. It sounds as if this whole thing can be solved by a coat of paint rather than by lawyers and legal fees. If it's acceptable to you, we'd be willing to close our file on this matter on your representation that at some point within the next three to six months, your "tired-looking personal emblem" will be replaced with something that not only you can be proud of but we will be happy with too.

If this is acceptable to you, please sign a copy of this letter and return it to me.

Very truly yours,

PLAYBOY ENTERPRISES, INC.

Howard Shapiro

■ The Media Reaction

The case of Bunny Browne's problem with Playboy spread throughout the community of Brookfield, the surrounding suburbs, and finally into Chicago. The newspapers reviewed the disagreement as a simple "attack" by big business against the "little guy." Articles quickly appeared in the local newspaper, and eventually editorials appeared by noted columnists Art Petacque and Hugh Hough of the *Chicago Sun-Times* and Mike Royko of the *Chicago Tribune*. (See excerpts here.)

> *Splitting Hares:* Bunny's Tavern, a neighborhood bar in west suburban Brookfield, has never been mistaken for a Playboy Club by its beer-quaffing customers. But that didn't stop Playboy Enterprises from threatening legal action against the bar's owner, John P. "Bunny" Browne. (Petacque & Hough—*Chicago Sun-Times*)
>
> There was a duel between Playboy Enterprises and a neighborhood tavern in Brookfield called Bunny's.
>
> For three decades, the Bunny's tavern had a big painting of a rabbit head on the side of its building.
>
> Then Playboy decided that the tavern's rabbit looked too much like Playboy's rabbit symbol and threatened to sue.
>
> It seemed unfair, because the tavern sells booze, not Hefner's kinky fantasies. . . .
> (Royko—*Chicago Tribune*)

By October 1982 the news had traveled as far as Natchez, Mississippi, where Bunny Browne had friends and acquaintances in the likes of Ben Chase Callun and Mayor Tony Byrne. After years of visits, Bunny Browne was fondly dubbed an "honorary citizen" of Natchez. Thus, the Natchez paper carried an article concerning Playboy's squabble over Bunny's emblem.

It wasn't long before the local television stations sent their minicams to film the tavern and interview Bunny over this incident with Playboy. While the television interviews were brief spots on the evening news, the interest in this little tavern in Brookfield, Illinois, was astounding.

Visitors came from all over the city and suburbs just to see this tavern and its rabbit head emblem that was upsetting Playboy Enterprises. To have a beer at Bunny's became something of a vogue—at least for a brief period of interest and curiosity.

■ Bunny's Dilemma

The fanfare subsided in a few weeks, and Bunny Browne's Tap returned to its normal routine and loyal clientele. They, being proud of Bunny's Tap in addition to being loyal, encouraged Bunny to take a stand against Playboy. "Let's fight 'em all the way,

Bunny!" they shouted. Bunny retorted, "Maybe I'll have to get in the ring and box with Playboy's best—like the old Golden Gloves days!" The bar cheered and toasted Bunny.

But the reality Bunny Browne faced was a different dilemma from the old Golden Gloves days—and he knew it. As he closed up the tavern on this late November evening, Bunny pondered about his rabbit head emblem that had for 30 years been a "friend" and now seemed to be the center of so much controversy. The now badly peeling painting had never been touched up in all those years. Bunny thought to himself that it never would be touched up if Playboy would simply let it fade away. Bunny said with an Irish grin, "I wish Playboy would just let my rabbit die a natural death—the way I'm doing." As he turned off the tavern lights, Bunny knew he must decide what to do.

Questions

1. If you were Bunny Browne, what exactly would you do? Why?

2. Explain what a trademark is and what rights it provides the owner.

3. Apply the "unfair competition" idea of trademark infringement to this case.

4. Do alternative solutions exist for Bunny Browne's tavern? If so, what are they?

5. What must a small business do to avoid infringing on the trademark rights of someone else?

6. Discuss the implications for Playboy Enterprises of pressuring a small business.

7. What lessons can be learned from Bunny Browne's situation?

8. Discuss the pros and cons of Bunny's decision (based on what you have recommended in question 1).

Part 4 Exercise

■ Angel Investor versus Venture Capitalist

Directions: Contact a local venture capital firm in order to schedule an interview with one of the partners. Then contact the local angel network in order to schedule an interview with an angel investor. If there is no local angel network, then contact one of the respected law firms in your area and ask for a recommended source that could serve as an angel investor for the purposes of this exercise. With each interview simply find out the answer to each component of the comparison table below.

TOTAL ANNUAL INVESTMENT IN START-UP VENTURES

	ANGEL	VENTURE CAPITALIST
Total Dollars		
Number of Investments		
Number of Investors		
Per Round		
Entities per Round		

INDIVIDUAL INVESTMENTS IN START-UP VENTURES

	ANGEL	VENTURE CAPITALIST
Investment Size per Round		
Each Investor		
Typical Investment Stage		

PART 5

Growth and Development of Entrepreneurial Ventures

15

Strategic Planning for Emerging Ventures

I have often heard it said that big companies, the corporate giants, are the ones that need to think about their business strategically. Smaller, more entrepreneurial companies, by contrast, do not need strategy; they can pursue other routes to business success. In my view, that is exactly backward. Unlike the giants, small businesses cannot rely on the inertia of the marketplace for their survival. Nor can they succeed on brute force, throwing resources at problems. On the contrary, they have to see their competitive environment with particular clarity, and they have to stake out and protect a position they can defend. That is what strategy is all about.

Michael E. Porter

Harvard Business School

Chapter Objectives

1 To introduce the importance of planning for an entrepreneurial venture

2 To discuss the nature of strategic planning

3 To examine the key dimensions that influence a firm's planning process

4 To discuss some of the reasons entrepreneurs do not carry out strategic planning

5 To relate some of the benefits of strategic planning

6 To examine four of the most common approaches entrepreneurs use to implement a strategic plan

7 To review the nature of operational planning for a venture

The Nature of Planning in Emerging Firms

Although most entrepreneurs do some form of planning for their ventures, it often tends to be informal and unsystematic.[1] The actual need for systematic planning will vary with the nature, size, and structure of the business. In other words, a small two-person operation may successfully use informal planning because little complexity is involved. But an emerging venture that is rapidly expanding with constantly increasing personnel size and market operations will need to formalize its planning because a great deal of complexity exists.

An entrepreneur's planning will need to shift from an informal to a formal systematic style for other reasons. First is the degree of uncertainty with which the venture is attempting to become established and to grow. With greater levels of uncertainty, entrepreneurs have a stronger need to deal with the challenges facing their venture, and a more formal planning effort can help them to do this. Second, the strength of the competition (in both numbers and quality of competitors) will add to the importance of more systematic planning in order for a new venture to monitor its operations and objectives more closely.[2] Finally, the amount and type of experience the entrepreneur has may be a factor in deciding the extent of formal planning. A lack of adequate experience, either technological or business, may constrain the entrepreneur's understanding and thus necessitate formal planning to help determine future paths for the organization.

Formal planning is usually divided into two major types: strategic and operational. We shall begin by examining the nature of strategic planning, and then we will discuss operational planning.

Strategic Planning

Strategic planning is the formulation of long-range plans for the effective management of environmental opportunities and threats in light of a venture's strengths and weaknesses. It includes defining the venture's mission, specifying achievable objectives, developing strategies, and setting policy guidelines. Dynamic in nature, the strategic management process (see Figure 15.1) is the full set of commitments, decisions, and actions required for a firm to achieve strategic competitiveness and earn above-average returns. Relevant strategic inputs derived from analyses of the internal and external environments are necessary for effective strategy formulation and implementation. In turn, effective strategic actions are a prerequisite to achieving the desired outcomes of strategic competitiveness and above-average returns. Thus, the strategic management process is used to match the conditions of an ever-changing market and competitive structure with a firm's continuously evolving resources, capabilities, and core competencies (the sources of strategic inputs). Effective strategic actions that take place in the context of carefully integrated strategy formulation and implementation actions result in desired strategic outcomes.[3] Thus, strategic planning is the primary step in determining the future direction of a business. The "best" strategic plan will be influenced by many factors, among them the abilities of the entrepreneur, the complexity of the

Figure 15.1 The Strategic Management Process

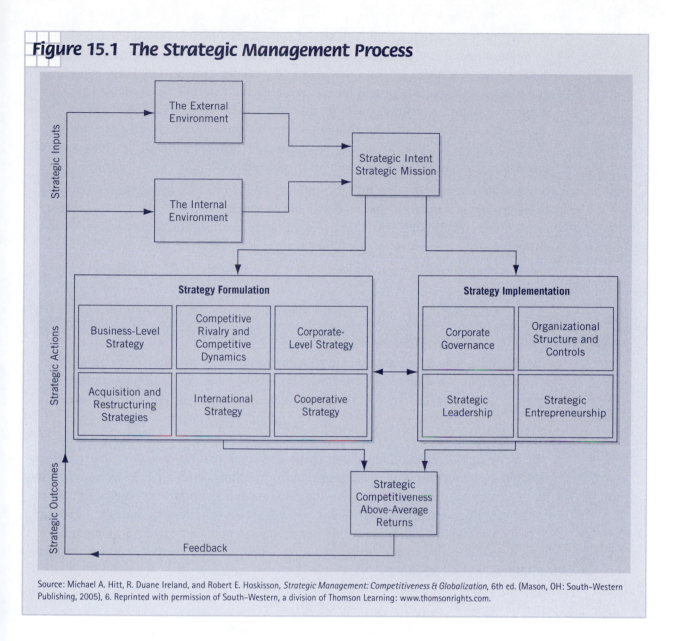

Source: Michael A. Hitt, R. Duane Ireland, and Robert E. Hoskisson, *Strategic Management: Competitiveness & Globalization*, 6th ed. (Mason, OH: South-Western Publishing, 2005), 6. Reprinted with permission of South-Western, a division of Thomson Learning: www.thomsonrights.com.

venture, and the nature of the industry. Yet, whatever the specific situation, five basic steps must be followed in strategic planning:

1. Examine the internal and external environments of the venture (strengths, weaknesses, opportunities, threats).

2. Formulate the venture's long-range and short-range strategies (mission, objectives, strategies, policies).

3. Implement the strategic plan (programs, budgets, procedures).

4. Evaluate the performance of the strategy.

5. Take follow-up action through continuous feedback.

(Figure 15.1 illustrates these basic steps in a flow diagram.)

The first step—examining the environment—can be one of the most critical for an emerging venture. Analyses of its external and internal environments provide a firm with the information required to develop its strategic intent and strategic mission. As shown in Figure 15.1, strategic intent and strategic mission influence strategy formulation and implementation actions. A clear review of a venture's internal and external factors is needed, and both sets of factors must be considered when performing an environmental analysis. This analysis is often called a **SWOT analysis**; *SWOT* is an acronym for a venture's internal strengths and weaknesses and its external opportunities and threats. The analysis should include not only the external factors most likely to occur and to have a serious impact on the company but also the internal factors most likely to affect the implementation of present and future strategic decisions. By focusing on this analysis, an emerging venture can proceed through the other steps of formulation, implementation, evaluation, and feedback.[4]

It should be remembered that the greatest value of the strategic planning process is the "strategic thinking" it promotes among business owners. Although not always articulated formally, strategic thinking synthesizes the intuition and creativity of an entrepreneur into a vision for the future.[5]

This chapter now examines the different aspects of strategic planning for emerging ventures.

Key Dimensions Influencing a Firm's Strategic Planning Activities

Five factors shape the strategic management activities of growing companies: (1) demand on strategic managers' time, (2) decision-making speed, (3) problems of internal politics, (4) environmental uncertainty, and (5) the entrepreneur's vision.

Demand on Strategic Managers' Time

The increasing demand on key owner-managers' time that accompanies the complexity brought on by growth of the entrepreneurial firm brings about a need for more rigorous strategic management practices. This logically appealing proposition has been offered in the past by many researchers. From their perspective, increased strategic planning activity provides the means to accommodate owner-managers' needs to maintain control and direction of the enterprise, while giving up some activities in recognition of increased time pressures.

Decision-Making Speed

As the firm expands, the decisions to be made can be expected to increase both in number and frequency. These pressures are referred to as "delegation demands" on the growing firm's management. More systematic strategic planning practices are needed for entrepreneurs to guide and control the increasing decision making within the firm.

Problems of Internal Politics

Strategic planning practices are seen as one way to alleviate difficulties associated with the dysfunctional effects of internal politics on organizational decision making. By providing a formal process by which to channel partisan organizational priorities, strategic planning helps to control the politics that emerge as an entrepreneurial firm grows and develops organizational power seekers.

Environmental Uncertainty

Research has suggested that the need for strategic planning is greater in the presence of increased environmental uncertainty. Thus, it appears likely that environmental uncertainty is a key factor influencing the strategic management activities of entrepreneurial firms with an increasingly life-cycle-diverse product and market base.[6]

The Entrepreneur's Vision

To a large degree, venture planning is an extension of the entrepreneurial ego. Planning is the process of transforming entrepreneurial vision and ideas into action. This process involves three basic steps:

☐ *Step 1: Commitment to an open planning process.* Many entrepreneurs are suspicious of planning. They fear the loss of control and of flexibility. Quite often this fear is the chief obstacle to future success because it blinds the entrepreneur to the ideas of other knowledgeable people. This, in turn, closes the door on new ideas and greatly limits the benefits associated with an open planning process.

☐ *Step 2: Accountability to a corporate conscience.* This often takes the form of an advisory board, which is a highly effective form of corporate conscience. It can substantially enhance the functioning of entrepreneurial ego. This committee differs from a board of directors by its lack of legal standing and the fact its primary objectives are to (1) increase the owner's sensitivity to larger issues of direction and (2) make the owner accountable, albeit on a voluntary basis.

☐ *Step 3: Establishment of a pattern of subordinate participation in the development of the strategic plan.* The planning process can create organizational energy, especially if key members of the organization are instrumental in creating it. Interviews with key subordinates have revealed that the absence of the organizational and personal guideposts needed to chart and monitor a successful course of executive action tend to result in little support for the plan.[7]

These three steps may seem obvious to any entrepreneur attempting to translate his or her vision into a planning process. The fact remains, however, that such planning is too often lacking in many new small ventures.

The Lack of Strategic Planning

The importance of new ventures to the economy is substantial in terms of innovation, employment, and sales, and effective planning can help these new firms survive and grow. Unfortunately, research has shown a distinct lack of planning on the part of new ventures. Five reasons for the lack of strategic planning have been found.

1. **Time scarcity.** Managers report that their time is scarce and difficult to allocate to planning in the face of day-to-day operating schedules.

2. **Lack of knowledge.** Small-firm owners/managers have minimal exposure to, and knowledge of, the planning process. They are uncertain of the components of the process and the sequence of those components. The entrepreneurs are also unfamiliar with many planning information sources and how they can be used.

3. **Lack of expertise/skills.** Small-business managers typically are generalists, and they often lack the specialized expertise necessary for the planning process.

4. **Lack of trust and openness.** Small-firm owners/managers are highly sensitive and guarded about their businesses and the decisions that affect them. Consequently, they are hesitant to formulate a strategic plan that requires participation by employees or outside consultants.

5. **Perception of high cost.** Small-business owners perceive the cost associated with planning to be very high. This fear of expensive planning causes many business owners to avoid or ignore planning as a viable process.[8]

In addition to these reasons, other factors have been reported as difficulties of the planning process. For example, both high-performing and low-performing small ventures have problems with long-range planning. Both time and expense are major obstacles. Additionally, low-performing firms report that a poor planning climate, inexperienced managers, and unfavorable economic conditions are problems. Quite obviously, strategic planning is no easy chore for new ventures. On the other hand, many benefits can be gained from such planning.

The Value of Strategic Planning

Does strategic planning pay off? Research shows it does. In one study in which the effects of planning on performance were examined, it was found that the extent of long-range planning was unrelated to company performance whether assessed by sales growth or by return on assets. However, when other factors, such as structure, attitude toward planning, implementation, time horizon, and the content of the planning were taken into consideration, the data strongly suggested that the smaller firms that performed financially better did a more thorough job in the planning process.[9] Although the time spent on planning may not have been apparent, the quality of planning was.

In another study, 357 Texas ventures were investigated.[10] Although only a minority of these firms reported engaging in detailed strategic planning, a large number did use some form of planning. The researchers were able to establish a five-level planning classification.

- *Strategy Level 0 (SL0):* no knowledge (predictive ability) of next year's sales, profitability, or profit implementation plans

- *Strategy Level 1 (SL1):* knowledge only of next year's sales, but no knowledge of upcoming industry sales, company profit, or profit implementation plans

- *Strategy Level 2 (SL2):* knowledge of next year's company and industry sales, but no knowledge of company profit or profit implementation plans

- *Strategy Level 3 (SL3):* knowledge of company and industry sales and anticipated profit, but no profit implementation plans

- *Strategy Level 4 (SL4):* knowledge of next year's company and industry sales, anticipated company profits, and profit implementation plans

When following this sample two years later, the researchers found that 20 percent of the firms that had no strategic planning (SL0) failed, while the same was true for only 8 percent of SL4 firms. The findings indicate a link between a small venture's success over time and its strategic planning. Yet the lack of strategic planning among small firms was prevalent in the early 1980s. Researchers Sexton and Van Auken stated, "Strategic planning appears to be a scarce, fragile commodity in the small business environment. Most small firms do not engage in true strategic planning at all, and the rest may do so only sporadically or temporarily, despite the evidence that strategic planning can help firms to survive and prosper."[11]

However, other researchers have found planning among small firms increasing. Researchers Ackelsburg and Arlow, in a study of 732 U.S. firms, found that most of the small businesses did plan and that planning firms engaged in more goal-setting activities, forecasting, and other planning procedures than nonplanners.[12] Researchers

Shuman, Shaw, and Sussman surveyed the planning practices of the *Inc.* 500 and found that a majority of the entrepreneurs did not have a business plan when they started their firms but as the firms grew the planning process became more prevalent and formalized.[13] CEO attitudes toward the impact of planning influenced the prevalence of strategic planning activities of this group. Seventy-two percent of the *Inc.* 500 CEOs surveyed perceived that planning leads to better decisions that in turn lead to increased profitability. The CEOs also believed that planning leads to increased time efficiency, company growth, and knowledge of the market.

A number of other studies have focused on the impact of planning on small firms.[14] These studies support the contention that strategic planning is of value to a venture. Most of the studies imply, if they do not directly state, that planning influences a venture's survival. As noted in Robinson and Pearce's study, a number of researchers found planning to be an important criterion for differentiating successful from unsuccessful firms.[15] In another study of 70,000 failed firms, lack of planning was identified as a major cause of failure,[16] and still another investigation demonstrated that firms engaged in strategic planning outperformed those that did not use such planning.[17]

In a more recent study of 220 small firms, Ibrahim established the importance of selecting an appropriate strategy (niche strategy) for a venture to build distinctive competence and a sustainable competitive advantage.[18] Another researcher, Mosakowski, examined the dynamic effects of strategies on company performance in the software industry. Her findings showed that when focus or differentiation strategies were established, performance by those firms was enhanced.[19]

One study tallied the benefits realized from long-range planning. In examining the responses from both high-performing firms and low-performing firms, researchers found a number of interesting similarities and differences. Both types of firms recognized cost savings, accurate forecasting, and faster decision making as a result of long-range planning. However, the high-performing firms also reported better resource allocation, an improvement of competitive position, a more thorough exploration of alternatives, and increased sales. Overall, it is clear that improved performance is often the result of better planning.

More specifically, a study conducted by Bracker and Pearson characterized the planning levels of small firms as structured strategic plans (SSP), structured operational plans (SOP), intuitive plans (IP), and unstructured plans (UP).[20] Table 15.1 illustrates the definitions associated with these types of plans. The research concentrated on a sample of homogeneous, small, mature firms in the dry-cleaning industry and revealed that firms using structured strategic planning outperformed all other planning categories with regard to overall financial performance. In a later application of the same planning categories to a sample of growth-oriented firms in the electronics industry, the results supported the previous research by showing firms with structured strategic planning outperforming all others.[21]

More recently, researchers Rue and Ibrahim examined 253 smaller firms to determine the relationship between performance and planning sophistication. They classified companies into these categories:

Category I: No written plan (101 firms, or 39.9 percent)

Category II: Moderately sophisticated planning, including a written plan and/or some quantified objectives, some specific plans and budgets, identification of some factors in the external environment, procedures for anticipating or detecting differences between the plan and actual performance (89 firms, or 35.2 percent).

Table 15.1 Strategic Planning Levels

Structured strategic plans (SSP): Formalized, written long-range plans covering the process of determining the major outside interest focused on the organization; expectations of dominant inside interests; information about past, current, and future performance; environmental analysis; and determination of strengths and weaknesses of the firm and feedback. Typically 3–15 years in nature.

Structured operational plans (SOP): Written short-range operational budgets and plans of action for current fiscal period. The typical plan of action would include basic output controls, such as production quotas, cost constraints, and personnel requirements.

Intuitive plans (IP): These formal plans are developed and implemented based on the intuition and experience of the firm's owner. They are not written and are stored in the memory of the owner. They are of a short-term duration, no longer than one year in nature. They depend on objectives of the owner and the firm's present environment.

Unstructured plans (UP): No measurable structured planning in the firm.

Source: Jeffrey S. Bracker and John N. Pearson, "Planning and Financial Performance in Small, Mature Firms," *Strategic Management Journal* 7 (1986): 507.

Category III: Sophisticated planning, including a written plan with all of the following: some quantified objectives, some specific plans and budgets, identification of some factors in the external environment, and procedures for anticipating or detecting differences between the plan and actual performance (63 firms, or 24.9 percent).

Their results demonstrated that more than 88 percent of firms with Category II or Category III planning performed at or above the industry average compared with only 40 percent of those firms with Category I planning.[22]

In summary, all of the research indicates that firms that engage in strategic planning are more effective than those that do not. Most important, the studies emphasize the significance of the planning process, rather than merely the plans, as a key to successful performance.[23]

Fatal Vision in Strategic Planning

The actual execution of a strategy is almost as important as the strategy itself. Many entrepreneurs make unintentional errors while applying a specific strategy to their own specific venture. Competitive situations differ, and the particular application of known strategies must be tailored to those unique situations.

Researcher Michael E. Porter has noted five fatal mistakes entrepreneurs continually fall prey to in their attempt to implement a strategy.[24] Outlined next are these flaws and their explanations.

☐ *Flaw 1: Misunderstanding industry attractiveness.* Too many entrepreneurs associate attractive industries with those that are growing the fastest, appear to be glamorous, or use the fanciest technology. This is wrong, because attractive industries have high barriers to entry and the fewest substitutes. The more high-tech or high-glamour a business is, the more likely a lot of new competitors will enter and make it unprofitable.

entrepreneurship IN PRACTICE

Mastering Competitive Intelligence

In general terms, competitive intelligence (CI) is defined as anything that could provide a competitive advantage. It is important for companies to learn competitors' information (and sometimes secrets) while protecting their own. According to experts, small companies tend to ignore the value of CI because the entrepreneur can't afford the time or because the entrepreneur thinks he or she knows everything there is to know about the environment. Fortunately, an aggressive CI effort doesn't require the work of a full-time employee. Part-time help or using customer service will provide enough feedback to make wise decisions. Competitive intelligence can help a company in many ways, including anticipating a competitor's next move, learning from a competitor's successes and failures, and identifying new opportunities.

Planning is critical for competitive intelligence, which requires three strategic approaches:

1. Collecting readily available information through databases, trade journals, trade shows, and public documents.

2. Researching facts buried in secondary sources, which can include details gained from the government on equipment and zoning.

3. Gleaning secrets from intermediate sources, such as professionals, trade organizations, or a salesperson from a supplier in the industry.

In the latter of the three approaches, entrepreneurs must think of three things when conducting an interview: offense, defense, and victory. They must think offensively when identifying competitor vulnerability, when exposing potential opportunities, and when assessing the impact that their strategic actions might make on competitors. They must think defensively when identifying competitors' technological development, distribution channels, marketing tactics, and financial information. Finally, they must fight for victory by using the competitive intelligence they've gathered, ranking the competition, and preparing an attacking strategy.

One entrepreneur, Jay Bloom, has his own ways of staying on top of what the competition is and isn't doing. Bloom, once in risk management, stumbled upon his business idea (pet insurance) when his pet Labrador was diagnosed with a disease for which treatment was not covered on the dog's health insurance policy. His work experience helped him to do more CI work than most business owners, ultimately enabling him to be the best. Bloom subscribes to periodicals tailored for the pet and veterinary industries. He reads *Cat Fancy*, *Dog Fancy*, and *Veterinary Economics* to find articles and advertisements about his rivals. Furthermore, Bloom employs a clipping agency that examines numerous publications and cuts out articles that contain predetermined words. As customer feedback is one of the most popular and useful ways to get information on what the competition is doing, Bloom gathers information collected by his customer service representatives and personally distributes it to the sales and marketing departments. His employees are also part of the ongoing pursuit for competitive intelligence: they sign up for the competition's policies. Lastly, PetAssure, Bloom's company, has financial backers keeping their eyes peeled and 2,000 member veterinarians calling to discuss competitors' offers.

Experts recommend remembering two key things about competitive intelligence. If Entrepreneur A can get Entrepreneur B's information, Entrepreneur B can get Entrepreneur A's valuable information, too. One must not forget to protect personal plans, strategies, and policies. Next, it is important to verify the material or data that is gathered. Knowledge is power only if it's accurate.

SOURCE: Edward Parker, "The Spy Fighters," *Success* (April 1994): 33–39; and Mark Henricks, "Spy Away," *Entrepreneur* (March 2000): 98–104.

entrepreneurship IN PRACTICE

Objections to Planning

Dr. John L. Ward of Loyola University is one of the leading authorities on family business. He stresses the critical importance of strategic planning for growing firms that desire to continue through future generations. However, business owners have continual "objections" to the planning process. Here are some of those objections with responses to each.

OBJECTION	RESPONSE
Planning is a "straitjacket" that limits flexibility.	Planning expands options and the ability to respond to change.
Too many uncertainties make planning impossible.	Planning generates more information and reduces uncertainty through better understanding.
Planning requires sharing sensitive information with others.	Planning motivates employees, increases the ability of the organization to understand how the business performs, and reduces unconstructive guessing as to what is going on.
Planning makes owners "go public" with ideas and prohibits them from changing their minds.	Planning allows owners to better understand the need for change; "going public" increases the organization's ability to reach its goals.
Planning implies change from the comfortable (and successful) to the uncomfortable (and unknown).	Planning anticipates inevitable change and better implements required change.
Planning often increases "focus" on certain markets at the expense of a broader strategy.	Planning helps conserve valuable resources.
Planning suggests changes that may "cannibalize" past success.	Planning suggests options to minimize that possibility while encouraging the business to compete.
Planning identifies changes that require moving managers beyond their current skills; therefore, it increases their dependence on others who can contribute or teach those skills.	Planning helps perpetuate the institution beyond the lives of key managers.
Planning challenges business assumptions that contribute to clarity, consistency, and effectiveness.	Planning confirms many assumptions while addressing those that must change with the times.

SOURCE: Adapted from John L. Ward, *Keeping the Family Business Healthy* (San Francisco: Jossey-Bass Inc., 1987), 5–6. Adapted with permission.

☐ *Flaw 2: No real competitive advantage.* Some entrepreneurs merely copy or imitate the strategy of their competitors. That may be an easy tactic, and it is certainly less risky, but it means an entrepreneur has no competitive advantage. To succeed, new ventures must develop unique ways to compete.

☐ *Flaw 3: Pursuing an unattainable competitive position.* Many aggressive entrepreneurs pursue a position of dominance in a fast-growing industry. However, they are so busy getting off the ground and finding people to buy their products that they forget what will happen if the venture succeeds. For example, a successful software program will be imitated quickly. So the advantage it alone gives cannot be sustained. Real competitive advantage in software comes from servicing and supporting buyers, providing regular upgrades, getting a company online with customers so their computer departments depend on the organization. That creates barriers to entry. Sometimes, small companies simply cannot sustain an advantage.

☐ *Flaw 4: Compromising strategy for growth.* A careful balance must exist between growth and the competitive strategy that makes a new venture successful. If an entrepreneur sacrifices his or her venture's unique strategy in order to have fast growth, then the venture may grow out of business. Although fast growth can be tempting in certain industries, it is imperative that entrepreneurs maintain and grow their strategic advantage also.

☐ *Flaw 5: Failure to explicitly communicate the venture's strategy to employees.* It is essential for every entrepreneur to clearly communicate the company's strategy to every employee. Never assume employees already know the strategy. Always be explicit.

"One of the fundamental benefits of developing a strategy is that it creates unity, or consistency of action, throughout a company. Every department in the organization works toward the same objectives. But if people do not know what the objectives are, how can they work toward them? If they do not have a clear sense that low cost, say, is your ultimate aim, then all their day-to-day actions are not going to be reinforcing that goal. In any company, employees are making critical choices every minute. An explicit strategy will help them make the right ones," Porter says.[25]

Entrepreneurial and Strategic Actions

Entrepreneurship and strategic management are both dynamic processes concerned with firm performance. Strategic management calls for firms to establish and exploit competitive advantages within a particular environmental context. Entrepreneurship promotes the search for competitive advantages through product, process, and market innovations. A new venture is typically created to pursue the marketplace promise from innovations.

Researchers Ireland, Hitt, Camp, and Sexton argue that entrepreneurial and strategic actions are often intended to find new market or competitive space for the firm to create wealth. Firms try to find fundamentally new ways of doing business that will disrupt an industry's existing competitive rules, leading to the development of new business models that create new competitive life forms. The degree to which the firm acts entrepreneurially in terms of innovativeness, risk-taking, and proactivity is related to dimensions of strategic management. From these commonalties between entrepreneurship and strategic management are specific domains of innovation, networks, internationalization, organizational learning, top management teams and governance, and growth (see Figure 15.2). Understanding the critical intersections of these specific domains allow entrepreneurs to increase their knowledge that, in turn, leads to higher quality entrepreneurial and strategic actions.[26]

Strategic Positioning: The Entrepreneurial Edge

Strategic competition can be thought of as the process of perceiving new positions that attract customers from established positions or draw new customers into the market. In

Figure 15.2 The Integration of Entrepreneurial and Strategic Actions

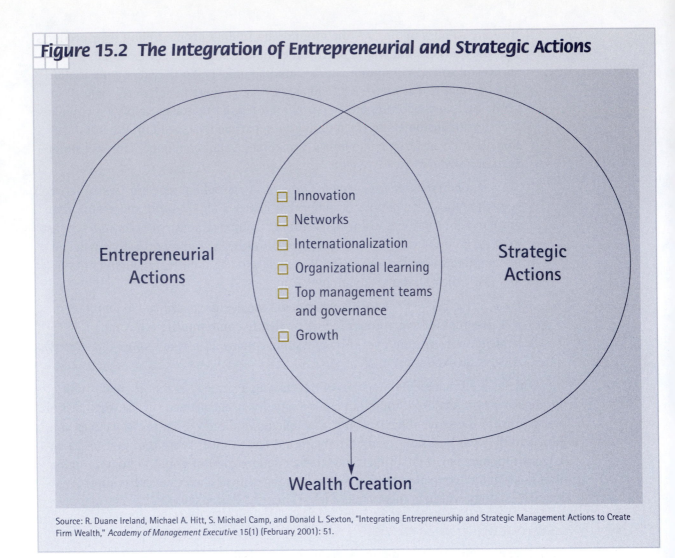

Entrepreneurial Actions

☐ Innovation
☐ Networks
☐ Internationalization
☐ Organizational learning
☐ Top management teams and governance
☐ Growth

Strategic Actions

Wealth Creation

Source: R. Duane Ireland, Michael A. Hitt, S. Michael Camp, and Donald L. Sexton, "Integrating Entrepreneurship and Strategic Management Actions to Create Firm Wealth," *Academy of Management Executive* 15(1) (February 2001): 51.

principle, incumbents and entrepreneurs face the same challenges in finding new strategic positions. In practice, entrepreneurs often have the edge.

Strategic positionings are often not obvious, and finding them requires creativity and insight. Entrepreneurs often discover unique positions that have been available but simply overlooked by established competitors. In addition, entrepreneurial ventures can prosper by occupying a position that a competitor once held but has ceded through years of imitation and straddling. (See Table 15.2 for alternative views of strategy.)

There are certain fundamental approaches to strategic positioning that include establishing and defending a defensible position, leveraging resources to dominate a market, and pursuing opportunities to establish new markets (see Table 15.3). Entrepreneurs must understand that the pursuit of opportunities provides the best choice for capitalizing on change.

Most commonly, new positions open up because of change. New customer groups or purchase occasions arise; new needs emerge as societies evolve; new distribution channels appear; new technologies are developed; new machinery or information systems become available. When such changes happen, entrepreneurial ventures unencumbered by a long history in the industry can often more easily perceive the potential for a new way of competing. Unlike incumbents, these organizations can be more flexible because they face no trade-offs with their existing activities.[27]

Table 15.2   Alternative Views of Strategy

THE IMPLICIT STRATEGY MODEL OF THE PAST DECADE

☐ One ideal competitive position in the industry

☐ Benchmarking of all activities and achieving best practice

☐ Aggressive outsourcing and partnering to gain efficiencies

☐ Advantages rest on a few key success factors, critical resources, and core competencies

☐ Flexibility and rapid responses to all competitive and market changes

SUSTAINABLE COMPETITIVE ADVANTAGE

☐ Unique competitive position for the company

☐ Activities tailored to strategy

☐ Clear trade-offs and choices vis-à-vis competitors

☐ Competitive advantage arises from fit across activities

☐ Sustainability comes from the activity system, not the parts

☐ Operational effectiveness a given

Table 15.3   Strategic Approaches: Position, Leverage, Opportunities

	POSITION	LEVERAGE	OPPORTUNITIES
STRATEGIC LOGIC	Establish position	Leverage resources	Pursue opportunities
STRATEGIC STEPS	Identify an attractive market Locate a defensible position Fortify and defend	Establish a vision Build resources Leverage across markets	Jump into the confusion Keep moving Seize opportunities Finish strong
STRATEGIC QUESTION	Where should we be?	What should we be?	How should we proceed?
SOURCE OF ADVANTAGE	Unique, valuable position with tightly integrated activity system	Unique, valuable, inimitable resources	Key processes and unique simple rules
WORKS BEST IN	Slowly changing, well-structured markets	Moderately changing, well-structured markets	Rapidly changing, ambiguous markets
DURATION OF ADVANTAGE	Sustained	Sustained	Unpredictable
RISK	It will be too difficult to alter position as conditions change	Company will be too slow to build new resources as conditions change	Managers will be too tentative in executing on promising opportunities
PERFORMANCE GOAL	Profitability	Long-term dominance	Growth

Implementing a Strategic Plan

New ventures can use a number of approaches to implement a strategic plan. The specific choice will be a function of the entrepreneur's personality and the environment in which the firm operates. Three basic approaches presented in this chapter are the milestone planning approach, the entrepreneurial strategy matrix, and the multistaged contingency approach. Each offers a comprehensive approach to strategic planning, although in practice entrepreneurs tend to draw the best elements from each rather than choose one and ignore the others.

Milestone Planning Approach

The **milestone planning approach** is based on the use of incremental goal attainment that takes a new venture from start-up through strategy reformulation.[28] Each important step is completed before moving on to the next one, and all are linked together into an overall strategic plan. Three major advantages of milestone planning are (1) the use of logical and practical milestones, (2) the avoidance of costly mistakes caused by failure to consider key parts of the plan, and (3) a methodology for replanning, based on continuous feedback from the environment.[29] Table 15.4 provides an example of a schedule that might be used in the milestone planning approach.

The milestone planning approach is popular with new ventures that are technical in nature, have multiple phases, or involve large sums of money. The approach is also used when close linkage between milestones or major objectives is needed.

An Entrepreneurial Strategy Matrix Model

Based upon the structure of traditional strategy matrices (such as the Boston Casualty Group [BCG] matrix) that have been used for portfolio analysis, researchers Sonfield and Lussier developed an **entrepreneurial strategy matrix** that measures risk and innovation.[30] For the purpose of this matrix, **innovation** is defined as the creation of something new and different. In terms of measurement, the newer and more different the proposed product or service is, the higher it would be scored on a measurement scale.

Risk is defined as the probability of major financial loss. What are the chances of the entrepreneurial venture failing? How serious would be the resulting financial loss? Whereas many ways exist to increase innovation, reducing risk largely focuses on financial factors, with a secondary consideration of self-image and ego.

The model allows even the most inexperienced entrepreneurs to characterize their new or existing venture situations and identify appropriate strategies. The model places innovation on the vertical axis, and risk on the horizontal axis. It denotes the levels of these two variables by using I and R for high levels and i and r for low levels (see Figure 15.3).

The value of the entrepreneurial strategy matrix is that it suggests appropriate avenues for different entrepreneurs. When the entrepreneur identifies the cell that best describes the new or existing venture being contemplated, then certain strategies are indicated as more likely to be effective (see Figure 15.4).

It should be obvious that certain cells are more advantageous than others. A high-innovation/low-risk venture is certainly preferable to a low-innovation/high-risk one. Yet for every venture found in *I-r*, large numbers of ventures can be found in *i-R*. Risk is more common than innovativeness in the business world.

Table 15.4   A Milestone Planning Approach

MILESTONE	DESCRIPTION	KEY QUESTIONS
1	Formulation of the basic idea for the new venture	Has a need for the new venture been established?
2	Completion of a prototype (in this case, a new product)	What initial assumptions were made about development time and costs, and how have they changed?
		What has been learned about labor, material, and equipment, and how does this affect pricing plans?
		Do the product's characteristics still fit with the original concept and plan?
3	Raising the seed capital	Is the venture acceptable to investors?
		How is the venture being perceived in the marketplace?
4	Conducting a pilot operation	Have any of the venture's basic assumptions been challenged in the initial operations?
		Check specifically:
		☐ Suitability and costs of materials
		☐ Processing costs and skills
		☐ Training needs for production personnel
		☐ Reject percentages and costs and quality-control requirements
5	Market testing	Why are customers buying the product?
		Why are they not buying the product?
		Is the product different from or superior to the competition?
		How should estimates of achievable market share and size be modified?
6	Start-up of operations	Are selling and delivery commitments accurate?
		Do the market and financing requirements make sense?
7	Sale to first major account	How does the product compare with that of the competition?
		Should the initial selling method be continued or changed?
8	Reaction to the competition	What countermoves should be taken in response to the competition?
		What changes in advertising, promotion, sales, inventory, or other operations are likely?
9	Redesign or redirection of strategy	What differences exist between the market and what the venture offers currently?
		What changes are needed in pricing, financing, design, marketing, or other aspects of the strategy?

Figure 15.3 The Entrepreneurial Strategy Matrix: Independent Variables

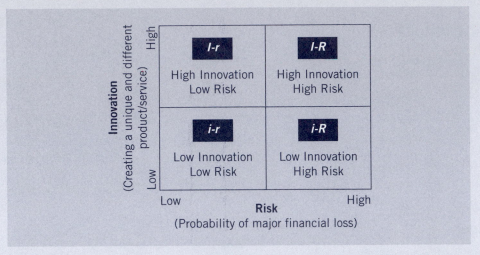

Figure 15.4 The Entrepreneurial Strategy Matrix: Appropriate Strategies

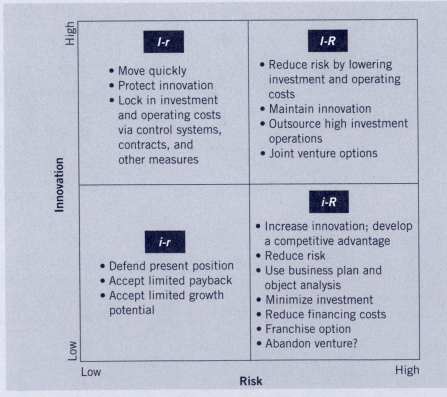

the entrepreneurial
PROCESS

Better Planning = Better Performance

Company executives repeatedly make the effort to buckle down behind closed doors once a year to pump out an operational plan to satisfy shareholders and investors. They take a snapshot of the business and put their projections on paper, but fail to follow up or use those projections as a benchmark throughout the year at hand. When done right, using strategic planning to support an operational plan provides a corporate weapon, positioning the company to overcome obstacles and succeed at their annual plan.

At Springfield Remanufacturing Corporation in Springfield, Missouri, strategic planning is a year-round practice. Around April, sales and marketing leaders receive outlines requesting certain information that they must compile and present to company leaders and board members in early summer. Following are the requirements that keep this company on track and employees involved throughout the year.

Market analysis. Current business conditions are laid out. New government regulations and technological advancements are addressed if they pertain to the operation and performance of the company.

Year-to-date performance. The first half of the year is reviewed, comparing original unit and dollar projections with actual numbers, and deviations are discussed.

May–December projections. Sales are projected for the remainder of the year and compared to the original second-half projections. Any deviations are once again discussed, as they are usually attributed to changes in the external or internal environment.

Price increases and decreases. Planned price changes are explained and justified.

Promotions/advertising. The success of executed programs and the potential of future plans are presented. The expenditure budget is also reviewed.

Budget review. Actual sales expenses are compared to planned sales expenses. The year-end status is altered or projected based on the current figures.

Competitive data. Detailed information about competitors' product lines and marketing programs is identified. SWOT analyses are discussed.

Contingency planning. Contingency plans, in the event of unexpected occurrences, are reviewed and summarized.

SOURCE: Karen Carney, "Mid-Year Planning Made Easy," *Open-Book Management: Bulletin* (May 1999).

The strategic implications of the matrix are twofold. First, entrepreneurs will find certain cells preferable to others, and one set of appropriate strategies involves moving from one cell to another. Second, such movement is not always possible for an entrepreneur, so the appropriate strategies involve reducing risk and increasing innovation within a cell.

Multistage Contingency Approach

A final approach presented here is the **multistage contingency approach**. This process was developed by reviewing the various approaches to entrepreneurship. Three distinct variables are critical to any strategic analysis: the individual, the venture, and the

Table 15.5 Entrepreneurial Strategy: A Contingency Multistage Approach

Strategic Entrepreneurial Assessment	New-Venture Initiation	Entrepreneurial Development and Continuation	Emerging Entrepreneurial Issues
Opportunity Evaluation	New-Venture Initiation • Creativity • Assessment Evaluation • Feasibility	Entrepreneurial Growth and Development • Understanding the Entrepreneurial Company	Corporate Entrepreneurship
		Managing Paradox and Contradiction	International: The Global Expansion
SWOT Analysis (Strengths/Weaknesses Opportunities/Threats)	The Business Plan Process • Definition • Benefits • Business Plan Development	Acquisition of a Venture	Women Entrepreneurs
		Valuation and Succession of Entrepreneurial Ventures • Methods of Valuation • Succession Strategy	Family Business
			Entrepreneurial Careers

Source: Donald F. Kuratko and Harold P. Welsch, *Entrepreneurial Strategy* (Fort Worth, TX: The Dryden Press, 1994), 10.

environment. However, the stages of any venture (idea, pre-venture, start-up, early growth, harvest) are also critical to strategic analysis. In addition, a career perspective should be considered, which means the entrepreneur's career stage (early, middle, or late) can be a decisive factor when differentiating the variables within the venture development stages. Thus, it may be necessary to visualize entrepreneurial strategies as contingencies. In other words, all of the evolving and emerging conditions involved with any entrepreneurial pursuit cause a constant dynamism. If newly emerging entrepreneurial issues such as global expansion, the growth in numbers of women entrepreneurs, and corporate entrepreneurship are also introduced, then a model of entrepreneurial strategy would be multidimensional, multistage, and contingency based. Table 15.5 attempts to capture all of these factors in a three-dimensional model that emphasizes the need for contingency strategies based on the evaluation and assessment of the various elements.[31]

Although all of these variables must be examined from a strategic perspective, the traditional strategic management process may provide assistance. As discussed earlier in the chapter, this perspective is summarized in the acronym SWOT (strengths, weaknesses, opportunities, and threats).[32] Thus, Table 15.5 shows entrepreneurial contingency issues for the purpose of entrepreneurial development and, eventually, entrepreneurial continuation.

The Nature Of Operational Planning

Having examined the various factors and theories relating to strategic planning, we now review some of the basic concepts involved in operational planning.

Operational planning, also referred to as *short-range planning* or *functional planning,* consists of the specific practices established to carry out the objectives set forth in the strategic plan. The operational plan is thus an outgrowth or extension of the strategic planning process. In the areas of finance, marketing, production, and management, functional policies need to be established in order to implement the goals determined in the strategy.

Research shows that small-business managers more commonly perform operational planning than strategic planning. In addition, operational planning has been established as a critical component in the overall planning process of a small firm.[33]

Operational Planning Process

The overall planning process incorporates all of the factors involved in strategic planning and the implementation tools of operational planning (see Figure 15.5). Specifically, the tools applied in the functional areas of the business will be a key to implementation of the planning process. Some of the tools most widely known and used are budgets, policies, and procedures.

Budgets are planning devices used to establish future plans in financial terms. They are valuable tools in the operational sense because they provide a set of measuring points by which the implemented plans can be evaluated. Effective budgeting is based on realistic estimates and appropriate allocations.

Policies are the fundamental guides for the venture as a whole. Each department or functional area needs to establish the policies that will guide its operations on a day-to-day basis. For example, sales policies, financial policies, credit policies, and manufacturing policies determine the daily course of business. Established policies allow

Figure 15.5 The Overall Planning Process for a Venture

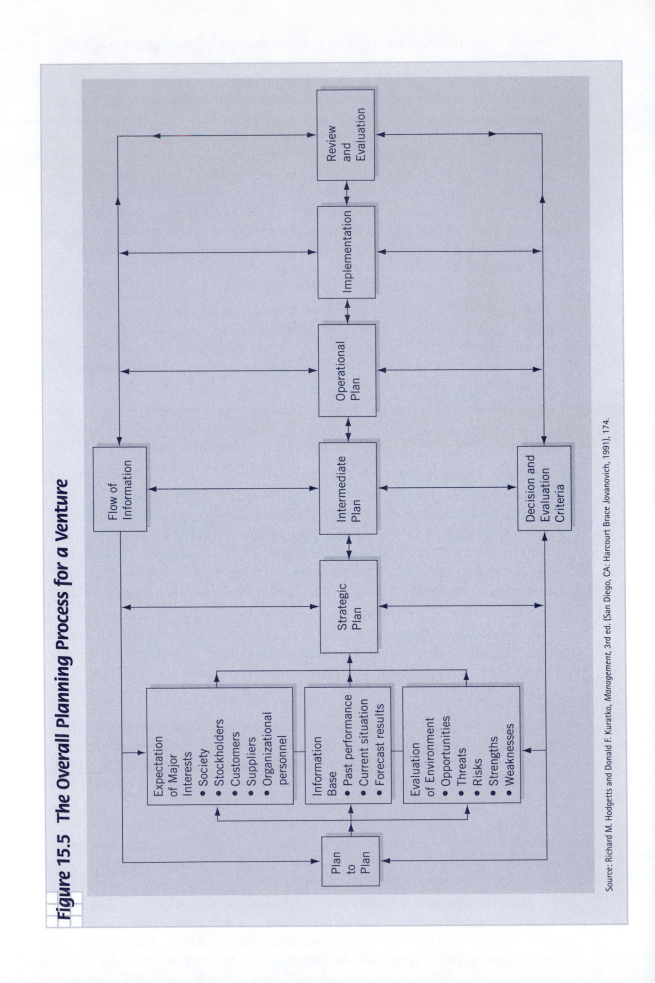

Source: Richard M. Hodgetts and Donald F. Kuratko, *Management*, 3rd ed. (San Diego, CA: Harcourt Brace Jovanovich, 1991), 174.

entrepreneurs the freedom to work more on strategy because each specific functional problem does not have to be analyzed. Policies are guidelines to decision making and action. They delimit the area a decision is made in and ensure that the decision is consistent with objectives.[34]

Although procedures are similar to policies, they are usually policies that have been standardized as a continuing method. For example, credit approval may follow specific credit policies, but eventually the steps that are followed can be completely standardized. Thus procedures are often referred to as *standard operating procedures*.

Each of these operating tools represents methods for implementing and evaluating the goals of strategic planning. Thus operational planning becomes the ongoing phase that brings a venture's strategic plan to action.

Summary

Although many ways of strategically planning a venture exist, all have one common element: Each is an extension of the entrepreneur's vision—each takes the owner's concept of the business and puts it into action.

Entrepreneurs do not use strategic planning for many reasons, among them scarcity of time, lack of knowledge about how to plan, lack of expertise in the planning process, and lack of trust in others.

A number of benefits to strategic planning exist. In particular, studies have shown that small firms that use this process tend to have better financial performance than those that do not. Other benefits are more efficient resource allocation, improved competitive position, higher employee morale, and more rapid decision making.

Four ways to carry out a strategic plan exist. The milestone planning approach is based on the use of incremental goal attainment that takes a new venture from start-up through strategy reformulation. Each major step is completed before moving on to the next one, and all are linked together in an overall strategic plan. The entrepreneurial strategy matrix model measures innovation and risk through a matrix that allows entrepreneurs to characterize their new or existing venture situations and identify appropriate strategies. Finally, the multistage contingency approach combines the stages of a venture with distinct variables that must be continually assessed for proper planning.

The operational plan is the implementation phase that includes specific tools for proper action. Sometimes referred to as functional planning, the operational plan uses budgets, policies, and procedures as methods for carrying out the objectives established in the strategic plan.

Key Terms and Concepts

entrepreneurial strategy matrix	operational planning
innovation	perception of high cost
lack of expertise/skills	policies
lack of knowledge	strategic planning
lack of trust and openness	strategic positioning
milestone planning approach	SWOT analysis
multistage contingency approach	time scarcity

Review and Discussion Questions

1. In what way does an entrepreneur's vision affect the company's strategic plan?

2. How is the strategic plan of an engineer/scientist entrepreneur likely to be different from that of an entrepreneur whose primary strength is in the manufacturing area? Be complete in your answer.

3. What are the three basic steps involved in transforming entrepreneurial vision and ideas into action?

4. Give three reasons why many entrepreneurs do not like to formulate strategic plans.

5. Describe five difficulties entrepreneurs face in long-range planning.

6. Does strategic planning really pay off for small ventures? Why or why not?

7. A new-venture entrepreneur is considering formulation of a strategic plan. However, he is concerned this effort will have little value for him. Is he right or wrong? Explain.

8. How does the milestone planning approach to strategic planning work?

9. What type of venture might profit from the use of a milestone planning approach? Defend your answer.

10. Describe the entrepreneurial strategy matrix and explain why it is effective for entrepreneurs.

11. What benefits does the multistage contingency approach offer to new-venture entrepreneurs?

12. What is operational planning? What specific tools are used?

13. How does operational planning fit with strategic planning?

Experiential Exercise

Strategic Planning in Action

Go to the library and look through the past 12 issues of *Entrepreneur* or *Inc.* Pick out two stories about new or growing ventures that have been involved in formulating a strategic plan. Gather as much information as you can, and then for each firm answer the following questions:

Firm 1

What did the company's strategic plan involve? Describe it in detail. _____

_____

_____

_____

How successful was the plan? Explain. _____

_____

_____

_____

What conclusions can you draw regarding the value of strategic planning to this company? Be complete in your answer. _____

_____

_____

_____

Firm 2

What did the company's strategic plan involve? Describe it in detail. _____

_____

_____

_____

How successful was the plan? Explain._____

_____

_____

_____

What conclusions can you draw regarding the value of strategic planning to this company? Be complete in your answer. _____

_____

_____

_____

Video Case 15.1

Strategic Planning in Emerging Firms
Modern Postcard with Steve Hoffman

> It's not about the complicated formula. You're really there to serve the customer and, really, to put them before yourself. Once you can get into that frame of mind, the rest of it falls into place. (Steve Hoffman)

In 1976, Steve Hoffman was a photographer who produced high-quality architectural photographs of properties for clients in the real estate industry. He was able to capture a significant portion of market share because he had developed a system to produce these images at a cost well below the going rate. He operated his business from a one-bedroom apartment.

Today, Steve is the owner and founder of Modern Postcard, a company employing over 250 people that creates promotional postcard products and solutions for a wide variety of business clients numbering over 250,000. After outgrowing several locations, his company is now based in a distinctively designed 75,000 square foot building overlooking the ocean in Carlsbad, California.

One of the important strategies that has made Modern Postcard a success is to harness and use various technologies. When Steve was working for real estate clients, he could rely on quality images to turn into postcards. With amateur photographers who also desire a top-notch postcard product, Steve has to rely on sophisticated technological processes.

Steve explains his customer challenges: "They send in one-hour photo prints and want you to reproduce them. And sometimes you get transparencies that are way overexposed, underexposed, off-color. . . . color separation . . . [is] very expensive, very time-consuming."

From the very beginning, Steve invested in digital technology. He built a system that automates all of the functions of the company, which traditionally had not seemed to lend itself to automation. This automation has resulted in a more efficient use of time and resources. Modern Postcard is able to price its products attractively to consumers and, consequently, has dominated the marketplace from its beginning.

Managing and still developing the company has been another strategic challenge. Steve relies on the "theory of constraints" to handle this challenge. He explains: "The theory of constraints is a system. It's basically a thinking process system in terms of how we think and how we can pull a lot of different, very complex ideas and concepts together into a single cohesive thought that everybody understands."

Steve notes that producing a postcard is a creative and complicated process involving useful client knowledge, a polished image, a solid marketing plan, and a reliable, expert production process. Modern Postcard employees work in teams, often brainstorming together in order to understand the parts of this process and to get group buy-in to their ideas. "We're continually pressing the limits . . . because it's a system-driven house."

One of the by-products of working within this system resulted in the decision to add mailing services for the postcard products. Customers can supply mailing lists of intended recipients for their cards on the same day that they submit their order, and, within a couple of days, the finished cards can be in the mail.

Arnie Cohen, mailing services manager, explains the importance of this innovation: "Our ability to think of this all under one roof and to come up with new ways to marry those technologies, both on the print and the mail side, is something that we've really emphasized, and something that really keeps us on the cutting edge." The company continues to search for innovations that will keep them on the cutting edge.

Steve maintains that his employees are an important asset in keeping the business dynamic. Jim Toya-Brown, senior vice president, explains: "Our business is very creative. . . . people are dealing with images all day, and these are creative people. They're young. They're psyched. I mean, they do a lot of different things, and this environment [of the building] was built and designed so it would stimulate them."

Modern Postcard is a success because Steve Hoffman has two operational standards: continually analyzing and improving processes and hiring creative people who can function in dynamic teams.

Questions

1. Describe the strategic planning at Modern Postcard.

2. What are the benefits of Hoffman's strategic planning for employees?

3. Identify operational policies that contribute to Modern Postcard's innovation and efficiency.

Case 15.2

The Banker's Request

Elizabeth Edwards opened her first restaurant three years ago. Since then she has opened two more. Elizabeth caters to family dining and has developed a loyal following. Many families come to her restaurant on a weekly basis. Friday, Saturday, and Sunday evenings are so popular that reservations are not accepted.

Last year Elizabeth's three units grossed $1.2 million. Her accountant estimates that this year the combined total will be in the neighborhood of $1.45 million.

The first restaurant was started with funds from her grandfather. Since then, internal profits have been sufficient to handle most of her operating needs. However, her expansion costs for the second and third restaurants were taken care of through a bank loan.

Elizabeth is now thinking of opening a fourth restaurant. Her banker is willing to lend her the necessary funds but thinks this would also be a good time for her to draw up a strategic plan. "You are getting too big to operate on a day-to-day basis," her banker said. "You need a long-range plan that will help you manage your overall operations. You need to start putting more focus on where you want to be in five years and how you are going to get there." Her banker would like Elizabeth to submit this plan with her new loan application. "With this plan and your excellent record here at the bank," he assured her, "I am sure your application will fly through the loan committee."

Elizabeth is not pleased with her banker's suggestion. First, she is unsure of how to draw up a strategic plan. It seems to her it would take a great deal of effort and probably not have any real value for her business. Second, she sees the banker's suggestion as nothing more than an attempt to cover himself should the loan fall into default. "I suppose when they lend you money they have to be able to justify the loan. In my case, they will have loaned me a substantial amount of money, so they want to cover their actions with the board of directors by showing that I have not only provided collateral for the loan but also provided them a detailed plan regarding the future operations of the enterprise. I can't say that I blame them, but I really don't think that plan has any practical value for me. Mostly it will be used to support the loan. Nevertheless, I want the loan, so I'll write the plan."

Elizabeth has tentatively scheduled construction of the new restaurant to begin in 90 days. She would like to have all of the paperwork associated with the application completed within 30 days. "I don't think it will be too difficult to write a strategic plan. I'll just pull together some of my current financial statements, write a brief description of the firm and its long-run objectives, and submit the plan along with the loan application sometime early next month."

Questions

1. In Elizabeth's case, what approach would you recommend she use for writing her plan? Why?

2. What specific steps should Elizabeth take for writing the plan? Will her current idea of what to include in the plan be of any value?

3. What benefits would a strategic plan have for Elizabeth's firm? Be complete in your answer.

Case 15.3

A Two-Phase Approach

Since its founding six months ago, Diego Sanchez's electronics repair shop has been booming. Diego repairs electronic household appliances, laptop computers, cell phones, VCRs, CD players, televisions, radios, and stereo equipment. Usually it does not take a great deal of time to make the repairs. For example, most cell phones have battery-related problems. All the repairer has to do is replace the battery and recharge the unit. The cost of a battery is around $50, service charges for other equipment repairs ranges from $35 to $150 depending on the complexity of the problem. So despite the fact the rent is high and the store has to keep a large supply of inventory on hand, profits are well over 40 percent.

Diego has been doing so well he has been thinking about opening a second store. However, he realizes that if this new venture does not pay off, he could be in financial straits. Before going any further, he has decided to sit down and plan his moves. The plan is going to have two major phases. The first phase will focus on areas such as the direction in which the store currently is heading, projected sales for the next two years, competitive countermoves, responses to these countermoves, and overall financial performance. Diego believes it will not be long before competitors begin to move into his market niche. "You can't make tremendous return on investment without attracting serious competition," he has told his wife. "If I want to continue being successful, I have to figure out how to stop these guys from invading my market. I have to have a game plan." The second phase of the plan will incorporate the new store and will examine the impact of this expansion on overall operations.

Diego believes this two-phase approach will help him plan for current operations and future expansion. He also feels it will be easier to plan for the expansion if he first lays the groundwork with a basic strategic plan. Diego's biggest problem right now is that he does not know much about strategic planning for new ventures. He is thinking he might drop by the local university and talk to one of the professors who teaches entrepreneurship or business strategy and get some advice on how to proceed.

Questions

1. If you were advising Diego, what approach would you recommend he use for putting together his strategic plan? Why?

2. What advantages would your proposed approach have over other approaches? Compare and contrast three approaches.

3. How would your approach allow Diego to incorporate expansion planning into the overall plan?

Notes

1. Douglas W. Naffziger and Donald F. Kuratko, "An Investigation into the Prevalence of Planning in Small Business," *Journal of Business and Entrepreneurship* 3(2) (October 1991): 99–110; see also Amar Bhide, "How Entrepreneurs Craft Strategies That Work," *Harvard Business Review* (March/April 1994): 150–161.

2. Radha Chaganti, Rajeswararo Chaganti, and Vijay Mahajan, "Profitable Small Business Strategies under Different Types of Competition," *Entrepreneurship Theory and Practice* (spring 1989): 21–36; see also Scott Shane and Frédéric Delmar, "Planning for the Market: Business Planning before Marketing and the Continuation of Organizing Efforts," *Journal of Business Venturing* 19(6) (November 2004): 767–785.

3. Michael A. Hitt, R. Duane Ireland, and Robert E. Hoskisson, *Strategic Management: Competitiveness and Globalization,* 6th ed. (Mason, OH: South-Western/Thomson Learning, 2005).

4. See James R. Lang, Roger J. Calantone, and Donald Gudmundson, "Small Firm Information Seeking as a Response to Environmental Threats and Opportunities," *Journal of Small Business Management* (January 1997): 11–23; and Reginald M. Beal, "Competing Effectively: Environmental Scanning, Competitive Strategy, and Organizational Performance in Small Manufacturing Firms," *Journal of Small Business Management* (January 2000): 27–47.

5. Henry Mintzberg, "The Fall and Rise of Strategic Planning," *Harvard Business Review* (January/February 1994): 107–114.

6. Richard B. Robinson, Jr., and John A. Pearce II, "Product Life-Cycle Considerations and the Nature of Strategic Activities in Entrepreneurial Firms," *Journal of Business Venturing* (spring 1986): 207–224; see also Charles H. Matthews and Susanne G. Scott, "Uncertainty and Planning in Small and Entrepreneurial Firms: An Empirical Assessment," *Journal of Small Business Management* (October 1995): 34–52.

7. Richard L. Osborne, "Planning: The Entrepreneurial Ego at Work," *Business Horizons* (January/February 1987): 20–24.

8. Richard B. Robinson, Jr., and John A. Pearce II, "Research Thrusts in Small Firm Strategic Planning," *Academy of Management Review* (January 1984): 129; and Charles B. Shrader, Charles L. Mumford, and Virginia L. Blackburn, "Strategic and Operational Planning, Uncertainty, and Performance in Small Firms," *Journal of Small Business Management* (October 1989): 52.

9. Christopher Orpen, "The Effects of Long-Range Planning on Small Business Performance: A Further Examination," *Journal of Small Business Management* (January 1985): 16–23.

10. Donald L. Sexton and Philip Van Auken, "A Longitudinal Study of Small Business Strategic Planning," *Journal of Small Business Management* (January 1985): 8.

11. Ibid., 15.

12. Robert Ackelsburg and Peter Arlow, "Small Businesses Do Plan and It Pays Off," *Long Range Planning* (October 1985): 61–67.

13. Jeffrey C. Shuman, John J. Shaw, and Gerald Sussman, "Strategic Planning in Smaller Rapid Growth Companies," *Long Range Planning* (December 1985): 48–53.

14. Robinson and Pearce, "Research Thrusts," 132–133.

15. Ibid.

16. "The Business Failure Record," *Dun & Bradstreet,* 1995.

17. Richard B. Robinson, "The Importance of Outsiders in Small Firm Strategic Planning," *Academy of Management Journal* (March 1982): 80–93.

18. A. Bakr Ibrahim, "Strategy Types and Small Firm's Performance: An Empirical Investigation," *Journal of Small Business Strategy* (spring 1993): 13–22.

19. Elaine Mosakowski, "A Resource-Based Perspective on the Dynamic Strategy–Performance Relationship: An Empirical Examination of the Focus and Differentiation Strategies in Entrepreneurial Firms," *Journal of Management* 19 (4) (1993): 819–839.

20. Jeffrey S. Bracker and John N. Pearson, "Planning and Financial Performances in Small Mature Firms," *Strategic Management Journal* 7 (1986): 503–522.

21. Jeffrey S. Bracker, Barbara W. Keats, John N. Pearson, "Planning and Financial Performance among Small Firms in a Growth Industry," *Strategic Management Journal* 9 (1988): 591–603.

22. Leslie W. Rue and Nabil A. Ibrahim, "The Relationship Between Planning Sophistication and Performance in Small Business," *Journal of Small Business Management* (October 1998): 24–32.

23. Charles R. Schwenk and Charles B. Shrader, "Effects of Formal Strategic Planning on Financial Performance in Small Firms: A Meta Analysis," *Entrepreneurship Theory and Practice* (spring 1993): 53–64; see also Philip D. Olson and Donald W. Bokor, "Strategy Process–Content Interaction: Effects on Growth Performance in Small, Startup Firms," *Journal of Small Business Management* (January 1995): 34–44.

24. Michael E. Porter, "Knowing Your Place–How to Assess the Attractiveness of Your Industry and Your Company's Position in It," *Inc.* (September 1991): 90–94.

25. Ibid., 93.

26. R. Duane Ireland, Michael A. Hitt, S. Michael Camp, and Donald L. Sexton, "Integrating Entrepreneurship and Strategic Management Actions to Create Firm Wealth," *Academy of Management Executive* 15(1) (February 2001): 49–63.

27. Michael E. Porter, "What Is Strategy?" *Harvard Business Review* (November–December 1996): 61–78.

28. See Zenas Block and Ian C. MacMillan, "Milestones for Successful Venture Planning," *Harvard Business Review* (September/October 1985): 184–196.

29. Ibid., 184.

30. Matthew C. Sonfield and Robert N. Lussier, "The Entrepreneurial Strategy Matrix: A Model for New and Ongoing Ventures," *Business Horizons* (May–June 1997): 73–77.

31. Donald F. Kuratko and Harold P. Welsch, *Entrepreneurial Strategy* (Fort Worth, TX: The Dryden Press, 1994), 11–12.

32. Thomas L. Wheelen and J. David Hunger, *Strategic Management and Business Policy*, 7th ed. (Upper Saddle River, NJ: Prentice Hall, 2000); see also William R. Sandberg, "Strategic Management's Potential Contribution to a Theory of Entrepreneurship," *Entrepreneurship Theory and Practice* (spring 1992): 73–90.

33. Charles B. Shrader, Charles L. Mumford, and Virginia L. Blackburn, "Strategic and Operational Planning, Uncertainty, and Performance in Small Firms," *Journal of Small Business Management* (October 1989): 45–60.

34. Richard M. Hodgetts and Donald F. Kuratko, *Management,* 3rd ed. (San Diego, CA: Harcourt Brace Jovanovich, 1991), 171.

16 Managing Entrepreneurial Growth

You often hear how companies have to 'cross the threshold to professional management' once they get beyond a certain size and stage of development. The implication is usually that you do it by changing leaders—that is, by getting rid of the entrepreneurial founders and replacing them with professional managers. Maybe that's because most of these theories come out of business schools and consulting firms.

There are hundreds of individuals, however, who make the transition successfully on their own, and some of them have names that are familiar to us all: Gates, Walton, Ford, Hewlett and Packard, Galvin, Watson, Marriott, and so on. They all built companies in which they played critically important roles—but the companies weren't dependent on them for survival. They each made sure the business could go on without them. It had a value of its own.

Jack Stack
A Stake in the Outcome

Chapter Objectives

1 To discuss the five stages of a typical venture life cycle: development, start-up, growth, stabilization, and innovation or decline

2 To explore the elements involved with an entrepreneurial firm

3 To examine the transition that occurs in the movement from an entrepreneurial style to a managerial approach

4 To identify the key factors that play a major role during the growth stage

5 To discuss the complex management of paradox and contradiction

6 To introduce the steps useful for breaking through the growth wall

7 To identify the unique managerial concerns of growing businesses

8 To examine the international market as an entrepreneurial growth opportunity

Figure 16.1 A Venture's Typical Life Cycle

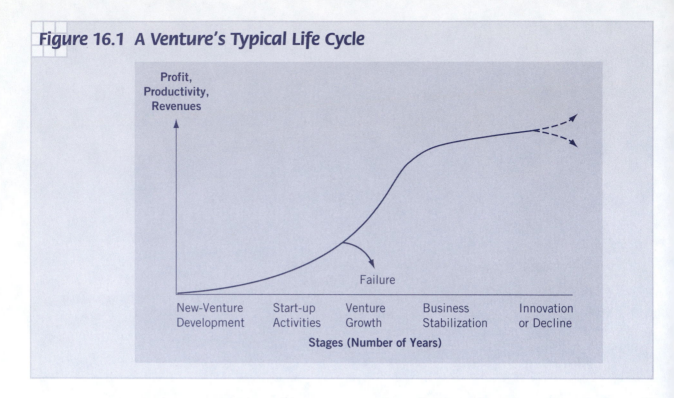

Managing entrepreneurial growth may be the most critical tactic for the future success of business enterprises. After initiation of a new venture, the entrepreneur needs to develop an understanding of management change. This is a great challenge, because it often encompasses the art of balancing mobile and dynamic factors.[1]

Thus, the survival and growth of a new venture require that the entrepreneur possess both strategic and tactical skills and abilities. Which specific skills and abilities are needed depend in part on the venture's current development. Figure 16.1 illustrates the typical venture life cycle.

The purpose of this chapter is to examine the venture characteristics, managerial abilities, and entrepreneurial needs and drives in relation to the stages of the venture's development. Specifically, attention is concentrated on the growth stage, since this is the phase during which a venture usually reaches major crossroads in the decisions that affect its future. Managing growth can be a formidable challenge to the successful development of any venture.

Venture Development Stages

As noted, Figure 16.1 presents the traditional **life–cycle stages** of an enterprise. These stages include new-venture development, start-up activities, growth, stabilization, and innovation or decline. Other authors have described these stages in different terms. For example, Alfred Chandler has presented a firm's evolution in the following stages:

1. Initial expansion and accumulation of resources

2. Rationalization of the use of resources

3. Expansion into new markets to assure the continued use of resources

4. Development of new structures to ensure continuing mobilization of resources[2]

These four phases are, in effect, the same major stages illustrated in Figure 16.1, with the exception of stabilization. In short, authors generally agree regarding a venture's life cycle. Presented next are the five major stages.

New-Venture Development

The first stage, **new-venture development**, consists of activities associated with the initial formulation of the venture. This initial phase is the foundation of the entrepreneurial process and requires creativity and assessment. In addition to the accumulation and expansion of resources, this is a creativity, assessment, and networking stage for initial entrepreneurial strategy formulation. The enterprise's general philosophy, mission, scope, and direction are determined during this stage.

Start-Up Activities

The second stage, **start-up activities**, encompasses the foundation work needed for creating a formal business plan, searching for capital, carrying out marketing activities, and developing an effective entrepreneurial team. These activities typically demand an aggressive entrepreneurial strategy with maximum efforts devoted to launching the venture. This stage is similar to Chandler's description of the rationalization of the use of resources. It is typified by strategic and operational planning steps designed to identify the firm's competitive advantage and to uncover funding sources. Marketing and financial considerations tend to be paramount during this stage.[3]

Growth

The **growth stage** often requires major changes in entrepreneurial strategy. Competition and other market forces call for the reformulation of strategies. For example, some firms find themselves "growing out" of business because they are unable to cope with the growth of their ventures.[4] Highly creative entrepreneurs sometimes are unable, or unwilling, to meet the administrative challenges that accompany this growth stage. As a result, they leave the enterprise and move on to other ventures. Steven Jobs of Apple Computer was forced out of his firm during this stage. His creative ideas were detrimental to the growth of the venture. The firm needed a managerial entrepreneur to run the operation; Jobs had neither the expertise nor the desire to assume this role.[5]

This growth stage presents newer and more substantial problems than those the entrepreneur faced during the start-up stage.[6] These newer challenges force the entrepreneur into developing a different set of skills while maintaining an "entrepreneurial perspective" for the organization.[7] The growth stage is a transition from entrepreneurial one-person leadership to managerial team-oriented leadership.

Business Stabilization

The **stabilization stage** is a result of both market conditions and the entrepreneur's efforts. During this stage a number of developments commonly occur, including increased competition, consumer indifference to the entrepreneur's good(s) or service(s), and saturation of the market with a host of "me too" look-alikes. Sales often begin to stabilize, and the entrepreneur must begin thinking about where the enterprise will go over the next three to five years. This stage is often a "swing" stage in that it precedes the period when the firm either swings into higher gear and greater profitability or swings toward decline and failure. During this stage innovation is often critical to future success.

Innovation or Decline

Firms that fail to innovate will die. Financially successful enterprises often will try to acquire other innovative firms, thereby ensuring their own growth. Also, many firms will work on new product/service development in order to complement current offerings.

All of a venture's life-cycle stages are important strategic points, and each requires a different set of strategies. However, this chapter concentrates specifically on the growth stage because entrepreneurs often ignore it. This happens not because of incompetence but rather because of the almost hypnotic effect a successful growth stage can cause. We shall now examine the key factors affecting the ability to manage this stage.

The Entrepreneurial Company in the Twenty-First Century

The pace and magnitude of change will continue to accelerate in the new millennium. Having the evolution and transformation of entrepreneurial firms match this pace will be critical. Building dynamic capabilities that are differentiated from those of the emerging competitors is the major challenge for growing firms that seek to adapt to the changing landscape. Two ways of building dynamic capabilities are internal—utilization of the creativity and knowledge from employees—and external[8]—the search for external competencies to complement the firm's existing capabilities.[9] The trend toward globalization, the advent of new technology, and the information movement are all examples of forces in this new millennium that are causing firms to examine their cultures, structures, and systems for flexibility and adaptability. Innovation and entrepreneurial thinking are essential elements in the strategies of growing ventures.

It has been noted that entrepreneurs (1) perceive an opportunity, (2) pursue this opportunity, and (3) believe that success of the venture is possible.[10] This belief is often due to the uniqueness of the idea, the strength of the product, or some special knowledge or skill the entrepreneur possesses. These same factors must be translated into the organization itself as the venture grows.

The Entrepreneurial Mind-Set

It is important for the venture's manager to maintain an entrepreneurial frame of mind. Figure 16.2 illustrates the danger of entrepreneurs evolving into bureaucrats who in turn stifle innovation. Table 16.1 provides a delineation of the differences between a managerial mind-set versus an entrepreneurial mind-set from the perspective of decision-making assumptions, values, beliefs, and approaches to problems.

In some cases, success will affect an entrepreneur's willingness to change and innovate. This is particularly true when the enterprise has developed a sense of complacency and the entrepreneur likes this environment. The person does not want to change. In fact, some entrepreneurs will create a bureaucratic environment where orders are issued from the top down and change initiated at the lower levels is not tolerated.[11] As a result, no one in the venture is willing (or encouraged) to

Figure 16.2 The Entrepreneurial Mind-Set

Future Goals

	Change	Status Quo
Perceived Capability — Possible	Entrepreneur	Satisfied manager
Perceived Capability — Blocked	Frustrated manager	Classic bureaucrat

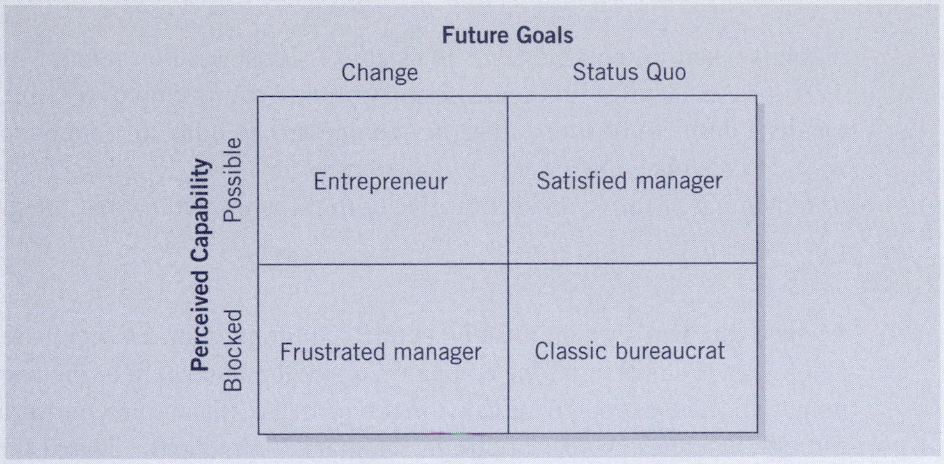

Table 16.1 The Managerial versus the Entrepreneurial Mind-Set

	MANAGERIAL MIND-SET	ENTREPRENEURIAL MIND-SET
Decision-making assumptions	The past is the best predictor of the future. Most business decisions can be quantified.	A new idea or an insight from a unique experience is likely to provide the best estimate of emerging trends.
Values	The best decisions are those based on quantitative analyses. Rigorous analyses are highly valued for making critical decisions.	New insights and real-world experiences are more highly valued than results based on historical data.
Beliefs	Law of large numbers: Chaos and uncertainty can be resolved by systematically analyzing the right data.	Law of small numbers: A single incident or several isolated incidents quickly become pivotal for making decisions regarding future trends.
Approach to problems	Problems represent an unfortunate turn of events that threaten financial projections. Problems must be resolved with substantiated analyses.	Problems represent an opportunity to detect emerging changes and possibly new business opportunities.

Source: Mike Wright, Robert E. Hoskisson, and Lowell W. Busenitz, "Firm Rebirth: Buyouts as Facilitators of Strategic Growth and Entrepreneurship," *Academy of Management Executive* 15(1): 114.

become innovative or entrepreneurial because the owner-founder stifles such activity.

One study found that the entrepreneur directly affects the firm's growth orientation as measured by profitability goals, product/market goals, human resource goals, and flexibility goals.[12] If the entrepreneur hopes to maintain the creative climate that helped launch the venture in the first place, specific steps or measures must be taken.

Building the Adaptive Firm

It is important for entrepreneurs to establish a business that remains flexible beyond start-up. An **adaptive firm** increases opportunity for its employees, initiates change, and instills a desire to be innovative. Entrepreneurs can build an adaptive firm in several ways.[13] The following are not inflexible rules, but they do enhance a venture's chance of remaining adaptive and innovative both through and beyond the growth stage.[14]

Share the Entrepreneur's Vision

The entrepreneur's vision must be permeated throughout the organization in order for employees to understand the company's direction and share in the responsibility for its growth. The entrepreneur can communicate the vision directly to the employees through meetings, conversations, or seminars. It also can be shared through symbolic events or activities such as social gatherings, recognition events, and displays. Whatever the format, having shared vision allows the venture's personnel to catch the dream and become an integral part of creating the future.[15]

Increase the Perception of Opportunity

This can be accomplished with careful job design. The work should have defined objectives for which people will be responsible. Each level of the hierarchy should be kept informed of its role in producing the final output of the product or service. This often is known as "staying close to the customer."[16] Another way to increase the perception of opportunity is through a careful coordination and integration of the functional areas. This allows employees in different functional areas to work together as a cohesive whole.

Institutionalize Change as the Venture's Goal

This entails a preference for innovation and change rather than preservation of the status quo. If opportunity is to be perceived, the environment of the enterprise must not only encourage it but also establish it as a goal. Within this context, a desire for opportunity can exist if resources are made available and departmental barriers are reduced.

Instill the Desire to Be Innovative

The desire of personnel to pursue opportunity must be carefully nurtured. Words alone will not create the innovative climate.[17] Specific steps such as the following should be taken.

A Reward System

Explicit forms of recognition should be given to individuals who pursue innovative opportunities. For example, bonuses, awards, salary advances, and promotions should be tied directly to the innovative attempts of personnel.

An Environment that Allows for Failure

The fear of failure must be minimized by the general recognition that often many attempts are needed before a success is achieved. This does not imply that failure is sought or desired. However, learning from failure, as opposed to expecting punishment entrepreneurship IN PRACTICE

Growing Too Fast

Bill Edlebeck, owner of the Heritage Bed & Breakfast Registry, had sales of more than $205,000 in 1999. His success didn't come without a few growing pains, however. The entrepreneur had enjoyed a moderate annual growth rate of 33 percent for 12 consecutive years. In 1998, he jumped on the bandwagon and put his business on the Internet. Life was never the same. Soon after the web page was established, Edlebeck recalls, nonstop phone calls prohibited him from leaving the office just to meet a friend for lunch. The number of phone calls to the "front desk for bed and breakfasts" increased five-fold and he became afraid of his own office. "I desperately needed new phone lines, phones, computers, a LAN, and a more efficient way of running the office."

Furthermore, Edlebeck's credit-card processor was taken aback by the sudden increase in the account's activity. Out of fear, the company ceased making deposits into the account. Unfortunately, the company did not inform Heritage of its action and left Edlebeck wondering why his firm had no money to cover its expenditures. Edlebeck was ill-prepared for the surplus of business, but was able to counteract the growth carefully and efficiently, by hiring more employees and obtaining the proper resources. "It wasn't until I started looking at our growth as the culmination of everything I'd been working for, as opposed to not being ready for all the new business, that I was able to start moving forward again."

By the time the realization and glories of success sink in, it may be too late to save the business. Maintain objectivity and downplay the desire to expand faster than your resources allow—large checkbooks do not always curb the effects of growing too fast. Growth Strategies' president Russ Holdstein emphasizes three key points to curbing detrimental growth:

1. **Stay aware.** Constantly take a step outside the business to gain and maintain an objective perspective. Inquire about the business at all levels—the part-time help will perceive the business in a whole new light. Involving others will serve two purposes: it will deter hindered decisions due to immersion in the business and it will encourage employee loyalty.

2. **Strategize.** Be proactive, not reactive. Assess the company's abilities and do not surpass them until the proper resources are in place. Have a plan of action ready for when sales hit a certain benchmark.

3. **Adapt.** Adapting is easier for the small-business owner. Red tape, bureaucratic management, and restrained budgets are minimal threats when making decisions and changes. Fluctuations in the business's economic and technological environment will necessitate policy and procedure adaptations.

SOURCE: Geoff Williams, "Crash Course," *Entrepreneur* (January 2000): 89–95.

for it, is promoted. When this type of environment exists, people become willing to accept the challenge of change and innovation.

Flexible Operations

Flexibility creates the possibility of change taking place and having a positive effect. If a venture remains too rigidly tied to plans or strategies, it will not be responsive to new technologies, customer changes, or environmental shifts. Innovation will not take place because it will not "fit in."

The Development of Venture Teams

In order for the environment to foster innovation, venture teams and team performance goals need to be established. These must be not just work groups but visionary, committed teams that have the authority to create new directions, set new standards, and challenge the status quo.[18]

The Transition from an Entrepreneurial Style to a Managerial Approach

The transitions between stages of a venture are complemented (or in some cases retarded) by the entrepreneur's ability to make a transition in style. A key transition occurs during the growth stage of a venture when the entrepreneur shifts into a managerial style. This is not easy to do. As researchers Hofer and Charan have noted, "Among the different transitions that are possible, probably the most difficult to achieve and also perhaps the most important for organizational development is that of moving from a one-person, entrepreneurially managed firm to one run by a functionally organized, professional management team."[19]

A number of problems can occur during this transition, especially if the enterprise is characterized by factors such as (1) a highly centralized decision-making system, (2) an overdependence on one or two key individuals, (3) an inadequate repertoire of managerial skills and training, and (4) a paternalistic atmosphere.[20] These characteristics, although often effective in the new venture's start-up and initial survival, pose a threat to the firm's development during the growth stage. Quite often these characteristics inhibit development by detracting from the entrepreneur's ability to manage the growth stage successfully.

In order to bring about the necessary transition, the entrepreneur must carefully plan and then gradually implement the process. Hofer and Charan have suggested a seven-step process:

1. The entrepreneur must want to make the change and must want it strongly enough to undertake major modifications in his or her own task behavior.

2. The day-to-day decision-making procedures of the organization must be changed. Specifically, participation in this process must be expanded. Greater emphasis also should be placed on the use of formal decision techniques.

3. The two or three key operating tasks that are primarily responsible for the organization's success must be institutionalized. This may involve the selection of new people to supplement or replace "indispensable" individuals who have performed these tasks in the past.

4. Middle-level management must be developed. Specialists must learn to become functional managers, while functional managers must learn to become general managers.

5. The firm's strategy should be evaluated and modified, if necessary, to achieve growth.

6. The organizational structure and its management systems and procedures must be slowly modified to fit the company's new strategy and senior managers.

7. The firm must develop a professional board of directors.[21]

Balancing the Focus (Entrepreneur and Manager)

In managing the growth stage, entrepreneurs must remember two important points. First, an adaptive firm needs to retain certain entrepreneurial characteristics in order to encourage innovation and creativity. Second, the entrepreneur needs to translate this spirit of innovation and creativity to his or her personnel while personally making a transition toward a more managerial style.[22] This critical entrepreneur/manager balance is extremely difficult to achieve. As researchers Stevenson and Gumpert have noted, "Everybody wants to be innovative, flexible, and creative. But for every Apple, Domino's, and Lotus, there are thousands of new restaurants, clothing stores, and consulting firms that presumably have tried to be innovative, to grow, and to show other characteristics that are entrepreneurial in the dynamic sense—but have failed."[23]

Remaining entrepreneurial while making the transition to some of the more administrative traits is vital to the successful growth of a venture. Table 16.2 provides a framework for comparing the entrepreneurial and administrative characteristics and pressures relative to five major factors: strategic orientation, commitment to seize opportunities, commitment of resources, control of resources, and management structure. Each of these five areas is critical to the balance needed for managing entrepreneurially. At the two ends of the continuum (from entrepreneurial focus to administrative focus) are specific points of view. Stevenson and Gumpert have characterized these in question format.

The Entrepreneur's Point of View

- Where is the opportunity?
- How do I capitalize on it?
- What resources do I need?
- How do I gain control over them?
- What structure is best?

The Administrative Point of View

- What resources do I control?
- What structure determines our organization's relationship to its market?
- How can I minimize the impact of others on my ability to perform?
- What opportunity is appropriate?[24]

The logic behind the variance in the direction of these questions can be presented in a number of different ways. For example, the commitment of resources in the entrepreneurial frame of mind responds to changing environmental needs, whereas the managerial point of view is focused on the reduction of risk. In the control of resources, entrepreneurs will avoid ownership because of the risk of obsolescence and the need for more flexibility, whereas managers will view ownership as a means to accomplish efficiency and stability. In terms of structure, the entrepreneurial emphasis is placed on a need for flexibility and independence, whereas the administrative focus is placed on ensuring integration with a complexity of tasks, a desire for order, and controlled reward systems.

These examples of differences in focus help establish the important issues involved at both ends of the managerial spectrum. Each point of view—entrepreneurial and administrative—has important considerations that need to be balanced if effective growth is going to take place.

Table 16.2 The Entrepreneurial Culture versus the Administrative Culture

| | ENTREPRENEURIAL FOCUS | | ADMINISTRATIVE FOCUS | |
	CHARACTERISTICS	PRESSURES	CHARACTERISTICS	PRESSURES
Strategic Orientation	Driven by perception of opportunity	Diminishing opportunities Rapidly changing technology, consumer economics, social values, and political rules	Driven by controlled resources	Social contracts Performance measurement criteria Planning systems and cycles
Commitment to Seize Opportunities	Revolutionary, with short duration	Action orientation Narrow decision windows Acceptance of reasonable risks Few decision constituencies	Evolutionary, with long duration	Acknowledgment of multiple constituencies Negotiation about strategic course Risk reduction Coordination with existing resource base
Commitment of Resources	Many stages, with minimal exposure at each stage	Lack of predictable resource needs Lack of control over the environment Social demands for appropriate use of resources Foreign competition Demands for more efficient use	A single stage, with complete commitment out of decision	Need to reduce risk Incentive compensation Turnover in managers Capital budgeting systems Formal planning systems
Control of Resources	Episodic use or rent of required resources	Increased resource specialization Long resource life compared with need Risk of obsolescence Risk inherent in the identified opportunity Inflexibility of permanent commitment to resources	Ownership or employment of required resources	Power, status, and financial rewards Coordination of activity Efficiency measures Inertia and cost of change Industry structures
Management Structure	Flat, with multiple informal networks	Coordination of key noncontrolled resources Challenge to hierarchy Employees' desire for independence	Hierarchy	Need for clearly defined authority and responsibility Organizational culture Reward systems Management theory

Source: Reprinted by permission of the *Harvard Business Review*. An exhibit from "The Heart of Entrepreneurship," by Howard H. Stevenson and David E. Gumpert, March/April 1985, 89. Copyright © 1985 by the President and Fellows of Harvard College; all rights reserved.

Understanding the Growth Stage

The growth stage often signals the beginning of a metamorphosis from a personal venture to a group-structured operation. Domination by the lead entrepreneur gives way to a team approach based heavily on coordination and flexibility.

Key Factors during the Growth Stage

Entrepreneurs must understand four key factors about the specific managerial actions necessary during the growth stage. These factors are control, responsibility, tolerance of failure, and change.

Control

Growth creates problems in command and control. When dealing with them, entrepreneurs need to answer three critical questions: Does the control system imply trust? Does the resource allocation system imply trust? Is it easier to ask permission than to ask forgiveness? These questions reveal a great deal about the control of a venture. If they are answered with "yes," the venture is moving toward a good blend of control and participation. If they are answered with "no," the reasons for each negative response should be closely examined.

Responsibility

As the company grows, the distinction between authority and responsibility becomes more apparent. This is because authority always can be delegated, but it is most important to create a sense of responsibility. This action establishes flexibility, innovation, and a supportive environment. People tend to look beyond the job alone if a sense of responsibility is developed, so the growth stage is better served by the innovative activity and shared responsibility of all of the firm's members.

Tolerance of Failure

Even though a venture has avoided the initial start-up pitfalls and has expanded to the growth stage, it is still important to maintain a tolerance of failure. The level of failure the entrepreneur experienced and learned from at the start of the venture should be the same level expected, tolerated, and learned from in the growth stage. Although no firm should seek failure, to continually innovate and grow it should tolerate a certain degree of failure as opposed to punishment for failure.

Three distinct forms of failure should be distinguished:

- □ *Moral failure.* This form of failure is a violation of internal trust. Since the firm is based on mutual expectations and trust, this violation is a serious failure that can result in negative consequences.

- □ *Personal failure.* This form of failure is brought about by a lack of skill or application. Usually responsibility for this form of failure is shared by the firm and the individual. Normally, therefore, an attempt is made to remedy the situation in a mutually beneficial way.

- □ *Uncontrollable failure.* This form of failure is caused by external factors and is the most difficult to prepare for or deal with. Resource limitations, strategic direction, and market changes are examples of forces outside the control of employees. Top management must carefully analyze the context of this form of failure and work to prevent its recurrence.

entrepreneurship IN PRACTICE

The Seven Secrets from the Fastest-Growing Companies

How fast do companies grow in today's environment? Here are the fastest-growth companies, based on revenues.

COMPANY	REVENUE GROWTH
Meritage	497%
Siebel Systems	218
Extended Stay America	213
SLI	158
Kellstron Industries	152
Jakks Pacific	143
Century Business Services	140
Citrix Systems	140
Arguss Holdings	139
Rainforest Café	125

The secrets to managing such hypergrowth? Here are seven traits of these fast-growth companies that keep them flying high:

☐ Never be late on orders or shipments.

☐ Do not overpromise.

☐ Do sweat the small stuff.

☐ Build a fortress through barriers to entry.

☐ Create a unique culture.

☐ Learn from mistakes.

☐ Get the message out—tell the story.

SOURCE: Nelson D. Schwartz, "Secrets of Fortune's Fastest-Growing Companies," *Fortune* (September 6, 1999): 72–86.

Change

Planning, operations, and implementation are all subject to continual changes as the venture moves through the growth stage and beyond. Retaining an innovative and opportunistic posture during growth requires a sense of change and variation from the norm. It should be realized, however, that change holds many implications for the enterprise in terms of resources, people, and structure. It is therefore important during growth that the flexibility regarding change be preserved. This allows for faster managerial response to environmental conditions.

Managing Paradox and Contradiction

When a venture experiences surges in growth, a number of structural factors begin to present multiple challenges. Entrepreneurs constantly struggle over whether to organize these factors, such as cultural elements, staffing and development of personnel, and appraisal and rewards, in a rigid, bureaucratic design or a flexible, organic design. Table 16.3 depicts the conflicting designs for each element.

Research has shown that new-venture managers experiencing growth, particularly in emerging industries, need to adopt flexible, organic structures.[25] Rigid, bureaucratic structures are best suited for mature, stabilized companies. Thus, the cultural elements need to follow a flexible design of autonomy, risk taking, and entrepreneurship. This type of culture is a renewal of the entrepreneur's original force that created the venture. Although the entrepreneur's focus makes a transition toward

Table 16.3 Conflicting Designs of Structural Factors

	FLEXIBLE DESIGN	BUREAUCRATIC DESIGN
Cultural Elements	Autonomous	Formalized
	Risk taking	Risk averse
	Entrepreneurial	Bureaucratic
Staffing and Development	Technical skills	Administrative skills
	Specialists	Generalists
	External hiring	Internal hiring
Appraisal and Rewards	Participative	Formalized
	Subjective	Objective
	Equity based	Incentive based

Source: Charles J. Fombrun and Stefan Wally, "Structuring Small Firms for Rapid Growth," *Journal of Business Venturing* (March 1989): 109.

a more administrative style, as mentioned earlier, the culture of the organization must be permeated with a constant renewal of the virtues of innovation and entrepreneurship.[26]

When designing a flexible structure for high growth, entrepreneurs must realize a number of contradictory forces are at work in certain other structural factors. Consider the following.

Bureaucratization versus Decentralization

Increased hiring stimulates bureaucracy: Firms formalize procedures as staffing doubles and triples. Employee participation and autonomy decline, and internal labor markets develop. Tied to growth, however, is also an increased diversity in product offering that favors less formalized decision processes, greater decentralization, and the recognition that the firm's existing human resources lack the necessary skills to manage the broadening portfolio.

Environment versus Strategy

High environmental turbulence and competitive conditions favor company cultures that support risk taking, autonomy, and employee participation in decision making. Firms confront competitors, however, through strategies whose implementation depends on the design of formal systems that inhibit risk taking and autonomy.

Strategic Emphases: Quality versus Cost versus Innovation

Rapidly growing firms strive to simultaneously control costs, enhance product quality, and improve product offerings. Minimizing costs and undercutting competitors' product prices, however, are best achieved by traditional hierarchical systems of decision making and evaluations. Yet these strategies conflict with the kinds of autonomous processes most likely to encourage the pursuit of product quality and innovation.[27]

These factors emphasize the importance of managing paradox and contradiction. Growth involves the multiple challenges of (1) the stresses and strains induced by attempts to control costs while simultaneously enhancing quality and creating new products to maintain competitive parity, and (2) centralizing to retain control while

the entrepreneurial
PROCESS

From Entrepreneur to Manager

For many entrepreneurs, one of the most difficult tasks is to make the successful transition from a creative, task-juggling entrepreneur to a business-skill-applying manager. A dozen top small-business experts were asked their advice on making this transition successfully. Their answers were consolidated into the following list of key management strategies to help entrepreneurs grow their companies and boost their bottom line.

1. **Don't be the company handyperson.** When starting a new business, the entrepreneur must be able to do every job in the company. But as the company grows, it becomes essential that the entrepreneur learn to delegate. If he or she continues to do every little task, the business will certainly suffer. Jay Conrad Levinson, coauthor of *Guerrilla Marketing Online Weapons,* has some advice on how to escape from the do-it-yourself trap. He suggests that the owner keep a log of all the things he or she does. "You'll see there are things you must do and things you don't have to do. Never do anything you can delegate," Levinson says. By delegating, the entrepreneur will have more time to concentrate on essential leadership functions, such as setting long-term strategic goals.

2. **Hire to your shortcomings.** Oftentimes the strong entrepreneurial characteristics of a small-business owner, such as willingness to take risks, can become a hazard to an established business, according to Ned Herrmann, author of *The Whole Brain Business Book.* "Many business owners keep entrepreneuring when they should be focusing on the quality of product, competition, receivables, the kind of stuff that's boring," Herrmann says. The best remedy is to hire managers that complement the owner by filling in knowledge gaps.

Herrmann explains that "Entrepreneurs tend to hire in their own image, so you get people who all think alike. But if you hire people who are different, it will lead to more innovative ideas."

3. **But don't overhire.** Today's labor market offers numerous staffing alternatives, such as temps, part-timers, and contract workers, that enable small businesses to keep taxes and insurance costs low. These alternatives also give businesses the flexibility to match their labor costs to the demand of their services, according to Irving Grousbeck, consulting professor of management at the Stanford Business School and cofounder of Continental Cablevision. In addition, "If one of your key people is sick or out for some other reason, you can bring in a trained person on an as-needed basis," Grousbeck says.

4. **Call out the "SWOT" team.** David H. Bangs, Jr., author of *The Business Planning Guide,* suggests that a SWOT meeting should be held at least once a year to keep an ongoing business on track. The meeting would evaluate the company's strengths, weaknesses, opportunities, and threats (SWOT) in order to set goals and objectives for the company. SWOT meetings should encourage frank, open discussions to be most productive. In addition, all employees should be required to attend, and the meeting should be facilitated by someone who is not involved in the company's day-to-day operations.

5. **Give employees a stake in the company's success.** In a small, lean business it is important to keep core employees motivated and loyal. "If you only have a small number of people working for you, obviously you count on these people for the success of the

company," Joanna T. Lau, president of Lau Technologies in Acton, Massachusetts, says. Lau, also Ernst & Young's 1995 Turnaround Entrepreneur of the Year award winner, adds, "You might want to provide some of those people with the opportunity for equity in the business to create better loyalty."

6. **Hold down expenses.** The math is simple. Regardless of how much business is done, if a company's costs are outweighing its revenues, hard times are sure to follow. William F. Williams, president and CEO of Glory Foods Inc. in Columbus, Ohio, which was *Black Enterprise* magazine's Emerging Company of the Year for 1996, makes a conscious effort to keep his costs down by consistently pressing for better deals from suppliers and service providers. "The most important thing is to negotiate the best possible cost reductions you can at the outset of every business relationship," Williams claims. Cost-cutting opportunities are everywhere, such as bargaining rent space and shopping for interest rates.

7. **Go global.** "If you have an established business and you're not pursuing the international market, you're probably missing out on potential sales," Tammy L. Flor, president and CEO of Laurel Engineering Inc. in Chula Vista, California, and the SBA's 1995 Exporter of the Year, says. Although many small businesses may be intimidated by the thought of global competition, real opportunities do exist in these markets for even the smallest of companies.

8. **Scratch the customer's itch.** All types of business, regardless of what they sell, should adopt a cradle-to-grave approach toward their customers. Tom Hopkins, author of *Selling for Dummies,* describes this as a commitment to a follow-up system that starts by figuring out the "itch cycle" for the company's customers and product. The itch cycle is Hopkins's term for the period of time after a purchase from a company during which the customer is particularly receptive to making another commitment to that company.

Hopkins's suggestion for benefiting from this cycle is to contact customers with hand-written letters expressing the company's hope that they are happy with their recent purchase. An example of this type of approach is a car salesperson who knows which customers usually buy a new car about every 30 months. "After about 28 months, the salesperson gets the latest model, drives it over to where the customer works, and invites him to drive it for a few days," Hopkins says. "And 85 percent of those cars are sold."

9. **Adapt to change.** "If customers want us to do things differently, we'll try to accommodate them. In fact, we ask them for suggestions," Peter Mendoza, Jr., president of MBE Electric, a contracting business in Riverside, California, says. Peter and his vice-president brother, Brian, agree that one of their biggest challenges in customer relations is staying abreast of changes. In 1994, when the earthquake destroyed the Santa Monica Freeway, the Mendozas were asked to design a new electrical system—promptly. Although changes were made in the original contract twice and the scope of the work tripled, the job was completed in 66 days. Adapting to change has paid off for the Mendoza brothers. MBE Electric has grown from $2.6 million in sales to $5.5 million in three years, and the Mendozas were named the SBA's Young Entrepreneurs of the Year in 1996.

10. **Seek customer advice.** According to Susan RoAne, author of *How to Work a Room* and *The Secrets of Savvy Networking,* "Small-business owners fail when they have no relationship with the people who buy their products." She suggests calling or sending personal notes (via regular or e-mail) to key customers at least once every three months to gather their advice. Another suggestion is to ask customers to fill out a customer survey. According to RoAne, the survey should be no longer than one page, it should offer a discount on customers' next purchase if it is completed, and it should ask customers to tell what the company does or does not do well,

in addition to providing space to include specific examples.

11. **Sniff out the silver linings.** The former president of Ben & Jerry's Ice Cream and author of *Ben & Jerry's: The Inside Scoop,* Fred Lager, says, "If I had one piece of advice, it would be to look for opportunities in the face of adversity." In his book, Lager describes the 1984 incident in which Pillsbury Company, owners of Häagan-Dazs, attempted to stop independent ice-cream dealers from offering Ben & Jerry's ice cream. "We were able to turn it to our advantage by asking 'What's the doughboy afraid of?' We got a lot of publicity. The result was that we got tremendous brand recognition—way beyond what we could have afforded with paid advertising," Lager recalls.

12. **Mix family and business with care.** Ross Nager, executive director of the Arthur Andersen Center for Family Business in Houston, Texas, says. "Don't forget your family." Small businesses can take advantage of the many roles family members can provide, such as a teenager's custodial work in the summers or the extended family's sales leads. Nager does suggest that to make the experience a positive one for everyone, relatives should be required to work somewhere else first, so their first job is not in the family business. This allows them to gain valuable outside experience, including realistic expectations, as well as increases their credibility among the other employees.

SOURCE: Stephen J. Simurda, "Instant MBA," *Small Business Computing* (February 1997): 60–63.

simultaneously decentralizing to encourage the contributions of autonomous, self-managed professionals to the embryonic corporate culture. Rapidly growing firms are challenged to strike a balance among these multiple pulls when designing their managerial systems.

Confronting the Growth Wall

In attempting to develop a managerial ability to deal with venture growth, many entrepreneurial owners confront a **growth wall** that seems too gigantic to overcome. Thus, they are unable to begin the process of handling the challenges that growth brings about.

Researchers have identified a number of fundamental changes that confront rapid-growth firms, including instant size increases, a sense of infallibility, internal turmoil, and extraordinary resource needs. In addressing these changes that can build a growth wall, successful growth-oriented firms have exhibited a few consistent themes:

- ☐ The entrepreneur is able to envision and anticipate the firm as a larger entity.
- ☐ The team needed for tomorrow is hired and developed today.
- ☐ The original core vision of the firm is constantly and zealously reinforced.
- ☐ New "big-company" processes are introduced gradually as supplements to, rather than replacements for, existing approaches.
- ☐ Hierarchy is minimized.
- ☐ Employees hold a financial stake in the firm.[28]

These themes are important for entrepreneurs to keep in mind as they develop their abilities to manage growth.

One researcher found that internal constraints such as lack of growth capital, limited spans of control, and loss of entrepreneurial vitality occur in growth firms that struggle to survive versus those that successfully achieve high growth. In addition, fundamental differences exist in the firms' approach to environmental changes and trends.[29] A six-step program was recommended as a process for breaking through the inability to handle environmental change or trends. These steps follow.

1. *Get the facts.* Develop an information base through competitor profiles, market studies, and technological analysis.

2. *Create a growth task force.* Develop a cross-functional team to organize and interpret the environmental data, to identify the venture's strengths and weaknesses, to brainstorm new ideas that leverage the firm's strengths, and to recommend key ideas that should be developed further.

3. *Plan for growth.* Develop a comprehensive plan for the recommended ideas that would be organized around four critical components: reasons for the stagnation in growth, the strategies to resolve the stagnation, a set of potential results, and identification of the necessary resources.

4. *Staff for growth.* Move beyond only the owner and key executives having responsibility for growth. Every manager needs to be charged with the constant challenge of responding to growth.

5. *Maintain a growth culture.* Create a corporate culture that encourages and rewards a growth-oriented attitude. Develop a core value statement that articulates the entrepreneur's commitment to growth.

6. *Use an advisory board.* Establish an outside board of advisors (directors) to become an integral part of the venture's growth. This board should help determine, design, and implement an organizational structure to enhance the desire for growth.[30]

Growth and Decision Making

The decision-making process is a critical issue in the growth stage of emerging ventures.[31] The focus and style of decision making are distinctive from the earlier or later stages that a venture goes through. Table 16.4 illustrates the primary decision-making focus for the growth stage compared to the early and later stages. Also, as depicted in the table, the organizational characteristics of successful early-stage firms and of successful mature firms are quite different, as indicated by differences in the problems

Table 16.4   Decision-Making Characteristics and Growth Stages

	EARLY STAGE(S)	GROWTH STAGE	LATER STAGE(S)
Primary Focus	Product business Definition Acquisition of resources Development of market position	Volume production Market share Viability	Cost control Profitability Future growth opportunity
Decision-Making Characteristics	Informal Centralized Nonspecialized Short time horizon	Transitional	Formal Decentralized Specialized Long and short time horizon

Source: Thomas N. Gilmore and Robert K. Kazanjian, "Clarifying Decision Making in High Growth Ventures: The Use of Responsibility Charting," *Journal of Business Venturing* (January 1989): 71.

they face. Early-stage firms usually face undefined tasks, such as technology or market development, characterized by high levels of uncertainty. As a result, their organizations typically demonstrate little structure in the form of job specialization, rules, or formality. Decision making is, in many instances, based solely on the owner communicating informally and face-to-face. The owner-founder integrates people, functions, and tasks in many instances through his or her own direct contact.

In contrast, mature firms that have attained a size of several hundred employees can no longer manage in such a fashion. They require some elements of formality, structure, and specialization to control and direct their organization effectively and efficiently. The transition of the decision-making process from that described for early-stage firms to that of later-stage firms must be effected during the growth stage. Timing is critical. Premature introduction of structure and formalities may dampen the venture's creative, entrepreneurial climate. However, if formality and structure are not adopted soon enough, management may lose control of the organization as its size increases, leading to major dislocations of the firm and even failure.[32]

Therefore, entrepreneurs need to recognize the important transition of decision-making style during growth and to learn to authorize others to make necessary decisions in order to address the simultaneous challenges of rapid growth. Methods for entrepreneurs to consider when handling decisions during growth have been suggested.

One method concentrates on the use of **external resources** through networking.[33] In other words, networking entails the establishment of external personal relationships that the entrepreneur may use for professional assistance. The idea is to gain a competitive advantage by extending decision making and resource availability beyond the assets under the domain and control of the venture. One example of such resource use is a firm that obtains a license to use a well-known name to market a product that could not achieve recognition otherwise and that does so by promising a royalty on future sales. This is obviously taking advantage of a series of resources—all the resources normally needed to create a national brand—that it does not own. "External resources" are assets—physical or otherwise—a firm uses in its pursuit of growth and over which it has no direct ownership.[34] Another example would be the use of outside consulting assistance in the areas of administrative or operating problems. Strategic planning, security financing, marketing, and day-to-day operational assistance are all areas in which emerging firms may seek outside assistance.[35]

Another method suggested to entrepreneurs for consideration when handling decisions during growth is **responsibility charting**.[36] The process assumes decision making involves multiple roles that come into play in various ways at different points of time. Therefore, its three major components are decisions, roles, and types of participation. These three components are combined to form a matrix, so a respondent can assign a type of participation to each of the roles for a specific decision. Responses are then analyzed either in a group setting with all participants present or by a facilitator alone when group size makes processing of the data unwieldy. The steps of responsibility charting are listed in Table 16.5.

When reporting the value of this process, researchers Gilmore and Kazanjian stated:

Responsibility charting enables better discussions of power and authority because it allows a rich range of potential solutions, rather than the win-lose dynamics that result from discussing these issues in terms of boxes and lines of a new structure.

In growth-stage ventures, team building often fails because of the influx of new executives. Once responsibility charting has been used to clarify major decisions, the

Table 16.5   *Steps of Responsibility Charting*

1. Establishment of initial parameters:
   Decision rules
   Common language
   Creating the matrix of key decisions and roles

2. Individual balloting and tabulation of patterns

3. Discussion, clarification, negotiation

4. Agreement on allocation of responsibility

5. Monitoring and renegotiation as needed

Source: Thomas N. Gilmore and Robert K. Kazanjian, "Clarifying Decision Making in High Growth Ventures: The Use of Responsibility Charting," *Journal of Business Venturing* (January 1989): 73.

results are a powerful way to orient new executives who step into key roles. Unlike a job description that only communicates one's duties, the chart shows how the role fits into many critical processes.[37]

Whether it's networking or responsibility charting, entrepreneurs need to develop methods for handling the increasing complexities of decision making in the growth stage. The key to any system may be the ability of the entrepreneur to delegate.

Unique Managerial Concerns of Growing Ventures

Emerging businesses differ in many ways from larger, more structured businesses. Several unique managerial concerns involve growing businesses in particular. These concerns may seem insignificant to the operation of a large business, but they do become important to many emerging entrepreneurs.

The Distinction of Small Size

The distinction of *smallness* gives emerging businesses certain disadvantages. The limited market, for example, restricts a small firm. Because a small size limits a company's ability to geographically extend throughout a region or state, the firm must recognize and service its available market. Another disadvantage is the higher ordering costs that burden many small firms. Because they do not order large lots of inventory from suppliers, small businesses usually do not receive quantity discounts and must pay higher prices. Finally, a smaller staff forces small firms to accept less specialization of labor. Thus, employees and managers are expected to perform numerous functions.

However, the distinction of small size is not all bad, and the advantages to smallness should be recognized and capitalized on. One advantage is greater flexibility. In smaller ventures, decisions can be made and implemented immediately, without the input of committees and the delay of bureaucratic layers. Production, marketing, and service are all areas that can be adjusted quickly for a competitive advantage over larger businesses in the same field. A second advantage is constant communication with the community.[38] An entrepreneur lives in the community and is personally involved in community affairs. The special insight of this involvement allows the entrepreneur to adjust products or services to suit the specific needs or desires of the particular community. This leads to the third and probably most important advantage of closeness to the customer: the ability to offer personal service. The personal service that an entrepreneur can provide is one of the key elements of success today. Major corporations work feverishly to duplicate or imitate the idea of personal service. Since the opportunity to provide personal service is an advantage emerging firms possess by nature of their size, it *must* be capitalized on.

The One-Person-Band Syndrome

Most entrepreneurs start their businesses alone or with a few family members or close associates. In effect, the business *is* the entrepreneur and the entrepreneur is the business.[39] However, a danger arises if the owner refuses to relinquish any authority as the emerging business grows. Some owners fail to delegate responsibility to employees, thereby retaining *all* decision-making authority. One study revealed that most planning in small firms is done by the owner alone, as are other operational activities.[40] This "syndrome" often is derived from the same pattern of independence that helped start the business in the first place. However, the owner who continues to perform as a one-person band can restrict the growth of the firm because the owner's ability is limited. How can proper planning for the business be accomplished if the owner is immersed in daily operations? Thus, the entrepreneur must recognize the importance of delegation. If the owner can break away from the natural tendency to do *everything,* then the business will benefit from a wider array of that person's abilities.

Time Management

Effective time management is not exclusively a challenge to entrepreneurs. However, limited size and staff force the entrepreneur to face this challenge most diligently. It has been said a person never will *find* time to do anything but must, in fact, *make* the time. In other words, entrepreneurs should learn to use time as a resource and not allow time to use them.[41] In order to perform daily managerial activities in the most time-efficient manner, owner-managers should follow four critical steps:

1. *Assessment.* The business owner should analyze his or her daily activities and rank them in order of importance. (A written list on a notepad is recommended.)

2. *Prioritization.* The owner should divide and categorize the day's activities based on his or her ability to devote the necessary time to the task that day. In other words, the owner should avoid a procrastination of duties.

3. *Creation of procedures.* Repetitive daily activities can be handled easily by an employee if instructions are provided. This organizing of tasks can be a major time saver for the owner that would allow the fourth and last step to be put into effect.

4. *Delegation.* Delegation can be accomplished after the owner creates procedures for various jobs. As mentioned in the description of the one-person-band syndrome, delegation is a critical skill entrepreneurs need to develop.

All of these steps in effective time management require self-discipline on the part of entrepreneurs.

Community Obligations

Proximity to the community was mentioned earlier as a size advantage for small business. However, unlike major corporations with public relations departments, the entrepreneur is involved with community activities directly. The community presents unique challenges to emerging business in three ways: participation, leadership, and donations.

Each of these expectations from the community requires entrepreneurs to plan and budget carefully. Many community members believe the entrepreneur has "excess" time because he or she owns the business. They also believe the owner has leadership abilities needed for various community activities. Although the latter may be true, the owner usually does not have excess time. Therefore, entrepreneurs need to plan carefully the activities they believe would be most beneficial. One consideration is the amount of advertising or recognition the business will receive for the owner's participation. When the owner can justify his or her community involvement, both the business and the community benefit.

Financial donations also require careful analysis and budgeting. Again, because consumers have access to the entrepreneur (as opposed to the chief executive officer of a major corporation), he or she may be inundated with requests for donations to charitable and community organizations. Although each organization may have a worthy cause, the entrepreneur cannot support every one and remain financially healthy. Thus, the owner needs to decide which of the organizations to assist and to budget a predetermined amount of money for annual donations. Any other solicitations for money must be placed in writing and submitted to the entrepreneur for consideration. This is the only way entrepreneurs can avoid giving constant cash donations without careful budget consideration.

The critical fact to remember is that time and money are extremely valuable resources for an entrepreneur. They should be budgeted in a meaningful way. Therefore, entrepreneurs need to analyze their community involvement and to continuously reassess the costs versus the benefits.[42]

Continuing Management Education

A final unique concern for the entrepreneur is continuation of management education. All of the previously mentioned concerns leave very little time left for owners to maintain or improve their managerial knowledge. However, the environment of the 1990s produced dramatic changes that can affect the procedures, processes, programs, philosophy, or even the product of a small business. The ancient Greek philosopher Epictetus once said, "It is impossible for a man to learn what he thinks he already knows." This quote illustrates the need for small-business people to dedicate time to learning new techniques and principles for their businesses. Trade associations, seminars, conferences, publications, and college courses all provide opportunities for entrepreneurs to continue their management education. Staying abreast of industry changes is another way for small-business people to maintain a competitive edge.

Effective Delegation

For making the transition from owner dominance of an entrepreneurial venture to the diversity of operations in a growth stage, **effective delegation** is a key component of success. This process entails three steps: (1) assigning specific duties, (2) granting authority to carry out these duties, and (3) creating the obligation of responsibility for necessary action.[43]

Why is delegation so essential to growth-oriented ventures? Because to continue growth and innovation, the entrepreneur needs to free up his or her time and to rely on others in the enterprise to carry on the day-to-day activities.[44] Timothy W. Firnstahl, an executive with a small growth-oriented firm, states:

> In start-up companies, the visions are usually the entrepreneurs'—they have the clear ideas about the product or service they plan to offer. Moreover, they often have to be in all places at all times, taking care of every detail. Unfortunately, this 100 percent hands-on

management does not permit an entrepreneur's staff to mature. Why think, if the boss has all the answers? Inadvertently, an entrepreneur usurps employees' responsibilities. Worse, people often perform well because they know the owner is right there.[45]

In addition to the three steps just outlined, two other delegation-related responsibilities arise.[46] The first is to hire the best employees—the basis of any effective entrepreneurial team. As a small venture grows into a larger enterprise, hiring becomes a major area of consideration. The organization needs to determine the proper skills so it can hire those who have the necessary skills (or abilities to learn these skills) to fill newly created jobs.

The second responsibility is to use delegation to free up time for thinking effectively. The entrepreneur needs to continually consider the basic philosophy and direction of the firm. Firnstahl put it this way:

> Thinking is not reading, meeting, routine reporting, listening, observing, or working. In a sense, thinking is dreaming the organization's future. It's the ability to see tomorrow and construct the company's ideal state. It's the ability to get excited about the possibilities of the future.[47]

In addition to the ideas presented thus far, other suggestions for thinking about the venture's future follow.

1. *View thinking as a strategy.* Thinking is the best way to resolve difficulties. The entrepreneur needs to maintain faith in his or her ability to think through problems. The individual also must recognize the difference between worrying and thinking. Worrying is repeated, needless problem analysis, whereas thinking is solution generation.

2. *Schedule large blocks of uninterrupted time.* Because thinking takes time, it must be scheduled. By carving out large blocks of uninterrupted time during periods when he or she is most productive, the entrepreneur makes effective use of time.

3. *Stay focused on relevant topics.* The entrepreneur must be prepared to work hard mentally until his or her mind produces the necessary quality. The ideas are there; it is a matter of ferreting them out.

4. *Record, sort, and save thoughts.* Ideas are the product of work; they should be recorded, sorted, and saved. Effective entrepreneurs write them on three-inch by five-inch cards, one idea per card, so they remain "mobile." Another approach is to use a handheld recorder to capture thoughts while driving and then to have these ideas written down. Files of ideas about the organization's future are a major source of information.[48]

The International Environment: Global Opportunities

The last decade witnessed a new breed of global entrepreneurs. They relied on global networks for resources, design, and distribution. The trend has escalated the global economy, allowing it to reach new heights. By all accounts, the pace and magnitude of this global economy are likely to continue to accelerate. Adept at recognizing opportunities, the new breed of global entrepreneurs recognizes that success in the new marketplace requires agility, certainty, and ingenuity with a global perspective. These entrepreneurs are the true vanguards in the new millennium.[49]

Therefore, one of the most exciting and promising avenues for entrepreneurs to expand their businesses is by participating in the global market. Each year thousands of small-business enterprises are actively engaged in the international arena. Two of the primary reasons for this emerging opportunity are the decline in trade barriers, especially among major trading nations, and the emergence of major trading blocs that have been brought about by the North American Free Trade Agreement and the European Union. In addition, over the past decade Asia has become a hotbed for entrepreneurial opportunity.

"Global thinking" is important because today's consumers can select products, ideas, and services from many nations and cultures. Entrepreneurs who expand into foreign markets must be global thinkers in order to design and adopt strategies for different countries.

Entrepreneurship has developed across the globe. As an example, research by the Kauffman Foundation entitled, *The Global Entrepreneurship Monitor*, examined 29 countries representing approximately 2.5 billion people. Approximately 56 percent (1.4 billion) were adults of working age. Random samples of at least 2,000 adults from each participating country were surveyed to ascertain several measures of entrepreneurial activity. From the more than 74,000 surveys conducted with those 18 to 64 years of age, about 10 percent of the adults were engaged in entrepreneurial activities.

Therefore, in the 29 countries, at any point in time, approximately 150 million people were involved in starting and growing new firms.

The overall level of entrepreneurial activity for each country is presented in Figure 16.3. The value depicted for each country shows the number per every 100 adult individuals who are trying to start a new firm or are the owner/manager of an active

Figure 16.3   Total Entrepreneurial Activity by Country

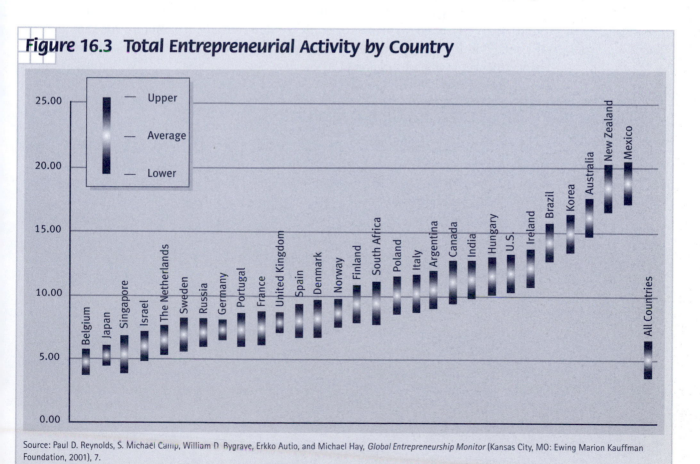

Source: Paul D. Reynolds, S. Michael Camp, William D. Bygrave, Erkko Autio, and Michael Hay, *Global Entrepreneurship Monitor* (Kansas City, MO: Ewing Marion Kauffman Foundation, 2001), 7.

business less than 42 months old (i.e., the Total Entrepreneurial Activity Index). The vertical bars represent the precision of each estimate based on the size of the sample in each country at the 95 percent confidence interval.[50]

Doing business globally is rapidly becoming a profitable and popular strategy for many entrepreneurial ventures.[51] The myth that international business is the province of giant multinational enterprises has long since been disproved by capable and opportunistic entrepreneurs.

Methods of Going International

The entrepreneur can actively engage in the international market in five ways: importing, exporting, joint ventures, direct foreign investment, and licensing.[52] Each of these methods involves increasing levels of risk. Figure 16.4 illustrates the continuum of risk each method falls within. The final choice will depend on the organization's needs and the risk it is willing to take.

Importing

Importing is buying and shipping foreign-produced goods for domestic consumption. Each year the United States imports an increasing amount of goods. During the 1980s, the United States imported more goods than it exported, marking the first time this country became a net debtor nation since World War II. This situation continues today, and several factors have played a role in this change of trade status. One has been the rising cost of energy. A second, and complementary, reason is the low labor costs in other countries, which make their products financially attractive. A third reason is that some products are not available or produced domestically. (Diamonds, for example, are not mined in the United States but mostly in Africa. As a result, American jewelry companies must import diamonds.)

Figure 16.4 Risk of Entering Global Markets

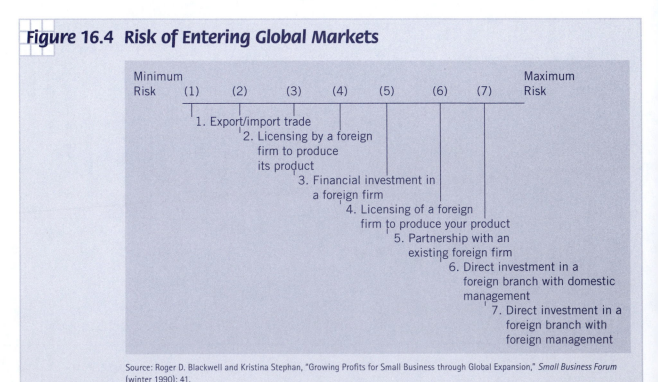

Source: Roger D. Blackwell and Kristina Stephan, "Growing Profits for Small Business through Global Expansion," *Small Business Forum* (winter 1990): 41.

How does an entrepreneur become aware of import opportunities? One way is to attend trade shows and fairs where firms gather to display their products and services. Some of these shows are international in flavor, with firms from different countries exhibiting their products and services. Basically, the trade show gives the prospective customer the opportunity to window-shop. Another way is to monitor trade publications. Often, firms will advertise in trade publications to make themselves known to potential customers.

Exporting

When an entrepreneurial firm decides to participate actively in the international arena as a seller, rather than a buyer, it becomes an exporter. **Exporting** is the shipping of a domestically produced good to a foreign destination for consumption. Exporting is important for entrepreneurs because it often means increased market potential. Instead of limiting its market to the United States, the firm now has a broader sales sphere. According to the **learning curve concept**, increased sales will lead to greater efficiencies along the cost curve, which in turn will lead to increased profits. (The learning curve essentially states that as more and more units are produced, the firm becomes more efficient at production of the units, thereby lowering the cost per unit. The lower unit cost thus enables the firm to compete more effectively in the marketplace.) It should be pointed out, however, that exporting normally will take three to five years to become profitable. Even if the firm is producing more units efficiently, it will take time to learn the intricacies and efficiencies of international business.

Exporting has been increasing as a method for venture growth and increased profitability among small firms. One study examined the types of export strategies small firms use to gain a competitive edge in their market.[53] It identified four key competitive strategies. The first involves market differentiation through competitive pricing, through the development of brand identification, or through innovation in marketing techniques. The second type is a focus strategy involving specialty products for particular customers or new-product development. The third strategy is achieving technological superiority of certain products. And the fourth key strategy is a product-oriented emphasis using the elements of customer service and high quality.[54] In order to pursue any of these strategies, entrepreneurs need to understand some of the ways to become involved in exporting that are presented in the following sections.

Export Management Company

Participation in the export market takes a variety of forms. One of the simplest is to engage the services of an **export management company**. An export management company is a private firm that serves as an export department for several manufacturers. The company solicits and transacts export business on behalf of its clients in return for a commission, salary, or retainer plus commission. In addition, some export management companies will purchase the product and sell it themselves to foreign customers. Export management companies can facilitate the export process by handling all of the details—from making the shipping arrangements to locating the customers. When approaching an export management company, however, entrepreneurs should exercise caution. Presented here is a list of questions that should be answered before making a commitment.

1. What is the reputation of the firm? Is it financially sound?
2. How long has the company been in business?

3. What expertise does the firm have in the specific product line the entrepreneur is offering? How many product lines does it have? Are they related?

4. What experience does the company have as an export management company?

5. What is its track record as an export management company?

6. Is it a full-time or part-time operation?

7. Does it have an adequate number of personnel to satisfactorily service all its clients, and what is the expertise of each?

8. What foreign language capability does it have?

9. What services does it offer—that is, can it buy and sell for its own account, or does it want to act only as a representative or agent to bring buyer and seller together?

10. Will it accept a nonexclusive contract?

11. Can it handle documentation and shipping requirements?

12. Is the company equally familiar with selling in all areas of the world, or does it concentrate in certain areas, such as Latin America, Europe, or the Middle East?

13. Who are its clients? Is the entrepreneur permitted to contact them?

14. What is the minimum term of contract it will accept?

15. Will it accept a performance clause in a contractual arrangement?

16. Do its personnel make trips overseas on behalf of its clients?

17. Does it participate in trade shows or fairs overseas?

18. What overseas marketing data can the company provide regarding the entrepreneur's product or products?

19. Does it have representatives overseas?[55]

One of the dangers the entrepreneur encounters when using an export management company is the possibility of losing control over the export function. It is easy for the novice exporter to permit the export management company to exercise complete control over the export function. In fact, often the exporter is unaware of the destination of the products. If the firm should ever decide to start exporting on its own, the entrepreneur would have no idea where its products have been successful. In addition, the firm may be unaware of the proper documentation that needs to be filed. As a result, the exporter becomes heavily dependent on the export management company. To prevent this problem, the entrepreneur should receive reports detailing the activities performed on its behalf by the export management company.

Freight Forwarder

Another method of exporting that entrepreneurs commonly use is to employ the services of a **freight forwarder**. A freight forwarder is an independent business that handles export shipments in return for compensation. Some of the services a freight forwarder can provide follow.

☐ Quoting inland, ocean, and air shipping costs

☐ Arranging inland shipping and reserving necessary space aboard an ocean vessel

☐ Advising on the requirements of international packing

☐ Preparing the necessary export documentation

☐ Seeing to it that the goods reach the port and tracing lost shipments[56]

entrepreneurship IN PRACTICE

The International Decision—Asking the Right Questions

If entrepreneurs are going to pursue the international marketplace, then a number of issues should be explored before they expand globally. The strategic options for small firms seeking to enter the international arena include three specific types: (1) Firms can choose to export products from the United States to foreign markets, (2) firms can establish a direct presence by setting up sales offices or manufacturing facilities in the foreign country they are interested in, and (3) firms can forge strategic alliances with foreign businesses.

Each of these options requires special preparations by the entrepreneur. However, general questions entrepreneurs need to answer in preparation for any global strategy include the following:

1. Is the product/service unique?

2. Is the entrepreneur flexible?

3. Who can use the product/service?

4. What are the costs?

5. What demands will international expansion place on the company's personnel?

6. Does serving the new foreign market fit with the company goals for growth and development?

7. Is the entrepreneur personally committed to international expansion?

8. Is the entrepreneur willing to invest enough money to initiate operations?

9. What analysis has been done on the competitors?

10. Can the entrepreneur be patient until global expansion begins to pay off?

SOURCE: Gary L. Keefe, "Helping Clients Prepare for Global Markets," *Journal of Accountancy* (July 1989): 54–64; Charles W. L. Hill, *International Business: Competing in the Global Marketplace* (Burr Ridge, IL: Irwin, 1994), Chapter 17; and Richard M. Hodgetts and Fred Luthans, *International Management* (Boston: McGraw-Hill/Irwin, 2003), Chapter 8.

Using a freight-forwarding service has several advantages. One is that this type of service does not cost as much as the services offered by an export management company. That is because an export management company handles all of the export-related activities, whereas the freight forwarder simply arranges for product shipment. Another advantage is that a freight forwarder can save the exporting firm many headaches. Shipping a product can be complex and confusing to the company. Arrangements must be made to ensure safe transportation from the departure point to the destination point, usually requiring more than one transportation mode. In addition, each country requires special forms and documentation when products are imported. If the forms are filled out incorrectly, payment—and quite possibly release of the goods—may be delayed indefinitely. The freight forwarder can obviate these potential nightmares by carefully monitoring the shipping process.

When selecting a freight forwarder, entrepreneurs should follow certain guidelines. First, if the cargo is to be shipped by sea, it is important that the freight forwarder be licensed by the Federal Maritime Commission. Such licensed freight forwarders are familiar with import rules and regulations, methods of shipping, U.S. government export regulations, and the documents connected with foreign trade. Second, references should be obtained from past customers. Third, the services to be provided and the associated costs to the firm should be determined. Fourth, the entrepreneur should talk with experienced exporters as well as with the potential overseas distributors in order to solicit their opinions of particular freight forwarders. Finally, the prospective exporter should check with current shippers of domestic products. Several freight companies are now expanding their operations into other countries and will handle all of the necessary shipping documentation and arrangements. This new service gives the entrepreneur the opportunity to contact a single shipper instead of maintaining information on many transportation companies.

Foreign Sales Corporation

Created by Congress as a replacement for the controversial **domestic international sales corporation (DISC)**, the **foreign sales corporation (FSC)** was developed in 1984 to combat an increasingly unfavorable trade balance and apparent inequities in the tax treatment of U.S. exporters compared with the tax treatment that other countries gave their exporters. The 1971 DISC regulation allowed companies to defer taxes on a portion of their export sales by forming a DISC subsidiary. By channeling export sales through the DISC, the organization could defer federal income taxes on 15 to 25 percent of its income from export sales. In addition, as long as the firm kept the earnings in the DISC and reinvested those funds in qualifying export assets, the deferral could become permanent. It was hoped this regulation would help spur additional export sales to improve the nation's balance of payments and to remove the incentive for U.S. companies to manufacture abroad.

U.S. trading partners objected to this legislation on the ground that it violated the General Agreement on Tariffs and Trade (GATT). Several GATT members contended that the DISC regulation was, in effect, a direct government subsidy on exports, which was prohibited by the agreement. After 12 years of discussion between the United States and the GATT Council, the Reagan administration sought to repeal the DISC legislation and replace it with the FSC regulation. The provisions of the FSC regulation were designed to comply more closely with the principal provisions of GATT. Accordingly, in 1984 Congress passed the FSC legislation, which allows tax-exempt treatment of a portion of export income. To qualify for this treatment, the exporter must meet three conditions.

1. *It must have a foreign presence.* This requirement can be satisfied by incorporating in a qualified foreign country or eligible U.S. possession, maintaining an office outside the United States, and retaining a permanent set of books at that office. The FSC also must be managed outside of the United States, which can be accomplished by holding shareholder and board meetings outside the United States, maintaining a principal bank account outside the United States, and disbursing dividends as well as certain fees and salaries from this account.

2. *It must have economic substance.* Certain direct costs of a transaction are grouped into one of five categories: advertising, processing customer orders and arranging for delivery, transportation, determination of final invoice and receipt of payment, and assumption of credit risk. At least half of these costs the FSC incurs must be outside the United States. An alternative to this is that 85 percent of the direct costs for two categories must be outside the United States.

3. *It must perform activities relating to its exporting income outside the United States.* In order to meet this requirement, the exporter must perform certain processes outside the United States. These processes are related to the solicitation, negotiation, and creation of a contract. At least one of the activities must be performed by the FSC or its agent outside the United States.

The income of a firm that satisfies these requirements is considered foreign trade income and is partially exempt from federal income tax.

In order to provide relief for the small exporter, Congress enacted a provision for the "small FSC" and the "interest-charge DISC." The small FSC is exempt from the foreign management and economic processes requirements, but it may take into consideration $5 million of export receipts for tax benefits. The interest-charge DISC is similar to the old DISC except that only $10 million of export receipts can be included, the amounts that qualify for shareholder distribution are different, and interest is charged on the amount of tax deferred by the interest-charge DISC.

Joint Venture

Another alternative available to the entrepreneur in the international arena is the **joint venture**.[57] A joint venture occurs when two or more firms analyze the benefits of creating a relationship,[58] pool their resources, and create a new entity to undertake productive economic activity. A joint venture thus implies the sharing of assets, profits, risks, and venture ownership with more than one firm.[59] A joint venture can take one of several different forms. In some countries, for example, it is not uncommon for a company to form a joint venture with the state or with a state-owned firm. This is particularly true in the case of petroleum companies with operations in the Middle East.[60]

Advantages and Disadvantages

A firm may decide to participate in a joint venture for several reasons.[61] One is that the firm would be able to gain an intimate knowledge of the local conditions and government where the facility is located. Another is that each participant would be able to use the resources of the other firms involved in the venture. This allows participating firms a chance to compensate for weaknesses they may possess. Finally, both the initial capital outlay and the overall risk would be lower than if the firm were setting up the operation alone.

Additional advantages of a joint venture relate to the strategic fit of the domestic firm with the foreign firm. One study examined the strategic fit of domestic firms (D-type) with Third World firms (TW-type) in a joint venture.[62] The dimensions of corporate-level advantages, operational-level advantages, and environmental advantages were all compared to the strategic fit of the partners in the joint venture.[63] Table 16.6 provides the complete listing of the advantages and their strategic fit.[64]

One of the disadvantages associated with joint ventures is the problem of fragmented control.[65] For example, a carefully planned logistics flow may be hampered if one of the firms decides to block the acquisition of new equipment. This type of problem can be avoided or diminished in a number of ways: (1) One party can control more than 50 percent of the voting rights. This will normally give formal control; however, even a minority opposing view can carry considerable influence. This can be particularly true if the differences of opinion reflect different nationalities. (2) Only one of the parties is made responsible for the actual management of the venture. This may be complemented by a buyout clause. In case of a disagreement among the owners, one party can purchase the equity of the other. (3) One of the parties can control either the input or the output, exerting significant control over the venture decisions, despite voting and ownership rights.

The joint venture can be a powerful tool for growth in the international market. If used properly, it will effectively combine the strengths of the partners involved and thereby increase its competitive position.[66]

Table 16.6   *Strategic Fit of Small D-Type Firms in Third-World Joint Ventures*

DIMENSION	STRATEGIC FIT
Corporate-Level Advantages	
Relevant/complementary technology	Meeting developing country's specific technology needs in cost-efficient manner; easier to adopt and integrate technology with local technological infrastructure
Match with D-type firm's strategy and long-range plans	Being the recommended strategic alternative for D-type firm
Venture strategy	Flexible structure; informal control mechanism; tolerance of deviation from set guidelines
Ownership-control relationship	Not overly demanding on level of control; flexible and less lopsided control-ownership nexus
TW firm type and capabilities	Type of firm; capabilities of the TW firm; historical record distinctive competencies
Conflict of interest between partners	Product related; market related; technology information related
Operational-Level Advantages	
Managerial resource allocation	Relevant managerial resource; low cost of managerial services
Decision-making and reporting systems	Formality, structure and policies; ability to solve crisis-oriented problems; flexibility
Approaches to organizational functioning	Close-knit operations of the firm; tolerance to low level of responsibility and accountability by the joint venture
Cultural differences between the parent firms	At the societal level; at the business level; at the corporate level
Local vested interests	Extent of damage that they can cause
Size of the D-type firm	Similar in "size" to the TW-type firm; similar problem-solving approaches; easier day-to-day operations
Environmental Advantages	
Local government incentives/constraints	Identifying relevant incentives and constraints; government approval and incentives may be easier to obtain because the smaller D-type firm may not be perceived as a threat
Market structure and distribution channels	Demand-supply nexus; substitute products and new entrants; ability to transfer expertise
Perceived host-country business climate	Business climate perceived as being good or bad

Source: Derrick E. D'Souza and Patricia P. McDougall, "Third World Joint Venturing: A Strategic Option for the Smaller Firm," *Entrepreneurship Theory and Practice* (summer 1989): 25. Reprinted with permission.

Direct Foreign Investment

A **direct foreign investment** is a domestically controlled foreign production facility. This does not mean the firm owns a majority of the operation. In some cases, less than 50 percent ownership can constitute effective control because the stock ownership is widely dispersed. On the other hand, the entrepreneur may own 100 percent of the

Doing European Business

The United States exports $210 billion worth of goods to the European Union and more than 60 percent is credited to small and mid-size businesses in America. The 25-member European Union has been known for excessive red tape and trade disputes, but for American entrepreneurs selling or operating on the continent there is dramatic growth. The advantage is in their maneuverability, aggressive sales approaches, and realistic pricing. They also are characterized as better at building relationships and will thusly benefit greater from the upswing in corporate European investment.

As the EU has become a reality and the entire continent of Europe continues to merge for economic trade purposes, entrepreneurs need to be aware of the differences of doing business among the European countries. Even though they are unified for economic purposes, the countries in Europe maintain their respective cultures. Depending on the particular country an entrepreneur seeks to do business with, differences should be understood before expanding operations there. For example, even though many experts consider English the international language of business, the French, Germans, and Spanish have a strong bias for their own languages. It has been pointed out that you can always "buy" in English, but you will have to "sell" in the other country's language.

In addition, each country has a valued culture with customs that should not be ignored. The following examples illustrate the importance of being culturally prepared for European business:

- ☐ Suit jackets must stay on in offices, in restaurants, and on the street, even during the summer months in Europe.

- ☐ First names are seldom used without invitation in Europe.

- ☐ Lighter handshakes are a greeting standard except for southern and eastern Europe.

- ☐ For all business introductions the exchange of business cards is expected.

- ☐ In Italy, handshakes are a national pastime, yet the Italians seldom remember names on first introduction.

- ☐ In Greece, handshakes, embraces, and kissing are all forms of business greetings.

- ☐ Punctuality is a *must* in Europe.

As these examples illustrate, in Europe socializing, etiquette, patience, and protocol are integral parts of doing business.

Entrepreneurs should contact the International Trade Administration (ITA) of the U.S. Department of Commerce in order to gain more information on specific countries.

SOURCE: Alan M. Rugman and Richard M. Hodgetts, *International Business* (New York: McGraw-Hill, 1995), Chapter 17; and David Fairlamb, "For U.S. Small Biz, Fertile Soil in Europe," *BusinessWeek Online* (spring 2002).

stock and not have control over the company. In some instances the government may dictate whom a firm may hire, what pricing structure the firm must use, and how earnings will be distributed. This causes some concern as to exactly who is in control of the organization. Because of the difficulty of identifying direct investments, governmental agencies have had to establish arbitrary definitions of the term. A direct foreign investment typically involves ownership of 10 to 25 percent of the voting stock in a foreign enterprise.[67]

A firm can make a direct foreign investment by several methods. One is to acquire an interest in an ongoing foreign operation. This initially may be a minority interest in the firm but enough to exert influence on the management of the operation. A second method is to obtain a majority interest in a foreign company. In this case the company becomes a subsidiary of the acquiring firm. Third, the acquiring firm may simply purchase part of the assets of a foreign concern in order to establish a direct investment. An additional alternative is to build a facility in a foreign country.

An entrepreneur may want to make a direct foreign investment for a number of reasons. One is the possibility of trade restrictions. Some countries have prohibitions or restrictive trade barriers on imports of certain products. These barriers can make exporting costly or impossible. In addition, foreign governments may grant tax incentives to a firm seeking direct investment in that country. These incentives can be attractive if the anticipated rate of return is estimated to be higher at the foreign location than domestically.

Direct investment can be an exciting venture for small firms making efforts to increase their sales and their competitive positions in the marketplace. However, it is sometimes not practical for a firm to make a direct investment in a foreign location. If the firm has a unique or proprietary product or manufacturing process, it may want to consider the concept of licensing.

Licensing

Licensing is a business arrangement in which the manufacturer of a product (or a firm with proprietary rights over certain technology or trademarks) grants permission to some other group or individual to manufacture that product in return for specified royalties or other payments. Foreign licensing covers myriad contractual arrangements in which the business (licenser) provides patents, trademarks, manufacturing expertise, or technical services to a foreign business (licensee). Under such an arrangement, the entrepreneur need not make an extensive capital outlay to participate in the international market. Nor does the licenser have to be concerned with the daily production, marketing, technical, or management requirements; the licensee will handle all of this. The foreign firm merely looks to the domestic firm for expertise and, perhaps, an additional opportunity to sell a product owned by the licenser.

For developing an international licensing arrangement, three basic types of programs are available:

1. *Patents.* If the entrepreneur decides to use the patent approach, he or she should begin with a valid U.S. patent. Within one year, the entrepreneur should then file for patents in the countries where business will be transacted. Although this step can be expensive, it is essential because this action will give him or her a stronger bargaining position. Keep in mind that the United States is trying to adjust its patent system from "first to invent" to the international system of "first to file." It's being referred to as "patent harmonization" in order to be compatible with the international marketplace. The new system includes safeguards for small inventors, such as an inexpensive system for provisional patents. The goals are to make the patent process more efficient and to offer better foreign protection for inventors.[68] Currently, a single patent filing could cost tens of thousands of dollars in fees if you include all the attorney fees. The entrepreneur must file multiple applications as a defense against competitors—particularly in a global economy. A rule of thumb is that gaining sufficient protection for a patent internationally could cost about $100,000. Filing ten related patents to create a protective "picket

fence" around his or her invention could cost the entrepreneur $1 million. Self-defense has increased the cost of international patent protection.[69]

2. *Trademarks.* Due to the difficulties that can occur in direct translations, it may be advisable for the entrepreneur to have more than one trademark licensed for the same product. The entrepreneur should keep in mind, however, that if the product is not well recognized in the international market, he or she will not be able to use it as a major incentive in the bargaining phase. Sometimes, licensees will want the patent rights but prefer to use their own trademarks. This can be particularly true if the foreign firm is well established.

3. *Technical Know-How.* This type of licensing is often the hardest to enforce since it depends on the security of secrecy agreements. (The licenser should sign an agreement to prevent the licensee from legally revealing trade secrets.) In some localities, governments have strict regulations governing the use of technical know-how licensing. Frequently, one may protect the technical capabilities for only five years before the licensee is free to use this know-how without paying royalties. However, keep in mind that this may differ from country to country, depending on the particular regulations. Because this is a complex process, the entrepreneur must continue to develop his or her technical capabilities to ensure an ongoing international need for the company's services.[70]

To arrange for licensing, these steps should be followed:

1. Obtain an enforceable and secured patent, trademark, or know-how position.
2. Allocate adequate resources for research, legal, and travel expenses.
3. Research interested foreign markets to be sure the product can be produced and marketed there.
4. Start with countries having a minimum of governmental regulation.
5. Make a tentative list of countries in order of preference.
6. Prepare attractive product catalogs and promotional brochures in different foreign languages.
7. Build a list of potential foreign licensees through consultation with trade associations, the U.S. Chamber of Commerce, the U.S. Department of Commerce, and commercial attachés at embassies in Washington, D.C., or at U.S. embassies in foreign countries.
8. Contact the high-potential licensees and arrange visits for exploratory meetings.
9. Develop criteria for selecting firms to become licensees. Some factors to evaluate are marketing, production, customer base, channel strength, service support, reputation, and financial capabilities.

Advantages and Disadvantages

Licensing can be an extremely attractive way to enter the international arena. It requires a minimal capital outlay and can generate savings in tariffs and transportation costs. Another advantage is that licensing is a more realistic means of expansion than exporting, particularly for the high-tech firm. In addition, access to the market is easier in comparison with equity investments, and foreign governments are more likely to give their approval because technology is being brought into the country. Finally, a potential exists for the licensees to become partners and contributors in improving the "learning curve" of technology.

Disadvantages to licensing also exist. First, it is possible the licensee will become a competitor after the contract expires. Second, the licenser must get the licensee to meet contractual obligations and to adjust products or services to fit the licensee's market. Third, the licensing entrepreneur must manage the relationship's conditions and circumstances, as well as resolve conflicts or misunderstandings as they occur. Finally, the integrity and independence of both the licenser and licensee must be maintained.

To be competitive with larger firms, small businesses have to be on the cutting edge of bringing in new and innovative technology. Moreover, some small firms may not have the financial resources available to participate in the international marketplace by exporting, joint venture, or direct investment. For many of these firms, international licensing is a viable and exciting method of expanding operations.[71]

Achieving Entrepreneurial Leadership in the New Millennium

Entrepreneurial leadership may be the most critical element in the management of high growth ventures. Terms such as "visionary" and "strategic" have been used when describing different types of leaders. Table 16.7 provides a comprehensive description of strategic leaders, visionary leaders, and managerial leaders. It is the concept behind strategic leadership that research has demonstrated to be the most effective in growing organizations.[72] Researchers Ireland and Hitt identified some of the most important concepts in effective strategic leadership.[73] This type of leadership can be classified as **entrepreneurial leadership**, which arises when an entrepreneur attempts to manage the fast-paced, growth-oriented company.[74]

Entrepreneurial leadership can be defined as the entrepreneur's ability to anticipate, envision, maintain flexibility, think strategically, and work with others to initiate changes that will create a viable future for the organization.[75] If these leadership processes are difficult for competitors to understand and, hence, to imitate, the firm will create a competitive advantage.

Today's fast-paced economy has created a new competitive landscape—one in which events change constantly and unpredictably. These changes are revolutionary in nature—that is, they happen swiftly and are relentless in their frequency, affecting virtually all parts of an organization simultaneously. The ambiguity resulting from revolutionary changes challenges firms and their strategic abilities to increase the speed of the decision-making processes through which strategies are formulated and implemented.[76] (Table 16.8 provides a list of key concepts that should be kept in mind as the firm grows.)

Growth-oriented firms need to adopt a new competitive mind-set—one in which flexibility, speed, innovation, and strategic leadership are valued highly. With this mind-set, firms can identify and completely exploit opportunities that emerge in the new competitive landscape. These opportunities surface primarily because of the disequilibrium that is created by continuous changes (especially technological changes). More specifically, although uncertainty and disequilibrium often result in seemingly hostile and intensely rivalrous conditions, these conditions may simultaneously yield significant product-driven growth opportunities. Through effective entrepreneurial leadership, growth firms can adapt their behaviors and exploit such opportunities.[77]

Table 16.7 Strategic, Visionary, and Managerial Leadership

STRATEGIC LEADERS

- ✓ synergistic combination of managerial and visionary leadership
- ✓ emphasis on ethical behavior and value-based decisions
- ✓ oversee operating (day-to-day) and strategic (long-term) responsibilities
- ✓ formulate and implement strategies for immediate impact and preservation of long-term goals to enhance organizational survival, growth, and long-term viability
- ✓ have strong, positive expectations of the performance they expect from their superiors, peers, subordinates, and themselves
- ✓ use strategic controls and financial controls, with emphasis on strategic controls
- ✓ use, and interchange, tacit and explicit knowledge on individual and organizational levels
- ✓ use linear and nonlinear thinking patterns
- ✓ believe in strategic choice, that is, their choices make a difference in their organizations and environment

VISIONARY LEADERS

- ✓ are proactive, shape ideas, change the way people think about what is desirable, possible, and necessary
- ✓ work to develop choices, fresh approaches to long standing problems; work from high-risk positions
- ✓ are concerned with ideas; relate to people in intuitive and empathetic ways
- ✓ feel separate from their environment; work in, but do not belong to, organizations; sense of who they are does not depend on work
- ✓ influence attitudes and opinions of others within the organization
- ✓ concerned with insuring future of organization, especially through development and management of people
- ✓ more embedded in complexity, ambiguity, and information overload; engage in multifunctional, integrative tasks
- ✓ know less than their functional area experts
- ✓ more likely to make decisions based on values
- ✓ more willing to invest in innovation, human capital, and creating and maintaining an effective culture to ensure long-term viability
- ✓ focus on tacit knowledge and develop strategies as communal forms of tacit knowledge that promote enactment of a vision
- ✓ utilize nonlinear thinking
- ✓ believe in strategic choice, that is, their choices make a difference in their organizations and environment

MANAGERIAL LEADERS

- ✓ are reactive; adopt passive attitudes toward goals; goals arise out of necessities, not desires and dreams; goals based on past
- ✓ view work as an enabling process involving some combination of ideas and people interacting to establish strategies
- ✓ relate to people according to their roles in the decision-making process
- ✓ see themselves as conservators and regulators of existing order; sense of who they are depends on their role in organization
- ✓ influence actions and decisions of those with whom they work
- ✓ involved in situations and contexts characteristic of day-to-day activities
- ✓ concerned with, and more comfortable in, functional areas of responsibilities
- ✓ expert in their functional area
- ✓ less likely to make value-based decisions
- ✓ engage in, and support, short-term, least-cost behavior to enhance financial performance figures
- ✓ focus on managing the exchange and combination of explicit knowledge and ensuring compliance to standard operating procedures
- ✓ utilize linear thinking
- ✓ believe in determinism, that is, the choices they make are determined by their internal and external environments

Source: W. Glenn Rowe, "Creating Wealth in Organizations: The Role of Strategic Leadership," *Academy of Management Executive* 15(1) (2001): 82.

Table 16.8 Components of Entrepreneurial Leadership

1. Determining the firm's purpose or vision
2. Exploiting and maintaining the core competencies
3. Developing human capital
4. Sustaining an effective organizational culture
5. Emphasizing ethical practices
6. Establishing balanced organizational controls

Source: R. Duane Ireland and Michael A. Hitt, "Achieving and Maintaining Competitiveness in the 21st Century: Role of Strategic Leadership," *Academy of Management Executive* 13(1): 43–57.

Summary

A typical life cycle of a venture has five stages: development, start-up, growth, stabilization, and innovation or decline. This chapter focused on ways to maintain an entrepreneurial frame of mind while making the necessary adjustments for dealing with the growth phase.

In building the desired adaptive firm, entrepreneurs need to be concerned with three important responsibilities: (1) increasing the perception of opportunity, (2) institutionalizing change as the venture's goals, and (3) instilling the desire to be innovative.

The transition from an entrepreneurial style to a managerial approach was reviewed. A seven-step process for achieving this transition was described. The balance between the entrepreneurial focus and the administrative focus was then considered. This balance was demonstrated by considering five major factors: strategic orientation, commitment to seize opportunities, commitment of resources, control of resources, and management structure. This differentiation of major factors is important for analyzing aspects of the venture that need either more administrative or more entrepreneurial emphasis.

The chapter then examined the importance of a venture's growth stage. Underscoring the metamorphosis a venture goes through, four factors were discussed: control, responsibility, tolerance of failure, and change.

In addition, the challenge of managing paradox and contradiction was presented. The myriad challenges resulting from entrepreneurial growth involve the conflicts between rigid, bureaucratic designs and flexible, organic designs. The focus and style of decision making differ in the early stages from those observed in the later stages of a venture. Networking for external resources may be one solution that satisfies the need for simultaneous decisions during rapid growth. Another solution for handling decisions during growth is responsibility charting, which involves assigning a type of participation to a particular role for a specific decision. The managerial skill of delegation was also examined to emphasize the importance of giving up specific managerial duties to free up the entrepreneur's time to think and to plan.

Doing business globally has rapidly become one of the most profitable and popular strategies for many entrepreneurial ventures. The North American Free Trade Agreement, forged among Canada, Mexico, and the United States, and the EU (European Union) are examples of the powerful economic forces that have created opportunities for entrepreneurs in the international marketplace. This chapter discussed five ways the entrepreneur can actively engage in the international market: *importing,* which involves buying goods from other countries; *exporting,* which takes a variety of forms including export management companies, freight forwarders, and foreign sales corporations; *joint ventures; direct foreign investment;* and *licensing,* which takes a number of different forms and has both advantages and disadvantages.

Finally, the concept of entrepreneurial leadership was introduced as a way for entrepreneurs to anticipate, envision, maintain flexibility, think strategically, and work with others to initiate changes that will create a viable future for the growth-oriented venture.

Key Terms and Concepts

adaptive firm	growth wall
direct foreign investment	importing
domestic international sales corporation (DISC)	joint venture
effective delegation	learning curve concept
entrepreneurial leadership	licensing
export management company	life-cycle stages
exporting	new-venture development
external resources	responsibility charting
foreign sales corporation (FSC)	stabilization stage
freight forwarder	start-up activities
growth stage	

Review and Discussion Questions

1. Briefly identify and describe the stages of development for a new venture.

2. Firms that fail to innovate will die. What does this statement mean in the context of new ventures?

3. What are the dangers of an entrepreneur evolving into a bureaucrat?

4. How can entrepreneurs build an adaptive firm? Be complete in your answer.

5. Successful ventures balance entrepreneurial characteristics with managerial style. What does this statement mean?

6. Comparing the entrepreneurial focus with the administrative focus involves five major areas of consideration. What are these areas?

7. Identify and describe the four key factors that need to be considered during the growth stage.

8. What is meant by managing paradox and contradiction?

9. Identify some examples of conflicting designs of structural factors. (Use Table 16.3.)

10. Describe the concepts of networking and responsibility charting, and explain their potential for improving entrepreneurs' decision-making abilities.

11. Identify five unique managerial concerns of small businesses.

12. What are some of the advantages and disadvantages associated with the distinction of small size?

13. Define the one-person-band syndrome.

14. Why is delegation so important to entrepreneurs who are making the transition from an entrepreneurial venture to the diversified operations of the growth stage? Explain in detail.

15. Describe some of the facts from the *Global Entrepreneurship Monitor* that indicate increasing global activity in entrepreneurship.

16. Identify the five most common methods for entrepreneurs to engage in the international marketplace.

17. How does a joint venture work? What are the advantages of this arrangement? What are the disadvantages?

18. How does a licensing arrangement work? What are the advantages and disadvantages of such an arrangement?

19. Explain the concept of entrepreneurial leadership and list some of its key components.

Experiential Exercise

The Venture Life Cycle

Listed below are the five basic phases or stages of the typical life cycle of a venture, labeled A through E. Rank these from *1* to *5*, beginning with the first phase and continuing to the last. Then examine the list of activities (a through j) and place a *1* next to those that happen during the first phase of the venture, on down to a *5* next to those that occur during the last phase. Answers are provided at the end of the exercise.

A. _____ Growth

B. _____ Innovation or decline

C. _____ Start-up

D. _____ Stabilization

E. _____ New-venture development

a. _____ Transition from one-person leadership to team management leadership

b. _____ New-product development

c. _____ Search for capital

d. _____ Increased competition

e. _____ Venture assessment

f. _____ Attempts to acquire other firms

g. _____ Consumer indifference to the entrepreneur's goods or services

h. _____ Accumulation of resources

i. _____ Major changes in entrepreneurial strategy

j. _____ Development of an effective entrepreneurial team

Answers:

A. 3	a. 3	f. 5
B. 5	b. 5	g. 4
C. 2	c. 2	h. 1
D. 4	d. 4	i. 3
E. 1	e. 1	j. 2

Case 16.1

Hendrick's Way

When Hendrick Harding started his consumer products firm, he was convinced he had a winning product. His small, compact industrial drill was easier to use than any other on the market and cost 30 percent less than any of the competitors' drills. The orders began to pour in, and within six months Hendrick's sales surpassed his first year's estimate. At the end of the first 12 months of operation his firm was grossing more than $50,000 a month, and he had a six-week backlog in filling orders.

The rapid growth of the firm continued for two years. Beginning about four months ago, however, Hendrick began to notice a dip in sales. The major reason appeared to be a competitive product that cost 10 percent less than Hendrick's drill and offered all the same benefits and features. Hendrick believes that with a couple of minor adjustments he can improve his product and continue to dominate the market.

On the other hand, Hendrick is somewhat disturbed by the comments of one of his salespeople, George Simonds. George spends most of his time on the road and gets to talk to a great many customers. Here is what he had to say to Hendrick: "Your industrial drill has really set the market on its ear. And we should be able to sell a modified version of it for at least another 36 months before making any additional changes. However, you need to start thinking about adding other products to the line. Let's face it; we are a one-product company. That's not good. We have to expand our product line if we are to grow. Otherwise, I can't see much future for us."

The problem with this advice is that Hendrick does not want to grow larger. He is happy selling just the industrial drill. He believes that if he continues to modify and change the drill, he can maintain a large market share and the company will continue to be profitable. As he explained to George, "I see the future as more of the past. I really don't think there will be a great many changes in this product. There will be modifications, sure, but nothing other than that. I think this firm can live off the industrial drill for at least the next 25 years. We've got a great thing going. I don't see any reason for change. And I certainly don't want to come out with a second product. There's no need for it."

Questions

1. What is the danger in Hendrick's thinking? Explain in detail.

2. Could the concept of understanding managerial versus entrepreneurial as described in the chapter be of any value to Hendrick? Why or why not?

3. Using Table 16.2 as your point of reference, how would you describe Hendrick's focus? Based on your evaluation, what recommendations would you make to him?

Case 16.2

Keeping Things Going

The Clayton Company has grown 115 percent in the past year and 600-plus percent in the past three years. A large portion of this growth is attributable to Jan Clayton's philosophy of hiring the best possible computer systems people and giving them the freedom they need to do their jobs.

Most of Jan's personnel operate as part of work teams that analyze, design, and implement computer systems for clients. The way the process works is this: First, the company will get a call from a potential client indicating that it needs to have a computer system installed or a special software written for its operations. Jan will send over one of her people to talk to the client and analyze the situation. If it turns out that the Clayton Company has the expertise and personnel to handle the job, the client will be quoted a price. If this price is acceptable, a Clayton group will be assigned the project.

An example of a typical project is the client who called three weeks ago and wanted to purchase five personal computers for the firm's engineering staff. The company wanted these machines hooked up to the main computer. Additionally, the firm wanted its computer-aided design software to be modified so the engineers could see their computer-generated drawings in a variety of colors, not just in monochrome. The Clayton group installed the entire system and modified the software in 10 working days.

Jan realizes that the growth of her enterprise will be determined by two factors. One is the creativity and ingenuity of her work force. The other is the ability to attract talented personnel. "This business is heavily labor intensive," she explained. "If someone wants a computer system installation, that may take 100 labor hours. If I don't have the people to handle the project, I have to turn it down. My expansion is heavily dependent on hiring and training talented people. Additionally, I need more than just hard workers. I need creative people who can figure out new approaches to handling complex problems. If I can do these two things, I can stay a jump ahead of the competition. Otherwise, I won't be able to survive."

In dealing with these key factors for success, Jan has initiated three changes. First, she has instituted a bonus system tied to sales; these bonuses are shared by all of the personnel. Second, she gives quarterly salary increases, with the greatest percentages going to employees who are most active in developing new programs and procedures for handling client problems. Third, she has retreats every six months in which the entire staff goes for a long weekend to a mountain area where they spend three days discussing current work-related problems and ways of dealing with them. Time is also devoted to social events and to working on developing an esprit de corps among the personnel.

Questions

1. In what phase of the venture life cycle is Jan's firm currently operating? Defend your answer.

2. How are Jan's actions helping to build an adaptive firm? Give three specific examples.

3. If Jan's firm continues to grow, what recommendations would you make for future action? What else should Jan be thinking about doing in order to keep things moving smoothly? Be specific in your answer.

Notes

1. Jeanie Daniel Duck, "Managing Change: The Art of Balancing," *Harvard Business Review* (November/December 1993): 109–118.

2. Alfred Chandler, *Strategy and Structure* (Cambridge, MA: MIT Press, 1962).

3. Jeffrey G. Covin, Dennis P. Slevin, and Michael B. Heeley, "Pioneers and Followers: Competitive Tactics, Environment, and Firm Growth," *Journal of Business Venturing* (March 2000): 175–210.

4. Hugh M. O'Neill, "How Entrepreneurs Manage Growth," *Long Range Planning* (February 1983): 117; and Donald F. Kuratko, "Managing Entrepreneurial Growth," *Entrepreneurship Development Review* (winter 1988): 1–5.

5. For more on this example, see E. Bruce Peters, "The Conflict at Apple Was Almost Inevitable," *Research & Development* (December 1985): 58–60; Richard E. Crandall, "Company Life Cycles: The Effects of Growth on Structure and Personnel," *Personnel* (September 1987): 28–36; and Kenneth E. Marino and Marc J. Dollinger, "Top Management Succession in Entrepreneurial Firms," *Journal of Management Case Studies* (spring 1987): 70–79.

6. David E. Terpstra and Philip D. Olson, "Entrepreneurial Start-up and Growth: A Classification of Problems," *Entrepreneurship Theory and Practice* (spring 1993): 5–20.

7. See Jacqueline N. Hood and John E. Young, "Entrepreneurship's Requisite Areas of Development: A Survey of Top Executives in Successful Entrepreneurial Firms," *Journal of Business Venturing* (March 1993): 115–135.

8. Morten T. Hansen, Nitin Nohria, and Thomas Tierney, "What's Your Strategy for Managing Knowledge?" *Harvard Business Review* 77(2) (1999): 106–116.

9. Shaker A. Zahra, "The Changing Rules of Global Competitiveness in the 21st Century," *Academy of Management Executive* 13(1) (1999): 36–42.

10. Howard H. Stevenson and Jose Carlos Jarillo-Mossi, "Preserving Entrepreneurship as Companies Grow," *Journal of Business Strategy* (summer 1986): 10.

11. Ibid., 11; see also Jill Kickul and Lisa K. Gundry, "Prospecting for Strategic Advantage: The Proactive Entrepreneurial Personality and Small Firm Innovation," *Journal of Small Business Management* 40(2) (2002): 85–97.

12. Vesa Routamaa and Jukka Vesalainen, "Types of Entrepreneurs and Strategic Level Goal Setting," *International Small Business Journal* (spring 1987): 19–29; see also Lanny Herron and Richard B. Robinson, Jr., "A Structural Model of the Effects of Entrepreneurial Characteristics on Venture Performance," *Journal of Business Venturing* (May 1993): 281–294.

13. Donald F. Kuratko, Jeffrey S. Hornsby, and Laura M. Corso, "Building an Adaptive Firm," *Small Business Forum* (spring 1996): 41–48.

14. Stevenson and Jarillo-Mossi, "Preserving Entrepreneurship," 13–16.

15. Steven H. Hanks and L. R. McCarrey, "Beyond Survival: Reshaping Entrepreneurial Vision in Successful Growing Ventures," *Journal of Small Business Strategy* (spring 1993): 1–12.

16. Thomas J. Peters and Robert H. Waterman, Jr., *In Search of Excellence* (New York: Harper & Row, 1982).

17. See Sanjay Prasad Thakur, "Size of Investment, Opportunity Choice and Human Resources in New Venture Growth: Some Typologies," *Journal of Business Venturing* (May 1999): 283–309.

18. Jon R. Katzenbach and Douglas K. Smith, "The Discipline of Teams," *Harvard Business Review* (March/April 1993): 111–120; and Alexander L. M. Dingee, Brian Haslett, and Leonard E. Smollen, "Characteristics of a Successful Entrepreneurial Management Team," in *Annual Editions 00/01* (Guilford, CT: Dushkin/McGraw Hill, 2000/2001), 71–75.

19. Charles W. Hofer and Ram Charan, "The Transition to Professional Management: Mission Impossible?" *American Journal of Small Business* (summer 1984): 3; see also William Lowell, "An Entrepreneur's Journey to the Next Level," *Small Business Forum* (spring 1996): 68–74.

20. Ibid., 4.

21. Ibid., 6.

22. John B. Miner, "Entrepreneurs, High Growth Entrepreneurs, and Managers: Contrasting and Over-lapping Motivational Patterns," *Journal of Business Venturing* (July 1990): 221–234; and Michael J. Roberts, "Managing Growth," in *New Business Ventures and the Entrepreneur* (New York: Irwin-McGraw Hill, 1999), 460–464.

23. Howard H. Stevenson and David E. Gumpert, "The Heart of Entrepreneurship," *Harvard Business Review* (March/April 1985): 85.

24. Ibid., 86–87.

25. Jeffrey G. Covin and Dennis P. Slevin, "New Venture Strategic Posture, Structure, and Performance: An Industry Life Cycle Analysis," *Journal of Business Venturing* (March 1990): 123–133.

26. Ikujiro Nonaka and Tervo Yamanovchi, "Managing Innovation as a Self-Renewing Process," *Journal of Business Venturing* (September 1989): 299–315.

27. Charles J. Fombrun and Stefan Wally, "Structuring Small Firms for Rapid Growth," *Journal of Business Venturing* (March 1989): 107–122; and Donna J. Kelley and Mark P. Rice, "Advantage Beyond Founding: The Strategic Use of Technologies," *Journal of Business Venturing* 17(1) (2002): 41–58.

28. Donald C. Hambrick and Lynn M. Crozier, "Stumblers and Stars in the Management of Rapid Growth," *Journal of Business Venturing* (January 1985): 31–45.

29. Richard L. Osborne, "Second Phase Entrepreneurship: Breaking Through the Growth Wall," *Business Horizons* (January/February 1994): 80–86.

30. Ibid., 82–85.

31. John W. Mullins and David Forlani, "Missing the Boat or Sinking the Boat: A Study of New Venture Decision Making," *Journal of Business Venturing* 20(1) (January 2005): 47–69.

32. Thomas N. Gilmore and Robert K. Kazanjian, "Clarifying Decision Making in High Growth Ventures: The Use of Responsibility Charting," *Journal of Business Venturing* (January 1989): 69–83.

33. Jose Carlos Jarillo-Mossi, "Entrepreneurship and Growth: The Strategic Use of External Resources," *Journal of Business Venturing* (March 1989): 133–147.

34. Ibid., 135.

35. James J. Chrisman and W. Ed McMullan, "Outsider Assistance as a Knowledge Resource of New Venture Survival," *Journal of Small Business Management* 42(3) (July 2004): 229–244.

36. Gilmore and Kazanjian, "Clarifying Decision Making in High Growth Ventures," 69–83.

37. Ibid., 81.

38. See Jerry R. Cornwell, "The Entrepreneur as a Building Block for Community," *Journal of Developmental Entrepreneurship* (fall/winter 1998): 141–148.

39. David E. Gumpert and David P. Boyd, "The Loneliness of the Small Business Owner," *Harvard Business Review* (November/December 1984): 19–24.

40. Douglas W. Naffziger and Donald F. Kuratko, "An Investigation into the Prevalence of Planning in Small Business," *Journal of Business and Entrepreneurship* 3(2) (October 1991): 99–110.

41. Charles R. Hobbs, "Time Power," *Small Business Reports* (January 1990): 46–55; and Jack Falvey, "New and Improved Time Management," *Small Business Reports* (July 1990): 14–17.

42. Terry L. Besser, "Community Involvement and the Perception of Success Among Small Business Operators in Small Towns," *Journal of Small Business Management* (October 1999): 16–29; and Rhonda Walker Mack, "Event Sponsorship: An Exploratory Study of Small Business Objectives, Practices, and Perceptions," *Journal of Small Business Management* (July 1999): 25–30.

43. See Richard M. Hodgetts and Donald F. Kuratko, *Management,* 3rd ed. (San Diego, CA: Harcourt Brace Jovanovich, 1991), 279–282.

44. Wayne C. Shannon, "Empowerment: The Catchword of the 90's," *Quality Progress* (July 1991): 62–63.

45. Timothy W. Firnstahl, "Letting Go," *Harvard Business Review* (September/October 1986): 15.

46. Ibid., 15–16.

47. Ibid., 16.

48.   Adapted from *Firnstahl*, "Letting Go," 18.

49.   Shaker A. Zahra, "The Changing Rules of Global Competitiveness in the 21st Century," *Academy of Management Executive* 13(1) (1999): 36–42; Rosebeth Moss Kanter, "Managing the Extended Enterprise in a Globally Connected World," *Organizational Dynamics* (summer 1999): 7–23; and Mike W. Peng, "How Entrepreneurs Create Wealth in Transition Economies," *Academy of Management Executive* 15(1) (2001): 95–110.

50.   Paul D. Reynolds, S. Michael Camp, William D. Bygrave, Erkko Autio, and Michael Hay, *Global Entrepreneurship Monitor* (Kansas City, MO: Kauffman Center for Entrepreneurial Leadership, 2001), 6.

51.   Shaker Zahra, James Hayton, Jeremy Marcel, and Hugh O'Neill, "Fostering Entrepreneurship During International Expansion: Managing Key Challenges," *European Management Journal* 19(4) (2001): 359–369.

52.   Richard M. Hodgetts and Donald F. Kuratko, *Management,* 3rd ed. (San Diego, CA: Harcourt Brace Jovanovich, 1991), 96–100.

53.   Nabuaki Namiki, "Export Strategy for Small Business," *Journal of Small Business Management* (April 1988): 32–37.

54.   Ibid., 35.

55.   *Seven Steps to Exporting* (Indianapolis: Indiana District Export Council, 1990), 15A; see also *A Basic Guide to Exporting,* (1998) http://www.export.gov.

56.   *Seven Steps to Exporting,* 16; and *A Basic Guide to Exporting.*

57.   For some useful joint-venture rules, see Carl F. Fey, "Success Strategies for Russian Foreign Joint Ventures," *Business Horizons* (November/December 1995): 49–54; and John A. Pearce II and Louise Hatfield, "Performance Effects of Alternate Joint Venture Resource Responsibility Structures," *Journal of Business Venturing* 17(4) (July 2002): 343–364.

58.   Keith W. Glaister and Peter J. Buckley, "Performance Relationships in U.K. International Alliances," *Management International Review* 39(2) (1999): 123–147.

59.   See also Geert Duysters, Ard-Pieter de Man, and Leo Wildeman, "A Network Approach to Alliance Management," *European Management Journal* (April 1999): 182–187.

60.   See also T. K. Das and Being Sheng Ten, "Managing Risks in Strategic Alliances," *Academy of Management Executive* (November 1999): 50–62.

61.   Robert L. Simison and Horihiko Shirouzu, "GM Pursues New Links with Japanese," *The Wall Street Journal* (December 3, 1999): A3.

62.   Derrick E. D'Souza and Patricia P. McDougall, "Third World Joint Venturing: A Strategic Option for the Smaller Firm," *Entrepreneurship Theory and Practice* (summer 1989): 20.

63.   Marina Papanastassiou and Robert Pearce, "Technology Sourcing and the Strategic Roles of Manufacturing Subsidiaries in the U.K.: Local Competencies and Global Competitiveness," *Management International Review* 37(1) (1997): 5–25.

64.   For more on this topic, see Jean-Marie Hiltrop, "The Quest for the Best: Human Resource Practices to Attract and Retain Talent," *European Management Journal* (August 1999): 422–430.

65.   See also Robert Bruner and Robert Spekman, "The Dark Side of Alliances: Lessons from Volvo–Renault," *European Management Journal* (April 1998): 136–150.

66.   See Kenneth J. Fedor and William B. Werther, Jr., "Making Sense of Cultural Factors in International Alliances," *Organizational Dynamics* (spring 1995): 33–47; and Walter Kuemmerle, "Home Base and Knowledge Management in International Ventures," *Journal of Business Venturing* 17(2) (2002): 99–122.

67.   Richard M. Hodgetts and Fred Luthans, *International Management* (Boston: McGraw-Hill/Irwin, 2003), 252–272.

68.   Peter Coy, "The Global Patent Race Picks Up Speed," *Business Week* (August 9, 1993): 57–62; and "Patent Harmonization: Bad News for Inventors?" *Inc.* (November 1993): 34.

69.   Michael S. Malone, "The Smother of Invention," *Forbes* (July 24, 2002): 33–40.

70.   See Shengliang Deng et al., "A Guide to Intellectual Property Rights in Southeast Asia and China," *Business Horizons* (November/December 1996): 43–56.

71. Paul Westhead, Mike Wright, and Deniz Ucbasaran, "The Internationalization of New and Small Firms: A Resource-Based View," *Journal of Business Venturing* 16(4) (2001): 333–358.

72. W. Glenn Rowe, "Creating Wealth in Organizations: The Role of Strategic Leadership," *Academy of Management Executive* 15(1) (2001): 81–94.

73. R. Duane Ireland and Michael A. Hitt, "Achieving and Maintaining Strategic Competitiveness in the 21st Century: The Role of Strategic Leadership," *Academy of Management Executive* 13(1) (1999): 43–57.

74. Michael A. Hitt, R. Duane Ireland, S. Michael Camp, and Donald L. Sexton, "Strategic Entrepreneurship: Entrepreneurial Strategies for Wealth Creation," *Strategic Management Journal* 22(6) (special issue, 2001): 479–492; see also John L. Thompson, "A Strategic Perspective of Entrepreneurship," *International Journal of Entrepreneurial Behavior & Research* 5(6) (1999): 279–296.

75. Michael A. Hitt, R. Duane Ireland, and Robert E. Hoskisson, *Strategic Management: Competitiveness and Globalization,* 4th ed. (Mason, OH: South-Western/Thomson Learning, 2001).

76. E. H. Kessler and A. K. Chakrabarti, "Innovation Speed: A Conceptual Model of Context, Antecedents, and Outcomes," *Academy of Management Review* 21 (1996): 1143–1191.

77. Shaker A. Zahra, "Environment, Corporate Entrepreneurship, and Financial Performance: A Taxonomic Approach," *Journal of Business Venturing* 8 (1993): 319–340; and Donald F. Kuratko, R. Duane Ireland, and Jeffrey S. Hornsby, "Improving Firm Performance Through Entrepreneurial Actions: Acordia's Corporate Entrepreneurship Strategy," *Academy of Management Executive* 15(4) (2001): 60–71.

17 Valuation of Entrepreneurial Ventures

The real fair market value of anything is defined as the price and terms agreed on between a willing seller and a willing buyer. However, in interpreting this definition, give careful consideration to the circumstances of the buyer and seller.

Douglas E. Kellogg

"How to Buy a Small Manufacturing Business"

Harvard Business Review

Chapter Objectives

1 To explain the importance of valuation

2 To describe the basic elements of due diligence

3 To outline ten key questions to ask when buying an ongoing venture

4 To examine the underlying issues involved in the acquisition process

5 To outline the various aspects of analyzing a business

6 To present the major points to consider when establishing a firm's value

7 To highlight the available methods of valuing a venture

8 To examine the three principal methods currently used in business valuations

9 To consider additional factors affecting a venture's valuation

10 To discuss the leveraged buyout (LBO) as a method of purchasing a business

The Importance of Business Valuation

Every entrepreneur should be able to calculate the value of his or her business and also should be able to determine the value of a competitor's operation. Such **business valuation** is essential in these situations:

- ☐ Buying or selling a business, division, or major asset
- ☐ Establishing an employee stock option plan (ESOP) or profit-sharing plan for employees
- ☐ Raising growth capital through stock warrants or convertible loans
- ☐ Determining inheritance tax liability (potential estate tax liability)
- ☐ Giving a gift of stock to family members
- ☐ Structuring a buy/sell agreement with stockholders
- ☐ Attempting to buy out a partner
- ☐ Going public with the company or privately placing the stock

Equally important is the entrepreneur's desire to know the real value of the venture. This valuation can provide a scorecard for periodically tracking the increases or decreases in the business's value.[1]

Acquisition of an Entrepreneurial Venture

A prospective entrepreneur may seek to purchase a business venture rather than start up an enterprise. This can be a successful method of getting into business, but numerous factors need to be analyzed. Purchasing a business venture is a complex transaction, and the advice of professionals always should be sought. However, a few basic steps that can be easily understood are presented here, including the entrepreneur's personal preferences, examination of opportunities, evaluation of the selected venture, and key questions to ask.

Personal Preferences

Entrepreneurs need to recognize certain personal factors and to limit their choices of ventures accordingly. An entrepreneur's background, skills, interests, and experience are all important factors in selecting the type of business to buy. In addition, personal preferences for location and size of a business should guide the selection process. If an entrepreneur always has desired to own a business in the South or West, then that is exactly where the search should begin.

Examination of Opportunities

Entrepreneurs in search of a possible venture to buy need to examine the available opportunities through various sources:

- ☐ *Business brokers.* Professionals specializing in business opportunities often can provide leads and assistance in finding a venture for sale. However, the buyer should evaluate the broker's reputation, services, and contacts. The entrepreneur also should remember that the broker usually represents—and gets a commission on the sale from—the seller.

☐ *Newspaper ads.* "Business Opportunity" classified ads are another source. Because an ad often will appear in one paper and not another, it may be necessary to check the classified sections of all the papers in the area.

☐ *Trade sources.* Suppliers, distributors, manufacturers, trade publications, trade associations, and trade schools may have information about businesses for sale.

☐ *Professional sources.* Professionals such as management consultants, attorneys, and accountants often know of businesses available for purchase.

Evaluation of the Selected Venture

After the entrepreneur considers personal preferences and examines information sources, the next step is to evaluate specific factors of the venture being offered for sale:

☐ The business environment. The local environment for business should be analyzed to establish the potential of the venture in its present location.

☐ *Profits, sales, and operating ratios.* The business's profit potential is a key factor in evaluating the venture's attractiveness and in later determining a reasonable price for it. To estimate the potential earning power of the business, the buyer should review past profits, sales, and operating ratios and project sales and profits for the next one to two years. Valuation will be further discussed later in the chapter.

☐ *The business assets.* The tangible (physical) and intangible (for example, reputation) assets of the business need to be assessed. These assets should be examined:

   ☐ Inventory (age, quality, salability, condition)

   ☐ Furniture, equipment, fixtures (value, condition, leased or owned)

   ☐ Accounts receivable (age of outstanding debts, past collection periods, credit standing of customers)

   ☐ Trademarks, patents, copyrights, business name (value, role in the business's success, degree of competitive edge)

   ☐ Goodwill (reputation, established clientele, trusted name)

Due Diligence

In addition to evaluating the major points just presented, the entrepreneur should perform a complete "due diligence," which means a thorough analysis of every facet of the existing business. Figure 17.1 provides a due diligence outline that is used in assessing the viability of a firm's business plan. Notice how each major segment is analyzed by applying specific questions to that part. A more general approach may also be applied by the entrepreneur in order to better assess the viability of the potential purchase. The following list of questions highlight some of the critical areas that need to be addressed.[2]

1. *Why is this business being sold?* It is important to establish the owner's motivation for selling. Although the reason may be very good, such as retirement or ill health, an entrepreneur needs to investigate and verify it. If at any time the owner's reason for selling does not appear to be the prime motivation, then further research must be done on that particular business.

Figure 17.1 *Due Diligence Evaluation*

Executive Summary

    A. Company name. *Does the management team have what it takes to implement the plan?*

    B. Product/Service Offering. *Is the idea viable?*

    C. Key considerations uncovered by external research. *Are there conditions in the industry, competitive environment, market, or other areas not addressed in the plan?*

    D. Key considerations discovered through analysis of the plan. *Is there something the plan does not uncover or that needs to be put into the plan?*

    E. Financial summary

        1. Funding request. *Is it appropriate for success?*

        2. Valuation (pre-money). *What is their starting point?*

        3. Burn rate. *Is it sufficient or excessive? Does their request take this into account?*

        4. Evaluation of the viability of the stated rate of return/investment potential. *When operations are adjusted by your analysis, is the stated return still there?*

Narrative Analysis

    I. **Introduction** *(May be presented in bullets)*

        A. Date

        B. Review team members

        C. Name of company

        D. Name of CEO

        E. Date founded

        F. Location

        G. Funding goal

        H. Founders investment

        I. Prior venture funding

            1. When?

            2. How much?

            3. From whom?

    II. **The Industry** (broad focus)

        A. General industry information

            1. What are the chief characteristics of the industry (economic, technological, political, social, change)?

            2. How does the plan address these? How is the proposed venture impacted by these?

            3. How attractive is the industry in terms of its prospects for above average profitability?

            4. What has the industry growth rate been for the past five years, and what is it projected to be for the next five? Give specific support or justification for these projections.

            5. Have there been any recent transactions in the industry, such as IPOs, LBOs, private placements, mergers, or acquisitions? Describe the transactions and provide a brief explanation of the financial arrangements of each transaction.

        B. Competitive environment

            1. What competitive forces (entry barriers, substitutes, power of buyers and suppliers—rivalry is addressed in next section) are at work in the industry, and how strong are they?

            2. Has the plan identified the competitive environment and how the company will fit into that environment?

            3. Calculate total market available in dollars.

            4. Calculate degree of market saturation.

Figure 17.1 (Continued)

C. Primary Competitor Analysis—*In-depth*
1. Compare and contrast *major* competitors (from the plan and your own research) along core competitive dimensions, including but not limited to:

Product/Service	Market Share
Pricing	Technology
Distribution	Financial Backing
Marketing	Financial Performance
Operations	P/E (if publicly traded) or revenue multiplier
Strategic Partnerships	
1st Mover	

2. Calculate market share available for this firm not already captured by competitors (dollars and users). Is this enough market share to achieve the financial projections in the plan?
3. Which companies are in the strongest/weakest competitive position?
4. Who will likely make what competitive moves next?
5. What key factors will determine competitive success or failure?

III. **Target Market/Customer Base** (narrow focus)
A. Describe the target market: size, scope, growth, growth potential, growth/demand drivers, price sensitivity, sales cycle.
B. What is the need or want that the company is satisfying?
C. What are the barriers that will keep competitors from copying this venture's product or service? What market inefficiencies exist?
D. How strong are competitive forces (rivalry, substitutes) within this target market?
E. What has the growth rate of the target market been for the past five years, and what is it projected to be for the next five? Provide support/justification for these projections.

IV. **The Company** (*This section asks you to evaluate the plan in terms of the industry and target market characteristics discussed.*)
A. Value proposition: What does the company do, and how does it provide value to its customers, investors?
B. Management team
1. Does this team have what it takes to make this venture a success?
2. Is success dependent on one key person? If so, is this recognized and dealt with in the plan (succession, key man replacement, etc.)?
3. HR gaps? Plans to address gaps?
C. Business model
1. How does the company make money?
2. How and when does it plan to be profitable?
3. Does the plan follow a demonstrated success formula? Support with 1 to 2 examples. For example, briefly discuss similar companies in terms of size (revenues/employees), operations, revenue model, and/or business model. These companies could be direct competitors or similar firms that are not in the same market, just a similar type of company/model.
D. Strategy
1. How does the company plan on achieving success in its business model?
2. What other strategic approaches might work well in this situation? Give examples.
E. Marketing plan
1. How will the company convert prospects into customers?
2. Who makes the customer's purchase decisions? When and how are the decisions made? What dimensions are critical to the customer in making the decisions? Is the plan specific in defining their strategy in this area?
3. Does the company have a base of current customers? Does their plan address customer retention?

Figure 17.1 (Continued)

      F.   Operations

          1.   Does the company's operating plan make sense in terms of supporting its strategy and business model?

  V. **Company Situation Analysis**

      A.   What are the company's strengths, weaknesses, opportunities, and threats?

      B.   Look at your competitor analysis; is the company competitive on cost? Is it differentiated compared to competitors? How?

      C.   How strong is the company's competitive position? Are there entry barriers that protect the company? What key strategic factors support this proposition? Which ones are counter to its success?

      D.   What strategic issues does the company face?

 VI. **Financial Analysis** *(Select the ones that apply to this plan. Provide the analysis if it is appropriate and especially note if it is not included in the plan.)*

      A.   Ratio analysis: liquidity, solvency, profitability, viability.

      B.   Compare projected growth rates versus historical industry growth rates. State why this company will be able to sustain the projected rate above that of its industry. If it is determined that the projections are too optimistic, what can be expected?

      C.   Valuation

          1.   Calculate pre-money valuation. What supports this valuation (number of shares $\times$ price per share, current audited balance sheet/accepted revenue multiples, etc.)?

          2.   Triangulate this valuation by (1) comparing the P/E ratios or revenue multiples of similar companies and (2) discounting the company's cash flow projections.

      D.   Other financial considerations:

          1.   Start-up cash spent or needed

          2.   Current burn rate

          3.   Cash needed years one to five

          4.   Five-year revenues

          5.   Five-year profits

          6.   Break even:

               a.   Revenues

               b.   When

      E.   Comments regarding financial statements such as:

          1.   Accuracy

          2.   Abnormalities. Is the budget in line or out of hand? Is the accounting correct?

          3.   Needed assumptions

          4.   Other

VII. **Additional Comments and Concerns**

      A.   Is the plan well written? Is it concise and to the point?

      B.   Can the "layperson" understand it?

      C.   Is the idea viable?

      D.   Is this appropriate for venture investing? Can we expect enough growth? What is the risk/reward relationship?

      E.   Other

Appendices

  I. Resources/Bibliography

 II. Other detailed support organized by section in order of reference

Source: Bethesda, MD: Beacon Venture Capital, 2002.

2. *What is the physical condition of the business?* The overall condition of the facilities needs to be carefully assessed in order to avoid major expenses after the purchase. Sometimes owners sell a business simply to avoid remodeling the entire location.

3. *How many key personnel will remain?* In order to conduct a smooth transition, a purchasing entrepreneur needs to be sure which personnel will remain after the sale. Certain key personnel may be extremely valuable to the continuity of the venture.

4. *What is the degree of competition?* The answer to this question must cover two distinct parts: the quantity and the quality of competitors. In other words, how many competitors are there, and how strong are they?

5. *What are the conditions of the lease?* When the business is being sold but not the building or property, it is vital to know all of the conditions of the present lease. In addition, the landlord's future plans should be established as far as future lease provisions are concerned.

6. *Do any liens against the business exist?* This refers to the position of creditors and the liabilities of the business. Entrepreneurs should check for any delinquent payments or outstanding debt of any kind by the business.

7. *Will the owner sign a covenant not to compete?* Legal restraint of trade is the actual purpose here, since a purchaser does not want the seller reopening a firm in direct competition. Thus, the law allows a reasonable covenant to cover the time and distance within which the seller agrees not to compete.

8. *Are any special licenses required?* The buyer needs to verify the federal, state, or local requirements, if any, that pertain to the type of business being purchased.

9. *What are the future trends of the business?* This is an overall look at the particular industry trends and how this business will fit into them. In addition, the financial health of the business needs to be projected.

10. *How much capital is needed to buy?* The final purchase price is not the only factor to consider. Repairs, new inventory, opening expenses, and working capital are just a few of the additional costs that should be considered. Table 17.1 illustrates how to calculate the total amount needed for buying a business venture.[3]

Underlying Issues

Three issues underlie the acquisition of a business: (1) the differing goals of the buyer and seller, (2) the emotional bias of the seller, and (3) the reasons for the acquisition.

Goals of the Buyer and Seller

It is important to remember one's reasons for valuing an enterprise. Both major parties to the transaction, buyer and seller, will assign different values to the enterprise because of their basic objectives. The seller will attempt to establish the highest possible value for the business and will not heed the realistic considerations of the market, the environment, or the economy. To the seller the enterprise may represent a

Table 17.1   Total Amount Needed to Buy a Business

Family Living Expenses	From last paycheck to takeover day	$_____
	Moving expense	_____
	For three months after takeover day	_____
Purchase Price	Total amount (or down payment plus three monthly installments)	_____
Sales Tax	On purchased furniture and equipment	_____
Professional Services	Escrow, accounting, legal	_____
Deposits, Prepayments, Licenses	Last month's rent (first month's rent in Operating Expense below)	_____
	Utility deposits	_____
	Sales tax deposit	_____
	Business licenses	_____
	Insurance premiums	_____
Takeover Announcements	Newspaper advertising	_____
	Mail announcements	_____
	Exterior sign changes	_____
	New stationery and forms	_____
New Inventory		_____
New Fixtures and Equipment		_____
Remodeling and Redecorating		_____
Three Months' Operating Expense	Including loan repayments	_____
Reserve to Carry Customer Accounts		_____
Cash	Petty cash, change, etc.	_____
	Total	$_____

Note: Money for living and business expenses for at least three months should be set aside in a bank savings account and not used for any other purpose. This is a cushion to help get through the start-up period with a minimum of worry. If expense money for a longer period can be provided, it will add to peace of mind and help the buyer concentrate on building the business.

lifetime investment—or at the very least one that took a lot of effort. The buyer, on the other hand, will try to determine the lowest possible price to be paid. The enterprise is regarded as an investment for the buyer, and he or she must assess the profit potential. As a result, a pessimistic view often is taken. An understanding of both positions in the valuation process is important.

Emotional Bias

The second issue in valuing a business is the **emotional bias** of the seller. Whenever someone starts a venture, nurtures it through early growth, and makes it a profitable business, the person tends to believe the enterprise is worth a great deal more than outsiders believe it is worth. Entrepreneurs therefore must try to be as objective as possible in determining a fair value for the enterprise (realizing this fair amount will be negotiable).

Reasons for the Acquisition

The third issue in valuing a business is the reason an entrepreneur's business is being acquired. The following are some of the most common reasons for acquisition:

- Developing more growth-phase products by acquiring a firm that has developed new products in the company's industry

- Increasing the number of customers by acquiring a firm whose current customers will broaden substantially the company's customer base

- Increasing market share by acquiring a firm in the company's industry

- Improving or changing distribution channels by acquiring a firm with recognized superiority in the company's current distribution channel

- Expanding the product line by acquiring a firm whose products complement and complete the company's product line

- Developing or improving customer service operations by acquiring a firm with an established service operation, as well as a customer service network that includes the company's products

- Reducing operating leverage and increasing absorption of fixed costs by acquiring a firm that has a lower degree of operating leverage and can absorb the company's fixed costs

- Using idle or excess plant capacity by acquiring a firm that can operate in the company's current plant facilities

- Integrating vertically, either backward or forward, by acquiring a firm that is a supplier or distributor

- Reducing inventory levels by acquiring a firm that is a customer (but not an end user) and adjusting the company's inventory levels to match the acquired firm's orders

- Reducing indirect operating costs by acquiring a firm that will allow elimination of duplicate operating costs (for example, warehousing, distribution)

- Reducing fixed costs by acquiring a firm that will permit elimination of duplicate fixed costs (for example, corporate and staff functional groups)[4]

In summary, it is important that the entrepreneur and all other parties involved objectively view the firm's operations and potential. An evaluation of the following points can assist in this process:

- A firm's potential to pay for itself during a reasonable period of time

- The difficulties the new owners face during the transition period

- The amount of security or risk involved in the transaction; changes in interest rates

- The effect on the company's value if a turnaround is required

- The number of potential buyers

- Current managers' intentions to remain with the firm

- The taxes associated with the purchase or sale of an enterprise[5]

A comprehensive business plan for an acquisition of an existing venture can be found on the website for this book: **http://kuratko.swlearning.com.** This

entrepreneurship IN PRACTICE

The "Rollup Frenzy": An Acquisition Nightmare

Big industry players such as AutoNation and the now defunct NationsRent characterized the acquisition spree of the 1990s. These "rollups" of mom-and-pop businesses into national chains were geared to provide a standardized and efficient system by trimming office costs and boosting purchasing power. Unfortunately, many former owners are now suffering big losses as the former moms-and-pops are buying back their businesses for sometimes less than half of what they were acquired for.

Brad Daniel built up his florist business into five stores throughout south Florida until deciding to sell out for $130 million to an industry rollup. The rollup quickly over-inflated and filed for Chapter 11 bankruptcy protection; Daniel gained back his business for less than half of the acquisition price. But many of the small-business owners were not as lucky. Entrepreneurs who sold their businesses often got burned by plunging share prices and were left to deal with unpaid workers and deteriorating services.

The rollups' cost savings never materialized because of conflicting office systems and people's reluctance to work together. In general, these rollups grew too fast and used too much debt during expansion. It is estimated that investors put $30 billion into rollups through stock offerings and private investments through the late 1990s. Since 1996 alone, rollups that had initial public offerings raised approximately $3.6 billion in equity while taking on $10 billion in debt.

Across the nation, the smartest entrepreneurs are digging through assets of failed rollups and finding treasures. The founders of Webshots, an online photo-sharing service, sold their company and 13 million registered users to Excite@Home, becoming instant millionaires. Now that the high-speed Internet provider liquidated in 2001, Webshots is back in the hands of its founders at a bargain price.

These rollups may have had the purchasing power and recognition to raise capital for further expansion, but they lost touch of what became their liabilities—service and experience.

SOURCE: Charles Haddad and Brian Grow, "Snapping Up the Spoils of Ruptured Rollups," *BusinessWeek Online: News Analysis* (March 5, 2002).

award-winning business plan by Jason B. Correll is entitled, "Rockwood Lodge & Canoe Outfitters." Based on an actual potential purchase, this plan demonstrates the thoroughness needed in examining every facet of the selling firm.

Analyzing the Business

In analyzing small, closely held businesses, entrepreneurs should not make comparisons with larger corporations. Many factors distinguish these types of corporations, and valuation factors that have no effect on large firms may be significantly important to smaller enterprises. For example, many closely held ventures have the following shortcomings:

☐ *Lack of management depth.* The degrees of skills, versatility, and competence are limited.

the entrepreneurial
PROCESS

Due Diligence

Hendrix F. C. Niemann was 37 years old, well educated, experienced in business, and out of work. He decided to use his severance pay and his savings to purchase a business of his own. For months Niemann analyzed numerous prospective businesses that were for sale: a hospital transcription service, a sandwich producer for vending machines, a sailboat dealership, and a food distribution company. None of these businesses seemed to be the opportunity Niemann wanted. He was married with three children, and this business opportunity had to be right.

Finally, he found an appropriate opportunity. Automatic Door Specialists, a manufacturer of security systems, had sales of $2 million, fairly good cash flow, a purchase price just above book value, and a 65-year-old owner ready to retire. After going through 17 business brokers, dozens of business ads, and four months of unemployment, Niemann believed this was it. He signed a letter of agreement contingent on a due-diligence process he would accomplish. (Due diligence is close examination of a firm's financial records, legal liabilities, and business questions.)

And what did the due-diligence inspection produce? A $36,000 loss occurred the first half of the fiscal year; half of the accounts receivable were more than 90 days old, and the majority dated back over a year; an overstated inventory caused a true loss year to date closer to $80,000; sales were down 50 percent; half of the net worth of the company was gone; and once the debt from the acquisition was added to the books, no money would be left for Niemann to draw a salary! It got worse as Niemann met with the key employees to find out the "inside" story of Automatic Door Specialists. Key people had left the company to work for competitors, parts and tools were in short supply, promises had been made to customers and then forgotten, and the building was a firetrap with no hot water.

All of this bad news provided Niemann with enough facts to demand a 50 percent reduction in the purchase price or to call the deal off. The seller accepted the new purchase price, and Automatic Door Specialists had a new owner. The due-diligence process paid off for Hendrix Niemann.

SOURCE: Hendrix F. C. Niemann, "Buying a Business," *Inc.* (February 1990): 28–38.

☐ *Undercapitalization.* The amount of equity investment is usually low (often indicating a high level of debt).

☐ *Insufficient controls.* Because of the lack of available management and extra capital, measures in place for monitoring and controlling operations are usually limited.

☐ *Divergent goals.* The entrepreneur often has a vision for the venture that differs from the investors' goals or stockholders' desires, thus causing internal conflicts in the firm.

These weaknesses indicate the need for careful analysis of the small business.

The checklist in Table 17.2, which is patterned after the information required for an effective business plan (see Chapter 11), provides a concise method for examining the various factors that differentiate one firm from another.

Table 17.2   Checklist for Analyzing a Business

History of the Business

The original name of business and any subsequent name changes

Date company was founded

Names of all subsidiaries and divisions; when they were formed and their function

States where company is incorporated

States where company is licensed to do business as a foreign corporation

Review of corporate charter, bylaws, and minutes

Company's original line of business and any subsequent changes

Market and Competition

Company's major business and market

Description of major projects

Sales literature on products

Growth potential of major markets in which company operates

Name, size, and market position of principal competitors

How does company's product differ from that of the competition?

Company's market niche

Information on brand, trade, product names

Sales pattern of product lines—that is, are sales seasonal or cyclical?

Review of any statistical information available on the market—for example, trade associations, government reports, Wall Street reports

Comparative product pricing

Gross profit margin on each product line (Analyze sales growth and profit changes for three years.)

Concentration of government business

Research and development expenditures—historical and projected

Sales and Distribution

How does company sell—own sales force or through manufacturer representatives?

Compensation of sales force

Details on advertising methods and expenditures

Details on branch sales offices, if any

Details on standard sales terms, discounts offered, return and allowance policies

Are any sales made on consignment?

Does company warehouse its inventory?

If company uses distributors, how are they paid, and what are their responsibilities? (For example, do they provide warranty services?)

Are company's products distributed nationwide or in a certain geographic area?

Names and addresses of company's principal customers

Sales volume of principal customers by product line for last few years

How long have customers been buying from company?

Credit rating of principal customers

Table 17.2   (Continued)

Historical bad-debt experience of company

Details on private-label business, if any

Do sales terms involve any maintenance agreements?

Do sales terms offer any express or implied warranties?

Has company experienced any product liability problems?

Does company lease, as well as sell, any of its products?

What is the percentage of foreign business? How is this business sold, financed, and delivered?

Have any new products come on the market that would make company's products obsolete or less competitive?

Have any big customers been lost? If so, why?

Size and nature of market—fragmented or controlled by large companies?

Manufacturing

Full list of all manufacturing facilities

Are facilities owned or leased?

Does company manufacture from basic raw materials, or is it an assembly-type operation?

Types and availability of materials required to manufacture the product

Time length of production cycle

Does company make a standard shelf-type product, manufacture to specification, or both?

How is quality control handled in the factory?

What is accounting system for work in process?

Are any licenses needed to manufacture product?

What is present sales capacity based on current manufacturing equipment?

Does company have a proprietary manufacturing process?

What is company's safety record in its factory operations?

Do any problems with OSHA or federal or state environmental regulations exist?

What is stability of company's supplier relationships?

Employees

Total number of employees by function

Does a union exist? If not, what is the probability of unionization? If a union exists, what have been its historical relations with company?

Any strikes or work stoppages?

Details on local labor market

Details on company's wage and personnel policies

Is employee level fixed, or can workforce be varied easily in terms of business volume?

What is company's historical labor turnover, especially in key management?

Analysis of working conditions

Analysis of general employee morale

Has the company ever been cited for a federal violation—for example, OSHA, Pregnancy Discrimination Act, Fair Labor Practices?

What are fringe benefits, vacation time, sick leave, and so on?

Table 17.2   (Continued)

Physical Facilities

List of all company-used facilities, giving location, square footage, and cost

Which facilities are owned? Which leased?

What is present condition of all facilities, including machinery and equipment?

If any facilities are leased, details of expiration term, cost, renewal options, and so forth

Are current facilities adequate for current and projected needs?

Will any major problems occur if expansion is needed?

Is adequate insurance maintained?

Are facilities adequately protected against casualty loss, such as fire damage, through sprinkler systems, burglar alarms, or other measures?

Are facilities modern and functional for work process and employees?

Are facilities air conditioned and do they have adequate electric, heat, gas, water, and sanitary service?

Are facilities easily accessible to required transportation?

What is cost, net book value, and replacement value for company-owned buildings and equipment?

Ownership

List of all current owners of the company's common and preferred stock, by class if applicable

List of all individuals and the number of their shares exercisable under stock option and warrant agreements with prices and expiration dates

Breakdown of ownership by shares and percentage: actual and pro forma (assuming warrants and stock options exercised)

Does common stock have preemptive rights or liquidation or dividend preference?

Do the shares carry an investment letter?

Do restrictions on the transferability of the shares or on their use as collateral exist?

Do any buy/sell agreements exist?

Does an employee stock ownership plan or stock bonus plan exist?

Are the shares fully paid for?

Are any shareholders' agreements outstanding?

Has any stock been sold below par or stated value?

Does cumulative voting exist?

With respect to the principal owner's stock, have any shares been gifted or placed in a trust?

How many shares does the principal stockholder own directly and beneficially (including family)?

If all stock options and warrants are exercised, will the principal stockholder still control 51 percent of the company?

If a business is being bought or sold, what percentage of the total outstanding shares is needed for approval?

Financial

Three years of financial statements

☐ Current ratio and net quick ratio

☐ Net working capital and net quick assets

Table 17.2   (Continued)

☐ Total debt as a percentage of stockholder's equity

☐ Source and application of funds schedules

Analysis of the company's basic liquidity and turnover ratios

☐ Cash as a percent of current liabilities

☐ Accounts receivable and inventory turnovers

☐ Age of accounts payable

☐ Sales to net working capital

If company has subsidiaries (or divisions), consolidating statements of profit and loss

Verification of the cash balance and maximum and minimum cash balances needed throughout year

If company owns marketable securities, what is their degree of liquidity (salability) and current market values?

Age of all accounts and notes receivable, any customer concentration, and the adequacy of bad debt reserve

Cost basis for recording inventories and any inventory reserves; age of inventory and relation to cost of sales (turnover)

Details on all fixed assets, including date of purchase, original cost, accumulated depreciation, and replacement value

Current market appraisals on all fixed assets, real estate, and machinery and equipment

Analysis of any prepaid expenses or deferred charges as to nature and as to amortization in or advance to affiliates; comparison of true value to book value; financial statements

Personal financial statements of principal stockholders

If company carries any goodwill or intangible items, such as patents or trademarks, what is their true value (to extent possible)? Does company have any intangible assets of value not carried on books (such as mailing lists in a publishing operation)?

Analysis of all current liabilities, including age of accounts payable, and details of all bank debt and lines of credit, including interest rate, term, and collateral; loan agreements

Details on all long-term debt by creditor, including loan agreement covenants that may affect future operations

Do any contingent liabilities or other outstanding commitments, such as long-term supplier agreements exist?

Details on franchise, lease, and royalty agreements

Income statement accounts for at least three years and analysis of any significant percentage variances, that is, cost of sales as percent of sales

Company's tax returns—do they differ from its financial statements? Which years still may be open for audit?

Three-year projection of income and cash flow for reasonableness of future sales and profits and to establish financing needs

Pension, profit-sharing, and stock bonus plans for contractual commitments and unfunded past-service liability costs

Table 17.2   (Continued)

Management

Details on all officers and directors—length of service, age, business background, compensation, and fringe benefits

Ownership positions: number of shares, stock options, and warrants

Similar details on other nonofficer/nondirector key management

Organizational chart

What compensation-type fringe benefits are offered to key management: bonuses, retirement-plan stock bonuses, company-paid insurance, deferred compensation?

What is management's reputation in its industry?

Does management have any personal interests in any other businesses? Does it have any other conflicts of interest?

Does key management devote 100 percent of its time to the business?

Any employment contracts—amount of salary, length of time, other terms

Has key management agreed to a noncompete clause and agreed not to divulge privileged information obtained while employed with company?

Establishing a Firm's Value

After using the checklist in Table 17.2, the entrepreneur can begin to examine the various methods used to valuate a business. It should be noted that the establishment of an actual value is more of an art than a science. Estimations, assumptions, and projections are all part of the process. The quantified figures are calculated based, in part, on such hidden values and costs as goodwill, personal expenses, family members on the payroll, planned losses, and the like.[6]

Several traditional valuation methods are presented here, each using a particular approach that covers these hidden values and costs. Employing these methods will provide the entrepreneur with a general understanding of how the financial analysis of a firm works. Remember, also, that many of these methods are used concurrently and that the *final* value determination will be the actual price agreed on by the buyer and seller.

Valuation Methods

Table 17.3 lists the various methods that may be used for business valuation. Each method listed is described and key points about them are presented. Specific attention here will be concentrated on the three methods that are considered the principal measures used in current business valuations: (1) adjusted tangible assets (balance sheet values), (2) price/earnings (multiple earnings value), and (3) discounted future earnings.

Adjusted Tangible Book Value

A common method of valuing a business is to compute its net worth as the difference between total assets and total liabilities. However, it is important to adjust for certain assets in order to assess true economic worth, since inflation and depreciation affect the value of some assets.

Table 17.3 Methods for Venture Valuation

METHOD	DESCRIPTION/EXPLANATION	NOTES/KEY POINTS
Fixed price	Two or more owners set initial value Based on what owners "think" business is worth Uses figures from any one or combination of methods Common for buy/sell agreements	Inaccuracies exist due to personal estimates Should allow periodic update
Book value (known as balance sheet method) 1. Tangible 2. Adjusted tangible	1. *Tangible book value:* Set by the business's balance sheet Reflects net worth of the firm Total assets less total liabilities (adjusted for intangible assets) 2. *Adjusted tangible book value:* Uses book value approach Reflects fair market value for certain assets Upward/downward adjustments in plant and equipment, inventory, and bad debt reserves	Some assets also appreciate or depreciate substantially; thus, not an accurate valuation Adjustments in assets eliminate some of the inaccuracies and reflect a fair market value of each asset
Multiple of earnings	Net income capitalized using a price/earnings ratio (net income multiplied by P/E number) 15% capitalization rate often used (equivalent to a P/E multiple of 6.7, which is 1 divided by 0.15) High-growth businesses use lower capitalization rate (e.g., 5%, which is a multiple of 20) Stable businesses use higher capitalization rate (e.g., 10%, which is a multiple of 10) Derived value divided by number of outstanding shares to obtain per-share value	Capitalization rates vary as to firm's growth; thus, estimates or P/E used must be taken from similar publicly traded corporation
Price/earnings ratio (P/E)	Similar to a return-on-investment approach Determined by price of common stock divided by after-tax earnings Closely held firms must multiply net income by an appropriate multiple, usually derived from similar publicly traded corporations Sensitive to market conditions (prices of stocks)	More common with public corporations Market conditions (stock prices) affect this ratio
Discounted future earnings (discounted cash flow)	Attempts to establish future earning power in current dollars Projects future earnings (5 years), calculates present value using a then discounted rate Based on projected "timing" of future income	Based on premise that cash flow is most important factor Effective method if (1) business being valued needs to generate a return greater than investment and (2) only cash receipts can provide the money for reinvesting in growth

Table 17.3   (Continued)

METHOD	DESCRIPTION/EXPLANATION	NOTES/KEY POINTS
Return on investment (ROI)	Net profit divided by investment Provides an earnings ratio Need to calculate probabilities of future earnings Combination of return ratio, present value tables, and weighted probabilities	Will *not* establish a value for the business Does not provide projected future earnings
Replacement value	Based on value of each asset if it had to be *replaced* at current cost Firm's worth calculated as if building from "scratch" Inflation and annual depreciation of assets are considered in raising the value above reported book value Does *not* reflect earning power or intangible assets	Useful for selling a company that's seeking to break into a new line of business Fails to consider earnings potential Does not include intangible assets (goodwill, patents, and so on)
Liquidation value	Assumes business ceases operation Sells assets and pays off liabilities Net amount after payment of all liabilities is distributed to shareholders Reflects "bottom value" of a firm Indicates amount of money that could be borrowed on a secured basis Tends to favor seller since all assets are valued as if converted to cash	Assumes each division of assets sold separately at auction Effective in giving absolute bottom value below which a firm should liquidate rather than sell
Excess earnings	Developed by the U.S. Treasury to determine a firm's intangible assets (for income tax purposes) Intent is for use only when no better method available Internal Revenue Service refers to this method as a last resort Method does not include intangibles with estimated useful lives (i.e., patents, copyrights)	Method of last resort (if no other method available) Very seldom used
Market value	Needs a "known" price paid for a similar business Difficult to find recent comparisons Methods of sale may differ—installment versus cash Should be used only as a reference point	Valuable only as a reference point Difficult to find recent, similar firms that have been sold

In the computation of the **adjusted tangible book** value, goodwill, patents, deferred financing costs, and other intangible assets are considered with the other assets and deducted from or added to net worth. This upward or downward adjustment reflects the excess of the fair market value of each asset above or below the value reported on the balance sheet. Here is an example:

	BOOK VALUE	FAIR MARKET VALUE
Inventory	$100,000	$125,000
Plant and equipment	400,000	600,000
Other intangibles		(50,000)
	—	—
	$500,000	$675,000

Excess = $175,000

Remember that in industry comparisons of adjusted values, only assets used in the actual operation of the business are included.

Other significant balance sheet and income statement adjustments include (1) bad debt reserves; (2) low-interest, long-term debt securities; (3) investments in affiliates; and (4) loans and advances to officers, employees, or other companies. Additionally, earnings should be adjusted. Only true earnings derived from the operations of the business should be considered. One-time items (from the sale of a company division or asset, for example) should be excluded. Also, if the company has been using a net operational loss carry forward, so its pretax income has not been fully taxed, this also should be considered.

Upward (or downward) income and balance sheet adjustments should be made for any unusually large bad-debt or inventory write-off, and for certain accounting practices, such as accelerated versus straight-line depreciation.

Price/Earnings Ratio (Multiple of Earnings) Method

The **price/earnings ratio (P/E)** is a common method used for valuing publicly held corporations. The valuation is determined by dividing the market price of the common stock by the earnings per share. A company with 100,000 shares of common stock and a net income of $100,000 would have earnings per share of $1. If the stock price rose to $5 per share, the P/E would be 5 ($5 divided by $1). Additionally, since the company has 100,000 shares of common stock, the valuation of the enterprise now would be $500,000 (100,000 shares $\times$ $5).

The primary advantage of a price/earnings approach is its simplicity. However, this advantage applies only to publicly traded corporations. Closely held companies do not have prices in the open market for their stock and thus must rely on the use of a multiple derived by comparing the firm to similar public corporations. This approach has four major drawbacks:[7]

1. The stock of a private company is not publicly traded. It is illiquid and may actually be restricted from sale (that is, not registered with the Securities and Exchange Commission). Thus any P/E multiple usually must, by definition, be subjective and lower than the multiple commanded by comparable publicly traded stocks.

2. The stated net income of a private company may not truly reflect its actual earning power. To avoid or defer paying taxes, most business owners prefer to keep pretax income down. In addition, the closely held business may be "overspending" on fringe benefits instituted primarily for the owner's benefit.

entrepreneurship IN PRACTICE

Buying a Business: Doing It Right

One reason entrepreneurs need to know how to valuate a business is that they may want to buy one someday. When this is the case, they should keep in mind a number of factors. Here are five of the most important:

1. Get a lawyer involved from the beginning. The purchase of assets often involves tax questions, unknown risks and, in some cases, the assumption of liabilities. A lawyer can help the entrepreneur be aware of these issues before they become problems.

2. Be aware of hidden risks that may not surface for 12 to 18 months. For example, a customer who was injured by a company-made product before the firm was sold may end up suing the new entrepreneur.

3. Have the old owner sign a noncompete clause whereby the individual promises not to reenter the business for a certain number of years (at least not in the local area). Be sure this clause is reasonable in terms of what is being promised; otherwise, the courts may set it aside.

4. Have a certified public accountant or an outside financial expert confirm all income and expenses as well as asset accounts. In this way, the entrepreneur knows what he or she is buying.

5. Before closing the deal, check out the seller. Why is the individual selling? Additionally, is the individual honest in business dealings? If not, the person may end up trying to walk away from the deal before the purchase has been finalized.

SOURCE: "Buying a Business: What to Watch Out For," *Financial Enterprise* (summer 1987): 13–14.

3. Common stock that is bought and sold in the public market normally reflects only a small portion of the business's total ownership. The sale of a large controlling block of stock (typical of closely held businesses) demands a premium.

4. It is very difficult to find a truly comparable publicly held company, even in the same industry. Growth rates, competition, dividend payments, and financial profiles (liquidity and leverage) rarely will be the same.

When applied to a closely held firm, here is an example of how the multiple-of-earnings method could be used:

Shares of common stock	=	100,000
2006 net income	=	$100,000
15% capitalization rate assumed	=	6.7 price/earnings multiple (derived by dividing 1 by 15 and multiplying the result by 100)
Price per share	=	$6.70
Value of company	=	100,000 × $6.70 = $670,000

Discounted Earnings Method

Most analysts agree that the real value of any venture is its potential earning power. The **discounted earnings method,** more than any other, determines the firm's true value. One example of a pricing formula using earning power as well as adjusted tangible book value is illustrated in Table 17.4.

Table 17.4 The Pricing Formula

Step 1. Determine the adjusted tangible net worth of the business. (The total market value of all current and long-term assets less liabilities.)

Step 2. Estimate how much the buyer could earn annually with an amount equal to the value of the tangible net worth invested elsewhere.

Step 3. Add to this a salary normal for an owner-operator of the business. This combined figure provides a reasonable estimate of the income the buyer can earn elsewhere with the investment and effort involved in working in the business.

Step 4. Determine the average annual net earnings of the business (net profit before subtracting owner's salary) over the past few years.

   This is before income taxes, to make it comparable with earnings from other sources or by individuals in different tax brackets. (The tax implications of alternative investments should be carefully considered.)

   This trend of earnings is a key factor. Have they been rising steadily, falling steadily, remaining constant, or fluctuating widely? The earnings figure should be adjusted to reflect these trends.

Step 5. Subtract the total of earning power (2) and reasonable salary (3) from this average net earnings figure (4). This gives the extra earning power of the business.

Step 6. Use this extra earnings figure to estimate the value of the intangibles. This is done by multiplying the extra earnings by what is termed the "years-of-profit" figure.

   This "years-of-profit" multiplier pivots on these points. How unique are the intangibles offered by the firm? How long would it take to set up a similar business and bring it to this stage of development? What expenses and risks would be involved? What is the price of goodwill in similar firms? Will the seller be signing an agreement with a covenant not to compete?

   If the business is well established, a factor of five or more might be used, especially if the firm has a valuable name, patent, or location. A multiplier of three might be reasonable for a moderately seasoned firm. A younger but profitable firm might merely have a one-year profit figure.

Step 7. Final price equals adjusted tangible net worth plus value of intangibles (extra earnings times "years of profit").

EXAMPLE

	BUSINESS A	BUSINESS B
1. Adjusted value of tangible net worth (assets less liabilities)	$100,000	$100,000
2. Earning power at 10%[a] of an amount equal to the adjusted tangible net worth, if invested in a comparable risk business	10,000	10,000
3. Reasonable salary for owner-operator in the business	18,000	18,000
4. Net earnings of the business over recent years (net profit before subtracting owner's salary)	30,000	23,350
5. Extra earning power of the business (line 4 minus lines 2 and 3)	2,000	(4,650)
6. Value of intangibles—using three-year profit figure for moderately well-established firm (3 times line 5)	6,000	None
7. Final price (lines 1 and 6)	$106,000	$100,000 (or less)

In *example A*, the seller receives a value for goodwill because the business is moderately well established and earning more than the buyer could earn elsewhere with similar risks and effort.

In *example B*, the seller receives no value for goodwill because the business, even though it may have existed for a considerable time, is not earning as much as the buyer could through outside investment and effort. In fact, the buyer may feel that even an investment of $100,000—the current appraised value of net assets—is too much because it cannot earn sufficient return.

[a] This is an arbitrary figure, used for illustration. A reasonable figure depends on the stability and relative risks of the business and the investment picture generally. The rate of return should be similar to that which could be earned elsewhere with the same approximate risk.

Source: Reprinted with permission from Bank of America NT&SA, "How to Buy and Sell a Business or Franchise," *Small Business Reporter,* copyright ©1987, 17.

IN PRACTICE

entrepreneurship

What Is This Business Worth?

Let's look at a business you wish to acquire. You will do the following:

1. Present the *net* cash-flow projections for this business for five years (2006 through 2010)

2. Change the format for presenting the data (You may find it easier to use.)

3. Use a present value rate of 24 percent

Assume you have an opportunity to buy a small division of a large company. Since you know the business intimately, you can accurately forecast the company's growth. Right now it's not profitable, but with your expertise and plans, you expect it can generate $380,000 net cash flow over five years and have a value (net worth) of $400,000 at the end of year five. (The $380,000 net cash flow is *after* all cash outlays.)

Question

Because you want to earn a minimum annual return of 24 percent on your investment (that is, the purchase price), how much should you pay for the division?

Here are the facts: Assume the acquisition will occur on December 31, 2006, and the projected annual net cash flow (the excess of all cash inflow over all cash outflow) looks like this:

	2006	2007	2008	2009	2010
Net cash flow (thousands)	$0	$40	$80	$110	$150

Answer

Because you want an annual return of 24 percent on your money, simply compute the present value of the projected net cash-flow stream. You also must compute the value of the $400,000 net worth position (projected assets less liabilities) at the end of year five.

Referring to present value tables in financial handbooks (or using a calculator), you can obtain the following data:

YEAR	PRESENT VALUE FACTOR FOR 24% RATE OF RETURN
Today	1.000
1	0.806
2	0.650
3	0.524
4	0.423
5	0.341

All that is needed now is to prepare a table showing the net cash flows for the five-year period. You then multiply the present value factor (for a 24 percent return) by the net cash flow for each year.

YEAR	NET CASH FLOW	PRESENT VALUE FACTOR	TODAY'S VALUE
2006	$ 0	0.806	$ 0
2007	40,000	0.650	26,000
2008	80,000	0.524	41,920
2009	110,000	0.423	46,530
2010	550,000[a]	0.341	187,550[a]
Totals	$780,000		$302,000

As computed, the total value of the projected net cash-flow stream is $302,000 today—and this includes the projected $400,000 net worth at the end of year five.

In other words, if the division were purchased *today* for its net cash-flow value of $302,000, and if the projected cash flows for the five years were generated (including the projected net worth value of $400,000), you would realize a 24 percent annual rate of return on your $302,000 investment over the five-year period.

[a]Includes $150,000 net cash flow and $400,000 net worth of division at end of fifth year.

SOURCE: Thomas J. Martin, *Valuation Reference Manual* (Hicksville, NY: Thomar Publications, 1987), 68. Figures updated, 2006.

The idea behind discounting the firm's cash flows is that dollars earned in the future (based on projections) are worth less than dollars earned today (due to the loss of purchasing power). With this in mind, the "timing" of projected income or cash flows is a critical factor.

The Entrepreneurship in Practice box on page 674 provides a step-by-step example of the process of discounting cash flows. Basically, the method uses a four-step process:

1. Expected cash flow is estimated. For long-established firms, historical data are effective indicators, although adjustments should be made when available data indicate that future cash flows will change.

2. An appropriate discount rate is determined. The buyer's viewpoint has to be considered in the calculation of this rate. The buyer and seller often disagree, because each requires a particular rate of return and will view the risks differently. Another point the seller often overlooks is that the buyer will have other investment opportunities to consider. The appropriate rate, therefore, must be weighed against these factors.

3. A reasonable life expectancy of the business must be determined. All firms have a life cycle that depends on such factors as whether the business is one product/one market or multiproduct/multimarket.

4. The firm's value is then determined by discounting the estimated cash flow by the appropriate discount rate over the expected life of the business.[8]

Other Factors to Consider

After reviewing these valuation methods, the entrepreneur needs to remember that additional factors intervene in the valuation process and that these should be given consideration. Presented next are three factors that may influence the final valuation of the venture.

Avoiding Start-Up Costs

Some buyers are willing to pay more for a business than what the valuation methods illustrate its worth to be. This is because buyers often are trying to avoid the costs associated with start-up and are willing to pay a little more for an existing firm. The higher price they pay will be still less than actual start-up costs and also avoids the problems associated with working to establish a clientele. Thus, for some buyers a known commodity may command a higher price.

Accuracy of Projections

The sales and earnings of a venture are always projected on the basis of historical financial and economic data. Short histories, fluctuating markets, and uncertain environments are all reasons for buyers to keep projections in perspective. It is critical they examine the trends, fluctuations, or patterns involved in projections for sales revenues (higher prices or more customers?), market potential (optimistic or realistic assumptions?), and earnings potential (accurate cost/revenue/market data?), because each area has specific factors that need to be either understood or measured for the accuracy of the projection.

Control Factor

The degree of control an owner legally has over the firm can affect its valuation. If the owner's interest is 100 percent or such that the complete operation of the firm is under his or her influence, then that value is equal to the enterprise's value. If the owner does not possess such control, then the value is less. For example, buying out a 49 percent shareholder will not be effective in controlling a 51 percent shareholder. Also, two 49 percent shareholders are equal until a 2 percent "swing vote" shareholder makes a move. Obviously, minority interests also must be discounted due to lack of liquidity—a minority interest in a privately held corporation is difficult to sell. Overall, it is important to look at the control factor as another facet in the purchase of any interest in a firm.

The Leveraged Buyout: An Alternative for Small Ventures

After the valuation procedures have been completed, the entrepreneur may have a problem securing the necessary cash for purchasing the business. One alternative allows the entrepreneur to finance the transaction by borrowing on the target company's assets. This method is the **leveraged buyout (LBO)**.

Entrepreneurs have used the LBO for a number of years to purchase small privately held firms whenever they lacked the needed funds by borrowing against assets such as accounts receivable, inventory, and equipment.

Issues Involved with LBOs

A great deal of literature is available about leveraged buyouts of multibillion-dollar firms. The 1990s brought about a huge increase in LBOs as a powerful financial tool for acquisition.[9] However, the new millennium witnessed a huge drop in the LBO activity. Leveraged buyouts accounted for only 2 percent of all acquisitions in 2001.[10] Figure 17.2 illustrates the drop off in LBO deals since 1999. A number of researchers have examined the long-run benefits of firms involved with LBOs.[11] However, it is most important for the entrepreneur to understand the smaller-scale LBO where ownership is concentrated in the hands of relatively few owners.

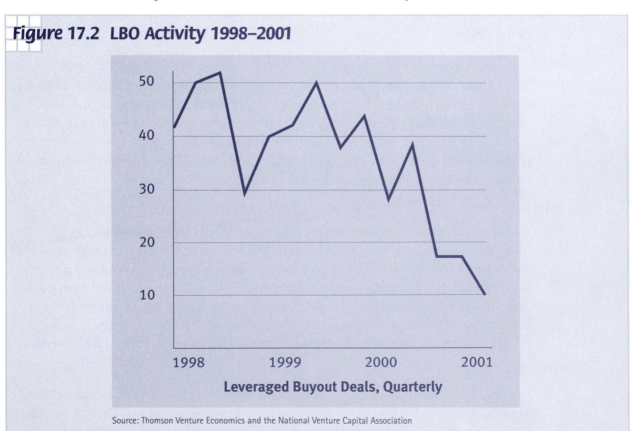

Figure 17.2 LBO Activity 1998–2001

Leveraged Buyout Deals, Quarterly

Source: Thomson Venture Economics and the National Venture Capital Association

Getting Your Money's Worth

Two years after deciding to sell their business, Doug Roberson and his partner instead merged their $18 million data communications company with an even larger one, gaining $5.7 million in stock and two five-year management contracts. A business valuation had put the overall picture in focus and allowed them to make the decision that best fit their interests. "The valuation was worth every penny for the added insight it gave us." Just as if they were preparing to purchase a business, Roberson and his partner knew early on that they needed to be as prepared as possible before getting involved in something they knew nothing about.

Corporate valuation, also known as business appraisal, is often ignored when it is needed the most: applying for a loan, selling out, and even entering bankruptcy, to name just a few situations. Business owners believe no one can know their businesses like they do, so they overlook the benefits that a valuation provides. Roberson rightly avoided that "tunnel vision." "What it did was allow us to prepare ourselves to respond to worries on the part of a prospective buyer. It helped us become stronger negotiators."

Roberson paid $15,000 for the resulting 25-page report that enabled him and his partner to see the business in a different light. Even though they were involved in the everyday operations of the business, the partners had been unaware how much the business's success was contingent on key employees and major customers. Such easily lost moneymakers are worrisome attributes for outside investors.

A valuation is a great business tool that comes in handy during various events. Generally, it is designed to assign a fair market value, but certain circumstances call for certain outcomes:

1. For estate- and gift-tax purposes, an ideal valuation is one that's as low as possible, so as to minimize tax liabilities. Expect the appraiser to look for any documentable factor that might lower your company's value.

2. For sale purposes, well-prepared sellers equip themselves with a valuation that documents the highest possible value.

3. For financing purposes, bankers will look for a valuation that focuses on liquidation value rather than a company's prospects as a going concern.

4. For litigation purposes, valuations are a "dog-eat-dog" business. Set your valuation goals according to the side of the case you're on, but remember that the best investment you can make is a comprehensive, fully defensible document from the most blue-chip appraiser you can afford.

SOURCE: Adapted from Jill Andresky Fraser, "What's Your Company Worth?" *Inc.* (November 1997): 111–112.

The **entrepreneurial leveraged buyout (E–LBO)** is characterized as having (1) at least two-thirds of the purchase price generated from borrowed funds, (2) more than 50 percent of the stock after acquisition owned by single individuals or their families, and (3) the majority investors devoting themselves to the active management of the company after acquisition.[12]

Generally, a company selected for a leveraged buyout has dependable cash flow from operations, a high ratio of fully depreciated fixed assets (plant, equipment, and so on), an established product line, and low current and long-term debt. This is because the traditional asset-based leveraged buyout bases the transaction on the presence of enough assets to loan against, as well as on the company's current position to take on more debt.

Another form of buyout is called the **cash-flow leveraged buyout (LBO)**.[13] This type is different because a cash-flow lender relies very heavily on the target company's cash receipts and on indicators of that positive cash flow continuing. These loans demand a higher yield than the traditional asset-based type, which are usually available at two or three points above the prime interest rate. In addition, many cash-flow lenders may require the current management team to remain with the business and retain some equity so that they have a vested interest in performance. The lender also may take some equity, leaving the purchasing entrepreneur paying high interest rates and giving up too much equity (in some cases 70 percent).[14] Since asset-based LBOs have lower interest rates, allow control to be with the purchasing entrepreneur, and usually leave all the stock with the entrepreneur, they remain the most popular form of leveraged buyouts.

The results of small-firm or entrepreneurial leveraged buyouts are interesting. One research study examined the current state of small-firm LBOs and the changes that occurred after the LBO took place.[15] The results indicated that most of the small-company LBOs occurred in industries far different from the high-growth, high-technology environments of the glamorous start-up. The cash-flow requirements of the high-debt component seemed to favor industries in which growth was very slow or even negative and in which the technology was stable. In addition, small LBOs were relatively immune from foreign competition.

The internal operating changes after the LBO did not include a shift in the decision-making power to the lead investor. The most common operating changes seemed to focus on such revenue-generating efforts as increased sales and marketing as well as on more stringent capital-budgeting requirements.

Overall, the research found that the once-stable environments in which the firms had operated became far more exciting. In addition, these small companies were being operated by owner-managers experienced in both the company and the industry. The financial requirements of the high-debt levels and the resulting emphasis on cash flow rather than profitability made these firms extremely fierce competitors.[16]

It should be noted that both the effects of government regulation and changes in tax structures impact the use and popularity of LBOs.[17] Tax considerations may have the most dramatic influence on the continued use of LBOs for small firms.

Many of the tax reform provisions took effect in different years, depending on a variety of clauses in the tax codes. Therefore, it is imperative that a tax accountant work closely with an entrepreneur on the various tax implications. In most transactions, the tax considerations will have a significant impact on the structure of the buyout or on the final negotiations. Either way, an entrepreneur needs to have the most current and favorable tax information.

Summary

Many entrepreneurs start by purchasing a venture already in existence. In this chapter, major steps were described that are critical to the purchase of any business. In addition, ten key questions were presented and described for evaluating a particular business that has been selected for purchase.

Entrepreneurs need to understand how to valuate a business for either purchase or sale. Many would like to know the value of their businesses. Sometimes this is strictly for informational purposes, and at other times it is for selling the operation. In either case, a number of ways of valuing an enterprise exist.

The first step is to analyze the business's overall operations, with a view to acquiring a comprehensive understanding of the firm's strong and weak points. Table 17.2 provided a checklist for this purpose. The second step is to establish a value for the firm. Table 17.3 set forth ten methods for the valuation of a venture. Three of the most commonly used are (1) adjusted tangible assets, (2) price/earnings ratio (multiple of earnings), and (3) discounted future earnings.

The adjusted tangible book value method computes the value of the business by revaluing the assets and then subtracting the liabilities. This is a fairly simple, straightforward process.

The price/earnings ratio method divides the market price of the common stock by the earnings per share and then multiplies by the number of shares issued. For example, a company with a price/earnings multiple of 10 and 100,000 shares of stock would be valued at $1 million.

The discounted earnings method takes the estimated cash flows for a predetermined number of years and discounts these sums back to the present using an appropriate discount rate. This is one of the most popular methods of valuing a business. Other factors to consider for valuing a business include start-up costs, accuracy of projections, and the control factor.

Finally, the concept of a leveraged buyout (LBO) was discussed as an alternative for entrepreneurs who lack the cash needed to purchase a business. Asset-based buyouts were described in comparison to cash-flow buyouts. The importance of tax implications and the need to use a skilled tax accountant in buyout situations were discussed.

Key Terms and Concepts

adjusted tangible book value	emotional bias
business valuation	entrepreneurial leveraged buyout (E-LBO)
cash-flow leveraged buyout (LBO)	leveraged buyout (LBO)
discounted earnings method	price/earnings ratio (P/E)

Review and Discussion Questions

1. What are the four basic steps to follow when buying a business?

2. Identify five (out of ten) key questions to ask when buying an ongoing venture.

3. Identify and discuss the three underlying issues in the evaluation of a business.

4. Define the term *due diligence*. How is it applied to the acquisition of an existing venture?

5. To analyze a business, what types of questions or concerns should the entrepreneur address in the following areas: history of the business, market and competition, sales and distribution, and manufacturing?

6. To analyze a business, what types of questions or concerns should the entrepreneur address in the following areas: employees, physical facilities, ownership, and trade and professional checks?

7. To analyze a business, what types of questions or concerns should the entrepreneur address in the following areas: financial, management?

8. One of the most popular methods of business valuation is the adjusted tangible book value. Describe how this method works.

9. Explain how the price/earnings ratio method of valuation works. Give an example.

10. What are the steps involved in using the discounted earnings method? Give an example.

11. How do the following methods of valuing a venture work: fixed price, multiple of earnings, return on investment, replacement value, liquidation value, excess earnings, and market value? In each case, give an example.

12. Explain why the following are important factors to consider when valuing a business: start-up costs, accuracy of projections, degree of control.

▌ Experiential Exercise

What Would You Recommend?

Jane Winfield would like to buy Ted Garner's company. She has conducted a detailed financial analysis of Ted's firm and has determined the following:

1. Book value of the inventory: $250,000

2. Discount rate on future earnings: 24 percent

3. Book value of the plant and equipment: $150,000

4. Fair market value of the inventory: $400,000

5. Fair market value of other intangibles: $60,000

6. Number of shares of common stock: 100,000

7. Fair market value of the plant and equipment: $400,000

8. Price/earnings multiple: 9

9. Book market value of other intangibles: $30,000

10. Estimated earnings over the next five years:

Year 1	$200,000
Year 2	300,000
Year 3	400,000
Year 4	500,000
Year 5	600,000

Based on this information, how much should Jane valuate the business according to each of the following methods: adjusted tangible assets, price/earnings ratio, and discounted future earnings? Based on your findings, recommend the valuation method she should use. Finally, given all of your calculations, estimate what the final price will be. Give reasons for this estimate. Enter your answers here.

a) Adjusted tangible assets valuation: _____

b) Price/earnings valuation: _____

c) Discounted future earnings valuation: _____

d) Final sales price: _____

▌ Case 17.1

A Valuation Matter

Charles Jackson has always been interested in determining the value of his small business. He started the operation five years ago with $1,500 of savings, and since then it has grown into a firm that has 15 employees and annual sales of $1.88 million.

Charles has talked to his accountant regarding methods that can be used in valuing his business. His accountant has briefly explained two of these to Charles: adjusted tangible book value and discounted earnings. Charles has decided to use both methods in arriving at a valuation. Here is the information he has gathered to help him use both methods:

ADJUSTED ASSETS AND TOTAL LIABILITIES		ESTIMATED EARNINGS OVER NEXT FIVE YEARS	
Total liabilities	$700,000	Year 1	$100,000
After revaluation:		Year 2	125,000
Inventory	600,000	Year 3	150,000
Plant and equipment	400,000	Year 4	200,000
Other assets	100,000	Year 5	250,000

Also, Charles believes that it is best to use a conservative discount rate. He has settled on 24 percent.

Questions

1. Under the adjusted tangible book value method, what is Charles's business worth? Show your calculations.

2. Under the discounted earnings method, what is Charles's business worth? Show your calculations.

3. Which of the two methods is more accurate? Why?

Case 17.2

Which Will It Be?

Georgia Isaacson and her son Rubin have been thinking about buying a business. After talking to seven entrepreneurs, all of whom have expressed an interest in selling their operations, the Isaacsons have decided to make an offer for a retail clothing store. The store is very well located, and its earnings over the past five years have been excellent. The current owner has told the Isaacsons he will sell for $500,000. The owner arrived at this value by projecting the earnings of the operation for the next seven years and then using a discount factor of 15 percent.

The Isaacsons are not sure the retail store is worth $500,000, but they do understand the method the owner used for arriving at this figure. Georgia feels that since the owner has been in business for only seven years, it is unrealistic to discount seven years of future earnings. A five-year estimate would be more realistic, in her opinion. Rubin feels that the discount factor is too low. He believes that 20 to 22 percent would be more realistic.

In addition to these concerns, the Isaacsons feel they would like to make an evaluation of the business using other methods. In particular, they would like to see what the value of the company would be when the adjusted tangible book value method is employed. They also would like to look at the replacement value and liquidation value methods.

"We know what the owner feels his business is worth," Georgia noted to her son. "However, we have to decide for ourselves what we think the operation is worth. From here on we can negotiate a final price. For the moment, I think we have to look at this valuation process from a number of different angles."

Questions

1. If the owner reduces the earnings estimates from seven to five years, what effect will this have on the final valuation? If the individual increases the discount factor from 15 percent to 20 to 22 percent, what effect will this have on the final valuation?

2. How do the replacement value and liquidation value methods work? Why would the Isaacsons want to examine these methods?

3. If the Isaacsons conclude that the business is worth $410,000, what will be the final selling price, assuming a sale is made? Defend your answer.

■ Notes

1. See, for example, W. G. Sanders and S. Bovie, "Sorting Things Out: Valuation of New Firms in Uncertain Markets," *Strategic Management Journal* 25(2) (February 2004): 167–186; and Saikat Chaudhuri and Behnam Tabrizi, "Capturing the Real Value in High-Tech Acquisitions," *Harvard Business Review* (September/October 1999): 123–130.

2. See Richard M. Hodgetts and Donald F. Kuratko, *Effective Small Business Management,* 7th ed. (New York: John Wiley & Sons, 2001), 110–113.

3. For additional insights, see Ted S. Front, "How to Be a Smart Buyer," *D & B Reports* (March/April 1990): 56–58; and Alfred Rappaport and Mark L. Sirower, "Stock or Cash? The Trade-Offs for Buyers and Sellers in Mergers and Acquisitions," *Harvard Business Review* (November/December 1999): 147–158.

4. "Acquisition Strategies—Part 1," *Small Business Reports* (January 1987): 34. Reprinted with permission from *Small Business Reports;* see also Laurence Capron, "The Long-Term Performance of Horizontal Acquisitions," *Strategic Management Journal* (November 1999): 987–1018.

5. "Valuing a Closely Held Business," *The Small Business Report* (November 1986): 30–31; see also Hal B. Heaton, "Valuing Small Businesses: The Cost of Capital," *The Appraisal Journal* (January 1998): 11–16; and Alan Mitchell, "How Much Is Your Company Really Worth?" *Management Today* (January 1999): 68–70.

6. Gary R. Trugman, *Understanding Business Valuation: A Practical Guide to Valuing Small to Medium-Sized Businesses* (New York: American Institute of Certified Public Accountants, 1998); and Robert W. Pricer and Alec C. Johnson, "The Accuracy of Valuation Methods in Predicting the Selling Price of Small Firms," *Journal of Small Business Management* (October 1997): 24–35.

7. Adapted from Albert N. Link and Michael B. Boger, *The Art and Science of Business Valuation* (Westport, CT: Quorum Books, 1999).

8. "Valuing a Closely Held Business," 34.

9. Matthew Schifrin, "LBO Madness," *Forbes* (March 1998): 128–134.

10. Riva D. Atlas, "What's an Aging Barbarian to Do?" *The New York Times* (August 26, 2001): Section 3, 1.

11. See, for example, Nancy Mohan, "Do LBOs Sustain Efficiency Gains?" *Akron Business and Economic Review* (fall 1990): 91–99; see also Tim Opler and Sheridan Titman, "The Determinants of Leveraged Buyout Activity: Free Cash Flow vs. Financial Distress Costs," *The Journal of Finance* (December 1993): 1985–1999; and "The LBO Market," *Mergers-and-Acquisitions* (March/April 1999): 65.

12. J. M. Kelly, R. A. Pitts, and B. Shin, "Entrepreneurship by Leveraged Buyout: Some Preliminary Hypotheses," *Frontiers of Entrepreneurship Research* (Wellesley, MA: Babson Center for Entrepreneurial Studies, 1986), 281–292.

13. James McNeill Stancill, "LBOs for Smaller Companies," *Harvard Business Review* (January/February 1988): 18–26; and Stanley L. Gaffin, "Evaluating Cash Flow: Key to a Successful Small Business LBO," *Credit and Financial Management* (December 1986): 16–20.

14. Ibid., 20.

15. Stewart C. Malone, "Characteristics of Smaller Company Buyouts," *Journal of Business Venturing* (September 1989): 349–359.

16. Ibid., 350.

17. Alan Gart, "Leveraged Buyouts: A Reexamination," *SAM Advanced Management Journal* (summer 1990): 38–46; see also John C. Easterwood, "Divestments and Financial Distress in Leveraged Buyouts," *Journal of Banking & Finance* (February 1998): 129–159.

18

Harvesting the Entrepreneurial Venture

Entrepreneurs tend to be control addicts. In a sense they have to be. They started their companies to be their own bosses, and at the start, they are usually in charge of everything. But as the company grows, being in charge of everything becomes increasingly impossible to manage. . . . Company building is a marathon, not a sprint. To avoid the loneliness of the long-distance runner, an entrepreneur needs to tap the support and experience of others. The entrepreneurial course is not only easier to traverse but also more enjoyable to run with others cheering one along!

Ray Smilor

Daring Visionaries

Chapter Objectives

1. To present the concept of "harvest" as a plan for the future.

2. To examine the key factors in the management succession of a venture.

3. To identify and describe some of the most important sources of succession

4. To discuss the potential impact of recent legislation on family business succession

5. To relate the ways to develop a succession strategy

6. To examine the specifics of an IPO as a potential harvest strategy

7. To present "selling out" as a final alternative in the harvest strategy

Harvesting the Venture: A Focus on the Future

Entrepreneurs must realize that the eventual success of their venture will lead them to a decision concerning the future operation and management of the business. A "harvest plan" defines how and when the owners and investors will realize an actual cash return on their investment. Note that "harvest" does not mean that the challenges and responsibility of the entrepreneur are over. There are challenging decisions to be made. It may be a decision regarding managerial control and succession for successful continued operations.[1] It may be a desire to initiate a "liquidity event" where the venture is able to generate a significant amount of cash for the investors. It may be that the venture has grown to a stage where now the possibility of an IPO (initial public offering) that we discussed in Chapter 14 is a reality. Or it may be that the most realistic opportunity is for the sale of the business. In any of these situations the entrepreneur is confronted with a myriad of choices and possibilities. While it is impossible for this chapter to answer all of the questions that an entrepreneur faces at this stage because each venture presents a unique set of circumstances, it is the goal of this final chapter to review some of the more common challenges confronting entrepreneurs at this stage. Thus, we examine the challenge of management succession and the two most notable harvest strategies for ventures: the initial public offering and the sale of the venture.

The Management Succession Challenge

Research shows that many privately held firms go out of existence after ten years; only three out of ten survive into a second generation. More significant, only 16 percent of all privately held enterprises make it to a third generation. One important study demonstrated these facts by examining the life expectancy of 200 successful manufacturing firms.[2] The average life expectancy for a privately held business is 24 years, which is also the average tenure for the founders of a business.[3] One of the major problems most privately held businesses have is the lack of preparation for passing managerial control to the next generation. The cruel fact is that one generation succeeds the other with biological inevitability, yet most privately held firms never formulate succession plans.

Management succession, which involves the transition of managerial decision making in a firm, is one of the greatest challenges confronting owners and entrepreneurs in privately held businesses. At first glance, succession would not seem to be a major problem. All an owner has to do is designate which heir will inherit the operation or, better yet, train one (or more) of them to take over the business during the founder's lifetime. Unfortunately, this is easier said than done. A number of problems exist. One of the major ones is the owner. To a large degree, the owner is the business. The individual's personality and talents make the operation what it is. If this person were to be removed from the picture, the company might be unable to continue. Additionally, this individual may not want to be removed. So if the owner-manager begins to have health problems or is unable to manage effectively, he or she may still hang on. The owner often views any outside attempt to get him or her to step aside as greedy efforts to plunder the operation for personal gain. What's more, the owner and

Table 18.1   Barriers to Succession Planning in Privately Held Businesses

FOUNDER/OWNER	FAMILY
Death anxiety	Death as taboo
Company as symbol	☐ Discussion is a hostile act
☐ Loss of identity	☐ Fear of loss/abandonment
☐ Concern about legacy	Fear of sibling rivalry
Dilemma of choice	Change of spouse's position
☐ Fiction of equality	
Generational envy	
☐ Loss of power	

Source: Manfred F. R. Kets de Vries, "The Dynamics of Family-Controlled Firms: The Good News and the Bad News," *Organizational Dynamics* (winter 1993): 68.

family members may feel anxiety over death, because discussing the topic of death conjures up a negative image in everyone's mind.

Other barriers to succession include sibling rivalry, family members' fear of losing status, or a complete aversion to death for fear of loss or abandonment.[4] Table 18.1 provides a list of barriers to succession attributed to the owner and to the family.

The basic rule for privately held businesses is this: The owner should develop a succession plan. Because many people want to keep the business in their families, decisions have to be made regarding heirs. This is often psychologically difficult. Choosing an heir can be like buying a cemetery plot. It is an admission of one's mortality. Owners who refuse to face the succession issue, however, place an unnecessary burden on those whom they leave behind. Successor problems are not insurmountable. For our consideration of these problems, the best place to begin is with an identification of the key factors in succession.

Key Factors in Succession

It has been said that the concept of "smooth succession" in a privately held business is a contradiction of terms. This contradiction is because succession is a highly charged emotional issue that requires not only structural changes but cultural changes as well.[5] Family succession includes the transfer of ethics, values, and traditions along with the actual business itself. The "family business" and the "business family" are two distinct components that must be dealt with and disentangled if progress toward succession is to be made.[6]

A number of considerations affect the succession issue.[7] One way to examine them is in terms of pressures and interests inside the firm and outside the firm. Another way is to examine forcing events. A third way is to examine the sources of succession. Finally we will discuss the legal restrictions that may affect succession decisions.

Pressures and Interests inside the Firm

Two types of succession pressures originate within the privately held business (see Figure 18.1). One comes from the family members. The other comes from nonfamily employees.[8]

Family Members

When members of the family are also employees, a number of succession-type problems can arise. One is that the family members may want to keep the business in existence so that they and their families will be able to manage it. Sometimes this results in the members wanting to get, or increase, control over operations. Another common development is pressure on the owner-manager to designate an heir. A third

Figure 18.1 Pressures and Interests in a Family Business

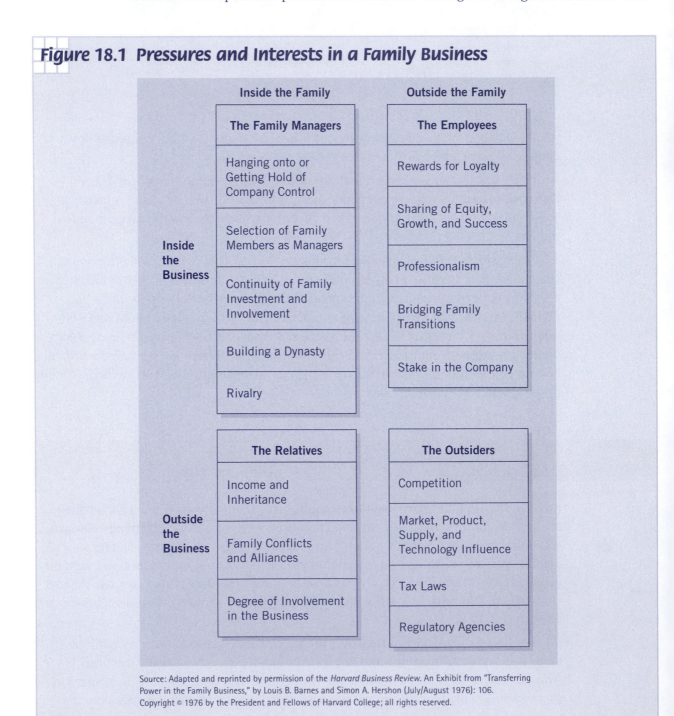

	Inside the Family	Outside the Family
Inside the Business	**The Family Managers** Hanging onto or Getting Hold of Company Control Selection of Family Members as Managers Continuity of Family Investment and Involvement Building a Dynasty Rivalry	**The Employees** Rewards for Loyalty Sharing of Equity, Growth, and Success Professionalism Bridging Family Transitions Stake in the Company
Outside the Business	**The Relatives** Income and Inheritance Family Conflicts and Alliances Degree of Involvement in the Business	**The Outsiders** Competition Market, Product, Supply, and Technology Influence Tax Laws Regulatory Agencies

Source: Adapted and reprinted by permission of the *Harvard Business Review*. An Exhibit from "Transferring Power in the Family Business," by Louis B. Barnes and Simon A. Hershon (July/August 1976): 106. Copyright © 1976 by the President and Fellows of Harvard College; all rights reserved.

possible development is rivalry among the various branches of the family. For example, each of the owner's children may feel that the owner should put him or her (or one of his or her children) in charge of the operation. Given that only one of the family branches can win this fight, the rivalry can lead to the sale or bankruptcy of the business.[9]

Nonfamily Employees

Nonfamily employees sometimes bring pressure on the owner-manager in an effort to protect their personal interests. For example, long-term employees often think the owner should give them an opportunity to buy a stake in the company, or they believe they should be given a percentage of the business in the owner's will. Such hopes and expectations are often conveyed to the owner and can result in pressure for some form of succession plan. Moreover, to the extent the nonfamily employees are critical to the enterprise's success, these demands cannot be ignored. The owner must reach some accommodation with these people if the business is to survive.

Pressures and Interests outside the Firm

Outside the firm, both family members and nonfamily elements exert pressure on and hold interest in the firm's succession.

Family Members

Even when family members do not play an active role in the business, they can apply pressure. Quite often these individuals are interested in ensuring that they inherit part of the operation, and they will put pressure on the owner-manager toward achieving that end. In some cases they pressure for getting involved in the business. Some family members will pressure the owner-manager to hire them. Quite often these appeals are resisted on the grounds of the firm not needing additional personnel or needing someone with specific expertise (sales ability or technical skills), and thus the owner sidesteps the request.

Nonfamily Elements

Another major source of pressure comes from external environmental factors. One of these is competitors who continually change strategy and force the owner-manager to adjust to new market considerations. Other factors include customers, technology, and new-product development. These forces continually change, and the entrepreneur must respond to them. Tax laws, regulatory agencies, and trends in management practices constitute still other elements with which the owner-manager must contend.[10]

Depending on the situation, any of these sources of pressure can prove troublesome.

Figure 18.2 illustrates the distinction of family and business issues in a systems model. At the interface of the family and business systems, both the family and the business respond to disruptions in their regular transaction patterns. These disruptions may come from either outside the family and business or from within them. Outside sources of disruption include public policy changes, economic upheavals, and technological innovation. Inside sources of disruption include marriage, birth, death, and divorce of family members. These disruptions may be either good or bad. In either case, they require a response from both the family and the business.

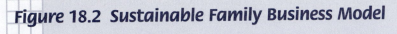

Figure 18.2 Sustainable Family Business Model

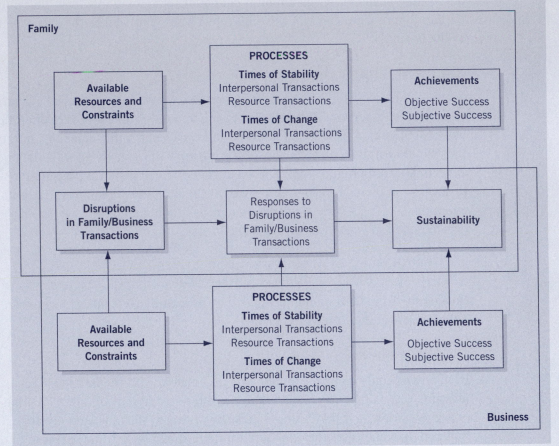

Source: Kathryn Stafford, Karen A. Duncan, Sharon Dane, Mary Winter, "A Research Model of Sustainable Family Business," *Family Business Review* (September 1999): 197–208.

The extent of overlap between the family and business systems will vary from family business to family business. In privately held businesses where the prevailing orientation is to keep the family and the business separate, there is little overlap—diagrammatically, this case is illustrated by a small area of interface between the two systems. Conversely, in family business characterized by great overlap, the area of interface between the family and business systems is considerable.

Sustainability results from the confluence of family success, business success, and appropriate responses to disruptions. In other words, sustainability requires consideration of the family as well as the business. It also requires consideration of the ability of the family and business to cooperate in responding to disruptions in a way that does not impede the success of either.[11]

Forcing Events

Forcing events are those happenings that cause the replacement of the owner-manager. These events require the entrepreneur to step aside and let someone else direct the operation. The following are typical examples:

- ☐ Death, resulting in the heirs immediately having to find a successor to run the operation
- ☐ Illness or some other form of nonterminal physical incapacitation

☐ Mental or psychological breakdown, resulting in the individual having to withdraw from the business

☐ Abrupt departure, such as when an entrepreneur decides, with no advance warning, to retire immediately

☐ Legal problems, such as incarceration for violation of the law (If this period of confinement is for more than a few weeks, succession usually becomes necessary if in name only.)

☐ Severe business decline, resulting in the owner-manager deciding to leave the helm

☐ Financial difficulties, resulting in lenders demanding the removal of the owner-manager before lending the necessary funds to the enterprise

These types of events are often unforeseen, and the family seldom has a contingency plan for dealing with them. As a result, when they occur they often create a major problem for the business.

These considerations influence the environment within which the successor will operate. Unless that individual and the environment fit well, the successor will be less than maximally effective.

Sources of Succession

An **entrepreneurial successor** is someone who is high in ingenuity, creativity, and drive. This person often provides the critical ideas for new-product development and future ventures. The **managerial successor** is someone who is interested in efficiency, internal control, and the effective use of resources. This individual often provides the stability and day-to-day direction needed to keep the enterprise going.

When looking for an inside successor, the entrepreneur usually focuses on a son or daughter or nephew or niece with the intent of gradually giving the person operational responsibilities followed by strategic power and ownership. An important factor in the venture's success is whether the founder and the heir can get along. The entrepreneur must be able to turn from being a leader to being a coach, from being a doer to being an advisor. The heir must respect the founder's attachment to the venture and be sensitive to this person's possessive feelings. At the same time the heir must be able to use his or her entrepreneurial flair to initiate necessary changes.[12]

When looking ahead toward choosing a successor from inside the organization, the founder often trains a team of executive managers consisting of both family and non-family members. This enables the individual to build an experienced management team capable of producing a successor. The founder assumes that, in time, a natural leader will emerge from the group.[13]

Two key strategies center on the entry of the inside younger generation and when the "power" actually changes hands. Table 18.2 illustrates the advantages and disadvantages of the **early entry strategy** versus the **delayed entry strategy**. The main question is the ability of the successor to gain credibility with the firm's employees. The actual transfer of power is a critical issue in the implementation of any succession plan.[14]

If the founder looks for a family member outside the firm, he or she usually prefers to have the heir first work for someone else. The hope is that the individual will make his or her initial mistakes early on, before assuming the family business reins.

the entrepreneurial
PROCESS

Family Business Concerns

In a survey conducted by Crowe, Chizek & Co. (a consulting and accounting firm) for *Family Business* magazine, 339 CEOs of family businesses responded to questions concerning the future. In comparing their level of concern of business factors and family factors from the previous ten years to the next ten years, the following results were found.

Looking back over the past ten years and ahead to the next ten years, rate your level of concern for the following business factors.

	PAST TEN YEARS		NEXT TEN YEARS	
	LITTLE	MODERATE TO GREAT	LITTLE	MODERATE TO GREAT
Business Factors				
Keeping up with technology	16%	80%	6%	94%
Attracting/keeping strong nonfamily executives	21	83	7	91
Lack of qualified employees	23	75	7	90
Customer pricing demands	17	80	12	90
Employee education	25	71	13	85
Government regulations	21	79	13	85
Increasing costs of labor and materials	22	76	14	83
Estate taxes	38	58	15	81
Consolidation in your industry	36	62	18	78
Access to capital	35	65	23	75
Greater competition from e-commerce/Internet	86	11	35	62
Foreign competition	73	24	57	40
Need to globalize business	76	20	54	37
Economic and political instability in other countries	74	21	54	33
Family Factors				
Choosing and preparing successors	35	65	12	79
Family employee compensation	43	55	29	66
Family conflict	38	58	30	65
Financial expectations of nonactive family	53	41	37	60
Lack of consensus on family values and mission	55	44	46	54
Creation of family council	61	31	37	52
Becoming ingrown	55	36	47	45

SOURCE: Edwin A. Hoover and Colette Lombard Hoover, "What You See Ahead," *Family Business* (autumn 1999): 33–41.

Table 18.2   Comparison of Entry Strategies for Succession in Family Business

	ADVANTAGES	DISADVANTAGES
Early Entry Strategy	Intimate familiarity with the nature of the business and employees is acquired. Skills specifically required by the business are developed. Exposure to others in the business facilitates acceptance and the achievement of credibility. Strong relationships with constituents are readily established.	Conflict results when the owner has difficulty with teaching or relinquishing control to the successor. Normal mistakes tend to be viewed as incompetence in the successor. Knowledge of the environment is limited, and risks of inbreeding are incurred.
Delayed Entry Strategy	The successor's skills are judged with greater objectivity. The development of self-confidence and growth independent of familial influence are achieved. Outside success establishes credibility and serves as a basis for accepting the successor as a competent executive. Perspective of the business environment is broadened.	Specific expertise and understanding of the organization's key success factors and culture may be lacking. Set patterns of outside activity may conflict with those prevailing in the family firm. Resentment may result when successors are advanced ahead of long-term employees.

Source: Jeffrey A. Barach, Joseph Ganitsky, James A. Carson, and Benjamin A. Doochin, "Entry of the Next Generation: Strategic Challenge for Family Firms," *Journal of Small Business Management* (April 1988): 53.

Sometimes the founder will look for a nonfamily outsider to be the successor, perhaps only temporarily. The entrepreneur may not see an immediate successor inside the firm and may decide to hire a professional manager, at least on an interim basis, while waiting for an heir to mature and take over.

Another form of nonfamily outsider is the specialist who is experienced in getting ventures out of financial difficulty. The founder then usually gives the specialist total control, and this person later hands the rejuvenated venture to another leader.

Still another nonfamily approach is for the founder to find a person with the right talents and to bring this individual into the venture as an assistant, with the understanding that he or she will eventually become president and owner of the venture. No heirs may exist, or perhaps no eligible family member is interested.

Legal Restrictions

The first source for succession often is family and in-house personnel prospects. However, such traditions of succession practices in privately held businesses have been challenged in the Oakland Scavenger Company case.

This suit was brought in 1984 by a group of black and Hispanic workers in the California-based **Oakland Scavenger Company** (a garbage collection firm), who complained of employment discrimination because of their race. The U.S. District Court of

Northern California dismissed the suit on the basis that it had no relation to antidiscrimination laws. However, the U.S. Court of Appeals for the Ninth Circuit reviewed the decision and held that "nepotistic concerns cannot supersede the nation's paramount goal of equal economic opportunity for all."[15]

According to Oakland Scavenger's legal brief, the question focused on the Fifth Amendment versus Title VII of the 1964 Civil Rights Act: If discrimination overrides the protection of life, liberty, and property from unreasonable interference from the state, then the rights of parents leaving their property and business to anyone can be abolished. This decision can have a major effect on the management succession plans of privately held businesses.

The case was appealed to the Supreme Court. However, before the Court could make a ruling, the Oakland Scavenger Company was purchased by the Waste Management Corporation, and an out-of-court settlement was reached. The company agreed to an $8 million settlement. The settlement allocated sums of at least $50,000 to 16 black and Hispanic plaintiffs, depending on their length of service, and also provided for payments to a class of more than 400 black and Hispanic workers Oakland Scavenger employed after January 10, 1972.[16]

As K. Peter Stalland, legal representative for the National Family Business Council, has stated, "The effect this case can have on small business is tremendous. It means, conceivably, that almost any small business can be sued by an employee of a different ethnic origin than the owner, based upon not being accorded the same treatment as a son or daughter. The precedent is dangerous."[17] Thus, **nepotism** is now something that must be considered seriously in light of the legal ramifications.

The Oakland Scavenger case has started a movement that is sure to result in more guidelines and limitations for family employment, and privately held businesses will have to be aware of this challenge when preparing succession plans. (See the Entrepreneurship in Practice box on legal concerns over nepotism.)

Developing a Succession Strategy

Developing a succession strategy involves several important steps: (1) understanding the contextual aspects, (2) identifying successor qualities, and (3) developing a written succession plan.[18]

Understanding the Contextual Aspects

The five key aspects that must be considered for an effective succession follow.

Time

The earlier the entrepreneur begins to plan for a successor, the better the chances of finding the right person. The biggest problem the owner faces is the prospect of events that force immediate action and result in inadequate time to find the best replacement.

Type of Venture

Some entrepreneurs are easy to replace; some cannot be replaced. To a large degree, this is determined by the type of venture. An entrepreneur who is the idea person in a high-tech operation is going to be difficult to replace. The same is true for an entrepreneur whose personal business contacts throughout the industry are the key factors for the venture's success. On the other hand, a person running an operation that requires a minimum of knowledge or expertise usually can be replaced without much trouble.

Capabilities of Managers

The skills, desires, and abilities of the replacement will dictate the future potential and direction of the enterprise. As the industry matures, the demands made on the entrepreneur also may change. Industries where high tech is the name of the game often go through a change in which marketing becomes increasingly important. A technologically skilled entrepreneur with an understanding of marketing, or with the ability to develop an orientation in this direction, will be more valuable to the enterprise than will a technologically skilled entrepreneur with no marketing interest or background.

Entrepreneur's Vision

Most entrepreneurs have expectations, hopes, and desires for their organization. A successor, it is hoped, will share this vision, except, of course, in cases where the entrepreneur's plans have gotten the organization in trouble and a new vision is needed. Examples are in plenty today because of the huge increase in life sciences ventures, high technology ventures, and other emerging technologies where the founding entrepreneur possesses the initial vision to launch the company but lacks the managerial experience to grow the venture. Outside executive experience is sought because the board of directors may feel that a more managerial, day-to-day entrepreneurial manager is needed to replace the highly conceptual, analytical entrepreneur who founded the company.

Environmental Factors

Sometimes a successor is needed because the business environment changes and a parallel change is needed at the top. An example is Edwin Land of Polaroid. Although his technological creativity had made the venture successful, Land eventually had to step aside for someone with more marketing skills. In some cases owners have had to allow financial types to assume control of the venture because internal efficiency was more critical to short-run survival than was market effectiveness.

Identifying Successor Qualities

Successors should possess many qualities or characteristics. Depending on the situation, some will be more important than others. In most cases, however, all will have some degree of importance. Some of the most common of these successor qualities are sufficient knowledge of the business or a good position (especially marketing or finance) from which to acquire this knowledge within an acceptable time; fundamental honesty and capability; good health; energy, alertness, and perception; enthusiasm about the enterprise; personality compatible with the business; high degree of perseverance; stability and maturity; reasonable amount of aggressiveness; thoroughness and a proper respect for detail; problem-solving ability; resourcefulness; ability to plan and organize; talent to develop people; personality of a starter and a finisher; and appropriate agreement with the owner's philosophy about the business.[19]

A Written Succession Strategy

These elements prepare the entrepreneur for developing a management continuity strategy and policy. A written policy can be established in one of the following strategies.

entrepreneurship IN PRACTICE

Legal Concerns over Nepotism

In certain cases, entrepreneurs may be in violation of the law if they employ too many family members. The law considers nepotism a neutral policy—that is, it's not discriminatory by itself. Such a policy is lawful unless it has an "adverse impact" on women or minority groups (as in the Oakland Scavenger Company case). In another case, the Supreme Court increased the burden of proving adverse impact to plaintiffs and, at the same time, made it easier for employers to defend such lawsuits. It is expected, however, that Congress will eventually enact a civil rights bill, with or without the president's signature, that will require employers to provide a strong business justification for a policy that results in racial or gender imbalance.

Nepotism is more vulnerable to attack for "disparate impact" by racial minorities than by women. As the U.S. Court of Appeals noted in *Platner v. Cash & Thomas*: "It is difficult to see how nepotism could mask systematic gender discrimination. While a person's relatives will usually be of the same race, men and women will presumably be equally represented both within and without the family."

The smallest companies—those with 15 or fewer employees—are specifically excluded from the provisions of the Civil Rights Law of 1964 dealing with employment discrimination. But many states have similar statutes with broader coverage. The following guidelines may help growing ventures avoid any charge of employment discrimination:

☐ Find out as much as you can about the racial and gender composition of the labor pool in your area, and try to bring your own shop in line with it.

☐ The argument that most hiring in your business is through industry connections or word of mouth is a weak defense, since these traditional sources often perpetuate an in-group.

☐ Avoid stereotyping in job assignments or communications. Jokes or epithets aimed at women or minority-group members will be taken in court as evidence of a "hostile environment" for these groups.

☐ When hiring or promoting a family member, explain the decision in job-related terms. If a disappointed applicant asks why he or she was passed over, emphasize the qualifications for the job, commitment to the long-term success of the company, and firsthand knowledge or skills—for whoever was selected.

☐ Never make or explain a hiring decision or promotion by reasoning that "our customers won't like it if we send them a black salesman or a woman." Customer preference is not a defense in a lawsuit based on a discrimination claim.

SOURCE: Howard Muson, "Dangerous Liaisons," *Family Business* (January/February 1991): 22–27.

1. The owner controls the *management continuity strategy* entirely. This is very common, yet legal advice is still needed and recommended.

2. The owner consults with selected family members. Here the legal advisor helps to establish a *liaison* between family and owner in constructing the succession mechanism.

3. The owner works with professional advisors. This is an actual board of advisors from various professional disciplines and industries that works with the owner to establish the mechanism for succession (sometimes referred to as a "quasi-board").[20]

4. The owner works with family involvement. This alternative allows the core family (blood members and spouses) to actively participate in and influence the decisions regarding succession.

If the owner is still reasonably healthy and the firm is in a viable condition, the following additional actions should be considered.

5. The owner formulates **buy/sell agreements** at the very outset of the company, or soon thereafter, and whenever a major change occurs. This is also the time to consider an appropriate insurance policy on key individuals that would provide the cash needed to acquire the equity of the deceased.

6. The owner considers **employee stock ownership plans (ESOPs)**. If the owner has no immediate successor in mind and respects the loyalty and competence of his or her employees, then an appropriate ESOP might be the best solution for passing control of the enterprise. After the owner's death, the employees could decide on the management hierarchy.

7. The owner sells or liquidates the business when losing enthusiasm for it but is still physically able to go on. This could provide the capital to launch another business. Whatever the owner's plans, the firm would be sold before it fails due to disinterest.

8. The owner sells or liquidates after discovering a terminal illness but still has time for the orderly transfer of management or ownership.[21]

For all of these strategies, legal advice is beneficial, but of greater benefit is having advisors (legal or otherwise) who understand the succession issues and are able to recommend a course of action.

Entrepreneurial founders of privately held businesses often reject thoughts of succession. Yet neither ignorance nor denial will change the inevitable. It is therefore crucial for entrepreneurs to design a plan for succession very carefully. Such plans prevent today's flourishing privately held businesses from becoming a statistic of diminishing family dynasties.

Consider Outside Help

Promotion from within is a morale-building philosophy. Sometimes, however, it is a mistake. When the top person does a poor job, does promoting the next individual in line solve the problem? The latter may be the owner-manager's clone. Or consider family-owned businesses that start to outgrow the managerial ability of the top person. Does anyone in the firm *really* have the requisite skills for managing the operation? The questions that must be answered are, How can the business be effectively run, and Who has the ability to do it? Sometimes answering these questions calls for an outside person. Privately held businesses also face the ever-present ego factor.[22] Does the owner-manager have the wisdom to step aside and the courage to let someone else make strategic decisions? Or is the desire for control so great that the owner prefers to run the risks associated with personally managing the operation? The lesson is clear to the dispassionate observer; unfortunately, it is one many owners have had to learn the hard way.[23]

IN PRACTICE

entrepreneurship

Buy/Sell Agreements for Succession

Many entrepreneurs owe their continued success to the combined skills of two or more owners. And when one of those owners dies, becomes disabled, or retires, it is imperative the transfer of his or her ownership interest is carried out in a way that protects the future of the business, the ownership interests of remaining shareholders, and the financial security of the departing owner's family. A buy/sell agreement can provide just such protection. It ensures that interest in a closely held business is transferred in a manner advantageous to all involved parties. This type of agreement can be designed to make certain the following:

1. The remaining shareholder(s) has the first right to retain the ownership interest.

2. The departing owner (or beneficiaries) receives a fair market price for the ownership interest.

3. Lawsuits and disputes that could threaten the company's existence are avoided.

4. Funds are available to purchase the ownership interest.

Legal counsel is necessary to ensure that a buy/sell agreement addresses all of the unique circumstances of a particular company.

The two basic types of agreements are the "cross-purchase agreement," in which the shareholders are obligated to purchase the departing owner's stock, and the "redemption agreement," in which the company is obligated to purchase the departing owner's stock. Each case has certain advantages, disadvantages, and tax implications that need to be considered. Thus, both a lawyer and a tax accountant should be consulted.

SOURCE: Thomas Owens, "Buy-Sell Agreements," *Small Business Reports* (January 1991): 57–61.

The Harvest Strategy: Liquidity Events

Many entrepreneurs choose to seek an exit from their firms in the form of what is referred to as a "liquidity event," which stands for the positioning of the venture for the realization of a cash return for the owners and the investors. This "event" is most often achieved through an initial public offering or complete sale of the venture. In either scenario the entrepreneur must seek professional advice and counsel due to the significant regulations and legal parameters involved. For our purposes we delve into the basic concepts involved with each of these liquidity events.

The Initial Public Offering (IPO)

As we covered in Chapter 14, many entrepreneurs have sought capital through the public markets. Just to reiterate here, the term *initial public offering (IPO)* is used to represent the registered public offering of a company's securities for the first time. In 2003 there were 81 IPOs, raising $13.5 billion. These figures reflect the tremendous *volatility* that exists within the stock market; however, entrepreneurs should be aware of the concerns confronting them when pursuing the IPO market. In addition, entrepreneurs have begun to recognize some of the complex requirements involved with going public.[24] Table 18.3 provides a complete illustration of the steps involved with an IPO.

Table 18.3   The IPO Process

The entire initial public offering process is at once fast-moving and highly structured, governed by an interlocking set of federal and state laws and regulations and self-regulatory organization rules. Each member of the IPO team has specific responsibilities to fulfill; however, the company ultimately calls the plays for the team.

The following steps in the IPO process apply to both U.S. and non-U.S. companies.

Present proposal to the board. The IPO process begins with management making a presentation to the company's board of directors, complete with business plan and financial projections, proposing their company enter the public market. The board should consider the proposal carefully.

Restate financial statements and refocus the company *(applies only to companies not in compliance with U.S. GAAP).* If the board approves the proposal to go public, the company's books and records should be reviewed for the past two to three years. Financial statements should be restated to adhere to GAAP in order for them to be certified. Any intracompany transactions, compensation arrangements, and relationships involving management or the board that are customary to a private enterprise—*but improper for a public company*—must be eliminated and the statements appropriately restated. Also, companies should consider whether any outside affiliations (operations tangential to the company's core business) will be perceived negatively by the market.

Find an underwriter and execute a "letter of intent." At this point, a company should select an underwriter, if it has not already engaged one. A company's relationship with an underwriter should then be formalized through a mutual "letter of intent," outlining fees, ranges for stock price and number of shares, and certain other conditions.

Draft prospectus. After a letter of intent is executed, the IPO attorneys can begin work on the prospectus.

Respond to due diligence. The next step is to ask your investment banker and accountant to begin an elaborate investigation of your company (the due diligence process). Your underwriter will examine your company's management, operations, financial conditions, performance, competitive position, and business plan. Other factors open to scrutiny are your labor force, suppliers, customers, creditors, and any other parties that have a bearing on the viability of the company as a public entity and could affect the proper, truthful, adequate disclosure of its condition in the prospectus. The accounting firm will examine financial information and such specific documents as contracts, billings, and receipts to ensure the accuracy and adequacy of financial statements.

Select a financial printer. Your company should select an experienced financial printer—one that is familiar with SEC regulations governing the graphic presentation of a prospectus and has the facilities to print sufficient quantities under severe time constraints.

Assemble the syndicate. After the preliminary prospectus has been filed with the SEC and is available for circulation among potential investors, your underwriter should assemble the "syndicate," consisting of additional investment bankers who will place portions of the offering to achieve the desired distribution. Your underwriter should also accumulate "indications of interest"—solicited through its efforts as well as those of the syndicate—from institutions and brokers that have approached their clients. These indications give assurance that the IPO is viable and help to determine the final number of shares to be offered and the allocations to investors.

Perform the road show. Next, your company and your investment banker should design and perform the "road show," a series of meetings held with potential investors and analysts in key cities across the

Table 18.3   (Continued)

country and, if appropriate, overseas. The road show has become increasingly important not only to communicate key information to investors, but also to display the managerial talent and expertise that will be leading the company.

Prepare, revise, and print the prospectus. In the meantime, the preliminary prospectus should have been prepared and revised according to SEC and NASDR (National Association of Securities Dealers Regulations) comments. Upon completion of these revisions, the company can expect NASDR to issue a letter stating that it has no objections to the underwriting compensation, terms, and arrangements, and the SEC to indicate its intent to declare their registration effective. The preliminary prospectus should be circulated to potential investors at least two days before the effective date, then the final version of the prospectus can be printed.

Price the offering. Just before the underwriting agreement is signed, on the day before the registration becomes effective and sales begin, the offering is priced. The investment banker should recommend a price per share for management's approval, taking into account the company's financial performance and competitive prospects, the stock price of comparable companies, general stock market conditions, and the success of the road show and ensuing expressions of interest. While the company will want to price the offering as high as possible, an offering that does not sell or sell completely will not be in its best interest or in the interest or the investors who find the share price declining in the market immediately after their initial purchase. In fact, investors look for at least a modest increase in the market price to reassure them about their investment decision.

Determine the offering size. The investment banking team should also consult with management regarding the offering size, taking into consideration how much capital the company needs to raise, the desired degree of corporate control, and investor demand. Often, the more shares outstanding, the greater the liquidity of the stock, which will increase institutional interest.

Source: Adapted from *Going Public* (New York: The NASDAQ Stock Market, Inc, 2000).

The SEC requires the filing of a registration statement that includes a complete prospectus on the company. The SEC then reviews the registration, ensuring that full disclosure is made before giving permission to proceed. (See Table 18.4 for a presentation of the registration process.)

The prospectus must disclose fully all pertinent information about a company and must present a fair representation of the firm's true prospects. All negative information must be clearly highlighted and explained. Some of the specific detailed information that must be presented follows.

- ☐ History and nature of the company
- ☐ Capital structure
- ☐ Description of any material contracts
- ☐ Description of securities being registered
- ☐ Salaries and security holdings of major officers and directors and the price they paid for holdings
- ☐ Underwriting arrangements
- ☐ Estimate and use of net proceeds

Table 18.4   The Registration Process

EVENT	PARTICIPANTS	AGENDA	TIMETABLE
Preliminary meeting to discuss issue	President, VP Finance, independent accountants, underwriters, counsel	Discuss financial needs; introduce and select type of issue to meet needs	1 July (Begin)
Form selection	Management, counsel	Select appropriate form for use in registration statement	3 July (3 days)
Initial meeting of working group	President, VP Finance, independent accountants, underwriter, counsel for underwriter, company counsel	Assign specific duties to each person in the working group; discuss underwriting problems with this issue; discuss accounting problems with the issue	8 July (8 days)
Second meeting of working group	Same as for initial meeting	Review work assignments; prepare presentation to board of directors	22 July (22 days)
Meeting of board of directors	Board of directors, members of working group	Approve proposed issue and increase of debt or equity; authorize preparation of materials	26 July (26 days)
Meeting of company counsel with underwriters	Company counsel, counsel for underwriters, underwriters	Discuss underwriting terms and blue-sky problems	30 July (30 days)
Meeting of working group	Members of working group	Review collected material and examine discrepancies	6 August (37 days)
Prefiling conference with SEC staff	Working group members, SEC staff, other experts as needed	Review proposed registration and associated problems: legal, financial, operative	9 August (40 days)
Additional meetings of working group	Members of working group	Prepare final registration statement and prospectuses	12–30 August (61 days)
Meeting with board of directors	Board of directors, members of working group	Approve registration statement and prospectuses; discuss related topics and problems	6 September (68 days)
Meeting of working group	Members of working group	Draft final corrected registration statement	10 September (72 days)
Filing registration statement with SEC	Company counsel or representative and SEC staff	File registration statement and pay fee	12 September (74 days)
Distribution of "red herring" prospectus	Underwriters	Publicize offering	16 September (78 days)

Table 18.4   (Continued)

EVENT	PARTICIPANTS	AGENDA	TIMETABLE
Receipt of letter of comments	Members of working group	Relate deficiencies in registration statement	15 October (107 days)
Meeting of working group	Members of working group	Correct deficiencies and submit amendments	21 October (113 days)
Due diligence meeting	Management representatives, independent accountants, company counsel, underwriter's counsel, underwriters, other professionals as needed	Exchange final information and discuss pertinent problems relating to underwriting and issue	24 October (116 days)
Pricing amendment	Management, underwriters	Add the amounts for the actual price, underwriter's discount or commission, and net proceeds to company to the amended registration statement	25 October (117 days)
Notice of acceptance	SEC staff	Report from SEC staff on acceptance status of price-amended registration statement	28 October (120 days)
Statement becomes effective			30 October (122 days)

Source: *From An Introduction to the SEC,* 5th ed. by K. Fred Skousen. Copyright © 1991. Reprinted by permission of South-Western, a division of Thomson Learning.

- ☐ Audited financial statements
- ☐ Information about the competition with an estimation of the chances of the company's survival

Some of the more important disclosure requirements for annual reports follow.

- ☐ Audited financial statements that include the balance sheets for the past two years and income and funds statements for the past three years
- ☐ Five years of selected financial data
- ☐ Management's discussion and analysis of financial conditions and results of operations
- ☐ A brief description of the business
- ☐ Line-of-business disclosures for the past three fiscal years
- ☐ Identification of directors and executive officers, with the principal occupation and employer of each
- ☐ Identification of the principal market in which the firm's securities are traded

- ☐ Range of market prices and dividends for each quarter of the two most recent fiscal years

- ☐ An offer to provide a free copy of the 10-K report to shareholders on written request unless the annual report complies with Form 10-K disclosure requirements[25]

Some of the forms the SEC requires follow.

- ☐ Form S-1 (information contained in the prospectus and other additional financial data)

- ☐ Form 10-Q (quarterly financial statements and a summary of all important events that took place during the three-month period)

- ☐ Form 8-K (a report of unscheduled material events or corporate changes deemed important to the shareholder and filed with the SEC within 15 days after the end of a month in which a significant material event transpired)

- ☐ Proxy statements (information given in connection with proxy solicitation)[26]

Entrepreneurs who pursue the public securities route should be prepared for these reporting requirements, disclosure statements, and the shared control and ownership with outside shareholders.

Complete Sale of the Venture

After considering the various succession ideas presented in this chapter as well as the potential for an initial public offering, many privately held business entrepreneurs choose a **harvest strategy** that involves complete sale of the venture. If this becomes the proper choice for an entrepreneur (and keep in mind it may be the best decision for an entrepreneur who has no interested family members or key employees), then the owner needs to review some important considerations. The idea of "selling out" actually should be viewed in the positive sense of "harvesting the investment."

Entrepreneurs consider selling their venture for numerous reasons. Based on 1,000 business owners surveyed, some of the motivations are (1) boredom and burnout, (2) lack of operating and growth capital, (3) no heirs to leave the business to, (4) desire for liquidity, (5) aging and health problems, and (6) desire to pursue other interests.[27]

Whether due to a career shift, poor health, a desire to start another venture, or retirement, many entrepreneurs face the sellout option during their entrepreneurial lifetime. This harvesting strategy needs to be carefully prepared in order to obtain the adequate financial rewards.[28]

Steps for Selling a Business

There are generally eight recommended steps for the proper preparation, development, and realization of the sale of a venture[29]

Step 1: Prepare a Financial Analysis

The purpose of such an analysis is to define priorities and forecast the next few years of the business. These fundamental questions must be answered:

- ☐ What will executive and other work force requirements be, and how will we pay for them?

☐ If the market potential is so limited that goals cannot be attained, should we plan an acquisition or develop new products to meet targets for sales and profits?

☐ Must we raise outside capital for continued growth? How much and when?[30]

Step 2: Segregate Assets

Tax accountants and lawyers may suggest the following steps to reduce taxes:

☐ Place real estate in a separate corporation, owned individually or by members of the family.

☐ Establish a leasing subsidiary with title to machinery and rolling stock. You can then lease this property to the operating company.

☐ Give some or all of the owner's shares to heirs when values are low, but have the owner retain voting rights. Thus, when a sale is made, part or all of the proceeds can go directly to another generation without double taxation.

☐ Hold management's salaries and fringe benefits at reasonable levels to maximize profits.[31]

Step 3: Value the Business

The various methods used to valuate a venture were discussed in Chapter 17. Obviously, establishing the valuation of a company constitutes a most important step in its sale.[32]

Step 4: Identify the Appropriate Timing

Knowing when to offer a business for sale is a critical factor. Timing can be everything. A few suggestions follow:

☐ Sell when business profits show a strong upward trend.

☐ Sell when the management team is complete and experienced.

☐ Sell when the business cycle is on the upswing, with potential buyers in the right mood and holding excess capital or credit for acquisitions.

☐ Sell when you are convinced that your company's future will be bright.[33]

Step 5: Publicize the Offer to Sell

A short prospectus on the company that provides enough information to interest potential investors should be prepared. This prospectus should be circulated through the proper professional channels: bankers, accountants, lawyers, consultants, and business brokers.

Step 6: Finalize the Prospective Buyers

Inquiries need to be made in the trade concerning the prospective buyers. Characters and managerial reputation should be assessed in order to find the best buyer.

Step 7: Remain Involved through the Closing

Meeting with the final potential buyers helps to eliminate areas of misunderstanding and to negotiate the major requirements more effectively. Also, the involvement of professionals such as attorneys and accountants usually precludes any major problems arising at the closing.

Step 8: Communicate after the Sale

Problems between the new owner and the remaining management team need to be resolved in order to build a solid transition. Communication between the seller and the buyer and between the buyer and the current management personnel is a key step.

In addition to these eight steps, an entrepreneur must be aware of the tax implications arising from the sale of a business. For professional advice, a tax accountant specializing in business valuations and sales should be consulted.

The eight steps outlined here, combined with the information on valuation in Chapter 17, will help entrepreneurs harvest their ventures. The steps provide a clear framework within which entrepreneurs can structure a fair negotiation leading to a sale. If the purpose of a valuation is to sell the business, then the entrepreneur must plan ahead and follow through with each step.

Summary

This chapter focused on the harvesting of the venture. Beginning with the issue of management succession as one of the greatest challenges for entrepreneurs, a number of considerations that affect succession were discussed. Using privately held firms as the focal point in this chapter, key issues such as family and nonfamily members, both within and outside the firm, were identified to show the unique pressures on the entrepreneur. Some family members will want to be put in charge of the operation; others simply want a stake in the enterprise.

Two types of successors exist: An entrepreneurial successor provides innovative ideas for new-product development, whereas a managerial successor provides stability for day-to-day operations. An entrepreneur may search inside or outside the family as well as inside or outside the business. The actual transfer of power is a critical issue, and the timing of entry for a successor can be strategic.

The Oakland Scavenger Company case revealed how legal concerns now exist about the hiring of only family members. Nepotism has been challenged in the courts on the basis of discrimination.

Developing a succession plan involves understanding these important contextual aspects: time, type of venture, capabilities of managers, the entrepreneur's vision, and environmental factors. Also, forcing events may require the implementation of a succession plan regardless of whether or not the firm is ready to implement one. This is why it is so important to identify successor qualities and carry out the succession plan.

The chapter closed with a discussion of the entrepreneur's decision to sell out. The process was viewed as a method to "harvest" the investment, and eight specific steps were presented for entrepreneurs to follow.

Key Terms and Concepts

buy/sell agreement	harvest strategy
delayed entry strategy	management succession
early entry strategy	managerial successor
employee stock ownership plans (ESOP)	nepotism
entrepreneurial successor	Oakland Scavenger Company
forcing events	

Review and Discussion Questions

1. What are the potential choices for an entrepreneur to examine as the venture matures?

2. A number of barriers to succession in privately held businesses exist. Using Table 18.1, identify some of the key barriers.

3. What pressures do entrepreneurs sometimes face from inside the family? (Use Figure 18.1 in your answer.)

4. What pressures do entrepreneurs sometimes face from outside the family? (Use Figure 18.1 in your answer.)

5. An entrepreneur can make a number of choices regarding a successor. Using Table 18.2 as a guide, discuss each of these choices.

6. How might the Oakland Scavenger case affect succession decisions in small businesses?

7. What are three of the contextual aspects that must be considered in an effective succession plan?

8. In what way can forcing events cause the replacement of an owner-manager? Cite three examples.

9. What are five qualities or characteristics successors should possess?

10. Why do entrepreneurs look forward to the day when they can take their company public?

11. What eight steps should be followed to harvest a business? Discuss each of these steps.

Experiential Exercise

Passing It On

Management succession and continuity are two of the critical concerns of most entrepreneurs. In your library, look through the past-year issues of these magazines: *Business Week, U.S. News & World Report, Inc., Fortune Small Business, Entrepreneur, Working Woman, Fast Company,* and *Family Business.* Focus on articles related to the management succession and continuity of specific firms. Then choose the two you find to be most interesting and informative and answer the following questions:

Firm 1

1. What business is this company in?_____

2. What difficulties did the owner have formulating a strategy regarding his or her succession?_____

    _____

    _____

    _____

3. What was the entrepreneur's final decision on how to handle the succession?____

    _____

    _____

    _____

4. What lessons can be learned from this individual's experience?_____

_____

_____

_____

Firm 2

1. What business is this company in?_____

_____

2. What difficulties did the owner have formulating a strategy regarding his or her succession?_____

_____

_____

_____

3. What was the entrepreneur's final decision on how to handle the succession?____

_____

_____

_____

4. What lessons can be learned from this individual's experience?_____

_____

_____

_____

In Conclusion

Based on what you have learned from these two cases, what recommendations would you give to an entrepreneur who is in the process of developing a succession plan? Be as helpful as possible.

Video Case 18.1

**Harvesting Strategy for Entrepreneurial Ventures
Advertising Arts College with Tracy Myers**

Always be thinking you're going to get a phone call saying, 'We're interested in buying you.' And are you ready? Because once someone asks you, they want to come and look at your books and look at your business and look at you right then. You don't have time to backtrack and change your reputation or change your revenue stream. Be always ready. (Tracy Myers)

In 1981, Tracy Myers and her partner, Gary Cantor, opened The Advertising Arts College in an 1,100 square foot location in La Jolla, California. The mission of the school was to prepare students for a career in advertising, and it became a fully accredited, private post-secondary, for-profit institution granting baccalaureate degrees. Over the next 19 years, the student population developed, the revenue flow increased, and the school moved to larger locations several times.

In 1987, they bought their own building to accommodate the growing enrollment; it was one of the few single-user buildings available in La Jolla at the time. Tracy believes this purchase represented a sound decision in growing the business. "The space comes before the customers. You have to . . . impress your customer with your location, with your facility."

Then, in 2001, out of the proverbial blue, Tracy received a phone call from The Art Institute, a publicly traded corporation that wanted to buy the school. Tracy remembers the call: "I think I was in shock at first. I kind of thought someday it would be nice to be able to sell the school, and everybody thinks about an exit strategy. . . . [but] I wasn't thinking about retiring. I thought, 'Oh, I'll work for maybe another ten years.'"

The Art Institute told Tracy and Gary that they wanted to have a school in San Diego County and that, if the partners weren't interested in selling their school, they would open one of their own. Tracy says this hardball approach did not make her fearful; she thought another school might create more local interest in the field. But the partners did decide to change the name of their school to The Art Institute of California. "In a strange way, it made us more valuable . . . because we secured the name that they wanted."

Tracy is clear about why The Art Institute wanted to buy her school. "It's about the numbers. It's about the revenue," she says. "They worked with our CPA that we had used for years and our bookkeeper. . . . There were about 400 students at the time that they bought it, and tuition was $10,000 a year at that time. And they could see, looking at the books over the years . . . that every year we acquired more and more students."

Another important factor that made the school saleable was its reputation in educating competent students and operating an efficient, honest business. The buyers did due diligence in the community to find out who hired the graduates and how well trained the graduates were. They asked the community what they thought about the school.

"We had a reputation that was so good . . . so sterling really. And it was a conscious decision my partner and I made when we started the school not to take shortcuts, to really care, to be honest about everything all the time, because when you own a school and you're dealing in federal funds, Title IV funds for student loans and grants, you are audited constantly . . . your reputation is so important . . . especially if you go to sell your business down the road. Don't cut corners from the very beginning."

Since Tracy and Gary had not considered harvesting their business, however, they did not know how to proceed with the sale. After a dialogue with The Art Institute started, Tracy quickly realized that she needed expert input on various legal and financial details, so she began a process of interviewing various appropriate experts. She was able to find a knowledgeable broker through a trade organization she belonged to, The California Association of Private Post-Secondary Schools. She explains: "I decided to choose the person that I felt would give me 100 percent of their time and energy and focus on my issues versus [someone considering] me basically [as] a small fish in a large pond." The broker turned out to be a skilled negotiator who worked well with the partners in evaluating the value of the school.

The sale's process started in February 2000, and ended in October of the same year. Tracy and Gary were paid in cash, 98 percent down and two percent a year later. "All the cards were stacked in our favor. And the more we went into the negotiating process, the more I realized how valuable this school was," Tracy says.

Now, looking back at the 19 years she spent growing the school from nothing, Tracy has a sense of accomplishment. "I feel good about [the sale]. . . . [I've] passed it on so it can grow and be better and bigger. I would love to find something else. I'm rested now. It's time. . . . I want to do it again."

Questions

1. Because Tracy and Gary had made no plans to sell their school, how would you describe their readiness to do so when they were approached by a buyer?

2. Because Tracy and Gary already employed a CPA and a bookkeeper, what more could a broker do for the partners in selling their business?

3. What relevant information about the buyers for the school should Tracy and Gary have gathered?

Case 18.2

Just as Good as Ever

When Pablo Rodriguez was found in the storage area, no one knew for sure how long he had been unconscious. Within 30 minutes he was in the emergency room of Mercy Hospital, and by early evening the doctors had determined that Pablo had suffered a mild heart attack.

During the first few days he was in the hospital, Pablo's family was more concerned with his health than anything else. However, as it became clear Pablo would be released within a week and would be allowed back at work within two weeks, family members talked about his stepping aside as president of the operation and allowing someone else to take over the reins.

Pablo is president of a successful auto-parts supply house. Gross sales last year were $3.7 million. Working with him in the business are his son, daughter, and two nephews. Pablo started the business 22 years ago when he was 33. After working for one of the large oil firms for ten years as a sales representative to auto-parts supply houses, Pablo broke away and started his own company. At first, he hired outside help. Over the past five years, however, he has been slowly bringing his family on board. It was Pablo's hope that his son would one day take over the business, but he did not see this happening for at least another 10 to 15 years.

Pablo's wife, Rebecca, believes that although he should continue to work, he should begin to train his son to run the business. On the day before he left the hospital, she broached this idea with him and asked him to think about it. He replied: "What is there to think about? I'm too young to retire and José does not know the business well enough to take over. It will take at least five more years before he is ready to run the operation. Besides, all I have to do is slow down a bit. I don't have to retire. What's the hurry to run me out of the company? I'm as good as ever."

Rebecca and José believe that over the next couple of months they must continue working on Pablo to slow down and to start training José to take over the reins.

Questions

1. Why is Pablo reluctant to turn over the reins to José? Include a discussion of Figure 18.1 in your answer.

2. Cite and discuss two reasons Pablo should begin thinking about succession planning.

3. What would you recommend Rebecca and José do to convince Pablo they are right? Offer at least three operative recommendations.

Case 18.3

Needing Some Help on This One

In the past, most people who wanted to get their foreign sports cars fixed had to turn to the dealer from which they had purchased the car. In recent years, however, auto repair shops that specialize in foreign sports cars have become popular in some areas of the country. When Jack Schultz started his company ten years ago, he was lucky if he had two cars a day to work on. Today, Jack has 15 people working for him, and he usually has a backlog of about five days' work. Some of this work is repairs caused by auto accidents; a lot of it is a result of improper maintenance by the owners.

Jack is 64 years old and feels he will work for about six more years before retiring. The business is very profitable, and Jack and his wife do not need to worry about retirement income. They have saved more than enough. However, Jack is concerned about what to do with the business. He has two children who work with him, Bob (31 years old) and Tim (29 years old). Jack has not asked either of them if they would want to take over the operation. He assumes they will. He also has a nephew, Richard (35 years old), working for him. All three of these relatives have been with Jack for nine years.

Jack believes that any one of the three could successfully head the venture. But he is concerned about in-fighting should he favor one over the others. On the other hand, if he turns the business over to all three of them collectively, will they be able to get along with one another? Jack has no reason to believe the three cannot work things out amicably, but he is unsure.

Jack has decided he cannot wait much longer to groom an heir. The major stumbling block is identifying who that person will be. Additionally, Jack really does not know anything about picking a successor. What characteristics should the individual possess? What types of training should the person be given? What other steps should be followed? Jack feels he needs to answer these questions as soon as possible. "I know how to plan business operations," he told his wife last week, "but I don't know how to go about planning for the succession of business operations. It's a whole different idea. I need some help on this one."

Questions

1. Identify and briefly describe four characteristics you would expect to find in a successful manager of this type of venture.

2. What steps does Jack need to follow to successfully identify and groom a successor? Be complete in your answer.

3. If you were going to advise Jack, what would you recommend he do first? How should he get started with his succession plan? What should he do next? Offer him some general guidance on how to handle this problem.

Notes

1. Tammi S. Feltham, Glenn Feltham, and James J. Barnett, "The Dependence of Family Businesses on a Single Decision-Maker," *Journal of Small Business Management* 43(1) (January 2005): 1–15; see also Timothy Bates, "Analysis of Young, Small Firms that Have Closed: Delineating Successful from Unsuccessful Closures," *Journal of Business Venturing* 20(3) (May 2005): 343–358.

2. John L. Ward, *Keeping the Family Business Healthy* (San Francisco: Jossey-Bass, 1987), 1–2.

3. Richard Beckhard and W. Gibb Dyer, Jr., "Managing Continuity in the Family-Owned Business," *Organizational Dynamics* (summer 1983): 7–8.

4. Manfred F. R. Kets de Vries, "The Dynamics of Family-Controlled Firms: The Good News and the Bad News," *Organizational Dynamics* (winter 1993): 59–71; and Richard A. Cosier and Michael Harvey, "The Hidden Strengths in Family Business: Functional Conflict," *Family Business Review* (March 1998): 75–79.

5. Peter Davis, "Realizing the Potential of the Family Business," *Organizational Dynamics* (summer 1983): 53–54; and Thomas Hubler, "Ten Most Prevalent Obstacles to Family Business Succession Planning," *Family Business Review* (June 1999): 117–122.

6. Phyllis G. Holland and William R. Boulton, "Balancing the 'Family' and the 'Business' in the Family Business," *Business Horizons* (March/April 1984): 19; Kathryn Stafford, Karen A. Duncan, Sharon Dane, and Mary Winter, "A Research Model of Sustainable Family Business," *Family Business Review* (September 1999): 197–208; and Michael D. Ensley and Allison W. Pearson, "An Exploratory Comparison of the Behavioral Dynamics of Top Management Teams in Family and Non-Family New Ventures: Cohesion, Conflict, Potency, and Consensus," *Entrepreneurship Theory & Practice* 29(3) (May 2005): 267–284.

7. See Donald F. Kuratko, "Understanding the Succession Challenge in Family Business," *Entrepreneurship, Innovation, and Change* (September 1995): 185–191; see also Heather A. Haveman and Mukti V. Khaire, "Survival Beyond Succession? The Contingent Impact of Founder Succession on Organizational Failure," *Journal of Business Venturing* 19(3) (May 2004): 437–463.

8. See Neil C. Churchill and Kenneth J. Hatten, "Non-Market-Based Transfers of Wealth and Power: A Research Framework for Family Business," *American Journal of Small Business* (fall 1987): 53–66; and Margaret A. Fitzgerald and Glenn Muske, "Copreneurs: An Exploration and Comparison to Other Family Businesses," *Family Business Review* 15(1) (2002): 1–16.

9. Peter S. Davis and Paula D. Harveston, "The Influence of Family on the Family Business Succession Process: A Multi-Generational Perspective," *Entrepreneurship Theory and Practice* (spring 1998): 31–54; Eleni T. Stavrou, "Succession in Family Business: Exploring the Effects of Demographic Factors on Offspring Intentions to Join and Take Over the Business," *Journal of Small Business Management* (July 1999): 43–61; and Sue Birley, "Attitudes of Owner-Managers' Children Toward Family and Business Issues," *Entrepreneurship Theory and Practice* 26(3) (2002): 5–19.

10. See Donald F. Kuratko, Helga B. Foss, and Lucinda L. VanAlst, "IRS Estate Freeze Rules: Implications for Family Business Succession Planning," *Family Business Review* (spring 1994): 61–72; and Joseph H. Astrachan and Roger Tutterow, "The Effect of Estate Taxes on Family Business: Survey Results," *Family Business Review* (fall 1996): 303–314.

11. Kathryn Stafford, Karen A. Duncan, Sharon Dane, and Mary Winter, "A Research Model of Sustainable Family Business," *Family Business Review* (September 1999): 197–208; see also Shaker A. Zahra, James C. Hayton, and Carlo Salvato, "Entrepreneurship in Family vs. Non-Family Firms: A Resource-Based Analysis of the Effect of Organizational Culture," *Entrepreneurship Theory and Practice* 28(4) (summer 2004): 363–382.

12. For an interesting perspective, see Sue Birley, "Succession in the Family Firm: The Inheritor's View," *Journal of Small Business Management* (July 1986): 36–43; T. Roger Peay and W. Gibb Dyer, "Power Orientations of Entrepreneurs and Succession Planning," *Journal of Small Business Management* (January 1989): 47–52; and Stavrou, "Succession in Family Business," 43–61.

13. See Kevin C. Seymour, "Intergenerational Relationships in the Family Firm: The Effect on Leadership Succession," *Family Business Review* (fall 1993): 263–282; and Eleni T. Stavrou and Paul Michael Swiercz, "Securing the Future of Family Enterprise: A Model of Offspring Intentions to Join the Business," *Entrepreneurship Theory and Practice* (winter 1998): 19–40.

14. Jeffrey A. Barach, Joseph Ganitsky, James A. Carson, and Benjamin A. Doochin, "Entry of the Next Generation: Strategic Challenge for Family Firms," *Journal of Small Business Management* (April 1988): 49–56.

15. "Nepotism on Trial," *Inc.* (July 1984): 29.

16. David Graulich, "You Can't Always Pay What You Want," *Family Business* (February 1990): 16–19.

17. "Feuding Families," *Inc.* (January 1985): 38.

18. Donald F. Kuratko and Richard M. Hodgetts, "Succession Strategies for Family Businesses," *Management Advisor* (spring 1989): 22–30; see also Mark Fischetti, *The Family Business Succession Handbook* (Philadelphia: Family Business Publishing Co., 1997).

19. James J. Chrisman, Jess H. Chua, and Pramodita Sharma, "Important Attributes of Successors in Family Business: An Exploratory Study," *Family Business Review* (March 1998): 19–34.

20. Adapted from Harold W. Fox, "Quasi-Boards: Useful Small Business Confidants," *Harvard Business Review* (January/February 1982): 64–72.

21. Glenn R. Ayres, "Rough Family Justice: Equity in Family Business Succession Planning," *Family Business Review* (spring 1990): 3–22; Ronald E. Berenbeim, "How Business Families Manage the Transition from Owner to Professional Management," *Family Business Review* (spring 1990): 69–110; and Michael H. Morris, Roy O. Williams, Jeffrey A. Allen, and Ramon A. Avila, "Correlates of Success in Family Business Transitions," *Journal of Business Venturing* (September 1997): 385–402.

22. Paul C. Rosenblatt, "Blood May Be Thicker, but in the Boardroom It Just Makes for Sticky Business," *Psychology Today* (July 1985): 55–56; and Ivan Lansberg, "Are You Ready for This Journey?" *Family Business* (winter 2000): 67–68.

23. Johannes H. M. Welsch, "The Impact of Family Ownership and Involvement on the Process of Management Succession," *Family Business Review* (spring 1993): 31–54.

24. See *Going Public* (New York: The NASDAQ Stock Market, Inc., 1999), 5–9; see also Richard C. Dorf and Thomas H. Beyers, *Technology Ventures: From Idea to Enterprise* (New York: McGraw Hill, 2005).

25. K. Fred Skousen, *An Introduction to the SEC,* 5th ed. (Mason, OH: South-Western/Thomson Learning), 157; see also Catherine M. Daily, S. Travis Certo, and Dan R. Dalton, "Investment Bankers and IPO Pricing: Does Prospectus Information Matter?" *Journal of Business Venturing* 20(1) (January 2005): 93–111.

26. For a complete listing, see Skousen, *An Introduction to the SEC,* 60; see also J. William Petty, Arthur J. Keown, David F. Scott, Jr., and John D. Martin, *Basic Financial Management,* 6th ed. (Englewood Cliffs, NJ: Prentice-Hall, 1993), 696–699.

27. Ellen Goldschmidt, "Selling Your Business Successfully," *Personal Finance* (December 1987): 62; see also James Fox and Steven Elek, "Selling Your Company," *Small Business Reports* (May 1992): 49–58.

28. See Donald Reinardy and Catherine Stover, "I Want to Sell My Business. Where Do I Begin?" *Small Business Forum* (fall 1991): 1–24; see also J. William Petty, "Harvesting Firm Value: Process and Results," *Entrepreneurship 2000* (Chicago: Upstart Publishing Company, 1997), 71–94.

29. From the *Harvard Business Review,* "Packaging Your Business for Sale," by Charles O'Conor, March/April 1985, 52–58. Copyright © 1985 by the President and Fellows of Harvard College; all rights reserved.

30. Ibid., 52.

31. Ibid., 56.

32. See Stephen Nelson, "When to Sell Your Company," *Inc.* (March 1988): 131–132.

33. O'Conor, "Packaging Your Business," 56.

Part 5

Acordia's "Little Giants"

■ Prologue

Overall, Acordia has redefined the notion of scale. Scale today is mostly associated with knowledge, not lumpy objects. The point of the individual Acordia company is to be a giant, not a dwarf. That is, within the collective heads of its 65 or so employees, an Acordia company will know more about its customers than bigger (total bodies, total assets) competitors. Moreover, through wise use of its overall network of inside and outside companies, it should be able to bring a wider set of resources to bear, more quickly, more efficiently, and more imaginatively than bigger competitors.

Tom Peters
Liberation Management (281–282)

■ Introduction

In 1986 The Associated Group (formerly known as Blue Cross/Blue Shield of Indiana) embarked on a critical 1,800-day strategic journey. During those days an ambitious transformation took place that changed one large, bureaucratic operation in health insurance into an entrepreneurial network of 50 companies involved with health insurance, life insurance, property and casualty insurance, insurance brokerage, government program administration, investment banking, computer software, and market research. This transformation took a company employing 2,800 people and serving only one state (Indiana) to a diversified "family" of companies that employs 7,000 people through 140 offices and serving 49 states. This remarkable restructuring strategy of "growing small" was made possible through the creation of new "Acordia" companies that would concentrate into specific market niches and operate as stand-alone entrepreneurial companies. It was an entrepreneurial vision transformed into entrepreneurial action, and the results have been an emotional, cultural, and financial success. In the fall of 1992 The Associated Group completed a successful initial public offering of Acordia, Inc.

This strategic journey spanned five years but sought to accomplish so much that early in its inception critics were quick to point out the "overambitious" ideals of creating an entrepreneurial climate in a traditionally rigid, bureaucratic organization. Some executives as well as some employees who didn't believe in the plan either left the company or took early retirement. Although the need to change was obvious to most of the employees, it was the dramatic challenge of restructuring into a network of entrepreneurial companies that scared away the weak of heart. Tearing away layer upon layer of bureaucracy is not easy in a well-entrenched, traditional culture. Yet the tearing away actually gave birth to a new breed of companies known as "Acordia." Through the creation of the Acordia concept, an actual network of companies was established that allowed an entrepreneurial structure to exist within a corporate giant. However, it is not the structure of Acordia that made such a difference as it is the vision and strategy behind it. The following section is intended to provide a short review of The Associated Group's past to better explain

Source: This case was prepared by Dr. Donald F. Kuratko of the Kelley School of Business at Indiana University–Bloomington and Michael D. Houk, CEO of Acordia Corporate Benefits, Inc., as a basis for class discussion rather than to illustrate either effective or ineffective handling of an administrative situation. All rights reserved to the author. Copyright © 1996 by Donald F. Kuratko. See also, Donald F. Kuratko, Michael D. Houk, and Richard M. Hodgetts, "Acordia, Inc. Leadership Through the Transformation of Growing Small," *The Journal of Leadership Studies* 5(2) (spring 1998): 152–162.

the present strategy of Acordia companies that is currently setting the stage for the future challenges.

Background: The Recent Past

One reason The Associated Group has been able to change and prosper when others in the insurance industry are struggling is that it has been different from the very beginning. It operated for many years as Blue Cross/Blue Shield of Indiana. Aggressiveness in the marketplace and conservative financial practices allowed it to become the largest health insurer in Indiana and the financially strongest Blue Cross/Blue Shield organization in the country. Unlike other Blue Cross and Blue Shield "plans," it was chartered as two separate mutual-property and casualty-insurance companies without state tax or regulatory advantages. Indiana treated prepaid health care as insurance.

Another unusual element was the cooperative arrangement between Indiana Blue Cross and Indiana Blue Shield. Early on, a unique structure was developed to allow the then-separate companies to share expenses and concentrate on their individual areas of expertise. This cooperation continued until the companies' merger in 1985.

What looked at the time to be detriments and oddities proved instead integral to success. Since The Associated Group was competing with and being regulated as commercial insurance companies, the development of both financial strength and marketing skill was essential.

In the late 1970s and early 1980s, the health care market began to undergo permanent change, with costs skyrocketing and competition intensifying. In Indiana, population, employment, and personal income growth all slowed or flattened. The local economy was shifting from manufacturing to a new service base. The auto and steel industries—traditionally the largest Blue Cross/Blue Shield of Indiana customers—began to reduce employment. And the Blue Cross/Blue Shield System as a whole started to lose national accounts.

While these changes to the current customer base were occurring, rising health care costs and deepening cycles of profit and loss in the health insurance business were fostering new competitors and new managed-care products. These rapid and permanent changes on both the market and product sides of the business made the need for internal change clear. In order to enhance the long-term success of The Associated Group, it was imperative to change the strategic direction.

The New Strategic Direction

In 1986, a newly developed strategic plan was set in motion. Its three primary objectives were to strengthen the core health insurance business; to diversify into other lines of insurance and financial services that are noncyclical or countercyclical to health insurance; and to expand outside Indiana into growing markets that have economies countercyclical to those in the Midwest, particularly in the South, Southwest, and West.

In pursuing these objectives, the organization's core competencies were used by matching expertise with growth opportunities in other fields. As a successful health insurance company, it had a desire to expand into areas where marketing ability, administrative skill, and computer competence could provide market advantages.

Familiarity and comfort with the assumption of actuarially predictable risk, as well as knowledge of how to work in regulated environments, provided existing strengths as the company set out its "enabling" objectives.

In order to meet the three original primary objectives stated earlier, the company had to set enabling objectives that would guide its efforts. These objectives included the following.

☐ Maintain a strong financial base and gain access to new sources of capital.

☐ Be recognized as an innovative product leader.

☐ Develop and maintain a strong management team.

☐ Make changes in corporate identity necessary to grow outside of Indiana and in new product lines.

However, as sincere as the enabling objectives sounded, the company still needed to *implement* the new direction, and two critical steps had to be taken. First, a restructuring through decentralizing operations had to occur, and second, a new corporate culture would have to be developed. Thus, in 1986 the new course was set and, as this case will illustrate, The Associated Group has never looked back.

Restructuring and Decentralization

The decentralization of operations and development of a more aggressive, entrepreneurial corporate culture were among the most challenging tasks, yet they were based on a few simple ideas: People do a better job when they are directly responsible for the results of their work; small work teams are more responsive than big organizations; customers have unique, definable needs; and service is more important than economies of scale.

These ideas are the antithesis of the assembly-line mentality that has dominated American business since the Industrial Revolution. As author and consultant Tom Peters has pointed out, assembly lines work in manufacturing, not in service businesses. Thus, instead of grouping employees by job function, the company divided them into smaller units organized around a specific type of customer with unique needs. These individual units became the nuclei for the Acordia companies, which today sell and service insurance and financial products to customers within specific industries, geographic areas, or demographic categories across the United States.

Restructuring went hand in hand with the philosophy of letting people do what they do best. Innovation was encouraged. The strategic plan was never a detailed route of how to get from here to there. It was a compass. As long as everyone moved in the same direction, each leader was free to find his or her own route, and every employee was free to be creative in fulfilling the requirements of his or her job. The Associated Group set about to attract a new breed of executive: experienced, well educated, aggressive, accustomed to taking risks. At The Associated Group, executives could run their own show with the spirit of an entrepreneur but have the resources and commitment of a large organization behind them.

The acquisition of new companies was an integral part of the restructuring, starting with Professional Administrators Limited and Raffensperger, Hughes & Co. and then American General Group Insurance Companies, a Texas-based life and health insurance company that instantly expanded the potential market into Florida, Texas, and California.

The diversification and expansion continued over the next two years with the addition of companies such as Novalis Corporation (a group of companies offering systems technology, software, and managed-care expertise to the insurance industry), Strategic Marketing and Research (a market research firm), and Robinson-Conner and The Shelby Insurance Group (acquired in 1991), which provided a strong presence in property and casualty brokerage and underwriting. (See Table 1 for year-by-year highlights of The Associated Group's development.)

The restructuring and diversification allowed The Associated Group to become a broad-based, diversified insurance and financial services company serving customers in 49 states with its business divided into seven major segments:

- *Health insurance and managed health care:* sold in Indiana under the trade name Blue Cross and Blue Shield of Indiana and in other states through Anthem Life, Anthem Health Plans, and Anthem Health Systems

- *Life insurance:* group policies provided through Anthem Life and personal life insurance and annuity products through The Shelby Insurance Group

- *Insurance brokerage and administration:* led by the growing network of Acordia companies

Table 1   Key Highlights of Building the Acordia Concept (Year by Year)

1986	1987
- The new strategic plan and corporate mission statement are conceived and adopted.	- A new market-focused corporate culture is created by restructuring claims systems and forming dedicated service units in preparation for strategic decentralization.
- A new corporate identity, The Associated Group, is created.	
- To diversify product lines, Professional Administrator Limited, a Kentucky-based insurance group specializing in products for the construction industry, and Raffensperger, Hughes & Co., an Indiana-based investment banking firm, are acquired.	- A Department of Defense contract to provide utilization review and quality assurance for the Civilian Health and Medical Program of the Uniformed Services (CHAMPUS) is won.
- To strengthen the core health insurance business, Key Care Health Resources, a health care management company specializing in case management and wellness products, is formed. Partnerships are also formed with Caremark to provide case management, home health care, and mail-order pharmacy services and with American Biodyne to provide mental health services to health maintenance organization (HMO) customers.	- Managed care becomes increasingly important. Health maintenance organization enrollment doubles. Premium income from managed care programs more than doubles.
	- Diversified insurance and financial services capabilities are demonstrated by providing risk management and employee benefits for the Tenth Pan Am Games, held in Indianapolis.
	- A decentralization plan is adopted.

Table 1   (Continued)

1988

- Market-focused strategic business units begin operating as independent companies, beginning decentralization.
- A second CHAMPUS contract to administer benefits for 900,000 military personnel and their dependents in 17 states is received.
- Digital Insurance Systems Corporation (DISCorp), a software development company, is acquired.
- Health Networks of America is created to develop new health insurance products and provider networks.

1989

- The purchase of American General Group Insurance Companies adds $600 million in health and life revenue and $750 million in assets, plus 17 sales offices in nine states.
- The marketing and administrative operations of the Indiana health insurance business are organized into eight independent, customer-oriented subsidiaries called Acordia companies.

1990

- American General Group Insurance Companies are renamed and placed in a holding company known as Anthem Companies, Inc.—the 3rd largest health insurer in Florida, 8th largest in Texas, and 13th largest in California.
- The Acordia companies begin selling products from several other insurance companies, becoming true insurance brokerage companies. Two new Acordia companies are created.
- The holding company, Novalis, is created to provide systems technology, benefit design, and clinical expertise to the managed care industry.

1991

- Robinson-Conner, the 21st largest property and casualty insurance brokerage firm in the United States, is acquired. Locations in 10 states provide a total of $40 million annually in commissions and fees.
- The Shelby Insurance Group, an Ohio-based property and casualty insurance underwriter with $197 million in revenue, is acquired.
- Seven new Acordia companies are created.
- Government services operations are consolidated in a company called AdminaStar and redirected for strategic expansion.

Source: The Associated Group *Annual Report*, 1991, 7.

- *Property and casualty insurance:* provided by The Shelby Insurance Group, the latest acquisition

- *Government program administration:* provided by AdminaStar and its affiliates

- *Service industry products:* software, research, and managed care services through Novalis and its companies, including Health Networks of America and DISCorp, and strategic marketing and research

- *Financial services:* provided through Raffensperger-Hughes & Co., an investment banking firm headquartered in Indiana

The Acordia Strategy

The Acordia vision is to become the nation's largest supplier of insurance products to midmarket clients. This is implemented by targeting cities of 100,000 to 1 million in population as well as by targeting employers with less than 5,000 employees and with $200,000 annually in property and casualty commissions and individuals with incomes greater than $50,000 and net worth greater than $500,000. Acordia seeks to become the "Wal-Mart" of insurance and brokerage administration. That vision, however, can become a reality only through the application of ten specific objectives.

Objective 1

"Product Customization" is to demonstrate that Acordia adds value to an employer or an individual by *selecting* an insurance or financial service product, by *tailoring* it to the client's needs, and by *servicing* the product after the sale. This can be done by continuing to structure and restructure the Acordia companies to focus on tight client niches that demonstrate unique insurance and financial service needs. However, each Acordia company must reduce its overall cost of distribution and administration that is included in the price of insurance and financial services products, and each must use core health, property, and casualty insurance products to pay the base costs of distribution and use innovative, profitable products to create added value. Finally, each Acordia Operating Company should attempt to develop "pioneer customers" willing to experiment with new forms of packaging and new products and services.

Objective 2

"Superior Performance" is to demonstrate superior financial performance to the shareholders in order to have capital available for expansion. This objective was expected to be achieved if each Acordia company could produce an average of 15 percent annual growth in earnings per share for 1992–1997 and maintain an above-average shareholder return on equity in the top half of comparable companies over the six-year period.

Objective 3

"Limited Exposure" is to minimize the risk to investors' principal by diversifying sources of net income. This is accomplished by expanding horizontally (new insurance products to the employer) and vertically (new individual products to employees in the workplace setting). In addition, each Acordia must diversify sources of net income by product line and seek to produce 10 percent of the 1997 net income from a combination of new markets, including the following:

☐ New Acordia industrial companies should be created in specific markets generally based on SIC code and where a significant presence can be achieved and in-depth knowledge of the client's business adds value to the products and services provided.

☐ New Acordia geographic markets should be created in "Main Street" cities where existing expertise can be leveraged and a significant presence can be achieved.

See Figure 1 for an illustration of the current Acordia structure.

Objective 4

"Main Street" is to concentrate marketing efforts in high population growth areas in which competitors do not have a dominant presence (cities of 100,000 to 1 million population). These areas should be selected based on territories where Acordia's existing expertise can be leveraged to become one of the top three brokers and administrators as measured by revenue.

Figure 1 The Acordia Structure

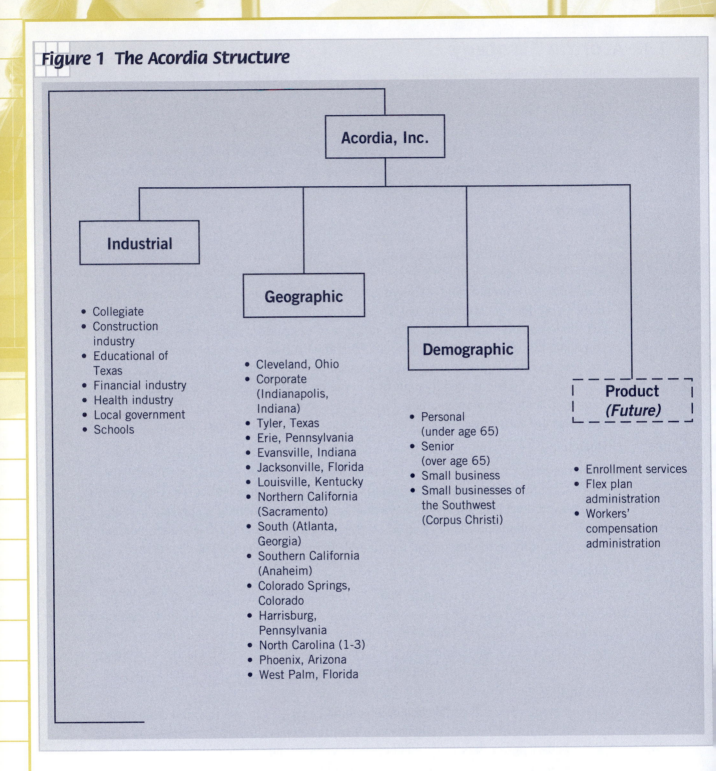

Acordia, Inc.

Industrial

- Collegiate
- Construction industry
- Educational of Texas
- Financial industry
- Health industry
- Local government
- Schools

Geographic

- Cleveland, Ohio
- Corporate (Indianapolis, Indiana)
- Tyler, Texas
- Erie, Pennsylvania
- Evansville, Indiana
- Jacksonville, Florida
- Louisville, Kentucky
- Northern California (Sacramento)
- South (Atlanta, Georgia)
- Southern California (Anaheim)
- Colorado Springs, Colorado
- Harrisburg, Pennsylvania
- North Carolina (1-3)
- Phoenix, Arizona
- West Palm, Florida

Demographic

- Personal (under age 65)
- Senior (over age 65)
- Small business
- Small businesses of the Southwest (Corpus Christi)

Product (Future)

- Enrollment services
- Flex plan administration
- Workers' compensation administration

Objective 5

"Mid-Market" clients are generally defined as employers with less than 5,000 employees and with $200,000 annually in property and casualty commissions and individuals with incomes greater than $50,000 annually and net worth greater than $500,000. The target customers are employers with 400 to 1,000 employees and $50,000 to $100,000 in property and casualty commissions and individuals who are self-employed or new retirees. Markets are segmented by industries and geographic and demographic factors based on customer buying preferences and similarities of product need.

Objective 6

"Concentrate and Divide" is to use a market segmentation strategy designed to continually refocus Acordia companies on increasingly specialized market segments. Thus, each Acordia company should be among the top three competitors in its market as measured by revenue. However, each Acordia should concentrate growth in a sub-segment that can create an Acordia spin-off and provide stock options to employees for new spin-offs.

Objective 7

"Targeted Acquisitions" is to target locations and product lines consistent with strategic diversification and growth objectives. Acquisitions will be made at the operating-company levels as well as by Acordia, Inc. However, acquired businesses must complement business in existing locations and product lines before expanding to new territories or product lines, and acquisitions should never dilute earnings per share. Thus, acquisitional searches should concentrate on candidates where the culture fits Acordia's strategy and culture.

Objective 8

"Management System" is to maintain small, highly entrepreneurial, and expense-sensitive Acordia companies. This can be accomplished, and is being accomplished, if each Acordia company maintains only two levels of management with an "outside" board of directors and a maximum size of 200 employees. Also, the high-speed electronic network information systems for inter/intracompany communications and reporting should be in place with a fully decentralized computer system for each Acordia operating company.

Objective 9

"Executive Talent" is to attract and retain the industry's best talent by offering the best benefits of being an entrepreneurial business owner and an executive with a large company. It is important to develop a program to recognize leaders among Acordia CEOs and to achieve a voluntary turnover of 5 percent or less among Acordia CEOs and vice presidents.

Objective 10

"Strategic Compensation" is to develop powerful incentives for all employees to foster growth, increase shareholder value, and successfully execute the strategic plan. This may be the critical component in the Acordia strategy. A new cash compensation system tied directly to growth in earnings, an Acordia stock ownership plan, and a new performance-driven benefit plan all have been introduced. The next section describes this compensation plan in greater detail.

The Acordia Compensation Plan

The compensation system for executives and officers designed for the Acordia companies is an integral part of the strategic plan and is needed to implement the aggressive entrepreneurial approach of each Acordia. As designed, the compensation system is competitive (in comparison to the market) and yet challenging (incentives are a critical component).

The compensation plan has three major segments (see Figure 2). First, cash wages are positioned at the market average. However, the market average is achieved through

Figure 2 Acordia Compensation System

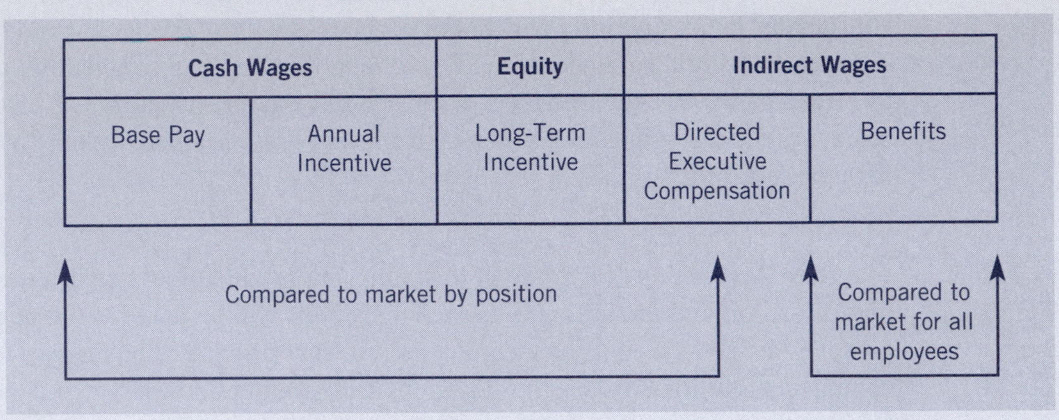

Cash Wages		Equity	Indirect Wages	
Base Pay	Annual Incentive	Long-Term Incentive	Directed Executive Compensation	Benefits

Compared to market by position

Compared to market for all employees

a combination of target base plus an annual incentive. Although base pay will be at the low end of market ranges, the annual incentive is positioned at the high end so that total wage potential can be well above the market. Actual payment of wages is based on performance.

The incentive determination is based on three elements: the individual Acordia company's financial performance for the year, the individual Acordia company's board-of-directors assessment, and Acordia, Inc.'s discretionary input. Each board of directors uses a worksheet similar to the one shown in Table 2 so that they have a clear understanding of the range of discretion to be applied. The goal is to create clear incentives tied directly to the firm's performance yet allowing for additional factors such as product and geographic diversification, customer satisfaction (identified through surveys), and employee satisfaction (identified through surveys). The second segment, aggressive long-term incentives, delivers significant compensation for performance above competitive levels, and the company's shareholders clearly benefit from such executive performance. The third segment involves benefits maintained at an appropriate competitive level and "directed executive compensation" (commonly known as "perks") designed in a cafeteria fashion, where each executive has a set pool of credits to apply toward his or her choice of items.

In addition, a stock option plan is designed to create long-term incentive and ownership opportunity for all Acordia companies' officers. The stock is, of course, Acordia, Inc., but its value is dependent on the performance of all the Acordia operating companies. The target pool is 1,800 shares of stock per year for each Acordia company, with a maximum individual officer award of 600 shares in any one year. Each Acordia company board of directors allocates the shares based on the following guidelines.

INDIVIDUAL PERFORMANCE	ACORDIA OPERATING COMPANY GROWTH RATE				
	12%		15%		16.5% AND ABOVE
Poor	0		0		0
Good	100	to	150	to	200
Excellent	200	to	400	to	500
Superior	300	to	500	to	600

Table 2 Annual Incentive Plan

AWARD CALCULATION GUIDE ($ EXPRESSED PER $10,000 OF TARGET AWARD)

FINANCIAL RESULT	FORMULA AWARD	INDIVIDUAL ACORDIA CO. BOARD DISCRETION RANGE[a]	ACORDIA, INC., DISCRETION RANGE[b]	TOTAL MAXIMUM AWARD
Less than Threshold 0–11.9% growth	Not eligible for incentive based on formula. Shareholder retains right but has no obligation to consider an appropriate payout after reviewing compelling mitigating factors affecting performance.			
Threshold = 12%	$6,000 (60% of target award)	+/− $2,000 (40–80% of target award)	Up to $2,000 (0–20% of target award)	$10,000 (100% of target)
Target = 15%	$8,000 (80% of target award)	+/− $2,000 (60–100% of target award)	Up to $5,000 (0–50% of target award)	$15,000 (150% of target)
Outstanding = 16.5%	$10,000 (100% of target award)	+/− $2,000 (80–120% of target award)	Up to $6,000 (0–60% of target award)	$18,000 (180% of target)

a Should decrease only for significant variances or events or to give a message; not intended for fine-tuning and creating precision in awards.

b Shareholder cannot reduce but may increase board award; 100% is normal award for fully meeting expected results. Increase only for exceptional performance, exceptional service to Acordia, Inc., overall, etc.

This unique approach to compensation seeks to add value to the overall entrepreneurial strategy by fostering and supporting an ownership perspective among the officers in all Acordia companies.

Acordia Corporate Benefits, Inc.

As an example of the implementation of the Acordia strategy, the following section describes the development and growth of one Acordia Company, Acordia Corporate Benefits, Inc.

Acordia Corporate Benefits, Inc., was incorporated as a Third Party Administrator and Insurance Agency in the State of Indiana effective December 1, 1990. Its approved mission was to market and administer insurance and insurance-related products to employers with 50 or more employees, excluding customers that fall within the missions of any other Acordia companies, such as schools, municipalities, and so forth (see Figure 1).

Generally speaking, employers in the manufacturing and service industries with fewer than 1,000 employees are targeted, while geographically it is restricted to employers located in the northern half of the United States.

Michael D. Houk, the company's CEO, described the company's birth.

On December 1, 1990, 97 employees staffed the new company and prepared to move to a new facility February 1, 1991. During that 60-day period, we began to build our new culture . . . the culture of a company whose future was totally dependent upon the results it produced.

From the first day, we eliminated the multiple levels of management that employees had been accustomed to. Each employee was hired by a vice president in our company who reported directly to the president . . . no more supervisors, managers, or directors to stagnate the communication channels. We also converted from a 37.5-hour work week to a 40-hour work week, added an Employee Profit Sharing Plan, a dress code, raised expectations, and set up our new facility with our new work flows in mind. . . . All these changes combined allowed us to eliminate over 30 positions from the operation that had been handling the business prior to December 1, 1990. Attitudes began to change, ever so slowly at first, but each day we saw some improvement. When we moved out of the old 15-story building to our new one-level facility on February 1, 1991, we realized a significant increase in the morale and excitement of our employees. Our employees began to take greater pride in where they worked and how they worked. . . . As a result, service to our customers improved! Our clients were no longer unknown employers and employees who generated work. . . . Now they were our clients upon whom our future would be built.

During that first year, we went on to add an employee advisory committee that meets monthly with the president to continually refine our corporate policies and practices . . . our culture! We've implemented a weight loss program for our employees, a totally no smoking facility, quarterly all-employee meetings, dress-down day every payday, an annual family picnic, a Christmas lunch, etc. . . . all organized and run by employees "elected" by their peers.

But have we been successful financially? In a word . . . Yes!

During 1991, Revenues exceeded $10 million and net income before taxes exceeded $1.8 million . . . a pretax return on revenue of over 18 percent. The second full year was even better . . . and pretax net exceeded $2.2 million . . . a 22 percent increase over 1991! During 1992, over 40 percent of net income came from outside Indiana, and over 20 percent of our net income was from nonhealth sources. Acordia Corporate Benefits was now licensed as a Third Party Administrator and Life and Health Insurance Agency in over 20 states, concentrating in the Midwest.

Acordia Corporate Benefits began to consider diversification geographically, by product, or into nonhealth products. In 1993, the company added a new product line, Flexible Benefits Administration, which increased revenues by more than $1 million in the first year. Also, Acordia Corporate Benefits acquired a large Indianapolis-based property and casualty insurance agency during the first quarter of 1993, increasing revenue an additional $3.5 million.

By the end of 1993, annual revenue increased to more than $16 million, with pretax net income approaching $3 million and an employment base of approximately 160 employees—all in a span of three years.

What's more, this particular Acordia made the transition from a business totally dependent on the health insurance business and employers in Indiana alone to a business operating in more than 20 states with more than one-third of its revenue from nonhealth products.

"We have become an employer of empowered employees who look forward to change, new products, and a promising future," Houk says. "We are no longer totally reliant upon a single product and a single state. However, growth brings new challenges to our management team. The Acordia Strategy requires that the companies remain small and focused. Our newest challenge is to look inward to determine what unique marketing niche will be best suited to provide the base of a new Acordia company. It may be a geographic segment of our company, or industrial segment of our current clients."

Future Considerations

Although The Associated Group achieved many of its strategic goals, its commitment to growth and diversification continues. By late 1997, The Associated Group plans to be more diversified, to serve more markets, and to continue to build successful businesses from its core competencies. Each time another building block is added the future is enhanced. The first 1,800 days (from 1986) provided a strong base to build on for the following 1,800 days.

Of course, no one can predict exactly what lies ahead. But guideposts exist: trends, movements, signs of the times. The following section outlines some of the most pressing areas.

Health Care

President Bill Clinton's health care reforms, announced in 1993, are now under way. Managed care is the future of health care. The nonmanaged segments of the health benefits industry are becoming smaller each year. The unlimited choices people have had regarding their own providers and providers have enjoyed when prescribing given courses of therapy will become more ordered as the industry responds to pay or cost pressures. Everyone in the health care system, from hospitals and physicians to insurance companies to the patients themselves, will become more informed and more involved in health care economics and decisions. The only companies to survive and prosper will be those that understand and deliver effective managed care. The Associated Group is positioned at the forefront of technology and product innovation in the managed care industry.

With regard to public policy, the health care industry will see more changes in the next decade than in any of the previous three. The Associated Group is an active participant, at both the state and federal levels, in the debate on health care costs and access and reflects the potential for different policy outcomes through its business strategy.

Trends within the Blue Cross/Blue Shield system also deserve attention due to the national prominence of this product line. Recent years have seen some of the 73 licensees struggling to meet the needs of traditional customers and to remain financially sound, with one even reaching the point of insolvency.

Aging America

The retirement boom is coming, and the next 1,800 days will find the United States at its leading edge. The population of America is slowly growing older and living longer; the 1990s has seen increases in two-generation geriatric families, with adult children in their 60s and 70s caring for parents in their 90s. By the year 2000, the number of Americans over age 75 will have grown by nearly 35 percent.

The pressures on our health care system become even more critical as the U.S. population ages and requires more medical attention. As one of America's leading health insurers, The Associated Group says it is committed to finding new ways to finance and deliver effective health care to older Americans.

Financial Services

Today, the lines separating the various segments of the financial services industry are more blurred than ever before. Institutions that once had little in common will continue to become more alike. Technological advances are changing the way people handle their money. Though a "checkless society" has been predicted since the 1960s, the idea is becoming reality. Electronic transactions are more efficient and accurate than paper transactions. And more people are gaining access to the technology required to completely automate their finances and investments. The Associated Group says it is committed to a future in financial services by continuing to successfully diversify operations to be in a position to offer a broader variety of products.

Continued Demassification

The trend toward specialization in U.S. society that marked The Associated Group's 1,800 days since 1986, a trend predicted by futurists such as Alvin Toffler more than a decade ago, has shown no signs of slowing. On the contrary, it seems to be accelerating. As the things we do, the choices we have, and the information we process become more specialized, uniform, traditional solutions make less sense. We have fewer mass needs that can be addressed with cookie-cutter products and services.

The ability to tailor products and services to niche markets is one of The Associated Group's new core competencies. For its following 1,800 days, Acordia companies continues to focus on even more tightly defined industry, demographic, and geographic market segments to try to deliver what customers want and need with great expertise and efficiency.

The Changing Role of the Corporation

The mirror image of the declining capability and credibility of government has meant a broadened role for corporations in meeting the noneconomic needs of U.S. society. Corporations, which must survive in increasingly competitive markets, have proven to be effective and highly adaptable entities. Not surprisingly, society has increasingly turned to the business community to solve problems traditionally viewed as public-sector issues.

The Associated Group has long acknowledged and accepted its obligations as a socially responsible corporation that is vitally interested in the communities where it does business.

Questions

1. Describe the significant changes that The Associated Group went through. Discuss how they are relevant to managing entrepreneurial growth.

2. What exactly is the Acordia strategy? How effective do you think it is?

3. Describe The Acordia Compensation Plan and how it helped the innovative strategy.

Part 5 Exercise

The TOWS Matrix

Directions: Using the concept of the SWOT Analysis presented in Chapter 15, the TOWS Matrix allows an analysis of a new venture based on the "strengths, weaknesses, opportunities, and threats as combined. Therefore, find a new start-up venture and work with the CEO in establishing the combinations of: strengths—in light of the opportunities; strengths—in light of the threats; weaknesses—in light of the opportunities; and weaknesses—in light of the threats. This combination of the SWOT Matrix will help you to understand the tactics a firm should develop in light of its own recognized strengths and weaknesses within the framework of the external environment.

TOWS MATRIX

	STRENGTH (S)	WEAKNESSES (W)
OPPORTUNITIES (O)	SO Strategies	WO Strategies
THREATS (T)	ST Strategies	WT Strategies

Glossary

The following are key terms and concepts that have been used in this book. In some cases, the description or definition has been expanded to provide information in addition to that presented in the text.

Abandonment Nonuse of a trademark for two consecutive years without justification or a statement regarding abandonment of the trademark.

Accounts payable Liabilities incurred by a business when goods or supplies are purchased on credit.

Accounts receivable Claims of a business against its customers for unpaid balances from the sale of merchandise or the performance of services.

Accounts receivable financing Short-term financing that involves either the pledge of receivables as collateral for a loan or the outright sale of receivables. (See also **Factoring.**)

Accredited purchaser A category used in Regulation D that includes institutional investors; any person who buys at least $150,000 of the offered security and whose net worth is in excess of $1 million; a person whose individual income was greater than $200,000 in each of the last two years; directors, partners, or executive officers selling securities; and certain tax-exempt organizations with more than $500,000 in assets.

Adaptive firm A venture that remains adaptive and innovative both through and beyond the growth stage.

Adjusted tangible book value A common method of valuing a business by computing its net worth as the difference between total assets and total liabilities.

Adjustment of debts Under Chapter 13 of the Bankruptcy Act, individuals are allowed to avoid a declaration of bankruptcy, have the opportunity to pay their debts in installments, and are protected by the federal court. (See also **Bankruptcy Act.**)

Administrative culture A culture typified by the presence of such characteristics as a hierarchical management structure, ownership of enterprise resources, a competitive commitment of resources, and a long-run time perspective. (See also **Entrepreneurial culture.**)

Administrative expenses Operating expenses not directly related to selling or borrowing.

Advisory board A board of professionals established to enhance a venture's growth.

Affiliation The specific interests that a business represents.

Amoral management Management is neither moral nor immoral, but decisions lie outside the sphere to which moral judgments apply.

Angel capital Investments in new ventures that come from wealthy individuals referred to as "business angels."

Appositional relationship A relationship among things and people existing in the world in relation to other things and other people.

Background or knowledge accumulation The first step in the creative thinking process, which involves investigation and information gathering related to the matter under analysis.

Balance sheet A financial statement that reports the assets, liabilities, and owners' equity in the venture at a particular point in time.

Balance sheet equation A basic accounting equation that states that assets equal liabilities plus owners' equity.

Bankruptcy A legal process for insolvent debtors who are unable to pay debts as they become due. For business this includes Chapters 7, 11, and 13 of the federal bankruptcy code.

Bankruptcy Act Federal law that provides for specific procedures in handling insolvent debtors.

Barriers to entry Elements restricting an emerging industry, such as proprietary technology, access to distribution channels, access to raw materials and other inputs, cost disadvantages due to lack of experience, and risk.

Better widget strategy Innovation that encompasses new or existing markets.

Book value The value of a business determined by subtracting total liabilities (adjusted for intangible assets) from total assets.

Bootlegging Secretly working on new ideas on company time as well as on personal time.

Break-even analysis A technique commonly used to assess expected product profitability, which helps to determine how many units must be sold in order to break even at a particular selling price.

Break-even point The point at which the company neither makes nor loses money on a particular project. The formula for computing this point (in units) is Fixed Cost/Selling Price per Unit–Variable Cost per Unit.

Budget A statement of estimated income and expenses over a specified period of time.

Business angel (informal risk capitalist) Wealthy people in the United States looking for investment opportunities.

Business assets The tangible (physical) and intangible (e.g., reputed) assets of the business.

Business description segment That segment of a business plan that provides a general description of the venture, industry background, company history or background, goals, potential of the venture, and uniqueness of the product or service.

Business environment The local environment for business that should be analyzed to establish the potential of the venture in its present location.

Business incubator A facility with adaptable space that small businesses can lease on flexible terms and at reduced rent.

Business plan The written document that details a proposed venture. It must illustrate current status, expected needs, and projected results of the new business.

Business valuation The calculated value of the business, used to track its increases or decreases.

Buy/sell agreement An agreement designed to handle situations in which one or more of the entrepreneurs wants to sell their interest in the venture.

Calculated risk taking Occurs when successful entrepreneurs carefully think out a venture and do everything possible to get the odds in their favor.

Cancellation proceedings A third party's challenge to the trademark's distinctiveness within five years of its issuance.

Capital budgeting A budgeting process used to determine investment decisions. It relies heavily on an evaluation of cash inflows.

Career risk Whether an entrepreneur will be able to find a job or go back to an old job if his or her venture fails.

Cash Coins, currency, and checks on hand. It also includes money the business has in its checking account and savings account.

Cash-flow budget A budget that provides an overview of inflows and outflows of cash during a specified period of time.

Cash-flow leveraged buyout (LBO) Type of buyout that relies heavily on the target company's cash receipts with indicators of that positive cash flow continuing.

Cash-flow statement A financial statement that sets forth the amount and timing of actual and/or expected cash inflows and outflows.

Champion A person with a vision and the ability to share it.

Claims A series of short paragraphs, each of which identifies a particular feature or combination of features, protected by a patent.

Cleaning-out procedure The failure of a trademark owner to file an affidavit stating that it is in use or justifying its lack of use within six years of registration.

Close corporation A corporation in which all shares of stock are held by one person or a small group of people and in which purchase of the stock is not available to the general public.

Code of conduct A statement of ethical practices or guidelines to which an enterprise adheres.

Collective entrepreneurship Individual skills integrated into a group wherein the collective capacity to innovate becomes something greater than the sum of its parts.

Common stock The most basic form of ownership, usually carrying the right to vote for the board of directors.

Community demographics The composition or makeup of consumers who live within a community.

Competitive analysis An analysis of both the quality and quantity of the competition, which needs to be carefully scrutinized by the entrepreneur.

Comprehensive feasibility approach A systematic analysis incorporating external factors.

Congressional Review Act Enacted in 1997, requires agencies to send their final regulations to Congress for review 60 days before they take effect. This mandatory review enables Congress to make the final decision on the need for specific regulations and makes agencies more sensitive to congressional intent.

Consumer-driven philosophy A marketing philosophy that relies on research to discover consumer preferences, desires, and needs before production actually begins. (See also **Production-driven philosophy** and **Sales-driven philosophy**.)

Consumer pricing Combining penetration and competitive pricing to gain market share; depends on consumer's perceived value of product.

Contribution margin approach A common approach to break-even analysis, determined by calculating the difference between the selling price and the variable cost per unit.

Convenience goods Goods that consumers want but are not willing to spend time shopping for.

Convertible debentures Unsecured loans that can be converted into stock.

Copyright A legal protection that provides exclusive rights to creative individuals for the protection of their literary or artistic productions.

Corporate entrepreneurship A new "corporate revolution" taking place due to the infusion of entrepreneurial thinking into bureaucratic structures.

Corporate Entrepreneurship Assessment Instrument (CEAI) A questionnaire designed to measure the key entrepreneurial climate factors.

Corporation An entity legally separate from the individuals who own it, created by the authority of state laws, and usually formed when a transfer of money or property by prospective shareholders takes place in exchange for capital stock in the corporation.

Corridor principle States that with every venture launched, new and unintended opportunities arise.

Creative process The four phases of creative development: background or knowledge accumulation, incubation process, idea experience, and evaluation or implementation.

Creativity The generation of ideas that results in an improvement in the efficiency or effectiveness of a system.

Critical factors Important new-venture assessments.

Critical risks segment The segment of the business plan that discusses potential problems, obstacles and risks, and alternative courses of action.

Customer availability Having customers available before a venture starts.

Dark side of entrepreneurship A destructive side existing within the energetic drive of successful entrepreneurs.

Debt financing Borrowing money for short- or long-term periods for working capital or for purchasing property and equipment.

Debtor-in-possession When a debtor involved in a Chapter 11 proceeding continues to operate the business.

Delayed entry strategy Entering the workforce at a later date.

Delegating Having trained people complete tasks for entrepreneurs to help them save time.

Demand-oriented pricing A flexible strategy that bases pricing decisions on the demand level for the product.

Deservedness The perception by the community that a venture deserves their support.

Design patent Gives the owner exclusive rights to hold, transfer, and/or license the production and sale of the product or process for 14 years.

Direct foreign investment A domestically controlled foreign production facility.

Discounted earnings method A method that determines the true value of the firm with a pricing formula that includes earning power as well as adjusted tangible book value.

Displacement school of thought A school of entrepreneurial thought that focuses on group phenomena such as the political, cultural, and economic environments.

Diversified marketing A marketing stage during which the organization focuses on decentralizing operations by examining individual product life cycles and developing portfolio management approaches to product lines.

Domain name The last part of a URL that includes the organization's unique name followed by a top-level domain name designating the type of organization, such as .com for "commercial" or .edu for "educational."

Domestic corporation A corporation doing business in the state in which it has been incorporated.

Domestic international sales corporation (DISC) A legal entity that provides special tax benefits for firms engaged in exporting, created by Congress to combat an increasingly unfavorable trade balance.

Drive to achieve A strong desire to compete, to excel against self-imposed standards, and to pursue and attain challenging goals.

Duplication A basic type of innovation involving the replication of an already existing product, service, or process.

Early entry strategy A succession strategy that encourages the younger generation to enter the business at an early age to gain experience.

E-commerce The marketing, promoting, buying, and selling of goods and services electronically, particularly via the Internet. The new wave in transacting business, it encompasses various models of Internet use: e-tailing (virtual storefronts), which is a site for shopping and making purchases; electronic data interchange (EDI), which is business-to-business exchange of data; e-mail and computer faxing; business-to-business buying and selling; ensuring the security of data transactions. It is simply the integration of business processes electronically via information and communication technologies.

Economic base The base that includes the nature of employment (which influences the size and distribution of income) and the purchasing trends of consumers in the area.

Ecovision Leadership style for innovative organizations. Encourages open and flexible structures that encompass the employees, the organization, and the environment, with attention to evolving social demands.

Effective delegation Assignment of specific duties, granting authority to carry out these duties, and creating the obligation of responsibility for necessary action.

Emotional bias The tendency to believe an enterprise is worth a great deal more than outsiders believe it is worth.

Employee stock ownership plan (ESOP) Passing control of the enterprise to the employees if the owner has no immediate successor in mind.

Entrepreneur An innovator or developer who recognizes and seizes opportunities; converts these opportunities into workable/marketable ideas; adds value through time, effort, money, or skills; assumes the risks of the competitive marketplace to implement these ideas; and realizes the rewards from these efforts.

Entrepreneurial assessment approach Stresses making assessments qualitatively, quantitatively, strategically, and ethically in regard to the entrepreneur, the venture, and the environment.

Entrepreneurial behavior An entrepreneur's decision to initiate the new-venture formation process.

Entrepreneurial culture A culture typified by the presence of characteristics such as a flat management structure with multiple informal networks, episodic use or rent of required resources, a long-run time perspective, and a strategic orientation driven by perception of opportunity. (See also **Administrative culture.**)

Entrepreneurial economy A new emphasis on entrepreneurial thinking that developed in the 1980s and 1990s.

Entrepreneurial leadership An entrepreneur's ability to anticipate, envision, maintain flexibility, think strategically, and work with others to initiate changes that will create a viable future for the organization.

Entrepreneurial leveraged buyout (E–LBO) Having at least two-thirds of the purchase price generated from borrowed funds, more than 50 percent of the stock after acquisition owned by a single individual or his or her family, and the majority investor devoted to the active management of the company after acquisition.

Entrepreneurial management The theme or discipline that suggests entrepreneurship is based on the same principles, whether the entrepreneur is an existing large institution or an individual starting his or her new venture single-handedly.

Entrepreneurial marketing A marketing stage in which the enterprise attempts to develop credibility in the marketplace by establishing a market niche.

Entrepreneurial mind–set All the characteristics and elements that compose the entrepreneurial potential in every individual.

Entrepreneurial motivation The willingness of an entrepreneur to sustain his or her entrepreneurial behavior.

Entrepreneurial Revolution The tremendous increase in entrepreneurial business and entrepreneurial thinking that has developed over the last 15 years. This revolution will be as powerful to the twenty-first century as the Industrial Revolution was to the twentieth century (if not more!).

Entrepreneurial strategy matrix Measures risk and innovation.

Entrepreneurial stress A function of discrepancies between one's expectations and one's ability to meet those demands.

Entrepreneurial successor A successor to a venture who is highly gifted with ingenuity, creativity, and drive.

Entrepreneurial trait school of thought A school of entrepreneurial thought that focuses on identifying traits that appear common to successful entrepreneurs.

Entrepreneurship The process of organizing, managing, and assuming the risks of a business.

Environmental assessment Entails evaluating the general economic environment, the government-regulating environment, and the industry.

Environmental awareness A reawakening of the need to preserve and protect our natural resources.

Environmental school of thought A school of entrepreneurial thought that focuses on the external factors and forces—values, mores, and institutions—that surround a potential entrepreneur's lifestyle.

Equal Access to Justice Act Federal law that provides greater equity between small business and regulatory bodies. It states, among other things, that if a small business challenges a regulatory agency and wins, then the agency must pay the legal costs of the small business.

Equity financing The sale of some ownership in a venture in order to gain capital for start-up.

Ethics A set of principles prescribing a behavioral code that explains what is good and right or bad and wrong.

Evaluation and implementation The fourth step in the creative thinking process, during which the individual makes adjustments in the approach so that it more closely approximates the necessary solution.

Excess earnings A method of determining a firm's intangible assets. It is a method of last resort that does not include intangibles with estimated useful lives such as patents and copyrights.

Expenses An expired cost; any item or class of cost of (or loss from) carrying on an activity; a present or past expenditure defraying a present operating cost or representing an irrecoverable cost or loss; an item of capital expenditures written down or off; or a term often used with some qualifying expression denoting function, organization, or time, such as a selling expense, factory expense, or monthly expense.

Experimentation A form of research that concentrates on investigating cause-and-effect relationships.

Export/Import Bank (Eximbank) Governmental agency that offers direct loans for large-project and equipment sales that require long-term financing. It also offers credit guarantees to commercial banks that finance export sales.

Export management company A firm that serves as an export department for a manufacturer by soliciting business and exporting the product(s) for the client in return for a commission, salary, or retainer plus commission.

Exporting Participating actively in the international arena as a seller rather than a buyer.

Extension A basic type of innovation that involves extending the life of a product, service, or process already in existence.

External locus of control A point of view in which external processes are sometimes beyond the control of the individual entrepreneur.

External optimism Ceaseless optimism emanating from entrepreneurs as a key factor in the drive toward success.

External problems Related to customer contact, market knowledge, marketing planning, location, pricing, product considerations, competitors, and expansion.

External resources Resources outside the venture.

Factoring The sale of accounts receivable.

Failure prediction model Based on financial data from newly founded ventures; assumes the financial failure process is characterized by too much initial indebtedness and too little revenue financing.

Fair use doctrine An exception to copyright protection that allows limited use of copyrighted materials.

Family and social risk Starting a new venture uses much of the entrepreneur's energy and time. Entrepreneurs who are married, and especially those with children, expose their families to the risks of an incomplete family experience and the possibility of permanent emotional scars. In addition, old friends may vanish slowly because of missed get-togethers.

Feasibility criteria approach A criteria selection list from which entrepreneurs can gain insights into the viability of their venture.

Finance company Asset-based lender that lends money against assets such as receivables, inventory, and equipment.

Financial/capital school of thought A school of entrepreneurial thought that focuses on the ways entrepreneurs seek seed capital and growth funds.

Financial expense The interest expense on long-term loans. Many companies also include their interest expense on short-term obligations as part of their financial expense.

Financial risk The money or resources at stake for a new venture.

Financial segment The segment of the business plan that discusses the financial forecast, the sources and uses of funds, budgeting plans, and stages of financing.

Five-minute reading A six-step process venture capitalists use when they are reviewing a business plan for potential investment.

Fixed assets These consist of land, building, equipment, and other assets expected to remain with the firm for an extended period.

Fixed cost A cost that does not change in response to changes in activity for a given period of time.

Forcing events Happenings that cause the replacement of the owner-manager.

Foreign corporation A corporation doing business in a state other than the one in which it is incorporated.

Foreign sales corporation (FSC) An entity, created by legislation to encourage exports, that receives tax-exempt treatment on a portion of its export income.

Franchise Any arrangement in which the owner of a trademark, trade name, or copyright has licensed others to use it to sell goods or services.

Free Trade Agreement (FTA) Global economic development that has provided new potential environments within which entrepreneurs could prosper.

Freight forwarder An independent business that handles export shipments in return for compensation.

Functional perspective Viewing things and people in terms of how they can be used to satisfy one's needs and to help complete a project.

Gazelle A business establishment with at least 20 percent sales growth every year, starting with a base of at least $100,000.

General Agreement on Tariffs and Trade (GATT) A major trade liberalization organization whose objectives are to create a basic set of rules under which trade negotiations take place.

General partner A person who is active in the business, is known to be a partner, and has unlimited liability.

Generic meaning Allowance of a trademark to represent a general grouping of products or services (for example, Kleenex has come to represent tissue).

Great chef strategies The skills or special talents of one or more individuals around whom a venture is built.

Growth of sales The growth pattern anticipated for new-venture sales and profits.

Growth stage The third stage of a new-venture life cycle, typically involving activities related to reformulating strategy in the light of competition.

Growth wall A psychological wall against change that prevents entrepreneurs from developing a managerial ability to deal with venture growth.

Harvest strategy Privately held business entrepreneurs' decision to sell the venture.

High-growth venture When sales and profit growth are expected to be significant enough to attract venture capital money and funds raised through public or private placements.

Horizontal analysis Looks at financial statements and ratios over time.

Idea experience The third step in the creative thinking process, during which the individual discovers the answers he or she has been pursuing.

Immersion in business When the successful entrepreneur devotes all of his or her time to the business rather than taking some time for leisure activities.

Immoral management Management decisions that imply a positive and active opposition to what is ethical.

Importing Buying and shipping foreign-produced goods for domestic consumption.

Income statement A financial document that reports the sales, expenses, and profits of the enterprise over a specified period, usually one year.

Incongruities Whenever a gap or difference exists between expectations and reality.

Incremental innovation The systematic evolution of a product or service into newer or larger markets.

Incubation process The second step in the creative thinking process during which one's subconscious is allowed to mull over the information gathered during the preparation phase.

Informal risk capitalists Wealthy people who invest capital in public and private placements but are not considered professional venture capitalists.

Infringement budget A realistic budget for prosecuting violations of the patent.

Initial public offering (IPO) A corporation's raising capital through the sale of securities on the public markets.

Innovation The process by which entrepreneurs convert opportunities into marketable ideas.

Intellectual property right Provides protection such as patents, trademarks, or copyrights against infringement by others.

Interactive learning Learning ideas within an innovative environment that cuts across traditional, functional lines in the organization.

Internal locus of control The viewpoint in which the potential entrepreneur has the ability or control to direct or adjust the outcome of each major influence.

Internal problems Involve adequate capital, cash flow, facilities/equipment, inventory control, human resources, leadership, organizational structure, and accounting systems.

Internal rate of return (IRR) method A capital-budgeting technique that involves discounting future cash flows to the present at a rate that makes the net present value of the project equal to zero.

Internet The major, worldwide distribution channel for goods, services, and for managerial and professional jobs.

Internet marketing Allows the firm to increase its presence and brand equity in the marketplace; allows the company to cultivate new customers, allows website visitors to match their needs with the offerings of the company and can improve customer service by allowing customers to serve themselves when and where they choose.

Intracapital Special capital set aside for the corporate entrepreneur to use whenever investment money is needed for further research ideas.

Intrapreneurship Entrepreneurial activities that receive organizational sanction and resource commitments for the purpose of innovative results.

Invention A basic type of innovation that involves the creation of a new product, service, or process that is often novel or untried.

Inventory Merchandise held by the company for resale to customers.

Joint venture An organization owned by more than one company—a popular approach to doing business overseas.

Lack of expertise/skills When small-business managers lack the specialized expertise/skills necessary for the planning process.

Lack of knowledge Small-firm owners/managers' uncertainty about the components of the planning process and their sequence due to minimal exposure to, and knowledge of, the process itself.

Lack of trust and openness When small-firm owners/managers are highly sensitive and guarded about their businesses and the decisions that affect them.

Learning curve concept The time needed for new methods or procedures to be learned and mastered.

Left brain The part of the brain that helps an individual analyze, verbalize, and use rational approaches to problem solving. (See also **Right brain.**)

Leveraged buyout (LBO) Allowing the entrepreneur to finance the transaction by borrowing on the target company's assets.

Liabilities The debts of a business, incurred either through normal operations or through the process of obtaining funds to finance operations. (See also **Short-term liabilities** and **Long-term liabilities.**)

Licensing A business arrangement in which the manufacturer of a product (or a firm with proprietary rights over technology or trademarks) grants permission to a group or an individual to manufacture that product in return for specified royalties or other payments.

Life-cycle stages The typical life cycle through which a venture progresses, including venture development, start-up, growth, stabilization, and innovation or decline.

Lifestyle venture A small venture where the primary driving forces include independence, autonomy, and control.

Limited liability A restriction on the amount of financial responsibility assumed by a partner or stockholder. (See also **Unlimited liability.**)

Limited liability company (LLC) A hybrid form of business enterprise that offers the limited liability of a corporation but the tax advantages of a partnership.

Limited liability partnership (LLP) A relatively new form of partnership that allows professionals the tax benefits of a partnership while avoiding personal liability for the malpractice of other partners.

Limited partnership Organizational arrangement that allows investors to put money into a partnership without assuming liability for any losses beyond this initial investment.

Liquidation See Bankruptcy.

Liquidation value A method of valuing a business in which the value of all assets is determined on the basis of their current sale value.

Loan payable The current installment on a long-term debt that must be paid this year.

Loan with warrants A loan that provides the investor (lender) with the right to buy stock at a fixed price at some future date.

Loneliness Isolation from persons with whom entrepreneurs can confide because of their long hours at work.

Long-term liabilities Business debts that are not due and payable within the next 12 months.

Loss leader pricing Pricing the product below cost in an attempt to attract customers to other products.

Macro view of entrepreneurship A broad array of factors that relate to success or failure in contemporary entrepreneurial ventures.

Management segment The segment of a business plan that discusses the management team, legal structure, board of directors, advisers, and consultants.

Management succession The transition of managerial decision making in a firm, one of the greatest challenges confronting owners and entrepreneurs in family businesses.

Managerial successor A successor to a venture who is interested in efficiency, internal control, and the effective use of resources.

Manufacturing segment The segment of a business plan that discusses location analysis, production needs, suppliers, transportation, labor supply, and manufacturing cost data.

Market A group of consumers (potential customers) who have purchasing power and unsatisfied needs. (See also **Market niche** and **Niche**.)

Market niche A homogeneous group of consumers with common characteristics.

Market planning The process of determining a clear, comprehensive approach to the creation of a consumer.

Market segmentation The process of identifying a specific set of characteristics that differentiate one group of consumers from the rest.

Market strategy A general marketing philosophy and strategy of the company developed from market research and evaluation data.

Market value A method of valuing a business that involves an estimation based on prices recently paid for similar enterprises as well as on the methods of sale.

Marketability Assembling and analyzing relevant information about a new venture to judge its potential success.

Marketing information system A system that compiles and organizes data relating to cost, revenues, and profit from the customer base.

Marketing research A gathering of information about a particular market, followed by an analysis of that information.

Marketing segment The segment of a business plan that describes aspects of the market such as the target market, the market size and trends, the competition, estimated market share, market strategy, pricing, and advertising and promotion.

Marketing strategy The general marketing philosophy of the company should be outlined to include the kinds of customer groups to be targeted by the initial intensive selling effort; the customer groups to be targeted for later selling efforts; methods of identifying and contracting potential customers in these groups; the features of the product or service (quality, price, delivery, warranty) to be emphasized to generate sales; and innovative or unusual marketing concepts that will enhance customer acceptance.

Microenvironmental assessment Analysis directed toward the community within which the new venture is to be launched.

Micro view of entrepreneurship Examines the factors specific to entrepreneurship and part of the internal locus of control.

Milestone planning approach A planning approach based on the use of incremental goal attainment that takes a new venture from start-up through strategy reformulation.

Milestone schedule segment The section of a business plan that provides investors with timetables for the accomplishment of various activities such as completion of prototypes, hiring of sales representatives, receipt of first orders, initial deliveries, and receipt of first accounts receivable payments.

Minority-owned business Business owned and operated by a minority, which may include blacks, Asians, Native Americans, and Hispanics.

Mixed costs A blend of fixed and variable costs.

Moral management Management activity that conforms to a standard of ethical behavior.

Mountain gap strategies Identifying major market segments as well as interstice (in-between) markets that arise from larger markets.

Muddling mind-sets When creative thinking is blocked or impeded.

Multidimensional approach Viewing entrepreneurship as a complex, multidimensional framework that emphasizes the individual, the environment, the organization, and the venture process.

Multiple of earnings A method of valuing a venture that consists of multiplying earnings by a predetermined multiple to arrive at a final value.

Multistage contingency approach Strategic analysis that includes the individual, the venture, and the environment in relation to a venture's stages as well as to the entrepreneur's career perspective.

National Federation of Independent Business (NFIB) The largest advocacy group representing small and independent businesses in Washington, D.C., and all 50 state capitals; has a membership of more than 600,000 business owners.

Need for control The strong desire entrepreneurs have to control both their ventures and their destinies.

Nepotism The hiring of relatives in preference to other, more qualified candidates.

Net income The excess of revenue over expenses during a particular period.

Net present value (NPV) method A capital-budgeting technique used to evaluate an investment that involves a determination of future cash flows and a discounting of these flows to arrive at a present value of these future dollars.

Networking Meeting key people in a particular field of business for purposes of gaining connections in the industry. Also valuable in sharing experiences with other business owners as a way to relieve loneliness.

New-venture development The first stage of a venture's life cycle that involves activities such as creativity and venture assessment.

Niche A homogeneous group with common characteristics, such as people who all have a need for a newly proposed good or service.

Nonprofit corporation A corporation whose main objective is not profit, such as a religious, charitable, or educational institution.

Nonprofit-sponsored incubator An incubator organized and managed through industrial development associations of private industry, chambers of commerce, or community-based organizations and whose primary objective is area development.

Nonrole Refers to unethical instances where the person is acting outside of his or her role as manager yet committing acts against the firm.

Note payable A promissory note given as tangible recognition of a supplier's claim or a note given in connection with an acquisition of funds, such as for a bank loan.

Oakland Scavenger Company A garbage collection firm based in California that was involved in a legal dispute over nepotism in a family business.

Observational methods Methods of collecting primary data that do not involve any direct contact with the respondents. (See also **Questioning methods**.)

Operating budget A budget that sets forth the projected sales forecast and expenses for an upcoming period.

Operating expenses The major expenses, exclusive of costs of goods sold, in generating revenue.

Operational planning Short-range or functional planning consisting of specific practices established to carry out the objective set forth in the strategic plan.

Opportunistic marketing A marketing stage in a growing venture in which the organization attempts to develop high sales volume through market penetration.

Opportunity orientation A pattern among successful, growth-minded entrepreneurs to focus on opportunity rather than on resources, structure, or strategy.

Owners' equity What remains after the firm's liabilities are subtracted from its assets.

Partnership An association of two or more persons acting as co-owners of a business for profit.

Patent An intellectual property right granted to an inventor giving him or her the exclusive right to make, use, or sell an invention for a limited time period (usually 20 years).

Patent and Trademark Office An office of the federal government where all patent and trademark applications are filed.

Payback method A capital-budgeting technique used to determine the length of time required to pay back an original investment.

Penetration Setting prices at such a low level that products are able to gain market share.

Perception of high cost When small-business owners perceive the cost associated with planning to be very high.

Planning The process of transforming entrepreneurial vision and ideas into action, involving three steps: (1) commitment to an open planning process, (2) accountability to a corporate conscience, and (3) establishment of a pattern of subordinate participation in the development of the strategic plan.

Policies Fundamental guides for the venture as a whole.

Prepaid expenses Expenses the firm already has paid but that have not yet been used.

Preferred stock Equity that gives investors a preferred place among the creditors in case the venture is dissolved.

Price/earnings ratio (P/E) A method of valuing a business that divides the price of the common stock in the market by the earnings per share and multiplies the result by the number of shares of stock issued.

Primary data New data that are often collected by using observational or questioning methods.

Private corporation A corporation created either wholly or in part for private benefits; another name for a close corporation or family corporation, where the rights of shareholders are restricted regarding transfer of shares.

Private offering The raising of capital through the private placement of securities to groups such as friends, employees, customers, relatives, and local professionals. (See also **Public offerings**.)

Private placement A method of raising capital through securities; often used by small ventures.

Privately sponsored incubators An incubator organized and managed by a private corporation for the purpose of making a profit for that corporation.

Pro forma financial statement A financial statement that projects the results of future business operations, such as a pro forma balance sheet, an income statement, or a cash-flow statement.

Pro forma statements Projections of a firm's financial position over a future period (pro forma income statement) or on a future date (pro forma balance sheet).

Probability thinking Relying on probability to make decisions in the struggle to achieve security.

Product availability The availability of a salable good or service at the time the venture opens its doors.

Production-driven philosophy A market philosophy based on the principle of producing efficiently and letting sales take care of themselves. (See also **Consumer-driven philosophy** and **Sales-driven philosophy**.)

Professional corporation A corporation made up of practicing professionals such as lawyers, accountants, or doctors.

Profits, sales, and operating ratios Used to estimate a business's potential earning power, which is a key factor in evaluating the attractiveness of the venture and in later determining a reasonable buying price.

Prompt Payments Act A federal law requiring that small businesses doing work for the federal government be paid within 30 days with an additional 15-day grace period; otherwise, interest penalty charges become retroactive from the 30-day point.

Psychic risk The great psychological impact on and the well-being of the entrepreneur who is creating a new venture.

Public corporation A corporation the government forms to meet a political or governmental purpose.

Public offerings The raising of capital through the sale of securities on public markets. (See also **Private offerings**.)

Publicly sponsored incubators An incubator set up by a public entity such as a municipal economic development department, urban renewal authority, or a regional planning and development department with the main objective of job creation.

Questioning methods Methods of collecting primary data directly from the respondents, such as surveys and telephone interviews. (See also **Observational methods**.)

R&D limited partnership A popular tool for funding research and development expenses in entrepreneurial ventures; it is a limited partnership in many ways.

Radical innovation The inaugural breakthroughs launched from experimentation and determined vision that are not necessarily managed but must be recognized and nurtured.

Ratio Designed to show relationships among financial statement accounts.

Ratio analysis Financial analysis designed to show relationships among financial statement accounts.

Rationalizations What managers use to justify questionable conduct.

Reach Relates to access and connection. It means, simply, how many customers with whom a business can connect and how many products it can offer to those customers.

Regulation D Regulation and exemption for reports and statements required for selling stock to private parties based on the amount of money being raised.

Regulatory Flexibility Act A federal law that puts the burden on government to ensure that legislation does not unfairly impact small business.

Reliance The strength of the community's need for the entrepreneur's venture and the entrepreneur's willingness to make a commitment to the community.

Reorganization A common form of bankruptcy in which the debtor attempts to formulate a plan to pay a portion of the debts, have the remaining sum discharged, and continue to stay in operation.

Replacement value A method of valuing a business in which the cost of replacing each asset is determined at current cost.

Research, design, and development segment The part of a business plan that discusses the development and design plan, technical research results, research assistance needs, and cost structure.

Responsibility charting Uses the three components of decisions, roles, and types of participation to form a matrix so that a respondent can assign a type of participation to each of the roles for a specific decision.

Responsive marketing A marketing stage during which the organization attempts to develop high customer satisfaction through product market development.

Retained earnings The accumulated net income over the life of the corporation to date.

Return on investment Net profit divided by investment.

Revenues The gross sales made by a business during a particular period under review.

Richness Focuses on the depth and detail of information that the business can give the customer, as well as the depth and detail of information it collects about the customer.

Right brain The part of the brain that helps an individual understand analogies, imagine things, and synthesize information. (See also **Left brain.**)

Risk Involves uncertain outcomes or events. The higher the rewards, the greater the risk entrepreneurs usually face.

Role assertion Unethical acts involving managers/entrepreneurs who represent the firm and who rationalize that they are in a position to help the firm's long-run interests are foremost.

Role distortion Unethical acts committed on the basis that they are "for the firm" even though they are not, and involving managers/entrepreneurs who commit individual acts and who rationalize that they are in the firm's long-run interests.

Role failure Unethical acts against the firm involving a person failing to perform his or her managerial role, including superficial performance appraisals (not being totally honest) and not confronting someone who is cheating on expense accounts.

S corporation A corporation that retains some of the benefits of the corporate form while being taxed similarly to a partnership.

Sales-driven philosophy A marketing philosophy that focuses on personal selling and advertising to persuade customers to buy the company's output. (See also **Consumer-driven philosophy** and **Product-driven philosophy.**)

Sales forecast The process of projecting future sales by applying statistical techniques to historical sales figures.

Secondary data Data that have already been compiled. Examples are periodicals, articles, trade association information, governmental publications, and company records.

Shopping goods Goods that consumers will take time to examine carefully and compare for quality and price.

Short-term liabilities Business debts that must be paid during the coming 12 months (also called *current liabilities*).

Simple linear regression A technique in which a linear equation states the relationship among three variables used to estimate the sales forecast.

Skimming Deliberately setting a high price to maximize short-term profits.

Skunkworks A highly innovative enterprise that uses groups functioning outside traditional lines of authority.

Small Business Administration A governmental agency that aids small business by providing financial, consulting, and managerial assistance.

Small Business Regulatory Enforcement Fairness Act Enacted in 1996, eases regulatory costs and burdens by requiring agencies issuing regulations and the SBA to assist small-business operators in understanding and complying with the rules.

Small profitable venture A venture in which the entrepreneur does not want venture sales to become so large that he or she must relinquish equity or ownership position and thus give up control over cash flows and profits, which it is hoped will be substantial.

Social obligation Reacting to social issues through obedience to the laws.

Social responsibility Reacting to social issues by accepting responsibility for various programs.

Social responsiveness Being proactive on social issues by being associated with various activities for the social good.

Sole proprietorship A business owned and operated by one person.

Specialty goods Products or services that consumers make a special effort to find and purchase.

Specification The text of a patent; it may include any accompanying illustrations.

Stabilization stage The fourth stage of a new-venture life cycle, typified by increased competition, consumer indifference to the entrepreneur's good(s) or service(s), and saturation of the market with a host of "me too" look-alikes. During this stage the entrepreneur begins planning the venture's direction over the next three to five years.

Start-up activities The second stage of a new-venture life cycle, encompassing the foundation work needed for creating a formal business plan, searching for capital, carrying out marketing activities, and developing an effective entrepreneurial team.

Start–up problems A perceived problem area in the start-up phase of a new venture, such as lack of business training, difficulty obtaining lines of credit, and inexperience in financial planning.

Stereotyping Refers to averages that people fabricate and then, ironically, base decisions on as if they were entities existing in the real world.

Stickiness A host of potential value-adds, features, functions, and "gimmies," all of which serves as electronic fly paper, of sorts, and make people want to stay at your website longer.

Straight bankruptcy A bankruptcy arrangement in which the debtor is required to surrender all property to a court-appointed trustee who sells the assets and turns the proceeds over to the creditors; sometimes known as liquidation.

Strategic formulation school of thought A school of entrepreneurial thought that focuses on the planning process used in successful venture formulation.

Strategic planning The primary step in determining the future direction of a business influenced by the abilities of the entrepreneur, the complexity of the venture, and the nature of the industry.

Strategic positioning The process of perceiving new positions that attract customers from established positions or draw new customers into the market.

Stress A function of discrepancies between a person's expectations and ability to meet demands, as well as discrepancies between the individual's expectations and personality. If a person is unable to fulfill role demands, then stress occurs.

Survey A method of collecting primary data, such as a mail, telephone, or personal interview.

Sustainable competitive advantage When a venture has implemented a strategy that other companies cannot duplicate or find it too costly to compete with a particular element. Every sustainable competitive advantage can only be maintained for a certain amount of time depending upon the speed with which competitors are able to duplicate or substitute.

SWOT analysis A strategic analysis that refers to strengths, weaknesses, opportunities, and threats.

Synthesis A basic type of innovation that involves combining existing concepts and factors into a new formulation.

Taxes payable Liabilities owed to the government—federal, state, and local.

Technical feasibility Producing a product or service that will satisfy the expectations of potential customers.

Telemarketing The use of telephone communications to directly contact and sell merchandise to consumers.

3–P Growth Model Introduced by Ernst & Young, defines three specific states for a venture pursuing the e-commerce route: presence (ramp-up) stage, penetration (hypergrowth) stage, and profitability (managed growth) stage.

Time scarcity Lack of time and the difficulty of allocating time for planning in the face of continual day-to-day operating problems.

Tolerance for ambiguity Ability of the entrepreneur to thrive on uncertainty and constant changes that introduce ambiguity and stress into every aspect of the enterprise.

Tolerance for failure The iterative, trial-and-error nature of a successful entrepreneur due to serious setbacks and disappointments that are an integral part of the entrepreneur's learning experience.

Top management support When upper-level managers in a corporation can concentrate on helping individuals within the system develop more entrepreneurial behavior.

Trade credit Credit given by a supplier who sells goods on account. A common arrangement calls for the bill to be settled within 30 to 90 days.

Trademark A distinctive name, mark, symbol, or motto identified with a company's product(s).

Trade secrets Customer lists, plans, research and development, pricing information, marketing techniques, and production techniques. Generally, anything that makes an individual company unique and has value to a competitor could be a trade secret.

Unfunded Mandates Reform Act Enacted in 1995, requires Congress and federal agencies to consider the actual costs of new federal mandates. Agencies must prepare cost-benefit and other analyses, unless prohibited by law, for any rule that will likely result in costs of $100 million or more in any year.

Uniform Franchise Offering Circular (UFOC) A disclosure form the Federal Trade Commission requires of all potential franchisors.

Uniform Limited Partnership Act (ULPA) The act contains 11 articles and 64 sections of guidelines. If a limited partnership appears to be the desired legal form of organization, the prospective partners must examine these ULPA guidelines.

Uniform Partnership Act Generally followed by most states as the guide for legal requirements of forming a partnership.

Uniqueness Special characteristics and/or design concepts that draw the customer to the venture and should provide performance or service superior to competitive offerings.

University–related incubators An incubator that is a spin-off of an academic research project with the major goal to transfer the findings of basic research and development into a new product or technology.

Unlimited liability A condition existing in sole proprietorships and partnerships wherein someone is responsible for all the enterprise's debts.

Unsought goods Goods that consumers neither currently need nor seek, such as encyclopedias and cemetery plots.

Value added A basic form of contribution analysis in which sales minus raw materials costs equals the value added.

Variable cost A cost that changes in the same direction as, and in direct proportion to, changes in operating activity.

Venture capitalist An individual who provides a full range of financial services for new or growing ventures, such as capital for start-ups and expansions, marketing research, management consulting, assistance with negotiating technical agreements, and assistance with employee recruitment and development of employee agreements.

Venture opportunity school of thought A school of entrepreneurial thought that focuses on the search for idea sources, on concept development, and on implementation of venture opportunities.

Venture team A small group of people who operate as a semiautonomous unit to create and develop a new idea.

Vertical analysis The application of ratio analysis to one set of financial statements.

Vision A concept of what the entrepreneur's idea can become.

Water well strategies The ability to gather or harness special resources (land, labor, capital, raw materials) over the long term.

Website A site (location) on the World Wide Web. Each website contains a home page, which is the first document users see when they enter the site. This site might also contain additional documents and files. Each site is owned and managed by an individual, company, or organization.

Women–owned businesses Businesses women own, the fastest-growing segment of small business in the nation.

Women's Business Ownership Act A law to establish programs and initiate efforts to help develop women-owned businesses.

Name Index

Subject Index